13 25

SEXUAL BEHAVIOR IN THE HUMAN FEMALE

CONSULTING EDITORS

SEXUAL BEHAVIOR IN THE HUMAN FEMALE

*By the Staff of the Institute for
Sex Research, Indiana University*

ALFRED C. KINSEY   WARDELL B. POMEROY

CLYDE E. MARTIN   PAUL H. GEBHARD
Research Associates

JEAN M. BROWN	Research Assistant, Library
CORNELIA V. CHRISTENSON	Research Assistant, in charge of Reference Research
DOROTHY COLLINS	Research Assistant, Statistical Calculator
RITCHIE G. DAVIS	Research Associate, Legal Studies
WILLIAM DELLENBACK	Research Assistant, Photographic Studies
ALICE W. FIELD	Research Associate, Legal Studies
HEDWIG G. LESER	Research Assistant, Translator
HENRY H. REMAK	Special Translator
ELEANOR L. ROEHR	Research Assistant, Secretary

W. B. SAUNDERS COMPANY

PHILADELPHIA AND LONDON

W. B. Saunders Company: West Washington Square
                         Philadelphia, Pa. 19105

                         12 Dyott Street
                         London, WC1A 1DB

                         833 Oxford Street
                         Toronto, Ontario M8Z 5T9, Canada

**Listed here is the latest translated edition of this
book together with the language of the translation
and the publisher.**

German *(Paperback)*—Gustav Fischer Verlag, Stuttgart-Hohenheim,
                    Germany

Portuguese *(1st Edition) (Reprint)*—Livraria Atheneu,
                              Rio de Janeiro, Brazil

Spanish *(1st Edition)*—Siglo Viento, Buenos Aires, Argentina

Swedish *(Paperback) (3 Vols.)*—Prisma A.B., Stockholm, Sweden

ISBN 0-7216-5450-9

LIBRARY OF CONGRESS CATALOG CARD NUMBER: 53-11127

Print No.:   9   8   7   6

To the nearly 8000 females
who contributed the data on
which this book is based

FOREWORD

It is the function of the National Research Council as an agency of the National Academy of Sciences to further in all feasible ways the development of science and the extension, perfecting, dissemination, and useful application of knowledge of natural phenomena. Thirty-two years ago when studies of sex were virtually taboo the Council created a special committee to initiate, organize and financially support the study of problems in sex and reproduction. During its long and active existence the Committee has sponsored and partially supported scores of investigations, including several long-range and long-continued programs of research. Among the best known of the Committee-supported projects have been studies in the field of endocrinology, where the discovery of hormones and their functions has proved of extraordinary importance. The Committee has supported studies in the sexual behavior of infra-human mammalian species, laboratory investigations of the neurologic bases of sexual behavior, some anthropological studies, and several case history studies of human sex behavior, including the Hamilton study which it sponsored in the late 1920's, and the studies made by Terman and Miles, and by Landis and Bolles in the late 1930's.

From the first the Committee sought an opportunity to initiate and support such human studies. But human sexual behavior is much more difficult to study objectively and scientifically than are reproductive mechanisms and processes. However skillful and wise, no investigator in this field can escape inhibiting and discouraging circumstances. The success of Dr. Kinsey and his corps of colleagues in meeting and overcoming these difficulties has therefore been notable. His project stands unique in its scope, methodological skills, degree of objectivity and history of progress and achievement.

It was in 1940, three years after he had begun his task, that Dr. Kinsey first applied to our Committee for financial aid. After preliminary inquiry, a small initial grant was made for 1941. During that year we gathered pertinent information about the institutional auspices of the project and by personal visits and interviews sought bases for an appraisal of Kinsey as a scientific investigator, his plans, his program, and his method. The inquiry was exceptionally thorough and painstaking because of the scope and the prospective demand of the undertaking for large resources of wisdom and tact, professional skill, energy, time, and funds. Assured by the outcome of the inquiry, we rapidly increased the annual allotment, and over the years the Committee aid has amounted to almost half of the total budget for the investigation.

From its inception in 1938, this project has had the staunch and generous support of the administration of Indiana University. Otherwise its rapid development, its expansion, and remarkable degree of success would have been impossible.

Now in its fifteenth year, the project has had to meet and resolve many problems of operation and some determined opposition; but in some respects

vii

it has been very fortunate. In the United States, the twentieth century has been a period of exceedingly rapid and revolutionary change in sex attitudes and practices. Whereas throughout the nineteenth century the puritanic attitude in sexual matters was dominant in the United States, since the turn of the century both mores and practices have been in flux. What fifty years ago could not have been mentioned in a social group—sexual and reproductive happenings and experiences—are now spoken of without inhibition. These changes are in part a product of (1) woman's progressive sexual and economic emancipation; (2) the all-pervasive influence of Freud's views and discoveries; and (3) the exposure during the World Wars of millions of American youth to cultures and peoples whose sex codes and practices differ greatly from those in which they had been reared. These changes made feasible the work of the Committee, and prepared the way for the Kinsey report. Only a few decades earlier, Henry Havelock Ellis (1859–1939), eminent student of sex in England, suffered severe censure and legal restriction of the publication of his scholarly findings. Only a little later, Sigmund Freud's (1856–1939) account of the role of sexuality in the etiology of the neuroses was rejected by his medical colleagues. But the Austrian psychiatrist persisted with his inquiry, and eventually proposed theories and formulated hypotheses which have fundamentally changed our conception of the role of sexuality in our mental and social lives.

Comparison of Freud and Kinsey is not implied, for the two men differed greatly in temperament, professional training and experience, and in their objectives; but what should be noted is the fact that Freud, on the basis of his clinical experience, proposed theories which laid the foundation for a task he was not fitted by nature or training to carry on. This is the great task of fact-finding through careful, patient, long-continued, objective research which Alfred Kinsey, the laboratory- and field-trained biologist, is now engaged in doing. From the Kinsey project, sufficiently extended, should come basic knowledge of sexual phenomena against which theory may be checked, modified and supplemented.

The current report makes a notable contribution of fact in replacement of ignorance and of inadequately verified surmise. We look forward to the possibility that the Institute for Sex Research may long serve to inform, enlighten and guide us in an area where knowledge and understanding may affect the very existence of the genus *Homo*. We, as scientists, have large faith in the values of knowledge, little faith in ignorance.

ROBERT M. YERKES, Chairman
Committee for Research
in Problems of Sex, 1922–1947

GEORGE W. CORNER, Chairman
Committee for Research
in Problems of Sex, 1947–date

ACKNOWLEDGEMENTS

The development of the present project on human sexual behavior has been possible only because of the cooperation which we have had from some thousands of persons who have contributed data, professional advice, and long-time encouragement toward a continuance of the program. Especial mention can be made of only a few of those who have been peculiarly involved in the support of the project.

Dr. Herman B Wells, President of Indiana University, Dr. Herman T. Briscoe, Vice President of the University, Dr. Fernandus Payne, formerly head of the Department of Zoology and Dean of the Graduate School, the Trustees of the University, and many others in the administration of Indiana University have believed in the importance of this research and constantly encouraged and materially supported it through a long period of years.

During the past twelve years, the National Research Council's Committee for Research in Problems of Sex has provided financial support, constant encouragement, and a considerable amount of professional guidance. We are especially indebted to Dr. Robert M. Yerkes and Dr. George W. Corner who have successively been chairmen of that Committee.

The Rockefeller Foundation has contributed through grants made to the National Research Council's Committee. We are especially indebted to Dr. Alan Gregg, formerly Director for the Medical Sciences of the Foundation, for his long-time interest and support of the project.

As consulting editors, Jerome Cornfield, Dr. Harold Dorn, Dr. Robert Laidlaw, Dr. Karl Lashley, and Dr. Emily Mudd have contributed from their backgrounds in statistics, psychiatry, psychology, neurophysiology, and marriage counseling. While the authors of this volume must assume full responsibility for whatever errors and misinterpretations have entered into the making of this book, credit for whatever quality it may have should be shared with these specialists who have contributed from their considerable experience in areas related to the subject matter of the present research.

Dr. William Breneman of the Zoology Department at Indiana University has served as a special consultant in regard to the endocrinological problems covered by the volume. Dr. Frank K. Edmondson, Head of the Department of Astronomy at Indiana University, has also advised on statistical procedures.

Dr. Frank Beach of the Department of Psychology at Yale University, Dr. Fred McKenzie of the Department of Animal Husbandry at the Oregon State College, and Dr. Albert Shadle of the Department of Biology at the University of Buffalo, have contributed to the data on animal behavior. Dr. Beach and Dr. Shadle have critically advised on those portions of the manuscript covering the mammalian data, and some of the anatomic, physiologic, neurophysiologic, and hormonal data presented in Chapters 14 to 18.

Among the many medically trained specialists who have helped, especial mention should be made of the several gynecologists who have contributed time, advice, and in many instances, specific data from their clinical experience. In this connection, we are especially indebted to: Dr. Robert L. Dickinson (now deceased), pioneer American student of human sexual problems, Dr. John O. Haman of San Francisco, Dr. Francis J. Hector of Bristol, England, Dr. Sophia Kleegman of New York City, Dr. Earle M. Marsh of San Francisco, Dr. Frances Shields of Monterey, California, and Dr. Abraham Stone of New York City.

Some hundreds of other specialists in other fields of medicine, biology, physiology, endocrinology, psychology, psychiatry, animal behavior, sociology, anthropology, statistics, literature, and the fine arts, have contributed important data and invaluable guidance on special aspects of our research. We trust that all who have so contributed will comprehend that we are deeply conscious of our obligation to them.

Dr. Jeannette Foster served as Librarian on this project for four years, and Dr. Hazel Toliver served for two years as Latin and Greek translator.

The wives and husbands of the several members of the staff deserve especial credit for the encouragement and support which they have contributed toward the pursuit of this research, and for their sharing of the burden imposed by the long hours of work which have gone into the preparation of the immediate volume.

Finally, we are indebted to the several thousand persons who have contributed to the case histories, the recorded data, the library, and the other resources of the Institute. We are indebted to several who, in addition to the chief sponsors of the research, have contributed toward the financial support of the general project, or of special aspects of the project. We are also indebted to the many thousands of those with whom we have had no direct contact, but who, in their expressed approval of a scientific study of human sexual behavior, have made it possible for us to undertake the exploration on which this volume has depended.

                                                    THE AUTHORS

Indiana University
Bloomington, Indiana

CONTENTS

PART III. COMPARISONS OF FEMALE AND MALE

LIST OF TABLES

PART I. HISTORY AND METHOD

PART II. TYPES OF SEXUAL ACTIVITY AMONG FEMALES

CHAPTER 6. NOCTURNAL SEX DREAMS

CHAPTER 9. MARITAL COITUS

LIST OF FIGURES

PART I. HISTORY AND METHOD

PART II. TYPES OF SEXUAL ACTIVITY AMONG FEMALES

PART III. COMPARISONS OF FEMALE AND MALE

CHAPTER 14. ANATOMY OF SEXUAL RESPONSE AND ORGASM

CHAPTER 15. PHYSIOLOGY OF SEXUAL RESPONSE AND ORGASM

CHAPTER 17. NEURAL MECHANISMS OF SEXUAL RESPONSE

Part I

HISTORY AND METHOD

Chapter 1

SCOPE OF THE STUDY

The present volume constitutes the second progress report from the study of human sex behavior which we have had under way here at Indiana University for some fifteen years. It has been a fact-finding survey in which an attempt has been made to discover what people do sexually, what factors may account for their patterns of sexual behavior, how their sexual experiences have affected their lives, and what social significance there may be in each type of behavior.

Our first report was based upon 5300 white males whose case histories provided most of the data which were statistically analyzed in our volume, Sexual Behavior in the Human Male.[1] The case histories of 5940 white females have similarly provided most of the statistical data in the present volume, but this volume also rests on a considerable body of material which has come from sources other than case histories (see Chapter 2).

Throughout the fifteen years involved in this research, it has had the support of Indiana University, and during the past twelve years it has been supported in part by grants from the National Research Council's Committee for Research in Problems of Sex. This Committee has been responsible for the administration of funds provided by the Medical Division of the Rockefeller Foundation. The present project is incorporated as the Institute for Sex Research. The Institute is the legal entity which holds title to the case histories, the library, and the other materials accumulated in connection with the research, receives all royalties from its publications, incomes from private contributions and other sources, and is responsible for the planning and administration of the research program. The staff of the Institute has included persons trained in biology, clinical psychology, anthropology, law, statistics, various language fields, and still other specialties. Sixteen persons have served on the staff of the Institute during the preparation of the present volume, and each of these has had a specific part in the making of this report.

We have also had the cooperation of a considerable group of specialists in various fields of medicine, biology, physiology, psychology,

---

[1] Kinsey, A. C., Pomeroy, W. B., and Martin, C. E., 1948. Sexual Behavior in the Human Male. Philadelphia and London, W. B. Saunders Co., xv+804 p.

psychiatry, statistics, animal behavior, neurophysiology, the social sciences, penology, marriage counseling, literature, the fine arts, and still other areas (see Chapter 2). Some of these consultants have contributed specific data which are included in the present volume, and a number of them have critically guided the interpretations of our findings in areas related to their specialties.

Our accumulation of female histories began with the inception of the research in July, 1938. Throughout the years, female histories have been added at approximately the same rate as the histories of males. It was possible, therefore, to utilize some female data in the preparation of our report on the male, and in the present volume we are now able to compare female and male data. In addition to the 5940 histories of the white females which are summarized in the present volume, we have the histories of 1849 additional females who, because they belong to special groups which we are not yet ready to analyze (pp. 22, 43), have not been included in the statistical analyses presented here. The records from these other females have, on the other hand, considerably extended our thinking, and provided bases for some of the more general statements in the present volume.

This is a study of sexual behavior in (*within*) certain groups of the human species, *Homo sapiens*.[2] It is obviously not a study of the sexual behavior of all cultures and of all races of man. At its best, the present volume can pretend to report behavior which may be typical of no more than a portion, although probably not an inconsiderable portion, of the white females living within the boundaries of the United States. Neither the title of our first volume on the male, nor the title of this volume on the female, should be taken to imply that the authors are unaware of the diversity which exists in patterns of sexual behavior in other parts of the world.

HISTORICAL BACKGROUND

The present study was undertaken because the senior author's students were bringing him, as a college teacher of biology, questions on matters of sex. They came to him because they hoped that he as a scientist would provide factual information which they might consider in working out their patterns of sexual behavior. Advice on the desirability or undesirability of particular patterns of sexual behavior

---

[2] This use of the preposition "in" is common throughout scientific writing, including studies in biology, physiology, psychology, medicine, public health, education, and sociology. There are studies on *Finger Sucking in Children, Sweating in Man, Blood Pressure Changes in Dogs, Academic Success in College Students, Superstition in the Pigeon.* For instance, typical pages of the Zoological Record may show three or four out of every ten English titles in this form. In volume 35 of the Journal of Genetics, twenty-five out of thirty-nine titles are in this form.

was available to them from a great many sources; they had found it more difficult to obtain strictly factual information which was not biased by moral, philosophic, or social interpretations.

In attempting to answer some of the questions which these students brought, we drew upon our general understanding of animal biology; but for a larger number of the answers we had to turn to the medical, psychologic, psychiatric, sociologic, and other literatures where one might have expected to find the desired data. In the course of this search, however, we discovered that scientific understanding of human sexual behavior was more poorly established than the understanding of almost any other function of the human body.

There seemed to be no sufficient studies of the basic anatomy or the physiology of sexual response and of orgasm. Both the biologists and the philosophers had confused reproductive function with sexual behavior, and had taken it for granted that the reproductive organs, and particularly the external reproductive organs (the genitalia), were the only parts of the anatomy that were involved with either of these functions. This was little better than the ancient belief which some persons still hold that sexual responses originate in the heart. There are others who locate the function "in the head," and believe that one may control his sexual responses if he sufficiently "puts his mind to the matter." In actuality, we now know (Chapters 14–17) that none of these structures —not even the external genitalia—are the organs which are chiefly concerned. Heretofore, in attempting to interpret sexual behavior, we have been as handicapped as one might be if he attempted to understand the processes of digestion before he knew anything of the anatomy of the digestive organs, or attempted to understand respiratory functions without realizing that the lungs and the circulatory system were involved.

Because of the limitations which are usually imposed on any consideration of sex, the scientist has been hesitant to investigate in this area. The average individual's understanding of these matters has had to be drawn largely from his or her own experience, from the desultory bits of information that could be obtained from a limited number of acquaintances, or from the increasing but still limited amount of information available in medical manuals. Even the clinician's understanding of the nature of human sexual behavior has had to depend primarily upon his own clinical experience, and no one has been certain how far the behavior of clinical patients may represent the behavior of the population as a whole. Psychologic and psychiatric interpretations have been based on specialized types of patients, and clinicians have usually been more concerned with alleviating their patients' immediate difficulties, or with redirecting their behavior, than they have with the systematic accumulation of complete sexual histories. The monumental work of Havelock Ellis and of Freud and of still others among the European pioneers did not involve a general survey of persons who did not have sexual problems which would lead them to professional sources for help.

There had been attempts to survey the behavior of non-clinical groups, beginning with Russian studies in the first decade of the present century, and with the studies made in this country prior to 1920 (see pp. 94–96). Case history studies of samples more typical of the general population had been undertaken by Katharine Davis, by Hamilton, by Dickinson, by Terman, and by Landis in the 1920's and 1930's. Some of these were excellent studies to which we shall always be indebted because they demonstrated the possibility as well as the desirability of securing sexual data by case history and interviewing techniques. But fifteen years ago the total number of individuals on which our knowledge of human sexual behavior was based was considerably less than the biologist would have considered necessary for an understanding of variation in any other species of animal. The published human material and our own initial exploration made it apparent that variation in human sexual behavior was greater than the variation which was to be observed in human anatomy or physiology; and it seemed apparent that any ultimate appreciation of sexual variation, and an understanding of the factors responsible for that variation, would have to come from extensive series of case histories drawn from diverse segments of the population.

During the past twenty years, there has been a considerable development of sampling theory and of statistical methods of analyzing population data. In consequence, studies in various fields of biology, medicine, economics, and the psychologic and social sciences have increasingly utilized statistical approaches. Persons interested in public health, public opinion, and market surveys have developed practical methods of obtaining extensive human samples (see the footnotes in Chapter 2). We have been able to utilize some of their experience. On the other hand, on the present project we have faced problems which are unique to a sex study (Chapter 2).

Because of the limited opportunities to observe sexual behavior, and because of our need to secure records of events which have taken place over long periods of years, we have had to depend primarily upon case history material for our data. But the information which we have tried to secure has concerned aspects of human behavior which most persons consider confidential and ordinarily do not discuss with' any except their most intimate friends. More than that, our openly expressed mores and the statute law (the overt culture) are so remote from the actual behavior (the covert culture) of the average citizen that there are few persons who can openly discuss their histories without risking social or legal difficulties. We have not, therefore, been able to utilize the statistically ideal techniques or the same procedures which have proved applicable in surveys dealing with material less intimate and less complex than human sexual behavior (see pp. 25–31, 58–64 for a discussion of the interviewing and sampling techniques which we have used).

But by guaranteeing the confidence of the record, and by abstaining from judgments or attempts to redirect the behavior of any of the subjects who have contributed to this study, we have so far been able to secure the histories of more than 16,000 persons who represent a diverse sample of many different groups. The sample has included both females and males, persons of all ages from the youngest to the oldest, persons with a variety of educational backgrounds, ranging from the illiterate and poorly educated to the best trained of the professional groups, persons belonging to a variety of occupational classes and rural and urban groups, persons belonging to various religious groups, persons representing various degrees of adherence and non-adherence to those religious groups, and persons who have lived in various parts of the United States. The sample is still, at many points, inadequate, but we have been able to secure a greater diversification of subjects than had been available in the previous studies.

THE SCIENTIFIC OBJECTIVE

It should be clearly understood that the original goal of our study was the extension of our knowledge in an area in which scientific information appeared to be limited. In the course of the years it has become apparent that the data we have acquired may prove of value in the consideration of some of our social problems, but that was not why we originally began this research.

It has been the history of science that any addition to our store of adequately established knowledge may ultimately contribute to man's mastery of the material universe. Not infrequently some of the most useful findings have come out of investigations that seemed to have no practical application when they were first begun.

On the other hand, when research has been confined to the solution of immediate problems, the investigator has not infrequently been so limited by the demands for immediate application that he has had no time to explore the basic elements of his problem. In the field of human sexual behavior, for instance, there have been direct attacks on the problems of sexual adjustment in marriage, but these have not proved as fruitful as they might have been because no one sufficiently understood the basic physiology of sexual response, or the basic psychologic differences between female and male responsiveness (Chapters 14–16). As another illustration, we have recently seen poorly established distinctions between normality and abnormality lead to the enactment of sexual psychopath laws which are unrealistic, unenforceable, and incapable of providing the protection which the social organization has been led to believe they can provide. There cannot be sound clinical practice, or sound planning of sex laws, until we understand more adequately the mammalian origins of human sexual behavior, the anatomy and physiology of response, the sexual patterns of human cultures outside of our own, and the factors which shape the behavioral patterns of children and of adolescent youth. We cannot reach ultimate solutions for our problems until legislators and public opinion allow the investigator sufficient time to discover the bases of those problems.

Some scientists hesitate to continue in a given field of research as soon as its application becomes apparent. This refusal to apply knowledge when it exists seems to us, however, to be as unrealistic as the attempt to apply knowledge before it exists. Consequently, as it became apparent that the data which we were accumulating in the present study might contribute to an understanding of some of our human problems, we have welcomed the opportunity to direct our survey into those areas. But such applications were not our original objectives, and we have not let the importance of any immediate application delimit the areas which we undertook to investigate.

THE RIGHT TO INVESTIGATE

With the right of the scientist to investigate most aspects of the material universe, most persons will agree; but there are some who have questioned the applicability of scientific methods to an investigation of human sexual behavior. Some persons, recognizing the importance of the psychologic aspects of that behavior, and the relation of the individual's sexual activity to the social organization as a whole, feel that this is an area which only psychologists or social philosophers should explore. In this insistence they seem to ignore the material origins of all behavior. It is as though the dietician and biochemist were denied the right to analyze foods and the processes of nutrition, because the cooking and proper serving of food may be rated a fine art, and because the eating of certain foods has been considered a matter for religious regulation.

Such protest at the scientific invasion of a field which has hitherto been considered the province of moral philosophers is nothing new in the history of science. There was a day when the organization of the universe, and the place of the earth, the sun, the moon, and the stars in it, were considered of such theologic import that the scientific investigation of those matters was bitterly opposed by the ruling forces of the day. The scientists who first attempted to explore the nature of matter, and the physical laws affecting the relationships of matter, were similarly condemned. The works of Kepler, Copernicus, Galileo, and Pascal were in the list of condemned books some two or three centuries ago. Within the past half century, biologists who attempted to investigate the processes by which offspring came to differ from their parents, and the processes by which whole populations of individuals or species came to differ from other species, were condemned because they had attempted to substitute scientific observation for the philosophic interpretations which had hitherto satisfied human vanity.

There is an honesty in science which demands that the best means be used for the determination of truth. Certainly there are many sorts of truth in the universe, and many aspects of truth must be taken into account if man is to live most effectively in the social organization to which he belongs. But in regard to matter—the stuff of which both non-living materials and living organisms are made—scientists believe that there is no better way of obtaining information than that provided by human sense organs. No theory, no philosophy, no body of theology, no political expediency, no wishful thinking, can provide a satisfactory substitute for the observation of material objects and of the way in which they behave. Whether the observations are made directly through one's sense organs, or indirectly through some instrument such as a telescope or a microscope, or whether the information is acquired, as in much of our present study, from the reports of the participants who were the observers of their own sexual activity, observation provides the information which the scientist most respects when material phenomena are involved.

There is an honesty in science which refuses to accept the idea that there are aspects of the material universe that are better not investigated, or better not known, or the knowledge of which should not be made available to the common man. There are, for instance, in this age, those who believe that it would have been better if we had never learned what we now know concerning atomic structure. One might be led to believe that there was something unique in the situation which atomic research has produced. But the history of science records that similar objections were raised as each new revolutionary discovery was made. It is, moreover, the record of science that greater knowledge, as it has become available, has increased man's capacity to live happily with himself and with his fellow men. We do not believe that the happiness of individual men, and the good of the total social organization, is ever furthered by the perpetuation of ignorance.

There is an honesty in science which leads to a certain acceptance of the reality. There are some who, finding the ocean an impediment to the pursuit of their designs, try to ignore its existence. If they are unable to ignore it because of its size, they try to legislate it out of existence, or try to dry it up with a sponge. They insist that the latter operation would be possible if enough sponges were available, and if enough persons would wield them.

There is no ocean of greater magnitude than the sexual function, and there are those who believe that we would do better if we ignored its existence, that we should not try to understand its material origins, and that if we sufficiently ignore it and mop at the flood of sexual activity with new laws, heavier penalties, more pronouncements, and greater intolerances, we may ultimately eliminate the reality. The scientist who observes and describes the reality is attacked as an enemy of the faith, and his acceptance of human limitations in modifying that reality is condemned as scientific materialism. But we believe that an increased understanding of the biologic and psychologic and social factors which account for each type of sexual activity may contribute to an ultimate adjustment between man's sexual nature and the needs of the total social organization.

THE INDIVIDUAL'S RIGHT TO KNOW

The right of the scientist to investigate is akin to the academic freedom which our American standards demand for scholars in every field, and not too remote from the freedom of speech which we have come to believe constitutes one of the foundation stones of our American way of living. Each of these privileges, however, carries with it an obligation—an obligation, in the case of the scientist, to investigate honestly, to observe and to record without prejudice, to observe as adequately as human sense organs or the most modern instruments may allow, to observe persistently and sufficiently in order that there may be an ultimate understanding of the basic nature of the matter which is involved. These are the obligations which the scientist assumes when he contracts with society for the right to investigate.

But there is another obligation which is also implicit in the contract between a scientist and the social organization which supports, protects, and encourages his research. We believe that the scientist who obtains his right to investigate from the citizens at large, is under obligation to make his findings available to all who can utilize his data. Any scientist who fails to report or to place his findings in channels where they may serve the maximum number of persons, fails to recognize the sources of his right to investigate and thereby jeopardizes the rights of all scientists to investigate in any field.

The scientist who investigates sexual behavior seems under especial obligation to make his findings available to the maximum number of persons, for there are few aspects of human biology with which more persons are more often concerned. Most men and women and adolescent children, and even pre-adolescent children in their youngest years, face, at times, problems which some greater knowledge of sex would help solve. As in other areas of science, the restriction of sexual knowledge to a limited number of professionally trained persons, to physicians, to priests, or to those who can read Latin, has not sufficiently served the millions of boys and girls, men and women who need such knowledge to guide them in their everyday affairs. It is for this reason, we believe, that some thousands of average American citizens have actively cooperated in the present research. It is for this reason, we believe, that our first volume, distributed by a medical publisher and described by a portion of the press as a dry and dull tome weighed down with forbidding statistical tables and charts, was taken out of the hands of those who claimed the exclusive right to knowledge in this area and made a part of the thinking of millions of persons, not only in this country but in countries spread all over the world. We believe that if we have any right to investigate in this field, we are under obligation to make the results of our investigations available to all who can read and understand and utilize our data.

PROBLEMS OF MARITAL ADJUSTMENT

As a specific instance of the need of the public at large, there is the problem of sexual adjustment in marriage. There are few married persons who have not, at least on occasion, recognized a serious need for additional information to meet some of the sexual problems which arise in their marriages. On the solution of these problems the stability of a marriage may sometimes depend, although we have previously said, and reassert in the present volume, that we do not believe that sexual factors are the elements which most often determine the fate of a marriage.

We have also said that there seems to be no single factor which is more important for the maintenance of a marriage than the determination, the will that that marriage shall be maintained. Where there is that determination, differences between the spouses may be overlooked or forgotten and minor disturbances may be viewed in a perspective which emphasizes the importance of maintaining the marital union. Where there is no such will, trivial and minor disturbances may grow until they appear important enough to warrant the dissolution of a marriage (Chapter 9).

But sexual factors are *among* those that may contribute to the happiness or the unhappiness, the maintenance or the dissolution of homes and marriages. Where there are common sexual interests, or some common understanding of each other's sexual interests, two persons who are married may be brought together at an emotional level which transcends that to be found in any other type of human contact. Where mutually satisfactory sexual relationships are regularly available, the spouses in a marriage may find the humdrum routines of a home less irritating, and may accept them in their stride.

But where the sexual relationships are not equally satisfactory to both of the partners in the marriage, disagreement and angry rebellion may invade not only the marital bed, but all other aspects of the marriage. Our data suggest that there may be as many as two-thirds of the marriages which, at least on occasion in the course of the years, run into serious disagreement over sexual relationships. In a considerable number, there is constant disagreement over sexual relationships. In perhaps three-quarters of the divorces recorded in our case histories, sexual factors were among those which had led to the divorce.

In nearly all societies, everywhere in the world, marriage and the maintenance of the home have been considered matters of major importance to the social organization as a whole. In the past half century, both in Europe and in this country, many persons, including pastors, teachers, physicians, and other clinicians dealing with human problems, have come to realize that improved sexual relationships might contribute to the improvement of our modern marriages.

But clinical advice has sometimes exceeded our scientifically established knowledge. It has been difficult to interpret the problems which are involved when we have not understood how nearly alike females and males may be in their sexual responses, and the extent to which they may differ. We have perpetuated the age-old traditions concerning the slower responsiveness of the female, the greater extent of the erogenous areas on the body of the female, the earlier sexual development of the female, the idea that there are basic differences in the nature of orgasm among females and males, the greater emotional content of the female's sexual response, and still other ideas which are not based on scientifically accumulated data—and all of which now appear to be incorrect (Chapters 14–18). It now appears that the very techniques which have been suggested in marriage manuals, both ancient and modern, have given rise to some of the differences that we have thought were inherent in females and males (p. 376). If we had undertaken, as an initial project in our study of human sexual behavior, to deal with the immediate problems of sexual adjustment in marriage, we might have been as inclined as others have been to accept the traditional interpretations of the nature of sexual response. But because we have spent these many years in accumulating information on all aspects of sexual behavior, it has now become possible to identify what seem to be the basic sources of some of these difficulties that arise during sexual relationships in marriage (Chapters 9, 14–16).

There are some who have feared that a scientific approach to the problems of sex might threaten the existence of the marital institution. There are some who advocate the perpetuation of our ignorance because they fear that science will undermine the mystical concepts that they have substituted for reality. But there appear to be more persons who believe that an extension of our knowledge may contribute to the establishment of better marriages.

SEXUAL PROBLEMS OF UNMARRIED YOUTH

As another instance of the everyday need for a wider general understanding of human sexual behavior, there are the sexual problems of unmarried individuals in our social organization, and particularly of unmarried youth. The problems are products of the fact that the human female and male become biologically adults some years before our social custom and the statute law recognize them as such, and of the fact that our culture has increasingly insisted that sexual functions should be confined to persons who are legally recognized as adults, and particularly to married adults.

This failure to recognize the mature capacities of teen-age youth is relatively recent. Prior to the last century or so, it was well understood that they were the ones who had the maximum sexual capacity, and the great romances of literature turned around the love affairs of teen-age boys and girls. Achilles' intrigue with Deidamia, by whom a son was born, had occurred some time before he was fifteen. Acis had just passed sixteen at the time of his love affair with Galatea. Chione was reputed to have had "a thousand suitors when she reached the marriageable age of fourteen." Narcissus had reached his sixteenth year when "many youths and many maidens sought his love." Helen was twelve years old when Theseus carried her off from Sparta. In one of the greatest of pastoral romances, Daphnis was fifteen and Chloe was thirteen. Heloise was eighteen when she fell in love with Abelard. Tristram was nineteen when he first met Isolde. Juliet was less than fourteen when Romeo made love to her. All of these youth, the great lovers of history, would be looked upon as immature adolescents and identified as juvenile delinquents if they were living today. It is the increasing inability of older persons to understand the sexual capacities of youth which is responsible for the opinion that there is a rise in juvenile delinquency, for there are few changes in the sexual behavior of the youth themselves.

There is an increasing opinion that these youths should ignore their sexual responses and should abstain from sexual activities prior to marriage—which means, for the average male and female in this country today, until they are somewhere between twenty-one and twenty-three years of age. But neither the law nor the custom can change the age of onset of adolescence, nor the development of the sexual capacities of teen-age youths. Consequently they continue to be aroused sexually, and to respond to the point of orgasm. There is no evidence that it is possible for any male who is adolescent, and not physically incapacitated, to get along without some kind of regular outlet until old age finally reduces his responsiveness and his capacity to function sexually.[3] While there are many females who appear to get along without such an outlet during their teens, the chances that a female can adjust sexually after marriage seem to be materially improved if she has experienced orgasm at an earlier age (pp. 385–391).

In actuality, the teen-age and twenty-year-old males respond more frequently than most older males; their responses are, on the whole, more intense than those of older males; and, in spite of their difficulty in finding socio-sexual outlets, they reach orgasm more frequently than most older males. Among unmarried males the frequency of orgasm is at a maximum somewhere between the ages of sixteen and eighteen. Similarly, among married males there is no age group in which sexual activity is, on an average, more frequent than it is among the males in their late teens and early twenties.[3]

The attempt to ignore and suppress the physiologic needs of the sexually most capable segment of the population has led to more complications than most persons are willing to recognize. This is why so many of our American youth, both females and males, depend upon masturbation instead of coitus as a pre-marital outlet. Restraints on pre-marital heterosexual contacts appear to be primary factors in the development of homosexual activities among both females and males (pp. 460, 465). The considerable development of pre-marital petting, which many foreigners consider one of the unique aspects of the sexual pattern in this country, is similarly an outgrowth of this restraint on pre-marital coitus (pp. 227–228). The law specifies the right of the married adult to have regular intercourse, but it makes no provision

---

[3] Kinsey, Pomeroy, and Martin, 1948: 218–262.

whatsoever for the approximately 40 per cent of the population which is sexually mature but unmarried. Many youths and older unmarried females and males are seriously disturbed because the only sources of sexual outlet available to them are either legally or socially disapproved.

Most unmarried males, and not a few of the unmarried females, would like to know how to resolve this conflict between their physiologic capacities and the legal and social codes. They would like to know whether masturbation will harm them physically or interfere with their subsequent responses to a marital partner; they would like to know whether they should or should not engage in petting; and, apart from the moral issues that may be involved, they would like to know what pre-marital petting experience may actually do to their marital adjustments. Should they or should they not have coitus before marriage? What effect will this sort of experience have on their subsequent marital adjustments? In any type of sexual activity, what things are normal and what things are abnormal? What has been the experience of other youth faced with these same problems? On all of these matters most youth are ready to consider the social and moral values, but they would also like to know what correlations the scientific data show between pre-marital and marital experience.

In an attempt to answer some of these questions, we have tried to discover the incidences and frequencies of non-marital activities among American females and males, and have attempted to discover what correlations there may be between pre-marital patterns of behavior and subsequent sexual adjustments in marriage (Chapters 5–9).

SEXUAL EDUCATION OF CHILDREN

Within the last thirty years, parents in increasing number have come to realize the importance of the early education of their children on matters of sex. But what things children should be taught, who should teach them, at what age they should be taught, and how the teaching should be conducted, are matters about which there has been much theory but few data on which to base any program of sex education. For some years we have, therefore, obtained information from our subjects in regard to the ages at which they acquired their first knowledge of various aspects of sex, the sources of their first knowledge, and the ages at which they first became involved in each type of sexual activity. In addition to obtaining this record from each adult, we have engaged in a more detailed study of younger children and particularly of children between two and five years of age. The study needs to be carried further before we are ready to report in detail, but some things already seem clear.

It is apparent that considerable factual knowledge about most sexual phenomena is acquired by most children before they become adolescent, but there is a considerable number who acquire their first information in their youngest years, as soon as they are able to talk. Although some persons insist that the sex education of the child should be undertaken only by the child's parents or religious mentors, not more than a few percent—perhaps not more than 5 per cent—of all the subjects in the present study recalled that they had received anything more than the most incidental sort of information from either of those sources. Most of the children had acquired their earliest information from other children. Whether it is more desirable, in terms of the ultimate effects upon their lives, that such information should come first from more experienced adults, or whether it is better that children should learn about sex from other children, is a question which we are not yet able to answer. At this stage in our study we are quite certain that no one has any sufficient information to evaluate objectively the relative merits of these diverse sources of sexual education.

It is apparent, however, that if parents or other adults are to be the sources of the child's first information on sex, they must give that information by the time the child is ten or twelve, and in many instances at some earlier age. Otherwise the child, whatever the parents may wish, will have previously acquired the information from its companions.

Our studies indicate, moreover, that the way in which a child reacts to the sexual information which it receives, and to the overt sexual activity in which it may become involved in later years, may depend upon attitudes which it develops while it is very young. Early attitudes in respect to nudity, to anatomic differences between the sexes, to the reproductive function, to verbal references to sex, to the qualities and prerequisites which our culture traditionally considers characteristic of females or males, and to still other aspects of sex are developed at very early ages. Emotional reactions on some of these matters have been discernible in some of the two-year-olds with which we have worked, and the three-year-old children have had pronounced reactions on most of these matters. When the child becomes older these early attitudes may influence its reactions to sexual manifestations in its own body, its capacity to meet sexual situations without serious disturbance, its acceptance or non-acceptance of socio-sexual contacts, and, as an adult, his or her capacity to adjust sexually in marriage. Because early training may be so significant, most parents would like to have information on the most effective methods of introducing the child to the realities of sex.

Most parents would like to know more about the significance of pre-adolescent sex play, about the sexual activities in which children actually engage, about the possibilities of their children becoming sexually involved with adults, and what effect such involvements may have upon a child's subsequent sexual adjustments. Most parents would like to know whether the sexual responses of a child are similar, physiologically, to those of an adult. They would like to know whether there are differences between the sexual problems of adolescent boys and those of adolescent girls; and if there are differences, they would like to know on what they depend. The data in the present volume will answer some of these questions.

In this study, we have had the excellent cooperation of a great many parents because they are concerned with the training of their children, and because they realize how few data there are on which to establish a sound program of sex education.

SOCIAL CONTROL OF SEXUAL BEHAVIOR

Most societies have recognized the necessity of protecting their members from those who impose sexual relationships on others by the use of force, and our own culture extends the same sort of restriction to those who use such intimidation as an adult may exercise over a child, or such undue influence as a social superior may exercise over an underling. In its encouragement of marriage society tries to provide a socially acceptable source of sexual outlet, and it considers that sexual activities which interfere with marriages and homes, and sexual activities which lead to the begetting of children outside of marriage, are socially undesirable. The social organization also tries to control persons who make nuisances of themselves, as the exhibitionist and voyeur may do, by departing from the generally approved custom. In addition our culture considers that social interests are involved when an individual departs from the Judeo-Christian sex codes by engaging in such sexual activities as masturbation, mouth-genital contacts, homosexual contacts, animal contacts, and other types of behavior which do not satisfy the procreative function of sex.

The Incidence of Sex Offenses. Within the last decade, there has been a growing concern in this country over an apparent increase in the number of persons who engage in sexual activities which are contrary to our law and custom. Reports in the press and the information which is officially released often suggest that the number of sex offenders is steadily increasing.

Unfortunately, however, there has been no good measure of the actual extent of the problem that is involved. The conclusion that the incidences of sex offense have increased is based primarily upon an increase in the number of arrests on sex charges, but it is not substantiated by our information on the incidences of various types of sexual activity among older and younger generations in the population as a whole. Statements concerning increasing incidences usually do not allow for the considerable increase in the total population of the country, the more complete reporting of sex crimes by the press and by the agencies which contribute to the official statistics, and the fact that the newer sex laws make felonies of some acts which were never penalized or which were treated as minor misdemeanors until a few years ago. Moreover, there has been no adequate recognition of the fact that fluctuations in the number of arrests may represent nothing more than fluctuations in the activities of law enforcement officers.

Preliminary analyses of our data indicate that only a minute fraction of one per cent of the persons who are involved in sexual behavior which is contrary to the law are ever apprehended, prosecuted, or convicted, and that there are many other factors besides the behavior of the apprehended individual which are responsible for the prosecution of the particular persons who are brought to court. The prodding of some reform group, a newspaper-generated hysteria over some local sex crime, a vice drive which is put on by the local authorities to distract attention from defects in their administration of the city government, or the addition to the law-enforcement group of a sadistic officer who is disturbed over his own sexual problems, may result in a doubling—a hundred percent increase—in the number of arrests on sex charges, even though there may have been no change in the actual behavior of the community, and even though the illicit sex acts that are apprehended and prosecuted may still represent no more than a fantastically minute part of the illicit activity which takes place every day in the community.

The Sex Offender. A primary fault in most studies of sex offenders is the fact that they are confined to the study of sex offenders. Just as the laboratory scientist needs a control group to interpret what he finds in his experimental animals, so we need to understand the sexual behavior of persons who have never been involved with the law.

Psychologists, psychiatrists, sociologists, and criminologists have given us some understanding of the personalities of criminals, including some sex offenders, but the studies have rarely compared convicted individuals with persons involved in similar behavior in the population at large. It does not suffice to find that sex offenders were breast fed, or bottle fed, without knowing how many other persons who were similarly fed did not become sex offenders. It does not suffice to discover that sex offenders come from disrupted homes without learning why so many other persons who come from similarly disrupted homes

do not end up as sex offenders. It does not suffice to find that the homosexual offenders preferred their mothers to their fathers, when a survey
of non-offenders shows that most children, for perfectly obvious reasons, are more closely associated with their mothers. We need to know
why certain individuals, rather than all of those who engage in similar
behavior, become involved with the law. We need to learn more about
the circumstances of the particular activities which led to their apprehension, and about the way they were handled by the arresting police
officer, the prosecutor, the court-attached psychiatrist, the judge, and
the local press.

In the course of this present study we have secured the histories of
some thirteen hundred persons who have been convicted and sentenced to penal institutions as sex offenders, but these histories would
be difficult to interpret if we had not gathered the histories of more
than fourteen thousand persons who have never been involved with
the law.[4]

We have been in a peculiarly favorable position to secure data from
persons serving time in penal institutions as sex offenders. We have
been able to guarantee the confidence of the record as no law enforcement officer, no clinician connected with the courts, and no institutional officer could guarantee. From coast to coast, the grapevine has
spread the word that we have not violated the confidences which we
have recorded in our histories, and that we have always refused to
work in any institution in which the administration has not agreed to
uphold our right to preserve such confidences. In addition to the information which we have secured directly from the prisoners, we have
had access to the institutional files on each inmate, and in many instances we have had access to the court records, the probation records,
and the records from the departments of public welfare or other agencies which had had contact with these cases.

Throughout our research, whether with persons who have been
convicted as sex offenders or with our subjects in the population at
large, we have tried to make it apparent that we wanted to understand
their activities as they understood them. Consequently we have not
found sex offenders prone to deny their guilt, or to rationalize their
behavior. In actuality, most of them have given us a record of activity
that far exceeded anything that had been brought out in the legal
proceedings or in the records of the penal institution.

Effective Sex Law. Out of this study of sex offenders, and of the
sexual behavior of females and males who have never been involved

---

[4] For a further description of the study we are making on sex offenders, see pages
93–94.

with the law, should come data which may some day be used by legislators in the development of a body of sex law that may provide society with more adequate protection against the more serious types of sex offenders. While we shall need to continue this part of our study before we are ready to summarize the data which we have been gathering, our present information seems to make it clear that the current sex laws are unenforced and are unenforceable because they are too completely out of accord with the realities of human behavior, and because they attempt too much in the way of social control. Such a high proportion of the females and males in our population is involved in sexual activities which are prohibited by the law of most of the states of the union, that it is inconceivable that the present laws could be administered in any fashion that even remotely approached systematic and complete enforcement (see pp. 261–263 in the present volume; and see the data in our volume on the male). The consequently capricious enforcement which these laws now receive offers an opportunity for mal-administration, for police and political graft, and for blackmail which is regularly imposed both by underworld groups and by the police themselves.

The Protection of the Individual. Many people, perhaps fortunately, have no conception that their everyday sexual activities may, in actuality, be contrary to the law. On the other hand, many other persons live in constant fear that certain of their sexual activities, even though they are typical of those which occur in the histories of most females and males, may be discovered and lead to social or possibly legal difficulties. In its attempt to protect itself from serious sex offenders, society has threatened the security of most of its members who are old enough to perform sexually. The efficiency of many individuals and their integration into the social organization is, thereby, seriously impaired. While this is especially true of persons with histories of extra-marital coitus, with homosexual histories, and with histories of animal contacts on the farm, it is also true of some persons who have pre-marital coitus, of many of those who engage in mouth-genital contacts, and even of some of those who engage in pre-marital petting. Because of the social taboos there are many individuals who, even in this generation, are disturbed over their masturbatory histories.

In many instances the law, in the course of punishing the offender, does more damage to more persons than was ever done by the individual in his illicit sexual activity. The histories which we have accumulated contain many such instances. The intoxicated male who accidentally exposes his genitalia before a child, may receive a prison sentence which leaves his family destitute for some period of years, breaks up his marriage, and leaves three or four children wards of the state and without the sort of guidance which the parents might well have supplied. The older, unmarried women who prosecute the male whom they find swimming nude, may ruin his business or professional career, bring his marriage to divorce, and do such damage to his children as the observation of his nudity could never have done to the woman who prosecuted him. The child who has been raised in fear of all strangers and all physical manifestations of affection, may ruin the lives of the married couple who had lived as useful and honorable citizens through half or more of a century, by giving her parents and the police a distorted version of the old man's attempt to bestow grandfatherly affection upon her.

The male who is convicted because he has made homosexual advances to other males, may be penalized by being sent to an institution where anywhere from half to three-quarters of the inmates are regularly having homosexual activity within the institution. The laws penalizing homosexual approaches as well as homosexual activities, and which offer the possibility in some states of an individual being incarcerated for life because he "shows homosexual tendencies," have developed a breed of teen-age law-breakers who first seek satisfaction in sexual contacts with these males, and then blackmail and assault and murder, if necessary, and escape legal punishment on the specious plea that they were protecting themselves from "indecent sexual advances." Still more serious is the utilization of the same sort of blackmail and physical assault by the police in many of our larger cities. The pre-adolescent boy who is convicted of some offense may be sent to a juvenile institution where he turns adolescent and reaches the peak of his sexual capacity in a community which is exclusively male, and where he can find no socio-sexual outlet except with other males. If kept in such an institution until he reaches his middle teens, he may find it difficult to make social and socio-sexual adjustments with girls when he gets out of the institution, and may continue his homosexual activities for the rest of his life. Then he may be penalized for being what society has made him.

Somehow, in an age which calls itself scientific and Christian, we should be able to discover more intelligent ways of protecting social interests without doing such irreparable damage to so many individuals and to the total social organization to which they belong.

We began our research, as we have said, for the sake of increasing knowledge in an area in which knowledge was limited. We have continued the research through these years, in part because we have come to understand that the total social organization, and many individuals in it, may benefit by an increase in our understanding of human sexual behavior.

Chapter 2

THE SAMPLE AND ITS STATISTICAL ANALYSIS

The present volume is based on reported, recorded, and observed data which we have accumulated in the course of the last fifteen years. As in our previous volume on the male, the reported data have been derived from case histories secured in personal interviews. The recorded data have included sexual calendars, diaries, personal correspondence, scrapbook and photographic collections, artists' paintings and drawings, and still other documentary material supplied by a series of our subjects (Chapter 3). Observations of sexual behavior in fourteen species of mammals, and clinical material supplied by a long list of medical consultants, have been the chief sources of the observed data (Chapter 3).

Over the course of the past fifteen years, 16,392 persons have contributed their histories to this study. To date, we have secured the histories of 7789 females and of 8603 males. Our more general information and thinking on female sexual behavior are based on this entire body of material, even though the statistical analyses have been restricted to a portion of the female sample. Because the sexual histories which we have of white females who had served prison sentences (915 cases) prove, upon analysis, to differ as a group from the histories of the females who have not become involved with the law, their inclusion in the present volume would have seriously distorted the calculations on the total sample. Neither has the non-white sample (934 cases) of females been included in the calculations, primarily because that sample is not large enough to warrant comparisons of the subgroups in it. The statistical analyses in the present volume have, therefore, been based on our 5940 cases of white, non-prison females. In order to standardize the statistical calculations, histories acquired since January 1, 1950, have not been used.

The 5940 females whose histories are statistically analyzed in the present volume represent something of the great diversity which exists among American females. Certain groups are well represented in the sample, and the conclusions based upon the data which we have obtained from those groups may, with some warrant, be extended to the comparable portions of the total American population. Certain other groups are not so well represented in the sample, and we can make no prediction at the present time as to the behavior of those portions of the population. A description of the sample which has been used in making the present volume, some discussion of the problems of sampling in general, and a discussion of some of the specific problems that have been involved in securing a sample for this study of human sexual behavior, are among the subjects contained in the present chapter.

PROBLEMS OF SAMPLING

Functions of a Sample. It should be emphasized that most of our everyday generalizations concerning matters which pertain to more than a limited number of individuals or specific circumstances are based upon some sort of sampling, since it is usually impossible to measure each and every individual in any large group before one attempts to generalize concerning the characteristics of the group. Everyday experience has taught all of us that an acquaintance with a smaller number of individuals may, within limits, give us a practical understanding of the larger group.

The ideas which most persons have concerning the sexual attitudes and behavior of the population as a whole are, for the most part, based upon their own personal experience, on fragmentary information picked up from contact with a relatively small number of friends, on newspaper and magazine reports, or on more general gossip. Our everyday knowledge of the capacities of the utensils and tools that we use, our likes and dislikes for particular kinds of food, the confidence or fear with which we cross a street in the face of moving traffic, our evaluations of our acquaintances and friends, and most of the other generalizations by which we live, are based upon a limited number of experiences which, nevertheless, most persons consider sufficient to warrant the generalizations which they draw.

Probability Sampling. The problem of securing a sample that may adequately represent the larger population from which it is drawn, has long been recognized. Innumerable systems have been devised for the selection of the individual elements that go into a sample, ranging from the casting of lots, the shaking up of slips of paper in a hat, the shuffling of a deck of cards, the tossing of coins, and the use of a roulette wheel, to the most refined methods of modern probability sampling. The basic concept of a probability sample involves the development of some method of selection which allows each individual in the population a known chance of being selected as a part of the sample, without the introduction of a bias which might lead to the inclusion of particular types of individuals more frequently than they occur, proportionately, in the population as a whole. Various modifications of simple, unrestricted sampling, such as stratified and still other types of sampling, are frequently employed without, however, changing the basic concept that lies back of all probability sampling.[1]

The selection of a probability sample usually begins with a listing of all the units, such as the dwelling units, the city blocks or the other sections of a city, the rural townships, the institutions, or the other units which make up the total area or universe which is the object of the study. Sometimes a published census or a city map or directory or some previous survey may provide the necessary information; sometimes a preliminary survey must be made by the investigators themselves. On the basis of the preliminary census, certain of the units are then selected by some mathematically controlled system of randomization, and the selected units are then intensively studied, or individuals from each of the selected units are chosen, again by an impersonal and mathematically objective process, for special study. After the selection of the sample, the problem becomes one of locating the chosen individuals and persuading them to cooperate. If the survey involves more than a few questions, there is the problem of persuading the interviewee to give sufficient time to the interviewer; and if the material covered by the survey has any considerable emotional significance, as in a study of sexual behavior, the interviewer's success will also depend upon his skill in getting the subject to frankly, fully, and freely contribute the desired information.

Properly selected, a probability sample should include its proper proportion of each type of individual in the population which is being studied. In a sex study, it should include proper proportions of persons with high levels of sexual activity, persons with low levels of activity, persons whose histories involve only the usual (the predominant) types of behavior, and persons whose histories include the less common types of behavior. The probability that each type of variant in the population will be proportionately represented in the sample will depend, to some extent, upon the size of the sample; and by increasing the size of the sample, the investigator may control the level of approximation which the sample may afford—provided, of course, that the selection of the individuals continues to be on a random basis.

With a probability sample, it should be possible to determine, mathematically, the probable limits of error which would be involved in extending generalizations from the sample to the total population from which it is drawn. This is a matter of very considerable importance, and the one which is primarily responsible for the increasing use of probability samples in government surveys—including the current

---

[1] For general discussions of sampling methods, see such statistical texts and articles as the following: U. S. Bureau of the Census 1947. Yates 1949. Deming 1950. Lorie and Roberts 1951. Cochran 1953.

population studies of the Bureau of the Census, many of the studies of
the U. S. Public Health Service, the Bureau of Labor Statistics, the
Department of Agriculture—, in some of the state surveys being conducted under university agencies, in some business surveys, and in an
increasing number of scientific research studies.[2] The predictive value
of a probability sample is of such importance that whenever its use is
feasible, and whenever the cost of such sampling is commensurate with
the function it may serve, there is good reason for using it in any statistical survey. Nevertheless, we have deliberately chosen not to use a
probability sample in the present study of human sexual behavior.

Probability Sampling in a Sex Study. Our first and most decisive
reason for not doing probability sampling on the present project has
been the necessity for obtaining cooperation from the individuals who
have served as the subjects for the study. It has been necessary to convince each individual to give the time necessary for the interview, and
to agree to answer questions on matters which many persons have
never discussed with anyone, even including their spouses and their
most intimate friends. We have asked for a record that was as frank
and full and honest as memory would allow.

The problem has been very different from the problem that is involved in random sampling which is done to determine, for example,
the incidences of an insect pest in a wheat field, or to determine the
occurrence of some physical phenomenon in a group of inanimate objects. It should be obvious that a considerable proportion of the persons
selected for study by the objective and impersonal processes of random
sampling, and confronted by an investigator of whom they had never
heard, would simply refuse to give information on as personal and
emotional a subject as sex. Even in surveys which have been concerned
with economic, social, or political issues, the refusal rates have often

---

[2] Probability sampling has been used, for instance, in the following, among other
surveys: Federal Reserve Bulletin 1946–1953 (annual surveys of consumer
finances). Dinerman 1949 (election predictions Elmira, N. Y.). Public Opinion
and Sociological Research Division, SCAP, 1950:452–453 (attitudes toward
foreign countries and questions on international affairs, Japan). Deming 1950:
372–398 (population study for Greek government). Washington Public Opinion Laboratory 1950 (attitudes on marriage and divorce, state of Washington). Belknap and Campbell 1951 (preferred presidential candidate, religion,
income, attitudes on sending troops to Korea, national sample). Crespi 1951
(German view of U. S. reorientation program). Crossley and Fink 1951 (satisfaction with living in Denver). Maccoby 1951 (television, its impact on school
children, in Cambridge, Mass.). Radvanyi 1951 (economic and cultural characteristics of rural population of Santiago Valley, Nayarit, Mexico). Hemphill
1952 (home injuries in Washtenaw Co., Mich.). Horvitz 1952 (Pittsburgh
morbidity survey). See also surveys by U. S. Bureau of Labor Statistics published in various Department of Labor bulletins, for example Nos. 956 (1949)
on family income, and 1065 (1952) on expenditures and savings. Examples
of other probability surveys may be found in the Journal of the American
Statistical Association and in the journal, Population Studies.

been high enough to cast doubt on the validity of the results.[3] Our experience leads us to predict that the attempt to secure sex histories from lone individuals who were not part of some group with which we were working, would have resulted in refusal rates so high that the sample would have been quite worthless.

Moreover, even among the persons who might have agreed to answer some of the questions, it is certain that many would not have given as full and complete information as we have been able to secure through winning the confidence of the community with which we were working, and then establishing rapport with each individual subject in the community (pp. 28–31, 58–64).

In this, as in many other studies of human populations, the requirements of accurate reporting and accurate sampling are to some extent antagonistic. Somehow one must decide upon a compromise between the two. We have desired neither a representative sample of unreliable answers, nor a set of reliable answers from respondents who represented nobody but themselves. For this reason we have been compelled to substitute for probability sampling a method of group sampling through which we have tried to secure representatives of each of the components of the larger population in which we were interested.

Our second chief reason for choosing to work with social units rather than with a sample chosen on a probability basis, has been the near impossibility of defining groups which could be sampled by some probability scheme. Since patterns of sexual behavior may be considerably affected by the individual's age, educational attainment, occupational class, religious background, and other social factors, we have needed samples from groups constituted on those bases; and it would have been very difficult or impossible to have secured any sort of census on a nationwide or even statewide scale which would have allowed us to choose the subjects for probability samples from such groups.

It should be pointed out that we have been concerned with much more than the problem of arriving at a single set of over-all figures on the incidences and frequencies of each type of sexual activity in the total American population. Scientists are more often concerned with analyzing the relationships between the phenomena which they study, than they are in tabulating the incidences of such phenomena. Causal relationships or parallel effects may be discovered by correlating the

---

[3] Reports on the rates of non-response in various studies may be found in: Dinerman 1949 (18 per cent failure to complete interviews). Heneman and Paterson 1949 (discussion of interviewer effectiveness vs. refusals). Crossley and Fink 1951 (14 per cent non-completion of interviews). U. S. Bureau of Labor Statistics (Bulletin 1065) 1952 (surveys, in a difficult problem, for 10 cities with non-completion rates from 2 per cent to 34 per cent; over-all non-completion 26 per cent).

relative incidences of phenomena in different groups of individuals and their distribution in relation to ecologic, geographic, or other factors. This is what the laboratory biologist does when he compares an experimental group with a "control" group which has not been operated upon or given the special feeding or drugs or hormones which were given to the experimental animals. This is what the taxonomist does when he attempts to analyze the evolutionary origins of the characters of a given species of plant or animal by measuring samples drawn from a variety of localities, or by measuring samples of related species. This is what the geneticist does when he compares the characters of a parental generation with the characters of their offspring, and thereby arrives at generalizations concerning the processes of heredity.

In the present study, it is true that we have been concerned with the incidences of masturbation, of pre-marital petting, of pre-marital coitus, and of various other types of sexual activity; but we have also been concerned with discovering the factors which contributed to the origin, the development, and the social outcome of each pattern of behavior. These things cannot be determined from a simple enumeration of the number (the incidences) of persons having such experience in the total population. Their exposition must depend upon comparing samples from each of the sub-groups in the total population—from groups which differ in their marital status, their educational levels, their occupational and religious connections, and their other social backgrounds.

If we had done any sort of proportionate sampling, it would not have given us adequate samples for analyzing each of these component groups. If, for instance, Negroes constitute only 10 per cent of the total U. S. population, a proportionate sample would have included only one-ninth as many Negroes as whites, and that would have constituted too small a sample for analyses of Negroes, unless we had secured an unnecessarily large sample of whites. It is true that if this had been the only difficulty it could have been overcome by taking equal-sized samples of each group and, wherever an over-all figure was desired, combining each component with an appropriate weight. Thus, in the present instance, an over-all figure could have been obtained by multiplying the Negro data by one, the white data by nine, and dividing the total by ten. Such a procedure, which is quite common, is still probability sampling and still possesses all of its advantages.

But to have secured such a probability sample from each segment of the population would have demanded such years of work and such financial resources as no one has yet proposed to put into a study of human sexual behavior; and while we might have secured better statistical data on the incidences of the various types of sexual activity, we would not have arrived at our present understanding of the other, non-statistical problems which we have considered of equal importance in the present study (see especially Chapters 14–18).

Group Sampling on Present Project. For these several reasons we have chosen to secure the subjects for the present study by working with the various social units to which they belonged. By winning the confidence of each group, we have ultimately obtained the cooperation of its individual members. Individuals in any cohesive group are more willing to contribute when they learn from their friends that such cooperation does not involve undue embarrassment, and when they observe in the course of time that none of their friends have gotten into difficulty because they have contributed. Many persons who, as lone individuals, see no particular advantage in giving their histories, are willing to do so when loyalty to a group project is involved. Thus it becomes more feasible to secure the histories of all members of a group than it is to secure the histories of single individuals chosen at random out of that group. No such group psychology is available to persuade the lone rancher living on the Western plain, the particular Negro in the swamps of Alabama, or the particular youth engaged in underworld activities in the heart of an Eastern city, when they are chosen, by the processes of randomization, as the ones who are to contribute their sex histories to a scientific study.

In principle, of course, it would have been desirable to have drawn a probability sample of the groups with which we wanted to work. But the limitations on the nature of the groups that can be used in a probability sample are so severe as to render them essentially inaccessible. For instance, the groups should be such that any individual belongs to one and to only one of the groups that enters the sample. This would immediately preclude the possibility of working with parent-teacher groups, church groups, sororities, and the like. The groups that best satisfy the ideal are groups that are confined to particular geographic areas. But since neighborhoods, particularly in large urban areas, may be among the least cohesive of all groups in our modern social organization, often involving no group loyalties and no effective means of communication, the problem of securing cooperation from neighborhood groups is sometimes insurmountable.

There are further difficulties in choosing the groups with which one works. It is not always possible, for instance, to secure a census of the individual units of certain groups, such as fraternal or service clubs, colleges of some particular type, parent-teacher organizations, church groups, underworld communities, local community clubs, and various others. Without such a census, the random selection of the particular groups with which one should work is impossible.

Moreover, to have secured the cooperation of a particular group chosen at random would, in many instances, have been as difficult as securing a sample of lone individuals chosen at random. For example, having selected a particular prison at random, the chances of securing entrance to the institution and of securing the necessary cooperation from the administration and inmate body of the institution would have been slight. On the other hand, working first in some institution that had become available through contact with an understanding warden or some state board official, it became possible to get into a second institution, and that in turn, after many years of labor, opened the doors of the very institution which would have barred us if it had been selected in the first place as the lone representative with which we wished to work. Similarly, our entrance into underworld groups has usually depended upon making some lone contact which was cultivated sometimes for months or a year or two before we secured any additional history from the area; but with such slow progress over a matter of two or three years, we finally were able to develop sufficient acquaintance in the community to make any and essentially all of its members accessible for study. We have gone into colleges, into church groups, and into many other groups where we would never have obtained entrance except for their relation to some other group with which we had previously worked. Such a method of choosing groups has undoubtedly introduced biases, but there are more practical difficulties involved in the application of sampling ideals than some theoreticians realize unless they have been faced with the actualities of obtaining data on a subject like human sex behavior.

Nevertheless, it has been possible in some instances to exercise some control over the choice of groups. For instance, in college communities it has been possible in a preliminary general lecture to emphasize the desire to work with groups and not with individuals who might volunteer histories. From a list of a score or more groups that were then suggested, we could choose one fraternity or more, a sorority or two, several student rooming houses, a large cooperative house for nonorganized students, the members of a student class or two in the local churches, a student social group, several classes in undergraduate courses, in graduate courses, in summer courses for older adults and professional persons returning for additional study, and still other types of groups. With each of the chosen groups it has then been possible to work intensively until we secured the histories of all the individuals or of a large proportion of all the individuals in each group. While it is still impossible to calculate the probable error on such a sample, it provides a diversification and a representativeness which far surpass that which might have been secured by depending on lone individuals who volunteered to contribute histories.

In a city community or in a rural area, the entrée may be obtained through some single individual, usually some significant individual in the community; but again we have tried to stay with each group until we have won the confidence of the whole community, and until we have obtained the histories of a high proportion of all the persons in the community. In one rural, sparsely settled western area an examination of the tax list showed that we had obtained the histories of 75 per cent of all the males and females in the community above fifteen years of age. In one church community, where less than ten persons had volunteered histories after the initial lecture to the assembled congregation, we ultimately obtained the histories of 180 out of the membership of 220. Most of the others in the group were out of town, ill, or inaccessible for other reasons and not because they refused to cooperate.

In one sense, everyone who has contributed to this study has been a volunteer, for no one can be forced into the disclosure of his full and complete sex history; but it should be emphasized that most of the persons who have contributed have not been volunteers in the sense in which the term is usually employed in sociologic studies and population surveys. The study has not been confined to or chiefly based on individuals who volunteer at the end of a public lecture, or who offer to contribute histories when they are introduced socially to some member of our staff. We have systematically refused to accept the histories of such volunteers unless we anticipated that they would lead to some group with which we wished to work, or would contribute particular material on which we were making a special study.

Some 28 per cent of all our histories, including 15 per cent of the female histories reported in the present volume, and 70 per cent of the prison and non-white females that have not been included in the calculations for the present volume, have come from groups where a hundred per cent of the members had contributed. While we have not systematically recorded the percentages obtained from incomplete groups, we may report that a considerable proportion of the rest of the sample has been drawn from groups in which something between 50 and 90 per cent of all the members had contributed histories. Such coverage should provide a good sample of those particular groups. It should eliminate a considerable portion of the bias which is introduced when a sample is based on individual volunteers. Hundred per cent groups, however, are still not ideal, for the groups that are thus available for intensive study may not constitute a fair cross section of the total population. The remainder of our sample, drawn from non-hundred per cent groups, has value of a different sort, and so we have not confined our study to the data obtained from the hundred per cent groups. For a further analysis of the value of hundred per cent and non-hundred per cent groups, and for comparisons of results obtained by each method of sampling, see our volume on the male (1948:93–102).

For our general sample, we have avoided groups that had been brought together by some particular sexual interest. On the other hand, such groups or communities may offer the easiest access to particular sorts of histories, and they will provide the material for subsequent, special studies on homosexual groups, on prison communities, on sex offenders, and on prostitutes. Except when such individuals belonged to some more general segment of the population, their histories have not been included in the incidence or frequency calculations in the present volume.

CONSTITUTION OF PRESENT SAMPLE

The distribution of the 5940 females who have supplied the data which have been statistically analyzed in the present volume is shown in Tables 1 and 2. The sample includes the following:

Age Range. The sample covers an age range of two to ninety years, with large or fairly adequate samples in the groups ranging from sixteen to fifty years at the time of reporting (Table 1). The still younger and still older groups are inadequately represented in the sample.

Educational Background. The sample includes females with diverse educational backgrounds. There are 17 per cent with some high school but no further education, 56 per cent with some college background, and 19 per cent who had gone beyond college into graduate work (Table 1). There is a much more limited sample (181 cases) of non-prison, white females who had some grade school but no additional education; but in connection with some other aspects of our total study we have secured the histories of 555 additional white females and 293 Negro females who had not gone beyond grade school, and these cases have contributed to some of the more general discussion of the grade school group, although they have not entered into the statistical calculations in the present volume.

The inadequacy of the educational distribution in the sample would be more serious if we had found that educational backgrounds affect the sexual patterns of females as materially as they affect the patterns of males. Comparisons of our high school, college, and graduate school samples of females show few differences in the behavior of these three

Table 1. Description of White, Non-prison Female Sample by Age at Reporting

Number of Cases

AGE at rpt.	TOTAL SAMPLE	EDUCATIONAL LEVEL					MARITAL STATUS		
		0–8	9–12	13–16	17+	Pre-school or in school	Never married	Ever married	Ever wid., sep., div.
PRE-ADOLESCENT FEMALES									
2–5	60					60	60		
6–10	61					61	61		
11–15	26	2				24	26		
Total pre-adol.	147	2				145	147		
ADOLESCENT AND ADULT FEMALES									
11–15	87	8	5			74	86	1	
16–20	1840	47	181	1533	10	69	1745	95	20
21–25	1211	6	168	800	237		833	378	49
26–30	709	9	199	298	203		214	495	102
31–35	582	20	171	218	173		136	446	138
36–40	494	25	114	183	172		117	377	136
41–45	361	21	57	132	151		70	291	124
46–50	239	14	41	72	112		49	190	91
51–55	134	13	33	36	52		33	101	50
56–60	80	8	23	20	29		20	60	40
61–65	25	4	6	5	10		5	20	15
66–70	21	3	8	6	4		5	16	10
71+	10	1	8	1				10	10
Total adol. + adult	5793	179	1014	3304	1153	143	3313	2480	785
Total sample	5940	181	1014	3304	1153	288	3460	2480	785
% of sample	100.0	3.0	17.1	55.7	19.4	4.8	58.2	41.8	13.2

AGE at rpt.	TOTAL SAMPLE	PROTESTANT			CATHOLIC			JEWISH		
		Dev.	Moder.	Inact.	Dev.	Moder.	Inact.	Dev.	Moder.	Inact.
PRE-ADOLESCENT FEMALES										
2–5	60	6	6	15	1	1			2	19
6–10	61	20	14	7	4	3	1	4	1	5
11–15	26	14	2	4	1				1	4
Total pre-ad.	147	40	22	26	6	4	1	4	4	28
ADOLESCENT AND ADULT FEMALES										
11–15	87	30	17	11	8	3	4	1	2	8
16–20	1840	392	342	173	128	43	32	63	296	380
21–25	1211	285	257	201	86	35	34	13	99	208
26–30	709	121	140	178	53	26	31	5	55	113
31–35	582	88	123	136	45	23	22	7	56	97
36–40	494	101	97	147	29	9	19	9	35	64
41–45	361	86	76	112	13	8	15	2	17	47
46–50	239	61	58	70	8	2	5	2	8	33
51–55	134	31	33	32	10	3	7	4	4	14
56–60	80	21	17	24	6	2	2		1	10
61–65	25	7	7	1	2		1	1	1	6
66–70	21	9	2	4	1					5
71+	10	3	2	2	1			1	1	1
Total adol. + adult	5793	1235	1171	1091	390	154	172	108	575	986
Total sample	5940	1275	1193	1117	396	158	173	112	579	1014
% of sample	100.0	21.5	20.1	18.8	6.7	2.7	2.9	1.9	9.7	17.1

Table 2. Description of White, Non-prison Female Sample by Age at Reporting

Number of Cases

AGE at rpt.	TOTAL SAMPLE	PARENTAL OCCUP. CLASS				SUBJECT'S OCCUP. CLASS				RURAL-URBAN BACKGROUND	
		2 + 3	4	5	6 + 7	2 + 3	4	5	6 + 7	Rural	Urban
PRE-ADOLESCENT FEMALES											
2–5	60	1	2	4	53	1	2	4	53		60
6–10	61	19	4	6	34	19	4	6	34		60
11–15	26	12	2	2	9	12	2	2	9	1	24
Total pre-adol.	147	32	8	12	96	32	8	12	96	1	144
ADOLESCENT AND ADULT FEMALES											
11–15	87	54	7	5	25	53	5	5	25	4	74
16–20	1840	261	238	507	920	188	18	766	910	96	1713
21–25	1211	178	172	330	587	45	22	597	638	49	1095
26–30	709	129	105	213	289	49	38	332	423	49	637
31–35	582	109	116	154	221	57	40	251	370	46	512
36–40	494	82	66	136	222	45	33	139	366	36	434
41–45	361	67	46	82	175	33	18	89	291	24	319
46–50	239	48	32	52	111	15	8	63	185	30	197
51–55	134	23	20	22	70	11	6	27	105	15	111
56–60	80	16	7	19	40	7	2	20	60	7	70
61–65	25	7	3	2	10	4	1	6	15	3	22
66–70	21	3	2	4	12	3	1	4	14	1	20
71 +	10	1	1	1	6	1	2	2	7		10
Total adol. + adult	5793	978	815	1527	2688	511	194	2301	3409	401	5214
Total sample	5940	1010	823	1539	2784	543	202	2313	3505	402	5358
% of sample	100.0	17.0	13.9	25.9	46.9	9.1	3.4	38.9	59.0	6.8	90.2

AGE at rpt.	TOTAL SAMPLE	DECADE OF BIRTH					AGE AT ONSET OF ADOL.				
		Bf. 1900	1900–1909	1910–1919	1920–1929	1930 +	–11	12	13	14	15 +
PRE-ADOLESCENT FEMALES											
2–5	60					60					
6–10	61					61					
11–15	26				3	23					
Total pre-adol.	147				3	144					
ADOLESCENT AND ADULT FEMALES											
11–15	87				42	45	24	27	27	8	1
16–20	1840			18	1735	87	422	585	570	187	75
21–25	1211			175	1036		276	382	351	156	45
26–30	709		2	444	263		153	230	184	102	39
31–35	582		59	523			101	165	196	79	41
36–40	494	1	308	185			94	111	160	93	36
41–45	361	41	320				55	87	106	69	44
46–50	239	144	95				37	46	73	55	27
51–55	134	134					26	20	41	30	17
56–60	80	80					9	21	28	13	9
61–65	25	25					6	2	9	3	5
66–70	21	21					1	6	5	3	6
71 +	10	10					2	2	2		4
Total adol. + adult	5793	456	784	1345	3076	132	1206	1684	1752	798	349
Total sample	5940	456	784	1345	3079	276	1206	1684	1752	798	349
% of sample	100.0	7.7	13.2	22.7	51.8	4.6	20.3	28.4	29.5	13.4	5.9

(Footnote to table on next page)

33

groups; but our limited samples of the grade school group suggest that their sexual behavior may be more different.

Marital Status. The sample includes many females who had never married, and many who had married (Table 1). There is a sizable although still inadequate sample (785 cases) of females who had been widowed, separated, or divorced.

Religious Background. The sample includes females associated with various religious faiths, and variously devoted in their adherence to those faiths (Table 1). We have samples of some size (over 500 cases in each) from religiously devout, moderately devout, and inactive Protestant groups, and from moderately devout and inactive Jewish groups. We have 727 histories of Catholic females, including devout, moderately devout, and inactive groups, but obviously need a larger sample of all Catholic groups. We have only 108 histories of devout Jewish females, and that has not been a sufficient sample to allow us to generalize concerning that group at more than a few points in the analyses.

Parental Occupational Class. The sample includes females raised in homes belonging to a variety of occupational classes (Table 2). Some 17 per cent of the sample had come from laboring groups, 14 per cent from the homes of skilled laborers, 26 per cent from lower white collar homes, and 47 per cent from upper white collar and professional groups.

Subject's Occupational Class. The sample includes females belonging to a variety of occupational classes either through their own occupational status or through the status of their husbands (Table 2). Out of the total sample, 9 per cent belonged to laboring groups, 3 per cent to the class of skilled workmen, 39 per cent to lower white collar groups, and 59 per cent to upper white collar and professional groups.

Rural-Urban Background. There are females from rural and urban groups (Table 2). Some 90 per cent of the total sample was urban.

Footnote to Table 2

For definitions of educational levels, occupational classes, rural-urban groups, religious groups, etc., see pp. 53–56.

The totals in the occupational and religious classifications amount to more than the totals shown for the entire sample because some individuals had belonged to more than one group in the course of their lives. In the rural-urban classification the totals fall short of the total number of cases because some 3 per cent of the females were not identifiable as either rural or urban. For slightly more than 1 per cent of the females in the sample, the data were incomplete and there were individuals who did not fall into the classifications shown above.

Children and dependents derive their occupational classification from that of their parents.

They had lived in a variety of smaller cities and towns, and in some of the larger cities of the United States. Only 7 per cent of the sample (402 cases) had lived on farms for the major portion of the years between the ages of twelve and eighteen. The sample is obviously inadequate for making any final comparisons of rural and urban groups, but such comparisons as we have made show few differences between the two.

Decade of Birth. The sample includes females born in five successive decades. Because they are more abundant in the population, we have secured a larger sample of persons born in more recent decades; but we also have 456 cases of females born before 1900, and 784 cases of females born in the first decade after 1900 (Table 2). It has, in consequence, been possible to make comparisons of females born in four successive decades; but in many instances the females born since 1930 had not yet developed their complete patterns of sexual behavior, and their histories therefore cannot be compared with those of the older generations.

Age at Onset of Adolescence. The sample includes females who had turned adolescent at various ages, beginning at some age before eleven and including some who had not turned adolescent until they were fifteen or older (Table 2). The age at onset of adolescence, however, has not proved as significant in determining the patterns of sexual behavior among females, as we found it among males.

Geographic Origin. The sample includes females who had lived in various states of the United States (Figures 1, 2). There are still many sections of the country from which we have only limited samples, but it is to be noted that the ten states from which we have our largest series (69 per cent of the total sample) include some 47 per cent of the total population of the United States. These ten states, in order of the size of each sample, are: New York, Pennsylvania, Illinois, Indiana, California, New Jersey, Ohio, Florida, Massachusetts, and Maryland. We need additional cases from the Southeastern quarter of the country, from the Pacific Northwest, and from the high plains and Rocky Mountain areas.

It has been assumed by many persons that we would find geographic differences in patterns of sexual behavior, but we have an impression, as yet unsubstantiated by specific calculations, that there are actually few differences in sex patterns between similar communities in different portions of the United States. The nature of the community in which the individual has lived, whether it be a large metropolitan center, a smaller city, a large or small town, a small farm, or a large ranch in a relatively uninhabited portion of the country, seems to be of greater significance than the geographic location of the area.

Inadequacies of Present Sample. To recapitulate, we may again point out that our present sample is inadequate at many points (Tables 1, 2), and the generalizations reached in the present volume are least

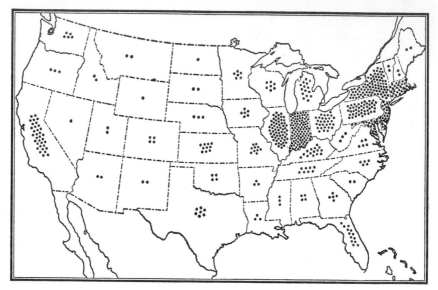

Figure 1. Geographic sources: total female and male sample

Each dot represents 50 individuals who had lived for a minimum of one year in the designated state. The total represents 16,392 cases.

likely to be applicable to the following groups:

Age groups over 50
Educational level 0–8 (with only grade school education)
Educational level 9–12 (high school), especially among individuals over 40 years of age
Previously married females, now widowed, separated, or divorced
All Catholic groups, especially among older females
Devoutly Jewish groups
Laboring groups (classes 2 and 3), especially among older females
All rural groups
Individuals born before 1900
Groups originating in the Southeastern quarter of the country, from the Pacific Northwest, and from the high plains and Rocky Mountain areas.

We have not been able to work with all of these groups, primarily because only four persons have been available to do the interviewing on this project, and two of us have done the interviewing which accounts for 81 per cent of the total number of histories in our files. We have not been able to find other persons who were available and qualified to meet the demands placed upon an interviewer on this project. In such a special field, an interviewer needs not only considerable pro-

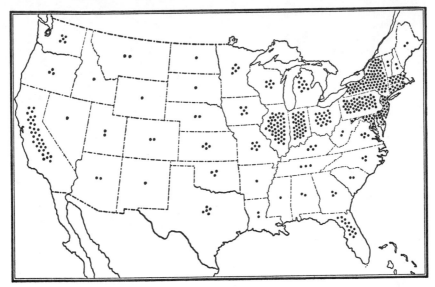

Figure 2. Geographic sources: female sample on which present volume is based

Each dot represents 25 individuals who had lived for a minimum of one year in the designated state. The total represents 5940 cases.

fessional training, but a personality which enables him to win rapport with persons of diverse social levels ranging from underworld and poorly educated or illiterate groups to socially superior and top professional groups. Moreover, the interviewer must be able to accept a record of any type of sexual activity, whether it is socially acceptable or taboo, or even damaging to the social organization, without passing judgment on the subject who is giving the record, and without wishing to control or redirect his behavior. This ability to accept without attempting to redirect the subject's behavior is the most difficult quality to find, particularly among clinically trained persons.

SPECIFIC SOURCES OF PRESENT SAMPLE

While the necessity for preserving confidence makes it impossible to identify the particular groups from which histories have been obtained in the present study, the following summary will show something of the diversity and limitations of the groups with which we have worked:

GROUPS INVOLVED

Armed Forces
   WAC
   WAVES
   Nurses
Artists
Business office groups
   Officers and administrators
   Clerks
   Technicians
Church congregations
Church organizations
City community groups
Clinical groups, patients and staff
   Hospitals
   Psychiatric clinics
   Psychologic clinics
   Mental hospitals
   Speech clinics
   Sterility clinics
   Social service groups
College classes in:
   Psychology
   Sociology
   Biology
   Chemistry
   Public health
   Family living
   Home economics
   English
College faculties
College student groups
   Sororities
   Social clubs
   Rooming houses
   Dormitories
   Cooperative houses
   Religious groups
Court officials
Detention homes
   Residents
   Staffs
Editorial staffs, magazines
Factory groups
Family groups
Grade school students
   Public schools
   Private schools

High school students
   Public schools
   Private schools
Housewives
   On farms
   In small towns
   In cities
Homes for unmarried mothers
Medical organizations
Medical school groups
Mothers' clubs
Museum staffs
Music schools
Nursery school children
Nurses' groups
Orphans' homes
Parent-teacher groups, in:
   Nursery schools
   Grade schools
   High schools
   Public schools
   Private schools
   Small towns
   Cities
Prison staffs
Professional organizations of:
   Marriage counselors
   Physicians
   Administrators of correctional institutions
Salvation Army
   Congregations
   Children's clubs
   Adult clubs
   Staff
Theatre groups
   Actors
   Managements
Union organizations
Women's clubs
   American Association of University Women
   Professional women's clubs
   Women's service clubs
   U.S.O.
Y.W.C.A. groups

An examination of the distribution of the sample shown in Tables 1 and 2 may be more informative than any listing of the groups or of the other characteristics of the persons with whom we have worked. Statistically still more valuable information about the sample may be obtained from an examination of the sample sizes shown in the ultimate breakdowns (the cells) in the various tables in the book.

On the other hand, from an examination of such statistics, one still may not comprehend how many different sorts of persons have been willing to contribute their histories to the present project. In order to emphasize the fact that persons in many walks of life have contributed to the statistics which are summarized and analyzed in the present volume, we submit the following lists showing (1) the occupations of the females in the sample, and (2) the occupations of the husbands of the married females in the sample:

OCCUPATIONS OF FEMALE SUBJECTS

Acrobat	Dentist
Actress	Designer
Advertiser	Dice girl
Airline hostess	Dietician
Anthropologist	Director of foundation
Archeologist	Director, religious educ.
Architect	Draftsman
Art critic	Dramatic critic
Art director	Dramatic teacher
Art model	Dress designer
Artificial flower maker	Drill press operator
Artist	Druggist
Auditor	Economist
Baby-sitter	Editor
Bacteriologist	Electrician
Baker	Elevator operator
Barmaid	Employment agent
Beautician	Expediter
Berry picker	Factory worker
Boardinghouse operator	Farmer
Bookbinder	Fashion model
Bookkeeper	Fashion publicist
Burlesque performer	Foreman
Bus girl	Garment worker
Business executive	Girl Scout executive
Buyer	Glass blower
Cafeteria manager	Governess
Camp counselor	Gymnasium instructor
Car hop	Hat check girl
Cartoonist	Hospital administrator
Cashier	Hospital attendant
Checker	Hostess
Chemist	Hotel manager
Cigarette girl	House mother
Circus rider	Housewife
Claim adjuster	Illustrator
Collector	Inspector
Comptometer operator	Insurance underwriter
Confectioner	Interior decorator
Cook	Interpreter
Copy writer	Interviewer
Dancer	Inventor
Dancing teacher	Job analyst
Dean of girls	Journalist
Dean of women	Judge
Dental assistant	Laboratory technician

Labor relations counselor
Laundress
Lawyer
Lecturer
Librarian
Linotype operator
Lobbyist
Machine operator
Maid
Male impersonator
Manicurist
Manikin maker
Marriage counselor
Master of ceremonies
Matron in orphans' home
Mechanic
Messenger
Milliner
Minister
Missionary
Movie editor
Movie scout
Museum guide
Music critic
Music teacher
Musician
Night club mgr.
Nurse, practical
Nurse, registered
Nurse's aide
Occupational therapist
Odd jobs
Office clerk
Office manager
OSS operative
Osteopath
Packer
Paleontologist
Parole officer
Personnel worker
Photographer
Physician
Physiotherapist
Poet
Policewoman
Politician
Potter
Press agent
Presser
Principal, grade school
Principal, high school
Probation officer
Producer (plays)
Professional ballplayer
Proofreader
Proprietor
Prostitute
Psychiatrist

Psychologist
Psychometrist
Public health nurse
Public relations worker
Publicity director
Publisher
Puppeteer
Radio announcer
Real estate agent
Receptionist
Recreation director
Reporter
Research assistant
Research worker
Riveter
Robber
Salesclerk
Sales demonstrator
Sales manager
Sales promoter
Salvation Army officer
Sculptress
Seamstress
Secretary
Shipping clerk
Singer
Social worker
Soda jerker
Speech therapist
Statistician
Steel burner
Stewardess
Student, college
Student, grade school
Student, graduate school
Student, high school
Student, nursery school
Stylist
Supt. of schools
Tavern proprietor
Taxi dancer
Taxi driver
Teacher, college
Teacher, grade school
Teacher, high school
Teacher, kindergarten
Teacher, nursery school
Telegrapher
Telephone operator
Teletype operator
Theatre director
Timekeeper
Traffic manager
Translator
Travel bureau mgr.
Truck driver
Tutor
Typist

U.N. employee
Unemployed
Union organizer
Usher
Vocational counselor
WAC
Waitress
WAVE

Weaver
Welder
Window decorator
WPA employee
Writer
X-ray technician
Y.W.C.A. executive
Y.W.C.A. staff

OCCUPATIONS OF HUSBANDS OF FEMALE SUBJECTS

Abortionist
Accountant
Actor
Advertiser
Agricultural agent
Anthropologist
Archeologist
Architect
Army, private to general
Art critic
Art director
Artist
Auto dealer
Aviation pilot
Bacteriologist
Bailiff
Baker
Ballplayer, professional
Banker
Bartender
Beautician
Bellhop
Bookbinder
Bootlegger
Boxer
Boys' club director
Boy Scout executive
Brewer
Bricklayer
Broker
Buffer
Burglar
Bus boy
Business executive
Business owner (small to large)
Butcher
Buyer
Camp director
Car dealer
Caretaker
Carnival worker
Carpenter
Cartographer
Cartoonist
CCC administrator
Chauffeur
Chef
Chemist

Chiropodist
Chiropractor
City manager
Claims adjustor
Clothier
Coach, athletic
Coast Guard
Collector, financial
College administrator
Comedian
Commercial artist
Composer
Comptroller
Concert manager
Contractor
Copy boy
Counselor
Crane operator
Credit manager
Croupier
Custom's collector
Cutter, dress
Cutter, metal
Dancer
Delivery boy
Dental technician
Dentist
Designer
Detective
Diamond cutter
Diplomat
Dispatcher
Doorman
Draftsman
Dramatic critic
Dramatic teacher
Druggist
Economist
Editor
Electrician
Electroplater
Engineer, aeronautic
Engineer, chemical
Engineer, civil
Engineer, electrical
Engineer, industrial
Engineer, mechanical
Engineer, radio

41

Engraver
Entomologist
Expediter
Explorer
Exporter
Factory manager
Factory worker
Farmer
Filling station attendant
Financier
Fireman, city
Fireman, industrial
Fisherman
Floor sander
Florist
Foreman
Forester
Funeral director
Furrier
Gambler
Garment worker
Geologist
Glass blower
Glazier
Golfer, professional
Grocer
Hairdresser
Handyman
Hat blocker
Horticulturist
Hospital administrator
Hospital attendant
Hotel manager
Hotel staff member
Importer
Insect exterminator
Inspector
Insurance adjuster
Insurance salesman
Interior decorator
Interpreter
Interviewer
Inventor
Investigator
Janitor
Jeweler
Jobber
Journalist
Judge
Laboratory technician
Labor negotiator
Landscape gardener
Lather
Lawyer
Layout artist
Lecturer
Lens grinder
Librarian
Linotype operator

Longshoreman
Lumberjack
Machinist
Mailman
Manufacturer
Market researcher
Mason
Mechanic
Merchant
Messenger
Metal worker
Metallurgist
Meteorologist
Mine superintendent
Miner
Minister
Missionary
Motorman
Movie agent
Movie director
Movie producer
Music critic
Music teacher
Musician
Mycologist
Narcotics inspector
Navy, seaman to commander
Office clerk
Office manager
Oil producer
Optometrist
Orchestra leader
OSS operative
Osteopath
Painter, house
Painter, sign
Park supervisor
Parole officer
Pattern maker
Pawnshop owner
Personnel worker
Photographer
Physical educ. instructor
Physician
Physicist
Physiologist
Piano tuner
Pile driver operator
Pilot trainer
Pimp
Pipe fitter
Plasterer
Plumber
Podiatrist
Poet
Policeman
Polisher
Politician
Porter

Postmaster
Press agent
Press operator
Presser
Principal, grade school
Principal, high school
Printer
Probation officer
Production manager
Promoter
Proofreader
Prosecutor
Prospector
Prostitute
Psychiatrist
Psychologist
Psychometrist
Public opinion research
Publicity man
Publisher
Racketeer
Radar expert
Radio announcer
Radio mechanic
Railroad conductor
Railroad engineer
Railroad fireman
Railroad section hand
Railroad yardmaster
Rancher
Real estate agent
Reporter
Research worker
Riveter
Roofer
Safety engineer
Sailor
Sales clerk
Sales manager
Salesman, city
Salesman, traveling
Salvation Army officer
School superintendent
Sculptor
Sea captain
Sewing machine operator
Sheet metal worker
Shipping clerk
Social worker

Speech therapist
Sprayer
Stationary engineer
Statistician
Steel worker
Steward
Stock boy
Street car conductor
Student
Subway conductor
Swimming instructor
Switchman
Tailor
Tax collector
Tax expert
Taxi driver
Teacher, college
Teacher, grade school
Teacher, high school
Teamster
Telegrapher
Telephone lineman
Telephone operator
Thief
Ticket agent
Tile setter
Timekeeper
Tire changer
Tool and die maker
Traffic manager
Tree surgeon
Truck driver
Tutor
Unemployed
Union organizer
Upholsterer
Veterinarian
Vocational adviser
Waiter
Watch repairman
Watchman
Weaver
Welder
Window designer
Wire tester
WPA employee
Writer
Y.M.C.A. executive
Y.M.C.A. staff

NUMBER OF CASES IN SAMPLE

Although we have so far taken 7789 histories of females, the statistical calculations in the present volume have been confined, as we have already noted, to the 5940 cases of white, non-prison females whose histories we had acquired prior to January 1, 1950. By closing the sample on that date, it has been possible to hold the total number of cases

43

(the N) more or less constant in the tabulations and calculations throughout the book; but the totals fall short of 5940 in most of the calculations for the following reasons:

1. Question Inapplicable. Very often a particular question does not apply to the entire sample. This is the chief reason for the occurrence of N's which are smaller than the N of the total sample. For instance, questions concerning marital coitus do not apply to single females; questions concerning menstruation do not apply to pre-adolescent females.

2. Uncertain Behavior. Sometimes there are uncertainties as to the nature of the behavior in which a subject has engaged. It may, for instance, be impossible to determine whether the incidental touching of genitalia should, in a given case, be considered masturbation or non-sexual activity. Sometimes it is difficult to determine whether there was erotic arousal in connection with the activity. There is usually no question whether the subject did or did not experience orgasm from masturbation or some other source, and, in consequence, the number of cases (the total N) on which the incidences of experience may be calculated is sometimes different from the number of cases on which we may calculate the incidences of experience to orgasm. Therefore the samples that are used for the two sorts of calculations are sometimes different, and for that reason there are a few places in the present volume where the active incidences of orgasm are a bit higher than the accumulative incidences of experience at the same age.

3. Question Not Asked. The N's are sometimes lower than 5940, and sometimes markedly lower than that number, when a particular question was not asked of all of the subjects in the study. From a very early point in the history of the research, a high proportion of all the questions have been uniformly asked on each interview, but something over 20 per cent of the present questions were not asked in the first year or two. Consequently the number of cases available for analyses on such items is lower than the number of cases in the total sample. Some additional questions have been introduced in more recent years, *e.g.*, questions concerning extra-marital petting, questions concerning the female's erotic response upon seeing male genitalia, and questions concerning the acceptance of homosexual friends. A few of the questions which were asked in the earlier part of the research were dropped from the interviews in the last few years because the answers were so uniform that there seemed no point in obtaining additional information.

4. Interviewer's Failure. The N's in some instances are lower than the total N because the interviewer failed to obtain information on the particular point. These failures have been relatively few because the standard form in which the interview is coded provides a simple check by which the interviewer at the end of an interview can make sure that all the questions have been answered. Interviewer failures have been most frequent in those periods in which new questions were being added, and when the interviewer had not yet become accustomed to exploring in those areas.

5. Refusal to Reply. This is responsible for only minor reductions in the total N's, and then on only a very few items. Unlike the experience of those engaged in public opinion and some other surveys, we find no difficulty in getting our subjects to answer all of the questions in an interview. In the course of the fourteen years, there have not been more than a half dozen subjects who have refused to complete the records after they had once agreed to be interviewed.

6. Insufficient Information. The interviewer's failure to secure sufficient or exactly pertinent information on certain items may account for some of the instances in which the available N's are lower than the total N. This sort of failure does the most damage when the final calculations are based upon some coordination of several answers. Then a failure to obtain data on any one of the points may make it impossible to use any of the answers in the group. For instance, the failure to secure a record of the frequencies of orgasm in pre-marital coitus would make it impossible to use the given history in correlating the pre-marital with the subsequent marital experience.

STATISTICAL ANALYSES

In our previous volume, nearly all of the statistical calculations were based upon the male's experience in sexual activity which had led to orgasm. Although the male is frequently aroused without completing his response, he rarely engages in such activities as masturbation or coitus without proceeding to the point of orgasm. On the other hand, a considerable portion of the female's sexual activity does not result in orgasm. In consequence, statistical calculations throughout the present volume have shown, wherever the data were available, the incidences and frequencies both of the female's sexual experience and of her experience in orgasm.

It is usually possible to secure data on the incidences of sexual experience that did not lead to orgasm, but it is often impossible to secure frequency data on such experience, because of the difficulty of distinguishing between non-erotic social activities—a simple kiss, for instance—and similar activities which do bring erotic arousal. On the other hand, orgasm is a distinct and specific phenomenon which is usually as identifiable in the female as in the male. It has served, therefore, as a concrete unit for determining both incidences and frequencies. The use of such a unit is justified by the fact that all orgasms, whether derived from masturbation, petting, marital coitus, or any other source, may provide a physiologic release from sexual arousal; but since there may be differences in the social significance of orgasms obtained from one or another type of activity, there has been some objection to the use of that phenomenon as a unit of measurement. The matter is further discussed in Chapter 13 (pp. 510–511). There seems, however, no better unit for measuring the incidences and frequencies of sexual activity. As we have already noted, a considerable portion of the present volume is concerned with reporting other aspects of sexual behavior which are not so readily quantified for statistical analyses.

The following definitions are designed to give the non-statistical reader an acquaintance with the meanings of some standard statistical terms. For the technically trained reader, these definitions will show the way in which the terms have been applied in the present volume.

Accumulative Incidence. An accumulative incidence curve shows, in terms of percentages, the number of persons who have ever engaged in the given type of activity by a given age. The calculations are, of course, based on the experience which the reporting subjects had had before contributing histories to the present study; but by securing information on the age at which each subject had first had experience, it is possible to determine the percentage of the total sample who had had experience at each age up to the time of interview. But an accumulative incidence curve may also be useful in indicating what percentages of any group might be expected to have experience if they were to live into the older age groups. A fuller explanation of the techniques involved in calculating these curves is given in our volume on the male (1948:114–119).

Most of the incidence data presented in research studies record the number of persons who are having experience in a given period of time, *e.g.*, the current incidences of venereal disease, or the current incidences of marriage in the U. S. population. The accumulative incidences, on the other hand, show how many persons have *ever* had experience by a given age. This answers a type of question that is very frequently asked. One may want to know how many persons *ever* masturbate, how many persons *ever* have coitus before marriage, how many persons *ever* have homosexual experience.

A subject's ability to report whether he has ever engaged in a given type of activity is not as liable to errors of memory and of judgment as his ability to recall frequencies of activity and to estimate the average frequencies of his activity (see also pp. 68–73). A subject's willingness to admit experience, however, may be affected by society's attitudes toward particular types of sexual activity—toward pre-marital coitus, extra-marital coitus, mouth-genital contacts, and homosexual contacts, for instance—; and in regard to such items, subjects may occasionally deny their experience. On the other hand, it is more difficult for a subject to exaggerate because of the difficulty in answering subsequent questions concerning the details of the professed experience. The accumulative incidence data are, therefore, probably a minimum record rather than an exaggeration of the experience actually had by the subjects in the study.

Active Incidence. As used in the present study, the active incidences represent, in terms of percentages, the number of persons who have engaged in each type of sexual activity in a particular period of their lives. In our previous and present volumes, these have been standardly expressed as five-year periods, covering in most instances the years between adolescence and fifteen, sixteen and twenty, twenty-one and twenty-five, etc. See our volume on the male (1948:76–77) for a further discussion.

The active incidences for the various age groups provide highly significant data in any sex study, because the number of persons involved in a given type of activity depends upon age more than upon most other factors. However, it should be recognized that any individual who has had a single experience within the five-year period raises the percentage shown in an active incidence. In most instances the active incidences would have been lower if they had been calculated for one-year instead of five-year periods. A better comprehension of the extent of any type of sexual activity may be had if one considers the active incidences in conjunction with the average frequencies among those who are having any experience (the active median frequencies).

Frequency of Activity. The frequency of each subject's activity is recorded as an average frequency for each of the five-year periods specified above. Throughout our previous and present volumes, frequencies have been expressed as average frequencies per week in each of those periods. The weeks or years in any five-year period which were without sexual activity have been averaged with the weeks or years in which there was activity, and in that way periods of inactivity have lowered the average rates in such a five-year period. Unless the data are specifically designated as applying to pre-adolescence, all of the frequency calculations in the present volume have been based upon activities which occurred after the onset of adolescence. In consequence, the first age period extends from adolescence to fifteen, and in that case the average frequencies are based on the number of adolescent years and are not reduced by being averaged with the pre-adolescent years. If the last age period—the one in which the subject contributes his or her history, or changes his marital status—is less than a full five-year period, it has been treated in the same fashion as the first adolescent period. No frequency calculations have been made for persons who belonged to a given age, adolescent, or marriage period for less than six months.

Because of the difficulties which most persons have in estimating average frequencies for experience which may have been sporadic or irregular in its occurrence, frequency data are subject to much greater error than incidence data. This explains why there have been few attempts in previous studies to determine the frequencies of sexual behavior. But even though considerable allowance must be made for errors in the frequency data, they show what appear to be significant correlations with age, the decade of birth, the religious associations, and still other social factors in the backgrounds of the females in the sample.

Frequency Classes. In all calculations in the present volume, individuals have been grouped in frequency classes which have been named, throughout both our previous and present volumes, for their upper limits. Since it is current practice in most statistical publication to name frequency classes for their lower limits, attention should be drawn to our different practice. The ranges and the mean values of the frequency classes as we have defined them in our preceding and present volumes, are as follows:

CLASS	RANGE	MEAN VALUE
0	0	0
0.09	0.01– 0.09	0.05
0.5	0.1 – 0.5	0.3
1.0	0.6 – 1.0	0.8
1.5	1.1 – 1.5	1.3
2.0	1.6 – 2.0	1.8
etc.		
10.0	9.6 –10.0	9.8
11.0	10.1 –11.0	10.5
12.0	11.1 –12.0	11.5
etc.		
28.0	27.1 –28.0	27.5
29.0+	28.1 and higher	28.5

Since most persons report frequencies in terms of whole integers, and since we have used the upper limits of each class to designate the frequency classes into which such reported data are placed, our calculations of both median and mean frequencies have, in actuality, been more conservative than they would have been if we had used the lower limits to designate each class. An individual who reported an average frequency of a given type of sexual activity at 2.0 per week would go, in our calculations, into a class which had a mean value of 1.8 per week. If the lower limits had been used to designate each class, that same individual would have gone into a group which had a mean frequency value of 2.2 per week. However, the differences in the averages obtained by these two methods of calculation are slight and usually immaterial in terms of the quantities being measured.

Median Frequency. When the individuals in any group are arranged in order according to the frequencies of their sexual experience, the individual who stands midway in the group, the median individual, may be located by the formula

$$Md = \frac{n + 1}{2}$$

Throughout such statistical formulae, the symbol N or n stands for the number of individuals in the group. While the median is an average which is not often calculated by people in their everyday affairs, it is a useful statistic because it is unaffected by the frequencies of activity of the extreme individuals in any sample. The mean, which is the sort of average that most persons ordinarily calculate, is affected by extreme individuals (p. 50). In consequence, median frequencies are the statistics which we have more often used in the present volume.

Active Median Frequency. In any group and especially in any group of females, there may be some individuals who are not having any sexual activity of the sort with which the calculation is concerned. That portion of the total sample which is actually having experience or reaching orgasm has been identified in the present study as the *active sample*. The median individual of this active sample has a frequency of experience or orgasm which we have identified throughout this volume as the *active median frequency*.

Total Median Frequency. The entire sample in any group, including both those individuals who are not having experience of the sort under consideration and those who are involved in that particular type of sexual activity, constitutes the *total sample* as we have used the term in the present study. The median individual in such a total sample has a frequency of activity which we have identified as the *total median frequency*.

Where less than half of the individuals in a sample are involved in a given type of activity—where, for instance, less than half of the individuals in a given group are petting to the point of orgasm—the median individual is, of course, not having any activity at all. In consequence, the median frequency for such a group is zero. Since the active incidences of many types of sexual activity among females are frequently less than 50 per cent, it has not been possible to calculate total median frequencies on more than a few of the types of sexual activity discussed in the present volume. They have been calculated chiefly for marital coitus and for the total sexual outlet, because more than 50 per cent of the females are actively involved in those activities in most of the age groups.

Mean Frequency. A mean frequency may be determined by totaling the measurements (in the present study, the total number of experiences or total number of orgasms) in each group, divided by the number of individuals in the group. The process is summarized in the formula:

$$M = \frac{\Sigma fv}{n}$$

The mean is the sort of average which is most commonly employed by most persons in their everyday affairs. If one wants to find the average price which has been paid for a number of articles, this is done by totaling the individual prices and dividing by the number of objects bought. Such an average is the mean of the various prices which were paid. Conversely, the total amount of money spent may be calculated by multiplying the mean price by the number of objects which were bought. In the same fashion the total number of orgasms experienced in any group may be determined by multiplying the mean frequencies of orgasm by the total number of persons in each group. The mean, therefore, serves a function which is not served by the median.

On the other hand, means often give a distorted picture because their values may be considerably raised by a few high-rating individuals in the group. Since there is usually a tremendous range of variation in the frequencies of sexual activity or of orgasm in any group of females, the mean frequencies are uniformly higher than the median frequencies of sexual activity (*e.g.*, see Tables 23, 43, 76, 114). Since the range of individual variation is more extreme among females than it is among males, mean frequencies calculated for females are even less adequate as measures of sexual activity than they are for males. Consequently mean frequencies have been used in the present volume only when we wished to calculate the total number of experiences, or the total number of orgasms occurring in a whole group.

Active Mean Frequency. The mean frequencies for the females in an active sample—those females who were having any experience, or experience to the point of orgasm—have been designated as the *active mean frequencies.*

Total Mean Frequency. The mean frequencies of the females in any total sample, including those who were not having experience or orgasm as well as those who were having such experience or orgasm, represent the total mean frequencies, as they are designated in the present volume.

Standard Error. What is known as the standard error or the standard deviation of the mean, the standard error of the mean, or the sigma of the mean, is a quantity which, when added to or subtracted from the mean, shows the limits within which the calculated mean might be expected to differ from the mean of the entire population approximately two-thirds of the time. In the present volume, the standard deviation of the mean has been calculated by using the formula

$$\sigma_m = \frac{\sigma}{\sqrt{n}} = \frac{\sqrt{\dfrac{\Sigma fv^2 - \dfrac{(\Sigma fv)^2}{n}}{n-1}}}{\sqrt{n}}$$

For the general reader it may be pointed out that the standard deviation is appended to the mean in the following form:

$$2.2 \pm 0.04$$
$$\text{Mean} \pm \quad \sigma_m$$

When the data involved comparisons of simple yes and no answers, as in Tables 3–5, the formula used for calculating the standard error was

$$\sigma_D = \sqrt{\frac{B + C - \dfrac{(C - B)^2}{N}}{N(N-1)}}$$

Significant Differences. Whether the differences between the calculations made for two or more groups—*e.g.*, the differences in the frequencies of orgasm calculated for two groups of different ages—are meaningful, or whether they fall within the range of variability that might be expected within either one of the groups, is a matter which may be tested by various statistical techniques. Within certain limits, it may thus be shown that the differences are or are not statistically significant. However, because most sexual data cannot be reported with the sort of precision which is obtainable in making physical measurements, and because the variations in sexual data almost never show normal frequency distributions, it has seemed undesirable to calculate the statistical significances of the differences in our data by methods which are often used for other sorts of data.

Whether a given difference is significant may, however, often be recognized without statistical calculation. This may be possible: (1) When the differences are of some magnitude, relative to the standard errors of the quantities being measured. (2) When the differences represent reasonably measurable quantities (*e.g.*, frequencies of one orgasm in a matter of a few weeks or a month, and not merely one orgasm in a year or two, which is such a small quantity that few persons could recall and report it with any precision). (3) When the variation in the one group lies entirely outside the range of the variation in the other group. (4) When the differences between the various groups which are in a series lie within a trend, *i.e.*, accumulate in a given direction between the extreme groups in the series. (5) When the differences between the contrasting groups in any pair, or the extreme groups in any series, lie consistently in the same direction, *e.g.*, for the different age groups, educational levels, decades of birth, levels of religious devotion, etc. For instance, when the incidences or frequencies of a given type of sexual activity are lower in all or essentially all of the devoutly religious groups, and higher in all the religiously inactive groups, whether Protestant, Catholic, or Jewish, the differences may be considered of some significance.

We have tried not to suggest that any of the differences shown between the groups in the present study are significant unless such a conclusion seemed warranted by this sort of direct inspection of the data.

Unfortunately the term *significant* has an older, non-statistical use which applies to situations that are *meaningful, important,* or in some fashion *indicative* of something. It has not been possible to avoid that use of the word in writing of matters that are so often *significant* to the individual, or *significant* to the social organization of which the individual is a part. Wherever this general use of the term might be confused with the more technical use, we have used the phrase *statistical significance* to distinguish the technical meaning of the term.

Percentage of Total Outlet. In the present volume we have systematically calculated what proportion of the orgasms experienced by each group had been derived from each type of sexual activity. Thus, in a given age group of white females of a particular educational, religious, or other background, we have calculated what proportion of the total number of orgasms occurring in the group had been derived from masturbation, from nocturnal dreams to orgasm, from pre-marital coitus, etc. Obviously, the sums of the percentages shown for the several types of sexual activity must constitute one hundred per cent of the total outlet (the total number of orgasms) of the group.

We have not calculated the percentage of the total outlet which was derived by each individual from each type of sexual activity, and then calculated averages based on those individual data, as we did at a few points in our volume on the male.

Coefficient of Correlation. In attempting to show the extent to which two phenomena may be correlated in their occurrence, it has been customary in certain fields to express such correlations by coefficients which are calculated by standard statistical formulae. In our volume on the male, we restricted the use of such coefficients to the comparisons of original histories and retakes, and to the comparisons of data contributed by paired spouses. However, our direct comparisons of the calculated incidences and frequencies seem more meaningful for the sorts of data we have in this study, and we have not used correlation coefficients at any point in the present volume.

Age. For each type of activity, the ages at first experience and the ages during which there was subsequent experience have been standardly recorded and calculated for each year in each history. However, as a matter of economy, and as an aid to the comprehension of the total picture, the accumulative incidence data have been published only for each fifth year, except when there were unusual or marked developments in the intervening years. In the latter event, we have published the record for those years.

Marital Status. In most calculations in this volume, sexual activities have been classified as occurring among single, married, or previously married females. Individuals were identified as single up to the time they were first married. They were identified as married if they were living with their spouses either in formally consummated legal marriages, or in common-law relationships which had lasted for at least a year. They were classified as previously married if they were no longer living with a spouse because they were widowed, divorced, or permanently separated. These definitions are more or less in accord with those used in the U. S. Census for 1950, except that common-law relationships have been more frequently accepted as marriages in our data, and we have considered any permanent separation of spouses the equivalent of a divorce.

Educational Level. On the basis of the educational levels which they had attained before completing their schooling, the females in the sample have been classified in four categories, as follows:

0– 8: those who had never gone beyond grade school
9–12: those who had gone into high school, but never beyond

13–16: those who had gone into college, but had not had more than
four years of college

17+: those who had gone beyond college into post-graduate or
professional training

It was obviously impossible to determine the educational level that
would ultimately be attained by subjects who were still in grade school
or high school at the time they contributed their histories, and they
were consequently unavailable for any calculation that involved an
educational breakdown. Persons still in college were classified among
those having 13 to 16 years of schooling, and this may have involved
a small error because a portion of them would ultimately go on into
graduate work.

Upon calculation, we find that educational backgrounds do not
seem to have been correlated with the patterns of sexual behavior
among females as they were among the males covered by our previous
volume. Consequently in the present volume we have published direct
correlations with most of the other factors, such as decade of birth
and religious background, without showing the preliminary classifications which we have made on the basis of the educational levels.

Occupational Class of Parental Home. Since the female's social
status after marriage depends on the occupational class of her husband
as well as upon her own social background, it has not proved feasible
to make correlations, as we did in the case of the male, with the
female's own occupational rating. However, in the present volume we
have correlated the incidences and frequencies of her sexual activities
with the occupational class of the parental home in which she was
raised. If the parental home had changed its social status during the
time that the female lived in it, she was given a rating in each of the
occupational classes. The occupational classes have been defined as
they were defined in the case of the male:

(1) Underworld: deriving a significant portion of the income from
illicit activities

(2) Unskilled laborers: persons employed by the hour for labor
which does not require special training

(3) Semi-skilled laborers: persons employed by the hour or on
other temporary bases for tasks involving some minimum of
training

(4) Skilled laborers: persons involved in manual activities which
require training and experience

(5) Lower white collar groups: persons involved in small busi-
nesses, or in clerical or similar work which is not primarily
manual and which depends upon some educational background

(6) Upper white collar groups: persons in more responsible, administrative white collar positions

(7) Professional groups: persons holding positions that depend upon professional training that is beyond the college level

(8) Persons holding important executive offices, or holding high social rank because of their financial status or hereditary family position

For further definitions and a discussion of these classes, see our volume on the male (1948:78–79).

Decade of Birth. Correlations with the decade of birth have been based, in the present volume, primarily on the four following groups:

Born before 1900
Born between 1900 and 1909
Born between 1910 and 1919
Born between 1920 and 1929

The decade of birth has proved to be one of the most significant social items correlating with the patterns of sexual behavior among American females. In many instances the youngest females in the sample, born since 1929, had not developed their patterns of sexual behavior far enough or been married long enough to warrant their inclusion in any of the comparisons of generations.

Age at Onset of Adolescence. Correlations have been made with the age at which the female showed the first adolescent developments (pp. 122–125). The classifications have been as follows:

Before and at 11 years of age
At 12 years of age
At 13 years of age
At 14 years of age
At 15 years of age or later

Rural-Urban Background. The subjects in the present study have been classified as having rural backgrounds if they lived on an operating farm for an appreciable portion of the time between the ages of twelve and eighteen. This is the pre-adolescent and adolescent period which is of maximum importance in the shaping of sexual patterns. The more extensive classification of rural and urban backgrounds given in our volume on the male (1948:79) would have provided a more satisfactory basis for correlations, but unfortunately we do not yet have enough histories of rural females to allow us to make such an intensive study.

Religious Background. Subjects in the present study have been classified as Protestant, Catholic, or Jewish, or as belonging to some other group. In these other groups (1.3 per cent of the total sample) the number of histories is too small to allow analyses. In each of the three religious groups, the subject has been classified as devout, moderately religious, or religiously inactive, in accordance with the following definitions:

(1) DEVOUT: if the subject is regularly attending church, and/or actively participating in church activities. If Catholic, frequent attendance at confession is a criterion; if Jewish, frequent attendance in the synagogue, or the observation of a significant portion of the Orthodox custom.

(2) MODERATELY RELIGIOUS: if the subject attends church or engages in church activities with fair frequency, or attends confession in the Catholic church, or follows the Orthodox custom to some degree which, however, is less than that of strictly devout groups.

(3) RELIGIOUSLY INACTIVE: if the subject only infrequently, or rarely, or never attends church or engages in church activities, or infrequently or never goes to confession, or observes few if any of the Orthodox Jewish customs. Such persons may still, however, be related to one or another of the religious groups through their parents, through their own earlier training, or through their own current thinking. There have been exceedingly few persons in the study who are as completely irreligious or agnostic as they often insist.

It has been possible to correlate the sexual data on these histories with the current religious status of each subject, but it has not yet been possible to make correlations with their earlier religious connections. The earlier connections may have been the more significant in affecting the subsequent patterns of sexual behavior, but we will need a more extensive series than we yet have before we can undertake further analyses.

There are obviously still other factors which affect patterns of sexual behavior and which deserve investigation. For instance, the age at which the female marries may markedly affect the nature and the extent of her pre-marital experience, particularly in pre-marital petting and in pre-marital coitus. Consequently we have made correlations with the age of marriage at certain points in the present volume. On the other hand, some of the other correlations that may ultimately deserve investigation, such as the correlation with the geographic location and the type of community in which the subject was raised, cannot be made until we have secured additional data.

U. S. Estimates. In our volume on the male we attempted to estimate the incidences and frequencies of the various types of sexual activity in the total U. S. population, by weighting and combining the data for the age groups, the single, married, and previously married groups, the educational groups, and the rural and urban groups in the sample, in accordance with the incidences of those groups in the United States Census of 1940. Such a correction seemed desirable in order to prevent the general reader from making his own extensions of the data without any correction for census distributions.

The research scientist may choose between two possible procedures in presenting his data. He may present the material as a description of his findings on the particular individuals with which he worked, and make no suggestion concerning any possible extension of his generalizations to any larger group; or he may attempt, by some statistical or other technique, to discuss the applicability of his findings to some group larger than the one with which he actually worked. If he follows the first procedure, he imposes upon the reader the task of deciding how far to extend the specific findings, and the reader is usually more poorly equipped than the scientist to decide that. For instance, if we had not attempted a U. S. correction in the male volume, our data on the incidences and frequencies of masturbation, because of the larger representation of college males in the sample, would have given an exaggerated picture to any reader who took them to be typical of American males in general; and our data on the incidences and frequencies of pre-marital coitus would have represented a gross understatement for the total population because of the lesser representation of grade school and high school groups in the sample.

We have not, however, undertaken to do U. S. corrections in the present volume, because our sample of females is even more inadequate than our sample of males in representing lower educational levels, rural groups, and some of the other segments of the population (p. 36). The generalizations made throughout the present volume have, therefore, been restricted to the particular samples that we have had available. Major changes might have been introduced into the generalizations if we had had a larger sample of females who had never gone beyond grade school, but we cannot suggest what those changes might have been. Meanwhile, the samples of high school, college, and post-graduate groups are of some size, and the generalizations drawn for the sample may not be too far from the actuality for those segments of the American population.

Chapter 3

SOURCES OF DATA

The specific sources of the reported, recorded, and observed data utilized in making this volume are described in the present chapter. The use that we have made of the previously published studies on human sexual behavior is also described. Since the data reported in our series of case histories constitute an important part of this volume, the nature of those data is described in some detail in this chapter, and critical tests of the reliability and validity of the case history data are also presented here.

CASE HISTORIES OBTAINED IN PERSONAL INTERVIEWS

All of the case histories in this study have been obtained through personal interviews conducted by our staff and chiefly by four of us during the period covered by this project. We have elected to use personal interviews rather than questionnaires because we believe that face-to-face interviews are better adapted for obtaining such personal and confidential material as may appear in a sex history.[1]

Establishing Rapport. We believe that much of the quality of the data presented in the present volume is a product of the rapport which we have been able to establish in these personal interviews. Most of the subjects of this study—whatever their original intentions in regard to distorting or withholding information, and whatever their original embarrassment at the idea of contributing a history—have helped make the interviews fact-finding sessions in which the interviewer and the subject have found equal satisfaction in exploring the accumulated record as far as memory would allow. Persons with many different sorts of backgrounds have cooperated in this fashion. Females have agreed to serve as subjects and, on the whole, have contributed as readily and as honestly (p. 73, Tables 3–8) as the males who were the subjects of our previous volume. Apart from rephrasing a few

---

[1] At many points in the United States, within the past five years, there have been impostors who have posed as interviewers connected with the present project. In most instances they have operated through telephone calls. It should be understood that our staff never conducts interviews over the telephone, that all of our interviews have been carried on in personal conference with each subject, that all of our staff carries identification both from Indiana University and from the National Research Council, and that the subjects of our interviewing have in most instances met us previous to the interview through the organized groups with which we were working, or through personal introductions made by their friends.

questions to allow for the anatomic and physiologic differences between the sexes, we have covered the same subject matter and utilized essentially the same methodology in interviewing females and males.[2]

Objectivity of the Investigator. In the course of our interviewing, we have constantly reassured our subjects that the interviewer was not passing judgment on any type of sexual activity, and that he was not interested in redirecting the subject's behavior. This has been explained in so many words at the beginning of each interview, but much of the reassurance has depended on the ease and objective manner of the interviewer, on the simple directness of his questions, on his failure to show any emotional objection to any part of the record, on his tone of voice, on his calm and steady eye, on his continued pursuit of the routine questioning, and on his evident interest in discovering what each type of experience may have meant to each subject. These things can be done in a face-to-face interview; they cannot be done as effectively on a questionnaire.

Confidence of the Record. In the interviews we have had the opportunity to convince the subjects that all of our records are kept confidential, that only four persons on our staff can read the code in which each history is recorded, that none of the staff has access to the files except the persons who have taken histories, that all of the histories are kept in locked and fireproof files in our laboratories at Indiana University, that no one except the interviewers ever prepares the data for subsequent analyses, that no part of the history is ever translated into words, that the data are placed directly onto punch cards by the same interviewing staff, that no individual history is ever discussed outside of the interviewing staff, and that no history will ever be published as an individual unit.

Recording the data in code in the presence of the subject has done a good deal to convince him or her of the confidence of the record. Even though anonymity is ordinarily guaranteed by the statement which caps most questionnaires, many persons still fear that there may be some means by which they can be identified if they write out answers to printed questions. They fear, and not without some justification in the history of such studies, that a record made in plain English may be read by other persons who obtain access to the file. It is not to be forgotten that our sex laws and public opinion are so far out of accord with common and everyday patterns of sexual behavior that many persons might become involved in social or legal difficulties if their sexual histories became publicly known.

---

[2] For a list of items covered by the questions in these interviews, and for a more detailed description of the interviewing techniques, see our 1948:35–82.

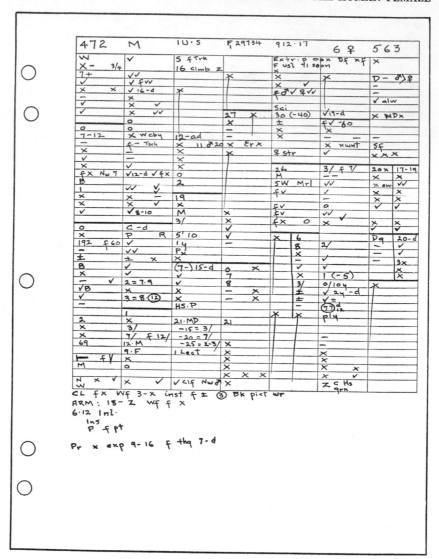

Figure 3. Sample of coded history

Flexibility in Form of Question. While the point of each question has been precisely defined throughout the history of the project, the wording of each question has been adapted to the vocabulary and experience of each subject. The study has included persons who were poorly educated and sometimes illiterate, technically trained medical and psychiatric groups, children of the age of two and adults as old as ninety, religiously devout and underworld groups, and persons with highly diverse sexual histories. We have constantly had to define terms and explain exactly what we have intended by our questions, for technically trained as well as for poorly educated subjects. This would not have been possible in a questionnaire study.

It is a mistake to believe that standard questions fed through diverse human machines can bring standard answers. The professionally trained subject may be offended at the use of anything but a precisely technical vocabulary for the anatomy and physiology of sex, but the poorly educated individual may have no sexual vocabulary beyond the four-letter English vernacular. Even the most technically trained person may not catch the meaning of some particular question, although it is phrased in a form that has proved effective for most of the others who have been interviewed.[3]

Vocabularies differ in different parts of the United States and there are differences among individuals belonging to different generations. Sexual vocabularies may differ among persons in different portions of a single city, depending upon their social levels, occupational backgrounds, racial origins, religious and educational backgrounds, and still other factors. In each community, we have had to discover the meanings that were being attached to particular terms, and learn which terms might be used without giving offense. In order to establish rapport one has to learn to use the local vocabulary with an ease and a skill that convinces the subject that we know something of the custom and mode of living in his or her type of community, and might be expected, therefore, to understand the viewpoint of such a community on matters of sex.

For instance, one has to learn that a person in a lower level community may live common-law, although he does not enter into a common-law marriage with a common-law wife. As we have noted in our volume on the male (1948:52), we have had to learn that a lower level individual is never ill or injured although he may be sick or hurt; he may not wish to do a thing although he may want to do it; he does not perceive although he may see; he may not be acquainted with a person although he may know him. Syphilis may be rare in such a community, although bad blood may be more common. At such a level an individual may not yet have learned about a particular type of sexual activity although he may have heard about it and even observed it many times; but he considers that he does not know about it until he has had

---

[3] This is illustrated by the misinterpretation of the question, "Are both testes descended?" which was used on a questionnaire with which we experimented at the beginning of the present project. While the question referred to the descent of the testes from the body cavity, it was regularly misinterpreted by those filling out the questionnaire, and even by a number of professionally trained zoologists and physicians, to apply to the relative position of the testes in the scrotum.

experience. Such an individual does not understand our question about seeing a burlesque although he can tell you about the burlesque show which he saw. The existence of prostitutes in the community may be denied, although it may be common knowledge that there are some females and males who are hustling. Inquiries about the frequency with which a prostitute robs her clients may not bring any admission that such a thing ever happens, although she may admit that she rolls some of her tricks. But the use of such terms with an upper level subject would leave him mystified or offended. At every level, inquiries about the circulation of pornographic literature might elicit very little information, although most teen-age boys may have seen eight-pagers. The adaptation of one's vocabulary in an interview thus not only contributes to the establishment of rapport, but brings out information which would be completely missed on a standardized questionnaire.

An interview may be restricted to the areas in which the subject has had sexual experience. By feeling his way, the interviewer may discover the limits of that experience, and not ask questions beyond that point. If the subject has not had masturbatory, or coital, or homosexual experience, questions concerning the detailed techniques of those activities are simply passed by. Thus it has been possible to interview children and inexperienced older individuals without mystifying or wearying them, or shocking them by discussing types of sexual activity about which they have had no previous information. But a questionnaire must cover all of the activities which the most experienced adult may have had, and there would be a variety of objections to undertaking such an exposition of all of the possibilities of human sexual behavior in the course of a single interview.

Consistency of Data. In a personal interview, the interviewer may check, on the spot, the consistency of the material covered in the history. He and the subject may then adjust, correct, and iron out contradictions which may have developed in the record. On occasion, the subject may have deliberately distorted the report; in other instances the subject's memory may have failed; but answers which develop later in the interview may allow the interviewer to return to the original statement and straighten out the inconsistencies, with the subject's help and without offending the subject by impugning his or her veracity. This would be difficult or impossible in most questionnaire studies.

Moreover, it has been possible for the interviewer to see that each and every item on the coded sheet was answered by the subject. The frequent failure to secure all of the answers on a questionnaire is a prime source of statistical difficulty which usually cannot be corrected after a subject has turned in a written record.

Determining the Quality of the Response. In a face-to-face interview, the interviewer has an opportunity to check the honesty, the certainty, and the exact meaning of the subject's reply. The speed of the subject's response, his tone of voice, the direction of his eye, the intonation and the directness or circumlocution of his statement, often provide a clue to the quality of the information which he is giving. When the subject seems uncertain in his reply, the interviewer may ask for additional information, sometimes on matters which are not covered by the standard interview. This may direct the inquiry toward important data which would have been overlooked if the interview had been confined to the minimum material. There are few such bases for determining the quality of the replies on a questionnaire, and little opportunity for extending the data beyond the set limits of a questionnaire.

Time Involved in Interview. The average interview of an adult contributing to the present study has required something between one and a half and two hours. When the subject had had more limited experience, as is frequently true of teen-age girls, the interviewing may have been accomplished in an hour or less; but when subjects had had more extensive experience the interviews have often extended beyond the two hours. Something over 300 questions have been minimum on the average history, but in special instances—where there had been extensive pre-marital or extra-marital experience, extensive homosexual experience, elaborate techniques in masturbation, coitus, or other types of sexual activity—the interviews have sometimes extended to 500 or more questions. It is doubtful whether it would have been possible to persuade many persons to give so much time to a questionnaire; and the quality of the answers on such a long questionnaire would probably have been lower.

The problem involved in a two-hour interview which covers 300 to 500 questions, many of which concern highly confidential material, is very different from the problem which is involved in most public opinion polls, and in most market, government, and other surveys which have utilized questionnaires. The claims made for the efficiency of the questionnaire have, to a large extent, been based upon studies that have covered relatively few questions and required relatively little time from each subject. Moreover, comparisons of questionnaire and interview techniques have usually been made on studies which dealt with subjects less sensitive than sexual behavior.[4]

----

[4] Attempts to assess the relative merits of questionnaire and interview techniques in sex studies have been presented in such studies as: Davis 1929:403–415. Bromley and Britten 1938:26–43. A. Ellis 1947, 1948. Finger 1947. Ross 1950. For a general discussion of questionnaire and interview techniques, see Young 1949:220–264.

It is possible that the quality of the data obtained in interview studies may be more variable than the quality of the data secured from questionnaire studies, because the effectiveness of an interview so largely depends on the ability and experience of the interviewer and on the quality of his interviewing. In our own study, the interviewing has been limited to a very small number of carefully trained and professionally equipped, full-time associates on the project. On the other hand, public opinion and market and government surveys which must be carried on and completed in a minimum period of time often have to utilize large corps of part-time interviewers, most of whom cannot be trained to do much more than locate the subjects of the study and deliver a set schedule which they wish to have answered. This has been a prime reason for the conclusion that questions on an interview should be strictly standardized and administered via a questionnaire which is filled out by the subject or by the interviewer.

REPORTED DATA FROM CASE HISTORIES

The items covered in our interviewing were listed in our previous volume on the male (1948:63–70). The histories obtained through the interviews provided most of the data which were statistically tabulated and correlated in that volume, and which we present now in this volume on the female. Specifically, the following statistics have been drawn from the data reported on the histories:

Accumulative Incidence. These show the number of females and males, in terms of the percentages of the total sample, who had ever, by a given age, had experience or reached orgasm in the various types of sexual activity. The data cover the pre-adolescent sex play, masturbation, nocturnal dreams, heterosexual petting, pre-marital coitus, marital coitus, extra-marital coitus, post-marital coitus, homosexual contacts, and animal contacts of each of the subjects in the study. See pages 46–47 for a further discussion.

The case histories have also provided accumulative incidence data showing the ages at which the subjects first acquired information concerning various aspects of sex, the ages of first erotic arousal, the ages at marriage, the techniques utilized in the various types of sexual activity, the nature and number of the partners in the socio-sexual contacts, the subject's attitudes toward particular types of sexual activity, and still other matters which are detailed later in this chapter.

Active Incidence. The case history data have made it possible to calculate the active incidences of the subjects—in terms of the percentages of the total sample—who were engaging in each type of sexual activity in each of the five-year age periods covered by the histories. See page 47 for a further discussion.

Frequency of Activity. The case history data have shown the frequencies with which each subject had engaged in each type of activity in each five-year period of his or her history. All frequencies have been calculated as average frequencies per week. See pages 47–48 for a further discussion.

Number of Years Involved. The case histories have shown the number of years during which each subject was involved in each type of sexual activity. At several points we have also obtained data on the continuity or discontinuity of certain types of sexual activity, noting those that had ordinarily occurred with some regularity and those which had occurred sporadically. We have stressed this point in the present volume, because sexual activities among females prove to be discontinuous more often than they are among males.

Techniques. Data on the incidences of the techniques used in the female's sexual activities have also been obtained from the case histories. The data have covered:

Masturbation: 12 items of technique
Heterosexual petting (pre-marital, marital, or extra-marital): 10 items of technique
Heterosexual coitus (pre-marital, marital, or extra-marital): 18 items of technique
Homosexual contacts: 24 items of technique
Animal contacts: 4 items of technique

Partners. Where there had been socio-sexual contacts, the case histories have shown the number and ages of the partners involved and, in the more extensive histories, the subject's preferences for particular types of partners, the way in which the partners first met, the marital status of each partner, the partner's occupational classification, and the frequencies of contact.

Motivations and Attitudes. In each interview there has been an attempt to identify the first sources of the subject's sexual knowledge, the factors that were originally responsible for the subject's involvement in each type of sexual activity, and the factors (such as erotic satisfactions) which were responsible for the continuation of the activity.

The subject's evaluation of his or her sexual experience, his or her intention to have or not to have additional experience, and his or her social and moral judgments of masturbation, pre-marital coitus, extra-marital coitus, and homosexual activities, have also been recorded, and are analyzed in the present volume.

Correlations with Biologic and Social Backgrounds. In each case history, we have obtained data on factors which might have affected the individual's choice of a pattern of sexual behavior, such as his or her age, marital status, educational level, parental occupational class, decade of birth, age at onset of adolescence, rural or urban background, religious background, and still other factors. See pages 53 to 56 for a further discussion.

Psychologic and Social Significance. In the interviewing, considerable information has been obtained on the psychologic and social significance of each type of sexual activity for the subject of each case history. Specific data have been secured on items of such obvious social concern as pregnancies consequent on pre-marital coitus, the effects of pre-adolescent sexual experience with adults, and the social and legal difficulties in which the subject may have become involved as a consequence of his or her sexual behavior. We have correlated the record on pre-marital sexual experience with the record of orgasm in the subsequent marital coitus. We have made special analyses of married couples, unmarried females, older females, females with homosexual histories, and still other special groups.

Much of the discussion of the social significance of each type of sexual activity has, however, been drawn from recorded and observed data, rather than from the case histories. These other sources of data are discussed below (pp. 83–92).

RELIABILITY AND VALIDITY OF REPORTED DATA

We are, of course, interested in knowing how far the events reported in an interview may represent an accurate account of what actually happened to the subject who has given the report. The record may be affected by: (1) a simple failure to recall, at the moment, events that should have been made a part of the record; (2) more specific errors (distortions) of memory; (3) some failure to comprehend the nature of the events when they originally took place; (4) emotional blockages which interfere with the subject's ability to make an objective report; (5) deliberate cover-up or misrepresentation of the fact; and (6) some deliberate exaggeration of the fact. There are some events that are less liable to these errors than some others on a sex history.

This problem of the reliability and validity of reported behavior is not unique to this study or even to case history studies in general. It is a problem which we all face in evaluating the statements made by our friends, the reports published in newspapers and magazines, and all other sources of information which does not come from our own direct observations. If we were to accept the extreme skepticism which some persons profess, we should rate all reports as worthless, and not be too certain that our own eyes do not deceive us. Obviously, we do not actually do this in our everyday lives, and we do not actually do this with a scientific report. What we do do is to try to find some means for determining the degree of reliability and the level of the validity of the reported data. We have learned to accept reports from persons who are reliable and sincere in their attempts to confine themselves to valid statements. We arrive at some opinion concerning the general reliability or unreliability of each of the local newspapers. We try to find out what experience lies back of the journalist who writes the magazine article, and we want to know how capable and cautious he may have been in separating well established data from mere gossip and emotionally biased interpretations. In a scientific study we attempt to develop a variety of tests to determine the reliability and validity of the reported and observed data.

By the *reliability* of a subject or of a report, we refer to the interlocking consistencies of the data, and the consistency with which the subject gives the same report on successive occasions. In our present study, we have given especial attention to the internal consistencies of the data which we get on each history, and before the end of an interview we requestion the subject in order to straighten out any apparent inconsistencies. We have further tested reliability by securing retakes of histories from subjects who had previously given us histories. Comparisons of the data secured from the original histories and the retakes are described on pages 68 to 74.

By *validity*, we refer to the conformance of the reported data with the event that actually occurred. The best test of validity would be a comparison of the report with recorded data made by qualified observers or recording machines. Short of that, we may test the validity of reported data by comparing the replies given independently by two or more participants in the same activity. We have, for instance, compared the reported data given us by several hundred pairs of spouses (pp. 74–76). More indirectly, we may test validity by comparing the replies obtained from one group with the replies obtained from a group that might be expected to have had similar sexual histories. For instance, we have compared the coital rates reported by males and the rates reported by females. The testing of the reliability and validity of our data is as yet insufficient, and we shall continue to make such tests as the research program allows; but it may be noted that this is the first time that tests of either reliability or validity have been made in any study of human sexual behavior, and that there are few other case history studies of any sort which have made as extensive tests as we have undertaken in the present study.

Retakes. Comparisons of the data secured in an original interview and the data secured from the same person at some subsequent date may test the reliability (the consistency) of the reports. In general, the test is more severe if an appreciable period of time has elapsed between the first and second interviews, for it then becomes more difficult to duplicate distortions which may have been accidentally, capriciously, or calculatedly introduced into the original record. If answers have been capricious, without a basis in fact, it becomes increasingly improbable that an exact duplicate could be produced after any considerable lapse of time. This is particularly likely to be true in the present study, where hundreds of details are covered on each history.

We have, in consequence, spent some time securing retakes from a series of subjects who had previously contributed their histories. In our previous volume we were able to report on 162 of these retakes, including both females and males. We can now report on 319 retakes, including 124 females and 195 males. We shall continue to accumulate such material as the total program allows, for we need to compare the reliability of the data which we secure from persons of various ages, various social levels, and various other groups.

While retakes do not provide a test of the validity of a report—the extent to which the reported behavior conforms with the event as it actually occurred—consistencies in answers on long-time retakes do suggest that they may have had some basis in fact.

With few exceptions, our retakes have been made only after a minimum lapse of 18 months. For some years we have demanded a minimum lapse of at least two years. The median lapse of time between the original histories and retakes reported in the present volume has been 35 months for the males, and 33 months for the females. In a number of instances, the retakes have not been made until 10 or 12 years after the original histories were obtained. This constitutes an extreme test of the capacity of an individual to reproduce the considerable detail which is involved in the more than 300 questions that have been covered on each history. Comparisons of the data secured on this series of original histories, and the data secured on the corresponding histories in the series of retakes (Tables 3 and 4), show the following:

In regard to the accumulative incidence data (the question of whether an individual has *ever* been involved in a particular type of activity), the number of identical replies on the original histories and the retakes ranges from 77 per cent on one of the items, to 97 per cent on two of the other items (Tables 3, 4, column 4). For most of the items, the incidences calculated on the whole group of retakes are not materially different from the incidences calculated on the original group of histories (Tables 3, 4, last column). On fourteen of the items, they are modified by something less than 3 per cent (of a possible 100 per cent) and on three more the modification amounts to something between 3 and 4 per cent. The modification amounts to more than that on only four items. It is most extreme (9 to 10 per cent) for the incidence of pre-adolescent heterosexual play among females and among males, and for the incidence of pre-adolescent homosexual play among females. The greater discrepancies on these latter items are probably due to errors of memory concerning such early events, and to some difficulty in identifying pre-adolescent play as sexual; they are less likely to be due to deliberate cover-up.

The differences between the means computed for the whole group of original histories, and for the whole group of retakes, are actually small in terms of the units of measurement (Tables 3, 4, column 2), and in most instances less than might have been expected from an examination of the percents of identical replies. This means that the discrepancies between the first and second reports do not lie in one direction more often than the other, and that the differences on the individual histories are to some extent ironed out in computing averages.

For the adult female activities, the retakes modify the incidences calculated on the original histories by less than 2 per cent (of a possible 100 per cent) in the case of masturbation, petting experience, petting to orgasm, pre-marital coitus, and homosexual experience (Tables 3, 4). They modify the incidences by something between 3 and 4 per cent in the case of nocturnal dreams which go to the point of orgasm, and in the case of extra-marital coitus. They modify the incidence of petting to the point of orgasm by nearly 6 per cent. For adult males, there is no activity for which the retakes modify the incidences calculated on the original histories by as much as 3 per cent, and in regard to five of the types of activity (nocturnal dreams to orgasm, petting to climax, coitus with prostitutes, extra-marital coitus, and animal contacts), they modify the incidences originally calculated by something less than 1 per cent.

It is to be noted that in regard to most types of activity both among females and males, the retakes raise the incidences calculated on the original histories. This confirms the impression we have acquired in the course of our interviewing, that the incidence data may be taken as minimum records, rather than exaggerations of the fact.

There were surprisingly few differences in the mean ages reported on the original histories and on the retakes for various items: for the

Table 3. Comparisons of Data Reported on Original Histories and Retakes of 124 Females

NO. OF CASES	ITEMS INVOLVED	UNIT OF CLASSI-FICATION	DISAGREE BY LESS THAN — One unit	Two units	Three units	RANGE OF DISAGREEMENT, 5th to 95th percentile	DIFFERENCE OF MEANS Retake minus original
	ACCUMULATIVE INCIDENCE		*Percent of females*				*Percentage points*
122	Masturb. to org.	Yes, No	86				+0.9 ± 3.39
118	Dreams to orgasm	Yes, No	90				−3.4 ± 2.93
123	Petting exper.	Yes, No	93				−1.6 ± 2.26
105	Petting to org.	Yes, No	77	*See*			+5.8 ± 4.66
121	Pre-mar. coitus	Yes, No	97				−1.7 ± 1.65
45	Pre-mar. coitus to orgasm	Yes, No	96	*last*			0.0
51	Extra-mar. coitus	Yes, No	90	*footnote*			+3.9 ± 4.42
121	Homosex. contacts to org.	Yes, No	95				+1.6 ± 1.98
122	Pre-ad. hetero. exper.	Yes, No	84				+9.9 ± 3.57
121	Pre-ad. homosex. exper.	Yes, No	79				+9.1 ± 4.07
	AVERAGE FREQUENCY		*Percent of females*			*Freq. per wk.*	*Freq. per wk.*
206	Total outlet	1.0/wk	63	78	86	+7.3 to −2.2	+1.03 ± 0.355
108	Masturb. to org.	0.5/wk	63	77	81	+0.9 to −2.6	−0.20 ± 0.161
21	Dreams to orgasm	0.1/wk	38	62	76	+0.2 to −1.5	−0.25 ± 0.163
32	Petting to org.	0.1/wk	44	59	63	+0.4 to −1.0	−0.16 ± 0.083
42	Pre-mar. coitus	0.5/wk	71	81	91	+1.4 to −0.2	+0.19 ± 0.085
41	Pre-mar. coitus to orgasm	0.5/wk	63	73	76	+1.8 to −0.6	+0.24 ± 0.164
21	Extra-mar. coitus	0.5/wk	91	100	100	+0.2 to −0.5	−0.05 ± 0.033
101	Marital coitus	0.5/wk	49	65	73	+2.1 to −2.7	+0.17 ± 0.290
14	Homosex. contacts to org.	0.5/wk	64	71	86	+1.8 to −1.5	+0.04 ± 0.290
	VITAL STATISTICS		*Percent of females*			*Per unit of classif.*	
121	Age of subject	1 year	88	97	98	+1.0 to −0.6	+0.15 ± 0.103
60	Age, male at marr.	1 year	52	82	85	+3.4 to −4.0	+0.13 ± 0.329
62	Age, female at marr.	1 year	58	82	90	+3.4 to −2.4	+0.10 ± 0.276
67	Age of father	1 year	28	69	79	+4.1 to −2.1	+0.61 ± 0.328
73	Age of mother	1 year	30	60	78	+6.4 to −2.8	+0.93 ± 0.406
120	No. of brothers	1	95	99	100	+0.5 to −0.5	−0.01 ± 0.026
120	No. of sisters	1	98	100	100	+0.4 to −0.5	−0.03 ± 0.015
123	Educational level	1 year	80	97	98	+1.0 to −1.2	−0.05 ± 0.060
	AGE, FIRST KNOWLEDGE OF:		*Percent of females*			*Per unit of classif.*	
92	Pregnancy	1 year	33	63	77	+2.4 to −4.4	−0.48 ± 0.240
84	Coitus	1 year	38	67	81	+4.2 to −5.1	−0.37 ± 0.268
57	Fertilization	1 year	28	59	75	+3.5 to −4.7	−0.19 ± 0.411
104	Menstruation	1 year	39	77	92	+2.1 to −2.9	−0.22 ± 0.150
53	Prostitution	1 year	23	51	70	+3.3 to −5.4	−0.26 ± 0.380
67	Venereal disease	1 year	19	49	66	+4.0 to −4.3	−0.42 ± 0.357
64	Condoms	1 year	30	67	73	+3.2 to −5.2	−0.50 ± 0.376
	AGE, FIRST EXPER. IN:		*Percent of females*			*Per unit of classif.*	
30	Pre-ad. hetero. exper.	1 year	47	80	93	+2.0 to −3.0	0.00
40	Pre-ad. homosex. exper.	1 year	28	65	85	+2.5 to −3.2	0.00
117	Adolescence	1 year	67	93	100	+1.4 to −1.4	+0.04 ± 0.067
73	Orgasm	1 year	40	71	80	+4.6 to −4.8	−0.27 ± 0.356
119	Menstruation	1 year	66	94	99	+1.4 to −1.2	+0.12 ± 0.081

(*Table continued on next page*)

Table 3 (continued)

NO. OF CASES	ITEMS INVOLVED	UNIT OF CLASSI-FICATION	DISAGREE BY LESS THAN			RANGE OF DISAGREEMENT, 5th to 95th percentile	DIFFERENCE OF MEANS Retake minus original
			One unit	Two units	Three units		
48	Masturb. to org.	1 year	29	63	77	+4.0 to −7.2	−0.52 ± 0.521
18	Dreams to orgasm	1 year	28	56	56	+18.8 to −13.1	−0.39 ± 2.443
22	Petting to org.	1 year	32	73	77	+3.9 to −3.4	−0.27 ± 0.629
66	Coitus, any	1 year	55	80	91	+1.7 to −3.0	−0.30 ± 0.164
52	Pre-mar. coitus	1 year	48	79	89	+1.7 to −3.3	−0.40 ± 0.198
36	Pre-mar. coitus to orgasm	1 year	47	86	92	+2.6 to −1.6	0.00
19	Extra-mar. coitus	1 year	37	63	68	+10.5 to −7.5	+0.05 ± 1.484
18	Homosex. contacts to orgasm	1 year	39	67	67	+3.6 to −10.8	−1.56 ± 1.212

Table is based on all available retakes, including both white and Negro females, and both prison and non-prison histories.

Comparisons have been made only for the period prior to the original interview. Activity reported as occurring after the first interview obviously cannot be used for comparisons.

The N's vary for the different items because: (1) in a few instances the question was not asked, or not asked in sufficient detail, in either the original or the retake interview; (2) comparisons of frequencies of activity apply only to persons actively engaged in such activity; (3) in some instances the questions were not applicable to the particular females.

The N's on the frequency data represent the number of five-year periods (rather than the number of individuals) on which calculations and comparisons could be made.

Italics indicate that the calculations are based on less than 50 cases.

In the original sample, the accumulative incidences for the items in this part of the table, in the sequence given here (from "Masturb. to org." to "Pre-ad. homosex. exper.") were as follows: 48, 27, 93, 37, 46, 32, 41, 17, 31, and 36 per cent, respectively.

ages involved in the vital statistics, for the ages at which the subjects had first acquired their knowledge of various sexual items, and for the ages at which they had first had experience in the various types of sexual activity. In 53 out of the 54 items (female plus male) covered in these calculations, the mean ages calculated on the original histories were modified by less than one year, and on 40 out of the 54 the modification would have amounted to less than four months (0.33 years). On 18 items, the retakes did not modify the means obtained on the original histories by more than one month. If one notes again that three years had, on the average, elapsed between the original histories and the retakes and, in some instances, there had been lapses of ten to twelve years, this high level of reliability is especially remarkable.

In general, the incidence data are more reliable than the frequency data. One may be expected to recall with considerable accuracy whether he has ever masturbated to orgasm, had pre-marital coitus, or been brought to orgasm in a homosexual relationship—although deliberate distortions may sometimes enter into such reports of incidence. Frequencies are more difficult to report with accuracy because most

Table 4. Comparisons of Data Reported on Original Histories and Retakes of 195 Males

NO. OF CASES	ITEMS INVOLVED	UNIT OF CLASSI-FICATION	DISAGREE BY LESS THAN			RANGE OF DISAGREEMENT, 5th to 95th percentile	DIFFERENCE OF MEANS Retake minus original
			One unit	Two units	Three units		
	ACCUMULATIVE INCIDENCE		*Percent of males*				*Percentage points*
192	Masturb. to org.	Yes, No	97				+2.0 ± 1.27
191	Dreams to orgasm	Yes, No	94				−0.5 ± 1.74
192	Petting exper.	Yes, No	93				+2.6 ± 1.87
186	Petting to org.	Yes, No	86				0.0
191	Pre-mar. coitus with companion	Yes, No	96	*See*			+2.6 ± 1.38
189	Pre-mar. coitus with prostitute	Yes, No	91	*last*			−0.5 ± 2.19
62	Extra-mar. coitus	Yes, No	87	*footnote*			0.0
191	Homosex. contacts to org.	Yes, No	88				+2.6 ± 2.62
192	Animal contacts	Yes, No	95				0.0
194	Pre-ad. hetero. exper.	Yes, No	88				+8.8 ± 2.49
195	Pre-ad. homosex. exper.	Yes, No	83				+3.5 ± 2.99
	AVERAGE FREQUENCY		*Percent of males*			*Freq. per wk.*	*Freq. per wk.*
570	Total outlet	1.0/wk	47	70	81	+4.5 to −3.4	+0.24 ± 0.147
454	Masturb. to org.	0.5/wk	39	60	71	+2.9 to −3.3	−0.06 ± 0.118
336	Dreams to orgasm	0.1/wk	61	72	78	+0.9 to −0.9	0.00
68	Petting to org.	0.1/wk	41	59	65	+0.7 to −0.9	−0.16 ± 0.098
151	Pre-mar. coitus with companion	0.5/wk	62	72	81	+3.6 to −2.1	+0.13 ± 0.178
107	Pre-mar. coitus with prostitute	0.5/wk	75	89	94	+0.6 to −1.0	−0.02 ± 0.070
36	Extra-mar. coitus	0.5/wk	*50*	*61*	*67*	*+4.8 to −3.9*	*−0.12 ± 0.380*
124	Marital coitus	0.5/wk	43	69	79	+3.6 to −2.1	+0.43 ± 0.244
152	Homosex. contacts to orgasm	0.5/wk	56	74	84	+2.8 to −1.4	+0.16 ± 0.102
	VITAL STATISTICS		*Percent of males*			*Per unit of classif.*	*Per unit of classif.*
195	Age of subject	1 year	89	100	100	+0.8 to −0.5	+0.03 ± 0.024
84	Age, male at marr.	1 year	56	81	83	+2.2 to −5.8	−0.57 ± 0.273
82	Age, female at marr.	1 year	45	72	78	+4.4 to −5.4	−0.15 ± 0.370
111	Age of father	1 year	27	56	70	+5.7 to −4.0	+0.54 ± 0.290
114	Age of mother	1 year	32	58	75	+6.2 to −3.4	+0.68 ± 0.260
193	No. of brothers	1	91	98	98	+0.5 to −0.5	−0.01 ± 0.051
193	No. of sisters	1	91	97	98	+0.5 to −0.5	+0.03 ± 0.053
192	Educational level	1 year	88	99	99	+0.5 to −0.9	−0.06 ± 0.050
	AGE, FIRST KNOWLEDGE OF:		*Percent of males*			*Per unit of classif.*	*Per unit of classif.*
152	Pregnancy	1 year	22	55	83	+3.1 to −4.4	−0.25 ± 0.174
127	Coitus	1 year	28	59	80	+3.9 to −4.0	−0.02 ± 0.198
108	Fertilization	1 year	32	61	78	+4.3 to −3.3	+0.31 ± 0.213
118	Menstruation	1 year	23	55	75	+3.5 to −4.2	−0.43 ± 0.225
66	Prostitution	1 year	24	59	73	+4.2 to −3.4	+0.02 ± 0.275
74	Venereal disease	1 year	28	61	78	+3.2 to −4.1	−0.28 ± 0.270
65	Condoms	1 year	20	49	74	+4.4 to −3.8	−0.08 ± 0.289
	AGE, FIRST EXPER. IN:		*Percent of males*			*Per unit of classif.*	*Per unit of classif.*
86	Pre-ad. hetero. exper.	1 year	33	69	85	+3.2 to −4.2	−0.24 ± 0.223
89	Pre-ad. homosex. exper.	1 year	25	70	90	+3.0 to −2.7	+0.02 ± 0.194
183	Adolescence	1 year	51	84	99	+2.0 to −1.8	+0.07 ± 0.077
184	Ejaculation	1 year	49	80	96	+2.1 to −2.1	−0.04 ± 0.114
175	Masturb. to org.	1 year	48	79	94	+2.1 to −2.4	−0.10 ± 0.137
147	Dreams to orgasm	1 year	24	56	75	+4.7 to −4.0	+0.09 ± 0.295
35	Petting to org.	1 year	*37*	*57*	*74*	*+4.7 to −3.7*	*+0.29 ± 0.508*
128	Coitus, any	1 year	43	70	84	+3.2 to −3.3	−0.12 ± 0.200
55	Coitus, prost.	1 year	35	64	82	+5.8 to −3.2	+0.29 ± 0.354
27	Extra-marit. coitus	1 year	*37*	*82*	*93*	*+2.3 to −2.1*	*+0.15 ± 0.248*
87	Homosex. contacts to orgasm	1 year	40	64	83	+4.1 to −4.7	−0.28 ± 0.326

(Footnote to table on next page)

72

persons are inexperienced in averaging any sort of activity which occurs sporadically. Moreover, in an interview in a sex study the subject is asked to estimate averages for events that may have occurred in the long-distant past (see also our 1948:124–125).

In connection with the frequencies of sexual activity, on 7 out of the 9 items reported by the females and on 8 out of the 9 items reported by the males, fewer than 70 per cent of the subjects had given identical replies (within the limits of the units designated in Tables 3, 4). For a number of the items less than half of the subjects had given identical replies. Moreover, something between 6 and 37 per cent of the subjects failed to give replies that lay within even two units of identity.

However, the utility of the frequency data appears to increase when we deal with the average frequencies for the whole group of subjects. The differences between the mean frequencies calculated for the original histories and the mean frequencies calculated for the retakes would amount to something less than one experience in five weeks for almost any type of activity, and to less than one experience in ten weeks for most of them.

Comparisons of the data presented in Tables 3 and 4 fail to show consistent differences in the reliability of the record secured from females and that secured from males. Females do not seem to have been more inclined, as some persons have suggested they might be, to distort the record on the material covered by the present study. In regard to the 45 items which the female and male histories have in common, the females gave identical replies more often than the males in 23 instances, identical replies as often as the males in 4 instances, and identical replies less often than the males in 18 instances. Comparisons of replies that were identical within one and within two units show about the same proportions of concurrence between the female and male replies. A further examination of Tables 3 and 4 shows that the reliability of the data on the specifically sexual items is as high as the reliability of the data on such non-sexual items as those covered by the vital statistics, and this seems remarkable.

It may be added that the reliability of the data which we have studied from our series of retakes is, with the exception of the frequency data, not particularly different from the reliability of reports obtained in other surveys which have dealt with much less personal

---

Footnote to Table 4

The footnotes for Table 3 also apply to this table.

In the original sample, the accumulative incidences for the items in this part of the table, in the sequence given here (from "Masturb. to org." to "Pre-ad. homosex. exper."), were as follows: 94, 89, 91, 39, 59, 34, 55, 51, 10, 51, and 59 per cent, respectively.

Table 5. Comparisons of Data Reported by 706 Paired Spouses

NO. OF CASES	ITEMS INVOLVED	UNIT OF CLASSI-FICATION	DISAGREE BY LESS THAN One unit	Two units	Three units	RANGE OF DISAGREEMENT, 5th to 95th percentile	DIFFERENCE OF MEANS Male minus female
	ACCUMUL. INCID., TECHNIQUES, COITAL FOREPLAY		*Percent of spouses*				*Percentage points*
702	Deep kissing	Yes, No	89				+1.3 ± 1.23
703	♀ breast, manual stim.	Yes, No	98				−0.1 ± 0.51
				See			
702	♀ breast, oral stim.	Yes, No	92				+1.1 ± 1.07
702	♀ genital, manual stim.	Yes, No	96	*last*			+0.3 ± 0.73
701	♂ genital, manual stim.	Yes, No	94	*footnote*			−0.1 ± 0.96
702	♀ genital, oral stim.	Yes, No	91				−3.4 ± 1.15
701	♂ genital, oral stim.	Yes, No	92				−2.3 ± 1.10
	ACCUMUL. INCID., COITAL TECHNIQUES		*Percent of spouses*				*Percentage points*
701	Male above	Yes, No	99				+0.6 ± 0.45
701	Female above	Yes, No	90				+2.9 ± 1.17
700	On side	Yes, No	82				+2.6 ± 1.59
696	Sitting	Yes, No	84	*See*			+3.6 ± 1.52
698	Standing	Yes, No	87				+1.6 ± 1.38
698	Rear entrance	Yes, No	87	*last*			+3.8 ± 1.38
649	Coitus nude	Yes, No	94				+1.5 ± 0.97
				footnote			
464	Male prefers light-dark	1 of 3	61				+0.10 ± 0.036
480	Female prefers light-dark	1 of 3	67				+0.01 ± 0.034
	COITUS		*Percent of spouses*				*Percentage points*
646	Incid. pre-mar. coitus with fiancé	Yes, No	93 (Incid. rep. by males = 53%)				+2.2 ± 1.07
647	Incid. of abortions	Yes, No	96 (Incid. rep. by males = 26%)				+0.2 ± 0.83
							Per unit of classif.
310	Lapse between 1st coitus with fiancé and marr.	6 mos.	65	79	89	+3.4 to −2.5	−0.10 ± 0.121
151	Number of abortions	1 event	76	95	98	+1.4 to −1.1	−0.04 ± 0.063
630	% of coitus with ♀ orgasm	10%	52	69	81	+3.3 to −5.8	+0.51 ± 0.102
						Freq. per wk.	*Freq. per wk.*
669	Max. freq., mar. coitus	2/wk	39	67	82	+8.2 to −7.8	+0.18 ± 0.186
494	Aver. freq., early marriage	1/wk	44	73	85	+4.0 to −2.3	−0.33 ± 0.087
654	Aver. freq. at age report	1/wk	67	89	95	+2.2 to −1.2	−0.24 ± 0.063
	VITAL STATISTICS		*Percent of spouses*			*Per unit of classif.*	
706	Years married	1 year	84	98	99	+1.1 to −0.8	−0.03 ± 0.022
682	Pre-mar. acquaint.	1 year	67	87	92	+2.1 to −2.0	0.00
705	Age of ♂ at marr.	1 year	65	96	98	+1.3 to −1.3	−0.01 ± 0.038
705	Age of ♀ at marr.	1 year	65	93	97	+1.4 to −1.4	+0.07 ± 0.041
704	No. of children	1	99	99	100	+0.5 to −0.4	0.00
678	Educ. level of ♂	1 year	72	91	97	+1.6 to −1.4	−0.03 ± 0.034
692	Educ. level of ♀	1 year	69	88	96	+2.0 to −1.5	−0.09 ± 0.042
703	Occup. class of ♂	1 of 9	73	96	99	+1.3 to −1.2	−0.02 ± 0.024
352	Lapse, marr. to 1st birth	6 mos.	72	88	98	+1.4 to −1.9	+0.12 ± 0.062

(Footnote to table on next page)

74

and much less emotional material than human sexual behavior. One might have anticipated a higher level of unreliability in a sex study. Even if one makes allowances of the sort indicated above, our generalizations concerning the nature of the sexual behavior of our female and male samples will still not be modified in any material respect, with the possible exception of some of the generalizations based on the frequency data.

Comparisons of Spouses. While comparisons of original histories and retakes provide some test of the consistency of reporting, a comparison of the data provided by the two spouses in a marriage, or by the sexual partners in any other type of relationship, may provide a test of the conformance between the reported data and the actual event—*i.e.,* the validity of the report. Even such a test, however, falls short of being a final test of validity, for there may have been some prior agreement between the sexual partners to distort their reports, or both of them may have had the same reason for consciously or subconsciously distorting the fact. Nevertheless, such comparisons provide information of some value in attempting to assess the quality of reported data.

In our previous volume we compared the responses received from 231 pairs of spouses. We now have the histories of 706 pairs of spouses (1412 individual spouses) which we have compared in regard to 33 items (Table 5). These items include certain of the vital statistics, data concerning coital relations in marriage, the incidences of various techniques in the pre-coital foreplay, and the incidences of various coital positions.

Footnote to Table 5

Table is based on all available paired spouses, including both white and Negro, and both prison and non-prison histories.

Because average frequencies of coitus are not well established in the first year of marriage, data from marriages which had extended for less than one year were not used in this table. Since the maximum frequencies reached in any week are usually attained early in the marriage, one-year marriages were included in the calculations on that point. In order to test recall that covered some years, the "average frequencies in early marriage" were based on marriages which had extended for at least three years.

Comparisons have been possible only for events occurring prior to the interview with the first spouse in each pair.

The N's vary for the different items because: (1) comparisons could not be made when a given question had not been asked, or had not been asked in sufficient detail, of either spouse; (2) a few of the questions did not apply to the experience of a particular female or male.

In the male sample, the accumulative incidences for the items in the first part of the table, in the sequence given here ("Deep kissing" to " ♂ genital, oral stim."), were as follows: 89, 99, 93, 97, 93, 54, and 52 per cent, respectively.

In the male sample, the accumulative incidences for the first six items in the second part of the table, in the sequence given here ("Male above" to "Rear entrance"), were as follows: 99, 83, 70, 41, 26, and 49 per cent, respectively.

The number of identical replies ranges from 39 per cent on one item (the maximum frequency of coitus in any single week of the marriage) to 99 per cent on another (the use of the male superior position in coitus). On 12 of the items, identical replies were received from 90 per cent or more of the pairs of spouses. On 18 out of the 33 items, identical replies were received from 80 per cent or more of the pairs of spouses.

Replies that were identical within a single unit were received from 90 per cent or more of the pairs of spouses, on 7 out of the 15 items on which such measurements could be made. Replies that were identical within two units were received from 90 per cent or more of the pairs of spouses on 11 out of the 15 items.

More important than the percentages of identical or near identical replies are the magnitudes of the differences between the means calculated for the female spouses, and the means calculated for the corresponding male spouses. With one exception the means of the replies of the female spouses on various items of the vital statistics do not differ from the means of the replies of the male spouses by as much as 10 per cent of the unit of measurement—*e.g.*, by one-tenth of a year. The incidences of the various techniques used in the pre-coital foreplay, and of the positions and other techniques of the actual coitus as reported by the female and male spouses, never differ by more than 4 percentage points on any item; and on 7 out of the 14 items they differ by only 1 percentage point or less.

This means that the disagreements that do appear in the replies received from the paired spouses do not lie predominantly in a single direction. This is even true for the frequencies of the marital coitus, where we previously (1948:127–128) found a tendency for the male to underrate the frequencies, and a tendency for the female to exaggerate the frequencies. The differences which we now find in our more than 700 pairs of spouses do lie in that direction, but they do not amount to more than one coital contact in three to five weeks.

Conformance of Female and Male Reports on Marital Coitus. Heterosexual coitus should, of course, involve females as frequently as it involves males. If the male and female samples are comparable, whether they are actually representative of the total population or not, and if the replies received from females and males are equally adequate, then the frequencies of marital coitus reported by each group of married females should be identical with the frequencies of marital coitus reported by the corresponding group of married males. The degree of conformance of the data which we have from our samples of

Table 6. Comparisons of Frequencies of Marital Coitus as Reported by Females and Males

By Age and Educational Level

AGE GROUP	MEDIAN FREQ. PER WK. Female	Male	MEAN FREQ. PER WK. Female	Male	NUMBER OF CASES Female	Male
TOTAL MARRIED SAMPLE						
16–20	2.8	2.6	3.7	3.7	578	272
21–25	2.5	2.3	3.0	3.2	1654	751
26–30	2.1	2.0	2.6	2.7	1663	737
31–35	1.9	1.8	2.3	2.2	1247	569
36–40	1.5	1.6	2.0	2.0	852	390
41–45	1.2	1.3	1.7	1.6	500	272
46–50	0.9	0.9	1.4	1.4	261	175
51–55	0.8	0.7	1.2	1.2	120	109
56–60	0.4	0.6	0.8	0.8	50	67
EDUCATIONAL LEVEL 0–8						
16–20	3.4	2.5	5.1	3.7	45	158
21–25	2.6	2.2	3.3	3.3	73	324
26–30	2.5	2.1	2.8	3.0	83	292
31–35	2.1	1.7	2.6	2.3	71	186
36–40	1.6	1.6	2.2	2.0	52	143
EDUCATIONAL LEVEL 9–12						
16–20	2.9	2.8	3.8	4.1	210	87
21–25	2.4	2.5	3.0	3.3	487	164
26–30	2.1	2.1	2.6	2.9	489	135
31–35	1.8	2.1	2.3	2.8	336	82
36–40	1.6	1.7	2.1	2.3	209	58
EDUCATIONAL LEVEL 13+						
16–20	2.7	2.6	3.4	3.5	323	46
21–25	2.5	2.5	2.9	3.1	1094	440
26–30	2.1	2.1	2.6	2.6	1091	532
31–35	1.9	1.7	2.3	2.1	840	301
36–40	1.5	1.6	2.0	1.9	591	189
41–45	1.1	1.2	1.7	1.5	345	138
46–50	0.8	0.9	1.5	1.2	167	81

Table based on total sample of white, non-prison females, and on total white male sample including prison and non-prison groups. It is based on the male sample rather than the "U. S. Corrections" reported in our 1948 volume, in order to secure a more comparable educational distribution of the females and males.

married females and males should, therefore, provide a test of the quality of each sample, and also some test of the validity of the replies received from the females and from the males.

An examination of Table 6 will show that there is, in actuality, a remarkable agreement between the frequencies of marital coitus reported by the females of the various age groups and educational levels in the sample, and by the males of the corresponding groups. This is true for both the median and mean frequencies. The discrepancies which do occur are for the most part very minor, and they do not lie in any single direction. Evidently the constitution of the married female sample closely parallels that of the married male sample; and there would seem to be considerable validity in the replies received from females and males.

Table 7. Comparisons of Frequencies of Pre-Marital Coitus as Reported by Females and Males

By Age and Educational Level

AGE GROUP	MEAN FREQ. PER WEEK Female	Male	NUMBER OF CASES Female	Male
TOTAL SAMPLE, SINGLE FEMALES				
Adol.–15	—	0.4	5678	3012
16–20	0.1	0.7	5614	2868
21–25	0.2	0.8	2811	1535
26–30	0.3	0.7	1064	550
31–35	0.3	0.6	540	195
36–40	0.4	0.4	316	97
EDUCATIONAL LEVEL 0–8				
Adol.–15	0.2	1.0	162	712
16–20	0.3	1.6	143	720
21–25	0.2	1.6	67	361
26–30		1.2		159
EDUCATIONAL LEVEL 9–12				
Adol.–15	—	0.8	983	606
16–20	0.2	1.4	976	607
21–25	0.3	1.1	537	263
26–30	0.4	0.8	181	117
EDUCATIONAL LEVEL 13+				
Adol.–15	—	0.1	4400	2799
16–20	0.1	0.2	4449	2861
21–25	0.2	0.5	2207	1898
26–30	0.3	0.6	844	487

Non-conformance of Female and Male Reports on Pre-Marital Coitus. In contrast to the foregoing, comparisons of the frequency data for pre-marital coitus reported by the females and males in the sample show discrepancies of considerable magnitude (Table 7). Quite consistently in every educational level and for every age group the males reported incidences and frequencies which were higher and in some cases considerably higher than those reported by the females. At this point we are not certain what factors are primarily responsible for these differences, but some of the following may be involved:

1. The discrepancies between the reports on pre-marital coitus by the females and the males are least for the college group and maximum for the grade school group. This suggests that the replies from the college males and females are more valid than the replies from the lower level groups; or it may suggest that the college sample is more representative than the grade school sample.

2. The data given in the present volume are based almost wholly on females of the high school, college, and graduate school levels; females from the grade school level are very poorly represented in the calculations. On the other hand, the record given in our volume on the male included a much larger sample of the grade school group and was probably more representative of that group of males.

3. The females may have covered up in reporting their pre-marital experience, or the males may have exaggerated their reports of such experience. It is quite possible that both things may have happened, but it is our judgment that the female record is more often an understatement of the fact.

4. The male sample included a considerable series of males, particularly of the grade school level, who had been involved with the law and had served time in penal institutions. The frequencies of pre-marital coitus in that group were definitely higher than the frequencies of pre-marital coitus among the grade school males who had never served time in penal institutions. In the case of the female, calculations show that the frequencies of pre-marital coitus were similarly higher among those who had served time in penal institutions. The group includes both prostitutes and the sort of promiscuous females who are most often involved in tavern pick-ups and in street approaches. The exclusion of the grade school sample, and particularly of the prison sample, from the male data, or the inclusion of the corresponding group of females in the present volume, would have brought the female and male data on pre-marital coitus closer together. It still would not have accounted for all the differences.

5. Males not infrequently have their pre-marital coitus with girls of social levels which are lower than their own. Consequently, a more adequate sample of lower level females would have accounted for some of the discrepancies among the better educated groups.

6. Males have a portion of their pre-marital coitus with prostitutes; and while we attempted to differentiate the male's contacts with prostitutes and with girls who were not prostitutes, it is possible that the distinction was not always made. None of the activities which females have had as prostitutes are included in any of the calculations in the present volume.

7. White males of all social levels may have pre-marital and extra-marital coitus with Negro females. White females very rarely have non-marital coitus with Negro males. Some small portion of the discrepancy between our female and male data may be accounted for by the fact that these interracial contacts were included in the male volume but are not accounted for in the present volume, because no Negro females are included in this volume. This correction, however, would account for only a small portion of the discrepancy.

8. Some of the pre-marital coitus recorded in the male volume represented contacts which males had had outside of the United States, chiefly while they were in the armed services during the first and second World Wars and on business trips. Essentially none of these contacts are covered in the present volume.

9. The coital frequencies reported for the males were based upon the frequencies of orgasm, whereas the frequencies shown for the females represent frequencies of experience, whether with or without orgasm. In the case of the males, the calculated frequencies were raised whenever there was multiple orgasm; in the case of

the females, multiple orgasm was not included in calculating the frequencies of the coitus. Recalculations on the basis of the frequencies of experience should bring the male data closer to those for the female; but the correction would not account for more than a portion of the discrepancy.

While most of these adjustments are small, their total would bring the female and male data much closer together. It is probable, however, that differences in the representativeness of the female and male samples, and the probability that the females have covered up some portion of their pre-marital coitus, are the two factors that are chiefly involved.

Memory vs. Physical Findings. The best test of validity is one which compares reported data with data obtained by direct observation from comparable samples. Unfortunately such comparisons are unavailable on most aspects of human sexual behavior. They are available, however, for comparisons of data on the ages at which physical developments first occurred at the onset of adolescence. Table 8 shows that the data which we have obtained by recall are amazingly close to the data which have been obtained by direct observation.

The first development of a physical character might be expected to pass unnoticed by a girl or boy, and recall after a great many years might be expected to be inaccurate on such non-discrete items. It is all the more surprising, therefore, to find that the data obtained by recall are remarkably close to those obtained by observation. The greatest discrepancy (Table 8) comes in the recall of the age at which pubic hair first developed. The observations on this character, reported in two studies, give median ages which are about a year earlier than our subjects recalled. Regarding breast development, one of the physical studies indicates earlier development while another study arrives at the very same median age which our females recalled. The median age of first menstruation obtained from the recall was 13.1 years, in comparison with ages ranging on the observational studies from 12.9 to 13.9 years. Four of the observational studies arrived at a median age which differed by only 0.1 years, plus or minus, from the median calculated in our own study. Since menstruation is a more discrete event than some other adolescent developments, it is understandable that this should have been recalled with greater precision by our older subjects. Even the median age of completion of height, which was recorded by our subjects as a bit under 16 years, very closely agrees with the age reported on three of the other studies.

No scientist would be inclined to consider that data obtained by recall were as valid as data obtained from the direct observation of a physical phenomenon; but recall has apparently not served too badly on these particular characters in our case history study.

Comparisons of Data in Present and Previous Studies. Conformance of the data obtained in two or more independent studies may suggest that there is some validity in the findings, or it may suggest that all of the studies have been affected by the same sources of error. Certainly both explanations are possible, but there is a strong presumption, both among scientists in their experimental work and among most people as they meet their everyday problems, to see some significance in conformant experience.

Table 8. Comparisons of Memory and Observation as Sources of Data on Physical Development of the Female in Adolescence

SOURCES OF DATA	MEAN AGE OF FIRST APPEARANCE			
	Pubic hair	Breast devel.	Menstruation	Completion of height
Data based on recall in present study	12.3	12.5	13.1	15.9
Data based on direct observation				
Abernethy 1925:539–546			13.5	
Gould and Gould 1932:1349–1352			13.6	
Engle and Shelesnyak 1934:431–453			13.5	
Shuttleworth 1937:212				
Harvard study			13.0	
Horace Mann School study			13.1	
Shuttleworth 1939:11				15–16
Hoffman 1944:293				
Englemann study			13.9	
Hooton 1946:235				14–16
Hyman 1946:2479			13.0	
Mazer and Israel 1946:66			13.2	
Reynolds and Wines 1949:95	11.0	10.8	12.9	
Shuttleworth 1951:Fig. 120	11.3	12.5		
Corner 1952:41				15

For what it is worth, then, it may be recorded that our findings on incidences, on ages of first experience, in some instances on frequencies, on the number of years involved in given types of activity, on the number of partners involved, and on still other aspects of human sexual behavior, are in striking accord with the findings in those relatively few other studies which have made statistical analyses of data systematically collected from samples of any size (Table 9). Even some of our findings which are most likely to surprise the readers of the present volume, such as the relatively low incidence of masturbation among females, the relative infrequency of fantasy in connection with female masturbation, the relatively low incidences of homosexual contacts among females, and many of the other statistics in this volume, agree with the findings in previous statistical studies. Detailed comparisons of certain of these items are shown in Table 9, and comparisons of many more are made in the footnotes throughout this volume, particularly in Chapters 4 through 13.

Table 9. Comparisons of Data in Present and Previous Studies

PREVIOUS STUDY	FEMALE GROUP INVOLVED	ACCUMULATIVE INCIDENCE Previous study	Present study
MASTURBATION			
Davis 1929	Single, college, aver. age 37	% 65	% 65
	Same, to orgasm	53	55
Hamilton 1929	Married, mostly college, aver. age in 30's	74	61
	Same, to orgasm	45	43
Landis 1940	Mostly high school, ages 18–35	54	53
DREAMS TO ORGASM			
Hamilton 1929	Married, mostly college, aver. age in 30's	37	27
PETTING			
Davis 1929	Married, mostly college, aver. age at marr. 26	60	97
Terman 1938	Petting in high school; mostly college, aver. age 36	67	65
Landis 1940	Normal group, mostly high school, ages 18–35	100	95
Gilbert Youth Res. 1951	Single, college, ages 17–22	96	95
PRE-MARITAL COITUS			
Davis 1929	Single, college, aver. age 37	11	36
Hamilton 1929	Married, mostly college, aver. age in 30's	35	37
Terman 1938	Married, mostly college, aver. age 36	37	32
Bromley and Britten 1938	Single, college, aver. age 20	24	22
Landis 1940	Married, mostly high school, ages 22–35	27	44
Gilbert Youth Res. 1951	Single, college, ages 17–22	25	26
EXTRA-MARITAL COITUS			
Hamilton 1929	Mostly college, aver. age in 30's	24	19
Landis 1940	Mostly high school, ages 18–35	4	15
HOMOSEXUAL CONTACT			
Davis 1929	Single, college, average age 37	26	26
Hamilton 1929	Married, mostly college, aver. age in 30's	26	16
Bromley and Britten 1938	Single, college, aver. age 20	4	9
Landis 1940	Single, mostly high school, mostly ages 18–30	4	8
Gilbert Youth Res. 1951	Single, college, ages 17–22	6	9

Percentages given are incidence of experience unless otherwise indicated. Comparisons are made with the nearest comparable groups, and recalculations on both our own and the previous studies had to be made in some instances to secure comparable groups. Such recalculations of data from previous studies are shown in italics.

It is very difficult to make comparisons between various studies in this area, because of the different ways in which the age groups, educational levels, and other portions of the samples have been classified, and because many of the important factors, like the decade of birth and the religious backgrounds, were not considered in most of the previous studies. In most previous studies the reported incidence data are neither accumulative nor active incidences, but the incidences of experience up to the point at which the subjects had contributed their histories to the study; and in most instances the published studies do not make specific correlations with the ages at which the subjects contributed their histories. Consequently the comparisons made both in Table 9 and in the footnotes throughout this volume cannot be more than approximate. It is all the more surprising, therefore, to find that they are in accord as often as they are.

RECORDED DATA AS SOURCES OF INFORMATION

Throughout the years of this study we have been accumulating recorded data on human sexual behavior, and these have been the bases for much of the non-statistical and more general discussions which appear in the present volume.

The recorded data to which we have had access represent calendars, diaries, correspondence, drawings, and various other types of material accumulated by a considerable number of our subjects and contributed to our files for preservation and study. Records made at the time of sexual activity or soon thereafter are valuable because they are not so liable to be affected by the errors of memory which may get into a case history obtained some years after the event. The recorded material may also contain a great deal more detail than can be obtained in an interview. Such records may still be distorted by deliberate or unconscious cover-up, and may show considerable bias in the choice of the material which the subject elects to preserve; but such a bias may in itself be significant, for it may reflect the subject's interests better than they can be described in an interview. In addition, the recorded data may reflect unconscious or unexpressed desires. Of some of these desires, the subject may not be sufficiently aware to report them in an interview. Not infrequently the recorded material concerns types of sexual behavior which the subject has never accepted as part of his or her overt activity, although the subject may be psychologically interested in them.

Even though it has been difficult to quantify and statistically treat most of this recorded material, it has been invaluable in its portrayal of the attitudes of the subjects in the study, the social, moral, and other factors which had influenced the development of their patterns of sexual behavior, details concerning the techniques of their socio-sexual approaches, the techniques of their overt relationships, their own evaluations of their sexual experience, and their reactions to the persons with whom they had been involved.

Specifically, the recorded data and documentary materials which are in the files of the Institute for Sex Research, and which have been utilized in the present study, include the following:

Calendars. Some 377 persons, representing 312 females and 65 males, have contributed sexual calendars which show, as a minimum, the dates on which their sexual activities had occurred. In many instances, the calendars distinguish the types of sexual activity, solitary or socio-sexual, in which the subject had engaged, and activities which led to orgasm are distinguished from those which did not lead to orgasm. Most of the female calendars show how the activities were related to periods of menstruation. In some instances there are data concerning other social activities, trips during which the subject was away from the spouse, periods of illness, and still other factors that had affected the frequencies of sexual contact.

The time covered by these calendars has ranged from six months to as long a period as thirty-eight years. The emphasis on the importance of such calendars, made by Havelock Ellis some years ago, inspired a number of persons to begin keeping records, and we have profited by having access to some of these.[5] Many of the calendars were started by females who were interested in becoming pregnant and who in consequence kept records of menstruation which they, at the physician's suggestion, had correlated with their coital activities. Many of the calendars have come from scientifically trained persons who have comprehended the importance of keeping systematic records. Many of the calendars are a product of our call for such material in the male volume. We are not yet certain whether the keeping of a calendar modifies an individual's sexual behavior, but we are inclined to believe that any such modification lasts for only a short period of time.

Persons who have kept calendars, or who are willing to begin keeping day-by-day calendars showing the sources and frequencies of their outlet, are urged to write us for instructions.

Diaries. Some scores of individuals, including both females and males, have kept more elaborate records of their sexual activities, either as occasional diaries, or as day-by-day diaries, or as tabulations in other forms which they have turned into our files. The diaries often

---

[5] For Havelock Ellis's use of calendars, see Ellis 1910(1):113–121. See also Mc-Cance et al. 1937 (a British study on sexual periodicity in women based on calendar records).

include detailed accounts of the situations and the techniques involved in sexual contacts, lists and descriptions of sexual partners, discussions of attitudes, and reports on the social consequences of the activities.

The journals and correspondence of literary persons, and of other persons in public positions, have always constituted a significant part of the world's published literature and have provided source material for the biographer and historian. The sexual portions of such journals usually do not reach publication, but in a number of instances they have been made available to us for our special study.[6] Persons who have kept diaries or journals which have included a record of their sexual activities, or who are willing to begin keeping such diaries, are urged to deposit them in the files of the Institute for Sex Research where they will be kept as confidentially as the case history material.

Correspondence. We have extensive files of correspondence between spouses and between other sexual partners. In addition to recording overt sexual contacts, such correspondence often shows the emotional backgrounds out of which the sexual activities emerged. Some of this correspondence has come from persons of some literary fame. It should be emphasized, however, that correspondence originating from a person with no literary ability may also give considerable insight into the author's thinking on matters of sex. Our file of correspondence carried on surreptitiously by prison inmates, for instance, has provided important information.

Original Fiction. Many persons, including some of considerable literary ability, may, on occasion, write fiction which is primarily intended to satisfy their erotic interests. In the choice of the subject matter of such fiction, in the choice of the characters who participate in the fictional action, and in the emphases placed upon particular details of the sexual activity, the writer often discloses interests and thinking which are brought to the surface only with difficulty in an interview. Such material has, consequently, been of considerable value in extending our understanding of some of the subjects of our case histories.

Erotic fiction, for reasons discussed in Chapter 16, is more frequently produced by males. As that chapter will show, it would be of considerable importance to secure additional material, whether it is openly erotic or more general and amatory material, written by females.

Scrapbooks and Photographic Collections. Many persons make scrapbooks which, inevitably, turn about their special sexual interests.

---

[6] For examples of the use of diaries for analyses of sexual material, see: Bühler 1928:35–41 (adolescents). Iovetz-Tereshchenko 1936 (with a further list of similar studies). Diary material for such use can also be found in: Diary of Samuel Pepys, 1659–1669. Boswell's London journal 1762–1763. Freud 1921, A young girl's diary. Anne Frank 1952, The diary of a young girl.

They collect newspaper or magazine clippings, or photographs and drawings cut from magazines, bought from commercial photographers, or gathered from their friends. Not a few persons photograph their sexual partners, or collect other materials which have been associated with their partners, and many such collections have been contributed for the present study. There are materials gathered from prison inmates, collections turned over to us by courts and police who have handled sex cases, collections of fine art, and still other types of material. Persons wishing to add such material to the files of the Institute would, consequently, be contributing to our basic understanding of human sexual behavior. Such collections are more frequently made by males (see Chapter 16), and it would be particularly valuable to secure additional material collected by females.

Art Materials. In an attempt to determine the extent to which erotic elements have contributed to the development of the world's fine art, we have been engaged for some years in obtaining the histories of living artists and in correlating each history with the character of the work done by the artist. Each artist has helped us accumulate originals or printed or photographic reproductions of his or her artistic output. We now have originals or copies of some 16,000 works of art, contemporary and non-contemporary, which are providing materials for this study.

The artist's drawing or painting provides something more than a photographic reproduction of the person or of the scene which he is depicting. In his emphasis on particular items, in his exaggeration of particular parts of the body, in his arrangement of the elements of the total composition, and in his selection of particular subject matter, he interprets his material in terms of his own special interests. The amateur is unable to introduce such emphases and exaggerations without making them so apparent that they become distortions instead of interpretations of the reality. For this very reason, however, amateur drawings are even more likely to expose conscious or sometimes subconscious sexual interests.[7] The doodlings which artists often do in their spare moments may give an especial insight into their thinking on matters of sex. Many artists have done more specifically erotic drawings or paintings. Since erotic art is more frequently produced by males (Chapter 16), we particularly need additional material done by females.

---

[7] Spontaneous drawings by both children and adults have been used increasingly as interpretive material, often with sexual implications. See such studies as the following: Berrien 1935. Elkisch 1945. Waehner 1946. Naumburg 1947; 1950. Jensen 1947. London and Caprio 1950. London 1952(2). Bender 1952: 104–184 (includes an excellent bibliography).

Toilet Wall Inscriptions. From the days of ancient Greece and Rome, it has been realized that uninhibited expressions of sexual desires may be found in the anonymous inscriptions scratched in out-of-the-way places by authors who may freely express themselves because they never expect to be identified. Students of anthropology, folklore, psychology, psychiatry, and the social sciences have found such graffiti (inscriptions, usually on walls and the like) a rich source of information.[8] In Chapter 16 we show that such material epitomizes some of the most basic differences between male and female sexual psychology. The importance of the toilet wall inscriptions which we have accumulated should become apparent upon examining the data presented in that chapter. Since males are more prone to produce such graffiti, we particularly need additional collections of material originating from females.

Other Erotic Materials. All erotic materials, whatever their nature, provide information on the interests of the persons who produce them, or of the public which consumes them. The sexual attitudes of whole cultures may be better exposed by their openly erotic drawings, paintings, and sculpture, than by their more inhibited art. The gross exaggerations of the erotic art of ancient Rome, the intensely emotional and religious approach to sex which is evident in Hindu erotic art, the emotionally undisturbed acceptance of sex in ancient Japanese art,

---

[8] The use of graffiti as sources of data is illustrated in: Corpus Inscriptionem Latinarum. Reiskel 1906. Diehl 1910. Luquet 1910, 1911. [Hirschfeld] Numa Praetorius 1911:410–422. Magaldi 1931. Read 1935. Bender 1952:46–49. Freud (1910, Anthropophyteia 7:472–474) pointed out the scientific value of collecting current erotic jokes and skits. In a letter which was sent to Dr. Krauss, editor of Anthropophyteia, in connection with a legal prosecution in which it was charged that that publication was an obscene or pornographic work, Freud stated that: The erotic jokes and skits that you present in the volumes of Anthropophyteia were invented and told solely because they gave erotic pleasure to narrators and listeners. It is easy to guess what components of the highly complex sexual instinct had found gratification. The stories give us specific information as to which aspects of the sexual instinct give pleasure to a certain group of people, and thus they confirm the conclusions to which the psychoanalytic examination of neurotic persons had led. Allow me to point up the most important example of this kind. Psychoanalysis has forced us to maintain that the anal region normally and even in non-perverted individuals is the seat of erogenous sensation and behaves in certain ways like the genitalia. Physicians and psychologists to whom "anal erotism" and "anal character" were mentioned have become highly indignant. Anthropophyteia comes to the rescue of psychoanalysis by showing how very commonly people dwell with pleasure on this bodily region, its function, and even the products of its function. If it were not so, all these stories would be nauseating to the listeners. . . . It would not be difficult to show by other examples how valuable the collected material is for psychosexual knowledge. . . . In my study of wit I have shown that the uncovering of the otherwise repressed unconscious can become a source of pleasure and therefore material for jokes. In psychoanalysis we call a fabric of ideas with the emotions attached to them a complex, and we are ready to maintain that many of the most valued jokes are "complex jokes" and owe their liberating and cheering effect to the adroit revelation of otherwise repressed complexes. . . . Thus erotic and other jokes current among people may give excellent help in the exploration of the unconscious psychology of man, just as dreams, myths, and legends do.

and the fine portrayals of sexual action in later Greek art, provide some of the best information which we have on the sexual mores and attitudes of those cultures.[9] The preoccupation of present-day erotic art with matters which do not occur so often in any overt form in the case histories, emphasizes the persistence of suppressed desires in our own culture.

Sado-Masochistic Material. As a particular instance of the erotic items which must be comprehended in any study of current social problems, there is the considerable body of literature, art, and other materials which reflect human interest in the giving and receiving of pain. It has long been recognized that there is a relationship between such sado-masochistic interests and sex, but the relationship is probably not as direct and invariable as current psychologic and psychiatric theory would have it.[10]

Because of the considerable interest which any social organization has in protecting itself from persons who force sexual relations upon others, and who inflict physical damage during such relationships, we are attempting to understand the exact nature of the sexual element in this sort of activity. This has involved the accumulation of the histories of persons with specifically sadistic or masochistic experience, the accumulation of correspondence, drawings, scrapbooks, collections of photographs, and other documentary materials, the accumulation of a considerable library of published and amateur writing, and a study of prison cases of individuals who have been convicted of sex crimes involving the use of force. In connection with this study, it has been inevitable that we should accumulate a library of the world's sado-masochistic literature, including the considerable body of religious

---

[9] A limited list of some of the richer sources of data on the erotic art of classical Greece and Rome would include the following: Famin 1832, 1871. Barré 1839–1861 (8v.). Lenormant 1867 (4v.). Furtwängler and Reichhold 1904. Vorberg 1921, 1926. Pfuhl 1923 (3v.). Licht 1925–1928 (3v.). Bilder-Lexikon 1928–1931 (I–IV). Richter 1936 (2v.), 1942. Brusendorff 1938 (3v.). See also: Ozaki, Hisaya 1928 (Japan). Krauss, Satow, and Ihm 1931 (Japan). W. E. Clark 1937 (2v.) (Tibet). Hara, Kōzan 1938 (Japan). Wassermann 1938 (Peru). Gichner 1949 (Hindu). Van Gulik 1952 (China). Originals or copies of Japanese pillow books and scrolls dating from the 12th to the 20th centuries are in the collections of the Institute for Sex Research, and have provided considerable insight into Oriental sex attitudes.

[10] The sado-masochistic problem is considered, for instance, in such studies in penology, criminology, psychoanalysis, psychology, and biography as the following: [Bloch] Dühren 1900 (biography). Schlichtegroll 1901 (biography). Eulenburg 1902, 1934 (medicine). Laurent 1904 (general). Rau 1903 (general). Havelock Ellis 1913(3):66–189 (psychology). Freud, A. 1923:89–102 (psychoanalysis). Freud, S. 1924(2):172–201 (psychoanalysis). Stekel 1929 (2v.) (psychoanalysis). Gorer 1934 (biography). Read 1941 (history). Lewinsky 1944 (psychoanalysis). Simon 1947:5–6 (criminology). Ludovici 1948 (general). Allen 1949:70–104 (psychiatry). Jackson 1949 (psychology). De River 1949:3–225 (criminology). London and Caprio 1950:384–461 (psychiatry). East 1951:156–162 (criminology). Praz 1951 (orig. 1933) (literary criticism). Cleugh 1951 (biography).

writing on the martyrdom of early Christians and the saints, technical, legal, and philosophic treatises on the subject, and the sometimes scholarly but more often amateur fiction on cruelty, flagellation, torture, subjugation, prison camps, and legalized punishment.[11] As a result of our study of the basic physiology of sexual response, we are acquiring some understanding of the relationship between responses to pain and the sexual syndrome (Chapters 14–15). From all of this we may, some day, come to understand some of the factors which account for the occurrence of sex crimes which involve the use of force.

OBSERVED DATA

All of the sciences depend upon observed data as their ultimate sources of information. Matter which may be observed with one's eyes, ears, nose, or other sense organs constitutes the part of the universe with which the scientist is best equipped to deal. Sometimes observations have to be made indirectly, as through a microscope or some more complex instrument, or when the existence of sub-microscopic units must be detected by their effects upon other, more observable phenomena. Nonetheless, it is still observation which provides most of our scientific knowledge. It is unfortunate that so much of our information on human sexual behavior must be acquired secondhand, through the reports of persons who have been involved in such behavior; but there is obviously no way in which anyone could observe the behavior of any other human being through all of the hours and years of a lifetime. In consequence, observation has not provided as much information as the reported and even the recorded materials in the present study; but data derived from the direct observation of mammalian sexual activities and human socio-sexual relationships have, nevertheless, constituted an important source of the information on which we have based the present study of human sexual behavior.

Community Studies. In securing case histories, we have spent many hours and sometimes days and weeks in various types of city communities, in rural communities, in schools, in homes for children, in university communities, in penal institutions, and in the still other areas from which we were securing histories. We have watched many individuals making socio-sexual approaches in taverns, on street corners, at dances, on college campuses, at swimming pools, on ocean beaches, and elsewhere. We have spent time in the homes of many of our sub-

---

[11] Basic data are provided by such sado-masochistic literature as the following, in church history: Gallonio 1591. Limborch 1692. Boileau 1700, 1732. Backhouse and Scott 1888. Walsh 1940. For the history of torture and corporal punishment: [Bertram] Cooper 1869. Quanter 1901. Kogon 1950. For literary material: Meibomius n.d. (ex. 1761). Swinburne 1888; 1952 (authorship of both now certain). Mirbeau 1931 (orig. 1899). Sade 1797; 1904. Sacher-Masoch 190–; 1902.

jects, visited with their friends, gone with them to taverns, night clubs, the theatre, and concerts, and become acquainted with the other places in which they were finding their recreation and in which many of them were finding their sexual partners. We have had an opportunity to listen to such discussions of sex as are characteristic of each community, and to observe the sorts of social situations which lead to sexual activity. Such observations have checked the adequacy of the records we were securing in the case histories. Our understanding, for instance, of the greater acceptability of pre-marital coitus in lower level groups, and its lesser acceptability in upper level groups, depends upon a considerable body of information which we have obtained in our community contacts, as well as upon the data in our case histories. It would be difficult to quantify and statistically tabulate the information which we have acquired from these community contacts, but they have constituted an integral part of the background out of which many of our generalizations have grown.[12]

Clinical Studies. Throughout this study on human sexual behavior we have spent considerable time with anatomists, gynecologists, obstetricians, urologists, neurologists, endocrinologists, clinical psychologists, psychiatrists, and other clinicians who have made their experience and in many instances their extensive records available to us for study. Thus we have had the benefit of the accumulated observations made by some scores of physicians in the course of their practice. We have had similar cooperation from criminologists, penologists, law enforcement officials, social workers, public health officers, laboratory physiologists, marriage counselors, anthropologists, geneticists, sociologists, students of animal behavior, students of child development, military and naval officers, students of law, and still others who have dealt with human problems. Many of these persons have served as special consultants in the preparation of the present volume.

A number of these clinicians have collaborated by gathering special data for our study. Thus the record which we present in the present volume (Chapter 14) on the sensitivity of the various areas of the female genitalia, is based upon observations made for us by a group of cooperating gynecologists on nearly nine hundred of their female patients.

Mammalian Studies. The opportunity to observe sexual activity either in the human or lower mammals is limited not only by the cus-

---

[12] The sociologic approach to community studies is illustrated in such volumes as the following: Lynd and Lynd 1929, 1937 (Middletown). Blumenthal 1932 (Mineville). Warner and Lunt 1941, 1942 (Yankee City). [Withers] West 1945 (Plainville). Hollingshead 1949 (Elmtown). Dollard 1949 [orig. 1937] (Southerntown). None of these, however, have included any detailed survey of sexual behavior.

tom, but by the fact that such activity occurs only occasionally, and then so briefly that there is usually little opportunity to analyze the activity in any detail. In consequence, careful studies of sexual behavior among mammals of even domesticated species have been surprisingly few. Most of the scientific studies have been confined to laboratory experiments on certain aspects of the physiology of sexual response; and while these have provided important data,[13] they have not given us the considerable body of observations which we have needed on the gross physiology of sexual response and orgasm. With this as an objective, we have undertaken observational studies on mammalian sexual behavior, and have gone to some lengths to accumulate data from other persons who have made such observations.

Since the human animal, in the course of its evolution, has acquired both its basic anatomy and its physiologic capacities from its mammalian ancestors, studies of sexual behavior in the lower mammals may contribute materially to our understanding of human sexual behavior (Chapters 14–18).

Because of the extreme rapidity of sexual response, and because the responses may involve every part of the animal's body, it is exceedingly difficult and usually impossible to observe all that is taking place in the few seconds or minute or two which are usually involved in sexual activity. We have, therefore, found it necessary to supplement our direct observations with moving picture records which we, and several others collaborating with the research, have now made on the sexual activities of some fourteen species of mammals.[14] With the photographic record, it is possible to examine and reexamine the identical performance any number of times and, if necessary, examine and measure the details on any single frame of the film. Thus we have been able to analyze the physiologic bases of the action in various parts of the animal body (Chapters 15, 17).

We have also been able to utilize records made by a number of persons who have had the opportunity to observe human sexual behavior. Parents who have observed their young children in sexual activities, and scientifically trained persons who, on occasion, have found the opportunity to observe adult performances in which they themselves were not participants, have reported some of these observations in the

---

[13] For references to studies on the neurology and physiology of sexual response in mammals, see footnotes in Chapters 14, 15, 17.

[14] In addition to the material which we ourselves have obtained on mammalian sexual activity, documentary films have been contributed by the following to whom we are especially indebted: Frank Beach of Yale University, Robert K. Enders of Swarthmore College, Fred McKenzie of Oregon State Agricultural College, Albert Shadle of the University of Buffalo, William Young of the University of Kansas.

technical literature (Chapters 14–15, 17). Most of the material which has been made available to us has never before been published. These and the observations on other mammals have provided, throughout the present volume, data which we have used for analyzing the physiologic bases of sexual response and orgasm, and for comparing the similarities and differences between the responses of human females and males (Chapters 14–16).

PREVIOUSLY PUBLISHED STUDIES

The research staff which has been responsible for the present volume has included persons trained in biology, psychology, anthropology, the social sciences, law, statistics, and still other areas. We have therefore been able to make a critical use of the previously published studies which have had a bearing on human sexual behavior.

Anthropologic Studies. Throughout the present volume we have presented comparative data on sexual behavior in some of the other cultures of the world. The anthropologic record of specifically sexual activity is, however, generally scant and highly inadequate. Aside from a limited number of biographies, there are practically no case histories made in pre-literate societies. Instead, the anthropologist has usually had to depend upon such general information as he could pick up in group discussions, upon a limited number of informants, or upon observation of that portion of the sexual behavior which is publicly displayed. As a result, he may obtain a general impression of what is openly advocated, expected, permitted, discouraged, or condemned within a given society (the overt culture), but how the people privately behave (the covert culture) is not accurately or fully revealed by such sources of information. The discrepancies that may exist between an overt and covert culture are, as anthropologists well know, often considerable.

The general inadequacy of the anthropologic record in sexual matters has been primarily due to the reluctance of the majority of the investigators to consider specific aspects of sex. Most of this reluctance stems from the anthropologist's inability to overcome his own cultural conditioning. Only too frequently he excuses himself on the grounds that sexual questioning would spoil rapport with his subjects, but the success of those few explorers who have seriously attempted to gather sexual information indicates that valid and reasonably extensive data may be collected without undue difficulty, provided that the interviewing is well done.

The lack of any systematic coverage in any of the studies makes it difficult to use them for establishing any broad generalizations. For instance, a report which contains data concerning pre-marital and extra-marital coitus may completely fail to mention masturbation or homosexuality. One acquires the impression that the investigator recorded the sexual data which were readily available and made no additional effort to secure the remainder of the record. In view of the highly systematized and minutely detailed studies accorded such things as kinship terminologies, canoe-building, and the like, the scant and random treatment of sexual behavior seems all the more remarkable.

The mistakes and omissions of the past are, unfortunately, embalmed in the literature and handicap the research of persons who merely depend on that literature, or on the "Human Relations Area Files" which are now being accumulated through the joint efforts of the anthropologists in a number of American universities. The anthropologic data reported in previous studies, as well as in the present volume, must therefore be viewed as illustrative of the behavior in which some individuals have engaged in each of these cultures, although they may not be adequate descriptions of patterns which are widespread in any of them.[15]

Legal Studies. Our study of sex law and sex offenders has utilized recorded, reported, and observed data as well as the published legal record in this area. We now have the histories of females and males who have been convicted of sex offenses in some 1300 instances. Our studies in penal institutions have been made with the whole-hearted cooperation of both the inmate bodies and the institutional administrations, and have given us an opportunity to understand the sorts of situations which brought the sex offender into conflict with the law and the problems which he now faces in reestablishing his position in the social organization.

We have spent time observing court processes and acquiring an acquaintance with the attitudes of judges, prosecutors, the police, penal administrators, and other officers who have handled sex offenders. We have secured the histories of some of these law enforcement officers, and thereby obtained some insight into the motivations which lie back of their policies in dealing with sex offenders. We have made intensive studies of the administration of the sex laws in a number of large cities and of some smaller towns scattered widely over the United States. Our legally trained associate is making an intensive study of the sex law of the forty-eight states, the interpretation of that law in published

---

[15] Important data on sexual behavior are found in the following anthropologic literature: Karsh-Haack 1911. Westermarck 1922. Crawley 1927. Malinowski 1929. Goodland 1931. Fortune 1932. Bryk 1933. Powdermaker 1933. Devereux 1936, 1937. Firth 1936. Gorer 1938. Mead 1939. Schapera 1941. Whiting 1941. DuBois 1944. Fehlinger 1945. Ford 1945. Elwin 1947. Goodenough 1949. Hallowell in Hoch and Zubin 1949. Henry in Hoch and Zubin 1949. Murdock in Hoch and Zubin 1949. Ford and Beach 1951 (a summary of the literature).

court decisions, the historical development of the statutes in each of the states, and something of the English and other European backgrounds of American sex law. Most of this material will be published later, but it has provided the brief summaries and the footnote annotations which appear throughout the present volume. These show the application of the laws in the various states to masturbation, petting, pre-marital coitus, extra-marital coitus, homosexual activities, and still other types of sexual behavior. We have also recorded data on the ways in which the sex laws are enforced.

Previous Statistical Studies. Most of the earlier studies which had systematically gathered data on the sexual behavior of American females and males and statistically analyzed those data were reviewed in our volume on the male (1948:21–34). The list, including the additions published since 1948, now stands as follows:

1. Achilles, P. S. 1923. The effectiveness of certain social hygiene literature. New York, American Social Hygiene Association, 116p.
2. Ackerson, L. 1931. Children's behavior problems. A statistical study based upon 5000 children examined consecutively at the Illinois Institute for Juvenile Research. I. Incidence, genetic and intellectual factors. Chicago, University of Chicago Press, xxi+268p.
3. Bromley, D. D., and Britten, F. H. 1938. Youth and sex. A study of 1300 college students. New York and London, Harper & Brothers, xiii+303p.
4. Davis, K. B. 1929. Factors in the sex life of twenty-two hundred women. New York and London, Harper & Brothers, xx+430p.
5. Dickinson, R. L., and Beam, L. 1931. A thousand marriages. A medical study of sex adjustment. Baltimore, Williams & Wilkins Company, xxv+482p.
6. Dickinson, R. L., and Beam, L. 1934. The single woman. A medical study in sex education. Baltimore, Williams & Wilkins Company, xix+469p.
7. Ehrmann, W. W. (in preparation). Pre-marital dating behavior. New York, Dryden Press.
8. Exner, M. J. 1915. Problems and principles of sex instruction. A study of 948 college men. New York, Association Press, 39p.
9. Finger, F. W. 1947. Sex beliefs and practices among male college students. J. Abnorm. & Soc. Psych. 42:57–67.
10. (Gilbert Youth Research.) 1951. How wild are college students? Pageant (Nov.), pp. 10–21.
11. Glueck, S., and Glueck, E. T. 1934. Five hundred delinquent women. New York, Alfred A. Knopf, xxiv+539+x p.
12. Hamilton, G. V. 1929. A research in marriage. New York, Albert & Charles Boni, xiii+570p.
13. Hohman, L. B., and Schaffner, B. 1947. The sex lives of unmarried men. Amer. J. Soc. 52:501–507.
14. Hughes, W. L. 1926. Sex experiences of boyhood. J. Soc. Hyg. 12:262–273.
15. Landis, C., et al. 1940. Sex in development. New York and London, Paul B. Hoeber, xx+329p.
16. Landis, C., and Bolles, M. M. 1942. Personality and sexuality of the physically handicapped woman. New York and London, Paul B. Hoeber, xii+171p.
17. Locke, H. J. 1951. Predicting adjustment in marriage: a comparison of a divorced and a happily married group. New York, Henry Holt and Co., xx+407p.

18. Merrill, L. 1918. A summary of findings in a study of sexualism among a group of one hundred delinquent boys. J. Delinquency 3:255–267.
19. Pearl, R. 1930, rev. ed. The biology of population growth. New York, Alfred A. Knopf, xiv+260p. (espec. pp. 178–207).
20. Peck, M. W., and Wells, F. L. 1923. On the psycho-sexuality of college graduate men. Ment. Hyg. 7:697–714.
21. Peck, M. W., and Wells, F. L. 1925. Further studies in the psycho-sexuality of college graduate men. Ment. Hyg. 9:502–520.
22. Peterson, K. M. 1938. Early sex information and its influence on later sex concepts. Unpublished manuscript in Library of University of Colorado, 136p.
23. Priester, H. M. 1941. The reported dating practices of one hundred and six high school seniors in an urban community. Ithaca, N. Y., Cornell University Master's Thesis, 115+xvii+5p.
24. Ramsey, G. V. 1943. The sex information of younger boys. Amer. J. Orthopsychiat. 13:347–352.
25. Ramsey, G. V. 1943. The sexual development of boys. Amer. J. Psych. 56:217–234.
26. Ross, R. T. 1950. Measures of the sex behavior of college males compared with Kinsey's results. J. Abnorm. & Soc. Psych. 45:753–755.
27. Smith, G. F. 1924. Certain aspects of the sex life of the adolescent girl. J. Applied Psych. 8:347–349.
28. Strakosch, F. M. 1934. Factors in the sex life of seven hundred psychopathic women. Utica, N. Y., State Hospitals Press, 102p.
29. Taylor, W. S. 1933. A critique of sublimation in males: a study of forty superior single men. Genet. Psych. Monogr. 13(1):1–115.
30. Terman, L. M. 1938. Psychological factors in marital happiness. New York and London, McGraw-Hill Book Co., xiv+474p.
31. Terman, L. M. 1951. Correlates of orgasm adequacy in a group of 556 wives. J. Psych. 32:115–172.

In addition to the American studies, there have been a number of European and Japanese studies which have presented statistical data on sexual behavior. The following may be listed:

1. Asayama, Sin-iti. 1949. Gendai gakusei no seikōdō. (Sex behavior of present-day Japanese students.) Kyoto, Usui Shobo, 346p.
2. Barash, M. 1926. Sex life of the workers of Moscow. J. Soc. Hyg. 12:274–288.
3. Dück, J. 1914. Aus dem Geschlechtsleben unserer Zeit. Sexual-Probleme 10: 545–556, 713–766.
4. Dück, J. 1941. Virginität und Ehe. München, priv. print., 11p.
5. England, L. R. 1949–1950. Little Kinsey: an outline of sex attitudes in Britain. Pub. Opin. Q. 13:587–600.
6. Feldhusen, F. 1909. Die Sexualenquete unter der Moskauer Studentenschaft. [Chlenov Study, 1904.] Ztschr. f. Bekämpfung der Geschlechtskrankh. 8:211–224, 245–255.
7. Friedeburg, L. von. [1950.] Ein Versuch ueber Meinung und Verhalten im Bereich der zwischengeschlechtlichen Beziehungen in Deutschland . . . Allensbach, Institut für Demoskopie, 40p. (mimeo.).
8. Gurewitsch, Z. A., and Grosser, F. J. 1929. Das Geschlechtsleben der Gegenwart, Charkov 1926. Ztschr. f. Sexualwiss. 15:513–546.
9. Gurewitsch, Z. A., and Woroschbit, A. J. 1931. Das Sexualleben der Bäuerin in Russland. Ztschr. f. Sexualwiss. u. Sexualpol. 18:51–74, 81–110.
10. Jonsson, G. 1951. Sexualvanor hos svensk ungdom. In: Wangson, Otto, et al., Ungdomen möter sämhallet. Stockholm, Justitiedepartmentet, Statens Offentliga Wredningar 1951:41 (Bilaga A.), pp. 160–204.

11. Shinozaki, N. 1951. Report on sexual life of Japanese. Tokyo, Research Institute of Population Problems, Ministry of Welfare, 38p. (mimeo.).
12. Weissenberg, S. 1924. Das Geschlechtsleben der russischen Studentinnen. [Schbankov Study, 1908. Reported, 1922.] Ztschr. f. Sexualwiss. 11:7–14.
13. Weissenberg, S. 1924. Das Geschlechtsleben des russischen Studententums der Revolutionszeit. [Hellmann Study, 1923.] Ztschr. f. Sexualwiss. 11:209–216.
14. Weissenberg, S. 1925. Weiteres über das Geschlechtsleben der russischen Studentinnen. [Golossowker Study, 1922–1923.] Ztschr. f. Sexualwiss. 12: 174–176.
15. Welander, E. 1908. Några ord om de veneriska sjukdomarnas bekämpande. Hygiea N:r 12:1–32.
16. Wolman, B. 1951. Sexual development in Israeli adolescents. Amer. J. Psychother. 5:531–559.

It has, of course, been significant to compare the findings on our own case histories with those reported in these previous statistical studies. Such comparisons are made throughout the present volume, primarily in the footnotes to the statistical sections in each chapter (see also pp. 81–83 and Table 9).

The Institute for Sex Research has become the repository for the original data from several of the previous studies on sexual behavior, including the Landis study, the study by Bromley and Britten, the Dickinson studies, and a number of smaller studies, including some that were never published. Access to these original data has made it possible to examine material that was not covered in publication. For the study by Katharine Davis and the study by Hamilton, we have had to recalculate some of the data in order to arrive at figures which were applicable to groups which paralleled those with which we have dealt; and such recalculations, rather than the data which were published, appear at various places in our footnotes.

Other Previous Studies. Human interest in matters of sex, and discussions of human sexual problems, have been recorded in nearly every field of literature. While the technical material lies largely in the literature of biology, medicine, psychology, psychiatry, anthropology, and the law, there is a considerable body of sexual material in the religious literature, in the Greek and Roman classics, in the Renaissance and later European literature, and in all of the world's fiction, European, American, and Oriental. There is a considerable publication of art which shows erotic elements.

Wherever the previously published material has a bearing upon the interpretation of our own data, or wherever it provides significant information supplementary to our own, it has been summarized in the present volume, chiefly in the footnotes. The literature has appeared in many languages, some dozen of which have been handled by the members of our staff, and some others of which have been made available to us through the help of persons outside of the staff. The previously published material which is in the library of the Institute for Sex Research constitutes some 15,000 volumes which are classified as follows:

SECTIONS	VOLUMES	SECTIONS	VOLUMES
Anthropology	250	Islamic and Near Eastern	
Art, by Artists	1049	Literature	116
Art, Collections	511	Journals	162
Art, Erotic	84	Law	565
Art, Graeco-Roman	115	Marriage and Sex Educ.	690
Art, Photography	92	Nudism	151
Art, Sittengeschichte	83	Oriental Literature	271
Bibliography	95	Physical Culture	182
Biography	637	Poetry	1138
Biology and Medicine	594	Prostitution	239
Classical Literature	413	Psychology and Psychiatry	1210
Dance	86	Reference Works	69
Dictionaries, Vernacular	72	Religion	299
Erotic Fiction	614	Sado-Masochism	597
Erotic Manuscripts	372	Social History	248
Fiction, Modern	1140	Statistics	137
Fiction, Pre-1900	1546	Symbolism	87
Galante Literature	379	Venereal Disease	115
General	288	Woman and Love	342
			15,038

By utilizing the data reported on our case histories, the recorded and observed data which have been made available to us, and the body of data which other students have previously published, we have attempted to survey the many aspects of human sexual behavior. It has seemed desirable to undertake such a broad survey in order to orient the subsequent, more intensive studies that we or others may undertake. We could have sampled the American population more thoroughly if that had been the only objective of our study. We might have concentrated on a study of the development of patterns of behavior among children, on a study of legal problems, on a study of particular aspects of the physiology of sex, on experimental studies of mammalian behavior, or on any of the dozens of other special problems. But we have had to be content with making a progress report on what we have been able to accomplish to date.

Part II

TYPES OF SEXUAL ACTIVITY AMONG FEMALES

Chapter 4

PRE-ADOLESCENT SEXUAL DEVELOPMENT

What an individual does sexually will depend on the nature of the stimulus with which he or she comes into contact, on the physical and physiologic capacities of the individual to respond to that stimulus, and on the nature and extent of the individual's previous experience with similar stimuli.

The child is born with a physical equipment and physiologic capacity which allows it to respond to various sorts of stimuli. As a newborn infant and even before birth it may react to touch, to pressure, to light, to warmth, and to still other types of physical stimulation. Some of its reactions may be of the sort which we call sexual. What distinguishes a sexual response from any other type of response is a matter which we shall not attempt to define until we can examine the nature of those responses in the pages which follow (especially in Chapters 14 and 15). Suffice it for the moment to point out that a sexual response in any mammal involves a considerable series of changes in the normal physiology of the body. In the course of those changes, there is a build-up of neuromuscular tensions which may culminate at a peak—from which there may be a sudden discharge of tensions, followed by a return to a normal physiologic state. This sudden release of neuromuscular tensions constitutes the phenomenon which we know as sexual climax or orgasm. Orgasm is distinct from any other phenomenon that occurs in the life of an animal, and its appearance can ordinarily if not invariably be taken as evidence of the sexual nature of an individual's response (Chapter 15).

Most of the physiologic changes which occur during sexual response are quite like those which occur during other responses to tactile stimuli and in other emotional situations; but sexual responses always involve a group of physiologic changes of a sort which ordinarily occur only in situations commonly recognized as sexual. They occur during actual coitus [1]—the union of the genitalia of two individuals of op-

---

[1] Coitus—pronounced co'i-tus, with the accent on the first syllable—refers to a union of male and female genitalia. The term intercourse, used without a modifier, is often intended as an exact synonym of coitus. On the other hand, there may be oral intercourse, anal intercourse, homosexual intercourse, and, in a totally non-sexual sense, social intercourse. The term coitus never carries more than the one meaning, which is genital intercourse between a female and male.

posite sex—but they may also occur in such non-coital situations as masturbation (Chapter 5), petting (Chapter 7), and homosexual contacts (Chapter 11).

PRE-ADOLESCENT SEXUAL RESPONSE AND ORGASM

At least some newborn mammals, including some human infants, both female and male, are capable of being stimulated by and responding to tactile stimulation in a way which is sexual in the strictest sense of the term. We now understand that this capacity to respond depends upon the existence of end organs of touch in the body surfaces, nerves connecting these organs with the spinal cord and brain, nerves which extend from the cord to various muscles in the body, and the autonomic nervous system through which still other parts of the body are brought into action (Chapter 17). All of these structures are present at birth, and the record supplied by the recall of the adult females and males who have contributed to the present study, and direct observations made by a number of qualified observers, indicate that some children are quite capable of responding in a way which may show all of the essential physiologic changes which characterize the sexual responses of an adult.

Among both young children and adults, there appear to be differences in the capacity to be aroused sexually. Some individuals respond quickly and frequently to a wide variety of physical and psychologic stimuli. Others respond more slowly and infrequently. Even in a single individual the levels of response may vary from time to time as his general health, nutritional state, fatigue, and still other circumstances may affect his physiologic capacities. Levels of response may also depend on the age of the individual. Although all individuals may be born with the necessary anatomy and capacity to respond to tactile stimulation, the capacity to respond in a way which is specifically sexual seems to increase as the child develops physically, and in many children it does not appear until near the time of adolescence. In some females it may not appear until some years after the onset of adolescence. We do not understand all of the factors which are involved, but some of the capacity to respond sexually seems to depend on certain hormones which develop in the body of the growing boy and girl (Chapter 18).

Whether the late appearance of sexual responsiveness in some individuals means that they were actually not capable of responding at an earlier age, or whether it means that they had not previously been subjected to sexual stimuli which were sufficient to bring response, is a matter which it has not yet been possible to determine. It is possible that some younger children are not at all capable of responding sexually, or at least incapable of responding to the sorts of stimuli which would arouse an adult, but of this we are not certain. It is certain, however, that there are children, both female and male, who are quite capable of true sexual response.[2]

Accumulative Incidence of Pre-Adolescent Response. What seem to be sexual responses have been observed in infants immediately at birth, and specifically sexual responses, involving the full display of physiologic changes which are typical of the responses of an adult, have been observed in both female and male infants as young as four months of age, and in infants and pre-adolescent children of every older age.

About one per cent of the older females who have contributed histories to the present study recalled that they were making specifically sexual responses to physical stimuli, and in some instances to psychologic stimuli, when they were as young as three years of age (Table 146, Figure 98). This, however, must represent only a portion of the children who were responding at that age, for many children would not recognize the sexual nature of their early responses.

About 4 per cent of the females in our sample thought they were responding sexually by five years of age. Nearly 16 per cent recalled such responses by ten years of age. All told, some 27 per cent recalled that they had been aroused erotically—sexually—at some time before the age of adolescence [3] which, for the average female, occurs some-

---

[2] That sexual activity and sexual response are often present in the normal female in childhood, is recognized by such authors as: Bell 1902 (an extensive pioneer study on emotional attachments in young children). Moll 1909, 1912 (an important volume with much original material). Freud 1910:34–58; 1938:580–603. Loewenfeld 1911:454, 525 (but he denies the occurrence of orgasm in childhood). Wulffen 1913:251. Sadger 1921:12, 14. Stekel 1923:14; 1950:26 ("coitus and onanism during childhood are neither signs of degeneration nor of depravity; . . . they are often merely the signs of the budding forth of a keen spirit, and disclose a strong natural endowment . . ."). Krafft-Ebing 1924:11 (genuine sexual arousal long before adolescence). Hodann 1929:33–37 (no asexual children; sex pleasure of a child is no way different from that gained in later life). Bauer 1929:198. Havelock Ellis 1936(I, 2):215 ff. Isaacs 1939:113–117 (nursery school observations of sexual interests and activity). Valentine 1942:331–352 (denies childhood sexuality, but has only limited data).

[3] For other specific data on pre-adolescent sexual arousal in females, see, for instance, the following: Achilles 1923:49 (10 per cent among 41 females aroused by age 13). Schbankov acc. Weissenberg 1924a:9 (20 per cent of 324 Russian females aroused before age 10, 42 per cent before menstruation). Hellmann acc. Weissenberg 1924b:210, 212 (among 338 Russian females, 15 per cent aroused by age 10, 23 per cent at ages 10–14, 30 per cent before menstruation). Gurewitsch and Grosser 1929:521–522 (5 per cent aroused by age 11, 25 per cent by age 14, 16 per cent before menstruation). Davis 1929:230 (46 per cent of 2000 females recalled "sex feelings" before age 14). Hamilton 1929:144, 210, 304–305, 333 (20 per cent of 91 females aroused before first menstruation). Willoughby 1937 (a summary of previous literature). Dück 1949 (24 of 31 females aroused by age 10). A. Ellis 1949:63.

time between her twelfth and thirteenth birthdays (see pp. 122–127). However, the number of pre-adolescent girls who are ever aroused sexually must be much higher than this record indicates.

Comparisons of the records contributed by subjects who had terminated their schooling at the grade school, high school, college, and graduate school levels, indicate that pre-adolescent erotic responses may have occurred in a higher percentage of the groups which subsequently obtained the most extensive schooling (Table 146); but this may simply reflect a greater capacity of the better educated females to recall their experience.

Nature of Pre-Adolescent Orgasm. Some of the sexual responses of pre-adolescent children, and even those of infants of a few months of age, may terminate in sexual orgasm. There is no essential aspect of the orgasm of an adult which has not been observed in the orgasms which young children may have. This seems to be equally true of the pre-adolescent female and the pre-adolescent male. The pre-adolescent boy does not ejaculate as adult males do when they reach orgasm, but ejaculation depends upon a relatively minor anatomic structure which is not yet developed in the boy; and the absence of ejaculation does not indicate that the boy does not reach orgasm, any more than the absence of ejaculation in the adult female indicates that she does not reach orgasm (see pp. 634–636).

We have previously (1948:175–181) given a detailed description of orgasm occurring among pre-adolescent boys. We may now extend the record to orgasm among pre-adolescent girls.

Masturbation (self-stimulation) is an essentially normal and quite frequent phenomenon among many children, both female and male (Chapter 5). Masturbation is not infrequently the source of orgasm among small girls. The typical reactions of a small girl in orgasm, made by an intelligent mother who had frequently observed her three-year-old in masturbation, were described as follows: "Lying face down on the bed, with her knees drawn up, she started rhythmic pelvic thrusts, about one second or less apart. The thrusts were primarily pelvic, with the legs tensed in a fixed position. The forward components of the thrusts were in a smooth and perfect rhythm which was unbroken except for momentary pauses during which the genitalia were readjusted against the doll on which they were pressed; the return from each thrust was convulsive, jerky. There were 44 thrusts in unbroken rhythm, a slight momentary pause, 87 thrusts followed by a slight momentary pause, then 10 thrusts, and then a cessation of all movement. There was marked concentration and intense breathing with abrupt jerks as orgasm approached. She was completely oblivious to everything during these later stages of the activity. Her eyes were glassy and fixed in a vacant stare. There was noticeable relief and relaxation after orgasm. A second series of reactions began two minutes later with series of 48, 18, and 57 thrusts, with slight momentary pauses between each series. With the mounting tensions, there were audible gasps, but immediately following the cessation of pelvic thrusts there was complete relaxation and only desultory movements thereafter."

We have similar records of observations made by some of our other subjects on a total of 7 pre-adolescent girls and 27 pre-adolescent boys under four years of age (see our 1948:175–181). These data indicate that the capacity to respond to the point of orgasm is certainly present in at least some young children, both female and male.

Accumulative Incidence of Pre-Adolescent Orgasm. About 14 per cent of all the females in our sample—nearly half of those who had been erotically aroused before adolescence—recalled that they had reached orgasm either in masturbation or in their sexual contacts with other children or older persons (*i.e.*, in their *socio-sexual* contacts) prior to adolescence. It is not at all impossible that a still higher percentage had actually had such experience without recognizing its nature.

On the basis of the adult recall and the observations which we have just recorded, we can report 4 cases of females under one year of age coming to orgasm, and a total of 23 cases of small girls three years of age or younger reaching orgasm. The incidences, based on our total female sample, show some 0.3 per cent (16 individuals) who recalled that they had reached orgasm by three years of age, 2 per cent by five years, 4 per cent by seven years, 9 per cent by eleven years, and 14 per cent by thirteen years of age (Table 10, Figure 98).[4] Thus, there had been a slow but steady increase in the number of girls in the sample who had reached orgasm prior to adolescence. In the case of the male, the percentages of those who had reached orgasm also rose steadily through the early pre-adolescent years, but they began to rise more abruptly in the later pre-adolescent years.

Sources of Early Arousal and Orgasm. One per cent of the females in our sample recalled that they were masturbating (in the strict sense of the term) by three years of age, and 13 per cent recalled masturbation by ten years of age (Table 21, Figure 10). The record does not show what percentage of the early masturbation had brought sexual arousal, but it does show 0.3 per cent of the females in the total sample

---

[4] See p. 513 in the present volume and footnote 6 on p. 106 for other data on early orgasm among females. See also Davis 1929:115 (6.5 per cent with orgasm in masturbation before twelve years of age).

masturbating to the point of orgasm by three years of age, and 8 per cent by ten years of age (Table 25, Figure 13).

Psychologic reactions or physical contacts with other girls were, in a few instances, the sources of sexual arousal at three years of age. About 3 per cent had been aroused by other girls by eleven years of age, and 6 per cent by thirteen years of age (Table 13, Figures 4, 82).

Reactions to or contacts with boys had brought similar arousal in a fraction of one per cent at three years of age, but in about 7 per cent of the sample by eleven, and in 12 per cent of the sample by thirteen years of age (Table 13, Figure 4).[5]

Out of the 659 females in the sample who had experienced orgasm before they were adolescent, 86 per cent had had their first experience in masturbation, some 7 per cent had discovered it in sexual contacts with other girls, 2 per cent in petting, and 1 per cent in coitus with boys or older males. Interestingly enough, 2 per cent had had their first orgasm in physical contacts with dogs or cats. Some 2 per cent had first reached orgasm under other circumstances, including the climbing of a rope.[6]

Orgasm had been discovered in self-masturbation more often by the girls than by the boys. In earlier pre-adolescence, the boy's first orgasms are frequently the product of physical and emotional situations which bring spontaneous sexual reactions; and although there is a great deal of incidental manipulation of genitalia among younger boys, it rarely brings orgasm. Among the adolescent boys in our sample, masturbation appears to have accounted for only 68 per cent of the first orgasms (see our 1948:190).

Some sort of finger manipulation of the genitalia, and particularly of the clitoris, seems to have been the commonest technique in the female's early masturbation. The second commonest technique had been one in which the child had lain face down on the bed, with her knees somewhat drawn up while she rhythmically moved her buttocks, building up the neuromuscular tensions which had ultimately led to orgasm (see Chapters 14–15). In many instances the genitalia were rubbed against a toy, a bed, a blanket, or some other object on which

---

[5] Sources of sexual arousal in pre-adolescent girls are also cited in: Schbankov acc. Weissenberg 1924a:9 (among 324 Russian females). Hellmann acc. Weissenberg 1924b:210 (among over 100 females who had been aroused, 19 per cent from a homosexual source, 13 per cent from a heterosexual source). Dück 1949 (among 31 females, 39 per cent aroused by girl schoolmates, 10 per cent by boy playmates, 16 per cent by older persons, 3 per cent by animals).

[6] Moll 1909:86; 1912:95, also gives nocturnal dreams as a frequent source of first orgasm in pre-adolescent girls, but our data do not bear this out. Hamilton 1929:313 reports only a single case out of 100 females who ever experienced pre-pubertal orgasm from nocturnal dreams.

the child lay face down. In those cases in which the child had failed to reach orgasm, the failure may have been due to lack of a physiologic capacity to respond to that point, but in many instances it may have been due to the child's failure to discover the necessary physical techniques for effective self-stimulation. The acquirement of these masturbatory techniques represents one of the learned aspects of sexual behavior (Chapter 16).

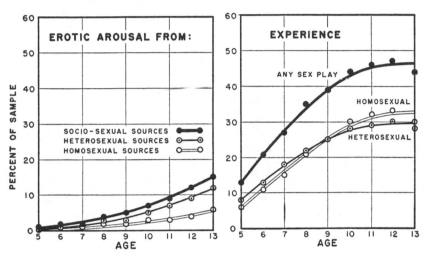

Figure 4. Accumulative incidence: pre-adolescent socio-sexual arousal

Including arousal from psychologic stimulation and overt socio-sexual play. Data from Table 13.

Figure 5. Accumulative incidence: pre-adolescent socio-sexual experience

Each dot indicates percent of sample with experience by the indicated age. Data from Table 11.

The child's initial attempts at self-masturbation had been inspired in some instances by the observation of other children who were engaged in such activity, or through the more deliberate instruction given by some older child or adult. These were quite commonly the first sources of information for most of the males in the sample; but in the great majority of instances females learn to masturbate, both in pre-adolescent and later years, by discovering the possibilities of such activity entirely on their own (Chapter 5).

PRE-ADOLESCENT HETEROSEXUAL PLAY

Although 30 per cent of the females in the sample recalled pre-adolescent heterosexual play, and 33 per cent recalled pre-adolescent homosexual play, only 48 per cent recalled any sort of socio-sexual play before adolescence (Table 11, Figure 5).[7] This means that 15

---

[7] Among the few previously published data on the incidences of pre-adolescent sex play, see: Davis 1929:56–58 (in 25 per cent of 1000 married females).

per cent had had sex play only with boys, 18 per cent had had it only with girls, and another 15 per cent had had it with both boys and girls.

Socio-Sexual Development. For both the females and males in the sample, the earliest sexual contacts with other individuals, either of their own or of the opposite sex, appear to have been the incidental outcome of other play activities, or the imitation of sexual behavior which they had observed among other children or even among adults. The anthropologic record indicates that there is a good deal of this imitative play among children of primitive groups where adult coitus is not as carefully guarded from observation as in our own culture.[8] More of the sex play among children in this country represents the perpetuation of age-old games commonly referred to as "mama and papa," and "doctor." These games were current in the generation which included our oldest subjects, and they still appear under these names in the youngest generation represented in the sample. The specifically sexual nature of these games is not always understood by the child; and even when the small boy lies on top of the small girl and makes what may resemble copulatory movements, there is often no realization that genital contacts might be made, or that there might be an erotic reward in such activity. However, in some communities, and in families where there are several children, it sometimes happens that an older child or some adult may give the girl or boy more extended information, or may even direct the physical contacts so they become specifically sexual.

A considerable portion of the child's pre-adolescent sex play, both with its own and with the opposite sex, is a product of curiosity concerning the playmate's anatomy (pp. 111–112).[9]

Landis et al. 1940:278 (36 per cent of 109 single females and 20 per cent of 44 married females). Individual cases describing pre-adolescent experience are in: Moll 1899:557; 1909:156, 245; 1912:174, 269. Liepmann 1922:250. Krafft-Ebing 1924:484. Robie 1925:62. Müller 1929:467–477 (5 girls under 12). Bühler 1931:637–638 (6 cases observed by Culp, ages 4 to 11).

[8] For anthropologic data on the female's pre-adolescent sex play, including coitus, see, for example: Malinowski 1929:55–59 (Trobriand Islanders, Melanesia). Powdermaker 1933:85 (Lesu, Melanesia; adults condone and approve). Devereux 1936:32 (Mohave, Calif.). Gorer 1938:310 (Lepcha, Northern India; adults encourage such activity and are amused). Landes 1938:21 (Ojibway, Ontario, Canada). Du Bois 1944:69–70 (Alor, Melanesia; condoned for young children). Elwin 1947:436–437 (Muria, India; children live in separate establishment until they eventually marry). Henry in Hoch and Zubin 1949:95–98 (Pilaga, Brazil; extremely free sex play permitted). Ford and Beach 1951:188–192 (summarizes various anthropologic studies).

[9] Hamilton 1929:454, 457 found 33 of 100 females curious to see male genitalia before age 12, 39 no curiosity at any age, 13 peeping before age 11. Dillon 1934:171–172 observed mutual genital inspection between a boy and girl in nursery school while fully dressed, although they were naked together during a daily 15 minute dressing period. Our own data include several more or less similar instances.

Accumulative Incidence of Heterosexual Play. Our data on the incidence and frequency of sex play among pre-adolescent children are drawn in part from the studies we have made of children of very young ages, but they depend largely upon the recall of the adults who have contributed to the present study. It has been apparent, however, that the adults have recalled only a portion of their pre-adolescent experience, for even children forget a high proportion of their experience within a matter of weeks or months. This is due sometimes to the incidental nature of the sex play, and in some instances to the fact that the child was emotionally disturbed by the experience and blocked psychologically in recalling a taboo activity. But even though the child may not be able to recall its experience, it is possible that it has acquired information and attitudes which will affect its subsequent patterns of behavior. While the records show that 48 per cent of the adult females in the sample had recalled some sort of pre-adolescent sex play (Table 11, Figure 5), we are inclined to believe, for the above reasons, that a much higher percentage must have had sexual contacts as young children.

About equal numbers of the females recalled contacts with girls and with boys. There is no evidence that their interest in their own sex (the homosexual interest) had developed either before or after their interest in the opposite sex (the heterosexual interest). Freudian hypotheses of psychosexual development proceeding, as a rule, from narcissistic (masturbatory) interests and activities to interests in other individuals whose bodies are similar (the homosexual interests), and finally to interests in individuals who are physically different (the heterosexual interests), are not substantiated by the pre-adolescent or adolescent histories of either the females or the males in the sample.[10]

Because of the restrictions which parents and our total social organization place upon the free intermingling of even small children of the opposite sex, it is not surprising to find that 52 per cent of the females in the sample had had more girls than boys as childhood companions, and that another 33 per cent had had boys and girls in about equal numbers as childhood companions. Only about 15 per cent had had more boys than girls as companions. This lesser significance of boys as the pre-adolescent companions of girls makes it all the more notable that the pre-adolescent sexual activities of the females in the sample were had with boys about as often as with girls. This had undoubtedly depended upon the fact that small boys are usually more aggressive than girls in their physical activities, and even at that age boys are more likely to initiate the sexual activities.

---

[10] Freud's theory of the stages of psychosexual development may be found in: Freud 1910:59–86; 1938:604–629. Fenichel 1945:40, 110–113.

One per cent of the adult females in the sample recalled childhood sex play with boys when they were as young as three, but 8 per cent recalled such play by five, and 18 per cent by seven years of age (Table 11, Figure 5). All told, some 30 per cent recalled some play with boys before they turned adolescent. The figures differed for the various educational levels represented in the sample: among those females who had never gone beyond high school, some 24 per cent recalled sex play with boys, but 30 per cent of those who had gone on into college, and 36 per cent of those who had gone still further into graduate school, recalled such pre-adolescent play.

The data indicate that the percentage of children engaging in any kind of pre-adolescent sex play had increased in the course of three of the decades represented in the sample. In comparison with the females born before 1900, some 10 per cent more of those born between 1910 and 1919 recalled pre-adolescent sex play (Table 12).

Active Incidence of Heterosexual Play. The incidence of pre-adolescent sex play at particular ages (the active incidence) seems to have been highest in the younger age groups. Some 8 per cent of the females in the sample recalled pre-adolescent heterosexual play at ages five and seven, but fewer recalled it for the later years of pre-adolescence. Only 3 per cent recalled that they were having heterosexual play just before adolescence (Table 14, Figure 6). On the contrary, among pre-adolescent boys we found that the number engaging in sex play had increased steadily throughout the pre-adolescent years. Near adolescence, some 20 per cent of the boys in the sample had been involved in heterosexual play. These differences between the incidences for boys and girls may depend in part upon the increasing restraints that are placed upon the girl as she approaches adolescence; but they undoubtedly depend to an even greater extent upon the fact that the pre-adolescent boy's capacities for specifically sexual responses develop rapidly as he nears adolescence. This is not matched by any similar rise in the sexual capacities of the female at the time of adolescence (Chapter 18).

With seven boys involved for every girl who is having any heterosexual play near the approach of adolescence, it is obvious that the girls who do accept contacts at that age must be having a variety of male partners. Not infrequently a number of boys may engage in group activities, most of which involve exhibitionistic masturbation or homosexual play, but some of which will include genital exhibitions or heterosexual contacts with one girl who is admitted to the largely male group.

Frequency of Heterosexual Play. For most of the females in the sample, the pre-adolescent play had been restricted to a single experience, or to a few stray experiences. Exceedingly few of the girls seem to have developed any pattern of frequent or regular activity. On the other hand, there are many reasons for believing, as we have already noted, that the extent of the pre-adolescent play was greater than these individuals recalled when they became adult.

Number of Years in Heterosexual Play. For 67 per cent of the females in the sample the pre-adolescent heterosexual play had been restricted, as far as they could recall, to a single year, and for another

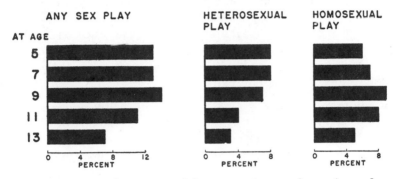

Figure 6. Active incidence: pre-adolescent socio-sexual experience, by age
Data from Table 14.

15 per cent to a couple of years (Table 15). There were only 11 per cent for whom the play had extended through five or more pre-adolescent years. Of those who had had pre-adolescent coitus, 61 per cent had had it in only a single year, and another 13 per cent in two different years. Some 9 per cent, however, had had coitus for five years or more before adolescence.

Techniques of Heterosexual Play. Genital exhibition had occurred in 99 per cent of the pre-adolescent sex play (Table 16). In perhaps 40 per cent of the histories that was all that was involved.[11]

Anatomic differences are of considerable interest to most children.[9] Their curiosity is whetted by the fact that they have in many instances been forbidden to expose their own nude bodies and have not had the opportunity to see the nude bodies of other children. Their curiosity is especially stimulated by the fact that they have been cautioned not to expose their own genitalia, or to look at the genitalia of other children. The genital explorations often amount to nothing more than

---

[11] Hamilton 1929:449 found 15 of 100 females recalled exhibition of male genitalia in pre-adolescent sex play. This is only half the incidence found in our sample.

comparisons of anatomy, in much the same way that children compare their hands, their noses or mouths, their hair, their clothing, or any of their other possessions. As we have noted in regard to the boy, it is probable that a good deal of the emotional content which such play may have for the small girl is not sexual as often as it is a reaction to the mysterious, to the forbidden, and to the socially dangerous performance.

On the other hand, we have the histories of females who were raised in homes that accepted nudity within the family circle, or who attended nursery schools or summer camps or engaged in other group activities where boys and girls of young, pre-adolescent ages used common toilets and freely bathed and played together without clothing. In such groups the children were still interested in examining the bodies of the other children, although they soon came to accept the nudity as commonplace and did not react as emotionally as they would have if nudity were the unusual thing.

A high proportion of our adult subjects rather precisely recalled the ages at which they had first seen the genitalia of the opposite sex. This emphasizes the importance which such experience has for the child in a culture which goes to such lengths as our culture does to conceal the anatomic differences between the sexes. Nevertheless, 60 per cent of our adult female subjects believed that they had first seen male genitalia at some very early age, and certainly between the ages of two and five, while another 24 per cent placed their first experience between the ages of five and eleven (Table 17). By adolescence, about 90 per cent had seen male genitalia.

Something more than a third (possibly 37 per cent) of the females in the sample recalled having seen the genitalia of adult males while they were still pre-adolescent (Table 17). Another third had seen adult male genitalia first between adolescence and twenty years of age. The first opportunity to observe adult male genitalia in pre-adolescence had come, in order of frequency, from the following (Table 18): the child's father (46 per cent), accidental exposure by a male who was not the child's father (19 per cent), deliberate exhibition by an adult male (22 per cent), the observation of relatives other than the father (9 per cent), the observation of the genitalia of the petting or coital partner (2 per cent), and miscellaneous sources (2 per cent). The children raised in homes of the better-educated groups had more often seen adult male genitalia at an earlier age, primarily because of the greater acceptance of nudity in homes of that level.

For 52 per cent of the females who had had any pre-adolescent heterosexual play, the play had involved manual manipulations of genitalia (Table 16). In a goodly number of instances, these had amounted to nothing more than incidental touching. The heterosexual contacts had been specifically masturbatory in only a small number of cases. There had been mouth-genital contacts among only 2 per cent of the girls, and insertions of various objects (chiefly fingers) into the female vagina in only 3 per cent of the cases.

There had been some sort of coitus in 17 per cent of the cases for which any heterosexual play was reported,[12] but it has been difficult to determine how much of the "coitus" of pre-adolescence involves the actual union of genitalia. In all instances recorded in the sample, there had been some apposition of the genitalia of the two children; and since erections frequently occur among even very young boys, penetrations may have been and certainly were effected in some of the pre-adolescent activity. However, the small size of the male genitalia at that age had usually limited the depth of penetration, and much of the childhood "coitus" had amounted to nothing more than genital apposition.

On the other hand, we have 29 cases of females who had had coitus as pre-adolescents with older boys or adult males with whom there had been complete genital union (p. 119).

PRE-ADOLESCENT HOMOSEXUAL PLAY

Pre-adolescent sex play with other girls was recalled by about the same number of females as had recalled pre-adolescent sex play with boys (Table 11, Figure 5). Although this sort of play seems not to have been particularly sexual among many of the females in the sample, it had either directly or indirectly taught a number of them how to masturbate. A few (5 per cent) of the girls had had their pre-adolescent homosexual contacts carry over into adolescence as more mature homosexual activity (p. 452).

Accumulative Incidence of Homosexual Play. Only a fraction of one per cent of the females in the sample recalled that they had had sex play with other girls as early as three years of age (Table 11, Figure 5). Some 6 per cent recalled such play by five years, and 15 per cent by seven years of age. The percentages who had ever had such experi-

---

[12] Pre-adolescent coitus is also reported in: Stekel 1895:247–248 (5 cases, ages 4–6). Forel 1905:207. Moll 1909:180; 1912:198. Stekel 1923:4; 1950:14 (pre-adolescent coitus far from rare). Schbankov acc. Weissenberg 1924a:13. Hellmann acc. Weissenberg 1924b:212 (3 out of 338 female Russian students had coitus by age 5, and 3 per cent by age 14). Davis 1929:56 (1.4 per cent of 1000 females reported coitus in childhood). Hamilton 1929:330–332 (10 of 100 married females reported coitus before puberty; 15 per cent had refused coitus).

ence (the accumulative incidence figures) then steadily rose, reaching a level of about 33 per cent by the onset of adolescence.[13]

Active Incidence of Homosexual Play. The number of girls who were having some sort of sex play with other girls at each age (the active incidence figures) similarly began at a fraction of one per cent in ages two and three, rose to 6 per cent by age five, and to 9 per cent by age nine (Table 14, Figure 6). Again it is to be noted that the actual occurrence of such activity was probably much higher than the adults in the sample had recalled. As with the heterosexual play, the active incidence of the homosexual play had declined as the girls approached adolescence.

Number of Years in Homosexual Play. Just as with the heterosexual play, the pre-adolescent homosexual activity had been confined to a single year, and in many cases to one or two experiences, for 61 per cent of the females who had had any such play (Table 15). Another 17 per cent had had the play extend into two years, and 8 per cent had had the play extend for five years or more.

Techniques of Homosexual Play. For 99 per cent of the females in the sample who had had any pre-adolescent homosexual play, the contacts had involved genital exhibitions and examinations, and for a third of them it had involved nothing more than that (Table 16). For 62 per cent the play had involved some manual manipulation of the genitalia of one or of both of the girls. It is interesting to note that genital manipulations between girls in pre-adolescent play had occurred in a larger percentage of the cases than genital manipulations between boys and girls in heterosexual play.

In the homosexual play, mouth-genital contacts were recalled by 3 per cent of the females who had had pre-adolescent play with other girls. Objects (at least fingers) had been inserted into the vaginas of the girls in 18 per cent of the cases—compared with 3 per cent receiving vaginal insertions in the heterosexual play.[13]

SIGNIFICANCE OF PRE-ADOLESCENT SEX PLAY

Significance in Psychosexual Development. In the course of their pre-adolescent sexual contacts with boys and with other girls, many of the females in the sample had acquired their first information about sex. They had acquired factual information about male and female genitalia and sometimes about reproduction, about masturbatory, pet-

---

[13] Additional data on pre-adolescent homosexual activity in the female are found in: Moll 1899:545–566 (ages 6–12, manual and oral techniques). Krafft-Ebing 1924:482–516 (ages 5 to 12, manual and oral techniques). Hamilton 1929:493 (10 out of 100 females with homosexual play before age 11; chiefly breast stimulation and thigh contacts with genitalia).

ting, and coital techniques, and about the significance of adult sexual activities. In fact, many of the contacts had been incidental to and not infrequently the direct outcome of the discussion of such matters. Most of the information so acquired represented a part of the necessary education which most parents carefully avoid giving their daughters at any age.

Effect on Adult Patterns. In the course of their pre-adolescent contacts, a significant portion of the females in the sample had discovered what it meant to be aroused erotically, and to be aroused to the point of orgasm. What was still more significant for their ultimate sexual adjustments, many of the females in the sample had learned how to respond in socio-sexual contacts. Some of the pre-adolescent contacts had provided emotional satisfactions which had conditioned the female for the acceptance of later sexual activities.

In not a few instances, guilt reactions had made the childhood experiences traumatic. This was especially true when the children had been discovered by adults, and when reprimands or physical punishment had been meted out to them. These guilt reactions had, in many instances, prevented the female from freely accepting sexual relations in her adult married relationships. When the parents had not become emotionally disturbed when they discovered the child in sex play, there was little evidence that the child's experience had done any damage to its later sexual adjustment.[14]

Interestingly enough the overt sex play of pre-adolescence had only infrequently carried over into the overt sexual activity of the adolescent or more adult female. Among the males a very much larger percentage had carried their pre-adolescent play directly into their adolescent and more adult activities. Among the females who had pre-adolescent sexual activity, the number who had continued the same type of activity into adolescence was as follows:

Pre-adolescent experience	Experience continued into adolescence			
	Percent		*Number of Cases*	
	FEMALE	MALE	FEMALE	MALE
Petting	13	65	807	1227
Coitus	8	55	247	628
Homosexual play	5	42	1071	1412

These discontinuities between the adolescent and pre-adolescent activity of the female appear to be products of the social custom and not of anything in the female's biologic or psychologic equipment. Such breaks do not occur between the early and more adult sexual

---

[14] Davis 1929:58–59 reports no significant correlation between pre-adolescent sex play and happiness in marriage.

activities of lower mammalian females; they do not occur among most of the primitive groups on which sexual data are available; and they do not occur among the females in lower level and less inhibited segments of our own American population.

As the child approaches adolescence, parents may increasingly restrict the female's contacts with the opposite sex. They may warn her against kissing, general body contacts, genital exposures, and more specific sexual relationships. In many cultures the girl is more restricted at this age than the boy. In Europe, in Latin America, and in this country, the opportunities for the girl to be alone with other children are fewer than those available to the developing boy. The cessation of pre-adolescent sex play in the later pre-adolescent years was taken by Freud and by many of his followers to represent a period of sexual latency. On the contrary, it seems to be a period of inactivity which is imposed by the culture upon the socio-sexual activities of a maturing child, especially if the child is female. Pre-adolescent masturbation is, on the other hand, usually carried over from the pre-adolescent to the adolescent and adult years, probably because it does not fall under the restraints which are imposed on a socio-sexual activity. This provides further evidence that no biologic latency is involved in the discontinuity of the socio-sexual activities.[15]

PRE-ADOLESCENT CONTACTS WITH ADULT MALES

There is a growing concern in our culture over the sexual contacts that pre-adolescent children sometimes have with adults. Most persons feel that all such contacts are undesirable because of the immediate disturbance they may cause the child, and because of the conditioning and possibly traumatic effects which they may have on the child's socio-sexual development and subsequent sexual adjustments in marriage. Press reports might lead one to conclude that an appreciable percentage of all children are subjected, and frequently subjected, to sexual approaches by adult males, and that physical injury is a frequent consequence of such contacts. But most of the published data are based on cases which come to the attention of physicians, the police, and other social agencies, and there has hitherto

---

[15] For general discussions of the Freudian concept of latency, see: Freud 1910:37–40; 1938:582–584 (latency organically determined although education contributes much to it). Sadger 1921:73 (no progress of sexuality between ages 6–12). Stekel 1923:12; 1950:25 (does not accept Freud's theory of latency). Sears 1943:45–47 (rejects concept, on basis of available data). Kinsey, Pomeroy and Martin 1948:180–181. Bender and Cramer in Eissler 1949:63. Fenichel 1945:62 concludes that latency might be either cultural or biologic. Kadis in Brower and Abt 1952:361–368, summarizing recent literature, points out the confusion in interpreting the term latency and our previous lack of adequate data on sexual activity between ages 5 to 10.

been no opportunity to know what proportion of all children is ever involved.[16]

Incidence and Frequency of Contacts with Adults. We have data from 4441 of our female subjects which allow us to determine the incidence of pre-adolescent sexual contacts with adult males, and the frequency of such contacts. For the sake of the present calculations we have defined an adult male as one who has turned adolescent and who is at least fifteen years of age; and, in order to eliminate experiences that amount to nothing more than adolescent sex play, we have considered only those cases in which the male was at least five years older than the female, while the female was still pre-adolescent. On this basis, we find that some 24 per cent (1075) of the females in the sample had been approached while they were pre-adolescent by adult males who appeared to be making sexual advances, or who had made sexual contacts with the child. Three-fourths of the females (76 per cent) had not recognized any such approach.[17]

Approaches had occurred most frequently in poorer city communities where the population was densely crowded in tenement districts; and while many of the subjects covered by the present volume were raised in such communities, we would have found higher incidences of pre-adolescent contacts with adults if we had had more cases from lower educational groups, or if we had included the data which we

---

[16] The following indicate the nature of the present concern over adult sexual approaches to children: Hoover, J. Edgar, "How Safe is Your Daughter?" American Magazine July, 1947:32 ("depraved human beings, more savage than beasts, are permitted to roam America almost at will"). Wittels, "What Can We Do About Sex Crimes?" Saturday Evening Post Dec. 11, 1948:31 ("at least tens of thousands of them [sex killers] are loose in the country today"). Frankfurter, Justice Felix, dissenting in Maryland v. Baltimore Radio Show 1950:338 U. S. 912 ("The impact of those two similar crimes [child sex murders] upon the public mind was terrific. The people throughout the city were outraged"). Levy, "Interaction of Institutions and Policy Groups: The Origin of Sex Crime Legislation," 1951:3. McDonald 1952 (a 31 page bedtime story book, which attempts to instill fear of all adults, both familiar and strange, as potential "sex perverts," utilizing a hobgoblin and witch technique in which friends turn into monsters with sexual intentions).

In 30 states the maximum punishment for sexual intercourse with a female child is death or life imprisonment. In 1952 alone, Calif., Mich., and Penn. made provision for life imprisonment for persons convicted of indecent or immoral practices with a child, and in recent years Ga., Ind., N. Y., N. J., Okla., and Texas have greatly increased their penalties for such activity. In 1949 the murder of Joyce Glucroft led to the convening of an extraordinary session of the California Legislature for the sole purpose of handling the problem of sex crimes against children.

[17] For the general population, there are data on the incidences and frequencies of sex aggressions against pre-adolescent girls (although the nature of the aggression is not exactly defined) in: Hamilton 1929:334–338 (20 of 100 females had 31 such experiences). Landis et al. 1940:278 (107 instances for 295 females). Data based entirely on cases that reach the clinic or court are in: Ackerson 1931:69–72. Apfelberg et al. 1944:763. Bowman 1952:49.

have on females who had served penal sentences, and on Negro females. These latter groups, however, were excluded from the calculations in the present volume for reasons which we have already explained (p. 22).

The **frequencies** of the pre-adolescent contacts with adults were actually low. Some 80 per cent of the females who were ever involved seem to have had only a lone experience in all of their pre-adolescent years. Another 12 per cent reported two such experiences, and 3 per cent reported something between three and six childhood experiences. On the other hand, 5 per cent of those who had been involved reported nine or more experiences during pre-adolescence. Repetition had most frequently occurred when the children were having their contacts with relatives who lived in the same household. In many instances, the experiences were repeated because the children had become interested in the sexual activity and had more or less actively sought repetitions of their experience.

Among the females who had been approached by adult males when they were pre-adolescent children, the ages at which they were approached were distributed as follows:

Ages of Females Having Adult Contacts

AGE	PERCENT OF ACTIVE SAMPLE	PERCENT OF TOTAL SAMPLE	AGE	PERCENT OF ACTIVE SAMPLE	PERCENT OF TOTAL SAMPLE
4	5	1	9	16	4
5	8	2	10	26	6
6	9	2	11	24	6
7	13	3	12	25	7
8	17	4	13	19	6
Cases				1039	4407

Adult Partners. The adult males who had approached these preadolescent children were identified as follows:

ADULT PARTNERS	PERCENT OF ACTIVE SAMPLE
Strangers	52
Friends and acquaintances	32
Uncles	9
Fathers	4
Brothers	3
Grandfathers	2
Other relatives	5
Cases reporting	609

Some 85 per cent of the subjects reported that only a single male had approached them when they were children. Some 13 per cent reported that two different males had made such approaches, 1 per cent reported three males, and another 1 per cent reported four or more males making such approaches.[18]

Nature of Contacts with Adults. The early experiences which the females in the sample had had with adult males had involved the following types of approaches and contacts:

NATURE OF CONTACT	PERCENT
Approach only	9
Exhibition, male genitalia	52
Exhibition, female genitalia	1
Fondling, no genital contact	31
Manipulation of female genitalia	22
Manipulation of male genitalia	5
Oral contact, female genitalia	1
Oral contact, male genitalia	1
Coitus	3
Number of cases with experience	1075

Nearly two-thirds (62 per cent) of these sexual approaches to children were verbal approaches or genital exhibition. In most of these cases the adult male had exhibited his genitalia, but in one per cent of the cases he had persuaded the small girl to exhibit her genitalia. It is difficult, in any given instance, to know the intent of an exhibiting male, but our histories from males who had been involved in such exhibitions and who, in a number of instances, had been prosecuted and given penal sentences for such exhibitions, include many males who would never have attempted any physical contact with a child. The data, therefore, do not warrant the assumption that any high percentage of these males would have proceeded to specifically sexual contacts. It is even more certain that it would have been an exceedingly small proportion of the exhibitionists who would have done any physical damage to the child. In all of the penal record, there are exceedingly few cases of rapists who start out as exhibitionists.[19]

[18] Hamilton 1929:337 found that relatives were the adults involved in 6 out of 31 cases (*i.e.*, 20 per cent compared to our figure of 23 per cent). Landis et al. 1940:278 (found members of the family or close relatives involved in 35 per cent of cases). Bowman 1952:49 reports that adult involved was a stranger in only 7 out of 46 cases, and a neighbor, family friend, or relative in the other instances.

[19] For further discussion of the role of the male exhibitionist and his pattern of sexual activity see: Henninger 1941:357 ff. (83 cases over a 2-year period). Arieff and Rotman 1942:523. New York Mayor's Committee 1944:56. Hirning 1947:557. Kelleher acc. Braude 1950:19–20. Rickles 1950:42 ("My personal experience and that of many other observers in the field, has shown conclusively that the public need have no fear of exhibitionists. They are not a physical threat to anyone"). Guttmacher 1951:31–33, 71–76. Guttmacher and Weihofen 1952:157.
That the progression from minor to major sex crimes rarely occurs, is also noted

The satisfaction which an adult male secures when he exhibits either to a pre-adolescent or to an adult, appears to depend, at least in part, upon the emotional excitation which he experiences when he observes the fright or surprise or embarrassment of the female whom he accosts. To an even greater degree, his satisfaction may depend upon the emotional arousal which he experiences when he risks social and legal difficulties by engaging in taboo behavior. In some cases there may be a narcissistic element in his display of his genital capacities. Not infrequently the adult male masturbates before the child. Sometimes, however, his exposure is quite accidental, as in the case of an intoxicated or urinating male, and the child is mistaken in believing that the exhibition is deliberate.

Some 31 per cent of these sexual contacts with adults had involved fondling and petting which, however, still had not involved genital contacts.

In 22 per cent of the cases the adult had touched or more specifically manipulated the genitalia of the child, and in 5 per cent of the cases the child had manipulated the male genitalia. Children, out of curiosity, sometimes initiate the manipulation of male genitalia, even before the male has made any exposure.

In about one per cent of the cases, the male had made oral contacts with the female genitalia, and in about the same percentage of cases the male had persuaded the child to make oral contacts with his genitalia.

Among the children who had had any sort of contact with adults, there were 3 per cent (*i.e.*, 0.7 per cent of the total female sample) who had had coitus with the adult.

Significance of Adult Contacts. There are as yet insufficient data, either in our own or in other studies, for reaching general conclusions on the significance of sexual contacts between children and adults. The females in the sample who had had pre-adolescent contacts with adults had been variously interested, curious, pleased, embarrassed, frightened, terrified, or disturbed with feelings of guilt. The adult contacts are a source of pleasure to some children, and sometimes may arouse

in: Tappan 1950:6. Guttmacher 1951:113–114 ("our investigations, as well as others, indicate first, that there is a low degree of recidivism among sexual offenders, and second, that there is no basis for the common belief that sex criminals engage in sex crimes of progressive malignancy"). Michigan Report 1951:4. Bowman in Brown 1951:151. Kelley acc. Guttmacher 1951:114 (only one case out of 100 reviewed in New York showed an increase in the amount of force used in the sex offense). Kelleher 1952:6 (in a study of 1328 sex offenders, concludes that "with few exceptions, a mild sexual offender remains mild, and . . . we could find little evidence of progression from mild to violent sex crimes within the individual").

the child erotically (5 per cent) and bring it to orgasm (1 per cent). The contacts had often involved considerable affection, and some of the older females in the sample felt that their pre-adolescent experience had contributed favorably to their later socio-sexual development.

On the other hand, some 80 per cent of the children had been emotionally upset or frightened by their contacts with adults. A small portion had been seriously disturbed; but in most instances the reported fright was nearer the level that children will show when they see insects, spiders, or other objects against which they have been adversely conditioned.[20] If a child were not culturally conditioned, it is doubtful if it would be disturbed by sexual approaches of the sort which had usually been involved in these histories. It is difficult to understand why a child, except for its cultural conditioning, should be disturbed at having its genitalia touched, or disturbed at seeing the genitalia of other persons, or disturbed at even more specific sexual contacts. When children are constantly warned by parents and teachers against contacts with adults, and when they receive no explanation of the exact nature of the forbidden contacts, they are ready to become hysterical as soon as any older person approaches, or stops and speaks to them in the street, or fondles them, or proposes to do something for them, even though the adult may have had no sexual objective in mind. Some of the more experienced students of juvenile problems have come to believe that the emotional reactions of the parents, police officers, and other adults who discover that the child has had such a contact, may disturb the child more seriously than the sexual contacts themselves. The current hysteria over sex offenders may very well have serious effects on the ability of many of these children to work out sexual adjustments some years later in their marriages.[21]

There are, of course, instances of adults who have done physical damage to children with whom they have attempted sexual contacts, and we have the histories of a few males who had been responsible for

---

[20] The effects on children of sexual contacts with adults are also discussed in: Abraham (1907) 1927:52–57 (such events often not reported to parents because of child's guilt feelings at pleasure in the experience). Bender and Blau 1937:500–513 (11 girls, ages 5 to 12, free of guilt and fear). Rasmussen 1934 (follow-up of 54 cases in Denmark showed little evidence of ill effects). Landis et al. 1940:279 (no unpleasant reactions in 44 per cent of 107 cases; worry, shock, or fright in 56 per cent). Bowman 1952:52–53, 61 (findings substantiate experience of other students). David M. Levy 1953 (communication) (concludes from experience with numerous cases that psychologic effects are primarily the result of the adult emotional disturbance, and are likely to be negligible if there is no physical harm to child).

[21] The following studies have investigated the possibility of a relationship between pre-adolescent traumatic experience and later sexual adjustment: Hamilton 1929:342 (data on 46 females, but pre-adolescent experience not distinguished from later pre-marital experience). Terman 1938:393, 397; 1951:136, 140, found no significant correlation between "sex shock" and orgasm adequacy.

such damage. But these cases are in the minority, and the public should learn to distinguish such serious contacts from other adult contacts which are not likely to do the child any appreciable harm if the child's parents do not become disturbed. The exceedingly small number of cases in which physical harm is ever done the child is to be measured by the fact that among the 4441 females on whom we have data, we have only one clear-cut case of serious injury done to the child, and a very few instances of vaginal bleeding which, however, did not appear to do any appreciable damage.

ADOLESCENT DEVELOPMENT

Physical Development. Shortly after the end of the first decade, the female begins to develop physically at a faster rate than she had before, and acquires pubic hair, hair under the arms, more mature breasts, and a body form more nearly like that of an adult. During this period of development, she menstruates for the first time. It is during this period that her ovaries mature and, for the first time, begin to release eggs which are capable of being fertilized and developing into new individuals.

This period in which there is an increased rate of physical growth and the final development of reproductive function is the period which has come to be known as adolescence. Various physical developments are involved in this adolescent growth, and they do not all begin or reach their conclusion simultaneously. Consequently, there is no single point at which adolescence may be said to begin, or any point at which it may be said to stop, but from the onset of the first adolescent development to the completion of all adolescent development, the time involved for the average (median) female is something between three and four years.

Corresponding adolescent developments in the male usually do not begin until a year or two after adolescence has begun in the female, and they usually take four years or more to reach their conclusion. In consequence, as far as physical development is concerned, the girl begins to "mature" at an earlier age, and reaches complete maturity before the average boy.[22]

Exact studies of adolescent development should, of course, be based upon the direct examination and measurement of developing children, and our own data, based upon the recall of adults, cannot be as certain; but the average ages at each stage of development, calculated from our

---

[22] Other data comparing physical developments of males and females at adolescence are, for example, in: Stratz 1909:298. Bühler in Stern 1927:155–169. Havelock Ellis 1929:138–142. Boas 1932:310. Westbrook et al. 1934:43–44 (Chinese boys and girls). Shuttleworth 1938a: fig. 8; 1939. Greulich in Henry ed. 1944:10–15. Hooton 1946:235–254. Reynolds 1946:124. Shuttleworth 1951: figs. 14, 118–120.

records, agree quite closely with those from the observational studies (Table 8).

It has been customary, both in general thinking and in technical studies, to consider that adolescence in the female begins at the time of first menstruation (barring any unusual disturbance of normal menstrual development). This is an error, and for several reasons an unfortunate error; for considerable physical growth which should be recognized as adolescent usually precedes the occurrence of the first menstruation. Most of the females in our sample reported the appearance of pubic hair as the first of the adolescent developments. Some of the females reported pubic hair development at ages as young as 8, but others did not recall that pubic hair had developed until the age of 18 (Table 19, Figure 7). For the median female in the sample, the hair had begun developing by 12.3 years of age.[23]

Almost simultaneously with the appearance of pubic hair, breast development became noticeable. The observational studies show that the very first signs of breast development may actually precede the appearance of the pubic hair. Among the females in our sample there were some who recalled such development by the age of 8, and some who did not recall breast development until the age of 25 (Table 19, Figure 7). The median age of breast development was 12.4 years for the females in the sample.[24]

Only a few of the adult females in the sample were able to recall the age at which a marked increase in the rate of growth had first begun. It is difficult to notice the onset of a process which is as continuous as this increase in rate of growth during adolescence. A much larger number of the females in the sample thought they could recall the ages at which they had completed their development in height. These ages ranged from 9 to 25 years, but for the median female growth seemed to have been completed by 15.8 years of age (Table 19, Figure 7).[25]

The age of first menstruation had ranged from 9 to 25 years in the sample (Table 19, Figure 7). For the median female it had been 13.0

---

[23] Observational studies on the average ages at first appearance of the pubic hair in females are: Marro 1922:31 (at 13 to 14 years). Priesel and Wagner 1930:337. Pryor 1936:60. Reynolds 1946:122 (at age 11.2). Reynolds and Wines 1949:94 (at age 11).

[24] Observational studies giving average ages at beginning of breast development in females include: Marro 1922:31. Priesel and Wagner 1930:342–345. Pryor 1936:61. Reynolds 1946:122 (at 10.7 years). Reynolds and Wines 1949:97. The following state that breast development is typically the first outward sign of adolescence: Stratz 1909:245. Moll 1909:33; 1912:36. Hoffman 1944:292. Hamblen 1945:117.

[25] There are a number of observational studies on increases in height and weight at adolescence, including, for instance: Stratz 1909:317. Boas 1932. Pryor 1936:56–59. Barker and Stone 1936. Stone and Barker 1937. Shuttleworth 1937, 1938b, 1951: figs. 118–120. Greulich in Henry ed. 1944:20. Reynolds

years.[26] For the median female, there had been a lapse of 8.4 months between the onset of pubic hair and breast development, and the first menstruation. The first menstruation is such a specific event and, in many instances, such a dramatic event in the girl's history, that its appearance is recalled more often than any other adolescent development. It is, therefore, quite natural that since the time of ancient Jewish law, menstruation should have been taken as the best single sign of sexual maturity in the female. Unfortunately, menstruation is a

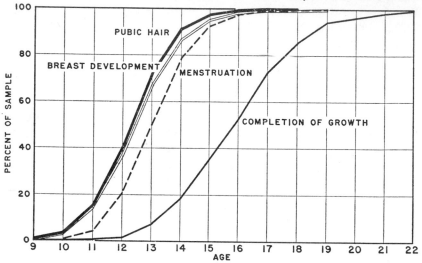

Figure 7. Cumulated percents: adolescent physical development in the female

Data from Table 19.

phenomenon which is affected by a larger number of factors, chiefly hormonal, than most of the other biologic developments at adolescence. In a few instances it may begin before there are any other adolescent developments. Not infrequently, however, it may be delayed for a considerable period of time, and in some instances for several years, after all of the other adolescent developments have been completed. It is customary today for parents to seek medical aid when first menstruation does not appear by the time the other adolescent developments are well under way; but among many of the older women in our histories, menstruation would have been a poor indicator of adolescent development.

1946:125. Dennis in Carmichael 1946:638–640 (a good survey, beginning with Bowditch 1891). Reynolds and Wines 1949:105–109.

[26] Average ages of 13 years for first menstruation are found in such studies as: Baldwin 1921:191. Bingham 1922:543. Abernethy 1925:540. Boas 1932:309. Engle and Shelesnyak 1934:434. Glueck and Glueck 1934:425. Mazer and Israel 1946:66. Other data on age at first menstruation are in: Mills 1937:48–56. Greulich 1938:52–53. Shuttleworth 1938a: figs. 108–114. Ito 1942:333–345 (effect of race and climate). Greulich in Henry ed. 1944:28–29. Ashley Montagu 1946:83. Dennis in Carmichael 1946:634, 641–643 (comprehensive survey). Dickinson 1949: fig. 46a.

It is popularly believed that the appearance of menstruation is an indication that a girl has become "sexually mature" enough to conceive and reproduce. On the basis of recent studies, it becomes clear, however, that the initial release of mature eggs from the ovaries is not always correlated with menstruation. There are known cases of fertile eggs and pregnancy occurring before menstruation had ever begun; and there is a considerable body of data indicating that the average female releases mature eggs only sporadically, if at all, during the first few years after she has begun to menstruate. This is the period of so-called adolescent sterility.[27] It is probable that the sterility is not complete, and more probable that eggs are occasionally released in that period; but regular ovulation in each menstrual cycle probably does not begin in the average female until she is sixteen to eighteen years of age. Precise studies on this point are still to be made.

Psychosexual Development in Adolescence. While these physical changes at adolescence are a fundamental part of the process by which the female becomes mature enough to reproduce, they seem to have little relation to the development of sexual responsiveness in the female. The steady increase in the accumulative incidence of erotic arousal and response to orgasm which we have seen in the pre-adolescent data continues into adolescence and for some years beyond. There is a slight but no marked upsurge in the incidence and frequency of arousal and orgasm during adolescence, but they do not reach their maximum development until the middle twenties or even thirties (Figures 98, 102).

In the case of the male, there is a sudden upsurge in sexual activity which may begin a year or more before adolescence, and usually reaches its peak within a year or two after the onset of adolescence (Figure 8). From that point the male's sexual responses and overt activity begin to drop and continue to drop steadily into old age (Figures 144–147). These striking differences between female and male psychosexual development may depend upon basic hormonal differences between the sexes (Chapter 18).

Because of the earlier appearance of adolescence in the female, and because of her more rapid physical development in that period, the opinion is generally held that the girl matures sexually more rapidly than the boy. Mature reproductive cells may appear in the average female before they appear in the average male, but the capacity to reproduce is not synonymous with the capacity to be aroused erotically

---

[27] For original data on adolescent sterility and for bibliographies of other studies see: Hartman 1931 (first use of term, data on monkeys). Yerkes 1935:542 (chimpanzee). Mills and Ogle 1936 (sterile period shorter if menstruation starts later). Greulich 1938:54. Siegler 1944:17–19. Ashley Montagu 1946:57–141 (most extensive summary of data). Dennis in Carmichael 1946:645 (summary of data). Shuttleworth 1951: figs. 125, 126 (summary of data) Webster and Young 1951 (in male guinea pigs).

and to respond to the point of orgasm. The irregular release of mature eggs from the ovaries during the years of adolescent sterility makes it uncertain whether the capacity for reproduction develops earlier in one sex than in the other, and in regard to sexual responsiveness the female matures much later than the male (Chapter 18).[28]

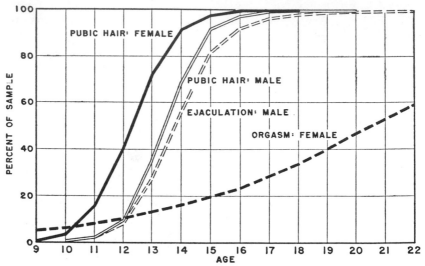

Figure 8. Cumulated percents, comparing female and male: onset of adolescence and sexual response

Taking appearance of pubic hair as first adolescent development, and orgasm or ejaculation as specific evidence of erotic response. Data from Tables 19 and 147, and our 1948:184.

We have found that the human female is born with the nervous equipment on which sexual responses depend, but we have found that only a portion of the females respond before the onset of adolescence. The acquirement of any full capacity for response depends upon the sort of sexual experience that the female has in pre-adolescence, adolescence, and the later years, and on the variety of social factors which may condition her psychologically (Chapter 16). The record of these developments during the adolescent and adult years is presented in the chapters that follow.

---

[28] It has usually been stated that girls show an earlier (6 months to 2 years) heterosexual interest than boys; see, for instance, Campbell 1939:470. Sadler 1948:338. Waller 1951:150. Such studies, however, do not clearly distinguish social interests from erotic responses. For studies recognizing the later erotic development of the female, which we find in our data, see: Kisch 1907:173 (also cites Loewenfeld). Bühler in Stern 1927:155–169. Hamilton 1929:488 (5 out of 100 married females, but 54 out of 100 married males had "longed for coitus" by age 15). Gurewitsch and Grosser 1929:521 (an important body of data on 536 females and 2280 males; reports arousal among females beginning on an average of 1.1 to 1.4 years later). Havelock Ellis 1936(I,2): 242–247 (generally recognizes later erotic development of female, cites literature beginning with Ovid). Pratt in Allen et al. 1939:1283 (complete response seldom possible for a woman before maturity).

Table 10. Accumulative Incidence: Pre-Adolescent Orgasm From Any Source

By Educational Level

AGE	TOTAL SAMPLE	EDUCATIONAL LEVEL 0–8	9–12	13–16	17+	TOTAL SAMPLE	EDUCATIONAL LEVEL 0–8	9–12	13–16	17+
	%		*Percent*			*Cases*			*Cases*	
3	—	0	—	—	—	5908	179	1013	3286	1144
5	2	0	2	1	3	5862	179	1013	3286	1144
7	4	2	4	3	6	5835	179	1013	3286	1144
9	6	4	6	5	9	5772	179	1009	3271	1137
11	9	5	11	8	13	4577	149	844	2533	928
13	14	8	14	13	20	1144	73	286	518	243

The data cover pre-adolescent orgasm from masturbation as well as from socio-sexual contacts.

Italic figures throughout the series of tables indicate that the calculations are based on less than 50 cases. No calculations are based on less than 11 cases.

The dash (—) indicates a percentage or frequency smaller than any quantity which would be shown by a figure in the given number of decimal places.

Table 11. Accumulative Incidence: Pre-Adolescent Socio-Sexual Experience

By Educational Level

AGE	TOTAL SAMPLE	EDUCATIONAL LEVEL 9–12	13–16	17+	TOTAL SAMPLE	EDUCATIONAL LEVEL 9–12	13–16	17+
			ANY SOCIO-SEXUAL EXPERIENCE					
	%		*Percent*		*Cases*		*Cases*	
3	1	—	1	2	5882	1013	3291	1146
5	13	10	12	18	5849	1013	3291	1146
7	27	21	27	36	5829	1013	3291	1146
9	39	33	39	50	5775	1009	3276	1139
11	46	41	46	57	4579	844	2536	928
13	44	40	46	54	1145	286	518	244
			HETEROSEXUAL EXPERIENCE					
	%		*Percent*		*Cases*		*Cases*	
3	1	—	—	1	5895	1014	3296	1147
5	8	7	9	14	5860	1014	3296	1147
7	18	15	19	26	5838	1014	3296	1147
9	25	23	26	36	5784	1010	3281	1140
11	29	26	28	39	4586	845	2540	929
13	28	24	30	36	1148	286	521	244
			HOMOSEXUAL EXPERIENCE					
	%		*Percent*		*Cases*		*Cases*	
3	—	0	—	1	5903	1013	3292	1149
5	6	5	6	8	5861	1013	3292	1149
7	15	11	15	19	5836	1013	3292	1149
9	25	20	25	30	5779	1009	3277	1142
11	32	29	31	38	4584	844	2538	931
13	30	29	31	36	1145	286	518	244

Table 12. Accumulative Incidence: Any Pre-Adolescent Socio-Sexual Experience

By Decade of Birth

AGE	TOTAL SAMPLE	DECADE OF BIRTH				TOTAL SAMPLE	DECADE OF BIRTH			
		Bf. 1900	1900–1909	1910–1919	1920–1929		Bf. 1900	1900–1909	1910–1919	1920–1929
	%	*Percent*				*Cases*	*Cases*			
3	1	1	1	1	1	5882	450	779	1338	3076
5	13	12	15	14	11	5849	450	779	1338	3076
7	27	23	30	30	26	5829	450	779	1338	3076
9	39	35	42	43	37	5775	448	775	1333	3061
11	46	40	50	52	43	4579	376	652	1067	2384
13	44	36	50	46	43	1145	151	232	261	484

Table 13. Accumulative Incidence: Pre-Adolescent Socio-Sexual Arousal

By Educational Level

AGE	TOTAL SAMPLE	EDUCATIONAL LEVEL				TOTAL SAMPLE	EDUCATIONAL LEVEL			
		0–8	9–12	13–16	17+		0–8	9–12	13–16	17+

ANY SOCIO-SEXUAL AROUSAL

AGE	%	*Percent*				*Cases*	*Cases*			
3	—	0	—	—	—	5865	177	1005	3261	1138
5	1	0	1	1	2	5818	177	1005	3261	1138
7	2	1	2	2	5	5790	177	1005	3261	1138
9	5	2	4	4	8	5729	177	1001	3246	1131
11	9	3	10	7	12	4539	147	838	2509	922
12	12	5	12	10	15	2867	118	571	1514	591
13	15	7	14	15	19	1131	72	283	510	242

HETEROSEXUAL AROUSAL

AGE	%	*Percent*				*Cases*	*Cases*			
3	—	0	—	—	—	5856	178	1003	3258	1134
5	1	0	1	1	1	5809	178	1003	3258	1134
7	2	1	2	1	3	5781	178	1003	3258	1134
9	3	2	3	3	6	5720	178	999	3243	1127
11	7	3	7	5	9	4533	148	836	2507	919
12	9	3	9	8	12	2863	119	569	1513	589
13	12	5	10	13	16	1128	73	281	508	242

HOMOSEXUAL AROUSAL

AGE	%	*Percent*				*Cases*	*Cases*			
3	—	0	0	—	—	5861	178	1005	3258	1135
5	—	0	0	—	—	5814	178	1005	3258	1135
7	1	0	—	1	2	5786	178	1005	3258	1135
9	2	1	2	2	3	5724	178	1001	3243	1128
11	3	1	4	3	4	4531	148	837	2504	919
12	4	2	5	4	4	2866	119	571	1511	592
13	6	1	6	4	5	1130	72	286	507	241

Table 14. Active Incidence: Pre-Adolescent Socio-Sexual Experience

AGE	TOTAL SAMPLE	EDUCATIONAL LEVEL 0–8	9–12	13–16	17+	TOTAL SAMPLE	EDUCATIONAL LEVEL 0–8	9–12	13–16	17+
		ANY SOCIO-SEXUAL EXPER.					HETEROSEXUAL EXPER.			
	%		Percent			%		Percent		
5	13	2	10	12	18	8	2	7	9	14
7	13	7	11	13	15	8	7	7	8	9
9	14	9	13	13	16	7	7	8	6	9
11	11	8	12	11	11	4	5	5	4	5
12	10	8	13	10	9	4	4	5	3	3
13	7	8	9	6	5	3	4	3	3	2
		HETEROSEXUAL COITAL EXPER.					HOMOSEXUAL EXPER.			
	%		Percent			%		Percent		
5	1	1	1	1	2	6	1	5	6	8
7	1	3	2	1	2	7	2	6	8	8
9	2	4	2	1	2	9	5	8	9	10
11	1	3	2	1	2	8	5	9	8	8
12	1	3	3	1	2	8	7	10	8	7
13	1	3	2	1	2	5	5	8	4	4
		CASES					CASES			
5	5895	178	1013	3300	1150	5895	178	1013	3300	1150
7	5842	179	1013	3299	1150	5842	179	1013	3299	1150
9	5791	179	1007	3281	1141	5791	179	1007	3281	1141
11	4597	149	844	2543	931	4597	149	844	2543	931
12	2908	120	573	1535	601	2908	120	573	1535	601
13	1154	73	286	523	244	1154	73	286	523	244

Table 15. Number of Years Involved In Pre-Adolescent Socio-Sexual Play

NUMBER OF YEARS	PERCENT OF ACTIVE SAMPLE IN: Any play	Hetero-sexual play	Hetero-sexual coitus	Homo-sexual play
1	54	67	61	61
2	19	15	13	17
3	10	7	9	9
4	6	4	8	5
5	4	3	2	3
6	3	2	3	2
7	2	1	3	2
8	1	1	1	1
9	1	—	—	—
10	—	—	—	—
Cases in active sample	2789	1805	312	1927
Mean no. of years	2.1	1.8	2.0	1.9
Median no. of years	1.4	1.2	1.3	1.3

129

Table 16. Techniques in Pre-Adolescent Socio-Sexual Play

TECHNIQUE	HETERO-SEXUAL	HOMO-SEXUAL	HETERO-SEXUAL	HOMO-SEXUAL
	Percent		*Cases*	
Any	100	100	1812	1934
Exhibition	99	99	1809	1930
Manual	52	62	1794	1914
Oral	2	3	1761	1831
Vaginal insertion	3	18	1566	1894
Coitus	17		1800	

Table 17. Accumulative Incidence: Females with Experience in Observing Male Genitalia

AGE	FEMALES WHO HAD OBSERVED GENITALIA OF:			
	Males of any age	Adult males	Males of any age	Adult males
	Percent		*Cases in total sample*	
5	60	17	5369	5186
7	70	20	5353	5151
9	78	24	5334	5134
11	84	30	5313	5119
13	89	37	5288	5093
15	92	45	5241	5047
20	97	69	3947	3803
25	99	88	2551	2496
30	99	94	1867	1825
35	99	95	1342	1314
40	100	96	868	836
45	100	95	525	493

Table 18. Source of First Opportunity to Observe Adult Male Genitalia

Among females with any experience

SOURCE	FEMALE'S AGE AT FIRST EXPERIENCE			
	Pre-adol.	Adol.–20	21–25	26+
	Percent of females			
Father	46	6	1	1
Other relative	9	6	1	1
Exhibitionist	22	18	3	3
Accidental	19	17	2	4
Petting experience	1	18	19	8
Coital experience	1	26	65	73
Non-marital	1	18	23	30
Marital	0	8	42	43
Miscellaneous	2	9	9	10
Number of cases	1651	1712	561	194

Table 19. Adolescent Physical Development
By Age

AGE	TOTAL SAMPLE	EDUCATIONAL LEVEL 0-8	9-12	13-16	17+	TOTAL SAMPLE	EDUCATIONAL LEVEL 0-8	9-12	13-16	17+
		PUBIC HAIR					BREAST DEVELOPMENT			
	%	Cumulated percent				%	Cumulated percent			
8-9	—	0	—	1	1	—	0	—	—	1
9-10	3	1	2	3	4	3	1	2	3	3
10-11	16	6	11	17	13	14	7	11	16	12
11-12	40	22	31	44	37	37	17	30	40	35
12-13	72	47	62	77	68	67	51	57	71	66
13-14	91	76	85	93	91	87	73	80	89	87
14-15	98	94	96	98	98	95	90	92	96	95
15-16	100	98	99	100	99	98	95	97	99	98
16-17		99	100		100	99	97	99	100	99
17-18		100				100	98	99		99
18-19							99	100		100
No. of cases	3850	123	648	2272	665	5081	150	882	2958	937
Mean age	12.3	13.1	12.7	12.2	12.4	12.5	13.2	12.8	12.4	12.6
Median age	12.3	13.1	12.6	12.2	12.4	12.4	13.0	12.7	12.3	12.5
		MENSTRUATION					COMPLETION OF HEIGHT			
	%	Cumulated percent				%	Cumulated percent			
9-10	1	0	1	1	1	—	0	0	—	0
10-11	4	3	3	5	4	—	0	0	—	—
11-12	21	17	17	23	19	2	1	1	2	1
12-13	50	33	43	53	48	7	2	4	9	7
13-14	79	59	71	82	77	18	8	11	21	19
14-15	92	81	89	94	92	35	22	26	38	37
15-16	97	94	96	98	96	53	45	43	56	52
16-17	99	98	99	99	99	73	66	64	76	72
17-18	100	99	99	100	100	85	74	79	88	82
18-19		100	100			94	88	91	96	93
19-20						97	93	94	98	96
20-21						98	97	97	99	98
21-22						99	100	98	99	99
22-23						100		99	100	100
No. of cases	5770	177	1012	3292	1149	5121	125	895	3013	1038
Mean age	13.1	13.6	13.3	13.0	13.1	15.9	16.5	16.4	15.7	16.0
Median age	13.0	13.7	13.2	12.9	13.1	15.8	16.3	16.3	15.7	15.9

Ages shown (*e.g.*, 8–9) include the lower limit (*e.g.*, 8), and extend to, but do not include, the upper limit (*e.g.*, 9). In each column, there may be cases lying beyond the age shown at the hundred per cent mark, but such extreme cases total less than 0.5 per cent in any column, and consequently would not affect the percentages shown without decimal places.

Chapter 5

MASTURBATION

Of the six possible types of sexual activity, heterosexual petting is the one in which the largest number of females engage before marriage, and marital coitus is the one in which the largest number of females engage after marriage. Masturbation is the one in which the second largest number of females engage both before and after marriage.

Among all types of sexual activity, masturbation is, however, the one in which the female most frequently reaches orgasm. Even in her marital coitus the average female fails to achieve orgasm in a fair proportion of her contacts (Tables 102 ff.), and this is true in most of the petting which she does prior to marriage; but in 95 per cent or more of all her masturbation, she does reach orgasm.[1]

This is due to the fact that the techniques of masturbation are especially effective in producing orgasm. Socio-sexual relationships usually demand some adjustment of the interests, the desires, the physical capacities, and the physiologic reactions of the partner in the activity. In coitus, a female who is not strongly aroused by the psychologic aspects of the relationship may find that some of the adjustments which she has to make interrupt the steady flow of her response, and she is, in consequence, delayed or completely prevented from reaching orgasm (pp. 385, 668). She may prefer the socio-sexual relationship because of its psychologic and social significance, and the delay in reaching orgasm may in actuality increase her pleasure, but the fact remains that the techniques of masturbation usually offer the female the most specific and quickest means for achieving orgasm. For this reason masturbation has provided the most clearly interpretable data which we have on the anatomy and the physiology of the female's sexual responses and orgasm (Chapters 14, 15).

Masturbation was accepted by a great many of the females in our sample as a desirable and often necessary source of outlet, but it had not been as frequent and as regular a source for the females as it had

---

[1] Davis 1929:97 shows 88 per cent of the unmarried women who masturbate reaching orgasm. Note that many of the data which we cite in the present volume from Davis and Hamilton represent our recalculations of their original data, and that these differ at several points from their published calculations (p. 96).

been for the males in the sample. Many males, projecting their own experience, are inclined to overestimate the incidences and frequencies of masturbation among females.[2] For the same reason, they poorly understand the techniques by which females masturbate, the anatomy which may be involved, the nature of the female's physiologic responses, and the part which fantasy plays in her masturbation. It has, therefore, been important to secure specific data on these points.

DEFINITION

Masturbation may be defined as deliberate self-stimulation which effects sexual arousal.[3] In the human animal, motivations for the activity lie in the conscious realization that erotic satisfactions and some release from erotic tensions may thus be obtained. Instances of orgasm induced by accidental self-stimulation are not, strictly speaking, masturbation. Masturbation may or may not be pursued to the point of orgasm, and it may or may not have orgasm as its objective. While the original forms of the word, *manusturbo* or *manustuprum*, associate the phenomenon with *manus*, the hand,[4] the techniques, particularly in the female, may also include other means of stimulating the genitalia or some other part of the body, stimulation by way of some of the other sense organs, and psychologic stimulation.

Since any form of tactile stimulation may initiate the physiologic responses which are to be observed in sexual behavior, it is sometimes difficult to determine how much of the self-stimulation which occurs in an animal's life is, in any strict sense, masturbatory. In much of the Freudian literature, and in still other studies,[5] all tactile stimulation of one's own body is interpreted as masturbation. This has been particularly true in reports on younger children, especially females. There

---

[2] Such overestimates of masturbatory incidences in the female, ranging from 98 to 100 per cent, may be found in: Berger (1876) acc. Rohleder 1902:45 (100 per cent). Guttzeit acc. Kisch 1907:108. Stekel 1920:22; 1950:39 (100 per cent). Cohn acc. Stekel 1920:23; 1950:40 (99 per cent). Lazarsfeld 1931:240. Lampl-deGroot 1950:155 (all children masturbate). Haire 1951: 500 (98 per cent). Young acc. Haire 1951:137 (100 per cent). See footnote 20.

[3] Other current writers generally agree with our definition. Autoerotism (used by Havelock Ellis) and onanism are frequently intended to be broader terms. See for example: Steiner 1912:129. Stekel 1920:18; 1950:31.

[4] The Latin verb *masturbare* appears, apparently for the first time, in Martial [1st cent. A.D.] IX,41,7; XI,104,13; XIV,203,2. Authorities disagree as to its exact derivation. Forcellini (Totius Latinitatis Lexicon) says it is from *manu* and *stupro*, to defile with the hand. Harper's Latin Dictionary gives the same. But Pierrugues (1826) 1908, and Rambach 1833 allow two origins: *manu* and *stuprare*, or *manu* and *turbare*, to disturb with the hand. Licht 1932:314 accepts this dual possibility. Murray, Oxford Dictionary, 1908, gives *manu* and *stuprare*, but cites one authority who suggests the Greek roots *mazdo* (the virile member) and *turba* (disturbance) as the basis for the word.

[5] Such extensions of the concept of masturbation to include most tactile stimulation may be found, for instance, in: Hirschfeld 1926:259. Meagher 1929:66. Meagher and Jelliffe 1936:66. Freud 1938:585–589. Stekel 1950:22.

has not been so much confusion in the identification of masturbation in the older boy or adult male where the techniques are usually genital and where erection is taken as evidence that the responses are sexual. But the term masturbation has often been extended to include all activities which bring satisfaction through the rubbing, scratching, pressing, or stroking of the breasts, thighs, legs, or other parts of the body including even the nose and ears, thumb sucking, the biting of one's fingernails, the chewing of gum, bed wetting, fast automobile driving, high diving, and still other activities.

In consequence, published incidences of masturbation, especially in the female, have often been unduly augmented by the inclusion of activities which we do not now consider sexual and which, as a matter of fact, few persons would consider masturbatory if they occurred in the adult male.[6] In most instances, the average person has no difficulty in determining whether particular activities are sexual. Technical attempts to identify masturbation have, on the other hand, proved less satisfactory because they have been based on the identification of the elements involved in the behavior rather than upon the nature of the syndrome as a whole.

We ourselves (1948:497–498) were formerly inclined to accept the Freudian interpretations. But as we have learned more about the basic physiology of sexual response (Chapters 14 and 15), it has become apparent that the individual elements in the response are not the factors that identify it as sexual—that the increased pulse rate, the increased blood pressure, the increase in peripheral circulation, the rise in surface temperatures, the loss of sensory perception, and even the genital erections are not in themselves sexual. Many of the same elements appear when a mammal becomes angry or afraid (Chapter 17), but that is no reason for synonymizing sex, anger, and fear. Each of these types of behavior is a group, a cluster, a constellation, a syndrome of elements which appear concomitantly whenever that type of response is involved. Many of the elements are common to all of the syndromes, but in each syndrome there are some elements which are not found in any other. Sexual behavior, as one of these syndromes, is a unique combination of elements which appears only when an animal has coitus or when it becomes involved in activities which, at least to some extent, duplicate some of the aspects of coitus.

MAMMALIAN AND PRIMITIVE HUMAN BACKGROUNDS

Masturbation among Mammals. Masturbation, sometimes to the point of orgasm, occurs widely among the males of most infra-human

---

[6] Other authors who also believe that the term should be restricted include: Moll 1912:172–173. Hamilton 1929:424. Valentine 1942:331–339.

mammalian species. It has been less often observed among the females of the infra-human species but it is recorded for the female rat, chinchilla, rabbit, porcupine, squirrel, ferret, horse, cow, elephant, dog, baboon, monkey, and chimpanzee.[7] The data on these infra-human mammals are, however, fragmentary, for the sexual activities of few of them outside of a limited number of laboratory species have ever been extensively observed. It is not impossible that more extended observations would greatly increase the list of species in which the female is known to masturbate.

The known distribution of masturbation among these several species is sufficient to make it clear, however, that the inclination to stimulate her own genitalia is one of the capacities which the human female shares with the females of the whole class Mammalia. But it should be recognized that masturbation among the females of most mammalian species occurs less frequently than among the males, perhaps because the incentives for masturbating are much less among the females. Outside of the human species, orgasm is infrequent and possibly absent among females of most species of mammals. The females of most of the species do show signs of erotic arousal during sexual activity, and some of them may be very much aroused, but it is not certain how many ever reach orgasm. This would considerably reduce the incentive for a lower mammalian female to masturbate. The capacity of most human females to achieve orgasm as the culmination of an appreciable proportion of their sexual activity is one which sharply distinguishes them from the females of most of the lower species of mammals.

Masturbation among Primitive Human Groups. The anthropologic record indicates that masturbation is widely known among the females of many human groups. It did not originate in our European culture. The published studies record masturbatory activity among the females of some thirty-five or forty primitive groups, including in particular those in the Pacific area and in Africa where the anthropologists have made the most extensive studies.[8] Once again, however, the record is

---

[7] Masturbation among the females of infra-human species of mammals is recorded in: Ellis 1910:165 (horse). Northcote 1916:420 (ferret). Zell 1921(1):237 (dog). Stone 1922:129 (rat). Zuckerman 1932:230 (baboon). Williams 1943: 445 (cow). Shadle, Smelzer, and Metz 1946:117–121 (porcupine), also cited in Ford and Beach 1951:161. Beach in Hoch and Zubin 1949:63 (elephant). Klein 1951 (verbal communic., rabbit). Ford and Beach 1951:162, 166 (monkey). Our own observations cover female dogs, chinchillas, rats, and chimpanzees. Shadle (verbal communic.) also has seen masturbation in the female racoon, skunk, and guinea pig. Data on the chimpanzee are in: Bingham 1928:148–150. Spragg 1940:87. Yerkes 1943:58. Ford and Beach 1951:163. Lashley, Nissen, Gavin, and the Brookfield Zoo keepers have observed the female chimpanzee masturbating (verbal communic.).

[8] To illustrate the widespread incidence of female masturbation in pre-literate societies, the following examples may be cited for Africa: Bryk 1933:224–225. Laubscher 1938:78. Ward 1938:46. Schapera 1941:183. For India: Elwin

notably fragmentary and probably gives no idea of the true spread of the phenomenon. The anthropologist's informant may neglect to refer to female masturbation, or only incidentally remark that it occurs, but a more systematic survey might disclose that the activity was widespread in many of these groups. Human males throughout history and among all peoples have been most often concerned with the sexual activities of the female when those activities served the male's own purposes, and her solitary and even homosexual activities (Chapter 11) have often been ignored.

Typical of this lack of interest in the female's solitary activities is the fact that practically none of the anthropologic literature ever records the presence or absence of orgasm in the female's masturbation, and sometimes leaves it uncertain whether she does anything more than touch her genitalia as she might touch any other part of her body. Certainly it would be unwarranted to conclude on the basis of the available information that the incidences or frequencies of masturbation among European and American females are any higher or any lower than they are in other cultures elsewhere in the world.[9]

Phylogenetic Interpretations. An animal inherits much of its morphologic structure and the physiologic capacities of those structures. Since its behavior may depend, to a considerable degree, upon the nature of its structure and its physiologic capacities, the ultimate bases of the behavior of any species or of any individual within the species may be a matter of heredity. This being so, it is not surprising to find that closely related species of animals show similar patterns of behavior. For instance, the rat, the guinea pig, the chinchilla, squirrels, and various other rodents assume similar positions in coitus, and make a relatively few pelvic thrusts, clean their genitalia with their mouths before they make a second series of thrusts, and continue to make such limited series of thrusts until they finally reach orgasm; and this pattern is more or less uniform throughout most of the species of the order

---

1947:447. For North American Indians: Devereux 1936:33. Hallowell in Hoch and Zubin 1949:109. Ford and Beach 1951:158. For South America: Nimuendajú 1939:73–74. For Oceania: Malinowski 1929:340, 476. Powdermaker 1933:276–277. Firth 1936:494–495. Mead 1949:216. For Siberia: Ford and Beach 1951:158.

[9] Descriptions of masturbation among females are to be found in classical, Biblical, and Oriental literature. Descriptions of the use of vaginal insertions (dildoes) are a chief feature of such accounts, as in: Ezekiel 16:17. Makurabunko (ca. 1840) (Japan). Karsch-Haack 1906:45 (China). Krauss 1911:ch. 14 (Japan). Stern 1933:295, 300–301.

For Greek and Roman literature, see: Aristophanes [5th–4th cent. B.C.]: Lysistrata, 108–110, 158 (1912(1):240, 243; 1924(3):15, 19). Aristotle [4th cent. B.C.]: 7(1):581b (Oxford 1910) (girls of 14 may develop habits of erotic indulgence). Herondas [3rd cent. B.C.]: 6(1921:83–92). Petronius [1st cent. A.D.]: Satyricon, 138 (1913:313; 1927(2):339). Vorberg 1926, pl. XXI, XXII, show female masturbation with dildoes in Greek art.

Rodentia because all of these species are evolutionarily related. On the other hand, the mink, ferret, marten, and skunk make very rapid copulatory movements with a perfect flutter of pelvic thrusts which may be carried through continuously to orgasm, because all of these species are members of the family Mustelidae and therefore evolutionarily related. Similarly, there are numerous other aspects of the sexual behavior of these related species which are remarkably similar.

Just which aspects of any behavioral pattern are inherited, which aspects are unique developments within the particular species, and which are the result of learned behavior in the pattern of a particular individual, may be determined by examining the distribution of the pattern among closely related species.

Whenever phenomena occur widely in an evolutionarily related group of species, and also occur widely among the individuals or groups of individuals within the species which is being examined, we have the best sort of evidence that those phenomena are part of the evolutionary heritage of the species. For that reason it has been exceedingly important in the present interpretations of human sexual behavior to examine the distribution of each phenomenon among the various species of the class Mammalia, which is the class to which the human species belongs. It has been similarly important to examine the distribution of each phenomenon, as far as anthropologic data will allow, in various cultural groups of the human species. Our present interpretations of the evolutionary backgrounds of masturbation in the female, and of the various other aspects of sexual behavior that will be considered in the later chapters of this volume, are based upon such phylogenetic (evolutionary) data. We shall find that a great many of the aspects of human sexual behavior, including many which various religious and cultural codes have considered the most abnormal, are, in actuality, basic to the whole mammalian stock. Moreover, by determining what are the basic mammalian characteristics in human behavior, it has become possible to identify the new phenomena which have developed in human evolution, and to identify which aspects of the behavior of any individual are a product of the learning and conditioning processes which have shaped the history of the particular individual (Chapter 16).

LEARNING TO MASTURBATE

Self-Discovery. Most of the females in our sample had discovered how to masturbate as a result of their exploration of their own genitalia. Since the child's experience from the day it is born has shown it that satisfactions may be secured from the tactile stimulation of various parts of its body, one might expect that all children would sooner or later discover, quite on their own, that the greatest satisfactions may be obtained from such genital stimulation as masturbation might afford.

A considerable portion of the masturbation which we have found among infants and young pre-adolescent girls in our sample appears to have been self-discovered. Some 70 per cent of the older pre-adolescent girls who had begun to masturbate before adolescence also appear to have discovered the possibilities through their own exploration (Table 20).[10] Although some of the adults who were the sources of our information had probably forgotten the part which other children and even adults played in inspiring their early experimentation, some 58 per cent of the females who had begun masturbation between eleven and twenty years of age reported that their activity had been self-discovered.[11] The figures were lower for the lower educational levels, and higher for the college and graduate school groups, but they were not particularly different in the several generations covered by the sample (Table 20).

Interestingly enough, many of the older individuals who did not begin to masturbate until they were well along in their twenties or thirties, and even in their forties and fifties, were still discovering the possibilities of such activity through their own exploration (Table 20).[12] This provides striking evidence of the ignorance which is frequent among females of sexual activities which are outside of their own experience, even though they may be common in the population as a whole. Some 28 per cent of the boys in our sample had discovered masturbation on their own, but 75 per cent of them had heard about masturbation, 40 per cent of them had actually observed it, and 9 per cent had been masturbated by other males before they began their own activities (p. 675). It is obvious that neither younger girls nor older women discuss their sexual experience in the open way that males do.

Not a few of the females in the sample had learned that masturbation occurred among males long before they learned that it was possible among females.

---

[10] The self-discovery of masturbation has been noted by many writers, including: Forel acc. Back 1910:112. Moll 1912:171. Hirschfeld 1916:122. Krafft-Ebing (Moll ed.) 1924:80. Rohleder in Stern 1927:283. Hoyer 1929:223. Hutton 1937:76.

[11] Other American studies show similar percentages learning to masturbate through self-discovery: Hamilton 1929:427 (65 per cent; records the circumstances). Davis 1929:109–110, 161 (51 per cent; records the circumstances). Dickinson and Beam 1931:350 (the majority). Landis and Bolles 1942:21 (69 per cent).

[12] Davis 1929:161 also mentions this late self-discovery in over a third of her married females who had started masturbation after age 14.

Among the females in the sample who had not begun masturbating until after age thirty, 19 per cent had not heard of it before they began their own masturbation (Table 20). However, 27 per cent of the graduate school group, from whom the professional counselors of youth most often come, had not known that masturbation was possible in the female until they discovered it in the course of their own experimentation after they were past thirty years of age. Since most of the males had begun masturbating before they became adolescent or soon after the onset of adolescence (see our 1948:502), most of them knew about masturbation and had actually been masturbating for ten or twenty years before some of their mothers and teachers ever learned that there was such a phenomenon.

Some females had masturbated for some years before they learned that the activity in which they had been engaged had any sexual connotation and constituted what is known as masturbation.[13]

Verbal and Printed Sources. Approximately 43 per cent of those females in the sample who had ever masturbated, had learned that such a thing was possible from information acquired through verbal and/or printed sources (Table 20).[14] This was the second most important source of first knowledge for those who had begun masturbation by age twenty. It was the most important source, surpassed by no other, for those who had begun masturbation after that age. In this regard, there were no significant differences between the generations born in the four decades covered by the sample (Table 20). On the other hand, 75 per cent of the males in our sample had acquired their first information about masturbation from verbal and/or printed sources, but chiefly from verbal sources (p. 675). The females in the sample had more often obtained their information from books—chiefly from moral and sex education literature, and from religious lectures which were designed to discourage masturbation.[15]

---

[13] For additional records of the female masturbating even to orgasm without realizing the sexual nature of the activity, see: Hirschfeld 1916:130. Meagher 1929:74. Davis 1929:400. Kelly 1930:174. Meagher and Jelliffe 1936:76.

[14] Learning from verbal and printed sources is also recorded in: Adler 1911:98, 101, 105. Achilles 1923:45 (about 50 per cent). Hellmann acc. Weissenberg 1924b:211 (friends, 35 per cent; literature, 16 per cent). Schbankov acc. Weissenberg 1924a:14 (servants, 13 per cent; literature and shows, 31 per cent). Golossowker acc. Weissenberg 1925:175 (friends, 39 per cent; literature, 10 per cent). Gurewitsch and Grosser 1929:528 (friends, 51 per cent; literature, 16 per cent). Davis 1929:109, 161 (30 per cent). Hamilton 1929:426 (25 per cent). Dickinson and Beam 1931:350. Landis and Bolles 1942:21 (15 per cent).

[15] Religious books as inspiration for masturbating are also cited in: Moraglia 1897:9. For the Bible and classics as sources, see: Wulffen 1913:257. G. S. Hall and Brill acc. Meagher and Jelliffe 1936:75 deny that serious books have such an influence, but our data do not support them.

Most of the females in the sample had begun to masturbate soon after they had learned that such a thing was possible, but some of them had waited months and even years after they learned of masturbation before they began their own activity. Males who hear of masturbation rarely delay their actual experimentation.

Petting Experience. The females in the sample had begun masturbation as a result of their petting or pre-coital experience with males in approximately 12 per cent of the cases.[16] There were very few males who had not known of masturbation before they ever engaged in heterosexual petting. Some of the females, even though they had had males manipulate their genitalia and bring them to orgasm in the course of a petting relationship, had not realized that self-manipulation could effect similar results. Although extensive heterosexual petting is somewhat more frequent in the younger generation (pp. 242 ff.), it seems to have provided an introduction to masturbation among older generations, forty years ago, fully as often as it does for the younger generation today (Table 20).

Observation. Observing other persons in masturbatory activities was the chief inspiration for the beginning of masturbation for only about 11 per cent of the females in the sample.[17] Such observation was the source of inspiration for the initial experimentation of some 40 per cent of the males. There appear to have been no changes in the importance of such observation over the last four decades (Table 20).

The direct observation of masturbation is most often possible during pre-adolescent or early adolescent years (Table 20). Not infrequently girls observe boys rather than other girls in masturbation, and subsequently explore their own capacities. There were even cases of older women who had found the initial stimulus for their masturbatory activities in their observation of infants and young pre-adolescent girls.

Homosexual Experience. About 3 per cent of the females in the sample had begun their masturbation as a result of their homosexual contacts in pre-adolescent, adolescent, or more adult years (Table 20).[18] In a few instances it was a nurse, housemaid, or female relative who had provided the first experience for the child. It was 9 per cent

---

[16] Hamilton 1929:426 found 18 per cent of his females reported masturbation which originated in petting, but did not distinguish between heterosexual and homosexual petting. Davis 1929:110 reported that 3 per cent of the unmarried females started masturbation from petting.

[17] Masturbation originating from imitation of others is recorded in: Hamilton 1929: 426 (6 per cent).

[18] Homosexual relationships as the origin of masturbation are also noted in: Adler 1911:101. Krafft-Ebing (Moll ed.) 1924:501. Davis 1929:110. Hamilton 1929:426.

of the boys in the sample who had learned of masturbation through their homosexual experience (p. 675).

RELATION TO AGE AND MARITAL STATUS

In our sample, masturbation had occurred among females of every group, from infancy to old age.

Among Children. We have records of 67 infants and small girls three years of age or younger who were observed in masturbation, or who as adults recalled that they had masturbated at that age. We have

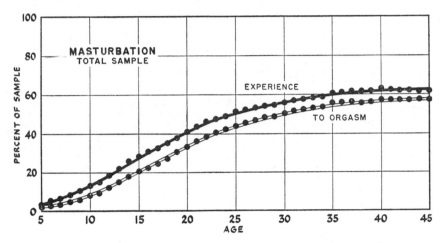

Figure 9. Accumulative incidence: masturbation, experience and orgasm

Each dot indicates percent of sample with experience or orgasm by the indicated age. Data from Tables 21, 25.

one record of a seven-month-old infant and records of 5 infants under one year of age who were observed in masturbation.[19] There were undoubtedly many more females who engaged in true masturbatory activities when they were young; but it has been impossible to calculate incidence figures from the available records.

---

[19] Similar cases of definitely erotic performances in masturbation in very young girls are reported by: Townsend 1896:186–189 (5 cases under 1 year of age). Moll 1909:52–53; 1912:57–58. Talmey 1910:92–93 (one 9 months, acc. Jacobi, and several 3-year-old girls). Stekel 1920:34; 1950:72 (at 4 years). Hirschsprung acc. Rohleder 1921:66 (at 4, 13, 18 months). Blache (1877) acc. Rohleder 1921:68 (at 17 months). Kraft acc. Rohleder 1921:66 (at 11 months). Krafft-Ebing 1922:55–56 (at 2, 3, 4 years). Krafft-Ebing (Moll ed.) 1924:81 (at 18 months). Riolan 1927:73 (at 3 years). Hodann 1929:28. Friedjung and Hetzer acc. Bühler 1931:616–617 (6, 11, 16 months). West acc. Havelock Ellis 1936 (II,1):155 (6–9 months). Spitz 1949:95 (rocking and genital play observed in over half of 248 children under one year of age). Levine 1951:118–121 ("typical orgasms even prior to the age of three"—sex not specified). Tactile stimulation, some of it genital but some of it less specifically sexual, is reported in Levy 1928:889. Dillon 1934:165–166. Koch 1935:145. Hattwick 1937:347.

Our records, however, include specific and repeated observations on several children whose responses were unmistakably erotic (see Chapter 4). We have records of 23 girls three years old or younger who reached orgasm in self-masturbation (p. 105). There are more records of small girls than there are of small boys masturbating to orgasm at such an early age (p. 106). It requires some experience and some development of muscular coordinations to effect the rhythmic manual movements on which masturbation depends, and the small boy does not so often manage to achieve that end. Some 19 per cent of the girls had masturbated prior to adolescence.

Accumulative Incidence. About 62 per cent of all the females in the sample had masturbated at some time in the course of their lives (Table 21, Figure 9).[20] About 58 per cent had masturbated at some time to the point of orgasm (Table 25, Figure 9). The 4 to 6 per cent which had masturbated without reaching orgasm was chiefly a group of females who had made only single or desultory and infrequent trials of their capacities, for nearly all of those who had seriously experimented soon learned to reach orgasm. The discussion in the present chapter is, therefore, confined (except in a few places expressly noted) to females whose masturbation had proceeded to the point of orgasm.

The incidences for those who had masturbated to the point of orgasm were 4 per cent by seven years of age, 12 per cent by twelve (which is the average age at which adolescence begins), and 15 per cent by age thirteen (which is the average age at which menstruation first occurs) (Table 25, Figures 9, 10).[21] The incidence curves for both experience and orgasm then rose more or less continuously from adolescence until age 35. The curves still continued to rise but more slowly after that, and there were still some females who began to masturbate for the first time after age forty. The steady development of the curves had not been affected by the ages at which the females had married.

---

[20] American data are also in: Davis 1929:98, 153 (65 per cent of single females; 52 per cent of all women; based, however, on an erroneous assumption that none began masturbation after marriage). Hamilton 1929:427 (74 per cent). Dickinson and Beam 1931:172 (49 per cent); 349 (41 per cent). Dickinson and Beam 1934:460 (76 per cent). Strakosch 1934:37 (66 per cent). Landis et al. 1940:59 (54 per cent). Dearborn 1952:51 (75–80 per cent). These American figures are very close to our own. The wide variation in accumulative incidence figures given by European authors depends for the most part on the fact that they are estimates, or data based on the select samples which go to clinics.

[21] Previous studies on masturbation show ages for beginning which are close to our own. See: Hamilton 1929:427 (15 per cent before adolescence). Davis 1929:106, 115 (12 per cent with orgasm by fourteen years of age). Ackerson 1931:224 (14 per cent by age 12). Harvey 1932a:98 (15 per cent by age 12 as the median of previous studies). Landis and Bolles 1942:21 (20 per cent by adolescence).

Active Incidence. Although 58 per cent of the females in our sample were masturbating to orgasm at some time in their lives, it was a much smaller percentage which had masturbated within any particular year or period of years. Because of the considerable discontinuity of most of the masturbatory histories, it is probable that not more than a fifth —20 per cent—of the females were masturbating within any particular year. It was perhaps 75 per cent of the single males and 30 per cent of the married males who were masturbating in any one year.

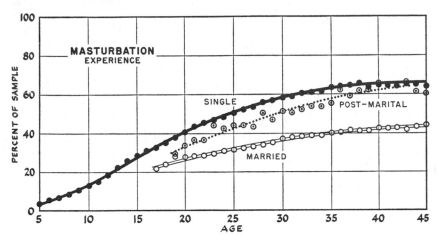

Figure 10. Accumulative incidence: experience in masturbation, by marital status

Showing percent of females with experience while single, married, or previously married. Data from Table 21.

The active incidences of masturbation were lowest in the younger groups, and highest in the older groups of females (Table 23, Figure 11). In the younger groups, as few as 20 per cent of the females were masturbating, while as many as 58 per cent of some of the older groups were having experience within a single five-year period (Table 23).[22] There may have been several explanations of these higher incidences of masturbation among the older females: (1) There may have been an actual increase in erotic responsiveness at the older ages. (2) The availability of socio-sexual outlets had been reduced at older ages, and this may have forced an increasing number of females to masturbate.

---

[22] Published figures which appear to be active incidence figures, whether with or without orgasm, are in: Achilles 1923:50. Schbankov acc. Weissenberg 1924a: 13. Hellmann acc. Weissenberg 1924b:211. Golossowker acc. Weissenberg 1925:175. Gurewitsch and Grosser 1929:525. Davis 1929:102–103. Hamilton 1929:425. Strakosch 1934:35–39. Landis and Bolles 1942:21. The higher incidence of masturbation among older females, whether single or married, is also noted in: Krafft-Ebing (Moll ed.) 1924:566. Hamilton 1929:439 (56 per cent for older married females). Davis 1929:100 (20 per cent at ages 22–27 rising to 39 per cent by ages 37–42, single females, active incidence at age of reporting). Hutton 1937:77.

(3) There was often a reduction of inhibitions among the older females. (4) The older females, having had more experience in petting and coitus, had learned, thereby, that similar satisfactions are obtainable through self-masturbation.

This increase in the incidence of masturbation among the older females sharply contrasts with the record for the single males where the active incidences reach their peak (88 per cent) in the mid-teens, and drop steadily from there into old age (see our 1948:240).[23]

The active incidences of masturbation to orgasm among the single females (ranging from 20 to 54 per cent) were somewhat higher than they were (23 to 36 per cent) among the corresponding married groups (Table 23, Figure 11). Many of those who had depended on this outlet before marriage had stopped masturbating when marital coitus became available. On the other hand, there were some females who had not begun masturbating until after they had learned from their pre-coital petting experience in marriage that self-stimulation could also bring sexual satisfaction. Some women who fail to reach orgasm in coitus are then stimulated manually by their husbands, or they masturbate themselves until they reach orgasm. Some of the married females, on the other hand, confine their masturbation to periods when their husbands are away from home.

Frequency to Orgasm. The average (active median and active mean) frequencies of masturbation were remarkably uniform among most of the groups of single females, from age twenty to the oldest age group in the sample (Table 23, Figure 11). The average frequencies among the married females and the previously married females were similarly uniform in most of the age groups in the sample. The frequencies of the married females were only a bit lower than the frequencies among the single females and among those who had been previously married.

Among the single females who were actually masturbating (the active sample), the average (median) individual was reaching orgasm about once in every two and a half to three weeks (between 0.3 and 0.4 per week) (Table 23). Among the married females the frequencies averaged about once in a month (0.2 per week).[24] Between the ages of sixteen and fifty among the single females, and between the ages of twenty-one and fifty-five among the married and previously married

---

[23] For incidences and frequencies of male masturbation, see: Kinsey, Pomeroy, and Martin 1948:218–262 and elsewhere.

[24] For other data on the frequency of masturbation, see: Davis 1929:122–123 (failed to categorize her data). Hamilton 1929:435–436 (for married females, a median frequency of less than once per month). Landis et al. 1940:288 (median frequency of 1 to 2 times a month, in 122 females).

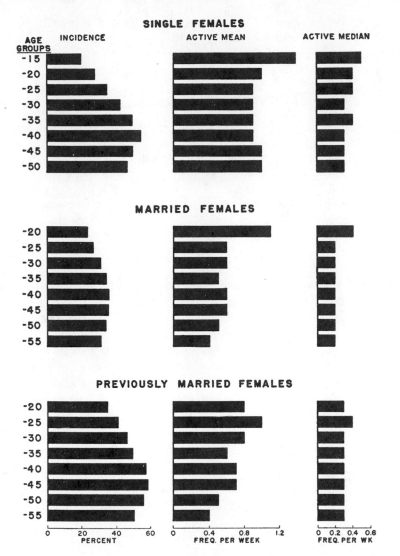

Figure 11. Active incidence, mean, median: masturbation to orgasm, by age and marital status

Data from Table 23.

females, there had been only slight changes in the active median frequencies of masturbation. We shall find that this is more or less true of the frequencies of several other types of female activity and of the total sexual outlet of single females (Chapters 6–13). This is one of the most remarkable aspects of female sexuality, and one which most sharply distinguishes it from the sexuality of the male. Hormonal factors may be involved (Chapter 18).

145

Since the frequencies of masturbation depend primarily on the physiologic state and the volition of the female, they may provide a significant measure of the level of her interest in sexual activity.[25] Heterosexual activities, on the other hand, are more often initiated by the male partner and, in consequence, they do not provide as good a measure of the female's innate capacities and sexual interests.

In some of the histories, there was a record of the female's masturbation being confined to the period just before the onset of her monthly menstruation. This is the period during which most human females are most responsive erotically (Chapter 15, pp. 608–610).

Individual Variation in Frequency. Among those females who had masturbated, some had not had such experience more than once or twice in a year. Most of them, however, had masturbated to the point of orgasm with frequencies which ranged from once in a month to once in a week. There were, however, about 4 per cent (Table 24, Figure 12) who had masturbated with frequencies of 14 or more per week at some period in their lives, and a few who had experienced orgasm from this source as often as 30 or more times per week. In the sample there were females who had regularly masturbated to the point of orgasm several times in immediate succession, and there were some who had masturbated to orgasm as often as 10, 20, and even 100 times within a single hour. This is an example of the individual variation which may occur in any type of sexual activity. While considerable individual variation also occurs among males (see our 1948:234), the range of variation in almost every type of sexual activity seems to be far greater among females.

Because there were some individuals who masturbated with very high rates, the mean frequencies of masturbation were two to three times as high as the corresponding median frequencies (Table 23).

Percentage of Total Outlet. In terms of the total number of orgasms which it had provided, masturbation was much the most important source of sexual outlet for the unmarried females in the sample. In the various age groups it had accounted for something between 37 and 85 per cent of the total pre-marital outlet (Table 23, Figure 110).

In contrast to the single females, the married females had derived, in most cases, something around 10 per cent of their total outlet from masturbation (Table 23). It had provided a somewhat lower percentage of the total outlet for the younger married females, and a somewhat higher percentage for the older females.

---

[25] Davis 1929:211–212 agrees that masturbation is a good index of strong sex desire in a single female.

Among those females who had been previously married but who were no longer living with their husbands, the percentage of the total outlet which was derived from masturbation rose in the sample, from 13 per cent in the younger age groups to 44 per cent in the older groups (Table 23).

Number of Years Involved. Masturbation was an activity of very short duration in the histories of some of the females, but it had ex-

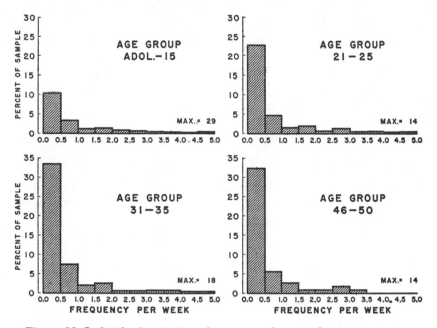

Figure 12. Individual variation: frequency of masturbation to orgasm

For four age groups of single females. Each class interval includes the upper but not the lower frequency. For incidences of females not masturbating or reaching orgasm, see Table 23.

tended throughout the lives of others in the sample. Confining our analyses to the older females in order to restrict the data to individuals who had had the maximum opportunity for developing long-time masturbatory histories, the record shows the following (Table 22): Among the females who were between thirty-one and thirty-five years of age at the time they contributed histories to the present study, 9 per cent of those who had ever masturbated had done so for only a single year or less than one year. About one-sixth (16 per cent) had extended their activities over a period of two to five years. For 16 per cent the activity had been continuous for something between six and ten years, and more than half (59 per cent) had masturbated for more than ten years. The average (median) female in this group had masturbated for something near fourteen years.[26] Among the females who had ever masturbated and who were over fifty years of age at the time they contributed their histories, 73 per cent had masturbated for more than ten years, and the median female in the group had masturbated for twenty-four years (Table 22).

In the histories of some 15 per cent of those females who had ever masturbated, the activity had been quite discontinuous. In such cases, masturbation had occurred a few times or regularly for some longer or shorter period, ceased entirely for a year or more, and then recurred at some later period. In some instances there had been as many as forty or more years between the periods of masturbation. In perhaps half of the cases, these breaks were due to the fact that other sexual outlets, particularly marital coitus, had become available. In some cases they were the product of moral restraint. In a few cases they were due to some dissatisfaction with masturbation as a source of outlet, or to a lack of interest in having any sexual outlet at all.

RELATION TO EDUCATIONAL LEVEL

Incidence to Orgasm. The number of females who had ever masturbated to the point of orgasm differed somewhat in the educational levels on which we have data. For instance, the **accumulative incidences** at age forty ranged from about 34 per cent among the females who had never gone beyond grade school, and 59 per cent for the females of the high school level, to 63 per cent among the females who had gone beyond college into graduate work (Table 25, Figure 13). The females of the grade school and high school levels had not begun masturbation as often at older ages, particularly after they were married.[27]

There are some differences in the **active incidences** of masturbation among unmarried females of the several educational levels (Table 27). For instance, in the late teens, the active incidences among single females were 27 per cent in the grade school group and 34 per cent in the graduate school group (Table 27, Figure 14). Among married females between twenty-one and twenty-five years of age, the active incidences ranged from 11 per cent for the grade school group to 31 per cent for the graduate school group (Table 27, Figure 14).

Frequency to Orgasm. In our sample, the average (active median) frequencies of masturbation had been remarkably constant (usually

---

[26] Data on duration of masturbation are also to be found in: Hirschfeld 1916:135. Hellmann acc. Weissenberg 1924b:211. Davis 1929:118–122, 162.

[27] Davis 1929:157–158 (found no significant difference between educational levels; the non-college group began earlier). Lazarsfeld 1931:235 (found no differences; clinical cases).

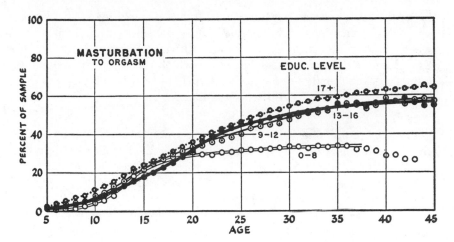

Figure 13. Accumulative incidence: masturbation to orgasm, by educational
level

Data from Table 25. For definitions of educational levels, see p. 53.

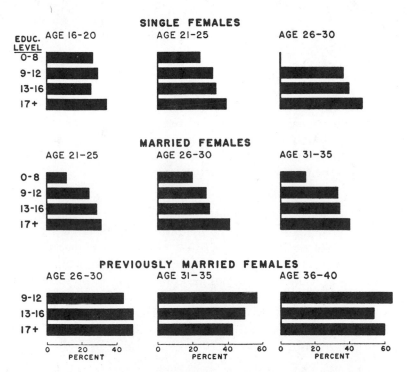

Figure 14. Active incidence: masturbation to orgasm, by educational level,
age, and marital status

Data from Table 27.

0.3 or 0.4 per week) among the single and previously married females of all the educational levels, and equally constant (usually 0.2 per week) among the married females of all the educational levels. Although the pattern of the social group to which she belonged may have influenced the female's decision to masturbate or not to masturbate, it had little if anything to do with establishing the frequencies of her masturbation after she had once begun.

Percentage of Total Outlet. Among the youngest adolescent girls in the sample, masturbation had accounted for half (52 per cent) of the total outlet of the grade school group, three-fourths (73 per cent) of the outlet of the high school group, and over 90 per cent of the outlet of the college and graduate school groups (Table 27). Females of the lower educational levels had more often depended on pre-marital coitus and less often accepted masturbation as a source of pre-marital outlet. They had more often feared that masturbation would do them physical harm, and more often considered it morally wrong and biologically abnormal. The girls who ultimately go on to college belong to a social group which considers masturbation more acceptable than pre-marital coitus. They are less often in conflict over the physical outcome or moral aspects of their masturbation, although they can become much disturbed at any consideration of coitus as a pre-marital activity.

The disparity between upper and lower educational levels was greatest in the youngest age groups, and much less among the older groups. As they grew older, there was a gradual reduction in the extent to which the unmarried, lower level females had depended on masturbation, but the reduction was more marked among those who had gone on into college. Consequently the differences were narrowed between the upper and lower educational groups.

RELATION TO PARENTAL OCCUPATIONAL CLASS

The social levels of the parental homes in which the females in the sample had been raised (particularly during their teens) seem to have had little effect on their masturbatory histories. Whether they were raised in laborers' homes, in the homes of skilled mechanics, in lower or upper level white collar homes, or in the homes of professional persons, the percentages which had ultimately masturbated (the accumulative incidence) and the percentages which were masturbating to orgasm in any given period (the active incidence) did not seem to vary in any consistent direction (Tables 28 and 29).[28]

---

[28] Estimates of incidences at different social levels are popular in European literature, for example in: Moraglia 1897:14 (more common in upper classes in Italy). Alibert n.d.:80–81 (rare among lower classes). Caufeynon 1902:32 (more in lower economic classes). Wulffen 1913:258 (most in lower level). Rohleder 1921:166 (most at upper level).

Similarly, the average (active median) frequencies with which the average female had masturbated did not seem to show any correlation with the occupational classes of the homes in which they were raised.

While there were greater differences in the percentages of the total outlet which various groups of females had derived from their masturbation, the variations did not seem to correlate with the occupational classes of the homes in which the girls were raised (Table 29).

RELATION TO DECADE OF BIRTH

The available histories are sufficient to allow a comparison of the masturbatory patterns of persons born in four successive decades. The

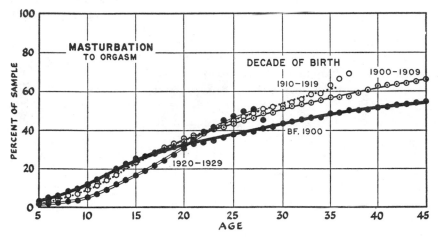

Figure 15. Accumulative incidence: masturbation to orgasm, by decade of birth

Data from Table 26.

oldest were born before 1900, the youngest between 1920 and 1929.

Incidence. The accumulative incidences of masturbation to the point of orgasm among the females in the sample had risen over the period of forty years. Compared with the females who were born before 1900, some 10 per cent more of the younger generations were masturbating in the course of their lives (Table 26, Figure 15). The accumulative incidence curves for those born in the intermediate decades lay between those extremes. For instance, by thirty years of age the curves had reached 44 per cent, 51 per cent, 53 per cent, and possibly 55 per cent in the four successive decades.[29] The youngest generation may

---

[29] Davis 1929:99 has data which, upon recalculation, show masturbation in 65 per cent of the single females born before 1900, and 64 per cent of those born in the next decade after 1900. This latter group was, however, still young when studied, and it could be expected that the accumulative incidence figure would rise above that of the older generation.

have started masturbating a year or two later than any of the preceding generations.

On the other hand, the number of females, either single or married, who were masturbating in any five-year period (the **active incidences**) had not particularly changed in the four decades (Table 30). This was true of the high school, college, and graduate school groups in the sample, in all of the age periods.

Frequency to Orgasm. Among those females in the sample who had actually masturbated, the active median frequencies in the younger generations were not particularly different from the frequencies with which the older generations had masturbated. Among the single females the median frequencies had averaged 0.3 to 0.4 per week. Among the married females they had averaged 0.2 to 0.3 per week.

Percentage of Total Outlet. Over the course of the four decades covered by the sample, the relative importance of masturbation among the single females had, with few exceptions, declined (Table 30). Since neither the active incidences nor the active median frequencies of total outlet had particularly changed in this period of years (Table 160), the decrease in the importance of masturbation must have been due to the increase which occurred in the frequencies of orgasm derived from petting (Table 66) and from pre-marital coitus (Table 84). Masturbation, petting, and pre-marital coitus are the only forms of activity whose relative importance had materially changed in those four decades.

RELATION TO AGE AT ONSET OF ADOLESCENCE

In the case of the male we recognized differences in the patterns of sexual behavior which correlated to a considerable extent with the age at which he became adolescent (1948:Ch. 9). In general, the males who turned adolescent at earlier ages more promptly became active sexually, became involved in more types of sexual activity, had higher frequency rates in each type of activity, and had higher rates of total outlet. Such correlations with the age of the female at the time she turns adolescent are, however, hardly observable in our data.

The number of females who ultimately masturbated (the accumulative incidences, Table 31) and the number who were masturbating in any single five-year period (the active incidences, Table 34) were not particularly different among the girls who had turned adolescent at twelve, thirteen, and fourteen years of age. A few more of the females who had turned adolescent by eleven may have masturbated, and a bit fewer of those who turned adolescent at fifteen.

The frequencies with which the average masturbating female had experienced self-induced orgasm (the active median frequencies), the average frequencies within the group (the active mean frequencies), and the averages for the total sample including both the masturbating and the non-masturbating females (the total mean frequencies), show little variation and no trend which correlates with the ages at which the females had turned adolescent.

Neither did the proportion of the female's total outlet which was derived from masturbation seem to depend upon the age at which she had turned adolescent (Table 34). The factors which are responsible for the correlations between the age at which the male turns adolescent and the nature of his subsequent sexual activity seem not to be operative in the female (Chapter 16).

RELATION TO RURAL-URBAN BACKGROUND

There are sufficient samples for comparing masturbation in rural and urban populations in only five age groups.

Incidence. In these samples, about 59 per cent of the city-bred females and 49 per cent of the rural females were ultimately involved in masturbation which had led to orgasm (the **accumulative incidence,** Table 32).[30] More of the city-bred females, and fewer of those raised on farms, had begun their masturbation after they had turned twenty (Table 32, Figure 16). In consequence, the accumulative incidence curves level off sooner for the rural groups, and continue to rise in later years among the urban groups. On the other hand, more of the urban group seemed to masturbate in each five-year period (the **active incidence**) after the age of twenty (Table 33).

Frequency to Orgasm. The average (both median and mean) frequencies of masturbation among those females who were actively masturbating (the active sample) show no consistent differences between the rural and urban groups which are available for comparison.

Percentage of Total Outlet. Among the city-bred females, the total outlet had depended on masturbation to a slightly lesser degree (in four out of the five instances) than it had among the rural females (Table 33). Since this is not due to any lower rate of masturbation, it obviously means that the total outlet of the city-bred females was higher, which is what the actual data show (Table 163). This was because they were having more coitus before marriage (Table 88).

---

[30] Studies on masturbation with a rural-urban breakdown are rare. Gurewitsch and Grosser 1929:529 found a somewhat higher percentage of masturbation among rural females in their sample of 280 Ukrainian students. Pure conjectures are in: Caufeynon 1902:31 (more in urban). Sturgis 1907:397 (more in rural). Rohleder 1921:62 (more in urban).

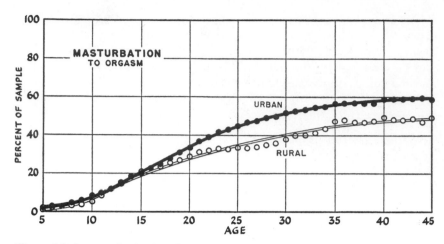

Figure 16. Accumulative incidence: masturbation to orgasm, by rural-urban background

Data from Table 32.

In cities in many parts of the United States, there have been increasingly objective discussions of masturbation among social, professional, and religious groups. This seems to have happened less often in rural areas. Rural populations may reflect more of the taboos which were formerly current among older generations in both rural and urban groups.

RELATION TO RELIGIOUS BACKGROUND

Since masturbation has always been severely condemned in Orthodox Jewish codes, and is similarly condemned in Catholic and some Protestant codes, it is not surprising to find in the case of the female, just as we did in the case of the male, that adherence to a religious faith may lower the incidences of masturbation.

Accumulative Incidence. Among the females in our sample, religious connections seem to have had an even greater effect upon the incidences of masturbation than they did among the males. In the high school, college, and post-graduate groups on which data are available, masturbation had ultimately occurred in an appreciably smaller number of those females who were religiously devout. In the non-religious groups the accumulative incidence figures had ultimately included some 10 to 25 per cent more of the entire sample (Table 35, Figures 17–19).

In some of the most devout groups, as few as 41 per cent had ultimately masturbated; in some of the least religious groups as many as 67 per cent had had such experience (Table 35, Figures 17–19).

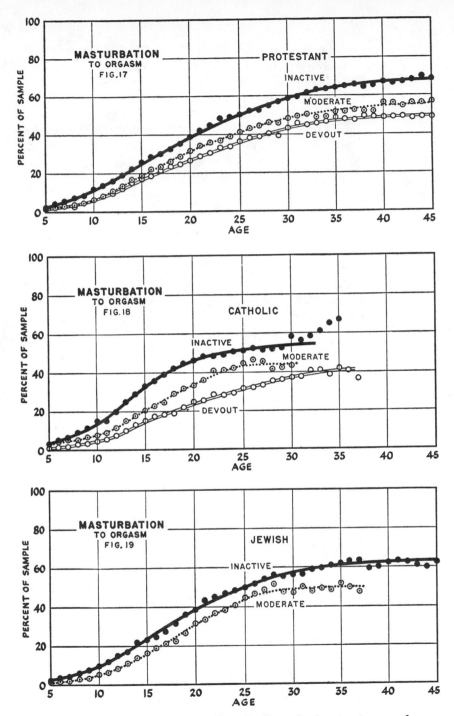

Figures 17–19. Accumulative incidence: masturbation to orgasm, by religious group

Data from Table 35.

155

As we previously found for the male (1948:485), there are relatively few distinctions between the accumulative incidences of masturbation among the Protestant, Catholic, and Jewish females of the same level of devotion. Inactive Protestant groups have much the same masturbatory histories as inactive Catholic and Jewish groups. Devout Protestant groups are close to the devout Catholic groups, and the limited data indicate that still fewer of the devout Jewish females in the sample had ever masturbated. It is the degree of the religious adherence, rather than the code of the particular sect, which most affects the pattern of sexual behavior.

All of these calculations have been based, perforce, on the degree of religious adherence which was current at the time that each subject contributed a history to this study. A high proportion of those who were religiously inactive at the time they were interviewed had been more religious in their earlier years. Nevertheless, even though this change in devotion could not be taken into account in the calculations, the incidences of masturbation shown for the early adolescent years and for the later teens distinguish the females who ultimately became inactive in their church affiliations, from those who were destined to remain devout. The differences between the two groups in their middle teens, for instance, were almost as great as the differences in the late thirties. This provides some evidence that females may to some extent match males in having their patterns of overt behavior established while they are in their teens.

Active Incidence. The active incidences of masturbation among the various religious groups show that more of the religiously inactive groups and fewer of the religiously devout groups were masturbating (Table 36, Figure 20). The differences were usually least for the younger age groups, and greatest for the older age groups. If they are not devout, older persons seem to become increasingly independent of religious influences on these matters.

Six of the seven devout Catholic groups and the two devout Jewish groups on which we have data show lower active incidences of masturbation than those shown for the corresponding, devout Protestant groups. The religiously inactive Catholic and Jewish groups had active incidences which were two to three times as high as those in the devout groups.

Frequency to Orgasm. Although the degree of adherence to a religious faith may constitute a prime factor in preventing females from beginning masturbation, it seems to have little effect on the frequencies with which they masturbate after they have once started such activity (Table 36). The total number of orgasms had by the average (median) female in the sample was surprisingly uniform throughout all of the religious groups. Technically phrased, the statement is that the degree of adherence to a religious faith shows an inverse correlation with the accumulative incidences (pp. 154–156), and an even more marked inverse correlation with the active incidences (p. 156), but it shows no clear-cut correlation with the frequencies of masturbation in the active sample.

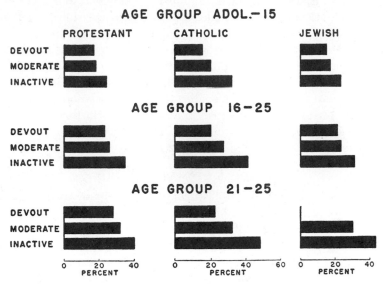

Figure 20. Active incidence: masturbation to orgasm, by religious group
Data on single females; see Table 36.

We have already pointed out that neither age nor educational level was of much importance in determining the rate of masturbation among the females in the sample. It is, therefore, especially significant to find that after the female had once started masturbation, her religious devotion usually ceased to have any particular influence on her. Just as with some other types of sexual activity, moral conflicts are often strongest among those who have never had sexual experience. After experience, most individuals find it difficult to understand why the acceptance of such activity should have seemed such a momentous matter.

Percentage of Total Outlet. Among the single females in the sample, with a few exceptions in certain of the age groups, masturbation had provided a larger proportion of the total outlet of the more devout Protestant, Catholic, and Jewish groups, and a smaller proportion of the outlet of the less devout groups (Table 36). For instance, in various groups, masturbation had provided 80 per cent of the outlet of the more devout females against 63 per cent of the outlet of the corresponding, inactive group; and, in other groups, 98 against 93 per cent, 58 against 38 per cent, and 54 against 45 per cent. This was similarly true of some of the married groups, but in a larger number of them the less devout had drawn more heavily on masturbation as a source of outlet.

While masturbation may be a religiously condemned source of outlet for the devout, unmarried female, it may seem less sinful than pre-marital petting to orgasm and pre-marital coitus; and the limited number of devout females who had reached orgasm from any source before marriage had evidently chosen to depend on masturbation as a primary source of outlet. After marriage, since the objections to coitus had disappeared, masturbation was relegated to a minor position (5 to 16 per cent) in the lives of the religiously inactive groups in the sample, and to a still less important position (4 to 11 per cent) among the religiously devout groups (Table 36).

TECHNIQUES OF MASTURBATION

Females may choose their masturbatory techniques from a longer list of techniques than males ordinarily utilize. Among the females in our sample, a half dozen different methods had been regularly or occasionally employed and still others appeared in some of the histories (Table 37). A half or more of those who had masturbated had depended upon a single technique, but in various groups a quarter to a half of the females had utilized a second or still additional technique.[31]

Clitoral and Labial Techniques. Masturbation among the females in the sample had most frequently involved some manipulation of the clitoris and/or the labia minora.[32] The clitoris is the small, bud-like structure—a homologue of the male penis—which is located near the outer surface at the upper end of the female genitalia (Figure 118). The labia minora are the paired and at times protrudent and prominent inner lips of the genitalia (see Chapter 14). Some 84 per cent of those females in the sample who had ever masturbated had depended primarily on labial and/or clitoral techniques (Table 37).

---

[31] The use of a greater variety of techniques by the females is also recognized in: Moraglia 1897:15. Riolan 1927:29. The continuous use of a single method of stimulation is considered typical in: Hirschfeld 1926(1):264–270. Dickinson and Beam 1934:231. Haire 1951:144.

[32] The dominance of labial and clitoral techniques is widely recognized in both the European and American literature. See, for instance: Anon., Histoire du Vice, n.d.:74. Rosenbaum 1845:137. Moraglia 1897:5–7. Kisch 1907:107. Moll 1909:82; 1912:90. Back 1910:112–113. Adler 1911:116. Rohleder 1921:14. Moll 1926(1):292. Riolan 1927:30. Bauer 1929:234. Kelly 1930:166, 169–170. Dickinson and Beam 1931:351 (66 per cent of more than 400 cases used vulvar friction). Meagher and Jelliffe 1936:70. Dearborn in Fishbein and Burgess 1947:365.

The clitoris and the inner surfaces of the labia minora are of about equal sensitivity and of equal importance as centers of stimulation (pp. 574, 576). In masturbation, the female usually moves a finger gently and rhythmically over the sensitive areas, or applies rhythmic or steady pressure with several of her fingers or with her whole hand. Frequently a single finger or two may be slowly or more rapidly moved forward between the labia in a manner which brings each stroke against the clitoris. Sometimes the labia are gently but still rhythmically pulled. This stimulates these structures and, because they are attached at their forward end to the clitoris, simultaneously stimulates that organ. Occasionally the subject's heel or some other object is used to press on the sensitive areas.

This concentration of stimulation on the clitoris and the labia minora in masturbation is a demonstration of the fact that they are the portions of the genitalia which are best supplied with end organs of touch. The minimum use of deep penetrations of the vagina in masturbation is a reflection of the fact that the walls of the vagina itself are practically without nerves in most females, although there may be some sensory nerves close to the entrance to the vagina in some individuals (pp. 579–584).

Labia Majora. The outer lips of the female genitalia are less often involved in female masturbation, although specific tests indicate that they are quite sensitive to touch.[33] Not all areas which are sensitive to tactile stimulation can be stimulated erotically (page 578). When the labia majora are concerned, the masturbatory techniques usually involve some sort of general pressure which is applied to the whole of the genital area.

Thigh Pressures. Nearly 10 per cent of the females in the available sample had masturbated at times by crossing their legs and appressing them to exert steady or more rhythmic pressures on the whole genital area (Table 37).[34] Such pressures affect the clitoris, the labia minora, and the labia majora, and again demonstrate the importance of those structures. Thigh pressures may be applied with or without simultaneous manipulations of the genitalia with the hand. The pressures effect tactile stimulation, but their effectiveness also depends in part upon

---

[33] The sensitivity of the labia majora is also noted in Rohleder 1921:48.

[34] Thigh friction or pressure as a masturbatory technique is frequently noted in the European and American literature. See, for example: Martineau 1886:70. Anon., Histoire du Vice, n.d.:76. Moraglia 1897:6. Alibert n.d.:61. Kisch 1907:108. Back 1910:110, 113. Moll 1921:618; 1926(1):256. Eberhard 1924:309. Riolan 1927:34. Bauer 1929:234. Hoyer 1929:222. Hodann 1929: 43. Kelly 1930:161. Dickinson and Beam 1931:351. Meagher and Jelliffe 1936:71. Hirschfeld 1944:123. Dearborn in Fishbein and Burgess 1947:365. Wirz in Hornstein and Faller 1950:132.

the fact that they contribute to the development of muscular tensions of the sort which are described below.

Muscular Tensions. A relatively infrequent but biologically important method of masturbation in the female is one which depends upon the development of muscular and nervous tensions throughout the body.[35] To accomplish this, the female may lie face down either in a prone position or with her knees drawn up against her belly. Her buttocks may then move rhythmically forward and against each other. The motion may be slow or faster. Sometimes it develops great speed, but it is always done with considerable tension and force. In such a prone position the female may press some portion of her genitalia against the bed on which she lies, or against a pillow or some other object which she has placed under her pelvis or between her legs. The clitoris and other portions of the genital area are consequently stimulated. Usually, however, the genital contacts are light. They do not involve more than the forward portions of the genitalia, and the effectiveness of such a technique depends chiefly upon the fact that a prone position offers an opportunity for pelvic movements and rhythmic contractions of the large muscles (the gluteal muscles) in the buttocks, and of the muscles (chiefly the adductors) which are located near the front and inner surfaces of the thighs. We have already given a description of such masturbation in a young child (pp. 104–105).

The muscular action which is involved when a female masturbates in this fashion is typical of the copulatory movements of the male, and of the movements which appear in an uninhibited female when she assumes a position on top of the male in coitus. The development of muscular and nervous tensions may be as effective as any direct stimulation of the genitalia. The speed with which orgasm is achieved through the use of such a technique is, in all the females on whom we have specific data, equal or superior to that with which orgasm may be achieved by any other method. Most individuals who have not used the technique may find it difficult to understand the source of its effectiveness, but this is because few persons understand that sexual responses involve a whole syndrome of physiologic reactions. Even when sexual arousal is initiated by the deliberate stimulation of the clitoris and the

[35] This type of masturbation has been referred to in the literature under a variety of titles: muscle eroticism, erotically accentuated tensions, rocking, onanistic rocking movements, and others. See: Stekel 1920:9; 1950:22–23. Hirschsprung acc. Rohleder 1921:66–67. Davis 1929:110. Hodann 1929:36–37 (says it is usual in children). Meagher 1929:71. Friedjung acc. Bühler 1931:616. Meagher and Jelliffe 1936:73. Hirschfeld 1944:121. Spitz 1949:95, 102 (rocking observed in 37 per cent of 248 infants; but we do not follow the interpretations of the significance of the parental backgrounds). Levine 1951:118, 120–121 (boys and girls). Anna Freud 1951:27–28 (to climax at ages 1 to 5). For additional observed cases of female infants reaching orgasm by this prone technique, see references in footnote 19.

labia minora in the female, or of the penis in the male, or by psychic stimulation, orgasm is the end product of all the physiologic changes which develop in the body. A rhythmic development of muscular tensions is probably the most important of all the physiologic changes which occur when an animal responds sexually (Chapter 15). These data on the build-up of such tensions in masturbation have, therefore, contributed materially to our understanding of the physiology of sexual response in general.

Similar developments of muscular tensions as a means of inducing orgasm are used by an occasional male who lies down or stands on his tip-toes and deliberately tenses or rhythmically moves his legs, buttocks, or whole body to secure orgasm without touching his genitalia. Similar tensions may contribute to the erotic arousal which sometimes develops in dancing. Some boys and girls react to the point of orgasm when they climb a pole or a rope, or chin themselves on a bar or some other support. Some boys and girls find their first experience in orgasm in this way, and some of them engage in such exercise with the deliberate intention of securing this sort of satisfaction. Some, on the other hand, are embarrassed and avoid climbing and other types of activities which might induce orgasm in public places, and then the gymnasium instructor may be puzzled to understand why these individuals rebel at engaging in the scheduled exercises. An occasional adult, female or male, may masturbate by pulling up on a door frame or on some other object.

While only 5 per cent of the females in the sample reported such a deliberate use of neuromuscular tensions as a means of masturbating (Table 37), there is reason for believing that its incidence is actually higher, for in the earlier years of our study we were not aware of its importance and did not systematically inquire about it.

Breasts. The breasts and especially the nipples of the breast are erotically sensitive in perhaps half of the females. They had provided some stimulation for about 11 per cent of the sample (Table 37). The female may stimulate them with her hand, or press them against the bed or some other object, usually while she simultaneously manipulates her genitalia. Breast stimulation alone, however, was not sufficient to effect orgasm in more than a very small percentage of the females.[36]

Vaginal Insertions. About 20 per cent of the females reported that they had sometimes used vaginal insertions in connection with their

---

[36] For various interpretations of breast eroticism, with few specific data, see, for example: Anon., Histoire du Vice, n.d.:74. Moraglia 1897:7–8. Alibert n.d.:50. Franz 1913:127 (nipple and areola relatively insensitive). Rohleder 1921:44. Moll 1921:618. Eberhard 1924:245–246, 316–319. Kind and Moreck 1930: 156. Dickinson and Beam 1931:352. Hirschfeld 1944:123.

masturbation (Table 37). Some had made vaginal insertions regularly; most of them had made such insertions only occasionally and usually in connection with other techniques of stimulation. However, many of those who reported "vaginal penetrations" in masturbation failed to distinguish the vestibule of the vagina (which is well equipped with nerve ends) from the vagina itself (which is poorly equipped or devoid of nerve ends). In many instances, the female's fingers had been inserted only far enough beyond the muscular ring which lies at the vaginal entrance (the introitus) to provide a firm hold for the rest of her hand while it was stimulating the outer portions of her genitalia.

Only a limited number of the females in the sample clearly indicated that they had used any object which had penetrated the vagina itself. Many males, however, basing their concepts on their understanding of coitus and upon their conceit as to the importance of the male genitalia in coitus, imagine that all female masturbation must involve an insertion of fingers or of some other object into the depths of the vagina.[37] For this reason, many a male who engages in petting may penetrate the female's vagina with his fingers, and the male-produced literature is frequently concerned with descriptions of dildoes—objects which serve as penis substitutes. But our data indicate that females who had used fingers or other objects in vaginal penetrations did so for a variety of reasons, including the following:

1. Because they actually derived erotic satisfaction from deep vaginal penetration. Such females may have nerve ends in the vaginal walls (p. 582), or they may be stimulated because of the psychologic association of vaginal penetration and coitus.

2. Because such penetrations had been recommended by some male friend, or by a male or female clinician whose interpretations of female anatomy and sexual physiology were based primarily on their misunderstanding of the nature of coitus.

3. Because they had not learned to masturbate until they had had considerable coital experience, and thought it necessary to imitate copulatory techniques while they were masturbating. In many of these cases, however, the insertions were not continued after the female had acquired a better understanding of her own anatomy and sexual capacities.

---

[37] The emphasis which male authors have placed on vaginal insertions and especially on the use of dildoes is illustrated in the following: Crouch (Bekker) 1741:4. Anon., Histoire du Vice, n.d.:74–75, 82–85. Moraglia 1897:4–5. Havelock Ellis 1910(1):167–172. Kisch 1907:108. Alibert n.d.:51–52. Back 1910:112–113. Adler 1911:108–109. Rohleder 1921:34. Moll 1921:617. Eberhard 1924:304–309. Bauer 1929:235–238. Hoyer 1929:223–227. Hirschfeld and Linsert 1930:273–278. Dickinson and Beam 1931:352. Windsor 1937:198 (in harems). Wirz in Hornstein and Faller 1950:132.

4. Because they wanted to entertain their male partners who found it erotically stimulating to observe this type of masturbatory activity.

Fantasy Alone. Some 2 per cent of the females in the sample had reached orgasm by fantasying erotic situations, without tactilely stimulating their genitalia or other parts of their bodies (Table 37).[38] Exceedingly few males are capable of reaching orgasm in this fashion while they are awake, although orgasm from psychic stimulation while asleep is a common enough phenomenon among males. Since less than two-thirds of the females fantasy while they are masturbating (Table 38), the individuals who achieve orgasm through fantasy alone represent an extreme among females.

Other Techniques. There were still other masturbatory techniques which were regularly or occasionally employed by some 11 per cent of the females in the sample (Table 37). Some had rubbed their genitalia against pillows, clothing, chairs, beds, or other objects. Douches, streams of running water, vibrators, urethral insertions, enemas, other anal insertions, sado-masochistic activity, and still other methods were occasionally employed, but none of them in any appreciable number of cases.[39]

Speed of Response to Orgasm. Some 45 per cent of all those females in the sample who had ever masturbated reported that they usually reached orgasm in three minutes or less, and another 25 per cent in something between four and five minutes. The median for the whole group was a few seconds under four minutes. Many of those who took longer to reach orgasm did so deliberately in order to prolong the pleasure of the activity and not because they were incapable of responding more quickly.

These data on the female's speed in reaching orgasm provide im-

---

[38] The ability to reach orgasm through fantasy alone is variously termed idealized coitus, mental cohabitation, moral or psychic masturbation, the mental vulva, and erotic day dreaming. It is recorded in: Bloch 1903:299–300 (gazing at pictures, statues). Kisch 1907:108–109. Back 1910:117. Hirschfeld 1916:129. Stekel 1920:18; 1950:31. Havelock Ellis in Moll 1921:611–612. Rohleder 1921:31–32 ("most noxious"). Hoyer 1929:227. Blanchard in Calverton and Schmalhausen 1929:559. Blanchard and Manasses 1930:35. Robinson 1931: 142. Dickinson and Beam 1934:230 (the physical stigmata of the "mental vulva"). Bleuler 1949:406. Klumbies and Kleinsorge 1950b:61. Several of these express the curious and certainly unfounded opinion that this is the "most noxious" of all forms of masturbation.

[39] Rubbing against objects to secure genital stimulation is also reported in: Rosenbaum 1845:122. Moraglia 1897:6. Moll 1909:81; 1912:89; 1921:618. Stekel 1920:84; 1950:172. Eberhard 1924:310. Urethral insertions are described in: Anon., Histoire du Vice, n.d.:75. Moraglia 1897:7 (most rare). Havelock Ellis 1910(1):172–173. Moll 1909:149; 1912:166. Bauer 1929:238–239. Dickinson and Beam 1931:351. Flagellation and sado-masochistic techniques are recorded in: Moll 1921:618. Eberhard 1924:314–319. Anal insertions are also noted in: Stekel 1920:68; 1950:136. Meagher 1929:71. Kind and Moreck 1930:231–232. Meagher and Jelliffe 1936:73.

portant information on her basic sexual capacities. There is a wide-spread opinion that the female is slower than the male in her sexual responses, but the masturbatory data do not support that opinion. The average male may take something between two and three minutes to reach orgasm unless he deliberately prolongs his activity, and a calculation of the median time required would probably show that he responds not more than some seconds faster than the average female. It is true that the average female responds more slowly than the average male in coitus, but this seems to be due to the ineffectiveness of the usual coital techniques (pp. 384–385).

FANTASY ACCOMPANYING MASTURBATION

Most of the stimulation which the female secures in masturbation is physical. For more than a third (36 per cent) of the masturbating females in the sample, nothing more than physical stimulation seemed to have been involved (Table 38).[40] For the remaining two-thirds (64 per cent), psychologic stimulation through fantasy concerning specifically sexual situations had sometimes accompanied the physical stimulation. For just about half (50 per cent) of the females, fantasies had occurred in connection with most of their masturbation, at least during certain periods of their lives. For a fair number, fantasies had not begun until some years after the masturbation had begun. In consequence, fantasies were more common among the older females, and less common among the younger females.

Masturbatory fantasies may concern heterosexual, homosexual, animal, sado-masochistic, or still other sorts of sexual contacts. With some of the females in the sample the fantasies had been confined to a single one of these categories. With other individuals, two or more types of fantasy had occurred, and with some, different sorts of fantasies had occurred during different periods of their lives.

The fantasies were heterosexual, at least on occasion, for about 60 per cent of those who had ever masturbated (Table 38). Some 10 per cent of them, on occasion, and some of them regularly, had had homosexual fantasies. Reflecting the limited occurrence of overt sexual relationships between human females and animals of other species (Chapter 12), only about 1 per cent of the females had had fantasies of such relationships. Over 4 per cent of the females had fantasied, at least on occasion, some sort of sado-masochistic situation.

The masturbatory fantasies were usually in accord with the overt experience of the individual. Males not infrequently have fantasies of

---

[40] This frequent dependence of the female on physical stimulation alone is also recognized by: Back 1910:112. Adler 1911:28, 109. Rohleder 1921:14, 48. Liepmann 1922:154. Eberhard 1924:302. Hamilton 1929:429, 430 (47 to 57 per cent). Decurtins in Hornstein and Faller 1950:136.

unfulfilled or repressed desires, but the fantasies among the females had less often concerned activities of a sort which they had not had: if kissing had been the limit of the female's petting experience, it was the limit of her fantasies; it was only after the petting had included genital manipulations that the fantasies went that far. The fantasies had rarely included coitus unless the female had had coital experience. On the other hand, many of the females who had had overt sexual contacts had never fantasied about them while they were masturbating.

The data on the fantasies were essentially alike in all of the age groups and in all of the educational levels represented in the sample (Table 38). In the male the maximum amount of fantasy is found among the better educated groups, but education does not seem to increase the female's inclination to fantasy.

Most males fantasy in connection with most of their masturbation (p. 667). Fantasies, as a matter of fact, often provide the stimulus which initiates the male's masturbation. Memories of past experience, the anticipation of renewed experience, and the contemplation of new types of activity are such significant factors in his arousal that it is usually difficult for a male to reach orgasm in masturbation without the aid of some sort of fantasy. Consequently, the female's ability to achieve orgasm without fantasy emphasizes her greater dependence upon physical and physiologic sources of erotic arousal.

Most males, projecting their own experience, take it for granted that females must similarly fantasy during their sexual activities. The male clinician, the male who writes in scientific, literary, and deliberately erotic literature, and most other males imagine that most females must be aroused as they would be in contemplating the possibilities of sexual activities. The male's failure to comprehend the lesser importance of psychologic stimulation for the female, and her failure to comprehend the greater importance of psychologic stimulation for him, are prime sources of the difficulty which so many men and women have in understanding each other sexually (Chapter 16).

SIGNIFICANCE OF MASTURBATION

Physiologic Significance. Most females masturbate for the sake of the immediate satisfactions which they may obtain, and as a means of resolving the physiologic disturbances which arise when they are aroused sexually and are restrained by the social custom from having socio-sexual contacts.[41]

---

[41] Masturbation as a substitute or additional outlet (the *Notonanie* of German authors) is also noted in: Moraglia 1897:8–9. Adler 1911:106. Hirschfeld 1916:127. Rohleder 1921:176–177. Moll 1926(1):292. Riolan 1927:41, 46. Hodann 1929:84–85. Remplein 1950:246–247.

We have already noted that a variety of physiologic disturbances, including a considerable development of neuromuscular tensions, are involved whenever there is sexual arousal. When the sexual responses lead to orgasm, these tensions are suddenly released and the individual thereupon returns to a physiologically normal or subnormal state (Chapter 15). Then she may function more efficiently in her everyday affairs. But without the release which orgasm can bring, most males and some females may continue to be disturbed for some period of time, and the prolongation of such a disturbance may distract or otherwise interfere with one's general efficiency. The individual may become nervous, irritable, incapable of concentrating on any sort of problem, and difficult to live with. Most persons live more happily with themselves and with other persons if their sexual arousal, whenever it is of any magnitude, may be carried through to the point of orgasm.

Lack of Physical Harm. Many persons believe that masturbation may harm one physically. Some of the females in the sample, for instance, had believed that masturbation was the cause of their facial pimples, mental dullness, poor posture, stomach upsets, ovarian pains, ovarian cysts, cancer, appendicitis, various infections, weak eyes, sterility, headaches, kidney troubles, weak hearts, lack of hormones, and other difficulties. But we have not been able to find evidence that any of these disturbances could have been caused by the masturbatory activities which were in the histories of these females. The fatigue which some of them recorded as an after-effect of masturbation appears to have been no greater than that which may follow any sort of sexual activity, solitary or socio-sexual. All sexual responses to the point of orgasm involve the utilization of a considerable amount of energy (Chapter 15), but most persons recover from their exhaustion within a matter of minutes or, at the most, after a night of sleep. An occasional female has reported some genital irritation resulting from her masturbation, but this is, again, no more than what happens to any part of the body when it is subjected to contacts to which it is not accustomed.

It is significant that those who had most often found moral objections to masturbation were the ones who most often insisted that physical and mental damage had resulted from their activity.[42] Such rationaliza-

---

[42] The following are a few examples from the hundreds of authors who over the past years have insisted, without scientific evidence, that physical harm can result from masturbation in the female: Crouch (Bekker) 1741:20. Tissot 1764:57–67; 1775:46–53; 1777:46–53; 1785:59–68. Rosenbaum 1845:220–229. Martineau 1886:57–74. Moraglia 1897:9–10, 18. Alibert n.d.:83–87. G. Stanley Hall 1904(1):442–445. Talmey 1910:190–191 (leads to undermining of health and possible nervous prostration in young girls). Jefferis and Nichols 1912:451 (results in slow and progressive derangement of her health). Winfield S. Hall 1920:83. Rohleder 1921:48. Coppens and Spalding 1921:114. Forel 1922:229–234 (especially dangerous in younger children). Marro (1900) 1922:83. Riolan 1927:48–54. Meyer 1929:32–33 ("jeopardizes

tions are of ancient standing, and they have been perpetuated into the present day by a surprising number of physicians, psychiatrists, psychologists, and educators.[43] But such arguments are obviously attempts to justify the moral code, and are not supported by any examination of the physical fact.[44]

On the basis of our previous review (1948:514) of more than five thousand cases of males who had masturbated, and on the basis of the data now available on nearly twenty-eight hundred cases of females with masturbatory experience, we may assert that we have recognized exceedingly few cases, if indeed there have been any outside of a few psychotics, in which either physical or mental damage had resulted from masturbatory activity.[45] We have, on the other hand, recognized

---

her entire physical growth and development"). Bauer 1929:240–241. Meagher 1929:95–96. Van der Hoog 1934:68. Meagher and Jelliffe 1936:103–104 (causes chronic pelvic congestion). Guze 1951:97–98 points out that the medical approach has been full of folklore and subjective emotional response. An extensive survey of authoritarian attitudes toward masturbation, with emphasis on the early medical literature, is found in Spitz 1952.

[43] More recently it has become customary to emphasize the physical or psychologic effects of *excessive* masturbation. Since the term "excessive" is entirely uninterpretable, the psychologic result of such condemnation is much the same. See: Moll 1909:163; 1912:181. Havelock Ellis 1910(1):259 (one of the first to discount the harm of moderate masturbation and to stress the possible damage of excessive masturbation). Gudden 1911:14. Adler 1911:94. Wulffen 1913:260–265. Sanger n.d.:40 ("never found anyone so repulsive as the chronic masturbator"). Vecki 1920:210. Menzies 1921:52. Fetscher 1928: 49 (leads to nervous exhaustion). Gerling 1928:49–51. Elliott and Bone 1929:77. Dickerson 1931:129–130. Dickinson and Beam 1934:251, 426. Meagher and Jelliffe 1936:82. Rosanoff 1938:153 (leads to use of too much physical and psychic energy, upsetting the balance of life). Steinhardt 1938: 72–73 (causes breakdown of physical health, with likelihood of end in asylum or early grave). Parker n.d. (American Social Hygiene Assoc.):9 (if excessive, may impair physical and mental energy). Bonnar 1941:149. Snow 1941:5 (if persistent or frequent, doctor should be consulted). Corner and Landis 1941:11 (if excessively frequent, the wise parent will seek medical advice and treatment). Keller 1942:7. Sidonie Gruenberg 1943:5–6 (children who masturbate may be told they will be happier if they do not do it very often). Thornton 1946:77. Boys' Clubs of America 1946:6 (affects general health). English in Fishbein and Burgess 1947:105. Everett 1948:18. Bleuler 1949: 406. Foster 1950:144 ("It does not ordinarily, if practiced only a short time as a young person or child, offset one's ability to marry and carry on normal sexual relations").

[44] Commendable examples of moral evaluations of masturbation which do not attempt to judge the physical outcome, are, for instance, in: Northcote 1916: 424–427. Weatherhead 1932:125–128. Ruland and Rattler 1934:308–310. Davis 1946(2):241–246. Remplein 1950:242–246.

[45] Others who agree that little or no physical harm results from masturbation in either sex include: Hunter 1786:200 ("I think I may affirm that this act in itself does less harm to the constitution in general than the natural [coitus]"). Moll 1909:162–167; 1912:180–185 (judgment based on many specific cases). Orsi 1913:141–148 (masturbation is a variant of love, and condemnatory attitude is unjustified). Stekel 1912:42 (in disagreement with many other psychoanalysts); 1920:53, 99; 1950:60, 204. Steiner 1912:130. Hodann 1929: 38–39. Davis 1929:96. Weatherhead 1932:123–125. Landis et al. 1940:58. Lees 1944:336 (as normal in children as eating and sleeping). Taylor acc. Brill 1946:102 (no harm at all; a good thing). Dearborn in Fishbein and Burgess 1947:361–364, 366 (an excellent discussion, pointing out lack of evidence of harm even when frequent). Strain 1948:181 (science has re-

a tremendous amount of damage which has been the result of worry over masturbation, and of attempts to abstain from such activity.

Moral Interpretations. The religious condemnation of masturbation in our culture is justified on the ground that it is a perversion of the "primary purpose" of sex, which is taken to be reproduction.[46] Since masturbation cannot lead to procreation, it constitutes a perversion which ranks with homosexual activity, intercourse between the human animal and animals of other species, all heterosexual techniques which stop short of coitus, and some other sorts of sexual activity. In Orthodox Jewish codes, masturbation constitutes a major sin and, at times in Jewish history, a sin which was penalized with death.[47] Catholic sex

---

pudiated its harmfulness). Stokes 1948:16, 94 (normal in childhood, harmless at all times). Bleuler 1949:123–124. Brown and Kempton 1950:212 (an acceptable outlet for the single woman). Levine 1951:123. Horrocks 1951:203. Dearborn 1952:51–53 (stresses need of informing general public regarding harmlessness). Specific mention of the beneficial effects of masturbation is found, for instance, in: Guttzeit acc. Adler 1911:96. Stekel 1920:24–25; 1950:43 (abstinence may bring neuroses). Moll 1921:623 (may be beneficial and soothing to nerves). Long 1922:125–126 (recommends it for brides to be, separated couples, widows, and spinsters). Eberhard 1924:304 (increases mental alertness in women). Robie 1925:133–136 (beneficial in many cases). Hoyer 1929:219–220 (especially beneficial for women). Blanchard and Manasses 1930:34 (may serve a useful purpose). Hirschfeld 1930:525 (moderate masturbation in adolescent is relaxing). Hutton 1937:78–80 (gives relief to the single woman). Bender 1939:578 (a very important part of the child's normal development). Adams 1946:32 (no reason for considering it an undesirable mode of sex release). Harper 1949:80–81 (serves as a tension release for many). Comfort 1950:96–101 (complete endorsement). Kellogg 1953:175 ("a normal and wholesome action for any person of any age").

[46] Historically, the disapproval of masturbation goes back at least as far as the Book of the Dead 1550–950 B.C.; see Pritchard 1950:34. It was only mildly condemned in Greece and Rome. See: Licht 1932:313–315. But also see: Aeschines [4th cent. B.C.]: Against Ctesiphon, 174 (1919:445). Martial [1st cent. A.D.] IX.41 (1920(2):101; 1921:245–246). Plutarch [1st–2nd cent. A.D.]: Contradictions of the Stoics, 21 (Clough and Goodwin, Plutarch's Essays and Miscellanies 1905(4):450). Juvenal [1st–2nd cent. A.D.]: 7:238–241 (1789(1):367–369; 1817(1):322). Landmarks in the early European literature are: Crouch 1741:20 (masturbation is an abominable custom, a horrible sin, results in black-yellowish and leaden complexion, paroxysm, desiccation, emaciation, sterility, frigidity; little chance of cure. This early German book appears to be a translation of Bekker's English volume of the same title. Both are little known forerunners of Tissot). Tissot 1764: This is the 3rd ed. of this French classic, "L'Onanisme," published originally in Latin in 1758 in Lausanne. Chapter 5 (pp. 57–67) is devoted to the evils of female masturbation which is said to result in hysteria, dizziness, jaundice, deformed figure, exhaustion, pain, and death. Other early European works which violently attack female masturbation, the whole volume in some cases being devoted to that one topic, are: Bienville 1771:142–143. Anon. 1829:57, 110–113. Dubois 1848. Garnier (1889) 1921:338–340. Pouillet 1897. Moldau 1911:47–51.

[47] For Jewish attitudes on masturbation, see the summary in: Epstein 1948:146–147 ("the severest sin of all recorded in the scriptures. The ethical literature of post-Talmudic days, down to the latest centuries, endlessly harps on the severity of this sin, exhorts its avoidance, points out its danger to health, threatens dire punishment in the day of reckoning, and pleads for penitence and expiation"). The Catholic code is specific in its condemnation of female masturbation as a gravely illicit act and a sin against nature, although it does not consider it as sinful as male pollution. See: Arregui 1927:151, 533. Davis 1946(4):256; 1946(2):237, 242. Masturbation is apparently permitted to a

codes originated among the Jewish founders of the early Church, and they similarly condemn masturbation as a carnal sin.[47] For some centuries Protestant groups accepted these same interpretations, although more recently some of them have attempted to utilize more scientific data.

Among the females in our sample who had never masturbated, 44 per cent said that they had not done so because they considered it morally wrong. It was apparent, however, that many of these females were so unresponsive sexually that they had found it a simple matter to accept the moral restrictions on their activity. More than three-fourths (81 per cent) who had never masturbated recognized that they had not done so because they had not felt any need for such an outlet. Some of them were already finding a sufficient release in some other type of activity, such as marital coitus, but many of them seemed to have a minimum of any capacity to be aroused sexually, and they had not recognized the need for any sort of regular outlet. More than a quarter (28 per cent) of those who had not masturbated, claimed that they had not done so because they did not know that masturbation was possible.

Legal Significance. While public opinion in Europe and America has largely accepted the Judeo-Christian attitudes toward masturbation, it is notable that these codes have never been accepted as part of the statute law. There are only two of the states, Indiana and Wyoming, which consider it a crime to encourage a person to masturbate, and no state makes it a criminal offense for an individual to engage in self-masturbation.[48] Society may be concerned when an individual procreates, but it has not always been so certain that social interests are involved when the individual engages in solitary sexual activities which do not lead to procreation.

Psychologic Significance. When no guilt, anxieties, or fears are involved, the physical satisfactions which may be found in any type of sexual activity, whether socio-sexual or solitary, should leave an individual well adjusted psychologically. But in view of the more than two thousand years of religious condemnation of masturbation, fortified by the ostensibly scientific opinions of physicians and other professionally trained groups, it is not surprising that many individuals,

---

married woman immediately before or after coitus in order to reach orgasm, according to Arregui 1927:533, and Davis 1946(4):252.

European examples of the more recent religious condemnation of masturbation are reviewed in: Hodann 1929:66–91; 1937:249–254, who cites such Catholic writers as Kapff, Schilgen, Gutmann, and Liertz. Among Protestant writers he names Seher 1925, Emsmann, various White Cross writers, Siedel, Levsen, Wondratschek, Hellwig, Vermeil.

[48] For state laws covering masturbation see: Ind. Stat. Ann. 1933:§10–4221. Wyo. Comp. Stat. 1945:§9–520.

both female and male, are considerably disturbed when they masturbate. Among the females in the sample who had ever masturbated,
approximately half had experienced some psychologic disturbance
over their experience (Table 39). Some of them were disturbed for
only a single year or two, but the average (median) female had been
disturbed for six and a half years. Some 30 per cent had been disturbed
for more than ten years. This means that some millions of the females
in the United States, and a larger number of the males, have had their
self-assurance, their social efficiency, and sometimes their sexual adjustments in marriage needlessly damaged—not by their masturbation,
but by the conflict between their practice and the moral codes.[49] There
is no other type of sexual activity which has worried so many women.

Freud and most of the psychoanalysts have recognized that masturbation does no physical harm, but they have introduced new sources
of psychologic disturbance by rating the activity infantile, immature,
and a personality defect which merits psychiatric attention when it
occurs in an adult.[50] But these objections merely perpetuate the Tal-

---

[49] That worry frequently does damage, while masturbation itself does none, is noted
in the following: Bloch 1902(1):132–134. Adler 1911:93–97. Stekel 1912:
29–35. Wulffen 1913:260. Marro 1922:509. Fetscher 1928:48–50. Gerling
1928:49–51. Bauer 1929:240–241. Hodann 1929:45–91. Davis 1929:130–146,
164. Hirschfeld and Bohm 1930:148. Kelly 1930:171–175. Lazarsfeld 1931:
240. Malamud and Palmer 1932 (includes a history of attitudes on masturbation). Meagher and Jelliffe 1936:106. Henry 1938:31 ("apprehensions regarding the consequences of masturbation are so deeply rooted that none can escape them"). Squier in Folsom 1938:137. Huschka 1938:347–352 (a list of
threats used to frighten children who masturbate). Butterfield 1939:62 (damage from cultural taboos). Haire 1940:97–111; 1951:165–166. Sidonie Gruenberg 1943:5–6 (only injury is worry and fear). Faegre 1943:18 (guilt because
of secrecy). Sadler and Sadler 1944:59. Wilhelm Reich 1945:110. Kirkendall
1947:32–33. Dearborn in Fishbein and Burgess 1947:361–367. Everett
1948:18. Allendy and Lobstein 1948:110 (harmfulness lies in mental conflict).
Bleuler 1949:123–124. Niedermeyer in Hornstein and Faller 1950:137, 154.
Remplein 1950:242–246. Levine 1951:123 (anxiety of parents has far reaching effect on children). Gollancz 1952:204–210 (a recent autobiographical
account of the mental hell created by the conflict over masturbation in an
adolescent boy). Much of the German literature suggests, curiously enough,
that self-searching would bring remorse, even if there were no moralistic
teaching. Lacking scientific evidence of the physical harm of masturbation,
some authors in the 1920's and 1930's turned to other interpretations, stating
that masturbation breaks down the individual's self-respect, destroys manliness
or womanhood, leads to loss of mental powers, self-control, self-confidence,
and in general interferes with the development of one's character, as in: B. C.
Gruenberg (for U. S. Public Health Service) 1922:51–52; (for Am. Soc. Hygiene Assoc.) 1932:45; B. C. Gruenberg and Kaukonen (for U. S. Public
Health Service) 1940:67. U. S. Public Health Service 1930(?):5; 1934:6;
1937:10. Indiana State Board of Health n.d.:8. Macfadden 1922:30–31.
[50] For psychoanalytic interpretations, see: Wiener psa. Ver., Die Onanie, 1912
(especially Freud:133–140, and Rank:107–129). Zeitschr. f. psa. Pädagogik
1927–1928 (4, 5, 6). Fenichel 1945:75–76, 371–372. Annie Reich 1951:
80–94. The latter is a historical survey of the shift in the psychoanalyst's attitude toward masturbation as represented by the 1912 and 1928 Vienna discussions. The early over-evaluation of the danger of masturbation which, Annie
Reich points out, grew in part from the sexual repression of the analysts themselves, was followed in 1928 (in Federn especially) by general approval. The

mudic traditions which are now being fortified with a new set of terms which appear to have scientific significance. Many adults who are not immature in any realistic sense do masturbate, and there is no science in refusing to recognize this fact.

Social Significance. Whatever may affect the efficiency of some millions of individuals may be considered of social concern. Whether masturbation provides a satisfactory source of sexual outlet or becomes a source of psychologic disturbance is, therefore, a question of some social import. Masturbation may be of still greater social importance if it affects an individual's sexual adjustments in marriage.

Some of the psychoanalysts have suggested that masturbation, because it depends primarily upon clitoral and labial stimulation, concentrates erotic response in the external genitalia and does not train the individual for the "vaginal responses" which they consider must be present before there is any "sexual maturity." But actually the vagina is, in most females, quite devoid of end organs of touch (p. 579). It is incapable of responding to tactile stimulation, and the areas primarily involved in the female's sensory responses during coitus are exactly those which are primarily involved in masturbation, namely the clitoris and the labia (Chapters 14, 15). We have seen very few cases of females who had encountered any difficulty in transferring their masturbatory experience to coitus, although we have seen some hundreds of cases of females who were considerably disturbed because they were unable to accomplish the anatomic impossibility of "transferring their clitoral reactions to vaginal responses."

It is true that the girl who has nothing but masturbatory experience prior to marriage encounters a new type of situation when vaginal insertions are first encountered in coitus. She would, however, have the same problem to meet if she had never masturbated.

It has been claimed that pre-marital masturbatory experience may so condition an individual that she may want to continue solitary activities in preference to having coital relations after marriage [51]; but we have seen very few histories of this sort. There are more cases of

---

author repudiates this stand, citing Fenichel's statement that masturbation is normal only in childhood and adolescence.

[51] The largely unsubstantiated claim that masturbation in the female leads to an aversion for coitus or does damage to the female's capacity for orgasm in marital intercourse is made, for instance, in: Crouch (Bekker) 1741:316. Tissot 1775:49. Hammond 1887:302. Sturgis 1908:25. Havelock Ellis 1910(1):261–262. Adler 1911:91–120. Talmey 1915:241. Eberhard 1924:257, 302. Stone 1924:50. Elliott and Bone 1929:78. Kelly 1930:171. Lazarsfeld 1931:245. Robinson 1931:135. Sanger n.d.:39. Bruckner 1937:29 (leaves no incentive to marry and rear a family). Keller 1942:15. Huhner 1945:224. Davis 1946 (2):252 (a Catholic code). Duvall 1950:92. Kroger and Freed 1951:387.

marital relations which were disturbed by some guilt which the wives had acquired during their pre-marital masturbatory experience.

Much more important is the evidence that pre-marital experience in masturbation may actually contribute to the female's capacity to respond in her coital relations in marriage.[51] It has been pointed out repeatedly, and our own data confirm the opinion, that a considerable portion of the sexual maladjustment in marriage arises from the fact that the average female is aroused sexually less often than the average male, and that she frequently has difficulty in reaching orgasm in her marital coitus (pp. 371 ff.). There are a variety of factors involved in this failure, the most significant of which seems to be the female's inexperience in orgasm prior to her marriage. Some 36 per cent of the females in our sample had not experienced orgasm on even a single occasion, from any type of sexual activity, prior to marriage (Table 150). Only half of them had had a regular outlet prior to marriage.

Calculations on the marital histories (Chapter 9) indicate that those females who had not responded to the point of orgasm prior to marriage, failed to respond after marriage three times as often as the females who had had a fair amount of orgasmic experience before marriage (p. 385, Table 108). It is true that there were many individuals who did respond promptly after marriage even though they had not experienced orgasm before then; but the chances of working out such adjustments seem to have been materially reduced for the girl who had not previously learned what it means to let herself go and respond uninhibitedly in sexual orgasm. The girl who has spent her pre-marital years withdrawing from physical contacts and tensing her muscles in order to avoid response has acquired a set of nervous and muscular coordinations which she does not unlearn easily after marriage.

The type of pre-marital activity in which the female had acquired her experience did not appear to have been as important as the fact that she had or had not experienced orgasm. This appears to have been true whether her pre-marital experience was in coitus, in petting to the point of orgasm, in homosexual relations, or in masturbation. Since masturbation was the activity in which the largest number of females had reached orgasm, it was of particular significance in these correlations.

Among those females in the sample who had never masturbated before marriage, or whose masturbation had never led to orgasm, about a third (31 to 37 per cent) had failed to reach orgasm in their coitus during the first year, and in most instances during the first five years of their marriages (Table 111). But among those who had masturbated to the point of orgasm before marriage, only 13 to 16 per cent had been totally unresponsive in the early years of marriage. A selective factor may have been involved. The more responsive females may have been the ones who masturbated before marriage, and the ones who responded more often in their marital coitus. On the other hand, a causal relationship seems also to have been involved. In many a specific history it appeared that the quality of the marital response was furthered by the female's previous knowledge of the nature of a sexual orgasm. In any event, it was certain that the capacity to respond in orgasm in marital coitus had not been lessened by the pre-marital masturbatory experience of the females in the sample.

SUMMARY AND COMPARISONS OF FEMALE AND MALE

MASTURBATION

	IN FEMALES	IN MALES
Mammalian and Human Backgrounds		
Masturbation in other mammals	In some species	In many species
Masturbation to orgasm in mammals	Uncertain	In some
Masturbation in primitive societies	Limited data	Some data
Learning to Masturbate		
Self-discovery	57%	28%
Verbal and printed sources	43%	75%
Petting	12%	—
Observation	11%	40%
Homosexual contact	3%	9%
Relation to Age and Marital Status		
Accumulative incidence		
Total: experience	62%	93%
Total: with orgasm	58%	92%
By age 12	12%	21%
By age 15	20%	82%
By age 20	33%	92%
Active incidence to orgasm	Increases to middle age	Decreases after teens
In various groups	20–58%	19–88%
Higher in married groups	No	No
Frequency (active median) to orgasm	Uniform to mid-fifties	Steady decrease after teens
Average, unmarried groups	0.3–0.4 per wk.	0.4–1.8 per wk.
Average, married groups	0.2 per wk.	0.1–0.2 per wk.
Individual variation	Very great	Less
Percentage of total outlet		
In unmarried groups	37–85%	31–70%
In married groups	About 10%	4–6%
In previously married groups	13–44%	8–18%
Number of years involved by age 31–35		
1 year or less	9%	Very few
For median individual	14 years	
Discontinuity	In 15%	Unusual

	IN FEMALES	IN MALES
Relation to Educational Level		
Accumulative incidence to orgasm		
Grade school group	34%	89%
High school group	59%	95%
College group	57%⎱	96%
Graduate group	63%⎰	
Active incidence, low in grade school, high in graduate group	Yes	Yes
Frequency (active median) to orgasm	No relation	Higher in college groups
Percentage of total outlet	Most in college groups	2 to 7 times more in college groups
Relation to Parental Occupational Class	Little or none	Little
Relation to Decade of Birth		
Accumulative incidence to orgasm	10% increase in later decades	Slight increase only in lower educ. level
Active incidence to orgasm	Little or no change	Small increase
Frequency (active median) to orgasm	Little or no change	Slight increase
Percentage of total outlet	Decrease in later decades	
Relation to Age at Onset of Adolescence		
Incidence and frequency to orgasm	No relation	Higher in early adol. groups
Relation to Rural-Urban Background		
Accumulative incidence to orgasm	Higher in urban	Little relation?
Active incidence to orgasm	Higher in older urban groups	Little relation
Frequency (active median) to orgasm	No relation	Little relation
Percentage of total outlet	Less in urban	Slightly less in urban
Relation to Religious Background		
Accumulative incidence to orgasm	Much lower in devout groups	
Active incidences to orgasm	Much lower in devout groups	Somewhat lower in devout groups
Frequency (active median) to orgasm	No relation	Somewhat lower in devout groups
Percentage of total outlet	Higher in more devout	Higher in devout groups?
Techniques of Masturbation		
Genital manipulation	84%	95%
Thigh pressures	10%	Rare
Muscular tensions	5%	Rare
Vaginal insertions, ever	20%	
Fantasy alone	2%	Extremely rare
Fantasy Accompanying Masturbation		
Almost always fantasy	50%	72%
Sometimes fantasy	14%	17%
Content	Occasionally surpasses experience	Usually surpasses experience
Relation to educational level	None	More frequent in better educated

Summary and Comparisons (*Continued*)

	IN FEMALES	IN MALES
Significance of Masturbation		
Physiologic significance		
Source of pleasure	Yes	Yes
Satisfies a physiologic need	Yes	Yes
Physical harm	None	None
Psychologic significance		
May contribute to psych. well-being	Yes	Yes
Worry, ever	47%	Majority
Social significance		
May increase efficiency	Yes	Yes
Contributes to higher rate of orgasm in marriage	Yes	No relation?

Table 20. Source of First Experience in Masturbation

By Age, Educational Level, and Decade of Birth

SOURCE	TOTAL ACTIVE SAMPLE	AGE AT FIRST EXPERIENCE			
		1–10	11–20	21–30	31+
	%	*Percent*			
Self-discovery	57	77	58	27	19
Verbal and printed sources	43	21	42	72	86
Petting experience	12	4	10	31	24
Observation	11	14	10	8	7
Homosexual experience	3	4	3	2	2
Number of cases	2675	757	1401	372	145

SOURCE	TOTAL ACTIVE SAMPLE	EDUCATIONAL LEVEL			
		0–8	9–12	13–16	17+
	%	*Percent*			
Self-discovery	57	37	50	61	56
Verbal and printed sources	43	60	49	39	43
Petting experience	12	13	13	11	13
Observation	11	27	12	9	11
Homosexual experience	3	0	4	2	4
Number of cases	2675	60	463	1372	723

SOURCE	TOTAL ACTIVE SAMPLE	DECADE OF BIRTH			
		Bf. 1900	1900–1909	1910–1919	1920–1929
	%	*Percent*			
Self-discovery	57	57	52	56	60
Verbal and printed sources	43	44	47	42	41
Petting experience	12	12	16	14	9
Observation	11	12	12	10	10
Homosexual experience	3	4	5	3	2
Number of cases	2675	268	506	739	1109

Two or more sources may be more or less simultaneously involved in an individual's first experience; the percentages in each group consequently add up to more than 100.

Table 21. Accumulative Incidence: Experience in Masturbation
By Marital Status

AGE	TOTAL SAMPLE	MARITAL STATUS While single	MARITAL STATUS While married	MARITAL STATUS Post-marital	TOTAL SAMPLE	MARITAL STATUS While single	MARITAL STATUS While married	MARITAL STATUS Post-marital
	%		Percent		Cases		Cases	
3	1	1			5913	5913		
5	4	4			5866	5866		
7	7	7			5841	5841		
10	13	13			5808	5808		
12	19	19			5784	5784		
15	28	28			5721	5717		
20	41	41	28	34	4344	3970	556	77
25	51	50	31	44	2793	1468	1338	174
30	56	58	37	51	2050	674	1216	221
35	61	63	40	55	1473	385	912	205
40	62	65	42	66	951	209	571	179
45	62	64	44	60	571	130	312	130

Table 22. Number of Years Involved in Masturbation
In active sample, including single and married females

NUMBER OF YEARS	AGE AT REPORTING 31–35	36–40	41–45	46–50	51+
			Percent		
1 year or less	9	6	10	6	4
2–3 years	11	10	6	5	6
4–5 years	5	5	7	5	7
6–10 years	16	13	11	8	10
11–20 years	31	32	25	22	17
21–30 years	27	27	22	16	19
31–40 years	1	7	17	21	12
41–50 years			2	17	17
51+ years					8
Number of cases	358	331	243	166	167
Median	14.0	16.0	17.5	23.9	24.1

Because the number of years involved may depend in part on the age of an individual, the table is confined to data reported by older females.

Table 23. Active Incidence, Frequency, and Percentage of Outlet Masturbation to Orgasm

By Age and Marital Status

AGE DURING ACTIVITY	ACTIVE SAMPLE			TOTAL SAMPLE		CASES IN TOTAL SAMPLE
	Active incid. %	Median freq. per wk.	Mean freq. per wk.	Mean freq. per wk.	% of total outlet	
SINGLE FEMALES						
Adol.–15	20	0.5	1.4 ± 0.08	0.3 ± 0.02	85	5677
16–20	28	0.4	1.0 ± 0.05	0.3 ± 0.0!	60	5613
21–25	35	0.4	0.9 ± 0.05	0.3 ± 0.02	16	2810
26–30	43	0.3	0.9 ± 0.09	0.4 ± 0.04	41	1064
31–35	49	0.4	0.9 ± 0.11	0.4 ± 0.06	42	539
36–40	54	0.3	0.9 ± 0.16	0.5 ± 0.09	37	315
41–45	50	0.3	1.0 ± 0.26	0.5 ± 0.13	45	179
46–50	47	0.3	1.0 ± 0.29	0.4 ± 0.14	52	109
51–55	40	*0.2*	*1.0 ± 0.59*	0.4 ± 0.24	70	58
56–60	*30*			*0.3 ± 0.22*	*78*	27
MARRIED FEMALES						
16–20	23	0.4	1.1 ± 0.15	0.2 ± 0.04	9	578
21–25	27	0.2	0.6 ± 0.08	0.2 ± 0.02	6	1654
26–30	31	0.2	0.6 ± 0.07	0.2 ± 0.02	7	1662
31–35	34	0.2	0.5 ± 0.04	0.2 ± 0.02	8	1246
36–40	36	0.2	0.6 ± 0.10	0.2 ± 0.04	10	851
41–45	36	0.2	0.6 ± 0.09	0.2 ± 0.03	11	497
46–50	34	0.2	0.5 ± 0.07	0.2 ± 0.03	11	260
51–55	31	*0.2*	*0.4 ± 0.11*	0.1 ± 0.04	13	118
56–60	*35*	*0.1*	*0.2 ± 0.08*	*0.1 ± 0.03*	*13*	49
PREVIOUSLY MARRIED FEMALES						
16–20	35	*0.3*	*0.8 ± 0.21*	0.3 ± 0.08	13	72
21–25	41	0.4	1.0 ± 0.17	0.4 ± 0.08	24	239
26–30	46	0.3	0.8 ± 0.12	0.4 ± 0.06	22	328
31–35	49	0.3	0.6 ± 0.11	0.3 ± 0.06	20	304
36–40	57	0.3	0.7 ± 0.08	0.4 ± 0.05	23	245
41–45	58	0.3	0.7 ± 0.11	0.4 ± 0.07	26	195
46–50	56	0.3	0.5 ± 0.09	0.3 ± 0.05	28	126
51–55	50	*0.3*	*0.4 ± 0.08*	0.2 ± 0.04	26	82
56–60	42	*0.2*	*0.4 ± 0.10*	0.2 ± 0.05	44	53

Italic figures throughout the series of tables indicate that the calculations are based on less than 50 cases. No calculations are based on less than 11 cases. The dash (—) indicates a percentage or frequency smaller than any quantity which would be shown by a real figure in the number of decimal places.

Table 24. Maximum Frequency of Masturbation Ever, in Any Single Week

MAXIMUM FREQUENCY, ANY WK.	TOTAL ACTIVE SAMPLE		EDUCATIONAL LEVEL			
	%	Cumul. %	0–8	9–12	13–16	17+
			Percent of females			
1	35	100	33	42	35	30
2	14	65	27	16	13	15
3	17	51	12	16	18	15
4	9	35	4	7	9	10
5	6	26	10	4	6	6
6	3	20		2	3	4
7	9	17	8	6	9	10
8	1	8		1	1	1
9	—	7			—	—
10	3	7		2	2	4
11	—	4		—		
12	—	4		1	—	1
13						
14	1	4	2	1	1	2
15	—	2		—	—	1
16	—	2		—	—	
17						
18	—	2			—	
19						
20	1	2	2		1	1
21	—	1			—	
22	—	1			—	
23						
24	—	1		—		
25	—	1		—	—	—
26						
27						
28	—	1			—	—
29+	1	1	2	1	1	—
Number of cases		2217	51	373	1131	623

Table 25. Accumulative Incidence: Masturbation to Orgasm

    By Educational Level

AGE	TOTAL SAMPLE	EDUCATIONAL LEVEL 0–8	9–12	13–16	17+	TOTAL SAMPLE	EDUCATIONAL LEVEL 0–8	9–12	13–16	17+
	%		*Percent*			*Cases*		*Cases*		
3	—	0	—	—	—	5913	179	1011	3290	1146
5	2	0	2	1	3	5866	179	1011	3290	1146
7	4	1	4	3	5	5838	179	1011	3290	1146
10	8	5	8	7	11	5802	179	1011	3290	1146
12	12	8	13	11	16	5778	179	1011	3290	1146
15	20	22	23	18	24	5715	173	1010	3290	1146
20	33	31	33	32	36	4342	127	859	2211	1145
25	44	32	40	45	46	2793	117	686	1042	948
30	50	34	48	50	55	2050	109	501	709	731
35	56	34	55	56	59	1473	91	322	495	565
40	58	28	59	57	63	951	67	193	305	386

The table is based on the total sample, including single, married, and previously married females.

Table 26. Accumulative Incidence: Masturbation to Orgasm

    By Decade of Birth

AGE	DECADE OF BIRTH Bf. 1900	1900–1909	1910–1919	1920–1929	Bf. 1900	DECADE OF BIRTH 1900–1909	1910–1919	1920–1929
		Percent				*Cases*		
5	3	3	2	1	452	780	1337	3079
10	12	12	10	6	452	780	1337	3079
15	25	25	24	17	452	780	1337	3061
20	33	34	36	30	452	780	1336	1775
25	38	43	46	47	452	780	1189	373
30	44	51	53		452	780	819	
35	49	57	63		452	751	270	
40	52	63			452	498		

Table based on total sample, including single, married, and previously married females.

Table 27. Active Incidence and Percentage of Outlet: Masturbation to Orgasm

By Educational Level and Marital Status

AGE DURING ACTIVITY	EDUC. LEVEL	SINGLE			MARRIED			PREVIOUSLY MARRIED		
		Active incid. %	% of total outlet	Cases in total sample	Active incid. %	% of total outlet	Cases in total sample	Active incid. %	% of total outlet	Cases in total sample
Adol.–15	0–8	21	52	162						
	9–12	23	73	983						
	13–16	17	93	3271						
	17+	24	90	1128						
16–20	0–8	27	48	143						
	9–12	29	44	976	16	8	210			
	13–16	25	66	3299	28	8	257			
	17+	34	67	1149	27	10	66			
21–25	0–8	24	39	67	11	9	72			
	9–12	31	35	537	24	5	487	36	17	89
	13–16	33	48	1204	28	7	727	45	29	89
	17+	39	47	1002	31	7	368			
26–30	0–8				20	6	81			
	9–12	36	38	181	27	5	489	44	14	100
	13–16	40	39	313	30	7	671	49	31	122
	17+	47	43	531	41	9	421	49	18	84
31–35	0–8				15	5	68			
	9–12	46	58	65	33	7	338	57	22	86
	13–16	47	30	139	34	7	480	50	19	107
	17+	53	47	309	40	9	360	42	19	88
36–40	0–8				22	6	50			
	9–12				31	9	210	65	27	62
	13–16	56	32	68	33	11	323	54	13	85
	17+	57	41	205	46	10	268	60	28	78
41–45	9–12				36	9	117			
	13–16				29	7	181	54	14	67
	17+	56	44	122	48	17	163	60	32	67
46–50	9–12				32	13	71			
	13–16				30	10	91			
	17+	51	50	80	43	13	76			

Table 28. Accumulative Incidence: Masturbation to Orgasm
By Parental Occupational Class and Ultimate Educational Level

| AGE | PARENTAL CLASS | | | | PARENTAL CLASS | | | |
	2 + 3	4	5	6 + 7	2 + 3	4	5	6 + 7
				TOTAL SAMPLE				
	Percent				*Cases*			
10	8	6	8	9	988	813	1524	2689
15	25	17	20	20	939	808	1518	2661
20	38	32	33	32	707	630	1136	2009
25	45	41	43	45	509	420	720	1220
30	52	45	51	51	376	312	504	905
35	57	51	57	57	265	197	343	690
40	54	53	60	59	171	119	205	468
			SUBJECT'S EDUCATIONAL LEVEL 9–12					
	Percent				*Cases*			
10	6	6	8	14	361	219	278	208
15	26	20	22	25	360	219	278	208
20	36	29	35	31	272	184	252	192
25	42	36	41	39	212	133	206	169
30	52	40	49	46	145	95	142	146
35	58	57	55	54	84	51	84	111
			SUBJECT'S EDUCATIONAL LEVEL 13–16					
	Percent				*Cases*			
10	9	5	7	7	279	414	940	1770
15	25	16	18	17	279	414	940	1770
20	43	32	31	30	219	283	594	1167
25	54	43	44	46	115	142	267	522
30	58	46	49	50	74	98	172	357
35	67	52	59	55	51	60	113	256
			SUBJECT'S EDUCATIONAL LEVEL 17+					
	Percent				*Cases*			
10	9	9	12	12	129	141	274	645
15	22	20	24	25	129	141	274	645
20	39	36	35	36	129	141	274	644
25	48	48	43	47	105	123	231	523
30	59	52	55	54	87	97	175	396
35	65	52	59	60	72	67	132	318

The occupational classes are as follows: 2 + 3 = unskilled and semi-skilled labor. 4 = skilled labor. 5 = lower white collar class. 6 + 7 = upper white collar and professional classes.

Table based on total sample, including single, married, and previously married females.

Table 29. Active Incidence and Percentage of Outlet: Masturbation to Orgasm

By Parental Occupational Class and Marital Status

AGE DURING ACTIVITY	PARENTAL CLASS	SINGLE			MARRIED		
		Active incid. %	% of total outlet	Cases in total sample	Active incid. %	% of total outlet	Cases in total sample
Adol.–15	2+3	24	70	947			
	4	17	87	796			
	5	19	94	1506			
	6+7	19	90	2654			
16–20	2+3	33	52	881	21	9	141
	4	28	55	796	20	12	86
	5	27	65	1512	19	6	150
	6+7	26	65	2649	27	9	225
21–25	2+3	37	44	461	23	6	309
	4	34	47	422	25	4	230
	5	30	48	734	26	5	425
	6+7	37	46	1283	30	8	732
26–30	2+3	44	42	195	27	6	307
	4	37	44	181	27	4	232
	5	42	50	275	31	6	408
	6+7	44	36	447	35	9	738
31–35	2+3	52	54	96	26	7	213
	4	45	64	91	29	4	177
	5	49	64	148	38	8	291
	6+7	50	31	224	38	9	572
36–40	2+3	50	37	62	27	8	134
	4				29	4	97
	5	52	49	85	36	8	208
	6+7	55	31	141	40	12	419
41–45	2+3				20	4	81
	4				38	7	63
	5				36	12	89
	6+7				40	12	261

The occupational classes are as follows: 2 + 3 = unskilled and semi-skilled labor. 4 = skilled labor. 5 = lower white collar class. 6 + 7 = upper white collar and professional classes.

Table 30. Active Incidence and Percentage of Outlet: Masturbation to Orgasm

By Decade of Birth and Marital Status

AGE DURING ACTIVITY	DECADE OF BIRTH	SINGLE			MARRIED		
		Active incid. %	% of total outlet	Cases in total sample	Active incid. %	% of total outlet	Cases in total sample
Adol.–15	Bf. 1900	25	88	436			
	1900–1909	24	91	760			
	1910–1919	23	92	1319			
	1920–1929	16	75	3049			
16–20	Bf. 1900	29	76	451	25	13	61
	1900–1909	31	68	772	22	9	114
	1910–1919	33	66	1328	23	13	172
	1920–1929	24	50	2999	24	4	230
21–25	Bf. 1900	30	55	366	19	7	206
	1900–1909	36	42	617	27	9	377
	1910–1919	37	46	986	29	6	624
	1920–1929	33	46	843	29	4	447
26–30	Bf. 1900	40	61	218	22	5	272
	1900–1909	45	34	344	33	10	507
	1910–1919	43	38	448	36	7	731
	1920–1929	31	51	54	21	2	153
31–35	Bf. 1900	46	56	151	30	5	290
	1900–1909	50	33	228	36	11	509
	1910–1919	51	40	160	36	7	448
36–40	Bf. 1900	48	42	123	30	6	283
	1900–1909	55	36	165	40	13	464
	1910–1919				34	10	105
41–45	Bf. 1900	48	47	116	33	10	273
	1900–1909	52	38	63	40	12	224

Table 31. Accumulative Incidence: Masturbation to Orgasm
By Age at Onset of Adolescence

AGE	ADOLESCENT					ADOLESCENT				
	By 11	At 12	At 13	At 14	At 15+	By 11	At 12	At 13	At 14	At 15+
	Percent					*Cases*				
5	2	2	2	2	2	1202	1675	1744	793	348
10	9	8	7	8	7	1202	1675	1744	793	348
15	22	19	21	22	18	1182	1659	1733	788	348
20	37	33	32	33	28	873	1222	1316	645	283
25	47	45	43	43	39	509	739	847	461	234
30	51	50	52	48	46	354	485	650	365	195
35	57	56	56	55	54	249	319	469	279	156
40	60	58	58	55	55	150	196	296	191	117

Table based on total sample, including single, married, and previously married females.

Table 32. Accumulative Incidence: Masturbation to Orgasm
By Rural-Urban Background

Age	Rural	Urban	Age	Rural	Urban	Age	Rural	Urban	Age	Rural	Urban
	Percent			*Percent*			*Cases*			*Cases*	
5	1	2	25	34	45	5	397	5286	25	221	2458
10	6	8	30	38	51	10	397	5223	30	167	1790
15	21	20	35	47	57	15	394	5147	35	123	1280
20	29	34	40	49	59	20	332	3860	40	83	822

Table based on total sample, including single, married and previously married females.

Table 33. Active Incidence and Percentage of Outlet: Masturbation to Orgasm
By Rural-Urban Background

Age during activity	Back-grnd.	Active incid. %	% of total outlet	Cases in total sample	Age during activity	Back-grnd.	Active incid. %	% of total outlet	Cases in total sample
Adol.–15	Rural	21	86	388	26–30	Rural	36	50	104
	Urban	20	86	5132		Urban	43	41	915
16–20	Rural	28	71	386	31–35	Rural	39	65	64
	Urban	28	60	5080		Urban	50	39	453
21–25	Rural	30	53	229					
	Urban	35	46	2483					

Table based on single females only.

Table 34. Active Incidence and Percentage of Outlet: Masturbation to Orgasm

By Age at Onset of Adolescence and Marital Status

AGE DURING ACTIVITY	AGE AT ADOL.	SINGLE			MARRIED		
		Active incid. %	% of total outlet	Cases in total sample	Active incid. %	% of total outlet	Cases in total sample
Adol.–15	8–11	21	76	1203			
	12	18	90	1684			
	13	20	86	1747			
	14	21	86	796			
	15+	17	83	262			
16–20	8–11	32	56	1166	24	7	139
	12	27	60	1638	24	9	153
	13	26	60	1700	25	10	169
	14	29	61	777	21	3	76
	15+	25	71	345			
21–25	8–11	39	43	526	29	7	333
	12	34	48	769	26	6	458
	13	34	48	851	28	7	487
	14	32	45	460	25	4	254
	15+	32	34	203	22	8	121
26–30	8–11	44	31	196	31	7	286
	12	39	37	266	31	6	426
	13	46	54	323	33	7	527
	14	40	34	192	29	6	275
	15+	44	48	87	31	11	147
31–35	8–11	54	32	99	36	8	185
	12	46	30	122	35	7	291
	13	49	60	162	36	8	415
	14	49	36	109	30	7	224
	15+				34	12	131
36–40	8–11	60	25	65	40	7	133
	12	50	30	66	34	10	187
	13	50	63	96	36	10	270
	14	60	29	62	33	10	168
	15+				41	12	93
41–45	8–11				38	10	78
	12				32	9	102
	13				35	10	144
	14				38	15	101
	15+				35	11	71

Table 35. Accumulative Incidence: Masturbation to Orgasm
By Religious Background

AGE	PROTESTANT Dev.	Moder.	Inact.	CATHOLIC Dev.	Moder.	Inact.	JEWISH Moder.	Inact.
				Percent				
5	1	1	3	1	3	4	1	2
10	7	7	12	5	8	15	6	10
15	17	19	26	15	21	33	17	23
20	26	31	39	25	33	46	31	39
25	37	41	50	32	45	51	44	50
30	43	48	58	37	43	58	47	56
35	49	51	64	42		67	51	62
40	48	57	67					62
				Cases				
5	1265	1186	1098	395	157	171	575	995
10	1250	1172	1088	390	153	170	574	985
15	1214	1156	1076	384	151	170	572	976
20	918	924	969	283	114	145	332	688
25	565	588	735	176	76	106	185	411
30	423	435	549	123	51	79	135	292
35	336	315	417	77		52	76	203
40	236	211	272					127

Table based on total sample, including single, married, and previously married females.

Table 36. Active Incidence, Frequency, and Percentage of Outlet Masturbation to Orgasm
By Religious Background

AGE	RELIGIOUS GROUP	SINGLE Active incid. %	Active median freq. per wk.	% of total outlet	Cases in total sample	MARRIED Active incid. %	Active median freq. per wk.	% of total outlet	Cases in total sample
Adol. −15	Protestant								
	Devout	17	0.4	83	1218				
	Moderate	18	0.4	81	1147				
	Inactive	24	0.5	91	1063				
	Catholic								
	Devout	15	0.4	80	382				
	Moderate	20	*0.4*	83	150				
	Inactive	32	0.5	63	169				
	Jewish								
	Devout	15	*0.4*	98	107				
	Moderate	17	0.5	92	571				
	Inactive	23	0.6	93	978				
16–20	Protestant								
	Devout	23	0.4	62	1197	17	*0.3*	5	92
	Moderate	26	0.3	58	1133	20	*0.4*	8	97
	Inactive	35	0.4	66	1065	28	*0.4*	9	139
	Catholic								
	Devout	20	0.4	58	372				
	Moderate	27	*0.3*	54	139				
	Inactive	41	0.5	38	160				
	Jewish								
	Devout	21	*0.4*	82	107				
	Moderate	23	0.5	68	571				
	Inactive	31	0.4	60	972	28	*0.3*	5	118

(*Table continued on next page*)

Table 36 (continued)

AGE	RELIGIOUS GROUP	SINGLE				MARRIED			
		Active incid. %	Active median freq. per wk.	% of total outlet	Cases in total sample	Active incid. %	Active median freq. per wk.	% of total outlet	Cases in total sample
21–25	Protestant								
	Devout	28	0.3	54	604	23	0.1	4	318
	Moderate	32	0.3	43	615	23	0.1	4	309
	Inactive	40	0.4	45	675	33	0.2	6	392
	Catholic								
	Devout	22	0.3	29	196	20	0.5	11	86
	Moderate	32	0.3	37	57	21	0.4	8	53
	Inactive	48	0.4	33	91	28	0.4	5	67
	Jewish								
	Moderate	30	0.6	54	192	22	0.3	7	145
	Inactive	43	0.4	44	396	31	0.2	5	319
26–30	Protestant								
	Devout	37	0.3	56	221	27	0.2	5	331
	Moderate	45	0.3	46	249	24	0.1	5	336
	Inactive	49	0.4	38	309	40	0.2	8	413
	Catholic								
	Devout	23	0.3	29	79	27	0.3	10	84
	Inactive					34	0.4	6	58
	Jewish								
	Moderate					29	0.3	7	140
	Inactive	52	0.4	39	110	36	0.2	7	275
31–35	Protestant								
	Devout	39	0.3	40	121	32	0.1	5	264
	Moderate	48	0.3	54	127	32	0.1	6	253
	Inactive	59	0.4	35	159	44	0.2	10	315
	Catholic								
	Devout					24	0.4	9	63
	Jewish								
	Moderate					29	0.3	7	102
	Inactive	63	0.5	36	51	36	0.2	8	199
36–40	Protestant								
	Devout	37	0.4	36	76	33	0.1	7	200
	Moderate	58	0.3	57	77	28	0.2	7	175
	Inactive	60	0.3	32	102	49	0.2	12	232
	Jewish								
	Moderate					33	0.3	7	58
	Inactive					34	0.3	8	132
41–45	Protestant								
	Devout					29	0.2	10	125
	Moderate					31	0.3	12	110
	Inactive					52	0.2	16	128
	Jewish								
	Inactive					29	0.3	8	79
46–50	Protestant								
	Devout					29	0.3	10	72
	Moderate					21	0.3	11	52
	Inactive					52	0.2	15	62

188

Table 37. Techniques in Masturbation

TECHNIQUES EVER USED	TOTAL ACTIVE SAMPLE	EDUCATIONAL LEVEL			
		0–8	9–12	13–16	17+
	%	*Percent*			
Clitoral and labial	84	82	86	83	88
Thigh pressure	10	6	8	10	10
Muscular tension	5	2	4	4	6
Breast stimulation	11	11	8	11	11
Vaginal insertion	20	25	18	18	25
Fantasy alone	2	2	2	2	3
Other techniques	11	11	9	11	11
Number of cases	2727	65	470	1393	737

Since each female may use more than one technique, the percentages in each group add up to more than 100.

Table 38. Fantasy in Masturbation
Among females with masturbatory experience

PRESENCE AND CONTENT	TOTAL SAMPLE	EDUCATIONAL LEVEL			
		0–8	9–12	13–16	17+
	%	*Percent*			
None, ever	36	32	35	38	32
At least sometimes	64	68	65	62	68
Sometimes none	14	12	13	14	15
Almost always	50	56	52	48	53
	%	*Percent*			
Heterosexual	60	63	61	58	64
Homosexual	10	20	10	8	10
Animal contacts	1	0	—	1	1
Sado-masochistic	4	0	2	4	7
Other content	3	0	1	5	3
Number of cases	2475	60	441	1230	694

Totals in portion of table showing content of fantasy exceed incidences of fantasy shown in first part of table, because many individuals fantasy more than one type of situation.

Table 39. Attitudes Toward Masturbation

EDUCATIONAL LEVEL	Bf. Adol.	Adol.–15	16–20	21–25	26–30	31–35	36–40	41–50
				AGE GROUP				

WORRY

	Bf. Adol.	Adol.–15	16–20	21–25	26–30	31–35	36–40	41–50
				Percent				
Total sample	38	46	42	32	30	27	21	17
Educ. 9–12	41	46	42	37	37	32	24	21
Educ. 13–16	38	47	43	32	29	27	23	22
Educ. 17+	36	44	41	29	25	22	18	11

ACCEPTANCE

	Bf. Adol.	Adol.–15	16–20	21–25	26–30	31–35	36–40	41–50
				Percent				
Total sample	35	43	61	67	69	73	78	81
Educ. 9–12	35	42	55	60	61	67	75	78
Educ. 13–16	33	42	63	68	72	75	80	80
Educ. 17+	38	46	61	70	73	76	81	86

NUMBER OF CASES

	Bf. Adol.	Adol.–15	16–20	21–25	26–30	31–35	36–40	41–50
Total sample	1023	1556	1979	1513	1118	881	637	430
Educ. 9–12	162	281	347	293	245	201	127	82
Educ. 13–16	511	833	1088	677	396	291	201	123
Educ. 17+	287	362	475	514	450	364	289	207

The sums of the total samples amount to less than 100 per cent in some age groups because some individuals masturbate without worry and without conscious decision to accept; they may amount to more than 100 per cent because some individuals worry over and consciously accept their masturbation in different portions of the same age period.

Table 40. Sources of Information Leading to Acceptance of Masturbation

SOURCES OF INFORMATION	TOTAL SAMPLE	EDUCATIONAL LEVEL		
		9–12	13–16	17+
	%	*Percent*		
Printed material	54	48	55	55
Professional consultants	30	23	31	33
Companions	11	17	11	8
Own observations	8	10	8	7
Parents	4	1	3	4
Other sources	—	0	0	1
Number of cases	459	69	238	146

The sums may amount to more than 100 per cent because more than one source of information may influence an individual's attitudes. The N's are small because the question was asked in only a portion of all cases.

Chapter 6

NOCTURNAL SEX DREAMS

The nocturnal sex dreams [1] of males have been the subject of extensive literary, pornographic, scientific, and religious discussion. The male, projecting his own experience, frequently assumes that females have similar dreams, and in erotic literature as well as in actual life he not infrequently expresses the hope that the female in whom he is interested may be dreaming of him at night. He may think it inevitable that anyone who is in love should dream of having overt sexual relations with her lover.[2] But relatively few records of female dreams have been available to establish such a thesis.[3] Even some of the best of the statistical studies of sexual behavior have failed to recognize the existence of nocturnal dreams in the female.[4]

This is curious, for it has not proved difficult to secure data on these matters. Females who have had nocturnal sex dreams seem to have no

---

[1] The term is generally used for all sex dreams in sleep, whether they occur in sleep at night or in sleep during the daytime.

[2] This projection of the male's hope that the female is dreaming of him is found as far back as Ovid in the first century B.C. See: Ovid: Heroides, 15:123–134; 19:55–66 (1921:188–190, 262–264).

[3] The existence of sex dreams in the human female has been recognized, however, in: Aristotle and Galen acc. Havelock Ellis 1936(I,1):199. Longus [Greek, 3rd cent. A.D.?]: Daphnis and Chloe, 1896:41; 1916:83 ("what they had not done in the day, they did in a dream"). Anon., The Fifteen Plagues of a Maiden-head, 1707:4, 6 ("as e'er I'm sleeping in my Bed, I dream I'm mingling with some Man my Thighs. . . . For dreams . . . at the present quench my Lechery." And, "Fancy some Gallant brings to my Arms . . . till breathless, faint, and softly sunk away, I all dissolved in reaking Pleasures lay"). Tissot 1785:233–234 (cites 2 cases). Guibout (1847) acc. Ellis 1936(I,1): 199 (an early French account). Roland 1864:66–69 (a diary account of preadolescent dreams with orgasm). Rosenthal (1875) acc. Kisch 1907:376 (probably the earliest medical discussion of sex dreams in women). Nelson 1888:390–391, 401. Kisch 1907. Rohleder 1907(1). Bloch 1908. Nystrom 1908:20. Moll 1909, 1912. Adler 1911. Talmey 1915:246. Hirschfeld 1920. Robie 1925. Marcuse in Moll 1926(2). Blanchard and Manasses 1930. Kelly 1930. Childers 1936:446 (Negro and white children). Ellis 1936(I,1):187–204 (the most detailed discussion of the psychologic aspects of nocturnal sex dreams among females). Stokes 1948. Ford and Beach 1951. Also see the other authors cited throughout the present chapter.

[4] Among the few studies which have included specific data on sex dreams among females, note the following: Heyn 1924:60–69 (452 women interviewed in a medical clinic in Germany). Hamilton 1929:313–320 (the most detailed investigation, with material on 100 married women, in 13 tables. The percentages cited here are recalculated from these tables, in order to make them comparable to the present data). But no investigation of such dreams was covered in such important studies of the female as: Davis 1929, Dickinson and Beam 1931, Dickinson and Beam 1934, Landis et al. 1940, and Landis and Bolles 1942.

more difficulty than males in recalling them, and do not seem to be hesitant in admitting their experience. Whether or not they reach orgasm in these dreams is a matter about which few of them have any doubt. Because the male may find tangible evidence that he has ejaculated during sleep, his record may be somewhat more accurate than the female's; but vaginal secretions often bear similar testimony to the female's arousal and/or orgasm during sleep. As with the male, the female is often awakened by the muscular spasms or convulsions which follow her orgasms. Consequently the record seems as trustworthy as her memory can make it, and the actual incidences and frequencies of nocturnal orgasms in the female are probably not much higher than the present calculations show. The violence of the female's reactions in orgasm is frequently sufficient to awaken the sexual partner with whom she may be sleeping, and from some of these partners we have been able to obtain descriptions of her reactions in the dreams. There can be no question that a female's responses in sleep are typical of those which she makes when she is awake.

Masturbation and nocturnal sex dreams to the point of orgasm are the activities which provide the best measure of a female's intrinsic sexuality. All other types of sexual activity involve other persons—the partners in the sexual relations—and the frequencies and circumstances of such socio-sexual contacts often depend upon some compromise of the desires of the two partners. The frequencies of the female's marital coitus, for instance, are often much higher than she would desire, and even those females who are most responsive in their sexual relations might not choose to have coitus as often as their spouses want it. Since other persons have a minimum effect upon the incidences and frequencies of masturbation and nocturnal sex dreams, these latter outlets provide a better measure of the basic interests and sexual capacities of the female.

ORIGINS OF NOCTURNAL DREAMS

Whether sexual responses originate through the physical stimulation of some body surface, or through some psychologic stimulation by way of the cerebrum, they are mediated primarily through lower spinal centers and the autonomic nervous system (Chapter 17). Ultimately all parts of the nervous system become involved; and all parts of the body which are nervously controlled, especially those which are controlled by the autonomic nervous system, may be affected. Whenever there is sexual arousal the muscles of the body respond, as we have already noted, with a rhythmic, involuntary flow of movement which is one of the most characteristic aspects of sexual behavior, and at orgasm the body may be thrown into localized or more general spasms or convulsions. All of this seems to be as true of sexual responses and orgasm reached during sleep as it is of sexual reponses and orgasm reached while one is awake.[5]

Sexual responses in sleep may differ, however, from the responses which one makes when awake, in the fact that the learned controls and inhibitions which an individual has acquired in the course of his or her lifetime are less likely to operate in sleep. The content of the dream, the speed of the response, and the abandon of the activity in orgasm may be less obstructed by rational controls. The dreams, particularly in the male, may include socially taboo types of behavior, unconventional sexual techniques, contacts with children and with relatives (incestuous relations), exhibitionistic performances, group activity, fantastic and physically impossible techniques, and still other types of activity and partners which the individual certainly would not accept if he or she were awake.[6] One of the most characteristic aspects of nocturnal sex dreams is the speed with which they carry the individual to orgasm, even though he or she may be quite slow in response while awake. An occasional female who finds it difficult to release her inhibitions and reach orgasm while awake may be able to reach it in sleep. There are some females (5 per cent), just as there are some males, who experience nocturnal dreams to orgasm before they have ever experienced orgasm from any other source while they are awake (Table 148).[7]

Among both females and males, nocturnal sex dreams, more than any other type of sexual outlet, appear to have their origins in what are primarily psychologic stimuli.[8] It seems true that the direct physical stimulation of an individual's body by night clothing, the bed covers, the bed partner, and other pressures on the reposing body may sometimes provide physical stimulation which is sufficient to produce

---

[5] Muscular movements in nocturnal orgasm are also noted in: Krafft-Ebing and Kisch acc. to Rohleder 1907(1):231. Heyn 1924:60–64.

[6] The inclusion of things in dreams which are not accepted when awake is elaborately discussed in Freud 1938:208 ff., and noted in Hamilton 1929:317–318, and Havelock Ellis 1936(I,1):195–196.

[7] The occurrence of orgasm in the nocturnal dreams of the female, before it occurs in any other sort of experience, is also noted in: Kisch 1907:576–577. Moll 1909:86; 1912:95. Heyn 1924:62–63. Robie 1925:205. Blanchard and Manasses 1930:32. Havelock Ellis 1936(I,1):197. Stekel 1950:158–159. See p. 213.

[8] Male paraplegics (Chapter 17) whose spinal cords have been severed may have nocturnal sex dreams and sometimes ejaculate. See: Shelden and Bors 1948: 388. Talbot 1949:266. Bors, Engle, Rosenquist, and Holliger 1950:393. In such paraplegics, psychologic stimulation of the genital area is impossible. Because of this, Ford and Beach 1951:164 state, "It seems more probable that sexual dreams associated with genital reflexes are a product of sensations arising in the tumescent phallus." With this interpretation we do not wholly agree. While the data from the paraplegics show that orgasm during sleep may be induced by physical stimulation alone, they do not disprove our contention that psychologic fantasies are, in the intact individual, the primary sources of the nocturnal responses.

orgasm. The physiologic condition of an individual, including her hormonal constitution, may also have a great deal to do with determining the frequencies of her sex dreams; and her nutritional state, her general health, her fatigue, the temperature of the room, and still other physical and physiologic factors may contribute to the origin of the dreams. Certainly there is a portion of the daytime sexual activity of the male and more of the daytime activity of the female which depends primarily on physical stimulation, with a minimum accompaniment of any psychologic imagery or fantasy; but the physical and physiologic stimuli which seem conducive to the development of orgasm in sleep are rarely of the sort which would be sufficient to produce orgasm when one is awake. It is not impossible, and it is even quite probable that a lowered threshold of response during sleep makes it possible for a lesser physical stimulus to precipitate sexual responses at that time; but if physical stimuli alone were sufficient, one might expect them to produce nocturnal orgasms with considerable regularity and with much greater frequency than they usually occur, for the necessary physical and physiologic conditions would appear to be present quite regularly under normal sleeping conditions. It seems probable, therefore, that psychologic stimuli are involved to a greater extent than any of the physical and physiologic factors.

One of the most characteristic aspects of the orgasms which occur while an individual sleeps is the fact that they are almost always accompanied by dreams, even among females who are rarely or never given to sexual fantasy while they masturbate or engage in any other type of daytime sexual activity. The amount of nocturnal orgasm which occurs in the female without any consciously remembered dream is small (p. 212). It involved something like one per cent of the females in the sample (Table 41), and there is some reason to doubt whether the failure to recall dreams is sufficient evidence that they did not occur. We are inclined to agree with most psychologists and psychiatrists in believing that the dreams are not only necessary factors in the great majority of cases, but the prime precipitating factors of most nocturnal orgasms; but the physiology of the matter is still poorly understood, and further studies must be made before we can be certain of the extent to which the dreams may actually dominate the situation. The elucidation of this problem should further our understanding of the psychology of female sexuality in general.

In respect to the male, the opinion is quite generally held that nocturnal emissions are the product of "accumulated pressures in reproductive glands." It is implied that semen accumulates in the testes (!), and that when those glands become full the resultant pressures touch off some mechanism which leads to orgasm and to seminal discharges in sleep.[9] The anatomy and physiology in any such explanation is, however, quite incorrect. As we have already noted in the volume on the male, semen consists primarily of secretions of the prostate gland and seminal vesicles, and it receives only a microscopic bit of sperm from the testes themselves (p. 612). There seem to be no sufficient data to show that pressures in the prostate and seminal vesicles, or in any other glands, actually stimulate the lower spinal centers which are concerned in sexual responses. The very fact that females, without testes, prostate glands, or seminal vesicles, still have nocturnal orgasms provides good evidence that glandular pressures probably have little or nothing to do with nocturnal emissions in the male. When mechanical stimulation results in nocturnal orgasms, it is more likely to be the tactile stimulation of some body surface which is involved.

At various points in the literature the opinion has been expressed that nocturnal dreams in the female are an expression of some neurotic disturbance,[10] and that "normal," well adjusted females do not dream to the point of orgasm. The very fact that nocturnal sex dreams are not as universal in the female as they are in the male seems to have contributed to the opinion that they are pathologic. There is a tendency to consider anything in human behavior that is unusual, not well known, or not well understood, as neurotic, psychopathic, immature, perverse, or an expression of some other sort of psychologic disturbance. Curiously enough, the persons who contend that sex dreams represent neurotic disturbances in the female admit that it is impossible to believe that 80 per cent or more of the male population is to be considered neurotic simply because that percentage has nocturnal sex dreams which effect orgasm.

It is true that we have few phylogenetic data to establish the evolutionary origin of these dreams in man, for we know of only two instances of nocturnal sex dreams among the females of any lower species of mammal, and only two or three instances in male mammals outside of man.[11] It is, however, very difficult to secure evidence of

---

[9] Instances of this opinion that accumulated pressures in various structures are responsible for nocturnal sex dreams in the male (and, by a parallelism, in the female) may be found in: Loewenfeld 1908:598 (discusses a hypothetic increase of arousability of the cortical sex centers determined by an accumulation of libido-genic matters in the blood). Hammer acc. Heyn 1924:61 (a discharge from over-strained mucous glands). Rice 1933:39, 41. Kahn 1939: 26. The erotic literature consistently refers to pressures in the testes.

[10] The opinion that females who have sex dreams are neurotic is expressed in: Kisch 1907:576. Krafft-Ebing acc. Kisch 1907:377. Loewenfeld 1908:596. Bloch 1908:439–440 (includes older references). Krafft-Ebing acc. Heyn 1924:60. Heyn 1924:63 objects to this neurotic interpretation.

[11] Nocturnal dreams among the males of lower mammals are reported in Ford and Beach 1951:165 for the cat (with ejaculation) and for the shrew (with erection only). We have observed erection in male dogs while they slept. From one of our subjects we have a clear-cut record of sex dreams in a female boxer

such dreams in an animal that cannot report its experience, and it is quite probable that further studies will show that such dreams not infrequently occur in other mammalian species. Consequently, one cannot conclude that the near absence of data proves that there is no evolutionary precedent for their occurrence in the human female.

Similarly, there are few records of nocturnal sex dreams among the females of any pre-literate people, although there are more records of sex dreams among males of such groups.[12] This probably proves nothing, although it may suggest that females among primitives, just as among present-day American groups, do not dream to the point of orgasm as frequently as males.

INCIDENCE AND FREQUENCY

General Summary. At some time prior to the contribution of their histories, approximately two-thirds (about 65 per cent) of the females in the sample had dreams that were overtly sexual (Table 41). For 20 per cent the dreams had proceeded to the point of orgasm, although these same individuals had sometimes had sex dreams without orgasm. Some 45 per cent reported having sex dreams which, however, had never reached orgasm. As with the male, the dreams often had a distressing way of stopping just short of the climax of the activity.[13]

The **accumulative incidence** curves indicate that 37 per cent of the females in the sample had experienced dreams which had led to orgasm by the age of 45 (Table 42, Figure 21). This means that 63 per cent had not dreamed to orgasm by that age. The data on the present sample indicate, however, that nearly half of this 63 per cent (*i.e.*, 34 per cent of the total female sample) had had dreams without orgasm. Including females of all ages, it may, therefore, be estimated that a total of more than 70 per cent have sex dreams in the course of their lives, whether with or without orgasm.[14]

---

dog. During periods of heat, the dog regularly showed signs of sexual disturbance while asleep, with body movements, vocalization, vaginal swellings, and the development of vaginal mucous secretions. Dr. Karl Lashley tells us of a female dachshund whining, making pelvic thrusts, and showing genital tumescence in sleep during periods of estrus.

[12] Nocturnal dreams among females of primitive peoples (in every instance without any record of orgasm) are reported in: Crawley 1927(1):233 (for the Yoruba in Africa). Malinowski 1929:339–340, 392 (for the Trobrianders in Melanesia). Blackwood 1935:549, 552, 559 (18 of 177 recorded dreams were sexual, among the Melanesians of Bougainville). Havelock Ellis 1936(I,1):199 (for the Hindu and Papua). Devereux 1936:32, 57 (for the Mohave Indians). Gorer 1938:185 (for the Lepcha). Laubscher 1938:10 (for the Tembu in South Africa). DuBois 1944:45, 69–70 (for the Alor in Melanesia). Elwin 1947:480 (for the Muria in India). Ford and Beach 1951:165 (give no cases; state it is rare in anthropologic literature).

[13] Dreams stopping short of orgasm are also noted in: Heyn 1924:65. Marcuse in Moll 1926(2):861 (in specifically neurotic females).

[14] Incidences of dreams to orgasm in the female are also reported in: Schbankov acc. Weissenberg 1924a:9 (in 12 per cent of 324 female Russian students).

The number of females in the sample who were experiencing nocturnal dreams to the point of orgasm (the **active incidence**) in any particular five-year period was, however, small. The incidences ranged from 2 to 38 per cent in the various age groups, but they were usually between 10 and 33 per cent (Table 43, Figure 22). Because of the low frequencies with which such dreams occur, it is probable that not much more than 10 per cent of the females in the population which is adolescent or older in age, have nocturnal dreams to the point of orgasm within any single year.

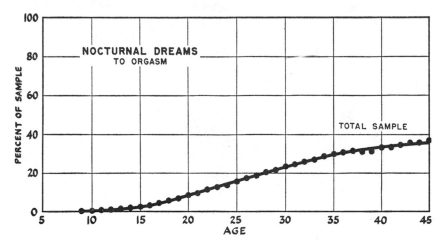

Figure 21. Accumulative incidence: nocturnal dreams to orgasm

Each dot indicates percent of sample with experience in orgasm by the indicated age. Data from Table 42.

In the sample, the average (median) female who had had sex dreams to the point of orgasm (Table 43) was having such dreams at a rate of 3 or 4 times per year (an **active median frequency** of 0.06 to 0.08 per week). For perhaps 25 per cent, the experience had not occurred more than 1 to 6 times in their lives (Figure 23). In the total female sample, regular frequencies had occurred as follow:[15]

        8% with frequencies over 5 per year
        3% with frequencies over 2 per month
        1% with frequencies over 1 per week

Heyn 1924:61 (about 50 per cent, slightly fewer in virgins). Hamilton 1929: 313 (37 per cent). Incidences are discussed, without specific data, in: Loewenfeld 1908:588. Eberhard 1924:263. Stokes 1948:18 (less frequent among females than males).

[15] Additional data on the frequencies of nocturnal orgasms may be found in Loewenfeld 1908:596 (individual variation). Heyn 1924:61–62 (frequency higher in females with "stronger sex drive"). Hamilton 1929:315–316 (12 out of 15 single females had frequencies of 3 per year or less. Of 41 females, 56 per cent had dreams only after marriage, 34 per cent had them both before and after marriage, and 10 per cent had them only before marriage).

The most extreme frequencies in any individual history were also low. There were only seven or eight histories among the nearly six thousand in which the dreams had occurred with average frequencies of more than 1.5 per week (three times in two weeks) during any five-

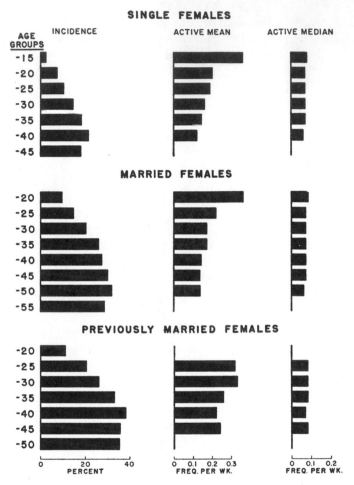

Figure 22. Active incidence, mean, median: nocturnal dreams to orgasm, by age and marital status

Data from Table 43.

year period. There were only one unmarried female over thirty years of age, two or three married females over forty years of age, and four previously married females over forty years of age who had had dreams which average more than once per week. For some other females, exceptional circumstances had produced several nocturnal dreams within a particular week, or even two or three times in a single night, but this was a very rare occurrence.[16] Such high frequencies had almost never extended over any prolonged period of time.

Among women who had been deprived of some drug to which they had been addicted, we have five cases of a considerable increase in the frequencies of sex dreams to orgasm for a matter of a few days or a week or two, but such withdrawal symptoms are more marked among men and less frequently seen among women.

In most male groups there are individuals who have nocturnal emissions with frequencies which average as high as four to seven, and in some instances as high as fourteen per week over some period of

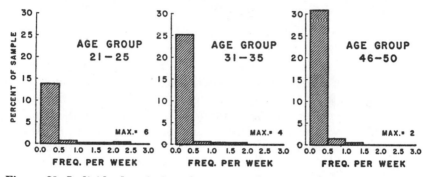

Figure 23. Individual variation: frequency of nocturnal dreams to orgasm

For three age groups of married females. Each class interval includes the upper but not the lower frequency. For incidences of females not dreaming to orgasm, see Table 43.

years (see our 1948:521). The range of the variation in the frequencies of nocturnal dreams to orgasm is, therefore, much more limited among females. This is the only instance of a sexual outlet in which the range of individual variation is more limited among females than it is among males. As we have already noted (Chapter 5), there are females who do not masturbate more than once or twice in a lifetime, and there are females who report masturbating to orgasm as frequently as a hundred times in an hour (p. 146); such exceedingly high rates are never approached by the male. In their pre-marital petting, there are some females who reach orgasm more frequently than any known male. Similarly, the maximum frequencies of orgasm among females in coitus may far exceed the maximum frequencies attained by any male (p. 350). It is only in the frequencies of nocturnal orgasms that the maximum frequencies for the females fall below the maximum frequencies for the males. In sexual responses which depend primarily

---

[16] Exceptional frequencies of more than one per night are also noted by: Stekel 1923:81; 1950:159. Heyn 1924:64. Hamilton 1929:315.

upon physical stimulation, the extreme females surpass the males; but in such responses as dreaming to orgasm, which depend primarily upon psychologic stimuli, the males surpass the females.

There were some females, including as many as 2 per cent of those with masturbation in their histories, who were capable of reaching orgasm through fantasy alone (Table 37), and this is beyond the capacity of almost any male. This would seem evidence of a high level of psychologic response in those particular females. But even these most responsive females do not have nocturnal orgasms with frequencies which approach those of the more responsive males or even of the average male. It is not immediately apparent why the psychologic responsiveness of a female when she is awake should not be correlated with a similar level of responsiveness when she is asleep.

The frequencies with which the average female in the sample had had nocturnal orgasms (the active median frequencies) were more or less constant for the single and married females of all age groups from adolescence to forty or fifty years of age; for the females of the grade school, high school, college, and graduate school levels; for the females of the various religious, occupational, and rural-urban groups on which we have sufficient data; for the females who became adolescent at various ages; and for the females of the several generations represented in the sample. This is one of the significant aspects of the record. The detailed data, with especial emphasis on the few groups in which there is any significant variation from the general rule, are discussed below.

Relation to Age and Marital Status. Nocturnal sex dreams had occurred among fewer of the younger females (the **active incidence**), and among many more of the older females in the sample. It was about 2 per cent who had had dreams to orgasm between adolescence and 15 years of age, but the percentages increased in the older groups.[17] Some 22 to 38 per cent of the females in the sample were having such dreams between the ages of forty and fifty (Table 43, Figure 22). After that the incidences began to decline. We have only one instance of a female over seventy years of age who was having sex dreams to orgasm.

In contrast to the above, the male peak in nocturnal dreams is reached in the late teens or twenties (see our 1948:242), some twenty or thirty years before the female reaches the peak of her dream activity.

---

[17] For correlations of nocturnal dreams with the age of the female, see also: Havelock Ellis and Moll in Moll 1911, 1921:614 (less commonly in the female, more often in the male during adolescence). Heyn 1924:63 (an occasional instance before first menstruation). Hamilton 1929:313, 320 (says 2 per cent by age 16, has 1 case before first menstruation; 21 out of 40 married women who had experienced sex dreams, had them more frequently in later marriage).

The later development in the female of an outlet which so largely depends upon psychologic stimuli is a matter that must be considered in any comparison of the female and the male (Chapter 16).

While the number of females who were dreaming to orgasm increased with advancing age, there was no correlation between the age of the individual and the frequencies with which she was having experience (Table 43, Figure 22). The average frequencies for those who were having dreams (the **active median frequencies**) remained around 3 to 4 times per year from adolescence to the oldest age groups on which we have good samples—at least to age sixty-five.

A somewhat lower proportion of the single females, a higher proportion of the married females, and a still higher proportion of the previously married females were having sex dreams to orgasm (the active incidences) (Table 43, Figure 22). The peak for the single females had come at age forty with 22 per cent involved; it had come for the married females at age fifty with 32 per cent involved. For the previously married females it had come at age fifty-five with 38 per cent involved.

Interesting to note, however, the average frequencies for the females who were having any nocturnal orgasms (the active median frequencies) remained quite constant, at something below 0.1 per week for all groups, including the single, married, and previously married females (Table 43, Figure 22). Marital experience had evidently developed the imaginative capacities of some females who had not had sex dreams before marriage, and of a still larger number of those who had become widowed, separated, or divorced; but even the greatly increased experience which regular coitus had provided had not succeeded in increasing the frequencies of the nocturnal fantasies for the average (median) female.

Relation to Educational Level. In the available sample, there seems to have been no correlation between the educational background of the female and the accumulative or active incidence of her nocturnal sex dreams (Tables 42, 44), or the frequency with which she had such dreams to the point of orgasm. Similarly, the portion of the total outlet which she had derived from her nocturnal orgasms did not seem to have been related to the female's educational level (Table 44).

The educational background of the male does seem to have a direct effect on the frequencies of his nocturnal emissions. The males who go furthest in their educational careers appear to have better developed imaginative capacities, and this seems to have an effect upon the development of their psychosexual responses. Unmarried males of the college level have nocturnal sex dreams with frequencies (medians) which are between three and four times those of the males who never go beyond grade school (see our 1948:342); but females who have college and graduate school training do not have sex dreams any more frequently than those who have not gone beyond grade school or high school.

Relation to Parental Occupational Class. There seems to be little correlation between the social levels of the homes in which the girls in our sample were raised, and the incidences and frequencies with which they ultimately had nocturnal dreams to the point of orgasm (Tables 45, 47).

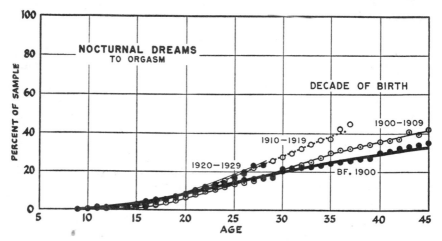

Figure 24. Accumulative incidence: nocturnal dreams to orgasm, by decade of birth

Data from Table 46.

Relation to Decade of Birth. In our sample, the number of teen-age females of the recent generations who were dreaming to the point of orgasm (both the accumulative and active incidences) was about what it had been among those who were born forty years earlier (Tables 46, 48, Figure 24). After the early twenties, however, a slightly higher percentage of the females of the younger generation were dreaming to orgasm. But the frequencies were not modified at all in the course of the forty years covered by the sample. If psychosexual development in the female were socially controlled, as it is ordinarily believed to be, we might have expected more change in the incidences and frequencies of nocturnal dreams over this period of years.

Within the last forty years the place of the female in our social organization has materially changed. Her position in the home has been considerably modified, her place in industry and in the business affairs of the nation has developed to an extent which was unimagined forty years ago, she has acquired some position in the political control of the nation, and become active in civic, state, and national affairs to an extent which her grandmother never anticipated. Forty years ago there were only about 7 per cent of the females who ever went to college, but the present generation is sending about 15 per cent of its girls into collegiate work.[18] The proportion who go on into graduate work and into professional programs has increased to an even greater extent. Even among those who do not go to college, the number of years of schooling has, on an average, tremendously increased: forty years ago there were two-thirds (67 per cent) who never got beyond grade school, today there are only 18 to 20 per cent who go no further than that in their schooling.[18] There has been a similarly marked change in the number who complete high school. In spite of this, the number of females who are ever stimulated by daytime fantasies (Chapter 5) or by sex dreams as they sleep, and the frequencies with which they have such dreams to the point of orgasm, remain just about what they were in their grandmothers' generation. The capacity to be aroused psychosexually evidently depends on something more innate than the culture (Chapters 16, 18). In the female, and not improbably in the male, there appears to be a limit beyond which psychosexual capacities cannot be developed within an individual's lifetime.

Relation to Age at Onset of Adolescence. There seems to have been no consistent correlation between the ages at which the females in the sample had turned adolescent, and their involvement in nocturnal dreams (the accumulative and active incidence figures), or the frequencies with which they had them (the active median and mean frequencies) (Tables 49, 52).

Relation to Rural-Urban Background. In the groups on which the data are available, there are some differences between the incidences of nocturnal dreams among the females who were raised in rural areas and those who were raised in urban areas (Tables 50, 51). However, none of these differences seem to lie in any constant direction, and we are inclined to credit them to the vagaries of sampling, or to the small sizes of some of the samples.

Relation to Religious Background. The number of females in the sample who had ever experienced nocturnal dreams to the point of orgasm (the accumulative incidence), and the number who were having such experience within any five-year period (the active incidence), did seem to have been affected by the degree of their religious devo-

---

[18] These data on educational attainment in the U. S. population are approximated from the Sixteenth Census of the U. S., 1940 (Population v. 4, pt. 1, U. S. Summary) 1943:79.

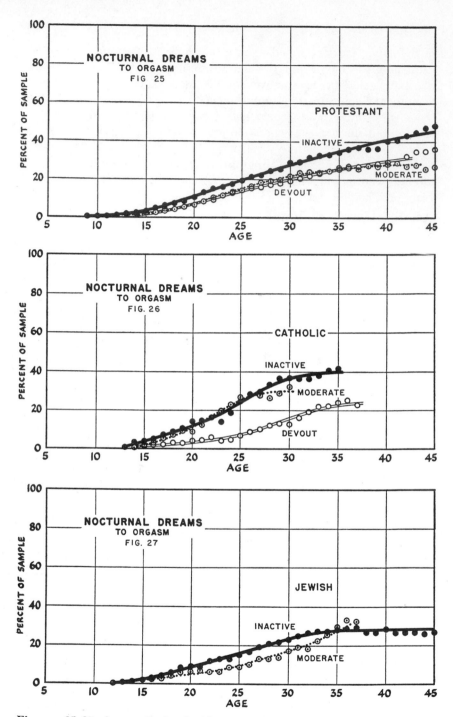

Figures 25–27. **Accumulative incidence: nocturnal dreams to orgasm, by religious group**

Data from Table 53.

tion (Tables 53, 54, Figures 25–28). The differences were not dependent on their Protestant, Catholic, or Jewish backgrounds, but
upon the degree of their devotion in their religion. In general, fewer of
the females who were active or devout religiously had dreamed to the
point of orgasm—perhaps because they had had the smallest amount
of overt sexual experience about which they could dream.

On the other hand, the frequencies with which the females had had
dreams after they had once started them did not seem to be affected
by the religious background (Table 54). It will be recalled that we

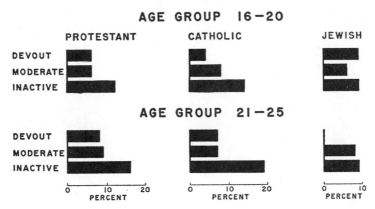

Figure 28. **Active incidence: nocturnal dreams to orgasm, by religious group**
Data on single females; see Table 54.

found a similar situation in regard to the masturbatory frequencies of
the females in the sample (Chapter 5). It is difficult to understand why
a religious background which has kept a female from dreaming of
sex for some period of years does not continue to influence her after
she has begun to have sex dreams.

PERCENTAGE OF TOTAL OUTLET

Nocturnal sex dreams carried to the point of orgasm appear to provide some physiologic outlet, albeit never more than a minor outlet,
for about a third of the females (Table 43).[19]

Nocturnal dreams had accounted for approximately 2 to 3 per cent
of the total number of orgasms experienced by the females in the total
sample, including both the single and married females of most of the
age groups (Table 170, Figure 109). The figure was low, in part because there were three-quarters or more of the females in each age
group who were not having any nocturnal orgasms, and in part because
the frequencies were always low.

---

[19] That dreams provide some physiologic release is also noted in Heyn 1924:64 ff.

Nocturnal dreams had provided only 2 per cent of the total outlet of the younger single females in the sample and 4 per cent of the total outlet of the unmarried older females (Table 171, Figure 110). Except for animal contacts, nocturnal dreams were, therefore, the least important of all the sources of outlet for the single females of every group under forty-five years of age. As sources of physiologic release for single females, they were surpassed in importance by masturbation, heterosexual petting, pre-marital coitus, and, especially in older groups, by homosexual contacts.

Among younger married females, the orgasms obtained through nocturnal dreams had accounted for only 1 per cent of the total sexual outlet (Table 171, Figure 111). However, the relative importance of the dreams had gradually increased as coital activities slowed up with advancing age, and the dreams had finally accounted for about 3 per cent of the outlet of the married females in their late forties. Animal contacts and homosexual relations were the least important sexual activities of the married females in all of the age groups, but nocturnal dreams were the next least important. Marital coitus, masturbation, and extra-marital coitus had provided larger proportions of the outlet for the married females.

In the histories of the females who had been previously married, and who in consequence had had their chief source of outlet, marital coitus, more or less suddenly withdrawn, orgasms derived from nocturnal dreams had accounted for a more significant part of the total picture. Among the younger females in the sample who had been previously married, and who were now widowed, separated, or divorced, the dreams had accounted for 4 or 5 per cent of the total number of orgasms. Among the older females who had been previously married, the dreams had accounted for as much as 14 per cent of the total outlet (Tables 43, 171, Figure 112).

None of these differences in the proportions of the total outlet derived from dreams were, however, the product of any variation in the frequencies of the dreams themselves. From the youngest to the oldest age groups, the frequencies (the active median frequencies) of the dreams of the single, married, and previously married females who were having any dreams at all were quite uniform. The variations in the proportions of the total outlet which were derived from dreams had depended primarily on the fact that the frequencies of petting, coitus, and homosexual relations varied in different age and marital groups. These other outlets were the ones in which other persons, the sexual partners of the female, had played a predominant role in determining the frequencies of contact. But the frequencies of the nocturnal dreams, which seem a better measure of the female's innate sexuality, had not changed in the long span of years between adolescence and fifty, or under any of the various social conditions imposed by marriage, education, rural-urban backgrounds, religion, and other factors.

CORRELATION WITH OTHER SEXUAL OUTLETS

There is a longstanding and widespread opinion that nocturnal orgasms provide a "natural" outlet for persons who abstain from other types of sexual activity. The frequencies of the dreams are supposed to have an inverse relation to the frequencies of other sexual activities, thus providing a safety valve for the "sexual energy" which accumulates when other outlets are unavailable or are not being utilized. Some authors, for instance, assert that orgasms in sleep occur only among unmarried virgins, or among married females when orgasm has not been reached in coitus, or when spouses are separated, or when marital coitus is for any other reason not available.[20]

The theory has considerable moral importance, for it recognizes nocturnal dreams as an acceptable form of sexual outlet—the only acceptable form outside of vaginal coitus. In both Jewish and Catholic codes, vaginal coitus in marriage, and such preliminary play as will lead to vaginal coitus, is considered the natural means of fulfilling what is taken to be the prime function of sex, namely procreation. Because other forms of sexual activity do not serve this procreative function, none of them except nocturnal dreaming to orgasm is morally acceptable. Orgasm resulting from nocturnal sex dreams is allowed as an exception because, if it is not deliberately induced, it is involuntary and a "natural" sort of "compensation" for the abstinence. The Catholic code, however, is precise in its condemnation of nocturnal orgasms which have been deliberately induced.[21]

---

[20] As examples of this concept of a compensatory function in the female's nocturnal sex dreams, see: Rohleder 1907(1):231. Kisch 1907:576–577 (dreams when frigid in coitus). Loewenfeld 1908:596 (dreams correlated with high erotic responsiveness). Adler 1911:129. Hammer and Mantegazza acc. Heyn 1924:60–61. Heyn 1924:62–63, 69 et passim (dreams correlated with high erotic responsiveness). Krafft-Ebing 1924:97. Marcuse in Moll 1926(2):861 (dreams because of cultural restraints on other outlets). Moll 1926(2):1076. Hamilton 1929:320 (of 42 females, 52 per cent found their dreams compensatory). Dickinson and Beam 1931:185, 285 (as a substitute for unsatisfactory coitus).

[21] The Catholic viewpoint on nocturnal dreams to orgasm is this: Such dreams are without fault or sin provided (1) they are not deliberately induced by thought or deed; (2) they are not consciously welcomed and enjoyed. See the following: Arregui 1927:6 (item 8, no. 3), 151 (item 257, no. 1, 2), who says: Pollution in sleep, following from improper thought, since it no longer belongs to the free will, is not in itself imputed to sin, but the placing of the cause from which it was foreseen to be about to follow is imputed to sin. Nocturnal pollution which is not at all voluntary, is free from all fault, although it pleases the one sleeping. To promote the dreams by touch, movement, etc., is grave

The belief that nocturnal dreams are compensatory carries the promise that undue physiologic tensions will be relieved if an individual remains abstinent. For those who accept the theory as an established fact, it is then possible to contend that there are no biologic or medical reasons which should make it impossible for anyone, female or male, to remain completely abstinent and chaste before marriage. But the compensatory function of nocturnal dreaming to orgasm has, as far as we have been able to discover, never been established by scientifically adequate data. If there are persons who, being abstinent, have specific records to contribute on this subject, it would be of considerable scientific and social value to have them made available for scientific study.

The moral significance of nocturnal sex dreams has most frequently been considered in connection with the male, but the principle has, on occasion, been extended to the female. Hammer,[20] for instance, asserts that the female who is deprived of other sexual outlets will find relief in nocturnal orgasms once every third day. Mantegazza,[20] however, says once in four or five days. No data are presented, and apparently the very positiveness of these statements is supposed to guarantee that they are based on specific evidence.

Because of the importance of this concept of a compensatory function served by nocturnal orgasms, we have gone to some pains to analyze the data on our total sample of 7789 females. From these analyses the following generalizations may be drawn:

1. Out of our total sample of 7789 females, including both Negro and white and both prison and non-prison cases, there are 1761 females who had dreamed at some time in their lives to the point of orgasm. However, only 251 of these cases, which is 14 per cent of all of those

---

. . . . not positively to hinder it is no sin provided the danger of consent be lacking. Pollution caused in sleep by chaste conversation held on the day before with a person of the opposite sex, by strongly seasoned foods, by liquors, or by a rather suitable position on the bed, is not imputed to sin, even though it was foreseen, provided, however, that it was not intended or, once having arisen, deliberately admitted.

Davis 1946(2):243, 246, says: Since pollution directly voluntary is a grave sin, it is not permitted even for the purpose of recovering health or for relieving pain, or for calming or destroying the temptations of the flesh. . . . nor is it permitted to give consent to it even though the ejaculation has arisen naturally. Nor is it permitted to release it, already begun, by completing any positive act. But indeed it is not a grave sin to hold oneself passively if no consent be given. Hence, respectable dancing, reasonable sport, moderate eating and drinking, kisses and embraces according to the custom of the country among those engaged and among friends are permitted, even though pollution may follow, be foreseen or permitted, but in no way intended, nor while it is going on considered as pleasing and welcome.

The Jewish interpretation is typified by the statement in Leviticus 15:15–16, that nocturnal emissions make one unclean, and one must wash and be unclean until the evening.

who had ever had nocturnal orgasms, seem to show a compensatory relationship between the dreams and the other outlets.

2. Such compensatory relationships seem to occur most frequently when other sexual outlets are drastically reduced or eliminated. When the female has not previously had nocturnal dreams, she may have them after the reduction of the other outlets. This was true in approximately 200 of our cases. When the female had previously had dreams, the frequencies may increase when the normal outlets are eliminated or reduced. This may occur, for instance, when divorce or separation from a spouse eliminates the coital sources on which the individual has been chiefly dependent (p. 536). Clear-cut cases also occur when a woman is committed to prison, which in most instances is synonymous with depriving her of the opportunity to have any regular sexual outlet. Out of our 208 prison cases of females who had ever in their lives had sex dreams to orgasm, 140 (68 per cent) showed marked changes in the incidences or frequencies of nocturnal sex dreams to orgasm after commitment to the penal institution. The specific data are as follows:

	Percent
Nocturnal sex dreams only while in prison	62
Nocturnal sex dreams began in prison, continued outside	6
Nocturnal sex dreams increased while in prison	23
Nocturnal sex dreams decreased or stopped in prison	9
Number of cases	140

3. Nocturnal orgasms seemed to occur, or increased in frequency, when socio-sexual outlets (as opposed to solitary outlets) were reduced or proved inadequate. The specific cases include instances of dreams which began only when petting, coitus, or homosexual outlets were eliminated or materially reduced in frequency. There are instances of nocturnal orgasms occurring after petting, or after premarital or marital coitus which had failed to bring the female to orgasm. Such cases, however, are not sufficiently frequent to warrant any statistical treatment here.

4. In nearly every instance the compensatory nature of the nocturnal dreams seemed quite inadequate. The increase in the frequencies of the nocturnal orgasms is usually not more than a few per year, although the outlets for which they were supposed to be compensating may have averaged several times per week.

5. In contrast to this group of cases in which the nocturnal experience seems to serve a compensatory function, there are some 117 cases (7 per cent of the 1761 females who had ever experienced nocturnal orgasms) in which the nocturnal orgasms seemed to correlate positively

with the occurrence of other sexual outlets. Nocturnal dreams seem to have occurred only when these individuals were most often involved in other types of sexual activity, or the dreams increased under such conditions (see our 1948:529). Instances of this are to be seen in the fact that the married females (in the same age groups) have higher rates of dreams than the single females.

6. For 183 females (10 per cent of the 1761 females who had ever experienced nocturnal orgasms), the nocturnal orgasms started in the same year that one or more of the other types of sexual activity had begun.

	% of females
Nocturnal dreams began when masturbation began	33
Nocturnal dreams began when petting began	34
Nocturnal dreams began when coitus began	48
Nocturnal dreams began when homosexual contacts began	8
Number of cases	183

7. In some instances nocturnal orgasms were superimposed on what would seem to have been quite adequate or even high rates of outlet. The most extreme instance was that of a female whose nocturnal orgasms were averaging twice a week, although (because of her ability in multiple orgasm) she was having an average outlet of nearly 70 orgasms per week.

8. In a portion of the cases, there seems to be a positive correlation between high levels of erotic responsiveness and the frequencies of nocturnal dreams to orgasm. For the 74 females in the sample whose nocturnal dreams had averaged at least once a week for at least five consecutive years, the record shows the following:

	% with nocturnal orgasms
Erotic responsiveness	
Above average	58
Average	30
Below average	12
Orgasmic response in coitus	
100% of contacts	89
With multiple orgasm (1.5 to 10 times each)	39

That 89 per cent of those with the highest dream frequency had reached orgasm regularly in their coitus, strikingly contrasts with the fact that not more than 47 per cent in any group of married females had ever reached orgasm one hundred per cent of the time, even after twenty years of marriage (Table 112). That 39 per cent of those who had most frequently dreamed, experienced multiple orgasm in coitus, similarly contrasts with the fact that only 14 per cent of the total sample had regularly experienced multiple orgasm (p. 375).

9. There is some correlation between the occurrence of masturbation and nocturnal dreams. There is also some correlation between the occurrence of fantasies in masturbation and nocturnal dreams. The data are as follows:

	% females with sex dreams	% females without sex dreams
Masturbation in history		
With fantasy in masturbation	35	19
Without fantasy in masturbation	18	13
Without masturbation in history	47	68
Number of cases	3423	1859

10. There are some individuals whose histories seem to show both compensatory and positive relationships between their nocturnal dreams and their other sexual activities. For instance, there are persons whose dreams began in the same year that coitus began, but when the coital rate was considerably stepped up in marriage, the dreams completely stopped. There are also cases of individuals whose dreams began only when their outlet was considerably increased through marriage, but whose dreams increased in frequency when their husbands were away from home.

It is quite possible that the different factors responsible for nocturnal dreams may operate in diverse ways. It is conceivable that physiologic factors may be responsible for the inverse or negative relationships which we have found. On the other hand, the psychologic factors which affect nocturnal dreams would more often produce positive correlations. This is indicated by the fact that there are cases in which the sexual experience of the previous evening supplies the subject matter of the nocturnal dream, leading to a repetition in sleep of the orgasm which had been had before retiring.

11. For 79 per cent of the 1761 females who had had sex dreams, there do not seem to be any obvious correlations between the occurrence or absence of nocturnal dreams and the magnitude of the total outlet. There are high rates of nocturnal dreams among females who have high rates of outlets from other sources, and similarly high rates of dreams among those who have very low rates of outlet from other sources. There are individuals representing every other level of outlet, who have never had any nocturnal dreams. There are even individuals who give evidence of high psychologic responsiveness in connection with their other sexual activities, who do not have nocturnal dreams. This means that a multiplicity of factors must, in the majority of in-

stances, determine the occurrence or non-occurrence of such nocturnal dreams, and that no single factor or small group of factors may account for their occurrence or non-occurrence in a history. What the present data do seem to show may be summed up as follows:

Relation Between Nocturnal Dreams and Other Sexual Outlets

	%
Inverse or compensatory relationship	14
Positive or parallel relationship	7
No marked relationship (among females with dream experience)	79
Number of cases with nocturnal dreams	1761

CONTENT OF NOCTURNAL DREAMS

About one per cent of the females in the sample reported nocturnal orgasms without dreams (Table 41).[22] Of the females who had had sex dreams, whether with or without orgasm, something between 85 and 90 per cent had had heterosexual dreams (Table 55). This closely matched the extent of the overt heterosexual activity in the same histories. Between 30 and 39 per cent of the females had dreamed, at least on occasion, of actual coitus,[23] while 17 to 38 per cent had dreamed on occasion of heterosexual petting which did not involve coitus.[24]

The sexual partners in these dreams were usually obscure and un-identifiable—an epitomization of some general type of person [25]; and even the actor in the dream was not always the dreamer, but a person who combined the capacities of an observer and a participant in the activity. More precise data are needed on this matter. Many of the heterosexual dreams had an indefinitely affectionate or generally social content which did not include overtly physical contacts. While such dreams may in actuality be sexual in significance, they are quite different from the overtly sexual dreams which males usually have.

Some 8 to 10 per cent of the females having dreams had had homosexual dreams (Table 55).[26] This again, was very close to the number

---

[22] Nocturnal orgasms without the recall of dreams are also noted by: Heyn 1924: 64. Hamilton 1929:315. Confusion of the dream with reality, especially in the female, is stressed in: Havelock Ellis and Moll in Moll 1911, 1921:615. Havelock Ellis 1936(I,1):200–205.

[23] Hamilton 1929:314–315 says 22 per cent of first dreams were of coitus. Our data range from 26 to 48 per cent in various groups.

[24] Petting in the dream content is also noted in: Heyn 1924:64. Hamilton 1929:314 (records only a few cases).

[25] That the dream partner is not the real lover and is often unidentified, is also noted in: Heyn 1924:64. Krafft-Ebing 1924:98 (no concrete persons). Hamilton 1929:318–319 (identifiable partner in about 50 per cent).

[26] Homosexual content of the dreams is also noted in: Krafft-Ebing 1901:26–27. Hirschfeld 1920:73, 317. Heyn 1924:65. Moraglia in Heyn 1924:65. Hamilton 1929:317. Kelly 1930:136.

who had had overt homosexual experience. There were dreams of pregnancies resulting from the homosexual relations.[27]

About 1 per cent of the females had dreamed of sexual relations with animals of other species. About 1.5 per cent had dreamed of sado-masochistic situations. Various other types of sex dreams had occurred in still other cases (Table 55).

Something between 1 and 3 per cent of the females had dreamed that they were pregnant or that they were giving birth to a child (Table 55). It is notable that these were reported as "sex dreams." For nine out of every ten of the females who had had such dreams, the dreams had not led to orgasm. Such dreams need further consideration, because the connection between the reproductive function and erotic arousal is probably not as well established as biologists and psychologists ordinarily assume. By association, many males and apparently some females may become erotically aroused when they contemplate any reproductive or excretory function, probably because it depends at least in part on genital anatomy, and this may explain why some females consider dreams of pregnancy as sexual. It is more likely they consider their pregnancy dreams as sexual simply because they know, intellectually, that there is a relationship between sexual behavior and reproduction. There are still other possible explanations in psychiatric theory.

Sex dreams, whether they occur in the female or the male, are often a reflection of experience which the individual has actually had. On the other hand, some 13 per cent of the females in the sample (Negro and white) who had ever dreamed, had had sex dreams which went beyond their actual experience.[28] The specific record is as follows:

Dream Content Without Overt Experience

	WITHOUT ORGASM %	WITH ORGASM %	WITH ANY DREAM %
Dreams of coitus (not rape)	36	10	46
Dreams of rape	4	2	6
Dreams of petting	6	1	7
Dreams of homosexual contacts	16	7	23
Dreams of animal contacts	2	4	6
Sado-masochistic dreams	2	1	3
Dreams of pregnancy and childbirth	13	2	15
Number of females whose dreams precede experience			622

[27] Dreams of pregnancies resulting from homosexual contacts are also noted in Hirschfeld 1920:74. This is what the Negro vernacular identifies as a *jelly baby*.

[28] The relation of the dreams to actual experience or the lack of experience is discussed in: Havelock Ellis and Moll in Moll 1911, 1921:615. Kelly 1930:163

The dreams which antedate experience may represent some desire to participate in an activity which has not yet been accepted in actual life, or which the female has not yet had the opportunity to engage in, or which she would always avoid in overt relationships. Freud and other psychoanalysts believe that the dream content is often a record of repressed desires.[29] Not a few individuals derive considerable pleasure from vicariously participating, through these dreams, in activities which, for one reason or another, are unattainable in actual life.

On the other hand, some of these dreams represent activities, like rape, which the individual may not desire and of which she may actually be afraid. It seems reasonable to believe that some of these dreams are nightmares rather than anything which the females would welcome either in or out of sleep.

The records which we have in the present study do not provide any original data for a discussion of the sexual symbolism of dreams.

The great majority of the females in the sample had accepted their nocturnal sex dreams without any disturbance. A smaller percentage had worried about the moral significance of their sex dreams. However, fewer females than males ever worry over their dreams, probably because some males are disturbed by their seminal emissions. In most instances the females had taken their experience as pleasurable, and had attached little other importance to it.[30]

SUMMARY AND COMPARISONS OF FEMALE AND MALE

Nocturnal Sex Dreams

	IN FEMALES	IN MALES
Origins of Sex Dreams		
Physical stimulation	Yes	Yes
Psychologic stimulation	Yes	Yes
Inhibitions lowered in sleep	Sometimes	More often
Dependent on glandular pressures	No	No evidence
Reflect neurotic disturbances	Rarely	Rarely
Evolutionary origin in lower mammals	Very few data	Few data
Evidence from primitive peoples	Very few data	Few data

(dreams can occur in inexperienced girls, but are more common in older women with masturbatory or coital experience). Dickinson and Beam 1934: 136. The following authors deny (incorrectly) that virgins are capable of reaching orgasm in nocturnal dreams: Rohleder 1907(1):231; 1918(1):135. Adler 1911:129. Loewenfeld 1911b:161. Reisinger 1916:344. Kahn 1937:346; 1939:404.

[29] The Freudian opinion on the nature of nocturnal dreams is summarized, for instance, in Freud 1935:116, 120; 1949:48 (dreams are sometimes an unconscious wish-fulfillment, sometimes represent unsatisfied conscious desires, but "the satisfaction in a pollution-dream can be real"). Heterosexual dreams among males who are completely homosexual are noted in Kinsey, Pomeroy, and Martin 1948:526–527.

[30] The wide acceptance by females of sex dreams without worry is also noted in: Heyn 1924:66. Hamilton 1929:316 (says 19 per cent worry).

Summary and Comparisons (*Continued*)

	IN FEMALES	IN MALES
Accumulative Incidence		
Dreams with or without orgasm	70%	Nearly 100%
Dreams with orgasm, by age 45	37%	83%
Dreams without orgasm	33%	Less than 17%
Active Incidence to Orgasm		
Range in various age groups	2–38%	28–81%
In any single year	10%?	40%?
Peak of activity	In forties	Teens–twenties
Frequencies (Active Median) to Orgasm		
Average, younger ages	3–4 per year	4–11 per year
Average, older ages	3–4 per year	3–5 per year
Regular in 5-year periods		
More than 5 per year	8%	48%
More than 2 per month	3%	14%
More than 1 per week	1%	5%
Range of variation	Limited	Much greater
Percentage of Total Outlet	2–3%	2–8%
Relation to Age and Marital Status		
Active incidences (at age 40) to orgasm		
Single	22%	60%
Married	28%	48%
Previously married	38%	54%
Frequency (active median) to orgasm	No relation	Highest in single
Percentage of total outlet		
Single	2–4%	5–12%
Married	1–3%	3–5%
Previously married	4–14%	4–6%
Relation to Educational Level	None	Much more in college group
Relation to Parental Occupational Class	None	None
Relation to Decade of Birth	None	Some increase
Relation to Age at Onset of Adolescence	None	Little
Relation to Religious Backgrounds		
Accumulative and active incidence	Fewer of devout are involved	Little relation
Frequency (active median)	No relation	No relation
Correlation with Other Sexual Outlets		
Dreams compensatory	In 14%	In some cases
But inadequate as a compensation	Yes	Yes
Correlation with other sexual activity	In 7%	In some cases
Correlation with erotic responsiveness	Yes	
Correlation between dreams and masturbation	Some	
Correlation btwn. dreams and fantasies in masturb.	Some	
Content of Nocturnal Dreams		
None recalled	1%	
Reflection of experience	Usually	Usually
Anticipated or desired experience	Occasionally	Sometimes

215

Table 41. Incidence of Nocturnal Sex Dreams

  By Age at Reporting

NATURE OF EXPERIENCE	TOTAL SAMPLE	AGE AT REPORTING		
		Adol.–30	31–40	41+
	%		*Percent*	
Never dreams, no nocturnal orgasms	34	38	24	26
Nocturnal orgasms, never dreams	1	1	2	2
Dreams, with or without orgasm	65	61	74	72
Dreams to orgasm, ever	20	12	34	39
Dreams, never to orgasm	45	49	40	33
Number of cases	5628	3706	1059	863

Table 42. Accumulative Incidence: Dreams to Orgasm

  By Educational Level

AGE	TOTAL SAMPLE	EDUCATIONAL LEVEL				TOTAL SAMPLE	EDUCATIONAL LEVEL			
		0–8	9–12	13–16	17+		0–8	9–12	13–16	17+
	%		*Percent*			*Cases*		*Cases*		
12	—	1	—	—	1	5720	175	1001	3255	1138
15	2	2	2	2	4	5658	169	1000	3255	1138
20	8	8	8	8	10	4291	123	850	2181	1137
25	16	13	16	14	17	2766	113	679	1032	942
30	23	21	24	23	24	2035	105	497	703	730
35	30	23	30	31	29	1464	87	319	492	566
40	33	32	30	34	34	944	63	193	300	388
45	37		33	41	36	570		126	165	236
50	40					308				

Table based on total sample, including single, married and previously married females.

Table 43. Active Incidence, Frequency, and Percentage of Outlet Dreams to Orgasm

By Age and Marital Status

AGE DURING ACTIVITY	ACTIVE SAMPLE			TOTAL SAMPLE		CASES IN TOTAL SAMPLE
	Incid. %	Median freq. per wk.	Mean frequency per wk.	Mean frequency per wk.	% of total outlet	
SINGLE FEMALES						
Adol.–15	2	0.08	0.36 ± 0.081	0.01 ± 0.002	2	5677
16–20	8	0.07	0.20 ± 0.022	0.02 ± 0.002	3	5613
21–25	11	0.07	0.18 ± 0.019	0.02 ± 0.002	3	2810
26–30	15	0.07	0.16 ± 0.025	0.02 ± 0.004	3	1064
31–35	19	0.07	0.14 ± 0.019	0.03 ± 0.004	3	539
36–40	22	0.06	0.12 ± 0.021	0.02 ± 0.005	2	315
41–45	18	*0.07*	*0.14 ± 0.033*	0.03 ± 0.007	2	179
46–50	18	*0.08*	*0.18 ± 0.054*	0.03 ± 0.011	4	109
51–55	14			0.03 ± 0.016	5	58
56–60	*7*			*0.06 ± 0.048*	*15*	27
MARRIED FEMALES						
16–20	10	0.08	0.36 ± 0.115	0.04 ± 0.012	1	578
21–25	15	0.07	0.22 ± 0.032	0.03 ± 0.005	1	1654
26–30	21	0.07	0.17 ± 0.016	0.04 ± 0.004	1	1662
31–35	26	0.07	0.17 ± 0.017	0.04 ± 0.005	2	1246
36–40	28	0.07	0.14 ± 0.014	0.04 ± 0.004	2	851
41–45	31	0.07	0.13 ± 0.017	0.04 ± 0.006	2	497
46–50	32	0.06	0.13 ± 0.022	0.04 ± 0.008	3	260
51–55	29	*0.07*	*0.21 ± 0.062*	0.06 ± 0.019	6	118
56–60	29	*0.08*	*0.19 ± 0.072*	*0.06 ± 0.024*	9	49
PREVIOUSLY MARRIED FEMALES						
16–20	11			0.01 ± 0.004	—	72
21–25	21	*0.08*	*0.32 ± 0.127*	0.07 ± 0.027	4	239
26–30	26	0.08	0.33 ± 0.088	0.09 ± 0.025	5	328
31–35	33	0.08	0.26 ± 0.066	0.09 ± 0.023	5	304
36–40	38	0.07	0.22 ± 0.054	0.08 ± 0.021	5	245
41–45	36	0.08	0.24 ± 0.060	0.08 ± 0.023	6	195
46–50	36	*0.09*	*0.41 ± 0.161*	0.14 ± 0.060	14	126
51–55	38	*0.08*	*0.24 ± 0.070*	0.09 ± 0.029	11	82
56–60	30	*0.09*	*0.16 ± 0.032*	0.05 ± 0.014	13	53

Italic figures throughout the series of tables indicate that the calculations are based on less than 50 cases. No calculations are based on less than 11 cases. The dash (—) indicates a percentage or frequency smaller than any quantity which would be shown by a figure in the given number of decimal places.

Table 44. Active Incidence and Percentage of Outlet: Dreams to Orgasm
By Educational Level and Marital Status

AGE DURING ACTIVITY	EDUC. LEVEL	SINGLE			MARRIED			PREVIOUSLY MARRIED		
		Active incid. %	% of total outlet	Cases in total sample	Active incid. %	% of total outlet	Cases in total sample	Active incid. %	% of total outlet	Cases in total sample
Adol.–15	0–8	2	3	162						
	9–12	2	1	983						
	13–16	2	2	3271						
	17+	3	3	1128						
16–20	0–8	5	4	143						
	9–12	7	2	976	9	1	210			
	13–16	7	4	3299	11	—	257			
	17+	10	4	1149	8	4	66			
21–25	0–8	9	15	67	18	4	72			
	9–12	9	2	537	16	1	487	20	4	89
	13–16	9	3	1204	13	1	727	18	4	89
	17+	13	2	1002	17	2	368			
26–30	0–8				23	4	81			
	9–12	12	2	181	22	2	489	24	7	100
	13–16	16	2	313	19	1	671	25	4	122
	17+	16	3	531	21	1	421	30	5	84
31–35	0–8				22	4	68			
	9–12	17	4	65	26	2	338	38	6	86
	13–16	15	2	139	27	1	480	30	4	107
	17+	22	3	309	26	2	360	32	7	88
36–40	0–8				22	3	50			
	9–12				27	3	210	34	7	62
	13–16	22	2	68	29	1	323	42	4	85
	17+	23	2	205	28	1	268	38	5	78
41–45	9–12				30	4	117			
	13–16				32	2	181	36	4	67
	17+	21	2	122	31	2	163	37	5	67
46–50	9–12				25	3	71			
	13–16				40	4	91			
	17+	19	4	80	29	1	76			

Table 45. Accumulative Incidence: Dreams to Orgasm
By Parental Occupational Class

AGE	OCCUPATIONAL CLASS				OCCUPATIONAL CLASS			
	2+3	4	5	6+7	2+3	4	5	6+7
	Percent				Cases			
12	—	—	—	1	962	801	1504	2652
15	2	2	1	3	932	799	1501	2638
20	8	9	6	10	701	622	1120	1987
25	15	16	14	18	507	415	710	1208
30	21	23	21	26	375	310	496	900
35	27	23	30	33	265	196	339	686
40	29	20	30	38	172	118	202	465
45	33	35	33	40	107	71	116	280

The occupational classes are as follows: 2 + 3 = unskilled and semi skilled labor.
4 = skilled labor. 5 = lower white collar class. 6 + 7 = upper white collar and
professional classes.
Table based on total sample, including single, married, and previously married
females.

Table 46. Accumulative Incidence: Dreams to Orgasm
By Decade of Birth

AGE	DECADE OF BIRTH				DECADE OF BIRTH			
	Bf. 1900	1900–1909	1910–1919	1920–1929	Bf. 1900	1900–1909	1910–1919	1920–1929
	Percent				Cases			
12	1	1	—	1	446	769	1304	3057
15	3	2	2	2	446	769	1304	3043
20	9	8	8	9	446	769	1304	1772
25	15	13	17	17	446	769	1179	372
30	21	20	28		446	769	820	
35	25	30	37		446	747	271	
40	30	36			446	497		
45	35	42			431	139		

Total based on total sample, including single, married, and previously married
females.

**Table 47. Active Incidence and Percentage of Outlet: Dreams to Orgasm
By Parental Occupational Class and Marital Status**

AGE DURING ACTIVITY	PAREN-TAL CLASS	SINGLE			MARRIED		
		Active incid. %	% of total outlet	Cases in total sample	Active incid. %	% of total outlet	Cases in total sample
Adol.–15	2+3	2	2	947			
	4	2	1	796			
	5	1	2	1506			
	6+7	2	3	2654			
16–20	2+3	7	3	881	6	1	141
	4	7	2	796	12	2	86
	5	6	3	1512	7	—	150
	6+7	9	4	2649	12	2	225
21–25	2+3	10	4	461	15	2	309
	4	9	3	422	16	1	230
	5	9	2	735	11	1	425
	6+7	12	3	1283	16	1	732
26–30	2+3	13	3	194	18	2	307
	4	12	2	181	20	2	232
	5	14	3	275	19	1	408
	6+7	17	3	447	23	1	738
31–35	2+3	10	1	96	21	2	213
	4	22	5	91	24	3	177
	5	19	4	148	26	1	291
	6+7	22	3	224	30	2	572
36–40	2+3	10	1	62	27	2	134
	4				16	2	97
	5	24	3	85	25	2	208
	6+7	27	2	141	31	2	419
41–45	2+3				25	3	81
	4				27	2	63
	5				29	2	89
	6+7				33	2	261

The occupational classes are as follows: 2 + 3 = unskilled and semi-skilled labor. 4 = skilled labor. 5 = lower white collar class. 6 + 7 = upper white collar and professional classes.

Table 48. Active Incidence and Percentage of Outlet: Dreams to Orgasm
By Decade of Birth and Marital Status

AGE DURING ACTIVITY	DECADE OF BIRTH	SINGLE			MARRIED		
		Active incid. %	% of total outlet	Cases in total sample	Active incid. %	% of total outlet	Cases in total sample
Adol.–15	Bf. 1900	3	4	436			
	1900–1909	2	3	760			
	1910–1919	2	1	1319			
	1920–1929	2	3	3049			
16–20	Bf. 1900	8	5	451	8	7	61
	1900–1909	8	4	772	9	1	114
	1910–1919	8	2	1328	8	1	172
	1920–1929	8	4	2999	12	—	230
21–25	Bf. 1900	9	3	366	16	3	206
	1900–1909	12	3	617	12	1	377
	1910–1919	12	2	987	17	2	624
	1920–1929	8	3	843	15	1	447
26–30	Bf. 1900	14	2	218	17	2	272
	1900–1909	15	3	344	18	1	507
	1910–1919	16	2	448	24	2	731
	1920–1929	7	2	54	16	1	153
31–35	Bf. 1900	15	2	151	19	2	290
	1900–1909	21	3	228	27	2	509
	1910–1919	19	3	160	29	2	448
36–40	Bf. 1900	20	1	123	23	2	283
	1900–1909	22	2	165	29	2	464
	1910–1919				33	2	105
41–45	Bf. 1900	18	2	116	27	2	273
	1900–1909	19	4	63	35	2	224

Table 49. Accumulative Incidence: Dreams to Orgasm
By Age at Onset of Adolescence

AGE	ADOLESCENT					ADOLESCENT				
	By 11	At 12	At 13	At 14	At 15+	By 11	At 12	At 13	At 14	At 15+
	Percent					*Cases*				
12	1	—	—	0	1	1194	1654	1727	786	342
15	3	2	2	2	1	1176	1638	1716	782	342
20	10	9	8	6	7	868	1202	1303	639	277
25	19	16	15	14	14	507	731	839	459	228
30	28	22	23	22	23	351	483	646	364	190
35	36	28	28	28	32	248	319	467	277	152
40	43	28	31	33	32	150	197	293	189	114
45	44	34	35	36	39	92	110	173	119	75

Table based on total sample, including single, married, and previously married females.

Table 50. Accumulative Incidence: Dreams to Orgasm
By Rural-Urban Background

Age	Rural	Urban	Age	Rural	Urban	Age	Rural	Urban	Age	Rural	Urban
	Percent			*Percent*			*Cases*			*Cases*	
12	1	—	30	22	23	12	388	5143	30	163	1780
15	2	2	35	28	31	15	386	5103	35	120	1274
20	7	9	40	34	33	20	324	3823	40	82	816
25	15	16	45	39	36	25	214	2439	45	59	485

Table based on total sample, including single, married, and previously married females.

Table 51. Active Incidence and Percentage of Outlet: Dreams to Orgasm
By Rural-Urban Background

Age during activity	Back-grnd.	Active incid. %	% of total outlet	Cases in total sample	Age during activity	Back-grnd.	Active incid. %	% of total outlet	Cases in total sample
Adol.–15	Rural	2	3	388	26–30	Rural	13	3	104
	Urban	2	2	5132		Urban	15	2	915
16–20	Rural	5	2	386	31–35	Rural	16	2	64
	Urban	8	3	5080		Urban	19	3	453
21–25	Rural	10	3	229					
	Urban	11	3	2484					

Table based on single females only.

**Table 52. Active Incidence and Percentage of Outlet: Dreams to Orgasm
By Age at Onset of Adolescence and Marital Status**

AGE DURING ACTIVITY	AGE AT ADOL.	SINGLE			MARRIED		
		Active incid. %	% of total outlet	Cases in total sample	Active incid. %	% of total outlet	Cases in total sample
Adol.–15	8–11	3	3	1203			
	12	2	1	1684			
	13	2	2	1747			
	14	2	2	796			
	15+	1	8	262			
16–20	8–11	9	4	1166	12	1	139
	12	8	4	1638	12	1	153
	13	7	3	1700	6	—	169
	14	6	2	777	5	—	76
	15+	7	6	345			
21–25	8–11	11	3	526	16	1	333
	12	11	3	770	17	1	458
	13	11	2	851	14	1	487
	14	9	2	460	12	1	254
	15+	11	4	203	15	5	121
26–30	8–11	21	2	196	21	1	286
	12	13	2	266	19	1	426
	13	12	2	323	21	1	527
	14	16	4	192	19	1	275
	15+	16	4	87	24	3	147
31–35	8–11	23	3	99	29	2	185
	12	20	2	122	25	2	291
	13	14	2	162	26	1	415
	14	25	5	109	24	2	224
	15+				29	4	131
36–40	8–11	26	1	65	38	2	133
	12	18	1	66	24	2	187
	13	17	2	96	26	2	270
	14	34	4	62	26	1	168
	15+				31	4	93
41–45	8–11				32	3	78
	12				29	2	102
	13				29	2	144
	14				32	2	101
	15+				32	4	71

Table 53. Accumulative Incidence: Dreams to Orgasm
By Religious Background

AGE	PROTESTANT			CATHOLIC			JEWISH	
	Devout	Moderate	Inactive	Devout	Moderate	Inactive	Moderate	Inactive
Percent								
12	1	1	1	0	0	0	0	—
15	2	2	4	1	1	5	2	1
20	7	7	11	5	9	15	7	9
25	15	14	20	7	27	25	9	15
30	19	22	29	13	32	36	18	24
35	25	27	35	24		41	30	28
40	29	28	40					28
45	36	27	48					27
Cases								
12	1213	1158	1061	386	149	168	573	981
15	1196	1148	1053	381	147	168	572	977
20	905	915	950	280	110	143	332	688
25	556	584	724	173	74	104	187	411
30	416	433	544	121	50	77	136	292
35	332	313	414	75		51	77	203
40	233	210	272					125
45	150	131	152					74

Table based on total sample, including single, married, and previously married females.

Table 54. Active Incidence, Frequency, and Percentage of Outlet: Dreams to Orgasm
By Religious Background and Marital Status

AGE	RELIGIOUS GROUP	SINGLE				MARRIED			
		Active incid. %	Active median freq. per wk.	% of total outlet	Cases in total sample	Active incid. %	Active median freq. per wk.	% of total outlet	Cases in total sample
Adol.–15									
	Protestant								
	Devout	2	*0.19*	4	1218				
	Moderate	2	*0.08*	1	1147				
	Inactive	3	*0.07*	2	1063				
	Catholic								
	Devout	1		2	382				
	Moderate	1		—	150				
	Inactive	5		2	169				
	Jewish								
	Devout	1		—	107				
	Moderate	2		1	571				
	Inactive	1	*0.09*	1	978				

(*Table continued on next page*)

Table 54 (continued)

		SINGLE				MARRIED			
AGE	RELIGIOUS GROUP	Active incid. %	Active median freq. per wk.	% of total outlet	Cases in total sample	Active incid. %	Active median freq. per wk.	% of total outlet	Cases in total sample
16–20	Protestant								
	Devout	6	0.07	4	1197	12	0.26	3	92
	Moderate	6	0.07	2	1133	8		1	97
	Inactive	10	0.07	3	1065	8	0.09	1	139
	Catholic								
	Devout	4	0.07	2	372				
	Moderate	8	0.06	2	139				
	Inactive	14	0.10	4	160				
	Jewish								
	Devout	9		1	107				
	Moderate	6	0.06	3	571				
	Inactive	9	0.07	3	972	12	0.06	—	118
21–25	Protestant								
	Devout	8	0.07	4	604	16	0.08	2	318
	Moderate	9	0.06	2	615	14	0.07	2	309
	Inactive	16	0.07	2	676	17	0.07	1	392
	Catholic								
	Devout	7	0.06	3	196	9		1	86
	Moderate	7		4	57	21	0.08	1	53
	Inactive	19	0.09	4	91	18	0.08	1	67
	Jewish								
	Moderate	8	0.09	3	192	3		—	145
	Inactive	9	0.08	2	396	14	0.07	1	319
26–30	Protestant								
	Devout	11	0.06	2	221	19	0.07	2	331
	Moderate	14	0.07	3	249	18	0.07	2	336
	Inactive	18	0.06	2	309	25	0.07	2	413
	Catholic								
	Devout	9		7	79	15	0.10	1	84
	Inactive					41	0.08	2	58
	Jewish								
	Moderate					14	0.08	1	140
	Inactive	18	0.07	3	110	17	0.07	1	275
31–35	Protestant								
	Devout	13	0.07	2	121	23	0.07	1	264
	Moderate	18	0.08	4	127	22	0.08	2	253
	Inactive	25	0.06	2	159	34	0.08	2	315
	Catholic								
	Devout					22	0.08	2	63
	Jewish								
	Moderate					22	0.07	1	102
	Inactive	16		2	51	23	0.06	1	199
36–40	Protestant								
	Devout	16	0.07	2	76	26	0.07	2	200
	Moderate	14	0.07	2	77	25	0.08	3	175
	Inactive	29	0.06	2	102	35	0.07	2	232
	Jewish								
	Moderate					24	0.06	1	58
	Inactive					22	0.07	1	132
41–45	Protestant								
	Devout					31	0.07	2	125
	Moderate					23	0.08	3	110
	Inactive					41	0.07	2	128
	Jewish								
	Inactive					22	0.08	2	79
46–50	Protestant								
	Devout					35	0.07	6	72
	Moderate					27	0.06	2	52
	Inactive					47	0.06	2	62

Table 55. Content of Nocturnal Sex Dreams

Percentage with experience prior to interview

CONTENT	DREAMS WITHOUT ORGASM				DREAMS WITH ORGASM			
	Total sample	Educational level			Total sample	Educational level		
		9–12	13–16	17+		9–12	13–16	17+
	%	Percent			%	Percent		
Heterosexual:								
Any kind	90	90	91	89	85	87	85	80
Coitus	30	44	26	28	39	48	38	31
Petting	38	41	38	32	17	24	19	11
Other	39	31	40	43	39	34	40	42
Homosexual	8	6	7	12	10	8	8	13
Animal contacts	1	1	1	1	1	1	1	2
Sado-masochistic	2	2	1	2	1	2	1	1
Pregnancy or child-birth	3	5	3	4	1	1	1	1
Other content	3	3	3	3	4	4	3	6
Not specified	6	5	6	6	9	9	9	11
Number of cases	2957	500	1749	601	1146	251	515	332

The totals of the various types of dreams always exceed 100 per cent because some individuals dream of more than one type of experience. Some individuals appear in both portions of the table, dreaming sometimes with and sometimes without orgasm.

Chapter 7

PRE-MARITAL PETTING

Sexual activities may be solitary, involving only the single individual, or they may be socio-sexual, involving two or more individuals. Masturbation (Chapter 5) and nocturnal dreams (Chapter 6) are the two chief types of solitary sexual activity. To judge on the basis of our sample, these solitary activities may provide about a quarter of the orgasms which females have (Table 170, Figure 109). Heterosexual petting, heterosexual coitus, and homosexual relationships are the three main types of socio-sexual activity. They may provide about three-quarters of the orgasms which females in the American population have; and because of their social significance, the socio-sexual outlets are more important than their frequencies might indicate. The interplay of stimulation and response which characterizes a socio-sexual relationship may make it of maximum significance for each of the partners, and give rise to situations which affect more than the immediate participants in the relationship. They may have, in consequence, considerable social significance.

DEFINITION

Sexual relationships between individuals of the same sex are homosexual; sexual relationships between individuals of opposite sexes are heterosexual. A heterosexual relationship which involves a union of female and male genitalia is identified as coitus. Physical contacts between females and males which do not involve a union of the genitalia of the two sexes constitute the socio-sexual behavior which American youth have come to know as necking or petting. Pre-marital petting is widespread among nearly all females and males of the younger generation in this country today, and not infrequent among many older unmarried persons.

In both pre-marital and marital histories, petting may provide a preliminary to actual coitus, but in the pre-marital histories of many American females and males it often serves as an end in itself. It may be sought for the sake of the immediate satisfactions which it can bring, and it may serve as a substitute for coitus. While pre-marital petting is often enough criticized by moral preceptors, it is not so severely condemned as pre-marital coitus, and petting is accepted by many females and males in order to avoid coitus. Moreover, it is not

always convenient to have coitus, while petting, as the younger generation takes it, may occur at almost any time and almost anywhere.
Coitus also introduces the possibility of a pregnancy; petting involves
no such problem. Moreover, in a social group in which petting is customary behavior, as, for instance, among most high school and college
students, petting may be accepted because of the social prestige which
it carries and because of the dancing, drinking, auto rides, and other
social activities which may precede or accompany it.[1]

The term petting is properly confined to physical contacts which
involve a deliberate attempt to effect erotic arousal.[2] Most females and
males who engage in petting frankly recognize its significance as a
source of erotic satisfaction. Accidental contacts do not constitute petting, even though they may be responsible for some erotic arousal.
While petting may not always result in arousal, we have considered
that the term was applicable if there was an attempt to achieve arousal,
and have so interpreted the records in making the calculations which
are presented in this chapter.

Distinctions between necking and petting, mild and heavy petting,
and still other classifications which are current among American youth,
appear to differentiate nothing more than various techniques, or the
parts of the body which are involved in the contacts, or the level of
the arousal which is effected. In the calculations in the present chapter,
all of these types of pre-marital petting have been included.

Some sort of petting almost invariably precedes coitus in marriage,
and not infrequently married spouses may engage in petting which
does not lead to coitus. There is also some extra-marital petting between married females and males who are not spouses, but none of this
marital or extra-marital petting is covered by the present chapter.

PHYLOGENETIC ORIGINS

Petting is not confined to adult human animals. Similar non-coital
contacts occur among mammals and among children of the human
species (Chapter 4) where such activity is usually identified as *sex*

---

[1] Reasons for petting are also discussed in: Smith 1924:349 (of 171 Purdue University females, 52 per cent cite infatuation, 40 per cent curiosity, 30 per
cent imitation, and 35 per cent various other reasons). Lynd and Lynd 1929:
139 (48 per cent of 159 high school girls petted for a good time, 36 per cent
because they feared unpopularity). Butterfield 1939:51–52 (lists admiration,
erotic gratification, curiosity, gratifying companion). Priester 1941:79 (51
high school girls). German studies emphasize that fear of pregnancy leads
to use of petting as a substitute for coitus: Adler 1911:164. Eberhard 1924:
433. Hirschfeld 1928:172. Hoyer 1929:68. For Russian data, see Schbankov
acc. Weissenberg 1924a:13.

[2] Definitions emphasizing the acceptance of all techniques except genital union
are, for instance, in: Forel 1905:93. Havelock Ellis 1936(II,3):518. Kahn
1937:163. Bromley and Britten 1938:141. Clark 1949:54.

play. While the specific activities involved in such play may be quite the same as those which are characterized as petting when they occur among adults, the adult human behavior differs in its more conscious pursuit of erotic satisfactions.

Among most species of mammals there is, in actuality, a great deal of sex play which never leads to coitus.[3] Most mammals, when sexually aroused, crowd together and nuzzle and explore with their noses, mouths, and feet over each other's bodies. They make lip-to-lip contacts and tongue-to-tongue contacts, and use their mouths to manipulate every part of the companion's body, including the genitalia. They may nip, bite, scratch, groom, pull at the fur of the other animal, pull out fur, urinate, and repeatedly mount without, however, making any serious attempt to effect a genital union. Such activity may contine for a matter of minutes, or hours, or even in some cases for days before there is any attempt at coitus. The student of mammalian mating behavior, interested in observing coitus in his animal stocks, sometimes may have to wait through hours and days of sex play before he has an opportunity to observe actual coitus, if, indeed, the animals do not finally separate without ever attempting a genital union.

Extensive sex play has been observed in such widely diverse mammals as cattle, horses, hogs, sheep, cats, lions, dogs, raccoon, rats, mice, guinea pigs, chinchillas, hamsters, porcupines, rabbits, mink, sable, ferrets, skunks, otter, monkeys, chimpanzees, and still other species. A wide variety of petting techniques is employed by many of these. There are few situations or techniques in human petting behavior which are not widespread among the other mammals.

Some individuals among the infra-human species may proceed quite directly to coitus whenever they find an acceptant partner. Other individuals may be more inclined to prolong their pre-coital activities. Some individuals rarely arrive at coitus at all, even though they may engage in a great deal of non-coital play. In these respects, all of the

---

[3] Significant studies and bibliographies on non-coital sex play among infra-human mammals include the following: Bölsche 1926(2):177. Jenkins in Warden 1931 (58 out of 79 rats pursued and licked females but failed to copulate). Zuckerman 1932:237. Young 1941 (an excellent survey and bibliography). Shadle, Smelzer, and Metz 1946 (porcupine). Reed 1946. Beach in Hoch and Zubin 1949. Hafez 1951. Ford and Beach 1951:42, 58, 66, *et passim.*
We are indebted especially to Frank Beach, Robert Bean, director of The Brookfield Zoo in Chicago, Robert Enders, Karl Lashley, Fred McKenzie, Henry Nissen, Albert Shadle, William Young, and a number of other students of mammalian sexual behavior for many of these data. Much of the material presented here is based on our study of the several thousand feet of moving picture film which we have made or acquired from other laboratories. Our own observations on non-coital sex play cover the baboon, chimpanzee, monkey, dog, chinchilla, hamster, rat, guinea pig, rabbit, porcupine, raccoon, cat, mare, cow, sheep, sow, and skunk.

variations in human petting behavior are matched by similar variations among the lower mammals.

Just as in the human animal, and even more often than in the human animal, petting among the other mammals is primarily, although not exclusively, male activity which is directed toward the female. As in the human species, it is the male which is more likely to be aroused psychologically and usually before he makes any physical contact. It is the male among most of the mammals which does most of the crowding, exploring, nipping, and biting, and which initiates most of the mouth-genital contacts.

Just as in the human species, it is the male among practically all of the mammals which initiates the ultimate genital union. Most of the females, however, reciprocate if they are in estrus or heat, i.e., at that state in the reproductive cycle when they are most responsive sexually, and the females of some species may then initiate petting and coital activities, and may even become quite aggressive, just as among some human females.

Just as in the human male, the non-coital sex play among other mammals may sometimes lead to ejaculation before coitus has been effected or even attempted; but there is no clear-cut evidence that the infrahuman female ever reaches orgasm in her non-coital sexual activities.

The anatomy of the human animal, particularly his hands, may allow him to utilize a wider variety of techniques than most other mammals can use, and the human activity may be more consciously planned, deliberately elaborated, and expertly prolonged. But it is obvious that the human animal behaves like the mammal which it is when it engages in petting before it begins coitus.

The wide distribution of non-coital sex play among all of the mammalian species on which there are sufficient data is evidence of the ancient origins of the anatomic and physiologic bases of such behavior some millions of years ago in the ancestral stocks of the class Mammalia. Indeed, some of the basic capacities on which petting behavior depends must have originated hundreds of millions of years ago among the ancient vertebrate stocks which gave rise to the Mammalia; for sensory satisfactions obtained from the crowding together of animal bodies, from tongue-to-tongue contacts, and from mouth contacts with other parts of the partner's body, are also evident in the behavior of some of the other vertebrates, including the lizards, still other reptiles, and the birds.[4] In a biologic sense, petting is a normal or natural sort

---

[4] For instances of tactile response in lower vertebrates, see: Bölsche 1926(2):177. Beach 1948:5. Ford and Beach 1951:58.

of behavior, and not the intellectually contrived perversion which it has sometimes been considered. In a biologic sense, the real perversion is the inhibition and suppression of such activities on the supposition that they represent "acts contrary to nature."

HISTORICAL OCCURRENCE

Many persons who are ignorant of the ancient mammalian origins of the phenomenon consider petting an invention of modern American youth—the product of an effete and morally degenerate, over-industrialized and over-educated, urban culture. It is taken by some to reflect the sort of moral bankruptcy which must lead to the collapse of any civilization.[5]

Older generations did, however, engage in flirting, flirtage, courting, bundling, spooning, mugging, smooching, larking, sparking, and other activities which were simply petting under another name.[6] The ancient origins of the extensive vocabulary by which the various techniques of petting have been designated provide some evidence that a considerable amount of such activity occurred in previous centuries of human history. A more specific record is supplied by the descriptive literature on human sexual relations. From the earliest art and writings in Sanskrit, Chinese, and Japanese literature, down through Greek and Roman history, and on through the earlier Arabic and European literature dealing with love and courting, all of the petting techniques known to modern generations are explicitly described.[7] The Mochican

---

[5] As examples of petting interpreted as moral bankruptcy, see: Hoyer 1929:64 (The demi-vierge represents the acme of sexual demoralization. She knows all shades of sex pleasure without having lost her virginity). Englisch 1931: 431 (The demi-vierge is vicious in body and soul). Lowry 1938:53–57 (the first kiss leads to intercourse and subsequent downfall. "If the young women of America only knew how lightly they are esteemed by those who so passionately seek their favors in this manner [*i.e.*, petting], they would certainly resist them if the effort cost them their lives").

[6] The many alternative and in many instances very old terms for petting may be found, for instance, in: Farmer and Henley 1890–1904 (see under toy, dally, play, spoon, etc.). Cary (1916?)1948. Justinian 1939. Niemoeller 1935.

[7] The ancient standing of all the non-coital petting techniques known to modern youth is detailed in the following rich and honorable literature: Pritchard 1950:39–40, 142, 496 (ancient Near Eastern documents dating back to the second millennium B.C.). The Ananga-Ranga [12th cent. A.D.?, Sanskrit], 1935:39–46, 165–189. Anon., Marriage—Love and Woman Amongst the Arabs otherwise entitled The Book of Exposition [orig. date?], 1896:10, 31, 59, 141. The Kama Sutra of Vatsyayana [between 1st and 6th cent. A.D., Sanskrit], 1883–1925:37–49, 61–63, 74–77, 110. Nefzawi: The Perfumed Garden [6th cent. A.D., Islamic], Librairie "Astra," n.d.:8, 53–54, 57, 76–79. Stern: The Scented Garden 1933:248–250 [Islamic]. Azama Otoko: Ikkyu Zenshi Shoshoku Monogatari [c. 1845, Japanese], Book I. Hikatsu-sho (Book of Secrets) [c. 1845, Japanese]. Jiiro Haya-shinan [c. 1850, Japanese]. Takara Bunko [c. 1885, Japanese], II (The Lower Part); III (The Upper Part); III (The Lower Part). Bible: The Song of Songs 1:2; 2:6; 4:11; 7:7–9; 8:3. Ezekiel 23:3. Proverbs 5:19–20. Aristophanes [5th–4th cent. B.C., Greek]: The Clouds, 51 (1912(1):307; 1924(1):271); The Knights, 1282–1289 (1912 (1):89–90; 1924(1):247); Peace, 863 (1912(1):201; 1924(2):79); 885

pottery of ancient Peru, which dates somewhere between 700 B.C. and 300 A.D., depicts practically every petting and coital technique known to modern youth. The condemnation in Judeo-Christian and other religious codes of sexual activities which are not coital or which do not serve as a preliminary to coitus, is sufficient evidence that there was petting behavior to be condemned when the codes were first originated.

Travelers' tales and anthropologists' reports on the customs of more primitive, pre-literate cultures provide a similar record of the world-wide occurrence of petting behavior. For one or another primitive group, the records include every conceivable form of non-coital sexual manipulation and contact. The independent but parallel development of such similar patterns in these widely scattered races is, again, further evidence of their phylogenetic origins in anatomic and physiologic characteristics which must have been part of the heritage of the ancient ancestors of all mankind.

If there is anything unique in the pre-marital petting behavior of American youth, it cannot be in its occurrence or in the techniques which are employed. If there is anything unique, it must be in the

(1912(1):203; 1924(2):81); Plutus, 1067–1068 (1912(2):459; 1924(3): 455); The Wasps, 737–740 (1912(2):41; 1924(1):481–483); 1341–1346 (1912(2):70–71; 1924(1):535). Theocritus [3rd cent. B.C., Greek]: II. 126 (1912:37); V. 132–133 (1912:79); XX. 1–5 (1912:239); XXVII. 49–51 (1912:341). Plautus [3rd–2nd cent. B.C., Roman]: Comedy of Asses, 891–892 (1916(1):221). Catullus [1st cent. B.C., Roman]: VIII. 18(1894:15; 1913: 11); LVIII (1894:100; 1913:67); LIX (1894:101; 1913:66). Virgil [1st cent. B.C., Roman]: Aeneid, VIII. 387–388 (1918(2):87). Horace [1st cent. B.C., Roman]: Epodes, VIII. 19–20(1914:416). Propertius [1st cent. B.C., Roman]: III. 6(1895:45). Tibullus [1st. cent. B.C., Roman]: I. 8. 25–26, 35–38 (1913:234). Priapeia 84:24–25 [attributed to Catullus?—1st cent. B.C., Roman] (1888:90). Ovid [1st cent. B.C., Roman]: Amores, I. 5.13–25(1921:335; May 1930:10); II. 5.23–26(1921:395; May 1930:40); II. 5.51–62(1921:397; May 1930:41); III. 7.7–10(1921:506; Young and Marlowe 1930:188); III. 7.73–74(1921:508; Young and Marlowe 1930:190); III. 14.21–26(1921:500; May 1930:92). Art of Love, II. 703–724(1929:115; May 1930:147–148). The Greek Anthology XI. 73 [1st cent. A.D.] (1918(4):107). Petronius [1st cent. A.D., Roman]: Satyricon, 127(1913:285; 1922(2):312–313); 131–132 (1913:293; 1922(2):323). Martial [1st cent. A.D., Roman]: VI. 23(1919(1): 370; 1921:153–154); XI. 29(1920(2):261; 1921:309–310); XI. 104 (1920 (2):310; 1921:329); XIV. 134(1920(2):486; 1921:400). Apuleius [2nd cent. A.D., Roman]: The Golden Ass, II. 10(1915:65; 1822:29; 1923:36). Longus [3rd cent. A.D.?, Greek]: Daphnis and Chloe, II. 9–11(1916:81–83; 1896:40– 41); III. 13(1916:149; 1896:84); III. 20(1916:157; 1896:91). The Greek Anthology [6th cent. A.D.] The Amatory Epigrams: 1916, No. 14, 21–22; No. 272, 117–118; No. 294, 129.
For references to older European and American Colonial customs see: Anon., The Fifteen Plagues . . . , 1707:6, 7 (England). Stiles 1869:14–35 (bundling). Fuchs 1912:276–278 (love courts in Russia). Bauer 1924:288 ff. (notes medieval, Hindu, German, and Swiss custom). Hoyer 1929:64 (Middle Ages, courtly love). Bloch acc. Marcuse 1924:144. Wikman 1937:223 ff. (European folk custom). Aurand 1938a, 1938b cites Naomi and Boaz (Ruth 3:6–14) as an early example of bundling, and describes survival of custom in early Amish communities in Pennsylvania.

incidences or in the frequencies of petting in this country, or in the significance of its position in the total pattern of American sexual behavior, or in the frankness with which such activity is accepted by modern American youth.

Although we will never be able to secure anything more than the most general idea of the incidences and frequencies of pre-marital petting in the United States prior to the turn of the present century, it probably occurred in an appreciable portion of the histories of earlier generations. The females in our sample who were born in the decade or so just before 1900, who belonged to a generation which by and large considered itself proper and sexually restrained, had some sort

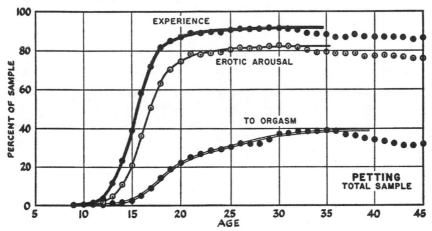

Figure 29. Accumulative incidence: petting experience, arousal, and orgasm

Each dot indicates percent of sample with experience, arousal, or orgasm by the indicated age. Data from Table 56.

of petting in about 80 per cent of their histories (Table 65). Even at that time petting must have been the most widespread type of pre-marital heterosexual activity (p. 243).

RELATION TO AGE

Accumulative Incidence. Approximately 40 per cent of the females in our sample had had heterosexual petting experience by fifteen years of age, which is near the average age at the beginning of the second year in high school. Between 69 and 95 per cent had had such experience by eighteen years of age, which is at about the end of high school. About 90 per cent of the entire sample, and nearly 100 per cent of those who had married, had had some sort of petting experience prior to marriage (Tables 56, 61, 62, Figures 29, 33, 34).[8]

---

[8] Previously published incidence data, not always distinguishable as incidence of experience or incidence of orgasm, are included in: Fuchs 1912:274. Schban-

However, only about 80 per cent of the total sample had ever become erotically aroused in the course of their petting experience. Some 97 per cent of those who had married had become erotically aroused in their petting. Some 39 per cent of the sample had responded to the point of orgasm on at least some occasion in the course of their experience (Tables 56, 61, Figures 29, 33).[9]

Active Incidence. Some sort of petting experience, whether with or without orgasm, had been had by a considerable proportion of the still unmarried females in the sample, in each and every age group (Figure 30). The active incidences were as follows:

AGE	% HAVING EXPERIENCE	AGE	% HAVING EXPERIENCE
Adol.–15	39	26–30	83
16–20	88	31–35	78
21–25	88	36–40	70

Petting had been carried to the point of orgasm by only 3 per cent of the females in the sample when they were between adolescence and fifteen years of age, but by as many as 23 per cent during their late teens (Table 57, Figure 31). About a third (31 to 32 per cent) of the unmarried females were reaching orgasm, at least on occasion, during their twenties and early thirties. After that the active incidences of those who were petting to orgasm began to drop until they included only 7 per cent of the females who were still unmarried in their late fifties.

While petting is clearly an activity of younger ages, it is not certain that the decrease in later years is due to biologic or psychologic aging. It is not clear that aging factors appear in the sexual history of the human female until she has passed fifty or even sixty years of age (p. 518). It is more likely that the lower figures for the older groups de-

---

kov acc. Weissenberg 1924a:13 (28 per cent of 324 Russian female students did petting, 7 per cent to orgasm). Smith 1924:348 (171 Purdue University females, median age of first petting 16–17). Golossowker acc. Weissenberg 1925:175 (Russian study of 550 female students, 77 per cent petting, 19 per cent heavy petting, half by age 17). Lynd and Lynd 1929:139 (78 per cent of 205 high school students). Davis 1929:60 (60 per cent of 972 females before marriage). Terman 1938:256 (67 per cent of 772 women had petted in high school). Landis et al. 1940:290 (100 per cent of 153 normal females, 80 per cent of 142 psychotics). Priester 1941:78. Landis and Bolles 1942:25 (63 per cent of handicapped females). Lederer acc. P. H. Landis 1945:263 (40 per cent petting at 12–15 years, 67 per cent between 16–18 years). Asayama 1949:131 (Japanese). England acc. Rosenthal 1951:59 (51 per cent of middle class British females). Wolman 1951:545 (49 per cent Israeli females by age 16). See also footnote 13.

[9] It is recognized in the following references that orgasm can occur in petting, although no specific data are given: Forel 1905:90. Talmey 1910:65. Long 1922:113, 123. Robie 1925:100, 102. Bauer 1929:254. Blanchard and Manasses 1930:60. Dickinson and Beam 1931:321. Dickinson and Beam 1934:135, 145. Havelock Ellis 1936(II,3):519. Bromley and Britten 1938:141. English in Fishbein and Burgess 1947:110.

pend primarily on the fact that they were born before the turn of the century and, as we shall record (p. 243), fewer of the females of that generation did any petting to orgasm (Table 65, Figure 36). Moreover, the girl who does not engage in petting because she considers it morally wrong, or does not engage because she is not attracted by males, or is not attractive to males, is the one who is most likely to remain unmarried at the older ages.[10] As she gets older, the number of unmarried males who are of her own age is sharply reduced; and she has little opportunity to do petting with younger males because many of them are

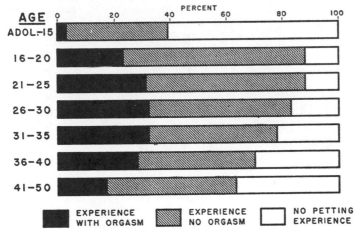

Figure 30. Active incidence: petting experience and orgasm, by age

Data from Table 57 and p. 234.

not interested in older females. Moreover, a quarter of the older unmarried males may be predominantly homosexual (our 1948:258–259). Finally, the unmarried, older males who are interested in heterosexual relations can secure coitus, and they are not likely to be interested in petting or even dating with females who will not accept coitus. It is a selective factor, rather than biologic aging, which accounts for the lowered incidences in the older age groups.

Frequency of Experience. We do not have records of the frequencies of the total petting experience of the females in the sample, although we do have specific data on the frequencies with which they engaged in petting which led to orgasm. There are gradations between merely social and socio-sexual contacts; and it has proved difficult for the subjects contributing to the present study to indicate how frequently their contacts were specifically erotic except when they had led to orgasm.

---

[10] Other students who have noted that restraints on petting may prove a handicap to marriage include: Fuchs 1912:273. Dickinson and Beam 1934:117.

Moreover, because petting often occurs sporadically, with several contacts in a week or even in a single afternoon or evening, and then possibly none for months at a stretch, it has proved too difficult for most of the subjects to estimate average frequencies, except for the petting which led to orgasm. Only a considerable series of day-by-day calendars could have supplied adequate data on this point.

For these reasons, we have had to be satisfied with rough estimates of the frequencies of petting experience. We have taken into account

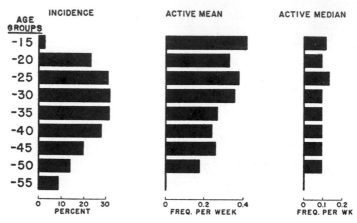

Figure 31. Active incidence, mean, median: petting to orgasm, by age
Data from Table 57.

the fact that some girls may date almost every night over a period of some weeks or months or even years, while others may go for many months between dates. Very few of them, however, even among the socially most limited groups, go for a year without at least some dates. Some females do some petting on practically every date. Others do petting on only a small portion of their dates. Many girls attend dances or other social activities where they may become involved in petting with several different males in a single evening. In many cases the petting is limited to simple kisses and caresses; in other cases it quickly turns to those techniques which are specifically calculated to bring sexual arousal and possibly orgasm. In any computation of averages, a week's record from a single one of the more active histories would balance the weeks and months of inactivity in the histories of some of the other females.

Taking these matters into account, it is our impression that the average frequencies of petting among unmarried females between the ages of fifteen and thirty-five (which is the period when the active incidences are at their highest) may range from about once in a week to once in a month. They may average once in two weeks for the typical female.[11] Even though these estimates may be considerably removed from the reality, they may prove useful when considered in connection with some other data.

Frequency of Orgasm. We have more specific data on the frequencies of orgasm achieved during petting. Consequently all of the *frequency* data in the remainder of the present chapter represent the frequencies of petting to the point of orgasm.

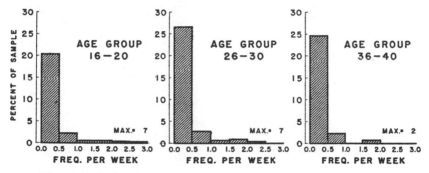

Figure 32. Individual variation: frequency of petting to orgasm

For three age groups. Each class interval includes the upper but not the lower frequency. For incidences of females not petting or reaching orgasm in petting, see Table 57.

The active median frequencies of petting to orgasm among the females in the sample were remarkably uniform in all groups between adolescence and fifty years of age (Table 57, Figure 31). They ranged from about 4 to 6 times per year (0.09 to 0.13 times per week). There was a slight decrease in the median frequencies from 0.11 per week at age fifteen to 0.09 per week at age fifty. It is possible, again, that the older, unmarried females were the less responsive individuals, and a selective factor rather than any biologic aging may have been involved.

Individual Variation in Frequency. There was, of course, marked variation in the frequencies among the individuals in any single group (Figure 32). Most of the females (61 per cent) had never experienced orgasm from pre-marital petting, some had not had such experience more than a single time before marriage, others had averaged as many as 7 to 10 orgasms per week for five or ten years or more before marriage. Most of the higher frequencies came from females who were capable of multiple orgasm (p. 375, Table 177).

---

[11] The only frequencies given in the literature are in very general terms, as in: Schbankov acc. Weissenberg 1924a:13 (very frequent, sometimes daily). Terman 1938:255–256 (recorded as very frequent, sometimes, rarely, etc.). Ehrmann 1952 (median frequencies of dating given as 16.9 per month; offers data for calculating petting frequencies).

Percentage of Total Outlet. Although petting had been the most widespread of all sexual activities among the single females in the sample, it had not been so often carried through to orgasm. Both masturbation and coitus had provided a larger proportion of the total number of orgasms which the females had experienced prior to marriage (Table 171).

Petting had accounted for only a small proportion (4 per cent) of the total outlet of the younger adolescent girls in the sample (Table 57). In the late teens and early twenties the importance of petting had increased; it had then provided about 18 per cent of the orgasms. In the late teens petting had been the most significant of the socio-sexual relations, but by the twenties it had been surpassed by pre-marital coitus as a source of heterosexual outlet (Table 171). After the middle twenties, the petting had become less and less significant. By age forty, only 5 per cent of the outlet of the females who were still single had come from petting and only 3 per cent by age fifty. Masturbation and coitus, between them, had provided 75 to 90 per cent of the orgasms of the older, unmarried females (Table 171).

Number of Years Involved. Basing the calculations on the females in the sample who were married and who, therefore, had completed their pre-marital experience, the record shows that 8 per cent had confined their petting to a single year or part of a year before marriage (Table 59). This seems to have been more often true of the girls who had never gone beyond grade school, but less often true of the females of the upper educational levels. Some 15 per cent of the females in the sample had done petting for two to three years before marriage, 23 per cent for four or five years, and nearly 40 per cent of the whole sample for something between six and ten years, inclusive. The median female had done petting for six or seven (6.6) years.

However, it is clear that the number of years, as well as the number of partners involved in pre-marital petting (p. 239), depends on the age at which the female marries, and therefore on the number of years that elapse between the high school age at which most females begin petting and the time of marriage. For instance, among the females who had not married until after thirty years of age, nearly three-quarters (73 per cent) had done pre-marital petting for eleven or more years.

Number of Partners. A considerable proportion of all the females in the sample had begun their petting while they were in the last two or three years of high school (Table 56, Figure 29), and it was at that period that most of them had had the greatest number of male partners per year. While the absolute number had actually increased after high school, this was due to the fact that a smaller number of high school years was involved, and a greater number of years between high school and marriage.

Basing the data on reports from females who were married and who, therefore, had completed their pre-marital histories, the records show that 10 per cent had confined themselves to a single petting partner before marriage (Table 60). About a third (32 per cent) had done petting with two to five males before they had married. Another quarter (23 per cent) had engaged in petting with six to ten males. Over a third (35 per cent) had engaged in petting with more than ten different males before marriage, and in a few instances with as many as a hundred or more. Nothing approaching this promiscuity in petting ever enters the female's history of pre-marital coitus (Table 78). But even among the most promiscuous females, there may be a restriction of petting activities to a single partner or two in the year or so which immediately precedes marriage.[12]

RELATION TO AGE AT MARRIAGE AND EDUCATIONAL LEVEL

Incidence. Simple correlations with the educational levels of the females in the sample suggest that there are slight differences in the accumulative incidences of petting experience in the grade school, high school, college, and graduate samples (Table 56). The differences appear to have been still more marked in the incidences of erotic responses to petting and in the incidences of petting to the point of orgasm.[13]

On the other hand, these differences prove to be primarily dependent upon the fact that females of the upper educational levels marry at later ages. For instance, by twenty years of age, marriage had occurred among 33 per cent of the grade school sample, 25 per cent of the high school sample, 13 per cent of the college sample, but only 6 per cent of the graduate group (Table 166). If the data for petting or pre-marital coitus (Chapter 8), are reexamined in terms of the ages at which the females had married, we find that almost exactly the same percentages in each educational level had done petting and petting to the point of orgasm before marriage (Table 62, Figures 33,

---

[12] Other data on number of partners in petting are in: Davis 1929:60 (of 583 married females who reported petting activity, 36 per cent petted with fiancé only). Daly 1951:150 (for high school females, estimates 4 to 50 partners, averaging 10).

[13] The following studies report the petting activities of females of the college level: Smith 1924:348 (171 females, 92 per cent petting incidence). Ehrmann 1952 (of 263 college females who dated, 98 per cent did petting). Gilbert Youth Research 1951:15 (96 per cent incidence). It is not clear what sort of petting was covered by the data in Bromley and Britten 1938:97. For the male data, see our 1948:534–537.

34). The apparent differences in patterns of petting in the several educational levels seem to depend upon these differences in the average
ages of marriage in each group. For instance, by eighteen years of age,
among the girls who married by the time they were twenty, some 94
per cent of the high school group, 97 per cent of the college group, and
93 per cent of the graduate group had had petting experience. Among
those who had married between twenty-one and twenty-five years of
age, similar incidences did not develop until the females were twenty
years of age (Table 62, Figures 33, 34). Either girls do not begin their
petting until a more or less uniform number of years before marriage,
or else a certain number of years of petting activity contributes to the
consummation of a marriage.

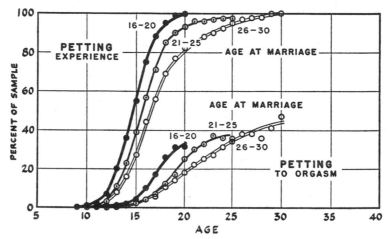

**Figure 33. Accumulative incidence: petting experience and orgasm, by age
at marriage**

Data from Table 61.

It will be recalled that we found (1948:377–381, 535–537) that
there were pronounced differences in the petting histories of males of
the different educational levels represented in the sample. For instance,
we found that petting to orgasm had occurred among 59 per cent of
the college males but in no more than 30 per cent of the high school
males and 16 per cent of the grade school males. While these figures
should also be corrected for differences in the average age of marriage
in these several groups, recalculations show that such corrections do
not account for more than a small proportion of the differences in the
petting records of the males of the different groups. On this point,
males seem to be more specifically controlled by the attitudes of the
social groups in which they are raised, and females are less often
controlled by the group attitudes. This is one of the most significant

differences between females and males (Chapter 16, especially p. 685).

In the sample, a distinctly smaller group of the females who had gone on into graduate work after college had ever married (Table 166). By forty-five years of age, when 91 per cent of the high school and 90 per cent of the college groups had married, only 59 per cent of the graduate group had married. In consequence, it is not surprising to find that the accumulative incidence of petting among females of the graduate group had never risen to the levels reached by the other educational levels.

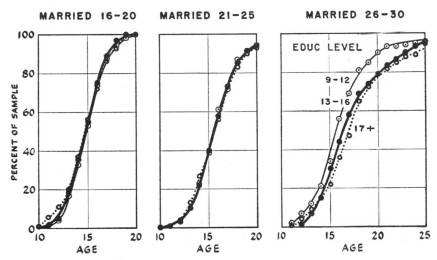

Figure 34. Accumulative incidence: petting experience, by age at marriage and educational level

Educational levels are not designated on first two curves because of near identity of data. Data from Table 62.

Frequency of Petting to Orgasm. However, the average (median) frequencies of petting to the point of orgasm were remarkably uniform for the females of all the educational levels represented in the sample (Table 58). Among those who had ever done any petting, the frequencies averaged about once in five to ten weeks (5 to 10 times per year), irrespective of the educational background. As in many other sexual activities, whatever effects the educational background, the generation in which the female was born, the religious background, or other social factors may have had in delaying the female's initial experience, they had disappeared as soon as she actually began petting.

Percentage of Total Outlet. If allowances are made for the differences in the age at marriage, there is no clear-cut distinction between the groups in regard to the extent to which their petting had contributed to their total sexual outlets (Table 58). For the sample as a whole, some 3 to 8 per cent of the total outlet had been derived from petting to orgasm between the ages of adolescence and fifteen, and some 18 per cent, more or less, in the late teens and early twenties. But at older ages, only a smaller proportion of the total sexual outlet had been derived from this type of sexual activity—amounting to not more than 4 to 5 per cent for those females who were still unmarried by the age of forty (Table 58).

RELATION TO PARENTAL OCCUPATIONAL CLASS

The social levels (occupational classes) of the parental homes in which the females in the sample had been raised seem to have had little effect on their petting behavior. The number of females in the sample who had ever had any sort of pre-marital petting experience—the **accumulative incidence** figure—was approximately 90 per cent, irrespective of whether the females had originated in laborers' homes, in homes of skilled mechanics, of white collar workers, or of business and professional men (Table 63). The accumulative incidence curves for the females who had done petting to the point of orgasm show only slightly greater differences, with the incidences after age eighteen only a bit higher for those who came from white collar homes (Table 63).

Similarly, the **active incidence**—the number of females who engaged in petting to the point of orgasm within any five-year period—seems to have been affected to only a minor extent by the social levels of the homes in which the females were raised (Table 64). A few more of those from white collar homes had engaged in petting which had led to orgasm in a given age period; but the differences were not great.

The **frequency** with which the average (active median) female in the sample had done petting to the point of orgasm did not show any consistent correlation with the occupational class of the home in which she had been raised.

Similarly, there does not seem to have been any consistent correlation between the home background and the **percentage of the total outlet** which these several groups had derived from petting (Table 64).

RELATION TO DECADE OF BIRTH

Although pre-marital petting of some sort certainly existed among American females of earlier decades and centuries in our history, it became more widely spread among those who were born after 1900, and its incidence has steadily increased down to the present day. This is one of the most clear-cut instances of social factors affecting the female's sexual behavior.

Accumulative Incidence. By thirty-five years of age, 80 per cent of the females in the sample who were born in the decade before 1900 had had some sort of pre-marital petting experience (Table 65, Figure 35). Of the females who were born in the first decade after 1900, 91 per cent had had pre-marital petting experience by that same age. Of those who were born in the next two decades (1910 to 1929), nearly 99 per cent had had experience. In this younger generation, only one out of a hundred of the females who were still unmarried by

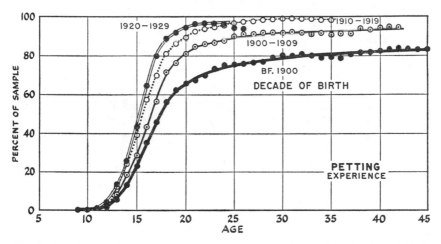

Figure 35. Accumulative incidence: petting experience, by decade of birth

Data from Table 65.

age thirty-five had failed to become involved in some sort of hetero-sexual petting. It was one out of every five of the females who were born before 1900.[14]

By age thirty-five, some 26 per cent of the females born before 1900 had done petting to the point of orgasm (Table 65, Figure 36). Of those born in the first decade after 1900, some 44 per cent had had such experience by that same age, and 53 per cent of those born in the next decade.

The younger generation had begun its petting at distinctly younger ages (Table 65, Figure 35). The females in the sample who were born before 1900 were 18 years of age before half of them had had experience; in the youngest generation, half of the girls had done petting

---

[14] Terman 1938:257 finds petting more accepted in recent decades, but notes its wide occurrence in older generations.

before they had reached 16 years of age. During the four decades on which we have data, no other aspects of the sexual behavior of the American female seem to have changed as much as petting and pre-marital coitus. The major change had occurred in the generation born in the first decade after 1900. This was the generation which was in its teens and early twenties during the first World War and in the years immediately following that war.[15]

Active Incidence. Not only were there fewer females who had done any sort of petting, among those who were born prior to 1900, but

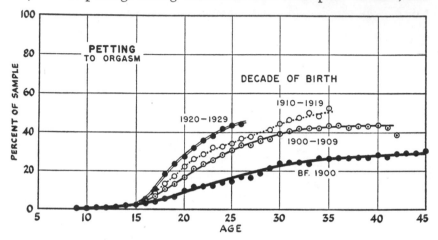

Figure 36. Accumulative incidence: petting to orgasm, by decade of birth
Data from Table 65.

fewer who were petting to the point of orgasm within any five-year period (Table 66, Figure 37). For instance, at ages sixteen to twenty, 10 per cent of the older generation in the sample, but 28 per cent of the generation born after 1920 were petting to orgasm. In the next five years, 15 per cent of the older and 37 per cent of the younger generation were involved. The development had occurred in both the high school and college groups, but it had been most marked in the college groups because they were the ones who had been most restrained in

---

[15] Something of the history and spirit of the 1920's is recorded in: Lindsey and Evans 1929. Allen 1931:ch. 5, especially 132–138, also 387–388 (an excellent although general picture, notes that there was no shift back at the end of the decade). Carpenter 1932:38–44. Mark Sullivan 1935, in "Our Times" v. 6, ch. 16, lists authors and books which epitomize the attitudes of the decade, including such authors as Scott Fitzgerald, Cyril Scott, Sherwood Anderson, Elinor Glyn, Carl Van Vechten, Edgar Lee Masters, Dorothy Parker, Edna St. Vincent Millay, Erskine Caldwell, Theodore Dreiser, Ben Hecht, and others. Lynd and Lynd 1937:168 ("It is our impression that no two genera-tions of Americans have ever faced each other across as wide a gap in their customary attitudes and behavior as have American parents and children since the World War"). McPartland 1947:37–52 (the change "was fairly perma-nent").

their behavior in the earlier generation. As a result of this post-war development, the petting records of the several educational levels do not particularly differ today.

Frequency of Orgasm. In contrast to this increase in the incidence of petting among younger generations, the average (active median) frequency of petting to orgasm does not seem to have changed among

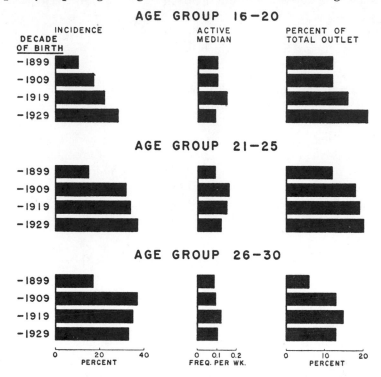

Figure 37. Active incidence, median, percent of total outlet: petting to orgasm, by decade of birth

Data from Table 66.

the females in the sample (Figure 37). In most groups, in all generations, the frequencies had usually been between 4 and 8 times a year. Even females of the oldest generation, when they had engaged in any petting which led to orgasm, had done so with about the same frequency as the females of the more recent generations.

Percentage of Total Outlet. As a consequence of the increase in the incidence of petting to orgasm after the first World War, this type of activity had contributed somewhat more to the total outlet of the younger generation in the sample (Table 66, Figure 37). The data show some variation in this regard, but among some of the graduate groups the part of the outlet which had been derived from petting to orgasm, by the females born in the first decade after 1900, had been two to four times what it had been for the group born before 1900.

RELATION TO AGE AT ONSET OF ADOLESCENCE

With two minor exceptions, the data fail to show any relation between the ages at which the females in the sample had turned adolescent, and the incidences of their petting experience, the incidences and frequencies with which they had reached orgasm in the course of their petting, the active incidences within any five-year period, or the proportion of their total outlet which had been derived from petting.

Those who had reached adolescence at earlier ages (by 11 or 12) had been the first to begin petting and petting to the point of orgasm, and those who had turned adolescent last were the last to begin petting and petting to orgasm (Tables 67, 68). Few males are interested in either petting or coitus with pre-adolescent girls, and this male reaction, rather than any physiologic development in the female, probably accounted for the ages at which the female's petting had begun. In some of the five-year age periods, somewhat more of the girls who had reached adolescence first were petting to orgasm (the active incidences), and fewer of the girls who had reached adolescence at some later age.[16]

There is, however, a striking contrast between the ages at which females and males begin petting. In most instances the male's activity begins quite promptly with or immediately after the onset of adolescence. We have reported (1948:534) that within the year after adolescence, some 55 per cent of the males had started petting. It was in that same period that most of the males had begun masturbating, had their first nocturnal orgasms, and in some cases begun coital or homosexual experience (Figure 148). In the median female, on the other hand, petting did not begin until 15 or 16 years of age, which is three or four years after the average female turns adolescent (Table 56, Figure 29). These differences between females and males may depend upon some hormonal factor (Chapter 18).

RELATION TO RURAL-URBAN BACKGROUND

The limited rural sample which is available does not show petting patterns which are markedly different from those in the much larger urban sample. The accumulative incidences of petting experience are essentially the same for the two groups (Table 69). Somewhat more of the urban group may begin petting to orgasm at an earlier age. In the five groups on which we have sufficient data to compare the active

---

[16] Terman 1938:254 similarly found early onset of adolescence (before 12) correlated positively (CR = 2.1) with high active incidences of petting.

incidences of petting to orgasm among rural and urban groups, a few more of the urban females may have been involved in some of the five-year periods (Table 70). The differences, however, are never great, and they do not seem to justify the assumption which is to be found in some of the literature that there must be marked differences between rural and urban patterns of sexual behavior because the opportunities for socio-sexual contacts differ in the two types of communities, and because the educational and religious backgrounds are generally different in the two.

RELATION TO RELIGIOUS BACKGROUND

Among the females in the sample, the chief restraint on petting and on petting which leads to orgasm seems to have been the religious

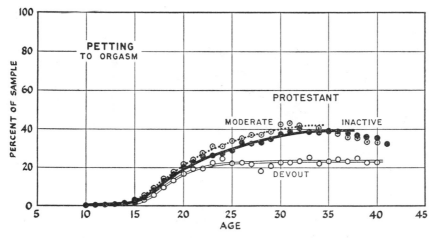

Figure 38. Accumulative incidence: petting to orgasm, in Protestant groups
Data from Table 71.

tradition against it. This appears to have limited the number of females who ever do any petting, and it appears to have limited the frequencies, the times and the places, and the techniques of the petting that was done. Because religious tradition has so largely shaped public thinking on these matters, its restraining influence is apparent not only among those who are devout, but, at least to some extent, among those who are not directly connected with any religious group.

Accumulative Incidence. The accumulative incidences of petting experience were more or less the same at early ages among the females of most of the religious groups on which we have data (Table 71). This was true of most of the devoutly Catholic and Protestant groups, the moderately devout Protestant, Catholic, and Jewish groups, and the inactive Protestant, Catholic, and Jewish groups. By age thirty-five, however, the accumulative incidences for petting experience had reached 96 per cent among the less devout Protestant females who were still unmarried, but had not gone much beyond 85 per cent among the devoutly religious Protestant females.

However, the accumulative incidences for petting to orgasm show strikingly negative correlations with the levels of religious devotion (Table 71, Figures 38, 39). The samples show more of the females of the less devout groups ever petting to the point of orgasm, and much

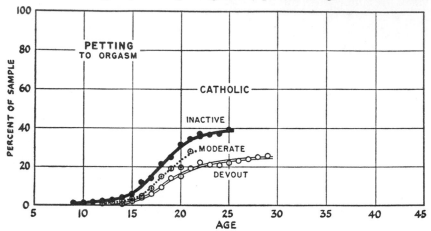

Figure 39. Accumulative incidence: petting to orgasm, in Catholic groups
Data from Table 71.

fewer of the more devout females. This depends on the fact that more of the devout females refuse to accept the techniques which are most likely to result in orgasm, or else they deliberately restrain themselves from responding to that point. Religious devotion may not prevent a female from engaging in some sort of petting activity, but it limits the point to which she will go in her petting.

Active Incidence. The number of individuals in the sample who were petting to the point of orgasm within any five-year period (the active incidence figure) was similarly affected by the degree of religious devotion (Table 72, Figure 40). Among Protestant, Catholic, and Jewish groups, fewer of the devoutly religious females were involved and more of the females of the religiously inactive groups. For instance, in the late teens the devout Protestant incidence was 19 per cent against 22 per cent for the inactive Protestants; in the corresponding Catholic groups it was 15 against 31 per cent, and in the Jewish groups it was 23 against 33 per cent.

Frequency of Orgasm. The religious codes seem to have had little effect on the frequencies of petting to orgasm, even among the most devout females in the sample (Table 72). Since the frequencies of orgasm attained in petting relationships are some measure of the effectiveness of the techniques which are used, and of the female's acceptance and reaction to those techniques, it is particularly significant to find that the devout female, after she has once accepted orgasm in a petting relationship, engages in such activity about as often as the average of the less devout females.

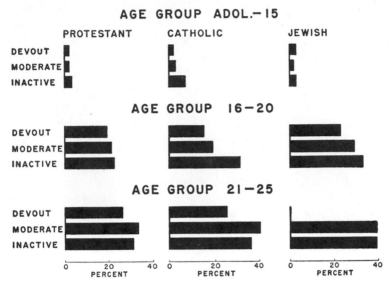

Figure 40. Active incidence: petting to orgasm, by religious group
Data from Table 72.

Why the responses of the devout females in the sample were not reduced in frequency, is a matter that merits some attention. In some instances it seems to have been because the petting situation, once having developed, had repeated itself with a regularity in which the individual was more or less unintentionally trapped. In some instances it appears to have been because experience had led to a frank acceptance of the satisfactions which were being obtained from the contacts. In some instances there had been a thoughtful conclusion that pre-marital petting provides a good means for learning to make social and marital adjustments.

Percentage of Total Outlet. The sample shows considerable variation (from 2 to 26 per cent) in the proportion of the total outlet which had been derived from petting to orgasm by the females of the various religious groups (Table 72). However, there does not seem to have been any consistent correlation with the sort of religious background which the female had had.

SOCIO-SEXUAL RELATIONS AS MEASURES OF FEMALE CAPACITIES

Such solitary activities as masturbation and nocturnal sex dreams, even though they may be accompanied by fantasies about other persons, depend primarily on an individual's own interests and capacities to respond sexually. On the other hand, such socio-sexual activities as petting, heterosexual coitus, and homosexual relations must depend upon some confluence of the capacities, interests, and desires of two individuals, and on the willingness of each to adjust to the other. The incidences and frequencies of such activities often represent, therefore, some compromise between an upper limit beyond which the less responsive partner will not agree to go, and a lower limit below which the more responsive partner will not allow the frequencies to drop if there is to be any continuance of the relationship. The incidences and frequencies of socio-sexual activities consequently do not provide a good measure of the sexual capacities of either the female or the male, although they may provide some measure of the willingness and ability of each to adjust to the other.

In most heterosexual relations, it is the male who is most interested in having more frequent contacts, and it is he, therefore, who establishes the minimal rates. Contrariwise, it is the female who is most likely to establish the upper limits beyond which she will not go; but occasionally the female is the more interested partner.

If, as we have previously estimated (p. 236), the median, unmarried female in the sample between the ages of fifteen and thirty-five had engaged in some kind of petting on an average of about once in two weeks, and if orgasm had occurred on an average of 4 to 6 times a year for something less than a third of those who were petting (Table 58), we may estimate that the average (median) female in the sample had reached orgasm in only 5 to 6 per cent of her contacts. Moreover, in a fair proportion of all her contacts, the female had not received any sort of erotic stimulation at all. Some of the females had engaged in petting for a year or two, or even for several years, before they had ever been aroused; and even after they had begun to respond, they had failed to find erotic significance in a high proportion of their contacts. The male therefore has to initiate fully half of all the petting activity, and takes the lead in initiating most of the other half of it [17]; and the incidences and frequencies of any heterosexual experience are largely a measure of his interests and capacities.

The female's responses to orgasm are, however, a measure of *her* interests and sexual capacities, and in considering the data for any

---

[17] Ehrmann 1952 finds that a heavy preponderance of the petting activity is initiated by the male partner.

heterosexual activity it is, therefore, important to distinguish between the female's experience and her responses to orgasm.

The accumulative incidence curves for the female's petting experience (whether with or without orgasm) develop rather abruptly between the ages of 12 and 18 and more or less level off by age 21 (Figure 29). As we shall subsequently see, the curves for the female's experience in coitus similarly develop in an abrupt way (Figure 149). They bear a striking resemblance to the male's accumulative incidence curves for masturbation, nocturnal emissions, pre-marital petting, pre-marital coitus, and, to a lesser extent, even his homosexual activities (Figure 148). The abrupt rise of these curves at the time that the male turns adolescent must be ascribed to factors which are related to his adolescent development—probably to some hormonal change which occurs in that period (Chapter 18).

On the other hand, the accumulative incidence curves which record the female's petting activities to the point of orgasm mount only gradually over a long period of years (Figure 29). Their slow rise probably depends on a gradual development of the biologic, psychologic, and social factors which account for sexual responses in the female (Chapters 15–18). This same gradual rise is also to be observed in the accumulative incidence curves for masturbation which leads to orgasm, and for nocturnal dreams in the female. The curve for orgasm in pre-marital coitus is very similar (Figure 150). These curves which show the development of activities which lead to orgasm are among the best measures we have of the female's basic sexual interests and capacities.

TECHNIQUES IN PETTING

The techniques which are utilized by American females and males in their pre-marital petting may, at one time or another, include every conceivable type of physical contact except genital unions which are, by definition, ruled out. In the sample, the petting had been most often prolonged and the techniques most varied among those who had had pre-marital coital experience, and particularly among those who had had the most coital experience. Table 73 and Figures 41 and 42 compare the techniques used by females who had never had coitus, by females who had had coitus less than twenty-five times, and by females who had had coitus twenty-five times or more.

Simple Kissing. General body contacts, hugging, and simple kissing are the usual first approaches in petting, and the individual who has not had previous experience may go no further than that. In our sample, nearly one hundred per cent of the females who had done any petting had included simple kissing in that experience (Table 73).[18] There were essentially no differences among the several generations represented in the sample. A few had been so conditioned against oral activities of any sort that they had not allowed kissing, even though they permitted some other types of contact. Simple kissing may bring erotic arousal, especially if pressure is involved in the lip contacts and the activity is prolonged. Some of the arousal may be ascribed to psychologic elements in the situation. For some females, simple kissing rarely or never effects arousal.

Deep Kissing. This is also known as soul kissing, tongue kissing, or French kissing. It may involve tongue-to-tongue contacts, lip and tongue sucking, tongue contacts with the inner surfaces of the lips and with the teeth, deep tongue explorations of the interior of the partner's mouth, contacts with the inner surfaces of the lips of the partner, and the nipping and gentle biting of the tongue and the lips. All of these techniques may be found among lower mammals, although the human female or male may elaborate them beyond the point to which the other species go. Because of the abundant nerve supply in the lips, the tongue, and the interior of the mouth, the stimulation of these areas may be very effective, and orgasm occasionally results from such deep kissing, even though no genital contact is involved.

Deep kissing was in the petting experience of approximately 70 per cent of the females in the sample who had not had pre-marital coitus (Table 73, Figure 42).[18] The incidences, however, rose with increased coital experience, and deep kissing was in the histories of something between 80 and 93 per cent of those who had had coitus before marriage. There were some differences between the educational levels on this point. For instance, among those who had had coitus some twenty-five times or more, deep kissing occurred in 83 per cent of the high school sample, and in 98 per cent of the graduate sample. As we have previously found for the male, there is a greater acceptance of the socially more taboo petting techniques in the better educated groups of females. Some individuals who are inhibited and unwilling to accept such techniques at the beginning of a sexual contact may lose their inhibitions and engage in deep kissing after they have become sufficiently aroused erotically.

[18] Simple kissing and deep kissing are, of course, noted in most of the literature. The references cover kissing which occurs in petting that does not lead to coitus, and kissing in connection with pre-marital or marital coitus. See: Anon. 1707:6 ("a tonguing kiss"). Robie 1925:107. Davis 1929:60. Hamilton 1929: 174, 177, 216. Van de Velde 1930:152–161. Dickinson and Beam 1931:66. Dickinson and Beam 1934:135. Stone and Stone 1937:222; 1952:182–183. Landis et al. 1940:290. Hutton 1942:96. Chesser 1947:130. Kelly in Fishbein and Burgess 1947:94. Brown and Kempton 1950:219. Ehrmann 1952 (of 263 female college students, 97 per cent incidence).

There were marked differences in the acceptance of deep kissing among the several generations in the sample. Among the females who had not had pre-marital coitus, those who were born before 1900 had done deep kissing in only 44 per cent of the cases, while those who were born in 1910 or later had had such experience in 74 per cent of the cases (Table 73). Among those whose coital experience totaled more than twenty-five times, 82 per cent of the older group had done deep kissing, as compared with 90 per cent of the younger generation.

Deep kissing, mouth-breast, and mouth-genital contacts were the most taboo of the petting techniques among older generations. Such taboos were sometimes rationalized on hygienic bases. The younger generation, ignoring the theoretic hygiene, more often accepts oral techniques—without any dire effects on their health.

Breast Stimulation. The stimulation of the whole female body by the male, and to a lesser degree of the male body by the female, constitute the primary activities in petting. Males, and particularly American males, may find considerable psychologic stimulation in touching and manipulating the female breast (Chapters 14, 16). Many males are more aroused erotically by observing female breasts, or by touching them, than they are by the sight of or manual contacts with female genitalia. In actuality, many females are not particularly stimulated by such breast manipulations, but some of them are aroused. A few may even reach orgasm as a result of such contacts.[19]

Among the females in the sample who had not yet had pre-marital coitus, some 72 per cent had allowed males to manipulate their covered or uncovered breasts (Table 73, Figure 41). Smaller percentages of the older generation and smaller percentages of the lower educational levels had been involved. Among the females who had had some limited experience in pre-marital coitus, the incidences rose to 95 per cent, while 98 per cent of those who had had more extensive coital experience had accepted such contacts.

Mouth-Breast Contacts. The male's manipulation of the unclothed female breast with his tongue or lips had been, in all the generations and in all of the educational levels represented in the sample, much more taboo than his manual manipulation of her breast. Many persons feel that the acceptance of any oral technique involves something that

---

[19] For additional comment on the erotic significance of the female breast, see for instance: Anon. 1707:3, 7. Long 1922:110. Robie 1925:99. Hamilton 1929: 173–177. Van de Velde 1930:163–164. Dickinson and Beam 1931:64, 66; 1934:135. Wright 1937:88. Stone and Stone 1937:221; 1952:182. Butterfield 1940:94. Himes 1940:325. Kelly in Fishbein and Burgess 1947:94. English in Fishbein and Burgess 1947:109. Clark 1949:54. Brown and Kempton 1950:220. Fromme 1950:99. Ehrmann 1952 (among 263 college females; 45 per cent incidence).

is peculiarly sexual, or that it represents an extreme break with the moral traditions of our culture. Among the females in the sample who had not had pre-marital coitus, only 30 per cent had accepted mouth-breast contacts (Table 73, Figure 42). On the other hand, among the females who had had even limited amounts of pre-marital coitus, such contacts had occurred in 68 per cent of the histories, and in 87 per cent of the histories of those who had had more extensive coitus. The ac-

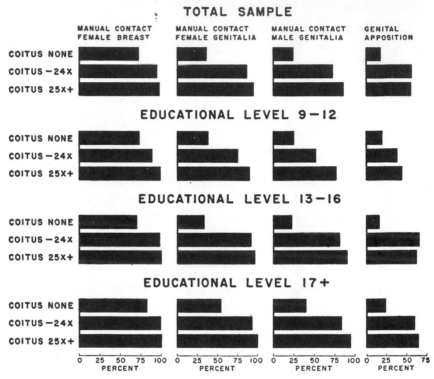

Figure 41. Incidence: manual techniques in petting, by coital experience and educational level

For females born after 1909; see Table 73.

ceptance was greatest among the females of the younger generation, particularly in the better educated groups. For instance, the females of the graduate level in the youngest generation had accepted mouth-breast contacts in 86 per cent of the cases where they had had limited amounts of coitus, and in 97 per cent of the cases where they had had more extensive coital experience.[19]

American males are said to be more interested than most European males in female breasts.[20] There is evidence of a greater interest in female buttocks in most European countries. According to the an-

---

[20] So claimed by Gorer 1948:77.

thropologic reports, there are pre-literate tribes in various parts of the world who pay little attention to female breasts. Our own observations in tropical America, where the breasts of females of all ages may be regularly exposed, indicate that female breasts there seem to have a minimum if any erotic significance for the males. For many centuries the Chinese seem to have considered any physical development of the

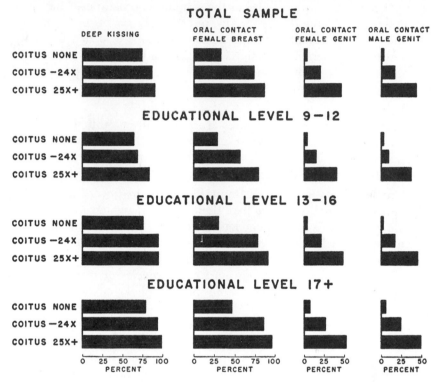

Figure 42. Incidence: oral techniques in petting, by coital experience and educational level

For females born after 1909; see Table 73.

female breast offensive and anti-erotic. Apparently psychologic conditioning and the cultural traditions are of considerable importance in these matters.

Among the lower mammals, the stimulation of the female breast by the male is relatively rare, although not completely unknown. We have observed male dogs licking the breasts of female dogs, in some cases for prolonged periods of time. Boars regularly nuzzle the breast of the sow when they are sexually aroused, and there are similar data for still other animals. A mouth-breast contact, however, constitutes the one technique in human petting behavior which is most distinctively human.

Manual Stimulation of Female Genitalia. Some sort of non-penile stimulation of the female genitalia is almost universal among the lower mammals where, however, the lack of prehensile hands places the burden of the activity on the nose and the mouth of the male. The manual manipulation of the female genitalia by the human male during petting contacts is recorded in the histories of a little more than a third (36 per cent) of those females in the sample who had never had pre-marital coitus (Table 73, Figure 41), but the figure is, of course, higher for those who had had coitus. Even among those who had had only limited coital experience, some 87 per cent had allowed the males to manipulate their genitalia, and among those who had had more extensive coital experience, some 95 per cent had accepted such contacts.[21]

Interestingly enough, the figures are practically no different for the several generations which are represented in the sample. The only markedly lower figures occur among those females who were born before 1900 and who did not have pre-marital coitus.

Manual Stimulation of Male Genitalia. There are fewer females who manipulate the male genitalia than there are males who manipulate the female genitalia. Even after she has accepted other petting techniques, the average female may delay for some time before she will touch the genitalia of the male. Since these same differences between males and females are to be found among most other species of mammals, one must conclude that they have some ancient phylogenetic origin (p. 228 ff.). Many females manipulate the male genitalia only at the request of the male, and the failure of the female to initiate such action is often noted by males who have had homosexual experience and are accustomed to the mutual genital manipulations which occur there. Most females seem to derive no particular satisfaction from their manipulations of the male. Some, however, do seem to find psychologic and probably sensory satisfaction in making such contacts. The evident responses of the male when he is stimulated may so arouse some females that they may experience orgasm as a result, even though their own genitalia have not been touched.[22]

In our sample of unmarried females who had not had coitus, only 24 per cent had ever touched the male genitalia (Table 73, Figure 41).

---

[21] Additional references to the male's stimulation of female genitalia may be found, for instance, in: Hamilton 1929:173, 175, 177, 217. Van de Velde 1930:165. Dickinson and Beam 1931:62; 1934:135. Wright 1937:89. Stone and Stone 1937:221; 1952:182. Himes 1940:325. Butterfield 1940:97. Hutton 1942:93. Clark 1949:54; 1952:29. Brown and Kempton 1950:220. Ehrmann 1952 (among 38 per cent of 263 college girls who did petting).

[22] The female's manipulation of the male genitalia is also noted, for example, in: Adler 1911:98. Long 1922:111. Hamilton 1929:177. Van de Velde 1930:166. Hartwich et al. 1931:118. Hutton 1942:92. Chesser 1947:135. Clark 1949:54; 1952:29. Ehrmann 1952:1.

The figure was as low as 12 per cent among the females who were born before 1900, but 31 per cent for those who were born between 1900 and 1909. Some 40 per cent of the younger generation of the graduate group had had such experience. Many older males, particularly of the lower educational levels, used to consider a female morally indecent if she touched the male genitalia. Few of the younger generation of the better educated males entertain any such attitudes today.

Where the pre-marital relations had proceeded to coitus, there were nearly three times as many females (in contrast to the above) who had manually stimulated the male genitalia. Among those in the younger generations who had had even limited experience in coitus, some 72 per cent had adopted such techniques (Table 73, Figure 41). Among those who had had more experience in coitus, some 86 per cent had so stimulated the male. There are some differences between the educational levels, but practically none between the generations. Certainly older persons who had pre-marital coitus when they were youths have no reason for being surprised at the petting techniques which are being employed by the younger generation today.

Oral Contacts with Female Genitalia. Although, as we have already noted, mouth-genital contacts are part of the pre-coital sex play of practically all mammals, such contacts are condemned in Judeo-Christian codes. In consequence, they are the last of the petting techniques to be accepted by males or females, for there are males as well as females who consider such activities biologically abnormal and perverse.

Among the younger females in the sample who had not had pre-marital coitus, only 3 per cent had allowed the male to touch their genitalia orally (Table 73, Figure 42). The figure was still lower— between 1 and 2 per cent—among the females who were born before 1900.[23]

But among those females who had had some, even though not extensive coital experience, some 20 per cent in the younger generations had accepted such oral stimulation; and among those who had had more extensive coital experience, 46 per cent had accepted such contacts. There were surprisingly few differences between the older and younger generations in these respects.

Oral Contacts with Male Genitalia. Oral stimulation of the male genitalia by the female occurs somewhat less frequently than oral stimulation of the female genitalia by the male. Often the female makes

---

[23] Oral contacts with the female genitalia are also noted in: Adler 1911:164. Hamilton 1929:177, 217. Van de Velde 1930:169. Dickinson and Beam 1931: 366. Strakosch 1934:84–85. Havelock Ellis 1936 (II,3):555–557. Stone and Stone 1937:222; 1952:183. Chesser 1947:139. Fromme 1950:99. **Brown and Kempton 1950:223.**

such contacts only because she is urged to do so by the male, but there are a few females who initiate such activity and some who may be much aroused by it. A few may even reach orgasm as they manipulate the male genitalia orally. This greater inclination of the human male toward oral activity is duplicated among other species of mammals. Contrary to our earlier thinking (1948:540), we now understand that there are basic psychologic differences between the sexes; and although cultural traditions may also be involved, the differences in oral behavior may depend primarily on the greater capacity of the male to be stimulated psychologically (Chapter 16).

In the younger generations in that portion of the sample which had not had pre-marital coitus, only 2 per cent had attempted to stimulate the male genitalia orally (Table 73, Figure 42). The incidence was lower for the group which was born before 1900, but it was higher for the younger generation in the upper educational levels. For instance, 5 per cent of the females who were born after 1910, and who had graduate school training, had had such experience.[24]

But among the females of the younger generations who had had some (even though limited) experience in coitus, 16 per cent had stimulated the male genitalia orally. And among those who had had more extensive pre-marital coitus, oral contacts with the male genitalia were recorded in 43 per cent of the petting histories. It is surprising to find that the figure was hardly lower (38 per cent) for the generation which was born before 1900. In the very youngest generation of the better educated groups, nearly two-thirds (62 per cent) of the females who had had extensive coital experience had made oral contacts with the male genitalia before marriage. Obviously experience in coitus leads to a considerable acceptance of petting techniques which sexually inexperienced persons often consider taboo.

Genital Apposition. In a surprising number of instances, male genitalia had been placed directly against female genitalia during the petting relationship, without any attempt to penetrate the vagina. In some instances this failure to effect actual coitus had depended upon the female's refusal to allow the male to go any farther; but in a larger number of instances, it had depended upon a mutual decision by the female and the male that there should be no penetration. To many individuals, the apposition of genitalia had appeared to be more acceptable than actual coitus, even though the stimulation provided by such apposition had not fallen far short of that which coitus would have provided. Some 17 per cent of the females who had never had

---

[24] Oral contacts with the male genitalia are also noted in: Hamilton 1929:177, 217. Van de Velde 1930:171. Hartwich et al. 1931:118. Dickinson and Beam 1931: 66, 366. Strakosch 1934:84–85.

coitus had allowed such genital apposition; but 56 per cent of those who had, on occasion, had actual coitus had made such genital contacts without penetration (Table 73, Figure 41).

Time Involved. Petting not infrequently begins at a high level of erotic arousal and reaches orgasm within a minute or two. More often it is deliberately extended to a quarter or a half hour or more if the situation permits. Sometimes it may be carried on for hours or through the whole of a night. Sometimes both individuals may be completely nude throughout the whole of even such a prolonged performance, although neither of them is willing to accept any sort of genital union.

Place. The place which is available for the petting may largely determine the time and the techniques that are utilized. A goodnight kiss on a street corner, on the steps of a girl's home, in the shrubbery outside of a dormitory, or in some out-of-the-way place adjacent to a dance hall, may develop into a short but distinctly erotic relationship. Most petting probably occurs in the girl's home, or in the rooming house or dormitory where she stays, or wherever else she may entertain her boy friends. A large part of the petting occurs in parked or moving automobiles, just as it used to occur in horse-drawn buggies among older generations. Much of the petting occurs out-of-doors on porches, in gardens, in parks, on swimming beaches, along unfrequented paths, in boats, or in the woods and the fields of more open country. Much petting occurs more or less openly within public view at dances, cocktail parties, or smaller social gatherings. Foreign travelers are sometimes amazed at the open display of such obviously erotic activity, and wrongly conclude that it indicates that most young persons in this country are having a great deal of pre-marital coitus. They fail to understand that petting often serves as a substitute for the pre-marital coitus which seems to be more prevalent in Europe. "Blanket parties" in secluded spots out-of-doors are modern versions of the ancient and widespread custom of "bundling." Moving picture theatres regularly provide opportunities for petting. There is an increasing amount of petting which is carried on in such public conveyances as buses, trains, and airplanes. The other passengers have learned to ignore such activities if they are pursued with some discretion. Orgasm is sometimes achieved in the petting which goes on in such public places.

SIGNIFICANCE OF PETTING

Moral Interpretations. Judeo-Christian codes specifically condemn the deliberate search for or acceptance of activities which bring erotic arousal without having procreation as their ultimate objective. The general disapproval of petting in this country and in much of Europe reflects this moral tradition. The strictly Orthodox Jewish code is extreme in condemning all nudity, either of the whole or of any part of the body except the face and the hands, in prohibiting the observation of such nudity, and in forbidding the exposure of nude bodies either in public or in the privacy of one's home—even during the coital relationships of married spouses, or in the solitude of changing one's clothing, or in bathing.[25] It consequently follows that physical contacts between nude bodies or nude parts of bodies, except for the limited genital contacts which are necessary for procreation, are forbidden.

While none of the petting techniques are in themselves identified as sinful in the Catholic moral philosophy, the code is specific in considering such activities sins if they constitute anything more than aids to marital coitus.[26] The coitus must be had in a fashion that offers a reasonable opportunity for a pregnancy to result.

Protestant groups have reflected many of the same attitudes, and most of them still condemn all pre-marital socio-sexual activities. Nevertheless, the Protestant clergy and laity have at times compromised with these demands. While the Catholic code allows no exception, some Protestant groups are inclined to accept petting between persons who are engaged or who are seriously considering the possibility of becoming engaged to marry. An increasing number of the Protestant

---

[25] The Jewish attitude toward nudity is admirably summarized in Epstein 1948: 25–67. See also: Bible: Ezekiel 16:36–39 (nudity among lovers condemned). The following are from the Babylonian Talmud, Epstein edit.: Kethuboth 72a–72b:448, 451 (uncovered head of female not to be exposed in public). Nedarim 30b:87 (woman's hair should be covered). Gittin 90b:438 (uncovered armpits unseemly for women). Baba Kamma 86b:496–497 (whether one who insults a naked person is liable). Sanhedrin 45a:295; 75a:505 (woman cannot stand nude before a man even to save his life).

[26] Catholic codes on petting may be summarized as follows: All sexual pleasure, complete or incomplete, can be lawfully desired or deliberately enjoyed only in marriage. Chaste touches are permitted to engaged couples if for pleasure of sensation but not for venereal pleasure. Petting in marriage likewise may not be for pleasure, but only as leading to coitus or as a sign of mutual love. The proper purposes of coitus are primarily generation of offspring, and secondarily faith owed to a spouse, calming of concupiscence, and fostering of conjugal affection. On sin of petting outside of marriage, see: Ballerini 1890(2):679, 683, 688, 703 (kisses, embraces, looks, touches, and similar things outside of marriage are venial or mortal sins). Arregui 1927:147–148 (any venereal pleasure outside of marriage is a sin). O'Brien 1950:221 ("sexual pleasure, be it complete or incomplete, may be lawfully desired, caused directly or deliberately enjoyed only by those in the state of matrimony"). On petting in marriage as a preliminary to coitus, see: Sanchez 1637:302, 313 (if for purposes of showing mutual love, it is legitimate; if for purposes of increasing pleasure in coitus, then a venial sin; but if for genital pleasure, it is a mortal sin. Every venereal act not related to coitus is mortal). Ballerini 1890(6):292. Arregui 1927:533. Davis 1946(4):252 (since marital coitus is honorable, all acts preceding which aid in having coitus forthwith are lawful. Hence, before coitus it is permitted to married persons to arouse sexual impulses, but one must beware that such acts do not provoke very near danger of pollution in either person. If, however, by chance, rarely, and beyond intention pollution should follow, there would be no sin). On purposes of marital coitus, see: Sanchez 1637:193. Arregui 1927:530. Davis 1946(4):253.

clergy and laity, moreover, have begun to believe that pre-marital petting may have some value in developing the emotional capacities of youth and in contributing to their future marital adjustments.

Evidently the religious and public condemnation of petting has had a minimal effect on the attitudes and behavior of the youth of more recent generations,[27] but many of those who engage in petting do so with some sense of guilt. There is probably no single aspect of sex about which American youth more often ask questions and seek scientific information. When the guilt reactions are extreme, they may give rise to a variety of personality problems, sexual maladjustments, difficulties in making social adjustments, various types of impotence, sometimes the substitution of homosexual activities, and still other difficulties which may do damage to the subsequent marital adjustments.

A great deal has been written about the damage that may be done by pre-marital sexual activities, and particularly by petting[28]; but relatively little has been said about the psychologic disturbances and subsequent marital difficulties which may develop when there is such condemnation and constant belaboring of any type of behavior which has become so nearly universal, and which is as likely to remain as universal, as petting is among American females and males.

Legal Implications. Anglo-American sex law is largely derived from and follows the religious codes on most issues.[29] While petting as a specific type of activity is not legally condemned, many of its particular techniques are punishable as misdemeanors or more serious crimes. When a minor is involved, petting may be prosecuted as juvenile delinquency or as a contribution to the delinquency of a minor.[30] For

---

[27] Our record on the incidences and frequencies of petting provides a measure of the attitudes of American youth themselves. Surveys of attitudes are also reported in: Blanchard and Manasses 1930:263. Pringle 1938:14. Bernard 1938:355. Christensen 1950:226. A. Ellis 1951:72–75. Christensen 1952:585.

[28] The dangers of petting are emphasized, for instance, in: Fowler 1875:544. Wood-Allen 1905:165. U. S. Public Health Service 1930:7. E. R. Groves 1933:114. Exner 1933:13–14. Edson 1936:8–9. Waller 1937:728. Crisp 1939: 21. G. H. Groves 1942:185. Popenoe 1943:76–82. Duvall and Hill 1945:54–56. Dickerson 1947:50–51. Duvall in Fishbein and Burgess 1947:41. Stephens in Fishbein and Burgess 1947:48–51. Kirkendall 1947:24–26. Landis and Landis 1948:72. Duvall 1950:242, 245. Bundesen 1951:86, 123–126.
A European and psychoanalytic viewpoint is available in Biederich and Dembicki 1951:84–90, which runs as follows: Petting is not genuine human sexuality, but a man-made act to produce orgasm. The problem is fairly new, although by now the United States is used to this double standard. Orgasm in petting is an orgasm "reached, not experienced." Petting may lead to disappointment in coitus, impotence, and premature ejaculation. Since it *does not occur in animals* [!], petting is the most unnatural of sexual activities.

[29] May 1931:ch. 5, 13.

[30] The genital manipulation of a female child may contribute to her delinquency. See: State v. Stone 1924:226 Pac. (Ore.) 430. But see: State v. Moore 1952: 241 P.2d (Ore.) 455 (hugging, kissing, and playing with breast insufficient under indictment charging "fondling of private parts"). In a court handling girls between 16 and 21 years of age, in one of our large cities, we have ob-

petting which an adult carries on with a very young minor, the laws in many states impose penalties which are among the most extreme in the criminal code.[31]

There are, however, few and only sporadic and capricious attempts to enforce such laws when the petting partners are of about the same age and when there has been mutual consent. There are a few instances of the prosecution of petting as assault and battery, particularly where the girl had not consented or was below the age of consent.[32] Most of the cases that get into court are instituted by irate parents or outraged neighbors. When the petting occurs in some public place, as in a moving picture theatre, on a beach, or in a car parked on some public highway, the police are more likely to take action. In most instances they simply put an end to the activity; in some instances they may make an arrest on a charge of public indecency or disorderly conduct. The charges are likely to be more severe if genital manipulations or mouth-genital contacts are involved, for the latter at least may be penalized as felonies in most of the forty-eight states.[33] Our histories

---

served many cases in which evidence of genital manipulation in petting was taken as sufficient grounds for judging the girls to be "morally depraved," and for committing them to institutions for relatively long terms.

[31] There are now 27 states having statutes which penalize indecent liberties with a child. Examples are: Penal Code of California:§288 (child under 14, offender over 18, penalty 1 year to life). Michigan Comp. Laws 1948:750.336 (child under 16, male offender over 16, improper and indecent liberties not amounting to intercourse, sodomy or gross indecency, maximum penalty 10 years or 1 day to life). Minnesota Statutes Ann. 1947:§617.08 (child under 16, age of offender not specified, maximum penalty 7 years). State v. Kocher 1941:119 P.2d (Mont.) 35 (attempting to remove dress as part of sexual play). State v. Gilmore 1926:150 N.E. (Ill.) 631 (putting hands under dress, tickling legs of 11 year old girl). But see: State v. Rounds 1933:248 N.W. (Ia.) 500 (hugging, kissing, not lewd and lascivious behavior).

[32] Interpretations of petting as assault and battery where the female had not given her consent are in: Moreland v. State 1916:188 S.W. (Ark.) 1. Corpus Juris Secundum (6):924. Arizona Code 1939:§43–603. Interpretations of petting as assault and battery because the female was below the age at which she was capable of consent, are in: People v. Gibson 1922:134 N.E. (N. Y.) 531. Hanes v. State 1900:57 N.E. (Ind.) 704. Snyder v. State 1915:110 N.E. (Ohio) 644. Miller v. State 1912:150 S.W. (Tex.) 635. Beausoliel v. U. S. 1939:107 F.(2d) 292. See also Burns Indiana Statutes 1933:§10–403 as amended in 1951 by ch. 277. Also see Ohio Criminal Code 1945:§12423–1. The reasoning of some of the courts seems to be that a female below the age of consent, being without capacity to consent to an act of coitus, is by analogy incapable of consenting to any touching of a sexual nature. There are some courts which have rejected this line of reasoning; see: N. Y. Law Revis. Comm. 1937:86.

[33] See: Michigan Comp. Laws 1948:§750.338b (forbidding a private grossly indecent heterosexual act) and New Jersey Statutes Ann. 1939:§2:140–1 (forbidding any lewd or carnally indecent act in private). Both of the above seem to include genital manipulation among the unmarried and provide maximum penalties of 5 and 3 years respectively. Indiana and Wyoming treat as sodomy any enticing, alluring, instigating, or aiding of a person under 21 to commit masturbation, and this has been interpreted to include any immoral act of sexual gratification which has a tendency to corrupt; see Burns Indiana Statutes:§10–4221. In Texas, permitting a person under 16 to handle or fondle one's sexual parts is sodomy, and in Oregon in addition to mouth-genital and anal contacts any "perverse" genital contact is the crime against

include cases of law enforcement officers blackmailing the apprehended youth into making a financial settlement to avoid arrest. The
utter caprice of such legal action provides an example of the impossibility of controlling behavior which is so nearly universal. Few American youth are aware that any legal question is involved; and if they
were aware, most of them would deliberately ignore the law. The
mores, rather than the legal mandates, provide whatever restraint
there is on the petting behavior of present-day American females and
males.

Physiologic Significance. As we have already noted, petting is most
often accepted because of the immediate satisfactions which it may
bring. We have seen that it had provided a physiologic release in the
form of orgasm for about 39 per cent of the females in the sample, and
nearer 45 per cent of the younger generation of females (Table 65).

However, physiologic difficulties may develop if there is considerable arousal in the petting and the activity is not carried through to
orgasm. In such a case, most males and some females find themselves
nervously upset, disturbed in their thinking, incapable of concentrating
on other matters, and inefficient in their motor reactions. They may
develop severe pains in the groin. Before they can resolve these disturbances, they may have to resort to strenuous physical exercise, and
not infrequently they masturbate or seek coitus or sometimes homosexual relations. While most females are not as disturbed as males
when petting activity stops short of orgasm, there are some who are as
disturbed as any of the males. Among the females in the sample who
had had any petting experience, half of them (51 per cent) recorded
that they had been disturbed on some occasion, although only a smaller
percentage had found themselves regularly disturbed (Table 74). A
quarter (26 per cent) reported pains in the groin which were similar
to those which males frequently experience when they are erotically
aroused and fail to reach orgasm. About a third of the females (35 per
cent) had masturbated, at least on some occasion, after the petting had
been concluded, just as many males do.[34]

---

nature. In Arizona, in addition to oral and anal intercourse any body contact
intended to arouse the sexual desires of a person in "any unnatural manner"
is a felony. Although historically sodomy was confined to anal intercourse,
today in most states some or all forms of mouth-genital contacts are specifically forbidden either as part of the sodomy statutes or in separate statutes.
In many of the other states some or all mouth-genital contacts are included
by judicial decision in the term "crime against nature" or sodomy; or mouth-
genital contacts have been considered to be "unnatural" or "perverse" or
"lascivious" or "grossly indecent" conduct under statutes forbidding such
conduct.

[34] It is notable that the female's masturbation following petting seems to be reported only in Talmey 1910:103 and Davis 1929:168. It is warned against in
Weatherhead 1932:38.

Such disturbances depend primarily on the fact that erotic arousal involves the development of neuromuscular tensions which may rise to a considerable peak in the course of sexual activity (Chapter 15). From that peak the tensions are suddenly released if orgasm occurs. For some reason which we do not yet understand, it is difficult for most males and some females to find release from any high level of sexual tension except through orgasm. If there is no orgasm, it may take some time and even hours to resolve these tensions. If there is orgasm, the tensions may be released in a matter of seconds or a minute or two, and the individual finds the comfort and peace which is characteristic of all completed sexual activity—unless it is contaminated with guilt reactions.

Social Significance. Among the females in the sample, petting had been significant because it had been the source of first arousal for about 34 per cent of those individuals who had ever been aroused erotically. Among those who had made their first responses in a heterosexual situation, petting had been the first source of arousal in 51 per cent of the cases (Table 148).

Petting was the first source of orgasm for about a quarter (24 per cent) of all those females in the sample who had ever experienced orgasm. It had been the first source of an orgasm attained in a heterosexual relationship for 46 per cent of the females in the sample. It was, therefore, nearly as important a first source of orgasm as all kinds of coitus combined, including pre-marital, marital, and extra-marital coitus (Table 148).

It is petting rather than the home, classroom or religious instruction, lectures or books, classes in biology, sociology, or philosophy, or actual coitus, that provides most females with their first real understanding of a heterosexual experience. They do not acquire such information from the general atmosphere of the homes in which they are raised, nor from specific instruction given by their mothers. On the contrary, the church, the home, and the school are the chief sources of the sexual inhibitions, the distaste for all aspects of sex, the fears of the physical difficulties that may be involved in a sexual relationship, and the feelings of guilt which many females carry with them into their marriages. Our records provide numerous illustrations of the problem which many females and males face when they try to learn in their late teens or twenties what they are biologically best equipped to learn soon after the onset of adolescence.[35]

---

[35] That pre-marital petting may provide an introduction to the emotional adjustments necessary in marriage is also suggested by: Dell 1930:298 (helps fit a girl for marriage). Terman 1938:257, 393 (somewhat higher frequency of climax in marriage where the pre-marital petting was most frequent—a CR

The failure of a female to reach orgasm in her marital coitus may be a considerable source of marital discord (Chapter 9). In an attempt to identify some of the sources of this difficulty, we have examined the possibility of a correlation between pre-marital experience in orgasm, and the frequencies with which the female responds to the point of orgasm in her subsequent marital coitus (see the detailed discussion in Chapter 9). The data indicate that among the females in our sample who had never experienced orgasm prior to marriage, 44 per cent had completely failed to reach orgasm in their first year of marital coitus (Table 108). On the other hand, among those who had had a fair amount of orgasmic experience prior to marriage, only 13 per cent had failed to reach orgasm in that first year of marriage. This is a difference of considerable magnitude. Differences which lay in the same direction were apparent in the later years, and even for fifteen years after marriage.[36]

The correlations between petting when it was the specific source of pre-marital orgasm, and orgasm in the subsequent marital coitus, are of a similarly high order. Among the females who had never done petting to the point of orgasm before marriage, 35 per cent had never reached orgasm in the first year of marriage (Table 110). On the other hand, among those who had reached orgasm in at least some of their pre-marital petting, only 10 per cent had failed to reach it in the first year of marriage. Similar differences were apparent for some fifteen years after marriage.

Selective factors are probably involved. The girls who respond to orgasm in pre-marital petting are probably those who are basically most responsive, and they, therefore, are the ones who are most likely to make better sexual adjustments after marriage. But we are inclined to believe that causal relationships are also involved, for our further analyses (Chapter 9) indicate that the sources of the pre-marital experience are not as important as the fact that the girl actually reaches orgasm before marriage.

But petting provides a great deal more than experience in orgasm. It introduces the female to the physical, psychologic, and social prob-

---

of 1.5). Levy and Munroe 1938:37 (a healthy preparation for marriage). Squier in Folsom 1938:135 ("within the confines of true affection petting is a part of the art of love, deserving intelligent and gentle cultivation"). Landis et al. 1940:101 (females with petting experience tend to have better sexual adjustment in marriage). Paul H. Landis 1945:265. Macandrew 1946:63–87 (suggested as a substitute for pre-marital coitus). Brown and Kempton 1950: 142 (a legitimate preparation for a normal sex life). Terman 1951:136.

[36] Attempts to analyze the relation between pre-marital petting experience and marital adjustments may be found in: Davis 1929:59–60 (116 wives of unhappy marriages showed higher incidence of petting than wives of happy marriages). Terman 1938:255–256 (marital happiness scores somewhat higher for females who never petted in high school).

lems that are involved in making emotional adjustments to other individuals. As a socializing agent, pre-marital petting had been of considerable significance to a great many of the females in the sample.[37]

The various petting techniques are, because of our social taboos, adopted only gradually in the course of the female's pre-marital experience. She may accept simple kissing long before she accepts deep kissing. It may be a considerable time before she accepts breast contacts, and genital contacts may seem unacceptable until there has been a considerable amount of experience. Mouth-genital contacts are accepted even more slowly. The pre-marital years provide a training period for learning these things. After marriage such gradual learning is not so often possible. Most males will not temporize and allow their wives months and years for the development of their sexual techniques. When difficulties arise in pre-marital relations because of the refusal of the female or sometimes the male partner to accept particular techniques, the relationships may be broken up; and while that may seem unfortunate, it is not as disastrous as breaking up a marriage. Even when a marriage is not dissolved by a sexual disagreement, it may be carried along at such a low level of satisfaction that the relationships are rarely mended.

Pre-marital petting experience provides an opportunity for the female to learn to adjust emotionally to various types of males. Thus she may acquire some wisdom in choosing the particular male with whom she hopes to make a permanent, life-long adjustment. A good deal has been said about the danger of allowing a satisfactory pre-marital sexual relationship to decide the choice of a partner without due regard for the other non-sexual qualities that should be taken into account, and we have seen a few marriages get into difficulties because they were based on sexual interests alone; but we have seen many hundreds of marriages ruined by the failure of the partners to learn before marriage that they could not adjust emotionally or sexually to each other.

It is sometimes said that pre-marital petting may make it difficult for the female to be satisfied with coitus in marriage.[38] The statement has never been supported by any accumulation of specific data, and we have not seen more than three or four such cases. On the other

---

[37] Petting as a socializing agency is noted in: Dell 1930:177. Blanchard and Manasses 1930:60, 191. Folsom 1938:109–111. Corner and Landis 1941:14 (strong interest in the opposite sex, a healthy sign of a development of personality; a certain amount of practical experimentation in petting, practically inevitable). Adams 1946:32–33. Harper 1949:81–83. Brown and Kempton 1950:142. Comfort 1950:96–98. Wangson 1951:107 (Swedish government report on sex problems of youth. Considers petting harmless and natural).
[38] The dangers of a fixation on petting are hypothesized in: E. R. Groves 1933:114. G. H. Groves 1942:185. Clark 1949:55–56. Brown and Kempton 1950:142. Duvall 1950:245.

hand, we have the histories of nearly a thousand females who had done pre-marital petting and who had then responded excellently in their marital coitus.

SUMMARY AND COMPARISONS OF FEMALE AND MALE

Pre-Marital Petting

	IN FEMALES	IN MALES
Phylogenetic Origins		
Occurs in all mammals	Yes	Yes
Techniques basically as in human	Yes	Yes
May prolong sex play without coitus	Yes	Yes
Sex play is initiated by:	Less often	More often
Orgasm may occur without coitus	Doubtful	Yes
Historically ancient in all cultures	Yes	Yes
Relation to Age		
Accumulative incidence		
Petting experience	Abrupt rise	Abrupt rise
By age 15	39%	57%
By age 18	81%	84%
By age 25	91%	89%
Petting with erotic response	83%	Almost all
Petting to orgasm	Gradual rise to 39%	Gradual rise to 31%
Active incidence of orgasm		
At adol.–15	3%	18%
At 16–20	23%	32%
At 21–25	31%	29%
Frequency (active median) to orgasm		
Average at ages 15–55	4–6 per year	3–5 per year
Maximum	7–10 per week	7 per week
Percentage of total outlet		
At adol.–15	4%	1%
At 16–25	18%	3%
At 36–40	5%	1%
Number of years involved		
1 year only	8%	
2–5 years	38%	
6 years or more	54%	
Median individual	6–7 years	
Number of partners		
1 only	10%	
2–5	32%	
6–10	23%	
Over 10	35%	
Relation to Age at Marriage and Educ. Level		
Accumulative incid. uniform for uniform age of marr.	Yes	No. Higher in high school and college groups
Active incidence of orgasm	Little relation	Marked relation
Frequency to orgasm	No relation	Some relation
Percentage of total outlet	Little relation	Marked relation

Summary and Comparisons (*Continued*)

	IN FEMALES	IN MALES
Relation to Parental Occupational Class	Little or none	Little or none
Relation to Decade of Birth	Marked	Some
Accumul. incid. petting experience (by age 35)	Steady increase	Some increase
Born before 1900	80%	
Born 1900–1909	91%	
Born 1910–1929	Nearly 99%	
First experience, median individ.		
Born before 1900	By age 18	
Born after 1920	Between ages 15–16	
Accum. incid., petting to orgasm (by age 35)	Increase from 26 to 53%	
Active incidence of orgasm (*e.g.* at ages 21–25)	Marked increase	
Born before 1900	15%	
Born 1900–1909	32%	
Born 1910–1919	34%	
Born 1920–1929	37%	
Frequency to orgasm	No relation	Some relation?
Relation to Age at Onset of Adolescence	Little or none	Little or none
Relation to Rural-Urban Background		
Accumulative incidence, experience	No relation	
Accumulative incidence, to orgasm	Urban higher	
Active incidence of orgasm	Little relation	Some relation
Relation to Religious Background		
Accumulative incidence, experience	Little relation	
Accumulative incidence, to orgasm	For less devout, twice as high as in devout	
Active incidence of orgasm	Little relation	Some relation
Frequency of orgasm (active median)	No relation	Little or no relation
Percentage of total outlet	No relation	Little or no relation
Petting as a Measure of Capacities		
Accumulative incidence		
Experience curve develops	Abruptly	Abruptly
Is a measure of sexual interest	Less often	More often
Petting to orgasm curve develops	Gradually in all groups	Abruptly in college group
Is a measure of sexual interest	Yes	
Frequency		
Maxima limited more often	Yes	No
Minima set more often	No	Yes
Techniques of Petting		
Most extended: college groups	Yes	Yes
Most extended: recent generations	Yes	Yes
Oral techniques most taboo	Yes	Yes
Maximum among those with most coital exper.	Markedly so	No

Summary and Comparisons (*Continued*)

	IN FEMALES	IN MALES
Moral and Legal Attitudes		
Religious codes condemn	Yes	Yes
Laws of most states condemn		
When minor is involved	?	Yes
As assault and battery	?	Yes
As public indecency	Yes	Yes
As disorderly conduct	Yes	Yes
As sodomy	Yes	Yes
Physiologic Significance of Petting		
Provides erotic satisfaction	Sometimes for 83%	Usually for 91%
Provides release in orgasm	Sometimes for 39%	Sometimes for 31%
Contributes to total outlet	4–18%	3% or less
Nervous disturbance if no orgasm	Sometimes for 51%	For many
Sometimes leads to masturbation in	35%	Many
Social Significance of Petting		
Source of first erotic arousal	34%	Rarely
Source of first orgasm	24%	1% or less
Educates in socio-sexual relations	Yes	Yes
Contributes to choice of a spouse	Yes	Yes
Contributes to improvement of marital coitus	Definitely	Yes, to some degree

Table 56. Accumulative Incidence: Petting Experience, Response, and Orgasm

By Educational Level

AGE	TOTAL SAMPLE	EDUCATIONAL LEVEL				TOTAL SAMPLE	EDUCATIONAL LEVEL			
		0–8	9–12	13–16	17+		0–8	9–12	13–16	17+

PETTING EXPERIENCE

AGE	%	Percent				Cases	Cases			
12	4	5	4	4	4	5764	176	1010	3291	1151
13	12	12	13	11	10	5761	175	1010	3291	1151
14	24	23	26	23	21	5751	175	1010	3291	1151
15	39	35	43	40	31	5723	171	1007	3291	1151
16	58	53	64	60	46	5680	163	998	3291	1150
17	72	62	76	75	59	5576	145	964	3275	1147
18	81	66	85	85	71	5305	123	903	3124	1140
20	88	78	91	91	81	3971	95	705	2061	1110
25	91		95	92	88	1474		272	485	668
30	91		95	94	90	674		98	186	362
35	88			89	88	383			87	241

PETTING WITH EROTIC RESPONSE

AGE	%	Percent				Cases	Cases			
12	2	3	2	2	2	5347	169	930	3050	1062
13	5	7	6	4	5	5334	168	930	3050	1062
14	11	15	12	10	10	5317	168	930	3050	1062
15	21	24	24	20	18	5287	164	928	3050	1062
16	36	35	42	36	31	5245	156	920	3050	1062
17	51	44	54	53	41	5142	138	886	3035	1059
18	64	51	67	67	53	4890	116	833	2889	1052
20	75	58	76	79	67	3638	89	647	1880	1026
25	80		81	84	79	1350		245	437	623
30	83		84	87	82	611		85	164	335
35	80			81	81	352			78	222

PETTING TO ORGASM

AGE	%	Percent				Cases	Cases			
12	—	1	—	—	—	5782	179	1014	3301	1148
13	1	2	1	—	1	5774	178	1014	3301	1148
14	1	3	1	1	1	5761	178	1014	3301	1148
15	3	4	5	2	2	5729	174	1011	3301	1148
16	6	5	8	5	4	5683	166	1001	3301	1147
17	9	9	12	9	7	5575	148	966	3285	1144
18	15	13	17	16	11	5308	126	905	3134	1137
20	23	13	24	24	19	3978	98	705	2068	1107
25	31	20	40	30	28	1471	51	270	486	664
30	38		43	42	36	675		97	186	362
35	39			44	39	385			87	241

Italic figures throughout the series of tables indicate that the calculations are based on less than 50 cases. No calculations are based on less than 11 cases. The dash (—) indicates a percentage or frequency smaller than any quantity which would be shown by a figure in the given number of decimal places.

Table 57. Active Incidence, Frequency, and Percentage of Outlet
Petting to Orgasm

By Age

AGE DURING ACTIVITY	ACTIVE SAMPLE			TOTAL SAMPLE		CASES IN TOTAL SAMPLE
	Active incid. %	Median freq. per wk.	Mean frequency per wk.	Mean frequency per wk.	% of total outlet	
Adol.–15	3	0.11	0.42 ± 0.055	0.01 ± 0.002	4	5677
16–20	23	0.09	0.33 ± 0.017	0.08 ± 0.004	18	5613
21–25	31	0.13	0.38 ± 0.024	0.12 ± 0.008	18	2810
26–30	32	0.09	0.36 ± 0.041	0.12 ± 0.014	13	1064
31–35	32	0.09	0.27 ± 0.038	0.09 ± 0.013	8	539
36–40	28	0.09	0.24 ± 0.034	0.07 ± 0.011	5	315
41–45	20	0.09	0.26 ± 0.054	0.05 ± 0.013	5	179
46–50	14	0.09	0.18 ± 0.054	0.03 ± 0.009	3	109
51–55	9			0.02 ± 0.013	3	58
56–60	7			0.00 ± 0.002	1	27

Table 58. Active Incidence, Frequency, and Percentage of Outlet
Petting to Orgasm

By Educational Level

Age	Educ. level	Active incid. %	Active median freq. per wk.	% of total outlet	Cases in total sample	Age	Educ. level	Active incid. %	Active median freq. per wk.	% of total outlet	Cases in total sample
Adol. –15 Total		3	0.1	4	5677	26–30 Total		32	0.1	13	1064
	0–8	4		8	162		9–12	33	0.1	16	181
	9–12	5	0.2	6	983		13–16	34	0.1	9	313
	13–16	2	0.1	3	3271		17+	31	0.1	14	531
	17+	2	0.1	3	1128	31–35 Total		32	0.1	8	539
16–20 Total		23	0.1	18	5613		9–12	31	0.1	9	65
	0–8	13	0.2	9	143		13–16	33	0.1	5	139
	9–12	24	0.1	21	976		17+	33	0.1	11	309
	13–16	26	0.1	18	3299	36–40 Total		28	0.1	5	315
	17+	19	0.2	16	1149		13–16	35	0.1	3	68
21–25 Total		31	0.1	18	2810		17+	26	0.1	6	205
	0–8	20	0.3	14	67	41–45 Total		20	0.1	5	179
	9–12	32	0.2	23	537		17+	19	0.1	4	122
	13–16	34	0.1	15	1204	46–50 Total		14	0.1	3	109
	17+	31	0.2	20	1002		17+	18	0.1	4	80

Table 59. Number of Years of Petting Experience
By Age at First Marriage

NUMBER OF YEARS INVOLVED	TOTAL MARRIED SAMPLE	AGE AT MARRIAGE			
		16–20	21–25	26–30	31–35
	%	*Percent*			
1 or less	8	16	5	4	3
2–3	15	32	8	7	11
4–5	23	34	26	4	4
6–10	39	18	56	40	9
11–20	15		5	45	73
Number of cases	2452	643	1211	431	111
Median number of years	6.6	4.1	7.0	10.3	14.2

Twenty females who were without petting experience before marriage were not included in this table.

Table 60. Number of Partners, Among Females with Petting Experience
By Age at First Marriage

NUMBER OF PARTNERS	PARTNERS BEFORE MARRIAGE					PARTNERS BEFORE GRAD. FROM HIGH SCHOOL	PARTNERS BETWEEN HIGH SCHOOL AND MARRIAGE
	Total married sample	Age at first marriage					
		16–20	21–25	26–30	31–35		
	%	*Percent of females*				*%*	*%*
1	10	13	9	8	8	15	16
2–5	32	35	31	32	29	31	39
6–10	23	23	26	17	19	10	21
11–20	16	17	16	17	16	6	12
21–30	8	6	8	11	12	2	6
31–50	6	3	6	7	7	1	3
51+	5	3	4	8	9	—	3
Number of cases	2415	631	1197	426	107	2099	2086
Median no. of partners	7.7	6.4	7.9	9.1	9.5	4.3	5.5

The data in the table are based on females who, because they were married by the time of the interview, had completed their pre-marital experience. In the calculation of the median, the number of partners have been treated as continuous data. The last two columns are based on females who had completed high school. Among the females who had done petting before marriage, 35 per cent had not done so before graduation from high school, and the median shown for the high school is based on the 65 per cent who did do petting in that period.

Table 61. Accumulative Incidence: Petting Experience and Orgasm

By Age at First Marriage

AGE	AGE AT FIRST MARRIAGE			AGE AT FIRST MARRIAGE		
	16–20	21–25	26–30	16–20	21–25	26–30

PETTING EXPERIENCE

	Percent			*Cases*		
12	7	3	3	650	1220	436
14	36	23	16	650	1220	436
16	75	57	44	650	1220	436
18	95	85	69	560	1220	436
20	100	93	82	236	1220	436
25		98	95		162	436
30			100			53

PETTING TO ORGASM

	Percent			*Cases*		
12	1	—	—	650	1224	436
14	2	1	1	650	1224	436
16	10	4	4	650	1224	436
18	26	12	10	560	1224	436
20	31	25	18	236	1224	436
25		34	36		161	436
30			47			53

Table 62. Accumulative Incidence: Petting Experience

By Age at First Marriage and Educational Level

AGE	EDUCATIONAL LEVEL			EDUCATIONAL LEVEL		
	9–12	13–16	17+	9–12	13–16	17+

AGE AT FIRST MARRIAGE: 16–20

	Percent			*Cases*		
12	4	5	11	226	309	71
14	33	36	37	226	309	71
16	74	75	72	226	309	71
18	94	97	93	188	284	61
20	100	100	*100*	64	128	32

AGE AT FIRST MARRIAGE: 21–25

	Percent			*Cases*		
12	3	3	4	319	547	320
14	23	22	27	319	547	320
16	61	58	56	319	547	320
18	87	85	83	319	547	320
20	94	94	93	319	547	320
25	*100*	95	*100*	43	64	48

AGE AT FIRST MARRIAGE: 26–30

	Percent			*Cases*		
12	7	1	4	106	151	164
14	21	15	15	106	151	164
16	56	44	36	106	151	164
18	81	69	65	106	151	164
20	90	79	79	106	151	164
25	96	96	95	106	151	164
28	*100*	98	97	48	57	76

273

Table 63. Accumulative Incidence: Petting Experience and Orgasm By Parental Occupational Class

AGE	PARENTAL CLASS 2+3	4	5	6+7	PARENTAL CLASS 2+3	4	5	6+7
	Percent				*Cases*			

PETTING EXPERIENCE

AGE	2+3	4	5	6+7	2+3	4	5	6+7
12	6	3	4	4	968	809	1522	2678
14	27	21	23	25	958	809	1520	2670
16	58	57	60	58	908	801	1516	2653
18	78	82	83	82	785	746	1435	2517
20	86	88	89	88	605	572	1036	1884
25	90	90	92	91	259	229	378	653
30	91	90	92	91	124	115	187	278
35	88	82	88	90	69	56	105	173

PETTING TO ORGASM

AGE	2+3	4	5	6+7	2+3	4	5	6+7
	Percent				*Cases*			
12	1	—	0	—	961	805	1509	2645
14	2	1	1	1	951	805	1507	2637
16	8	5	4	6	901	797	1503	2620
18	15	12	14	15	777	743	1423	2484
20	20	18	22	24	599	569	1024	1857
25	29	27	30	32	256	225	374	642
30	34	33	36	41	122	114	183	273
35	35	27	42	42	69	55	102	170

Table 64. Active Incidence and Percentage of Outlet: Petting to Orgasm By Parental Occupational Class

Age	Parental class	Active incid. %	% of total outlet	Cases in total sample	Age	Parental class	Active incid. %	% of total outlet	Cases in total sample
Adol.–15					26–30				
	2+3	5	5	947		2+3	30	16	195
	4	3	6	796		4	27	10	181
	5	2	2	1506		5	29	12	275
	6+7	3	3	2654		6+7	35	13	447
16–20					31–35				
	2+3	20	14	881		2+3	31	14	96
	4	21	22	796		4	24	11	91
	5	22	19	1512		5	33	6	148
	6+7	26	17	2649		6+7	32	8	224
21–25					36–40				
	2+3	29	22	461		2+3	24	16	62
	4	27	18	422		5	31	7	85
	5	30	18	734		6+7	26	3	141
	6+7	34	17	1283					

The occupational classes are as follows: 2 + 3 = unskilled and semi-skilled labor. 4 = skilled labor. 5 = lower white collar class. 6 + 7 = upper white collar and professional classes. For an explanation of the discrepancies between certain of these active incidences and the accumulative incidences shown for the same ages, see p. 44.

Table 65. Accumulative Incidence: Petting Experience and Orgasm By Decade of Birth

AGE	Bf. 1900	DECADE OF BIRTH 1900–1909	1910–1919	1920–1929	Bf. 1900	DECADE OF BIRTH 1900–1909	1910–1919	1920–1929
		PETTING EXPERIENCE						
		Percent				*Cases*		
12	1	3	4	4	454	782	1334	3066
14	13	19	24	26	454	782	1333	3066
16	35	44	58	65	454	778	1330	3020
18	56	71	81	89	445	762	1301	2750
20	66	81	90	94	418	705	1209	1639
25	76	90	97	94	274	432	614	154
30	80	91	99		172	257	245	
35	80	91	98		132	189	62	
		PETTING TO ORGASM						
		Percent				*Cases*		
12	—	—	—	—	452	774	1306	3051
14	1	1	1	1	452	774	1305	3051
16	3	5	6	6	452	770	1302	3005
18	6	10	13	18	443	755	1274	2734
20	10	17	22	28	416	698	1183	1629
25	15	30	34	43	271	424	605	154
30	24	39	45		169	252	242	
35	26	44	53		129	186	61	

Table 66. Active Incidence and Percentage of Outlet: Petting to Orgasm By Decade of Birth

Age	Decade of birth	Active incid. %	% of total outlet	Cases in total sample	Age	Decade of birth	Active incid. %	% of total outlet	Cases in total sample
Adol. –15	Bf. 1900	3	4	436	31–35	Bf. 1900	21	7	151
	1900–1909	2	1	760		1900–1909	36	8	228
	1910–1919	3	3	1319		1910–1919	34	10	160
	1920–1929	3	5	3049					
16–20	Bf. 1900	10	12	451	36–40	Bf. 1900	19	4	123
	1900–1909	17	12	772		1900–1909	33	6	165
	1910–1919	22	16	1328					
	1920–1929	28	21	2999					
21–25	Bf. 1900	15	12	366	41–45	Bf. 1900	13	3	116
	1900–1909	32	18	617		1900–1909	32	10	63
	1910–1919	34	19	986					
	1920–1929	37	20	843					
26–30	Bf. 1900	17	6	218					
	1900–1909	37	13	344					
	1910–1919	35	15	448					
	1920–1929	33	13	54					

For an explanation of the discrepancies between certain of these active incidences and the accumulative incidences shown for the same ages, see p. 44.

Table 67. Accumulative Incidence: Petting Experience and Orgasm
By Age at Onset of Adolescence

AGE	ADOLESCENT					ADOLESCENT				
	By 11	At 12	At 13	At 14	At 15+	By 11	At 12	At 13	At 14	At 15+
					PETTING EXPERIENCE					
			Percent					Cases		
12	11	6				1198	1678			
14	31	27	23	18		1185	1673	1743	794	
16	62	63	57	53	41	1171	1650	1712	787	344
18	83	84	82	76	75	1100	1535	1607	726	322
20	87	90	88	84	83	787	1118	1213	599	250
25	91	92	90	89	91	252	383	455	259	121
30	91	94	89	90	95	127	152	207	128	59
35	90	90	83	88		79	82	116	74	
					PETTING TO ORGASM					
			Percent					Cases		
12	1	—				1187	1656			
14	2	1	1	1		1174	1651	1731	786	
16	7	5	5	5	3	1160	1628	1700	779	345
18	19	15	14	13	9	1088	1514	1595	719	323
20	26	23	23	18	14	778	1100	1202	594	251
25	33	30	31	30	25	251	378	449	255	118
30	38	32	40	37	42	127	150	203	126	57
35	46	35	40	36		79	81	114	72	

Table 68. Active Incidence and Percentage of Outlet: Petting to Orgasm
By Age at Onset of Adolescence

Age during activity	Age at adol.	Active incid. %	% of total outlet	Cases in total sample	Age during activity	Age at adol.	Active incid. %	% of total outlet	Cases in total sample
Adol. −15	8–11	4	6	1203	26–30	8–11	35	15	196
	12	2	3	1684		12	27	12	266
	13	3	4	1747		13	34	9	323
	14	3	3	796		14	32	17	192
	15+	—	—	262		15+	32	12	87
16–20	8–11	28	18	1166	31–35	8–11	38	10	99
	12	23	21	1638		12	31	7	122
	13	25	18	1700		13	32	7	162
	14	18	15	777		14	25	9	109
	15+	14	8	345					
21–25	8–11	33	18	526	36–40	8–11	32	3	65
	12	32	21	769		12	29	6	66
	13	33	18	851		13	26	6	96
	14	30	17	460		14	24	5	62
	15+	27	19	203					

For an explanation of the discrepancies between certain of these active incidences and the accumulative incidences shown for the same ages, see p. 44.

Table 69. Accumulative Incidence: Petting Experience and Orgasm By Rural-Urban Background

AGE	PETTING EXPERIENCE				PETTING TO ORGASM			
	Rural	Urban	Rural	Urban	Rural	Urban	Rural	Urban
	Percent		*Cases*		*Percent*		*Cases*	
12	3	4	398	5185	—	—	387	5151
14	20	24	397	5171	1	1	386	5137
16	55	58	392	5106	3	6	381	5072
18	77	82	366	4766	9	15	355	4733
20	87	88	307	3527	13	23	296	3502
25	90	91	134	1275	23	31	129	1263
30	91	91	70	575	36	38	67	568
35		88		321		41		315

Table 70. Active Incidence and Percentage of Outlet: Petting to Orgasm By Rural-Urban Background

Age during activity	Back-grnd.	Active incid. %	% of total outlet	Cases in total sample	Age during activity	Back-grnd.	Active incid. %	% of total outlet	Cases in total sample
Adol.–15	Rural	2	3	388	26–30	Rural	32	17	104
	Urban	3	4	5132		Urban	32	12	915
16–20	Rural	17	13	386	31–35	Rural	27	12	64
	Urban	25	18	5080		Urban	32	8	453
21–25	Rural	29	26	229					
	Urban	31	18	2483					

For an explanation of the discrepancies between certain of these active incidences and the accumulative incidences shown for the same ages, see p. 44.

Table 71. Accumulative Incidence: Petting Experience and Orgasm By Religious Background

AGE	PROTESTANT			CATHOLIC			JEWISH	
	Dev.	Moder.	Inact.	Dev.	Moder.	Inact.	Moder.	Inact.
PETTING EXPERIENCE—PERCENT								
12	3	5	4	2	5	10	3	5
14	22	23	26	20	28	37	20	26
16	56	59	56	53	63	62	61	62
18	78	82	79	74	84	82	88	86
20	86	88	85	85	86	89	92	92
25	86	93	90	88		92	97	95
30	85	89	94					99
35	80	84	96					
PETTING TO ORGASM—PERCENT								
12	—	—	—	0	1	2	—	—
14	1	1	1	—	1	4	1	1
16	3	6	5	4	5	12	6	8
18	10	15	14	10	15	22	19	21
20	17	21	20	15	20	31	27	33
25	21	34	29	22		40	44	42
30	23	43	38					53
35	23	39	39					
PETTING EXPERIENCE—CASES								
12	1228	1164	1087	388	153	171	575	984
14	1223	1159	1086	385	152	171	575	981
16	1197	1143	1075	379	148	165	573	977
18	1115	1094	1027	346	123	147	529	902
20	856	851	885	260	84	122	305	624
25	304	334	407	110		59	71	174
30	141	159	197					73
35	86	93	121					
PETTING TO ORGASM—CASES								
12	1217	1154	1066	386	151	168	573	977
14	1212	1149	1065	383	150	168	573	974
16	1186	1133	1054	377	146	162	571	970
18	1103	1085	1007	344	121	144	528	895
20	846	842	868	259	82	119	305	619
25	302	329	398	109		58	71	170
30	141	155	192					70
35	86	91	117					

Table 72. Active Incidence, Frequency, and Percentage of Outlet: Petting to Orgasm

By Religious Background

Age during activity	Religious group	Active incid. %	Active median freq. per wk.	% of total outlet	Cases in total sample
Adol.–15	Protestant				
	Devout	2	0.10	3	1218
	Moderate	3	0.10	5	1147
	Inactive	3	0.18	3	1063
	Catholic				
	Devout	2		2	382
	Moderate	3		7	150
	Inactive	7	0.43	4	169
	Jewish				
	Devout	3		2	107
	Moderate	2	0.45	7	571
	Inactive	3	0.09	2	978
16–20	Protestant				
	Devout	19	0.09	18	1197
	Moderate	21	0.09	21	1133
	Inactive	22	0.10	13	1065
	Catholic				
	Devout	15	0.11	11	372
	Moderate	19	0.10	18	139
	Inactive	31	0.28	11	160
	Jewish				
	Devout	23	0.08	12	107
	Moderate	29	0.09	23	571
	Inactive	33	0.09	21	972
21–25	Protestant				
	Devout	26	0.11	20	604
	Moderate	33	0.10	23	615
	Inactive	31	0.12	14	675
	Catholic				
	Devout	25	0.16	26	196
	Moderate	40	0.20	21	57
	Inactive	36	0.25	14	91
	Jewish				
	Moderate	39	0.21	24	192
	Inactive	39	0.15	17	396
26–30	Protestant				
	Devout	20	0.11	11	221
	Moderate	37	0.09	19	249
	Inactive	31	0.09	10	309
	Catholic				
	Devout	20	0.13	12	79
31–35	Protestant				
	Devout	21	0.19	7	121
	Moderate	35	0.08	10	127
	Inactive	32	0.08	8	159
36–40	Protestant				
	Devout	18	0.19	4	76
	Moderate	29	0.16	9	77
	Inactive	27	0.08	4	102

For an explanation of the discrepancies between certain of these active incidences and the accumulative incidences shown for the same ages, see p. 44.

Table 73. Incidence: Pre-Marital Petting Techniques

Percentage with experience prior to interview

EDUC. LEVEL	BORN BEFORE 1900		BORN BETWEEN 1900–1909			BORN 1910 AND AFTER		
	Coital Experience		Coital Experience			Coital Experience		
	None	Over 25 times	None	Less than 25 times	Over 25 times	None	Less than 25 times	Over 25 times
SIMPLE KISSING								
Total	100	100	100	99	100	100	100	100
9–12	99		100			100	100	100
13–16	100		100	100	100	100	100	100
17+	100	100	100	98	100	100	100	100
DEEP KISSING								
Total	44	82	63	78	93	74	87	90
9–12	49		57			64	68	83
13–16	50		63	82	91	76	95	95
17+	38	82	71	79	95	79	94	98
MANUAL·STIMULATION OF FEMALE BREAST								
Total	65	96	77	93	98	72	95	98
9–12	61		76			73	89	98
13–16	70		77	97	98	70	98	99
17+	66	96	81	93	99	82	99	100
ORAL STIMULATION OF FEMALE BREAST								
Total	19	78	33	59	87	32	73	87
9–12	16		39			28	56	79
13–16	20		32	58	87	30	78	91
17+	23	82	35	70	90	46	86	97
MANUAL STIMULATION OF FEMALE GENITALIA								
Total	20	93	44	87	95	36	87	95
9–12	20		54			38	75	90
13–16	21		42	86	93	33	92	97
17+	24	96	46	91	97	54	93	100
MANUAL STIMULATION OF MALE GENITALIA								
Total	12	87	31	59	87	24	72	86
9–12	14		35			25	52	77
13–16	11		31	59	88	22	81	90
17+	14	92	31	70	91	40	83	94

(*Table continued on next page*)

Table 73 (continued)

| EDUC. LEVEL | BORN BEFORE 1900 | | BORN BETWEEN 1900–1909 | | | BORN 1910 AND AFTER | | |
| | Coital Experience | | Coital Experience | | | Coital Experience | | |
	None	Over 25 times	None	Less than 25 times	Over 25 times	None	Less than 25 times	Over 25 times
ORAL STIMULATION OF FEMALE GENITALIA								
Total	1	50	4	9	51	3	20	46
9–12	1		5			3	15	40
13–16	0		4	8	45	3	21	48
17+	3	56	5	14	57	7	26	52
ORAL STIMULATION OF MALE GENITALIA								
Total	—	38	3	5	42	2	16	43
9–12	1		1			2	8	37
13–16	0		4	3	40	2	17	45
17+	0	40	3	7	47	5	23	49
APPOSITION OF GENITALIA								
Total	8	38	22	40	52	17	56	55
9–12	9		18			19	38	44
13–16	5		25	47	51	16	65	62
17+	10	40	24	43	53	23	59	64
NUMBER OF CASES								
Total	286	89	353	150	263	2662	705	831
9–12	74		74			383	158	215
13–16	80		132	59	89	1936	386	391
17+	107	50	129	57	124	313	134	187

Table 74. After-Effects of Petting Without Orgasm

| NATURE OF AFTER-EFFECTS | TOTAL SAMPLE | EDUCATIONAL LEVEL | | | TOTAL SAMPLE | EDUCATIONAL LEVEL | | |
		9–12	13–16	17+		9–12	13–16	17+
	%	*Percent of females*			Cases	*Cases*		
Nervous, ever	51	48	54	51	4878	875	2801	1018
Masturbate, ever	35	31	35	39	1005	229	508	240
Ache in groin, ever	26	27	24	30	1723	417	910	359

Chapter 8

PRE-MARITAL COITUS

About two-thirds (64 per cent) of the married females in our sample had experienced sexual orgasm prior to their marriage. Some of them had had limited experience, some of them had had frequent and regular experience in orgasm. Masturbation, nocturnal dreams, heterosexual petting, heterosexual coitus, and homosexual contacts were the five sources of essentially all of this pre-marital outlet (Table 171).

Coitus had provided only a sixth (17 per cent) of the orgasms which these females had had before marriage. Although many persons think of "intercourse" and "sexual relations" as synonymous terms, true vaginal intercourse had accounted for only a part, albeit a significant part, of the sexual activity before marriage. The social significance of the coitus was, of course, more important than its function in providing a physiologic outlet for the female. In our culture, its significance has been enhanced by the moral and legal condemnation of such activity before marriage, and this has made it difficult to secure any objective evaluation of the relation of pre-marital coitus to the individual's sexual needs and to society's intrinsic interests.

There have been few scientific data to show what effect pre-marital coitus may have on a female's subsequent sexual adjustments in marriage. It is to be hoped that the data which we now have on the pre-marital and marital histories of the females in the present sample may contribute to our understanding of the meaning of coitus before marriage.

HISTORICAL ORIGINS

Mammalian Backgrounds. Most mammals, both female and male, engage in coitus or try to engage in coitus as soon as they are able to make the necessary physical coordinations. This happens within a matter of weeks after birth in the case of most of the rodents and in some of the other smaller mammals, and within the first year among the larger mammals. Similarly early activity is found even in such large and higher primates as the chimpanzee and the orang-utang where adolescence does not appear until some seven to ten years after birth, which is not much earlier than it appears in the human species.[1]

---

[1] There are data on the attempts of very young or pre-adolescent mammals to effect coitus in the following, among other references: Stone 1922 (rat).

The males of all the lower mammals are erotically responsive and become aggressive in initiating sex play and actual coitus at a somewhat earlier age than the females of the same species.[2] It is not surprising, therefore, to find that the pre-adolescent human female is not so often involved in sex play and actual coitus as the average pre-adolescent male (Table 14; see our 1948:162).

Since there is no institution of marriage among the lower mammals, and since coitus for them is a direct outgrowth of early infantile and pre-adolescent play, there can be, strictly speaking, no distinction between pre-marital and marital activity in any group lower than man. While human custom and man-made law may make a sharp distinction between coitus which occurs before marriage and the identical physical acts when they occur within a marriage, it is important to realize that physically and physiologically they are one and the same thing in man, just as they are in the lower mammals.

Anthropologic Data. In most human cultures outside of our own, sex play starts, just as it does among the lower mammals, as soon as there is a sufficient muscular coordination and any sort of social integration.[3] Children as young as two or three may engage in some sort of play, and by five or six they may regularly engage in play which at least imitates coitus (Chapter 4). Much of the play may amount to nothing more than inter-femoral or inter-labial intercourse (placing the penis between the thighs or the genital lips of the female), but vaginal penetrations can be effected by some young boys. Sometimes this play receives the admiring encouragement of the adults of the community. The techniques of adult coitus are gradually developed out of this early play. This is precisely what we have found among younger children of the more uninhibited segments of our own American population.

Bingham 1928:82–86, 89–112 (chimpanzee). Louttit 1929 (guinea pig). Zuckerman 1932:259, 272–274, 289 (baboon). Boling et al. 1939 (guinea pig). Beach 1948; Beach in Hoch and Zubin 1949:43 (rat, hamster, guinea pig, bull). Ford and Beach 1951:192–193 (lamb, bull, monkey, orang-utang). We have data from the personnel of the Brookfield Zoological Park in Chicago (antelope and orang-utang), and our own observations cover the guinea pig, porcupine, and bull. Our observations on coitus among adult mammals include, in addition, the baboon, chimpanzee, monkey, dog, cat, mink, guinea pig, rat, rabbit, chinchilla, hamster, skunk, horse, cattle, pig, and sheep.

[2] The earlier sexual development of the mammalian male has been confirmed in personal communication with a number of students of sexual behavior in the lower mammals. See also the careful observations of Louttit 1929 on the guinea pig.

[3] Early sex play in children is described in the following, for example: Malinowski 1929:55–59 (for the Trobrianders in Melanesia). Powdermaker 1933:85 (for the Lesu of Melanesia). Devereux 1936:31–32 (for the Mohave Indians). Gorer 1938:310 (for the Lepcha in India). Henry in Hoch and Zubin 1949:94–98 (for the Pilaga in Brazil). See our 1948:ch. 5, and the present volume (Chapter 4).

In some cultures pre-adolescent sex play continues without a break into adolescent and teen-age relationships. In other cultures there are social restrictions on the continuation of such play as adolescence approaches.[4] In many primitive groups, and in some Asiatic and European groups including, for instance, some Mediterranean and Latin American groups, complete nudity and at least some open sex play may be allowed among younger pre-adolescent girls until they are five or six years of age. Until they are nearly adolescent, boys may go nude in rural and small urban areas and sometimes even on city streets which are not frequented by European or American tourists. With the approach of adolescence, however, social contacts between boys and girls in such cultures may be restricted, and mature sexual activities subsequently start as more or less new developments.

In nearly every culture in the world except our own, there is at least some acceptance of coital activities among unmarried adolescent and teen-age youth, both female and male. About 70 per cent of the cultures are overtly permissive to at least some degree.[5] There are usually tribal restrictions on relations between relatives, or between members of the same clan or of particular clans, but in the majority of instances it is considered socially desirable that there should be pre-marital coitus. In some groups, places are provided in which coitus may occur, as in the bachelors' huts which are customary in some tribes, or in the temporary homes which other groups provide for courting couples.

In ancient Greece and Rome, and in Mediterranean, Moslem, and Oriental cultures, there has been a widespread acceptance of coitus for unmarried males, even though usually there have been sharp restrictions on such activities for females, or at least for females of the middle and upper classes.[6] Consequently the unmarried males in such cultures

---

[4] For attitudes toward sex play at the approach of adolescence, see, for example: Du Bois 1944:69–70, 83, 98 (for the Alor in Melanesia). Elwin 1947:436–437 (for the Muria in India). Ford and Beach 1951:183 (for the Hopi Indians).

[5] Summarizations of the data on the acceptance of pre-marital coitus in primitive cultures may be found in: Hobhouse, Wheeler, and Ginsberg acc. Westermarck 1922(1):157 (found 50 per cent permissive in 120 cultures). Ford 1945:100 (says 40 per cent are overtly permissive). Murdock 1949:264–265 (estimates less than 5 per cent of the peoples of the earth have over-all prohibitions on sexual relations outside of marriage, finds 70 per cent of 158 cultures are definitely permissive to some degree).

[6] The extent and acceptance of pre-marital coitus for the male, with restrictions on the female, is noted *for Europe,* for instance, in: Lecky 1881(2):345. Bloch 1908:237. Michels 1914:134–142. Eberhard 1924:406–408. Beauvoir 1949; 1952. *For Arabia:* Dickson 1949:202–206. *For Japan:* Becker 1899. Krauss, Satow, and Ihm 1931. Azama Otoko, Ikkyū Zenshi Shoshoku Monogatari [ca. 1845]: Book I, III. Takara Bunko [ca. 1885]: I (The Lower Part). *For Greece and Rome:* Aristophanes [5th–4th cent. B.C.]: Peace, 887–899 (1912(1):203; 1924(2):81); The Wasps, 500–502 (1912(2):32; 1924(1): 455). Theocritus [3rd cent. B.C.]: II.40–41 (1912:29); II.138–143 (1912: 37); XXVII.53–71 (1912:343–345). Ovid [1st cent. B.C.]: Amores, I.5. 13–25 (1921:335). Lucian [2nd cent. A.D.]: Lucius, or the Ass, 8–10 (1895:12–

must find their heterosexual contacts among prostitutes or among other lower level females, or clandestinely on occasion among girls of their own social levels. In some European countries, particularly in Scandinavia and in parts of Central Europe, there has been some wider acceptance of pre-marital coitus for both females and males of all social levels.[7]

In American Cultures. There are curiously mixed attitudes in our own country concerning coitus. Religious and legal codes, the psychologic and social sciences, psychiatric and other clinical theory, and public attitudes in general, agree in extolling heterosexual coitus as the most desirable, the most mature, and the socially most acceptable type of sexual activity. Simultaneously, however, the religious and legal codes and much clinical theory condemn such activity when it occurs outside of marriage and thereby, to a greater extent than most persons ordinarily comprehend, negate all of these claims concerning the desirability of coitus. Such conflicting appraisals of similar if not identical acts often constitute a source of considerable disturbance in the psychosexual development of American youth. These disturbances may have far-reaching effects upon subsequent adjustments in marriage. Our case histories show that this disapproval of heterosexual coitus and of nearly every other type of heterosexual activity before marriage is often an important factor in the development of homosexual activity.

Because of this public condemnation of pre-marital coitus, one might believe that such contacts would be rare among American females and males. But this is only the overt culture, the things that people openly profess to believe and to do. Our previous report (1948) on the male has indicated how far publicly expressed attitudes may depart from the realities of behavior—the covert culture, what males actually do. We may now examine the pre-marital coital behavior of the female sample which has been available for this study.

RELATION TO AGE

As we have already noted, the term coitus, as used in the present volume, refers to a union of female and male genitalia. The term intercourse, when used without a modifier, is often intended as an exact

15). Apuleius [2nd cent. A.D.]: The Golden Ass, 16–17 (1935:72–74; 1822: 33).

[7] The acceptance of pre-marital coitus for the female as well as for the male in parts of Europe is noted, for instance, in: Sundt 1857:51–58 (night courting in Norway). Stiles 1869 and later editions (Scotland, Holland). Rohleder 1907:237 (East Prussia). Henz 1910:743–750. Bauer 1924:77, 287–290 (Germany, Switzerland). Gurewitsch and Woroschbit 1930:68–74 (Russia). Wikman 1937 (an outstanding survey). Jonsson in Wangson 1951 (Sweden). See footnote 16.

synonym of coitus; but the term intercourse may also be used with a modifier, as in the phrases oral or anal intercourse, to refer to the union of the genitalia of one individual with some non-genital portion of another individual's body. In this broader sense it is possible for two individuals of the same sex, as well as two of the opposite sex, to have intercourse; but coitus can be had only between individuals of opposite sex. The data in the present chapter are limited to coital activities, meaning heterosexual, vaginal intercourse between females and males. The data are further limited to the coital activities of females who were

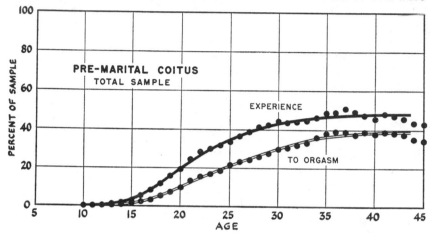

Figure 43. Accumulative incidence: pre-marital coitus, experience and orgasm

Each dot indicates percent of sample with experience or orgasm, by the indicated age. Data from Table 75.

past the age at which they began adolescence, but had not yet been married. The data do not cover pre-adolescent activities, or the activities of females who were again single because they were widowed or divorced.

Accumulative Incidence of Experience. Nearly 50 per cent of the females in our sample had had coitus before they were married (Tables 75, 79, Figure 43).[8] A considerable portion of the pre-marital coitus had been had in the year or two immediately preceding marriage, with a portion of it confined to the fiancé in a period just before marriage. Consequently the incidences had depended upon the age of

---

[8] The incidences of pre-marital coitus reported in previous surveys are highly diverse because of the limited and selected samples on which the studies were based. The data represent accumulative incidences only when they are based on married females for whom the pre-marital period was, in consequence, complete. The following American studies were so based: Hamilton 1929:347 (35 per cent of 100 upper level females). Strakosch 1934:53 (22 per cent of 298 psychopaths). Glueck and Glueck 1934:88 (74 per cent of 254 females who were married before commitment to a reformatory). Terman 1938:320 (37 per cent of 777 females). Landis et al. 1940:290 (36 per cent of 85

marriage (Table 79, Figure 47). The females who married at earlier ages had had pre-marital coitus when they were younger; the females who married at later ages had not begun coitus until much later. There is an obvious correlation between the two phenomena and it is a question whether early experience in coitus leads to early marriage, or whether the possibility of a forthcoming marriage leads, as it certainly does in some cases, to an acceptance of coitus just before marriage.

Very nearly 50 per cent of the females who were married by age twenty had had pre-marital coitus. Similarly those who were married between ages twenty-one and twenty-five had had pre-marital coitus in nearly 50 per cent of the cases. Those who were married between the ages of twenty-six and thirty had had pre-marital coitus in something between 40 and 66 per cent of the cases. If the data are calculated for the entire sample without respect to the age of marriage, the total number of unmarried females who had had coitus by any one of these ages would be very much smaller (Table 75, Figure 43), but it is statistically incorrect to determine the number of persons who ultimately have pre-marital experience by the use of such an accumulative incidence curve.

Except among the females who had married earlier, pre-marital coitus was relatively rare in the early teens. This may have depended in part upon the fact that only a small number of the younger girls are sexually responsive. It must also have depended on the fact that public opinion and the law in this country impose especially heavy penalties on the males who have sex relations with younger girls.[9]

---

married females). Warner 1943:295 (42 per cent of 402 brides who sought medical consultation). Locke 1951:134 (35 per cent of 200 happily married females, and 41 per cent of 201 divorced females).

The data in the following are incomplete because they were based on single females: Achilles 1923:50 (24 per cent). Dickinson and Beam 1934:32, 425–426, 459 (12 to 33 per cent). Strakosch 1934:53 (19 per cent of 402 single psychopathic females). Landis et al. 1940:64 (25 per cent of 210 single females). Warner 1940:6 (38 per cent of 93 engaged females). Clark 1952:27 (63 per cent of a clinical sample of 107 females).

Because the data were not systematically gathered, the figures in the following American studies are quite inadequate: Davis 1929:19 (7 per cent). Dickinson and Beam 1931:81 (8 per cent).

Non-American incidence data on pre-marital coitus may be found in: Schbankov acc. Weissenberg 1924a:13 (10 per cent of 263 single Russian students). Hellmann acc. Weissenberg 1924b:212 (67 per cent of 104 married, middle class Russian females). Golossowker acc. Weissenberg 1925:175 (16 per cent of 107 married Russian females). Gurewitsch and Woroschbit 1930:66 (23 per cent of 1696 married Russian peasants). Dück 1941:11 (80 per cent of 500 German females). Asayama 1949:175 (5 per cent of 282 Japanese college females). Brattgård 1950:1678 (74 per cent of 114 Swedish females). Friedeburg 1950:12 (69 per cent of 517 German females). Fink 1950:34 (44 per cent of 100 Australian females). Jonsson in Wangson 1951:195–196 (52 per cent of 132 single Swedish females and 80 per cent of 182½ married Swedish females). England acc. Rosenthal 1951:56 (39 per cent of single British females, and 47 per cent of married British females). Slater and Woodside 1951:288 (40 per cent of 172 British working class wives).

[9] The maximum penalties for "statutory" rape (coitus by a man with a consenting

Accumulative Incidence to Orgasm. In any sort of coitus there are many females who do not reach orgasm in more than a portion of their contacts. This is true whether the coitus be pre-marital, marital, or extra-marital. The accumulative incidence curve of females who had responded to the point of orgasm more or less parallels the accumulative incidence curve for experience in pre-marital coitus, but at a somewhat lower level. Approximately two-thirds of the females in the active sample had reached orgasm, on at least some occasion, in their pre-marital coitus (Table 75, Figure 43). Interestingly enough, the percentage of the pre-marital coitus which had led to orgasm for the females in the sample seems not to have been materially different from the percentage of marital coitus which had led to orgasm.

Active Incidence. The data show that 3 per cent of the females in the total sample, irrespective of the age at which they had married, had had coital experience by fifteen years of age, 20 per cent had had it between the ages of sixteen and twenty years, and 35 per cent had had it between twenty-one and twenty-five years of age. In the next twenty years something over 40 per cent of the unmarried females were having some pre-marital coitus (Table 76, Figure 44).[10]

Frequency. Pre-marital coitus is had much less frequently than marital coitus, partly because unmarried youth may have some difficulty in locating sexual partners and the places where coitus may be comfortably had, but primarily because of the social restrictions on

---

girl who is below a certain age fixed by statute) are only exceeded by those for murder. They are only equaled by those for forcible rape and kidnapping. Unless the jury recommends mercy, the death sentence is mandatory in 6 states (Del., Fla., Ga., La., N.C., S.C.). A capital sentence is possible in an additional 10 states (Ala., Ky., Md., Miss., Mo., Okla., Tenn., Tex., Va., W. Va.). A life sentence is possible under some circumstances in another 19 states (Ariz., Cal., Colo., Ida., Ill., Ind., Ia., Me., Mass., Minn., Nev., N. M., N. Dak., Ore., S. Dak., Utah, Wash., Wyo.). In the other 13 states the maxima range from 10 years in New York to 99 years in Montana. When the girl is under ten or twelve years of age, the minimum is life imprisonment in several states (*e.g.*, Minn., N. M., Wash.).

[10] What are apparently active incidences of pre-marital coitus are in the following American studies: Ackerson 1931:172 (for 689 girls at Ill. Inst. for Juv. Res., ages 13–18, 26 per cent). Glueck and Glueck 1934:430 (ages of first coitus for 448 delinquent females). Bromley and Britten 1938:287 (7 per cent by end of high school, 25 per cent by college age for 618 females). Lion et al. 1945: 23 (ages of first pre-marital coitus of 365 "promiscuous" females of lower educational levels; one-third before age 16, two-thirds before age 18). In non-American studies, see the following: Hellmann acc. Weissenberg 1924b:212 (13 per cent first coitus by age 16, 82 per cent at ages 17–25, 5 per cent after 25, among 124 Russian females). Schbankov acc. Weissenberg 1924a:13 (26 Russian females). Gurewitsch and Woroschbit 1930:67 (among Russian peasants, note higher incidences of pre-marital coitus in later marriages: 27 per cent if married at 15–19, 43 per cent if married at 25–33). Asayama 1949:175 (13 Japanese college girls). Fink 1950:34 (among 100 Australian girls who married at ages 17–23, 20 per cent had pre-marital coitus; among those married after age 30, 70 per cent were experienced). Wolman 1951:551 (9 per cent of 207 Israeli females had coitus by age 19).

such pre-marital activity (Table 76, Figure 44). Nevertheless, the females in the sample who were having any pre-marital coitus were
having it at an average (active median) frequency of about once in
five or ten weeks if they were under twenty years of age, and about
once in three weeks if they were over twenty years of age. As with
most other sorts of sexual activity among females, the frequencies had
not reached their peak until the twenties. Then they had stayed remarkably level without any evident aging effect until the middle fifties
or even later.[11]

There was, of course, considerable variation in the frequencies of
pre-marital coitus among the females in any particular group (Figure

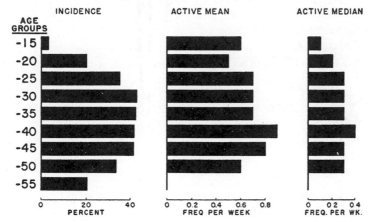

Figure 44. Active incidence, mean, median: experience in pre-marital
coitus, by age
Data from Table 76.

45), and for most of them the activity was sporadic. Outside of marriage relatively few females have coitus with anything like the regularity that is typical of the male. Half or more of the females in the
sample had had pre-marital coitus as often as three or more times in
some single week (Table 77), although often they had not had it again
for weeks or months or even years. Some 20 per cent of the females
had had coitus as often as every day in some single week and 7 per
cent had had it as often as 14 times or more in a single week—but
usually with periods of inactivity occurring between the periods of
coitus. All of the medians and other averages which are presented in
the present chapter represent average frequencies for whole groups,
calculated as though the activity were evenly distributed over the
whole period of time; but it should be understood that such averages
do not sufficiently emphasize the range of the individual variation, and

[11] The very limited material in Dickinson and Beam 1934:171 seems to provide
the only previously published data on frequencies of pre-marital coitus.

the averages are particularly misleading because they fail to emphasize the sporadic nature of such an activity as pre-marital coitus.

Individual variation in the frequency of orgasm was even greater than the variation in the frequency of experience. Some females had never reached orgasm in any of their coitus, some of them had reached orgasm in some portion of it, and some of them had reached orgasm

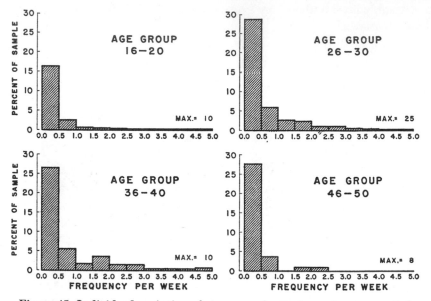

Figure 45. Individual variation: frequency of experience in pre-marital coitus

For four age groups. Each class interval includes the upper but not the lower frequency. For incidences of females not having pre-marital coitus, see Table 76.

one hundred per cent of the time. Some of them had regularly reached orgasm two or more times whenever they had had coitus. Such multiple orgasm is similarly found in marital and post-marital coitus (p. 375). About 14 per cent of the females regularly experience multiple orgasm (Table 177, Figure 151). It is notable that this capacity appears immediately among a portion of the girls who have pre-marital coitus.

Percentage of Total Outlet. Orgasms achieved in pre-marital coitus had accounted for 6 per cent of the total number of orgasms (total sexual outlet) which the younger, teen-age girls in the sample had had. In the late teens between the ages of sixteen and twenty, 15 per cent of the total outlet of the unmarried sample was coming from pre-marital coitus, and for those who were still unmarried in their early twenties, some 26 per cent of the outlet was coming from that source (Table 76). The importance of coitus as a source of the pre-marital outlet had continued to increase until it reached 43 per cent in the mid-forties. After that, its significance had declined among the females who were still unmarried in the late forties and fifties.

Throughout all age groups, masturbation had provided more of the pre-marital outlet, and in the late teens pre-marital petting was still providing somewhat more orgasms than coitus provided. After the early twenties, however, pre-marital coitus had become more important than petting, and after the mid-twenties it was not far inferior to masturbation as a source of outlet (Table 171, Figure 110).

Number of Years Involved. If the calculations are based on the females in the sample who were married and who, in consequence, had completed their pre-marital histories, the record shows that more than a quarter (29 per cent) of those who had had any pre-marital coitus had had it only ten times or less before they were married (Table 78). In many instances it had not occurred more than once before marriage. For 44 per cent of those who had had pre-marital coitus, the entire experience had been confined to a single year or to a portion of a year. For nearly a third (30 per cent), the coitus had extended over a period of two or three years, and for 26 per cent it had extended over four or more years. However, only a very few females had had pre-marital coitus with any continuity over such periods of time.

It is interesting to note that the periods over which the pre-marital experience had extended were remarkably similar in the several generations represented in the sample (Table 78). In this respect, the behavior of the females in the more recent generations had not differed particularly from the behavior of their mothers and grandmothers.

There is, inevitably, a marked correlation between the age at which a female marries and the length of time over which she has pre-marital coitus. Among the females who had married by age twenty, 60 per cent had had such coitus for only one year or less; but among those who had not married until they were past thirty, only 27 per cent had confined their coitus to a single year (Table 78). This means that among the younger females, experience in coitus may, conceivably, be a factor in precipitating an early marriage; but since many of those who do not marry until their late twenties or thirties had been having coitus for several years, and in nearly half of the cases for something more than six years, it is apparent that the mere fact that a female has pre-marital coitus is not sufficient to lead her, in all cases, to any immediate marriage.

Pre-marital coitus with the future spouse had not usually extended over such long periods of time as the coitus with other males (Table

78). For three-quarters (75 per cent) of those females who had had pre-marital relations, the coitus with the fiancé had been confined to a single year or less. The record shows that only a few of the females had become engaged because they had had coitus with the male. On the other hand, there is some evidence that coitus between engaged couples is not infrequently a factor in leading them to fix an early date for their marriage. In at least some of the cases, this is because they wish to secure an opportunity for more complete sexual relationships than they are able to manage before they are married.

Number of Partners. Restricting our data to the married females in the sample, because they had completed their pre-marital histories, the record shows that 53 per cent had had coitus with only a single partner prior to marriage. A third (34 per cent) had had coitus with two to five partners, and 13 per cent had had coitus with six or more (Table 78).[12] However, it should be pointed out again that the sample does not adequately represent the lower educational levels, and we do not have sufficient information to predict whether the data from those groups would show a greater or lesser promiscuity. Neither does the sample include histories of females who had done time in penal institutions, and our calculations show that that group is much more promiscuous in its pre-marital activity. Consequently, the present record is based on only middle class and upper social level females. While the promiscuity in these groups may surprise some persons, it does not approach the promiscuity of the male.

Among the married females in the sample who had had pre-marital coitus, 87 per cent had had at least a portion of it with the men whom they subsequently married (Table 78). Some 46 per cent had confined their coitus to the fiancé.[13] This means that 41 per cent of all the females who had had any such coitus had had it with both the fiancé and with other males. Some 13 per cent had had it with other males but

---

[12] The nature and number of the female's partners in pre-marital coitus are also discussed in the following American studies: Davis 1929:20 (75 per cent of 63 females had one partner, 25 per cent had more than one). Hamilton 1929: 350 (of 35 upper level females with pre-marital experience, 43 to 54 per cent had a single partner, 46 to 57 per cent had 2 or more partners). Bromley and Britten 1938:104 (14 per cent of 185 college females with pre-coital experience are "promiscuous"). Clark 1952:281 (of 34 single females, 64 per cent had 1 partner, 15 per cent, 2–5 partners, and 21 per cent more than 5). European data on pre-marital partners are in Gurewitsch and Woroschbit 1930:72 (31 per cent of 84 Russian females had more than one partner). Brattgård 1950:1678 (in Sweden, finds larger percentage of casual partners at earlier ages).

[13] Data on the fiancé as a pre-marital partner are also given in: Schbankov acc. Weissenberg 1924a:13 (44 per cent of 34 Russian females had coitus with fiancé). Davis 1929:20 (56 per cent of 63 females, with fiancé only). Glueck and Glueck 1934:431 (15 per cent of 328 delinquent women had first coitus with fiancé). Jonsson 1951:200 (of 210 Swedish females, 64 per cent had first coitus with fiancé). England acc. Rosenthal 1951:57 (in Britain, 49 per cent of married females had pre-marital coitus with future spouse).

not with the fiancé. In this respect, females of the older and younger generations represented in the sample had not been particularly different. Among the females who had married at an earlier age, a somewhat higher percentage (54 per cent) had had pre-marital coitus with the fiancé only, while among those who did not marry until they were past thirty, only 28 per cent had confined their coitus to the fiancé.

There is some inclination, even in groups that consider all non-marital coitus wrong, to make some allowance for pre-marital coitus which is had with the subsequent spouse. Even those who administer the law may excuse a certain amount of pre-marital activity if the couple intend to marry and if marriage does in actuality occur. The point of this acceptance is emphasized by the fact that even though such activity may be condoned where there is an intent to marry, legal penalties may subsequently be imposed if the couple fails to marry.[14]

RELATION TO AGE AT MARRIAGE AND EDUCATIONAL LEVEL

Accumulative Incidence. If calculations of the accumulative incidences of pre-marital coitus are based upon the total sample, irrespective of the age of marriage, there appears to have been a marked correlation between the educational levels which the females had ultimately attained, the ages at which they began their pre-marital coitus, and the percentages which were ultimately involved (Table 75, Figure 46). The females in the grade school sample had started coitus five or six years before the females in the graduate sample. Ultimately only 30 per cent of the grade school group had had pre-marital coitus, in contrast to 47 per cent of the high school group and more than 60 per cent of the girls who had gone on into college.[15] Strangely enough, these findings appear to be diametrically contrary to the record which we secured (1948:551) from the pre-marital coital histories of the males in our sample. For instance, about 67 per cent of the males who had gone on to college, but 98 per cent of certain of the male groups which had never gone beyond grade school, had had coitus before marriage.

---

[14] The subsequent intermarriage of the parties is a defense to charges of seduction in most states; of adultery and fornication in Ga., Hawaii, Mont., and N. D.; of statutory rape in Va.; and even of rape in Ill. In some of the states the marriage must be carried on by cohabitation and support for a period of time before it becomes a complete defense. See particularly New Mexico Statutes 1941:41–702.

[15] Data on pre-marital coitus correlated with educational levels may also be found in: Hellmann acc. Weissenberg 1924b:212 (53 per cent of 338 female students in Moscow). Davis 1929:335 (13 per cent of 1064 still unmarried college graduates averaging 37 years of age). Bromley and Britten 1938:289 (24 per cent of 772 college females). Adams 1946:33 (estimated less than one-third of college level have experience). England 1950:152 (in Britain, found a "noticeable lessening of moral strictness amongst those with more education"). Gilbert Youth Research 1951:15 (25 per cent of females in 14 universities). Ehrmann 1952 (12 per cent of 265 females and 14 per cent of 50 females still in college).

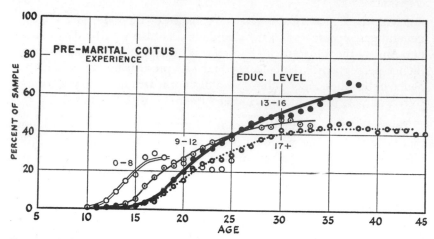

Figure 46. Accumulative incidence: pre-marital coitus, by educational level

Data from Table 75.

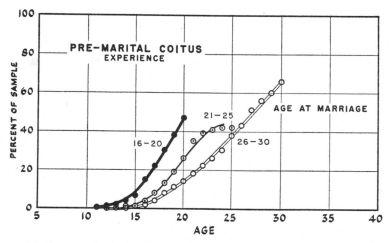

Figure 47. Accumulative incidence: pre-marital coitus, by age at marriage

Data from Table 79.

Further analyses indicate, however, that these correlations between the female's pre-marital coital history and her educational background are wholly dependent upon the fact that marriage occurs, on an average, at quite different ages in these several educational levels (Table 166).

Among the females who had married at a given age, approximately the same percentages had had pre-marital coitus, irrespective of whether they belonged to high school, college, or graduate groups (Table 79). This was true for the females who had married between the ages of sixteen and twenty, for the females who had married between the ages of twenty-one and twenty-five, and for those who had married between the ages of twenty-six and thirty. The close conformance of the incidence figures within any one of these groups is very striking. It emphasizes the fact that most social factors had had a minimum effect upon the pattern of sexual behavior among the females in the sample, but whether they had or had not had pre-marital coitus had been definitely correlated with the age at which they had married.

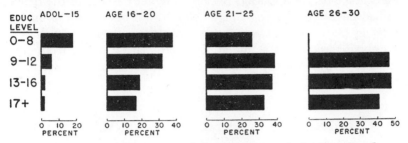

Figure 48. Active incidence: experience in pre-marital coitus, by educational level

Data from Table 80.

We reported (1948:Ch. 10) that social factors do affect the male's pattern of sexual behavior, and a recalculation of our data on the basis of the ages at which the males had married indicates that the correlations with the educational backgrounds of the male are still real and are not eliminated by any corrections for their ages at marriage.

Active Incidence. Because females of the grade school and high school groups marry earlier than females of the college and graduate groups, higher percentages of the lower educational levels were having coitus in the early and late teens, and lower percentages of the upper educational groups. In our limited sample of grade school females, 18 per cent was having coitus by fifteen years of age, as against one per cent of the college and graduate groups (Table 80, Figure 48). Between the ages of sixteen and twenty, 38 per cent of the grade school group and 32 per cent of the high school group were having coitus as against 17 to 19 per cent of the college-educated groups. But after the age of twenty, the active incidences were much the same for the females of all the educational levels. Social restraints and the parental supervision exercised over the girls of the better educated groups may delay their participation in coital activities for some period of years, but such restraints do not appear to have any great influence on their pre-marital activities in later years. This contrasts with the record for the male where the active incidences of pre-marital coitus remain higher among the more poorly educated groups, and lower among the better educated groups, until at least thirty years of age (see our 1948: 348).

Frequency. In contrast to these incidence data, the frequencies of pre-marital coitus do not show consistent correlations with the educational levels of the females, or with the ages at which they had married. These factors may prevent a girl from beginning coitus or some other type of sexual activity, but they do not affect the frequencies with which she engages in pre-marital coitus.

Percentage of Total Outlet. Because a larger number of the females who had never gone beyond high school were having coitus in their late teens, that group, in comparison with the college group, had derived about three times as much of its pre-marital outlet from coitus (Table 80). After twenty years of age, however, these discrepancies had been reduced.

RELATION TO PARENTAL OCCUPATIONAL CLASS

Accumulative Incidence. In the available sample more of the girls who were raised in the homes of parents who were laborers were having pre-marital coitus in their teens, and fewer of those who came from other social levels (Table 81, Figure 49). This again depended upon the fact that the females of the lower social levels had married earlier than the females of the white collar groups; and, as we have already noted (p. 286), pre-marital coitus is most likely to occur in the year or so before marriage.

Among the females who were not married by age twenty-three, almost exactly the same percentages (about 30 per cent) were having pre-marital coitus, irrespective of the occupational classes from which they had come. Because of the selective processes which appear to lead the more responsive females into earlier marriage among the lower social levels, only 38 per cent of those in the sample who had come from laborers' homes had ultimately had pre-marital coitus. On the other hand, among the females who had come from white collar homes, by age thirty-five some 56 per cent had had pre-marital coitus.[16] This record of earlier coital activity among females from the laboring groups supports the popular opinion that there is more pre-marital coitus at those levels; but as far as the older unmarried females are

---

[16] Additional data on pre-marital experience correlated with the female's social background may be found in: Sundt 1857:88–132, Table 4 (for 9000 couples in Norway, reports births of children conceived out of wedlock in 30 per cent of the "property class" and in 50 per cent of the worker class). Dück 1941:8 (in 500 German females, incidence higher and experience earlier in lower classes). Jonsson in Wangson 1951:197 (in Sweden, 50 per cent in two upper social levels, 65 per cent in lowest social level, before age 21). Statements that pre-marital coitus is generally accepted among lower levels in Europe may be found in Rohleder 1907(1):333. Fuchs 1912(3):286–287. Scheuer in Marcuse 1923:242. Eberhard 1924:406.

concerned, it is a much higher percentage of the white collar group that ultimately has pre-marital coitus.

Additional analyses indicate that among the females who had gone on into graduate work, those who were most restrained in regard to pre-marital coitus had come from the homes of skilled mechanics (Class 4). By age thirty, for instance, only 27 per cent of that group had had pre-marital coital experience while 39 per cent of the girls who had come from lower white collar homes and 47 per cent of the ·

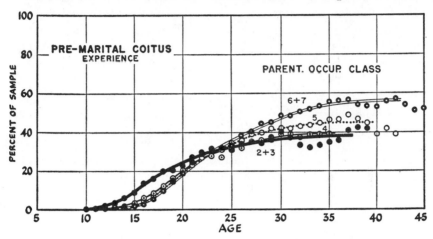

Figure 49. Accumulative incidence: pre-marital coitus, by parental occupational class

Data from Table 81. See pp. 54–55 for definitions of occupational classes.

girls who had come from upper white collar and professional homes had had coital experience (Table 81). Just as we found in the case of the male (1948:427–433), the female who rises from a lower level home and moves up into an upper educational level is likely to be more restrained sexually than the female who originates in an upper level and stays there. The lower level girl seems to be less secure in her newly acquired position, and is consequently more impressed with the importance of following the pattern of behavior which she thinks is most acceptable to the group into which she has moved.

Active Incidence. The percentages who were having coitus in any single five-year period (the active incidence) reflect the situation which we have described for the accumulative incidences. In the younger age groups, 11 per cent of the girls who had come from laborers' homes were having coitus (Table 82), but only 2 per cent of those who had come from white collar homes. Similarly, in the late teens, 31 per cent of the girls from laborers' homes were having coitus, but only 19 per cent of the girls from white collar homes. But after age twenty the differences had disappeared, and by the thirties and forties among the females who were still unmarried, those who came from white collar homes were most often having coitus.

Percentage of Total Outlet. Reflecting the earlier activity of girls from laboring homes, a much higher percentage (15 per cent) of the total sexual outlet of that group was being derived from coitus between adolescence and fifteen years of age, but only 2 per cent of the total outlet of the girls who had originated in white collar homes (Table 82). All the differences were eliminated, however, by the early twenties, and among the females who were still unmarried in their thirties, the upper white collar group, in comparison with the laboring group, was deriving fully twice as much of its total sexual outlet from coitus. Between the ages of thirty-one and forty the females who had originated in upper white collar homes were deriving as much as 41 per cent of their total outlet from coitus.

RELATION TO DECADE OF BIRTH

In contrast to the limited importance of the female's educational and parental home backgrounds, the decade in which she was born shows a marked influence on the incidences and frequencies of her premarital coitus.

Accumulative Incidence. Among the females in the sample who were born before 1900, less than half as many had had pre-marital coitus as among the females born in any subsequent decade (Table 83, Figure 50). For instance, among those who were still unmarried by age twenty-five, 14 per cent of the older generation had had coitus, and 36 per cent of those born in the next decade. This increase in the incidence of pre-marital coitus, and the similar increase in the incidence of pre-marital petting, constitute the greatest changes which we have found between the patterns of sexual behavior in the older and younger generations of American females.[17]

---

[17] Data comparing incidences of non-marital coitus in different generations may also be found in: Hamilton 1929:384 (an increase in such coitus among females born before 1891 and those born later; sample limited). Gurewitsch and Woroschbit 1930:66 (among 1696 married Russian women, pre-marital coitus among 16 per cent of those born before 1900, 37 per cent of those born 1905–1909). Terman 1938:321–323 (finds increasingly more pre-marital coitus in younger generations). Dearborn in Fishbein and Burgess 1947:163 (on 18 older females). Jonsson in Wangson 1951:198 (for Sweden, first coitus before age 18 for 25 per cent of older and 37 per cent of younger females). Locke 1951:136 (shows same trend on small sample). Vigman 1952:90–91 (coitus now begins at an earlier age). The change in attitude after the first World War and later is discussed in: Scheuer in Marcuse 1923: 243. Moreck 1929:77–82. Lynd and Lynd 1929:112. Dickinson and Beam 1931:443–444. Allen 1931:ch.5 (a good general description of changes in manners and morals in the 1920's). Baber 1936:121 (survey of attitudes of 321 college men and 105 fathers). Buck 1936:14–17. Fortune Survey 1937:

As in the case of pre-marital petting (Table 65, Figure 35), practically all of this increase had occurred in the generation that was born in the first decade of the present century and, therefore, in the generation which had had most of its pre-marital experience in the late teens and in the 1920's following the first World War. The later generations appear to have accepted the new pattern and maintained or extended it.

An examination of the possible correlations indicates that changes in the age of marriage of the females in the sample were not responsible for these decade effects. The great change in the incidences of pre-

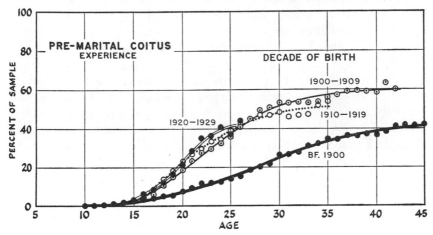

Figure 50. Accumulative incidence: pre-marital coitus, by decade of birth
Data from Table 83.

marital coitus seems to have been a product of a change in attitudes in the generation born in the first decade after 1900. The changes reflected more deliberate approaches to sexual problems by the post-war generation. The development of public interest in the work of Havelock Ellis and Sigmund Freud had helped break down many a traditional barrier to the free consideration of human sexual behavior. The changes were correlated with a developing emancipation of the female, and especially of the unmarried female in our American culture. They were certainly hastened by the war itself. Never before in American history had so many college and lower level males lived together as they did in the first draft army. Never before had so many Americans come into contact with a foreign culture, and especially with one in which the sexual patterns differ as much as Central European patterns do from our own. American youth returning from war service reevaluated the traditional codes as they had not done in any preceding

168; 1943:20. Pringle 1938:14. Himes 1940:31 (suggests factors responsible for the change).

decade, and their adoption of new patterns of behavior in many cases represented an intellectual as well as a hedonistic response to realities which American thinking had previously tried to ignore.

The increased knowledge of contraception, and an increase in the proportion of persons living under the greater anonymity provided by urban centers, may have contributed to the increase in the incidence of pre-marital coitus. Not the least of the contributing factors was the drive against organized prostitution which was stimulated in part by the experience with venereal disease in the first World War. While the number of prostitutes does not seem to have been materially reduced by that drive, and while the number of males who had some experience with prostitutes did not seem to change materially, the frequencies with which American males went to prostitutes had been reduced to about half of what they were in the pre-war generation.[18] Our data indicate, however, that the frequencies of the total amount of pre-marital coitus were not materially modified for the males, because the frequencies of coitus with females who were not prostitutes had increased to an extent which largely compensated for the decreased frequencies with prostitutes. The data which we now have on the female confirm the male data. This increase seems to have occurred among all of the educational and social levels represented in the sample.

It has been suggested that the economic depression of the 1930's and the discovery of penicillin in the mid-forties as a means of controlling venereal infections were factors which contributed to this increase in pre-marital coitus; but these cannot have been more than very minor factors, for the data show clearly that the increase came between 1916 and 1930, a decade or two earlier than either the depression or the discovery of penicillin. There have been only minor increases since 1930.

There has been a general understanding that some sort of change had occurred in the attitudes and sexual behavior of American youth in the so-called "roaring twenties," and the present data show the extent of those changes. Interestingly enough, however, there has been little recognition that the pre-marital petting and coital patterns which were established then are still with us. In the 1920's, older persons were much disturbed at the behavior of the younger generation. Today older persons seem less disturbed about the younger generation. The reason

---

[18] The reduced importance of prostitution is also noted in: Lynd and Lynd 1929: 113–114. Parshley 1933:301. Hohman and Schaffner 1947:505 (56 per cent of 4100 male draftees had coitus with "nice girls," and 23 per cent with prostitutes only). Sylvanus Duvall 1952:207–212. See the specific data in our 1948:411.

seems patent if we realize that the parents and grandparents of today were the youth who introduced the new patterns of sexual behavior thirty years ago.[19]

Active Incidence. The changes in the active incidences of pre-marital coitus, between the pre-war and post-war generations, were similar to those which had occurred in the accumulative incidences. In this sam-

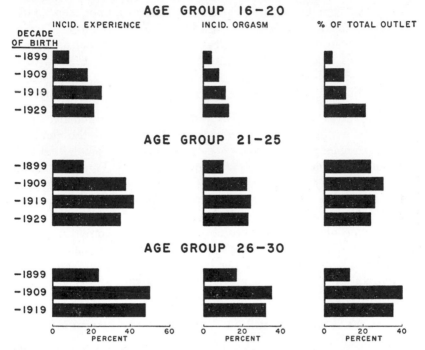

Figure 51. Active incidence: pre-marital coital experience, orgasm, percent of total outlet, by decade of birth

Data from Table 84.

ple, two to three times as many of the females of the younger generations were having pre-marital coitus within a five-year period (Table 84, Figure 51). In examining the specific data in Tables 83 and 84, it should be noted that the lower incidences in the youngest generation do not represent changes in behavior, because a high proportion of the females of the youngest group were not yet married and had not, therefore, completed their pre-marital experience. They may be expected to match the record established for them by the preceding generations.

However, the proportion of females in the sample who ever reached orgasm in their pre-marital coitus had remained remarkably constant,

---

[19] That the sexual patterns of the 1920's survived into the next decade was also recognized by: Lynd and Lynd 1937:170. Newcomb 1937:667 (but behavior today is more realistic and spontaneous, and less compulsive).

from the oldest to the youngest generations (Table 84). The proportion ranged from about 50 per cent at age twenty to more than 75 per cent by age thirty-five.

Frequency. Similarly, the frequency of coitus for the average female who was having any experience (the active median frequency) seems to have been remarkably constant in all generations. The factors which may have accounted for the increased incidences do not seem to have had any comparable effect on the frequencies of pre-marital coitus. The increase in the amount of coitus which American males now have with females who are not prostitutes depends on an increase in the number of females who are having such activity, and not on any increase in the frequencies for the average female (see our 1948:411).

Percentage of Total Outlet. Because the number of females having pre-marital coitus to the point of orgasm had increased, the number of orgasms derived from that source in the sample as a whole had materially increased in the last four decades (Table 84, Figure 51). Since there had not been any comparable increase in the incidences or frequencies of most other sources of sexual outlet—masturbation, nocturnal dreams to orgasm, and homosexual activities—pre-marital petting and pre-marital coitus had become relatively more important sources of outlet. For instance, at ages sixteen to twenty, the females born before 1900 had derived only 4 per cent of their total outlet from pre-marital coitus, while the females born after 1920 had derived 21 per cent of their outlet from that source.

RELATION TO AGE AT ONSET OF ADOLESCENCE

A larger number of the males who had turned adolescent at younger ages had had pre-marital coitus, and a smaller number of the males who had turned adolescent at later ages (see our 1948:313, 315). In the female sample, there is only a slight indication that more of those who had matured at earlier ages (11 or 12) had become involved in pre-marital coitus (the **accumulative incidence** figure), and that those who had not turned adolescent until they were 13 or 14 (and 15?) had not become involved so often (Table 85). The percentages which had ever reached orgasm in their pre-marital coitus were also slightly higher for those who had turned adolescent at earlier ages, and lower for those who became adolescent at later ages.[20] The differences are not great, but an examination of the data shows that they had not been dependent upon the age at which the female had married.

For half of the five-year groups, the **active incidences** were highest

---

[20] Apparently the only other data correlating the female's age at menarche with her pre-marital coitus are in Terman 1938:333 (45 per cent incidence for 103 females adolescent before 12, 34 per cent for 88 females adolescent after 14).

among those females who had turned adolescent by 11 years of age, but this was not true of the other half of the groups (Table 86). The **frequencies** of the pre-marital coitus, and the frequencies of the coitus which had led to orgasm, do not seem to have been correlated with the ages at which the females had turned adolescent.

RELATION TO RURAL-URBAN BACKGROUND

Our samples of rural females are much smaller than the samples of urban females, but in the available material there is an indication that the total number of urban females who had been involved in pre-mari-

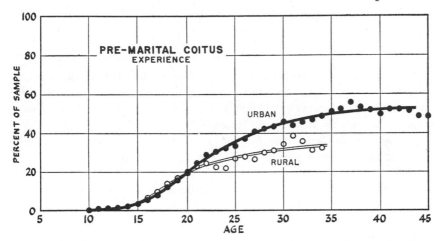

Figure 52. Accumulative incidence: pre-marital coitus, by rural-urban background

Data from Table 87.

tal coitus (the **accumulative incidence** figure) was higher than the number of rural females who had been involved (Table 87, Figure 52).

In the younger age groups, the numbers involved in any single five-year period (the **active incidence** figures) were essentially the same among the rural and urban groups, but after age twenty they were somewhat higher for the urban groups (Table 88).[21]

The average **frequencies** with which the rural and urban females had engaged in pre-marital coitus did not seem to differ in any consistent way in the available sample. Neither had the frequencies with which the rural and urban females reached orgasm.

---

[21] Rural and urban attitudes toward pre-marital coitus are compared in: Fortune Survey 1943:20 (urban twice as liberal as rural females). Rockwood and Ford 1945:43 (of 364 college students, urban group more liberal in attitudes). In Europe, rural areas are reputed to have earlier and more pre-marital coitus, as in: Welander 1908:12 (Swedish; in first coitus of 462 males, the females were under 21 in 44 per cent of Stockholm cases and in 80 per cent of rural cases). Hoyer 1929: 51–59. Remplein 1950:396. Also see footnote 7.

In all five of the groups which are available for comparisons, the **percentage of the total outlet** which was derived from pre-marital coitus was higher among the urban groups (Table 88). This seems to have depended upon the fact that the active mean frequencies were higher in the urban groups, even though the active median frequencies were not. This means that the frequencies of the mid-individuals of the urban population were about the same as the frequencies of the mid-individuals of the rural population, but there were more individuals with higher frequencies in the urban sample. This, however, may have depended on nothing more than the fact that the urban samples were larger and consequently were more likely to include high-rating females.

RELATION TO RELIGIOUS BACKGROUND

Incidence. The accumulative and active incidences of pre-marital coitus had been distinctly higher among those females in the sample who were less actively connected with religious groups, and lower among those who were most devout (Tables 89, 90, Figures 53–56). This, in general, was true for the Protestant, Catholic, and Jewish groups. In many instances the differences between devout and inactive members of particular groups were very marked. The differences between Protestant, Catholic, and Jewish females of the same degree of devoutness were usually less than the differences between the various levels within any one religion. There appear to be no other factors which affect the female's pattern of pre-marital behavior as markedly as the decade in which she was born and her religious background.

The **accumulative incidence** curves for the females in the sample who had not yet married had risen at thirty-five years of age to about 63 per cent among the religiously inactive Protestants, to nearly the same point among the non-devout Jewish females, and to perhaps 55 per cent among the inactive Catholic females (Table 89, Figures 53–55). In contrast, hardly more than 30 per cent of the devout Protestants and 24 per cent of the devout Catholics had become involved. The females who were intermediate in their religious devotion stood midway between the devout and the less devout groups.[22]

Differences of the same general sort and of the same considerable magnitude were found in the number of females who had had pre-marital coitus within any five-year period (the **active incidences of experience**). To take typical examples, the differences between the active

---

[22] The importance of religious backgrounds is also noted in: Landis et al. 1940:64, 312 (19 per cent with pre-marital experience among Jewish females, 29 per cent among Catholics, 45 per cent among Protestants; but degree of devoutness was not taken into account). Fortune Survey 1943:24. England 1949/50:591. Fink 1950:33.

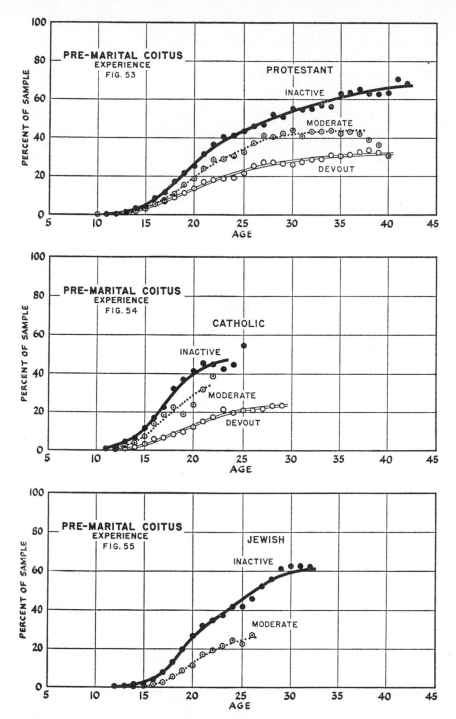

Figures 53–55. Accumulative incidence: pre-marital coitus, by religious group

Data from Table 89.

incidences had varied from 17 per cent in one of the more devout groups to 29 per cent in the corresponding least devout group, from 22 to 48 per cent in another instance, and from 15 to 43 per cent and from 21 to 56 per cent in still other instances (Table 90, Figure 56).

The same sorts of differences are to be observed in the **active incidences of orgasm** achieved in pre-marital coitus. The differences are not so marked in the Protestant groups; they are more marked in the two extreme Catholic groups, especially at younger ages (Table 90).

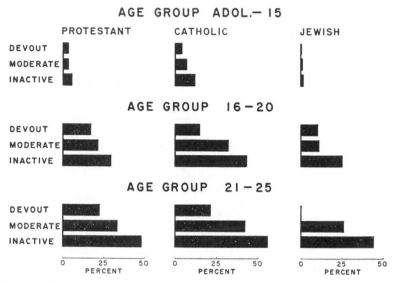

Figure 56. Active incidence: experience in pre-marital coitus, by religious group

Data from Table 90.

For instance, between sixteen and twenty years of age, 40 per cent of the devout Catholic females who were having coital experience were reaching orgasm in at least some of the coitus, but 68 per cent of the females in the religiously inactive group were reaching some orgasm. This may mean that the feelings of guilt which were experienced by the more devout females had reduced the satisfaction of the pre-marital coitus (pp. 318–319).

Frequency. Devoutly religious backgrounds had had a marked effect in preventing the females in the sample from starting various types of sexual activity, and they also seem to have had an effect on the frequencies of the pre-marital coital experience after the females had begun their activity (Table 90). For 21 out of the 38 religious groups on which we have samples, the average (active median) frequencies of pre-marital coitus had ranged from once in three to once in five weeks (0.3 and 0.2 per week). Lower frequencies had occurred chiefly in the younger age groups. In 10 out of the 11 groups on which we have sufficient data for comparing more devout and less devout females, the differences in frequencies were inversely correlated with the degree of the religious devotion.

Percentage of Total Outlet. Because of the lower incidences of pre-marital coitus among the more devout groups, and because of the lower frequencies in those groups, the proportion of the total pre-marital outlet which had been derived from coitus by the females in the sample had been definitely lower in the more devout groups, and definitely higher in the less devout groups (Table 90). Apart from the very youngest Protestant group, there were no exceptions to this generalization. For instance, the percentages of total outlet had ranged from 12 per cent in one devout group to 31 per cent in the corresponding less devout group, from 14 to 39 per cent in another group, and from 21 to 44 per cent in another. It should be emphasized again that these percentages are relative to the contribution of the other outlets, masturbation, petting to orgasm, and the homosexual, which contribute to the total pre-marital outlet.

SIGNIFICANCE OF PRE-MARITAL COITUS

Arguments for or against the acceptance of coitus before marriage have been based, for the most part, on emotional reactions which reflect the cultural tradition. However, these reactions are ordinarily supported or rationalized by arguments which may be summarized as follows:

Against Pre-Marital Coitus. Most marriage manuals, treatises on sex education, moral philosophies, and much of the technical literature agree in emphasizing the disadvantages and general undesirability of pre-marital coitus.[23] They point out the damage it may do to the indi-

---

[23] Examples of strictly and strongly moral interpretations may be found in: Neumann 1936:105 (Ethical Culture approach). Banning 1937:1–10 (a widely circulated article full of unsubstantiated generalizations and exaggerated warnings). Kuhn in Becker and Hill 1942:226 (finds Terman data a "shocking picture"). Popenoe 1943:113–118. Duvall and Hill 1945:141–163. Kirkendall 1947:26–31. Dickerson 1947:57–69. Landis and Landis 1948:124–131. Christensen 1950:149–158. Foster 1950:66–69. Bundesen 1951:88–120.

Examples of tolerant attitudes are presented in: Michels 1914:177–190. Gerling 1928:109–111 (German). Guyon 1933:124–133. Levy and Munroe 1938:1–46. Wilhelm Reich 1945:111–115 (child and adolescent training). Comfort 1950:89 ff. (English). Farnham 1951:130–135. Stone and Stone 1952:246–259.

Examples of mixed reactions or a middle ground in moral interpretations are in: Himes 1940:29–43. Folsom in Becker and Hill 1942:187. Bowman 1942:219–236 (lists arguments pro and con). Fenichel 1945:111 (the psychoanalytic attitude). Leuba 1948:94–104 (disposes of many false arguments). Stokes 1948:19. Harper 1949:83–87. Brown and Kempton 1950:134–139. Fromme 1950:80. Speigel 1951:385 (the psychoanalytic attitude). Sylvanus Duvall 1952:ch.9. Am. Assoc. Marr. Counselors, Round Table 1952:229–238.

vidual, to the sexual partner, and to the social organization. Specifically, they emphasize:

1. The danger of pregnancy
2. The danger if abortion is used to terminate a pregnancy
3. The possibility of contracting a venereal disease
4. The undesirability of a marriage which is forced by a pre-marital pregnancy
5. The traumatic effects of coitus which is had under the inadequate circumstances which are supposed to attend most pre-marital relations
6. The damage done by the participant's guilt over the infringement of the moral law
7. The guilt at the loss of virginity, and its subsequent effect on marriage
8. The fear that males lose respect for and will not marry a female with whom they have had coitus
9. The damage done when guilt feelings are reawakened after marriage
10. The guilt resulting from fear of public disapproval
11. The risk and fear of social difficulties that may follow discovery of the relationship
12. The risk and fear of legal difficulties that may follow any discovery of the relationship
13. The possibility that pre-marital coitus which is satisfactory may delay or altogether prevent the individual from marrying
14. The possibility that the coitus may make one feel obligated to marry the sexual partner
15. The possibility that guilt over the coitus may break up an otherwise desirable friendship with the sexual partner
16. The overemphasis which pre-marital experience may place on the physical aspects of friendship and marriage
17. The likelihood that pre-marital irregularities will lead to later extra-marital infidelities, with consequent damage to the marriage
18. The possibility that the female will be less capable of responding satisfactorily in her marital coitus because of the traumatic effects of pre-marital experience
19. The fact that pre-marital coitus is morally wrong
20. The principle that abstinence from such activities may develop one's will power

For Pre-Marital Coitus. The reasons for having pre-marital coitus have rarely been marshaled in any comparable order, perhaps because of the general disapproval in our culture of any extenuation of such behavior, or perhaps because those who do not disapprove consider that the reasons for having any coitus are self-evident. Nevertheless, the following advantages have been claimed for such experience: [23]

1. It may satisfy a physiologic need for a sexual outlet
2. It may become a source of immediate physical and psychologic satisfaction
3. If there is no guilt, it may increase one's ability to function more effectively in other, non-sexual fields
4. It is more valuable than solitary sexual activity for developing one's capacity to make emotional adjustments with other persons
5. It may develop one's capacity to make the particular sorts of emotional adjustments which are needed in marital relationships
6. It may provide training in the sorts of physical techniques that may be involved in marital coitus

7. It may test the capacities of two persons to make satisfactory sexual adjustments after marriage
8. It is easier to learn to make emotional and physical adjustments at an earlier age; they are learned with greater difficulty after marriage
9. Failure in a pre-marital relationship is socially less disastrous than failure after marriage
10. Heterosexual experience may prevent the development of a homosexual pattern of behavior
11. Pre-marital coitus may lead to marriage
12. In at least some social groups, an individual may acquire status by fitting into the group pattern of behavior

All of these arguments, pro and con, are met by denials from those who believe to the contrary. There are obvious biases on both sides of the fence. On the one hand, it is claimed that the objections to pre-marital coitus are primarily moral, even when they are presented in ostensibly technical manuals emanating from professionally trained persons.[23] On the other hand, it is claimed that arguments for pre-marital coitus are based on hedonistic desires rather than upon any consideration for the ultimate good of the participating partners or of the social organization. On the one hand, there is an insistence that the mores were born out of ancient experience which remains valid for the present day. On the other hand, it is claimed that conditions have changed, and that many of the older objections to pre-marital coitus are no longer valid in a world which has acquired the means of controlling conception and venereal disease, and some scientific understanding of the nature of the emotions and of the problems that underlie human relationships. There have been few attempts to accumulate anything like scientific data.

The resolution of these conflicting claims can come only through some recognition that certain of these problems lie in areas which belong to the biologic, psychologic, and social sciences, while others are moral problems which the student of moral philosophies must solve.[24]

---

[24] Attitudes on pre-marital coitus for the female are also surveyed in: Blanchard and Manasses 1930:262 (accepted by 55 per cent of 252 middle class females). Katz and Allport 1931:252 (30 per cent of more than 3000 female and male students at Syracuse University support double standard). Baber 1936:118 (accepted by 29 per cent of 321 college males). Fortune Survey 1937:188 (accepted by 17 per cent of females and 28 per cent of males). Bernard 1938:356 (accepted by 3 per cent of 250 females and 4 per cent of 250 males at University of Colorado). Pringle 1938:15, 49 (14 per cent of women accept, more often in urban, non-religious, single, and younger groups). Bromley and Britten 1938.71 (62 per cent of 772 college females accept). Cuber and Pell 1941:21 (22 per cent of 11 females and 53 per cent of 106 males accept). Fortune Survey 1943:20 (36 per cent of women accept). Rockwood and Ford 1945:40 (28 per cent of 191 males and females, 26 per cent of 73 males, and 12 per cent of 100 females at Cornell accept). Landis and Landis 1948:121 (at Michigan State, among 2000 students, 9 per cent of females and 31 per cent of males approve for female). Lanval 1950: 118 (82 per cent of 500 French and Belgian women accept). Christensen 1950:226 (a study of 234 college students). Friedeburg 1950:12 (65 per cent of 493 German females and males accept).

Even the scientific aspects are too many for any immediate solution; but the data brought together in the present chapter may contribute to a more objective understanding of certain aspects of the problem.

NATURE AND CONDITIONS OF PRE-MARITAL COITUS

There is a general impression that pre-marital coitus is of necessity had under inadequate and often distinctly inadequate conditions which must make the experience unsatisfactory or even traumatic in its effect on subsequent marital adjustments; but this impression is not supported by any accumulation of data in the literature. It has, there-fore, seemed significant to analyze the specific data on the experience of the females in our sample.

Place of Coitus. In this sample more than half (58 per cent) of the females who had any pre-marital experience in coitus had had at least a portion of it within their own homes (Table 78). In terms of frequencies our less specifically tabulated data indicate that the female's parental home or other residence was the place in which a high proportion of all the contacts had occurred. For instance, the data indicate that girls living away from home while attending college have a smaller proportion of their pre-marital coitus in the college town, and a larger proportion of it while they are at home, during vacations. This is no new development, for it seems to have been equally true of all generations for the past forty years, including the generation born before 1900.

Some 48 per cent of the females had had a portion of their coitus in the male's home (Table 78). This, again, was more or less equally true of all the generations represented in the sample. The record indicates, however, that the frequencies of contacts in such places were considerably lower than the frequencies of contacts in the girl's home.

Some 40 per cent of the females reported that some of their pre-marital coitus had occurred in hotel rooms or in some other type of rented room (Table 78). In spite of the increased amount of traveling which the present generation does, and the increasing use of facilities like tourist camps, the number of girls who had coitus in rented facilities had, in terms of percentages, remained more or less constant for all of the generations included in the sample.

Within recent decades, the automobile parked on some side road out of town, or moving along a highway, has provided an opportunity for pre-marital coitus. Some 41 per cent of the females in the sample had had such experience (Table 78). The data indicate that the importance of the car had more than doubled in the thirty years covered by the sample. In earlier generations in both European and American history, the buggy or other horse-drawn conveyance appears to have served the function which the automobile now serves in connection with pre-marital coitus.

A variety of other places had been utilized by some of the females (Table 78). The diverse nature of such places has been the source of the general opinion that pre-marital coitus is usually had under unfavorable circumstances; but it may be noted again that half to three-quarters of all the coitus had by the females in the sample seems to have occurred in the home of the female or male.[25]

Techniques of Pre-Coital Foreplay. The foreplay which may accompany pre-marital coitus may involve the same techniques which appear in pre-marital petting that does not lead to coitus (pp. 251–259).[26] We have already noted that the pre-coital petting techniques were more limited among those females in the sample who had had the least experience in coitus, and more diverse among those who had had more extensive coital experience (Table 73, Figures 41, 42).

Time Involved in Foreplay. Among the females in the sample, the petting which had preceded the pre-marital coitus had often been more extensive than the petting which preceded marital coitus. Of those who had had extended experience in pre-marital coitus, only 9 per cent reported that the foreplay was ordinarily restricted to something between one and five minutes, while 23 per cent of the married females reported such limitations of the foreplay. For the pre-marital activity, 75 per cent of the females reported that something between eleven minutes and an hour or more had regularly been involved in petting before any genital union occurred, while only 53 per cent of the married females reported such extended play. Certainly the data do not justify the general opinion that pre-marital coitus is, of necessity, more hurried and consequently less satisfactory than coitus usually is in marriage.

There must be courting if the male intends to secure or continue pre-marital or extra-marital coitus, but such courting is often absent from marital relationships. In marriage the male more or less assumes that coitus is his privilege, and the law confirms him in this interpretation (p. 368 ff.). Moreover, the higher frequencies of marital coitus, and the ease of obtaining it, may in time reduce its attraction and its capacity to stimulate. In consequence, many of the females and males in the

---

[25] Only a few studies have included data on the places where pre-marital coitus occurs, but see: Welander 1908:20 (for 628 European males with venereal disease). Schbankov acc. Weissenberg 1924a:13 (European). Hoyer 1929: 53–59. Dickinson and Beam 1934:170. Banning 1937:6 ("Being clandestine, it is rarely either well housed or comfortable"). Clark 1952:31.

[26] There is a detailed analysis of petting and pre-marital pre-coital techniques among college students in Ehrmann 1952 (unpublished data).

sample had found the foreplay in pre-marital activity, common-law marriages, and extra-marital relationships more stimulating than similar activity in legal marriages.

Positions in Coitus. In the sample, the positions utilized in the pre-marital coitus appear to have been more restricted than those utilized in marital coitus (Table 101). Just as in marriage, the coitus had most frequently involved a position in which the male was placed above the female. That was the only position which had been utilized by some 21 per cent of those females in the sample who had had more extensive pre-marital experience. Only 9 per cent of the married females had been so restricted in their positions.

In order of use, other positions included one in which the female was above the male in 35 per cent of the pre-marital histories and in 45 per cent of the marital histories; a side position with the partners facing each other in some 19 per cent of the pre-marital activity and in some 31 per cent of the marital activity; a sitting position on occasion in 8 per cent of the pre-marital sample and in 9 per cent of the marital sample; less often a position which allowed a rear vaginal entrance; and still more rarely a standing position.

It is generally believed that a high proportion of the pre-marital coitus is had in uncomfortable sitting positions in back seats of cars, or in standing positions when the relationships are more hurried. It is, therefore, significant to note that a number of the married spouses use sitting and standing positions, evidently from choice rather than from some force of circumstance. While the variety used in pre-marital coitus is not as great as the variety used in some of the older marital histories, the pre-marital techniques actually come near matching and in many instances surpass the techniques utilized by newly-wed couples.

Nudity. A large proportion of the pre-marital coitus of the females in the sample had occurred under circumstances in which it had been possible for the participants to become completely nude. About 64 per cent of those who had had pre-marital coitus twenty-five times or more had had a large proportion of it nude (Table 101). Another 15 per cent reported some less frequent use of nudity. The figures were still higher for the better educated females, where as many as 78 per cent had frequently had their pre-marital coitus without clothing, while another 13 per cent had had some portion of it nude.

As we have already pointed out for the male (1948:366), there are considerable differences in attitudes toward nudity at different social levels. This is now confirmed by the data for the female. Some 33 per cent of the females in the sample who had never gone beyond high school, but only 15 per cent of the females who had college backgrounds and only 9 per cent of those who ultimately went on into graduate work, reported that they had never been nude in their pre-marital experience. This is no new development, for the trends are present in the four decades on which we have data. The lower level and high school females who reported that they had never been nude during their pre-marital coitus probably had retained their clothing because they shared the attitudes of their social level, and not because circumstances forced them to do so.

PHYSIOLOGIC SIGNIFICANCE

There is no doubt that coitus, both before and after marriage, is had primarily because it may satisfy a physiologic need and may serve as a source of pleasure for one or both of the individuals who are involved. No appreciable part of the coitus, either in or out of marriage, is consciously undertaken as a means of effecting reproduction.[27]

Our understanding of the physiology of sexual arousal and response (Chapter 15) makes it clear that most males and perhaps a third of the females find it difficult to resolve any considerable sexual arousal which is not carried through to orgasm. As we have already indicated, pre-marital coitus had provided the sort of resolution which orgasm can bring for the 20 per cent of the females in the sample who were having coitus with an average frequency of once in three to ten weeks during a period of some years before marriage.

Basing the calculations on the females who were married, and who, in consequence, had completed their pre-marital histories, we find that pre-marital coitus had been the source of the first orgasm experienced by some 8 per cent of the sample (Table 148). The figure was lower for those females who were born before 1900, but ranged from 8 to 10 per cent in all the generations born since then. Among those females who had reached their first orgasm during a heterosexual contact, some 14 per cent had reached it in pre-marital coitus.

PSYCHOLOGIC SIGNIFICANCE

By many persons, the psychologic effects of pre-marital coitus are considered more significant than the physical or physiologic aspects of such experience. As measures of these psychologic significances, we have data on the attitudes of the females in our sample toward having pre-marital coitus, the extent and nature of any regret which had been

---

[27] Some writers have tried to minimize physical satisfactions as a motivation for pre-marital coitus among females. They see such factors as inferiority feelings, a desire to be popular, excessive restrictions at home, crowded living conditions, and unhappy family situations, as the real reasons for coitus. See, for example: Popenoe 1943:121. Lion et al. 1945:63–64. Strain 1948:185.

consequent on their coital experience, and the extent to which they had accepted their experience.

Attitudes. Whether a female decides to begin pre-marital coitus, or to continue it after she has once had it, must depend on a multiplicity of physical, situational, social, and other factors, on some of which we have specific information and on others of which we do not yet have sufficient data for analyses. Interestingly enough, the most significant correlation seems to have been with the presence or absence of experience. Among the unmarried females who had never had coital experience, 80 per cent insisted that they did not intend to have it before marriage; but among those who had already had such experience, only 30 per cent said that they did not intend to have more (Table 91, Figure 57). A selective factor must have been involved; but it may be

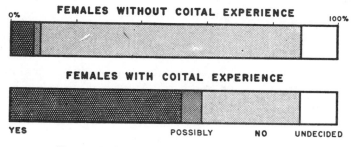

Figure 57. Intent to have pre-marital coitus

Among females with and without previous experience. Data from Table 91.

noted again that experience dispels many of the fears that gather about the unknown, especially when it is an unknown type of sexual activity.

In their own analyses of the factors which had restricted their pre-marital coitus, 89 per cent of the females in the sample said that moral considerations had been of primary importance (Table 91, Figure 58). Some of these individuals had identified these factors as moral. However, some of them insisted that they were not accepting the traditional codes just because they were the codes, and believed that they had developed their attitudes as a result of their own rational analyses of what they considered to be expedient, decent, respectable, fine, sensible, right or wrong, better or best. This represented an interesting attempt on the part of the younger generation to proclaim its emancipation from the religious tradition, but most of them were still following the traditions without having found new bases for defending them. It is to be noted that the females of the younger generations had recognized moral restraints on their pre-marital activities about as often as the females born some thirty or forty years before. But the increased incidences of coital activity, more than the expressed opinions, indicated that the moral codes had been less effective among the younger generations.

Some 45 per cent of the females in the sample recognized that their lack of sexual responsiveness had been a factor in limiting their pre-marital activity (Table 91, Figure 58); but it seems clear that a lack of responsiveness or an inability to respond was even more important than the females themselves understood. As someone long ago recog-

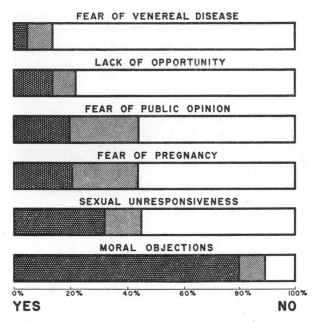

Figure 58. Factors restricting pre-marital coitus

Intermediate shading indicates replies falling between "yes" and "no," including data from females with and without coital experience. Based on total sample, including single and married females. Data from Table 91.

nized, it is easier to abstain from sin when one is not physically or physiologically endowed with the capacity—or with much capacity—to sin.

Fear of pregnancy ranked next, with 44 per cent of the females considering that this had been one of the factors which had limited their pre-marital coitus (Table 91, Figure 58).

As many females (44 per cent) said that fear of public opinion had been an important factor in limiting their behavior (Table 91, Figure 58). On the other hand, most of them were confident that no one except their sexual partners would know of any coitus which they might have.

Some 22 per cent frankly recognized that they had abstained from coitus, at least in part, because they had not encountered the opportunity to have it (Table 91, Figure 58).

Fear of venereal disease had been only a minor factor in limiting the pre-marital coitus of the females in the sample. It was reported as a factor in only 14 per cent of the sample (Table 91, Figure 58).

These were the expressed reasons which the females gave for their lack of coitus, or for their decisions to limit their further coitus.[28] In many cases, these probably were the factors which had been involved; but in some cases these appeared to be nothing more than rationalizations of the real reasons. Taking all of our experience into account, we are inclined to list, in order of importance, the following as the primary factors which had limited the pre-marital activity of the females in the sample:

1. The sexual unresponsiveness of many younger females
2. The moral tradition of our American culture
3. Lack of experience, and the individual's fear of engaging in an unfamiliar activity.

Regret After Experience. That pre-marital coitus is often unsatisfactory is commonly believed by most persons and asserted with considerable positiveness by many who consider such activity morally wrong. Many of those who have written on the subject (*e.g.*, Margaret Culkin Banning, Robert Foster, Evelyn Duvall, and others noted elsewhere) [23] assert that pre-marital activity always brings psychologic disturbance and lasting regrets. The positiveness of these assertions might lead one to believe that they were based on sufficient investigations of the fact, but data which might sufficiently support such statements have never been accumulated by these writers or by other students in this field.

As a matter of fact, some 69 per cent of the still unmarried females in the sample who had had coitus insisted that they did not regret their experience (Table 92). Another 13 per cent recorded some minor regret. An even larger proportion, some 77 per cent of the married females, looking back from the vantage point of their more mature experience, saw no reason to regret their pre-marital coitus. Another 12 per cent of the married females had some minor regret. These figures

---

[28] Various reasons given for avoiding coitus are also recorded by: Blanchard and Manasses 1930:262 (252 females, reporting parental disapproval, fear of venereal disease, later regrets, fear of pregnancy, future spouse's disturbance, supposedly lessened chances to marry, loss of self-respect, social disapproval, etc.). Bromley and Britten 1938:64 (among 375 college females, 50 per cent feared pregnancy, 45 per cent had moral and religious scruples, 34 per cent wished to avoid any serious relationship).

differ considerably from those usually presented in public discussions
of such pre-marital activity. They illustrate the difference between
wishful thinking and scientifically accumulated data. There are, of
course, more cases of regret among the disturbed persons who go to
clinicians for help.

The regret registered by a portion of the sample appeared to depend
on the nature of the pre-marital experience (Table 92). For the most
part, those who regretted it most were the females who had had the
least experience.[29] Our data, for instance, show that 25 per cent of those
who had had the smallest amount of pre-marital coitus seriously regretted their experience, while only 14 per cent of those who had had
such experience for two or three years, and only 10 per cent of those
who had had it for something between four and ten years, registered
such regret (Table 92, Figure 59). This is borne out by the fact that
the married females, with their more extended coital experience, regretted their pre-marital coitus in only 11 per cent of the cases. This is
especially interesting because the statement is often made that the
quality of a marital relationship is so far superior to a pre-marital relationship that married women usually regret such experience. That
statement is not confirmed by our data.

Similarly, regrets were inversely correlated with the extent of the
promiscuity in the pre-marital activity (Table 92). Among the females
in the sample who had confined their coital contacts to a single male,
15 per cent seriously regretted their experience. On the other hand, of
those who had extended their coitus to something between eleven and
twenty males, only 6 per cent regretted their experience. It may be that
experience reduces the psychologic disturbance, or it may be that those
females who are least inclined to worry are the ones who become most
promiscuous. It is probable that both factors contribute to these correlations.

Whether pre-marital experience was regretted or not did not, interestingly enough, seem to depend upon the generation to which the
individual belonged (Table 92). Actually, the data show a larger number of the youngest generation regretting their pre-marital coitus, but
this probably depends on the fact that they had had more limited experience at the time they contributed their histories. Initial regrets are
often resolved as an individual matures and acquires more experience.

Whether one regrets her pre-marital experience seems to depend to
only a small degree upon the complications which a pregnancy may

---

[29] The relation of lack of experience to guilt is also noted in: Landis et al. 1940:66,
291 (12 per cent of 266 females with guilt, especially if experience was limited). The data in Hamilton 1929:349 are not clearly interpretable.

produce. In the sample, some 17 per cent of those who had become pregnant (p. 326) as a result of their pre-marital experience seriously regretted that they had had coitus, while 13 per cent of those who had not become pregnant registered such regret (Table 92). It is more surprising to find that 83 per cent of those who had become pregnant registered little or no regret.

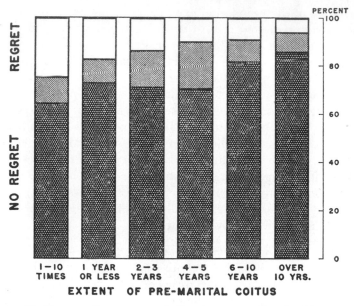

Figure 59. Regret after pre-marital coitus, correlated with extent of experience

Intermediate shading indicates some lesser degree of regret. Data from Table 92.

Regrets were correlated to only a small extent with the complications which venereal infections had introduced. Although 16 per cent of the females who had had infections seriously regretted their pre-marital coitus, some 13 per cent of those who had not been infected registered similar levels of regret (Table 92).

Pre-marital coitus which was had with the future spouse was least often regretted. Serious regret had occurred in only 9 per cent of the histories of the females who had had at least some of their pre-marital coitus with the males whom they subsequently married (Table 92). But if the pre-marital coitus had not included the fiancé, there had been serious regret in 28 per cent of the cases.

There were no factors which were more closely correlated with guilt, among the females in the sample who had had pre-marital coitus, than their religious backgrounds, and the extent to which they felt that such experience was morally wrong. The data show, for instance, that 23 per cent of the devout Protestants but only 10 per cent of the inactive Protestants seriously regretted their pre-marital experience (Table 92, Figure 60). Some 35 per cent of the devout Catholics but only 9 per cent of the inactive Catholics in the sample recorded such regrets. The more limited sample of Jewish females showed the same trends. The

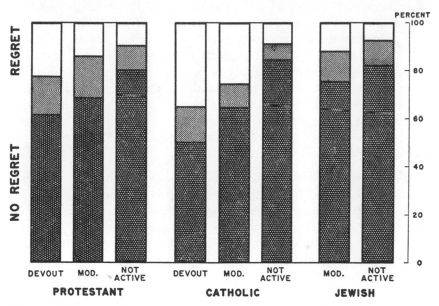

Figure 60. Regret after pre-marital coitus, correlated with religious background

Intermediate shading indicates some lesser degree of regret. Data from Table 92.

clinician might very well advise the individual who is strongly convinced that coitus before marriage is morally wrong to hesitate about having such experience, for she is more likely to be emotionally disturbed by it. We have also shown (p. 306) that the possibility of the pre-marital coitus reaching a satisfactory conclusion in orgasm is definitely lower for females who are religiously devout. It might be argued, however, that the religious attitudes were as responsible as the coitus for these psychologic disturbances.

Acceptance. That a considerable portion of the pre-marital coitus is psychologically satisfactory is, of course, evidenced by its continuation and considerable prolongation in the histories of many of the females who begin such activities. We have already noted that 69 per cent of the single females in the sample had accepted their coital experience, and 77 per cent of the married females had recalled their pre-marital experience without evident psychologic disturbance (Table 92).

The psychologic significance of any type of sexual activity very largely depends upon what the individual and his social group choose to make of it. The disturbances which may sometimes follow coitus rarely depend on the nature of the activity itself, or upon its physical outcome. An occasional unwanted pregnancy, a rare instance of venereal disease, or a very rare instance of physical damage are about the only undesirable physical after-effects. But if the behavior leads to some open conflict with the social organization of which the individual is a part, then the consequences may be serious and sometimes disastrous. The so-called traumatic effects of sexual experience often depend on the individual's inability or refusal to recognize the satisfaction that he or she actually found in the experience, or on his or her persistence in believing that the experience should not have been satisfactory, or that it must, in some way, have undesirable consequences; but these, again, reflect the attitudes of the community in which the individual was raised.

The truth of this thesis is abundantly evidenced by our thousands of histories which, among them, include every conceivable type of sexual behavior without subsequent psychologic disturbance, while the same sort of behavior in other histories may bring shame, remorse, despair, desperation, and attempted suicide. The simplest matter can be built into an affair of gigantic proportions. Failing to comprehend that their own attitudes and the social codes generated these disturbances, most persons identify them as direct evidence of the intrinsic wrongness or abnormality of the sexual act itself.

In one or another of the cultures of the world, nearly every type of sexual behavior has been condemned, while in other cultures the same activities have been considered desirable sources of pleasure and socially valuable. Heterosexual coitus is extolled in most cultures, but forbidden to Buddhist and Catholic priests. Homosexual activity is condemned in some cultures, tacitly accepted in others, honored as a religious rite in others, and allowed to Buddhist priests. Behavior which is accepted by the culture does not generate psychologic conflicts in the individual or unmanageable social problems. The same behavior, censored, condemned, tabooed, or criminally punished in the next culture, may generate guilt and neurotic disturbances in the non-conforming individual and serious conflict with the social organism. This seems to be the source of most of the disturbances which we have found in the histories of American females and males who masturbate, who engage in heterosexual petting, or in homosexual relations or animal contacts, or utilize sexual techniques which, biologically normal enough in themselves, are taboo in our particular culture. This is the explanation of most of the psychologic disturbances that come out of pre-marital coitus.

MORAL ASPECTS

Under strictly Orthodox Jewish codes and the codes of a consider able segment of the Christian church, all coitus outside of marriage is judged to be morally wrong.[30] For many persons that is an absolute which is not subject to scientific or any other type of logical debate. Like other principles in absolutist philosophies, such judgments are supposed to emanate from the innate capacities of the intelligent, moral man to know what is right and what is wrong; and there are many persons who are convinced that this is a valid method of dealing with moral problems.

That relatively few persons are absolutists in any realistic sense is evidenced by the fact that they rarely discuss the right or wrong of pre-marital coitus or, indeed, of any other type of sexual activity, without seeking some justification of their interpretations in practical or scientific experience. Anyone who considers pre-marital coitus in terms of possible pregnancies, abortion, or venereal disease, or the ultimate effects upon subsequent marital adjustments, demonstrates his or her belief in a moral philosophy which is the product of experience, and which continues to be justified only as long as it proves to be the best way of life for the individual and for the total social organization.

---

[30] Jewish attitudes, with citations of sources, are well summarized in: Epstein 1948:167–170 (the code emphasizes the importance of virginity at marriage; although there has been no actual law against it, in Jewish history there has been a very strong public condemnation of pre-marital coitus for both female and male). See Deuteronomy 22:13–21. The Catholic viewpoint is presented in the following: Sanchez 1637:312 (And then it is evident among all, that contacts had on account of venereal pleasure arising from coitus are deadly sins between persons neither married nor betrothed, as also is coitus itself). Ballerini 1890(2):715–716 (It is generally the opinion of the DD. that rape offered to a virgin willing and consenting does not differ in species from fornication. For it is in fact the same wickedness of wantonness: intercourse, namely, which is outside of marriage. For the fact that the virginal seal, if there is any, is broken by means of the virile member, the virgin consenting, is not contrary to the special end of nature but rather is according to it; since this member was destined by nature for the use previously mentioned: therefore nature is offended only because the said rupture happens outside of marriage). Hieronymus Noldin, Summa Theologiae Moralis, 1905(2):472, 473; 1904(3):600, 609 (fornication is a sin, virginity is a blessing, coitus between betrothed persons is a sin. Fornication by an engaged man with a third party is not considered "notable"; fornication by the engaged woman with a third party is so considered and her fiancé may withdraw from the betrothal). Arregui 1927:147–150 (any venereal pleasure outside of marriage is a sin). Davis 1946(2):238, 241 (fornication is bad because it is contrary to the order of nature and connotes an unstable union of parents which will lead to the neglect of offspring and is therefore opposed to the propagation of the human race. Rape is, in canonical law, called simple if it is the illicit deflowering of a virgin, but it is a sin against chastity and justice regardless of whether the woman is a virgin or not).

Actually, most persons compromise between an absolutist approach to the morality of pre-marital coitus and a practical consideration of the realities of human nature. In most cultures, throughout history, everywhere in the world, some sort of distinction has been made between the acceptability of pre-marital coitus for the male and the acceptability of such coitus for the female. This undoubtedly stems from the fact that it has always proved impossible to prevent the majority of males from having coitus before marriage; while females, who are less often sexually responsive at early ages and less often stimulated psychologically at any age, have proved to be more controllable. They are, therefore, the ones who are most often expected to adhere to the moral and social codes. This "double standard" is based in part on a recognition of actual differences between the sexes rather than on an absolutist's determination of what is right or wrong.

These differences in the social attitudes toward pre-marital coitus among males and among females are also rooted historically in certain economic factors. Sexual activities for the female before marriage were proscribed in ancient codes primarily because they threatened the male's property rights in the female whom he was taking as a wife. The demand that the female be virgin at the time of her marriage was comparable to the demand that cattle or other goods that he bought should be perfect, according to the standards of the culture in which he lived. In the ancient Chaldean, Jewish, and other codes, the prohibitions were directed primarily against the female's activity after she had become betrothed, and penalties for the violation of her sexual integrity involved the payment of goods equivalent to those which the fiancé had already turned over to the girl's father. Goods were also demanded as compensation to the husband, father, or fiancé for the depreciation in value of his interests in the female.[31] At some points English marriage law still recognizes the property rights which the male has in the female whom he is planning to marry, or in his wife, but American law has more or less completely broken away from this concept of the husband having any property rights in his wife or prospective wife. Our moral judgments of pre-marital coitus for the female are, however, still affected by this economic principle which developed among the Chaldeans and other ancient peoples, three or four thousand years ago.

---

[31] The property rights which the father and the fiancé had in the female are illustrated by the following ancient codes: Exodus 22:16–17. Pritchard 1950: 162, Law of Eshunna [2000–1000 B.C., Mesopotamia] ¶31 (a fine for coitus with another man's virgin slave girl). Pritchard 1950:171, Code of Hammurabi [2000 B.C.?] ¶130 (death for the male having coitus with a betrothed female, no punishment for female). Pritchard 1950:185, Middle Assyrian Laws [1500–1200 B.C.] ¶55–56 (male seducing a virgin must pay three times her value to the father).

Many a male, particularly in certain social levels and in certain parts of the United States, is prone to seek coitus from every available girl, while insisting that the girl he marries should be virgin when he first has coitus with her. It is the male, rather than the female, who imposes this incongruity on the social code. He will defend his right and any other man's right to try to secure coitus from another man's sister or wife, but he may fight or kill the man who attempts to secure coitus from his own sister, fiancée, daughter, or wife. Interestingly enough, juries and the statute law in certain parts of the country are still inclined to grant him the privilege of defending what he now calls his honor, although it originated in the ancient codes as a property right.[32]

Females are less inclined to demand that their husbands be virgins when they marry. In our own sample, something over 40 per cent of the males wanted to marry virgins (see our 1948:364), while only 23 per cent of the females expressed the same desire (Table 91). There was a larger number of females (32 per cent) who were inclined to marry non-virgins, and another 42 per cent who were indifferent on the point.[33]

In this attempt to resolve the conflict between the sexual nature of the human male and the pattern imposed by his code on the human female, the age-old institution of heterosexual prostitution has been widely accepted throughout history and in most parts of the world. A considerable portion of the pre-marital coitus which males secure in most Oriental, North African, Continental European, Mediterranean, and Latin American cultures is, apparently, secured from prostitutes rather than from girls who plan to marry males who have any social status. The strict way in which girls of socially respectable families are guarded by parents or by dueñas in Spanish and Latin American countries forces the male to become better acquainted with the ways of prostitutes and the sort of coitus that prostitutes provide than he ever

---

[32] The special interest of a male in the sexual sanctity of his close female relatives or fiancée is even today generally recognized by juries (see Wharton 1932(1): 809) and judges, and even some state legislative bodies. See Texas Penal Code 1925:Art. 1220. See especially the Georgia Code 1933:Title 26 §1015 and 1016 and numerous cases decided under these sections. At common law and in many states, if a man takes the law into his own hands in defense or in vindication of his wife's, sister's, daughter's, or fiancée's "honor," strong evidence of the seduction is considered sufficient provocation to reduce a killing from murder to manslaughter, and to mitigate the sentence or completely excuse mild assault and battery. See Clark and Marshall 1940:318.

[33] Data on preferences for marrying a virgin are also in: Neely 1940:516–519 (1600 college students; between 1929 and 1936, a lessening of desire to marry a virgin. Shift more marked among males, but virginity in mate still more important to males than to females). Landis and Landis 1948:85 (among students at Michigan State College, 48 per cent of females, 67 per cent of males willing to marry a non-virgin). Gilbert Youth Research 1951:20 (72 per cent of females and 27 per cent of males in college survey willing to marry non-virgin).

does with the girl that he marries. So strict is the tradition against pre-marital coitus for girls of better families that we have histories of Spanish and some other European males who find it difficult to have coitus with their wives, because they hold them in something of the same respect that they held their mothers, sisters, and all "decent" girls before marriage. Consequently some males in such cultures may continue to secure much of their coitus after marriage from prostitutes or mistresses, rather than from their wives.

The second most widespread plan for controlling pre-marital coitus has been the attempt in Judeo-Christian cultures to impose pre-marital chastity upon both males and females. This has been the most important factor in restricting pre-marital activity in the United States; but the limits of the possible effectiveness of such suppression are shown by the incidence and frequency data which we have now given for the American male and female. Objections to a double standard have usually implied that the male should accept the same restraints which our culture has been imposing upon the female. The record indicates, however, that the double standard is being resolved by the development of a single standard in which pre-marital coital activities have become extended among females to levels which are more nearly comparable to those in the male.

LEGAL ASPECTS

The statute law on pre-marital coitus largely reflects the moral codes from which it originated. This means that it is the product of the Jewish and Christian heritage in medieval and Renaissance Europe, of the sex law which evolved in the English ecclesiastic courts, and of the resultant laws and customs of the early American colonies.

While our forty-eight bodies of state law are derived largely from a single basic pattern, there is considerable diversity in the extent to which they try to limit pre-marital coitus, and the means by which they attempt to implement those laws. Almost universally throughout the United States coitus is prohibited for juveniles, both female and male.[34] The age at which an individual ceases to be a juvenile varies in the several states from 14 to 21; it is set at 18 in some 23 of the states.[35] While the court processes and subsequent confinement for juvenile delinquency are not supposed to be penal, in their actual administration they are often more severe and the penalties may be more extreme than those imposed upon adults. It is possible in most states for the judge to hold a delinquent in a juvenile institution—which is often

---

[34] The definitions of delinquency in all states include "immoral" conduct, acts, or life, or some such phrase; and even in the states where fornication is no crime, non-marital coitus is considered immoral.

[35] For detailed data on varying juvenile jurisdictions, see: Tappan 1949:14.

more severely administered than the average institution for older persons—for the entire period between the child's delinquency and the time he or she becomes adult. This in some instances may amount to six or eight years, and is not infrequently a matter of three or four years.

Some 35 of the states of the Union attempt to penalize as fornication pre-marital coitus which occurs between the age at which the individual becomes an adult and the age at which he or she marries. There are, however, 13 of the states which attach no criminal penalty to coitus which occurs in that period, provided that the activity is the product of mutual consent, and provided that no fraud, force, public display, or payment of money is involved.[36]

But whatever the statutes, the administration of the laws on pre-marital coitus differs widely at different times and places within any state, depending largely on local attitudes and upon the social backgrounds and moral codes of the law enforcement officers and of the judges in the courts. Courts are most inclined to become severe when the coitus involves youths under 20 years of age, when it involves persons of different social levels, and particularly when it involves persons of different racial groups, or an adult male and a minor girl. There are some jurists, chiefly among those who have originated from lower social strata, who comprehend the realities and who in consequence attach little significance to the cases which reach their courts. There are other jurists, chiefly those who come from upper level, better educated, or religiously more devout groups, who regularly denounce the girl or boy, or older female or male who stands before them on delinquency or fornication charges. Neither the judges, nor state legislators, nor the public at large seem willing to believe that it is only a minute fraction of one per cent of all pre-marital coitus which is ever brought to the attention of the court. It is difficult to convince any one except persons who have actually been involved with the law that it is usually nothing more than some caprice of circumstances which leads to the apprehension and trial of a certain few individuals out of all those who engage in such sexual activity.

The truth of this matter must become apparent if one (using the incidence and frequency data which we have given here) contemplates the considerable amount of coitus that must occur among his or her unmarried friends in the course of a year, or the total amount that oc-

---

[36] The 13 states, containing more than 30 per cent of the U. S. population, which have no statute prohibiting fornication, are: Calif., Del., La., Md., Mich., Mo., N.M., N.Y., Okla., S.D., Tenn., Vt., and Wash. Sixteen states require aggravating circumstances such as cohabitation or repetition. There are only 19 which penalize any single act of coitus. In 6 of these 19, however, fines are the sole penalties. See Bensing 1951:69.

curs in one's immediate neighborhood, or in the whole town, and considers how little of the activity is ever observed or in any other way comprehended by anyone except the immediate participants. The record in classical, later European, Oriental, and modern fiction would lead one to believe that persons involved in illicit coitus are frequently apprehended in the midst of their activities; but in actuality in a series of 2020 histories we have only 29 instances of the accidental discovery and observation of pre-marital coitus. This means that not more than 6 cases out of each 100,000 pre-marital copulations in our records were discovered while in progress. More surprising even than that is the fact that we have no instance of legal difficulty arising from the actual discovery of pre-marital coitus while in progress, although we do have histories of both females and males who were convicted and served penal sentences on the basis of other sorts of evidence that the coitus had occurred.

There is no aspect of American sex law which surprises visitors from other countries as much as this legal attempt to penalize pre-marital activity to which both of the participating parties have consented and in which no force has been involved. As we have already noted, there is practically no other culture, anywhere in the world, in which all non-marital coitus, even between adults, is considered criminal.[5] Certainly most American youth do not consider it so, whatever they may think of it as a moral issue.

SOCIAL SIGNIFICANCE

The possibilities of pregnancies and venereal disease resulting from pre-marital coitus, and the emotional significance of pre-marital experience and its subsequent effects on sexual adjustments in marriage, are matters which many persons will consider of paramount importance.

Pre-Marital Pregnancy. Official estimates allow some 130,000 births out of wedlock each year in the United States. The actual facts might multiply the official figures several times. This problem is apparently more acute in various European and Asiatic areas, and was a factor of still greater importance in past periods of history.[37] Attempts to

---

[37] The present and past extent of illegitimate births is only suggested in European and American studies. The figures range from 7 to 45 per cent, the higher incidences appearing in surveys based on percent of first born to younger females. See, for example: Käser 1830:75–76, Tables A, B (8 to 42 per cent of all births, Southern Germany, 1770–1829). Fletcher 1849:205 (7 per cent of registered births, England and Wales, 1845). Sundt 1857:Table 4, Sec. 5 (43 per cent of first born, Norway, 1850–1851). Eberhard 1924:40 (cites Klumker, 38 per cent of first born; Geissler, 45 per cent of first born, Germany, 1875–1885). Comfort 1950:90 (20 to 40 per cent among brides under 21, Great Britain, 1938). For the United States, see: 16th Census of U. S., 1940 (Population, Differential Fertility, Women by Number of Children Ever Born)

control such pregnancies and to provide that children should have responsible parents were undoubtedly factors of considerable moment in the development of society's interest in controlling coitus outside of wedlock.

We have a sample of 2094 single, white females (adolescent to forty years of age) who had had coitus and on whom we have data concerning pregnancy. They had had 476 pregnancies. Nearly 18 per cent had become pregnant. A fair number of the pregnancies had occurred after the couples had become engaged. Some 15 per cent of those who had become pregnant had become pregnant more than once.

However, the probability that a pregnancy may result from any particular act of coitus is actually low. The 2094 single females who had had coitus had had it approximately 460,000 times. This means, approximately, that one pregnancy had resulted from each 1000 copulations. But considering the effectiveness of modern contraceptives and the exceedingly few failures which we have recorded for the condom or diaphragm when properly used, there is, today, practically no necessity for such a pregnancy rate in pre-marital coitus.

Venereal Infection. In spite of the fact that our sample included older females who had had their pre-marital experience in the days before there were adequate controls of venereal disease, the incidences of such disease in the sample were exceedingly low. Among the white females in the sample who had had coitus before marriage, we have venereal disease data on 1753 cases. Of this group, only 44 females had ever had any type of venereal infection (Table 92). Present methods of simple and rapid cures for both syphilis and gonorrhea make their spread through pre-marital coitus a relatively unimportant matter today. The incidences may be higher in some lower level groups, but even then the medical techniques which are now available can prevent venereal disease from becoming a matter of much social importance.

Emotional Significance. Because of its emotional connotations, pre-marital coitus, like any other type of socio-sexual experience, may have long-range effects which are of considerable social significance. In socio-sexual contacts, individuals may become acquainted with each other, learn to adjust physically and emotionally, come to understand each other, and come to appreciate each other's qualities in a way which is not possible in any other type of social relationship. Learning to respond emotionally to a sexual partner may contribute to the effectiveness of one's other, non-sexual, social relationships.

1945:2 (reports over 74,000 illegitimate births registered per year, and emphasizes the total inadequacy of the data). Dublin 1951:20 (an estimated 131,900 illegitimate births in U. S. in 1947, equaling 4 per cent of all births).

Effect on Marriage. As we have pointed out in our volume on the male, the child is born with an uninhibited capacity to make physical contacts and to snuggle against other persons. Such contacts may contribute to its emotional development. As children grow, however, it is customary in our culture to teach them that they must no longer make physical contacts, and must inhibit their emotional responses to persons outside of the immediate family. Many persons believe that this restraint should be maintained until the time of marriage. Then, after marriage, the husband and wife are supposed to break down all of their inhibitions and make physical and emotional adjustments which will contribute to the solidarity of the marital relationship. Unfortunately there is no magic in a marriage ceremony which can accomplish this. The record indicates that a very high proportion of the females, in particular, and a considerable number of the males find it difficult after marriage to redevelop the sort of freedom with which they made contacts as children, and to learn again how to respond without inhibition to physical and emotional contacts with other persons.[38]

At least theoretically, pre-marital socio-sexual experience, whether in petting or in coitus, should contribute to this development of emotional capacities. In this as in other areas, learning at an early age may be more effective than learning at any later age after marriage. But many persons believe that pre-marital experience cannot be as rich emotionally as marital experience. It is even insisted that pre-marital experience distinctly decreases a female's chance to make satisfactory sexual adjustments in marriage.[39]

It is impossible, at this point, to attempt an over-all evaluation of the effects of pre-marital coitus on marriage, but we have been able to make correlations between the incidences and frequencies of the female's pre-marital experience in orgasm, and her subsequent capacity to respond to the point of orgasm in her marital coitus. The detailed correlations are presented more fully in Chapter 9, but we may summarize briefly at this point.

The record on our sample of married females shows that there was a marked, positive correlation between experience in orgasm obtained from pre-marital coitus, and the capacity to reach orgasm after marriage (Table 109, Figure 71).[40] Among those females who had never reached orgasm from any source prior to marriage, 44 per cent had failed to reach orgasm in any of their coitus in the first year of mar-

---

[38] The difficulty of eliminating the effects of pre-marital restraint is also noted, for example, in: Michels 1914:180–181. Lynd and Lynd 1929:112. Fisher in Folsom 1938:20. Popenoe 1938:5.

[39] See footnote 34 in Chapter 9.

[40] See footnote 33 in Chapter 9.

riage (Table 108). Among those who had had pre-marital coitus but had failed to reach orgasm in that coitus, between 38 and 56 per cent had failed to reach orgasm in that first year of marriage (Table 109). But among the females who had had pre-marital coitus in which they had reached orgasm at least twenty-five times before marriage, only 3 per cent had failed to achieve at least some orgasm in their coitus during the first year of marriage. Similar correlations were evident as long as fifteen years after marriage.

Well over half (50 to 57 per cent) of the females who had had pre-marital coital experience which had led to orgasm, had reached orgasm in practically all of their coitus during the first year of marriage (Table 109). Of those who had had no pre-marital coital experience and had not reached orgasm from any source before marriage, only 29 per cent had approached a hundred per cent response in the first year of marriage.

These correlations may have depended on selective factors, or they may have depended on causal relationships. The most responsive females may have been the ones who had had the largest amount of pre-marital experience and, because they were responsive, they were the ones who had most often reached orgasm in marriage. The females who had abstained before marriage may have been the physiologically less responsive individuals who, therefore, were the ones who had most often remained chaste, both before and after marriage.

But there are several reasons for believing that such selective factors could not have accounted for the whole of these correlations. There are psychologic and sociologic data which show the importance of early experience in the establishment of habits of thought and attitudes which are very difficult to alter or counteract in later years. That the capacity to respond to the point of orgasm may be developed is evidenced by a variety of data, but particularly by the fact that some women who are unresponsive in their early marriages may improve in the course of some years in their capacities to reach orgasm. There are women in our histories who were unresponsive for several years, and in some cases for as long as twenty-eight years after their marriages, before they began to respond to the point of orgasm (Table 113).

There is the further evidence that the failure to respond sexually is often the product of inhibitions which prevent an individual from entering a sexual relationship with the abandon which is necessary before orgasm can be achieved. Inhibitions represent the development of habits of behavior, patterns of negative response, or intellectual processes which interfere with the autonomic and involuntary functions on which satisfactory sexual relations most depend (Chapter 17).

When there are long years of abstinence and restraint, and an avoidance of physical contacts and emotional responses before marriage, acquired inhibitions may do such damage to the capacity to respond that it may take some years to get rid of them after marriage, if indeed they are ever dissipated. While pre-marital experience in orgasm attained in masturbation and petting also shows a positive correlation with the capacity to reach orgasm in marital coitus (Tables 110, 111), there is no sort of experience which shows a higher positive correlation with orgasmic success in marriage than coitus before marriage.

Any determination of the social desirability or undesirability of pre-marital coitus might, then, take into account the emotional effects on the individual whenever he or she engages in any type of socially taboo behavior, the actual damage that such activity may do to the social organization, the desirability of resolving some of the conflicts between the biologically normal urge to have coitus and the social insistence on pre-marital chastity, and the effects of abstinence or of pre-marital experience on the ultimate success of a marriage.

SUMMARY AND COMPARISONS OF FEMALE AND MALE

Pre-Marital Coitus

	IN FEMALE	IN MALE
Mammalian Origins: Coitus attempted as soon as neuromuscular coordination permits	Less often and later	More often and earlier
Anthropologic Background		
In most primitive societies, coital play among children permitted or tolerated	Yes	Yes
In primitive societies, some adolescent coitus permitted	In about 70%	In virtually all
Relation to Age		
Accumulative incidence		
Experience	50%	Educ. 0–8 = 98% Educ. 9–12 = 85% Educ. 13+ = 68%
Experience with orgasm	±40%	±always
Active incidence, experience		
Age: adol.–15	3%	40%
Age: 16–20	20%	71%
Age: 21–25	35%	68%
Frequency of exper. (act. med.), per week		
Age: adol.–20	0.1–0.2	0.6
After age 20	0.3	0.4
Regularity	Little	Some
Percentage of total outlet		
In early twenties	26%	33%
In mid-forties	43%	34%
Number of years involved		
1 year or less	44%	
2 to 3 years	30%	

	IN FEMALE	IN MALE
Pre-marital partners (in active sample)		
With one partner	53%	
Coitus with fiancé only	46%	
Coitus with fiancé and others	41%	
Relation to Age at Marr. and Educ. Level	Some	Very marked
Accumul. incid. uniform for uniform age of marr.	Yes	No. Higher in less educated
Active incid., experience		
Age: 16–20		
Grade school	38%	85%
High school	32%	76%
College and graduate	17–19%	42%
After age 20	No relation	Persistent relation
Frequency	No relation	Highest in lower educ. levels
Percentage of total outlet		
Age: 16–20	Lowest in college group	Lowest in college group
After age 20	No relation	Persistent relation
Relation to Parental Occupational Class	Little	Little
Relation to Decade of Birth		
Accumulative incid., (*e.g.* at age 25)		
Born before 1900	14% }	Little. Younger
Born after 1900	36–39% }	gener. starts earlier
Active incidence, exper.		
Born before 1900	Lower }	Higher in younger
Born after 1900	2–3 times as high }	generation of grade school, high school sample
Frequency	No relation	Some relation
Percentage of total outlet	Marked increase since 1900	
Relation to Age at Onset of Adolescence		
Accumulative and active incidence	Little relation	Some relation
Frequency	No relation	Little or no relation
Relation to Rural-Urban Background		
Accumulative incidence	Higher in urban	Higher in urban
Active incidence	Higher in urban after age 20	Higher in urban
Frequency	No relation	Higher in urban
Relation to Religious Background		
Accumulative incidence, experience		
Devout	24–30%	Lower
Less devout	55–63%	Higher
Active incidence	Lower in devout	Lower in devout
Frequency	Somewhat lower in devout	Markedly lower in devout
Percentage of total outlet	Lower in devout	Lower in devout

	IN FEMALE	IN MALE
Nature and Conditions of Pre-Marital Coitus		
Place: most often in own home	Yes	No
Techniques		
More extended when coital experience most extensive	Yes	
Oral contacts more accepted by younger generation	Yes	Yes
Time involved often greater than in marital coitus	Yes	Yes
Coital positions more limited than in marital coitus	Yes	Yes
Nudity more common in upper educ. levels	Yes	Yes
Physiologic Significance: provides release of sexual tension	Sometimes for 40%	±always for 68–98%
Psychologic Aspects		
Intention to avoid coitus		
Among virgins	80%	
Among non-virgins	30%	Almost none
Factors restraining coitus:		
Moral	89%	21–61%
Lack of desire	45%	19–45%
Fear of pregnancy	44%	18–28%
Fear of discovery	44%	14–23%
Fear of venereal disease	14%	25–29%
Lack of opportunity	22%	35–52%
Regret following coitus		
No regret	69–77%	Most
Most often regret if:		
Experience limited	Yes	
Not with fiancé	Yes	
Devoutly religious	Yes	
Desire to marry virgin	23%	39–47%
Acceptance depends primarily on social custom	Yes	Yes
Judeo-Christian codes condemn	Yes	Yes
Legal Aspects		
Coitus among juveniles prohibited in nearly all states	Yes	Yes
Coitus among unmarried adults penalized in 35 states	Yes	Yes
Social Significance		
Pregnancies as a result	18%	
Venereal infections as a result	2–3%	Low in college level, higher in lower educ. level
Effect on Marriage		
Pre-marital restraint creates inhibitions, difficult to break after marriage	Yes	Yes, to lesser degree
No orgasm, first year of marr., if:		
No pre-marital coitus or orgasm	40%	
Pre-marital coitus without orgasm	46–56%	
Pre-marital coitus with frequent orgasm	3%	
Orgasm ± always, first year of marr., if:		
No pre-marital coitus or orgasm	29%	
Pre-marital coitus without orgasm	17%	
Pre-marital coitus with freq. orgasm	57%	

Table 75. Accumulative Incidence: Pre-Marital Coitus
By Educational Level

AGE	TOTAL SAMPLE	EDUCATIONAL LEVEL				TOTAL SAMPLE	EDUCATIONAL LEVEL			
		0–8	9–12	13–16	17+		0–8	9–12	13–16	17+

COITAL EXPERIENCE

AGE	%	Percent				Cases	Cases			
13	1	9	1	—	1	5774	177	1014	3303	1151
15	3	18	5	2	1	5732	173	1011	3303	1151
20	20	25	26	20	15	3982	97	705	2070	1110
25	33	26	37	39	28	1476	50	271	487	668
30	44		47	49	42	674		97	186	362
35	48			60	45	384			87	241

COITUS TO ORGASM

AGE	%	Percent				Cases	Cases			
13	—	3	—	0	—	5738	174	1005	3286	1143
15	1	11	3	1	—	5694	170	1002	3286	1143
20	10	13	13	10	8	3955	95	700	2058	1102
25	21	14	23	24	19	1467	50	271	484	662
30	30		27	35	28	671		97	185	360
35	38			49	35	383			86	241

Italic figures throughout the series of tables indicate that the calculations are based on less than 50 cases. No calculations are based on less than 11 cases. The dash (—) indicates a percentage or frequency smaller than any quantity which would be shown by a figure in the given number of decimal places.

Table 76. Active Incidence, Frequency, and Percentage of Outlet Pre-Marital Coitus

By Age

AGE DURING ACTIVITY	ACTIVE SAMPLE			TOTAL SAMPLE		CASES IN TOTAL SAMPLE
	Active incid. %	Median freq. per wk.	Mean frequency per wk.	Mean freq. per wk.	% of total outlet	
COITAL EXPERIENCE						
Adol.–15	3	0.1	0.6 ± 0.09	—		5678
16–20	20	0.2	0.5 ± 0.03	0.1 ± 0.01		5614
21–25	35	0.3	0.7 ± 0.04	0.2 ± 0.01		2811
26–30	43	0.3	0.7 ± 0.07	0.3 ± 0.03		1064
31–35	43	0.3	0.7 ± 0.08	0.3 ± 0.04		540
36–40	42	0.4	0.9 ± 0.13	0.4 ± 0.06		316
41–45	42	0.3	0.8 ± 0.16	0.3 ± 0.07		180
46–50	34	0.3	0.6 ± 0.21	0.2 ± 0.08		109
51–55	21	0.3	0.4 ± 0.18	0.1 ± 0.04		58
56–60	15			—		27
COITUS TO ORGASM						
Adol.–15	1	0.2	1.3 ± 0.35	—	6	5677
16–20	10	0.1	0.6 ± 0.07	0.1 ± 0.01	15	5613
21–25	21	0.3	0.8 ± 0.07	0.2 ± 0.02	26	2810
26–30	30	0.3	1.0 ± 0.15	0.3 ± 0.05	32	1064
31–35	34	0.2	1.0 ± 0.22	0.3 ± 0.08	33	539
36–40	36	0.4	1.3 ± 0.29	0.5 ± 0.11	36	315
41–45	35	0.4	1.4 ± 0.49	0.5 ± 0.18	43	179
46–50	27	0.3	1.2 ± 0.50	0.3 ± 0.14	37	109
51–55	19	0.3	0.7 ± 0.37	0.1 ± 0.08	22	58
56–60	15			—	6	27

Table 77. Maximum Frequency of Pre-Marital Coital Experience
Ever, in Any Single Week

MAXIMUM FREQ. IN ANY WEEK	TOTAL SAMPLE		EDUCATIONAL LEVEL		
	%	Cumul. %	9–12	13–16	17+
			Percent of females		
1	30	100	38	28	20
2	16	70	17	16	17
3	13	55	11	14	14
4	10	41	12	9	11
5	6	31	2	8	8
6	4	25	3	4	6
7	7	20	5	7	6
8	2	14		1	4
9	1	12		—	1
10	3	11	3	4	2
11	—	8	—		
12	1	8		1	3
13					
14	1	7	1	—	2
15	1	6		2	1
16	—	4	1		
17	—	4		1	
18	—	4	1		—
19	—	4		—	
20	2	4	2	1	2
21	—	2	1	—	
22					
23					
24	—	2			—
25	1	2	1	1	1
26					
27					
28					
29+	1	1	2	—	1
Number of cases		783	131	363	210

Table 78. Nature and Conditions of Pre-Marital Coitus

Percents, among females with experience in coitus before marriage

ITEM	TOTAL SAMPLE	DECADE OF BIRTH			AGE AT MARRIAGE			
		Bf. 1900	1900– 1909	1910– 1919	16–20	21–25	26–30	31–35
Extent of total experience								
1 to 10 times	29	27	30	25	32	31	20	17
1 year or less	44	40	44	38	60	45	27	27
2–3 years	30	26	27	33	29	33	30	14
4–5 years	13	14	11	14	10	15	16	7
6–10 years	10	10	13	13	1	7	23	29
11 years or more	3	10	5	2	0	0	4	23
Number of cases	1230	92	312	504	296	600	226	66
Number of coital partners								
1 only	53	56	55	48	63	57	39	36
2–5	34	33	31	38	28	33	42	39
6–10	7	9	6	8	6	5	11	14
11–20	4	1	5	4	2	4	6	8
21 or more	2	1	3	2	1	1	2	3
Number of cases	1220	90	311	500	292	598	224	66
Pre-mar. coitus with fiancé								
With fiancé only	46	40	48	42	54	50	32	28
With other males only	13	20	11	12	14	12	13	15
With both fiancé and other males	41	40	41	46	32	38	55	57
Number of cases	1229	91	310	501	296	599	226	65
Extent of exper. with fiancé								
1 to 10 times	36	30	34	35	41	37	31	30
1 year or less	75	68	73	76	85	75	68	54
2–3 years	20	24	22	18	12	21	22	33
4–5 years	4	4	4	4	3	4	6	6
6 years or more	1	4	1	2	0	—	4	7
Number of cases	1071	71	276	437	253	521	193	54
Places of pre-mar. coitus								
In female's home	58	52	58	60	55	57	65	62
In male's home	48	40	43	53	43	50	49	44
In friend's home	9	6	7	9	9	10	6	8
In automobiles	41	18	38	44	47	40	38	35
In hotel or rented room	40	35	42	44	29	39	51	60
Out-of-doors	36	40	39	36	34	37	37	35
Other places	15	29	13	17	14	14	18	17
Number of cases	983	65	228	402	235	490	179	52

The data in the table are based on females who, because they were married by the time of the interview, had completed their pre-marital experience. "Fiancé" as used in this table refers only to the male whom the female ultimately married.

Table 79. Accumulative Incidence: Pre-Marital Coital Experience By Age at First Marriage and Educational Level

AGE	TOTAL MARRIED SAMPLE	EDUCATIONAL LEVEL 9-12	13-16	17+	TOTAL MARRIED SAMPLE	EDUCATIONAL LEVEL 9-12	13-16	17+
		AGE AT FIRST MARRIAGE 16-20						
	%		Percent		Cases		Cases	
14	4	3	3	1	650	226	309	72
16	15	20	10	10	650	226	309	71
18	30	32	27	34	560	188	284	61
20	47	44	48		236	64	128	
		AGE AT FIRST MARRIAGE 21-25						
	%		Percent		Cases		Cases	
16	4	5	4	3	1224	319	551	319
18	13	17	11	12	1224	319	551	319
20	26	27	27	24	1224	319	551	319
22	39	37	40	39	909	230	397	259
25	42		47	46	162		64	48
		AGE AT FIRST MARRIAGE 26-30						
	%		Percent		Cases		Cases	
16	2	3	4	1	437	106	152	164
18	8	14	7	5	437	106	152	164
20	14	21	12	13	437	106	152	164
22	22	26	21	20	437	106	152	164
24	30	34	36	23	437	106	152	164
26	43	47	48	37	437	106	152	164
28	56		61	55	190		57	76

Table 80. Active Incidence and Percentage of Outlet: Pre-Marital Coitus By Educational Level

Age during activity	Educ. level	Active incid. exper. %	Active incid. orgasm %	% of total outlet	Cases in total sample	Age during activity	Educ. level	Active incid. exper. %	Active incid. orgasm %	% of total outlet	Cases in total sample
Adol. −15	Total	3	1	6	5677	26-30	Total	43	30	32	1064
	0-8	18	9	23	162		9-12	46	27	32	181
	9-12	5	3	14	983		13-16	47	34	39	313
	13-16	1	1	1	3271		17+	40	28	27	531
	17+	1	1	2	1129	31-35	Total	43	34	33	540
16-20	Total	20	10	15	5614		9-12	38	26	23	65
	0-8	38	22	29	143		13-16	47	37	52	139
	9-12	32	17	29	976		17+	43	35	21	310
	13-16	19	10	10	3299	36-40	Total	42	36	36	316
	17+	17	8	8	1150		13-16	59	50	46	68
21-25	Total	35	21	26	2811		17+	36	32	31	205
	0-8	26	19	29	67	41-45	Total	42	35	43	180
	9-12	39	23	32	537		17+	38	31	42	123
	13-16	37	23	26	1204	46-50	Total	34	27	38	109
	17+	33	22	23	1003		17+	31	24	38	80

For an explanation of the discrepancies between certain of these active incidences and the accumulative incidences shown for the same ages, see p. 44.

Table 81. Accumulative Incidence: Pre-Marital Coitus
By Parental Occupational Class

AGE	PARENTAL CLASS 2+3	4	5	6+7	PARENTAL CLASS 2+3	4	5	6+7
	COITAL EXPERIENCE—ALL EDUCATIONAL LEVELS							
	Percent				*Cases*			
13	4	1	—	—	972	812	1523	2680
15	9	3	2	2	943	809	1521	2670
20	23	20	19	19	608	575	1035	1889
25	31	32	34	33	260	229	378	655
30	40	39	42	49	124	115	187	279
35	35	39	47	56	69	56	105	174
	COITUS TO ORGASM—ALL EDUCATIONAL LEVELS							
	Percent				*Cases*			
13	1	—	—	—	964	807	1515	2665
15	5	1	—	1	935	804	1513	2655
20	13	10	9	10	606	571	1029	1873
25	18	20	19	23	260	228	376	648
30	23	26	30	33	124	115	187	275
35	23	36	39	43	69	56	105	173
	COITAL EXPERIENCE—SUBJECT'S EDUCATIONAL LEVEL 17+							
	Percent				*Cases*			
13	0	2	1	1	130	141	275	648
15	0	2	1	1	130	141	275	648
20	14	15	14	16	125	136	265	626
25	26	24	29	29	78	93	167	355
30		27	39	47		55	98	177
35			42	51			67	120

Table 82. Active Incidence and Percentage of Outlet: Pre-Marital Coitus
By Parental Occupational Class

Age	Parental class	Active incid. exper. %	Active incid. orgasm %	% of total outlet	Cases in total sample	Age	Parental class	Active incid. exper. %	Active incid. orgasm %	% of total outlet	Cases in total sample
Adol. −15	2+3	11	5	15	948	26–30	2+3	39	23	28	196
	4	3	1	3	796		4	39	28	36	181
	5	2	—	—	1506		5	40	27	29	275
	6+7	2	1	2	2654		6+7	47	33	34	447
16–20	2+3	31	19	26	882	31–35	2+3	27	21	17	97
	4	20	10	17	796		4	33	27	19	91
	5	19	9	10	1513		5	43	35	15	149
	6+7	19	10	10	2649		6+7	51	42	41	224
21–25	2+3	36	23	27	463	36–40	2+3	27	26	21	63
	4	32	20	26	422		5	37	31	35	86
	5	34	19	28	735		6+7	50	42	41	141
	6+7	36	23	25	1283						

The occupational classes are as follows: 2 + 3 = unskilled and semi-skilled labor. 4 = skilled labor. 5 = lower white collar class. 6 + 7 = upper white collar and professional classes.

For an explanation of the discrepancies between certain of these active incidences and the accumulative incidences shown for the same ages, see p. 44.

338

Table 83. Accumulative Incidence: Pre-Marital Coitus
By Decade of Birth

AGE		DECADE OF BIRTH			Bf. 1900	DECADE OF BIRTH		
	Bf. 1900	1900–1909	1910–1919	1920–1929		1900–1909	1910–1919	1920–1929
COITAL EXPERIENCE								
	Percent				*Cases*			
13	1	1	1	1	455	783	1342	3071
15	2	2	3	4	455	782	1342	3056
20	8	18	23	21	419	706	1219	1639
25	14	36	39	37	274	432	617	154
30	26	53	48		172	257	246	
35	35	56	54		132	189	63	
COITUS TO ORGASM								
	Percent				*Cases*			
13	—	0	—	—	452	778	1322	3067
15	1	—	1	2	452	777	1322	3052
20	4	8	11	11	417	702	1202	1636
25	10	22	24	27	274	428	613	152
30	19	37	30		172	255	244	
35	25	45	45		132	189	62	

Table 84. Active Incidence and Percentage of Outlet: Pre-Marital Coitus
By Decade of Birth

Age	Decade of birth	Active incid. exper. %	Active incid. or-gasm %	% of total outlet	Cases in total sample	Age	Decade of birth	Active incid. exper. %	Active incid. or-gasm %	% of total outlet	Cases in total sample
Adol. −15	Bf. 1900	2	1	3	437	31–35	Bf. 1900	33	25	16	152
	1900–1909	2	—	2	760		1900–1909	49	40	42	228
	1910–1919	2	1	1	1320		1910–1919	43	33	39	160
	1920–1929	4	2	11	3049						
16–20	Bf. 1900	8	4	4	452	36–40	Bf. 1900	32	25	34	124
	1900–1909	18	8	10	772		1900–1909	48	44	39	165
	1910–1919	25	11	11	1329						
	1920–1929	21	13	21	2999						
21–25	Bf. 1900	16	10	24	367	41–45	Bf. 1900	36	29	42	117
	1900–1909	38	22	30	617		1900–1909	52	46	45	63
	1910–1919	42	24	26	987						
	1920–1929	35	23	24	843						
26–30	Bf. 1900	24	17	13	219						
	1900–1909	50	35	40	344						
	1910–1919	48	32	35	448						

For an explanation of the discrepancies between certain of these active incidences and the accumulative incidences shown for the same ages, see p. 44.

Table 85. Accumulative Incidence: Pre-Marital Coitus

    By Age at Onset of Adolescence

AGE	ADOLESCENT					ADOLESCENT				
	By 11	At 12	At 13	At 14	At 15+	By 11	At 12	At 13	At 14	At 15+
					COITAL EXPERIENCE					
		Percent						*Cases*		
13	1	1	1			1198	1680	1749		
15	3	3	3	3	1	1183	1667	1737	791	349
20	22	22	18	19	13	789	1120	1216	600	254
25	34	37	32	32	30	253	385	455	259	121
30	48	51	37	45	44	128	152	207	128	59
35	55	60	37	45		80	82	116	74	
					COITUS TO ORGASM					
		Percent						*Cases*		
13	1	—	1			1185	1673	1740		
15	2	1	1	1	1	1170	1660	1728	787	345
20	13	10	8	10	7	780	1114	1210	598	250
25	23	23	20	21	16	252	382	453	258	119
30	32	34	27	29	25	128	152	205	127	59
35	41	49	29	38		80	82	115	74	

Table 86. Active Incidence and Percentage of Outlet: Pre-Marital Coitus

    By Age at Onset of Adolescence

Age	Age at adol.	Active incid. exper. %	Active incid. orgasm %	% of total outlet	Cases in total sample	Age	Age at adol.	Active incid. exper. %	Active incid. orgasm %	% of total outlet	Cases in total sample
Adol. –15	8–11	3	2	9	1204	26–30	8–11	47	32	40	196
	12	3	1	3	1685		12	44	30	26	266
	13	3	2	6	1747		13	41	30	30	324
	14	3	1	3	796		14	40	29	34	192
	15+	1	1	6	262		15+	45	28	30	87
16–20	8–11	24	13	18	1167	31–35	8–11	49	39	44	99
	12	22	10	12	1639		12	55	45	34	122
	13	18	8	15	1700		13	34	29	28	163
	14	21	13	16	777		14	36	28	34	109
	15+	19	10	11	345						
21–25	8–11	34	22	25	526	36–40	8–11	52	45	62	65
	12	37	23	24	771		12	45	42	18	66
	13	32	20	25	852		13	40	31	27	97
	14	34	23	28	460		14	31	27	38	62
	15+	40	21	38	203						

For an explanation of the discrepancies between certain of these active incidences and the accumulative incidences shown for the same ages, see p. 44.

Table 87. Accumulative Incidence: Pre-Marital Coitus
   By Rural-Urban Background

AGE	COITAL EXPERIENCE				COITUS TO ORGASM			
	Rural	Urban	Rural	Urban	Rural	Urban	Rural	Urban
	Percent		*Cases*		*Percent*		*Cases*	
10	0	0	400	5202	0	0	392	5179
15	4	3	398	5159	1	1	390	5136
20	20	20	309	3537	7	10	303	3520
25	27	34	134	1278	15	22	132	1272
30	34	46	70	576	22	31	68	575
35		51		322		41		321

Table 88. Active Incidence and Percentage of Outlet: Pre-Marital Coitus
   By Rural-Urban Background

Age	Back-grnd.	Active incid. exper. %	Active incid. orgasm %	% of total outlet	Cases in total sample	Age	Back-grnd.	Active incid. exper. %	Active incid. orgasm %	% of total outlet	Cases in total sample
Adol. −15	Rural	4	1	1	388	26–30	Rural	31	24	28	104
	Urban	3	1	4	5133		Urban	44	31	33	915
16–20	Rural	20	10	9	386	31–35	Rural	30	23	21	64
	Urban	20	12	15	5081		Urban	45	36	35	454
21–25	Rural	30	19	15	229						
	Urban	36	23	26	2487						

For an explanation of the discrepancies between certain of these active incidences and the accumulative incidences shown for the same ages, see p. 44.

Table 89. Accumulative Incidence: Pre-Marital Coitus
By Religious Background

AGE	PROTESTANT			CATHOLIC			JEWISH	
	Dev.	Moder.	Inact.	Dev.	Moder.	Inact.	Moder.	Inact.
COITAL EXPERIENCE—Percent								
13	1	1	2	1	3	5	0	—
15	3	3	5	3	7	12	—	2
20	14	19	25	12	24	41	11	27
25	22	33	44	21		54	23	42
30	26	44	55					62
35	30	42	63					
COITUS TO ORGASM—Percent								
13	—	—	—	0	1	4	0	0
15	1	1	2	2	4	7	0	1
20	6	9	12	3	10	26	7	16
25	12	20	28	11		45	20	27
30	18	26	38					43
35	20	34	51					
COITAL EXPERIENCE—Cases								
13	1232	1165	1088	388	153	172	575	985
15	1217	1155	1081	384	152	171	574	981
20	860	853	887	261	84	122	305	625
25	305	335	407	110		59	71	175
30	141	159	197					74
35	86	93	121					
COITUS TO ORGASM—Cases								
13	1224	1156	1079	386	151	170	573	979
15	1209	1146	1072	382	150	169	572	975
20	855	845	879	259	83	121	304	621
25	304	331	405	109		58	71	172
30	141	156	197					72
35	86	93	121					

Table 90. Active Incidence, Frequency, and Percentage of Outlet Pre-Marital Coitus

By Religious Background

AGE DURING ACTIVITY	RELIGIOUS GROUP	COITAL EXPERIENCE		COITUS TO ORGASM			CASES IN TOTAL SAMPLE
		Active incid. %	Active median freq. per wk.	Active incid. %	Active median freq. per wk.	% of total outlet	
Adol.–15	Protestant						
	Devout	3	0.1	1	0.2	4	1218
	Moderate	3	0.1	1	0.1	9	1148
	Inactive	5	0.2	2	0.1	2	1064
	Catholic						
	Devout	4	0.3	2		3	382
	Moderate	7	0.1	3		4	150
	Inactive	12	0.3	7	2.2	25	169
	Jewish						
	Devout	0		0		0	107
	Moderate	—		0		0	571
	Inactive	1	0.2	1		2	978
16–20	Protestant						
	Devout	17	0.1	9	0.1	10	1197
	Moderate	21	0.1	11	0.1	17	1134
	Inactive	29	0.2	14	0.2	13	1066
	Catholic						
	Devout	15	0.2	6	0.5	14	372
	Moderate	32	0.2	17	0.2	20	139
	Inactive	43	0.5	29	0.5	39	160
	Jewish						
	Devout	10	0.1	5		5	107
	Moderate	11	0.1	6	0.2	6	571
	Inactive	25	0.2	15	0.2	14	972
21–25	Protestant						
	Devout	22	0.2	12	0.2	12	604
	Moderate	33	0.2	20	0.2	28	615
	Inactive	48	0.3	31	0.3	31	677
	Catholic						
	Devout	21	0.2	10	0.2	27	196
	Moderate	42	0.5	25	0.4	26	57
	Inactive	56	0.5	42	0.5	36	91
	Jewish						
	Moderate	26	0.3	18	0.3	19	192
	Inactive	44	0.4	27	0.4	31	396
26–30	Protestant						
	Devout	26	0.2	17	0.2	14	221
	Moderate	43	0.3	30	0.3	28	250
	Inactive	54	0.4	38	0.3	37	309
	Catholic						
	Devout	23	0.2	13		23	79
31–35	Protestant						
	Devout	23	0.2	17	0.2	17	121
	Moderate	39	0.2	35	0.1	30	128
	Inactive	57	0.3	45	0.2	44	159
36–40	Protestant						
	Devout	26	0.2	24	0.2	21	76
	Moderate	36	0.3	31	0.3	30	78
	Inactive	53	0.4	41	0.4	44	102

For an explanation of the discrepancies between certain of these active incidences and the accumulative incidences shown for the same ages, see p. 44.

343

Table 91. Attitudes Toward Pre-Marital Coitus

INDICATORS OF ATTITUDES	RESPONSES GIVEN				CASES IN SAMPLE
	Yes	More or less	No	Un-decided	
	Percent				
Intent to have, or to have more coitus					
Single females without experience	7	2	80	11	2288
Single females with experience	53	6	30	11	879
Factors accounting for restraint					
Moral objections	80	9	11		5735
Sexual unresponsiveness	32	13	55		4831
Fear of pregnancy	21	23	56		5727
Fear of public opinion	20	24	56		5646
Lack of opportunity	14	8	78		5653
Fear of venereal disease	5	9	86		5720
Desire to marry a virgin male	Yes	No pref-erence	No	Un-decided	
Total sample	23	42	32	3	5449
Females born bf. 1900	29	45	15	11	365
Females born 1900–1909	22	45	28	5	708
Females born 1910–1919	17	45	36	2	1267
Females born 1920–1929	24	41	32	3	2985

Table 92. Regret After Pre-Marital Coitus

Factors correlated with regret	No regret	Some regret	Definite regret	Cases in sample
	Percent			
Marital status				
Single	69	13	18	751
Married	77	12	11	1039
Extent of pre-marital experience				
10 times or less	64	11	25	528
1 year or less	73	10	17	693
2–3 years	71	15	14	545
4–5 years	70	20	10	244
6–10 years	81	9	10	195
11–20 years	86	8	6	96
Number of pre-marital partners				
1 partner	75	10	15	844
2–5 partners	69	17	14	646
6–10 partners	81	9	10	160
11–20 partners	77	17	6	82
Decade of birth				
Before 1900	80	10	10	104
1900–1909	79	9	12	327
1910–1919	76	14	10	572
1920–1929	69	13	18	769
Pregnancy, a result				
Yes	70	13	17	333
No	74	13	13	1444
Venereal infection, a result				
Yes	*66*	*18*	*16*	44
No	74	13	13	1709
Coitus with fiancé				
With fiancé only	81	10	9	465
With other males only	62	10	28	124
With both fiancé and other males	78	13	9	913
Religious background				
Protestant				
Devout	62	15	23	295
Moderate	69	17	14	376
Inactive	80	10	10	490
Catholic				
Devout	50	15	35	86
Moderate	65	10	25	51
Inactive	84	7	9	90
Jewish				
Moderate	75	13	12	93
Inactive	82	11	7	331

"Fiancé" as used in this table refers to the male whom the female ultimately married.

Chapter 9

MARITAL COITUS

For most females and males, coitus in marriage provides, in the course of their lives, a larger proportion of their total sexual outlet than any other single type of activity (Tables 170, 171). Moreover, marital coitus is socially the most important of all sexual activities, because of its significance in the origin and maintenance of the home.

Throughout most human groups, everywhere in the world, the home has been recognized as the basic unit of the social organization. In only a few instances have there been serious attempts to abandon the family organization, and to substitute some state-centered institution which would abolish the long-time associations of adults and their offspring. Such an abandonment of the family was attempted in ancient Sparta, and in the communal groups such as the Brook Farm Colony, the New Harmony Colony, the Oneida Colony, and the various other experimental societies which developed in the United States a century or more ago. Something of the sort has been attempted more recently in Nazi Germany, Soviet Russia, and Communist China. None of these schemes, however, has provided satisfactory substitutes for the home, and most of them have been short-lived. History confirms the importance of the family, even though it does not justify some of the other customs which are a part of our culture.

As we pointed out in our volume on the male (1948:563), "Society is interested in maintaining the family as a way for men and women to live together in partnerships that may make for more effective functioning than solitary living may allow. Society is interested in maintaining the family as a means of providing homes for children that result from coitus; and in Jewish and many Christian philosophies, this is made a prime end of marriage. Society is also interested in maintaining families as a means of providing a regular sexual outlet for adults, and as a means of controlling promiscuous sexual activity."

Some persons fear that the family as an institution is in imminent danger in our present-day American social organization. They are disturbed over the increasing divorce rate. They see the traditional relation between the sexes upset by the female's growing emancipation from her former role in the home, and by the increasing importance of her position in the social organization outside of the home. They see organized social events, moving pictures, and the automobile taking the family away from the fireside circle for its recreational and intellectual development. They feel that the integrity of the family organization is threatened by the younger generation's rebellion against parental controls.

On the other hand, the proportion of married persons in the total population is higher than ever before in American history, there is a higher proportion who live in separate housing units, and there are more persons who own their own homes. Many persons feel that some of these developments are contributing to a type of family which is better than the patriarchal, autocratically controlled organization which our grandparents knew.

The primate family, roaming the wild, is dominated by the physical brawn of its male head, and there is a minimum of anything which resembles a partnership between the adults in such an organization. The primate offspring depend upon their mother for most of the care and protection which they receive. Until a half century ago, many human families in Europe and in this country were as nearly male-dominated as the primate family is in the wild. But with the emergence of the female as a significant force in the political, industrial, and intellectual life of our Western culture, marriage is increasingly becoming a partnership in which the duties, responsibilities, and privileges are more equally shared by or divided between the two spouses. Similarly, an increased understanding of human psychology, with its emphasis upon the importance of the early years in the life of an individual, has made the child a partner in the home, as it rarely was in Europe or America a century ago.

As a result of this awakened interest in more human and more substantial family partnerships, there is developing in this country, as well as in some other parts of the world, an increasing interest in understanding some of the factors which contribute to the effectiveness of a home, and an increasing emphasis on training modern youth and adults to be more effective marital partners. It is in these terms that the significance of sex education, of pre-marital sexual outlets, of non-marital sexual activities for adults, and of the techniques and frequencies of marital coitus are being evaluated today.

The place which marital coitus had held in the lives of the married females in our sample, and the factors which had contributed to the success or failure of that coitus, are the subject matter of the present chapter.

RELATION TO AGE

In our sample of American females, the incidences and frequencies of marital coitus had reached their maxima in the first year or two after marriage. From that point, they had steadily dropped into minimum frequencies in the oldest age groups. There is no other type of sexual activity among females which shows such a steady decline with advancing age.

Incidence of Experience. Unlike any other type of sexual activity, the accumulative incidence of marital coitus had nearly reached its maximum, which was close to one hundred per cent, immediately after marriage. But neither the accumulative nor active incidences had quite reached a hundred per cent, for there were a few (an exceeding few) of the married couples who had delayed their first coitus for some months or a year or more after marriage, and there were a few (an exceeding few) who had not had coitus at all after marriage. Some of the females in the sample had not actually lived with their husbands, and some of them were physically handicapped and incapable of having coitus. A few had married homosexual males as a matter of social convenience, and they were among the very few who had completely abstained from coitus in marriage.

The active incidence of marital coitus had included more than 99 per cent of all the married females in the younger age groups (Table 93, Figure 62). After thirty years of age, the figure began to drop. Between thirty-one and thirty-five years of age, 98 per cent of the married females were still having coitus, but after age fifty-five, only 80 per cent of the sample were having coitus in their marriages.[1] Our male sample showed a similar decline in active incidences in the older age groups (see our 1948:252), but the decline recorded by the females was a bit steeper than that recorded by the males. At fifty years of age, for instance, 97 per cent of the males reported that they were still having coitus, while only 93 per cent of the females reported such experience. By sixty years of age the record included 94 per cent of the males in contrast to 80 per cent of the females. These differences may be due to differences in the composition of the samples, or to the usual discrepancies in the ages of the married partners, or to differences in the way in which the males and females had reported coitus which occurred at very low frequencies.

Frequency of Experience. The average (active median) frequencies of marital coitus in the sample had begun at nearly three (2.8) per week for the females who were married in their late teens (Table 93,

---

[1] A material drop in the percentage having marital coitus in the later age groups was also reported by Terman 1938:270 (98 per cent in the twenties, 65 per cent by age 60).

Figure 62). They had dropped to 2.2 per week by thirty years of age, to 1.5 per week by forty years of age, to 1.0 per week by fifty years of age, and to once in about twelve days (0.6 per week) by age sixty.[2] These figures are closely comparable to the frequencies indicated by the males in the sample (Table 6). We have already noted that studies of paired spouses indicate that females estimate the frequencies of

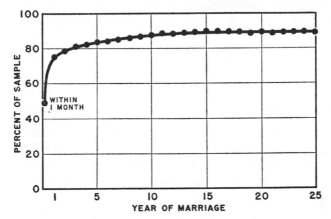

Figure 61. Accumulative incidence: orgasm in marital coitus, by length of marriage

Data from Table 113.

their marital coitus a bit higher than males estimate them (Table 5), evidently because some females object to the frequencies of coitus and therefore overestimate the amount they are actually having. Males, on the other hand, often wish that they were having coitus more frequently, and consequently may underestimate the amount they actually have.

---

[2] The best data on coital rates in marriage in the previously published studies are in Terman 1938:270–271, who reports a median frequency of 7.2 per month under age 25, 4.1 per month at ages 35 to 44, and 1.2 per month after age 55. Dickinson and Beam 1931:58, and Bernard 1935:433, fail to find any consistent variation in frequency correlated with age, apparently because they had not systematically gathered the data. In nearly all the other studies, the frequency data are calculated for total samples, without respect to age, e.g.: Schbankov acc. Weissenberg 1924a:12 (6 to 8 times per month, for 42 Russian wives). Hamilton 1929:374 (recalculates 1.7 per week as a median for 84 cases). Davis 1929:21 (1 to 2 per week for 1000 cases). Gurewitsch and Grosser 1929:539 (1 to 3 per week, for 124 Russian women). Dickinson and Beam 1931:219 (nearly 2 per week, for 205 couples). Harvey 1932b:65, 70 (summarizes earlier studies, with a composite rate of 8 per month). Kopp 1933:94 (twice a week, median among 8671 females). McCance, et al. 1937: 598, 608 (1.2 per week, for 56 British wives, ages 20–47). Woodside 1950:134 (2 per week, for 44 cases). Slater and Woodside 1951:165 (2 per week, for 200 English couples). Havelock Ellis 1936(II,3):532–536, in a comprehensive survey of historical and religious pronouncements on appropriate frequencies of marital coitus, cites: Zoroaster (once in 9 days), Hindu authorities (3 to 6 times a month), Solon (3 times a month), the Koran (once a week), Talmud (once a day to once a week depending on occupation), Luther (twice a week).

Because there are some individuals who have coitus with frequencies which are much higher than the averages given above, the mean frequencies are higher than the median frequencies in all age groups (Table 93, Figure 62). Because such a high proportion of all of the females were having coitus in each age period, the median and mean frequencies calculated for the total sample are essentially the same as those calculated for the active sample.

The day-by-day calendars which we have on some hundreds of cases of married females and males show a remarkable regularity in the occurrence of marital coitus. There are, of course, periods of illness,

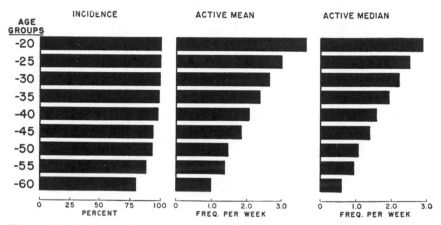

Figure 62. Active incidence, mean, median: experience in marital coitus, by age

Data from Table 93.

periods of menstruation or pregnancy, periods when the spouses are separated, and other interruptions in the regular sequence of coital rates. But, by and large, coitus in marriage occurs with a regularity which is not equaled by any other type of sexual activity in the female, although it may be matched by the masturbatory, coital, and sometimes homosexual activity of the male. This suggests that it is the male rather than the female partner who is chiefly responsible for the regularity of marital coitus.

Individual Variation in Frequency. The individual variation in the frequencies of marital coitus had been considerable (Figure 63). This had undoubtedly depended on differences in the interests and capacities of the individual females, but it had also depended on the great variation which exists in the interests and capacities of the male spouses.

The most common frequencies in the sample (the mode of the variation curve) had been close to the median frequencies. They lay between two and four times per week for the younger age groups, but had dropped to about once a week by age forty. In the younger groups, only a few individuals had had coitus less often than once in two weeks. The number of those who were having such low rates of contact had increased in the older age groups (Figure 63), and the per-

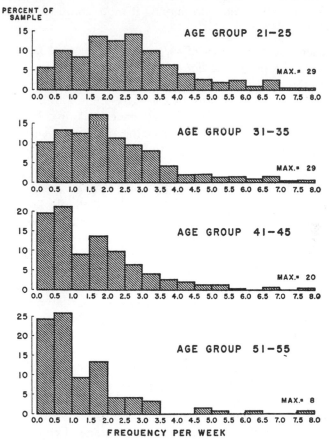

Figure 63. Individual variation: frequency of experience in marital coitus

For four age groups. Each class interval includes the upper but not the lower frequency. For incidences of females not having marital coitus, see Table 93.

centages with such low rates had begun to dominate by the middle forties.

The maximum frequencies in all of the age groups had extended considerably beyond the median or modal values. Some 14 per cent of the married females in the sample had had marital coitus with frequencies of seven or more per week during their late teens. By thirty years of age it was only 5 per cent, and by forty years of age it was only 3 per cent who were having coitus with average frequencies of seven or more per week. However, in each age group, from the youngest to age forty, there were some individuals who were having coitus in their marriages on an average of four times a day, every day in the week.[3] By fifty-five years of age there were only two individuals in the sample who were having coitus as frequently as seven or eight times per week, and none who were having it more frequently (Figure 63; see also Table 94).

Incidence and Frequency of Orgasm. The married female reaches orgasm in only a portion of her coitus, and some 10 per cent of all the females in the available sample had never reached orgasm at any time, in any of their marital coitus (Table 113, Figure 61). Some 75 per cent had responded to orgasm at least once in their coitus within the first year of marriage. The accumulative incidence curve had ultimately risen to 90 per cent by the time the females had been married some twenty years.

Similarly, the number of females who had ever reached orgasm within any particular age period had been distinctly lower than the number who were having coitus (Table 93). For instance, only 71 per cent (the active incidence) of the married females in the sample had ever reached orgasm in marital coitus while they were between sixteen and twenty years of age, when nearly one hundred per cent were having coitus. After that, the percentages responding to orgasm had gradually increased. The highest active incidences lay between thirty-one and forty years of age, when 90 per cent of the married females in the sample were reaching orgasm, at least on occasion, in their coitus. This means that there were still 10 per cent who were not reaching orgasm in their coitus even during the period when the largest number of females were responding. From age forty-one the number of females who were reaching orgasm had begun to drop. Only 78 per cent were reaching orgasm in their early fifties, and only 65 per cent by the late fifties. A more detailed analysis of the percentage of copulations which had led to orgasm, and of the factors that may have affected the oc-

---

[3] High frequencies in marital coitus are also noted in: Davis 1929:29–31. Hamilton 1929:374 (20 per cent with daily coitus in first year of marriage). McCance et al. 1937:598. Terman 1938:270. The supposed dangers of over-frequent coitus are luridly portrayed in some of the older literature. A loss of mental grip, backache, lassitude, giddiness, dimness of sight, noises in the ears, numbness of fingers, loss of memory, and paralysis are ascribed to frequent coital activity, as, for instance, in: Marinello 1563:5–6 (an early Italian medical book with remedies for ills caused by too frequent coitus in the female). Pomeroy 1888:79–80 ("It is wise to abide by temperance and duty in the marital relation. . . . We may drink the nectar as we will . . . if we drink too deeply she [nature] adds water . . . then gall, and finally, it may be, deadly poison"). Stall 1897:95 ("no man of average health . . . can exceed the bounds of once a week without . . . danger of having entered upon a life of excess both for himself and for his wife").

currence of orgasm in the sample, is presented in the latter portion of this chapter.

Apparent Aging Effect in Incidence and Frequency. It must be emphasized that these declines in the incidences and frequencies of marital coitus, and of coitus to the point of orgasm, do not provide any evidence that the female ages in her sexual capacities. We have previously pointed out (Chapters 5 and 6) that in such solitary activities as masturbation and nocturnal dreams to orgasm, the female frequencies rise gradually to their maximum point and then stay more or less on a level until after fifty-five or sixty years of age (Figures 143–144). Since the female's participation in masturbation is largely a matter of her own choosing, the frequencies of such an activity are probably a good measure of her sexual interests and intrinsic capacities. We have, on the other hand, pointed out (p. 234) that in such a socio-sexual activity as pre-marital petting, the frequencies of the female's experience reach a peak at some early age and then do decline; but this pattern is certainly controlled by the male's desires, and it is primarily his aging rather than the female's loss of interest or capacity which is reflected in the decline.

In exactly the same way, the steady decline in the incidences and frequencies of marital coitus, from the younger to the older age groups, must be the product of aging processes in the male (see our 1948:253–257). There is little evidence of any aging in the sexual capacities of the female until late in her life (Chapter 18, Figures 143–150).

One of the tragedies which appears in a number of the marriages originates in the fact that the male may be most desirous of sexual contact in his early years, while the responses of the female are still undeveloped and while she is still struggling to free herself from the acquired inhibitions which prevent her from participating freely in the marital activity. But over the years most females become less inhibited and develop an interest in sexual relations which they may then maintain until they are in their fifties or even sixties. But by then the responses of the average male may have dropped so considerably that his interest in coitus, and especially in coitus with a wife who has previously objected to the frequencies of his requests, may have sharply declined. Many of the husbands in the sample reported that early in their marriages they had wanted coitus more often than their wives had wanted it. Many of the younger married females reported that they would be satisfied with lower coital rates than their husbands wanted. On the other hand, in the later years of marriage, many of the females had expressed the wish that they could have coitus more frequently than their husbands were then desiring it.[4] Most of the decline in the male's interest may have represented physiologic aging; part of it may have been the product of a failure to work out effective relations in the earlier years of marriage; and part of it may have been a product of the fact that a number of the males—especially the better-educated males—were engaging in extra-marital coitus or other extra-marital sexual activities in their forties and fifties at the expense of coitus with their wives (see our 1948:259, 587–588).

Percentage of Total Outlet. Something between 72 and 89 per cent of the total outlet of the married females in the sample had been derived from their marital coitus (Table 93). In the late teens, 84 per cent of the outlet of these females had come from this coitus. The maximum figure, 89 per cent, had been reached between the ages of twenty-one and twenty-five, after which the percentage had steadily dropped. At sixty years of age, only 72 per cent of the total outlet of the married females was being derived from the coitus in marriage.

This decline in the significance of marital coitus had depended in part upon the considerable reduction in coital frequencies in the older age groups and its replacement by other outlets. An examination of Tables 171 and 173 will show that masturbation and extra-marital coitus had again become important sources of outlet for the married females in these later years. The decline had further depended upon the fact that only a smaller percentage of the females were reaching orgasm in the later years of their marriages.

RELATION TO EDUCATIONAL LEVEL

There were surprisingly few differences between the incidences and frequencies of marital coitus among the females of the several educational levels represented in the sample (Table 95, Figure 64). The widespread opinion that coitus is most frequent among the economically poorest segments of the population receives corroboration in only a very minor way in this sample which, however, inadequately represents the grade school group.

The active incidences of coital experience in marriage had been essentially the same in all of the educational levels (Table 95).

But in almost every age group, and particularly in the younger age groups, fewer of the females of the lower educational levels had reached orgasm in their marital coitus (the active incidences). In the younger groups, as many as 10 per cent more of the females of the upper educational levels had experienced some orgasm in their coitus.

---

[4] The wife's preference for lower rates of coitus early in marriage is also reported in Davis 1929:74 (64 per cent of 968 marriages). The same preference in early marriage, and the wife's desire for more coitus in the later years of marriage, are also reported in Terman 1938:272–273.

The differences, however, were not so marked after age thirty, where they amounted to something between 1 and 6 per cent. However, these data merely show the number of females who had ever reached orgasm in any five-year period. The percentages of the copulations which had led to orgasm are discussed in a later section of this chapter, where the data show that a distinctly higher proportion of the better educated females, in contrast to the grade school and high school females, had actually reached orgasm in a higher percentage of their marital coitus (p. 378, Table 102).

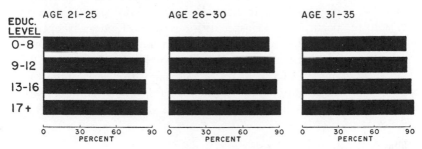

Figure 64. **Active incidence: marital coitus to orgasm, by educational level**
Data from Table 95.

In the younger age groups, the active median frequencies of marital coitus had averaged a bit higher among the females of the grade school group in the sample; but the differences did not amount to more than one orgasm in two to five weeks, and they had more or less completely disappeared by the middle thirties (Table 6).

The percentage of the total outlet which was drawn from marital coitus by the females of the various educational levels represented in the sample did not seem to have been consistently different in the earlier age groups (Table 95). But after age twenty-five the females of the college and graduate groups seem to have derived a slightly smaller proportion of their total outlet from coitus. In the forties, for instance, the high school sample had derived something between 73 and 80 per cent of its outlet from marital coitus, while the graduate group had derived only 60 to 65 per cent of its outlet from that source. This so closely parallels the situation which we have already reported for the male (1948:355–357, 567) that we are inclined to believe that these differences are significant. The decreasing dependence upon marital coitus in the older female is, however, not a product of her desire to substitute masturbation or extra-marital relations for her marital outlet, but of the fact that the older upper level male is no longer as interested in having coitus with such high frequencies, or has become dependent on extra-marital contacts and masturbation. The lower level male does not so often turn to these alternative outlets in his later years, and consequently the lower level female continues to find her chief outlet in coitus with her husband.

RELATION TO PARENTAL OCCUPATIONAL CLASS

The active incidences of marital coitus were, within any single age period, essentially the same for the females raised in homes of the various occupational classes which were represented in the sample (Table 96).

Similarly, the number of females who, in any five-year period, had ever reached orgasm in their marital coitus did not show any correlation with the occupational classes of the parental homes; except that a slightly smaller number of the females from the lower level homes had reached orgasm in the age group sixteen to twenty (Table 96). Similarly, throughout all of the years of marriage, the percentage of the copulations which had led to orgasm (Table 103) had been lower among the females who had originated in the laboring groups (pp. 379–380).

The percentage of the total outlet which the females in the sample had derived from their marital coitus, had been correlated in much the same way with the occupational classes of the homes in which they had been raised (Table 96). A smaller percentage of the total outlet of the females who had come from the laboring groups, had been derived from their marital coitus while they were between sixteen and twenty years of age. After age twenty, the differences had disappeared, and after age thirty the females who had come from upper white collar homes, in contrast to all other groups, had derived less of their outlet from their marital coitus.

RELATION TO DECADE OF BIRTH

There had been significant changes in the frequencies of coitus in marriage, and in the incidences of orgasm reached in that coitus, within the four decades covered by the available sample (Table 97, Figure 65). We have already shown that there had been considerable change in the patterns of pre-marital masturbation, pre-marital heterosexual petting, and pre-marital coitus. There was more social significance to the fact that there had been changes in the patterns of marital coitus during the four decades.

Active Incidence of Orgasm. There had been no changes in the accumulative or active incidences of coital experience in marriage during the four decades covered by the available sample (Table 97). There had, however, been a distinct and steady increase in the number (the incidences) of females reaching orgasm in their marital coitus (Table 97, Figure 65). This, of course, meant that there had been a corresponding decrease in the number of females who were completely frigid in their marital relationships (Table 104, Figure 67). While the changes had begun with the generation which was born between 1900 and 1909, and which was therefore marrying in the late teens and 1920's, they had continued in the same direction through the succeeding generations, down to and including the youngest generation in the sample. This had been true of eighteen out of the twenty

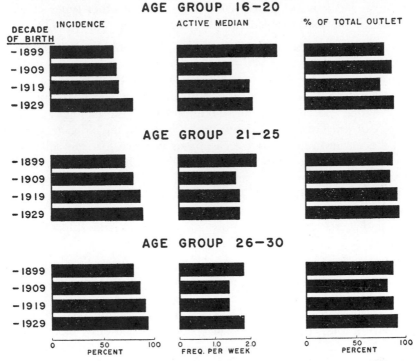

Figure 65. **Active incidence, median, percent of total outlet: marital coitus to orgasm, by decade of birth**
Data from Table 97.

groups on which we have data (Table 97). The increases had been considerable—from 72 to 80, 87, and 89 per cent in the successive decades in one age group and from 80 to 86, 91, and 93 per cent in another age group—to cite typical examples. In these two series, for instance, complete frigidity for as much as a five-year period had been reduced from 28 to 11 per cent in the one case, and from 20 to 7 per cent in the other case.[5]

The incidence of orgasm in the average marital history (the number of copulations which had led to orgasm) had also increased in the

---

[5] Terman 1938:375–376, 407, found no significant difference in rates of orgasm correlated with decade of birth. From this he infers that constitutional factors are a likely basis for "frigidity."

four decades covered by the sample (Table 104, Figure 67). The correlations are discussed at a later point in this chapter (p. 380).

While orgasm is not the final test of the effectiveness of a sexual
relationship, and while there may be considerable significance and
satisfaction in coital relationships which do not lead to orgasm, the
female's failure to respond to orgasm in her sexual relationships is,
nonetheless, one of the most frequent sources of dissatisfaction in
marriage, and it is not infrequently the source of other types of conflict which may lead to the dissolution of a marriage (see p. 371).

To have frigidity so reduced in the course of four decades is, therefore, a considerable achievement which may be credited, in part, to
the franker attitudes and the freer discussion of sex which we have had
in the United States during the past twenty years, and to the increasing scientific and clinical understanding of the basic biology and psychology of sex. There were wives and husbands in the older generation
who did not even know that orgasm was possible for a female; or if
they knew it was possible, they did not comprehend that it could be
pleasurable, or believe it proper for a well-bred female to respond even
in her marital relationships. The average female and male today are
more often aware of the significance of mutual relationships in marriage and increasingly desirous of making such relationships satisfactory.

The reduction in female frigidity may also be a product of the increase in the amount of pre-marital socio-sexual experience which
younger generations of American females have had. We have already
pointed this out in connection with pre-marital petting (p. 265) and
pre-marital coitus (pp. 328 ff.). The specific correlations which demonstrate the relationships between pre-marital experience in orgasm and
the frequency with which the marital coitus had led to orgasm, are
given in a later section of the present chapter (Table 108, Figure 70,
p. 385).

Frequency of Experience. Interestingly enough, this improvement in
the quality of the coitus in marriage had occurred coincidentally with
some reduction in the frequencies of marital coitus in the course of
the four decades covered by the available sample (Table 97). In
the youngest age group, the median frequencies of the coitus in marriage had dropped from 3.2 per week in the group born before 1900
to 2.6 in the first generation born after 1900. In the next age group
they had dropped from 2.8 per week to 2.4 per week. The differences
had persisted through most of the later years of marriage.[6]

---

[6] Henry Seidel Canby 1934, in a pungent article on "Sex and Marriage in the
    Nineties," stated that he believed coital frequencies in marriage had not
    changed over a period of years, but presented no specific data.

The mean frequencies in the sample (the averages of all the frequencies in the individual histories) had dropped to a still greater extent—for instance, from 3.7 to 2.9 within a single decade in one of the age groups, and from 3.3 to 2.3 in another age group. This means that there were fewer individuals in the younger generation who were having coitus with such extreme frequencies as sometimes occurred in the older generation. Various factors may have contributed to this situation, but the data confirm our impression that many of the males of the older generation were less often inclined to consider the wife's desires in regard to the frequencies of coitus and were less often interested in seeing that she reached orgasm in that coitus. It is our impression that today the males of the younger generation more often limit their contacts to the frequencies which their wives desire.

Percentage of Total Outlet. In general, the proportion of the total outlet which the females in the sample had derived from the marital coitus had increased in the last forty years. This appeared to be due to the increased incidences and relative frequencies of orgasm in the marital coitus. The significance of the marital relationships had increased as a result of the more honest handling of sex problems among the younger generations.

RELATION TO AGE AT ONSET OF ADOLESCENCE

There seems to have been very little relation between the ages at which the females in the sample had turned adolescent and the incidences and frequencies of their marital coitus or the incidences and frequencies of their coitus to the point of orgasm (Table 98). This might have been expected, considering the control which the male spouse exercises over the rates of coitus in marriage. Similarly, the proportion of the total outlet which was derived from the coitus did not show any consistent correlation with the ages at which the females in the sample had turned adolescent.

RELATION TO RELIGIOUS BACKGROUND

As we have already shown, the accumulative incidences of masturbation (p. 154), pre-marital petting (p. 247), and pre-marital coitus (p. 304) were considerably affected by the female's religious background. In general, these pre-marital activities had occurred among a larger number of the least devout Protestant, Catholic, and Jewish females, and among a smaller number of the more devout females. But after a female had become involved in one of these pre-marital activities, the frequencies of her activity, and of her response to orgasm, had been little if at all affected by her religious background.

Since coitus between wedded spouses is a form of sexual activity which the law and the church codes allow and, in many instances, encourage or impose as a duty, it is not surprising to find that the accumulative and active incidences of marital coitus were essentially the same among all of the groups of females in the sample, irrespective of their levels of religious devotion (Table 99). Just as with the premarital activities, after the marital activities had started, the frequencies of activity and the frequencies of activity to the point of orgasm had not significantly differed in the various religious groups. There are only a few points in the younger age groups at which there seems to be some indication that the more devout groups were a bit slower in developing any frequency in their marital coitus. For most of the groups the degree of religious devotion had not determined the frequency of their responses to orgasm, *i.e.*, the percentage of the copulations which had led to orgasm; but the more devout Catholic groups had been more restrained than the inactive Catholic groups (Table 106). See page 381 for a further discussion.

Actually, since it is the male who has most to do with determining the rate of coitus in marriage, and since our data have shown (1948:482) that the more devout males do carry over their moral attitudes and keep the coital rates low in marriage, it is not surprising to find that the level of the male's devotion affects the rates of the marital coitus while the female's level of devotion does not.

In contrast to the uniformity of the incidences and frequencies in the various religious groups, we do find a correlation between the female's religious background and the percentage of the total outlet which she derives from her marital coitus (Table 99). In 8 out of the 9 groups on which we have sufficient data to compare religiously devout and inactive groups, we find that the more devout females were deriving a somewhat higher percentage of their total sexual outlet from their marital coitus. The differences were rather marked—a matter of 12 to 14 per cent in some cases, and of 4 to 12 per cent in most cases. This means that the religiously inactive groups among the married females were reaching orgasm more often than the devout groups in such non-marital activities as masturbation and extra-marital coitus.

COITAL TECHNIQUES IN MARRIAGE

There is considerable variation in the techniques which are utilized by human females and males in connection with their coitus. The choice depends in part upon the custom of the cultural group to which the individuals belong; in part upon their knowledge of and preferences for particular sexual techniques; in part upon their physical and physiologic capacities; and in part upon their age, health, energy, and psychologic state.

Pre-Coital Petting Techniques. Among most females and males, no union of genitalia is attempted before there has been a certain amount of sex play. We have pointed out (p. 229) that this is true of most of the infra-human species of mammals, as well as most human females and males. However, at some social levels in our own culture, and in some cultures elsewhere in the world, there may be a studied avoidance of pre-coital play, and a social mandate that sexual contacts be limited to genital unions which are directly carried through to orgasm for the male, with little if any attempt to arouse the female sexually.

In our own sample, it was only a very small portion (0.2 per cent) of the females who reported that they had abstained from any sort of petting in connection with their marital coitus. All of these cases represented females who were born before 1909. This they had done sometimes because their husbands had wanted it so, sometimes because they, the females, were psychologically offended by such activities, sometimes because neither the husband nor the wife recognized any advantage in such pre-coital play, and sometimes because one or both of the partners had adhered to some moral code which justified only those sexual activities which were specifically necessary for the accomplishment of procreation.

The pre-coital techniques in marriage are, as we have already noted, quite the same as those found in pre-marital petting which may or may not lead to coitus (Chapter 7). In the sample, simple lip kissing between the spouses had almost always (99.4 per cent) been an accompaniment to the marital coitus. In order of descending incidences, the other techniques which were used at least on occasion had included the manual stimulation of the female breast by the male (in 98 per cent); the manual stimulation of the female genitalia by the male (in 95 per cent); the oral stimulation of the female breast (in 93 per cent); the manual stimulation of the male genitalia by the female (in 91 per cent); extended oral techniques in deep kissing (in 87 per cent); and finally the oral stimulation of the female genitalia by the male (in 54 per cent) and of the male genitalia by the female (in 49 per cent) (Table 100). Still other techniques had sometimes been utilized.

The incidences of the petting techniques in marriage had closely paralleled the incidences of the same techniques in pre-marital petting (Table 73, Figures 41, 42). In general, the pre-marital petting among the females who had had pre-marital coitus with some appreciable frequency had been more prolonged than the pre-coital petting in marriage. Marital coitus is more readily available and there is, in consequence, not as much reason for extending each contact indefinitely.

The most notable differences between pre-marital and the marital procedures lay in the fact that the female was more inclined to manipulate the male genitalia with her hand after marriage, and mouth-genital contacts with the male and female genitalia had become a bit more common after marriage.

The techniques of pre-coital petting had changed in the course of the forty years covered by the sample (Table 100). Fewer (80 per cent) of the females of the generation born before 1900 had manipulated the male genitalia manually, and more (95 per cent) of the younger generation had done so. In the sample of females born before 1900, some 29 per cent had made oral contacts with the male genitalia, while 57 per cent of the females born between 1920 and 1929 had made such contacts. The oral techniques had become much more frequent in the generation that was born immediately after the turn of the century.

In general the differences between the petting techniques employed by the females of the four educational levels represented in the sample were not so great as the differences between females of the same educational level who were born in different decades (Table 100). A better sample of the grade school group might have shown a more restricted use of petting techniques there.

Coital Positions. Nearly all of the females in the sample recorded that they had most frequently used a coital position in which the male was above while the female lay supine beneath, facing the male. As we have pointed out in our volume on the male (1948:372–374), this is the traditional position throughout European and American cultures, and to many persons it may seem to be the only biologically normal position. But it is exceedingly rare among the other mammals and is only doubtfully recorded for the orang-utan and young chimpanzee. There is some evidence that it may not have been used as commonly in ancient Greece and Rome as it is today, and there are other positions that are regularly used in parts of Asia and Africa and in various Pacific areas.[7] The near restriction of coitus in our European-American

---

[7] There are literary references and frequent portrayals of coital positions in the ancient art. It is difficult to know whether such representations record the usual, or whether they record the unusual and therefore the repressed desires of a culture. Whatever they may mean, references to various coital positions are, for instance, in: Aristophanes [5th–4th cent. B.C., Greek]: Lysistrata, 229–232 (1912(1):248; 1924(3):25); 678 (1912(1):269; 1924(3):71); 773 (1912(1):274; 1924(3):79). Peace, 887–899 (1912(1):203; 1924(2): 81). Horace [1st cent. B.C., Roman]: Satires, II.7.49–50 (1926:229). Ovid [1st cent. B.C., Roman]: Art of Love, 771–808 (1929:173; May 1930:178–179). Martial [1st cent. A.D., Roman]: XI.104 (1920(2):311; 1921:329). Lucian [2nd cent. A.D., Greek]: Lucius, or the Ass, 8–10 (1895:12–15). Apuleius [2nd cent. A.D., Roman]: The Golden Ass, II.16–17 (1915:72–75; 1822:33). III.20 (1915:131; 1822:60).

culture to the single position must represent a cultural development rather than a biologically determined phenomenon. It would be interesting to discover how our culture ever came to believe that this is the only normal position for coitus.

In the available sample, the generations born after 1900 showed a trend toward an increasing use of a variety of coital positions (Table 101). Among the females born before 1900, some 16 per cent reported that they had never tried any position except the one with the male above, but only 6 per cent of the females born between 1920 and 1929 reported that their coitus had been so confined.[8]

About a third (35 per cent) of the older generation and over a half (52 per cent) of the younger generation reported that they had frequently had coitus in a position in which the female lay above the male (Table 101). Some moral philosophers and philosophically inclined clinicians think they see evidence of a personality disturbance when the "normal" male and female roles are so reversed. On the other hand, some of the gynecologists, impressed with the mechanics of coitus, have been inclined to recommend that the female should be above in order to effect the anatomic relationships which are most likely to bring her to orgasm. Certainly our histories include instances of females who were unable to achieve orgasm in any other position, but we are now inclined to believe that the effectiveness of the position depends not so much on an anatomic relation as upon three other factors: (1) the female who will assume such a position is already less inhibited in her sexual activity; (2) she may reduce her inhibitions by accepting a non-traditional technique; and (3) the utilization of such a position makes it possible for her to move more spontaneously than when she is lying under the male. In fact, when she lies above, she is more or less forced into actively participating in the coital movements.

Positions in which the sexual partners lay on their sides facing each other had been used by about a third (31 per cent) of the females in the sample. Vaginal entrance from behind had occurred in about 15

For Islamic and Oriental discussions of positions and other techniques in coitus, see, for instance: Vatsyayana, Kama Sutra [between 1st and 6th cent. A.D., Sanskrit] 1883–1925:50–53, 57–59. Ananga-Ranga [12th cent. A.D.(?), Sanskrit] 1935:191–195. Anon., Marriage, Love and Women Amongst the Arabs [orig. date?], 1896:56–59, 100–102, 139–143. Nefzawi, The Perfumed Garden [6th cent. A.D., Islamic], n.d.:8, 58–75. Stern 1933:249, 262–264 [Islamic]. Hikatsu-sho (Book of Secrets), ca. 1845 [Japanese]. Jiiro Haya-shinan ca. 1850 [Japanese].

For anthropologic data, see: Malinowski 1929:336–337 (Trobriand Islanders). Devereux 1936:8 (Mohave of Arizona and California). Schapera 1941:188–189 (Kgatla of Africa). DuBois 1944:98–99 (Alor Islanders). Ford 1945:27. Elwin 1947:438 (Muria of India). Ford and Beach 1951:24–25 (a summary of the literature).

[8] For the limited data in the previous statistical studies on coital positions, see: Hamilton 1929:178. Dickinson and Beam 1931:66. Landis et al. 1940:92.

per cent of the histories. Sitting and standing positions had been less frequently used (Table 101). The widest experimentation had occurred in the earlier years of marriage. Most of the married couples in the sample had ultimately adopted a limited number of positions or a single position in later years.

There are many males and some females who are psychologically stimulated by considering the possibilities of the positions which two human bodies can assume in coitus. From the time of the most ancient Sanskrit literature, through Ovid and the Arabic treatises, down to the marriage manuals of the present day, there have been numerous attempts to calculate the mathematic possibilities of the combinations and recombinations of human forms in coital relationships. Descriptions of a score, or of several score, or even of a couple of hundred positions have been seriously undertaken in various literatures. Artists in many cultures have attempted to portray the full panoply of the conceivable variety. In view of the lack of evidence that any of these positions have any particular mechanical advantage in producing orgasm in either the female or the male, they must be significant primarily because they serve as psychologic stimulants.

And though it may be doubtful whether any particular position is of any advantage as a means of inducing orgasm, the use of a variety reflects a psychologic acceptance of sex which is of some import. The clinician, discovering what positions his patient has used in coitus, may thereby obtain some insight into her attitudes on sex.

Time Involved in Foreplay. In some of the marriages (11 per cent) the petting had ordinarily been limited to some three minutes or less. In more than a third (36 per cent) of the histories, the petting had been extended for some four to ten minutes, and in another third (31 per cent) for some eleven to twenty minutes. A fair number (22 per cent) had regularly extended their petting beyond twenty minutes and sometimes to a half hour or an hour or more, especially among the better educated groups. There are some husbands and wives who may spend two to three hours out of each day in incidental or even intense erotic play.

We are not convinced that the data demonstrate that any limitations or extensions of pre-coital petting are of primary importance in establishing the effectiveness or satisfactoriness of coitus (p. 384). The duration of the petting reflects the personalities of the sexual partners, and the patterns of behavior which they happen to have adopted. Some persons derive considerable enjoyment from any technique which can contribute to the prolongation of the erotic activity. Many persons also feel that the intensity of the ultimate orgasm is heightened by extended foreplay. But there are many females and males, particularly in the lower educational levels, who find the indefinite continuation of any type of sexual activity disturbing or even offensive, and their interest in coitus may be reduced by the use of such techniques. Marriage manuals have not sufficiently allowed for these differences in preferences, and have consistently recommended extended foreplay, primarily because they incorrectly believe that it increases the female's chances of reaching orgasm.[9]

Nudity in Sleep and in Coitus. Since sexual arousal does not depend solely upon genital stimulation, and may in many cases develop from the stimulation of other parts of the body, it is inevitable that most persons should find coitus more effective when they are nude and can make maximum body contacts. Nudity may also provide an opportunity for the one partner to be stimulated psychologically (particularly in the case of the male) by observing the nude body of the other partner. Considering these advantages in nude coitus—and not forgetting the evolutionary emergence of the human species out of unclothed mammalian stocks—it seems reasonable to conclude that the avoidance of nudity during coitus is a perversion of what is, in a biologic sense, normal sexuality.

Some of the females in the sample reported, however, that they were usually or always clothed during their coitus. This was true of a full third (33 per cent) of those who were born before 1900 (Table 101). But there had been a considerable change in attitudes among the females who were born immediately after 1900 and who, in consequence, were married in the late teens or 1920's, immediately after the first World War. Since then the incidences of nude coitus have continued to increase, and only 8 per cent of the females of the youngest generation reported that they were clothed in most of their coitus.

Half of the married females in the sample had regularly slept nude (Table 101). Some 37 per cent of the females born before 1900 recorded such experience; but there had been a considerable development of this practice within more recent years, and 59 per cent of the

---

[9] For examples of the emphasis placed on the importance of pre-coital foreplay, see: Sturgis ca. 1908:3. Otto Adler 1911:194. Long 1922:68–69, 136. Fetscher 1928:70. Van de Velde 1930:167, 187. Hodann 1932:31–34. Stone and Stone 1937:219–222; 1951:205, 211, 214. Groves, Groves, and Groves 1943:176, 190. Kelly in Fishbein and Burgess 1947:94, 98. Faller in Hornstein and Faller 1950:239. Haire 1951:303.

Reflecting this emphasis on prolonged activity, the usual time of intromission is reported as follows in: Dickinson and Beam 1931:221 (length of intromission: 0–3 minutes, 31 cases; 5–10 minutes, 57 cases; 15 minutes or more, 39 cases). Popenoe 1938:13 cites 5–10 minutes as typical of the duration of coitus in American marriages, but suggests that a longer time is probably desirable. Popenoe 1952:6 (10–15 minutes average duration based on case histories from Institute of Family Relations). Terman 1938:295 (a mean duration of 12.2 minutes for 698 wives).

females in the sample who had been born after 1920 recorded nudity in sleep. There is every indication that the percentages are still increasing, much to the consternation of the manufacturers of night clothing.

The fear of observing the nude human body constitutes one of the most curious phenomena in human history.[10] The strictly Orthodox Jewish Code has forbidden nude coitus for some 2000 years. It represents a considerable break with our cultural past when we find 92 per cent of the younger generation forgetting its offense at the sight of a nude sexual partner and its fear of physical contact with that nude body (Table 101). This sort of change is, of course, reflected in the styles of clothing, in swimming costumes, in an increasing spread of near nudity in all sorts of outdoor activities, in an increased acceptance of nude art, in freer discussions of the nude form, in an increase in nudity within the household circle, and in a variety of other developments in our present-day American patterns of living. In view of recently intensified attempts by censoring agencies to impose stricter controls on the exposure of the human body, and on its portrayal in photography or in art, it is especially interesting to find this increase in the acceptance of nudity in marital relationships. Evidently most persons are not in sympathy with the censorship which a small but vigorous minority has been attempting to impose on the whole American population.

MORAL AND LEGAL CONSIDERATIONS

In nearly all moral codes, the world round, coitus between wedded spouses is accepted even though all other types of sexual activity may be condemned. In most instances, coitus is considered not only a privilege but an obligation which is imposed on both parties in the marriage. Marital coitus is accepted primarily because it may lead to procreation; and in both Jewish and Catholic codes, and in some others elsewhere in the world, this is taken to be the prime function of marriage and of coitus in marriage.[11] But as we have already noted, there is, today, an increasing recognition of the fact that sexual relationships in marriage may also serve a moral function when they contribute to the emotional well-being of the spouses, and for these several reasons nearly all religions insist that marriage be solemnized in a religious ceremony over which a priest presides. Thus it becomes a religious

---

[10] For the Jewish requirements that coitus be in the dark or semi-dark, and the rule against observing the nude female or female genitalia, even though the female be the wife, see: Ganzfried 1927(4):14. Epstein 1948:25–31.

[11] For a summary statement on the Jewish concept of procreation as the only legitimate function of coitus, see: Epstein 1948:18. Cohen 1949:164. The Catholic interpretation recognizes procreation as the primary end of coitus in marriage, but also recognizes its function in allaying concupiscence, in the yielding of his right to a partner, in promoting mutual love, and in contributing to the health of the body. See: Davis 1946(4):253.

covenant or sacrament among most peoples, in most parts of the world. In our own culture, the substitution of a civil ceremony and the civil control of marriage is a relatively recent development.

Some restrictions, however, may be placed by religious and legal codes on an individual's right to marry and on his or her right to have coitus in marriage.[12] Various groups, both within ancient and modern times, have restricted the right of their priests to marry. Not infrequently complete sexual abstinence is demanded of those taking religious orders, and in not a few groups religious castrations have been performed. The Russian Skopts and certain of the Coptics of Egypt and Ethiopia consider self-castration a Christian virtue. There have been several religious sects, including not only the Skopts of Russia but such American pioneer groups as those who built the New Harmony Colony, which forbid coitus to all of their members. Even the sacred duty to procreate may, in such religious codes, be transcended by these higher fidelities.

That many religious groups still find an immorality in marital coitus is also evidenced by the continued insistence that all persons are "conceived in wickedness and sin," and by the restrictions which are placed on conjugal relationships under certain conditions. At various times in European and American history, for instance, coitus has been forbidden during Lent or the forty days preceding Easter, the forty days preceding Christmas, three days before taking communion, on Sunday, on the two fast days of the week (Wednesday and Friday), and (particularly in Jewish and Mohammedan codes) during the time of menstruation, during a period of a week before and sometimes after menstruation, during certain phases of the moon, sometimes at seed-planting and harvesting times, and from the time of the discovery of a pregnancy until forty days after parturition. In some codes the restrictions have been such that coitus was not acceptable for more than a single week out of each lunar month. The Jewish and Mohammedan

---

[12] For a discussion of the restrictions imposed on marital coitus by primitives, see: Ford 1945:12–13, 28–29. Ford and Beach 1951:75–77, 211–220. The Jewish code forbids coitus for seven days following the cessation of the menstrual flow and sometimes for a short period before. For this and other Jewish restrictions, see: Leviticus 18:19; 20:18. Talmud, Yebamoth:418–419; Kethuboth 369, 374–375. Ganzfried 1927(4):16, 21–30. The Mohammedan restriction is limited to the period of menstrual flow, and this must be followed by a cleansing; see: Koran, pt.2,ch.2:222. For a recent Catholic interpretation, see Davis 1946(4):255 (coitus during menstruation is not unlawful if it can be done with mutual consent and without grave harm). Note also in the Catholic code, Davis 1946(4):258–259 (Immoderate requesting is unlawful. Request is immoderate if it would harm health. After the first months of a marriage it is asked moderately if in the sufficiently strong it is sought twice in seven days on different nights. But temperance in sexual matters is relative; therefore with mutual consent and without danger to health (a thing that will have to be established by experience, especially if fatigue or weakness should follow), to have intercourse almost every night will not be immoderate).

codes place severe restrictions on the activities of the male and female who have engaged in any sort of coitus, and forbid their entrance into any religious service until they have been "cleansed" by a suitable ceremony. At one time in New England coitus on Sunday was considered a sin, and a child born on Sunday might have been refused baptism because of the erroneous belief that its birth on that day proved that it had been conceived on Sunday.[13]

On the other hand there have been many religious groups which have extolled the beauty and sacred nature of all sexual activity, and have incorporated sexual symbolism and sexual ceremonies into their worship. The ancient Sanskrit love books were sacred literature. The temple worship in ancient Athens and in certain Roman and Hindu cults, and religious ceremonies among primitive groups in many parts of the world, recognized the morality of both marital and non-marital sexual activities.

Both Hebrew and Christian codes have emphasized the obligation of the wife, and to some lesser degree the obligation of the husband, to engage in coitus with the lawfully wedded spouse. Among the impediments which might deny an individual the right to marry, and which in some instances have allowed the dissolution of a marriage which had already been contracted, the physical inability to engage in coitus, or the refusal to engage in coitus after marriage, was, and still is in some codes, of outstanding importance. In medieval and Renaissance Europe, the one complaint which offered the wife the best promise of a legal annulment of a marriage, was evidence that her husband had been physically incapable of performing coitus ever since the marriage ceremony.

In keeping with the more ancient concept of the wife as property acquired by the husband in a lawful transaction, the older emphasis was placed on her obligation to accept coitus as and when her husband desired it; but gradually, through the centuries, the wife came to share the husband's privilege of securing ecclesiastic or legal redress when her husband refused to cohabit with her. In Anglo-American law, such a refusal on the part of either spouse has sometimes been interpreted as desertion or cruelty, and consequently in many states as grounds for a divorce.[14] A spouse's refusal to have coitus in marriage is still a matter for confession in the Catholic code.[15]

---

[13] The New England practice relating to children born on Sunday is cited in May 1931:254.

[14] In law, the wife's right to marital coitus was first recognized in Orme v. Orme 1824:2 Add. 382. Only recently, and contrary to the common law doctrine, she has been given money damages for the loss of her husband's "consortium." See Hitaffer v. Argonne Co. 1950:183 F.(2d)811. The codes of Calif., N.D., and S.D. provide that "persistent refusal to have reasonable matrimonial

The formerly subordinate position of the wife in a marriage is reflected in the traditional attitude of English and American law which rules that she, in consenting to marry, has thereby given her irrevocable consent to accept coitus under any conditions from her husband, even though he may use extreme force or violence to achieve his ends. Even under present-day American penal codes, a husband's coitus with his wife can never be interpreted as rape, no matter how much the coitus may be against her wishes and no matter how much force he may use; but in nearly every state a husband can be prosecuted for assault and battery if he uses undue force, and he may be penalized indirectly, not by criminal action, but by having such forceful relations considered grounds for a divorce.[16]

The frequencies of coitus have been the subject of court review at various times, including recent divorce cases in American courts in which the judges were called upon to consider the reasonableness of the coital frequencies which the husband had demanded. Even near daily coitus has been ruled by the bench to be unreasonable and cruel and sufficient grounds for securing a divorce. This is another example of the law's failure to allow for the fact that such high rates of coitus are maintained by a not inconsiderable portion of the population.[17]

intercourse as husband and wife when health or physical condition does not make such refusal reasonably necessary . . . is desertion." There are decisions in some ten states (Ark., Colo., Ga., Ky., Md., Miss., N. J., Ore., Va., and W. Va.), which have considered refusal to have intercourse to constitute sufficient or contributory bases for establishing desertion; but there are contrary decisions in a greater number of states. North Carolina formerly made twelve months' persistent refusal of conjugal intercourse sufficient grounds for divorce. A very few states treat such refusal as cruelty, and as a basis for divorce on those grounds; see: Campbell v. Campbell 1907:112 N.W. (Mich.) 481. Hudgins v. Hudgins 1943:23 S.E.2d (Va.)774. Fruehaut v. Fruehaut 1946:170 P.2d (Wash.)309. Two states (N. H. and Ky.) specifically provide that joining a religious organization which holds marital intercourse to be unlawful is grounds for divorce, and in Ohio it is a criminal offense to induce a married person to join such a religious organization.

[15] The obligation of both spouses to engage in coitus is set forth in the Catholic code; see: Arregui 1927:531–532 (each spouse bound to render marital dues, except rarely; a trivial inconvenience does not excuse from rendering it; to deny marital dues is a trivial sin if denied only rarely, and not a grave sin if denied at one time or another to one seeking often). Davis 1946(4):257–258. Kelly 1951:79–81, 94. For the Jewish code, see: Ganzfried 1927(4):15–16 (the wife cannot be deprived of her rights to coitus except by her consent, but the male cannot consort with his wife unless it be with her consent, and it is forbidden to force her).

[16] The general tenor of the legal opinions indicates that the husband has a duty of forbearance just as the wife has a duty of submission; see: Himes v. Himes 1921:185 N.W. (Ia.)91. Hockman v. Hockman 1945:41 A.2d (Md.)510. American Law Reports 1922(18):1063.

[17] For legal decisions involving the legitimate frequencies of coitus, see: Harnish v. Harnish 1946:60 N.Y.S.2d 153 (unreasonable demands, particularly if the wife is older, are grounds for legal separation). Rudnick v. Rudnick 1934:192 N.E. (Mass.)501 (ungovernable lust or unreasonable exercise of marital rights is cruelty). But see: Cappazzoli v. Cappazzoli 1949:64 A.2d (N. J.)440 where the wife complained of continuous, unreasonable demands for intercourse without abatement or variation for twenty years as follows: "He abused me

It is not often realized that the coital techniques which are employed in marriage may be subject to the same legal restrictions which are placed on those techniques when they occur between persons who are not wedded spouses. Coital positions were regulated by older codes, and the early Catholic codes considered the use of any except the prone position with the male above as a matter for confession and, in the days when the church's authority was backed by the civil administration, as a matter for punishment. Jewish codes, on the other hand, did not condemn the use of a variety of coital positions.[18]

In most states the sodomy acts are so worded that they would apply to mouth-genital contacts and to anal coitus between married spouses, as well as to both heterosexual and homosexual relations outside of marriage. Surprisingly few persons including very few attorneys are aware that the sodomy acts can be extended to married partners. The penalties for such acts may in some jurisdictions be exceeded only by the penalties for murder, kidnapping, and rape. There are court statements on the applicability of these sodomy statutes, and one case even goes so far as to uphold the conviction of a man for soliciting his wife to commit sodomy. We have cases of persons who were convicted because one of the spouses objected, or because some other person became aware that oral or anal play had been included in the marital activities. There are, however, few prosecutions under these laws, but as long as they remain on the books, they are subject to capricious enforcement and become tools for blackmailers. In those states where the definition of cruelty as one of the grounds for divorce includes "personal indignities" or "mental cruelty," divorce cases involving either the husband's or the wife's desires or demands for the use of oral techniques are not infrequent.[19]

---

with sexual intercourse at all times. . . . If I refused he would bribe me with money"; but the court denied her a divorce because there was no showing of danger to her health. In Dittrick v. Brown County 1943:9 N.W.(2d) 510 the Supreme Court of Minnesota upheld the commitment as a sexual psychopath of a 42-year-old father of six who "was mentally bright, capable, and a good worker," because of his uncontrollable craving for sexual intercourse with his wife, amounting in the year before his commitment to approximately 3 or 4 times a week!

[18] A Jewish rule regarding appropriate coital positions in marriage is found in: Ganzfried 1927(4):14 ("He should have intercourse in the most possible modest manner"; female above considered unchaste, improper). For more current Catholic interpretations, see: Arregui 1927:531 (unnatural position does not exceed a venial sin, and from a just cause is free from all fault). Davis 1946(4):254 (wife on back most suitable, but other positions, if conception is not hindered, are permitted). But see also Ellis 1936(II,3):555– 556 (states that Aquinas took a serious view of deviations, while Sanchez was more indulgent, but that the Christian theologians were generally opposed to a position with the female above).

[19] For the application of the criminal law on sodomy to similar activities between married spouses, see, for instance: Regina v. Jellyman 1838:8 Carr and Payne 604 (jury so charged but verdict not guilty). Smith v. State 1934:234 S.W. (Ark.)32 (upheld conviction on charge of carnally knowing and abusing

SIGNIFICANCE OF ORGASM

It cannot be emphasized too often that orgasm cannot be taken as the sole criterion for determining the degree of satisfaction which a female may derive from sexual activity. Considerable pleasure may be found in sexual arousal which does not proceed to the point of orgasm, and in the social aspects of a sexual relationship. Whether or not she herself reaches orgasm, many a female finds satisfaction in knowing that her husband or other sexual partner has enjoyed the contact, and in realizing that she has contributed to the male's pleasure. We have histories of persons who have been married for a great many years, in the course of which the wife never responded to the point of orgasm, but the marriage had been maintained because of the high quality of the other adjustments in the home.

Although we may use orgasm as a measure of the frequency of female activity, and may emphasize the significance of orgasm as a source of physiologic outlet and of social interchange for the female, it must always be understood that we are well aware that this is not the only significant part of a satisfactory sexual relationship. This is much more true for the female than it would be for the male. It is inconceivable that males who were not reaching orgasm would continue their marital coitus for any length of time.

Nevertheless our data confirm what many clinicians have regularly seen, that the persistent failure of the female to reach orgasm in her marital coitus, or even to respond with fair frequency, may do considerable damage to a marriage. If the coitus fails to bring the satisfaction and physiologic release which the female might obtain from completed activity, and if the female is disappointed because of her inability to accomplish what she thinks she should, she may develop a sense of

his wife, by "disregarding the laws of nature"). Commonwealth v. Schiff 1944: 29 North. Co. Rep. (Pa.)283 (conviction on counts of sodomy, solicitation to commit sodomy, and assault and battery). Commonwealth v. Wiesner 1945:21 Leh. L.J. (Pa.)284 (forced anal intercourse, new trial granted because wife's testimony improbable). For court dicta to the same effect see: Houselman v. People 1897:48 N.E. (Ill.)304. State v. Nelson 1937:271 N.W. (Minn.)114. For sodomy in divorce proceedings see: Ploscowe 1951:203. Glick v. Glick 1951:84 A.2d (Pa.)248 (wife asked for the relations). Kranch v. Kranch 1951:84 A.2d (Pa.)230 (wife in same appellate court, same day as above). For tables showing the criminal penalties involved see: Sherwin 1949(1):82. Bensing 1951:63. The statement in Sherwin 1950:24, that "cunnilingual activity . . . even when practiced by married couples, is still a felony in all forty-eight states," is not exactly correct. In Kentucky and South Carolina the law does not apply to any mouth-genital contact in marriage, and in New York it is a misdemeanor only. Oral contact with the female genitalia, because it does not involve any penetration by the male organ, is not an offense in Illinois, Wisconsin, Mississippi, and Ohio. The seven states above have a combined population of over 40 million. It is also possible that higher courts in still other states would not, if presented with the problem, consider such activity within marriage as "indecent, lascivious, or unnatural," even though it is considered to be so when it occurs between persons not married.

inferiority which further reduces the possibilities of her ever having satisfactory relationships.

The failure of the female to reach orgasm may also be a source of considerable disappointment to the male. Today most males, especially among better educated groups, feel under some obligation to see that the female secures gratification comparable to their own in coitus. To such a male, the failure of the wife may seem an indication of some incapacity on his part and he, in consequence, may develop a sense of inferiority which, again, may compound the difficulties. Far from contributing to the solidarity of the marriage, the coitus may then become a source of disappointment, friction, and more serious discord.

Mutual responses in a socio-sexual relationship are also significant because the one partner may respond sympathetically (p. 648) to the reactions of the other partner. The male may become emotionally aroused when he observes that his wife is aroused, and he is particularly liable to be aroused when he is in physical contact with her and can feel her responding. It is this interplay of physical, psychologic, and emotional responses which makes coitus one of the most completely mutual activities in which two individuals may engage.

Simultaneous orgasm for the two partners in a coital relationship derives its significance chiefly from the fact that the intense responses which the one partner makes at the moment of orgasm may stimulate the other partner to similarly intense response. Consequently simultaneous orgasm represents, for many persons, the maximum achievement which is possible in a sexual relationship.

The failure of an unresponding sexual partner to provide these physical or emotional stimuli may, on the other hand, do considerable damage to the effectiveness of the relationship. The responding male, especially if he has had previous experience and understands what effective coitus may be, will sense the lack of cooperation, and his responses may be inhibited or stopped. Such failures lead not only to disappointment, frustration, and a sense of defeat, but sometimes to contrary emotional responses which become anger and rage.

A good many females, more particularly of the older generation, contribute little or nothing to the pre-coital petting activities with which the males are inclined to preface their coitus. The female's abstinence may be based on a trained modesty; it may be based, in part, on the theory that the male is normally so aroused that he does not need additional physical stimulation; and it may be based in part on the theory that in a culture which considers that sex should always be associated with romanticism and gallantry, it becomes the duty of the male to provide for the pleasure of the female. This, of course, is something very different from the sort of cooperation which may make a sexual relationship a mutual undertaking.

Similarly, there are many females who remain relatively immobile during their coitus. As the old phrase puts it, instead of enthusiastic cooperation there is nothing but condescending acquiescence on the part of such a female. In the younger generations, on the other hand, there is an increasing proportion of the females who have become aware of the fact that active participation in coitus may contribute not only to the satisfaction which the husbands receive, but to their own satisfaction in coital activity.[20]

OCCURRENCE OF ORGASM IN THE FEMALE

Incidence of Female Orgasm. About 36 per cent of the married females in the sample had never experienced orgasm from any source prior to marriage. In their early adolescent years, when 95 per cent of the boys of corresponding age were experiencing orgasm with average frequencies of 2.3 per week (see our 1948:226), only 22 per cent of the girls in the sample were reaching orgasm in any sort of activity, either solitary, heterosexual, or homosexual (Table 153). In the later teens, when over 99 per cent of the males were responding sexually to orgasm with average (median) frequencies of over 2.2 per week if they were single, and 3.2 per week if they were married—at a period when the average male was at the peak of his sexual capacity and activity—, there was still nearly a half (47 per cent) of the females who had not had their first orgasm (Table 147). With this relatively limited background of experience and limited understanding of the nature and significance and desirability of orgasm, it is not surprising to find that a goodly number of the married females never or rarely reach orgasm in their marital coitus (Table 112).

The failure of a female to be aroused or to reach orgasm during coitus is commonly identified in the popular and technical literature as "sexual frigidity." We dislike the term, for it has come to connote either an unwillingness or an incapacity to function sexually. In most circumstances neither of these implications is correct. It is doubtful whether there is ever a complete lack of capacity, although individuals do appear to differ in their levels of response. In general, females and males appear to be equally responsive to the whole range of physical stimuli which may initiate erotic reactions (Chapters 14–15), and the

---

[20] The post-Victorian development of the idea that respectable women should enjoy marital coitus is well set forth in Sylvanus Duvall 1952:70–71. But Slater and Woodside 1951:167 still found evidence in the British working class that responsiveness in the wife was hardly expected, and if too marked was disapproved.

specific data show that the average female is no slower in response than the average male when she is sufficiently stimulated and when she is not inhibited in her activity (p. 163). Females may not be so often aroused by psychologic stimuli (Chapter 16); but if there is any sufficient physical stimulation, it is probable that all females are physiologically capable of responding and of responding to the point of orgasm.[21]

While there are many cases of quite unresponsive females reported in the literature, and while we have found such cases in the present study, we do not find evidence in any of them that the individual, rid of her inhibitions, would not be capable of response. We have histories of women who had been married to a single husband for many years, in some instances for as long as twenty-eight years, before they ever reached their first orgasm (footnote to Table 113). We have histories of females who had been married and divorced two or three or four times before they finally effected a marriage in which they were able to reach orgasm in their coitus. Anyone examining the histories of such women before they had ever responded would have pronounced them frigid and probably incapable of response; but their subsequent performance proved that they were not basically incapable. In fact, in some of these cases, the formerly unresponsive females developed patterns of response which included orgasm and even multiple orgasm whenever they engaged in coitus. It should be added, however, that many unresponsive individuals need clinical help to overcome the psychologic blockages and considerable inhibitions which are the sources of their difficulties.

There has, of course, been widespread interest in discovering what proportion of the coitus of the average female does lead to orgasm, and in discovering some of the factors which account for such success or failure in coitus. Unfortunately, it is not a statistically simple matter to calculate what percentage of the copulations in any particular sample leads to orgasm. Before adding together the data on any series of females, one must take into account the age of each individual, the age at which she married, the number of years that she has been married, the frequencies of her coital relationships, the techniques that have been employed in the coitus, and changes in the incidences of orgasm at various periods in the history. No significant correlations can be demonstrated unless the data are considered from all of these angles.

---

[21] As examples of authors who seem to suggest that there are some females who may be incapable of response, see: Terman 1938:407–408. Hutton 1942:94. Sylvanus Duvall 1952:71–72. Authors who doubt, as we do, any total incapability on the part of the female, include, for instance: Stekel 1926(1):117. Weiss and English 1949:585. Brown and Kempton 1950:118.

Taking these several factors into account, we find that the average (median) female in the sample had reached orgasm in something between 70 and 77 per cent of her marital coitus. The percentages had varied considerably in different periods of the marriage. In the earliest years of marriage, not more than 63 per cent of the coitus of the average (median) female had resulted in orgasm, but the percentages had increased as the marriages became more extended. The data, calculated from Table 112, are as follows:

In the first year   63% of coitus resulted in orgasm
By the fifth year   71% of coitus resulted in orgasm
By the tenth year   77% of coitus resulted in orgasm
By the fifteenth year   81% of coitus resulted in orgasm
By the twentieth year   85% of coitus resulted in orgasm

This means that something between 36 and 44 per cent of the females in the sample had responded to orgasm in a part but not in all of their coitus in marriage. About one-third of those females had responded only a small part of the time, another third had responded more or less half of the time, and the other third had responded a major portion of the time, even though it was not a hundred per cent of the time (Table 112).[22]

Multiple Orgasm. There were some 14 per cent of the females in the sample who had regularly responded with multiple orgasm (Table 176, Figure 151). This, interestingly enough, was true not only of the females who responded every time they had coitus, but also of some of the females who had responded to orgasm only part of the time (see also p. 626). In either event the female may have had two or three or

---

[22] Other studies which report specific data on the percent of females responding in marital coitus, include: Heyn 1921:406 (among 512 females, 52 per cent always responding, 31 per cent part of the time, 17 per cent never). Hamilton 1929:171 (38 per cent of 100 wives usually or always, 21 per cent sometimes). Dickinson and Beam 1931:221 (61 per cent of 164 wives usually reached orgasm). Kopp 1933:101 (34 per cent usually, 46 per cent occasionally, 20 per cent never, among 8500 women). Yarros 1933:213 (51 per cent of 174 females had satisfactory orgasm). Terman 1938:300–301 (among 760 wives, 22 per cent always, 45 per cent usually, 25 per cent sometimes, 8 per cent never). Landis et al. 1940:302 (of 44 cases, 38 per cent usually, 32 per cent sometimes). Woodside 1950:135 (75 per cent of small sample reached orgasm always or often). England acc. Rosenthal 1951:55 (65 per cent usually or always, in British survey). Terman 1951:117 (among 556 wives, 70 per cent always or usually, 30 per cent sometimes or never). Slater and Woodside 1951:168 (over 50 per cent adequate among 200 working class wives in Britain). Stone and Stone 1952:208 (41 per cent regularly, 43 per cent occasionally or rarely, 16 per cent never, among 3000 women).
Unsubstantiated and exaggerated estimates of 50 per cent or higher failure in marital orgasm may be found in: Hammond 1887:300 (90 per cent no pleasurable sensation). Stekel 1926(1):97. Squier in Folsom 1938:120. Sylvanus Duvall 1952:71. Knight 1943:25 ("Gynecologists and psychiatrists . . . are aware that perhaps 75 per cent of all married women derive little or no pleasure from the sexual act"). Kroger and Freed 1951:294 ("majority of women derive little or no pleasure from the sex act").

even as many as a dozen or more orgasms in a relationship in which her husband had ejaculated only once.[23]

Among the younger males, some 8 to 15 per cent in the sample had been capable of multiple orgasm, but the capacity had decreased among the older males. The accidents of mating in human marriages had rarely brought together two individuals who were equally capable of multiple orgasm; and whether it was the female or the male who had been most capable, it had often been difficult for a couple to work out satisfactory coital techniques when one but only one of them was accustomed to having several orgasms in each contact. Many males are incapable of maintaining an erection and continuing coitus after they have reached orgasm, and many males become so hypersensitive that it is painful and sometimes excruciatingly painful for them to continue movement after orgasm. If the female has not yet reached orgasm, or if she is capable of multiple orgasm and is not yet satisfied sexually, the male who is incapable of proceeding may leave his wife much disturbed. Some males, therefore, regularly carry their wives to orgasm by manually or orally manipulating their genitalia. More expert males have learned to bring their wives to a number of orgasms in their coitus, before they allow themselves to ejaculate for the first time.

NATURE OF FACTORS AFFECTING ORGASM

As we have already pointed out, and ought to emphasize again, the nature of an animal's sexual response must depend on the nature of the stimulus which it meets, the nature of the living stuff of which it is made, and the nature and extent of its previous experience. Considerable attention has been given in marriage manuals and in other medical literature to the possibility that the female's response may depend very largely upon the effectiveness of the techniques of the coitus; and since the male so often controls the pattern of the petting and coital activity, it has been too easily assumed that the success or failure of the female to reach orgasm must depend primarily upon the male's knowledge and utilization of effective coital techniques.[24] But such an interpretation emphasizes the nature of the stimulus and ignores the nature of the responding matter.

---

[23] For other references to multiple orgasm in the female, see: Dickinson and Beam 1931:64. Ellis 1936(II,3):536–537. Popenoe 1938:13. Stokes 1948:38. Stekel 1950:103. Hamilton 1929:154, 385 (considered multiple orgasm related to clitoral orgasm, and labeled it non-terminative minor climaxes, and in actuality an orgasmic incapacity). Kelly 1930:104–105 and Clark 1937:146–148 follow Hamilton's interpretation.

[24] As typical examples of the emphasis placed on coital techniques, see: Van de Velde 1930:144–252. Dickinson and Beam 1931:56–70. Dickinson 1933:84–109, Figs. 145–157. Clinton 1935:125–134. Thornton and Thornton 1939:106–130. Himes 1940:328. Evans 1941:99–106. Hutton 1942:86–117. Griffith 1947:139–162. Chesser 1947:125–162. Dickinson 1949:84–109, Figs. 145–159d. Stone and Stone 1952:188–192.

Psychiatrists and clinical psychologists, on the other hand, have centered their attention on the background of the responding female, her subconscious motivations, and the sources of her inhibitions. They minimize the significance of the stimuli in the immediate situation and sometimes imply that all individuals would be equally capable of sexual response if their early experience had been uniform. Many of them ignore possible variations in the intrinsic capacities of different individuals to respond to the same sort of sexual stimuli.[25] In any attempt to analyze the factors which account for the considerable variation which exists in female responses to orgasm, it is imperative that we consider these three groups of factors: the stimuli, the capacity of the responding individual, and the nature and extent of the individual's previous experience.

1. Intrinsic Capacity of the Female. Our understanding of individual variation in morphologic and physiologic characters, among all plant and animal species, makes it probable that differences in the physical and physiologic capacities of the structures which are concerned in sexual response (Chapter 14) may account for some of the individual variation which we observe in human sexual behavior.[26] Portions of the central nervous system, of the autonomic nervous system, of other parts of the nervous system, and of the musculatory and other systems are involved. Variations in these structures may be responsible for some of the more striking variations, as well as a multitude of the lesser variations which are to be observed in the sexual responses of different individuals.

For instance, the exceedingly rapid responses of certain females who are able to reach orgasm within a matter of seconds from the time they are first stimulated, and the remarkable ability of some females to reach orgasm repeatedly within a short period of time, are capacities which most other individuals could not conceivably acquire through training, childhood experience, or any sort of psychiatric therapy. Similarly, it seems reasonable to believe that at least some of the females who are

---

[25] For psychoanalytic interpretations of the factors, such as penis envy, castration fear, defense against incestuous wishes, fixations at the clitoral level of development, aversions to menstruation, coitus, and childbearing, which may account for female frigidity see, for instance: Stekel 1920; 1926(1,2). Rado 1933:440–442. Bonaparte 1935:327–330. Hitschmann and Bergler 1936:21ff. Karl A. Menninger 1938:341–350. Knight 1943:26–29. Bergler 1944:374–390. Fenichel 1945:113,173ff. Weiss and English 1949:566–572. Freud (1931)1950(5):257–269. Kroger and Freed 1951:294–312.

[26] Terman 1938:376 suggests that biologic factors may determine orgasmic capacity; and in Terman 1951:168 is the statement: "The relative influence of biological and cultural or experiential factors on a woman's orgasm adequacy remains unknown; conceivably both the adequacy and the personality traits associated with adequacy could be largely determined by either of the two factors operating singly, or the outcome could be the result of their joint influence."

slower in their responses are not equipped anatomically or physiologically in the same way as those who respond more rapidly. Unfortunately, however, we do not yet know enough about the anatomy and
physiology of sexual response (Chapters 14 and 15) to understand the
exact origins of such individual variation.

2. Orgasm in Relation to Age of Female. While incidences and
frequencies of marital coitus and of the female's orgasm in that coitus
had reached their peak in the earlier years and dropped steadily in the
later years of marriage (Table 93), the percentage of the marital contacts which had led to orgasm was lowest in the youngest groups. It
had then steadily risen in the older age groups (cf. Tables 107, 112,
Figures 68, 69). The sample available for these analyses had extended
into groups that were in their forties and fifties in age, but it is inadequate for analyses of the still older females.

3. Orgasm in Relation to Educational Level. We have already
indicated (p. 354) that the accumulative incidences and the frequencies of marital coitus had been essentially the same among females of
the several educational levels represented in the sample. On the other
hand, we found (p. 354) that the number of females reaching orgasm
within any five-year period was rather distinctly higher among those
with upper educational backgrounds. There were still more marked
differences in the percentages of the copulations which had led to
orgasm in the different educational levels (Table 102). In every period
of marriage, from the first until at least the fifteenth year, a larger
number of the females in the sample who had more limited educational
backgrounds had completely failed to respond to orgasm in their marital coitus, and a smaller number of the better educated females had so
completely failed (Table 102, Figure 66). For instance, in the first year
of marriage, 34 per cent of the grade school sample and 28 per cent of
the high school sample, but only 22 per cent of the graduate school
sample had completely failed to reach orgasm. Fifteen years later the
differences had been reduced but still lay in the same direction. The
average ages at marriage had differed in these several educational
groups (Table 166, Figure 100), and this may have accounted for some
of the differences in the responses of these educational groups (Table
107, Figure 68).

On the other hand, a distinctly smaller number of the females of the
lower educational levels and a distinctly larger number of the better
educated females had responded nearly 100 per cent of the time in
their marital coitus (Table 102, Figure 66), and these differences were
in excess of those which could be accounted for on the basis of the age
at which marriage had occurred in the several groups (Table 107,

Figure 68). For instance, in the first year of marriage, only 31 per cent of the grade school sample and 35 per cent of the high school sample had responded in all or nearly all of their coitus, but 43 per cent of the females who had gone on into graduate work after college had so responded. The differential had also been maintained throughout the later years, even into the fifteenth year of marriage.[27]

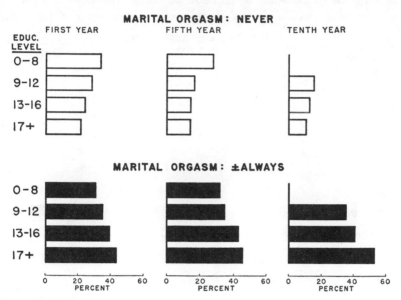

Figure 66. Educational level vs. percent of marital coitus leading to orgasm
In the first, fifth, and tenth years of marriage. Data from Table 102.

These data are not in accord with a preliminary, unpublished calculation which we made some years ago. On the basis of a smaller sample, and on the basis of a less adequate method of calculation, we seemed to find a larger number of the females of the lower educational levels responding to orgasm in their marital coitus. Those data now need correction in the light of our more extensive sample and more adequate method of analysis.

4. Orgasm in Relation to Parental Occupational Class. In the available sample, a smaller percentage of the females who had come from lower level homes had reached orgasm in all or nearly all of their coitus during the first year of marriage, and a larger percentage of those who had come from upper white collar or professional homes (Table 103). The differences were not great—34 per cent among the females who had come from laborers' homes, and 40 per cent among

---

[27] Terman 1938:390, 394, and 1951:131, reported, however, that he found no relationship between orgasmic adequacy and educational level.

the females who had come from upper white collar homes. But the differences had persisted for at least fifteen years in the married sample; and they accord with our finding (p. 378) that females from the upper educational levels respond in more of their coitus than females from the lower educational levels.

5. **Orgasm in Relation to Decade of Birth.** We have shown that the number of females in the sample who had responded to orgasm

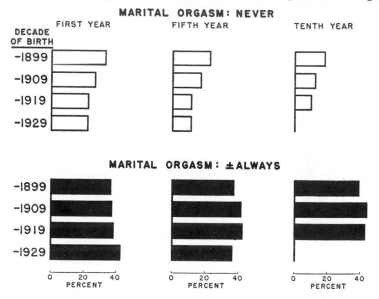

Figure 67. Decade of birth vs. percent of marital coitus leading to orgasm

In the first, fifth, and tenth years of marriage. Data from Table 104.

in their coitus within any five-year period (the active incidences) had increased in the last four decades (Table 97, Figure 65, p. 356). It is, socially, even more significant to find that the percentages of the copulations which had led to orgasm had steadily increased in that same period of time (Table 104, Figure 67). The number of females who had never responded to the point of orgasm in the first year of marriage was 33 per cent among those born before 1900, but only 22 or 23 per cent among those born after 1909. Differences of this same general order had held for at least fifteen years in the marriages in the sample.

Conversely, the number of females who had responded in all or nearly all of their marital contacts during the first years of marriage had risen from 37 per cent in the older generation to 43 per cent in the younger generation. Again, differences of this order had been maintained for ten years or more. This is evidence that the attitudes and publicly accepted mores of the group to which a female belongs may influence her attitudes and sexual performance.[28] Often an individual's difficulties in making sexual adjustments originate in the thinking of the whole generation and of the whole cultural group in which she is reared. Any true resolution of her problems may involve the acceptance of attitudes and patterns of behavior which differ from those of the social organization to which she belongs, and this may introduce new difficulties. But millions of women appear to have made such an adjustment, without serious disturbance, because the sexual attitudes of large segments of the population had materially changed in these United States in the course of the forty years covered by the sample. As a result, many of the women had functioned more effectively in their marital coitus.

6. Orgasm in Relation to Age at Onset of Adolescence. We have already found that the age at which a female turns adolescent seems to have little to do with the active incidences or the frequencies of her marital coitus (Table 98, p. 359). In regard to the proportion of the copulations which had led to orgasm, the data also indicated that there are practically no correlations with the ages at which the females in the sample had turned adolescent (Table 105).[29] A possible exception was in the group which did not turn adolescent until fifteen or later. There the number of females who had never reached orgasm seemed to be a bit higher, and the number who had reached orgasm in all or nearly all of their coitus seemed to have been a bit lower than in any of the other groups.

7. Orgasm in Relation to Religious Background. We found (p. 360) little evidence that the active incidences or frequencies of marital coitus among the females in the sample had depended on their religious background. Similarly the data indicate that the proportion of the copulations which had led to orgasm in marriage did not seem to have differed significantly between most of the religiously devout, moderate, and inactive groups of females (Table 106).[30] Only the more devout Catholic groups seem to have been more restrained in their

---

[28] Mead 1949:217–222 cites two contrasting primitive civilizations, the Mundugumor and Arapesh, with high and negative evaluations of orgasm for the female, and suggests that capacity for orgasm is a "potentiality that may or may not be developed by a given culture."

[29] Hamilton 1929:155, 195, reported that late menarche (first menstruation) increased orgasmic capacity in his sample of 100 wives, and suggested that late puberty may lessen negative conditioning on sex attitudes; but his rating of multiple orgasm as an "inadequate capacity" makes the interpretation of his data on orgasm uncertain. Terman 1938:254, 393; 1951:140, in a much larger sample, found no relationship between age at onset of adolescence and orgasmic capacity.

[30] Terman 1938:395, and 1951:139, also failed to find any correlation between the wife's religious training and her capacity in orgasm, but he did find a negative correlation with the husband's religious training, *i.e.*, the wives of strictly trained husbands tended to have lower orgasm rates.

first year of marriage, with a distinctly higher percentage completely failing to reach orgasm, and a distinctly lower percentage reaching orgasm in most of their coitus.

8. Orgasm in Relation to Age at Marriage. Responses to orgasm in coitus among the females in the sample show some correlation with the ages at which the females in the sample had married (Table 107, Figure 68). Those who had least frequently responded to orgasm were

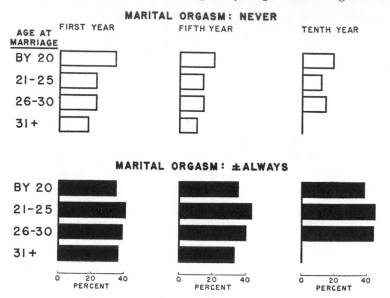

Figure 68. Age at first marriage vs. percent of marital coitus leading to orgasm

In the first, fifth, and tenth years of marriage. Data from Table 107.

the females who had married by twenty years of age. In that group some 34 per cent had never reached orgasm in the first year of marriage. This had been true of only 22 per cent of those who had married between twenty-one and thirty, and of only 17 per cent of those who had not married until after thirty years of age. The differences were still apparent ten and fifteen years after marriage.

In the first year of marriage, the females who had responded to orgasm in all or nearly all of their coitus represented 35 per cent of those who had married by twenty years of age, but 41 per cent of those who were married between ages twenty-one and twenty-five. The percentages had not increased, however, and they had apparently decreased among those who had married when they were past twenty-five years of age; but there is some evidence of the original trend continuing some five or ten years (but not later) after marriage.

The somewhat lower capacity of the teen-age female to reach orgasm in marriage may depend in part upon the fact that there are many females who are never aroused sexually or reach orgasm until they are past twenty years of age (Tables 146, 147, Figure 98). This slow appearance of sexual responsiveness may depend on basic biologic factors, or it may be the product of the individual's failure to make socio-sexual adjustments at an earlier age. The capacity of the twenty-year-old and older females to respond to orgasm more immediately when they marry may depend upon the fact that they have then had, in the average instance, more pre-marital experience in orgasm from masturbation, petting, or actual coitus; and the data presented below indicate that such pre-marital experience is definitely correlated with responses in marriage.

9. Orgasm in Relation to Length of Marriage. Nearly half (49 per cent) of the females in the sample had experienced orgasm in their coitus within the first month of marriage (Table 113, Figure 61). The number who had so responded then steadily rose, and 67 per cent had made at least some response to orgasm within the first six months of marriage. By the end of the first year, 75 per cent had experienced orgasm in at least some of their coitus. For three-quarters of the females in the sample, the ability to respond to the point of orgasm—which meant learning through experience, and freeing themselves of some of the inhibitions that had prevented their earlier participation in sexual activity and response—had been acquired in the first year of marriage. After the first year, however, the reconditioning process had slowed up, but had continued steadily for some women into the fifteenth and even later years of marriage. By the fifteenth year of marriage there were still some 10 per cent of the females who had never reached orgasm in their marital coitus, but there were cases of females who had not reached their first orgasm in marital coitus until twenty-eight years after marriage.[31]

In the sample, the maximum failure to respond to orgasm had come in the first year of marriage, irrespective of the age at which the marriage had occurred (Table 112, Figure 69). While it was 25 per cent of the females who had never reached orgasm by the end of the first

---

[31] Additional data as to timing of first orgasm in marital coitus are found in: Heyn 1921:406. Schbankov acc. Weissenberg 1924a:12. Hamilton 1929:149, 194 (49 per cent of 86 wives by end of first year, 13 per cent later; 10 out of 18 wives who reached climax only after first year of marriage, had orgasm rates of 90 to 100 per cent later). Terman 1938:306 (shows 77 per cent reaching orgasm by first year of marriage, 16 per cent after a year or more, and 7 per cent never). Slater and Woodside 1951:174 (chances of satisfactory adjustment improve with length of marriage). But Terman 1938:376, and 1951:133, concludes that ability to experience orgasm does not improve after the first years of marriage.

year of marriage, it was 17 per cent who were not reaching orgasm in the fifth year, and 11 per cent who were not reaching orgasm in the twentieth year of marriage.

On the other hand, 39 per cent of the females were reaching orgasm in all or nearly all of their marital coitus during the first year of marriage. This percentage had gradually increased over the years. By the end of twenty years of continuous marriage, the number so responding had risen to 47 per cent—nearly half!—of all the females in the sample. These data provide impressive evidence that experience and psychologic reconditioning may, in the course of time, improve the ability of the female to respond to the point of orgasm in her marital coitus.

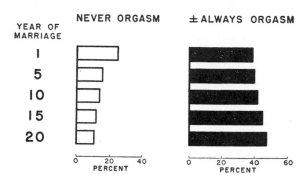

Figure 69. Length of marriage vs. percent of marital coitus leading to orgasm

In the first, fifth, tenth, fifteenth, and twentieth years of marriage. Data from Table 112.

10. Orgasm in Relation to Techniques of Marital Coitus. From the days of the most ancient love literature, down to present-day marriage manuals, there has been a considerable interest in the anatomy and mechanics of sexual stimulation and response. Throughout these several thousand years the idea has been widely accepted that the effectiveness of a sexual relationship must depend primarily upon the skill and the art of the male partner in physically stimulating the female.[24]

On the other hand, it now appears that we have misunderstood the way in which these techniques operate. Attention has been concentrated on the end organs (the sensory organs) which are directly involved in such techniques, and on those parts of the body in which the end organs are located; but our present understanding (Chapter 15) indicates that sexual response always involves a group of physiologic reactions, of which the development of muscular tensions throughout the animal's body may be among the most important. Response in the female, and for that matter in many a male, may not depend on elaborated, varied, and prolonged petting techniques as often as upon brief but uninterrupted pressures and/or continuous rhythmic stimulation which leads directly toward orgasm.[32]

Our data even suggest (p. 132) that the use of extended and varied techniques may, in not a few cases, interfere with the female's attainment of orgasm. Most females are able to masturbate to orgasm in much less time than it takes them to reach orgasm in coitus which is preceded with extended foreplay, because masturbation is usually continuous and uninterrupted in its build-up to orgasm.

11. Orgasm in Marital Coitus vs. Pre-Marital Orgasm. In the available sample, there was no factor which showed a higher correlation with the frequency of orgasm in marital coitus than the presence or absence of pre-marital experience in orgasm. Some 36 per cent of the females in the sample had married without having had such previous experience in orgasm. They had not found such pre-marital experience in masturbation, in nocturnal dreams, in petting, in pre-marital coitus, or in pre-marital homosexual relationships. Among those who had had no previous experience, 44 per cent had failed to respond to the point of orgasm in the first year of marriage (Table 108, Figure 70). But among the females who had had even limited pre-marital experience in orgasm, only 19 per cent had failed to reach orgasm in the first year of marriage; and among those who had experienced orgasm at least twenty-five times before marriage, only 13 per cent had failed to reach orgasm in the first year of marriage.

Among those females who had never experienced pre-marital orgasm from any source prior to marriage, 25 per cent did respond in all or nearly all of their contacts during the first year of marriage; but 45 to 47 per cent of the females who had had pre-marital experience responded to orgasm in all or nearly all of their coitus during the first year of marriage. Similar trends had been evident throughout the later years of marriage, and even for fifteen years in the continuous marriages in the sample. It is doubtful if any type of therapy has ever been as effective as early experience in orgasm, in reducing the incidences

---

[32] The value of continuous activity in effecting orgasm for the female is also noted in: Anon. 1707:2, The Fifteen Plagues of a Maiden-head, in which the female says: "But bid him boldly march, not grant me leisure/Of Parley, for 'tis Speed augments the pleasure." Hamilton 1929:168, 205–206, interestingly enough found 63 per cent of the husbands believing that their climax came too quickly for the partner's pleasure, but only 48 per cent of the wives so believe; he also presents data showing no relationship between the extent of the sex play and variations used in marital coitus, and the orgasmic capacity of the wives; but he points out that those who find orgasm difficult to reach may for that reason practice such techniques more extensively. Terman 1951:125, 128–129, reporting on 556 married females, concluded that the prolongation of coitus is "a less important factor in orgasm adequacy than commonly supposed." Also see footnote 9.

of unresponsiveness in marital coitus, and in increasing the frequencies of response to orgasm in that coitus.

These correlations may depend upon selective factors, or upon causal relationships through which the pre-marital experiences contribute to the marital experience. Both types of factors are probably involved. The more responsive females may have been the ones who discovered orgasm in their pre-marital years, either in solitary or socio-sexual activities, and they were the ones who had most often responded in marriage. On the other hand, we have already presented data (p. 383) which show that the female can learn through experience to re-

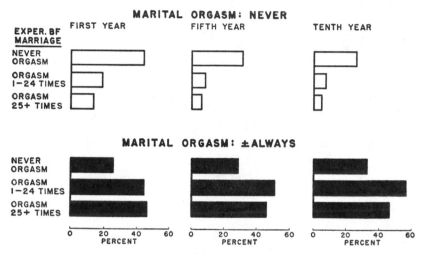

Figure 70. Pre-marital orgasm from any source vs. percent of marital coitus leading to orgasm

In the first, fifth, and tenth years of marriage. Data from Table 108.

spond in orgasm, and we have also emphasized (p. 266) the fact that such learning is most effective in the early years, when inhibitions have not yet developed or have not yet become too firmly fixed. Early orgasmic experience may, therefore, contribute directly to the sexual effectiveness of a marriage.

12. Orgasm in Marital Coitus vs. Pre-Marital Coital Experience. The type of pre-marital experience which correlates most specifically with the responses of the female in marital coitus is pre-marital coitus —*provided that that coitus leads to orgasm* (Table 109, Figure 71). For instance, among the females in the sample who had had pre-marital coitus but who had not reached orgasm in the coitus, 38 to 56 per cent failed to reach orgasm in the first year of marriage. While the percentages had decreased in the later years, there were still 11 to 30 per cent of the pre-maritally unresponsive females who had remained unresponsive in their coitus ten years after marriage. On the other hand, among the females who had had pre-marital coitus in which they had reached orgasm at least twenty-five times, only 3 per cent were totally unresponsive in the first year of marriage, and only 1 per cent in the later years of marriage. For more than half of the females in the sample, coitus without orgasm had been correlated with orgasmic failure in marriage. They had been unresponsive in marriage ten to twenty times as often as the females who had had fairly frequent pre-marital coitus in which they had reached orgasm.

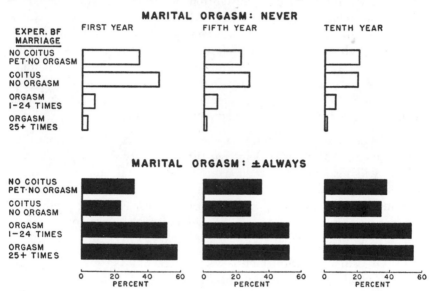

Figure 71. Pre-marital coital experience vs. percent of marital coitus leading to orgasm

In the first, fifth, and tenth years of marriage. Data from Table 109.

Furthermore, the record indicates that two or three times as many of the females in the sample had reached orgasm in all or nearly all of their marital contacts if their pre-marital coitus had led to orgasm. In the first year of marriage, 17 to 29 per cent of those whose pre-marital coitus had not led to orgasm did respond with regularity in their marital relations; but 50 to 57 per cent of those who had had pre-marital experience which had led to orgasm were regularly responsive in all or nearly all of their coitus in marriage. Similar correlations had extended through the first five years of marriage; and although the disparity was narrowed in later years, the pre-maritally experienced females were still more responsive ten years after marriage.

It should be emphasized that pre-marital coital experience which had not led to orgasm had not correlated with successful sexual relations in marriage (Table 109, Figure 71). On the contrary, it showed a high correlation with failure in the marital coitus. A basic error has been involved in some of the previous studies which have attempted to assay the relation of pre-marital coitus with successful coitus in marriage, because the distinction has not been made between pre-marital coitus that had led to orgasm, and pre-marital coitus that had not led to orgasm.[33]

Whether these correlations are the product of some selection which leads the innately more responsive females to engage in pre-marital coitus in which they reach orgasm, or whether the correlations between the pre-marital and marital records represent causal relationships, are matters which we cannot now determine. In general, it seems probable that selective factors are more often responsible. On the other hand, a girl who becomes involved in pre-marital coitus in which she does not respond may be traumatically affected by such experience, and thus be handicapped in her later adjustments in marriage.

But whether selective factors or causal relationships are responsible for these correlations, it is clear that the possibility that any particular female will respond with regularity in her marital coitus can, other things being equal, be predicted with considerable confidence by examining her orgasm record in pre-marital coitus. For such predictions the pre-marital coitus seems more significant than any other single sexual item, or any social factor in the background of the female.[34]

13. Orgasm in Marital Coitus vs. Pre-Marital Petting to Orgasm. In the available sample, pre-marital petting which led to orgasm also showed a high correlation with sexual performance after marriage. Among the females who had never done petting to the point of orgasm before marriage, 35 per cent had never reached orgasm in the first year of marriage; but only 10 per cent of those who had reached orgasm in at least some of their pre-marital petting were unresponsive in marriage (Table 110, Figure 72). The same sorts of differences held for at least fifteen years after marriage.

---

[33] See the following attempts to analyze the possible relationship between pre-marital coital experience and orgasm or happiness in marriage: Davis 1929:59 (of 71 females who had had pre-marital coitus, an undue number was in the unhappily married group). Hamilton 1929:388 (pre-marital coitus showed no relationship to orgasm in marriage, unless with future spouse, where it was favorable). Terman 1938:383, 387 (a positive relationship between pre-marital experience and orgasm in marriage). Landis et al. 1940:97, 315 (a higher incidence of pre-marital coitus among females with "good general sexual adjustment" in marriage).

[34] Examples of writers who, on the other hand, have stressed the unfavorable effects which pre-marital coitus might have on later marital adjustments, include: Banning 1937:4–8. Popenoe 1938:15–16. Bowman 1942:232–236. Duvall and Hill 1945:141. Kirkendall 1947:29. Dickerson 1947:68–69. Stokes 1948:19. Landis and Landis 1948:124–131. Foster 1950:69. Christensen 1950:156.

On the positive side, 32 per cent of those who had not experienced orgasm in petting (or in coital experience) before marriage did respond regularly to orgasm in the first year of marriage; but some 46 to 52 per cent of those who had reached orgasm in pre-marital petting had responded in all or nearly all of their coitus during the first year of marriage. A similar correlation is apparent for at least fifteen years after marriage, although the comparisons are not as extreme as in the earlier years of marriage.[35]

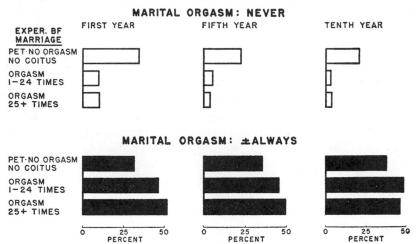

Figure 72. Pre-marital petting vs. percent of marital coitus leading to orgasm

In the first, fifth, and tenth years of marriage. Data from Table 110.

Again, these correlations may be the product of selective factors or of some causal relationship between pre-marital and marital experience. The most responsive females may be the ones who most often pet to orgasm before marriage, and who similarly respond best in their marital coitus. Or petting to orgasm may have provided the experience which helped the female respond to orgasm after marriage. But whatever the explanation, there are three, five, or more chances to one that a girl who has not done pre-marital petting in which she reaches orgasm will not respond to orgasm after she marries (Table 110). If she has reached orgasm in her pre-marital petting, there is a much better chance that she will respond in all or nearly all of her marital intercourse during the early years of her marriage and also in the later years of her marriage.

---

[35] Other data showing the relationship of petting, to orgasm in marriage, or to other marital adjustments, are found in: Davis 1929:59 (a negative relationship between "spooning" and happiness in marriage). Hamilton 1929:389 (lack of guilt feelings in early petting positively related to orgasm capacity). Terman 1938:393, 397, and 1951:136 (a slight positive relationship between adolescent petting and adequacy in marital orgasm). See also Chapter 7, footnotes 35–38.

We have already noted (p. 264) that pre-marital petting is significant because it provides the first experience in orgasm for some 18 to
24 per cent of the females, particularly among the younger generations
(Table 148). We have also pointed out (p. 265) that petting is even
more significant because it introduces the female to the meaning of
physical contacts with individuals of the opposite sex. The unresponsiveness of many of the married females who had little or next to no
experience in pre-marital petting is sometimes due to nothing more
than their refusal to allow physical contacts which would be sufficient
to effect erotic arousal. Experience in pre-marital petting may help
educate the girl in the significance of such contacts.

   14. Orgasm in Marital Coitus vs. Pre-Marital Experience in Masturbation. Although the correlations between pre-marital masturbatory experience that had led to orgasm and the female's subsequent
responses in coitus in marriage were not as marked as the correlations
with coital or petting experience, the masturbatory experience did
show a definite correlation with the marital performance (Table 111,
Figure 73). Among the females who had never masturbated before
marriage, or whose masturbation had never led to orgasm, about a
third (31 to 37 per cent) had failed to reach orgasm in the first year,
and nearly as many had failed in the first five years of their marital
coitus. Among those who had previously masturbated to the point of
orgasm, only 13 to 16 per cent were totally unresponsive in the first
year of marriage.

   Although more than a third (35 per cent) of the females who had
had no pre-marital experience in masturbation did respond in all or
nearly all of their marital coitus in the first year of marriage, a larger
number—42 to 49 per cent—of those with pre-marital masturbatory
experience which had led to orgasm had responded regularly in the
early years of their marriage. The differences became less, but were
still apparent some fifteen or twenty years after marriage.[36]

   Once again, the correlations may have depended upon the fact that
those who had masturbated were the more responsive females, and
therefore the ones who had responded most frequently in marriage.
The correlations may also have been the result of causal relationships;
but since the techniques of masturbation in the female (Chapter 5)
are so different from the techniques of coitus, it is probable that the
significance of the pre-marital masturbatory experience lay primarily
in the fact that it had acquainted the girl with the nature of an orgasmic response. Even after marriage, and even among females who

---

[36] The contrary opinion, that much of the lack of response by the female in marital
   coitus can be blamed on previous masturbation, is found, for instance, in:
   Rohleder 1907(1):220, 222. Zikel 1909:46, 47. Back 1910(1):144. See also
   footnote 51 (p. 171) for additional data.

are in their thirties and forties, difficulties in coital responses are some-times cleared up if they learn how to masturbate to the point of or-gasm. The techniques of masturbation and of petting are more spe-cifically calculated to effect orgasm than the techniques of coitus itself, and for that reason it is sometimes possible for a female to learn to masturbate to orgasm even though she has difficulty in effecting the same end in coitus. Having learned what it means to suppress inhibi-tions, and to abandon herself to the spontaneous physical reactions which represent orgasm in masturbation, she may become more capa-

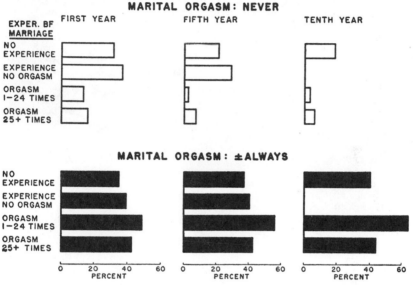

Figure 73. Pre-marital masturbation vs. percent of marital coitus leading to orgasm

In the first, fifth, and tenth years of marriage. Data from Table 111.

ble of responding in the same way in coitus. There are very few in-stances, among our several thousand histories, of females who were able to masturbate to orgasm without becoming capable of similar responses in coitus.

There are legal and social responsibilities in any marriage; there are economic problems to be solved; above all, there are psychologic ad-justments to be made between the wedded partners. Sexual adjust-ments represent only one aspect and not necessarily the most important aspect of marriage. No balanced program for American youth can be confined to preparing them for sexual relationships in marriage. But it is inconceivable that anyone who is objectively and scientifically in-terested in successful marriages should fail to appreciate the signifi-cance of coitus in marriage, or wholly ignore the correlations which exist between pre-marital activities and the sexual adjustments which are made in marriage.

SUMMARY AND COMPARISONS IN FEMALE AND MALE

Marital Coitus

	IN FEMALES	IN MALES
Historical Origins		
Family a basic unit in all cultures		
Family formerly dominated by male, now becoming more of a partnership		
Relation to Age		
Accumulative incidence		
Experience	±100%	±100%
Exper. to orgasm, first year of marr.	75%	±100%
Exper. to orgasm, 20th year of marr.	90%	±100%
Active incidence		
Experience		
Before age 30	99%	±100%
By age 50	93%	97%
By age 60	80%	94%
Experience to orgasm		
Age 16–20	71%	±100%
Age 31–40	90%	±100%
Age 51–55	78%	±100%
Frequency (active median) per week		
By age 20	2.8	2.6
By age 40	1.5	1.6
By age 60	0.6	0.6
With freq. of 7 or more per week		
By age 20	14%	16%
By age 40	3%	4%
Most interest in coitus in:	Later marr.	Early marr.
Percentage of total outlet		
Age 16–20	84%	81%
Age 21–25	89%	81%
Age 60	72%	±78%
Relation to Educational Level		
Active incidence		
Experience	No relation	No relation
Experience to orgasm	Higher in better educ.	No relation
Frequency	Little or no relation	Little or no relation
Percentage of total outlet		
Grade and high school groups	Decrease after age 25	Steady increase
College and graduate groups	Marked decrease after 25	Steady decrease
Relation to Parental Occupational Class	Little or none	Little or none
Relation to Decade of Birth		
Active incidence		
Experience	No relation	No relation
Orgasm	Material increase after 1900	No relation
Frequency	Lower in younger generations	?
Percentage of total outlet	Steady increase	
Relation to Age at Onset of Adolescence	Little or none	?

	IN FEMALES	IN MALES
Relation to Religious Background		
Incidence	No relation	No relation
Frequency	No relation	Less devout 20–30% higher
Percent of total outlet higher in devout	Yes	Yes
Techniques		
Foreplay		
Manual techniques most common	Yes	Yes
Oral techniques more accepted by younger generations	Yes	Yes
Time involved in foreplay		
3 minutes or less	11%	Unpubl.
4–10 minutes	36%	calcul. give es-
11–20 minutes	31%	sentially same
Over 20 minutes	22%	percents
Coital positions		
Male above, commonest	Yes	Yes
Female above, frequently	45%	Vary with social
Side by side, frequently	31%	level
Other positions less frequent	Yes	Yes
More variation in younger generation	Yes	Yes
Nudity		
Increase in coitus, in successive generations	67 to 92%	
Increase in sleeping, in successive generations	37 to 59%	
Moral and Legal Aspects		
Marital coitus a moral and legal obligation	Yes, always	Yes, more recently
Marital coitus often restricted by religious and secular injunctions	Yes	Yes
Techniques and other aspects may be restricted by law	Yes	Yes
Occurrence of Orgasm in Coitus		
Percentage (aver.) of copulations leading to orgasm	70–77%	±100%
Multiple orgasm		
Younger ages	±14%	8–15%
Older ages	±14%	2–3%
Persistent failure of female to reach orgasm may damage marriage	Yes	Yes
Orgasm positively correlated with:		
Intrinsic physiologic capacity	Marked	
Age	Some	
Educational level	Some	
Parental occupational class	Some	
Decade of birth	Marked	
Age at marriage	Some	
Length of marriage	Marked	
Pre-marital experience in orgasm	Marked	
Pre-marital coitus to orgasm	Marked	
Pre-marital petting to orgasm	Marked	
Pre-marital masturbation to orgasm	Marked	
Orgasm not correlated with:		
Age at onset of adolescence		
Religious background		
Techniques of foreplay and coitus		

Table 93. Active Incidence, Frequency, and Percentage of Outlet Marital Coitus

By Age

AGE DURING ACTIVITY	ACTIVE SAMPLE			TOTAL SAMPLE			CASES IN TOTAL SAMPLE
	Active incid. %	Median freq. per wk.	Mean frequency per wk.	Median freq. per wk.	Mean frequency per wk.	% of total outlet	
COITAL EXPERIENCE							
16–20	100	2.8	3.7 ± 0.15	2.8	3.7 ± 0.15		578
21–25	99	2.5	3.0 ± 0.06	2.5	3.0 ± 0.06		1654
26–30	99	2.2	2.6 ± 0.06	2.1	2.6 ± 0.06		1663
31–35	98	1.9	2.4 ± 0.06	1.9	2.3 ± 0.06		1247
36–40	98	1.5	2.1 ± 0.07	1.5	2.0 ± 0.07		852
41–45	94	1.3	1.8 ± 0.09	1.2	1.7 ± 0.08		500
46–50	93	1.0	1.5 ± 0.08	0.9	1.4 ± 0.08		261
51–55	88	0.9	1.3 ± 0.13	0.8	1.2 ± 0.12		120
56–60	80	*0.6*	*1.0 ± 0.16*	0.4	0.8 ± 0.14		50
COITUS TO ORGASM							
16–20	71	2.0	3.4 ± 0.21	0.9	2.4 ± 0.17	84	578
21–25	84	1.7	2.7 ± 0.09	1.3	2.3 ± 0.08	89	1654
26–30	88	1.5	2.4 ± 0.08	1.2	2.1 ± 0.08	85	1661
31–35	90	1.3	2.1 ± 0.09	1.1	1.9 ± 0.08	84	1245
36–40	90	1.0	1.8 ± 0.10	0.9	1.7 ± 0.09	78	850
41–45	85	0.8	1.6 ± 0.13	0.6	1.4 ± 0.11	74	497
46–50	85	0.7	1.2 ± 0.11	0.5	1.0 ± 0.09	72	260
51–55	78	0.5	1.0 ± 0.16	0.4	0.8 ± 0.13	76	118
56–60	*65*	*0.4*	*0.7 ± 0.14*	0.2	0.5 ± 0.10	72	49

Italic figures throughout the series of tables indicate that the calculations are based on less than 50 cases. No calculations are based on less than 11 cases. The dash (—) indicates a percentage or frequency smaller than any quantity which would be shown by a figure in the given number of decimal places.

Table 94. Maximum Frequency of Marital Coitus Ever, in Any Single Week

MAXIMUM FREQUENCY IN ANY WEEK	TOTAL SAMPLE		EDUCATIONAL LEVEL			
	%	Cumul. %	0–8	9–12	13–16	17+
			Percent of females			
1	1	100	2	1	1	1
2	2	99	4	2	2	3
3	7	97	9	7	6	7
4	12	90	14	13	11	11
5	13	78	15	13	14	11
6	7	65	4	7	6	7
7	23	59	32	25	22	21
8	5	36	1	4	6	6
9	3	31		2	3	4
10	9	28	6	8	9	10
11	—	19		—	—	—
12	3	19	1	3	4	3
13	—	15				—
14	5	15	8	5	5	4
15	2	11	1	2	2	4
16	1	8		—	1	1
17	—	8			—	
18	1	8		1	1	1
19		7				
20	3	7	2	2	3	4
21	1	3		2	1	1
22	—	2			—	
23	—	2		—	—	
24	—	2			—	
25	1	2		1	1	—
26		2				
27	—	2		—		
28	—	2			—	—
29+	1	1	1	2	1	1
Number of cases		2372	96	648	1026	601

Table 95. Active Incidence and Percentage of Outlet: Marital Coitus By Educational Level

Age	Educ. level	Active incid. exper. %	Active incid. orgasm %	% of total outlet	Cases in total sample	Age	Educ. level	Active incid. exper. %	Active incid. orgasm %	% of total outlet	Cases in total sample
16–20	9–12	100	66	89	210	36–40	0–8	100	90	86	52
	13–16	100	75	90	257		9–12	97	87	83	210
	17+	98	76	86	66		13–16	98	90	74	323
21–25	0–8	100	78	81	73		17+	98	91	79	268
	9–12	99	84	91	487	41–45	9–12	92	81	73	117
	13–16	100	84	89	727		13–16	94	86	82	182
	17+	99	86	90	368		17+	94	87	65	163
26–30	0–8	100	81	86	83	46–50	9–12	92	83	80	71
	9–12	99	86	90	489		13–16	93	86	76	91
	13–16	99	88	84	670		17+	93	86	60	76
	17+	99	91	83	421						
31–35	0–8	99	87	90	71						
	9–12	96	87	87	338						
	13–16	99	91	82	480						
	17+	99	93	82	360						

Table 96. Active Incidence and Percentage of Outlet: Marital Coitus By Parental Occupational Class

Age	Parental class	Active incid. exper. %	Active incid. orgasm %	% of total outlet	Cases in total sample	Age	Parental class	Active incid. exper. %	Active incid. orgasm %	% of total outlet	Cases in total sample
16–20	2+3	99	68	75	141	31–35	2+3	99	92	88	216
	4	100	60	86	86		4	97	92	89	177
	5	99	71	92	150		5	99	90	88	291
	6+7	100	75	86	225		6+7	99	90	80	572
21–25	2+3	100	86	89	310	36–40	2+3	99	92	88	136
	4	100	85	93	230		4	95	88	93	97
	5	99	86	92	427		5	97	91	85	208
	6+7	99	83	88	733		6+7	98	89	74	420
26–30	2+3	99	89	87	309	41–45	2+3	96	88	85	83
	4	100	88	90	232		4	90	83	81	63
	5	99	89	86	409		5	94	85	78	90
	6+7	99	88	84	738		6+7	94	85	70	262

The occupational classes are as follows: 2 + 3 = unskilled and semi-skilled labor. 4 = skilled labor. 5 = lower white collar class. 6 + 7 = upper white collar and professional classes.

Table 97. Active Incidence, Frequency, and Percentage of Outlet
Marital Coitus

By Decade of Birth

AGE DURING ACTIVITY	DECADE OF BIRTH	COITAL EXPERIENCE		COITUS TO ORGASM			CASES IN TOTAL SAMPLE
		Active incid. %	Active median freq. per wk.	Active incid. %	Active median freq. per wk.	% of total outlet	
16–20	Bf. 1900	100	3.2	61	2.8	79	61
	1900–1909	99	2.6	64	1.5	87	114
	1910–1919	99	2.8	66	2.0	75	173
	1920–1929	100	2.8	80	2.1	88	230
21–25	Bf. 1900	99	2.8	72	2.2	87	207
	1900–1909	99	2.5	80	1.6	84	378
	1910–1919	100	2.5	87	1.7	91	625
	1920–1929	100	2.4	89	1.7	93	447
26–30	Bf. 1900	100	2.5	80	1.8	87	274
	1900–1909	99	2.2	86	1.4	81	507
	1910–1919	99	2.1	91	1.4	87	731
	1920–1929	100	2.0	93	1.8	91	153
31–35	Bf. 1900	98	2.2	85	1.3	85	292
	1900–1909	98	1.9	92	1.3	79	508
	1910–1919	99	1.7	92	1.2	85	448
36–40	Bf. 1900	98	1.9	86	1.2	82	285
	1900–1909	98	1.3	92	0.9	75	463
	1910–1919	98	1.5	91	1.1	85	105
41–45	Bf. 1900	93	1.6	84	0.9	77	275
	1900–1909	94	0.9	88	0.8	72	225

Table 98. Active Incidence and Percentage of Outlet: Marital Coitus

By Age at Onset of Adolescence

Age	Age at adol.	Active incid. exper. %	Active incid. orgasm %	% of total out-let	Cases in total sample	Age	Age at adol.	Active incid. exper. %	Active incid. orgasm %	% of total out-let	Cases in total sample
16–20	8–11	100	72	84	139	31–35	8–11	99	91	82	185
	12	99	72	88	153		12	98	90	85	291
	13	100	72	83	169		13	99	94	83	416
	14	99	79	89	76		14	98	84	88	224
							15+	96	87	72	132
21–25	8–11	99	85	90	333	36–40	8–11	99	91	79	133
	12	100	83	91	458		12	97	90	79	187
	13	99	86	88	488		13	99	94	75	270
	14	99	83	92	255		14	96	85	83	169
	15+	99	79	82	122		15+	97	85	76	93
26–30	8–11	100	87	84	286	41–45	8–11	92	82	62	78
	12	99	87	87	426		12	94	85	78	103
	13	100	92	84	527		13	97	91	78	145
	14	98	84	89	276		14	91	83	77	102
	15+	99	86	81	148		15+	93	80	72	71

Table 99. Active Incidence, Frequency, and Percentage of Outlet
Marital Coitus

By Religious Background

AGE DURING ACTIVITY	RELIGIOUS GROUP	COITAL EXPERIENCE		COITUS TO ORGASM			CASES IN TOTAL SAMPLE
		Active incid. %	Active median freq. per wk.	Active incid. %	Active median freq. per wk.	% of total outlet	
16–20	Protestant						
	Devout	100	2.6	72	2.0	92	93
	Moderate	100	2.9	72	1.6	91	98
	Inactive	99	2.8	69	1.9	88	139
21–25	Protestant						
	Devout	100	2.3	82	1.7	92	319
	Moderate	100	2.5	85	1.7	94	311
	Inactive	99	2.6	83	1.7	89	393
	Catholic						
	Devout	99	2.3	78	0.9	81	86
	Moderate	100	2.9	85	1.8	90	53
	Inactive	97	2.7	84	2.3	86	68
	Jewish						
	Moderate	100	2.4	86	1.7	92	145
	Inactive	99	2.5	87	1.8	91	321
26–30	Protestant						
	Devout	100	2.2	89	1.5	90	332
	Moderate	99	2.1	87	1.6	92	336
	Inactive	99	2.1	86	1.5	81	413
	Catholic						
	Devout	100	2.2	85	1.2	88	84
	Inactive	100	2.1	90	1.5	87	58
	Jewish						
	Moderate	99	2.2	89	1.6	82	140
	Inactive	99	2.2	91	1.7	85	277
31–35	Protestant						
	Devout	99	1.9	90	1.3	94	265
	Moderate	99	1.9	90	1.3	88	253
	Inactive	98	1.8	90	1.3	82	315
	Catholic						
	Devout	98	1.7	86	1.0	89	63
	Jewish						
	Moderate	98	2.0	91	1.2	75	102
	Inactive	98	2.0	90	1.4	81	200
36–40	Protestant						
	Devout	97	1.5	89	1.1	89	200
	Moderate	98	1.6	90	1.0	78	175
	Inactive	97	1.4	88	1.0	80	232
	Jewish						
	Moderate	98	1.8	93	0.9	66	58
	Inactive	97	1.7	92	1.1	75	132
41–45	Protestant						
	Devout	97	1.2	84	0.7	83	126
	Moderate	94	1.3	84	0.9	71	110
	Inactive	91	1.2	86	0.8	69	129
46–50	Protestant						
	Devout	96	0.8	83	0.5	84	72
	Moderate	92	1.0	85	0.7	81	52
	Inactive	95	1.4	90	0.8	71	62

Table 100. Pre-Coital Techniques in Marriage

Percent of females utilizing each type of technique

EDUC. LEVEL	TOTAL SAMPLE	DECADE OF BIRTH Bf. 1900	1900– 1909	1910– 1919	1920– 1929	TOTAL SAMPLE	DECADE OF BIRTH Bf. 1900	1900– 1909	1910– 1919	1920– 1929
		SIMPLE KISSING					DEEP KISSING			
Total	99	99	99	100	100	87	74	85	90	92
9–12	100	99	99	100	100	85	74	82	87	88
13–16	100	99	99	100	100	90	82	85	91	94
17+	99	100	99	100	100	89	79	87	93	96
		MANUAL STIMUL., FEMALE BREAST					ORAL STIMUL., FEMALE BREAST			
Total	98	93	97	99	100	93	83	90	96	97
9–12	97	91	95	99	99	92	82	89	95	95
13–16	99	96	98	100	100	96	90	93	97	99
17+	98	96	98	100	100	93	87	88	97	99
		MANUAL STIMUL., FEMALE GENITALIA					MANUAL STIMUL., MALE GENITALIA			
Total	95	88	95	97	97	91	80	91	93	95
9–12	95	88	95	94	98	90	76	93	91	94
13–16	97	94	93	97	98	93	86	90	94	97
17+	96	88	97	99	98	93	84	94	97	95
		ORAL STIMUL., FEMALE GENITALIA					ORAL STIMUL., MALE GENITALIA			
Total	54	42	53	58	57	49	29	46	53	57
9–12	50	44	48	54	49	46	30	44	49	52
13–16	58	44	54	60	64	52	24	47	54	62
17+	57	44	56	67	51	52	35	50	62	52
		NUMBER OF CASES					NUMBER OF CASES			
Total	2470	346	606	895	621	2470	346	606	895	621
9–12	583	89	126	279	189	583	89	126	279	189
13–16	1058	109	241	378	330	1058	109	241	378	330
17+	618	113	208	206	91	618	113	208	206	91

Table 101. Positions and Nudity in Pre-Marital and Marital Coitus

	IN PRE-MAR. COITUS	IN MARITAL COITUS				
	Total sample	Total sample	Bf. 1900	Decade of birth 1900–1909	1910–1919	1920–1929
	%	%	Percent of females			
POSITIONS FREQUENTLY USED						
Male above	usual	100	100	100	100	100
Male above: only position used	21	9	16	10	7	6
Female above	35	45	35	38	48	52
Side	19	31	27	31	34	29
Sitting	8	9	6	9	9	10
Rear entrance	6	15	10	12	18	16
Standing	4	4	4	4	5	4
Number of cases	478	2451	345	603	894	607
	%	%	Percent of females			
NUDITY FREQUENT IN COITUS						
Total sample	64	84	67	85	85	92
Educ. 9–12	49	77	59	77	76	86
Educ. 13–16	68	89	74	87	89	96
Educ. 17+	78	90	78	90	92	94
Number of cases in total sample	1033	2337	319	571	846	599
	%	%	Percent of females			
Nudity frequent in sleep	27	50	37	43	54	59
Number of cases	3116	2394	325	590	859	618

The pre-marital data are based on females whose experience in coitus had totaled 25 times or more; the marital data are similarly based on females who had had marital coitus 25 times or more.

Table 102. Educational Level vs. Percentage of Marital Coitus Leading to Orgasm

% OF MARITAL COITUS WITH ORGASM	EDUCATIONAL LEVEL				EDUCATIONAL LEVEL			
	0–8	9–12	13–16	17+	0–8	9–12	13–16	17+
	IN 1ST YEAR OF MARRIAGE				IN 5TH YEAR OF MARRIAGE			
	Percent of females				*Percent of females*			
None	34	28	24	22	28	17	15	15
1–29	18	9	13	9	17	15	13	13
30–59	12	14	12	14	17	15	15	14
60–89	5	14	12	12	6	18	15	13
90–100	31	35	39	43	32	35	42	45
Number of cases	97	630	944	574	69	410	585	384
	IN 10TH YEAR OF MARRIAGE				IN 15TH YEAR OF MARRIAGE			
	Percent of females				*Percent of females*			
None		16	13	10		12	12	10
1–29		16	14	11		16	16	13
30–59		11	13	15		11	11	12
60–89		22	19	11		18	19	12
90–100		35	41	53		43	42	53
Number of cases		225	346	238		131	199	143

In this and the following tables, all calculations are based on continuous, first marriages (without separation or divorce), with a minimum duration of 6 months. Calculations for the first year of marriage are based on the performance in the last 6 months of that year. Because of the irregularities of coital rates and frequent delay in reaching the first orgasm in the earlier months of marriage, the percentages of marital coitus leading to orgasm in that period are lower than those shown for the last six months of that first year.

Table 103. Parental Occupational Class vs. Percentage of Marital Coitus Leading to Orgasm

% OF MARITAL COITUS WITH ORGASM	PARENTAL OCCUPATIONAL CLASS				PARENTAL OCCUPATIONAL CLASS			
	2+3	4	5	6+7	2+3	4	5	6+7
	IN 1ST YEAR OF MARRIAGE				IN 5TH YEAR OF MARRIAGE			
	Percent of females				*Percent of females*			
None	28	27	26	24	16	12	14	17
1–29	12	10	12	11	16	13	17	12
30–59	16	12	12	12	18	18	13	14
60–89	10	13	13	13	14	16	15	15
90–100	34	38	37	40	36	41	41	42
Number of cases	426	309	563	994	250	201	347	665
	IN 10TH YEAR OF MARRIAGE				IN 15TH YEAR OF MARRIAGE			
	Percent of females				*Percent of females*			
None	14	13	13	15	8	12	12	13
1–29	17	12	19	11	19	13	21	13
30–59	15	16	14	12	18	12	12	10
60–89	17	18	17	16	17	16	12	18
90–100	37	41	37	46	38	47	43	46
Number of cases	136	113	198	419	78	61	102	262

The occupational classes are as follows: 2 + 3 = unskilled and semi-skilled labor. 4 = skilled labor. 5 = lower white collar class. 6 + 7 = upper white collar and professional classes.

Table 104. Decade of Birth vs. Percentage of Marital Coitus Leading to Orgasm

% OF MARITAL COITUS WITH ORGASM	DECADE OF BIRTH				DECADE OF BIRTH			
	Bf. 1900	1900–1909	1910–1919	1920–1929	Bf. 1900	1900–1909	1910–1919	1920–1929
	IN 1ST YEAR OF MARRIAGE				IN 5TH YEAR OF MARRIAGE			
	Percent of females				Percent of females			
None	33	27	23	22	23	17	12	12
1–29	9	13	12	8	14	15	13	14
30–59	10	12	15	12	14	13	16	19
60–89	11	11	12	15	12	13	17	19
90–100	37	37	38	43	37	42	42	36
Number of cases	331	589	834	484	302	489	528	130
	IN 10TH YEAR OF MARRIAGE				IN 15TH YEAR OF MARRIAGE			
	Percent of females				Percent of females			
None	19	13	10		15	9		
1–29	15	14	13		17	14		
30–59	13	12	14		13	11		
60–89	13	17	19		12	20		
90–100	40	44	44		43	46		
Number of cases	261	376	216		219	251		

Table 105. Age at Onset of Adolescence vs. Percentage of Marital Coitus Leading to Orgasm

% OF MARITAL COITUS WITH ORGASM	AGE AT ADOLESCENCE					AGE AT ADOLESCENCE				
	8–11	12	13	14	15+	8–11	12	13	14	15+
	IN 1ST YEAR OF MARRIAGE					IN 5TH YEAR OF MARRIAGE				
	Percent of females					Percent of females				
None	25	24	25	25	29	17	16	12	19	21
1–29	12	10	11	11	9	14	13	14	15	10
30–59	11	15	12	12	11	14	15	16	13	19
60–89	14	12	12	11	14	14	15	16	13	15
90–100	38	39	40	41	37	41	41	42	40	35
Number of cases	429	579	690	364	180	243	350	469	247	139
	IN 10TH YEAR OF MARRIAGE					IN 15TH YEAR OF MARRIAGE				
	Percent of females					Percent of females				
None	18	14	8	19	18	9	15	7	15	16
1–29	15	12	15	15	14	20	12	15	19	15
30–59	12	14	13	11	16	13	9	13	7	18
60–89	16	20	18	13	14	12	18	17	17	15
90–100	39	40	46	42	38	46	46	48	42	36
Number of cases	136	198	281	153	89	75	114	157	96	62

Table 106. Religious Background vs. Percentage of Marital Coitus Leading to Orgasm

% OF MARITAL COITUS WITH ORGASM	PROTESTANT			CATHOLIC			JEWISH	
	Dev.	Moder.	Inact.	Dev.	Moder.	Inact.	Moder.	Inact.
IN 1ST YEAR OF MARRIAGE								
	Percent of females			*Percent of females*			*Percent of females*	
None	27	25	26	32	37	22	20	24
1–29	10	11	12	18	5	7	9	11
30–59	13	14	10	13	18	11	17	11
60–89	10	11	13	5	9	14	14	14
90–100	40	39	39	32	31	46	40	40
Number of cases	430	435	564	112	67	88	191	398
IN 5TH YEAR OF MARRIAGE								
	Percent of females						*Percent of females*	
None	16	15	18				14	15
1–29	12	16	14				15	12
30–59	15	12	13				19	16
60–89	14	13	14				12	18
90–100	43	44	41				40	39
Number of cases	305	280	363				129	240
IN 10TH YEAR OF MARRIAGE								
	Percent of females						*Percent of females*	
None	13	14	14				13	15
1–29	15	13	13				20	13
30–59	12	13	10				16	13
60–89	15	14	19				10	20
90–100	45	46	44				41	39
Number of cases	213	178	202				67	127
IN 15TH YEAR OF MARRIAGE								
	Percent of females							
None	14	10	14					
1–29	15	14	15					
30–59	8	15	6					
60–89	20	11	20					
90–100	43	50	45					
Number of cases	132	106	121					

Table 107. Age at First Marriage vs. Percentage of Marital Coitus Leading to Orgasm

% OF MARITAL COITUS WITH ORGASM	AGE AT FIRST MARRIAGE				AGE AT FIRST MARRIAGE			
	By 20	21–25	26–30	31+	By 20	21–25	26–30	31+
	IN FIRST YEAR OF MARRIAGE				IN FIFTH YEAR OF MARRIAGE			
	Percent of females				*Percent of females*			
None	34	22	22	17	21	15	15	11
1–29	9	11	12	17	14	12	15	23
30–59	10	13	16	17	13	15	15	23
60–89	12	13	11	12	16	15	15	9
90–100	35	41	39	37	36	43	40	34
Number of cases	575	1118	407	144	333	742	287	86
	IN TENTH YEAR OF MARRIAGE				IN FIFTEENTH YEAR OF MARRIAGE			
	Percent of females				*Percent of females*			
None	19	12	15		17	11	8	
1–29	13	14	12		11	14	18	
30–59	12	12	15		9	12	11	
60–89	18	18	14		14	17	18	
90–100	38	44	44		49	46	45	
Number of cases	183	452	177		106	270	99	

Table 108. Pre-Marital Orgasm from Any Source vs. Percentage of Marital Coitus Leading to Orgasm

% OF MARITAL COITUS WITH ORGASM	PRE-MARITAL ORGASM			PRE-MARITAL ORGASM		
	Never	1–24 times	25+ times	Never	1–24 times	25+ times
	IN 1ST YEAR OF MARRIAGE			IN 5TH YEAR OF MARRIAGE		
	Percent of females			*Percent of females*		
None	44	19	13	32	9	6
1–29	10	12	11	14	14	13
30–59	11	13	14	14	15	16
60–89	10	11	15	11	11	19
90–100	25	45	47	29	51	46
Number of cases	788	339	1093	529	219	688
	IN 10TH YEAR OF MARRIAGE			IN 15TH YEAR OF MARRIAGE		
	Percent of females			*Percent of females*		
None	26	7	5	20	3	5
1–29	14	15	13	17	14	15
30–59	15	11	11	14	11	9
60–89	12	10	24	13	12	21
90–100	33	57	47	36	60	50
Number of cases	347	125	379	230	73	197

Table 109. Pre-Marital Coital Experience vs. Percentage of Marital Coitus Leading to Orgasm

% OF MARITAL COITUS WITH ORGASM	WITHOUT PRE-MAR. COITUS		WITH PRE-MARITAL COITAL EXPERIENCE			
			No orgasm in pre-mar. coitus		With orgasm in pre-mar. coitus	
	No orgasm from any source	Orgasm from other sources	No orgasm, any source	Orgasm from other sources only	Orgasm in coitus 1–24 times	Orgasm in coitus 25+ times
IN FIRST YEAR OF MARRIAGE						
	% of females		*% of females*		*% of females*	
None	40	15	56	38	8	3
1–29	10	12	10	12	16	8
30–59	11	14	10	13	14	15
60–89	10	15	7	8	12	17
90–100	29	44	17	29	50	57
Number of cases	563	566	223	245	258	356
IN FIFTH YEAR OF MARRIAGE						
	% of females		*% of females*		*% of females*	
None	28	6	43	14	8	1
1–29	14	11	14	22	14	11
30–59	16	15	9	17	14	16
60–89	11	19	11	14	12	19
90–100	31	49	23	33	52	53
Number of cases	399	385	129	154	146	217
IN TENTH YEAR OF MARRIAGE						
	% of females		*% of females*		*% of females*	
None	25	6	30	11	6	1
1–29	14	13	13	22	14	8
30–59	15	10	15	10	14	13
60–89	12	22	11	19	13	24
90–100	34	49	31	38	53	54
Number of cases	272	231	74	80	79	112

Table 110. Pre-Marital Petting vs. Percentage of Marital Coitus Leading to Orgasm

% OF MARITAL COITUS WITH ORGASM	PETTING EXPERIENCE			PETTING EXPERIENCE		
	Without orgasm (no coitus)	With orgasm 1–24 times	With orgasm 25 + times	Without orgasm (no coitus)	With orgasm 1–24 times	With orgasm 25 + times
	IN 1ST YEAR OF MARRIAGE			IN 5TH YEAR OF MARRIAGE		
	Percent of females			*Percent of females*		
None	35	10	10	22	6	4
1–29	11	13	8	14	12	11
30–59	11	16	15	16	18	16
60–89	11	15	15	13	19	20
90–100	32	46	52	35	45	49
Number of cases	752	417	401	535	261	262
	IN 10TH YEAR OF MARRIAGE			IN 15TH YEAR OF MARRIAGE		
	Percent of females			*Percent of females*		
None	20	3	3	15	3	3
1–29	14	13	14	15	11	20
30–59	14	15	11	15	13	9
60–89	14	21	25	15	26	18
90–100	38	48	47	40	47	50
Number of cases	360	135	147	251	72	66

Calculations for the group which had petting experience "without orgasm" were based on females who had not had experience in pre-marital coitus.

Table 111. Pre-Marital Masturbation vs. Percentage of Marital Coitus Leading to Orgasm

% OF MARITAL COITUS WITH ORGASM	EXPERIENCE IN MASTURBATION				EXPERIENCE IN MASTURBATION			
	None	Exper. without orgasm	With orgasm 1–24 times	With orgasm 25 + times	None	Exper. without orgasm	With orgasm 1–24 times	With orgasm 25 + times
	IN 1ST YEAR OF MARRIAGE				IN 5TH YEAR OF MARRIAGE			
	Percent of females				*Percent of females*			
None	31	37	13	16	21	29	3	7
1–29	11	5	13	12	14	9	15	14
30–59	12	8	12	15	15	11	10	17
60–89	11	11	13	15	13	10	17	19
90–100	35	39	49	42	37	41	55	43
Number of cases	1159	128	186	722	770	79	114	459
	IN 10TH YEAR OF MARRIAGE				IN 15TH YEAR OF MARRIAGE			
	Percent of females				*Percent of females*			
None	19		3	6	16			6
1–29	14		13	14	16			16
30–59	14		6	12	13			9
60–89	13		14	24	13			20
90–100	40		64	44	42			49
Number of cases	473		70	261	294			151

Table 112. Length of Marriage vs. Percentage of Marital Coitus Leading to Orgasm

% OF MARITAL COITUS WITH ORGASM	YEAR OF MARRIAGE				
	First	Fifth	Tenth	Fifteenth	Twentieth
	Percent of females				
None	25	17	14	12	11
1–29	11	13	14	16	13
30–59	13	15	13	11	12
60–89	12	15	17	16	17
90–100	39	40	42	45	47
Number of cases	2244	1448	858	505	261

Based on females who had been married for at least six months and continuously (without separation or divorce) for the indicated number of years.

Table 113. Accumulative Incidence: Orgasm in Marital Coitus

Time after marriage	Accum. incid. %	Cases	Time after marriage	Accum. incid. %	Cases
			Year		
Within first year of marriage:		*See footnote*	1	75	2354
			2	78	2029
			3	81	1827
Month			4	82	1681
1	49		5	83	1548
2	55		6	84	1420
3	59		7	85	1291
4	61		8	86	1190
5	62		9	87	1076
6	67		10	87	980
7	68		11	88	883
8	68		12	88	798
9	69		13	89	715
10	69		14	89	649
11	69		15	90	584

There were 1010 females who experienced their first marital orgasm within the first year of marriage and who reported the exact month of that experience. Percentages shown for the months of the first year are based on these 1010 cases. There were 764 additional females who reported orgasm within the first year without specifying the exact month, and the total of 1774 accounts for the 75 per cent incidence shown for the first year.

Between the fifteenth and twenty-eighth years of marriage, 11 of the females in our sample of 2354 experienced their first orgasm. The accumulative incidence figures, however, never rose above 90 per cent, even in the thirtieth year of marriage.

Chapter 10

EXTRA-MARITAL COITUS

It is widely understood that many males fail to be satisfied with sexual relations that are confined to their wives and would like to make at least occasional contacts with females to whom they are not married. While it is generally realized that there are some females who similarly desire and actually engage in extra-marital coitus, public opinion is less certain about the inclination and behavior of the average female in this regard.

Most males can immediately understand why most males want extra-marital coitus. Although many of them refrain from engaging in such activity because they consider it morally unacceptable or socially undesirable, even such abstinent individuals can usually understand that sexual variety, new situations, and new partners might provide satisfactions which are no longer found in coitus which has been confined for some period of years to a single sexual partner. To most males the desire for variety in sexual activity seems as reasonable as the desire for variety in the books that one reads, the music that one hears, the recreations in which one engages, and the friends with whom one associates socially. On the other hand, many females find it difficult to understand why any male who is happily married should want to have coitus with any female other than his wife. The fact that there are females who ask such questions seems, to most males, the best sort of evidence that there are basic differences between the two sexes (Chapter 16).

As we have remarked in our volume on the male, the preoccupation of the world's biography and fiction, through all ages and in all human cultures, with the non-marital sexual activities of married females and males, is evidence of the universality of human desires in these matters, and of the universal failure of the existent social regulations to resolve the basic issues which are involved. The record of extra-marital coitus in our sample of American females, and our examination of the outcome of their experience, may contribute to an understanding of the nature and magnitude of the problem; and an examination of the anthropologic and more ancient mammalian backgrounds of this aspect of human behavior may show something of the origins of the conflict between the individual's personal desires and the social regulation of individual behavior.

409

MAMMALIAN ORIGINS

Since extra-marital coitus can exist only where there is an institution of marriage, there is nothing strictly comparable to it among man's mammalian ancestors, although a rather similar phenomenon may develop in any species of animal which establishes sexual partnerships that last through at least one full breeding season. Such more or less prolonged relationships exist among many of the primates (the monkeys and apes) and among some of the other larger mammals such as sea lions, elephants, some of the dogs, beaver, horses, deer, and still other species. These animals travel in family groups or packs, or herds which may include several or many adult females and their offspring but only a limited number of adult males. It is usually a single male, however, which dominates the whole group.

The dominant male in such a mammalian family claims exclusive sexual rights to all of the females in his group, and attempts to prevent other males from having access to them even when he himself is sexually satiated. The females are property which he has acquired, maintains, and can defend because of his physical strength and aggressiveness, and less aggressive males usually find it difficult or impossible to invade his domain. In the same way, many animals consider certain geographic locations as their own, and will fight to keep other animals from invading their territory.[1] Similarly, a gorged animal may still try to prevent other individuals from eating his food, even though he no longer wants or needs it. The maintenance of a sexual monopoly appears to emanate from a similar attempt to maintain the exclusive possession of one's property, and this appears to be as true in the human species as in the lower mammals.

Both the females and the males in these mammalian mateships are quite ready to accept coitus with individuals who are not their established mates; but females are deterred by their male mates, and males are limited in their promiscuity by other males who bar them from their groups. Sometimes males are also deterred from becoming promiscuous by the fact that they are already satiated by the coitus which they have had with their own mates.

In both the baboon and the rhesus monkey, females soliciting new sexual partners have been known to utilize a remarkably human procedure to escape the anger of their established mates. When the mates discover them in coitus with other males, or seem about to discover them, the females may cease their sexual activities and attack the new male partners. A high proportion of the human "rape" cases which we

---

[1] An excellent description of animal territories, and the possessive attitudes toward them, is in: Hediger 1950:7–18.

have had the opportunity to examine involve something of the same motifs. In the case of the infra-human primates, such action diverts the anger of the established mates who turn on the other males and drive them away, often with the help of the unfaithful females. After such an episode, the females may then present themselves to their own mates for coitus.[2]

There are occasional records of infra-human females objecting to other females having coitus with their mates, but this is not the rule.[3] Males among these other mammals, just as in the human species, are the ones who are most often and most violently disturbed at any sexual infidelity on the part of their mates. While cultural traditions may account for some of the human male's behavior, his jealousies so closely parallel those of the lower species that one is forced to conclude that his mammalian heritage may be partly responsible for his attitudes.

Among most species of mammals, sexual response is likely to become most vigorous when the animal encounters a new situation or meets a new sexual partner. Many species become psychologically fatigued when relationships with a single partner are maintained over any long period of time. The introduction of a new partner will then revive the sexual interest. Among cattle, for instance, a new bull brought into the corral may incite the other bulls to a renewal of the heterosexual or homosexual activities which had subsided before the new animal was introduced.[4] Among monkeys it has been noted that animals caged together gradually become less aroused by each other, the preliminary sex play must be more extended before they are stimulated enough to attempt coitus, and the subsequent copulation is less vigorous. With the introduction of new partners, both the female and the male may become more aroused and copulate with them more vigorously and with a minimum of foreplay.[5] Psychologic fatigue must be a prime source of the difficulty in keeping married human mates strictly monogamous.

But even among those mammals which have reasonably durable sexual partnerships, coitus outside of the partnership is still a definite part of the life pattern. The sexual history of the male in such a species (e.g., the seal, elephant, gibbon, or baboon) usually passes through three

---

[2] Escaping the anger of an offended mate by offering coitus is described by: Hamilton 1914:304–305. Zuckerman 1932:228.

[3] One of the few cases of females fighting over the possession of a male, is recorded for the monkey by: Hamilton 1914:304. Carpenter 1942:passim believes that the female gibbon drives other adult females away from her mate.

[4] That there may be a renewal of sexual activity among bulls following the introduction of a new bull is common knowledge among cattle breeders, and we have frequently observed such behavior.

[5] The increased vigor in copulation, and the reduction of foreplay which characterizes sexual activity with a new partner, are described for monkeys in: Hamilton 1914:303. Kempf 1917:143.

phases. First, as a young adolescent he is a bachelor, primarily because he is not yet dominant enough to keep a female from other male aspirants. He hunts for the occasional, unattached female, or hangs around a family unit (which may be his own parental family group or some other family group) and surreptitiously secures coitus from whatever females are available. Periodically he has to fight the older, more dominant males who discover him while he is trying to secure sexual relations with their mates.

But as the young male becomes more mature and physically and psychologically more dominant, he may succeed in taking some other male's mate, or in obtaining or keeping a just-adult female which has not been mated. This constitutes the second period of his career, and the one in which he is sexually most active. If he is very dominant he collects several females as mates; if he is less dominant he has fewer chances to accumulate female mates. At this stage he must periodically fight off the current group of bachelors, including his own sons who try to secure coitus from his mates. For some years he may succeed in dominating the situation, but finally, as an old and physically less powerful animal, he begins to lose his females to younger males and he himself eventually ends up as a bachelor again. Now he hangs around other family units trying to obtain sexual relations or, in many instances, he may have to go away and live alone for the rest of his life.[6]

There are obvious parallels between the situation in these other mammalian families, and the course of marital infidelity in the human species. Not all of the human problems are cultural developments or the product of particular social philosophies. It is evident that interest in a variety of sexual partners is of ancient standing in the mammalian stocks, and occurs among both females and males. The human male's interest in maintaining his property rights in his female mate, his objection to his wife's extra-marital coitus, and her lesser objection to his extra-marital activity, are mammalian heritages. These heritages, human females and males must accept, or rise above them if they intend to control their patterns of sexual behavior.

ANTHROPOLOGIC DATA

In the course of human history, and in various cultures, there has been some recognition of the human mammal's desire for coitus with individuals to whom he or she is not wedded, and various means have been devised to cope with these demands for non-marital sexual experience.[7] All cultures recognize the desirability of maintaining the

---

[6] The rise from youthful bachelorhood to adult mateship, and the subsequent return to bachelorhood, is well known for animals such as the elephant and stallion. It is described for the baboon by: Zuckerman 1932.

[7] The omnipresent desire for extra-marital coitus is noted, for instance, by Reichard

family as a stabilizing unit in the social organization, but it still remains to decide whether it is necessary to forbid and try to prevent all non-marital activity, or whether it is possible to accept and regulate such activity so it will do a minimum of damage to the institution of the family.

In no society, anywhere in the world, does there seem to have been any serious acceptance of complete sexual freedom as a substitute for the arrangements of a formal marriage. On the other hand, some cultures allow considerable freedom for both females and males in non-marital relationships. This is primarily true in groups which do not associate sex with social goals, with love, and with other emotional values. Thus, one anthropologist records for the Lepcha that "sexual activity is practically divorced from emotion; it is a pleasant and amusing experience, and as much a necessity as food and drink; and like food and drink it does not matter from whom you receive it, as long as you get it; although you are naturally grateful to the people who provide you with either regularly." [8] Another records for a second group that "intercourse is among all people whatsoever regarded essentially as a pleasure, and among the Arunta . . . there is no evidence that it is invested with any more meaning than that." [9]

The anthropologists find that most societies recognize the necessity for accepting at least some extra-marital coitus as an escape valve for the male, to relieve him from the pressures put on him by society's insistence on stable marital partnerships. These same societies, however, less often permit it for the female. But most societies have also recognized that some restraint on extra-marital activities is necessary if marriages and homes are to be maintained and if the social organization is to function effectively. As one anthropologist puts it, "unrestrained competition over food, drink, and sexual partners would soon involve the destruction of any society." [10] As another puts it, "Prohibitory regulations curb the socially more disruptive forms of social competition. Permissive regulations allow at least the minimum impulse gratification required for individual well-being." [11] And a third sums up the significance of a permissive attitude by pointing out that "Pre-nuptial license and the relaxation of the matrimonial bonds must not be regarded as a

---

in Boas 1938:435 ("There is probably no tribe in which formal marriage alone is sexually satisfactory"). The checking of this desire by various social devices is noted by Linton 1936:136 ("All societies inhibit the male's tendency to collect females to some degree, setting limits to the competition for them and, through marriage, assuring the male of the possession of those which he has already gathered").

[8] Gorer 1938:170.
[9] Ashley Montagu 1937:236.
[10] Ford 1945:93.
[11] Murdock 1949:261.

denial of marriage, as its abrogation, but rather as its complement. The function of license is not to upset but rather to maintain marriage." [12]

Most societies, in consequence, permit or condone extra-marital coitus for the male if he is reasonably circumspect about it, and if he does not carry it to extremes which would break up his home, lead to any neglect of his family, outrage his in-laws, stir up public scandal, or start difficulties with the husbands or other relatives of the women with whom he has his extra-marital relationships. Even in those societies which overtly forbid all non-marital coitus, there is a covert toleration of occasional lapses if social difficulties do not arise from such acts. There are few if any human societies in which the male's extra-marital coitus is very stringently suppressed or very severely punished.[13]

On the other hand, such extra-marital activity is much less frequently permitted or condoned for the female. Only 10 per cent of the cultures freely permit it. In another 40 per cent, the female may be allowed extra-marital experience on special occasions or with particular persons.[14] For instance, non-marital activity may be permitted at certain orgiastic ceremonies which are recurrent and usually seasonal events. It may be permitted or even required for the new bride as part of the marriage ceremony.[15] In a few instances it is the customary means of entertaining the husband's guests, but in this case it is the male who lends his wife to the guests. Occasionally non-marital coitus is allowed and sometimes required of siblings-in-law. Occasionally non-marital coitus has been allowed and even required when a marriage was barren.

In many of these societies, extra-marital coitus is overtly forbidden for the female, although it may be covertly condoned if it is not too

---

[12] Malinowski in Marcuse 1928:104.

[13] This lesser social concern in the majority of primitive societies over extra-marital coitus for the male is noted by: Ford 1945:29–30.

[14] Using the "Cross Cultural Survey" files, Ford 1945:29–30, 101, found under one-third of the societies permitting extra-marital coitus. In a later work, Ford and Beach 1951:113 estimated 39 per cent. Utilizing the same files, Murdock 1949:265 reports a smaller percentage but adds: "A substantial majority of all societies . . . permit extra-marital relations with certain affinal relatives." Considering these sources and still additional data, and defining a "permissive" society as one which permits female extra-marital coitus under *any* situation, including wife-lending and orgiastic ceremonies or festivities, we arrive at our figures of 10 per cent and 40 per cent. A broad definition is imperative if one is to avoid such complications as arise, for example, in the case of the Yakut who are listed as forbidding female extra-marital coitus (Ford and Beach 1951:115), and who also demand extra-marital coitus for females in the form of wife-lending (Ford 1945:30).

[15] The widespread practice of defloration or coitus with a bride by someone other than the groom, throughout European and derivative cultures, is the so-called "Jus primae noctis" or "Droit du seigneur." Its history is excellently covered by: Schmidt 1881. Foras 1886. Westermarck 1922(1):ch.5. The custom is also listed for almost a score of primitive groups, as in: Crawley 1927(2):66, 255.

flagrant and if the husband is not particularly disturbed.[16] As our later data may indicate, this seems to be the direction toward which American attitudes may be moving.

In about half of the known human societies, extra-marital coitus is completely prohibited for the female, and in many of them she may be rigorously and severely punished for such activity. In not a few cultures it is the husband's privilege and often his obligation to kill the offending wife. In many cultures, his failure to exact such a penalty from his wife and/or the offending suitor is taken as disgraceful evidence of his insufficient masculinity. He loses caste if he does not seek revenge from those who threaten his conjugal rights. Even in cultures where there is no established law or custom allowing such retribution, the male would, nevertheless, be supported by public opinion if he took the law into his own hands, and he would not be penalized for doing so. In our own European and American past, this attitude predominated; but the privilege of the husband to exact any severe penalty from either the unfaithful wife or her paramour has largely disappeared in all but a few parts of the United States.

Nevertheless, even in those cultures which most rigorously attempt to control the female's extra-marital coitus, it is perfectly clear that such activity does occur, and in many instances it occurs with considerable regularity. Even those males who disapprove of extra-marital coitus for their own wives may be interested in securing such contacts for themselves, and this in most instances means securing coitus with the wives of other males. Such inconsistencies would be unexplainable if we did not understand the mammalian backgrounds of human male behavior.

The reasons given in any particular society for the prohibition of the female's extra-marital coitus may appear logical. It is, for instance, pointed out that such activity represents a defiance of social convention and threatens a husband's right to sufficiently frequent and regular coitus with his spouse. It is said that the wife's involvement in such activity would spoil the prestige of her husband and his kin. It is pointed out that such non-marital activity may cause her to neglect her duties and obligations in her home, and social interests are clearly involved if the coitus leads to extra-marital pregnancies. It is generally believed that extra-marital coitus invariably leads to marital discord and/or divorce, with all of their consequent social implications. In many instances there is an insistence that any coitus outside of marriage is, intrinsically, in itself, morally wrong; and irrespective of the social

---

[16] Covert toleration of female extra-marital coitus in societies forbidding such coitus, is not uncommon. See: Ford 1945:30. Ford and Beach 1951:116.

consequences of such activity, it constitutes a profanation of the sacrament of marriage and consequently a sin against God and against society. These considerations have all been part of the rationale by which various societies have supported their condemnation of extramarital activities for the female. The arguments would be more impressive if they led to any resolution of behavior which does not appear in the unreasoned behavior of the males of the lower mammalian groups.

In the light of these mammalian and historic backgrounds, it has been significant to examine the status of extra-marital coitus among the females in our sample.

RELATION TO AGE

Among the married females in the sample, about a quarter (26 per cent) had had extra-marital coitus by age forty (Table 115, Figure 74). Between the ages of twenty-six and fifty, something between one in six and one in ten was having extra-marital coitus (Table 114, Figure 75). Both the accumulative and active incidences of extra-marital coitus were remarkably uniform for many of the subdivisions of the sample, but they had varied in relation to the ages, the educational levels, the decades of birth, and the religious backgrounds of the various groups. The frequencies had increased somewhat with advancing age.

Since the cover-up on any socially disapproved sexual activity may be greater than the cover-up on more accepted activities, it is possible that the incidences and frequencies of extra-marital coitus in the sample had been higher than our interviewing disclosed.

Accumulative Incidence. In their late teens, 7 per cent of the married females in the sample were having coitus with males other than their husbands. The accumulative incidences did not materially increase in the next five years, but after age twenty-six they gradually and steadily rose until they reached their maximum of 26 per cent by forty years of age (Table 115, Figure 74). After that age only a few females began for the first time to have extra-marital coitus.[17]

---

[17] American data on incidences of extra-marital activities among females are also found in: Hamilton 1929:350. Dickinson and Beam 1931:313, 315, 394. Strakosch 1934:77. Glueck and Glueck 1934:432. Landis et al. 1940:97. Dearborn in Fishbein and Burgess 1947:168. Locke 1951:152. The findings in these studies range from the low figure of 1.2 per cent in Locke's happily married sample to a 24 per cent figure in the studies of Hamilton and Glueck. The European studies show the following: Schbankov acc. Weissenberg 1924a:13 (6 per cent of 53 Russian students). Golossowker acc. Weissenberg 1925:176 (30 per cent of 107 Russian students). Gurewitsch and Grosser 1929:535 (18 per cent of 166 Russian female students). Gurewitsch and Woroschbit 1931:91 (8 per cent of over 1500 Russian peasant women, but 12 per cent in the 35–40 age group). Friedeburg 1950:13 (10 per cent of 517 German women in a questionnaire survey). England acc. Rosenthal 1951:59 (18 per cent of British middle-class women).

Active Incidence. The number of females in the sample who were having extra-marital coitus in any particular five-year period had been lowest in the youngest and in the oldest age groups (Table 114, Figure 75). The incidences had reached their maxima somewhere in the thirties and early forties. For the total sample the active incidences had begun at about 6 per cent in the late teens, increased to 14 per cent by the late twenties, and reached 17 per cent by the thirties. They began to decrease after the early forties. They had dropped to 6 per cent by the early fifties.

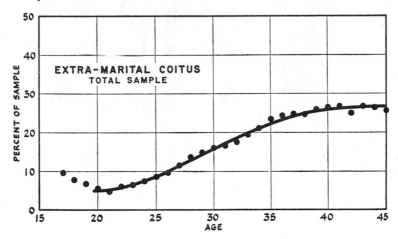

Figure 74. Accumulative incidence: experience in extra-marital coitus
Data from Table 115.

The younger married females had not so often engaged in extra-marital coitus, partly because they were still very much interested in their husbands and partly because the young husbands were particularly jealous of their marital rights. Moreover, at that age both the male and the female were more often concerned over the morality of non-marital sexual relationships. In time, however, many of these factors had seemed less important, and the middle-aged and older females had become more inclined to accept extra-marital coitus, and at least some of the husbands no longer objected if their wives engaged in such activities.

Although it is commonly believed that most males prefer sexual relations with distinctly younger partners, and although most males are attracted by the physical charms of younger females, data which we have on our histories show that many of them actually prefer to have coitus with middle-aged or older females. Many younger females become much disturbed over non-marital irregularities in which they may have engaged, and many males fear the social difficulties that may arise from such disturbances. Older females are not so likely to become disturbed, and often have a better knowledge of sexual techniques. In consequence many males find the older females more effective as sexual partners. All of these factors probably contributed to the fact that the peak of the extra-marital activities of the females in the sample had come in the mid-thirties and early forties.

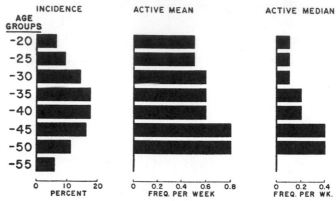

Figure 75. Active incidence, mean, median: experience in extra-marital coitus, by age

Data from Table 114.

Incidence of Orgasm. In the available sample, about 85 per cent (in most groups 78 to 100 per cent) of all those who were engaging in extra-marital activity were responding, at least on occasion, to orgasm (compare the incidences of experience and orgasm in Table 114). For most age groups the incidences of response were about the same as those in marital coitus.

On the other hand, comparisons of the median frequencies of experience and of experience to the point of orgasm indicate that orgasm in the extra-marital relationships had occurred in a high proportion of the contacts (Table 114). In some cases, this had been more often than those same females were reaching orgasm in their marital coitus. Some of the females had experienced multiple orgasms, and the total number of orgasms had actually exceeded the number of contacts in some of the groups. Selective factors may have been involved, and the more responsive females may have been the ones who had most often accepted extra-marital coitus; but the high rate of response appears to have depended also on the fact that the extra-marital experience had provided a new situation, a new partner, and a new type of relationship which had been as stimulating to some of the females as it would have been to most males. Some females who had never or rarely reached orgasm with their husbands had responded regularly in their extra-marital relationships (p. 432).

Frequency. In that segment of the sample which was having extra-marital coitus (the active sample), the frequencies had begun at the rate of once in ten weeks (0.1 per week) in the married teen-age and twenty-year-old groups (Table 114, Figure 75). They had steadily increased in the later age groups. By the forties, the extra-marital coitus was occurring once in two to three weeks for those who were having any experience at all. This means that the active median frequencies

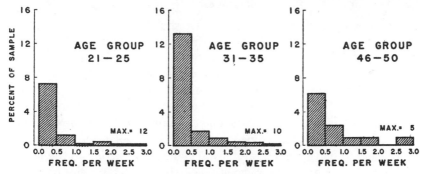

Figure 76. Individual variation: frequency of experience in extra-marital coitus

Each class interval includes the upper but not the lower frequency. For incidences of females not having extra-marital coitus, see Table 114.

of the extra-marital coitus were of about the same order as the active median frequencies of masturbation and twice as high as the frequencies of nocturnal dreams in marriage. The frequencies of the extra-marital coitus were in actuality second only to the frequencies of marital coitus in the sample of middle-aged and older married females.

Because there were some individuals in each age group who were having extra-marital experience much more frequently than the average female in the sample, the active mean frequencies were much higher than the active median frequencies. The active mean frequencies had begun at once in two weeks (0.5 per week) among the teen-aged, married females, and had risen to about once in eight or nine days (0.8 per week) among the females in their forties (Table 114, Figure 75).

However, since the incidences of the extra-marital coitus were relatively low, the mean frequencies for the total sample, including those who were having and those who were not having experience, were very low. They had not averaged more than one extra-marital contact in something like ten weeks (the total mean frequencies), even during their peak between the ages of thirty and forty (Table 114).

Sporadic Nature of Frequency. There are few types of sexual activity which occur more irregularly than extra-marital coitus. This is because the opportunities to make such contacts usually occur only sporadically, and it is often difficult to find the time and place where the coitus may be had without the spouse or someone else becoming aware of the activity. Married persons may find more difficulty in arranging their non-marital activities than single persons find in arranging their pre-marital activities. Moreover, many married persons sharply limit their extra-marital activities in order to avoid emotional relationships which might break up their marriages.

Consequently the average frequencies shown in our calculations are misleading if they suggest that the extra-marital contacts had occurred with any weekly or monthly regularity. It is a prime weakness of statistical averages that they suggest a regularity in the occurrence of activities which do not actually occur with any regularity. A dozen sexual contacts which are made in two weeks of a summer vacation may show up as frequencies of once per month for the whole of a year, and such an even distribution of activity does not often occur. It is more usual to find several non-marital contacts occurring in the matter of a few days or in a single week when the spouse is away on a trip, or when the female is traveling and putting up at a hotel, or at a summer resort, or on an ocean voyage, or visiting at a friend's home; and then there may be no further contacts for months or for a year or more. Only a smaller proportion of the females in the sample had ever developed regular and long-time relationships with males who were not their husbands.

Among the females in the available sample, the highest average frequencies of extra-marital coitus had occurred in the twenties, when three individuals were averaging seven contacts, one was averaging twelve, and one was averaging nearly thirty contacts per week over a five-year period. The maximum frequencies for particular individuals had dropped in the older groups. By fifty years of age, only one female in the total sample of 261 was having extra-marital coitus with a frequency which averaged more than three times per week (Figure 76). Just as with pre-marital coitus, the high frequencies were often attained by assured and socially effective individuals who had not been emotionally disturbed by their departures from the social code and who, therefore, had not gotten into difficulties because of their non-marital sexual activities.

Percentage of Total Outlet. Because of the relatively low incidences and low average frequencies of the extra-marital coitus, only a relatively small proportion of the sexual outlet of the total female sample had been derived from that source. Such activity had accounted for only 3 per cent of the orgasms of the females who were in their early twenties, but an increasing proportion of the outlet in the later age groups, until 13 per cent of the outlet had come from the non-marital activity by the late forties (Table 114). At that age in many of the marriages there had been some drop in the frequencies of the marital coitus, and the female who was still as responsive as or even more responsive than she had been in her earlier years had become more inclined to accept extra-marital coitus as a substitute for her reduced marital outlet.

RELATION TO EDUCATIONAL LEVEL

There had been only minor differences in the accumulative incidences of extra-marital coitus among the females of the different edu-

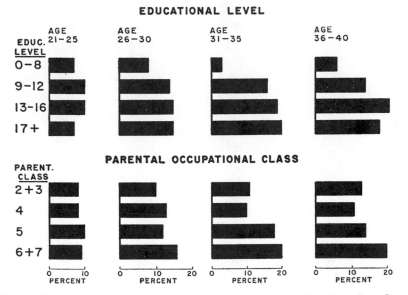

Figure 77. Active incidence: experience in extra-marital coitus, by educational level and parental occupational class

Data from Tables 116 and 117.

cational levels (Table 115). Some 31 per cent of the females in the college sample had had some extra-marital coitus by age forty. Some 27 per cent of those who had done graduate work, and about 24 per cent of those who had gone into but not beyond high school had had such experience. The differences had not been great.[18]

The active incidences had hardly differed among the females of the several educational levels during their late teens (Table 116), but after age twenty-five the limited grade school sample showed definitely lower incidences than the rest of the sample (Table 116, Figure 77).

---

[18] In the several Russian studies (see footnote 17), the incidence of extra-marital coitus among peasant women is lower than the incidence among students, as in: Gurewitsch and Woroschbit 1931:91.

The active incidences of the extra-marital coitus had steadily become higher in the older age groups, often because of the more deliberate acceptance of such activity among the older husbands and wives, especially in the better educated groups.

None of the differences in the average frequencies of the extra-marital coitus seemed to have been related in any significant way with the educational backgrounds of the females in the sample.

RELATION TO PARENTAL OCCUPATIONAL CLASS

In the late teens, the active incidences of extra-marital coital experience and orgasm had not significantly differed among the females in the sample who had come from laborers' homes, from the homes of skilled mechanics, and from the homes of lower and upper white collar and professional groups. But after age twenty-five more of the females who had come from upper white collar and professional homes were having extra-marital coitus, and extra-marital coitus in which they had reached orgasm (Table 117, Figure 77).

The average frequencies of the extra-marital coitus had not varied in any way which seemed significantly correlated with the occupational classes of the homes in which the females had been raised.

RELATION TO DECADE OF BIRTH

The number of married females who were ultimately involved in extra-marital coitus (the accumulative incidences), and the number who were involved in any particular five-year period (the active incidences), appear to have been more or less markedly affected by the increased acceptance of sexual activities which began in this country with the generation that was born immediately after the turn of the century and which was, therefore, sexually most active immediately after the first World War or in the 1920's (Tables 119, 120, Figures 78, 79).

The accumulative incidences of extra-marital coitus among the females in the sample who were born before 1900 had reached 22 per cent by forty years of age. The incidences among the females who were born in the first decade after 1900 had reached 30 per cent by that same age. The later generations seem to be maintaining that level of incidence.[19]

The lowest active incidences of extra-marital coitus had been among

---

[19] These changes in patterns of marital fidelity are commented on by: Kühn 1932: 228–229 (increase is product of freer life of women). Folsom 1937:720–723 (increase due to revaluation of importance of pleasure in sexual experience). Locke 1951:149–150 (reported no differences in incidences of extra-marital coitus among females born in four successive decades; but based his findings on an active sample of not more than 12 cases).

the females who were born before 1900. Most of the groups born after that showed a somewhat and, in many instances, a markedly increased incidence (Table 120, Figure 79). For instance, in the sample of females between twenty-one and twenty-five years of age, 4 per cent of

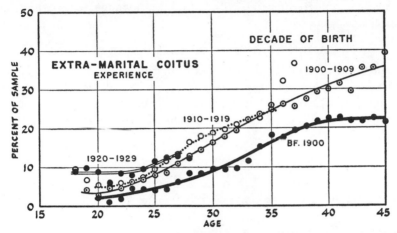

Figure 78. Accumulative incidence: experience in extra-marital coitus, by decade of birth

Data from Table 119.

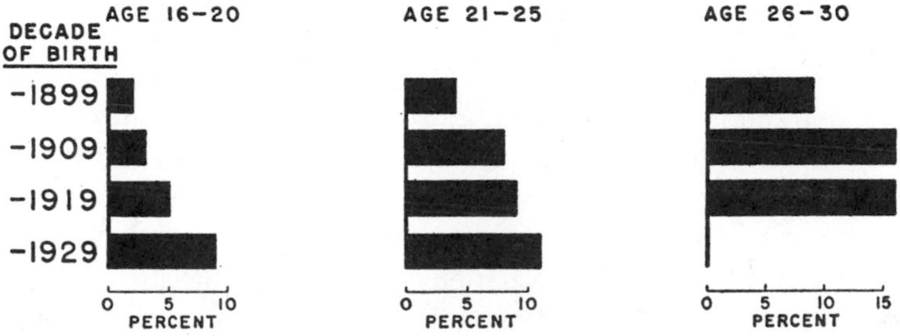

Figure 79. Active incidence: experience in extra-marital coitus, by decade of birth

Data from Table 120. Incidence for ages 26–30 in youngest generation not shown because their marriages are of such short duration that data are incomplete.

the generation that was born before 1900, but 8 per cent of those who were born in the first decade after 1900, had been involved in extra-marital coitus. For the age group twenty-six to thirty, the figures were 9 per cent for the older generation and 16 per cent for the next generation. These increased active incidences of extra-marital coitus had paralleled the increases which had occurred in pre-marital petting (p. 244) and pre-marital coitus (p. 301) in the post-war generation of American females.

There were, however, no consistent differences in the active median frequencies of extra-marital coitus among the females of the several generations in the sample. It is important to note again, as we already have in connection with the other sexual activities which became more prevalent after the first World War, that the increases in extra-marital coitus lay in the number of females who were involved, and not in any increase in the frequencies with which the average female had had experience.

RELATION TO AGE AT ONSET OF ADOLESCENCE

The incidences of the female's extra-marital coitus in particular periods of her marriage (the active incidences) (Table 118), and the frequencies with which she had had such coitus (the active median frequencies), did not seem to have been affected by the age at which she had turned adolescent.

RELATION TO RELIGIOUS BACKGROUND

The active incidences of extra-marital coitus had been more affected by the religious backgrounds of the females in the sample than by any other factor which we have examined. In every group in which we have sufficient cases for comparing females of different levels of religious devoutness, the lowest incidences of extra-marital coitus had occurred among those who were most devoutly religious, and the highest incidences among those who were least closely connected with any church activity. This was true of all the Protestant, Jewish, and Catholic groups in the sample. The differences in incidences were well enough marked in the younger age groups, but they become even more striking in the older Protestant groups. For example, in the Protestant groups aged twenty-one to twenty-five, some 5 per cent of the religiously active females had had extra-marital coitus, while 13 per cent of the inactive group had had such experience. But during the early thirties the differences lay between 7 per cent for the active Protestants and 28 per cent for the inactive Protestants (Table 121, Figure 80).[20]

While the frequencies of extra-marital experience had varied in the different groups, the variation did not show consistent trends which would warrant the opinion that the differences were related to the degree of religious devotion.

NATURE AND CONDITIONS OF EXTRA-MARITAL COITUS

The times and places and detailed circumstances of extra-marital relationships have been the subject of so much literature throughout written history and fiction, that they need little additional analysis

---

[20] Friedeburg 1950:31 found an inverse relationship between the incidence of extra-marital coitus and regularity of church attendance in a German survey of 579 males and females. The figures ranged from 9 per cent reporting extra-marital experience among those who attended church regularly, to 27 per cent reported by those who never attended church.

in the present context. Because of their previous marital experience, those who engage in extra-marital coitus usually see to it that the contacts are had under conditions which are similar to those usual in marital contacts.[21]

Partners. The extra-marital partners of the females in the sample had, for the most part, been married males somewhat near the females in age; but sometimes they were younger or older males who had not been married or who were widowed or divorced. Not a few of the younger, unmarried males had had their pre-marital coital experience with married females, some of whom were the aggressors in starting the relationships.

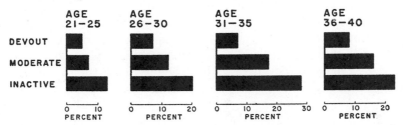

Figure 80. Active incidence: experience in extra-marital coitus, in Protestant groups

Data from Table 121.

Up to the time at which they contributed their histories, some 41 per cent of the females in the active sample had confined their extra-marital coitus to a single partner; another 40 per cent had had contacts with something between two and five partners (Table 122). This means that 19 per cent had had more than five partners and some 3 per cent had had more than twenty partners in their extra-marital relationships.[22] This is a somewhat higher degree of promiscuity than we found in the pre-marital coital histories, primarily because more years had been involved in the extra-marital activity.

Number of Years Involved. Of those females in the sample who had had any experience at all, nearly a third (32 per cent) had had extra-marital coitus ten times or less, up to the date at which they contributed their histories to the present study (Table 123). Some 42 per cent had confined their activity to a single year or less; nearly a quarter (23 per cent) had confined it to two or three years. About a third (35 per cent) had had the coitus for some four years or more, including 10 per cent

---

[21] Sylvanus Duvall 1952:161 also recognizes that conditions for extra-marital coitus may be better than for pre-marital coitus.

[22] Data on number of partners in extra-marital relations are also to be found in: Hamilton 1929:350–351 (among 24 females, 38 per cent had had only one partner). Gurewitsch and Woroschbit 1931:92 (among 1516 Russian peasant women, 53 per cent had had one partner, 25 per cent had had two, 10 per cent had had three).

who had carried on their extra-marital relationships for more than ten years and in a few instances for more than twenty years.

The length of time over which extra-marital coital activities had been carried on and the number of partners involved were, of course, dependent on the number of years that the females had been married. At the time she contributed her history, the median female in the sample was 34 years old, and had been married 7.1 years (12.5 years among those who had had extra-marital coitus). If the females in the sample had been married longer, they would have had more extensive extra-marital histories. Basing the calculations on the number of years that the females in the active sample had been married, we find that 36 per cent of those who had been married six to ten years had had extra-marital coitus one to ten times; but among those who had been married over twenty years, only 23 per cent had been so confined in their experience (Table 123). Among those in the active sample who had been married six to ten years, 4 per cent had been having extra-marital coitus for six to ten years; but among those who had been married more than twenty years, 19 per cent had been having extra-marital coitus for as long a period of years, and 31 per cent had been having it for more than ten years.

Extra-Marital Petting. There were not a few of the married females and males in the sample who had accepted extra-marital petting even though they had refused to accept vaginal coitus. Such extra-marital petting seems to have increased within recent years,[23] although we do not have sufficient data to establish this point statistically. However, such petting is not confined to younger persons, for it occurs not infrequently in middle-aged histories and even in some of the older married histories. Just as with pre-marital petting, extra-marital petting is accepted because of the satisfactions which are peculiar to it, or in order to avoid a possible pregnancy, or sometimes because the available facilities are inadequate for coitus but sufficient for petting. In fact, at dinner parties, cocktail parties, in automobiles, on picnics, and at dances, a considerable amount of public petting is allowed between married adults when coitus would be unacceptable. Apparently petting is considered less immoral than coitus, even though the petting techniques may be as effective in bringing erotic response and orgasm. Extra-marital petting is not infrequently carried on in social groups which may include the female's husband, and he would usually be less inclined to allow the extra-marital relationships if coitus were involved.

Unfortunately our record on extra-marital petting is incomplete, for we did not realize the extent of such activity when this study first be-

---

[23] Bernard 1938:357 found 49 per cent of females and 59 per cent of males, among 500 college students, tolerant of extra-marital petting.

gan. Information on this point is available, however, on 1090 of the married females in the sample. Of these, some 16 per cent had engaged in extra-marital petting although they had never allowed extra-marital coitus.

The techniques of the extra-marital petting are, of course, identical with those which are used in pre-marital petting (pp. 251 ff.) and in the petting which precedes coitus both in marital (p. 361) and in non-marital (p. 311) relationships. Of those females who had done extra-marital petting without coitus, more than half had accepted breast and genital contacts. In some cases they had accepted mouth-genital contacts. Something short of 15 per cent of the females in the sample had reached orgasm in this extra-marital petting, including 2 per cent who had petted to orgasm although they had never allowed extra-marital coitus. The accumulative incidences of all these activities would undoubtedly have proved to be higher, if our data had been more complete.

Relation to Pre-Marital Coitus. Among the 514 females in the sample who had had extra-marital coitus up to the date at which they contributed their histories, over 68 per cent had also had coitus before marriage (Table 122). Since only 50 per cent of all the married females in the sample had had pre-marital coitus, it would appear that the pre-maritally experienced females were somewhat more inclined to accept coitus with males other than their husbands after marriage.

To put it in another way, 29 per cent of the females with histories of pre-marital coitus had had extra-marital coitus by the time they contributed their histories to this study, but only 13 per cent of those who had not had pre-marital coital experience.

This greater inclination of the females with pre-coital experience to accept extra-marital coitus after marriage, is even more strikingly shown by the accumulative incidences of experienced females, calculated as follows:

By age	% of sample with extra-mar. coitus		Number of cases	
	FEMALES WITHOUT PRE-MAR. COITUS	FEMALES WITH PRE-MAR. COITUS	FEMALES WITHOUT PRE-MAR. COITUS	FEMALES WITH PRE-MAR. COITUS
35	16	33	513	399
40	20	39	364	207
45	20	40	225	87

These correlations between pre-marital and extra-marital experience may have depended in part upon a selective factor: the females who were inclined to accept coitus before marriage may have been the ones who were more inclined to accept non-marital coitus after marriage. A causal relationship may also have been involved, for it is not impossible that non-marital coital experience before marriage had persuaded those females that non-marital coitus might be acceptable after marriage.[24]

However, the females who had had pre-marital coitus seemed to have been no more promiscuous in their extra-marital relationships than the females who had had no pre-marital coitus (Table 122). Among those who had had coitus before they were married, 81 per cent had had extra-marital contacts with one to five partners; and among those who had had no pre-marital experience, 80 per cent had had coitus with that number of partners.

MORAL AND LEGAL STATUS

In nearly all societies and all moral codes, everywhere in the world, extra-marital coitus is restricted more severely than pre-marital coitus.[25] The Jewish, Mohammedan, and more ancient codes attached considerable significance to the virginity of the female at the time of marriage; but the morality of having coitus after marriage with an individual who was not one's spouse was a matter of still more serious concern. In a general way this is true of Christian codes and of the Anglo-American law that grew out of them.

Anglo-American Law. The specific legal restrictions on extra-marital coitus, or *adultery* as it is known in Anglo-American law, largely originate in Jewish and Roman codes, but acquire their force more particularly from the Catholic Church codes which allow fewer exceptions than the original Jewish codes.[26] While there is a general prohibition of extra-marital coitus in Jewish law, there were exceptional circumstances which made such activity acceptable. As we have seen, the code allowed and even required extra-marital activity of the husband

---

[24] A positive relationship between pre-marital and extra-marital coital experience was also reported by: Hamilton 1929:346. Landis et al. 1940:98. Terman 1938:340 reported a similar correlation with *desire* for extra-marital relations.

[25] This greater restriction on extra-marital coitus, in comparison to the restrictions on pre-marital coitus, is surveyed and documented in: Donohue 1931:4. Ohlson 1937:330. Ford and Beach 1951:115.

[26] Extra-marital coitus is penalized in the ancient codes, some of which date back to the 2nd millennium B.C. See: Pritchard 1950:35, Book of the Dead. Pritchard 1950:160, Lipit-Ishtar law code (with some provisions for second wives). Pritchard 1950:171–172, Code of Hammurabi. Pritchard 1950:181–182, Middle Assyrian laws (including the following: "If he has kissed her [the wife of another], they shall draw his lower lip along the edge of the blade of an ax and cut it off"). Pritchard 1950:196, Hittite code. For the Jewish code, see Epstein 1948:201–214. Biblical references are plentiful, ranging from the specific prohibitions in Exodus 20:14, Leviticus 20:10, and Deuteronomy 22:22, to the colorful descriptions in II Samuel 11:4, Proverbs 7:6–23, and Ezekiel 23:1–45. Also see the Koran pt.18, ch. 24:2–20. For the Catholic code, see Davis 1946(2):237–239.

whose wife was sterile, and required the male to take unto himself as an additional wife the wife of his brother who had died.[27]

American law has tended toward the proscription of all extra-marital sexual relationships; but in recognition of the realities of human nature, the penalties for adultery in most states are usually mild and the laws are only infrequently enforced. In 5 of the states the maximum penalty is a fine. There are 3 states which attach no criminal penalty at all to adultery, but civil penalties may be involved in these and in many other states.[28] In every state of the Union proof of adultery is allowed as sufficient grounds for divorce. Adultery is often taken as evidence of desertion or failure to support or a contribution to the delinquency of the children in the home. Both females and males may sometimes be penalized in this indirect fashion. In some states the right of the female to share in the husband's property may be threatened by her adulterous behavior. The broadest definitions of adultery and the heaviest penalties are concentrated in the northeastern section of the United States, all 10 of those states being among the 17 which may impose prison terms for a single act of extra-marital coitus.

In actual practice, such extra-marital coitus is rarely prosecuted because its existence rarely becomes known to any third party. Even when it does become known, the matter is rarely taken to criminal court. Most of the cases which we have seen in penal institutions were prosecuted because of some social disturbance that had grown out of the extra-marital activity, as when a wife had complained, or when the family had been neglected or deserted as a result of the extra-marital relationships, or when arguments, physical fights, or murder was the product of the discovery of the relationships. Not infrequently the prosecutions represented attempts on the part of neighbors or relatives to work off grudges that had developed over other matters. In this, as in many other areas, the law is most often utilized by persons who have ulterior motives for causing difficulties for the non-conformant individuals. Not infrequently the prosecutions represent attempts by sheriffs, prosecutors, or other law enforcement officers to work off personal or political grudges by taking advantage of extra-marital relationships which they may have known about and ignored for some

---

[27] Talmudic students searched assiduously for other special circumstances which might justify exceptions to the rule against extra-marital coitus—as, for instance, when a male, looking over a parapet, accidentally fell onto a passing female, and accidentally effected a genital union as he fell. In such a case the male would be absolved of any blame for having broken the rule against extra-marital coitus. See the Talmud, Yebamoth 54a.

[28] The states in which the maximum penalty for adultery is a fine are: Ky., Md., Tex., Va., and W. Va. The states in which there is no criminal penalty are: La., N. M. (but see §41–702 N.M.Stat. 1941), and Tenn. Also see Bensing 1951:67. In 6 states (Ia., Mich., Minn., N. D., Ore., and Wash.), adultery can be prosecuted only on the complaint of the spouse.

time before they became interested in prosecuting. In Boston, which is the only large city in which there is an active use of the adultery law, the statute appears to serve chiefly as a means of placing heavier penalties on simple prostitution.[29]

In some 14 states, which include a third of the total population of the country, the law specifies that adultery is punishable only when it represents regular contacts or notorious or open cohabitation between two persons who are not lawfully wedded as spouses.[30] Higher courts in such states have consistently pointed out that lone or occasional contacts are not covered by the law. However, in dealing with cases which do not have experienced attorneys to defend them, the lower courts and law enforcement officers in general usually ignore these qualifications in the law.

Social Attitudes. There is a surprising paucity of any open and frank discussion of extra-marital coitus in the serious literature.[31] Public opinion in regard to such coitus represents a mixture of professed disapproval, and spite and malice in which a considerable undercurrent of envy and suppressed desire may become apparent. As we have seen, this envy is more often apparent in the male. The female is more often tolerant of other persons having extra-marital coitus unless it concerns her own spouse. Then her disapproval may represent envy of the female who has distracted her husband's attention, or a general moral disapproval of all such non-marital activity. More often it reflects some fear that the extra-marital relationships will interfere with her own marriage.

As with other types of sexual activity, the most serious objections to extra-marital coitus come from females and males who have never had such experience. Those who have had experience are more often inclined to indicate that they intend to have more. In the sample, when the extra-marital experience had been satisfactory and had not gotten the females into personal or social difficulties, most of the experienced individuals were inclined to continue their activities.

---

[29] This use of the law in Boston is clearly evident from Ploscowe 1951:157, and from Reiman and Schroeter 1951:75.

[30] The states in which the prosecution of adultery is limited to instances where there has been regular, notorious, or open cohabitation are: Ala., Ark., Calif., Colo., Fla., Ill., Ind., Miss., Mo., Mont., Nev., N. C., Ohio, and Wyo. In Arizona and Oklahoma, single acts can be prosecuted only on the complaint of the injured spouse.

[31] The traditional social disapproval is reflected, for instance, in: Inge 1930:366–374. Neumann 1936:109. Fromme 1950:207–225. Sylvanus Duvall 1952:150–171, 292–296. More liberal interpretations may be found in: Bertrand Russell 1929:139–144. Guyon 1948:138. Haire 1948:195. Comfort 1950:103–105. Havelock Ellis 1952:84–90. That extra-marital coitus is less acceptable for females than for males is noted, for instance, in: Talmey 1910:241. Michels 1914:136, 223. Kisch 1918(1):4–6.

Thus, among the married females in the sample who had not had extra-marital experience, some 83 per cent indicated that they did not intend to have it, but in a sample of those who had had extra-marital experience, only 44 per cent indicated that they did not intend to renew their experience (Table 124, Figure 81). Some 5 per cent of those who had not had extra-marital coitus indicated that they wanted to have it, while another 12 per cent indicated that they might at some time consider the possibility of having it. This gave a total of 17 per cent who were not seriously opposed to the idea. In contrast, however, among

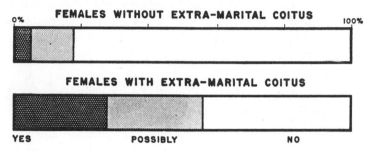

Figure 81. Intent to have extra-marital coitus
Based on females married at time of interview. Data from Table 124.

those who had already had extra-marital coital experience, some 56 per cent indicated that they intended to have more or would consider the possibility of having more.[32]

SOCIAL SIGNIFICANCE

To weigh the social significance of extra-marital sexual activity will require considerable objectivity in order to avoid, on the one hand, the traditional moral interpretations and, on the other hand, biases which are introduced by the human animal's desire for a variety of sexual experience. Certainly any scientific analysis must take into account the fact that there are both advantages and disadvantages to engaging in such activity. We do not yet have sufficient data to undertake an over-all appraisal of the problem, but the following aspects of extra-marital activity are pointed up by the experience of the females who have contributed histories to this study:

---

[32] Specific data on the female's desire to have extra-marital coitus are also in: Davis 1929:409 (16 per cent). Hamilton 1929:368 (35 per cent). Terman 1938: 336 (27 per cent). Locke 1951:149 (4 per cent and 12 per cent). For surveys of attitudes, see: Davis 1929:356 (21 per cent of 955 women saw possible justifications for extra-marital relations). Hamilton 1929:364 (73 per cent of 100 married women saw possible justification). Bernard 1938:357–358 (80 per cent of 500 college males and females stated they would pardon one act of infidelity in their spouse). Friedeburg 1950:13 (in German questionnaire survey, found 38 per cent approve some extra-marital relations). Lanval 1950:123 (among 552 chiefly French and Belgian women, 36 per cent considered faithfulness after marriage unimportant).

1. Extra-marital coitus had attracted some of the participants because of the variety of experience it afforded them with new and sometimes superior sexual partners.[33] As in pre-marital coitus, the males in the extra-marital relationships had usually engaged in more extensive courting, in more extended sex play, and in more extended coital techniques than the same males had ordinarily employed in their marital relationships. In consequence many of the females had found the extra-marital coitus particularly satisfactory. It is true that 24 per cent of the females in the sample had not reached orgasm in their extra-marital coitus as often as they had reached it in their marital coitus; but 34 per cent had reached it with about equal frequency in the two types of activity; and 42 per cent reported that orgasm had occurred more often in the extra-marital relations.

2. In many instances the female or male had engaged in the extra-marital coitus in a conscious or unconscious attempt to acquire social status through the socio-sexual contacts.

3. In some instances the extra-marital coitus had been accepted as an accommodation to a respected friend, even though the female herself was not particularly interested in the relationship.

4. In some instances the female or male had engaged in extra-marital coitus in retaliation for the spouse's involvement in similar activity. Sometimes the extra-marital activity was in retaliation for some sort of non-sexual mistreatment, real or imagined, by the other spouse.

5. In some instances, both among the females and males, the extra-marital coitus had provided a means for the one spouse to assert his or her independence of the other, or of the social code.[34]

6. For some of the females the extra-marital relationships had provided a new source of emotional satisfactions. Some of them had found it possible to develop such emotional relationships, while maintaining good relationships with their husbands. Others, however, had found it impossible to share such emotional relationships with more than one partner. In a culture which considers marital fidelity to be the symbol

---

[33] That a low orgasm rate, or other dissatisfactions in marital coitus, may develop a desire for extra-marital coitus is implied by: Hamilton 1929:389, 395. Strakosch 1934:78. Terman 1938:337, 340, 387. But Landis et al. 1940:172 found wives with extra-marital experience (14 cases) had made fairly adequate sexual adjustments with their husbands.

[34] Reasons for extra-marital coitus are also listed in: Hamilton 1929:362. Gurewitsch and Woroschbit 1931:92. Maslow 1942:279. Sylvanus Duvall 1952:158. These list such factors as unsatisfactoriness of the marital relationship, absence or illness of husband, financial advantage, desire for variety, need for emotional reassurance, emotional attachment to new partner, and attempt to help the marriage.

and proof of such other things as social conformance, law abidingness, and love, many of the females had found it difficult to engage in non-marital sexual activities without becoming involved in guilt reactions and consequent social difficulties.[35] The females who had accepted their extra-marital activity as another form of pleasure to be shared, did not so often get into difficulties over their extra-marital relationships.

7. Not infrequently the extra-marital activities had led to the development of emotional relationships which had interfered with the relations with the lawfully wedded spouses. This had caused neglect and disagreement which had seriously affected some of the marriages. This is the aspect of extra-marital activity which most societies, throughout the world, have been most anxious to control. We doubt whether such disturbances are inevitable, for there are cases of extra-marital relationships which do not seem to get into difficulties. There are strong-minded and determined individuals who can plan and control their extra-marital relationships in such a way that they avoid possible ill consequences. In such a case, however, the strong-minded spouse has to keep his or her activity from becoming known to the other spouse, unless the other spouse is equally strong-minded and willing to accept the extra-marital activity. Such persons do not constitute a majority in our present-day social organization.

8. Sometimes sexual adjustments with the spouse had improved as a result of the female's extra-marital experience.[36]

9. Extra-marital relationships had least often caused difficulty when the other spouse had not known of them. They had most often caused difficulty at the time that the spouse first discovered them. Some of the extra-marital relationships had been carried on for long periods of years without ill effects on the marital adjustments; but when the other spouse discovered them, difficulties and in some instances divorce proceedings had been immediately begun. In such instances, the extra-marital coitus had not appeared to do as much damage as the knowledge that it had occurred. The difficulties were obviously compounded by the attitudes of our culture toward such non-marital activity.

---

[35] Landis et al. 1940:174 found fewer guilt reactions in extra-marital coitus than in pre-marital coitus.

[36] An actual improvement of the marital relationship following extra-marital experience is also reported in: Landis et al. 1940:98 (in 4 cases out of 12). It is suggested by: Bell 1921:31. Folsom 1937:723. See also Pepys 1668: Nov. 14, who wrote that he had had coitus with his wife "as a husband more times since this falling out [twenty days ago] than in I believe twelve months before. And with more pleasure to her than I think in all the time of our marriage before." Assertions that extra-marital relationships will inevitably do damage to a marriage are typified by the statement in: Kirkendall 1947:29.

The females who had had extra-marital coitus believed that their husbands knew of it, or suspected it, as follows:

	Percent
Husband knew	40
Husband suspected	9
Husband presumably did not know	51
Number of cases	470

The females in the sample reported as follows on the difficulties which developed when their husbands learned of or suspected their wives' extra-marital activities:

	Percent
Serious difficulty	42
Minor difficulty	16
No difficulty	42
Number of cases	221

Adding these cases in which there had been no difficulty to the cases in which the husbands did not know of the extra-marital relationships, it is a total of 71 per cent for whom no difficulty had yet developed.[37]

It is, of course, not impossible that the extra-marital activities may have become sources of marital difficulties at some later date. We have seen instances of what appeared to be a frank and whole-hearted acceptance of the spouse's extra-marital activity when it first began and even for some period after it had begun, with considerable conflict growing out of the activity at some later period. Sometimes extraneous circumstances, such as a new economic situation, the development of some insecurity on the part of the other spouse, or the appearance of a new extra-marital partner, had reopened the issues of extra-marital relationships some five or even ten years after they had begun.

10. Among 16 females we have a record of 18 pregnancies resulting from the extra-marital coitus. The actual incidences of such pregnancies are probably higher than that. In most cases the pregnancies had been terminated by abortions. In some instances the child had been raised in its mother's home, either with or without the husband's knowledge of the child's parentage. In other instances, the pregnancy had led to a divorce.

11. There is a not inconsiderable group of cases in the sample in which the husbands had encouraged their wives to engage in extra-marital activities. This represented a notable break with the centuries-old cultural tradition. In some instances it represented a deliberate

---

[37] Locke 1951:152 reported that 5 per cent of the happily married wives believed their mates knew or suspected that they had had extra-marital relations, while 17 per cent of the divorced wives believed so.

effort to extend the wife's opportunity to find satisfaction in sexual relations. In not a few instances the husband's attitude had originated in his desire to find an excuse for his own extra-marital activity. What is sometimes known as wife swapping usually involves this situation. In another group of cases the husband had encouraged extra-marital relations in order to secure the opportunity for the sort of group activity in which he desired to participate. Sometimes his interest in group participation involved a homosexual element which was satisfied by seeing another male in sexual action, or which he, on occasion, had satisfied by extending his contacts to the male who was having coitus with his wife. Much the same elements were involved when the husband sought the opportunity, through peeping, to surreptitiously observe his wife's extra-marital coitus. In some lower level histories, but infrequently in the better educated or economically better placed groups, the husband had encouraged his wife's extra-marital activity as a form of prostitution which had added to the prestige or the financial income of the family. There were a few instances of husbands who had encouraged their male friends and strangers to have coitus with their wives because of the sadistic satisfaction which they had obtained by forcing their wives into such relationships.

It should, however, be emphasized again that most of the husbands who accepted or encouraged their wives' extra-marital activity had done so in an honest attempt to give them the opportunity for additional sexual satisfaction.

12. Extra-marital coitus had figured as a factor in the divorces of a fair number of the females and males in our histories. We have data on 907 individuals (female and male) who had had extra-marital experience and whose marriages had been terminated by divorce. We have the subjects' judgments of the significance of their extra-marital coitus in 415 cases. In nearly two-thirds (61 per cent) of these cases, the subject did not believe that his or her own extra-marital activity had been any factor in leading to that divorce (Table 125). Some 14 per cent of the females and 18 per cent of the males believed that their extra-marital experience had been prime factors in the disruption of the marriage, and something between 21 and 25 per cent more believed that it had been a contributing factor. It is to be noted, however, that these were the subjects' own estimates of the significance and, as clinicians well know, it is not unlikely that the extra-marital experience had contributed to the divorces in more ways and to a greater extent than the subjects themselves realized.

The subjects' estimates of the importance of the spouses' extra-marital activity were handicapped, both in the case of the females and the males, by the fact that they were ignorant in perhaps half of the cases that the extra-marital activity had occurred (p. 434).

It is particularly notable that the males rated their wives' extra-marital activities as prime factors in their divorces twice as often as the wives made such evaluations of their husbands' activities. Some 51 per cent of the males considered that their wives' non-marital relations had been chief factors in precipitating the divorces, and another 32 per cent considered them factors of some importance. Only 17 per cent considered them minor factors (Table 125). In contrast to this, the females considered that the husbands' extra-marital activities were prime factors in only 27 per cent of the divorces, moderate factors in 49 per cent, and minor factors in a full 24 per cent. It may be a fact that the males' extra-marital activities do not do so much damage to a marriage, or the wives may be more tolerant of their husbands' extra-marital relations, or the wives may not comprehend the extent to which the male activities are actually affecting the stability of their marriages. Contrariwise, like the true mammal that he is, the male shows himself more disturbed and jealous and more ready to take drastic action if he discovers that his wife is having extra-marital relations.

These data once again emphasize the fact that the reconciliation of the married individual's desire for coitus with a variety of sexual partners, and the maintenance of a stable marriage, presents a problem which has not been satisfactorily resolved in our culture. It is not likely to be resolved until man moves more completely away from his mammalian ancestry.

SUMMARY AND COMPARISONS OF FEMALE AND MALE

Extra-Marital Coitus

	IN FEMALES	IN MALES
Mammalian Origins		
Dominant animal acquires several mates	No	Yes
Less dominant animal has difficulty in finding a mate	No	Yes
Seeks coitus with animals other than mate	Sometimes	Yes
More responsive with new partner	Yes	Yes
Prevented from coitus with others by	Mate	Other males
Anthropologic Data		
All societies concerned with maintenance of family		
All societies use marriage to restrain disruptive sexual competition		
In primitive societies, extra-marital coitus		
Permitted rather freely	±10%	
Permitted in special circumstances	±40%	Majority
Completely prohibited	±50%	Minority
Object to extra-marital coitus primarily on social rather than religious grounds	Yes	Yes

	IN FEMALES	IN MALES
Relation to Age		
Accumulative incidence, experience		
By age 20	6%	
By age 30	16%	
By age 40	26%	±50%
Active incidence, experience		
Age 16–20	6%	35%
Age 36–40	17%	28%
Age 51–55	6%	22%
Incidence of orgasm in extra-marital coitus	±85%	±100%
Frequency (active med.), exper., per wk.		
Age 16–20	0.1	0.4
Age 31–35	0.2	0.2
Age 41–45	0.4	0.2
Regularity	Little	Some?
Percentage of total outlet		
Age 21–25	3%	7%
Age 36–40	10%	8%
Age 46–50	13%	9%
Relation to Educational Level		
Accumulative incidence, experience	Little relation	
Active incidence, experience		
Before age 25	No relation	Higher in less educ.
After age 25	Higher in better educ.	Little difference
Frequency	No relation	Higher in less educ.
Relation to Parental Occupational Class	Little or none	
Relation to Decade of Birth		
Accumulative incidence, experience		
By age 25		
Born before 1900	4%	
Born 1900–1909	8%	
Born 1910–1919	10%	
Born 1920–1929	12%	
By age 40		
Born before 1900	22%	
Born 1900–1909	30%	
Active incidence, higher in more recent generat.	Yes	Yes in all but college males
Frequency	No relation	± higher in younger generat.
Relation to Age at Onset of Adolescence	None	None?
Relation to Religious Background		
Active incidence of exper. higher among less devout	Yes	Yes
Frequency	No relation	Higher in less devout
Nature and Conditions of Extra-Marital Coitus		
Partners		
One	41%	
Two to five	40%	

Summary and Comparisons (*Continued*)

	IN FEMALES	IN MALES
Number of years involved		
Depends on length of marriage	Yes	Yes
One year or less	42%	
Over ten years	10%	
Extra-marital petting		
Petting but no extra-marital coitus	16%	
Petting to orgasm	15%	
Petting to orgasm but never coitus	2%	
Extra-marital vs. pre-marital coitus		
Among those without pre-marital coitus	13%	
Among those with pre-marital coitus	29%	
Number of extra-marital partners	No relation	
Moral and Legal Status		
Most societies restrict extra-mar. more than pre-mar. coitus	Yes	Yes
In Anglo-American law:		
Penalties mild and infrequently enforced	Yes	Yes
Adultery grounds for divorce in all states	Yes	Yes
In 14 states, not punishable unless regular and publicly known	Yes	Yes
Acceptance greater if individual has had exper.	Yes	Yes
Indiv. without exper. intend to or may have	17%	
Indiv. with exper. intend to have more	56%	
Social Significance		
May provide new types of sexual exper.	Yes	Yes
May be done to raise social status	Yes	Yes
May be done as a favor to a friend	Yes	
May be done as retaliation	Yes	Yes
May be done to assert independence	Yes	Yes
May provide emotional satisfaction	Yes	Yes
Emotional involvement may cause diffic.	Yes	Yes
May improve marital adjustment	Yes	Yes
Less often diffic. if spouse unaware	Yes	Yes
Serious difficulty when known	42%	
No difficulty when known	42%	
Pregnancy rarely results	Yes	
Husband may encourage wife's extra-mar. coitus	Yes	Yes
May be a factor in divorce	Yes	Yes
Subject rates own extra-marital coitus a major factor in divorce	14%	18%
Subject rates spouse's extra-marital coitus a major factor in divorce	27%	51%

Table 114. Active Incidence, Frequency, and Percentage of Outlet
Extra-Marital Coitus

By Age

AGE DURING ACTIVITY	ACTIVE SAMPLE			TOTAL SAMPLE		CASES IN TOTAL SAMPLE
	Active incid. %	Median freq. per wk.	Mean frequency per wk.	Mean frequency per wk.	% of total outlet	
COITAL EXPERIENCE						
16–20	6	_0.1_	_0.5 ± 0.18_	—		579
21–25	9	0.1	0.5 ± 0.11	—		1654
26–30	14	0.1	0.6 ± 0.14	0.1 ± 0.02		1664
31–35	17	0.2	0.6 ± 0.09	0.1 ± 0.02		1248
36–40	17	0.2	0.6 ± 0.11	0.1 ± 0.02		853
41–45	16	0.4	0.8 ± 0.12	0.1 ± 0.02		500
46–50	11	_0.4_	_0.8 ± 0.20_	0.1 ± 0.03		261
51–55	6			0.1 ± 0.03		119
56–60	_4_			—		49
COITUS TO ORGASM						
16–20	5	_0.2_	_0.6 ± 0.25_	—	5	577
21–25	7	0.1	0.9 ± 0.25	0.1 ± 0.02	3	1654
26–30	11	0.2	1.2 ± 0.30	0.1 ± 0.03	6	1662
31–35	14	0.2	1.0 ± 0.25	0.1 ± 0.04	6	1244
36–40	14	0.3	1.4 ± 0.37	0.2 ± 0.06	10	851
41–45	14	0.4	1.6 ± 0.45	0.2 ± 0.07	12	497
46–50	9	_0.3_	_2.0 ± 1.18_	0.2 ± 0.11	13	260
51–55	_4_			0.1 ± 0.03	5	118
56–60	_4_			—	_4_	49

Italic figures throughout the series of tables indicate that the calculations are based on less than 50 cases. No calculations are based on less than 11 cases. The dash (—) indicates a percentage or frequency smaller than any quantity which would be shown by a figure in the given number of decimal places.

Table 115. Accumulative Incidence: Extra-Marital Coital Experience By Educational Level

AGE	TOTAL SAMPLE	EDUCATIONAL LEVEL			TOTAL SAMPLE	EDUCATIONAL LEVEL		
		9–12	13–16	17+		9–12	13–16	17+
	%		*Percent*		*Cases*		*Cases*	
18	8	6	6		190	86	67	
19	7	8	4		375	149	161	
20	6	7	6	6	556	195	260	64
25	9	10	10	7	1338	412	566	294
30	16	16	16	17	1216	343	476	331
35	23	21	26	25	912	238	346	271
40	26	24	31	27	571	140	205	188
45	26	22	29	27	312	85	111	92

For an explanation of the discrepancies between certain of these active incidences and the accumulative incidences shown for the same ages, see p. 44.

Table 116. Active Incidence and Percentage of Outlet: Extra-Marital Coitus By Educational Level

Age during activity	Educ. level	Active incid. exper. %	Active incid. orgasm %	% of total outlet	Cases in total sample	Age during activity	Educ. level	Active incid. exper. %	Active incid. orgasm %	% of total outlet	Cases in total sample
16–20	9–12	7	5	2	210	36–40	0–8	6	4	5	52
	13–16	6	5	1	257		9–12	14	11	5	210
	17+	6	5	—	66		13–16	21	18	13	323
21–25	0–8	7	3	6	74		17+	18	15	9	268
	9–12	10	6	3	487	41–45	9–12	16	15	14	117
	13–16	10	9	3	727		13–16	18	15	9	182
	17+	7	6	1	368		17+	14	13	16	163
26–30	0–8	8	6	4	84	46–50	9–12	8	7	4	71
	9–12	14	10	3	489		13–16	15	12	10	91
	13–16	15	12	7	671		17+	11	11	25	76
	17+	15	11	7	421						
31–35	0–8	3	0	0	71						
	9–12	16	12	3	338						
	13–16	19	14	8	480						
	17+	20	17	7	360						

Table 117. Active Incidence and Percentage of Outlet: Extra-Marital Coitus
By Parental Occupational Class

Age during activity	Parental class	Active incid. exper. %	Active incid. orgasm %	% of total outlet	Cases in total sample	Age during activity	Parental class	Active incid. exper. %	Active incid. orgasm %	% of total outlet	Cases in total sample
16–20	2+3	11	9	15	142	31–35	2+3	11	8	1	216
	4	7	5	—	86		4	10	8	4	177
	5	7	5	1	150		5	18	11	3	292
	6+7	6	5	2	225		6+7	20	19	9	572
21–25	2+3	8	7	3	311	36–40	2+3	13	10	2	136
	4	8	6	1	230		4	11	7	1	97
	5	10	7	2	427		5	14	11	5	209
	6+7	9	7	3	732		6+7	20	18	12	420
26–30	2+3	10	8	3	310	41–45	2+3	7	6	8	83
	4	13	10	3	232		4	11	10	10	63
	5	12	9	7	409		5	17	15	8	90
	6+7	16	14	6	738		6+7	18	16	16	262

The occupational classes are as follows: 2+3 = unskilled and semi-skilled labor. 4 = skilled labor. 5 = lower white collar class. 6+7 = upper white collar and professional classes.

Table 118. Active Incidence and Percentage of Outlet: Extra-Marital Coitus
By Age at Onset of Adolescence

Age during activity	Age at adol.	Active incid. exper. %	Active incid. orgasm %	% of total outlet	Cases in total sample	Age during activity	Age at adol.	Active incid. exper. %	Active incid. orgasm %	% of total outlet	Cases in total sample
16–20	8–11	8	6	8	139	31–35	8–11	17	14	8	185
	12	6	5	1	153		12	19	15	5	291
	13	7	6	7	169		13	17	15	7	415
	14	8	7	6	77		14	16	11	3	225
							15+	18	15	12	132
21–25	8–11	10	7	1	333	36–40	8–11	15	14	12	133
	12	10	7	1	458		12	18	14	8	188
	13	8	7	4	488		13	17	16	12	270
	14	7	5	3	254		14	20	14	5	169
	15+	15	10	5	122		15+	19	14	8	93
26–30	8–11	13	11	6	286	41–45	8–11	17	15	25	78
	12	15	11	6	426		12	17	17	11	103
	13	14	12	7	527		13	15	15	10	145
	14	12	8	4	276		14	14	11	7	102
	15+	18	16	5	148		15+	15	13	13	71

Table 119. Accumulative Incidence: Extra-Marital Coital Experience
By Decade of Birth

| AGE | DECADE OF BIRTH | | | | DECADE OF BIRTH | | | |
	Bf. 1900	1900–1909	1910–1919	1920–1929	Bf. 1900	1900–1909	1910–1919	1920–1929
	Percent				*Cases*			
18			10	9			63	79
19		4	7	10		72	116	153
20	2	3	5	9	63	107	172	214
25	4	8	10	12	197	357	568	216
30	10	16	19		250	453	513	
35	18	26	25		282	453	177	
40	22	30			268	303		
45	21	40			236	76		

For an explanation of the discrepancies between certain of these active incidences and the accumulative incidences shown for the same ages, see p. 44.

Table 120. Active Incidence and Percentage of Outlet: Extra-Marital Coitus
By Decade of Birth

Age	Decade of birth	Active incid. exper. %	Active incid. orgasm %	% of total outlet	Cases in total sample	Age	Decade of birth	Active incid. exper. %	Active incid. orgasm %	% of total outlet	Cases in total sample
16–20	Bf. 1900	2	2	1	62	31–35	Bf. 1900	15	13	8	293
	1900–1909	3	2	3	114		1900–1909	21	16	8	509
	1910–1919	5	4	11	172		1910–1919	16	13	5	448
	1920–1929	9	8	7	230						
21–25	Bf. 1900	4	3	2	208	36–40	Bf. 1900	15	13	10	285
	1900–1909	8	7	6	378		1900–1909	19	16	10	464
	1910–1919	9	7	1	624		1910–1919	16	12	3	105
	1920–1929	11	9	2	447						
26–30	Bf. 1900	9	7	6	275	41–45	Bf. 1900	13	12	11	275
	1900–1909	16	12	8	507		1900–1909	19	17	14	225
	1910–1919	16	13	4	731						
	1920–1929	8	6	2	153						

Table 121. Active Incidence, Frequency, and Percentage of Outlet
Extra-Marital Coitus

By Religious Background

AGE DURING ACTIVITY	RELIGIOUS GROUP	COITAL EXPERIENCE		COITUS TO ORGASM			CASES IN TOTAL SAMPLE
		Active incid. %	Active median freq. per wk.	Active incid. %	Active median freq. per wk.	% of total outlet	
16–20	Protestant						
	Devout	2		2		—	93
	Moderate	2		2		—	97
	Inactive	9	0.1	6		1	139
	Jewish						
	Inactive	8		6		3	119
21–25	Protestant						
	Devout	5	0.1	4	0.1	2	319
	Moderate	7	0.1	5	0.1	—	309
	Inactive	13	0.1	9	0.1	3	392
	Catholic						
	Devout	8		5		7	86
	Moderate	15		11		1	54
	Inactive	25	0.1	19	1.0	6	68
	Jewish						
	Moderate	5		3		1	145
	Inactive	12	0.2	9	0.1	3	321
26–30	Protestant						
	Devout	7	0.1	5	0.1	3	332
	Moderate	12	0.1	9	0.1	1	336
	Inactive	20	0.1	15	0.1	7	413
	Catholic						
	Devout	10		7		1	84
	Inactive	16		12		3	58
	Jewish						
	Moderate	11	0.3	9	0.3	10	140
	Inactive	19	0.3	16	0.3	7	277
31–35	Protestant						
	Devout	7	0.1	6	0.1	—	265
	Moderate	17	0.1	13	0.1	3	253
	Inactive	28	0.2	22	0.2	6	315
	Catholic						
	Devout	10		5		—	63
	Jewish						
	Moderate	17	0.3	15	0.4	17	102
	Inactive	21	0.4	19	0.4	10	201
36–40	Protestant						
	Devout	8	0.1	7	0.2	2	201
	Moderate	16	0.2	13	0.2	12	175
	Inactive	23	0.2	19	0.1	5	233
	Jewish						
	Moderate	21	0.3	19	0.5	26	58
	Inactive	23	0.4	20	0.8	16	132
41–45	Protestant						
	Devout	6		6		5	126
	Moderate	18	0.3	17	0.3	14	110
	Inactive	21	0.3	20	0.4	13	129
46–50	Protestant						
	Devout	3		1		—	72
	Moderate	13		12		6	52
	Inactive	16		15		12	62

Table 122. Number of Extra-Marital Partners, Correlated with History of Pre-Marital Coitus

Number of extra-marital partners	Total sample	Females without pre-marital coitus	Females with pre-marital coitus
	%	Percent	
1 only	41	46	38
2–5	40	34	43
6–10	11	12	11
11–20	5	4	5
21–30	1	2	1
31+	2	2	2
Number of cases	514	163	351

Table 123. Number of Years Involved: Extra-Marital Coital Experience

YEARS INVOLVED	TOTAL SAMPLE	YEARS MARRIED			
		6–10	11–15	16–20	21–30
	%	Percent			
1–10 times	32	36	28	20	23
1 year or less	42	51	37	27	21
2–3 years	23	29	26	16	23
4–5 years	11	16	9	14	6
6–10 years	14	4	22	25	19
11–20 years	8		6	18	21
21+ years	2				10
Number of cases	507	116	128	80	80

"Years married" represents the number of years that the spouses actually lived together.

Table 124. Intent to Have Extra-Marital Coitus

Intend to have or to continue	Total sample	Females without extra-marital coitus	Females with extra-marital coitus
	%	*Percent*	
Yes	7	5	28
Doubtful	14	12	28
No	79	83	44
Number of cases	1702	1537	165

The table is based on females who were married at the time of interview.

Table 125. Reported Significance of Extra-Marital Coitus in Divorce

SIGNIFICANCE IN DIVORCE	SUBJECT'S ESTIMATE, OWN EXTRA-MARITAL EXPER. REPORTED BY		SUBJECT'S ESTIMATE, SPOUSE'S EXTRA-MARITAL EXPER. REPORTED BY	
	Females	Males	Females	Males
	Percent		*Percent*	
Major	14	18	27	51
Moderate	15	9	49	32
Minor	10	12	24	17
None	61	61		
Number of cases	234	181	181	82

Chapter 11

HOMOSEXUAL RESPONSES AND CONTACTS

The classification of sexual behavior as masturbatory, heterosexual, or homosexual is based upon the nature of the stimulus which initiates the behavior. The present chapter, dealing with the homosexual behavior of the females in our sample, records the sexual responses which they had made to other females, and the overt contacts which they had had with other females in the course of their sexual histories.

The term homosexual comes from the Greek prefix *homo,* referring to the sameness of the individuals involved, and not from the Latin word *homo* which means man. It contrasts with the term heterosexual which refers to responses or contacts between individuals of different (*hetero*) sexes.

While the term homosexual is quite regularly applied by clinicians and by the public at large to relations between males, there is a growing tendency to refer to sexual relationships between females as *lesbian* or *sapphic.* Both of these terms reflect the homosexual history of Sappho who lived on the Isle of Lesbos in ancient Greece. While there is some advantage in having a terminology which distinguishes homosexual relations which occur between females from those which occur between males, there is a distinct disadvantage in using a terminology which suggests that there are fundamental differences between the homosexual responses and activities of females and of males.

PHYSIOLOGIC AND PSYCHOLOGIC BASES

It cannot be too frequently emphasized that the behavior of any animal must depend upon the nature of the stimulus which it meets, its anatomic and physiologic capacities, and its background of previous experience. Unless it has been conditioned by previous experience, an animal should respond identically to identical stimuli, whether they emanate from some part of its own body, from another individual of the same sex, or from an individual of the opposite sex.

The classification of sexual behavior as masturbatory, heterosexual, or homosexual is, therefore, unfortunate if it suggests that three different types of responses are involved, or suggests that only different types of persons seek out or accept each kind of sexual activity. There is nothing known in the anatomy or physiology of sexual response and orgasm which distinguishes masturbatory, heterosexual, or homosexual reactions (Chapters 14–15). The terms are of value only because they describe the source of the sexual stimulation, and they should not be taken as descriptions of the individuals who respond to the various stimuli. It would clarify our thinking if the terms could be dropped completely out of our vocabulary, for then socio-sexual behavior could be described as activity between a female and a male, or between two females, or between two males, and this would constitute a more objective record of the fact. For the present, however, we shall have to use the term homosexual in something of its standard meaning, except that we shall use it primarily to describe sexual *relationships,* and shall prefer not to use it to describe the *individuals* who were involved in those relationships.

The inherent physiologic capacity of an animal to respond to any sufficient stimulus seems, then, the basic explanation of the fact that some individuals respond to stimuli originating in other individuals of their own sex—and it appears to indicate that every individual could so respond if the opportunity offered and one were not conditioned against making such responses. There is no need of hypothesizing peculiar hormonal factors that make certain individuals especially liable to engage in homosexual activity, and we know of no data which prove the existence of such hormonal factors (p. 758). There are no sufficient data to show that specific hereditary factors are involved. Theories of childhood attachments to one or the other parent, theories of fixation at some infantile level of sexual development, interpretations of homosexuality as neurotic or psychopathic behavior or moral degeneracy, and other philosophic interpretations are not supported by scientific research, and are contrary to the specific data on our series of female and male histories. The data indicate that the factors leading to homosexual behavior are (1) the basic physiologic capacity of every mammal to respond to any sufficient stimulus; (2) the accident which leads an individual into his or her first sexual experience with a person of the same sex; (3) the conditioning effects of such experience; and (4) the indirect but powerful conditioning which the opinions of other persons and the social codes may have on an individual's decision to accept or reject this type of sexual contact.[1]

[1] Various factors which have been supposed to cause or contribute to female homosexual activity are the following: *Fear of pregnancy or venereal disease:* Talmey 1910:149. Krafft-Ebing 1922:397. Norton 1949:62. Cory 1951:88. *Heterosexual trauma or disappointment:* Havelock Ellis 1915(2):323. Stekel 1922:292–305. Krafft-Ebing 1922:397–398. Marañón 1932:200. Caufeynon 1934:31. Hutton 1937:139. Kahn 1939:268. Beauvoir 1952:418. *Sated with males:* Bloch 1908:546–547. Krafft-Ebing 1922:398. Moreck 1929:286. *Society's heterosexual taboos:* Hutton 1937:139–140. Henry 1941(2):1026. English and Pearson 1945:378. Strain 1948:179. *Seeing parents in coitus:* Farnham

MAMMALIAN BACKGROUND

The impression that infra-human mammals more or less confine themselves to heterosexual activities is a distortion of the fact which appears to have originated in a man-made philosophy, rather than in specific observations of mammalian behavior. Biologists and psychologists who have accepted the doctrine that the only natural function of sex is reproduction, have simply ignored the existence of sexual activity which is not reproductive. They have assumed that heterosexual responses are a part of an animal's innate, "instinctive" equipment, and that all other types of sexual activity represent "perversions" of the "normal instincts." Such interpretations are, however, mystical. They do not originate in our knowledge of the physiology of sexual response (Chapter 15), and can be maintained only if one assumes that sexual function is in some fashion divorced from the physiologic processes which control other functions of the animal body. It may be true that heterosexual contacts outnumber homosexual contacts in most species of mammals, but it would be hard to demonstrate that this depends upon the "normality" of heterosexual responses, and the "abnormality" of homosexual responses.

In actuality, sexual contacts between individuals of the same sex are known to occur in practically every species of mammal which has been extensively studied. In many species, homosexual contacts may

1951:168. *Seduction by older females:* Moll 1912:314. Havelock Ellis 1915 (2):322. Moreck 1929:302. English and Pearson 1945:378. Norton 1949:62. Farnham 1951:167. *Masturbation which leads to homosexuality:* Havelock Ellis 1915(2):277. Krafft-Ebing 1922:286. *This factor is also mentioned for males by:* Taylor 1933:63, and Remplein 1950:246–247. *Endocrine imbalance:* Havelock Ellis 1915 (2): 316. Lipschütz 1924:371. S. Kahn 1937:135. Hyman 1946(3):2491. Negri 1949:197. *Penis envy and castration complex:* Chideckel 1935:14. Brody 1943:56. Deutsch 1944:347. Fenichel 1945:338. Freud 1950 (5):257. *Father-fixation or hatred toward mother:* Blanchard and Manasses 1930:104, 106. Hesnard 1933:208–209. S. Kahn 1937:20. Bergler 1943:48. Fenichel 1945:338–339. *Mother-fixation:* S. Kahn 1937:20. Deutsch 1944: 347–348. Fenichel 1945:338. Farnham 1951:169. *A continuation of a childhood "bisexual" phase, or a fixation at, or a regression to, an early adolescent stage of psychosexual development:* Moll 1912:60–61, 125. Havelock Ellis 1915(2):309–310. Stekel 1922:39. Marañón 1929:172–174. Blanchard and Manasses 1930:104. Hesnard 1933:188. Freud 1933:177–178. Hamilton in Robinson 1936:336, 341. S. Kahn 1937:18–19. Deutsch 1944:330–331. Sadler 1944:91. English and Pearson 1945:379. Negri 1949:203–204. Hutton in Neville-Rolfe 1950:429. London and Caprio 1950:635. Farnham 1951:166, 175. Kallmann 1952:295. Brody 1943:58 (adds that a homosexual would be neurotic even in a society which accepted homosexuality). *A defense against or a flight from incestuous desires:* Hamilton in Robinson 1936:341. Farnham 1951:175. *Constitutional, congenital, or inherited traits or tendencies:* Parke 1906:320. Bloch 1908:489. Carpenter 1908:55. Moll 1912:125, 130; 1931:234. Havelock Ellis 1915(2):308–311, 317. Krafft-Ebing 1922:285, 288. Kelly 1930:132–133, 220. Robinson 1931:230–231. Freud 1933:178. Potter 1933: 151. Caufeynon 1934:34. Hirschfeld in Robinson 1936:326. S. Kahn 1937:89. Henry 1941(2):1023–1026. Sadler 1944:106. Hirschfeld 1944:281. Thornton 1946:94. Negri 1949:163, 187. Benvenuti 1950:168. Kallmann 1952:295 (in a study of twins).

occur with considerable frequency, although never as frequently as heterosexual contacts. Heterosexual contacts occur more frequently because they are facilitated (1) by the greater submissiveness of the female and the greater aggressiveness of the male, and this seems to be a prime factor in determining the roles which the two sexes play in heterosexual relationships; (2) by the more or less similar levels of aggressiveness between individuals of the same sex, which may account for the fact that not all animals will submit to being mounted by individuals of their own sex; (3) by the greater ease of intromission into the female vagina and the greater difficulty of penetrating the male anus; (4) by the lack of intromission when contacts occur between two females, and the consequent lack of those satisfactions which intromission may bring in a heterosexual relationship; (5) by olfactory and other anatomic and physiologic characteristics which differentiate the sexes in certain mammalian species; (6) by the psychologic conditioning which is provided by the more frequently successful heterosexual contacts.

Homosexual contacts in infra-human species of mammals occur among both females and males. Homosexual contacts between females have been observed in such widely separated species as rats, mice, hamsters, guinea pigs, rabbits, porcupines, marten, cattle, antelope, goats, horses, pigs, lions, sheep, monkeys, and chimpanzees.[2] The homosexual contacts between these infra-human females are apparently never completed in the sense that they reach orgasm, but it is not certain how often infra-human females ever reach orgasm in any type of sexual relationship. On the other hand, sexual contacts between males of the lower mammalian species do proceed to the point of orgasm, at least for the male that mounts another male.[3]

In some species the homosexual contacts between females may occur as frequently as the homosexual contacts between males.[4] Every farmer

---

[2] We have observed homosexual behavior in male monkeys, male dogs, bulls, cows, male and female rats, male porcupines, and male and female guinea pigs. Homosexual activities in other animals are noted by: Karsch 1900:128–129 (female antelope, male and female goat, ram, stallion). Féré 1904:78 (male donkey). Havelock Ellis 1910(1):165 (male elephant, male hyena). Hamilton 1914:307 (female monkey). Bingham 1928:126–127 (female chimpanzee). Marshall and Hammond 1944:39 (doe rabbit). Reed 1946:200 (male bat). Beach 1947a:41 (female cat). Beach 1948:36 (male mouse). Beach in Hoch and Zubin 1949:63–64 (female marten, female porcupine, male lion, male rabbit). Gantt in Wolff 1950:1036 (male cat). Ford and Beach 1951:139 (male porpoise), 141 (lioness, mare, sow, ewe, female hamster, female mouse, female dog). Shadle, verbal communication (male porcupine, male raccoon).

[3] Ejaculation resulting from homosexual contact between males of lower mammalian species has been noted in: Karsch 1900:129 (ram and goat). Kempf 1917:134–135 (monkey). Moll 1931:17 (dog). Beach 1948:36 (mouse). Ford and Beach 1951:139 (rat). Brookfield Zoo, verbal communication (baboon). We have observed such ejaculation in the bull.

[4] For the sub-primates, Beach 1947a:40 states that "the occurrence of masculine sexual responses in female animals is more common than is the appearance

who has raised cattle knows, for instance, that cows quite regularly mount cows. He may be less familiar with the fact that bulls mount bulls, but this is because cows are commonly kept together while bulls are not so often kept together in the same pasture.

It is generally believed that females of the infra-human species of mammals are sexually responsive only during the so-called periods of heat, or what is technically referred to as the estrus period. This, however, is not strictly so. The chief effect of estrus seems to be the preparation of the animal to accept the approaches of another animal which tries to mount it. The cows that are mounted in the pasture are those that are in estrus, but the cows that do the mounting are in most instances individuals which are not in estrus (p. 737).[5]

Whether sexual relationships among the infra-human species are heterosexual or homosexual appears to depend on the nature of the immediate circumstances and the availability of a partner of one or the other sex. It depends to a lesser degree upon the animal's previous experience, but no other mammalian species is so affected by its experience as the human animal may be. There is, however, some suggestion, but as yet an insufficient record, that the males among the lower mammalian species are more likely than the females to become conditioned to exclusively homosexual behavior; but even then such exclusive behavior appears to be rare.[6]

The mammalian record thus confirms our statement that any animal which is not too strongly conditioned by some special sort of experience is capable of responding to any adequate stimulus. This is what we find in the more uninhibited segments of our own human species, and this is what we find among young children who are not too rigorously restrained in their early sex play. Exclusive preferences and patterns of behavior, heterosexual or homosexual, come only with experience, or as a result of social pressures which tend to force an individual into an exclusive pattern of one or the other sort. Psychologists and psychiatrists, reflecting the mores of the culture in which they have been

---

of feminine behavior in males." Ford and Beach 1951:143 note, however, that in the class Mammalia taken as a whole, homosexual behavior among males is more frequent than homosexual behavior among females.

[5] Two situations may be involved: (1) the estrual female may be receptive to being mounted and often attempts to elicit such mounting (see Beach in Hoch and Zubin 1949:64; Rice and Andrews 1951:151). (2) If she is not mounted the estrual female may mount another animal of the same or opposite sex. For the latter, see: Beach 1948:66–68 (cow, sow, rabbit, cat, shrew). Ford and Beach 1951:141–142 (rabbit, sow, mare, cow, guinea pig).

[6] Exclusive, although usually temporary male homosexuality is noted in: Hamilton 1914:307–308 (monkey). Beach in Hoch and Zubin 1949:64–65 (lion). Ford and Beach 1951:136, 139 (baboon and porpoise). Shadle, verbal communication (porcupine). No exclusively homosexual patterns have been reported for female mammals.

raised, have spent a good deal of time trying to explain the origins of homosexual activity; but considering the physiology of sexual response and the mammalian backgrounds of human behavior, it is not so difficult to explain why a human animal does a particular thing sexually. It is more difficult to explain why each and every individual is not involved in every type of sexual activity.

ANTHROPOLOGIC BACKGROUND

In the course of human history, distinctions between the acceptability of heterosexual and of homosexual activities have not been confined to our European and American cultures. Most cultures are less acceptant of homosexual, and more acceptant of heterosexual contacts. There are some which are not particularly disturbed over male homosexual activity, and some which expect and openly condone such behavior among young males before marriage and even to some degree after marriage; but there are no cultures in which homosexual activity among males seems to be more acceptable than heterosexual activity.[7] It is probable that in some Moslem, Buddhist, and other areas male homosexual contacts occur more frequently than they do in our European or American cultures, and in certain age groups they may occur more frequently than heterosexual contacts; but heterosexual relationships are, at least overtly, more acceptable even in those cultures.

Records of male homosexual activity are also common enough among more primitive human groups, but there are fewer records of homosexual activity among females in primitive groups. We find some sixty pre-literate societies from which some female homosexual activity has been reported, but the majority of the reports imply that such activity is rare. There appears to be only one pre-literate group, namely the Mohave Indians of our Southwest, for whom there are records of exclusively homosexual patterns among females. That same group is the only one for which there are reports that female homosexual activity is openly sanctioned.[8] For ten or a dozen groups, there are records of female transvestites—i.e., anatomic females who dress and assume the position of the male in their social organization—but transvestism and homosexuality are different phenomena, and our data show that only a portion of the transvestites have homosexual histories (p. 679).

There is some question whether the scant record of female homosexuality among pre-literate groups adequately reflects the fact. It may merely reflect the taboos of the European or American anthropologists who accumulated the data, and the fact that they have been notably

---

[7] Ford and Beach 1951:130 note that 64 per cent of a sample of 76 societies consider homosexuality acceptable for certain persons.

[8] The sexual life of the Mohave was intensively studied by Devereux 1936, 1937.

reticent in inquiring about sexual practices which are not considered
"normal" by Judeo-Christian standards. Moreover, the informants in
the anthropologic studies have usually been males, and they would
be less likely to know the extent of female homosexual activities in
their cultures. It is, nonetheless, quite possible that such activities are
actually limited among the females of these pre-literate groups, possibly because of the wide acceptance of pre-marital heterosexual relationships, and probably because of the social importance of marriage
in most primitive groups.[9]

RELATION TO AGE AND MARITAL STATUS

As in any other type of sexual situation, there are: (1) individuals
who have been erotically aroused by other individuals of the same

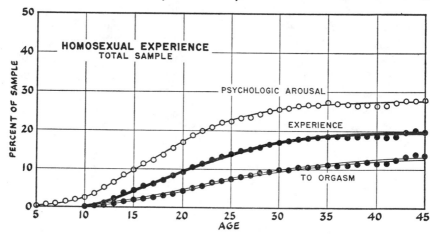

**Figure 82. Accumulative incidence: homosexual experience, arousal, and
orgasm**

Data from Table 131.

sex, whether or no they had physical contact with them; (2) individuals who have had physical contacts of a sexual sort with other individuals of the same sex, whether or no they were erotically aroused in
those contacts; and (3) individuals who have been aroused to the point
of orgasm by their physical contacts with individuals of the same sex.
These three types of situations are carefully distinguished in the statistics given here.

Accumulative Incidence in Total Sample. Some of the females in
the sample had been conscious of specifically erotic responses to other
females when they were as young as three and four (Table 13). The
percentages of those who had been erotically aroused had then steadily

---

[9] Ford and Beach 1951:133, 143, also note that female homosexuality seems less
frequent than male homosexuality among pre-literates.

risen, without any abrupt development, to about thirty years of age. By that time, a quarter (25 per cent) of all the females had recognized erotic responses to other females. The accumulative incidence figures had risen only gradually after age thirty. They had finally reached a level at about 28 per cent (Table 131, Figure 82).[10]

The number of females in the sample who had made specifically sexual contacts with other females also rose gradually, again without any abrupt development, from the age of ten to about thirty. By then some 17 per cent of the females had had such experience (Tables 126, 131, Figure 82). By age forty, 19 per cent of the females in the total sample had had some physical contact with other females which was deliberately and consciously, at least on the part of one of the partners, intended to be sexual.[11]

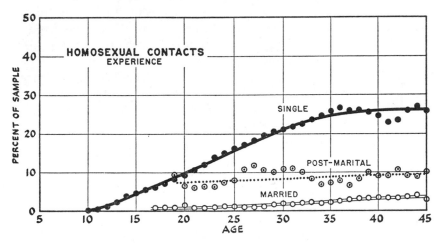

Figure 83. Accumulative incidence: homosexual experience, by marital status

Data from Table 126.

Homosexual activity among the females in the sample had been largely confined to the single females and, to a lesser extent, to previously married females who had been widowed, separated, or divorced. Both the incidences and frequencies were distinctly low among the married females (Table 126, Figure 83). Thus, while the accumu-

---

[10] Our accumulative incidence figures for homosexual responses among females are close to those in two other studies: Davis 1929:247 (26 per cent at age 36). Gilbert Youth Research 1951 (13 per cent, college students).

[11] Our accumulative incidence figures for overt homosexual contacts among females are of the same general order as those from other studies: Davis 1929:247 (20 per cent, unmarried college and graduate females, average age 36). Bromley and Britten 1938:117 (4 per cent, college females). Landis et al. 1940:262, 286 (4 per cent, single females). England acc. Rosenthal 1951:58 (20 per cent, British females). Gilbert Youth Research 1951 (6 per cent, college females).

lative incidences of homosexual contacts had reached 19 per cent in the total sample by age forty, they were 24 per cent for the females who had never been married by that age, 3 per cent for the married females, and 9 per cent for the previously married females. The age at which the females had married seemed to have had no effect on the pre-marital incidences of homosexual activity, even though we found that the pre-marital heterosexual activities (petting and pre-marital coitus) had been stepped up in anticipation of an approaching marriage. The chief effect of marriage had been to stop the homosexual activities, thereby lowering the active incidences and frequencies in the sample of married females.

A half to two-thirds of the females who had had sexual contacts with other females had reached orgasm in at least some of those contacts. By twenty years of age there were only 4 per cent of the total sample who had experienced orgasm in homosexual relations, and by age thirty-five there were still only 11 per cent with such experience (Table 131, Figure 82). The accumulative incidences finally reached 13 per cent in the middle forties. Since there were differences in the incidences among females of the various educational levels (Table 131, Figure 85), and since our sample includes a disproportionate number of the females of the college and graduate groups where the incidences seem to be higher than in the grade school and high school groups, the figures for this sample are probably higher than those which might be expected in the U. S. population as a whole.

Active Incidence to Orgasm. Since there is every gradation between the casual, non-erotic physical contacts which females regularly make and the contacts which bring some erotic response, it has not been possible to secure active incidence or frequency data on homosexual contacts among the females in the sample except where they led to orgasm. However, comparisons of the accumulative incidence data for experience and for orgasm (Table 131, Figure 82) suggest that the active incidences of the homosexual contacts may, at least in the younger groups, have been nearly twice as high as the active incidences of the contacts which led to orgasm.

In the total sample, not more than 2 to 3 per cent had reached orgasm in their homosexual relations during adolescence and their teens (Table 128), although five times that many may have been conscious of homosexual arousal and three times that many may have had physical contacts with other girls which were specifically sexual. After age twenty, the active incidences of the contacts which led to orgasm had gradually increased among the females who were still unmarried, reaching their peak, which was 10 per cent, at age forty. Then they began to drop. Between the ages of forty-six and fifty, about 4 per cent of the still unmarried females were actively involved in homosexual relations that led to orgasm. We do not have complete histories of single females who were reaching orgasm in homosexual relations after fifty years of age, but we do have incomplete information on still older women who were making such contacts with responses to orgasm while they were in their fifties, sixties, and even seventies.

Among the married females, slightly more than 1 per cent had been actively involved in homosexual activities which reached orgasm in each and every age group between sixteen and forty-five (Table 128).

On the other hand, among the females who had been previously married and who were then separated, widowed, or divorced, something around 6 per cent were having homosexual contacts which led to orgasm in each of the groups from ages sixteen to thirty-five (Table 128). After that some 3 to 4 per cent were involved, but by the middle fifties, only 1 per cent of the previously married females were having contacts which were complete enough to effect orgasm.

Frequency to Orgasm. Among the unmarried females in the sample who had ever experienced orgasm from contacts with other females, the average (active median) frequencies of orgasm among the younger adolescent girls who were having contacts had averaged nearly once in five weeks (about 0.2 per week), and they had increased in frequency among the older females who were not yet married (Table 128). In the late twenties they had averaged once in two and a half weeks (0.4 per week), and had stayed on about that level for the next ten years. This means that the active median frequencies of orgasm derived from the homosexual contacts had been higher than the active median frequencies of orgasm derived from nocturnal dreams and from heterosexual petting, and about the same as the active median frequencies of orgasm attained in masturbation.[12]

The active mean frequencies were three to six times higher than the active median frequencies, because of the fact that there were some females in each age group whose frequencies were notably higher than those of the median females (Table 128). The individual variation had depended in part upon the fact that the frequencies of contact had varied, and in part upon the fact that some of these females had regularly experienced multiple orgasms in their homosexual contacts.

In most age groups, three-quarters or more of the single females who were having homosexual experience to the point of orgasm were having it with average frequencies of once or less per week (Figure

---

[12] The limited frequency data previously published were not calculated on any basis comparable to our 5-year calculations.

84). There were individuals, however, in every age group from adolescence to forty-five, who were having homosexual contacts which
had led to orgasm on an average of seven or more per week. From ages
twenty-one to forty there were a few individuals who had averaged
ten or more and in one instance as many as twenty-nine orgasms per
week from homosexual sources. In contrast to the record for most other
types of sexual activities, the most extreme variation in the homosexual
relationships had not occurred in the youngest groups, but in the
groups aged thirty-one to forty.

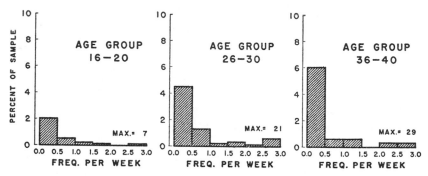

Figure 84. Individual variation: frequency of homosexual contacts to orgasm

For three age groups of single females. Each class interval includes the upper but
not the lower frequency. For incidences of females not having homosexual experience
or reaching orgasm in such contacts, see Table 128.

As in most other types of sexual activity among females (except
coitus in marriage), the homosexual contacts had often occurred sporadically. Several contacts might be made within a matter of a few
days, and then there might be no such contacts for a matter of weeks
or months. In not a few instances the record was one of intense and
frequently repeated contacts over a short period of days or weeks, with
a lapse of several years before there were any more. On the other hand,
there were a fair number of histories in which the homosexual partners
had lived together and maintained regular sexual relationships for
many years, and in some instances for as long as ten or fifteen years or
even longer, and had had sexual contacts with considerable regularity
throughout those years. Such long-time homosexual associations are
rare among males. A steady association between two females is much
more acceptable to our culture and it is, in consequence, a simpler
matter for females to continue relationships for some period of years.
The extended female associations are, however, also a product of differences in the basic psychology of females and males (Chapter 16).

Among the married females in the sample, there were a few in each
age group—usually not more than one in a hundred or so—who were

having homosexual contacts to the point of orgasm (Table 128). Even in those small active samples, however, the range of individual variation was considerable. Most of the married females had never had more than a few such contacts, but in nearly every age group there were married females who were having contacts with regular frequencies of once or twice or more per week. There were a few histories of married females who were completely homosexual and who were not having coitus with their husbands, although they continued to live with them as a matter of social convenience. In some of these cases there were good social adjustments between the spouses even though the sexual lives of each lay outside of the marriage.

Among the females in the sample who had been previously married and who were then widowed, separated, or divorced, the frequencies of homosexual experience were distinctly higher than among the married females (Table 128). In some cases these females, after the dissolution of their marriages, had established homes with other women with whom they had then had their first homosexual contacts and with whom they subsequently maintained regular homosexual relationships. Some of the women had been divorced because of their homosexual interests, although homosexuality in the female is only rarely a factor in divorce. It should be emphasized, however, that a high proportion of the unmarried females who live together never have contacts which are in any sense sexual.

Percentage of Total Outlet. Homosexual contacts are highly effective in bringing the female to orgasm (p. 467). In spite of their relatively low incidence, they had accounted for an appreciable proportion of the total number of orgasms of the entire sample of unmarried females. Before fifteen years of age, the homosexual contacts had been surpassed only by masturbation and heterosexual coitus as sources of outlet, and they were again in that position among the still single females after age thirty (Table 171, Figure 110). Among these single females, orgasms obtained from homosexual contacts had accounted for some 4 per cent of the total outlet of the younger adolescent females, some 7 per cent of the outlet of the unmarried females in their early twenties, and some 19 per cent of the total outlet of the females who were still unmarried in their late thirties (Table 128).

Among the married females in the sample, homosexual contacts had usually accounted for less than one-half of one per cent of all their orgasms (Table 128).

However, among the females who had been previously married, homosexual contacts had become somewhat more important again as a source of outlet. They had accounted for something around 2 per cent of the total outlet of the younger females in the group, and for nearly 10 per cent of the outlet of the females who were in their early thirties (Table 128).

Number of Years Involved. For most of the females in the sample, the homosexual activity had been limited to a relatively short period of time (Table 129). For nearly a third (32 per cent) of those who had had any experience, the experience had not occurred more than ten times, and for many it had occurred only once or twice. For nearly a half (47 per cent, including part of the above 32 per cent), the experience had been confined to a single year or to a part of a single year. For another quarter (25 per cent), the activity had been spread through two or three years. These totals, interesting to note, had not materially differed between females who were in the younger, and females who were in the older age groups at the time they contributed their histories. This means that for most of them, most of the homosexual activity had occurred in the younger years. There were a quarter (28 per cent) whose homosexual experience had extended for more than three years. There were histories of a few females whose activities had extended for as many as thirty or forty years, and more extended samples of older females would undoubtedly show cases which had continued for still longer periods of time.

Number of Partners. In the sample of single females, a high proportion (51 per cent) of those who had had any homosexual experience had had it with only a single partner, up to the time at which they had contributed their histories to the record. Another 20 per cent had had it with two different partners. Only 29 per cent had had three or more partners in their homosexual relations, and only 4 per cent had had more than ten partners (Table 130).[13]

In this respect, the female homosexual record contrasts sharply with that for the male. Of the males in the sample who had had homosexual experience, a high proportion had had it with several different persons, and 22 per cent had had it with more than ten partners (p. 683). Some of them had had experience with scores and in many instances with hundreds of different partners. Apparently, basic psychologic factors account for these differences in the extent of the promiscuity of the female and the male (Chapter 16).

---

[13] Davis 1929:251 gives closely parallel data (63 per cent with one partner, 18 per cent with two partners, 19 per cent with three or more partners). Statistically unsupported impressions of a high degree of promiscuity in female homosexuality may be found in: Bloch 1908:530 (female homosexuals change partners more frequently than male homosexuals). Alibert 1926:22. Kisch 1926:192. Chideckel 1935:122. But the greater durability of relationships among female homosexuals is also noted in: Smitt 1951:102.

RELATION TO EDUCATIONAL LEVEL

The incidences of homosexual activity among the females in the sample had been definitely correlated with their educational backgrounds. This was more true than with any of their other sexual activities.

Accumulative Incidence. Homosexual responses had occurred among a smaller number of the females of the grade school and high school sample, a distinctly larger number of the college sample, and still more

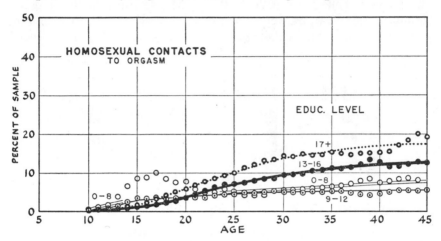

Figure 85. Accumulative incidence: homosexual contacts to orgasm, by educational level

Based on total sample, including single, married, and previously married females. Data from Table 131.

of the females who had gone on into graduate work (Table 131). At thirty years of age, for instance, there were 10 per cent of the grade school sample, 18 per cent of the high school sample, 25 per cent of the college sample, and 33 per cent of the graduate group who had recognized that they had been erotically aroused by other females.[14]

Overt contacts had similarly occurred in a smaller number of the females of the lower educational levels and a larger number of those of the upper educational levels. At thirty years of age, the accumulative incidence figures had reached 9 per cent, 10 per cent, 17 per cent, and 24 per cent in the grade school, high school, college, and graduate groups, respectively.

At thirty years of age, homosexual experience to the point of orgasm had occurred in 6 per cent of the grade school sample, 5 per cent of

---

[14] Davis 1929:308 also finds a higher incidence of adult homosexual responses among better educated females (38 per cent of college group, 15 per cent of non-college group).

the high school sample, 10 per cent of the college sample, and 14 per cent of the graduate sample (Table 131, Figure 85).

We have only hypotheses to account for the extension of this type of sexual activity in the better educated groups. We are inclined to believe that moral restraint on pre-marital heterosexual activity is the most important single factor contributing to the development of a homosexual history, and such restraint is probably most marked among the younger and teen-age girls of those social levels that send their daughters to college. In college, these girls are further restricted by administrators who are very conscious of parental concern over the heterosexual morality of their offspring. The prolongation of the years

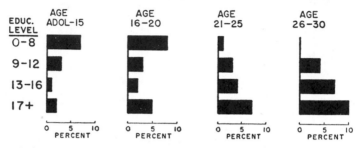

Figure 86. Active incidence: homosexual contacts to orgasm, by educational level

Data based on single females; see Table 127.

of schooling, and the consequent delay in marriage (Figure 46), interfere with any early heterosexual development of these girls. This is particularly true if they go on into graduate work. All of these factors contribute to the development of homosexual histories. There may also be a franker acceptance and a somewhat lesser social concern over homosexuality in the upper educational levels.

Active Incidence to Orgasm. Between adolescence and fifteen years of age, homosexual contacts to orgasm were more common in the sample of high school females and in the limited sample of grade school females (Table 127, Figure 86). However, between the ages of twenty-one and thirty-five, while the active incidences stood at something between 3 and 6 per cent among the high school females, they had risen to something between 7 and 11 per cent in the college and graduate school groups.

Frequency to Orgasm. Between adolescence and fifteen years of age, the active median frequencies of homosexual contacts to orgasm among the females in the sample were higher in the grade school and high school groups, and lower among the sexually more restrained young females of the upper educational levels (Table 127). Subsequently these discrepancies had more or less disappeared, and after age twenty the frequencies had averaged once in two or three weeks for the median females of all the educational levels represented in the sample.

Percentage of Total Outlet. Among the younger teen-age girls, 14 per cent of the orgasms of the grade school group had come from homosexual contacts, while only 1 or 2 per cent of the orgasms of the college and graduate groups had come from such sources (Table 127). Subsequently, these differences were reversed, and between thirty and forty years of age the still unmarried females of the graduate group were deriving 18 to 21 per cent of their total outlet from homosexual sources. If one-fifth of the outlet of this group came from homosexual sources, and only a little more than one-tenth (11 per cent) of the females in the group were having such activity, it is evident that the females who were having homosexual experience were reaching orgasm more frequently than those who were depending on other types of sexual activity for their outlet.

RELATION TO PARENTAL OCCUPATIONAL CLASS

In the available sample there seems to be little or nothing in the accumulative or active incidences, or the frequencies of the homosexual contacts, which suggests that there is any correlation with the occupational classes of the homes in which the females were raised (Tables 132, 133). There is only minor evidence that the accumulative incidences of contacts to the point of orgasm may have involved a slightly higher percentage of the females who came from upper white collar homes, and a smaller percentage of those who came from the homes of laboring groups—at age forty, a matter of 14 per cent in the first instance, and under 10 per cent in the second instance (Table 132).

The active incidences in the younger age groups were higher among the females who had come from the homes of laborers; but after the age of twenty the differences had largely disappeared, and after the age of twenty-five the females who had come from upper white collar homes were the ones most often involved (Table 133).

RELATION TO DECADE OF BIRTH

In the available sample, the accumulative incidences of homosexual contacts to the point of orgasm had been very much the same for the females who were born in the four decades on which we have data. There is no evidence that there are any more females involved in homosexual contacts today than there were in the generation born before

1900 or in any of the intermediate decades (Table 134, Figure 87).[15] Similarly, the number of females having homosexual contacts in particular five-year periods of their lives (the active incidences), the frequencies of such contacts, and the percentages of the total outlet which had been derived from homosexual contacts, do not seem to have varied in any consistent fashion during the four decades covered by the sample (Table 135).

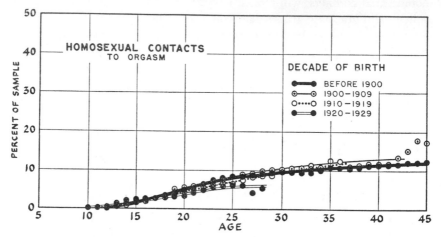

Figure 87. Accumulative incidence: homosexual contacts to orgasm, by decade of birth

Based on total sample, including single, married, and previously married females. Data from Table 134.

It is not immediately obvious why this, among all other types of sexual activity, should have been unaffected by the social forces which led to the marked increase in the incidences of masturbation, heterosexual petting, pre-marital coitus, and even nocturnal dreams among American females immediately after the first World War, and which have kept these other activities on the new levels or have continued to keep them rising since then.

RELATION TO AGE AT ONSET OF ADOLESCENCE

There do not seem to be any consistent correlations between either the accumulative incidences, the active incidences, or the frequencies of homosexual contacts, and the ages at which the females in the sample had turned adolescent (Tables 136, 137). Among males we found (1948:320) that those who turned adolescent at earlier ages were more often involved in homosexual contacts as well as in mastur-

---

[15] Statistically unsubstantiated statements that female homosexuality is on the increase may be found, for instance, in: Parke 1906:319. Havelock Ellis 1915 (2):261–262. Potter 1933:6–9, 150. McPartland 1947:143, 150. Norton 1949: 61.

bation and pre-marital heterosexual contacts. The absence of such a correlation among females may be significant (see Chapter 18).

RELATION TO RURAL-URBAN BACKGROUND

The accumulative incidences of homosexual contacts to the point of orgasm were a bit higher among the city-bred females in the sample (Table 138, Figure 88). The active incidences appear to have been a

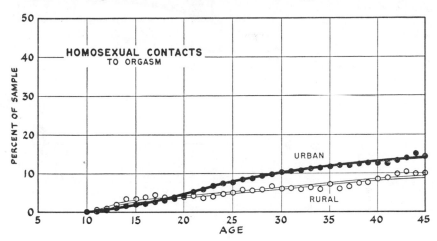

Figure 88. Accumulative incidence: homosexual contacts to orgasm, by rural-urban background

Based on total sample, including single, married, and previously married females. Data from Table 138.

bit higher among the rural females in their teens, but they were higher among urban females after the age of twenty (Table 139). The data, however, are insufficient to warrant final conclusions.

RELATION TO RELIGIOUS BACKGROUND

The educational levels and religious backgrounds of the females in the sample were the social factors which were most markedly correlated with the incidences of their homosexual activity.

Accumulative Incidence. In the Protestant, Catholic, and Jewish groups on which we have samples, fewer of the devout females were involved in homosexual contacts to the point of orgasm, and distinctly more of the females who were least devout religiously (Table 140, Figures 89–91). For instance, by thirty-five years of age among the Protestant females some 7 per cent of the religiously devout had had homosexual relations to orgasm, but 17 per cent of those who were least actively identified with the church had had such relations. The differences were even more marked in the Catholic groups: by thirty-five

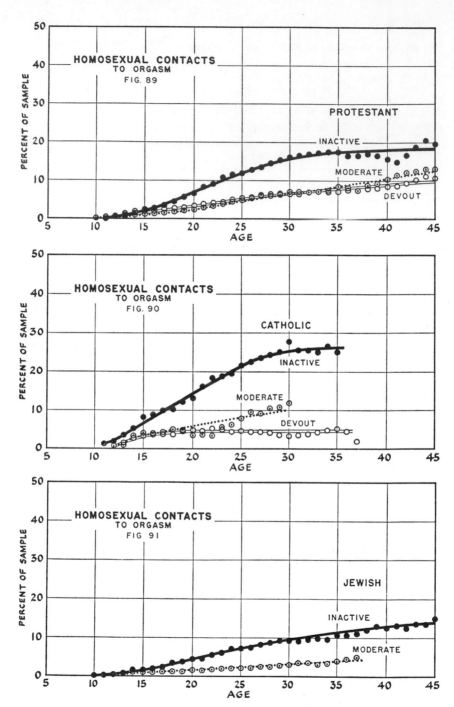

Figures 89–91. Accumulative incidence: homosexual contacts to orgasm, by religious background

Based on total sample, including single, married, and previously married females. Data from Table 140.

years of age, only 5 per cent of the devoutly Catholic females had had homosexual relations to the point of orgasm, but some 25 per cent of those who were only nominally connected with the church. The differences between the Jewish groups lay in the same direction.

There is little doubt that moral restraints, particularly among those who were most actively connected with the church, had kept many of the females in the sample from beginning homosexual contacts, just as some were kept from beginning heterosexual activities. On the other

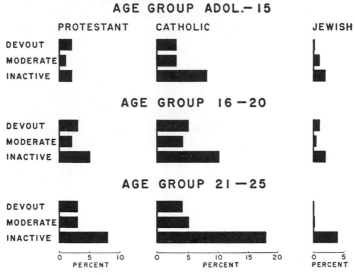

Figure 92. Active incidence: homosexual contacts to orgasm, by religious background

Data based on single females; see Table 141.

hand, as we have already noted, some of the females had become involved in homosexual activities because they were restrained by the religious codes from making pre-marital heterosexual contacts, and such devout individuals had sometimes become so disturbed in their attempt to reconcile their behavior and their moral codes that they had left the church, thereby increasing the incidences of homosexual activity among the religiously inactive groups.

Active Incidence. In eleven out of the twelve groups on which we have data available for comparisons, the active incidences of homosexual contacts to the point of orgasm were lower among the more devout females and higher among those who were religiously least devout (Table 141, Figure 92). For instance, among the younger adolescent groups, there were 3 per cent of the devoutly Catholic females who were having homosexual relations to the point of orgasm, but 8 per cent of the inactive Catholics. Similarly, at ages twenty-six to thirty, among the still unmarried Protestant groups, 5 per cent of the more devout females were involved, but 13 per cent of the least devout females (Table 141).

Active Median Frequency to Orgasm. In the sample, there does not seem to have been any consistent correlation between the active median frequencies of homosexual activities and the religious backgrounds of the females in the various groups (Table 141).

Percentage of Total Outlet. The percentage of the total outlet which had been derived by the various groups of females from their homosexual relations was, in most instances, correlated with the number of females (the active incidences) who were involved in such activity (Table 141); but among the religiously more devout females, and especially in the older age groups, the percentage of the total outlet derived from homosexual sources was in excess and often in considerable excess of what the incidences might have led one to expect. This had depended in part upon the fact that an unusually large number of the religiously devout were not reaching orgasm in any sort of sexual activity (Table 165), and for those who had accepted homosexual relations and reached orgasm in them, those relations had become a chief source of all the orgasms experienced by the group. It is also possible that a selective factor was involved, and that the sexually more responsive females were the ones who had most often accepted homosexual relations.

TECHNIQUES IN HOMOSEXUAL CONTACTS

The techniques utilized in the homosexual relations among the females in the sample were the techniques that are ordinarily utilized in heterosexual petting which precedes coitus, or which may serve as an end in itself. The homosexual techniques had differed primarily in the fact that they had not included vaginal penetrations with a true phallus.

The physical contacts between the females in the homosexual relations had often depended on little more than simple lip kissing and generalized body contacts (Table 130). In some cases the contacts, even among the females who had long and exclusively homosexual histories, had not gone beyond this. In many instances the homosexual partners had not extended their techniques to breast and genital stimulation for some time and in some cases for some period of years after the relationships had begun. Ultimately, however, among the females in the sample who had had more extensive homosexual experience, simple kissing and manual manipulation of the breast and genitalia had become nearly universal (in 95 to 98 per cent); and deep kissing (in 77 per cent), more specific oral stimulation of the female breast (in 85 per cent), and oral stimulation of the genitalia (in 78 per cent) had become common techniques. In something more than half of the histories (56 per cent), there had been genital appositions which were designed to provide specific and mutual stimulation (Table 130). But vaginal penetrations with objects which had served as substitutes for the male penis had been quite rare in the histories.[16]

It is not generally understood, either by males or by females who have not had homosexual experience, that the techniques of sexual relations between two females may be as effective as or even more effective than the petting or coital techniques ordinarily utilized in heterosexual contacts. But if it is recalled that the clitoris of the female, the inner surfaces of the labia minora, and the entrance to the vagina are the areas which are chiefly stimulated by the male penetrations in coitus (pp. 574 ff.), it may be understood that similar tactile or oral stimulation of those structures may be sufficient to bring orgasm. However, for females who find satisfaction in having the deeper portions of the vagina penetrated during coitus (pp. 579–584), the lack of this sort of physical stimulation may make the physical satisfactions of homosexual relationships inferior to those which are available in coitus.

Nevertheless, comparisons of the percentages of contacts which had brought orgasm in marital coitus among the females who had been married for five years, and in the homosexual relations of females who had had about the same number of years of homosexual experience, show the following:

% of contacts leading to orgasm	In fifth year of marital coitus	In more extensive homosexual experience
	Percent of females	
0	17	7
1–29	13	7
30–59	15	8
60–89	15	10
90–100	40	68
Number of cases	1448	133

The higher frequency of orgasm in the homosexual contacts may have depended in part upon the considerable psychologic stimulation provided by such relationships, but there is reason for believing that it may also have depended on the fact that two individuals of the same

[16] Further data on the nature of female homosexual techniques may be found in: Forberg 1884(2):113–115, 135, 141, 143. Parke 1906:322. Rohleder 1907(2): 466, 484, 494. Bloch 1908:529. Talmey 1910:154–155. Havelock Ellis 1915(2):257–258. Krafft-Ebing 1922:400. Kronfeld 1923:58. Kisch 1926: 195–196. Eberhard 1927:354, 360. Kelly 1930:137. Deutsch 1933:40; 1944: 348. Sadler 1944:96. Hirschfeld 1944:232–233. Bergler 1948:200. See also the classical references in footnote 22.

sex are likely to understand the anatomy and the physiologic responses and psychology of their own sex better than they understand that of the opposite sex. Most males are likely to approach females as they, the males, would like to be approached by a sexual partner. They are likely to begin by providing immediate genital stimulation. They are inclined to utilize a variety of psychologic stimuli which may mean little to most females (Chapter 16). Females in their heterosexual relationships are actually more likely to prefer techniques which are closer to those which are commonly utilized in homosexual relationships. They would prefer a considerable amount of generalized emotional stimulation before there is any specific sexual contact. They usually want physical stimulation of the whole body before there is any specifically genital contact. They may especially want stimulation of the clitoris and the labia minora, and stimulation which, after it has once begun, is followed through to orgasm without the interruptions which males, depending to a greater degree than most females do upon psychologic stimuli, often introduce into their heterosexual relationships (p. 668).

It is, of course, quite possible for males to learn enough about female sexual responses to make their heterosexual contacts as effective as females make most homosexual contacts. With the additional possibilities which a union of male and female genitalia may offer in a heterosexual contact, and with public opinion and the mores encouraging heterosexual contacts and disapproving of homosexual contacts, relationships between females and males will seem, to most persons, to be more satisfactory than homosexual relationships can ever be. Heterosexual relationships could, however, become more satisfactory if they more often utilized the sort of knowledge which most homosexual females have of female sexual anatomy and female psychology.

THE HETEROSEXUAL-HOMOSEXUAL BALANCE

There are some persons whose sexual reactions and socio-sexual activities are directed only toward individuals of their own sex. There are others whose psychosexual reactions and socio-sexual activities are directed, throughout their lives, only toward individuals of the opposite sex. These are the extreme patterns which are labeled homosexuality and heterosexuality. There remain, however, among both females and males, a considerable number of persons who include both homosexual and heterosexual responses and/or activities in their histories. Sometimes their homosexual and heterosexual responses and contacts occur at different periods in their lives; sometimes they occur coincidentally. This group of persons is identified in the literature as bisexual.

That there are individuals who react psychologically to both females and males, and who have overt sexual relations with both females and males in the course of their lives, or in any single period of their lives, is a fact of which many persons are unaware; and many of those who are academically aware of it still fail to comprehend the realities of the situation. It is a characteristic of the human mind that it tries to dichotomize in its classification of phenomena. Things either are so, or they are not so. Sexual behavior is either normal or abnormal, socially acceptable or unacceptable, heterosexual or homosexual; and many persons do not want to believe that there are gradations in these matters from one to the other extreme.[17]

In regard to sexual behavior it has been possible to maintain this dichotomy only by placing all persons who are exclusively heterosexual in a heterosexual category, and all persons who have any amount of experience with their own sex, even including those with the slightest experience, in a homosexual category. The group that is identified in the public mind as heterosexual is the group which, as far as public knowledge goes, has never had any homosexual experience. But the group that is commonly identified as homosexual includes not only those who are known or believed to be exclusively homosexual, but also those who are known to have had any homosexual experience at all. Legal penalties, public disapproval, and ostracism are likely to be leveled against a person who has had limited homosexual experience as quickly as they are leveled against those who have had exclusive experience. It would be as reasonable to rate all individuals heterosexual if they have any heterosexual experience, and irrespective of the amount of homosexual experience which they may be having. The attempt to maintain a simple dichotomy on these matters exposes the traditional biases which are likely to enter whenever the heterosexual or homosexual classification of an individual is involved.

Heterosexual-Homosexual Rating. Only a small proportion of the females in the available sample had had exclusively homosexual histories. An adequate understanding of the data must, therefore, depend upon some balancing of the heterosexual and homosexual elements in each history. This we have attempted to do by rating each individual on a heterosexual-homosexual scale which shows what proportion of

---

[17] Attempts to categorize female homosexuality as congenital, real, genuine, acquired, situational, temporary, latent, partial, complete, total, absolute, regressive, progressive, pseudo-homosexuality, psychosexual hermaphroditism, bisexuality, inversion, perversity, etc., may be found, for instance, in: Féré 1904: 188. Parke 1906:320. Bloch 1908:489. Carpenter 1908:55. Freud 1910:2. Talmey 1910:143, 152. Moll 1912:125–130. Krafft-Ebing 1922:285–289, 336. Kelly 1930:136, 220. Robinson 1931:230–231. Marañón 1932:199. Potter 1933:151. Henry 1941(2):1023–1026. Hirschfeld 1944:281–282. Negri 1949: 163, 187. The concept of a continuum from exclusive heterosexuality to exclusive homosexuality is less often encountered, but is suggested, for instance, in: Freud 1924(2):207–208. Marañón 1929:170. Blanchard and Manasses 1930:109.

her psychologic reactions and/or overt behavior was heterosexual, and what proportion of her psychologic reactions and/or overt behavior was homosexual (Figure 93). We have done this for each year for which there is any record. This heterosexual-homosexual rating scale was explained in our volume on the male (1948:636–659), but before applying it to the data on the female it seems desirable to summarize again the principles involved in the construction and use of the scale.

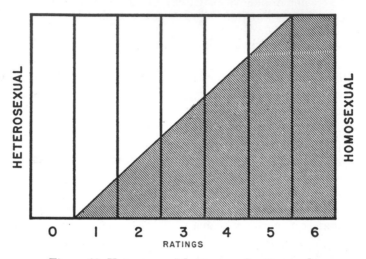

Figure 93. Heterosexual-homosexual rating scale

Definitions of the ratings are as follows: 0 = entirely heterosexual. 1 = largely heterosexual, but with incidental homosexual history. 2 = largely heterosexual, but with a distinct homosexual history. 3 = equally heterosexual and homosexual. 4 = largely homosexual, but with distinct heterosexual history. 5 = largely homosexual, but with incidental heterosexual history. 6 = entirely homosexual.

¶ The ratings represent a balance between the homosexual and heterosexual aspects of an individual's history, rather than the intensity of his or her psychosexual reactions or the absolute amount of his or her overt experience.

¶ Individuals who fall into any particular classification may have had various and diverse amounts of overt experience. An individual who has had little or no experience may receive the same classification as one who has had an abundance of experience, provided that the heterosexual and homosexual elements in each history bear the same relation to each other.

¶ The ratings depend on the psychologic reactions of the individual and on the amount of his or her overt experience. An individual may receive a rating on the scale even if he or she has had no overt heterosexual or homosexual experience.

¶ Since the psychologic and overt aspects of any history often parallel each other, they may be given equal weight in many cases in determining a rating. But in some cases one aspect may seem more significant than the other, and then some evaluation of the relative importance of the two must be made. We find, however, that most persons agree in their ratings of most histories after they have had some experience in the use of the scale. In our own research, where each year of each individual history has been rated independently by two of us, we find that our independent ratings differ in less than one per cent of the year-by-year classifications.

¶ An individual may receive a rating for any particular period of his or her life, whether it be the whole life span or some smaller portion of it. In the present study it has proved important to give ratings to each individual year, for some individuals may materially change their psychosexual orientation in successive years.

¶ While the scale provides seven categories, it should be recognized that the reality includes individuals of every intermediate type, lying in a continuum between the two extremes and between each and every category on the scale.

The categories on the heterosexual-homosexual scale (Figure 93) may be defined as follows:

0. Individuals are rated as 0's if all of their psychologic responses and all of their overt sexual activities are directed toward persons of the opposite sex. Such individuals do not recognize any homosexual responses and do not engage in specifically homosexual activities. While more extensive analyses might show that all persons may on occasion respond to homosexual stimuli, or are capable of such responses, the individuals who are rated 0 are those who are ordinarily considered to be completely heterosexual.

1. Individuals are rated as 1's if their psychosexual responses and/or overt experience are directed almost entirely toward individuals of the opposite sex, although they incidentally make psychosexual responses to their own sex, and/or have incidental sexual contacts with individuals of their own sex. The homosexual reactions and/or experiences are usually infrequent, or may mean little psychologically, or may be initiated quite accidentally. Such persons make few if any deliberate attempts to renew their homosexual contacts. Consequently the homosexual reactions and experience are far surpassed by the heterosexual reactions and/or experience in the history.

2. Individuals are rated as 2's if the preponderance of their psychosexual responses and/or overt experiences are heterosexual, although they respond rather definitely to homosexual stimuli and/or have more than incidental homosexual experience. Some of these individuals may have had only a small amount of homosexual experience, or they may have had a considerable amount of it, but the heterosexual element always predominates. Some of them may turn all of their overt experience in one direction while their psychosexual responses turn largely in the opposite direction; but they are always erotically aroused by anticipating homosexual experience and/or in their physical contacts with individuals of their own sex.

3. Individuals are rated as **3**'s if they stand midway on the heterosexual-homosexual scale. They are about equally heterosexual and homosexual in their psychologic responses and/or in their overt experience. They accept or equally enjoy both types of contact and have no strong preferences for the one or the other.

4. Individuals are rated as **4**'s if their psychologic responses are more often directed toward other individuals of their own sex and/or if their sexual contacts are more often had with their own sex. While they prefer contacts with their own sex, they, nevertheless, definitely respond toward and/or maintain a fair amount of overt contact with individuals of the opposite sex.

5. Individuals are rated as **5**'s if they are almost entirely homosexual in their psychologic responses and/or their overt activities. They respond only incidentally to individuals of the opposite sex, and/or have only incidental overt experience with the opposite sex.

6. Individuals are rated as **6**'s if they are exclusively homosexual in their psychologic responses, and in any overt experience in which they give any evidence of responding. Some individuals may be rated as **6**'s because of their psychologic responses, even though they may never have overt homosexual contacts. None of these individuals, however, ever respond psychologically toward, or have overt sexual contacts in which they respond to individuals of the opposite sex.

X. Finally, individuals are rated as **X**'s if they do not respond erotically to either heterosexual or homosexual stimuli, and do not have overt physical contacts with individuals of either sex in which there is evidence of any response. After early adolescence there are very few males in this classification (see our 1948:658), but a goodly number of females belong in this category in every age group (Table 142, Figure 95). It is not impossible that further analyses of these individuals might show that they do sometimes respond to socio-sexual stimuli, but they are unresponsive and inexperienced as far as it is possible to determine by any ordinary means.

Percentage With Each Rating. It should again be pointed out, as we did in our volume on the male (1948:650), that it is impossible to determine the number of persons who are "homosexual" or "heterosexual." It is only possible to determine how many persons belong, at any particular time, to each of the classifications on a heterosexual-homosexual scale. The distribution of the available female sample on the heterosexual-homosexual scale is shown in Table 142 and Figure 94. These incidence figures differ from the incidence figures presented in the earlier part of this chapter, because the heterosexual-homosexual ratings are based on psychologic responses and overt experience, while the accumulative and active incidences previously shown are (with the exception of Table 131 and Figure 82) based solely on overt contacts.

The following generalizations may be made concerning the experience of the females in the sample, up to the time at which they contributed their histories to the present study.

Something between 11 and 20 per cent of the unmarried females and 8 to 10 per cent of the married females in the sample were making at least incidental homosexual responses, or making incidental or more specific homosexual contacts—*i.e.*, **rated 1 to 6**—in each of the years between twenty and thirty-five years of age. Among the previously married females, 14 to 17 per cent were in that category (Table 142).

Something between 6 and 14 per cent of the unmarried females, and 2 to 3 per cent of the married females, were making more than incidental responses, and/or making more than incidental homosexual contacts —*i.e.*, **rated 2 to 6**—in each of the years between twenty and thirty-five years of age. Among the previously married females, 8 to 10 per cent were in that category (Table 142).

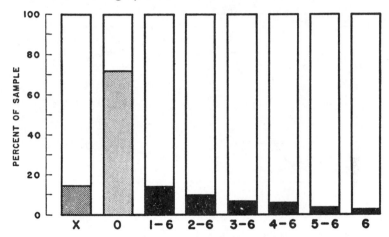

Figure 94. Active incidence: heterosexual-homosexual ratings, single females, age twenty-five

For definitions of the ratings, see p. 471. Data from Table 142.

Between 4 and 11 per cent of the unmarried females in the sample, and 1 to 2 per cent of the married females, had made homosexual responses, and/or had homosexual experience, at least as frequently as they had made heterosexual responses and/or had heterosexual experience—*i.e.*, **rated 3 to 6**—in each of the years between twenty and thirty-five years of age. Among the previously married females, 5 to 7 per cent were in that category (Table 142).

Between 3 and 8 per cent of the unmarried females in the sample, and something under 1 per cent of the married females, had made homosexual responses and/or had homosexual experience more often than they had responded heterosexually and/or had heterosexual experience—*i.e.*, **rated 4 to 6**—in each of the years between twenty and thirty-five years of age. Among the previously married females, 4 to 7 per cent were in that category (Table 142).

Between 2 and 6 per cent of the unmarried females in the sample, but less than 1 per cent of the married females, had been more or less

exclusively homosexual in their responses and/or overt experience
—*i.e.*, rated **5 or 6**—in each of the years between twenty and thirty-
five years of age. Among the previously married females, 1 to 6 per
cent were in that category (Table 142).[18]

Between 1 and 3 per cent of the unmarried females in the sample,
but less than three in a thousand of the married females, had been
exclusively homosexual in their psychologic responses and/or overt

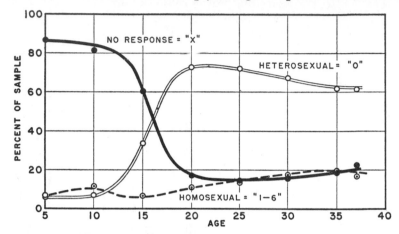

Figure 95. Active incidence: heterosexual-homosexual ratings, single females
For definitions of the ratings, X, 0, and 1–6, see p. 471. Data from Table 142.

experience—*i.e.*, rated **6**—in each of the years between twenty and
thirty-five years of age. Among the previously married females, 1 to 3
per cent were in that category (Table 142).

Between 14 and 19 per cent of the unmarried females in the sample,
and 1 to 3 per cent of the married females, had not made any socio-
sexual responses (either heterosexual or homosexual)—*i.e.*, rated **X**—
in each of the years between twenty and thirty-five years of age. Among
the previously married females, 5 to 8 per cent were in that category
(Table 142).

Extent of Female vs. Male Homosexuality. The incidences and frequencies of homosexual responses and contacts, and consequently the
incidences of the homosexual ratings, were much lower among the
females in our sample than they were among the males on whom we
have previously reported (see our 1948:650–651). Among the females,
the accumulative incidences of homosexual responses had ultimately
reached 28 per cent; they had reached 50 per cent in the males. The

---

[18] That fewer females than males are exclusively homosexual is also noted in:
Havelock Ellis 1915(2):195. Potter 1933:151. Hesnard 1933:189. Cory
1951:88.

accumulative incidences of overt contacts to the point of orgasm among the females had reached 13 per cent (Table 131, Figure 82); among the males they had reached 37 per cent. This means that homosexual responses had occurred in about half as many females as males, and contacts which had proceeded to orgasm had occurred in about a third as many females as males. Moreover, compared with the males, there were only about a half to a third as many of the females who were, in any age period, primarily or exclusively homosexual.

A much smaller proportion of the females had continued their homosexual activities for as many years as most of the males in the sample.

A much larger proportion (71 per cent) of the females who had had any homosexual contact had restricted their homosexual activities to a single partner or two; only 51 per cent of the males who had had homosexual experience had so restricted their contacts. Many of the males had been highly promiscuous, sometimes finding scores or hundreds of sexual partners.

There is a widespread opinion which is held both by clinicians and the public at large, that homosexual responses and completed contacts occur among more females than males.[19] This opinion is not borne out by our data, and it is not supported by previous studies which have been based on specific data.[20] This opinion may have originated in the fact that females are more openly affectionate than males in our culture. Women may hold hands in public, put arms about each other, publicly fondle and kiss each other, and openly express their admiration and affection for other females without being accused of homosexual interests, as men would be if they made such an open display of their interests in other men. Males, interpreting what they observe in terms of male psychology, are inclined to believe that the female behavior reflects emotional interests that must develop sooner or later into overt sexual relationships. Nevertheless, our data indicate that a high proportion of this show of affection on the part of the female does not reflect any psychosexual interest, and rarely leads to overt homosexual activity.

Not a few heterosexual males are erotically aroused in contemplating the possibilities of two females in a homosexual relation; and the opin-

[19] For instance, Clark 1937:70, and Bergler 1951:317, feel that the incidences of homosexuality among females exceed those among males. Others differentiate various types of homosexuality, and feel that incidental or temporary homosexuality is commoner in the female, as in: Bloch 1908:525, and Hirschfeld 1944:281. Others who estimate that homosexuality is equally common in both sexes include: Havelock Ellis 1915(2):195. Krafft-Ebing 1922:397. Freud 1924(2):202. Kelly 1930:143. Sadler 1944:92.

[20] All specific studies have arrived at incidence figures for the male which exceed those for the female: Hamilton 1929: 492–493 (57 per cent male, 37 per cent

ion that females are involved in such relationships more frequently than males may represent wishful thinking on the part of such heterosexual males. Psychoanalysts may also see in it an attempt among males to justify or deny their own homosexual interests.

The considerable amount of discussion and bantering which goes on among males in regard to their own sexual activities, the interest which many males show in their own genitalia and in the genitalia of other males, the amount of exhibitionistic display which so many males put on in locker rooms, in shower rooms, at swimming pools, and at informal swimming holes, the male's interest in photographs and drawings of genitalia and sexual action, in erotic fiction which describes male as well as female sexual prowess, and in toilet wall inscriptions portraying male genitalia and male genital functions, may reflect homosexual interests which are only infrequently found in female histories. The institutions which have developed around male homosexual interests include cafes, taverns, night clubs, public baths, gymnasia, swimming pools, physical culture and more specifically homosexual magazines, and organized homosexual discussion groups; they rarely have any counterpart among females. Many of these male institutions, such as the homosexually oriented baths and gymnasia, are of ancient historic origin, but there do not seem to have been such institutions for females at any time in history. The street and institutionalized homosexual prostitution which is everywhere available for males, in all parts of the world, is rarely available for females, anywhere in the world.[21] All of these differences between female and male homosexuality depend on basic psychosexual differences between the two sexes.

SOCIAL SIGNIFICANCE OF HOMOSEXUALITY

Society may properly be concerned with the behavior of its individual members when that behavior affects the persons or property of other members of the social oganization, or the security of the whole group. For these reasons, practically all societies everywhere in the world attempt to control sexual relations which are secured through the use of force or undue intimidation, sexual relations which lead to unwanted pregnancies, and sexual activities which may disrupt or prevent marriages or otherwise threaten the existence of the social organization itself. In various societies, however, and particularly in our own Judeo-

female). Bromley and Britten 1938:117, 210 (13 per cent male, 4 per cent female). Gilbert Youth Research 1951 (12 per cent male, 6 per cent female).
[21] In addition to our own data, female homosexual clubs and bars are recorded in: Bloch 1908:530. Caufeynon 1934:22. Hirschfeld 1944:285. McPartland 1947:149–150. Cory 1951:122 (more rare than male homosexual clubs and bars). Female homosexual prostitution is also noted, for example, in: Martineau 1886:31. Parke 1906:313. Rohleder 1907(2):493; 1925:338–339. Bloch 1908:530. Hirschfeld 1944:282.

Christian culture, still other types of sexual activity are condemned by religious codes, public opinion, and the law because they are contrary to the custom of the particular culture or because they are considered intrinsically sinful or wrong, and not because they do damage to other persons, their property, or the security of the total group.

The social condemnation and legal penalties for any departure from the custom are often more severe than the penalties for material damage done to persons or to the social organization. In our American culture there are no types of sexual activity which are as frequently condemned because they depart from the mores and the publicly pretended custom, as mouth-genital contacts and homosexual activities. There are practically no European groups, unless it be in England, and few if any other cultures elsewhere in the world which have become as disturbed over male homosexuality as we have here in the United States. Interestingly enough, there is much less public concern over homosexual activities among females, and this is true in the United States and in Europe and in still other parts of the world.[22]

In an attempt to secure a specific measure of attitudes toward homosexual activity, all persons contributing histories to the present study were asked whether they would accept such contacts for themselves, and whether they approved or disapproved of other females or males engaging in such activity. As might have been expected, the replies to these questions were affected by the individual's own background of experience or lack of experience in homosexual activity, and the following analyses are broken down on that basis.

Acceptance for Oneself. Of the 142 females in the sample who had had the most extensive homosexual experience, some regretted their experience and some had few or no regrets. The record is as follows:

Regret	Percent
None	71
Slight	6
More or less	3
Yes	20
Number of cases	142

---

[22] For ancient Greece, Rome, and India, female homosexuality is recorded in: Ovid [1st cent. B.C., Roman]: Heroides, XV, 15–20, 201 (1921:183, 195) (Sappho recounts her past loves). Plutarch [1st cent. A.D., Greek]: Lycurgus, 18.4 (1914:(1)265). Martial [1st cent. A.D., Roman]: I,90(1919(1):85–87; 1921:33); VII, 67 (1919(1):469–471; 1921:193–194); VII, 70 (1919(1):471; 1921:194). Juvenal [1st–2nd cent. A.D., Roman]: Satires, VI, 308–325 (1789:272–275; 1817:239–240). Lucian [2nd cent. A.D., Greek]: Amores (1895:190); Dialogues of Courtesans, V (1895:100–105). Kama Sutra of Vatsyayana [1st–6th cent. A.D., Sanskrit] 1883–1925:62, 124. For additional accounts of Sappho of Lesbos, see: Wharton 1885, 1895. Miller and Robinson 1925. Weigall 1932.

Among the females who had never had homosexual experience, there were only 1 per cent who indicated that they intended to have it, and 4 per cent more who indicated that they might accept it if the opportunity were offered (Table 144).

But among the females who had already had some homosexual experience, 18 per cent indicated that they expected to have more. Another 20 per cent were uncertain what they would do, and some 62 per cent asserted that they did not intend to continue their activity. Some of the 18 per cent who indicated that they would continue were making a conscious and deliberate choice based upon their experience and their decision that the homosexual activity was more satisfactory than any other type of sexual contact which was available to them. Some of the others were simply following the path of least resistance, or accepting a pattern which was more or less forced upon them.

The group which had had homosexual experience and who expected to continue with it represented every social and economic level, from the best placed to the lowest in the social organization. The list included store clerks, factory workers, nurses, secretaries, social workers, and prostitutes. Among the older women, it included many assured individuals who were happy and successful in their homosexual adjustments, economically and socially well established in their communities and, in many instances, persons of considerable significance in the social organization. Not a few of them were professionally trained women who had been preoccupied with their education or other matters in the day when social relations with males and marriage might have been available, and who in subsequent years had found homosexual contacts more readily available than heterosexual contacts. The group included women who were in business, sometimes in high positions as business executives, in teaching positions in schools and colleges, in scientific research for large and important corporations, women physicians, psychiatrists, psychologists, women in the auxiliary branches of the Armed Forces, writers, artists, actresses, musicians, and women in every other sort of important and less important position in the social organization.[23] For many of these women, heterosexual relations or marriage would have been difficult while they maintained their professional careers. For many of the older women no sort of socio-sexual contacts would have been available if they had not worked out sexual adjustments with the companions with whom they had lived, in some instances for many years. Considerable affection or strong emotional attachments were involved in many of these relationships.

---

[23] As examples of the statistically unsupported opinion that homosexuality is more common among females in aesthetic professions, see: Eberhard 1924:548. Rohleder 1925:381–382. Moreck 1929:312. Hesnard 1933:189. Chesser 1947:257. Martinez 1947:103. McPartland 1947:154. Beauvoir 1952:411.

On the other hand, some of the females in the sample who had had homosexual experience had become much disturbed over that experience. Often there was a feeling of guilt in having engaged in an activity which is socially, legally, and religiously disapproved, and such individuals were usually sincere in their intention not to continue their activities. Some of them, however, were dissatisfied with their homosexual relations merely because they had had conflicts with some particular sexual partner, or because they had gotten into social difficulties as a result of their homosexual activities.

Some 27 per cent of those who had had more extensive homosexual experience had gotten into difficulty because of it (Table 145). Some of these females were disturbed because they had found it physically or socially impossible to continue relationships with the partner in whom they were most interested, and refused to contemplate the possibility of establishing new relationships with another partner. In a full half of these cases, the difficulties had originated in the refusal of parents or other members of their families to accept them after they had learned of their homosexual histories.

On the other hand, among those who had had homosexual experience, as well as among those who had not had experience, there were some who denied that they intended to have or to continue such activity, because it seemed to be the socially expected thing to disavow any such intention. Some of these females would actually accept such contacts if the opportunity came and circumstances were propitious. It is very difficult to know what an individual will do when confronted with an opportunity for sexual contact.

Approval for Others. As a further measure of female reactions to homosexual activity, each subject was asked whether she approved or disapproved or was neutral in regard to other persons, of her own or of the opposite sex, having homosexual activity. Each of the female subjects was also asked to indicate whether she would keep friends, female or male, after she had discovered that they had had homosexual experience. Since the question applied to persons whom they had previously accepted as friends, it provided a significant test of current attitudes toward homosexual behavior. From these data the following generalizations may be drawn:

1. The approval of homosexual activity for other females was much higher among the females in the sample who had had homosexual experience of their own. Some 23 per cent of those females recorded definite approval, and only 15 per cent definitely disapproved of other females having homosexual activity (Table 144, Figure 96).

2. Females who had had experience of their own approved of homosexual activity for males less often than they approved of it for females. Only 18 per cent completely approved of the male activity, and 22 per cent definitely disapproved (Table 144, Figure 96).

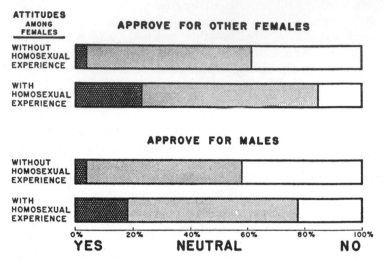

Figure 96. Attitudes of females toward homosexual contacts for others
Data from Table 144.

3. The females who had never had homosexual experience were less often inclined to approve of it for other persons. Some 4 per cent expressed approval of homosexual activity for males, but approximately 42 per cent definitely disapproved (Table 144). Some 4 per cent approved of activities for females, and 39 per cent disapproved.

4. Among the females who had had homosexual experience, some 88 per cent indicated that they would keep female friends after they had discovered their homosexual histories; 4 per cent said they would not (Table 144, Figure 97). Some of these latter responses reflected the subject's dissatisfaction with her own homosexual experience, but some represented the subject's determination to avoid persons who might tempt her into renewing her own activities.

5. Among the females who had had homosexual experience, 74 per cent indicated that they would continue to keep male friends after they had discovered that they had homosexual histories, and 10 per cent said they would not (Table 144, Figure 97). The disapproval of males with homosexual histories often depends upon the opinion that such males have undesirable characteristics, but this objection could not have been a factor in the present statistics because the question had concerned males whom the subject had previously accepted as friends.

6. Females who had never had homosexual experience were less often willing to accept homosexual female friends. Only 55 per cent said they would keep such friends, and 22 per cent were certain that they would not keep them (Table 144, Figure 97). This is a measure of the intolerance with which our Judeo-Christian culture views any type of sexual activity which departs from the custom.

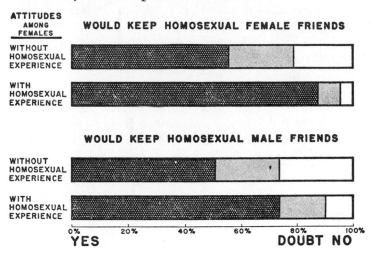

Figure 97. Attitudes of females toward keeping homosexual friends
Data from Table 144.

7. Some 51 per cent of the females who had never had homosexual experience said that they would keep homosexual males as friends, 26 per cent said they would not, and 23 per cent were doubtful (Table 144, Figure 97). As we have noted before (1948:663–664), this sort of ostracism by females often becomes a factor of considerable moment in forcing the male who has had some homosexual experience into exclusively homosexual patterns of behavior.

Moral Interpretations. The general condemnation of homosexuality in our particular culture apparently traces to a series of historical circumstances which had little to do with the protection of the individual or the preservation of the social organization of the day. In Hittite, Chaldean, and early Jewish codes there were no over-all condemnations of such activity, although there were penalties for homosexual activities between persons of particular social status or blood relationships, or homosexual relationships under other particular circumstances, especially when force was involved.[24] The more general condemnation of

---

[24] For the rather broad acceptance of homosexuality in many parts of the ancient Near East, see: Pritchard 1950:73–74, 98–99, for the Gilgamesh Epic (2nd millennium B.C. or earlier) which contains passages suggesting homosexual relations between the heroes Gilgamesh and Enkidu. Homosexuality is not

all homosexual relationships originated in Jewish history in about the seventh century B.C., upon the return from the Babylonian exile. Both mouth-genital contacts and homosexual activities had previously been associated with the Jewish religious service, as they had been with the religious services of most of the other peoples of that part of Asia, and just as they have been in many other cultures elsewhere in the world.[25] In the wave of nationalism which was then developing among the Jewish people, there was an attempt to dis-identify themselves with their neighbors by breaking with many of the customs which they had previously shared with them. Many of the Talmudic condemnations were based on the fact that such activities represented the way of the Canaanite, the way of the Chaldean, the way of the pagan, and they were originally condemned as a form of idolatry rather than a sexual crime. Throughout the middle ages homosexuality was associated with heresy.[26] The reform in the custom (the mores) soon, however, became a matter of morals, and finally a question for action under criminal law.

Jewish sex codes were brought over into Christian codes by the early adherents of the Church, including St. Paul, who had been raised in the Jewish tradition on matters of sex.[27] The Catholic sex code is an almost precise continuation of the more ancient Jewish code.[28] For centuries in Medieval Europe, the ecclesiastic law dominated on all questions of morals and subsequently became the basis for the English common law, the statute laws of England, and the laws of the various states of the United States. This accounts for the considerable conformity between

---

mentioned in the codes of Lipit-Ishtar or Hammurabi, and the injunction in the Hittite code (Pritchard 1950:196) is aimed only at men who have contact with their sons. The Middle Assyrian laws (12th century B.C. or earlier) likewise mention male homosexuality which was punishable by castration (see: Barton 1925:Chapter 15, item 19), but a more modern translation suggests that this punishment was preceded by homosexual contact between the convicted man and his punishers (Pritchard 1950:181). Epstein 1948:135–136 assumes a general taboo on male homosexuality among the ancient Hebrews, but admits that this taboo is not to be found in the Covenant Code or in Deuteronomy, but only in the somewhat later Leviticus 18:22 and 20:13. See also Genesis 19:1–25, and Judges 19:17–25, for the protection of a male guest from forced homosexual relations. Deuteronomy 23:17–18 simply prohibits men of the Israelites from becoming temple prostitutes, but goes no further.

[25] Male homosexual temple prostitutes, "kadesh," were at one time a part of Jewish religion, as may be gathered from II Kings 23:7, and from the warning in Deuteronomy 23:17–18. This is discussed by Westermarck 1917(2):488, and by Epstein 1948:135–136. The subsequent condemnation of homosexuality occurs repeatedly, as in: I Kings 14:24; 15:12; 22:46. Leviticus 18:22; 20:13. See also the Talmud, Sanhedrin 54a, 78a, 82a. Yebamoth 25a, 54b. Sotah 26b, etc.

[26] The condemnation of homosexuality as idolatry is noted by Westermarck 1917(2):487–488, and by Epstein 1948:136.

[27] For St. Paul's condemnation of homosexuality, see: Romans 1:26–27. I Corinthians 6:9. I Timothy 1:10.

[28] The Catholic codes explicitly condemn male and female homosexuality. See such accepted Catholic sources as: Arregui 1927:153. Davis 1946(2):246.

the Talmudic and Catholic codes and the present-day statute law on sex, including the laws on homosexual activity.[29]

Condemnations of homosexual as well as some other types of sexual activity are based on the argument that they do not serve the prime function of sex, which is interpreted to be procreation, and in that sense represent a perversion of what is taken to be "normal" sexual behavior. It is contended that the general spread of homosexuality would threaten the existence of the human species, and that the integrity of the home and of the social organization could not be maintained if homosexual activity were not condemned by moral codes and public opinion and made punishable under the statute law. The argument ignores the fact that the existent mammalian species have managed to survive in spite of their widespread homosexual activity, and that sexual relations between males seem to be widespread in certain cultures (for instance, Moslem and Buddhist cultures) which are more seriously concerned with problems of overpopulation than they are with any threat of underpopulation. Interestingly enough these are also cultures in which the institution of the family is very strong.

Legal Attitudes. While it is, of course, impossible for laws to prohibit homosexual interests or reactions, they penalize, in every state of the Union, some or all of the types of contact which are ordinarily employed in homosexual relations. The laws are variously identified as statues against sodomy, buggery, perverse or unnatural acts, crimes against nature, public and in some instances private indecencies, grossly indecent behavior, and unnatural or lewd and lascivious behavior. The penalties in most of the states are severe, and in many states as severe as the penalties against the most serious crimes of violence.[30] The penalties are particularly severe when the homosexual relationships involve an adult with a young minor.[31] There is only one state, New York, which, by an indirection in the wording of its statute, appears to attach no penalty to homosexual relations which are carried on between adults in private and with the consent of both of the participating parties; and this sort of exemption also appears in Scandinavia and in many other European countries. There appears to be no other major culture in the world in which public opinion and the statute law so severely penalize homosexual relationships as they do in the United States today.

It might be expected that the moral and legal condemnations of homosexual activity would apply with equal force to both females and

---

[29] For the relationship between Jewish and Catholic codes, and the statute law, see also: Westermarck 1917 (2): 480–489. May 1931: ch. 2, 3.

[30] For a convenient and almost complete summary of the statutes concerning homosexuality in the forty-eight states, see:Cory 1951:appendix B.

[31] For the problem involved in the relationships of adults and minors, see: Guttmacher and Weihofen 1952:156.

males. The ancient Hittite code, however, condemned only male homosexual activity and then only when it occurred under certain circumstances, and made no mention of homosexual activity among females.[24] Similarly the references to homosexual activity in the Bible and in the Talmud apply primarily to the male. The condemnations were severe and usually called for the death of the transgressing male, but they rarely mentioned female activity, and when they did, no severe penalties were proposed.[32] In medieval European history there are abundant records of death imposed upon males for sexual activities with other males, but very few recorded cases of similar action against females.[33] In modern English and other European law, the statutes continue to apply only to males [31]; but in American law, the phrasing of the statutes would usually make them applicable to both female and male homosexual contacts.[35] The penalties are usually invoked against "all persons," "any person," "whoever," "one who," or "any human being" without distinction of sex. Actually there are only five states [36] in the United States where the statutes do not cover female homosexual relationships, and it is probable that the courts would interpret the statutes in nearly all of the other states to apply to females as well as to males.

These American statutes appear, however, to have gone beyond public opinion in their condemnation of homosexual relations between females, for practically no females seem to have been prosecuted or convicted anywhere in the United States under these laws. In our total sample of several hundred females who had had homosexual experience, only three had had minor difficulties and only one had had more serious difficulty with the police (Table 145), and none of the cases had been brought to court. We have cases of females who were

---

[32] The stringent penalty for homosexuality given in Leviticus 18:22 and 20:13 applies only to the male. Reference to female homosexuality does not appear until much later: Romans 1:26, where it is considered a "vile affection." The Talmud is relatively lenient regarding females, stating that female homosexual activity is a "mere obscenity" disqualifying a woman from marrying a priest. See Yebamoth 76a. Maimonides, according to Epstein 1948:138, felt that a female guilty of homosexuality should be flogged and excluded from the company of decent women, which is a penalty far less severe than the death penalty required for the male.

[33] Such medieval penalties for homosexuality are mentioned, for instance, in: Havelock Ellis 1915(2):346–347. Westermarck 1917(2):481–482. For a case of capital punishment levied on a female, see: Wharton 1932(1):1036–1037, footnote 18.

[34] There are specific statutes against female homosexuality only in Austria, Greece, Finland, and Switzerland.

[35] The applicability of the laws to both females and males are also noted in: Sherwin 1951:13. Ploscowe 1951:204. Pilpel and Zavin 1952:220.

[36] The states in which the statutes apparently do not apply to female homosexuality are: Conn., Ga., Ky., S. C., and Wis. Heterosexual cunnilingus has been held not "the crime against nature" in Illinois, Mississippi, and Ohio, and the decisions would supposedly apply to homosexual cunnilingus. In Arkansas, Colorado, Iowa, and Nebraska there is also some doubt as to the status of female homosexuality.

disciplined or more severely penalized for their homosexual activities in penal or other institutions, or while they were members of the Armed Forces of the United States, and we have cases in which social reactions constituted a severe penalty, but no cases of action in the courts.

Our search through the several hundred sodomy opinions which have been reported in this country between 1696 and 1952 has failed to reveal a single case sustaining the conviction of a female for homosexual activity. Our examination of the records of all the females admitted to the Indiana Women's Prison between 1874 and 1944 indicates that only one was sentenced for homosexual activity, and that was for activity which had taken place within the walls of another institution. Even in such a large city as New York, the records covering the years 1930 to 1939 show only one case of a woman convicted of homosexual sodomy, while there were over 700 convictions of males on homosexual charges, and several thousand cases of males prosecuted for public indecency, or for solicitation, or for other activity which was homosexual.[37] In our own more recent study of the enforcement of sex law in New York City we find three arrests of females on homosexual charges in the last ten years, but all of those cases were dismissed, although there were some tens of thousands of arrests and convictions of males charged with homosexual activity in that same period of time.

It is not altogether clear why there are such differences in the social and legal attitudes toward sexual activities between females and sexual activities between males. They may depend upon some of the following, and probably upon still other factors:

1. In Hittite, Jewish and other ancient cultures, women were socially less important than males, and their private activities were more or less ignored.

2. Both the incidences and frequencies of homosexual activity among females are in actuality much lower than among males. Nevertheless, the number of male cases which are brought to court are, even proportionately, tremendously higher than the number of female cases that reach court.

3. Male homosexual activity more often comes to public attention in street solicitation, public prostitution, and still other ways.

4. Male homosexual activity is condemned not only because it is homosexual, but because it may involve mouth-genital or anal contacts. It is not so widely understood that female homosexual techniques may also involve mouth-genital contacts.

---

[37] New York City data are to be found in the report of the Mayor's Committee on Sex Offenses 1944:75.

5. Homosexual activities more often interfere with the male's, less often interfere with the female's marrying or maintaining a marriage.

6. The Catholic Code emphasizes the sin involved in the wastage of semen in all male activities that are non-coital; it admits that female non-coital activities do not involve the same species of sin.

7. There is public objection to the effeminacy and some of the other personality traits of certain males who have homosexual histories; there is less often objection to the personalities of females who have homosexual histories.[38]

8. The public at large has some sympathy for females, especially older females, who are not married and who would have difficulty in finding sexual contacts if they did not engage in homosexual relations.

9. Many heterosexual males are erotically aroused when they consider the possibilities of two females in sexual activities. In not a few instances they may even encourage sexual contacts between females. There are fewer cases in our records of females being aroused by the contemplation of activities between males.

10. There are probably more males and fewer females who fear their own capacities to respond homosexually. For this reason, many males condemn homosexual activities in their own sex more severely than they condemn them among females.

11. Our social organization is presently much concerned over sexual relationships between adults and young children. This is the basis for a considerable portion of the action which is taken against male homosexual contacts; but relationships between older women and very young girls do not so often occur.

Basic Social Interests. When a female's homosexual experience interferes with her becoming married or maintaining a marriage into which she has entered, social interests may be involved. On the other hand, our social organization has never indicated that it is ready to penalize, by law, all persons who fail to become married.

When sexual relationships between adult females do not involve force

---

[38] The statistically unsupported opinion that females with homosexual histories frequently or usually exhibit masculine physical characters, behavior, or tastes appears, however, in such authors as the following: Féré 1904:189. Parke 1906:266, 300–301, 321. Bloch 1908:526. Carpenter 1908:30–31. Talmey 1910:158–161. Freud 1910:11. Havelock Ellis 1915(2):251–254. Krafft-Ebing 1922:336, 398–399. Kisch 1926:192. Kelly 1930:138. Moll 1931:226 ff. Potter 1933:158. Hesnard 1933:186. Caufeynon 1934:132. S. Kahn 1937:69, 134. Hutton 1937:126, 129. Henry 1941(2):1062, 1075, 1081. Deutsch 1944:325. Negri 1949:187. Keiser and Schaffer 1949:287, 289. Bergler 1951:318. Higher "masculinity" ratings on masculinity-femininity tests are reported by: Terman and Miles 1936:577–578. Henry 1941(2):1033–1034.

or undue coercion, and do not interfere with marital adjustments that might have been made, many persons, both in Europe and in our American culture, appear to be fairly tolerant of female homosexual activities. At any rate, many of those who feel that a question of morality may be involved, fail to believe that the basic social interests are sufficient to warrant any rigorous legal action against females who find a physiologic outlet and satisfy their emotional needs in sexual contacts with other females.

SUMMARY AND COMPARISONS OF FEMALE AND MALE

HOMOSEXUAL RESPONSES AND CONTACTS

	IN FEMALES	IN MALES
Physiologic and Psychologic Bases		
Inherent capacity to respond to any sufficient stimulus	Yes	Yes
Preference developed by psychologic conditioning	Yes	Yes
Among mammals homosexual behavior widespread	Yes	Yes
Anthropologic Background		
Data on homosexual behavior	Very few	Some
Heterosexual more acceptable in most cultures	Yes	Yes
Homosexual behavior sometimes permitted	Yes	Yes
Social concern over homosexual behavior	Less	More
Relation to Age and Marital Status		
Accumulative incidence		
Homosexual response, by age 45	28%	±50%
Homosexual experience, by age 45	20%	
Single	26%	±50%
Married	3%	±10%
Previously married	10%	
Homo. exper. to orgasm, by age 45	13%	±37%
Active incidence, to orgasm		
Single		
Age 16–20	3%	22%
Age 36–40	10%	40%
Age 46–50	4%	36%
Married	1–2%	2–8%
Previously married, age 16–50	3–7%	5–28%
Frequency to orgasm, per week		
Single		
Age Adol.–15	0.2	0.1
Age 21–30	0.3–0.4	0.4–0.7
Age 31–40	0.3–0.4	0.7–1.0
Married freq. lower than in single	Somewhat	Markedly
Percent of total outlet, before age 40		
Single, gradual increase	4–19%	5–22%
Married	Under 1%	Under 1%
Previously married, gradual increase	2–10%	9–26%
Number of years involved		
1 year or less	47%	
2 to 3 years	25%	

	IN FEMALES	IN MALES
Number of partners		
1–2	71%	51%
Over 10	4%	22%
Relation to Educational Level *		
Accumul. incid. to orgasm, by age 30		
Grade school	6%	27%
High school	5%	39%
College	10%⎫	34%
Graduate	14%⎭	
Act. incid. and % of outlet, higher		
Before age 20	In less educ.	In less educ.
After age 20	In better educ.	In less educ.
Frequency to orgasm higher	In less educ.	In less educ.
Relation to Parental Occupational Class	Little	Little or none
Relation to Decade of Birth	None	Little or none
Relation to Age at Onset of Adolescence	None	Higher incid. and freq. in early-adol.
Relation to Rural-Urban Background	Little	Incid. and freq. higher in urban
Relation to Religious Background		
Accum. and act. incid. higher among less dev.	Yes	Yes
Frequency to orgasm (active median)	No relation	Little relation
Percentage of total outlet	Higher among devout	No relation
Techniques in Homosexual Contacts		
Essentially same as in hetero. petting	Yes	Yes
Kissing and general body contacts	Extensive	
Genital techniques utilized	Later or never	Early and ± always
More effective than marital coitus	Yes	No
Hetero.-Homo. Ratings, *e.g.*, ages 20–35		
X: no socio-sexual response		
Single	14–19%	3–4%
Married	1–3%	0%
Previously married	5–8%	1–2%
0: entirely heterosexual experience		
Single	61–72%	53–78%
Married	89–90%	90–92%
Previously married	75–80%	
1–6: at least some homosexual	11–20%	18–42%
2–6: more than incidental homosexual	6–14%	13–38%
3–6: homo. as much or more than hetero.	4–11%	9–32%
4–6: mostly homosexual	3–8%	7–26%
5–6: ± exclusively homosexual	2–6%	5–22%
6: exclusively homosexual	1–3%	3–16%
Social Significance of Homosexuality		
Social concern in Anglo-Amer. culture	Little	Great
Most exper. indiv. regret least	Yes	Yes
Intent to have, highest among those with exper.	Yes	

* Beginning at this point, the data apply to single females and males only, unless otherwise indicated.

Summary and Comparisons (*Continued*)

	IN FEMALES	IN MALES
Approval for others, most often:		
By those with experience	Yes	Yes
For own sex	Yes	No
Moral and Legal Aspects of Homosexuality		
Injunction against, in:		
Ancient Near Eastern codes	No	Sometimes
Old Testament	No	Yes
Talmud	Yes	Yes
St. Paul and Christian codes	Yes	Yes
Formerly considered heresy	Yes	Yes
Death in ancient and medieval hist.	Rarely	Yes
Legally punishable in	43 states	48 states
Laws enforced	Almost never	Frequently

Table 126. Accumulative Incidence: Homosexual Contacts By Marital Status

Age	Total sample	While single	While married	Post-marital	Total sample	While single	While married	Post-marital
	%	*Percent*				*Cases*		
12	1	1			5733	5732		
15	5	5			5685	5681		
20	9	9	1	7	4318	3941	556	77
25	14	16	1	8	2779	1464	1338	174
30	17	21	2	11	2045	670	1216	221
35	19	26	2	7	1470	381	912	205
40	19	24	3	9	951	207	571	179
45	20	26	3	10	572	128	312	130

Table based on total sample, including single, married, and previously married females.

Table 127. Active Incidence, Frequency, and Percentage of Outlet Homosexual Contacts to Orgasm

Single Females, by Educational Level

Age during activity	Educ. level	Active incid. %	Active median freq. per wk.	% of total outlet	Cases in total sample	Age during activity	Educ. level	Active incid. %	Active median freq. per wk.	% of total outlet	Cases in total sample
Adol. –15	0–8	7	*0.7*	14	162	26–30	9–12	4		12	181
	9–12	3	*0.3*	6	983		13–16	7	*0.5*	10	313
	13–16	1	*0.1*	1	3271		17+	10	0.3	13	531
	17+	2	*0.2*	2	1128	31–35	9–12	6		6	65
16–20	0–8	8	*0.7*	9	143		13–16	7		11	139
	9–12	3	*0.3*	4	976		17+	11	*0.3*	18	309
	13–16	2	0.1	3	3299	36–40	13–16	12		17	68
	17+	5	0.3	6	1149		17+	11	*0.3*	21	205
21–25	9–12	3	*0.5*	7	537	41–45	17+	7		7	122
	13–16	4	*0.4*	8	1204	46–50	17+	5		5	80
	17+	7	0.3	7	1002						

Italic figures throughout the series of tables indicate that the calculations are based on less than 50 cases. No calculations are based on less than 11 cases. The dash (—) indicates a percentage or frequency smaller than any quantity which would be shown by a figure in the given number of decimal places.

Table 128. Active Incidence, Frequency, and Percentage of Outlet Homosexual Contacts to Orgasm

By Age and Marital Status

AGE DURING ACTIVITY	ACTIVE SAMPLE			TOTAL SAMPLE		CASES IN TOTAL SAMPLE
	Active incid. %	Median freq. per wk.	Mean frequency per wk.	Mean freq. per wk.	% of total outlet	
SINGLE FEMALES						
Adol.–15	2	0.2	0.6 ± 0.09	—	4	5677
16–20	3	0.2	0.6 ± 0.08	—	4	5613
21–25	5	0.3	1.0 ± 0.16	—	7	2810
26–30	8	0.4	1.3 ± 0.30	0.1 ± 0.03	11	1064
31–35	9	0.3	1.6 ± 0.63	0.1 ± 0.06	14	539
36–40	10	0.4	2.5 ± 0.96	0.3 ± 0.10	19	315
41–45	6			0.1 ± 0.04	6	179
46–50	4			—	4	109
51–55	0			0.0	0	58
56–60	0			0.0	0	27
MARRIED FEMALES						
16–20	1			—	—	578
21–25	1	0.3	0.9 ± 0.29	—	—	1654
26–30	1	0.2	1.2 ± 0.64	—	1	1662
31–35	1	0.3	1.0 ± 0.51	—	—	1246
36–40	2	0.1	0.4 ± 0.19	—	—	851
41–45	1			—	—	497
46–50	—			—	—	260
51–55	1			—	1	118
56–60	2			—	3	49
PREVIOUSLY MARRIED FEMALES						
16–20	6			—	2	72
21–25	6	0.7	1.1 ± 0.38	0.1 ± 0.03	4	239
26–30	6	2.0	2.3 ± 0.59	0.1 ± 0.05	9	328
31–35	7	1.1	2.4 ± 0.80	0.2 ± 0.06	10	304
36–40	3			—	2	245
41–45	4			0.1 ± 0.05	6	195
46–50	4			—	3	126
51–55	1			—	—	82
56–60	0			0.0	0	53

Table 129. Number of Years Involved in Homosexual Contacts

Including activity with and without orgasm

NUMBER OF TIMES OR YEARS	TOTAL SAMPLE	AGE AT REPORTING			
		Adol.–20	21–30	31–40	41–50
		Percent			
1–10 times	32	26	35	32	33
1 year or less	47	48	51	44	44
2–3 years	25	26	27	21	25
4–5 years	10	15	7	9	9
6–10 years	9	11	11	8	7
11–20 years	7		4	14	8
21+ years	2			4	7
Number of cases	709	137	202	202	122

Table 130. Partners and Techniques in Homosexual Contacts

PARTNERS		TECHNIQUES		
Number	%	Technique utilized	By females with limited exper.	By females with extensive exper.
			%	%
1 only	51	Kissing: simple		95
2	20	Kissing: deep		77
3	9	Breast: manual stimul.	27	97
4	5	Breast: oral stimul.	7	85
5	4	Genital: manual stimul.	67	98
6–10	7	Genital: oral stimul.	16	78
11–20	3	Genital apposition	24	56
21+	1			
Cases with exper.	591		499	145

Data on kissing unavailable on females with limited experience.

Table 131. Accumulative Incidence: Homosexual Arousal, Experience, and Orgasm

By Educational Level

AGE	TOTAL SAMPLE	EDUCATIONAL LEVEL				TOTAL SAMPLE	EDUCATIONAL LEVEL			
		0–8	9–12	13–16	17+		0–8	9–12	13–16	17+
HOMOSEXUAL AROUSAL										
	%	*Percent*				*Cases*	*Cases*			
8	2	1	1	1	2	5720	179	999	3226	1124
10	3	2	3	2	4	5699	179	999	3226	1124
12	5	3	6	4	6	5674	179	999	3226	1124
15	10	11	10	9	11	5614	173	998	3226	1124
20	17	13	14	17	21	4267	127	849	2168	1123
25	23	9	16	24	28	2743	117	678	1020	928
30	25	10	18	25	33	2017	109	494	697	717
35	27	10	21	28	33	1447	91	317	487	552
40	27	10	18	28	32	937	67	189	301	380
45	28		17	28	36	565		124	165	231
HOMOSEXUAL CONTACTS: EXPERIENCE										
	%	*Percent*				*Cases*	*Cases*			
12	1	2	1	1	1	5733	179	1007	3267	1142
15	5	9	5	4	4	5685	175	1006	3267	1142
20	9	11	7	9	12	4318	129	854	2194	1141
25	14	8	8	14	19	2779	119	683	1035	942
30	17	9	10	17	24	2045	111	500	707	727
35	19	9	12	17	25	1470	93	322	493	562
40	19	10	10	19	24	951	68	193	304	386
45	20		8	20	27	572		127	166	234
HOMOSEXUAL CONTACTS TO ORGASM										
	%	*Percent*				*Cases*	*Cases*			
12	1	2	1	—	—	5779	178	1012	3301	1152
15	2	9	3	1	2	5733	174	1011	3301	1152
20	4	8	4	3	6	4359	128	860	2220	1151
25	7	5	5	7	10	2803	118	687	1046	952
30	10	6	5	10	14	2058	110	502	713	733
35	11	7	5	11	15	1480	92	323	498	567
40	12	7	5	13	15	956	68	194	305	389
45	13		6	13	19	574		127	166	236

Table based on total sample, including single, married, and previously married females.

Table 132. Accumulative Incidence: Homosexual Contacts to Orgasm
By Parental Occupational Class

AGE	PARENTAL CLASS				PARENTAL CLASS			
	2+3	4	5	6+7	2+3	4	5	6+7
	Percent				Cases			
12	1	—	—	1	973	812	1526	2684
15	5	2	1	2	943	810	1523	2671
20	5	3	4	4	711	631	1139	2018
25	6	6	7	9	511	421	722	1225
30	9	6	9	12	379	313	506	907
35	10	6	9	13	268	197	345	692
40	9	4	10	14	174	119	206	470
45	7	4	15	17	108	71	117	282

Table based on total sample, including single, married, and previously married
females.
The occupational classes are as follows: 2+3 = unskilled and semi-skilled labor.
4 = skilled labor. 5 = lower white collar class. 6+7 = upper white collar and
professional classes.

Table 133. Active Incidence and Percentage of Outlet
Homosexual Contacts to Orgasm

Single Females, by Parental Occupational Class

Age	Parental class	Active incid. %	% of total outlet	Cases in total sample	Age	Parental class	Active incid. %	% of total outlet	Cases in total sample
Adol.									
–15	2+3	5	8	947	26–30	2+3	5	11	195
	4	2	3	796		4	6	8	181
	5	2	2	1506		5	7	6	275
	6+7	1	2	2654		6+7	10	14	447
16–20	2+3	5	5	881	31–35	2+3	4	14	96
	4	3	4	796		4	3	1	91
	5	2	3	1512		5	9	11	148
	6+7	?	4	2649		6+7	13	17	224
21–25	2+3	4	3	461	36–40	2+3	5	25	62
	4	4	6	422		5	9	6	85
	5	4	4	735		6+7	12	23	141
	6+7	5	9	1283					

Table 134. Accumulative Incidence: Homosexual Contacts to Orgasm

By Decade of Birth

AGE	DECADE OF BIRTH				Bf. 1900	DECADE OF BIRTH		
	Bf. 1900	1900–1909	1910–1919	1920–1929		1900–1909	1910–1919	1920–1929
	Percent					*Cases*		
12	—	—	—	1	456	783	1341	3072
15	2	2	2	3	456	783	1341	3058
20	5	6	4	3	456	783	1340	1780
25	8	9	7	6	456	783	1191	373
30	9	10	10		456	783	819	
35	11	11	13		456	754	270	
40	11	12			456	499		
45	12	17			435	139		

Table based on total sample, including single, married, and previously married females.

Table 135. Active Incidence and Percentage of Outlet
Homosexual Contacts to Orgasm

Single Females, by Decade of Birth

Age	Decade of birth	Active incid. %	% of total outlet	Cases in total sample	Age	Decade of birth	Active incid. %	% of total outlet	Cases in total sample
Adol.									
–15	Bf. 1900	2	1	436	26–30	Bf. 1900	6	18	218
	1900–1909	1	3	760		1900–1909	8	10	344
	1910–1919	2	3	1319		1910–1919	9	10	448
	1920–1929	2	6	3049		1920–1929	7	9	54
16–20	Bf. 1900	4	3	451	31–35	Bf. 1900	8	19	151
	1900–1909	5	6	772		1900–1909	8	14	228
	1910–1919	3	5	1328		1910–1919	11	8	160
	1920–1929	2	4	2999	36–40	Bf. 1900	8	19	123
21–25	Bf. 1900	5	6	366		1900–1909	9	17	165
	1900–1909	6	7	617					
	1910–1919	6	7	987	41–45	Bf. 1900	4	6	116
	1920–1929	3	7	843		1900–1909	8	3	63

Table 136. Accumulative Incidence: Homosexual Contacts to Orgasm
By Age at Onset of Adolescence

AGE	ADOLESCENT					ADOLESCENT				
	By 11	At 12	At 13	At 14	At 15+	By 11	At 12	At 13	At 14	At 15+
	Percent					*Cases*				
12	2	1				1203	1681			
15	3	2	2	2	2	1185	1666	1738	792	348
20	5	3	5	5	4	876	1227	1321	649	283
25	8	6	8	8	8	511	741	848	465	235
30	11	9	9	11	10	355	488	650	368	196
35	12	11	11	11	11	250	322	470	281	156
40	14	11	12	12	10	151	199	297	191	117
45	13	14	14	13	11	93	111	174	119	76

Table based on total sample, including single, married, and previously married females.

Table 137. Active Incidence and Percentage of Outlet
Homosexual Contacts to Orgasm
Single Females, by Age at Onset of Adolescence

Age during activity	Age at adol.	Active incid. %	% of total outlet	Cases in total sample	Age during activity	Age at adol.	Active incid. %	% of total outlet	Cases in total sample
Adol.–15	8–11	3	6	1203	26–30	8–11	10	12	196
	12	2	3	1684		12	9	24	266
	13	2	2	1747		13	5	5	323
	14	2	6	796		14	10	11	192
	15+	2	3	262		15+	7	6	87
16–20	8–11	3	4	1166	31–35	8–11	10	11	99
	12	2	4	1638		12	7	28	122
	13	3	4	1700		13	8	2	162
	14	5	6	777		14	13	16	109
	15+	3	4	345					
21–25	8–11	5	11	526	36–40	8–11	11	9	65
	12	3	5	770		12	14	45	66
	13	5	6	851		13	6	2	96
	14	7	7	460		14	13	25	62
	15+	6	5	203					

Table 138. Accumulative Incidence: Homosexual Contacts to Orgasm By Rural-Urban Background

Age	Rural	Urban	Rural	Urban	Age	Rural	Urban	Rural	Urban
	Percent		*Cases*			*Percent*		*Cases*	
12	1	1	399	5200	30	6	10	168	1796
15	3	2	397	5161	35	7	12	124	1285
20	4	4	335	3873	40	8	13	84	825
25	5	8	223	2465	45	10	14	60	488

Table based on total sample, including single, married, and previously married females.

Table 139. Active Incidence and Percentage of Outlet Homosexual Contacts to Orgasm

Single Females, by Rural-Urban Background

Age during activity	Back-grnd.	Active incid. %	% of total outlet	Cases in total sample	Age during activity	Back-grnd.	Active incid. %	% of total outlet	Cases in total sample
Adol.–15	Rural	3	7	388	26–30	Rural	2	2	104
	Urban	2	4	5132		Urban	9	12	915
16–20	Rural	4	5	386	31–35	Rural	2	—	64
	Urban	3	4	5080		Urban	10	15	453
21–25	Rural	3	3	229					
	Urban	5	7	2484					

Table 140. Accumulative Incidence: Homosexual Contacts to Orgasm By Religious Background

AGE	PROTESTANT			CATHOLIC			JEWISH	
	Dev.	Moder.	Inact.	Dev.	Moder.	Inact.	Moder.	Inact.
				Percent				
12	1	1	1	1	1	2	—	—
15	2	1	2	3	4	8	1	2
20	3	2	7	5	4	13	2	5
25	5	5	12	5	8	22	2	7
30	7	6	16	3	12	28	3	9
35	7	9	17	5		25	4	11
40	8	10	16					13
45	11	13	20					15
				Cases				
12	1234	1166	1090	390	153	171	575	985
15	1217	1156	1083	385	151	171	574	981
20	922	923	976	284	114	146	334	692
25	566	587	739	177	76	107	187	413
30	424	435	552	124	51	79	136	294
35	337	315	419	78		52	77	205
40	237	212	274					127
45	150	132	153					74

Table based on total sample, including single, married, and previously married females.

Table 141. Active Incidence, Frequency, and Percentage of Outlet

Homosexual Contacts to Orgasm

Single Females, by Religious Background

Age during activity	Religious group	Active incid. %	Active median freq. per wk.	% of total outlet	Cases in total sample
Adol.–15	Protestant				
	Devout	2	0.3	6	1218
	Moderate	1	0.4	4	1147
	Inactive	2	0.2	2	1063
	Catholic				
	Devout	3	0.3	13	382
	Moderate	3		6	150
	Inactive	8	0.4	6	169
	Jewish				
	Devout	0		0	107
	Moderate	1		—	571
	Inactive	2	0.1	2	978
16–20	Protestant				
	Devout	3	0.2	6	1197
	Moderate	2	0.2	2	1133
	Inactive	5	0.2	5	1065
	Catholic				
	Devout	5	0.6	15	372
	Moderate	4		6	139
	Inactive	10	0.7	8	160
	Jewish				
	Devout	1		—	107
	Moderate	—		—	571
	Inactive	2	0.2	2	972
21–25	Protestant				
	Devout	3	0.3	10	604
	Moderate	3	0.4	4	615
	Inactive	8	0.4	8	676
	Catholic				
	Devout	4		15	196
	Moderate	5		12	57
	Inactive	18	0.5	13	91
	Jewish				
	Moderate	0		0	192
	Inactive	4	0.3	6	396
26–30	Protestant				
	Devout	5	0.4	17	221
	Moderate	4	0.4	4	249
	Inactive	13	0.5	13	309
	Catholic				
	Devout	5		29	79
31–35	Protestant				
	Devout	7		34	121
	Moderate	6		2	127
	Inactive	15	0.4	11	159
36–40	Protestant				
	Devout	7		37	76
	Moderate	6		2	77
	Inactive	16	0.5	18	102

Table 142. Active Incidence: Heterosexual-Homosexual Ratings By Marital Status

AGE	0	1–6	1	2	3	4	5	6	X	
					RATING					

SINGLE FEMALES

AGE	Percent				Percent				%	Cases
	0	1–6	1	2	3	4	5	6	X	
5	7	6	—	—	2	—	—	3	87	5914
10	7	11	—	1	2	—	—	8	82	5820
15	34	6	2	1	1	—	—	2	60	5714
20	72	11	5	2	1	1	1	1	17	3746
25	72	14	4	3	1	3	1	2	14	1315
30	67	18	5	4	2	3	2	2	15	622
35	61	20	6	3	3	2	3	3	19	370
37	61	17	5	3	2	2	2	3	22	290

MARRIED FEMALES

AGE	Percent				Percent				%	Cases
	0	1–6	1	2	3	4	5	6	X	
17	80	11	9	1	0	0	0	1	9	89
20	89	8	5	1	1	—	—	—	3	545
25	90	8	6	1	—	—	—	—	2	1331
30	90	9	6	2	—	—	—	—	1	1215
35	89	10	7	2	—	—	—	—	1	908
40	89	9	6	2	—	0	—	—	2	569
45	89	9	6	2	—	0	—	1	2	311
50	88	8	4	3	0	0	1	0	4	154

PREVIOUSLY MARRIED FEMALES

AGE	Percent				Percent				%	Cases
	0	1–6	1	2	3	4	5	6	X	
20	80	14	6	1	3	3	0	1	6	81
25	75	17	7	3	0	1	3	3	8	178
30	78	14	6	2	1	2	1	2	8	224
35	78	17	9	3	0	1	2	2	5	204
40	76	14	8	2	2	0	1	1	10	177

Definitions of the ratings are as follows: 0 = entirely heterosexual. 1–6 = with homosexual history, of any sort. 1 = largely heterosexual, but with incidental homosexual history. 2 = largely heterosexual, but with a distinct homosexual history. 3 = equally heterosexual and homosexual. 4 = largely homosexual, but with distinct heterosexual history. 5 = largely homosexual, but with incidental heterosexual history. 6 = entirely homosexual. X = without either. See p. 471.

Table 143. Active Incidence: Females with Some Homosexual Rating By Educational Level and Marital Status

AGE	TOTAL SAMPLE	EDUCATIONAL LEVEL			TOTAL SAMPLE	EDUCATIONAL LEVEL		
		9–12	13–16	17+		9–12	13–16	17+
			SINGLE FEMALES					
	%		Percent		Cases		Cases	
5	6	5	6	8	5914	1014	3302	1152
10	11	12	11	12	5820	1014	3301	1151
15	6	6	5	8	5714	1005	3299	1150
20	11	7	10	13	3746	641	1943	1079
25	14	8	14	17	1315	229	423	621
30	18	8	17	21	622	85	167	343
35	20		28	20	370		82	237
			MARRIED FEMALES					
	%		Percent		Cases		Cases	
20	8	7	9	11	545	194	253	63
25	8	5	10	11	1331	408	563	296
30	9	6	10	11	1215	342	475	331
35	10	6	11	13	908	235	346	271
40	9	4	12	10	569	139	204	188
45	9	4	10	13	311	83	111	93
			PREVIOUSLY MARRIED FEMALES					
	%		Percent		Cases		Cases	
25	17	11	18		178	64	65	
30	14	14	12	16	224	76	73	61
35	17	16	20	17	204	55	72	60
40	14		13	18	177		61	62

The table includes all females with heterosexual-homosexual ratings of 1 to 6. These females had had some homosexual history, either psychologic or overt, in the particular year shown. Those with a rating of 1 had minimum homosexual histories; those with a rating of 6 had the maximum and therefore exclusive homosexual histories. See Table 142.

Table 144. Attitudes of Females Toward Homosexual Activity

Correlation of attitudes with subject's own homosexual experience

ATTITUDES	ACCEPT FOR SELF		APPROVE HOMOSEXUAL ACTIVITY				WOULD KEEP FRIENDS WHO HAD HOMOSEXUAL EXPERIENCE			
			For other females		For males		Female friends		Male friends	
	Subject		Subject		Subject		Subject		Subject	
	With exp.	No exp.	With exp.	No exp.	With exp.	No exp.	With exp.	No exp.	With exp.	No exp.
	%	%	%	%	%	%	%	%	%	%
Yes	18	1	23	4	18	4	88	55	74	51
Uncertain	20	4	62	57	60	54	8	23	16	23
No	62	95	15	39	22	42	4	22	10	26
Number of cases	683	4500	653	4758	616	4718	251	941	122	935

Table 145. Social Difficulties Resulting from Homosexual Experience

Source of difficulty	Total cases	Cases of major difficulty	Cases of minor difficulty
Home	21	13	8
School	8	4	4
Business	6	2	4
Police	4	1	3
Institutional	3	1	2
No. of cases of difficulties	42	21	21
No. of females with diffic.	38		
No. of females without diffic.	104		
% of females with diffic.	27		

There were 710 females in the sample with homosexual experience, but only the 142 with the most extensive experience are included in these calculations. None of those with more minor experience had run into such social difficulties.

Chapter 12

ANIMAL CONTACTS

Universally, human males have shown a considerable interest in unusual, rare, and sometimes fantastically impossible types of sexual activity. In consequence there is a great deal more discussion and a more extensive literature about such things as incest, transvestism, necrophilia, extreme forms of fetishism, sado-masochism, and animal contacts than the actual occurrence of any of these phenomena would justify.

From the earliest recorded history, and from the still more ancient archives of folklore and mythology, there are man-made tales of sexual relations between the human female and no end of other species of animals. The mythology of primitive, pre-literate peoples in every part of the world has included such tales.[1] Classic Greek and Roman mythology had accounts of lovers appearing as asses, Zeus appearing as a swan, females having sexual relations with bears, apes, bulls, goats, horses, ponies, wolves, snakes, crocodiles, and still lower vertebrates. The literary and artistic efforts of more recent centuries have never abandoned these themes; erotic literature and drawings, including some of the world's great art, have repeatedly come back to the same idea.[2]

Much of this interest in rare or non-existent forms of sexual performance may represent the male's wishful thinking, a projection of his own desire to engage in a variety of sexual activities, or his erotic response to the idea that other persons, especially females, may be involved in such activities. This stems from the male's capacity to be aroused erotically by a variety of psychosexual stimuli (Chapter 16). Females, because of their lesser dependence on psychologic stimulation, are less inclined to be interested in activities which lie beyond the immediately available techniques, and rarely, either in their conversation, in their written literature, or in their art, deal with fantastic or impossible sorts of sexual activity. Human males, and not the females themselves, are the ones who imagine that females are frequently involved in sexual contacts with animals of other species. In fact, human males may be

---

[1] Folk tales and myths of human females in contact with male animals are summarized in: Dubois-Desaulle 1933:31–47. Ford 1945:31. Leach and Fried 1949(1):61.

[2] As examples of the persistence of this theme into more modern life, note the hundreds of representations of "Leda and the Swan," the magazine cartoons showing a female abducted by an ape, the still-current "Prince Charming" nursery tale, and motion pictures of gorillas interested in human females.

responsible for initiating some of the animal contacts and especially the exhibitionistic contacts in which some females (particularly prostitutes) engage.[3]

Considerable confusion has been introduced into our thinking by this failure to distinguish between sexual activities that are frequent and a fundamental part of the pattern of behavior, and sexual activities which are rare and of significance only to a limited number of persons. Psychologic and psychiatric texts are as likely to give as much space to overt sado-masochistic or necrophilic activity as they give to homosexual and mouth-genital activities, but the last two are widespread and significant parts of the lives of many females and males, while many of the other types of behavior are in actuality rare.

BASES OF INTER-SPECIFIC SEXUAL CONTACTS

As we have already seen, males may be more often involved than females in a variety of non-coital sexual activities. Sexual contacts between the human male and animals of other species are not rare in the rural segments of our American population, and probably not infrequent in other parts of the world. Some 17 per cent of the farm boys in our sample had had some sexual contact with farm animals to the point of orgasm, while half or more of the boys from certain rural areas of the United States had had such experience (see our 1948:671–673). It will be profitable to try to analyze the factors which account for the lesser frequencies of animal contacts among the females in the present sample.

In discussing this matter in our volume on the male (1948:667–668), we pointed out that there is no sufficient explanation, either in biologic or psychologic science, for the confinement of sexual activity to contacts between females and males of the same species. We have no sufficient knowledge to explain why an insect of one species should not mate or attempt to mate with many other species, why different species of birds do not indiscriminately interbreed, or why any species of mammal should confine its sexual activity as often as it does. There are obvious anatomic problems which prevent the indiscriminate, interspecific mating of some forms, but no known anatomic or psychologic factors which would prevent most of the more closely related species from trying to make inter-specific matings.[4] We have also pointed out

---

[3] The observation of exhibitions of coitus between prostitutes and animals is frequently recorded in our male histories; they are also mentioned in: Kisch 1907:201. Bloch 1908:644, 646. Krafft-Ebing 1922:562. Rohleder 1925:370. Kelly 1930:184–185. Robinson 1936:46. Negri 1949:217. London and Caprio 1950:21–22.

[4] But records of sexual activity attempted between animals of gross morphologic disparity are in: Karsch 1900:129 (female eland with ostrich). Féré 1904:79–80 (male dog with chicken). Hamilton 1914:308 (male monkey with snake). Zell 1921(1):238 (stallion with human). Bingham 1928:71–72 (female chimpanzee with cat). Williams 1943:445 (cow with human).

that evidence is beginning to accumulate that individuals of quite un-related species do make inter-specific contacts more often than biologists have heretofore allowed. The intensive study of the movements of individual birds, which bird-banding techniques have made possible, has shown that there is a great deal more inter-specific mating among birds than we have previously realized. More intensive taxonomic and genetic work in the field has shown the existence of a large number of inter-specific hybrids, and these provide evidence that inter-specific mating occurred at some time or other and, more than that, that such matings were viable and gave rise to fertile offspring. The successful matings must represent only a small proportion of the inter-specific contacts which are actually attempted or made.

It is not a problem of explaining why individuals of different species should be attracted to each other sexually. The real problem lies in explaining why individuals do not regularly make contacts with species other than their own. In actuality, it is probable that the human animal makes inter-specific sexual contacts less often than some of the other species of mammals, primarily because he has no close relative among the other mammals, and secondarily because of the considerable significance which psychologic stimuli have in limiting his sexual activity.

We have previously pointed out (1948:675–676) that the farm boy may begin his sexual contacts with animals because he responds sympathetically upon observing their sexual activities. With the mating animals he can, to a considerable degree, identify his own anatomic and physiologic capacities. Moreover, the boy may come into contact with freer discussions of sex at an earlier age than most boys who are not raised on farms, and in many instances he has an example set for him by other boys whom he discovers having sexual contacts with the farm animals. Not infrequently he hears adults in the community discuss such matters. The comments are usually bantering and not too severely condemnatory.

But none of these factors are of equal significance to the female. At earlier ages, girls do not discuss sexual activities as freely or as frequently as boys do (p. 675), and they less often observe sexual activity among other girls or even among the farm animals. The specific record (p. 663) shows that some 32 per cent of the adult males in the sample had been erotically aroused when they saw animals in coitus, while only 16 per cent of the females had been so aroused. The histories indicate that many of the farm-bred females had been oblivious to the coital activities which went on about them. Quite frequently they had been kept away from breeding animals by their parents, and we find that a good many of the rural females in the sample had not learned that coitus was possible in any animal, let alone the human, until they were adolescent or still older. As a result, the animal contacts which the females had made were usually the consequence of their own discovery of such possibilities, whether the first experiences were had in pre-adolescence or in more adult years. Most of the farm boys had acquired that much information some years before adolescence.

It is not surprising then, to find that the incidences and frequencies of the animal contacts made by the females in the sample were much lower than the incidences and frequencies which we found among the males in the sample.[5]

INCIDENCES AND FREQUENCIES

In Pre-Adolescence. A few of the females—1.5 per cent of the total sample—had had some sort of sexual relation with other animals in pre-adolescence, usually as a result of some accidental physical contact with the household pet, a cat or a dog, or as a result of curiosity which had led to the exploration of the animal's anatomy, or through some deliberate approach on the part of the animal itself. Among the pre-adolescent females who had had any such experience, the contacts were incidental in 38 per cent of the cases. In most of the pre-adolescent cases (92 per cent), however, the girl had had contacts which had aroused her erotically, and in 20 per cent of these pre-adolescent cases she had reached orgasm. Among the 659 females in the total sample who had reached orgasm prior to adolescence, 1.7 per cent had experienced their first orgasm in contact with other species of animals.

Among the 89 females who had had pre-adolescent animal experience, general body contacts and masturbation of the animal had been involved in most cases. But out of the 5940 females in the sample, 23 had had dogs put their mouths on their genitalia, 6 had had cats similarly perform, and 2 had had coitus with dogs.

Among Adult Females. Some 3.6 per cent of the females in the sample had had sexual contacts of some sort with animals of other species after they had become adolescent. Some 3.0 per cent of the females in the total sample had been erotically aroused by their animal contacts. In only 1.2 per cent of the total sample had there been repeated genital contacts which aroused the female erotically, or mouth-genital relations or actual coitus. This means that only one female in each eighty in the sample had had such specific sexual contacts with animals after the onset of adolescence. In addition to the overt experience with animals,

---

[5] A number of other authors have also recognized that females make animal contacts less often than males. See, for instance: Casañ ca.1900(4):67. Bloch 1908:642; 1909:704. Kelly 1930:183. Dubois-Desaulle 1933:143. Chideckel 1935:312.

1 per cent of the females had fantasied such contacts while they masturbated (Table 38), and 1 per cent had dreamt of having animal contacts (Table 55).

Half of the females had had their contacts with animals after the
onset of adolescence and before the age of twenty-one, but there were
95 older females who had had such contacts, in some instances even
in their late forties. Most of the contacts had occurred among single
females, although there were 44 cases among married or previously
married females.[6] Contacts had occurred among females of every educational level, although most of them (81 per cent) had occurred in
the better educated segments of the sample, largely because that group
is better represented in the sample.

Nearly all of the contacts had occurred with dogs or cats which were
household pets. Nearly three-quarters (74 per cent) of the females had
had contacts with dogs.[7] Over half of the relationships had involved
only general body contacts with the animal. In some instances, the
females had only touched the animal's genitalia; in other instances,
there had been more specific masturbation of the animal. For some 21
per cent of the females, the animal had manipulated the human
genitalia with its mouth, but in only one of the adult cases had there
been actual coitus with the animal. There were, however, additional
cases of coitus in other segments of the female sample which were not
utilized in the calculations for the present volume (p. 22).

In 25 out of the 5793 adult histories on which we have data concerning animal contacts, the human female had been brought to orgasm
by her sexual contacts with the animal, chiefly as a result of the animal's
manipulation of her genitalia with its mouth.

The frequencies of the animal contacts had been low, amounting
to only a single experience in about half of the cases. In 47 per cent of
the 91 cases which had involved the most specific sort of contact there
had been two or more experiences, and in 23 per cent of the cases there
had been six or more contacts. There were only 13 females in the sample of 5793 who had reached orgasm by contact with an animal of another species more than three times up to the age at which they contributed their records to the study. There were 6 females, each of whom

---

[6] Talmey 1910:162 notes that animal contacts are commoner among unmarried
females. Bloch 1933:185 feels that the married and unmarried are equal in this
respect.

[7] That the majority of female contacts with animals are had with dogs is also noted
in: Mantegazza 1885:128–131. Moraglia 1897:6. Féré 1904:184. Havelock
Ellis 1906(5):83. Hoyer 1929:252. Kelly 1930:184. Chideckel 1935:315.
Haire 1937:484. Hirschfeld 1940:138.

had reached orgasm more than 125 times in her animal contacts, and there was one female who had reached orgasm perhaps 900 times in such contacts.

SIGNIFICANCE OF ANIMAL CONTACTS

The incidences and frequencies and significance of animal contacts as a source of outlet for the human female are obviously a minute fraction of what most human males have guessed them to be. The present data consequently illuminate some of the basic differences between the sexual psychology of the human female and male, and show something of the effects that such differences in psychology may have on the overt behavior of the two sexes.

In ancient codes and laws, there were frequent references to human males having animal contacts, and judgments and penalties were prescribed for such activity. The more ancient codes, however, appear to have ignored the possibilities of females having sexual contacts with animals,[8] and there are apparently only two references, both of them in Leviticus (parts of which represent a later development in Biblical law), concerning females who have sexual contacts with animals.[9] The Biblical references involve the prohibition of such acts, and demand death as the penalty for both the female and the animal. The Talmud, however, makes more frequent reference to such female activity, repeating the Biblical injunctions against it and imposing the same penalties. Finally the Talmud goes so far as to prohibit a female being alone with an animal because of the possible suspicion that she might have sexual contact with it, and this is unusual because it gives the matter more attention than is ordinarily given it in any of the other codes.[10]

The Catholic code on animal contacts logically follows the general concept that sexual function is justified only as a means of procreation, primarily in marriage, and all contacts between the human female or male and an animal of another species are consequently contrary to nature, a perversion of the primary function of sex, and sinful in deed or desire. The judgment would appear to apply to female as well as to

---

[8] See: Pritchard 1950:196–197. The code of Lipit-Ishtar, the code of Hammurabi, the Middle Assyrian Laws, and the Neo-Babylonian Laws contain no references to animal contacts, but the Hittite Laws have five references to male contacts with animals. Since the Hittite Laws are in essential agreement with other Near-Eastern codes, it may well be that the makers of these codes held the same opinion as the Hittites in regard to animal contacts. It must be recalled, however, that some of these codes are not known *in toto*.

[9] The injunction against and penalty for contact between a human female and an animal is in Leviticus 18:23 and 20:16. Also Exodus 22:19 might be considered as applying to both sexes.

[10] The Talmudic references to female contacts with animals are in: Kethuboth 65a, Yebamoth 59b, Sanhedrin 2a, 15a, 53a, and 55a, Abodah Zarah 22b–23a.

male contacts.[11] Touching the genitalia of an animal even out of curiosity may be a sin, and touching it with lust may be a grave sin.[12] The opinion is expressed that experience in animal contacts might be sufficient grounds for a separation.[13]

The legal codes of essentially all of the states prohibit sexual relations between the human animal and animals of other species, usually rating them as bestiality or sodomy, and usually attaching the same penalties that are attached to homosexual relations. In a few instances the penalties are lower than those for homosexual relations; in some instances they are very severe.[14] When there is no specific statute covering the matter, the common law ruling against bestiality would sometimes apply.[15] In some instances the statutes specifically indicate that they are applicable to both females and males.[16] In many instances they do not specifically designate the sex to which they apply, but in most such cases they would be interpreted to cover both sexes. It is probable, however, that the lawmakers in most instances had male activity in mind when they framed their statutes; and the question is quite academic, for cases of females who have been prosecuted for animal contacts are practically unknown in the legal record.

There are in the older literature a few records of females receiving the death penalty for such contacts, particularly in medieval history.[17]

---

[11] Catholic interpretations of animal contacts are in: Arregui 1927:153–154, and Davis 1946(2):247, who specifically include the female. The "penitentials," partially secular and partially religious codes dating before the 13th century, occasionally refer to contacts between human females and animals. According to Havelock Ellis 1906(5):87–88, Burchard's penitential stipulates a seven-year penance for a female who has had sexual contact with a horse.

[12] Touching an animal's genitalia may vary from a light to a grave sin depending on the motivation, according to Davis 1946(2):249. Arregui 1927:156 adds that when such touching is necessary, as in animal breeding, it is best that it be done by older or married persons.

[13] Using the term "divorce" to mean permanent separation with "the conjugal bond remaining," Noldin 1904(3):sec. 665 states: According to the probable opinion of learned men any alien sexual intercourse, even that which happens through sodomy or bestiality, suffices for instituting a divorce.

[14] Forty-four states specifically forbid sex relations with animals, and cases in three of the remaining (Ark., Del., and Vt.) indicate it is a crime, leaving only New Hampshire where any such activity is not a felony or its equivalent. In Georgia up until 1949 the minimum penalty for the crime against nature when committed with another human was "imprisonment at labor in the penitentiary for and during the natural life of the person convicted," whereas the penalty for "bestiality" was five to twenty years imprisonment. In eight states (Calif., Colo., Ida., Mo., Mont., Nev., N. M., and S. C.) the possible maximum sentence is life imprisonment.

[15] For the application of the common law ruling, see: State v. LaForrest 1899:45 Atl. (Vt.) 225.

[16] For the application of the statutes to both female and male, see, for example: Georgia Code 1933:Title 26 §5903. Maryland Code 1951:Article 27 §627.

[17] The death penalty for females making contacts with animals in medieval times is noted in: Mantegazza 1885:128–131. Havelock Ellis 1906(5):88. Hernandez [Fleuret and Perceau] 1920:83–94. Dubois-Desaulle 1933:58, 81–89. Robinson 1936:42–44.

We do not have any instance of legal action against any of the cases in our sample, and we find only one case in the published court records here in the United States.[18]

Considering the rarity of sexual contacts between females and animals of other species, it is interesting to find specific recognition of such contacts in the moral and legal codes.

SUMMARY AND COMPARISONS OF FEMALE AND MALE

ANIMAL CONTACTS

	IN FEMALES	IN MALES
Among mammals, inter-specific contacts common	Yes	Yes
Anthropologic Background		
Animal contacts in other cultures	Rare in all	Occasional in some
Animal contacts in myth and folklore	Commonly	Less often
Incidence and Frequency		
Accumulative incid. in pre-adol.	1.5%	3%
Erotic response	1.4%	
Orgasm	0.3%	Rare
As source of first orgasm	Rare	Rare
Accumulative incid. in adult	3.6%	8% to orgasm
Erotic response	3.0%	
Orgasm	0.4%	8%
Primarily before age 21	50%	Yes
Frequency, active sample, bf. age 21	Usually 1–2 times	0.1 per wk.
Animals chiefly involved	Dog, cat	Farm animals, pets
Techniques		
General body contact	Common	Some
Masturbation of animal	Some	Common
Anim. mouth on human genit.	Some	Some
Coitus	Very rare	Common
Social Significance		
As a source of outlet	Insignif.	1%
Legal and religious injunctions		
In Hammurabi's code	No	No
In Hittite code	No	Yes
In Old Testament	No	Yes
In Talmud	Yes	Yes
In American statute law	Yes	Yes

---

[18] The only published case in the U.S. of a female convicted because she had had contact with an animal is in: State v. Tarrant 1949:80 N.E.2d (Ohio) 509.

Chapter 13

TOTAL SEXUAL OUTLET

In the present study, we have tried to secure data on (1) the incidences and frequencies of sexual activities among the females in the available sample; (2) the incidences and frequencies of their responses to socio-sexual contacts and to psychosexual stimuli; and (3) the incidences and frequencies of the responses which led to orgasm.

From most of the subjects it has been possible to secure incidence data on the overt, physical contacts which were recognizably sexual because they were genital or because they brought specific erotic response. From most of the subjects it has also been possible to secure frequency data on most of those contacts, but this has not always been possible because there are situations in which the genital anatomy is not involved, and then it is sometimes difficult to determine whether the contacts or emotional responses are sexual in any real sense of the term (Chapter 15). It has been difficult, for instance, to secure exact data on the incidences and frequencies of self-stimulation which was non-genital, on the frequencies of sexual dreams which did not lead to orgasm, and on the incidences and frequencies of the non-genital socio-sexual contacts. As we have already pointed out (p. 235), there is every gradation between a simple good night kiss or a friendly embrace, and a kiss or an embrace which is definitely sexual in its intent and consequences.

But whenever physical contacts or psychologic stimuli had led to orgasm, there was rarely any doubt of the sexual nature of the situation, and it has in consequence been possible to secure incidence and frequency data which were as reliable as the interview technique would allow. For these reasons, the statistical data in the present volume, just as in our volume on the male, have been largely concerned with the incidences and frequencies of sexual activities that led to orgasm. The procedure may have overemphasized the importance of orgasm, but it would have been impossible in any large-scale survey to have secured as precise records on some of the other, less certainly identifiable aspects of sexual behavior.

For these same reasons, we have defined the total sexual outlet of an individual as the sum of the orgasms derived from the various types

510

of sexual activity in which that individual had engaged. Since all sexual responses, whether they are the product of psychologic stimulation or of some physical contact, may involve some sort of physiologic change (Chapter 15) and therefore some expenditure of energy, all sexual responses might be considered a part of the individual's total sexual outlet; but the term *total outlet* as we have used it has covered only those contacts and/or responses which had led to orgasm.

There is, moreover, a reality involved in any such summation of orgasms, for all orgasms appear to be physiologically similar quantities, whether they are derived from masturbatory, heterosexual, homosexual, or other sorts of activity (Chapters 14–15). For most females and males, there appear to be basic physiologic needs which are satisfied by sexual orgasm, whatever the source, and the sum total of such orgasms may constitute a significant entity in the life of an individual.[1]

It is, of course, true that sexual experience may have a significance which lies beyond the physiologic release that it provides, and each type of sexual experience may have its own peculiar significance. For instance, many persons will consider the psychologic significance of an orgasm attained in masturbation very different from the psychologic significance of an orgasm derived from a socio-sexual source. The social significance of orgasms attained in non-marital coitus may be different from those attained in marital coitus. In many ways, it may be more significant to know the frequencies and incidences of the particular types of sexual activity (Chapters 5–12) than it is to total them as we do in the present chapter. But social interests are still involved when an individual finds satisfaction for a physiologic and psychologic need; and the data on total sexual outlets may, therefore, deserve as much consideration as any of the data on particular types of sexual activity.

DEVELOPMENT OF SEXUAL RESPONSIVENESS

As we have previously indicated, specifically erotic responses and sometimes orgasm may be observed in very young infants, both female and male (Chapter 4, and our 1948:175). Among infant females, the incidences of response and completed orgasm were about as high as they were among infant males; but the number of males who had responded sexually had gradually and steadily increased through the early pre-adolescent years, and then had risen abruptly in the later pre-adolescent years. On the other hand, the number of females who had been aroused erotically appears to have increased somewhat more

---

[1] The concept of a total sexual outlet appears not to have been employed in other studies. The nearest approximation seems to be in Davis 1929:233, who classifies her sample on the basis of the number of sources of outlet which they were utilizing.

gradually through the pre-adolescent and adolescent years (Table 146, Figure 98).

First Erotic Response in the Female. The average female in the available sample had begun to turn adolescent by twelve years and four months of age (p. 123). By that age *about* 30 per cent had been aroused erotically by some sort of psychologic stimulation or physical contact, and under conditions which they subsequently recalled as definitely sexual (Table 146, Figure 98). First menstruation for the average fe-

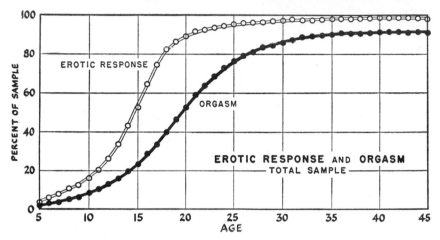

Figure 98. Accumulative incidence: erotic response and orgasm from any source

Data from Tables 146 and 147.

male in the sample had come just as she was turning thirteen (p. 123); and by that age about a third (34 per cent) of the sample had recognized some sort of erotic arousal. By fifteen years of age, half (53 per cent) of the females had been aroused erotically in some form or fashion. By twenty years of age, 89 per cent had been so aroused, but there were some who had not recognized their first arousal until some later age.

Ultimately 98 per cent of the females in the sample had had at least one experience in which they recognized arousal, but even in the late forties there were still some 2 per cent who had never recognized any sexual arousal, under any sort of condition (Table 146, Figure 98). These females reported that they had never been aroused by self-stimulation of their own genitalia or of any other part of their bodies, they had not been aroused by thinking of sexual situations or by dreaming of them at night, and they had not been aroused by any other sort of psychologic stimulation. Neither had they been aroused by physical contacts with other persons, and in most instances they had never had any contacts which could be identified as sexual. It is, of course, not impossible that some of them had reacted erotically without being aware of the nature of their emotional responses; and it is possible that some other method of gathering data, or specific physiologic measurements, might have shown that some of these females had, on occasion, responded to erotic stimuli. On the other hand, their responses must have been so mild, infrequent, or non-specific that it would have been difficult to have identified them as sexual.[2]

Sources of First Arousal. A third of the females (30 to 34 per cent) had first been aroused erotically in heterosexual petting (Table 148). Nearly as many (27 to 30 per cent) had first become aware of the meaning of erotic arousal as a result of their own self-masturbation. Another third (30 to 32 per cent) had first been aroused through psychologic stimulation, chiefly in connection with their social contacts with male friends. Nocturnal dreams, pre-marital coitus, marital coitus, and homosexual and animal contacts had been only minor sources of first arousal.

The sources of first arousal had remained remarkably constant through the four decades represented in the sample (Table 148). They had, however, been more affected by the age at which the female had married: 37 per cent of the females who married between the ages of sixteen and twenty had been aroused first in petting, in contrast to 28 per cent of those who married after age thirty. Those who married at later ages had more often found their first arousal in masturbation or psychologic stimulation. There may have been some causal relationship between the occurrence of the first arousal in heterosexual contacts and the earlier age of marriage among those females.

Age at First Orgasm in the Female. The percentages of females who had experienced orgasm (the accumulative incidences) had risen steadily during pre-adolescence, but they were still relatively low (about 14 per cent) at the onset of adolescence (Table 147, Figure 98). There was some increase after the onset of adolescence, but less than a quarter (23 per cent) of the sample had had such experience by fifteen years of age. A little more than a half (53 per cent) had had orgasm by twenty, three-quarters (77 per cent) by twenty-five, and about 90 per cent by thirty-five years of age. The accumulative incidence curves had leveled off at that point, and there appear to be some 9 per cent who would probably not reach orgasm in the course of their lives. Some 64 per cent of the females in the sample had experienced their first orgasm prior to marriage (Table 150). About 33

---

[2] Discussions of females who had never been erotically aroused are also in: Dickinson and Beam 1931:128 (found no such cases among 100 frigid wives). Landis and Bolles 1942:96 (cases among physically handicapped females).

per cent of the females who had married had experienced their first orgasm after they were married.

The females who had never reached orgasm had, in many instances, been aroused erotically, but none of them had recognized the high levels of tension which ordinarily precede orgasm, the sudden release which is orgasm, and the physical relaxation which follows orgasm (Chapter 15). Most of them had had socio-sexual contacts, and some of them were married and had had coitus regularly for some period of years—but none of them seem ever to have experienced orgasm. For a further discussion of this so-called frigidity, see pages 373 ff.

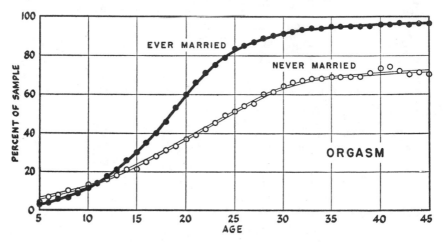

Figure 99. Accumulative incidence: orgasm from any source, by marital status

The second curve is based on those who had never married and were age forty or over at time of interview. Data from Table 150.

Factors Affecting Age at First Orgasm. The age of the female at marriage had been the prime factor affecting the age at which she first experienced orgasm, primarily because marital coitus had provided the first orgasmic experience for most of those who had not had such experience prior to marriage. Before marriage, and until the age of fifteen, there were few differences in the several groups. At fifteen, only 31 per cent of the females who were to marry in the next five years had experienced orgasm, but by the age of twenty, 82 per cent of that group had responded to orgasm, chiefly after marriage (Table 151, Figure 101). Similarly, among those who married at later ages, there were rather definite rises in the curves just before or after the age of marriage.

There seem to have been no significant differences in the accumulative incidence curves for the first experience in orgasm, between the females of the high school, college, and graduate school groups; but the curve for the females who had never gone beyond grade school was definitely lower at nearly every point (Table 147). In the younger age groups, more of the females who were raised in parental homes of the lower occupational classes had experienced orgasm, fewer of the girls who were raised in upper white collar homes (Table 152).

Before the age of twenty, there were no significant differences in the percentages reaching orgasm among the females who were born in the several decades covered by the sample (Table 157, Figure 103). After the age of twenty, the generation which was born before 1900 seems to have included a larger number of females who were slower in reaching their first orgasm and a larger number who had never responded to orgasm, even by the age of forty-five. Some 5 to 10 per cent more of the females who were born after 1900 had ultimately experienced orgasm, and at an earlier age. The females of the generation born after 1920 seem to have been somewhat slower in having experience prior to the age of eighteen, but after that a larger proportion of the group had experienced orgasm, and experienced it at an earlier age than the females born in the previous decades (p. 522). The present generation will probably complete its history with a much smaller percentage of females who remain totally inexperienced in orgasm throughout their lives.

The accumulative incidence data do not indicate that there was any correlation between the ages of the females when they first responded to orgasm, and the ages at which they had turned adolescent (Table 159).

The accumulative incidence curves for first orgasm were generally lower for the rural sample and higher for the urban females (Table 162); but the differences were not great, and the rural sample is not large enough to allow any final conclusions.

The religious factors were of considerable importance in determining the ages at which the females in the sample had first responded to orgasm. For instance, the females who were devoutly Catholic had, on an average, not reached their first orgasm until some six or seven years after the females who were only nominally Catholic (Table 164, Figure 107). There were 21 per cent of the devoutly Catholic females who had not reached orgasm by thirty-five years of age, even though most of them were then married and regularly having coitus in their marriages. It was not more than 2 per cent of the nominal, non-religious Catholics who had not reached orgasm by that age.

The differences were not so extreme between the religiously active and inactive Protestants, but they lay in the same direction (Table 164.

Figure 106). For instance, at forty-five years of age there were still 15 per cent of the devout Protestant females who had never experienced orgasm in their lives, but only 5 per cent of the inactive Protestants who belonged in that category. As far as the more limited record goes, the differences between the religiously devout and inactive Jewish groups appear to have been of about the same order (Table 164). There seems no doubt that the moral restraints which lead a female to avoid sexual contacts before marriage, and to inhibit her responses when she does make contacts, may also affect her capacity to respond erotically later in her life. We shall not solve the problem of female "frigidity" until we realize that it is a man-made situation, and not the product of innate physiologic incapacities in those females.

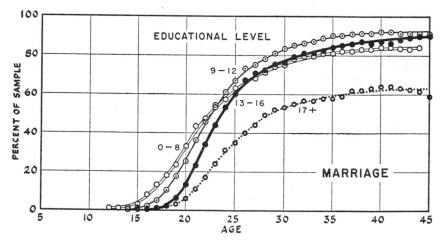

Figure 100. Accumulative incidence: age at first marriage, by educational level

Data from Table 166.

Sources of First Orgasm. If we base our calculations on the females in the sample who had been married, and who therefore had had a maximum opportunity to experience orgasm, the sources of such experience were as follows (Table 148): Some 37 per cent had reached their first orgasm in masturbation. Some 18 per cent had reached their first orgasm in pre-marital petting, and 30 per cent in coitus after marriage. Only smaller percentages had reached their first orgasm in nocturnal dreams, pre-marital coitus, homosexual relations, animal contacts, or psychologic stimulation.

The source of first orgasm had depended somewhat on the age of the female at the time she married (Table 148). Masturbation had been the source of first orgasm for some 32 per cent of the females who married between the ages of sixteen and twenty, but for 41 per cent of

those who had married after the age of twenty-five. The first orgasm
had been reached in marital coitus among 33 per cent of those who
were married between the ages of sixteen and twenty, but among only
21 per cent of those who had been married between thirty-one and
thirty-five. There were essentially no differences between the educational levels when the comparisons were made for females who had
married at the same age.

The sources of first orgasm had differed somewhat among the females
who were born in the different decades represented in the sample
(Table 148). There had been no essential differences between the
generations when the first orgasms were derived from masturbation;

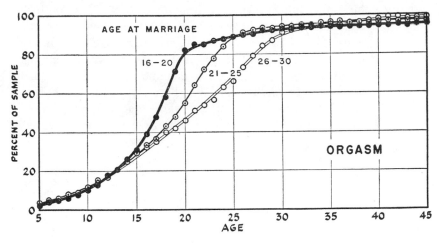

**Figure 101. Accumulative incidence: orgasm from any source, by age at
first marriage**

Data from Table 150.

but when the first orgasm had come from pre-marital petting, 10 per
cent of those born before 1900, but 25 per cent of those born between
1920 and 1929, had been involved. From pre-marital coitus, some 3
per cent of the older generation, but 10 per cent of the generation born
between 1920 and 1929, had derived their first orgasm. On the other
hand, the first orgasm had come from coitus after marriage among 37
per cent of the older generation, but among only 26 per cent of the
group born between 1920 and 1929. These figures are an interesting reflection of changes in the patterns of female behavior during the four
decades. In the younger generations, there had been a rise in the importance of pre-marital petting and pre-marital coitus as sources of
first orgasm, and some drop in the importance of masturbation. There
had been a marked decrease in the number of females who had waited
until after marriage to secure their first experience in orgasm.

SINGLE FEMALES: TOTAL OUTLET

Accumulative Incidence. Among the unmarried females in the sample, the accumulative incidence curve for those who had ever responded to orgasm had included 14 per cent by twelve years and four months of age, which was the average age at the onset of adolescence. It had risen to 23 per cent by age fifteen, and to 49 per cent by age twenty (Table 149). It had approached its ultimate level of about 75 per cent among the still unmarried females near thirty-five years of age.

Active Incidence. Among the single females in the sample, the active incidences had rather definitely risen during pre-adolescence and through adolescence into the mid-twenties (Table 154, Figure 102). Some 22 per cent were responding to the point of orgasm between the ages of adolescence and fifteen. Some 47 per cent were responding in the later teens, and 60 per cent between the ages of twenty-one and twenty-five. Between the ages of twenty-one and fifty, the active incidences among the single females had stood between 60 and 71 per cent. The peak had come between the ages of thirty-one and forty, where 70 to 71 per cent of the still unmarried females were reaching orgasm.

There was some decline in the active incidences after the age of forty, and a steady decline through the fifties (Table 154), but no marked decline until after the age of sixty. In the white, non-prison sample which has been used in the making of the present volume, we have no instance of a female experiencing orgasm after the age of seventy-five; but among our prison and non-white histories we have cases of females responding in their seventies and eighties and, in one instance, responding to the point of orgasm with frequencies which averaged between once a month and once a week at the age of ninety.

Relation of Frequency to Age. The frequencies of orgasm among the single females in the sample who were having any experience at all, had stayed more or less on a level from the youngest to the oldest age group. The median females in the active samples had averaged one orgasm in two weeks (0.5 per week) between adolescence and fifteen years of age (Table 154, Figures 102, 143). The average frequencies then lay between 0.3 and 0.5 per week in every subsequent group up to the age of sixty. We have previously found that the frequencies of female masturbatory activities, nocturnal dreams, petting to the point of orgasm, and still other activities similarly remain near a level throughout this same period of years. This is in marked contrast to the steady decline in the frequencies of total outlet among the males, from their late teens into old age (Figure 143). Hormonal factors probably contribute to these differences between the sexes (Chapter 18).

Female vs. Male Frequency Prior to Marriage. These differences in frequencies of orgasm between unmarried females and unmarried males are of considerable social significance. To summarize again: at the age of marriage there were some 36 per cent of the females in the sample who had not yet responded to orgasm (Table 150), while all of the

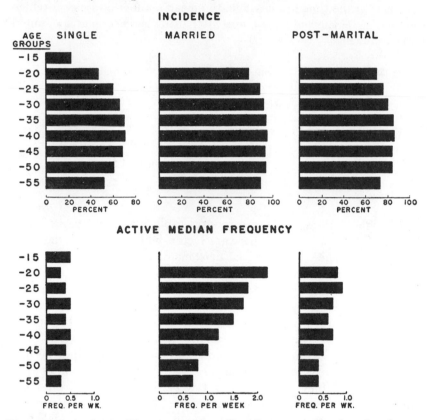

Figure 102. Active incidence, active median frequency: total outlet, by age and marital status

Data from Table 154.

males (essentially 100 per cent) at marriage had not only long since had their first experience in orgasm, but had already passed the peak of their sexual capacity. Among those born after 1910, the average male had experienced orgasm over 1500 times (the mean frequencies) before marriage; the average female appears not to have experienced orgasm more than about 223 times before her marriage. Practically all of the males born since 1910 had had a regular sexual outlet before marriage, with mean frequencies of about 2.9 orgasms per week for ten and a half years. There were not more than 10 to 20 per cent of the females who were having any outlet from any source which averaged as much as once per week for as long as five years before marriage. Between the ages of sixteen and twenty, the average (median) male was having experience with more than three (3.4) different types of sexual activity (our 1948:228), while the average female in that age period was having experience with less than half as many (1.4) types of activity (Table 169). At the time of marriage, the mean number of orgasms which the average female and male (born after 1910) had ever had, amounted to the following:

Activity to orgasm	Accumulative incidence % to orgasm		Mean number of orgasms	
	FEMALE	MALE	FEMALE	MALE
Total outlet	64	100	223	1523
Masturbation	41	94	130	872
Nocturnal dreams	12	82	6	175
Petting	37	26	37	64
Coitus	27	80	39	330
Homosexual	5	30	11	75
Animal contacts	—	8	—	7

Although there is, of course, considerable individual variation in these matters, and although there are factors which often lead the more responsive females to marry earlier, many marriages involve even greater differences than those which we have just shown between the average female and male. Many males are disappointed after marriage to find that their wives are not responding regularly and are not as interested in having as frequent sexual contact as they, the males, would like to have; and a great many of the married females may be disappointed and seriously disturbed when they find that they are not responding in their coitus, and not enjoying sexual relations as they had anticipated they would. Not a few of the divorces which occur within the first year or two of marriage are the product of these discrepancies between the sexual backgrounds of the average female and the average male. However, in view of the diverse pre-marital backgrounds of the spouses in the average marriage, it is not surprising that they sometimes find it difficult to adjust sexually. It is more surprising that so many married couples are ever able to work out a satisfactory sexual arrangement (p. 375).

Other Factors Affecting Incidence and Frequency. The educational backgrounds of the unmarried high school and college-bred females in the sample seem to have had no consistent effect upon the active incidences or active median frequencies of their total outlet (Table 155), even though they had had some definite effect upon the incidences of masturbation and homosexual contacts. The grade school sample is too small for certain interpretation.

The occupational classes of the parents in whose homes the females were raised had not been particularly correlated with the active incidences or active median frequencies of their total outlet before marriage (Table 156). At younger ages, the incidences had been a bit higher among those females who were raised in homes of laboring groups (Parental Classes 2 and 3). Apparently, girls from these lower level homes get started earlier in their sexual activity, but by the twenties their total outlets were not particularly different from the total outlets of the females in the other groups.

There were more definite differences among the females born in the successive decades represented in the sample (Table 160, Figure 105). Except in the youngest age group, the active incidences were lower among the unmarried females who were born before 1900. For instance, between the ages of twenty-one and twenty-five, 45 per cent of the older generation were experiencing some orgasm, as against something between 61 and 63 per cent of the later generations. After age thirty the differences were less extreme, even though they lay in the same direction. There were no significant differences in the active median frequencies of the females born in the four decades covered by the sample.

The active incidences of total outlet were correlated with the ages at which the females in the sample had turned adolescent, only for the group which had turned adolescent by eleven—where the active incidences were higher—, and for the group which turned adolescent at fifteen or later—where the active incidences were lower (Table 161). The age at onset of adolescence did not seem to have any effect on the frequencies of total outlet among the unmarried females in the sample (Table 161).

Because of the small size of the rural sample we cannot be certain of our comparisons of the total outlets of the single females of the rural and urban groups. What data we do have, however, indicate that the active incidences were somewhat higher among the unmarried urban females after age fifteen, and the active frequencies of orgasm were a bit higher among the unmarried urban groups after age twenty (Table 163).

Active Incidence and Frequency, and Religious Background. In contrast to the above, the religious backgrounds of the single females in the sample had consistently affected the active incidences and active median frequencies of their total sexual outlet. In every one of the eleven groups which are available for comparisons, definitely smaller percentages of the religiously devout females and higher percentages of the religiously less devout or inactive females were experiencing orgasm from any source prior to marriage (Table 165, Figure 108). This was more or less equally true of the Protestant, Catholic, and Jewish groups in the sample. It was true in every age group, from the youngest to the oldest single females on whom we have sufficient data.

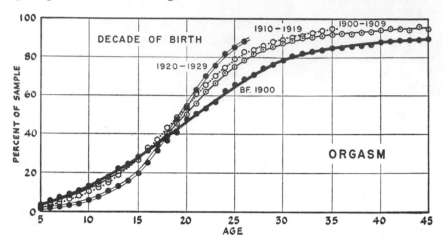

Figure 103. Accumulative incidence: orgasm from any source, by decade of birth

Data from Table 157.

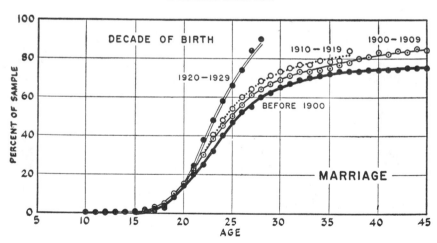

Figure 104. Accumulative incidence: age at first marriage, by decade of birth

Data from Table 167.

For instance, between the ages of sixteen and twenty, 41 per cent of the more devout Protestant females were experiencing some orgasm, in contrast to 53 per cent of the inactive Protestants. In the same age period, 34 per cent of the devout Catholics, but 70 per cent of the inactive Catholics were experiencing some orgasm. Also in that age period, 46 per cent of the devout Jewish females but 56 per cent of the inactive Jewish females were having some experience in orgasm. In older age groups, among the still unmarried females, the differences were not obliterated and, in general, were as great as those just cited.

Similarly, the active median frequencies for the unmarried females in the devout groups were always lower than those in the religiously

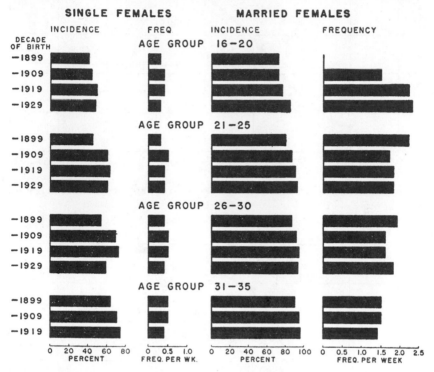

Figure 105. Active incidence, active median frequency: total outlet, by marital status and decade of birth

Data from Table 160.

inactive groups, and in some instances the differences were considerable. For instance, between the ages of twenty-one and twenty-five, the median frequency of orgasm for the devout Protestant group was 0.3 per week against 0.5 per week for the inactive Protestants (Table 165). For the Catholic group in the same age period it was 0.4 for the devout, in contrast to 1.0 per week for the inactive Catholics.

We have seen that the age of the female had affected her total outlet only in the youngest and the very oldest groups; we have seen that the total outlet of the unmarried females in the sample had not been particularly affected by their educational level, the occupational level of the home in which they had been raised, the decade in which they had been born, the age at which they had turned adolescent, or their rural-urban background. Among all of the cultural and biologic factors which might affect their sexual activity, and which in actuality had consid-

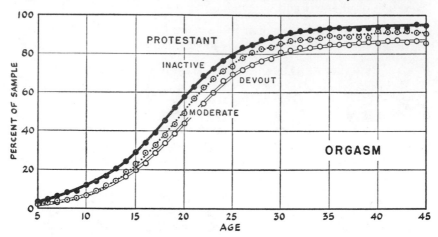

Figure 106. Accumulative incidence: orgasm from any source, in Protestant groups

Data from Table 164.

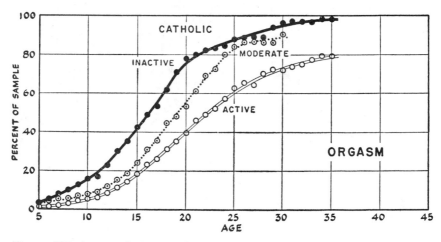

Figure 107. Accumulative incidence: orgasm from any source, in Catholic groups

Data from Table 164.

erably affected the sexual activities of the males in the sample, only the religious backgrounds of the unmarried females had had any material relation to their acceptance of either solitary or socio-sexual contacts.

Sources of Total Outlet for Single Females. The sources from which the single females in the sample had derived their total outlet had varied considerably in the different age groups (Table 171, Figure 110). As examples, the following tabulation will show the three most important outlets in four of the age groups:

AGE: ADOL.–15	%	AGE: 21–25	%
Masturbation	84	Masturbation	46
Pre-marital coitus	6	Pre-marital coitus	26
Homosexual contacts	4	Petting to orgasm	18
AGE: 16–20		AGE: 31–35	
Masturbation	60	Masturbation	42
Petting to orgasm	18	Pre-marital coitus	33
Pre-marital coitus	15	Homosexual contacts	14

AGE GROUP ADOL.– 15

PROTESTANT   CATHOLIC   JEWISH

DEVOUT
MODERATE
INACTIVE

AGE GROUP 16 – 20

DEVOUT
MODERATE
INACTIVE

AGE GROUP 21 – 25

DEVOUT
MODERATE
INACTIVE

Figure 108. Active incidence: total outlet, by religious background, among single females

Data from Table 165.

At all ages, masturbation had been the most important source of total outlet for the unmarried females in the sample (Table 171, Figure 110). Coitus had been the second chief source of the pre-marital outlet in all of the groups after age twenty, and for those females who were still unmarried in their late thirties and forties, it was nearly as important a source of outlet as masturbation. Homosexual contacts had provided a rather important portion of the total outlet for the unmarried females in the sample between the ages of twenty-six and forty. Petting to orgasm had been an important source of pre-marital outlet for the females between the ages of sixteen and thirty, but it had become much less important after that age. Nocturnal dreams to orgasm had never accounted for more than 2 to 4 per cent of the total outlet of the unmarried females in any of the age groups.

Single Females Without Orgasm. A considerable portion of the unmarried females in the sample, in each and every age group, was not
experiencing orgasm from any source. Thus, between adolescence and
fifteen years of age there were 78 per cent, and among the older teen-
age girls there were 53 per cent who were not reaching orgasm in any
type of sexual activity (Table 171). Although the incidences of unresponding individuals had dropped steadily from that point, there were
29 per cent of the still unmarried females who were not reaching orgasm from any source between the ages of thirty-six and forty, and
there were higher percentages again in the still older groups. Some 39
per cent of the unmarried females were without such experience between the ages of forty-six and fifty. There were more than a quarter
(28 per cent) of the older unmarried females who had never experienced orgasm at any time in their lives (Table 150, Figure 99).

This existence of such a large group of females who are not having
any sexual outlet poses a problem of some social importance. Some of
these females in the sample had been frustrated in their attempts to
make social adjustments, and resented the fact that they had not been
able to marry. Many of them were sexually responsive enough, but they
were inhibited, chiefly by their moral training, and had not allowed
themselves to respond to the point of orgasm. Many of them had been
psychologically disturbed as a result of this blockage of their sexual
responses.[3] But others, including many of the 28 per cent who had
never reached orgasm, were sexually unresponsive individuals who had
not felt the lack of a sexual outlet. All of these females, however, were
limited in their understanding of the nature of sexual responses and
orgasm, and many of them seemed unable to comprehend what sexual
activity could mean to other persons. They disapproved of the sexual
activities of females who had high rates of outlet, and they were particularly incapable of understanding the rates of response which we
have reported (1948) for the males in the population.[4]

When such frustrated or sexually unresponsive, unmarried females
attempt to direct the behavior of other persons, they may do considerable damage. There were grade school, high school, and college teachers among these unresponsive or unresponding females. Some of them
had been directors of organizations for youth, some of them had been

[3] Discussions of the sexual problems of the mature single female may be found in:
Hellmann acc. Weissenberg 1924b:213 (notes diverse types of cases). Parshley 1933:300. Van der Hoog 1934:47–58. Hutton 1935:168. Smith 1951:48
(continence and health not workable for majority). Sylvanus Duvall 1952:186–
188.

[4] An attitude found among some females was expressed by one woman who in-
dignantly wrote, after the publication of our volume on the male, that the study
was a waste of effort for it merely confirmed her previous opinion "that the
male population is a herd of prancing, leering goats."

directors of institutions for girls or older women, many of them had
been active in women's clubs and service organizations, and not a few
of them had had a part in establishing public policies. Some of them
had been responsible for some of the more extreme sex laws which
state legislatures had passed. Not a few of them were active in religious

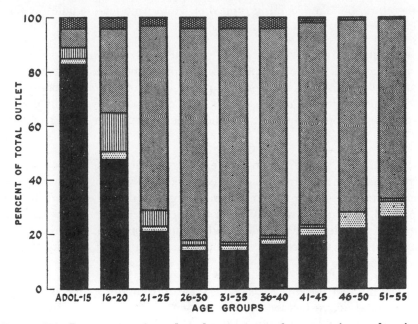

Figure 109. Percentage of total outlet: sources of orgasm, in total active
sample

Data from Table 170.

Masturbation   Nocturnal Orgasms

                                                Petting

Coitus   Homosexual

work, directing the sexual education and trying to direct the sexual
behavior of other persons. Some of them were medically trained, but
as physicians they were still shocked to learn of the sexual activities
of even their average patients. If it were realized that something between a third and a half of the unmarried females over twenty years of
age have never had a completed sexual experience (Table 149), parents
and particularly the males in the population might debate the wisdom
of making such women responsible for the guidance of youth. There
were, however, another half to two-thirds of the unmarried females
who did understand the significance of sex, and were not living the
blank or sexually frustrated lives which our culture, paradoxically, had
expected them to live.

MARRIED FEMALES: TOTAL OUTLET

The median female in our white, non-prison sample had married at the age of twenty-three. The median age given by the U. S. Census for the *total* female population (white and non-white) for the last forty years was about twenty-one. In this respect our sample may, therefore, be taken as fairly typical of white American females in general.

Among the females in the sample, about 97 per cent had experienced erotic arousal before marriage, but 3 per cent had never been so aroused before marriage. Some 64 per cent had experienced orgasm at least once before marriage, but 36 per cent married without understanding, through actual experience, the meaning of sexual orgasm (Table 150).

Relation to Age. After marriage the frequencies of total outlet for the females in the sample had increased considerably over the frequencies which single females of the same age would have had. This depended, of course, primarily upon the fact that marital coitus had begun to provide such a regular and frequent source of sexual activity and outlet as few females had found in any type of activity before marriage.

The number of females reaching orgasm from any source after marriage (the active incidences) had begun at 78 per cent between the ages of sixteen and twenty (Table 154, Figure 102). They had then increased steadily to 95 per cent at ages thirty-six to forty, after which they had begun to drop, reaching 89 per cent by age fifty-five and, to judge by our small sample, 82 per cent by age sixty.

The median frequencies of total outlet for the married females who were ever reaching orgasm show marked "aging effects." The active median frequencies between sixteen and twenty had amounted to 2.2 orgasms per week, from which point they had steadily declined, reaching 1.0 per week between the ages of forty-one and forty-five, and 0.5 per week by age sixty (Table 154, Figure 102).

The mean frequencies were much higher than the corresponding median frequencies because they included the activities of a few highly responsive and unusually active females. This had been true in all of the age groups, from the youngest to the oldest. These "aging effects," however, must be largely dependent, as we have noted elsewhere (p. 353), upon the aging processes which occur in the male, and not upon any physiologic or psychologic aging in the female between the ages of twenty and fifty-five.

Relation to Decade of Birth. In the chapter on marital coitus, we found that the percentages of married females who were responding to the point of orgasm in that coitus (the active incidences) had risen more or less steadily in the four decades represented in the sample. This accounted for the fact that the active incidences of the total outlet of the married females in the sample had steadily risen in that period of time. For instance, among the females in the sample who were between the ages of twenty-one and twenty-five, some 80 per cent of those born before 1900 had reached orgasm; but of those who were born in the successive decades, 86, 90, and 92 per cent had so responded (Table 160, Figure 105). Something of the same differences had been maintained in the subsequent age groups.

We have also pointed out (p. 358) that the frequencies of marital coitus had been reduced during the four decades represented in the sample. Consequently the active median frequencies of total outlet were, for the most part, reduced in that period of time (Table 160, Figure 105). There were some inconsistencies in the data and the reductions were not great. For instance, between the ages of twenty-one and twenty-five, the active median frequencies had been 2.2 in the generation born before 1900, but they had dropped to 1.8 in the generation born after 1920.

Relation to Other Factors. The incidences of total outlet for the married females in the sample had generally been a bit higher for the better educated groups, and lower for the grade school and high school groups (Table 155). There seem to have been no consistent correlations between the active median frequencies of the total outlet among the married females in the sample and their educational backgrounds, except that the graduate school group had slightly higher frequencies up to the age of thirty-five (Table 155).

There seem to have been no correlations at all between the occupational classes of the parental homes in which the females in the sample had been raised and the incidences and frequencies of their total outlet (Table 156).

On the other hand, the religious backgrounds of the females in the sample had definitely and consistently affected their total outlet after marriage. In nearly every age group, and in nearly all the samples that we have from Protestant, Catholic, and Jewish females, smaller percentages of the more devout and larger percentages of the inactive groups had responded to orgasm after marriage (Table 165). Similarly, the median frequencies of orgasm for those who were responding at all were, in most instances, lower for those who were devout and higher for those who were religiously inactive. In many groups the differences

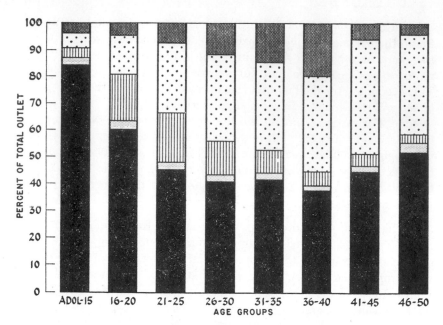

Figure 110. Percentage of total outlet: sources of orgasm, among single females

Data from Table 171.

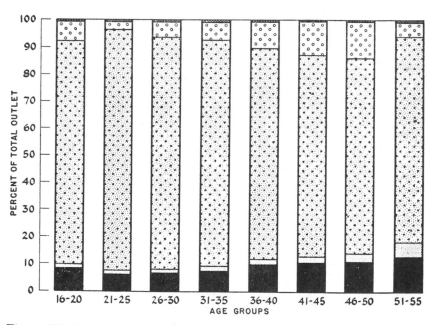

Figure 111. Percentage of total outlet: sources of orgasm, among married females

Data from Table 171.

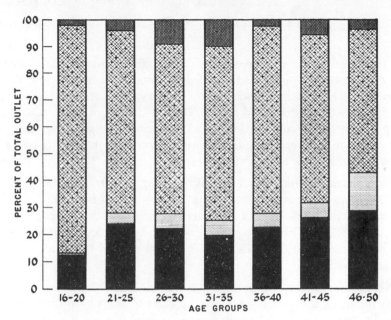

Figure 112. Percentage of total outlet: sources of orgasm, among previously married females

Data from Table 171.

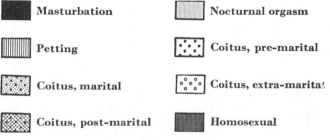

Key to figures 110–112

had not been great; but in some instances, as among the Catholic females who were married between the ages of twenty-one and twenty-five, the differences were of some magnitude: an active median frequency of 1.1 orgasms per week for the devoutly Catholic females, and 2.4 for the inactive Catholic females.

Sources of Total Outlet. Coitus in marriage had accounted for something between 84 and 89 per cent of the total outlet of the married females in the sample who were between the ages of sixteen and thirty-five (Table 171, Figure 111). After the middle thirties, the importance of marital coitus had decreased. In the age group forty-six to fifty, only

73 per cent of the total number of orgasms were coming from that source.

Masturbation was the second most important source of sexual outlet for the married females in the sample, providing something between 7 and 10 per cent of the total number of orgasms for each of the age groups between sixteen and forty (Table 171, Figure 111). Although 11 per cent of the total outlet had come from this source in the next ten years, the increase in importance of extra-marital coitus had reduced masturbation to a third place in the list.

Extra-marital coitus and orgasms derived in extra-marital petting had accounted, in various age groups, for something between 3 and 13 per cent of the total outlet of the married females in the sample (Table 171, Figure 111). This had become the second most important source of outlet after age forty, providing 12 to 13 per cent of the total orgasms in that period.

Nocturnal dreams had provided between 1 and 3 per cent of the total outlet of the married females in each of the age groups in the sample. Homosexual contacts had never provided more than a fraction of 1 per cent of the orgasms experienced by the married females in the sample (Table 171, Figure 111).

Married Females Without Orgasm. There had been an appreciable percentage of the married females who were not reaching orgasm either in their marital coitus or in any other type of sexual activity while they were married. The percentage had been highest in the younger age groups where 22 per cent of the married females between the ages of sixteen and twenty, and 12 per cent of the married females between the ages of twenty-one and twenty-five, had never experienced any orgasm from any source (Table 171). The number of unresponsive individuals had dropped steadily in the successive age groups, reaching 5 per cent in the late thirties; but it had risen again to 6 and 7 per cent in the forties.

PREVIOUSLY MARRIED FEMALES: TOTAL OUTLET

According to the 1950 census, there are some 15 per cent of the females in the United States who have been previously married and who are no longer living with their husbands because they are widowed, separated, or divorced. Many persons, both clinicians and the public at large, have realized that women who have previously had coitus with some frequency in marriage may be faced with a problem of readjustment when they are left without any legalized or socially approved source of sexual outlet.[5] It is generally presumed that the problem is

---

[5] That previously married females, whether widowed or divorced, often face distinctive sexual problems, is also recognized in: Bienville 1771:13. Tissot

more extreme for a female who has been previously married than for one who has never been married. Our sample of previously married females is not large, but it may be sufficient to warrant some generalizations concerning the group.

There was, of course, considerable individual variation in the problems which these previously married females had faced. Some of them who were not particularly responsive seem not to have missed the regular outlet which coitus had provided, and they had been quite satisfied with the outlet which masturbation or homosexual contacts had afforded. Some of them had even been satisfied to live without any sort of sexual outlet. Many of them had, however, faced difficult problems of adjustment. Even when they had not been physiologically disturbed, they had felt a lack of socio-sexual contacts. On the other hand, a fair number of these previously married females had had socio-sexual contacts as frequently, in some instances, as they had had them in their marriages. Some of the females had welcomed the opportunity that divorce had provided to secure a wider variety of sexual experience than was possible while they were married.

The most notable aspect of the histories of these previously married females was the fact that their frequencies of activity had not dropped to the levels which they had known as single females, before they had ever married. It will be recalled that the median frequencies of orgasm for the single females in the sample lay between 0.3 and 0.5 per week in every age group between adolescence and age fifty-five (Table 154, Figure 102). The median frequencies of total outlet for the females who had been previously married had ranged between 0.4 and 0.9 per week. In every age group, however, they were well below those of the married females in the sample.

Relation to Age. Among the females who were still in their teens or early twenties when they were widowed, separated, or divorced, 70 to 76 per cent had still found some source of sexual outlet (Table 154, Figure 102). Just as in the single and married females, the highest incidences had not developed until after age twenty-five, by which time they leveled off at something between 80 and 86 per cent between ages twenty-six and fifty.

The active median frequencies of orgasm among these previously married females had declined gradually from the youngest to the oldest age groups in the sample. Between the ages of sixteen and twenty-five, the median frequencies had been 0.8 or 0.9 per week. They had

---

1773(1):52. Forel 1922:96. Dickinson and Beam 1931:270–287. Baber 1939: 487. Goode 1949:396 (450 divorced mothers, no consistent trauma). Shultz 1949:243–265. Waller 1951:553–559 (trauma following divorce or death of spouse).

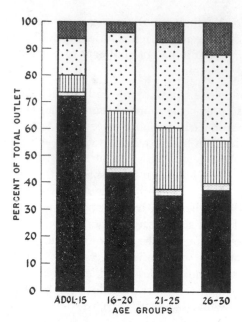

Figure 113. Percentage of total outlet: sources of orgasm, among single females of high school level

Data from Table 172.

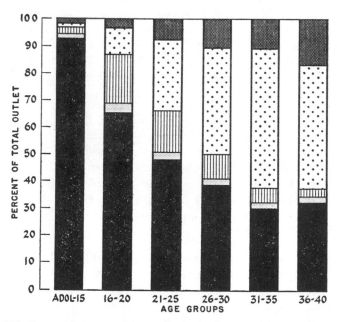

Figure 114. Percentage of total outlet: sources of orgasm, among single females of college level

Data from Table 172.

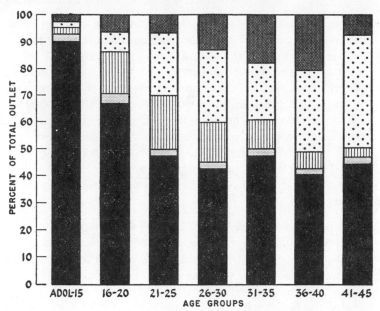

Figure 115. Percentage of total outlet: sources of orgasm, among single females of graduate level

Data from Table 172.

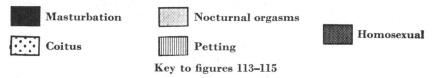

■ **Masturbation**   ▦ **Nocturnal orgasms**   ▨ **Homosexual**

⦂⦂ **Coitus**   ‖‖ **Petting**

Key to figures 113–115

dropped in the middle age groups, reaching 0.4 by fifty, and 0.3 by sixty years of age (Table 154, Figure 102). In all of these groups, however, there were some females who were engaging in sexual activities which had brought orgasm with much higher frequencies, and the active mean frequencies and the total mean frequencies were in consequence definitely higher than the corresponding median frequencies.

Relation to Educational Level. There seem to have been no important correlations between the educational levels of the previously married females in the sample and the incidences and median frequencies of their total outlet (Table 155). During the twenties the active median frequencies of orgasm had been higher for the previously married females of the high school sample, and lower for those of the college and graduate samples; but the differences had not been maintained in all of the age groups.

We do not have sufficient material for analyzing the effects of the other background factors on the total outlet of the previously married females in the sample.

Sources of Total Outlet. Among these previously married females, the active median frequencies of the post-marital coital contacts had ranged from once in two and a half weeks to nearly twice in three weeks (0.4 to 0.6 per week) in most of the age groups (Table 168). Consequently heterosexual coitus and/or petting to orgasm had, in many of the groups, provided three-quarters as much of the total outlet as it had for the females who were married (Table 171, Figures 111, 112). For the previously married females between the ages of sixteen and twenty, about 85 per cent of the outlet had been derived from the heterosexual contacts. The percentage of the outlet which had come from those sources had, however, then dropped, reaching 54 per cent by fifty years of age.

We have previously found (1948:294–296) that the post-marital patterns for the male had approached those of the married males, just as the post-marital patterns for the females are rather close to those of the married females. The patterns clearly reflect the marital experience of the previously married females and males, and they suggest that some of the females had been more interested in coitus than one would have concluded from an examination of their histories prior to divorce. In some instances, however, these females may have been more interested in the social aspects of the post-marital coital contacts than in the sexual experience itself.

In every age group, masturbation had been the second most important source of outlet and in actuality a material source of outlet for most of the previously married females (Table 171, Figure 112). For those who were still in their teens, 13 per cent of the outlet had come from masturbation, but the importance of this source of orgasm had increased in later age groups until it had accounted for 29 per cent of the total outlet of the previously married females between the ages of forty-six and fifty.

The third most important source of outlet for the previously married females had been either nocturnal dreams to orgasm or homosexual contacts. In some of the older groups, nocturnal dreams had accounted for two to three times as much of the outlet as such dreams had provided for the single or married females. This had been due to the slightly higher active median frequencies and the much higher incidences of dreams to orgasm in the previously married group. The previously married females may have dreamt of sex more often because of their desire, conscious or unconscious, for a more active sex life.

The homosexual activities of the previously married females seem to have been most important between the ages of twenty-six and thirty-five, at which time they had provided between 9 and 10 per cent of the

total outlet for each of the age groups. The importance of the homosexual contacts had then declined, but the samples for the older age
groups are so small that we cannot be sure that this conclusion is generally applicable.

In the earlier age groups, as much as 87 per cent of the outlet of
these previously married females had been derived from socio-sexual
contacts, either heterosexual or homosexual; but by age fifty only 57
per cent of the contacts were socio-sexual. This provides a measure
of the considerable problem which many an older individual has in
making a sexual adjustment after the termination of a marriage. Although sexual relationships may be significant because they satisfy a
physiologic need, they are more significant as factors in the development and the maintenance of an individual's personality and, consequently, may contribute to her value in the total social organization.

Previously Married Females Without Orgasm. In the teen-age group
in the sample, some 30 per cent of the previously married females had
found no outlet in any type of sexual activity. This was not markedly
higher than the percentage among the married females of that age, but
it was only half as high as the percentage of unresponsive individuals
among the single females in the teen-aged sample. In the older age
groups, however, the number of previously married females who had
lived without orgasm had decreased, reaching 20 per cent by age thirty
and 16 per cent by age fifty. Some of these previously married females
seemed almost as unresponsive, and as incapable of understanding responsive females, as though they had never been married. This, however, had been less often true than it had been for the single females
in the sample. Consequently, some of these previously married women
had shown a considerable understanding of the problems involved
when they had become responsible as teachers, counselors, or institutional administrators for directing the behavior of other persons.

INDIVIDUAL VARIATION

It is obvious, but it needs to be pointed out again, that no population
of variant individuals can ever have their behavior characterized by
any simple description. It is more nearly possible to write anatomic
descriptions which cover a whole group of individuals, but physiologic
functions are usually more variable than anatomic structures, and behavioral characters are still more variable than physiologic functions.

In our previous volume (1948) we have shown the extent of the
sexual variation that occurs among males, and in the present volume
we have recorded the variation that occurs in the sexual behavior of
the female. We have noted that the range of variation in the female

far exceeds the range of variation in the male. Consequently, it would be unfortunate if any of the comparisons made in the present volume should be taken to indicate that there are sexual qualities which are found only in one or the other sex. The record will have misled the reader if he fails to note this emphasis on the range of variation, and fails to realize that he or she probably does not fit any calculated median or mean, and may in actuality depart to a considerable degree from all of the averages which have been presented. The difficulty lies in the fact that one has to deal with averages in order to compare the most characteristic aspects of two different groups, but such averages do not adequately emphasize the individual variation which is the most persistent reality in human sexual behavior (Figures 116, 117).

Since sexual matters are less frequently discussed among females than other aspects of their lives (p. 675), most females have little knowledge of the sexual habits of any large number of other females. Only clinicians who have seen a considerable variety of sexual histories, and are able to think in terms of statistical averages, can have foreseen the sort of record which we have presented here.

Interestingly enough, we may predict that the persons who will be most often incapable of accepting our description of American females will be some of the promiscuous males who have had the largest amount of sexual contact with females. Most of these males do not realize that it is only a select group of females, and usually the more responsive females, who will accept pre-marital or extra-marital relationships. Some of these males will find it difficult to believe that the incidences of extra-marital coitus are as low as our data indicate; some of them will not easily be persuaded that there is such a percentage of females who fail to reach orgasm in their coitus; some of them will find it difficult to believe that there is such a large proportion of the female population which is not aroused in anticipation of a sexual relationship, and which is not dependent upon having a regular sexual outlet. They will fail to take into account the large number of females who never make socio-sexual contacts, and never become involved in the sort of non-marital relationships from which these males have acquired most of their information about females.

Because there is such wide variation in the sexual responsiveness and frequencies of overt activity among females, many females are incapable of understanding other females. There are fewer males who are incapable of understanding other males.[6] Even the sexually least re-

---

[6] Cases of females who fail to comprehend the sexuality of other females are frequently noted in psychiatric and sociologic literature, as in: Burgess and Cottrell 1939:230 (female at twenty-one shocked to find there are women who

sponsive of the males can comprehend something of the meaning of the frequent and continuous arousal which some other males experience. But the female who goes through life or for any long period of years with little or no experience in orgasm, finds it very difficult to comprehend the female who is capable of several orgasms every time she has sexual contact, and who may, on occasion, have a score or more orgasms in an hour. To the third or more of the females who have rarely been aroused by psychologic stimuli, it may seem fantastic to believe that there are females who come to orgasm as the result of sexual fantasy, without any physical stimulation of their genitalia or of any other part of their body. Sensing something of this variation in capacities and experience, many females—although not all—hesitate to discuss their sexual histories with other females, and may prefer to carry their sexual problems to male clinicians. Because they fail to comprehend this variation in female sexual capacities, some of the females in positions of authority in schools and penal and other institutions may be more harsh than males are in their judgments of other females. There are many social problems which cannot be understood unless one comprehends the tremendous range of variation which is to be found in sexual behavior among both females and males, but particularly among females.

As a conclusion to this section of the present volume, it seems appropriate, therefore, to summarize the record of individual variation which has thus far been presented.

1. **Incidences and Frequencies of Erotic Response.** We have noted that there were 2 per cent of the females in the sample who had never been aroused erotically (Table 146, Figure 98). There were some who had been aroused only once or twice or a very few times in their lives. At the other extreme there were females who had been aroused almost daily, and sometimes many times per day, for long periods of years. There was, of course, every gradation between those extremes.

2. **Intensity of Erotic Response.** The same degree of tactile or psychologic stimulation had brought very different responses from different females. There were individuals who had responded mildly, with only mild physiologic reactions and without reaching orgasm; but there

desire coitus). Kroger and Freed 1951:382 (female of forty-three asks if women "actually enjoyed sex or were just talking"). Two contrasting statements may be found in: Gray 1951:193, 195–196 (a female author who states "There is no such thing, in a women at least, as 'sex starvation.' . . . There is no hunger for sex in the sense that there is hunger for food. . . . lack of a sex life will not hurt you no matter how young you are"). English and Pearson 1945:364 (male authors who state that when coitus occurs only once or twice a month, "if the wife is sexually normal, she is bound to find incompatibility in such a marriage").

were other females who had responded instantaneously to a wide variety of stimuli, with intense physiologic reactions which had quickly led to orgasm.

3. **Physical vs. Psychologic Sources of Arousal.** Among those who had ever been aroused, there was no female who had been totally unre-

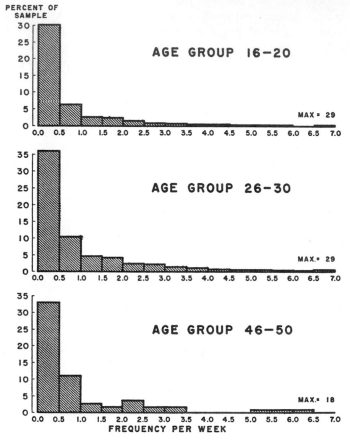

Figure 116. Individual variation: frequency of total outlet, among single females

For three age groups. Each class interval includes the upper but not the lower frequency. For incidences of females not reaching orgasm from any source, see Table 154.

sponsive to tactile stimulation, but there were females in the sample who appear to have never been aroused by any sort of psychosexual stimuli (Chapter 16). At the other extreme there were females who had been aroused by a great variety of psychologic stimuli, and some who had responded to the point of orgasm from psychologic stimulation alone. There were females in the sample who had been more responsive to psychologic stimulation than any male we have known.

4. **Sources of Psychologic Stimulation.** Among those females who had been aroused by psychologic stimuli, there were some who had responded to only a single sort of situation, and some who had responded to every conceivable sort of psychologic stimulation, including the observation of other persons, the observation of sexual objects or activity, fantasies of sexual objects or activity, recall of past experience, and the anticipation of new experience (Chapter 16). There was every

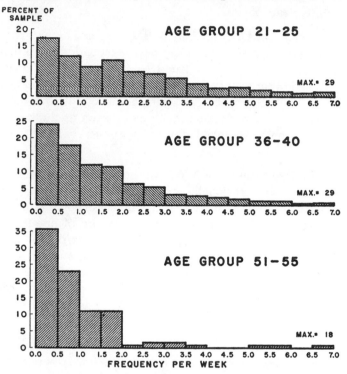

Figure 117. **Individual variation: frequency of total outlet, among married females**

For three age groups. Each class interval includes the upper but not the lower frequency. For incidences of females not reaching orgasm from any source, see Table 154.

gradation between females who had responded only occasionally to a single sort of psychologic stimulus, and females who had responded regularly to every item of psychosexual stimulation.

5. **Age at First Erotic Response.** We have reported female infants showing erotic responses at birth and specific responses by four months of age, we have reported the various ages at which other females first responded, and we have reported that there were some females who had not experienced their first erotic arousal until they were over thirty years of age (Table 146, Figure 98).

6. **Age at First Response to Orgasm.** We have recorded female infants reaching orgasm as early as four months of age, and we have indicated that there were some 9 per cent of the females in the sample who had lived into their late forties without reaching orgasm (Table 147, Figure 98). There were females in the sample who had reached their first orgasm at every age between these extremes, including three who had not reached their first orgasm until they were between forty-eight and fifty years of age.

7. **Frequencies of Orgasm.** Among the females who had responded to orgasm, there were some who had never responded more than once or twice in their lives. This was true even of some of the females who had been married for long periods of years. There were others who had responded in 1 or 2 per cent of their marital coitus, but there were many more who had responded much more often, including some 40 to 50 per cent who had responded to orgasm in nearly all of their coitus (Table 112).

8. **Continuity of Response.** We have shown that there were females who had been only occasionally aroused to the point of orgasm, with lapses of weeks or months and in some instances of some years between periods of arousal or orgasm. We have the record of one female who had gone for twenty-eight years between periods of coitus, with a masturbatory outlet of not more than one orgasm every two years in that long period. On the other hand, there were cases of females who had responded with high frequencies and great regularity throughout their lives, and there were cases with every conceivable pattern of discontinuity.

9. **Aging Effects.** There were females in the sample who had responded earlier in their lives but who had ceased to experience orgasm and, in some instances, to be aroused erotically after their late thirties or forties. More of the females had responded until they were in their fifties or sixties, and we have recorded the case of one ninety-year-old female who was still responding regularly.

10. **Sources of Outlet.** There were females in the sample who had derived their entire sexual outlet from a single source, which was sometimes masturbation, or petting to climax, pre-marital coitus, marital coitus, or some homosexual contact. There were a few instances of females who had never experienced orgasm except in nocturnal dreams, and instances of married females who had never experienced orgasm except in extra-marital coitus. There were females in the sample who, in the course of their lives, had utilized all six of the possible sources of outlet, and some who were utilizing all six in a single five-year period (Table 169). After the age of fifteen, something between 27 and 44

per cent of the females in the sample were depending upon a single source of outlet within each five-year period; something between 16 and 33 per cent were utilizing two sources of outlet more or less simultaneously; something between 6 and 16 per cent were utilizing three sources, and a smaller percentage was utilizing four to six sources within single age periods. There had been every conceivable combination of the possible types of sexual outlet.

11. **The Combination of Variables.** The sexual history of each individual represents a unique combination of these variables. There is little chance that such a combination has ever existed before, or ever will exist again. We have never found any individual who was a composite of all of the averages on all of the aspects of sexual response and overt activity which we have analyzed in the present volume. This is the most important fact which we can report on the sexual histories of the females who have contributed to the present study.

Table 146. Accumulative Incidence: Erotic Arousal From Any Source By Educational Level

AGE	TOTAL SAMPLE	EDUCATIONAL LEVEL				TOTAL SAMPLE	EDUCATIONAL LEVEL			
		0–8	9–12	13–16	17+		0–8	9–12	13–16	17+
	%		*Percent*			*Cases*		*Cases*		
3	1	0	—	1	1	5846	176	1002	3245	1137
5	4	0	3	3	6	5799	176	1002	3245	1137
10	16	10	15	15	22	5735	176	1002	3245	1137
12	27	15	26	25	33	5711	176	1002	3245	1137
13	34	25	32	32	41	5697	176	1002	3245	1137
15	53	43	52	52	56	5648	170	1001	3245	1137
20	89	78	90	92	86	4293	124	851	2182	1136
25	95	86	96	98	94	2751	114	678	1021	938
30	97	91	98	99	97	2019	107	494	694	724
35	98	90	99	99	98	1446	89	316	483	558
40	98	92	99	100	98	933	65	188	298	382
45	98		98	100	97	557		121	161	232

Table based on total sample, including single, married, and previously married females.

Italic figures throughout the series of tables indicate that the calculations are based on less than 50 cases. No calculations are based on less than 11 cases. The dash (—) indicates a percentage or frequency smaller than any quantity which would be shown by a figure in the given number of decimal places.

Table 147. Accumulative Incidence: Orgasm From Any Source By Educational Level

AGE	TOTAL SAMPLE	EDUCATIONAL LEVEL				TOTAL SAMPLE	EDUCATIONAL LEVEL			
		0–8	9–12	13–16	17+		0–8	9–12	13–16	17+
	%		*Percent*			*Cases*		*Cases*		
3	—	0	—	—	—	5873	177	1004	3269	1137
5	2	0	2	1	3	5826	177	1004	3269	1137
10	8	6	8	7	12	5762	177	1004	3269	1137
12	13	10	14	12	17	5738	177	1004	3269	1137
15	23	29	27	20	27	5675	171	1003	3269	1137
20	53	52	58	52	51	4309	125	854	2194	1136
25	77	67	80	79	72	2774	115	683	1034	942
30	86	73	87	88	85	2037	107	499	703	728
35	90	74	93	93	89	1463	89	320	491	563
40	91	79	94	95	89	945	65	192	303	385
45	91		93	95	89	568		125	165	234
48	91		91	99	88	402		98	105	164

Table based on total sample, including single, married, and previously married females.

Table 148. Sources of First Erotic Arousal and Orgasm

SOURCES	TOTAL SAM-PLE	TOTAL MARR. SAM-PLE	AGE AT MARRIAGE				DECADE OF BIRTH			
			16–20	21–25	26–30	31–35	Bf. 1900	1900–1909	1910–1919	1920–1929
FIRST EROTIC AROUSAL										
	%	%	*Percent*				*Percent*			
Masturbation	27	30	26	31	31	33	26	33	31	26
Dreams	1	1	1	1	1	3	1	1	1	1
Petting	34	30	37	30	29	28	31	31	30	33
Coitus	2	3	3	2	3	0	5	4	2	1
Homosexual	3	4	3	4	4	3	5	3	3	5
Animal contacts	1	2	2	1	2	2	2	1	2	2
Psych. stim.	32	30	28	31	30	31	30	27	31	32
Number of cases	4444	1972	515	976	351	93	284	476	720	490
FIRST ORGASM										
	%	%	*Percent*				*Percent*			
Masturbation	40	37	32	37	41	41	38	40	38	33
Dreams	5	4	5	4	4	6	7	4	4	3
Petting	24	18	18	18	17	20	10	15	18	25
Pre-mar. coitus	10	8	9	8	8	8	3	8	9	10
Mar. coitus	17	30	33	30	25	21	37	30	28	26
Homosexual	3	3	2	3	4	3	4	3	2	2
Animal contacts	—	—	1	—	0	1	1	—	—	1
Psych. stim.	1	—	—	—	1	0	0	0	1	—
Number of cases	3826	2181	568	1077	387	101	316	544	789	530

The first column is based on the total sample, single and married. All of the other calculations are based on married females, because they had had a maximum opportunity to have been aroused erotically or to have experienced orgasm.

Table 149. Accumulative Incidence: Pre-Marital Orgasm From Any Source By Educational Level

AGE	TOTAL SAMPLE	EDUCATIONAL LEVEL 0–8	9–12	13–16	17+	TOTAL SAMPLE	EDUCATIONAL LEVEL 0–8	9–12	13–16	17+
	%		Percent			Cases		Cases		
3	—	0	—	—	—	5864	176	1003	3264	1135
5	2	0	2	1	3	5817	176	1003	3264	1135
10	8	6	8	7	12	5753	176	1003	3264	1135
12	13	10	14	12	17	5728	176	1003	3264	1135
15	23	29	27	20	27	5662	169	1000	3264	1135
20	49	39	50	48	50	3926	95	699	2038	1094
25	62		64	62	62	1460		270	480	661
30	70		66	70	74	670		97	184	360
35	75			79	77	380			85	239
40	73				75	206				138
45	70				76	128				94

Table 150. Accumulative Incidence: Orgasm From Any Source By Age at First Marriage

AGE	NEVER MARR. BY AGE 40	TOTAL MARR. SAMPLE	AGE AT FIRST MARRIAGE 16–20	21–25	26–30	NEVER MARR. BY AGE 40	TOTAL MARR. SAMPLE	AGE AT FIRST MARRIAGE 16–20	21–25	26–30
	Percent			Percent		Cases			Cases	
3	1	—	—	—	0	191	2453	646	1208	432
5	4	3	2	2	3	191	2453	646	1208	432
10	13	12	10	12	12	191	2453	646	1208	432
12	16	18	18	17	18	191	2453	646	1208	432
15	21	30	31	29	29	191	2453	646	1208	432
20	37	60	82	55	46	191	2402	600	1208	432
25	51	83	89	89	66	191	2056	428	1036	432
30	64	91	93	94	91	191	1570	308	727	378
35	69	95	94	96	95	191	1138	213	514	266
40	73	96	94	96	98	191	754	144	332	180
45	70	97	95	97	98	126	442	85	193	100

In the total married sample available for the present study, 36 per cent of the females had not experienced orgasm from any source prior to marriage; 15 per cent had experienced orgasm from 1 to 25 times, and 49 per cent had experienced orgasm more than 25 times.

Table 151. Accumulative Incidence: Orgasm From Any Source
By Age at First Marriage and Educational Level

AGE	TOTAL MARRIED SAMPLE	EDUCATIONAL LEVEL			TOTAL MARRIED SAMPLE	EDUCATIONAL LEVEL		
		9–12	13–16	17+		9–12	13–16	17+

AGE AT FIRST MARRIAGE 16–20

AGE	%	Percent			Cases	Cases		
5	2	1	3	3	646	225	308	71
10	10	6	15	11	646	225	308	71
15	31	26	34	34	646	225	308	71
20	82	79	84	86	600	213	279	71
25	89	87	90	97	428	165	169	60
30	93	92	96	100	308	120	106	51
35	94	95	97		213	76	79	

AGE AT FIRST MARRIAGE 21–25

AGE	%	Percent			Cases	Cases		
5	2	3	1	3	1208	315	544	316
10	12	12	11	15	1208	315	544	316
15	29	31	27	31	1208	315	544	316
20	55	55	53	59	1208	315	544	316
25	89	90	89	90	1036	287	448	268
30	94	94	93	95	727	202	301	192
35	96	97	96	97	514	132	202	152

AGE AT FIRST MARRIAGE 26–30

AGE	%	Percent			Cases	Cases		
5	3	4	3	3	432	104	149	163
10	12	12	11	12	432	104	149	163
15	29	29	32	28	432	104	149	163
20	46	50	46	44	432	104	149	163
25	66	66	69	64	432	104	149	163
30	91	83	92	95	378	90	130	144
35	95	94	95	97	266	51	100	103
40	98		98	99	180		66	77

547

Table 152. Accumulative Incidence: Orgasm From Any Source
By Parental Occupational Class

AGE	PARENTAL CLASS				PARENTAL CLASS			
	2+3	4	5	6+7	2+3	4	5	6+7
	Percent				*Cases*			
5	2	—	2	2	996	808	1520	2712
10	8	6	8	9	983	805	1515	2670
15	30	21	23	23	934	800	1509	2642
20	57	50	53	53	703	622	1127	1994
25	77	72	78	77	505	415	716	1208
30	85	83	88	86	375	308	501	899
35	89	88	92	91	264	194	342	685
40	89	88	90	93	170	117	205	465
45	88	89	88	94	105	70	116	280

Table based on total sample, including single, married, and previously married females.

The occupational classes are as follows: 2+3 = unskilled and semi-skilled labor. 4 = skilled labor. 5 = lower white collar class. 6+7 = upper white collar and professional classes.

Table 153. Active Incidence and Frequency: Total Outlet to Orgasm
By Age

AGE DURING ACTIVITY	ACTIVE SAMPLE			TOTAL SAMPLE		CASES IN TOTAL SAMPLE
	Active incid. %	Median freq. per wk.	Mean frequency per wk.	Median freq. per wk.	Mean frequency per wk.	
Adol.–15	22	0.5	1.4 ± 0.08	0.0	0.3 ± 0.02	5677
16–20	50	0.4	1.1 ± 0.04	0.0	0.5 ± 0.02	5649
21–25	72	0.8	1.7 ± 0.05	0.4	1.2 ± 0.04	3607
26–30	84	1.1	2.2 ± 0.07	0.8	1.8 ± 0.06	2554
31–35	88	1.1	2.1 ± 0.08	0.9	1.8 ± 0.07	1855
36–40	89	1.0	2.0 ± 0.10	0.8	1.8 ± 0.09	1301
41–45	87	0.8	1.9 ± 0.12	0.6	1.6 ± 0.11	810
46–50	84	0.6	1.4 ± 0.12	0.4	1.2 ± 0.10	469
51–55	77	0.5	1.1 ± 0.16	0.3	0.9 ± 0.13	240
56–60	66	0.4	0.7 ± 0.11	0.2	0.5 ± 0.08	121
61–65	47	*0.3*	*0.5 ± 0.11*	0.0	0.2 ± 0.06	53
66–70	*37*			*0.0*	*0.1 ± 0.04*	27
71–75	*30*			*0.0*	*0.1 ± 0.04*	10
76–80	*0*			*0.0*	*0.0*	3
81–85	*0*			*0.0*	*0.0*	2
86–90	*0*			*0.0*	*0.0*	1

While there are fewer than 11 cases in each of the oldest age groups, the data are included because of the importance of information on those groups.

**Table 154. Active Incidence and Frequency: Total Outlet to Orgasm
By Age and Marital Status**

| AGE DURING ACTIVITY | ACTIVE SAMPLE | | | TOTAL SAMPLE | | CASES IN TOTAL SAMPLE |
	Active incid. %	Median freq. per wk.	Mean frequency per wk.	Median freq. per wk.	Mean frequency per wk.	
			SINGLE FEMALES			
Adol.–15	22	0.5	1.4 ± 0.08	0.0	0.3 ± 0.02	5677
16–20	47	0.3	0.9 ± 0.04	0.0	0.4 ± 0.02	5613
21–25	60	0.4	1.1 ± 0.05	0.1	0.6 ± 0.03	2810
26–30	66	0.5	1.4 ± 0.10	0.2	0.9 ± 0.07	1064
31–35	70	0.4	1.4 ± 0.16	0.2	1.0 ± 0.12	539
36–40	71	0.5	1.7 ± 0.23	0.3	1.2 ± 0.17	315
41–45	68	0.4	1.6 ± 0.34	0.2	1.1 ± 0.24	179
46–50	61	0.5	1.4 ± 0.35	0.1	0.9 ± 0.22	109
51–55	52	0.3	1.1 ± 0.48	—	0.6 ± 0.25	58
56–60	44	0.4	0.9 ± 0.48	0.0	0.4 ± 0.23	27
			MARRIED FEMALES			
16–20	78	2.2	3.6 ± 0.22	1.3	2.8 ± 0.18	578
21–25	88	1.8	2.8 ± 0.10	1.5	2.5 ± 0.09	1654
26–30	92	1.7	2.6 ± 0.09	1.5	2.4 ± 0.09	1661
31–35	94	1.5	2.4 ± 0.10	1.3	2.3 ± 0.09	1245
36–40	95	1.2	2.2 ± 0.11	1.1	2.1 ± 0.11	850
41–45	93	1.0	2.0 ± 0.15	0.9	1.9 ± 0.14	497
46–50	94	0.8	1.5 ± 0.16	0.7	1.4 ± 0.15	260
51–55	89	0.7	1.2 ± 0.19	0.6	1.1 ± 0.17	118
56–60	82	0.5	0.8 ± 0.13	0.4	0.6 ± 0.11	49
			PREVIOUSLY MARRIED FEMALES			
16–20	70	0.8	2.9 ± 0.85	0.2	2.1 ± 0.62	71
21–25	76	0.9	2.3 ± 0.29	0.4	1.7 ± 0.23	238
26–30	80	0.7	2.0 ± 0.21	0.4	1.6 ± 0.18	328
31–35	85	0.6	1.9 ± 0.20	0.4	1.6 ± 0.18	303
36–40	86	0.7	1.9 ± 0.23	0.5	1.7 ± 0.20	245
41–45	84	0.5	1.8 ± 0.24	0.4	1.5 ± 0.21	195
46–50	84	0.4	1.2 ± 0.16	0.3	1.0 ± 0.14	126
51–55	73	0.4	1.1 ± 0.27	0.2	0.8 ± 0.21	82
56–60	55	0.3	0.6 ± 0.15	—	0.3 ± 0.09	53

Table 155. Active Incidence and Frequency: Total Outlet to Orgasm
By Educational Level and Marital Status

AGE	EDUC. LEVEL	SINGLE			MARRIED			PREVIOUSLY MARRIED		
		Active incid. %	Active median freq. per wk.	Cases in total sample	Active incid. %	Active median freq. per wk.	Cases in total sample	Active incid. %	Active median freq. per wk.	Cases in total sample
Adol. −15	0–8	27	0.8	162						
	9–12	27	0.4	983						
	13–16	19	0.5	3271						
	17+	27	0.5	1128						
16–20	0–8	45	0.7	143						
	9–12	51	0.4	976	73	2.1	210			
	13–16	46	0.3	3299	82	2.1	257			
	17+	48	0.4	1149	83	2.5	66			
21–25	0–8	46	0.6	67	81	1.8	72			
	9–12	60	0.4	537	89	1.7	487	74	1.1	88
	13–16	59	0.4	1204	88	1.7	727	75	0.8	89
	17+	61	0.4	1002	89	2.1	368			
26–30	0–8				84	1.5	81			
	9–12	62	0.5	181	91	1.7	489	76	1.0	100
	13–16	68	0.4	313	92	1.6	670	82	0.6	122
	17+	69	0.4	531	94	1.8	421	88	0.8	84
31–35	0–8				87	1.2	68			
	9–12	65	0.5	65	93	1.3	338	88	0.8	86
	13–16	69	0.5	139	96	1.4	479	84	0.6	106
	17+	75	0.4	309	95	1.7	360	83	0.8	88
36–40	0–8				90	1.0	50			
	9–12				92	1.4	210	87	1.0	62
	13–16	78	0.8	68	96	1.2	322	87	0.6	85
	17+	72	0.5	205	96	1.3	268	90	0.8	78
41–45	9–12				93	1.1	117			
	13–16				92	1.0	181	85	0.4	67
	17+	70	0.4	122	96	1.1	163	84	0.5	67
46–50	9–12				92	1.0	71			
	13–16				96	0.8	91			
	17+	65	0.4	80	95	0.8	76			

Table 156. Active Incidence and Frequency: Total Outlet to Orgasm
By Parental Occupational Class and Marital Status

AGE DURING ACTIVITY	PARENTAL CLASS	SINGLE			MARRIED		
		Active incid. %	Active median freq. per wk.	Cases in total sample	Active incid. %	Active median freq. per wk.	Cases in total sample
Adol.–15	2+3	29	0.6	947			
	4	21	0.4	796			
	5	22	0.4	1506			
	6+7	22	0.5	2654			
16–20	2+3	53	0.4	881	77	2.5	141
	4	45	0.3	796	67	1.6	86
	5	46	0.3	1512	78	2.1	150
	6+7	47	0.3	2648	81	2.2	225
21–25	2+3	62	0.5	460	89	1.7	309
	4	58	0.4	422	89	1.6	230
	5	57	0.4	734	90	1.8	425
	6+7	61	0.4	1283	87	1.9	732
26–30	2+3	65	0.5	195	91	1.6	307
	4	63	0.4	181	92	1.5	232
	5	67	0.4	275	92	1.6	408
	6+7	68	0.5	447	92	1.8	738
31–35	2+3	69	0.4	96	93	1.3	213
	4	62	0.4	91	94	1.2	177
	5	73	0.4	148	96	1.4	291
	6+7	73	0.5	224	95	1.6	572
36–40	2+3	61	0.6	62	93	1.3	134
	4				91	1.0	97
	5	72	0.5	85	96	1.2	208
	6+7	76	0.7	141	95	1.4	419
41–45	2+3				90	0.8	81
	4				90	0.7	63
	5				91	1.1	89
	6+7				95	1.1	261

The occupational classes are as follows: 2+3 = unskilled and semi-skilled labor. 4 = skilled labor. 5 = lower white collar class. 6+7 = upper white collar and professional classes.

Table 157. Accumulative Incidence: Orgasm From Any Source
By Decade of Birth

AGE	DECADE OF BIRTH Bf. 1900	1900–1909	1910–1919	1920–1929	Bf. 1900	DECADE OF BIRTH 1900–1909	1910–1919	1920–1929
	Percent				*Cases*			
5	3	3	2	1	447	771	1319	3058
10	13	13	10	6	447	771	1319	3058
15	28	27	28	20	447	771	1319	3041
20	47	50	55	54	447	771	1318	1771
25	66	75	79	85	447	771	1181	373
30	78	87	89		447	771	818	
35	85	92	95		447	746	270	
40	88	94			447	497		
45	90	95			429	139		

Table based on total sample, including single, married, and previously married females.

Table 158. Accumulative Incidence: Orgasm From Any Source
By Age at Marriage and Decade of Birth

AGE	TOTAL MARR. SAMPLE	Bf. 1900	DECADE OF BIRTH 1900–1909	1910–1919	1920–1929	TOTAL MARR. SAMPLE	Bf. 1900	DECADE OF BIRTH 1900–1909	1910–1919	1920–1929
		AGE AT FIRST MARRIAGE 16–20								
	%		*Percent*			*Cases*		*Cases*		
5	2	0	4	3	1	646	64	113	185	283
10	10	13	12	10	10	646	64	113	185	283
15	31	34	34	31	29	646	64	113	185	283
20	82	75	74	82	86	600	64	113	185	239
25	89	83	85	91	95	428	64	113	177	75
30	93	88	95	93		308	64	113	131	
35	94	89	95			213	64	110		
		AGE AT FIRST MARRIAGE 21–25								
	%		*Percent*			*Cases*		*Cases*		
5	2	4	3	2	2	1208	145	267	475	321
10	12	12	15	12	12	1208	145	267	475	321
15	29	28	30	31	26	1208	145	267	475	321
20	55	43	52	59	57	1208	145	267	475	321
25	89	81	89	91	93	1036	145	267	457	167
30	94	88	95	96		727	145	267	315	
35	96	93	97	100		514	145	265	104	
		AGE AT FIRST MARRIAGE 26–30								
	%		*Percent*			*Cases*		*Cases*		
5	3	4	1	4		432	79	150	190	
10	12	13	12	11		432	79	150	190	
15	29	30	28	28		432	79	150	190	
20	46	42	44	48		432	79	150	190	
25	66	52	64	72		432	79	150	190	
30	91	87	91	92		378	79	150	149	
35	95	94	96			266	79	143		
40	98	97	99			180	79	101		

Table 159. Accumulative Incidence: Orgasm From Any Source
By Age at Onset of Adolescence

| AGE | ADOLESCENT | | | | | ADOLESCENT | | | | |
	By 11	At 12	At 13	At 14	At 15+	By 11	At 12	At 13	At 14	At 15+
	Percent					*Cases*				
5	2	2	2	3	2	1196	1659	1735	789	346
10	10	8	8	9	7	1196	1659	1735	789	346
15	26	22	23	25	19	1176	1643	1724	784	346
20	58	52	53	51	44	868	1209	1309	640	281
25	79	77	76	75	73	508	735	840	457	232
30	85	87	87	84	84	353	483	646	361	193
35	89	94	90	89	88	248	318	467	275	155
40	90	95	91	90	87	150	196	294	188	116
45	90	92	92	92	86	93	108	172	118	76

Table based on total sample, including single, married, and previously married females.

Table 160. Active Incidence and Frequency: Total Outlet to Orgasm
By Decade of Birth and Marital Status

| AGE DURING ACTIVITY | DECADE OF BIRTH | SINGLE | | | MARRIED | | |
		Active incid. %	Active median freq. per wk.	Cases in total sample	Active incid. %	Active median freq. per wk.	Cases in total sample
Adol.–15	Bf. 1900	27	0.4	436			
	1900–1909	26	0.4	760			
	1910–1919	27	0.5	1319			
	1920–1929	19	0.4	3049			
16–20	Bf. 1900	41	0.3	451	72	*3.2*	61
	1900–1909	44	0.4	772	72	1.5	114
	1910–1919	50	0.4	1328	76	2.2	172
	1920–1929	48	0.3	2999	84	2.3	230
21–25	Bf. 1900	45	0.3	366	80	2.2	206
	1900–1909	61	0.5	617	86	1.7	377
	1910–1919	63	0.4	985	90	1.8	624
	1920–1929	61	0.4	843	92	1.8	447
26–30	Bf. 1900	54	0.4	218	86	1.9	272
	1900–1909	69	0.5	344	91	1.6	506
	1910–1919	72	0.5	448	94	1.6	731
	1920–1929	59	*0.4*	54	93	1.8	153
31–35	Bf. 1900	64	0.5	151	90	1.5	290
	1900–1909	71	0.5	228	95	1.5	508
	1910–1919	74	0.4	160	96	1.4	448
36–40	Bf. 1900	66	0.5	123	93	1.4	283
	1900–1909	72	0.6	165	95	1.2	463
	1910–1919				97	1.2	105
41–45	Bf. 1900	64	0.5	116	93	1.0	273
	1900–1909	75	*0.4*	63	94	0.9	224

Table 161. Active Incidence and Frequency: Total Outlet to Orgasm
By Age at Onset of Adolescence and Marital Status

AGE DURING ACTIVITY	AGE AT ADOL.	SINGLE			MARRIED		
		Active incid. %	Active median freq. per wk.	Cases in total sample	Active incid. %	Active median freq. per wk.	Cases in total sample
Adol.–15	8–11	25	0.5	1203			
	12	21	0.4	1684			
	13	22	0.5	1747			
	14	24	0.5	796			
	15+	18	*0.8*	262			
16–20	8–11	53	0.4	1166	80	2.9	139
	12	47	0.3	1638	80	1.8	153
	13	45	0.3	1700	77	2.4	169
	14	46	0.3	777	86	2.1	76
	15+	41	0.3	345			
21–25	8–11	63	0.4	526	88	1.9	333
	12	58	0.4	769	88	1.7	458
	13	60	0.4	850	90	1.8	487
	14	58	0.5	460	87	1.8	254
	15+	57	0.4	203	83	2.2	121
26–30	8–11	69	0.5	196	92	1.7	286
	12	64	0.4	266	92	1.6	426
	13	68	0.5	323	94	1.7	526
	14	66	0.5	192	88	1.7	275
	15+	66	0.3	87	89	1.7	147
31–35	8–11	77	0.4	99	95	1.6	185
	12	76	0.4	122	96	1.3	291
	13	67	0.4	162	96	1.6	414
	14	66	0.7	109	90	1.3	224
	15+				92	1.4	131
36–40	8–11	77	0.7	65	96	1.8	133
	12	77	0.5	66	96	0.9	187
	13	66	0.5	96	97	1.3	269
	14	74	*0.5*	62	90	1.3	168
	15+				91	1.2	93
41–45	8–11				91	1.3	78
	12				94	0.9	102
	13				97	1.0	144
	14				93	0.8	101
	15+				87	1.2	71

Table 162. Accumulative Incidence: Orgasm
From Any Source

By Rural-Urban Background

AGE	RURAL	URBAN	RURAL	URBAN
	Percent		*Cases*	
5	1	2	391	5261
10	6	9	391	5198
15	23	23	388	5122
20	45	53	325	3841
25	70	77	217	2447
30	80	86	163	1783
35	83	91	121	1274
40	84	92	82	818
45	81	92	58	484

Table based on total sample, including single, married, and previously married females.

Table 163. Active Incidence and Frequency: Total Outlet to Orgasm

By Rural-Urban Background

Age	Back-grnd.	Active incid. %	Active median freq. per wk.	Cases in total sample	Age	Back-grnd.	Active incid. %	Active median freq. per wk.	Cases in total sample
Adol. −15	Rural	23	0.5	388	26–30	Rural	57	0.4	104
	Urban	22	0.5	5132		Urban	67	0.5	915
16–20	Rural	42	0.3	386	31–35	Rural	56	0.4	64
	Urban	48	0.3	5080		Urban	72	0.5	453
21–25	Rural	54	0.3	229					
	Urban	60	0.4	2482					

Table based on single females only.

Table 164. Accumulative Incidence: Orgasm From Any Source
By Religious Background

AGE	PROTESTANT			CATHOLIC			JEWISH		
	Dev.	Moder.	Inact.	Dev.	Moder.	Inact.	Dev.	Moder.	Inact.
					Percent				
5	1	1	3	1	3	4	1	1	2
10	7	7	12	5	8	16	3	6	10
15	20	23	29	18	24	42	20	18	26
20	44	49	58	40	53	78	57	55	63
25	69	74	79	63	84	88		83	85
30	81	85	89	72	90	96		89	92
35	85	90	94	79		98		95	95
40	86	92	94						98
45	85	90	95						97
					Cases				
5	1250	1182	1083	393	156	171	112	574	993
10	1235	1168	1073	388	152	170	109	573	983
15	1199	1152	1061	382	150	170	107	571	974
20	906	920	956	282	113	145	54	331	687
25	559	587	727	176	75	106		184	408
30	418	434	544	123	51	79		134	289
35	334	314	413	77		52		75	200
40	234	211	270						125
45	149	132	150						74

Table based on total sample, including single, married, and previously married females.

Table 165. Active Incidence and Frequency: Total Outlet to Orgasm
By Religious Background and Marital Status

AGE DURING ACTIVITY	RELIGIOUS GROUP	SINGLE			MARRIED		
		Active incid. %	Active median freq. per wk.	Cases in total sample	Active incid. %	Active median freq. per wk.	Cases in total sample
Adol.–15	Protestant						
	Devout	19	0.4	1218			
	Moderate	21	0.4	1147			
	Inactive	28	0.5	1063			
	Catholic						
	Devout	17	0.4	382			
	Moderate	23	0.4	150			
	Inactive	41	0.8	169			
	Jewish						
	Devout	19	0.3	107			
	Moderate	18	0.5	571			
	Inactive	25	0.6	978			

(*Table continued on next page*)

Table 165 (continued)

AGE DURING ACTIVITY	RELIGIOUS GROUP	SINGLE			MARRIED		
		Active incid. %	Active median freq. per wk.	Cases in total sample	Active incid. %	Active median freq. per wk.	Cases in total sample
16–20	Protestant						
	Devout	41	0.3	1197	74	2.3	92
	Moderate	43	0.3	1133	77	1.5	97
	Inactive	53	0.4	1065	81	1.8	139
	Catholic						
	Devout	34	0.4	372			
	Moderate	45	0.4	139			
	Inactive	70	0.7	160			
	Jewish						
	Devout	46	0.1	107			
	Moderate	46	0.3	571			
	Inactive	56	0.4	972	79	2.4	118
21–25	Protestant						
	Devout	51	0.3	604	86	1.7	318
	Moderate	57	0.3	615	87	1.7	309
	Inactive	67	0.5	675	89	1.9	392
	Catholic						
	Devout	44	0.4	196	83	1.1	86
	Moderate	60	0.5	57	92	1.7	53
	Inactive	78	1.0	91	94	2.4	67
	Jewish						
	Moderate	62	0.4	192	88	1.8	145
	Inactive	67	0.5	396	91	1.9	319
26–30	Protestant						
	Devout	51	0.4	221	93	1.6	331
	Moderate	70	0.4	249	90	1.6	336
	Inactive	75	0.5	309	90	1.8	413
	Catholic						
	Devout	49	0.3	79	87	1.3	84
	Inactive				97	1.8	58
	Jewish						
	Moderate				91	1.9	140
	Inactive	73	0.7	110	94	1.8	274
31–35	Protestant						
	Devout	54	0.4	121	94	1.4	264
	Moderate	72	0.4	127	93	1.4	253
	Inactive	82	0.5	159	96	1.6	315
	Catholic						
	Devout				86	1.3	63
	Jewish						
	Moderate				94	1.4	102
	Inactive	78	1.1	51	94	1.6	198
36–40	Protestant						
	Devout	50	0.4	76	94	1.1	200
	Moderate	74	0.4	77	95	1.2	175
	Inactive	80	0.5	102	93	1.3	232
	Jewish						
	Moderate				95	1.5	58
	Inactive				98	1.4	131
41–45	Protestant						
	Devout				92	0.8	125
	Moderate				90	1.0	110
	Inactive				95	1.0	128
	Jewish						
	Inactive				95	1.3	79
46–50	Protestant						
	Devout				93	0.5	72
	Moderate				92	0.7	52
	Inactive				94	1.0	62

Table 166. Accumulative Incidence: Percentage of Females Ever Married
      By Educational Level

AGE	TOTAL SAMPLE	EDUCATIONAL LEVEL				TOTAL SAMPLE	EDUCATIONAL LEVEL			
		0–8	9–12	13–16	17+		0–8	9–12	13–16	17+
	%		*Percent*			*Cases*		*Cases*		
15	—	3	1	0	—	5645	175	1013	3304	1153
20	14	33	25	13	6	4364	129	860	2223	1152
25	53	63	67	60	35	2807	119	687	1048	953
30	70	75	83	76	53	2061	111	502	714	734
35	75	81	90	84	58	1483	93	323	498	568
40	78	84	92	87	64	957	68	194	305	389
45	77		91	90	59	575		127	166	236
50	76		87	88	60	311		82	77	122

Data based on age at first marriage, whether legal or common-law.

Table 167. Accumulative Incidence: Percentage of Females Ever Married
      By Decade of Birth

AGE	TOTAL SAMPLE	DECADE OF BIRTH				TOTAL SAMPLE	DECADE OF BIRTH			
		Bf. 1900	1900–1909	1910–1919	1920–1929		Bf. 1900	1900–1909	1910–1919	1920–1929
	%		*Percent*			*Cases*		*Cases*		
15	—	0	1	—	—	5645	456	784	1345	3056
20	14	14	15	14	14	4364	456	784	1344	1775
25	53	47	50	54	66	2807	456	784	1194	368
30	70	65	69	73		2061	456	784	821	
35	75	72	75	78		1483	456	754	272	
40	78	74	83			957	456	499		
45	77	75	84			575	435	139		
50	76	76				311	311			

Data based on age at first marriage, whether legal or common-law.

Table 168. Active Incidence, Frequency, and Percentage of Outlet
Post-Marital Coital Experience and Orgasm

By Age

AGE DURING ACTIVITY	ACTIVE SAMPLE			TOTAL SAMPLE		CASES IN TOTAL SAMPLE
	Active incid. %	Median freq. per wk.	Mean frequency per wk.	Mean frequency per wk.	% of total outlet	
COITAL EXPERIENCE						
16–20	61	0.4	1.3 ± 0.31	0.8 ± 0.20		70
21–25	69	0.8	1.5 ± 0.14	1.0 ± 0.10		238
26–30	68	0.6	1.3 ± 0.13	0.9 ± 0.09		328
31–35	72	0.5	1.3 ± 0.12	0.9 ± 0.09		305
36–40	68	0.6	1.3 ± 0.14	0.9 ± 0.10		246
41–45	59	0.4	0.9 ± 0.12	0.5 ± 0.08		197
46–50	47	0.5	1.0 ± 0.16	0.5 ± 0.09		128
51–55	36	0.4	1.2 ± 0.41	0.4 ± 0.16		83
56–60	25	0.3	0.6 ± 0.28	0.2 ± 0.08		53
COITUS TO ORGASM						
16–20	44	0.3	1.7 ± 0.51	0.7 ± 0.24	83	71
21–25	54	0.7	1.9 ± 0.30	1.0 ± 0.17	66	237
26–30	58	0.5	1.7 ± 0.25	1.0 ± 0.15	63	328
31–35	62	0.5	1.6 ± 0.21	1.0 ± 0.14	62	303
36–40	63	0.5	1.8 ± 0.30	1.2 ± 0.20	69	245
41–45	54	0.4	1.7 ± 0.34	0.9 ± 0.19	61	195
46–50	45	0.4	1.2 ± 0.21	0.6 ± 0.11	54	126
51–55	32	0.4	1.6 ± 0.49	0.5 ± 0.17	63	82
56–60	21	0.4	0.7 ± 0.28	0.2 ± 0.07	43	53

Table 169. Number of Sources of Sexual Experience and Orgasm By Five-Year Age Groups

| AGE GROUP | ANY SOURCE % | NUMBER OF SOURCES | | | | | ACTIVE SAMPLE | | CASES IN TOTAL SAMPLE |
		1	2	3	4	5+6	Mean number of sources	Median number of sources	

PERCENTAGE OF TOTAL SAMPLE HAVING EXPERIENCE

AGE GROUP	ANY SOURCE %	1	2	3	4	5+6	Mean	Median	CASES
Adol.–15	57	38	15	3	1	—	1.4	1.2	5703
16–20	93	41	34	15	3	—	1.8	1.7	5672
21–25	97	32	35	23	6	1	2.0	2.0	3658
26–30	97	36	36	19	5	1	1.9	1.8	2569
31–35	96	38	35	19	4	—	1.9	1.8	1871
36–40	95	36	36	18	4	1	1.9	1.8	1313
41–45	94	40	32	20	2	—	1.9	1.8	818
46–50	90	39	31	17	3	0	1.8	1.7	474
51–55	84	43	28	11	2	0	1.7	1.5	245
56+	76	41	25	9	1	0	1.6	1.4	123

PERCENTAGE OF TOTAL SAMPLE REACHING ORGASM

AGE GROUP	ANY SOURCE %	1	2	3	4	5+6	Mean	Median	CASES
Adol.–15	22	18	3	1	—	—	1.3	1.1	5706
16–20	50	27	16	6	1	—	1.6	1.4	5669
21–25	72	34	24	11	3	—	1.8	1.6	3654
26–30	84	40	30	12	2	—	1.7	1.6	2567
31–35	88	39	33	14	2	—	1.8	1.7	1869
36–40	89	39	33	15	2	—	1.8	1.7	1311
41–45	87	39	31	16	1	—	1.8	1.7	816
46–50	84	38	32	13	1	0	1.7	1.6	476
51–55	77	44	22	10	1	0	1.6	1.4	245
56+	66	36	21	8	1	0	1.6	1.4	123

The possible sources of sexual experience are masturbation, nocturnal sex dreams, petting, coitus, homosexual contacts, and animal contacts. For the calculation of means and medians, the data were treated as continuous data.

Table 170. Percentage of Total Outlet, by Source

   In Total Active Sample

Source	Adol. −15	16–20	21–25	26–30	31–35	36–40	41–45	46–50	51–55
Masturbation	83	48	21	14	14	16	19	22	26
Nocturnal orgasm	2	3	2	2	2	2	3	6	6
Petting to orgasm	4	14	6	2	1	1	1	—	1
Coitus, any	7	31	68	78	79	77	75	71	67
Pre-marital	6	11	9	6	5	6	6	6	3
Marital	—	17	53	63	62	54	49	44	42
Extra-marital	—	1	2	4	5	7	8	9	3
Post-marital	0	2	4	5	7	10	12	12	19
Homosexual	4	4	3	4	4	4	2	1	—
Total outlet	100	100	100	100	100	100	100	100	100
Total solitary	85	51	23	16	16	18	22	28	32
Total heterosexual	11	45	74	80	80	78	76	71	68
Total homosexual	4	4	3	4	4	4	2	1	—
% with any orgasm	22	50	72	84	88	89	87	84	77
Number of cases in total sample	5677	5649	3607	2554	1855	1301	810	469	240

Table based on total sample, including single, married, and previously married females. "Active sample" refers to those experiencing orgasm from any source.

Table 171. Percentage of Total Outlet, by Source
In Active Sample, by Marital Status

Source	Adol.–15	16–20	21–25	26–30	31–35	36–40	41–45	46–50
			SINGLE FEMALES					
Masturbation	84	60	46	41	42	37	45	52
Nocturnal orgasm	2	3	3	3	3	2	2	4
Petting to orgasm	4	18	18	13	8	5	4	3
Coitus	6	15	26	32	33	37	43	37
Homosexual outlet	4	4	7	11	14	19	6	4
Total outlet	100	100	100	100	100	100	100	100
Total solitary	86	63	49	44	45	39	47	56
Total heterosexual	10	33	44	45	41	42	47	40
Total homosexual	4	4	7	11	14	19	6	4
% with any orgasm	22	47	60	66	70	71	68	61
Number of cases in total sample	5677	5613	2810	1064	539	315	179	109
			MARRIED FEMALES					
Masturbation		9	7	7	8	10	11	11
Nocturnal orgasm		1	1	1	2	2	2	3
Coitus, marital		85	89	85	84	78	75	73
Coitus + Petting, extra-marital		5	3	6	6	10	12	13
Homosexual outlet		—	—	1	—	—	—	—
Total outlet		100	100	100	100	100	100	100
Total solitary		10	8	8	10	12	13	14
Total heterosexual		90	92	91	90	88	87	86
Total homosexual		—	—	1	—	—	—	—
% with any orgasm		78	88	92	94	95	93	94
Number of cases in total sample		578	1654	1661	1245	850	497	260
			PREVIOUSLY MARRIED FEMALES					
Masturbation		13	24	23	20	23	26	29
Nocturnal orgasm		—	4	5	5	5	6	14
Coitus + Pet. to orgasm		85	68	63	65	70	62	54
Homosexual outlet		2	4	9	10	2	6	3
Total outlet		100	100	100	100	100	100	100
Total solitary		13	28	28	25	28	32	43
Total heterosexual		85	68	63	65	70	62	54
Total homosexual		2	4	9	10	2	6	3
% with any orgasm		70	76	80	85	86	84	84
Number of cases in total sample		71	238	328	303	245	195	126

"Active sample" refers to those experiencing orgasm from any source.

Table 172. Percentage of Total Outlet, by Source

In Active Sample of Single Females, by Educational Level

Source	Adol.–15	16–20	21–25	26–30	31–35	36–40	41–45
EDUCATIONAL LEVEL 9–12							
Masturbation	73	44	36	38	58		
Nocturnal orgasm	1	2	2	2	4		
Petting to orgasm	6	21	23	16	9		
Coitus	14	29	32	32	23		
Homosexual	6	4	7	12	6		
Total outlet	100	100	100	100	100		
Total solitary	74	46	38	40	62		
Total heterosexual	20	50	55	48	32		
Total homosexual	6	4	7	12	6		
% with any orgasm	27	51	60	62	65		
Number of cases in total sample	983	976	537	181	65		
EDUCATIONAL LEVEL 13–16							
Masturbation	93	65	48	39	30	32	
Nocturnal orgasm	2	4	3	2	2	2	
Petting to orgasm	3	18	15	9	5	3	
Coitus	1	10	26	40	52	46	
Homosexual	1	3	8	10	11	17	
Total outlet	100	100	100	100	100	100	
Total solitary	95	69	51	41	32	34	
Total heterosexual	4	28	41	49	57	49	
Total homosexual	1	3	8	10	11	17	
% with any orgasm	19	46	59	68	69	78	
Number of cases in total sample	3271	3299	1204	313	139	68	
EDUCATIONAL LEVEL 17+							
Masturbation	90	66	47	43	47	40	45
Nocturnal orgasm	3	4	3	3	3	2	2
Petting to orgasm	3	16	20	14	11	6	4
Coitus	2	8	23	27	21	31	42
Homosexual	2	6	7	13	18	21	7
Total outlet	100	100	100	100	100	100	100
Total solitary	93	70	50	46	50	42	47
Total heterosexual	5	24	43	41	32	37	46
Total homosexual	2	6	7	13	18	21	7
% with any orgasm	27	48	61	69	75	72	70
Number of cases in total sample	1128	1149	1002	531	309	205	122

"Active sample" refers to those experiencing orgasm from any source.

Table 173. Percentage of Total Outlet, by Source
In Active Sample of Married Females, by Educational Level

Source	16–20	21–25	26–30	31–35	36–40	41–45	46–50
EDUCATIONAL LEVEL 9–12							
Masturbation	8	5	5	7	9	9	13
Nocturnal org.	1	1	2	2	3	4	3
Coitus, marital	89	91	90	88	83	73	80
Coitus + Pet., extra-marit.	2	3	3	3	5	14	4
Homosexual	—	—	—	0	—	0	0
Total outlet	100	100	100	100	100	100	100
Total solitary	9	6	7	9	12	13	16
Total hetero.	91	94	93	91	88	87	84
Total homosex.	—	—	—	0	—	0	0
% with any orgasm	73	89	91	93	92	93	92
Number of cases in total sample	210	487	489	338	210	117	71
EDUCATIONAL LEVEL 13–16							
Masturbation	8	7	7	7	11	7	10
Nocturnal org.	—	—	1	2	1	2	4
Coitus, marital	90	89	84	82	74	82	76
Coitus + Pet., extra-marit.	1	3	7	8	13	9	10
Homosexual	1	1	1	1	1	0	0
Total outlet	100	100	100	100	100	100	100
Total solitary	8	7	8	9	12	9	14
Total hetero.	91	92	91	90	87	91	86
Total homosex.	1	1	1	1	1	0	0
% with any orgasm	82	88	92	96	96	92	96
Number of cases in total sample	257	727	670	479	322	181	91
EDUCATIONAL LEVEL 17 +							
Masturbation	10	7	9	9	10	17	13
Nocturnal org.	4	2	1	1	1	2	1
Coitus, marital	86	90	83	83	79	65	60
Coitus + Pet., extra-marit.	—	1	7	7	10	16	25
Homosexual	—	—	—	—	—	—	1
Total outlet	100	100	100	100	100	100	100
Total solitary	14	9	10	10	11	19	14
Total hetero.	86	91	90	90	89	81	85
Total homosex.	—	—	—	—	—	—	1
% with any orgasm	83	89	94	95	96	96	95
Number of cases in total sample	66	368	421	360	268	163	76

"Active sample" refers to those experiencing orgasm from any source.

Part III

COMPARISONS OF FEMALE AND MALE

Chapter 14

ANATOMY OF SEXUAL RESPONSE AND ORGASM

In our previous volume (1948) we presented data on the incidences and frequencies of the various types of sexual activity in the human male, and attempted to analyze some of the biologic and social factors which affect those activities. In the previous section of the present volume we have presented similar data for the female. Now it is possible to make comparisons of the sexual activities of the human female and male, and in such comparisons it should be possible to discover some of the basic factors which account for the similarities and the differences between the two sexes.

In view of the historical backgrounds of our Judeo-Christian culture, comparisons of females and males must be undertaken with some trepidation and a considerable sense of responsibility. It should not be forgotten that the social status of women under early Jewish and Christian rule was not much above that which women still hold in the older Asiatic cultures. Their current position in our present-day social organization has been acquired only after some centuries of conflict between the sexes. There were early bans on the female's participation in most of the activities of the social organization; in later centuries there were chivalrous and galante attempts to place her in a unique position in the cultural life of the day. There are still male antagonisms to her emergence as a co-equal in the home and in social affairs. There are romantic rationalizations which obscure the real problems that are involved and, down to the present day, there is more heat than logic in most attempts to show that women are the equal of men, or that the human female differs in some fundamental way from the human male. It would be surprising if we, the present investigators, should have wholly freed ourselves from such century-old biases and succeeded in comparing the two sexes with the complete objectivity which is possible in areas of science that are of less direct import in human affairs. We have, however, tried to accumulate the data with a minimum of pre-judgment, and attempted to make interpretations which would fit those data.

It takes two sexes to carry on the business of our human social organization; but men will never learn to get along better with women, or women with men, until each understands the other as they are and not

567

as they hope or imagine them to be. We cannot believe that social relations between the sexes, and sexual relations in particular, can ever be improved if we continue to be deluded by the longstanding fictions about the similarities, identities, and differences which are supposed to exist between men and women.

BASIC SIGNIFICANCE OF ANATOMIC DATA

It must be emphasized again that what any animal does depends upon the nature of the stimulus which it receives, its physical structure, the capacity of that structure to respond to the given stimulus, and the nature of its previous experience. Its anatomy, its physiology, and its psychology must all be considered before one can adequately understand why the animal behaves as it does.

It is the physical structure which receives the stimulus and responds to it. Some knowledge of the anatomy of that structure and of the way in which it functions must be had before one can make adequate psychologic or social interpretations of any type of behavior. But, conversely, no knowledge of structures can completely explain the behavior unless psychologic factors are taken into account. From the lowest to the highest organism, psychologic factors—the animal's previous experience, what it has learned, and the extent to which its present behavior is conditioned by its previous activity—will determine the way in which its structures function.

Psychologic factors become most significant among those species which have the most highly developed nervous systems. Among mammals, with their highly complex brains, the psychologic aspects of behavior may become of primary importance. This is true of sexual as well as of other types of behavior. It is, of course, particularly true of man, the most complex of all the mammals; and this provides some justification for the considerable attention which has, heretofore, been given to the psychologic and social aspects of human sexual behavior. Nothing we have said or may subsequently say in this chapter or in any other part of our report should be construed to mean that we are unaware of the importance of psychologic factors in human sexual behavior.

Much of the psychologic theory about sex has, however, been developed without any adequate appreciation of the anatomy which is involved whenever there is sexual response. In the human species, there have been anatomic studies of the external genitalia, primarily of the female; there have been studies of the way in which stimulation of those genitalia may be transmitted to the lower levels of the spinal cord, and of the mechanisms by which those portions of the cord then effect genital erection, pelvic thrusts, and orgasm. There have been studies of the significance of the cerebral cortex when there is psychologic stimulation which leads to sexual response (p. 710). But this is about the limit of the sexual anatomy and physiology which has been investigated, and this represents only a small portion of the anatomy and physiology which is actually involved. There has been hardly any investigation of the physiologic changes which occur throughout the body of the animal whenever it is aroused sexually. In fact, there has been a considerable failure to comprehend that sexual responses ever involve anything more than genital responses. We no longer consider the heart the seat of love, or an inflammation of the brain the source of the drive which impels the human creature to perform carnal acts; but we fall almost as far short of the fact when we think of the genitalia as the only structures or even the primary structures which are involved in a sexual response.

Some years ago we realized that it would be impossible to make significant interpretations of our data on human sexual behavior, and especially on the sexual behavior of the human female, or to make significant comparisons of female and male sexuality, until we obtained some better understanding of the anatomy and physiology of sexual response and orgasm. We could never have understood the female's responses in masturbation, in nocturnal dreams, in petting, in coitus, and in homosexual relations, as they are presented in the previous chapters of this volume, and we could never have understood the basic similarities and differences between females and males, if we had not first become acquainted with the anatomy and physiology on which sexual functions depend.

SOURCES OF DATA

There have been six chief sources of the data which we now have on the nature of sexual response and orgasm. These have been:

1. Reports from individuals who, in the course of contributing their histories to this study, have attempted to describe and analyze their own sexual reactions.

2. An invaluable record from scientifically trained persons who have observed human sexual activities in which they themselves were not involved, and who have kept records of their observations.

3. Observations which we and other students have made on the sexual activities of some of the infra-human species of mammals, and a great library of documentary film which we have accumulated for this study of animal behavior.

4. Published clinical data and a body of unpublished gynecologic data that have been made available for the present project.

5. Published data on the gross anatomy of those parts of the body which are involved in sexual response, and some special data on the histology (the detailed anatomy) of some of those structures.

6. The published record of physiologic experiments on the sexual activities of lower mammals and, to a lesser extent, of the human animal.

It is difficult, although not impossible, to acquire any adequate understanding of the physiology of sexual response from clinical records or case history data, for they constitute secondhand reports which depend for their validity upon the capacity of the individual to observe his or her own activity, and upon his or her ability to analyze the physical and physiologic bases of those activities. In no other area have the physiologist and the student of behavior had to rely upon such secondhand sources, while having so little access to direct observation.

This difficulty is particularly acute in the study of sexual behavior because the participant in a sexual relationship becomes physiologically incapacitated as an observer. Sexual arousal reduces one's capacities to see, to hear, to smell, to taste, or to feel with anything like normal acuity, and at the moment of orgasm one's sensory capacities may completely fail (Chapter 15). It is for this reason that most persons are unaware that orgasm is anything more than a genital response and that all parts of their bodies as well as their genitalia are involved when they respond sexually. Persons who have tried to describe their experiences in orgasm may produce literary or artistic descriptions, but they rarely contribute to any understanding of the physiology which is involved.

The usefulness of the observed data to which we have had access depends in no small degree upon the fact that the observations were made in every instance by scientifically trained observers. Moreover, in the interpretation of these data we have had the cooperation of a considerable group of anatomists, physiologists, neurologists, endocrinologists, gynecologists, psychiatrists, and other specialists. The materials are still scant and additional physiologic studies will need to be made.

STIMULATION THROUGH END ORGANS OF TOUCH

Among the mammals, tactile stimulation from touch, pressure, or more general contact is the sort of physical stimulation which most often brings sexual response. In some other groups of animals, sexual responses are more often evoked by other sorts of sensory stimuli.

Among the insects, for instance, the organs of smell and taste are most often involved. In such vertebrates as the fish it becomes difficult to distinguish between responses to sound and responses to pressure. It is true that among mammals, sexual responses may also be initiated through the organs of sight, hearing, smell, and taste; but tactile stimuli account for most mammalian sexual responses.

It has long been recognized that tactile responses are akin to sexual responses,[1] but we now understand that sexual responses amount to something more than simple tactile responses. A sexual response is one which leads the animal to engage in mating behavior, or to manifest some portion of the reactions which are shown in mating behavior. Mating behavior always involves a whole series of physiologic changes, only a small portion of which ordinarily develop when an individual is simply touched. The matter will become apparent as we analyze the data in this and the next chapter.

The organs which make the animal aware that it has been touched, and which at times may lead it to make more specifically sexual responses, are the end organs of touch (nerve endings) that are located in the skin, and some of the deeper nerves of the body. Certain areas of the body which are richly supplied with end organs have long been recognized as "erogenous zones."[2] In the petting techniques which many females and males regularly utilize (Chapter 7), the sexual significance of these areas is commonly recognized. It is, in consequence, surprising to find how many persons still think of the external reproductive organs, the genitalia, as the only true "sex organs," and believe that arousal sufficient to effect orgasm can be achieved only when those structures are directly stimulated.

The data that are given here on the sensitivity of certain structures must, therefore, be considered in relation to the fact that the tactile stimulation of all other surfaces which contain end organs of touch may also produce some degree of erotic arousal.

Penis. In the female and male mammal the external reproductive organs, the genitalia, develop embryologically from a common pattern.[3] They are, therefore, homologous structures in the technical meaning of the term. In spite of considerable dissimilarities in the gross anatomy of the adult female and male genitalia, each structure in the one sex

---

[1] As examples of this association of tactile and sexual responses, see: Bloch 1908:30. Havelock Ellis 1936(I,3):3–8. Freud 1938:599–600.

[2] As examples of such lists of erogenous zones, see: The Kama Sutra of Vatsyayana [between 1st and 6th cent. A.D., Sanskrit]. The Ananga Ranga [12th cent. A.D.?, Sanskrit]. Van de Velde 1930:45–46. Havelock Ellis 1936(II,1):143. Haire 1951:304–306.

[3] For the embryology of the genitalia, see, for instance: Arey 1946:283–308. Patten 1946:575–607. Hamilton, Boyd, and Mossman 1947:193–223.

is homologous to some structure in the other sex. During the first two months of human embryonic development, the differences between the male and the female structures are so slight that it is very difficult to identify the sex of the embryo. In any consideration of the functions of the adult genitalia, and especially of their liability to sensory stimulation, it is important and imperative that one take into account the homologous origins of the structures in the two sexes.

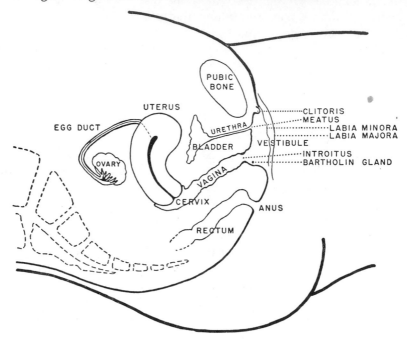

Figure 118. Female reproductive and genital anatomy

The embryonic phallus becomes the penis of the male or the clitoris of the female (Figures 118, 119). The adult structures in both cases are richly supplied with nerves which terminate in what seem to be specialized sorts of end organs of touch—some of which are called Meissner's corpuscles, and some Krause's genital corpuscles.[4]

It is commonly understood that the lower edge of the head (the glans) of the penis, or what is technically known as the corona of the glans, is the area that is most sensitive to tactile stimulation. The area on the under surface of the penis directly below the cleft of the glans

[4] Recent authors are inclined to discard the concept of Krause's corpuscles as end organs of touch and emphasize other end organs, especially Meissner's. See: Fulton 1949:3–6, 17. Ruch in Howell (Fulton edit.) 1949:304–306. Houssay et al. 1951:836. Blake and Ramsey 1951:29. For data on Krause's corpuscles, see: Eberth 1904:249. Jordan 1934:147, 149, 438, 467. Wharton 1947:10. Bailey 1948:585, 630. Dickinson 1949:58. Fulton 1949:6. Maximow and Bloom 1952:181, 524.

is similarly sensitive to stimulation. This latter area lies directly beneath the longitudinal fold (the frenum) by which the loose foreskin is attached if it has not been removed by circumcision.

It appears, however, that there is a minimum of sensation in the main shaft of the penis or in the skin covering it. When the frenum is moved to one side or cut away, pressure on the original point shows that it is as sensitive as it was before the removal of the skin. Stimulation applied by inserting a probe into the urethra similarly shows that the sensory nerves are not located between the urethra and the under surface of the organ, but between the urethra and the spongy mass which forms the shaft of the penis. It remains for the neurologist and the student of male anatomy to identify the exact nerves which are involved, but the present evidence seems to show that they end deep in the shaft of the penis and not in its epidermal covering.

In addition to reactions to sensory stimulation, mechanical reactions also appear to be involved in the erection of the penis. It has been generally assumed that the increased flow of blood into the organ during sexual arousal depends entirely upon circulatory changes which are effected by tactile or other sorts of erotic stimulation; but the possibility that mechanical effects may have something to do with the erection needs consideration. Forward pressures exerted on the corona of the glans not only effect sensory stimulation but, just as in stripping a wet piece of sponge rubber, also help crowd blood into the glans. Similarly, downward pressures on the upper (the distal) ends of the two spongy bodies (the corpora cavernosa) which constitute the shaft of the penis, and especially pressures on the upper edges of the spongy bodies at the point where they meet directly under the frenum, may stimulate the deep-seated nerves; but they may also have some mechanical effect in crowding blood into the corpora.

The effects of any direct stimulation of the penis are so obvious that the organ has assumed a significance which probably exceeds its real importance. The male is likely to localize most of his sexual reactions in his genitalia, and his sexual partner is also likely to consider that this is the part of the body which must be stimulated if the male is to be aroused. This overemphasis on genital action has served, more than anything else, to divert attention from the activities which go on in other parts of the body during sexual response. It has even been suggested that the larger size of the male phallus accounts for most of the differences between female and male sexual responses, and that a female who had a phallus as large as the average penis might respond as quickly, as frequently, and as intensely as the average male. But this is not in accord with our understanding of the basic factors in sexual response. There are fundamental psychologic differences between the two sexes (Chapter 16) which could not be affected by any genital transformation. This opinion is further confirmed by the fact that among several of the other primates, including the gibbon and some of the monkeys, the clitoris of the female is about as large as the penis of the male, but the basic psychosexual differences between the female and male are still present.[5]

Clitoris. The clitoris, which is the phallus of the female, is the homologue of the penis of the male (Figures 118, 119). The shaft of the clitoris may average something over an inch in length. It has a diameter which is less than that of a pencil. Most of the clitoris is embedded in the soft tissue which constitutes the upper (*i.e.*, the anterior) wall of the vestibule to the vagina. The head (glans) of the clitoris is ordinarily the only portion which protrudes beyond the body. In many females the foreskin (the hood) of the clitoris completely covers the head and adheres to it, and then no portion of the clitoris is readily apparent. Because of the small size of any protrudent portions, no localizations of sensitive areas on the corona or on other parts of the clitoris have been recorded.

Also because of its small size and the limited protrusion of the clitoris, many males do not understand that it may be as important a center of stimulation for females as the penis is for males. However, most females consciously or subconsciously recognize the importance of this structure in sexual response. There are many females who are incapable of maximum arousal unless the clitoris is sufficiently stimulated.

In connection with the present study, five gynecologists have cooperated by testing the sensitivity of the clitoris and other parts of the genitalia of nearly nine hundred females. The results, shown in Table 174, constitute a precise and important body of data on a matter which has heretofore been poorly understood and vigorously debated. The record shows that there is some individual variation in the sensitivity of the clitoris: 2 per cent of the tested women seemed to be unaware of tactile stimulation, but 98 per cent were aware of such tactile stimulation of the organ. Similarly, there is considerable evidence that most females respond erotically, often with considerable intensity and immediacy, whenever the clitoris is tactilely stimulated.

We have already noted (p. 158, Table 37) that a high percentage of all the females who masturbate use techniques which involve some

---

[5] For data on the large clitoris of some primates, see: Hooton 1942:175, 231, 252, 273. Ford and Beach 1951:21. In examining spider monkeys we find the clitoris may be as long as or longer than the penis, although not as large in diameter.

sort of rhythmic stimulation of the clitoris, usually with a finger or several fingers or the whole hand. Such techniques often involve the stimulation of the inner surfaces of the labia minora as well, but then each digital stroke usually ends against the clitoris. When the technique includes rhythmic pressure on those structures, the effectiveness of the action may still depend upon the sensitivity of the clitoris and of the labia minora. Even direct penetrations of the vagina during mas-

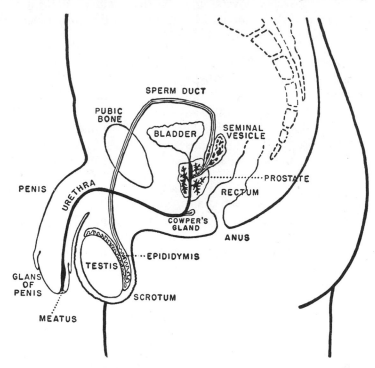

Figure 119. Male reproductive and genital anatomy

turbation may depend for their effectiveness on the fact that the base of the clitoris, which is located in the anterior wall of the vagina, may be stimulated by the penetrating object.

Whenever female homosexual relations include genital techniques, the clitoris is usually involved (Table 130). This is particularly significant because the partners in such contacts often know more about female genital function than either of the partners in a heterosexual relation. While there are more females than males who achieve orgasm through the stimulation of some area other than their genitalia, certainly there are no structures in the female which are more sensitive than the clitoris, the labia minora, and the extension of the labia into the vestibule of the vagina.

The male who comprehends the importance of the clitoris regularly provides manual or other mechanical stimulation of that structure during pre-coital petting. In coitus, he sees to it that the clitoris makes contact with his pubic area, the base of his penis, or some other part of his body. Oral stimulation of the female genitalia is most often directed toward the labia minora or the clitoris.

Some of the psychoanalysts, ignoring the anatomic data, minimize the importance of the clitoris while insisting on the importance of the vagina in female sexual response (p. 582).

Urethra and Meatus. The penis of the male is normally penetrated for its full length by the urethra (Figure 119). The urethra of the female does not penetrate the clitoris; instead it lies in the soft tissues which constitute the upper (the anterior) wall of the vagina (Figure 118). The opening of the urethra of the male (the meatus) is normally on the tip of the head of the penis (Figure 119); in the female it is located between the clitoris and the entrance to the vagina (Figure 118).

A few persons, females and males, employ masturbatory techniques which include insertions of objects into the urethra.[6] The urethral lining which has not become accustomed to such penetration is so sensitive that most individuals, upon initial experimentation, desist from further activity. More experienced persons claim that they receive some erotic stimulation from the penetrations. The recorded satisfactions may include reactions to pain, and sometimes they may be wholly psychologic in origin. Urethral insertions may also stimulate the nerves which lie in the tissue about the urethra of the female, or deep in the shaft of the penis of the male.

There is evidence that the area surrounding the meatus is supplied in some individuals with an accumulation of nerves.[7] Consequently, direct stimulation of the meatus is sometimes included in the masturbatory procedures. This may happen more often in the female than in the male.

Labia Minora. The inner lips of the female genitalia, the labia minora (Figure 118), are homologous with a portion of the skin covering the shaft of the penis of the male. Both the outer and the inner surfaces of the labia minora appear to be supplied with more nerves than most other skin-covered parts of the body, and are highly sensi-

---

[6] Urethral insertions are also noted, for instance, in: Bloch 1908:411. Havelock Ellis 1936(I,1):171–173. Dickinson 1949:63, 69. Grafenberg 1950:146. Haire 1951:147.

[7] For nerve endings located about the urethral meatus of the female, see, for instance: Lewis 1942:8. Dickinson 1949:62.

tive to tactile stimulation. The gynecologic examinations made for this study showed that some 98 per cent of the tested women were conscious of tactile stimulation when it was applied to *either* the out-

Table 174. Responses to Tactile Stimulation and to Pressure, in Female Genital Structures

Structures	% Responding	Total no. of cases	Typical variation in response in 15 cases														
			1	2	3	4	5	6	7	8	9	10	11	12	13	14	15
AREA OF TACTILE STIMULATION																	
Labia majora																	
Right	92	854	x	x	√	√	x	x	√		√	√	√		√	√	x
Left	87	854	x	x	√	√	√	x	√		x	√	√		√	√	x
Clitoris	98	879	√	x	√	√	√	√	√	√	x	√	√	x	√	√	√
Labia minora																	
Right, outer surf.	97	879	x	x	√	√	x	√	√	√	√	√	√	x	√	√	√
Right, inner surf.	98	879	x	x	√	√	x	√	√	√	√	√	√	x	√	√	√
Left, outer surf.	95	879	√	x	√	√	x	√	√	√	x	√	√	x	√	√	√
Left, inner surf.	96	879	√	x	√	√	x	√	√	√	√	√	√	x	√	√	√
Vestibule																	
Anterior surf.	92	650	x	x	x	√	√			√	√	√	√	√	√	√	√
Posterior surf.	96	879	√	√	√	√	√	√	√	√	√	√	√	x	√	√	√
Right surf.	98	879	√	√	√	√	√	√	√	√	√	√	x	√	√	√	√
Left surf.	98	879	√	√	√	√	√	√	√	√	√	√	x	√	√	x	√
Vagina																	
Anterior wall	11	578	x	x	x	√	x	x	x	√	x	√	x	x	√	x	
Posterior wall	13	578	x	x	x	√	x	x	x	√	x	x	x	x	√	x	
Right wall	14	578	x	x	x	√	√	x	x	√	x	√	x	x	√	x	
Left wall	14	578	x	x	x	√	√	x	x	√	x	√	x	x	√	x	
Cervix	5	878	x	x	x	√	√	√	x	x	x	x	x	x	x	x	x
AREA OF PRESSURE																	
Vagina																	
Anterior wall	89	878	x	√	√	√	√	√	√	√	√	√	x	x	x	x	√
Posterior wall	93	878	√	√	√	√	√	√	√	√	√	√	√	x	x	√	√
Cervix	84	878	x	√	√	√	√	√	√	√	√	√	x	√	x	x	√

The check (√) shows response, x shows lack of response to stimulation in the designated area. The tests were made by five experienced gynecologists, two of them female, on a total of 879 females. In all of the tests, the vagina was spread with a speculum, and all testing of internal structures was done with especial care not to provide any simultaneous stimulation of the external areas. The tests of tactile responsiveness were made with a glass, metal, or cotton-tipped probe with which the indicated areas were gently stroked. Awareness of pressure was tested by exerting distinct pressure at the indicated points with an object larger than a probe. Finer standardizations of the tests proved impractical under the office conditions. It should be noted that awareness of tactile stimulation or of pressure does not demonstrate the capacity to be aroused erotically by similar stimuli; but it seems probable that any area which is not responsive to tactile stimulation or pressure cannot be involved in erotic response.

side or inside surfaces of the labia, and about equally responsive to stimulation of either the left or right labium (Table 174).

As sources of erotic arousal, the labia minora seem to be fully as important as the clitoris. Consequently, masturbation in the female usually involves some sort of stimulation of the inner surfaces of these labia. Sometimes this is accomplished through digital strokes which may be confined to the labial surfaces; usually the strokes extend to the clitoris which is located at the upper (the anterior) end of the genital area where the two labia minora unite to form a clitoral hood. However, manipulation of the labia may also involve nerves that lie deep within their tissues. This is suggested by the fact that digital stimulation of the labia is often effected while the thighs are tightly pressed together so pressure may be exerted on the labia. Sometimes the technique may involve nothing more than a tightening of the thighs or a crossing of the legs, without digital stimulation. Sometimes the labia are rhythmically pulled in masturbation. During coitus, the entrance of the male organ into the vagina may provide considerable stimulation for the labia minora. All of these techniques are also significant in producing the muscular tensions which are of prime importance in the development of sexual responses (p. 618).

Labia Majora and Scrotum. The solid, outer lips (the labia majora) of the female genitalia are (at least in part) homologues of the skin which forms the scrotum of the male (Figures 118, 119). Both structures develop from the two swollen ridges which lie on the sides of the genital area in the developing embryo. They form the lateral limits of the adult female genitalia. The homologous ridges in the male embryo become hollow during their development. Finally their two cavities unite to form a single cavity in a single sac, the scrotum of the male. In the human male, shortly before the completion of embryonic development, the testes, which have previously been located in the body cavity, descend through the inguinal canals (which lie in the groins) and take up their permanent locations in the scrotum.

The labia majora of the female are sensitive to tactile stimulation. This was so in some 92 per cent of the women who were tested by the gynecologists (Table 174). But there is a difference between the capacity to respond to tactile stimulation and the capacity to respond erotically. Although it is improbable that any area which is insensitive to tactile manipulation could be stimulated erotically, some areas which are tactilely sensitive (e.g., the backs of the hands, the shoulders) are of no especial importance as sources of erotic response. We do not yet have evidence that the labia majora contribute in any important way to the erotic responses of the female.

Neither do we have any evidence that the skin of the scrotum is more sensitive than any other skin-covered surface of the body, and the scrotum does not seem an important source of erotic arousal.[8] There are quite a few males who react erotically, and a small number who

---

[8] Havelock Ellis 1936(II,1):123 also states that the scrotum "is not the seat of any voluptuous sensation."

may respond to the point of orgasm when there is some stimulation or more active manipulation of the testes; but this response is not due to the stimulation of the skin of the scrotum.

Vestibule of Vagina. The labia minora continue inward to form a broad, funnel-shaped vestibule which leads to the actual entrance (the orifice or introitus) of the vagina (Figure 118). The structure represents an in-pocketing of external epidermis which is well supplied with end organs of touch. Nearly all females—about 97 per cent according to the gynecologic tests (Table 174)—are distinctly conscious of tactile stimulation applied *anywhere* in this vestibule, and only a very occasional female out of the 879 who were tested proved to be entirely insensitive in the area. For nearly all women the vestibule is as important a source of erotic stimulation as the labia minora or the clitoris. Since the vestibule must be penetrated by the penis of the male in coitus, it is of considerable importance as a source of erotic stimulation for the female.

The hymen of the virgin female is a more or less thin membrane which lies at the inner limits of the vestibule. It is attached by its outer rim, partially blocking the entrance to the vagina. It usually has a natural opening of some diameter located in the center of the membrane, but this may, of course, be enlarged either by coitus or by the insertion of fingers, tampons, or other objects. An unusually thick or tough hymen which might cause considerable pain if it were first stretched or torn in coitus, may be more easily stretched or cut by the physician who makes a pre-marital examination. Remnants of the hymen almost always persist even after long years of coital experience, and the remnant of the tissue is sometimes sensitive. It is not clear whether the sensitivity depends on nerves in the remnants of the tissue or on the fact that movements of the tissue may stimulate the underlying nerves.

A ring of powerful muscles (the levator muscles) lies just beyond the vaginal entrance. The cavity of the vagina extends beyond this point. The female may be very conscious of pressure on the levators. The muscles may respond reflexly when they are stimulated by pressure, and most females are erotically aroused when they are so stimulated.

Interior of Vagina. The vagina is the internal cavity which lies beyond the external genitalia of the female (Figure 118). Unlike its vestibule, the vagina is derived embryologically from the primitive egg ducts which, like nearly all other internal body structures, are poorly supplied with end organs of touch. The internal (entodermal) origin of the lining of the vagina makes it similar in this respect to the rectum and other parts of the digestive tract. There is no functional homologue of the vagina in the male.

In most females the walls of the vagina are devoid of end organs of touch and are quite insensitive when they are gently stroked or lightly pressed. For most individuals the insensitivity extends to every part of the vagina. Among the women who were tested in our gynecologic sample, less than 14 per cent were at all conscious that they had been touched (Table 174). Most of those who did make some response had the sensitivity confined to certain points, in most cases on the upper (anterior) walls of the vagina just inside the vaginal entrance. The limited histologic studies of vaginal tissues confirm this experimental evidence that end organs of touch are in most cases lacking in the walls of the vagina, although some nerves have been found at spots in the vaginal walls of some individuals.[9]

This insensitivity of the vagina has been recognized by gynecologists who regularly probe and do surface operations in this area without using anesthesia.[10] Under such conditions most patients show little if any awareness of pain. There is some individual variation in this regard, and clinicians are aware of this, for they ordinarily stand prepared to administer a local anesthetic if the patient does register pain.

The relative unimportance of the vagina as a center of erotic stimulation is further attested by the fact that relatively few females masturbate by making deep vaginal insertions (p. 161, Table 37). Fully 84 per cent of the females in the sample who had masturbated had depended chiefly on labial and clitorial stimulation. Although some 20 per cent had masturbated on occasion by inserting their fingers or other objects into the vagina, only a small portion had regularly used that technique. Moreover, the majority of those who had made insertions did so primarily for the sake of providing additional pressure on the introital ring of muscles, or to stimulate the anterior wall of the vagina at the base of the clitoris, and they had not made deeper insertions. As we shall note below, there is satisfaction to be obtained from deeper penetration of the vagina by way of nerve masses that lie outside of the vaginal wall itself, but all the evidence indicates that the vaginal walls are quite insensitive in the great majority of females.[11]

---

[9] Relative lack of nerves and end organs in the vaginal surface is noted by: Dahl acc. Kuntz 1945:319. Undeutsch 1950:447. Dr. F. J. Hector (Bristol, England) and Dr. K. E. Krantz (University of Vermont) have furnished us with histologic data on this point. Vaginal sensitivity applying primarily to the area on the anterior wall at the base of the clitoris is also noted in: Lewis 1942:8. Grafenberg 1950:146, 148.

[10] From our gynecologic consultants, we have abundant data on the limited necessity of using anesthesia in vaginal operations. See also Döderlein and Krönig 1907:88.

[11] Simone de Beauvoir 1952:373 says vaginal pleasure certainly exists, and pro-

In most of the homosexual relations had by females, there is no attempt at deep vaginal insertions (Table 130). Once again, the insertions that are made are usually confined to the introitus or intended to stimulate the anterior wall of the vagina at the base of the clitoris. Occasionally there are deeper penetrations in order to reach the perineal nerves (p. 584). This restriction of so much of the homosexual technique is especially significant because, as we have already noted, homosexual females have a better than average understanding of female genital anatomy.

On the other hand, many females, and perhaps a majority of them, find that when coitus involves deep vaginal penetrations, they secure a type of satisfaction which differs from that provided by the stimulation of the labia or clitoris alone. In view of the evidence that the walls of the vagina are ordinarily insensitive, it is obvious that the satisfactions obtained from vaginal penetration must depend on some mechanism that lies outside of the vaginal walls themselves.

There is a parallel situation in anal coitus. The anus, like the entrance to the vagina, is richly supplied with nerves, but the rectum, like the depths of the vagina, is a tube which is poorly supplied with sensory nerves. However, the receiving partner, female or male, often reports that the deep penetration of the rectum may bring satisfaction which is, in many respects, comparable to that which may be obtained from a deep vaginal insertion.

There may be six or more sources of the satisfactions obtainable from deep vaginal penetrations, and several or all of these may be involved in any particular case. The six sources are:

1. Psychologic satisfaction in knowing that a sexual union and deep penetration have been effected. The realization that the partner is being satisfied may be a factor of considerable importance here.

2. Tactile stimulation coming from the full body contact with the partner, and from his weight. This may result in pressures on various internal organs which can produce "referred sensations." These may be incorrectly interpreted as coming from surface stimulation.

3. Tactile stimulation by the male genitalia or body pressing against the labia minora, the clitoris, or the vestibule of the vagina. This alone would provide sufficient stimulation to bring most females to orgasm. The location of this stimulation may be correctly recognized, or it may be incorrectly attributed to the interior of the vagina (see p. 584).

poses (without specific data) that vaginal masturbation seems more common than we have indicated.

4. Stimulation of the levator ring of muscles in coitus. Such stimulation may bring reflex spasms which may have distinctly erotic significance.

5. Stimulation of the nerves that lie on the perineal muscle mass (the so-called pelvic sling), which is located between the rectum and the vagina (see the discussion of the perineum, below).

6. The direct stimulation, in some females, of end organs in the walls of the vagina itself. But this can be true only of the 14 per cent who are conscious of tactile stimulation of the area. There is, however, no evidence that the vagina is ever the sole source of arousal, or even the primary source of erotic arousal in any female.

Some of the psychoanalysts and some other clinicians insist that only vaginal stimulation and a "vaginal orgasm" can provide a psychologically satisfactory culmination to the activity of a "sexually mature" female. It is difficult, however, in the light of our present understanding of the anatomy and physiology of sexual response, to understand what can be meant by a "vaginal orgasm." The literature usually implies that the vagina itself should be the center of sensory stimulation, and this as we have seen is a physical and physiologic impossibility for nearly all females. Freud recognized that the clitoris is highly sensitive and the vagina insensitive in the younger female, but he contended that psychosexual maturation involved a subordination of clitoral reactions and a development of sensitivity within the vagina itself; but there are no anatomic data to indicate that such a physical transformation has ever been observed or is possible.[12]

---

[12] For Freud's interpretation of the relative importance of the clitoris and vagina, and the adoption of this interpretation by many of the psychoanalysts, see, for instance: Freud 1933:161 (". . . in the phallic phase of the girl, the clitoris is the dominant erotogenic zone. But it is not destined to remain so; with the change to femininity, the clitoris must give up to the vagina its sensitivity, and, with it, its importance, either wholly or in part"). Freud 1935:278 ("The clitoris in the girl, moreover, is in every way equivalent during childhood to the penis. . . . In the transition to womanhood very much depends upon the early and complete relegation of this sensitivity from the clitoris over to the vaginal orifice"). Hitschmann and Bergler 1936:15 (". . . the girl . . . must undertake a *removal of the leading sexual zone* from the clitoris to the vagina. . . . If this transition is not successful, then the woman cannot experience satisfaction in the sexual act. . . . *The first and decisive requisite of a normal orgasm is vaginal sensitivity*"). Deutsch 1945(2):80 (". . . the clitoris preserves its excitability during the latency period and is unwilling to cede its function smoothly, while the vagina for its part does not prove completely willing to take over both functions, reproduction and sexual pleasure"). Fenichel 1945:82 ("The significance of the phallic period for the female sex is associated with the fact that the feminine genitals have two leading erogenous zones: the clitoris and the vagina. In the infantile genital period the former and in the adult period the latter is in the foreground. The change from the clitoris as the leading zone to the vagina is a step that definitely occurs in or after puberty only"). Kroger and Freed 1950:528 ("Hence, in the child the clitoris gives sexual satisfaction, while in

The concept of a vaginal orgasm may mean, on the other hand, that the spasms that accompany or follow orgasm involve the vagina; and in much of the psychoanalytic literature there is an implication that the vagina must be chiefly involved before one may expect any maximum and "mature" psychosexual satisfaction.[13] This is an equally untenable interpretation for, as we shall see in Chapter 15, most parts of the nervous system, and all parts of the body which are controlled by those parts of the nervous system, are involved whenever there is sexual response and orgasm. In some individuals the spasms or convulsions that follow orgasm are intense and prolonged, and in others they are mild and of short duration. The individual differences in patterns of response are quite persistent throughout an individual's lifetime, and probably depend upon inherent capacities more than upon learned acquirements. Those females who have extensive spasms throughout their bodies when they reach orgasm are the ones who are likely to have vaginal convulsions of some magnitude at the same time. Those who make few gross body responses in orgasm are not likely to show intense vaginal contractions. No question of "maturity" seems to be involved, and there is no evidence that the vagina responds in orgasm as a separate organ and apart from the total body. Whether a female or male derives more or less intense sensory or psychologic satisfaction when the vaginal spasms are more or less extreme is a matter which it would be very difficult to analyze.

---

the normal adult woman the vagina is supposed to be the principal sexual organ . . . . in frigid women the transference of sexual satisfaction and excitement from the clitoris to the vagina, which usually occurs with emotional maturation, does not take place). See also: Chideckel 1935:39. Ferenczi 1936: 255–256. Knight 1943:28. Abraham (1927) 1948:284.

[13] The shift from clitoris to vagina is sometimes stated to be psychologic rather than physiologic, and in psychoanalytic theory the failure to effect this change is frequently considered the chief cause of frigidity. For example, see: Freud 1935:278 ("In those women who are sexually anaesthetic, as it is called, the clitoris has stubbornly retained this sensitivity"). Hitschmann and Bergler 1936:20 ("Under frigidity we understand the incapacity of woman to have a *vaginal orgasm.* . . . The sole criterion of frigidity is the absence of the vaginal orgasm"). Deutsch 1944(1):233 ("The competition of the clitoris, which intercepts the excitations unable to reach the vagina, and the genital trauma then create the dispositional basis of a permanent sexual inhibition, *i.e.,* frigidity"). Abraham (1927) 1948:359 ("In . . . frigidity the pleasurable sensation is as a rule situated in the clitoris and the vaginal zone has none"). Kroger and Freed 1950:526 ("However, as a general rule, the question of what constitutes true frigidity depends on whether clitoric or vaginal response is achieved. It is believed that the clitoris does not often come into contact with the male organ during intercourse, and, if a transfer in sensation occurs from the clitoris to the vagina, it is purely psychologic and unconscious. In completely frigid women this psychologic transmission is always disturbed. Therefore, the problem of frigidity is reduced to a psychologic basis"). See also: Lundberg and Farnham 1947:266. Stokes 1948:39. Bergler 1951:216 (transfer is purely psychologic). Beauvoir 1952:372 ("the clitorid orgasm . . . is a kind of detumescence . . . only indirectly connected with normal coition, and it plays no part in procreation").

This question is one of considerable importance because much of the literature and many of the clinicians, including psychoanalysts and some of the clinical psychologists and marriage counselors, have expended considerable effort trying to teach their patients to transfer "clitoral responses" into "vaginal responses." Some hundreds of the women in our own study and many thousands of the patients of certain clinicians have consequently been much disturbed by their failure to accomplish this biologic impossibility.

Cervix. The cervix is the lower portion of the uterus (Figure 118). It protrudes into the deeper recesses of the vaginal cavity, and stands out from the vaginal wall as a rounded and blunt tip about as large or larger than the tip of a thumb. It has been identified by some of our subjects, as well as by many of the patients who go to gynecologists, as an area which must be stimulated by the penetrating male organ before they can achieve full and complete satisfaction in orgasm; but most females are incapable of localizing the sources of their sexual arousal, and gynecologic patients may insist that they feel the clinician touching the cervix when, in reality, the stimulation had been applied to the upper (anterior) wall of the vestibule to the vagina near the clitoris. All of the clinical and experimental data show that the surface of the cervix is the most completely insensitive part of the female genital anatomy. Some 95 per cent of the 879 women tested by the gynecologists for the present study were totally unaware that they had been touched when the cervix was stroked or even lightly pressed (Table 174). Less than 5 per cent were more or less conscious of such stimulation, and only 2 per cent of the group showed anything more than localized and vague responses.

Histologic studies show that there are essentially no tactile nerve ends in the surfaces of the cervix. This is further confirmed by gynecologic experience, for the surfaces are regularly cauterized and operated upon in other ways without the use of any anesthesia—and nearly all such patients are unaware that they have been touched. Cutting deeper into the tissue of the cervix may lead an occasional patient to register pain, and the dilation of the cervical canal causes most patients to feel intense pain. In none of these instances, however, is there any evidence of erotic response.[14]

Perineum. The perineal area includes and lies between the lower portions of the digestive and the reproductive tracts. The area is essentially the same in the female and the male. The surface of the perineum includes the anal and genital areas and all of the space between.

---

[14] Our data on the insensitivity of the cervix come from the abundant experience of our gynecologic consultants. See our Table 174. See also: Döderlein and Krönig 1907:88. Malchow 1923:183. Lewis 1942:8. Dickinson ms.

This surface is highly sensitive to touch, and tactile stimulation of the area may provide considerable erotic arousal.

The perineal area is occupied for the most part by layers of muscles, the so-called pelvic sling. Within and on this muscular mass there are nerves, and the area is, in consequence, definitely sensitive when it is stimulated with any sufficiently strong pressure. Many males are quickly brought to erection when pressure is applied on the perineal surface at a point which is about midway between the anus and the scrotum. In the case of the female, strong pressure applied from inside on the posterior (lower) wall at the back of the vagina may stimulate these same nerves, and this is one of the sources of the satisfaction which many females experience when the vagina is penetrated in coitus. Deep penetrations of the rectum may stimulate the same perineal nerves, and prove to be similarly erotic.

Anus. The anal area is erotically responsive in some individuals. In others it appears to have no particular erotic significance even though it may be highly sensitive to tactile stimulation. As many as half or more of the population may find some degree of erotic satisfaction in anal stimulation, but good incidence data are not available. There are some females and males who may be as aroused erotically by anal stimulation as they are by stimulation of the genitalia, or who may be more intensely aroused.

The erotic sensitivity of the anal area depends in part upon the fact that there are abundant end organs of touch throughout the anal surfaces, and in part upon the fact that reactions of the muscles (the anal sphincters) which normally keep the anus closed may be erotically stimulating. Some persons are psychologically aroused while others respond negatively to the idea of anal intercourse, and psychologic factors may have a good deal to do with the erotic or non-erotic significance of such contacts. These generalizations apply to both females and males.

Penetration of the anus may cause pain, and this may intensify the sexual responses for some persons.

The anus is particularly significant in sexual responses because the anal and genital areas share some muscles in common, and the activity of either area may bring the other area into action. Stimulation of the genitalia, both in the female and the male, may cause anal constrictions. Gynecologists frequently observe that stimulation of the clitoris, or of the areas about the clitoris and the urethral meatus, may cause contractions of the anus,[15] the hymenal ring, and the vaginal and peri-

---

[15] An early reference to anal contractions during coitus is found in Aristotle [4th cent. B.C.]: Problems, Bk.IV:879b.

neal muscles. As rhythmic muscular movements develop during sexual responses, and particularly in the spasms that follow orgasm, the anal sphincter may rhythmically open and close. The incentives for anal insertions of various sorts and for anal intercourse lie partly in the significance of these rhythmic responses of the anal sphincters.

Conversely, contractions of the anal sphincter, whether they be voluntary or initiated by erotic stimulation, may bring contractions of the muscles that extend into the genitalia and produce erection in the male or movement of the genital parts in the female. As a matter of fact, contractions of the anal sphincter appear to produce contractions of muscles in various remote parts of the body, including areas as far away as the throat and the nose. Anal contractions may cause the sides of the nose to flare, and the subject is inclined to inhale deeply—both of which are characteristic aspects of an individual who is responding sexually. When the clinician has difficulty in bringing a patient out of anesthesia, he may start deep breathing by inserting a gloved finger into the anus of the patient. Anal contractions may also be associated with contractions of still other muscles elsewhere in the body; for the contraction of any muscle, anywhere in the body, may develop tensions in every other muscle in the body (p. 618).

Apparently the abdominal diaphragm is involved when there is anal contraction, for it is very difficult for an individual to exhale as long as the anal sphincters are under any considerable tension.

In brief, anal contractions, perineal responses, genital responses, and nasal and oral responses are so closely associated that one may believe that some sort of simple and direct reflex arc is involved. We do not yet understand the neural bases of such a connection.

Breasts. The breasts of both the male and the female may be more sensitive than some other parts of the body. Because of the greater size of the female breast its reactions to tactile stimulation are quite generally known. Among the infra-human mammals, the breast rarely plays a part in sexual activity,[16] but among human animals there may be a considerable amount of manual or oral stimulation of the female breast. In American patterns of sexual behavior, breast stimulation most regularly occurs among the better educated groups where nearly all of the males (99%) manually manipulate the female breast, and about 93 per cent orally stimulate the female breast during heterosexual petting or pre-coital play (Tables 73, 100). All of this usually stimulates the male erotically, but the significance for the female has probably been

---

[16] The relative infrequency of breast stimulation in the sexual activity of the infra-human mammal is also noted by Ford and Beach 1951:48. See also p. 255 of the present volume.

overestimated. There are some females who appear to find no erotic satisfaction in having their breasts manipulated; perhaps half of them do derive some distinct satisfaction, but not more than a very small percentage ever respond intensely enough to reach orgasm as a result of such stimulation (Chapter 5).[17] Some females hold their own breasts during masturbation, coitus, or homosexual activities, evidently deriving some satisfaction from the pressure so applied; but there were only 11 per cent of the females in our sample who recorded any frequent use of breast stimulation as an aid to masturbation (Table 37).

Because of their smaller size the sensitivity of the male breasts has not so often been recognized except among some of the males who have had homosexual experience. This is undoubtedly not due to differences between heterosexual and homosexual males, but to the fact that relatively few females ever try to stimulate the breasts of their male partners, whereas such behavior is rather frequent in male homosexual relations. Our homosexual histories suggest that there may be as many males as there are females whose breasts are distinctly sensitive. A few males may even reach orgasm as a result of breast stimulation.[18]

Mouth. The lips, the tongue, and the whole interior of the mouth constitute or could constitute for most individuals an erogenous area of nearly as great significance as the genitalia. Erotic arousal always involves the entire nervous system, and there appears to be some oral response whenever there is sexual arousal. We have already noted (p. 586) the apparently reflex connections between contractions of the genital, anal, nasal, and oral musculatures. Most uninhibited individuals become quite conscious of their oral responses, particularly if they accept deep kissing, mouth-breast contacts, or mouth-genital contacts as part of their sexual play.

The significance of the mouth depends, of course, upon the fact that all of its parts are richly supplied with nerves. This is true throughout the class Mammalia, and also true of some of the other vertebrates. Fish, lizards, many birds, and practically all of the mammalian species which have been studied are likely to place their mouths on some part of the partner's body during pre-coital play or actual coitus (see p. 229). Mouth-to-mouth contacts between some of the birds and mammals may occasionally be continued for hours. The sexual significance

---

[17] Records of females reaching orgasm from breast stimulation alone are rare. In addition to our own data (p. 161), we note: Moraglia 1897:7–8. Rohleder 1921:44. Eberhard 1924:246. Kind and Moreck 1930:156. Dickinson 1949: 66–67. Grafenberg 1950:146.

[18] The sensitivity of male breasts is recorded in our 1948:575. It is also recorded in: Van de Velde 1930:164. Féré 1932:105. Pillay 1950:81.

of the mouth is obviously of long phylogenetic standing.[19] The human
animal testifies to its origin when it engages in mouth activity during
sexual relationships. The human is exceptional among the mammals
when it abstains from oral activities because of learned social proprieties, moral restraints, or exaggerated ideas of sanitation.

In the course of mammalian oral activity, the lips may be pressed
against the mouth or against some other portion of the partner's body;
tongues are brought into contact or used to lick the body; the lips and
the teeth may nibble, or the teeth may bite more severely somewhere
on the partner's body. In some of the lower mammals (*e.g.*, the mink)
such biting may penetrate the skin of the partner,[20] and while this is
the means by which the males of these species hold the females in
position for coitus, the immediate source of such behavior probably
lies in the sensory satisfaction which the male secures by making these
contacts. Even such large animals as stallions, which are ill-equipped
to make contacts with their mouths, keep their lips in constant motion
during sexual activity and constantly attempt to nibble or bite over the
surface of the body of the mare. In many mammalian species, where
the tip of the nose may be as sensitive as the lips of the mouth, the lips
and the nose are used indiscriminately to make contacts with all parts
of the body.[21] All of these things also happen during sexual activity in
an uninhibited human animal.

It is not surprising that the two areas of the body which are most
sensitive erotically, namely the mouth and the genitalia, should frequently be brought into direct contact. The high incidence of such
mouth-genital contacts in all species of mammals, from one to the other
end of the class Mammalia, and the high frequency of mouth-genital
contacts in the human animal have been detailed in our volume on
the male (1948: especially pages 368–373, 573–578), and in the present
volume (pp. 229, 257).

Ears. The lobe of the ear and the inner cavity leading from it are
points of especial sensitivity for at least some persons.[22] The ear lobes

---

[19] For our own data on oral activity among the lower mammals, see p. 229 including footnotes 3 and 4. Also see: Yerkes 1929:296. Zuckerman 1932:123,
147, 227, 230. Yerkes and Elder 1936a:10–11. Havelock Ellis 1936(1,2):85.
Reed 1946:*passim*. Beach in Hoch and Zubin 1949:55–62. Ford and Beach
1951:46–55.

[20] Biting through the skin of the sexual partner's neck is recorded for the mink,
ferret, marten, and sable. See also: Ford and Beach 1951:58–59.

[21] Manipulation of the sexual partner's body with the nose and lips has occurred
among nearly all of the species of mammals which we have observed (see p.
229). See also: Stone 1922 (rat). Louttit 1927 (guinea pig). Shadle 1946
(porcupine). Reed 1946 (various mammals).

[22] The erotic sensitivity of the ear is quite common knowledge. In the literature
see: Van de Velde 1930:45. Havelock Ellis 1936(II,1):143. Stone and Stone
1937:221; 1952:182. Beach 1947b:246.

become engorged with blood during sexual arousal, and become increasingly sensitive at that time. An occasional female or male may reach orgasm as a result of the stimulation of the ears.

Buttocks. Tactile stimulation and heavier pressure on the buttocks may elicit unusually strong responses from the gluteal muscles.[23] These are the largest and the chief muscles on the back surface of the upper part of the leg. Contractions of these muscles reflect, more than any other one factor, the development of the nervous and muscular tensions which are involved in erotic arousal. Some persons, both female and male, deliberately contract these gluteal muscles to build up their erotic responses. Movements of vertebral muscles in conjunction with contractions of the gluteal muscles are the chief means by which the pelvis is thrown forward in rhythmic thrusts during copulation.

Thighs. The thin-skinned, inner surfaces of the thighs, particularly on their midlines, are richly supplied with nerves. Any tactile stimulation of these areas may contribute to erotic arousal.[24] Such stimulation may bring responses of the adductor muscles on the inner faces of the thighs, and of the abductor muscles which are located on the outer surfaces of the legs, and as a result the thighs may be rolled together or thrown apart with distinctive movements that are characteristic of much coital, masturbatory, and other sexual activity. These movements of the adductors and abductors are also involved in the build-up of nervous tensions throughout the whole body (see p. 618).

Other Body Surfaces. The areas just listed are the ones which are most often concerned in erotic stimulation and response. Other parts of the body may, however, be involved, and for some individuals these other parts may be as significant as any of the particular areas listed.

The nape of the neck, the throat, the soles of the feet, the palms of the hand, the armpits, the tips of the fingers, the toes, the navel area, the midline at the lower end of the back, the whole abdominal area, the whole pubic area, the groin, and still other parts have been recognized as areas which may be erotically sensitive under tactile stimulation. Even non-sensitive, non-living structures like teeth and hair may sometimes become sources of erotic stimulation, because movements of those structures stimulate the sensitive nerves that lie at their bases. There are females in our histories who have been brought to orgasm

---

[23] Contraction of the buttocks was once considered the mechanism by which semen was expelled during coitus. See Aristotle [4th cent. B.C.]: Problems, Bk.IV: 876b.

[24] There are abundant data in our records on the erotic sensitivity of the inner surfaces of the thigh. There are few references in the published studies, but see: Van de Velde 1930:45. Havelock Ellis 1936(II,2):113. Kahn 1939:70. Fulton 1949:140 records that manipulation of this area can cause penile erection in dogs, cats, monkeys, and humans whose spinal cords are severed.

by having their eyebrows stroked, or by having the hairs on some other part of their bodies gently blown, or by having pressure applied on the teeth alone. This may be a factor in the biting which often accompanies sexual activities. Such stimuli are most effective when there is some accompanying and significant psychologic stimulation. Acting alone, these unusual sorts of stimuli would rarely be sufficient to effect any considerable arousal. Acting in conjunction with other physical and psychologic stimuli, they may, on occasion, provide the additional impetus which is necessary to carry the individual on to orgasm.

STIMULATION THROUGH OTHER SENSE ORGANS

Many persons are conscious of the fact that they are sexually stimulated by things that they see, smell, taste, or hear. Oriental, Islamic, Classical Greek and Roman, Medieval, Galante, and more modern European sex literatures regularly refer to odors and to other chemical stimuli which are "aphrodisiacs" capable of exciting sexual responses.

But it is not certain that stimuli received through these other sense organs effect erotic arousal in the same direct fashion that tactile stimuli do. It is conceivable that great intensities of light, lights of particular colors, or movements of lights of different intensities or of different colors, do have some direct effect upon an animal's sexual responses; but specific investigations have not yet been made.

It is also not impossible and even probable that strong odors, spices, and loud noises have direct effects upon the nervous system and thus start the physiologic changes which constitute sexual response. It is rather clear that particular sorts of rhythms (*e.g.*, march and waltz time), variations of tempo, particular sequences of pitch (*e.g.*, continued repetitions of one note or chord, alternations of tones which lie an exact octave apart), and variations in volume (*e.g.*, crescendos and diminuendos, sudden and sharp notes, heavy chords) produce physiologic effects on the human and on some other animals which have some affinity to sexual responses. But on none of these points have there been sufficient scientific studies to warrant further discussion here.

It is more certain that stimuli received through these other sense organs operate primarily through the psychic associations which they evoke (p. 647). The arousal which the average male and some females experience in seeing persons with whom they have had previous sexual contacts, in seeing potential new partners, or in seeing articles of clothing or other objects which have been connected with some previous experience, must depend largely upon the fact that they are reacting, consciously or subconsciously, to memories of the past events. In the same fashion one may be aroused by entering a room, seeing a beach, a mountain top, or a sunset which, by its similarity to some situation associated with the previous sexual contact, brings arousal through recall of that experience. Sexual arousal from the taste of some particular food, through particular odors, or from hearing particular birds sing, particular tones of ringing bells, certain words spoken, the tones of particular voices, particular musical themes sung or played, or any other particular sounds, appears to depend largely upon associations of those things with previous sexual experience.

All of this is a picture of psychologic learning and conditioning, and not one of direct mechanical stimulation of the sort which tactile stimuli provide. In considering the erotic significances of things that are seen, smelled, tasted, or heard, the possibility that both psychologic and sensory factors are involved should, therefore, always be taken into account.

SUMMARY AND COMPARISONS OF FEMALE AND MALE

The physical differences between the genitalia and reproductive functions of the mammalian female and male have been the chief basis for the longstanding opinion that there must be similarly great differences in the sexual physiology and psychology of the two sexes. In view of the considerable significance of such concepts in human social relations, it has, therefore, been important to reexamine and reevaluate the similarities and differences in the anatomic structures which are involved in sexual responses and orgasm in the two sexes. Specifically we have found that:

1. In both sexes, end organs of touch are the chief physical bases of sexual response. There seems to be no reason for believing that these organs are located differently in the two sexes, that they are on the whole more or less abundant in either sex, or that there are basic differences in the capacities of the two sexes to respond to the stimulation of these end organs.

2. The genitalia of the female and the male originate embryologically from essentially identical structures and, as adult structures, their homologous parts serve very similar functions. The penis, in spite of its greater size, is not known to be better equipped with sensory nerves than the much smaller clitoris. Both structures are of considerable significance in sexual arousal. The chief consequence of the larger size of the penis is the fact that sexual stimulation is more often directed specifically toward it. Its larger size accounts in part for the greater psychologic significance of the penis to the male.

3. The labia minora and the vestibule of the vagina provide more extensive sensitive areas in the female than are to be found in any

homologous structure of the male. Any advantage which the larger size of the male phallus may provide is equalled or surpassed by the greater extension of the tactilely sensitive areas in the female genitalia.

4. The larger and more protrudent and more extensible phallus of the male, and the more internal anatomy of the female, are factors which may determine the roles which the two sexes assume in coitus. The female may find psychologic satisfaction in her function in receiving, while the male may find satisfaction in his capacity to penetrate during coitus, but it is not clear that this could account for the more aggressive part which the average male plays, and the less aggressive part which the average female plays in sexual activity. The differences in aggressiveness of the average female and male appear to depend upon something more than the differences in their genital anatomy (see Chapters 16 and 18).

5. The vagina of the female is not matched by any functioning structure in the male, but it is of minimum importance in contributing to the erotic responses of the female. It may even contribute more to the sexual arousal of the male than it does to the arousal of the female.

6. The perineal area provides a considerable source of stimulation for both the female and the male. In the male, nerves located among the perineal muscles may be stimulated through direct pressure on the external surface of the perineum or through the rectum; in the female, the area may be stimulated in exactly the same fashion or through vaginal penetrations.

7. Because female breasts are larger, they may appear to be more significant to the female than male breasts are to the male. But since most males are aroused by seeing female breasts, and because most females are, in actuality, only moderately aroused by having their breasts tactilely stimulated, female breasts may be more important sources of erotic stimulation to males than they are to females.

8. The mouth, which is one of the most important erotic areas of the mammalian body, appears to be equally sensitive in the female and the male.

9. Tactile stimulation of the buttocks and of the inner surfaces of the thighs may play a significant part in the picture of sexual response. Responses to such stimulation seem to be essentially the same in the female and the male.

10. All of the other body surfaces which respond to tactile stimuli seem to function, as far as the specific evidence goes, identically in the two sexes.

11. There are no data to indicate that there are any differences in female and male responses which depend directly on the senses of sight, smell, taste, or hearing.

12. In brief, we conclude that the anatomic structures which are most essential to sexual response and orgasm are nearly identical in the human female and male. The differences are relatively few. They are associated with the different functions of the sexes in reproductive processes, but they are of no great significance in the origins and development of sexual response and orgasm. If females and males differ sexually in any basic way, those differences must originate in some other aspect of the biology or psychology of the two sexes (see Chapters 16 and 18). They do not originate in any of the anatomic structures which have been considered here.

Chapter 15

PHYSIOLOGY OF SEXUAL RESPONSE AND ORGASM

The responses which an animal makes when it is stimulated sexually constitute one of the most elaborate and in many respects one of the most remarkable complexes (syndromes) of physiologic phenomena in the whole gamut of mammalian behavior. The reactions may involve changes in pulse rates, blood pressure, breathing rates, peripheral circulation of blood, glandular secretions, changes in sensory capacities, muscular activity, and still other physiologic events which are described in the present chapter. As a climax to all these responses, the reacting individual may experience what we identify as sexual orgasm. There is every reason for believing that most of the physiologic changes which are described in the present chapter take place even in the mildest sexual response, even though the gross movements of the body may be limited and the individual fails to reach orgasm.

The gross aspects of sexual response and orgasm may differ considerably in different individuals. The stimuli which initiate the response may vary in intensity, continuity, and duration, and the animal's responses may depend not only on such variation in the nature of the stimuli, but upon its physiologic state and psychologic background. There is nothing more characteristic of sexual response than the fact that it is not the same in any two individuals. On the other hand, the most obvious variations lie in the gross body movements which are part of the response, and particularly in the spasms or convulsions which follow orgasm; and while these variations are striking and sometimes very prominent, the basic physiologic patterns of response are remarkably uniform among all the mammals, including both man and the infra-human species. Even more significant is the fact that the basic physiology of sexual response is essentially the same among females and males, at least in the human species.

The record in the present chapter emphasizes the physical reality of any sexual response. Whatever the poetry and romance of sex, and whatever the moral and social significance of human sexual behavior, sexual responses involve real and material changes in the physiologic functioning of an animal. The present chapter describes the gross physiologic changes which occur whenever there is sexual response;

the neural and hormonal mechanisms which may be responsible for these changes are discussed in Chapters 17 and 18.

PHYSIOLOGIC CHANGES DURING SEXUAL RESPONSE

1. **Tactile and Pressure Responses.** One of the most characteristic qualities of living matter, plant or animal, is its capacity to respond to touch. The normal, first reaction of an organism is to press against any object with which it may come into contact. One-celled animals mass against objects. Multicellular bodies like cockroaches crowd into corners. Infants and small children spontaneously snuggle against other human bodies. Uninhibited human adults do the same thing whenever the opportunity affords.

When the contact causes pain, or subjects the animal to extreme temperatures, the organism may respond negatively and pull away from the stimulus. Higher animals become conditioned by experience and may learn to react negatively to the mere possibility of repeating such a contact. Moral codes and social custom aid in this conditioning, and the human adult, in consequence, often reacts adversely to contacts with other living bodies. It is probable, however, that most negative responses are learned responses, and they do not represent the innate qualities of uneducated protoplasm. Sexual difficulties in marriages, and personal maladjustments, are not infrequently the product of this sort of perversion of the biologically normal reactions to tactile stimuli.

If an animal pulls away from the stimulating object, little else may happen to it physiologically. If it responds by pressing against the object, a considerable series of physiologic events may follow. If the tactile stimulation becomes rhythmic, or the pressure is long-continued, the level of response may increase and build up neuromuscular tensions which become recognizable as sexual responses.

2. **Pulse Rate.** A rise in pulse rate is one of the most obvious and widely recognized results of a mammal's reaction to tactile stimulation or to any sort of erotic stimulation.[1] Such changes in pulse rate are probably an invariable outcome of sexual arousal, although we cannot be certain of this until more extensive studies are made. Unfortunately, exact measurements of these changes are rare in the literature, although they could easily be obtained with automatic recording devices.

---

[1] Such an increase in pulse rate is widely recognized in the literature, as in: Roubaud 1876:16. Caufeynon 1903:57. Bloch 1908:49. Talmey 1912:61; 1915:92. Krafft-Ebing 1922:40. Kisch 1926:288, 344. Bauer 1927(1):154. Van de Velde 1930:245. Dickinson 1933, 1949:fig. 126. Havelock Ellis 1936 (II,1):149, 151. Haire 1937:200. Reich 1942:82. Podolsky 1942:49. Sadler 1944:41. Negri 1949:97. Faller in Hornstein and Faller 1950:234, 237. Ford and Beach 1951:244–246. Stone and Stone 1952:173.

The few records which are available on the human animal indicate
that a pulse which normally runs at something between 70 and 80 per
minute may be raised to as much as 150 or more when there is erotic
arousal, and particularly if the reaction proceeds to the point of orgasm
(Figures 120–125).[2] This may approach the pulse rate of an athlete

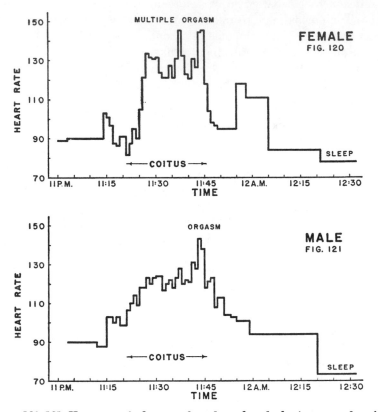

Figures 120–121. Heart rate in human female and male during sexual activity

Showing erotic responses before, during, and after coitus between husband and
wife. The female had four orgasms. Data from Boas and Goldschmidt 1932.

---

[2] Precise measurements on the increase in pulse rate during arousal are few.
Mendelsohn 1896:381–384 reproduces graphs of the pulse of human males
and females before, during, and after coitus, showing a maximum pulse of
150. Boas and Goldschmidt 1932:99–100 record pulses in human coitus reaching points between 128 and 146 in four consecutive orgasms in a human
female, and a pulse of 143 at orgasm in a male. Gantt 1944:128–129, and
Gantt in Hoch and Zubin 1949:44, graph the pulses of three male dogs, showing increases at orgasm more marked than those found under other emotional
situations. Klumbies and Kleinsorge 1950a:953–956; 1950b:61–66, report on
one human male and one female who masturbated to orgasm, finding a maximum pulse of 142 at orgasm in the male, while the female's normal pulse of
63 rose to something between 85 and 97 in five successive orgasms. Polatin
and Douglas (ms. 1951) record spontaneous orgasm in a female with a pulse
rising from 60 to 140 at orgasm.

during his maximum effort, or that of a man involved in heavy labor.[3] But sometimes the rise is less than this. There is considerable individual variation in this regard, and there may be variation in the same individual on different occasions. We have records which show that an individual whose pulse ordinarily rises to 150 or more during maximum arousal, and who normally does not experience orgasm unless his pulse reaches that height, may sometimes reach orgasm after a less intense

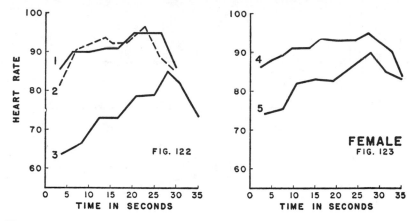

Figures 122–123. Heart rate in human female in five consecutive orgasms

The female masturbated to orgasm by fantasy alone, without genital manipulation. Data from Klumbies and Kleinsorge 1950.

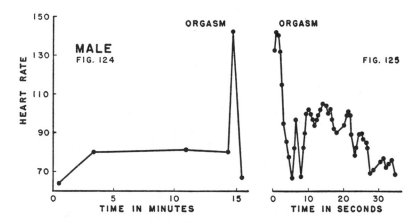

Figures 124–125. Heart rate in human male in orgasm

Orgasm reached in manual masturbation; Figure 125 shows the detail of the aftereffects following orgasm. Data from Klumbies and Kleinsorge 1950.

---

[3] Pulse rates during violent exertion are given in: Boas and Goldschmidt 1932:83, 91. Robinson 1938:253–266. Hoff in Howell (Fulton edit.) 1949:661–663. Houssay et al. 1951:475, 481. Pulses in violent exercise varied between 160 and 195 among boys, and 160 to 170 in adults. The maximum pulses of 10 young men ranged from 182 to 208 while running on a treadmill.

experience during which his pulse does not rise above 100. Fatigue, starvation, ill health, psychologic blockages and distractions, and other factors may account for the occasionally lower rates at the time of orgasm. There are similar data on the rise in pulse rate among some other animals, including dogs, during sexual activity (Figures 126–128).

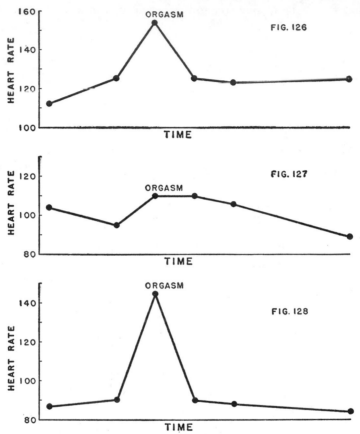

Figures 126–128. Heart rate in three male dogs during sexual activity
Data from Gantt 1944, and Gantt in Hoch and Zubin 1949.

This rise in pulse rate is one of the products of sexual response which many persons may observe in themselves and in their sexual partners. Consequently this has provided one means for determining the nature of the experience of the subjects of the present study. There has been doubt on the part of some persons whether all females are able to recognize erotic arousal, and whether all of them could correctly report their experience for the present study. To those of us who have done the interviewing, this apprehension has seemed for the most part unnecessary. It is impossible to believe that any male would ever be unconscious of the fact that he was aroused sexually, even if he did not have a penis to bear testimony to that effect; and neither does there appear to be any uncertainty in the minds of most women as to whether or when or where they have responded to sexual stimulation. It is true that some younger girls and some of the less experienced older women do, on occasion, hesitate to record their experience until the nature of sexual arousal has been defined for them. It has, therefore, been our standard procedure to explain that arousal is ordinarily accompanied by the realization that "one's pulse is beating faster, one's heart is thumping, and one's breathing has become deeper." This description has almost invariably brought an instantaneous reply from the subject to the effect that she had or had not had such experience during a sexual contact. We venture the opinion that normally intelligent persons who have never become conscious of at least the circulatory disturbances which occur during sexual contacts have never, in actuality, been very much aroused.

3. **Blood Pressure.** The blood pressure of an animal may rise materially when it is sexually aroused. There are few measurements on the human female or male, but these indicate that diastolic blood pressures which have normally been as low as 65 may be raised to 160, and systolic pressures may be raised from 120 to 250 or more at the time of orgasm (Figures 137, 138). There are similar findings in an excellent study on dogs (Figures 129–136).[4] However, even these few records indicate that there is considerable variation among different individuals, and it is probable that there is variation within the history of any single individual. This is another matter on which it would be highly desirable and quite possible to secure further data.

Hemiplegia, stroke, or death may occasionally occur, although not at all frequently, during coital and other sexual activities. The average physician may see a few such cases during a lifetime of practice. In such instances the fatality may be the consequence of this rise in blood pressure which accompanies sexual activity. The increased pressure may lead to a rupture of blood vessels, especially in older individuals

---

[4] A rise in blood pressure during sexual arousal is also mentioned in: Mendelsohn 1896:383–384 (in human). Urbach 1921:126. Bauer 1927(1):154. Hirschfeld 1928(2):242. Van de Velde 1930:245. Sadler 1944:41. Faller in Hornstein and Faller 1950:237. Ford and Beach 1951:244–245. Exact measurements are in: Pussep 1922:61 ff. (in male dogs, 215 mm. at orgasm, in female dogs, 195 mm. at moment of intromission). Scott 1930:97 ff. (nearly all of 100 medical students responded to an erotic moving picture with increases in blood pressure of 5 to 15 mm., and in some cases of 45 mm.). Havelock Ellis 1936(II,1):151–152 (a rise from 65 mm. to 160 mm. in a human female during erotic arousal). Klumbies and Kleinsorge 1950a:953, 955; 1950b:61–62, 64 (in masturbation, an increase in systolic pressure from 120 to 250 mm. in the human male, and from 110 to 160 mm. (and once to 200 mm.) in the female; in diastolic pressure an increase from 80 to 120 in the male, and 80 to 105 in the female).

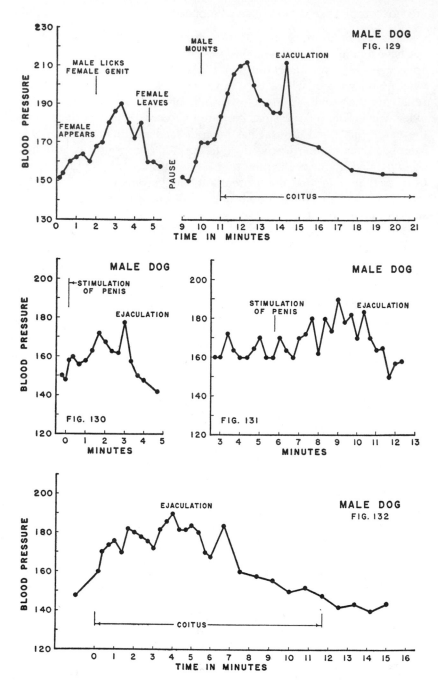

Figures 129–132. Blood pressure in three male dogs during sexual activity

Figures 129, 130 represent two different experiences for the same dog. Figures 129, 132 represent responses in coitus; Figures 130, 131 represent responses in masturbation. Data from Pussep in Weil 1922.

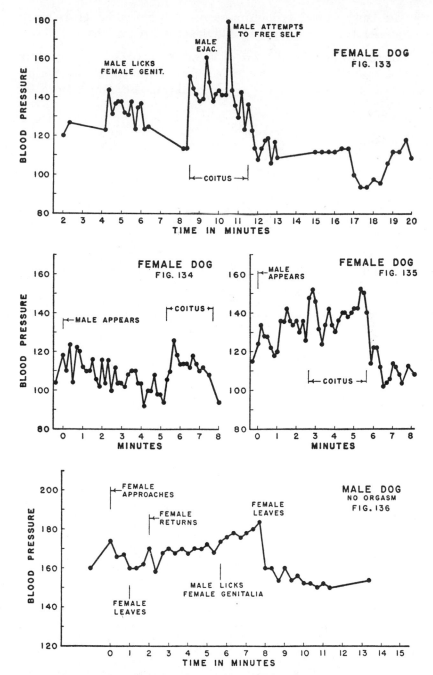

Figures 133–136. Blood pressure in three female dogs and one male dog during sexual activity

The recession from the peak of response in the female bears a striking resemblance to orgasm in the male. Data from Pussep in Weil 1922.

who are handicapped by high pressures to begin with.[5] There would be considerable value in having additional records on this point.

4. **Increased Peripheral Flow of Blood.** Probably as a result of the direct neural stimulation of arterioles, blood is forced into the peripheral areas of the whole body during sexual response. For instance, the

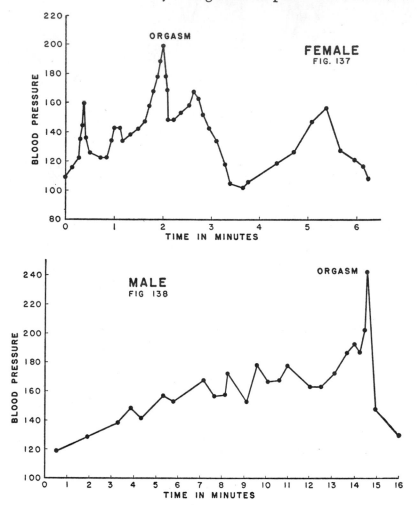

Figures 137–138. Blood pressure in human female and male during sexual activity

The female fantasied, the male masturbated to orgasm. Data from Klumbies and Kleinsorge 1950.

---

[5] Death during sexual activity has been reported from Pliny [23–79 A.D.]: Natural History, Bk. 7, LIII, 184, to the following, for instance: Mendelsohn 1896:384. Rohleder 1907(1):372. Hirschfeld 1928(2):242. Van de Velde 1930:245. Havelock Ellis 1936(II,1):168–169. Klumbies and Kleinsorge 1950a:957–958; 1950b:63, 66.

face of the sexually aroused individual usually becomes flushed. Such changes in coloration may be marked enough to be noticeable to other persons, even when the responses represent nothing more than the mildly erotic reactions which one may experience in meeting a friend. At maximum arousal, the faces of some individuals radically change color, the whole chest and throat may become brilliant or dark red or deep reddish purple, and the genital area may become deeply colored.

One may become conscious of an increase in temperature in his own or the sexual partner's body surfaces, partly due to this peripheral circulation of blood, and perhaps in part due to the neuromuscular tensions which develop when there is any sexual response. Even very cold feet may become warm during sexual activity. The identification of sexual arousal as a fever, a glow, a fire, heat, or warmth, testifies to the widespread understanding that there is this rise in surface temperatures [6]; but there seem to be no precise measurements of the extent of these temperature changes. There seem to be no data which indicate whether there is any rise in the temperature of the body as a whole, as a result of sexual arousal, even though there are these changes in surface temperatures.

The peripheral circulation of blood which occurs during sexual response is paralleled in other emotional situations. The face of the person who is embarrassed, angry, or excited in some other way (but not frightened) may become flushed and red. Since the parasympathetic nervous system is known to be the source of this vasodilation in the other emotional situations, it is probable that the same system is involved in sexual responses. Sexual flushing cannot be the outcome of adrenal or sympathetic nervous stimulation, for both of these agencies effect the sort of vasoconstriction which is responsible for the white and cold body surfaces of most frightened persons.

5. **Tumescence.** In consequence of this increase in the peripheral circulation of blood, all distensible parts of the body become swollen (tumescent) in an individual who is sexually stimulated. This tumescence provides some of the most obvious evidences of sexual arousal.

Almost instantly, or within a matter of seconds or a minute or so after the initiation of a sexual contact, certain areas of the body may become swollen, enlarged, and stiff with an excess of blood. This is equally true of the human and lower mammalian species, both female and male. In some of the most distensible areas, such as the penis, blood is forced in by the arteries faster than the capillaries and the

---

[6] Records of an increase in skin temperature during sexual arousal are also given, for instance, in: Roubaud 1876:16. Bloch 1908:49. Urbach 1921:133. Bauer 1927(1):157. Hirschfeld 1935:44. Havelock Ellis 1936(II,1):149, 167. Haire 1937:200.

veins can carry it away. This engorgement may in itself aid in the process by closing the veins so they cannot carry blood away as rapidly as they normally do.[7] The penis, clitoris, some of the tissues near the entrance to the vagina, the nipples of the breast, and the side walls of the nose contain a spongy *erectile* tissue which makes those structures especially liable to enlargement during sexual arousal. Blood is carried by small arterioles into the spaces of the spongy tissue, or actually forced through the walls of the capillaries into the cavities, and the whole structure consequently enlarges. The penis, for instance, may become from half again to double its usual length, and become turgid and stand forward or up in erection when it is tumescent. The clitoris may become swollen and erect. The labia minora, which are usually limp and folded, may become swollen and prominently protrudent. In both the female and the male, the nipples of the breast may become enlarged, hard, and erect. The soft parts of the nose, the alae, may become swollen and the nostrils in consequence become expanded.

While the phenomenon of tumescence is commonly recognized in connection with the penis, and sometimes with these other erectile organs, it is not so often realized that a considerable tumescence may also occur during sexual arousal in all other parts of the body, even though these other parts do not contain erectile tissues. The surface outlines of the whole body of one who is sexually aroused become quite different from the outlines of one who is not so aroused. The lobes of the ears may become thickened and swollen. The lips of the mouth may become filled with blood and, in most individuals, more protrudent than under ordinary circumstances. The whole breast, particularly of the female, may become swollen, enlarged, and more protrudent, and the general outline of the breast may become more rounded.[8] The anal area may become turgid. The arms and the legs may have their outlines altered. The tumescence is so apparent everywhere over the body that it alone is sufficient evidence of the presence of erotic arousal. Women who pretend arousal when there is none may, to some degree, simulate the motions of coitus; but they cannot voluntarily produce the peripheral circulation of blood and the consequent tumescence of the lips, the breasts, the nipples, the labia minora, and

---

[7] Entrapment of blood in the penis as a result of venous compression in erection is also noted in: Eberth 1904:253. Dickinson 1933, 1949:78–80. Hirsch 1949: 66 (locked). Hooker in Howell (Fulton edit.) 1949:1203 (veins possess funnel-like valves). Maximow and Bloom 1952:487.

[8] Tumescence of various parts of the body during arousal has also been noted by: Rohleder 1907(1):372. Bauer 1927(1):157. Van de Velde 1930:245. Dickinson 1933, 1949:65–68, figs. 103–104 (recognized the tumescence of the whole breast). Havelock Ellis 1936(II,1):144 ff. Sadler 1944:37. Faller in Hornstein and Faller 1950:237. Stone and Stone 1952:173.

the whole body contour which are the unmistakable and almost invariable evidences of erotic arousal.

In some males the erection of the penis may occur in a matter of seconds—even three or four seconds—and in some females the clitoris and the labia minora may respond as quickly. In many species of lower mammals the reactions are even more nearly instantaneous. Stallions, bulls, rams, rats, guinea pigs, porcupines, cats, dogs, apes, and males of other species may come to full erection almost instantaneously upon contact with a sexual object.[9] Rapid tumescence in the human animal occurs most frequently among vigorous, younger persons in whom erectile capacities far exceed those of most older persons, although some older females and males may still retain their capacities for rapid response.

6. **Respiration.** As a correlate of the increase in pulse rate and blood pressure which occurs in the sexually responding individual, there is an increase in breathing rate. In the earlier stages of arousal the breathing becomes deeper and faster, but with the approach of orgasm the respiration becomes interrupted. Inspiration is then effected with prolonged gasps, and expiration follows with a forceful collapse of the lungs (Figure 139). There is some popular understanding of this, as is evidenced by the fact that the panting of the actor in the old-time melodrama became a stylized representation of sexual passion. Some of the gasping and sucking sounds and some of the more specific vocalizations which may occur during the climax of sexual activity result from this forced type of breathing.[10] The tortured facial expressions of persons who are sexually aroused, and particularly of those who are near the point of orgasm, usually include expanded nostrils, an open mouth, and pursed lips which suggest that the individuals are struggling to secure air to satisfy the demands of the increased pulse rates and high blood pressures.

7. **Anoxia.** The facial conspectus of a sexually responding individual, especially at the time of orgasm, suggests that he or she may be suffering from a shortage of oxygen—an anoxia. This sort of shortage is

---

[9] We have observed almost instantaneous erection in all of the animals listed above. Root and Bard 1947:82 mention this in the cat, and other authors imply rapid erection in their descriptions of the brevity of coitus—for example, in: Ford and Beach 1951:35–37.

[10] Modifications in respiratory rate as a result of sexual arousal are matters of common knowledge, and are also recorded by various authors: Roubaud 1876:17. Rohleder 1907(1):372. Talmey 1912:61. Kisch 1926:288, 345. Bauer 1927 (1):154, 157. Van de Velde 1930:245. Havelock Ellis 1936(II,1):150–151. Reich 1942:82. Podolsky 1942:49. Negri 1949:97. Brown and Kempton 1950: 207. Faller in Hornstein and Faller 1950:237. Stone and Stone 1952:173. Actual measurements have been made less often, but see: Gantt in Hoch and Zubin 1949:37, 42–43. Klumbies and Kleinsorge 1950a:954; 1950b:61 ff.

characteristic of the athlete at the peak of his performance, or of the person involved in heavy labor; and the face of the human female or male who is approaching sexual climax often bears a striking resemblance to that of the runner who is making a supreme effort to finish his race.[11]

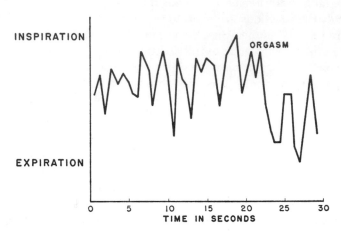

Figure 139. Respiration in human female during sexual activity

Record on the same female shown in Figures 122, 123, 137. Data from Klumbies and Kleinsorge 1950.

The face of the individual who is approaching orgasm similarly and for the same reason presents the traditional aspect of a person who is being tortured. Prostitutes who attempt to deceive (jive) their patrons, or unresponsive wives who similarly attempt to make their husbands believe that they are enjoying their coitus, fall into an error because they assume that an erotically aroused person should look happy and pleased and should smile and become increasingly alert as he or she approaches the culmination of the act. On the contrary, an individual who is really responding is as incapable of looking happy as the individual who is being tortured.

It would not be difficult to investigate the possibility that an anoxia is actually involved during sexual response. Such an anoxia could be detected with simple mechanical devices, and this is one of the first

[11] The possibility of an anoxia during sexual response is further suggested by the following: Cannon 1920:205, 209 states that great exertion and strong emotions may cause "asphyxia." Van de Velde 1930:245 mentions an excess of CO_2 in the blood at orgasm. Rossen, Kabat, and Anderson 1943:513–515 list the following symptoms of anoxia: fixation of the eyes, narrowed and blurring of vision, loss of consciousness, mild convulsion—all of which we have found in the sexual syndrome. Shock in Reymert 1950:279 speaks of hyperventilation leading to "local tissue anoxia" and cerebral vasoconstriction. Klumbies and Kleinsorge 1950a:956; 1950b:63, show that sexual activity increases oxygen consumption.

aspects of the physiology of sexual response which might well be studied.

8. Bleeding. There are limited data which indicate that bleeding from cut blood vessels is much reduced during sexual arousal. Skin abrasions, accidental cuts and even cuts on the genitalia and on other tumescent parts of the body, and the injuries that may be incurred during sado-masochistic activity, seem to be remarkably free from extensive bleeding. We have records of menstrual flow being slowed up when there is erotic stimulation, although the physical activity in coitus might be expected to induce an increased flow.[12] The records include data on an increase in the flow of blood from wounds after an individual experiences orgasm and returns to a normal physiologic state.

9. Female Genital Secretions. The glands connected with the female reproductive tract increase their activity during sexual arousal. The Bartholin glands, which open in the vestibule just outside the entrance to the vagina (Figure 118), are the source of a clear, quite liquid, and somewhat slippery secretion. This secretion should not be confused with the usually thicker and often more colored secretions which frequently come from vaginal or cervical infections, or which constitute the so-called uterine discharges. During sexual activity, an increase in Bartholin secretions provides one of the best indicators of erotic response. Of this fact many observant participants in sexual activities are well aware.[13] The absence of such a secretion is ordinarily evidence that there is no arousal, except among some older women in whom all secretions may be limited, and in occasional instances of anatomic abnormalities. In addition to providing lubrication, the alkaline Bartholin secretions may neutralize the normal acidity of the vagina and prevent that acidity from killing the sperm which are ejaculated in coitus.[14]

The cervix, which is the tip of the uterus which projects into the vagina (Figure 118), also secretes a mucus, and when there is arousal this secretion may become even more copious than the Bartholin secretions. In clinical practice, when it has been necessary to remove the

---

[12] Assertions that the menstrual flow is increased during coitus, are also in: Malchow 1923:136. Van de Velde 1930:292. Stone and Stone 1952:241–242.

[13] Secretions of the Bartholin glands during sexual arousal are commonly recognized. In the literature, they are mentioned, for instance, by: Rohleder 1907 (1):310. Bloch 1908:50. Talmey 1912:60. Moll 1912:25. Malchow 1923: 133. Kisch 1926:290–291. Hirschfeld 1928(2):225, 231. Van de Velde 1930: 195. Dickinson 1933, 1949:48. Havelock Ellis 1936(II,1):145. Kahn 1939:74, 85. Sadler 1944:14, 39. Negri 1949:82. Brown and Kempton 1950:19. Faller in Hornstein and Faller 1950:236. Stone and Stone 1952:61, 173.

[14] The function of the Bartholin secretions in reducing the acidity of the vagina, thus giving the sperm greater longevity, was suggested some years ago (e.g., Talmey 1912:58), and is treated more fully by Siegler 1944:223.

Bartholin glands, it is found that the cervical glands still supply enough mucus for vaginal lubrication. On the other hand, extirpation of the cervical glands, even while the Bartholin glands are still functioning, may so reduce the vaginal secretions as to interfere with coitus.[15] This indicates that the cervical secretions are more important than they have sometimes been considered.

The cervical secretions are also important because they may loosen the mucous plug which ordinarily lies in the opening (the os) of the cervix.[16] Unless the cervical canal is opened, sperm which have been deposited in the vagina cannot move into the uterus and egg ducts (Fallopian tubes), and fertilization may therefore be prevented.[17]

There is considerable variation in the quantity of the vaginal secretions among different females. There may also be variation in the quantity of the secretion at different times in the same individual. This depends upon the intensity of her sexual response, upon her physiologic state, and, interestingly enough, upon the timing of the activity within the menstrual month. About 59 per cent of our sample of women with coital experience recognized such a monthly fluctuation in their vaginal secretions during erotic arousal. About 69 per cent of those who recognized such a fluctuation reported that the mucus was most abundant when sexual activity occurred one to four (or more) days before the onset of menstruation. Some 39 per cent reported that the maximum secretion during arousal occurred soon after the menstrual flow had ceased. About 10 per cent reported that it occurred in the course of the menstrual flow itself, and 11 per cent reported that it occurred in the middle of the month near the time of ovulation. These percentages total more than one hundred because some of the women reported that the increased secretion had occurred both before and after menstruation.

In interviewing for the present study, we have inquired about fluctuations in vaginal mucous secretions before we have discussed fluctuations in erotic responsiveness. The data so obtained indicate that the time of maximum mucous secretion and the time of maximum erotic responsiveness are almost always the same. The record of fluctuations in erotic response is therefore of especial significance, since it

---

[15] Data from Dr. Sophia Kleegman *in litt.*
[16] Cervical secretions are discussed in: Bloch 1908:50. Talmey 1912:60; 1915:91. Urbach 1921:133. Kisch 1926:287, 296. Bauer 1927(2):159. Hirschfeld 1928 (2):225. Van de Velde 1930:194. Dickinson 1933, 1949:fig. 102. Havelock Ellis 1936(II,1):162. Brown and Kempton 1950:18. In an unpublished ms., Dickinson estimates a cervical secretion of 1 to 4 cc. during arousal.
[17] That the cervical os may be opened to the passage of sperm, through cervical secretory activity, is discussed by: Dickinson 1933, 1949:92–94. Weisman 1941:111–113, 130–131. Siegler 1944:229–231. Gardner in Howell (Fulton edit.) 1949:1179.

originated in questions concerning a physical reality, the vaginal secretions, which could be precisely identified. If it had been based on questions concerning erotic arousal, the answers might have represented more subjective judgments.

However, these records on the human female do not fit the laboratory data on the periods of sexual responsiveness in some other mammals. These periods of response, the so-called periods of heat or estrus, occur periodically, and in many of the mammals (but not in all of them) the females rarely accept the males for coitus except during these periods of heat.[18] Ovulation, the release of an egg from the ovary preparatory to its passage down the egg ducts where fertilization may occur (Figure 118), takes place during this period of heat, and at no other time in the female's cycle. This means that the infra-human female has coitus near the time of ovulation, and therefore at the period in which coitus is most likely to lead to fertilization and reproduction. Among the monkeys and apes, which are practically the only animals besides the human which menstruate, the period of maximum sexual arousal may also come just before or concurrently with the time of ovulation, which is about midway between the periods of menstrual flow.[19]

The location of the period of heat near the time of ovulation is, obviously, advantageous to the propagation of any species. The occurrence of the period of maximum sexual responsiveness in the human female just before the onset of menstruation and therefore at her most sterile period, does not appear so advantageous for the accomplishment of fertilization. To those who believe that the evolutionary origins of new structures and physiologic characters are determined by their advantage or disadvantage (*i.e.*, by Darwinian adaptation and selection), it seems proper and correct that a period of arousal should occur close to the time of ovulation. Therefore some laboratory students,

[18] Since heat or estrus is often defined as a period in which the female accepts the male, the acceptance of copulation outside of estrus is not often mentioned. Williams 1943:125 says "Copulation in female domestic animals is physiologically limited to the period of estrum . . . outside these periods the female absolutely refuses the sexual advances of the male." But also see: Miller 1931: 384, 387. McKenzie and Terrill 1937:10. Andrews and McKenzie 1941:7, 11, 20–22. Hartman 1945:23 ff. Asdell 1946:*passim*. Roark and Herman 1950: 7–11. Whitney; Farris; and Bissonette in Farris 1950b:199, 246–247, 264. A general summary of the data on periodicity is to be found in Marshall 1936. See also Chapter 18, footnote 39.

[19] The close relationship between ovulation and estrus is discussed by: Ball and Hartman 1935. Marshall 1936:447–448. Corner 1942:70. Yerkes 1943:62–66. Hartman 1945:23 ff. Asdell 1946:13–25. Beach 1947b:272–274, 292, 293. Gardner in Howell (Fulton edit.) 1949:1170. Ford and Beach 1951:201–204, 273. Houssay 1951:639. There may be some slight discharge of blood at the time of ovulation in some human females and in the females of some other species. This *Mittelschmerz* is more pronounced in the dog, but it is an ovulatory discharge and not menstruation.

working with lower mammals, have been loath to accept the human data.[20] On the other hand, most of the research on human subjects has produced data which accord with our own.[21] They are confirmed by observations which have been made by a number of the husbands who have contributed histories to the present study. Some of the women who masturbate only once in a month do so in the period just before or immediately after menstruation. Evidently the human female, in the course of evolution, has departed from her mammalian ancestors and developed new characteristics which have relocated the period of maximum sexual arousal near the time of menstruation.

10. **Male Genital Secretions.** In the male the so-called Cowper's glands connect with the urethra near the base of the penis (Figure 119). These glands in the male and the Bartholin glands in the female originate from the same embryonic tissues. They are, therefore, actual homologues. The clear and slippery Cowper's secretions supply a pre-coital or pre-ejaculatory mucus (the glad-come of the Negro vernacular), which may exude from the urethral opening at the tip of the penis of some males when they are sexually aroused.[22] In many species of mammals the Cowper's glands are well developed and in some species (*e.g.*, the boar) they are enormous.[23] Stallions, rams, boars, male goats, and some others may dribble or run continuous streams of such secretions as soon as they approach a female in which they are sexually interested. In the human species, the Cowper's glands are much more poorly developed. Most human males do not secrete more than a drop of mucus during sexual activity, and perhaps a third, especially at older ages, do not secrete enough mucus to have it ever exude from the urethra. Another third, however, may develop enough of the Cow-

---

[20] Reluctance to believe that the human female's maximal arousal does not coincide with ovulation is noted or discussed in: Tinklepaugh 1933:335. Hartman 1936:77–86. Yerkes and Elder 1936a:38. Stone in Allen et al. 1939:1228–1230, 1258. Benedek and Rubenstein 1942:4. Ford and Beach 1951:210–213.

[21] Others who find that the period of maximum responsiveness in the human female is close to the time of menstruation, are: Sturgis ca.1908:23. Schbankov acc. Weissenberg 1924a:10. Robie 1925:124. Hamilton 1929:197–198. Hamilton and Macgowan 1929:91. Hoyer 1929:20–21. Davis 1929:220–229. Kelly 1930:222. Van de Velde 1930:285–286. Kopp 1933:98–100. McCance et al. 1937:597–599, 609. Terman 1938:351. Popenoe 1938:17. Dickinson ms. Stone and Stone 1952:239. The outstanding exception is Benedek and Rubenstein 1942 and Benedek 1952:6–12, 144–159. This latter work, which combines psychoanalytic and endocrine data, concludes that sexual desire in the human female is highest at mid-month, immediately preceding ovulation. No understandable interpretation is given as to why other studies fail to concur.

[22] That there is a secretion from Cowper's glands as a result of sexual arousal is, of course, commonly known, and is noted in: Roubaud 1876:26. Rohleder 1907(1):310. Moll 1912:22. Hirschfeld 1928(2):231. Dickinson 1933, 1949:81. Havelock Ellis 1936(II,1):153. Sadler 1944:4, 14. Faller in Hornstein and Faller 1950:92, 236.

[23] The boar possesses enormous Cowper's glands measuring in some cases 4 to 5 inches in length and 1 to 2 inches in diameter, according to McKenzie, Miller, and Bauguess 1938:6–7, 37–41.

per's secretion to wet the head of the penis during sexual arousal, and there are a few human males who secrete Cowper's mucus in such quantity that it may pour copiously from the urethra whenever they are erotically stimulated. When there are pre-coital mucous secretions they do provide evidence of erotic arousal; but the absence of such secretions in a human male cannot be taken as evidence that he is not aroused.

Cowper's secretion usually appears before orgasm. It is, therefore, a pre-coital mucus, although there is an occasional male in whom secretion does not develop until after orgasm. Since these secretions are alkaline, it is commonly pointed out that they may neutralize the acidity of urine in the urethra. Sperm should in consequence have a better chance to survive their passage through the urethra. The secretions may also provide lubrication for genitalia which are in copulo.[24] But the fact remains that few human males secrete enough of this mucus to accomplish either of these ends, and most males do manage to copulate and to effect fertilization without especial difficulty.

In addition to the Cowper's secretions, the liquids which exude from the male's penis during sexual arousal may contain secretions from the lining of the urethra.

The largest gland contributing to the male genital secretions is the prostate. It is located at and around the base of the penis (Figure 119). It provides the major portion of the liquid semen which is ejaculated by the male at the time of orgasm.

Most of the remainder of the semen comes from two seminal vesicles, which are expanded portions of the two ducts (vas deferens) which carry sperm from the testes to the seminal vesicles (Figure 119). Sperm are continually moving up from the testes and into the seminal vesicles. There they are stored until there is sexual arousal and orgasm and then, along with other sperm which have been accumulating in the upper ends of the sperm ducts, they are thrown out as a microscopic part of the ejaculate. While the cavities of the seminal vesicles serve as storehouses for the sperm, their spongy walls are glandular, and these are the structures which contribute their secretions to the semen. Both the prostate and seminal vesicles are probably stimulated into secretion as soon as erotic arousal starts, and by the time orgasm occurs a considerable quantity of liquid, averaging about 3 cc. or the equivalent of a teaspoonful in volume, is ready for ejaculation.

---

[24] That Cowper's secretion may neutralize the urethral acidity is suggested in: Dickinson 1933, 1949:72. Hotchkiss 1944:55. Farris 1950b:14. On the other hand, Hooker in Howell (Fulton edit.) 1949:1202 feels that the prostatic secretion is the neutralizing agent and that Cowper's secretion is merely a lubricant.

There is a popular opinion that the testes are the sources of the semen which the male ejaculates. The testes are supposed to become swollen with accumulated secretions between the times of sexual activity, and periodic ejaculation is supposed to be necessary in order to relieve these pressures. Many males claim that their testes ache if they do not find regular sources of outlet, and throughout the history of erotic literature and in some psychoanalytic literature the satisfactions of orgasm are considered to depend upon the release of pressures in the "glands"—meaning the testes.[25] Most of these opinions are, however, quite unfounded. The prostate, seminal vesicles, and Cowper's are the only glands which contribute any quantity of material to the semen, and they are the only structures which accumulate secretions which could create pressures that would need to be relieved. Although there is some evidence that the testes may secrete a bit of liquid when the male is erotically aroused, the amount of their secretion is too small to create any pressure. The testes may seem to hurt when there is unrelieved erotic arousal (the so-called stone-ache of the vernacular), but the pain probably comes from muscular tensions in the perineal area, and possibly from tensions in the sperm ducts, especially at the lower ends (the epididymis) where they are wrapped about the testes (Figure 119).[26] Such aches are usually relieved in orgasm because the muscular tensions are relieved—but not because of the release of any pressures which have accumulated in the testes. Exactly similar pains may develop in the groins of the female when sexual arousal is prolonged for some time before there is any release in orgasm.

In both the female and the male, a considerable congestion of the whole pelvic area may be the consequence of sexual arousal. This depends both upon the tumescence and upon the muscular tensions which have developed. Whenever there is prolonged or repeated arousal without orgasm, this pelvic congestion may become chronic (as in the "engagement pelvis") and lead to the continual discomfort or more acute pain which the clinician sometimes meets in his practice.

The prostate gland and seminal vesicles of the male do have embryonic equivalents in the female embryo, but they never develop in the adult female and do not produce any secretions equivalent to those of the male.

---

[25] For examples of the carry-over of the popular concept of full male "glands" accounting for sexual interest, see such material as: Bauer 1929:234. Haire 1937:150. Freud 1938:608–609. Deutsch 1945(2):85.

[26] Pain in the genital region as a result of unrelieved sexual arousal is, of course, common knowledge. Curiously enough, it is mentioned infrequently in the literature, but see: Malchow 1923:252. Haire 1948:109. Weisman 1948:137–138. Negri 1949:114–115.

11. Nasal and Salivary Secretions. When there is sexual arousal, the membranes which line the nostrils may secrete more than their usual amounts of mucus. This mucus may contribute to the generally swollen state of the nose during sexual activity.

In the mouth, the salivary glands may also increase their secretions during sexual arousal. This is particularly true at the approach of orgasm. Then the glands may spurt quantities of saliva into the mouth. This is often sufficient to provide an abundant lubrication when there is uninhibited kissing or mouth-genital contact. The secretions are often so copious that one's mouth may in actuality "water" in anticipation of a sexual relationship, and one who is erotically aroused may have to swallow repeatedly to clear his mouth of the overabundant supply of saliva. If one's mouth is open when there is a sudden upsurge of erotic stimulation and response, saliva may be spurted some distance out of the mouth. Such behavior becomes especially characteristic at the approach of orgasm. Some of this may be due to difficulty in swallowing because of the muscular tensions which develop in the throat during erotic arousal.[27]

12. Reduction in Sensory Perception. There is a general impression that one who is aroused erotically becomes more sensitive to tactile and other types of sensory stimuli.[28] Quite on the contrary, all of our evidence indicates that there is a considerable and developing loss of sensory capacity which begins immediately upon the onset of sexual stimulation, and which becomes more or less complete, sometimes with complete unconsciousness, during the maximum of sexual arousal and orgasm. At orgasm some individuals may remain unconscious for a matter of seconds or even for some minutes.[29] There are French terms,

---

[27] We have abundant data from recorded observations on the increase in salivation with sexual arousal, but the phenomenon has not often been reported in the literature. See, however, Van de Velde 1930:244. Havelock Ellis 1936(II,1): 153, 166. Lashley 1916:487–488, on the contrary, found that in three human subjects sexual arousal inhibited parotid salivation; but swallowing was also inhibited so that drooling resulted despite the decreased salivation. Our data, however, apply to the increased secretions from the sublingual glands.

[28] The idea that sexually aroused individuals are more sensitive to stimuli is a common one, appearing in such references as: Roubaud 1876:12. Caufeynon 1903:56. Rohleder 1907(1):310. Urbach 1921:127. Malchow 1923:181. Bauer 1927(1):155. Havelock Ellis 1936(I,2):236. Van de Velde 1930:178, 246–247. But the latter author adds: "There is here a profound contradiction. In spite of this magnified receptiveness to sensory impressions during sexual excitement, an individual under its immediate impact, will pay no attention to extraneous things which would otherwise rouse most violent reactions. He is deaf and blind to the world."

[29] Loss of sensory capacity or even of consciousness during extreme emotion or sexual arousal is also noted by: Roubaud 1876:16–17. Caufeynon 1903:57. Talmey 1912:61–62; 1915:92–93. Prince 1914:491. Kantor 1924(1):103. Bauer 1927(2):159–160. Hirschfeld 1928(2):241. Van de Velde 1930:247. Hirschfeld 1935:44. Havelock Ellis 1936(II,1):149–150. Kahn 1939:86. W. Reich 1942:83. Negri 1949:97. Brown and Kempton 1950:207.

"La petite mort" (the little death), and "La mort douce" (the sweet death), which indicate that some persons do understand that unconsciousness may enter at this point. Most persons, however, including technically and professionally trained persons, have failed to comprehend the considerable loss of sensitivity which actually occurs, and the matter therefore needs discussion.

This loss of sensory capacity was first brought to our attention by prostitutes who were contributing histories to this study. Many of the prostitutes rob (roll) their patrons during their sexual contacts. They well understand that their confederates (the creepers) can move about a room without the victim hearing or seeing them if they do not pass directly in front of him; and they can touch him without his being conscious of their presence—providing they confine their activities to the period when he is erotically aroused.

The situation may involve some psychologic distraction. The attention of the individual may be so centered on the sexual activities that he is not consciously aware of other sensory stimulation; but there is some evidence that an actual anesthesia of the sensory structures may occur. It is possible and not improbable that both distraction and anesthesia may be involved. Similar situations are recognized in anger, in fear, and in epilepsy—all of which are phenomena that are physiologically related to sexual response. It is popularly understood that a person may become "too mad to see straight"; "so excited he did not hear the train coming"; or "too angry to know what was happening to him." Love too appears to be blind, and probably more blind than the poets realized when they wrote about it.[30]

Specific observations and experimental data indicate that the whole body of the individual who is sexually aroused becomes increasingly insensitive to tactile stimulation and even to sharp blows and severe injury. Any stimulation which is maintained at a constant level becomes ineffective; and it is quite usual for the participants in a sexual relationship, even though they are unaware of the physiology which is involved, to progressively increase the speed and the force of their techniques. Toward the peak of sexual arousal there may be considerable slapping and heavier blows, biting and scratching, and other activities which the recipient never remembers and which appear to have a minimum if any effect upon him at the time they occur. Not only does

---

[30] The physiology of such a sensory loss, and of the loss of consciousness, is ill understood and probably very complex. One factor may be the reduction of the blood supply to the brain which may result from excessive vasodilation (Engel 1950:19) or hyperventilation (Engel 1950:76; Shock in Reymert 1950:279). Hyperventilation, according to Houssay et al. 1951:287, also may cause dizziness with muscular hyperexcitability, muscular contractions, and tetany. These symptoms resemble some of those in the sexual syndrome.

the sense of touch diminish, but the sense of pain is largely lost. If the blows begin mildly and do not become severe until there is definite erotic response, the recipient in flagellation or other types of sado-masochistic behavior may receive extreme punishment without being aware that he is being subjected to more than mild tactile stimulation.

There is also evidence that even the genitalia, contrary to the general opinion, become anesthetic as the sexual relationships progress. It is not impossible that precise measurements might show that the genital structures preserve their sensitivity longer than some other parts of the body, but there are no data to establish that point. Since so much of the stimulation during a sexual contact is directed toward the genitalia, and since their pronounced turgidity may increase one's awareness of those structures, it is understandable that there should be some concentration of attention on those organs during sexual arousal.

It may take only mild stimulation and sometimes only the slightest touch of the genitalia at the peak of sexual arousal to precipitate orgasm. This, however, does not seem to be evidence of increasing sensitivity, but evidence of the high level to which the physiologic changes may have proceeded before the final touch brings the individual to the point of climax. A drop of water cannot fill an empty cup, but a single drop can make an already filled cup overflow. The effectiveness of the minor tactile stimulation which may precipitate orgasm may emphasize nothing more than the fact that there has been a previous build-up of physiologic changes which are now ready to culminate in orgasm.

Not only the sense of touch but all of the other senses become increasingly ineffective during erotic arousal. The sense of sight is considerably contracted during sexual activity.[31] The pupils dilate,[32] and the range of vision is so narrowed that the individual loses his capacity to observe things that lie to the side and can see only those objects which are directly ahead (p. 614). Some persons become so blind at the peak of sexual arousal that they do not see lights which are moved directly in front of them or recognize other sorts of visual stimuli. Such a loss of visual capacity is one of the known effects of anoxia; and since an anoxia may be involved in sexual response, this is one possible explanation of the sensory loss here.

---

[31] The reduction of visual capacity during arousal is also noted by several authors, including: Roubaud 1876:17. Talmey 1912:61. Bauer 1927(2):159. Goldstein and Steinfeld 1942:44.

[32] Dilation of the pupil of the eye during arousal is also described by: Van de Velde 1930:247. Havelock Ellis 1936(II,1):166–167. Haire 1937:200. Sadler 1944:42. Faller in Hornstein and Faller 1950:237. Stone and Stone 1952:173. Note that the injection of adrenaline may also produce such a dilation (Cannon 1920:37).

The sense of hearing is similarly impaired during erotic arousal. Minor sounds are completely overlooked by the sexually responding individual. The wife who hears the shade flapping or the baby crying after coitus has begun, simply registers the fact that she is not responding erotically. The occasional records of persons being apprehended by police or other intruders when they are engaged in sexual activity may depend on the fact that sexually occupied persons do not hear with their normal acuity. The sense of hearing may be so completely lost during maximum sexual response that very loud noises close at hand and voices at their maximum are not heard.[33]

The senses of smell and taste may similarly be reduced and ultimately more or less lost whenever there is real sexual arousal. Contacts which would be offensive to an individual who was not sexually stimulated, no longer offend. Data on the reception of semen in the performance of fellatio indicate that there may be considerable consciousness and some offense when the sexual relation is not sufficiently stimulating, but that there is a reduction of consciousness of both the contact and the taste when the sexual relation is had between persons who are erotically aroused.

The temperature sense is similarly diminished and may become quite lost during sexual activity. In the earlier stages of arousal there is, as we have already noted, a considerable recognition of the surface warmth of the body which develops as a result of the peripheral circulation of blood. But the sexual arousal may progress to a point at which most persons become unconscious of the extreme temperatures of summer or of winter, of an overheated or a very cold room, or even of objects like cigarettes which may actually burn them.

Since few persons are aware of these losses of sensory capacities, they do not comprehend that they are incapable of giving a coherent account of the physiologic events which transpire during their sexual activities. There is usually some recognition of the fact that one becomes "hot" when there is sexual arousal (because of the peripheral flow of blood), "bothered" (because of the neuromuscular tensions), and "aroused" (by the change in physiologic state). But that is usually the limit of awareness of one's own reactions. Persons whose sexual reactions regularly involve the most vigorous sorts of body movements, such as rhythmic or propulsive extensions of the arms and legs and movements and torsions of the back and neck, are amazed to learn from other persons who have observed them that they have ever behaved so.

---

[33] The impairment of hearing during arousal is also noted in: Bauer 1927(2):159. Van de Velde 1930:247 manufactures a paradox by deciding that while hearing becomes more acute, the aroused person is nevertheless "deaf and blind to the world."

Some insight into the effects of sexual arousal comes from our histories of amputees who have lost arms or lower limbs. It is well known that such individuals frequently experience what have always been considered to be phantom pains in their non-existent limbs. It is, however, sometimes possible to stop such phantom pains by blocking the spinal centers which would control those areas in a normal limb. The spinal centers are still connected with the remnants of the nerves that belong to those areas, and the localization of the pains in the non-existent portion of the limb is due to the fact that no one, amputee or non-amputee, is able to localize the point of origin of any stimulation when the stimulus is applied to the basal portion of a nerve.

From the standpoint of the sexual physiology which is involved, it is notable that our data indicate that amputees rarely if ever experience phantom pains when they are aroused sexually. On the other hand, such pains may suddenly return after orgasm, thereby emphasizing the fact that they were absent during the period of arousal. This appears to be another instance of a loss of sensory perception, or of the distraction of perception during sexual arousal.

13. **Central Nervous System.** There is evidence that the whole central nervous system is affected whenever there is sexual arousal. The data are fragmentary, but sufficient to indicate some of the points which the neurophysiologist should investigate.

During sexual arousal, inhibitions and psychologic blockages are relieved or completely eliminated. A considerable series of histories indicate that stutterers are not likely to stutter when they are with a companion to whom they are sexually responsive. Similarly, gagging may be eliminated, even among individuals who are quite prone to gag when objects are placed deep in their mouths. If sufficiently aroused, these individuals do not gag even when they perform fellatio, although that may involve deep penetration of the mouth. Some persons have their hay fever and sinus congestions relieved when they are sexually aroused, and this may depend in part on the relief of some psychologic state by the arousal. Some persons break out into nervous sweating when they are aroused sexually, although it is more usual for the skin to stay dry or normally moist during sexual activity.[34]

Interferences with the free action of the musculatory system may be relieved during sexual arousal. We have histories which indicate that spastics are able to move more freely when they are sexually aroused, and they may be surprisingly capable in coitus. The improved condition does not persist, however, after the cessation of the sexual arousal.

---

[34] Increased perspiration as a result of sexual arousal is also noted by: Van de Velde 1930:244. Havelock Ellis 1936(II,1):153. Sadler 1944:42. Negri 1949:97.

There is also some information to the effect that some partial paraplegics may be improved when they are aroused sexually (p. 700).

Most persons display unusual muscular strength during sexual arousal, and may become capable of performing feats that require abilities which they do not ordinarily exhibit. This is not because they actually acquire strength, but because they are released from the inhibitions which normally prevent them from utilizing their full capacities. The possibility of a rapist doing unusual damage may depend on this fact; and many another male becomes unexpectedly strong and handles his partner roughly during sexual activity. When there is arousal, many persons become capable of bending and distorting the body to an extent which would be impossible if there were no arousal. The doubling of the body which is necessary in self-fellation, for instance, may be impossible before arousal, but may become possible for some males as they approach orgasm.

14. **Movements in Buttocks and Pelvis.** One of the most striking aspects of a sexual performance is the development of neuromuscular tensions throughout the body of the responding individual, female or male. From head to toe, the muscles contract and relax, involuntarily, in steady or more convulsive rhythms. The movements may vary at various times in the experience of each individual, but they may vary even more between different individuals. Sometimes the muscular action is sufficient to effect major movements of the limbs and of still other parts of the body. Sometimes the movements are violent. Sometimes they are so limited that they are hardly noticeable; but in even the most quiescent individuals, whenever there is sexual response there is likely to be some evidence that muscles are rhythmically tensing and relaxing, everywhere in the body. There may be occasional moments when the movements cease and the muscles are held in continuous tension; but in an uninhibited and responding individual there is usually a flow of continuous muscular movement, from the first moment of arousal to the moment of orgasm.

The most prominent of these muscular activities effect rhythmic movements of the buttocks and of the whole pelvis, and the consequent rhythmic pelvic thrusts during sexual activity are among the distinctive characteristics of the class Mammalia. Without the capacity to make these rhythmic movements, mammalian coitus could not occur. Simple intromission of a male organ into a vagina occurs among a few of the birds and reptiles and among some of the insects, and this is copulation, but it is not coitus in the mammalian sense. The mammals are nearly the only animals in which there are rhythmic alternations of in-and-out movements of the male copulatory organ and, in at least some cases, correspondingly rhythmic movements of the pelvis of the female partner.

Coital movements depend in part upon the gluteal muscles, which are the large muscles in the buttocks, working in conjunction with certain lower vertebral muscles. Even when there is no gross movement of the pelvis, the gluteal muscles may rhythmically contract during erotic arousal. More extended movements of these muscles may crowd or crush the two halves of the buttocks together. Since tensions in these gluteal muscles are correlated with or contribute to a rise in neuromuscular tensions throughout the body, some persons begin their sexual activities by voluntarily moving their buttocks, and thus they may build up their erotic responses.

The erotic significance of gluteal contractions may depend in part upon the fact that movements of the buttocks can stimulate the perineal area, with its abundant supply of nerves. Movements of the buttocks may also stimulate the anal area, which is erotically sensitive in many individuals. In addition, gluteal contractions may stimulate a flow of blood into the genitalia, thereby contributing to the erection of the genital structures. Some males are able to effect full erection by voluntarily tensing and moving their buttocks, and may occasionally reach orgasm without the genitalia being touched. Not a few females have also learned that voluntary contractions of their buttocks and movements of the pelvis may develop their erotic reactions and even effect orgasm in masturbation, petting, coitus, and homosexual activities.

The muscular movements which occur during sexual response are usually involuntary. While most of the muscles which are involved are ordinarily under voluntary control, no such control could effect the coordinated flow of movement which occurs throughout the body of one who is sexually aroused, or the extraordinary rapidity of some of the rhythmic movements which may occur during sexual activity.

15. **Movements of Thighs.** Coordinated with the gluteal contractions, there may be movements of the adductor and/or abductor muscles in the upper portions of the legs. The adductor muscles lie toward the front, on the inner surfaces of the thighs, and the abductors lie toward the sides. Rhythmic contractions of the adductors during sexual activity may pull the upper halves of the legs together rhythmically or, sometimes, quite convulsively. Contractions of the abductors may, on the contrary, roll the legs out. The coordination of the gluteal and adductor contractions may bring the buttocks and thighs together simultaneously in rhythmic sweeps of movement. Many persons intensify the force with which the upper halves of the legs come together by crossing their feet, or by placing objects between their legs to in-

crease the muscular tensions. The sexual partner, placed between the legs of an intensely reacting individual, may be caught in a vise of considerable force.

16. **Movements of Feet and Toes.** Outside of the movements of gluteal, adductor, and abductor muscles, the muscular reactions which are next most noticeable during sexual activity may involve the feet and the toes. The whole foot may be extended until it falls in line with the rest of the lower leg, thereby assuming a position which is impossible in non-erotic situations for most persons who are not trained as ballet dancers. The toes of most individuals become curled or, contrariwise, spread when there is erotic arousal. Many persons divide their toes, turning their large toes up or down while the remaining toes curl in the opposite direction. Such activity is rarely recognized by the individual who is sexually aroused and actually doing these things, but the near universality of such action is attested by the graphic record of coitus in the erotic art of the world. For instance, in Japanese erotic art curled toes have, for at least eight centuries, been one of the stylized symbols of erotic response.

Some persons tense so severely during sexual activity that their feet and toes develop cramps as soon as they have experienced orgasm. They rarely recognize such cramps during the sexual activity itself, but upon the sudden release of the tensions at orgasm, they may have to rise and shake their legs to rid themselves of the cramps.[35] Dramatic instances of the development of such tensions are found in the histories of some of the amputees who have contributed to the present study. Although these persons may have nothing but remnants of the nerves that would have served the muscles of their lower limbs, they may build up neuromuscular tensions in the non-existent portions of those limbs which are quite like those of persons who have complete limbs. Consequently the amputee may also have to rise after orgasm and shake the cramps out of his non-existent toes.

17. **Movements of Arms and Legs.** The legs of a person who is involved in sexual activity may be thrust out in a straight line and held there with considerable tension.[36] The arms may be thrust into similar positions. Or the arms and legs may be bent at the elbows and knees in angular positions which may be rigidly maintained throughout the period of maximum arousal. Contractions of the individual muscles

---

[35] Cramps in the feet or limbs are noted in: Roubaud 1876:17. Van de Velde 1930:246.

[36] Roubaud 1876:17 (who is also quoted by Kisch 1926:288 and Havelock Ellis 1936(II,1):149–150) describes the limbs at the approach of orgasm as becoming "stiff like iron bars." See also Faller in Hornstein and Faller 1950: 238.

usually become distinctly visible, standing out from the body surfaces as they do in an athlete who is demonstrating his muscular capacities.

The upper halves of the arms and of the legs may move rhythmically, sometimes in a slow rhythm, but often with an increase in speed as orgasm is approached. In amputees, the remaining portions of the arms and legs, being unimpeded by the weight of the limbs, may move in an even more distinctive fashion.

18. **Movements of Hands and Fingers.** In the midst of intense sexual activity the hands and fingers may move and curl in a manner which is comparable to the movements of the feet and toes. In some cases the fingers curl under and clench into a tight fist. In other cases the fingers spread in somewhat the same fashion that the toes may spread. Many persons clasp some object when they approach the point of maximum arousal. This may be the side of a chair, some part of the bed, the bed covers, or some other solid object which is available. It may be the body of the sexual companion. Usually the hands and the fingers move rhythmically. Often the movements become spasmodic as the tensions increase, and then the hand may grab objects with considerable force. The tensions are often so great that the sexual partner who is caught in such a situation may be bruised or cut by the fingernails of the reacting individual.

19. **Abdominal Muscles.** During sexual arousal the abdominal muscles may contract with considerable force. The "stomach" is pulled in, sometimes being held in continuous tension, but more often contracting with spasmodic jerks which may rock the whole body. In persons with well trained muscles, such as weight-lifters and dancers, the contractions may be phenomenal in their magnitude and intensity. Sometimes the contractions build up to the very moment of orgasm with increasingly prolonged periods of continuous tension. In other cases, the contractions cease to be spasmodic and become more evenly rhythmic at the approach of orgasm. Sometimes the final contractions are slow, but often they become faster. In a few persons, both female and male, the movements immediately before, during, and after orgasm become so fast that the individual elements are no longer discernible to the human eye. The speed of some of these abdominal movements at the approach of orgasm may approach the most rapid rhythmic movements of which the human body is capable. Such rapid abdominal and pelvic movements regularly occur among many human females and males, and in a number of infra-human mammalian species during coitus.

20. **Thoracic Muscles.** Because of the fixed skeleton which lies under the thoracic muscles, their movements during sexual arousal are

not as prominent as the muscular movements in some other parts of the body. Nevertheless, the tensions of the muscles on the chest and on the sides often become apparent enough to outline the ribs with a typically washboard effect. That these muscles are tensed during sexual response becomes most apparent when they are relaxed after orgasm. Then the thorax assumes a smoothed-out appearance which it did not have during sexual arousal.

The pectoral muscles, on the chest, may protrude prominently under erotic tension. They become so prominent on some males that they may assume something of the appearance of female breasts. The increased prominence of the female breast during sexual arousal may also depend on some protrusion of the underlying pectorals, as well as upon the increased tumescence of the tissue in the breast itself.

21. **Neck Muscles.** In most persons the neck becomes rigid during sexual arousal. The tensions may cause the muscles and the tendons to stand out prominently.[37] Under maximum tensions, at the approach of orgasm, the neck may shift in position, moving the head either forward or backward, but often poising it in a fixed position which is maintained until the tensions are released in orgasm. The prolonged maintenance of such a rigid position may account for some of the "rheumatic neck pains" which an occasional patient takes to the physician for treatment.

22. **Facial Muscles.** Some degree of muscular tension is usually apparent in the face of the person who is reacting sexually, and in some individuals such tensions become extreme at the moment of orgasm. This, combined with the fact that the mouth is open to secure air, may cause the face to take on a drawn, tense, and tortured expression which is paralleled only in the facial expressions of persons who are suffering intense pain and agony (see p. 606).

23. **Eye Muscles.** The eyes of sexually aroused persons acquire a distinctive glare, particularly at the moment of orgasm. This glare cannot be mistaken, and is one of the things that the sexual partner may sometimes report; but it is difficult to analyze exactly what is involved. The pupil of the eye becomes dilated. The lids are held in a fixed position, and the eyes stare without being focused. This gives them something of the blankness which is evident in the eye of a blind person. The eyeball appears to protrude and the eye glistens to a greater degree than usual, in part because there is an increased lachry-

---

[37] During extreme arousal the muscular tensions in the neck become quite prominent, especially in the sternocleidomastoid muscle. This phenomenon was also described by Roubaud 1876:17.

mal secretion.[38] There may be some tumescence of the tissues about the eye. Often, however, the eyelids are kept closed.

24. **Scrotum and Testes.** During sexual arousal, and especially at the moment of maximum tension, the testes are usually pulled up by their supporting cremaster muscles. The walls of the scrotum also contract and in many males the testes are pulled tight against the shaft of the penis, against the perineal surfaces, or into the groins. In a few human males in whom the inguinal canals are pathologically open, and among some other species of mammals in which the inguinal canals are normally open, the testes may be pulled high enough to enter the canals or even to enter the abdominal cavity. This accounts for the near (or more rarely complete) disappearance of the testes of some human males when they are engaged in sexual activity.[39]

25. **Other Structures.** Sexual responses obviously involve a great deal more than genital structures. In actuality, every part of the mammalian body may be involved whenever there is sexual response, and many parts of the body may respond as notably as the genitalia during sexual contact. The activities of any of these other parts of the body may be as useful as the genital activities for the identification of the onset of the response, the continuity or discontinuity of the response, the gradual rise in the level of response, the sudden approach of the ultimate peak in orgasm, and the moment of release in orgasm. The progress of the response may be as obvious in the neck tensions, the aspect of the eye, the behavior of the fingers or toes, or the movements of the buttocks or abdominal muscles, as it is in the genitalia themselves.

THE APPROACH TO ORGASM

The Build-up. With continued and uninterrupted stimulation, the physiologic changes which characterize sexual response may progress and build up in intensity until they approach some maximum point of departure from their normal physiologic states. While exact measurements of these progressive developments are available on only a few of the phenomena which are involved—most specifically on pulse rates and blood pressures, as we have already shown (Figures 120–138)—the more general observations on tumescence, the development of muscular and nervous tensions, the loss in sensory perception, the

---

[38] Changes in the appearance of the eye during sexual arousal have also been noted by: Anon. 1772: The Virgin's Dream, 143–144 ("My Body was all Pulse, my Breath near gone:/ My Cheeks inflam'd, distorted were my eyes . . ."). Roubaud 1876:17. Talmey 1912:61. Moll 1912:164. Kisch 1926:288, 297. Bauer 1927(1):157. Havelock Ellis 1936(II,1):167. Sadler 1944:43.

[39] The drawing up of the testes in coitus was noted as long ago as Aristotle [4th cent. B.C.]: Problems, Bk. 4, 879a and Bk. 27, 949a.

rates of respiration, glandular secretions, and still other phenomena make it apparent that in all of its aspects sexual response may be an accumulative phenomenon which is most effectively concluded by the occurrence of orgasm.

In most human females and males, sexual responses usually develop irregularly, with sudden upsurges of arousal and the development of preliminary peaks and periods of regression in the course of an over-all rise to continually higher levels of response (again see Figures 120–138). The maximum peak may be reached only after a sudden rise which is more abrupt than any of the previous rises, and the level of the final peak may be much higher than the level of any of the preceding peaks of response.

Some persons, particularly younger males, may respond instantaneously to sexual stimulation and proceed quite immediately, with sharp peaks and regressions which follow rapidly upon each other, until they suddenly surge to the maximum level of response at the moment of orgasm. Some persons, particularly older persons, experience more even and more steady rises in their responses, and reach their maxima without the abrupt developments which characterize the approach to orgasm in many other individuals. There are, however, some older persons, including both females and males, who continue to react in an abrupt fashion throughout their lives.[40]

The speed of reaction to sexual stimuli, the speed with which physiologic changes progress toward the peak of arousal, the presence or absence of preliminary peaks and regressions, the abruptness of the approach toward orgasm, the level at which orgasm occurs, and the pattern of the muscular reactions which may follow orgasm are likely to remain more or less uniform throughout most of an individual's life. This is established by specific records which we have on the nature of the responses of a limited number of persons who had been observed over long periods of years—over as many as sixteen years in one case, and in some cases from pre-adolescence into the late teens or twenties. These individual patterns of response may depend at least to some extent on the physiologic equipment with which an individual is born, for clinicians report striking individual variation in the responses of even very young infants to general contact, to pressure, to specific tactile stimuli, and to genital stimulation. There is, however, considerable reason for believing that some aspects of the behavioral pattern

---

[40] For examples of variation in the build-up to orgasm, see the diagrams and charts in: Boas and Goldschmidt 1932:99. Dickinson 1933, 1949:figs. 126–127. Klumbies and Kleinsorge 1950a:952–958; 1950b:64–66. Ford and Beach 1951:245–248 (Fig. 16 is theoretic and inadequate).

represent learned behavior which has become habitual after early experience (pp. 643 ff.).

Many persons may exert some deliberate control over the normal course of their sexual responses in order to modify or prolong the activity or particularly pleasurable aspects of it. By regulating the frequency of sexual contacts, by controlling the breathing rate, by holding muscles in continuous tension, by avoiding continuous stimulation, by avoiding fantasies or other controllable sources of psychosexual stimulation, and by still other means, it is possible to extend the period of preliminary activity and delay the upsurge of response which carries the physiologic developments to climax. The sexual literature for at least four thousand years, from early Sanskrit to current marriage manuals, has recommended that the male in particular delay his responses in order that the female may reach orgasm simultaneously with him. There are, however, many persons who, at least on occasion, find greater satisfaction in sexual relations which proceed directly to the point of orgasm.

Coitus reservatus, the *Karezza* of the Sanskrit and Hindu literature, represents a maximum sophistication of such deliberate control. It has been practiced by whole communities, like the Oneida Colony in the nineteenth century in New York State. In this technique it is common for the individual to experience as many as a dozen or twenty peaks of response which, while closely approaching the sexual climax, deliberately avoid what we should interpret as actual orgasm. Persons who practice such techniques commonly insist that they experience orgasm at each and every peak even though each is held to something below full response and, in the case of the male, ejaculation is avoided. We now interpret the supposed orgasms as preliminary peaks of arousal. The possibility of prolonging this sort of experience, especially at any high level of response, apparently depends on the very fact that there is no orgasm.[41]

Speed of Response. There is a longstanding and widespread opinion that the female is slower than the male in her sexual responses and needs more extended stimulation in order to reach orgasm. This opinion is accepted and is the basis of much clinical practice today.[42]

---

[41] Coitus reservatus, or *Karezza*, is the subject of some literature, including two volumes: Stockham 1901(?). Lloyd 1931. For the history of the Oneida colony, see Parker 1935.

[42] The idea that the female is inherently slower than the male in sexual response occurs repeatedly in the literature, as in: Rohleder 1907(1):312. Moll 1912: 26. Talmey 1912:63; 1915:94. Urbach 1921:124 ff. Malchow 1923:164, 231. Hirschfeld 1928(2):230. Stopes 1931:74. Rutgers 1934:135–136. Havelock Ellis 1936(I,2):236. Wright 1937:85. Clark 1937:46–49. Kahn 1939:fig.31. Butterfield 1940:94. Podolsky 1942:52. Magoun 1948:216–220. Hirsch 1949: 134. Faller in Hornstein and Faller 1950:238–239. Stone and Stone 1952:180.

Certain it is that many males reach orgasm before their wives do in their marital coitus, and many females experience orgasm in only a portion of their coitus (Chapter 9). On the other hand, a high proportion of the males could ejaculate soon after coitus begins. These facts seem to substantiate the general opinion that the female is slower than the male, but our analyses now make it appear that this opinion is based on a misinterpretation of the facts.

This becomes apparent when we examine the time which the average female needs to reach orgasm in masturbation. Apparently many females, even though they may be slow to respond in coitus, may masturbate to orgasm in a matter of a minute or two. Masturbation thus appears to be a better test than coitus of the female's actual capacities; and there seems to be something in the coital technique which is responsible for her slower responses there.

The crux of the matter seems to lie in the fact that the female in masturbation usually proceeds directly to orgasm and is not interrupted or distracted as she often is in coitus. The record indicates that the average (median) female ordinarily takes a bit less than four minutes to reach orgasm in masturbation, although she may need ten or twenty minutes or more to reach that point in coitus. Similar records show that the average male needs something between two and four minutes to reach orgasm in masturbation although, in order to increase his pleasure, he often delays his performance. The record indicates, therefore, that the female is not appreciably slower than the male in her capacity to reach orgasm.

Actually there are some females who regularly reach orgasm within a matter of fifteen to thirty seconds in their petting or coital activities. Some regularly have multiple orgasms (p. 375) which may come in rapid succession, with lapses of only a minute or two, or in some instances of only a few seconds between orgasms. Such speed is found in only a small percentage of the females, but it is found, similarly, in only a small percentage of the males. Of the 2114 females in our sample who supplied data on the time usually taken to reach orgasm in masturbation, some 45 per cent had regularly done so in something between one and three minutes, and another 24 per cent had averaged four to five minutes. About 19 per cent had averaged something between six and ten minutes, and only 12 per cent regularly took longer than that to reach orgasm. In all of these groups there were, of course, females who had deliberately taken longer than necessary to reach orgasm, in order to prolong the pleasure of the experience.

The slower responses of the female in coitus appear to depend in part upon the fact that she frequently does not begin to respond as promptly as the male, because psychologic stimuli usually play a more important role in the arousal of the average male, and a less important role in the sexual arousal of the average female (Chapter 16). The average male is aroused in anticipation of a sexual relationship, and he usually comes to erection and is ready to proceed directly to orgasm as soon as or even before he makes any actual contact. The average female, on the contrary, is less often aroused by such anticipation, and sometimes she does not begin to respond until there has been a considerable amount of physical stimulation.

Moreover, because she is less aroused by psychologic stimuli, the female is more easily distracted than the male in the course of her coital relationships (Chapter 9). The male may be continuously stimulated by seeing the female, by engaging in erotic conversation with her, by thinking of the sexual techniques he may use, by remembering some previous sexual experience, by planning later contacts with the same female or some other sexual partner, and by any number of other psychologic stimuli which keep him aroused even though he may interrupt his coital contacts. Perhaps two-thirds of the females find little if any arousal in such psychologic stimuli. Consequently, when the steady build-up of the female's response is interrupted by the male's cessation of movement, changes of position, conversation, or temporary withdrawal from the genital union, she drops back to or toward a normal physiologic state from which she has to start again when the physical contacts are renewed. It is this, rather than any innate incapacity, which may account for the female's slower responses in coitus.[43]

ORGASM

As the responding individual approaches the peak of sexual activity, he or she may suddenly become tense—momentarily maintain a high level of tension—rise to a new peak of maximum tension—and then abruptly and instantaneously release all tensions and plunge into a series of muscular spasms or convulsions through which, in a matter of seconds or a minute or two, he or she returns to a normal or even subnormal physiologic state (Figures 120–138).

This explosive discharge of neuromuscular tensions at the peak of sexual response is what we identify as orgasm. The spasms into which the individual is thrown as a result of that release, we consider the after-effects of that orgasm. Many psychologists and psychiatrists, emphasizing the satisfactions that may result from sexual experience,

---

[43] We have had access to a considerable body of data on the continuous nature of male response and the discontinuous nature of female response. Although this situation has rarely been recognized in the literature, it is noted in Urbach 1921:132.

suggest that the after-effects of this release from sexual tensions may be a chief source of those satisfactions. They are, therefore, inclined to extend the term orgasm to cover both the release from tensions and the after-effects of that release. There are, however, several advantages in restricting the concept of orgasm to the sudden and abrupt release itself, and it is in that sense that we have used the term throughout the present volume.[44]

Some, and perhaps most persons may become momentarily unconscious at the moment of orgasm, and some may remain unconscious or only vaguely aware of reality throughout the spasms or convulsions which follow orgasm. Consequently few persons realize how they behave at and immediately after orgasm, and they are quite incapable of describing their experiences in any informative way.

Sometimes the recession from the high peak of orgasm is accomplished in a single great sweep. Sometimes there are momentary pauses in the recession, or some brief resurgence to a subsidiary peak or peaks which are, however, always lower than the maximum at which orgasm occurred (Figures 120–138). The return to the physiologically normal or subnormal state is, however, usually accomplished in a short period of time.

The abrupt cessation of the ofttimes strenuous movements and extreme tensions of the previous sexual activity, and the peace of the resulting state, provide in their contrast the most obvious evidence that orgasm has occurred. It is the best means of identifying orgasm in the human female, and it is the best means of identifying orgasm in the human male in instances in which ejaculation cannot be observed. Because this sudden release is not often seen among females of infra-human species of mammals, we conclude that they are not reaching orgasm. In coital relations, the neuromuscular tensions of the responding infra-human female are usually maintained after the cessation of coitus, and they disappear only gradually, without the explosive discharge which characterizes orgasm. Moreover, after coitus the females of the infra-human species are usually as responsive as they were before coitus, and this is not generally true of animals that have experienced orgasm.

On the other hand, the statement that orgasm never occurs among the females of any of the infra-human species does not seem to be

---

[44] The concept of orgasm as the period of time during which the spasms (and, in the male, ejaculation) occur is implicit in various works, as in: Adler 1911: 30 ff. Van de Velde 1930:173, 184–188. Kuntz 1945:312–313, 323. Hardenbergh 1949:226. Stone and Stone 1952:185–186. On the other hand, the concept of orgasm as a sudden release of neuromuscular tensions is supported by such measurements as those in: Pussep 1922:61 ff. Boas and Goldschmidt 1932:99. Klumbies and Kleinsorge 1950a:955, 957; 1950b:61–66.

entirely correct, although it apparently applies to most individuals of most of the species. Reference to Figures 133 to 135 will show that blood pressures among female dogs build up in essentially the same way as they do among male dogs in coitus (Figures 129–132), and the females similarly show a sudden return from the high peak of tension to normal levels of blood pressure. If measurements of other aspects of the physiology of responding female dogs parallel the data shown for blood pressure, it is difficult to understand why this should not be identified as a record of orgasm.

The difficulty has originated in the fact that there have not been well understood criteria for interpreting orgasm when it appears in these infra-human females. However, looking at the specific record which some of the students of mammalian behavior have been able to provide, we find descriptions of what appear to be good cases of orgasm among rabbits and among chimpanzees. There is a record of masturbation in a female chimpanzee which has apparently been reaching orgasm regularly over a considerable period of years. We ourselves have had the opportunity to observe another female chimpanzee in a physiologic reaction which may well have been orgasm.

While most cows who mount other cows give evidence of erotic arousal, they do not ordinarily show any build-up to peaks of tension, from which there is the sort of sudden release which is characteristic of the bull at the time of orgasm. On the other hand, we have reports of mounting cows giving a sudden lunge at the peak of response, and then dropping back into inactivity as though they had experienced orgasm.[45]

The very strenuous activities which the females of all species of cats, including the house cat, the tiger, and the lion, regularly display after coitus, may involve a most strenuous series of convulsive movements which turn the body in a wild succession of circles for some moments or some minutes after the cessation of coitus. While we have

---

[45] Dr. Marc Klein of the Université de Strasbourg informs us that he believes orgasm occurs in the female rabbit. In a letter of February, 1952 he states: "I have very often observed a quite definite peak of response with climax, from which the female falls back abruptly into a quiet state . . . . the two partners fall together on one side; . . . the female is shrieking and sometimes even the male is shrieking himself. The female thrusts the male aside by a sudden movement of the pelvis and the two animals at once come back to the normal stature on the four limbs . . . . it is an individual response of the female which is far from appearing in all females even of a definite strain . . . . there are enormous individual differences in this behavior." Our chimpanzee data come from the observations of Dr. Henry Nissen of the Yerkes Primate Laboratory at Orange Park, Florida, and concern primarily the adult female Alpha. We have observed an additional female in what seemed to be orgasm. The data on completed thrusts in cows mounting other cows come from Dr. Albert Shadle of the University of Buffalo.

PHASE I

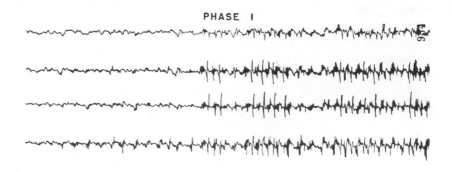

PHASE 2

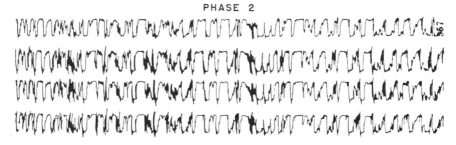

PHASE 3

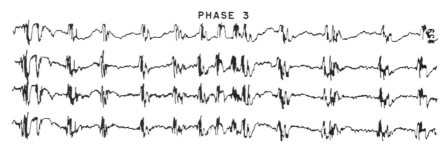

Figure 140. Electroencephalogram of human subject in sexual activity

From unpublished data provided by courtesy of Dr. Abraham Mosovich. Four electrodes, attached to the head at different points, recorded four lines simultaneously. The three sets of lines are not continuous, but represent samples from three phases of the record. For example, the sample of phase 2 begins approximately half a minute after the end of the sample of phase 1. Read from left to right.

PHASE 1: With the beginning of sexual stimulation, rapid, low voltage (small) waves develop in the brain. Such waves are known to occur during excitement. These are subsequently obscured by spikes resulting from muscle contraction and tremor.

PHASE 2: With orgasm, very high voltage, slow (large) waves develop in the brain. These appear to be flat-topped only because the machine was not set to record waves of such height. Interspersed with and partially obscuring the large slow waves are spikes resulting from muscle spasm. This phase resembles petit mal epilepsy or the later stages of grand mal when the subject is passing from tonic rigidity to clonic spasms.

PHASE 3: Later, the large slow waves vanish and the low voltage, rapid (small) waves reappear. These are periodically interrupted by spikes from rhythmic clonic muscular spasm.

previously been uncertain of the interpretation of this phenomenon, it may represent the after-effects of a true orgasm.

It is true, however, that there are no records of orgasm among the females of most of the infra-human species of mammals, and apparently most individuals among most of the species just cited do not appear to reach orgasm in any of their sexual activities, even though some individual females may do so. The matter will not be finally settled until extensive physiologic measurements are made on these infra-human species; but as far as our knowledge yet goes, the human female is unique among the mammals in her capacity to reach orgasm with some frequency and regularity when she is aroused sexually.

Sexual orgasm constitutes one of the most amazing aspects of human behavior. There is only one other phenomenon, namely sneezing, which is physiologically close in its summation and explosive discharge of tension. Sneezing is, however, a localized event, while sexual orgasm involves the whole of the reacting body. While the summation of neuromuscular tensions is a phenomenon with which neurophysiologists are well acquainted, the mechanism of the explosive discharge of such tension is not understood.

AFTER-EFFECTS OF ORGASM

Muscular Spasms and Convulsions. Muscular spasms or more intense convulsions are the usual product of the sudden release of tension in orgasm. Sometimes these spasms are localized and mild, amounting to nothing more than slight movements of some particular part of the body. Usually they are more pronounced and extend to all parts of the body. Sometimes they may involve the entire body in extreme convulsions.[46]

In some persons the spasms which follow orgasm may subside within a moment or two. They may be so mild and pass so quickly that it would be difficult to observe that there had been any spasms at all. The average individual, however, may be in spasm for a half minute or a minute or more before subsiding into a normal physiologic state. Some persons may experience spasms or more extreme convulsions for two or three minutes, or in rare cases for as long as five minutes after the moment of orgasm.

The more extreme convulsive movements into which some individuals are thrown after orgasm bear a striking resemblance to those which may be observed in epilepsy (Figure 140). There may be some

---

[46] We have had access to a considerable body of observed data on the involvement of the entire body in the spasms following orgasm. The situation was graphically described by Roubaud 1876:17, whose description has not been surpassed by later authors.

common physiologic mechanism which accounts for the resemblances between the spasms or convulsions in epilepsy and those following orgasm, but the mechanisms are not yet understood. The convulsions following orgasm also resemble those which follow an electric shock. This makes it all the more amazing that most persons consider that sexual orgasm with its after-effects may provide one of the most supreme of physical satisfactions.

In the most extreme types of sexual reaction, an individual who has experienced orgasm may double and throw his whole body into continuous and violent motion, arch his back, throw his hips, twist his head, thrust out his arms and legs, verbalize, moan, groan, or scream [47] in much the same way as a person who is suffering the extremes of torture. In all of these respects, human females and males may react in essentially the same way. In some individuals the whole body may be thrown, or tossed, or rolled over a distance of several feet or yards. On occasion the sexual partner may be crushed, pounded, violently punched, or kicked during the uncontrolled responses of an intensely reactive individual. The movements are obviously involuntary, and they are for the most part beyond voluntary control. Some persons whose responses are mild can control their movements if there is some social advantage in reacting without attracting attention; but for those whose responses are more extreme, any deliberate control is nearly impossible.

Genital Spasms and Convulsions. The genitalia of both the female and the male are usually included in the spasms or convulsions which follow orgasm. In the female the perineal muscles may go into convulsion, and the levator muscles of the vagina may also move convulsively and sometimes may grab the male's penis or any other object which has been inserted into the entrance to the vagina.[48] The fact that some women experience vaginal spasms or convulsions may provide some basis for the references in the psychiatric literature to a "vaginal orgasm." These vaginal spasms are, however, simply an extension of the spasms which may involve the whole body after orgasm.

While the vaginal contractions may prove a source of considerable pleasure both for the female and for her male partner, it is a more

---

[47] Involuntary vocalization at orgasm is, of course, a matter.of common knowledge. It is also reported in: Roubaud 1876:17. Bloch 1908:50. Talmey 1912:62; 1915:93. Bauer 1927(1):157. Van de Velde 1930:246. Havelock Ellis 1936(II,1):150, 166. Haire 1937:200. Brown and Kempton 1950:207.

[48] Genital spasms at or immediately following orgasm are also noted by: Roubaud 1876:13. Rohleder 1907(1):310–311. Bloch 1908:50. Moll 1912:25. Urbach 1921:125–126. Malchow 1923:135. Kisch 1926:295–296. Bauer 1927(1):156. Dickinson 1933, 1949:98. Van de Velde 1930:199. Havelock Ellis 1936(II,1): 159. W. Reich 1942:83. Hardenbergh 1949:228. Faller in Hornstein and Faller 1950:238.

difficult matter to determine whether the lack of vaginal spasms represents any loss of pleasure for a female. The absence of vaginal contractions in a woman who customarily has them may, however, provide some evidence that she is not responding in that particular relationship.

Strong rhythmic contractions of the abdominal muscles sometimes push the uterus and the attached walls of the vagina closer to the vaginal entrance (Figure 118) if it is not blocked by the inserted penis. Recently the action of the uterus has been studied with electrical instruments which can follow the movements of fine particles that are inserted in the cavity of the organ. These studies show that the upper end of the uterus goes into rhythmic contractions of considerable frequency whenever there is sexual arousal. The rate of movement, however, decreases in the body of the uterus, and the cervix at the lower end of the uterus shows a minimum of movement. There is, in consequence, an actual sucking effect which may pull semen through the cervix into the uterus.[49]

In the male, spasms or convulsions following orgasm may involve both the penis and the scrotum. The scrotal walls may suddenly relax, or expand and contract in rhythmic movements; and the testes, which have been drawn up into the groins during sexual arousal, may undergo considerable movement within the scrotum as a specific after-effect of orgasm.

In most males there are only limited gross movements of the penis following orgasm, but in some individuals the movements may become spasmodic jerks of some magnitude. The most pronounced movements appear to depend upon contractions of the muscular attachments of the two spongy bodies (the corpora cavernosa) which constitute the main shaft of the penis. For most of their length the two spongy bodies are joined to form a single body, but at the base of the penis the two corpora separate into divergent roots which are fastened at their tips (the crura of the penis) to the pelvic bones. Movements of either the flaccid or erect penis may be effected by voluntary contractions of these crura, and at orgasm there may be strong and violently convul-

---

[49] The descent and/or sucking of the uterus is mentioned in: Rohleder 1907(1): 531. Talmey 1912:56–57; 1915:87–89. Urbach 1921:133. Malchow 1923: 135–136. Kisch 1926:295–300. Hirschfeld 1928(2):226. Dickinson 1933, 1949:90–93. Havelock Ellis 1936(II,1):160–162. Haire 1937:199, 202, 283. Kahn 1939:85, fig. 17. Weisman 1941:109–110 (a good summary of opinions). Hutton 1942:71. Huhner 1945:454–455. Gardner in Howell (Fulton edit.) 1949:1179. Faller in Hornstein and Faller 1950:238. Such uterine action has been described in animals (e.g., Marshall 1922:173–174, and Baker 1926:32), and data on its occurrence in human females are brought together in Colmeiro-Laforet 1952:125–126. Extensive work done under the direction of Carl Hartman is not yet published.

sive contractions of the crura. In consequence, the whole penis may sometimes move in strong jerks; but sometimes there is hardly any gross movement of the penis even though the crural contractions may be strong. Ejaculation may depend in part upon these contractions of the corpora cavernosa, as well as upon contractions of the urethra.

Any contraction of the muscles in the crura simultaneously contracts the anal sphincters, and the anus may open and close in violent convulsion as an after-effect of orgasm. Most persons are unconscious of this anal action unless they have had anal intercourse or utilized anal insertions as a source of erotic stimulation.

Ejaculation. Ejaculation is one of the most characteristic products of the spasms or convulsions which follow orgasm in the male. The prostate and seminal vesicles are thrown into spasms which press their liquid secretions into the urethra, and urethral contractions and contractions of muscle tissues in the crura of the penis may propel the semen with a force which is sufficient to carry it at least to the meatus (the opening of the urethra).

It is generally believed that semen is usually ejaculated with a force which is sufficient to propel it for some distance beyond the tip of the penis. Some clinicians have considered that the force with which the semen is thrown against the cervix in vaginal coitus may be a factor in determining whether fertilization occurs.[50] However, a considerable body of data to which we have had access, based on observations of some hundreds of males, indicates that there is considerable individual variation in this regard and some lesser variation in the experience of any single individual. In perhaps three-quarters of the males the semen merely exudes from the meatus or is propelled with so little force that the liquid is not carried more than a minute distance beyond the tip of the glans of the penis. In other males the semen may be propelled for a matter of some inches, or a foot or two, or even as far as five or six (or rarely eight) feet. This variation in function may depend upon anatomic or physiologic variations, for the pattern of ejaculation is largely fixed for each individual except as fatigue and, ultimately, age may reduce the intensity of all the physiologic responses.

Since the prostate gland and seminal vesicles are only vestigial structures in the female, she does not actually ejaculate. Muscular contractions of the vagina following orgasm may squeeze out some of the genital secretions, and in a few cases eject them with some force.[51] This

---

[50] Ejaculation against or into the cervix is mentioned by: Roubaud 1876:45. Rohleder 1907(1):311. Friedlaender 1921:27–28. Forel 1922:57. Hirschfeld 1928(2):226. This idea is, however, denied by Dickinson 1933, 1949:93–94.
[51] The expulsion of genital secretions by the female at orgasm, which is the so-called "female ejaculation," is popularly known and talked about. In the

is frequently referred to, particularly in the deliberately erotic literature, as an ejaculation in the female; but the term cannot be strictly
used in that connection. Ejaculation is, in fact, the only phenomenon
in the physiology of sexual response which is not identically matched
in the male and the female, or represented by closely homologous
functions.

Because ejaculation is almost invariably and immediately associated
with orgasm, it is often considered as the orgasm of the male. This
interpretation is not acceptable, for the following reasons:

1. The data already presented show that sexual arousal and orgasm
involve the whole nervous system and, therefore, all parts of the body.
Ejaculation is only one of the events that may follow the release of
nervous tensions at orgasm.

2. Orgasm in the female matches the orgasm of the male in every
physiologic detail except for the fact that it occurs without ejaculation.

3. Pre-adolescent boys may experience orgasm, duplicating the
experience of the adult male in every respect except for the fact that
they do not ejaculate. This simply depends on the fact that the prostate
gland and seminal vesicles of the younger boy are not sufficiently
developed to secrete seminal fluids.

4. Adult males who are capable of multiple orgasm may have several
experiences with ejaculation and then, when the secretions of the prostate and seminal vesicles are exhausted, they may have further orgasms without semen. The later orgasms may be duplicates of the
earlier ones, except that they do not lead to ejaculation. Physiologically
and psychologically they may be as satisfactory as those in which
ejaculation occurred.

5. There are some males in whom ejaculation does not occur until
some seconds after orgasm, and in whom, therefore, it is possible to
distinguish orgasm and ejaculation as two separate events.

6. There are a few adult males (perhaps one in four thousand) who
are anatomically incapable of ejaculation, although they may experience orgasms which are in all other respects similar to those which
are accompanied by ejaculation.

7. Males who have had their prostate glands or a portion of the
sympathetic system removed by surgical operation (a prostatectomy
or a sympathectomy) are no longer capable of ejaculation, although
they may still be capable of orgasm if no other complications have

---

literature it is described, for instance, in: Van de Velde 1930:195–196. Havelock Ellis 1936(II,1):145. Grafenberg 1950:147.

been involved in the operation. Although the males of some of the lower mammalian species (*e.g.*, rats) may have their capacity to reach orgasm stopped by such a prostatic operation, they may again become capable of reaching orgasm if they are given male hormones (androgens); and such orgasms may be typical in every respect of orgasm in the normal rat except that they occur without ejaculation.

Because of this mistaken identification of ejaculation as orgasm, many persons have concluded that orgasm in the female is something different from orgasm in the male. On the contrary, we find that orgasm in the female is, physiologically, quite the same as orgasm in the male. Ejaculation may constitute a spectacular and biologically significant event which is unique to the male, but it is an event which depends on relatively simple anatomic differences, rather than upon differences in the basic physiology of sexual response in the female and male.

Other Readjustments. In addition to the physiologic readjustments noted above, all other functions which have been distorted during sexual response are quickly restored by orgasm to their normal or even subnormal states.

Pulse rates which had reached 150 or more at the moment of orgasm are, within a matter of seconds or a few minutes at the most, returned to their normal 75 or 80 (Figures 120–128).[52] Blood pressures similarly drop (Figures 129–138). The increase in the peripheral circulation of the blood quickly subsides, and tumescence may be abruptly reduced, although the speed of detumescence may vary considerably in different individuals. Younger males may maintain erection for several minutes after orgasm; most older males begin to lose erection immediately. If there is any continuing excitation, some younger individuals and even some older males may maintain full erection for five or ten minutes or even for a half hour or more after orgasm. It is sometimes possible for such a male to renew sexual activity and attain another orgasm without having experienced flaccidity between performances.

After the cessation of the respiratory convulsions which are the immediate after-effects of orgasm, the respiratory rate in most individuals quickly drops to normal or, in case the individual is already fatigued, to something lower than normal frequency (Figure 139).

Wounds which were acquired during the sexual activity, and which exhibited a surprisingly scant flow of blood at that time, may begin to

---

[52] The rapidity of the decrease in pulse following orgasm is shown in Boas and Goldschmidt 1932:99, where the female's pulse fell from 146 to 117 in a matter of seconds, and the male's from 143 to 117 within a minute. In Klumbies and Kleinsorge 1950a:953, 955; 1950b:62, the male's pulse fell from 142 to 67 in four seconds.

flow more freely after orgasm. The menstrual flow, which may have been slowed up during erotic response, is resumed at its normal rate.

Even more remarkable is the sudden return of sensory acuity (or the reorientation of sensory perception) which may follow orgasm. While the increased capacity may amount to nothing more than a return to normal sensitivity, the contrast with the previous insensitive state may be enough to cause the individual considerable discomfort. Many males—perhaps a majority of them—become so sensitive after orgasm that they may experience considerable pain if there is any additional stimulation of the penis at that time. Marriage manuals frequently recommend that the male who reaches orgasm before his female partner does, should continue coital movements until she has been satisfied; but it should be recognized that such continued activity would be excruciatingly painful to many males, and for many of them a physical impossibility. There is some record of a similar hypersensitivity among females, although the specific data are more limited.

Various parts of the body may itch after orgasm. Many individuals become especially conscious of a full bladder after orgasm.[53] Muscles, such as those of the groin, the legs, the calf, the fingers, and the neck, may go into cramps during sexual activity, but one may not be conscious of that fact until after he or she has experienced orgasm (p. 620).

Some persons become conscious of the fact that they are hungry and thirsty after sexual activity. Sometimes such hunger or thirst simply reflects a return to normal perceptive capacities; but hunger, thirst, a general restlessness, a desire to get away from other people, a desire to smoke, and still other nervous types of behavior may, on occasion, be the product of the psychologic disturbance which is engendered by doubts over the moral propriety or the social acceptability of the act in which one has just engaged. Sometimes there are increased movements of the digestive tract following sexual activity, and an occasional individual may defecate or vomit in the course of sexual activity, or immediately after it. Such disturbances are not infrequently credited to the supposedly unsanitary nature of some sexual technique, but the true explanation of such activity is certainly psychologic.

A marked quiescence of the total body is the most widely recognized outcome of orgasm. The famous aphorism, *post coitum triste*—one is sad following coitus—, is not only a distortion of Galen's original statement, but an inadequate description of the usually quiescent state of

---

[53] The secretion of urine, or desire to urinate during sexual excitement, is also noted by: Van de Velde 1930:244. Havelock Ellis 1936(II,1):154. Hardenbergh 1949:227.

a person who has experienced orgasm.[54] There is neither regret nor conflict nor any tinge of sadness for most persons who have experienced orgasm. There is, on the contrary, a quiescence, a calm, a peace, a satisfaction with the world which, in the minds of many persons, is the most notable aspect of any type of sexual activity.

Sometimes, especially in youth, the post-orgasmic relaxation is hardly more than momentary. There are some individuals who, within a matter of seconds or minutes after the cessation of the orgasmic spasms, are ready for any type of vigorous exercise or mental activity. The average individual may require four or five minutes of repose before coming back to a normal state. Many persons promptly fall asleep after the termination of sexual activity, especially if it occurs in the evening when they are already fatigued.

It has been said that sexual excitement after orgasm recedes more slowly in the female than in the male. We do not know of data which warrant such a generalization, although it frequently recurs in the literature, sometimes with impressive but wholly imaginary charts to illustrate the concept.[55] The small body of actual measurements that are available (Figures 120–138) do not warrant any general distinction between females and males.

A few persons may be fatigued for some hours, and a rare individual may be exhausted for some days following orgasm, but such cases represent ill health which is overtaxed by the additional expenditure of energy required by sexual activity. The physical exhaustion which is usually ascribed to sexual excess is probably the outcome of the late hours, the lack of sleep, the alcoholic dissipation, or other excesses which may accompany the sexual activity. Sexual activity itself is limited by a self-regulating mechanism which controls the possible frequencies of orgasm. When sexual performance has reached the limits of one's nervous capacity, one is no longer interested erotically, and no longer responds to sexual stimuli. Once or twice in a lifetime, each male may deliberately attempt to set a record and force himself to

---

[54] Galen [ca. 130–200 A.D.] actually said: *Triste est omne animal post coitum, praeter mulierem gallumque* (every animal is sad after coitus, except the human female and the rooster).

[55] That excitement after orgasm diminishes more slowly in the female is often asserted in the literature, as in: Roubaud 1876:17. Rohleder 1907(1):313. Moll 1912:26. Talmey 1912:63; 1915:94. Urbach 1921:129 ff. Krafft-Ebing 1922:41. Bauer 1927(1):158. Hirschfeld 1928(2):230. Van de Velde 1930: 181, 248. Havelock Ellis 1936(II,1):168. Haire 1937:200, 211. Kahn 1939: fig.31. Faller in Hornstein and Faller 1950:239. Stone and Stone 1952:186. Few of the references give exact measurements. Klumbies and Kleinsorge 1950a:956; 1950b:61, found no difference between the female and male in this respect, but the case is complicated by the fact that the female had several consecutive orgasms. On the other hand, the Boas and Goldschmidt female case (1932:99) returned to a physiologic norm somewhat more rapidly than the male.

perform beyond the limits of his spontaneous erotic responses; but such performances are infrequent in the histories of most males. Similarly, females do not respond in sexual activities which go beyond their physiologic capacities, although they may, of course, be forced into physical relationships in which they do not respond.

Individual Variation. To summarize the data which have already been presented, we note that variations in the gross aspects of sexual response and orgasm may involve the following: (1) the amplitude of the muscular movements; (2) the particular parts of the body which are most prominently involved in the responses; (3) the speed of the muscular movements; (4) the number of pelvic thrusts or other movements which are made prior to orgasm; (5) the time which may elapse from the beginning of the activity to the peak at orgasm (and this may vary from ten seconds to an hour or two); (6) the magnitude and duration of the spasms which follow orgasm.

These variations offer endless possibilities for combination and recombination.[56] Consequently the responses of each individual may be quite unlike those of any other individual, although the basic physiologic patterns of sexual response and orgasm are remarkably uniform among all individuals, both female and male, and throughout all of the species of mammals.

Conscious Satisfactions. Even though sensory perception and intellectual activity may be at a minimum during sexual activity, there is usually enough conscious realization of satisfaction to provide a considerable stimulus for a continuation of the activity, usually to the point of orgasm. Although it is not entirely clear what the sources of those satisfactions may be, they appear to be influenced by the following:

¶ The nature and the intensity of the physical and psychologic stimuli which effect the sexual response.

¶ The innate physiologic capacities of the responding individual.

¶ The psychologic capacities of the individual, such as his or her ability to win sexual partners, to develop effective psychologic situations during the overt activity, and to respond sympathetically to the partner's performance.

¶ The physiologic level which is attained at orgasm. It is possible that orgasm which is accompanied by a pulse running at 150 may be

---

[56] It is commonly understood that there is individual variation in the conspectus of sexual response and orgasm, although it is only occasionally mentioned in the literature. But see: Roubaud 1876:16. Talmey 1915:95. Negri 1949:78, 82–83. Brown and Kempton 1950:207. Stone and Stone 1952:186.

more stimulating than orgasm which is reached with the pulse running at 100 or so; but the data are not conclusive. Similarly, other physiologic changes may be more important when they represent a maximum departure from the normal state.

¶ The previous sexual experience of the individual, and the manner in which he or she has been conditioned by such experience.

¶ The individual's previous experience with the particular sexual partner. The satisfactions to be obtained from relationships which are continued over long periods of years may steadily increase because of the increasing appreciation of the partner's psychologic and physiologic needs, and his or her preferences in sexual matters.

¶ The novelty of the sexual situation, which may stimulate when old situations have lost some of their former attraction.

¶ The directness and the speed with which orgasm is attained. Some individuals prefer direct and uninterrupted activity, others prefer a leisurely, long-drawn-out performance in which there are deliberate interruptions for the sake of delaying orgasm.

¶ The extent to which the sexual activities are accepted psychologically. The presence or absence of guilt feelings is, for many persons, the most important factor in determining the level of the satisfactions which may be obtained from a sexual relationship.

SUMMARY AND COMPARISONS OF FEMALE AND MALE

1. More than a score of the elements which have been recognized in the physiology of sexual response have been discussed in the present chapter. Females and males do not differ in regard to any of these basic elements. Because of differences in anatomy, the processes in the two sexes may differ in details. Tumescence, for instance, is most noticeable in the male in the erection of his penis, and most noticeable in the female in the erection of the nipples of her breasts and of the clitoris and labia minora; but the physiologic bases of these several events are essentially identical. The female and male are quite alike, as far as the data yet show, in regard to the changes in pulse rate, the changes in blood pressure, the peripheral circulation of blood, the tumescence, the increase in respiration, the possible development of an anoxia, the loss of sensory perception, and the development of rhythmic muscular movements, even including rhythmic pelvic thrusts.

2. Orgasm is a phenomenon which appears to be essentially the same in the human female and male. This is somewhat surprising, since orgasm appears to occur only infrequently among the females of the infra-human mammalian species.

3. Females appear to be capable of responding to the point of orgasm as quickly as males, and there are some females who respond more rapidly than any male. The usual statement that the female is slower in her capacity to reach orgasm is unsubstantiated by any data which we have been able to secure. But because females are less often stimulated by psychologic factors, they may not respond as quickly or as continuously as males in socio-sexual relationships.

4. In general, the after-effects of orgasm in the female do not differ in any essential way from those in the male. Ejaculation occurs in the adult male, and there is no such phenomenon in the female; but ejaculation depends upon a minor anatomic distinction between the female and male, and not upon any fundamental differences in the physiology of the two sexes.

In spite of the widespread and oft-repeated emphasis on the supposed differences between female and male sexuality, we fail to find any anatomic or physiologic basis for such differences. Although we shall subsequently find differences in the psychologic and hormonal factors which affect the responses of the two sexes (Chapters 16, 18), males would be better prepared to understand females, and females to understand males, if they realized that they are alike in their basic anatomy and physiology.

Chapter 16

PSYCHOLOGIC FACTORS IN SEXUAL RESPONSE

It might properly be contended that all functions of living matter are physiologic, but it is customary to distinguish certain aspects of animal behavior as psychologic functions. The distinctions can never be sharp, and they probably do not represent reality; but they are convenient distinctions to make, particularly in regard to human behavior.

Usually physiologists have been concerned with the functions of particular parts of the plant or animal, and with an attempt to discover the physical and chemical bases of such functions. Psychologists, on the other hand, have more often been concerned with the functioning—the behavior—of the organism as a whole. Many of the psychologic studies record—and properly record—the behavior of an animal without being able to explain the bases of that behavior in the known physics or chemistry of living matter. When psychologists try to explain behavior in physico-chemical terms, it is difficult to say, and quite pointless to try to say, whether such studies lie in the field of psychology or physiology.

It is important to understand how nebulous the distinctions are between the psychologic and physiologic aspects of behavior, for there are some who seem to believe that there are three universes: an animal's anatomy, its physiology, and its psychology. Such a misinterpretation formerly led biologists to think of a dualistic relationship between the physiologic capacities of an organism and its form and structure. The same sort of misinterpretation has led to the dualistic distinction of mind and body to which many persons have been inclined. But form and function are coordinate qualities of any living cell, and of any more complex assemblage of living cells.

Such specious distinctions between form and function have, unfortunately, lent encouragement to the opinion that the psychologic aspects of human sexual behavior are of a different order from, and perhaps more significant than, the anatomy or physiology of sexual response and orgasm. Such thinking easily becomes mystical, and quickly identifies any consideration of anatomic form and physiologic function as a scientific materialism which misses the "basic," the "human," and the "real" problems in behavior. This, however, seems an unnecessary judgment. Whatever we may learn of the anatomy and physiology and of the basic chemistry of an animal's responses, must contribute to our understanding of the totality which we call behavior. Those aspects of behavior which we identify as psychologic can be nothing but certain aspects of that same basic anatomy and physiology.

This, however, will not prevent us from recognizing the existence of many phenomena, such as the processes of learning and conditioning, the development of preferences in the choice of sexual objects, and the development of whole patterns of behavior, which cannot yet be explained in terms of the physics and chemistry which may be involved. Indeed, some of the aspects of sexual behavior which most critically affect the lives of human animals, and which are most often involved in the relations between human females and males, are among these still unexplained phenomena.

LEARNING AND CONDITIONING

One of the best known and distinctive qualities of living matter, although it is one which is still unexplainable in terms of physics and chemistry, is its capacity to be modified by its experience. The first time that an animal meets a given situation, its reactions may represent little more than direct responses to immediate stimuli; but in its subsequent contacts with similar stimuli, the organism may react differently from the way it did on the first occasion. In some fashion which no biologist or biochemist understands, living plant and animal cells, and groups of cells and tissues and organs in more complex animal bodies, are modified by their experience. The organism's later behavior represents a composite of its reactions to the stimuli which are immediately present, and its reactions to the memory of its previous experience. This depends on the processes which are known, in psychologic terminology, as learning and conditioning.

Learning and conditioning are, of course, familiar parts of the everyday experience of the human animal. Other things being equal, the first experiences, the most intense experiences, and the latest experiences may have the maximum effect on an individual's subsequent behavior. Freud and the psychiatrists, and psychologists in general, have correctly emphasized the importance of one's early experience, but it should not be forgotten that one may continue to learn and continue to be conditioned by new types of situations at any time during one's life. It is incorrect to minimize the importance of all except childhood experiences in the development of adult patterns of behavior.

Learning and conditioning in connection with human sexual behavior involve the same sorts of processes as learning and conditioning in other types of behavior. But man, because of his highly developed forebrain, may be more conditionable than any of the other mammals. The variations which exist in adult sexual behavior probably depend more upon conditioning than upon variations in the gross anatomy or physiology of the sexual mechanisms.

The sexual capacities which an individual inherits at birth appear to be nothing more than the necessary anatomy and the physiologic capacity to respond to a sufficient physical or psychologic stimulus. All human females and males who are not too greatly incapacitated physically appear to be born with such capacities. No one has to learn to become tumescent, to build up the neuromuscular tensions which lead to the rhythmic pelvic thrusts of coitus, or to develop any of the other responses which lead to orgasm.

But apart from these few inherent capacities, most other aspects of human sexual behavior appear to be the product of learning and conditioning. From the time it is born, and probably before it is born, the infant comes into contact with some of the elements that enter into its later sexual experience. From its first physical contacts with other objects, and particularly from its contacts with other human bodies, the child learns that there are satisfactions which may be obtained through tactile stimulation. In its early sexual experience with other individuals, the child begins to learn something of the rewards and penalties which may be attached to socio-sexual activities. From its parents, from other adults, from other children, and from the community at large, it begins to acquire its attitudes toward such things as nudity, the anatomic differences between males and females, and the reproductive functions; and these attitudes may have considerable significance in determining its subsequent acceptance or avoidance of particular types of overt sexual activity.

The type of person who first introduces an individual to particular types of socio-sexual activities may have a great deal to do with his or her subsequent attitudes, his or her interest in continuing such activity, and his or her dissatisfactions with other types of activity. Above all, experience develops a certain amount of technical facility, and an individual *learns* how to masturbate and *learns* how to utilize particular techniques in petting, in coitus, or in homosexual or other relations. As we shall subsequently see (Chapter 17), we may sharply distinguish the inherent sexual capacities with which an animal is born, from those aspects of its sexual behavior which are acquired by the processes of learning and conditioning.

DEVELOPMENT OF PREFERENCES

As a result of its experience, an animal acquires certain patterns of behavior which lead it to react positively to certain sorts of stimuli, and to react negatively to other sorts of stimuli. But there are also various degrees of response, and an animal learns to react toward or against certain stimuli more intensely than it does to others.[1] When there is any possibility of choosing, the animal may show strong preferences for one rather than another type of activity.

An individual may come to prefer particular types of individuals as sexual partners; may prefer tall persons or short persons; may prefer blondes or brunettes; may prefer sexual partners who are much younger or much older, or of his or her own age [2]; may develop an incapacity to respond to any except a single sexual partner, or a preference for variety in sexual experience; may prefer a heterosexual or a homosexual pattern of behavior; may prefer masturbation to the pursuit of socio-sexual contacts; may prefer a considerable amount of petting prior to actual coitus, or immediate coitus without preliminary play; may find satisfaction or be offended by the use of certain genital, oral, or anal techniques; may come to desire a variety of positions in coitus, or the more or less exclusive use of a single position; may choose a farm animal instead of a human partner for sexual relationships. All of these choices and reactions to particular stimuli may seem reasonable enough and more or less inevitable to the person who is involved, even though some of them may seem un-understandable, unnatural, and abnormal to the individual who has not been conditioned by the same sort of experience.

Even some of the most extremely variant types of human sexual behavior may need no more explanation than is provided by our understanding of the processes of learning and conditioning. Behavior which may appear bizarre, perverse, or unthinkably unacceptable to some persons, and even to most persons, may have significance for other individuals because of the way in which they have been conditioned.

---

[1] Students of animal behavior have noted that if a male's initial coital experience involves pain or fright, the male may become reluctant to mate thereafter. See, for example: Beach 1947b:265. Rice and Andrews 1951:180–181.

[2] The extreme variation which may be found among both men and women in the types of preferred sexual partners, is well illustrated in the listing in Hamilton 1929:502–505. That the males of infra-human species often develop strong preferences for particular females or types of females, is recorded in: Tinklepaugh 1928:296–300 (rhesus monkey). Yerkes and Elder 1936a:32–34, 38 (chimpanzee). Carpenter 1942:139 (monkey). Enders 1945 (fox). Hafez 1951 (ram). Ford and Beach 1951:91–93 (general discussion). Shadle (verbal communic.) records two porcupines, each of which developed strong preferences for a particular female. That estrual females of sub-primate species almost never show strong preferences, even in species in which preferences are strongly marked in the male, is noted in: Rowlands and Parkes 1935 (fox). Enders 1945.

Flagellation, masochism, transvestism, and the wide variety of fetishes appear to be products of conditioning, fortified sometimes by some other aspect of an individual's personality and by inherent or acquired anatomic and physiologic capacities. Sexual reactions to stockings, to underclothing, to other articles of clothing, to shoes, or to long hair may be no more difficult to explain than attractions to the body of a sexual partner, or to particular parts of that body, to the legs of females, to the breasts of females, to male genitalia, to buttocks, or to other portions of the human anatomy.

The male who reacts sexually and comes to erection upon seeing a streetcar, may merely reflect some early experience in which a streetcar was associated with a desirable sexual partner; and his behavior may be no more difficult to explain than the behavior of the male who reacts at the sight of his wife undressing for bed. There may be more social advantage in the one type of behavior than in the other. In rare instances some of the so-called aberrant types of behavior, meaning the less usual types of conditioned responses, may be definitely disadvantageous, but in most instances they are of no social concern. The prominence given to classifications of behavior as normal or abnormal, and the long list of special terms used for classifying such behavior, usually represent moralistic classifications rather than any scientific attempt to discover the origins of such behavior, or to determine their real social significance.

VICARIOUS SHARING OF EXPERIENCE

A fair amount of the conditioning which occurs in connection with human sexual behavior depends upon the fact that the human animal, with its extraordinary capacity for communication through verbal interchange, through the printed word and pictorial material, and through other modern devices, may vicariously share the sexual experience of many other persons. Learning of their satisfactions or difficulties in particular types of sexual activity may influence one's own decision to engage or not to engage in similar types of activity.

Many persons find considerable stimulation in listening to accounts of the sexual experience of other persons, in hearing fictional tales of sexual exploits, in reading of such experience, and in seeing photographs and drawings of sexual objects and activities. Many individuals become strongly conditioned toward or against having particular types of sexual activity, before they have ever had any actual experience of the sort.

An individual's pattern of sexual behavior usually depends to a great extent upon the longstanding and sometimes ancient social codes concerning the various types of sexual activity. The social attitudes may begin to condition the child at a very early age, and may force it to confine its attitudes, its responses, and its overt activities to sexual expressions which are acceptable to the particular culture.

REACTIONS TO ASSOCIATED OBJECTS

An animal may become conditioned to respond not only to particular stimuli, but to objects and other phenomena which were associated with the original experience. Pavlov's classic experiment with the dog which was so conditioned that it salivated upon hearing a dinner bell, as well as when it came in contact with the food with which the bell was originally associated, stands as the prototype of such associative conditioning.[3]

Sexual behavior, among all species of mammals, may involve a great deal of conditioning by phenomena which were associated with previous experience. Male cats and dogs and many other mammals respond sexually when they approach places in which they have had previous experience [4]; male rabbits, guinea pigs, skunks, raccoons, bulls, and horses may respond to odors left by female secretions.[5] They often respond to the odor of the urine of a female, especially if the female is in estrus. In the laboratory, male animals may respond to particular dishes, to particular boards, or to particular pieces of other furniture with which some female has had contact. They may respond more intensely to particular animals with which they have had previous sexual contact, they may respond less intensely to animals with which they have not had previous contact—although another phenomenon, psychologic fatigue, may lead to an exact reversal of this pattern of response.[6]

If satisfactory relations were previously had with an individual of the opposite sex, animals are more likely to respond to other individu-

---

[3] For descriptions of Pavlov's experiments with dogs, see: Woodworth and Marquis 1947:525–530. Andrews 1948:44. Freeman 1948:180.

[4] Male animals which showed sexual arousal on returning to a place where they had previously had coitus are described by: McKenzie and Berliner 1937:18 (ram). Zitrin and Beach in Hartman 1945:42–44 (cat). That a strange environment may prevent or handicap a male in having coitus although the female may not be thus affected, is recorded in: Marshall and Hammond 1944:12. Beach 1947b:264. Root and Bard 1947:81.

[5] One of the best illustrations of a male's interest in odors left by females is recorded for the porcupine by: Shadle, Smelzer, and Metz 1946:118, 120. Shadle 1946:159–160. See also: Beach and Gilmore 1949:391–392.

[6] That some male animals will copulate only with familiar females and ignore strange females is recorded in: Hartman 1945:39 (monkey). Shadle 1946:160–161 (porcupine). Beach 1947b:264–265 (general statement). That estrual females, on the contrary, will usually accept any male, familiar or strange, is recorded by: Bean, director of Brookfield Zoo (verbal communic.). Beach 1947b:264. Psychologic fatigue, the lessening of sexual response through prolonged living together, has been noted in animals by: Hamilton 1914:301–302. Miller 1931:397–398, 406.

als of that sex. If the previous experience was with an individual of their own sex, they are, because of the association with the previous experience, more likely to respond again to individuals of their own sex. If the laboratory investigator was present when the animal was previously involved in sexual activity, it is likely to react more intensely on later occasions if the investigator is again present. A dog which has been masturbated by its owner may subsequently come to full erection whenever it sees the human agent, move toward him, and try to renew the relationship. We have the record of one dog which did not go to its owner when it saw him, but ran to the place where it had been previously masturbated and there awaited a renewal of that experience.

We have already pointed out (p. 590) that sexual stimulation by things that one sees, hears, smells, or tastes often depends upon the associations which they evoke, rather than upon the direct physical stimulation of the sense organs through which those things are perceived. While this is true of all the higher mammals, it is particularly true of the human animal. From its earliest years the child comes to associate a considerable number of particular objects and phenomena with things that make him comfortable or in some other way prove satisfying. In the course of time, an adult comes to associate sexual activities with warmth, tactile satisfactions, particular types of food, alcoholic drinks, furniture, the clothing of the sexual partner, particular odors, particular intensities of light, particular sounds, certain musical compositions, particular sorts of voices, particular words which have been used to describe particular types of sexual performance, the sort of room or outdoor setting in which satisfactory sexual relations previously occurred, the use of particular techniques in a sexual relationship, and an endless list of other particular things.

Sometimes an individual may reach a point at which he reacts to these associated phenomena as intensely or more intensely than he reacts to the physical stimulation of a sexual contact. Not a few individuals find that they are more intensely aroused by the anticipation of an opportunity to engage in sexual activity than they are when they arrive at the activity itself.

SYMPATHETIC RESPONSES

Among most species of mammals, most males and some females become erotically aroused when they observe other individuals engaging in sexual activity. Animals which have not reacted to the mere presence of the other animals may become interested if the other animals begin sexual activity. Most males are likely to respond quite immediately to such stimuli, to come to erection, and to seek the opportunity for sexual activity of their own. This is as true of the human male as it is of the males of other species of mammals.[7]

These are, technically speaking, **sympathetic responses.** The one animal feels or reacts (*pathos*) with (*sym*) the other. Of all the situations to which an animal may become conditioned, none is as likely to evoke sexual responses as sexual activity itself. The restrictions which most human societies place upon the public performance of sexual acts probably did not arise out of any innate perception of what was shameful or wrong, but from an attempt to control the sympathetic responses of the bystanders and the social consequences of group sexual activity. Among laboratory animals and animals in the wild, vigorous competition and violent conflict are the usual outcome of group sexual activity. They are as likely to be the outcome of group activity in the human species, unless the individuals control their jealousies in a conscious attempt to obtain the especial stimulation which may be found in group activity.

In a socio-sexual relationship, the sexual partners may respond to each other and to the responses made by each other. For this reason, most persons find socio-sexual relationships more satisfactory than solitary sexual activities.

When there is physical contact, all of one's sense organs may aid in making one aware of the responses of the partner and of the movements of the partner's body, particularly when there are such extensive contacts as completely nude bodies may provide. Tensions developing in the body of the one partner may be reflected instantaneously in the reactions of the other partner's body. As the one partner approaches orgasm, his or her extreme reactions may stimulate the other partner into simultaneous orgasm. Such a simultaneity of response may occasionally originate in the fact that the two partners are so constituted that they respond in exactly the same period of time, but it usually depends upon some sympathetic interaction between the two.

SIGNIFICANCE OF CONDITIONING IN FEMALES AND IN MALES

In general, males are more often conditioned by their sexual experience, and by a greater variety of associated factors, than females. While there is great individual variation in this respect among both females and males, there is considerable evidence that the sexual re-

---

[7] Sympathetic responses in mammals are also noted in Ford and Beach 1951:71. Such responses are, of course, not invariable; for example, a herd of grazing ruminants may ignore a copulating couple in their midst, acc. Bean, director of Brookfield Zoo (verbal communic.). It should be noted that the sight of coitus is without effect upon inexperienced chimpanzees, but is sexually arousing to experienced animals of both sexes, acc. Nissen (verbal communic.).

sponses and behavior of the average male are, on the whole, more often determined by the male's previous experience, by his association with objects that were connected with his previous sexual experience, by his vicarious sharing of another individual's sexual experience, and by his sympathetic reactions to the sexual responses of other individuals. The average female is less often affected by such psychologic factors. It is highly significant to find that there are evidences of such differences between the females and males of infra-human mammalian species, as well as between human females and males.[8]

While we found no basic differences in the anatomy which is involved in the sexual responses of females and of males, and no differences in the physiologic phenomena which are involved when females and males respond sexually, we do find, in these responses to psychologic stimuli, an explanation of some of the differences that we have reported in the incidences and frequencies and the patterns of sexual behavior among females and males. We shall subsequently find (Chapter 18) that hormonal differences between the human female and male may account for certain other differences between the two sexes.

It cannot be too strongly emphasized that there is tremendous individual variation in the way in which different individuals may be affected by psychologic stimuli. We have already pointed out some of these differences. For instance, we have shown (p. 164) that there is a considerable proportion of the females who masturbate without associated fantasies, and a considerable proportion of our female sample who had never had specifically sexual dreams while they slept. In this respect, such a female differs considerably from the average male, for nearly all males do fantasy while masturbating, and nearly all of them have nocturnal sex dreams. On the other hand, we have also recorded (p. 164) that there are some females who invariably fantasy while they are masturbating, who have an abundance of sex dreams, and who have daytime fantasies which may so arouse them that they reach orgasm without any physical stimulation of any part of their bodies. It is only one male in a thousand or two who can fantasy to orgasm. In our sample, the range of variation in responses to psychologic stimuli is, therefore, much greater among females than it is among males. While we may emphasize the differences which exist between the average female and the average male, it should constantly be borne in mind that there are many individuals, and particularly many females, who widely depart from these averages.

---

[8] In summing up the situation among infra-human mammals, Ford and Beach 1951:241 state: "We are strongly impressed with the evidence for sexual learning and conditioning in the male and the relative absence of such processes in the female."

1. Observing the Opposite Sex. A third (32 per cent) of the males in the sample reported that they were considerably and regularly aroused by observing certain females (clothed or nude), including their wives, girl friends, and other females of the sort with whom they would like to have sexual relations. Another 40 per cent recorded some response. Only half as many of the females (17 per cent) in the sample reported that they were particularly aroused upon observing males, whether they were their husbands, boy friends, or other males, and another 41 per cent recorded some response. The specific data are as follows:

Observing the opposite sex

EROTIC RESPONSE	BY FEMALES	BY MALES
	%	%
Definite and/or frequent	17	32
Some response	41	40
Never	42	28
Number of cases	5772	4226

The responses of these males upon observing females were the physiologic responses characteristic of sexual arousal; they often included genital reactions, and often led the male to approach the female for physical contact. Females who had been aroused with similar intensities did occur in the sample, but most of the females who had been aroused had not responded with such marked physiologic reactions.

Responses upon observing potential sexual partners are also characteristic of the males of most of the infra-human species of mammals, but the females of most of the mammalian species less frequently show signs of erotic arousal before they have made physical contact with the sexual partner (p. 230). Psychologic arousal in the female occurs most frequently when she is in estrus. Female dogs, female chimpanzees, sometimes cows, female porcupines, and the females of some other species may become quite aroused while they are in estrus and become aggressive in making sexual approaches to the male; although among even these species the females are not aggressive as often as the males.[9]

---

[9] That aggressive sexual behavior is common among estrual females of infra-human mammalian species, is recorded by: Elliott acc. Miller 1931:382, 405 (fur seal; the male is so busy guarding his harem that the female must take the initiative). Zuckerman 1932:227–229, 243 (baboon). Carpenter 1942:131, 136, 154 (monkey; the female may repeatedly approach the male despite having been driven off and wounded). Yerkes and Elder 1936a:25–26 (chimpanzee; female almost always goes to the male, not the male to the female). Roark and Herman 1950:7 (cows sometimes pursue the bull). McKenzie (verbal communic., says between 10 and 30 per cent of mares may pursue stallions). Carpenter 1942:129 (in gibbon, both sexes are about equally aggressive in pugnacity and reproductive behavior). We have also observed such female aggressiveness in the dog and porcupine.

2. Observing One's Own Sex. The recognition of erotic arousal upon observing other individuals of one's own sex is, of course, a basically homosexual phenomenon. In our culture, with its strong condemnation of male homosexuality, most males who want to think of themselves as completely heterosexual are therefore afraid to admit that they see even esthetic merit in other males. On the other hand, females are allowed to find esthetic satisfactions in observing the nude female form, or in observing well dressed females, and our cultural traditions make it possible for a female to express her admiration of another female without being suspected of homosexual interests. Actually, the female's interest in other females is often a matter of identification with a person she admires, and lacks any erotic element.

In view of this lesser social acceptance of male interests in males, and of the readier acceptance of female interests in females, it is particularly interesting to find that males recognize and admit their erotic responses to other males as often or even more often than females recognize and admit their erotic responses to other females. The record is as follows:

Observing one's own sex

EROTIC RESPONSE	BY FEMALES	BY MALES
	%	%
Definite and/or frequent	3	7
Some response	9	9
Never	88	84
Number of cases	5754	4220

3. Observing Portrayals of Nude Figures. Something more than half (54 per cent) of the males in our sample had been erotically aroused by seeing photographs or drawings or paintings of nude females, just as they were aroused upon observing living females. Most homosexual males are similarly aroused by seeing portrayals of nude males. Fewer (12 per cent) of the females in the sample had ever been aroused by seeing photographs or drawings or paintings of either male or female nudes. The specific record is as follows:

Observing portrayals of nude figures

EROTIC RESPONSE	BY FEMALES	BY MALES
	%	%
Definite and/or frequent	3	18
Some response	9	36
Never	88	46
Number of cases	5698	4191

It is difficult for the average female to comprehend why males are aroused by seeing photographs or portrayals of nudes when they cannot possibly have overt sexual relations with them. Males on the other hand, cannot comprehend why females who have had satisfactory sexual relations should not be aroused by nude portrayals of the same person, or of the sort of person with whom they have had sexual relations. We have histories of males who have attempted to arouse their female partners by showing them nude photographs or drawings, and most of these males could not comprehend that their female partners were not in actuality being aroused by such material. When a male does realize that his wife or girl friend fails to respond to such stimuli, he may conclude that she no longer loves him and is no longer willing to allow herself to respond in his presence. He fails to comprehend that it is a characteristic of females in general, rather than the reaction of the specific female, which is involved in this lack of response.

Striking evidence of the differences in the reactions of females and males is to be found in the commercial distribution of portrayals of nude human figures. There is a tremendous business of this sort, including the sale of good nude art, of photographic prints, and of moving picture, physical culture, and nudist magazines. There are nude or near nude figures in the main pages and in the advertising sections of nearly all illustrated magazines. Much of this material is distributed without any deliberate intent to provide erotic stimulation, and much of it has artistic and other serious value; but all of it may provide erotic stimulation for many of the male consumers.[10]

Photographs of female nudes and magazines exhibiting nude or near nude females are produced primarily for the consumption of males. There are, however, photographs and magazines portraying nude and near nude males—but these are also produced for the consumption of males. There are almost no male or female nudes which are produced for the consumption of females. The failure of nearly all females to find erotic arousal in such portrayals is so well known to the distributors of nude photographs and nude magazines that they have considered that it would not be financially profitable to produce such material for a primarily female audience.

4. Erotic Fine Art. There may be a diversity of erotic elements in art, but the most obvious is the portrayal of the human body or portions of the human body in a fashion which gives evidence of the

---

[10] A survey and discussion of the popularity of near nudity in magazines and in advertising is in: A. Ellis 1951:104–107. He recognizes that females are not aroused by portrayals of male nudity, but explains it on the basis of the lack of taboo. For other recognition of the lack of female arousal from erotic pictures, see: Brettschneider in Wulffen et al. 1931:106. Wallace 1948:22. Friedeburg 1950:24 (47 per cent males, 11 per cent females erotically aroused by photographs or pictures in German survey).

artist's erotic interest in his or her subject matter, or provides erotic stimulation for the individual observing the work.[11]

An extensive study which we are making of the erotic element in art indicates that a very high proportion of the male artists who portray the human form, either female or male, do so in a fashion which indicates an erotic interest in that form. Even though there may be no portrayal of genitalia and no suggestion of sexual action, the nude body itself may be drawn or painted in a fashion which is erotic to the artist and to most males who subsequently observe the drawing or painting. Such artists as Michelangelo, Leonardo da Vinci, Raphael in his drawings, Rubens, Rodin, Renoir, and Maillol—to cite a few specific cases—rarely drew nudes which, in the judgment of the qualified artists whom we have consulted, did not show such an erotic element.

It is, of course, possible to portray the nude form, as was regularly done in Egyptian art, for instance, in a way which is not erotic; but among the males who have drawn or painted nude figures, it is rare to find any in European or American art who have done so without evident erotic interest. We have not found more than a half dozen male artists of moment who have regularly drawn nudes which have not shown an erotic content.

While the number of female artists has been much less than the number of males who have done painting or drawing, there are many hundreds of them in the history of European and American art. But in some years of searching, we have been able to find only eight instances of important female artists who have drawn the human figure in a fashion which qualified artists, female or male, judge to be erotic.[12] In conjunction with the data (p. 652) which indicate that relatively few females are aroused upon observing nude paintings or drawings, it is understandable that female artists themselves should not be erotically responsive to the nude subjects which they are drawing or painting; and this is evident in their finished work.

[11] Freud 1922:78–79 in his study of Leonardo da Vinci recognized this in the following words: "A kindly nature has bestowed upon the artist the capacity to express in artistic productions his most secret psychic feelings hidden even to himself, which powerfully affect outsiders who are strangers to the artist. . . ."

[12] For encyclopedic lists of artists, the standard works are: Thieme and Becker 1907–1947, 35 v. Mallett 1935; 1940. Bénézit 1948–1952, 5 v. For a convenient anthology, see: Sparrow 1905, Women painters of the world. Bulliet in McDermott and Taft 1932:233–252 lists 40 artists, all of whom are male, known for their female nudes. Havelock Ellis 1929:376–378 (cites Ferrero who explains the small part played by women in art as due to their less keen sexual emotions. Ellis, however, interprets male power of creation in fine arts as compensation for the male's lesser role in producing and moulding the race). Wallace 1948:21 recognizes that female painters and sculptors do not use nude subjects as frequently as male artists.

It is to be noted that seven out of the eight female artists whose work seems erotic had confined themselves to portraying the nude female form.

5. Observing Genitalia. Most heterosexual males are aroused by observing female breasts or legs, or some other part of the female body. They are usually aroused when they see female genitalia. A smaller percentage of the females in the sample (of 617 to whom the question was put) reported erotic arousal as a product of their observation of male genitalia, and more than half (52 per cent) reported that they had never been aroused by observing male genitalia. The record is as follows:

Observing genitalia of opposite sex

EROTIC RESPONSE	BY FEMALES	BY MALES
	%	%
Definite and/or frequent	21	many
Some response	27	many
Never	52	few
Number of cases	617	

Many females are surprised to learn that there is anyone who finds the observation of male genitalia erotically stimulating. Many females consider that male genitalia are ugly and repulsive in appearance, and the observation of male genitalia may actually inhibit their erotic responses. It may be true, as psychoanalysts suggest, that the negative reactions of females to male genitalia may originate in unpleasant sexual experiences with males; but there seems no doubt that these reactions largely depend upon the fact that most females are not psychologically stimulated, as males are, by objects which are associated with sex.

Among the infra-human species of mammals there seem to be something of the same differences between the reactions of females and males to the genitalia of the opposite sex. For instance, a female monkey or ape grooming the body of a male who may become aroused erotically, may pay no attention to the male's erect genitalia. On the other hand, when male apes and monkeys groom females, they usually show considerable interest in the female genitalia, and explore around and within the genital cavity. Male rats, guinea pigs, dogs, raccoons, skunks, porcupines, and many other male animals may similarly explore at considerable length about the genitalia of the female, but the females of these species less often explore about the genitalia of the male.[13] Any interpretation of the human female's lack of interest in

[13] We base this statement on our own observations and on discussions with several who have been on the staff of the Yerkes Laboratories at Orange Park,

male genitalia must take into account the similar situation among
these infra-human species.

Most human males with homosexual interests are aroused, and in
most instances strongly aroused, by seeing male genitalia. Genital exposures and genital exhibitions are frequently employed to interest
other males in homosexual contacts. In the course of a homosexual relationship among males, considerable attention may be given to the
genital anatomy and genital reactions. Moreover, many males who are
not conscious of homosexual reactions are interested in their own
genitalia and in the genitalia of other males. But only a small percentage of the homosexual females is ever aroused erotically by seeing
the genitalia of other females.

6. Observing Own Genitalia. A great many of the males in the
sample (56 per cent) had been aroused by observing their own genitalia as they masturbated, or by viewing their genitalia in a mirror.
Few (9 per cent) of the females in the sample had found any erotic
stimulation in looking at their own genitalia. The specific data are as
follows:

Observing own genitalia

EROTIC RESPONSE	BY FEMALES	BY MALES
	%	%
Definite and/or frequent	1	25
Some response	8	31
Never	91	44
Number of cases	5725	3332

There were more males (56 per cent) who were aroused by observing their own genitalia than there were females (48 per cent) who
were aroused by observing male genitalia. The male's arousal may
have a homosexual element in it, but many of the males who have
never consciously recognized any other homosexual interests and have
never had homosexual contacts may be aroused at seeing their own
genitalia or the genitalia of other males.

7. Exhibitionism. Because of their interest in their own genitalia
and their arousal upon seeing the genitalia of other persons, males
quite generally believe that other persons would be aroused by seeing
their genitalia. This seems to be the prime factor which leads many

Florida. Dr. Nissen of that staff sums up their data by observing that in the
chimpanzee the head, back, limbs, and anus of the male receive the most
grooming attention by the grooming partner (whether female or male), and
that the ventral body surface and genitalia receive the least. When the
male grooms the female he concentrates considerable attention upon the
sexual skin and anal area, and may make anal or vaginal insertions occasionally. Shadle (verbal communic.) is the source of the data on the skunk
and porcupine.

males to exhibit their genitalia to their wives, to other female partners, and to male partners in homosexual relationships.[14]

It is difficult for most males to comprehend that females are not aroused by seeing male genitalia. Some males never come to comprehend this. Many a male is greatly disappointed when his wife fails to react to such a display, and concludes that she is no longer in love with him. On the contrary, many females feel that their husbands are vulgar, or perverted, or mentally disturbed, because they want to display their genitalia. We have seen difficulties develop in marital histories because of this failure of females to understand male psychology, and of males to understand female psychology. Divorces had grown out of some of these misunderstandings.

The male who exposes himself in a public place similarly secures erotic satisfaction primarily because he believes that the females who observe him are going to be aroused as he would be at seeing a genital exhibition. Sometimes the exhibitionist is aroused by the evident fright or confusion or other emotional reactions of the females who see him and, responding sympathetically, he may be stimulated by such an emotional display. But a considerable portion of the erotic arousal which the exhibitionist finds is a product of his anticipation that the female will be aroused, and this is evidenced by the fact that he is usually in erection before any passerby sees him. His reactions, therefore, may not depend entirely or even primarily upon the responses of the passing female (p. 655).

There are some females who will show their genitalia to the male partner because they intellectually realize that this may mean something to him. But only an occasional female among those who exhibit receives any erotic arousal from this anticipation of the male's responses. There are no cases in our sample, and practically none in the literature, of females publicly exhibiting their genitalia because they derived erotic satisfaction from such an exhibition.[15]

Stage, night club, burlesque and other commercial exhibitions of female nudity almost never, as far as our sample indicates, provide erotic

[14] The male chimpanzee frequently solicits the female by coming to erection, spontaneously or by masturbation, and exhibiting the erection to the female, according to: Yerkes and Elder 1936a:9. Nissen, verbal communic. Our observation.

[15] That exhibitionism is infrequent among females in comparison to males, has also been recognized by: [Jacolliot] Jacobus X 1900:347. Hirschfeld 1920(3):319; 1948:504. Kronfeld in Marcuse 1923:121. Bilder-Lexikon 1930(1):241. Brown 1940:383. Guyon 1948:319. Allen 1949:108. Exhibitionism is considered non-existent among females by: Walker and Strauss 1939:177–178. Fenichel 1945:346. Rickles 1950:49 (considers it due to the fact that women "have nothing to expose"). In a few pre-literate cultures, women may solicit men by deliberately exposing their own genitalia; see: Ford and Beach 1951:93.

stimulation for the exhibiting females. Our specific data provide no physiologic evidence (Chapter 15) of arousal among the females staging such exhibitions, although some of them may acquire considerable facility in making body movements which are taken by many of the males in the audience to indicate that the exhibiting females are tremendously aroused. Most of the females in our histories who had been involved in such stage exhibitions, were highly disdainful of males who could so easily be misled into believing that there was any real eroticism in such a performance.

8. **Interest in Genital Techniques.** While the genitalia may be the chief focus of a considerable amount of sexual activity, this does not depend wholly on the fact that these organs are well supplied with end organs of touch. There are many other parts of the body which are similarly supplied with end organs, and the importance attached to the genitalia in a sexual relationship must partly depend upon the fact that most males and some females are psychologically conditioned to consider the genitalia as *the* structures which are primarily associated with sexual response.

This interpretation is favored by the fact that males attach much more importance to the genitalia than females do in a sexual relationship. But there is no reason for believing that the genitalia of the male are more richly supplied with end organs than the genitalia of the female. While genital erection may draw the male's attention to his own genitalia, this does not suffice to interest most females in his genitalia.

Most males, whether heterosexual or homosexual, are inclined to initiate a sexual relationship through some genital exposure or genital manipulation. Most females prefer to be stimulated tactilely in various other parts of the body before the activity is concentrated on the genitalia. It is the constant complaint of married females that their husbands are interested in "nothing but the intercourse," and by that they mean that he is primarily concerned with genital stimulation and an immediate genital union. On the other hand, it is the constant complaint of the married male that his wife "will do nothing to him," which means, in most instances, that she does not tactilely stimulate his genitalia.

These same differences in the significance of genital activities are to be found in the homosexual activities of females and males. A high proportion of the homosexual contacts among males is initiated through some genital exposure or some sort of genital manipulation (groping). During the actual relationships most homosexual males are likely to prefer more genital than non-genital stimulation. But in female homosexual relationships, the stimulation of all parts of the body may proceed for some period of time before there is any concentration of attention on the genitalia. We have histories of exclusively homosexual females who had had overt relationships for ten or fifteen years before they attempted any sort of genital stimulation.

Homosexual females frequently criticize homosexual males because they are interested in nothing but genitalia; homosexual males, in turn, may criticize homosexual females because "they do nothing" in a homosexual relationship. The idea that homosexuality is a sexual inversion is dispelled when one hears homosexual females criticizing homosexual males for exactly the same reasons which lead many wives to criticize their husbands, and when one hears homosexual males criticize homosexual females for exactly the things which husbands criticize in their wives. In fact, homosexual males, in their intensified interest in male genitalia and genital activity, often exhibit the most extreme examples of a typically male type of conditioning.

9. Observing Commercial Moving Pictures. Portrayals of more or less erotic situations are so common in present-day commercial moving pictures that their significance as sources of erotic arousal, for either females or males, is probably less than it was in an earlier day and certainly much less than most official and unofficial censors would believe. It is not impossible that many males would more often respond erotically to love scenes, to close-ups of petting and kissing, and to exhibitionistic displays of semi-nude bodies if they were to observe such pictures in the privacy of their homes or in conjunction with some sexual partner. In the average public theatre, however, the openly expressed reactions of the audience suggest that they are more amused than aroused by the sort of eroticism which is usually presented. However, their vocal responses, cat calls, and whistling may indicate that they are reacting emotionally and trying to deny it by way of a contrary response.

The males and females in our sample recorded their reactions to commercial moving pictures as follows:

Observing moving pictures

EROTIC RESPONSE	BY FEMALES	BY MALES
	%	%
Definite and/or frequent	9	6
Some response	39	30
Never	52	64
Number of cases	5411	3231

This means that the females found the moving pictures erotically stimulating somewhat more often than the males. This is one of the few sources of psychologic stimulation which seem to have been more significant for the females in the sample.

Some of the stimulation provided by a moving picture may depend on the romantic action which it portrays, and some of it may depend on the portrayal of some particular person. In a larger number of instances, the erotic stimulation may depend on the emotional atmosphere created by the picture as a whole, just as viewing a landscape, reading a book, or sitting with another person before an open fire may lead to emotional responses which then become erotic. Sometimes the erotic element in the picture may have no obvious sexual meaning except to the individual who has been conditioned by the particular element. Sometimes the erotic arousal may depend upon the presence of the companion with whom one is attending the performance.

10. Observing Burlesque and Floor Shows. Burlesque shows more or less openly attempt to provide erotic stimulation for the attending audience, and a considerable proportion of those who go to such shows do so with the anticipation that they are going to be aroused erotically. More skilled versions of the burlesque routines are the chief elements of the average night club's floor show.

Most males are aroused by the advertisements at the entrance to a burlesque show, and considerably aroused by anticipating what they are going to see. Most of the males (62 per cent) in our sample had been aroused by the show itself upon their first visit or two, but most of them had not found the shows particularly stimulating after that. Since some of these males had continued to attend such shows, it may be that they did receive some generalized erotic satisfaction from them even though it was not as specific as on the first occasion. Some of them may have gone because they were attracted by the humorous elements in such performances; but in many instances they continued to go because they hoped that they would again be stimulated as they had been on their first few visits.

The erotic reactions of those females and males in our sample who had ever seen a burlesque or night club floor show were reported as follows:

Observing burlesque and floor shows

EROTIC RESPONSE	BY FEMALES	BY MALES
	%	%
Definite and/or frequent	4	28
Some response	10	34
Never	86	38
Number of cases	2550	3377

A decade or two ago the burlesque audiences were almost exclusively male; today the audiences may include a more equal number of females and males. It is difficult, however, to explain this attendance by females in view of the fact that so few of them (14 per cent in our sample) are aroused erotically by such shows. Apparently most females attend burlesque shows because they are social functions about which they are curious, and which they may share with their male companions. They may find some pleasure in the humorous elements in such a show. Only a very few of them are seeking homosexual stimulation from observing the females in the show.

11. Observing Sexual Action. A considerable proportion of those males in our sample who had had the opportunity to observe other persons in sexual activity had responded sympathetically during their observation. The females in the sample who had had the opportunity to observe sexual activity rarely reported such sympathetic responses. Most of them had been indifferent in their responses, if they had not been offended by the social impropriety of such an exhibition.

It is, therefore, no accident, and not merely the product of the cultural tradition, that commercialized exhibitions of sexual activity, since the days of ancient Rome, have been provided for male but almost never for female audiences. There are many males who would not accept an opportunity to attend such exhibitions because they consider them morally objectionable, but even they usually recognize that they would be aroused if they were to observe them.

There is an inclination to explain these differences in the responses of females and of males as products of the cultural tradition, and there is a widespread opinion that females are more inclined to accept the social proprieties because they are basically more moral than males. On the other hand, the same sorts of differences between the sympathetic responses of females and of males may be observed in other species of mammals. The males of practically all infra-human species may become aroused when they observe other animals in sexual activity.[16] Of this fact farmers, animal breeders, scientists experimenting with laboratory animals, and many persons who have kept household pets are abundantly aware. The females of the infra-human species less often show such sympathetic responses when they observe other animals in sexual activity. These data suggest that human females are

---

[16] The sight of coitus between animals of the same species arouses such diverse animals as the bull (our observation, and McKenzie, verbal communic.), and chimpanzee (Nissen, verbal communic.). Zitrin and Beach in Hartman 1945:43–44 report that male cats become aroused by seeing female cats reacting to being masturbated by a human experimenter.

more often inclined to accept the social proprieties because they are stimulated psychologically and respond sympathetically less often than most males do.

12. Observing Portrayals of Sexual Action. In spite of state and federal laws, and in spite of the considerable effort which law enforcement officers periodically make to prevent the distribution of photographs, drawings, moving pictures, and other portrayals of sexual action, such materials exist in considerable abundance in this country and probably in greater abundance in most other countries. Graphic portrayals of sexual action have existed in most cultures, throughout history. This is a measure of the considerable significance which such materials may have for the consuming public which, however, is largely male.

Practically all of the males in the sample had had the opportunity to observe portrayals of sexual action, and had taken the opportunity to observe them. Most of the males (77 per cent) who had seen such material indicated that they had been aroused erotically by seeing it. A smaller proportion of the females in the sample had had the opportunity to see, or had taken the opportunity to see such portrayals of sexual action.[17] Only a third of them (32 per cent) had found any erotic arousal in observing such material. The specific record is as follows:

Observing portrayals of sexual action

EROTIC RESPONSE	BY FEMALES	BY MALES
	%	%
Definite and/or frequent	14	42
Some response	18	35
Never	68	23
Number of cases	2242	3868

Many females, of course, report that they are offended by portrayals of sexual action, and denounce them on moral, social, and aesthetic grounds. This is ordinarily taken as evidence of the female's greater sense of propriety; but in the light of our other data on the relative significance of psychologic stimulation for females and for males, it seems more likely that most females are indifferent or antagonistic to the existence of such material because it means nothing to them erotically.

---

[17] Clark and Treichler 1950 report an increase in acid phosphatase (an enzyme found in the urine) in four males aroused by erotic pictures, a decrease in a male who was repelled by them, and no change in two females who saw the pictures.

Most males find it difficult to comprehend why females are not aroused by such graphic representations of sexual action, and not infrequently males essay to show such materials to their wives or other female partners, thinking thereby to arouse them prior to their sexual contacts.[18] The wives, on the other hand, are often at a loss to understand why a male who is having satisfactory sexual relations at home should seek additional stimulation in portrayals of sexual action. They are hurt to find that their husbands desire any stimulation in addition to what they, the wives, can provide, and not a few of the wives think of it as a kind of infidelity which offends them. We have seen considerable disturbance in some of the married histories because of such disagreements over the husband's use of erotic objects, and there are cases of wives who instituted divorce proceedings because they had discovered that their husbands possessed photographs or drawings of sexual action.

Local drives against so-called obscene materials, and state, federal, and international moves against the distribution of such materials, are not infrequently instituted by females who not only find the material morally and socially objectionable, but probably fail to comprehend the significance that it may have for most males and for some females.

13. Observing Animals in Coitus. Many human males and some females respond sympathetically upon observing animals of other species in coitus. The specific data show that 32 per cent of the males in our sample had so responded. Watching dogs or cattle in coitus had been the inspiration for the involvement of some of the farm boys in sexual relationships with the animals themselves. There were some females but fewer (16 per cent) who were aroused by observing the sexual activities of other animals. The data are as follows:

Observing animals in coitus

EROTIC RESPONSE	BY FEMALES	BY MALES
	%	%
Definite and/or frequent	5	11
Some response	11	21
Never	84	68
Number of cases	5250	4082

14. Peeping and Voyeurism. There are probably very few heterosexual males who would not take advantage of the opportunity to ob-

---

[18] This masculine misconception is not new. Brantome (16th century, "Lives of Fair and Gallant Ladies," First Discourse, ch. 5 (1901:55), tells of a prince who served wine to women in a cup covered with copulatory figures. He would then ask, "Now feel ye not a something that doth prick you in the mid part of the body, ladies, at the sight?" and the women would reply, "Nay!, never a one of all these droll images hath had power enow to stir me!"

serve a nude female, or to observe heterosexual activity, particularly if it were possible to do so surreptitiously so they would not suffer the social disgrace that the discovery of their behavior might bring. To many males, the observation of a female who is undressing may be erotically more stimulating than observing her when she is fully nude, for the undressing suggests, in fantasy, what they may ultimately be able to observe. Consequently, we have the peeper who gets into difficulty with the law, the peep show which was formerly common in this country and which is still available in many other countries, and the more surreptitious and unpublicized peeping in which most males engage, at some time in their lives, from the windows of their homes, from hotel windows, and from wherever they find the opportunity to observe. Our data are insufficient for determining what percentage of the male population is ever involved, but Hamilton found some 65 per cent of the males in his study admitting that they had done some peeping.[19] The percentages for the population as a whole are probably higher.

The erotic significance of what the peeper observes obviously depends on his capacity to be stimulated psychologically. But there are few instances in our own study, or in other studies, or in the medical and psychiatric literature, of females as peepers. Out of curiosity some females are undoubtedly sometimes involved, and a few of them may find erotic stimulation in such peeping; but such behavior is certainly rare among females.

15. Preferences for Light or Dark. We have previously (1948:581–582) pointed out that many (40 per cent) of the males in our sample preferred to have their coitus or other sexual activities where there was at least some light. Fewer (19 per cent) of the females in the sample preferred sexual relations in the light. This, again, is ordinarily taken to represent the greater modesty of the female, but it seems to depend upon the fact that the male is stimulated by seeing the sexual partner, by seeing the genitalia or other parts of the body of the sexual partner, by getting some chance to observe, as a voyeur, something of his own sexual action, and by the opportunity to observe various objects with which he comes to associate sexual action. Females, as we have already shown, are much less often attracted by observing the male partner, his genitalia, or other objects associated with the sexual performance. The specific data are as follows:

---

[19] Hamilton 1929:456 found 16 per cent of females and 83 per cent of males had had desire to peep as adults; 20 per cent of females and 65 per cent of males had done actual peeping.

Preferences for Light or Dark

Preferences	Report on own preferences		Subject's report on	
	BY FEMALES	BY MALES	FEMALE SPOUSE	MALE SPOUSE
	Percent		*Percent*	
Definitely prefer light	8	21	11	21
Prefer some light	11	19	13	10
Prefer dark	55	35	58	34
No preference	26	25	18	35
Number of cases	2042	798	662	1633

Anthropologic data indicate that there are different customs in regard to having coitus in the light or dark in various cultural groups,[20] and the cultural tradition may be a factor in determining the practice in our own culture; but this does not explain why, within our own single culture, males are more likely than females to prefer some light during their sexual activities. The differences provide another illustration of the greater capacity of the male to be conditioned by experience.

16. Fantasies Concerning Opposite Sex. Practically all males who are not exclusively homosexual may be erotically aroused by thinking of certain females, or of females in general. Fewer males of the lower educational levels are aroused by such fantasies, and older males sometimes lose their capacity to be stimulated by fantasies, and males who are exclusively homosexual may not fantasy concerning females. But most of the males in our sample (84 per cent) indicated that they were at least sometimes, and in most instances often aroused by thinking of sexual relations with females—by thinking of the sexual relations that they had previously had, or by thinking of the sexual relations that they anticipated they might have or would like to have. Such erotic stimulation probably occurs more often than any other single type of psychologic stimulation among males.

A smaller percentage (69 per cent) of the females in the sample reported that they had ever had erotic fantasies about males, and nearly a third (31 per cent) insisted that they had never been aroused by thinking about males or of sexual relations with them. They had not even been aroused by thinking of their husbands or of their boy friends. Most of the females who were not aroused by the contemplation of males were heterosexual, and most of them had had sexual relations with males in which they had regularly responded to the point

---

[20] For varying practices in various cultures in regard to day or night preferences for coitus, see Ford and Beach 1951:73.

of orgasm; but even some of the females who were most responsive in physical relationships had never been aroused by fantasies about males.

The specific data showing these differences between the females and males in the sample are as follows:

Fantasies concerning opposite sex

EROTIC RESPONSE	BY FEMALES	BY MALES
	%	%
Definite and/or frequent	22	37
Some response	47	47
Never	31	16
Number of cases	5772	4214

These differences between females and males have a great deal to do with the fact that more males search for overt sexual experience, and fewer females search for such experience. These differences provide one explanation of the fact that males are usually aroused and often intensely aroused before the beginning of a sexual relationship and before they have made any physical contact with the female partner. These differences account for the male's desire for frequent sexual contact, his difficulty in getting along without regular sexual contact, and his disturbance when he fails to secure the contact which he has sought. The differences often account for the female's inability to comprehend why her husband finds it difficult to get along with less frequent sexual contacts, or to abandon his plans for coitus when household duties or social activities interfere.

Too many husbands, on the other hand, fail to comprehend that their wives are not aroused as they are in the anticipation of a sexual relationship, and fail to comprehend that their wives may need general physical stimulation before they are sufficiently aroused to want a genital union or completed coitus. Too often the male considers the wife's lesser interest at the beginning of a sexual relationship as evidence that she has lost her affection for him. Sexual adjustments between husbands and wives could be worked out more often if males more often understood that the reactions of their particular wives represent characteristics which are typical of females in general, and if females more often understood that the sexual interests shown by their particular husbands represent qualities which are typical of most males.

17. Fantasies Concerning Own Sex. Sexual arousal from fantasies about other males, or of sexual relations with other males, is as frequent among homosexual males as heterosexual fantasies are among heterosexual males. Such erotic fantasies are less frequent among homosexual females, but they do occur in as high or a higher percentage of the homosexual females (74 per cent) as heterosexual fantasies occur among heterosexual females. The specific data are as follows:

Fantasies concerning own sex

EROTIC RESPONSE	BY FEMALES
	%
Definite and/or frequent	28
Some response	46
Never	26
Cases with homosexual history	194

18. **Fantasies During Masturbation.** Some 89 per cent of the males in our sample had utilized erotic fantasies as one of their sources of stimulation during masturbation. Some 72 per cent had more or less always fantasied while masturbating. Such fantasies usually turn around memories of previous sexual experience, around sexual experience that the male hopes to have in the future, or around sexual experience which he may never allow himself to have but which he anticipates might bring erotic satisfaction if the law and the social custom made it possible for him to engage in such activity. In not a few instances males develop rather elaborate fictional situations which they regularly review as they masturbate. Quite a few males, particularly among the better educated groups, may, at least on occasion, utilize erotic photographs or drawings, or make their own erotic drawings, or read erotic literature, or write their own erotic stories which they use as sources of stimulation during masturbation. Some 56 per cent of the males in the sample indicated that they observed their own genitalia at least on occasion during masturbation, and while this is more likely to be true of males with homosexual histories, it is also true of many others who give no other evidence of homosexual interests. But in any event, these males find the observation of their own genitalia an additional source of erotic stimulation. So dependent are many males on psychologic stimuli in connection with masturbation that it is probable that many of them, especially middle-aged and older males, would have difficulty in reaching orgasm if they did not fantasy while masturbating.

Fantasies during masturbation

FANTASIES PRESENT	AMONG FEMALES	AMONG MALES
	%	%
Almost always	50	72
Sometimes	14	17
Never	36	11
Number of cases	2475	2815

The record shows (p. 164) that only 64 per cent of the females in our sample who had ever masturbated, had fantasied while masturbating.[21] Only 50 per cent of the females who had masturbated, had regularly fantasied for any period of their lives. We have nearly no cases of females utilizing erotic books or pictures as sources of stimulation during masturbation.

19. Nocturnal Sex Dreams. Nearly all males have nocturnal sex dreams which are erotically stimulating to them. Ultimately some 75 per cent of the females (p. 196) may have such nocturnal dreams.

To judge from our sample, approximately 83 per cent of the males (the accumulative incidence figure) ultimately have sex dreams which are erotically stimulating enough to bring them to orgasm during sleep. The corresponding figure for the females in the sample was 37 per cent (p. 196).[22]

The frequencies of sex dreams show similar differences between males and females. Among those males in the sample who were having any sex dreams (the active sample), the median frequencies averaged about 10 times per year in the younger age groups, and about 5 times per year in the older age groups. The median female in the sample had had sex dreams which were sufficiently erotic to bring her to orgasm with frequencies of 3 to 4 per year (p. 197). For perhaps 25 per cent of the females who had had any dreams which had resulted in orgasm, the experience had not occurred more often than 1 to 6 times in their lives. These differences depend, again, on differences in the significance of psychologic stimulation for the average female and the average male.

20. Diversion During Coitus. We have already pointed out (p. 384) that effective female responses during coitus may depend, in many cases, upon the continuity of physical stimulation. If that stimulation is interrupted, orgasm is delayed, primarily because the female may return to normal physiologic levels in such periods of inactivity. This appears to be due to the fact that she is not sufficiently aroused by psychologic stimuli to maintain her arousal when there is no physical stimulation. We have pointed out that the male, on the contrary, may go through a period in which physical activity is interrupted without losing erection or the other evidences of his erotic arousal, primarily because he continues to be stimulated psychologically during those periods.

---

[21] Hamilton 1929:429 reports 36 per cent of females, 69 per cent of males record fantasies during masturbation.

[22] Hamilton 1929:318–319 reports 66 per cent of females, 42 per cent of males without nocturnal sex dreams.

Similarly, because the male is more strongly stimulated by psychologic factors during sexual activities, he cannot be distracted from his performance as easily as the female. Many females are easily diverted, and may turn from coitus when a baby cries, when children enter the house, when the doorbell rings, when they recall household duties which they intended to take care of before they retired for the night, and when music, conversation, food, a desire to smoke, or other non-sexual activities present themselves. The male himself is sometimes responsible for the introduction of the conversation, cigarettes, music, and other diversions, and he, unwittingly, may be responsible for the female's distraction because he does not understand that the sources of her responses may be different from his.

It is a standard complaint of males that their female partners in coitus "do not put their minds to it." This is an incorrect appraisal of the situation, for what is involved is the female's lack of stimulation by the sorts of psychologic stimuli which are of importance to the male. Such differences between females and males have been known for centuries, and are pointed out in the classic and Oriental literature. From the most ancient to the most modern erotic art, the female has been portrayed on occasion as reading a book, eating, or engaging in other activities while she is in coitus; but no artist seems to have portrayed males engaged in such extraneous activities while in coitus.

Various interpretations may be offered of these differences between females and males. Many persons would, again, be inclined to look for cultural influences which might be responsible. But some sort of basic biologic factor must be involved, for at least some of the infra-human species of mammals show these same differences. Cheese crumbs spread in front of a copulating pair of rats may distract the female, but not the male. A mouse running in front of a copulating pair of cats may distract the female, but not the male. When cattle are interrupted during coitus, it is the cow that is more likely to be disturbed while the bull may try to continue with coitus.[23] It explains nothing to suggest that this is due to differences in levels of "sex drive" in the two sexes. There are probably more basic neurologic explanations of these differences between females and males (p. 712).

21. Stimulation by Literary Materials. Erotic responses while reading novels, essays, poetry, or other literary materials may depend upon the general emotional content of the work, upon specifically romantic

---

[23] As examples of the fact that the female is more easily distracted, see: Beach 1947b:264 (bitches will eat during coitus, most male dogs refuse food in this situation; female cats may investigate mouse holes during coitus). Robert Bean, director of Brookfield Zoo, reports (verbal communic.) females of various species eating during coitus.

material in it, upon its sexual vocabulary (particularly if it is a vernacular vocabulary), or upon its more specific descriptions of sexual activity. The reader may thus, vicariously, share the experience of the characters portrayed in the book, and reactions to such literary material are some measure of the reader's capacity to be aroused psychologically.

The reactions of the females and males in our sample were as follows:

Reading literary materials

EROTIC RESPONSE	BY FEMALES	BY MALES
	%	%
Definite and/or frequent	16	21
Some response	44	38
Never	40	41
Number of cases	5699	3952

It will be noted that the females and males in the sample had responded erotically in nearly the same numbers while reading literary materials.[24] Twice as many of the females in the sample had responded to literary materials as had ever responded to the observation of portrayals of sexual action (p. 662), and five times as many as had responded to photographs or other portrayals of nude human figures (p. 652). At this point we do not clearly understand why this should be so. There are possible psychoanalytic interpretations, but in view of all the evidence that there may be basic neurophysiologic differences between females and males, we hesitate to offer any explanation of the present data.

22. Stimulation by Erotic Stories. Practically all of the males in the sample, even including the youngest adolescent boys, had heard stories that were deliberately intended to be erotically stimulating, usually through their descriptions of sexual action. Nearly half (47 per cent) of the males in the sample reported that they had been aroused, at least on occasion, by such stories. There had been differences in the responses among males of the various educational levels. Most of the better educated males had responded, while fewer of the males of the lower educational levels were aroused by such stimuli. Some 53 per cent of the males in the total sample said that they had never been aroused by such stories.

Some 95 per cent of the females in the sample had heard or read stories that were deliberately intended to bring erotic response, but

---

[24] That the erotic stimulation which females derive from reading romantic stories or seeing moving pictures equals or exceeds that which is derived from those sources by males, is also recognized by: Friedeburg 1950:24. See also Dickinson and Beam 1934:111, 427.

only 14 per cent recalled that they had ever been aroused by such stories. The specific record is as follows:

Stimulation by erotic stories

EROTIC RESPONSE	BY FEMALES	BY MALES
	%	%
Definite and/or frequent	2	16
Some response	12	31
Never	86	53
Number of cases	5523	4202

Note that some 86 per cent of the females who had heard obscene stories had never received any erotic arousal from them. Some of the females had been offended by the stories, and it is not impossible that their failure to be aroused represented a perverse attitude which they had developed in consequence of the general opinion that such stories are indecent and immoral. On the other hand, a surprising proportion of the females in the sample indicated that they enjoyed such stories, usually because of their intrinsic humor. Sometimes their interest in the stories represented a defiance of the social convention. There is some indication, although we do not have the data to establish it, that there is an increasing acceptance of such stories among females in this country today. The older tradition which restricted the telling of such stories in the presence of a female has largely broken down within the last decade or two, and since there is this freer acceptance of such stories by many females, it is all the more surprising to find how few ever find erotic stimulation in them.

23. Erotic Writing and Drawing. What is commonly identified as pornography is literature or drawing which has the erotic arousal of the reader or observer as its deliberate and primary or sole objective. Erotic elements may be involved in the production of other literary material and in the fine arts; but in the opinion of most students, and in various court decisions, such literary and fine art materials are distinguished by the fact that they have literary or artistic merit as their prime objective, and depend only secondarily on erotic elements to accomplish those ends.[25]

---

[25] For examples of court decisions holding that despite certain obscene or indecent passages the books themselves were not obscene; see: In re Worthington Co. 1894:30 N.Y. Supp. 361. Halsey v. N.Y.Soc. for the Suppression of Vice 1922:136 N.E.(N.Y.) 219 ("It contains many paragraphs, however, which taken by themselves are undoubtedly vulgar and indecent. . . . Printed by themselves they might, as a matter of law, come within the prohibition of the statute. So might a similar selection from Aristophanes or Chaucer or Boccaccio or even from the Bible. The book, however, must be considered broadly as a whole"). U.S. v. One Book Entitled Ulysses 1934:72F(2d)705. Com. v. Gordon 1949:66 D. and C. (Pa.) 101 (Judge Bok's scholarly discussion of the changing concepts of obscenity, citing our male volume on 116). But cf. Com. v. Isenstadt 1945:62 N.E.2d (Mass.)840. Detailed discussions are found in: Alpert 1938, and Jenkins 1944.

In every modern language, the amount of deliberately pornographic material that has been produced is beyond ready calculation. Some thousands of such documents have been printed in European languages alone, and the literature of the Orient and other parts of the world is replete with such material. Similarly, there is an unlimited amount of pornographic drawing and painting which has been produced by artists of some ability in every part of the world, and there is no end to the amateur portrayals of sexual action.

But in all this quantity of pornographic production, it is exceedingly difficult to find any material that has been produced by females. In the published material, there are probably not more than two or three documents that were actually written by females. It is true that there is a considerable portion of the pornographic material which pretends to be written by females who are recounting their personal experience, but in many instances it is known that the authors were male, and in nearly every instance the internal content of the material indicates a male author. A great deal of the pornographic literature turns around detailed descriptions of genital activity, and descriptions of male genital performance. These are elements in which females, according to our data, are not ordinarily interested. The females in such literature extol the male's genital and copulatory capacity, and there is considerable emphasis on the intensity of the female's response and the insatiability of her sexual desires. All of these represent the kind of female which most males wish all females to be. They represent typically masculine misinterpretations of the average female's capacity to respond to psychologic stimuli. Such elements are introduced because they are of erotic significance to the male writers, and because they are of erotic significance to the consuming public, which is almost exclusively male.

Among the hundreds and probably thousands of unpublished, amateur documents which we have seen during the past fifteen years, we have been able to find only three manuscripts written by females which contain erotic elements of the sort ordinarily found in documents written by males. Similarly, out of the thousands of erotic drawings which we have seen, some of them by artists of note and some of them by lesser artists and amateurs, we have been able to find less than a half dozen series done by females.

Females produce another, more extensive literature which is called erotic, and do drawings which are called erotic; but most of these deal with more general emotional situations, affectional relationships, and love. These things do not bring specifically erotic responses from males, and we cannot discover that they bring more than minimal responses from females.

24. Wall Inscriptions. Making inscriptions (graffiti—literally, *writings*) of various sorts on walls of buildings, walls lining country lanes, walls in public toilets, and walls in still other public places, is a custom of long and ancient standing. Among the inscriptions made by males, an exceedingly high proportion is sexual and obviously intended to provide erotic stimulation for the inscribers as well as for the persons who may subsequently observe them.

Relatively few females, on the contrary, ever make wall inscriptions.[26] When they do, fewer of the inscriptions are sexual, and only a small proportion of the sexual material seems to be intended to provide erotic stimulation for the inscribers or for the persons who observe the inscriptions.

With the collaboration of a number of other persons, we have accumulated some hundreds of wall inscriptions from public toilets, making sure that the record in each case covered all of the inscriptions, sexual or non-sexual, heterosexual or homosexual, which were on the walls in the place (p. 87). The record is as follows:

Incidences of sexual inscriptions

	FEMALE %	MALE %
Places with any sexual inscription	50	58
% of inscriptions which were erotic	25	86
Number of places surveyed	94	259
Number of sexual inscriptions	331	1048

A high proportion (86 per cent) of the inscriptions on the walls of the male toilets were sexual. The sexual materials were drawings, lone words, phrases, and sometimes more extended writing. There were three chief subjects in these inscriptions: genitalia (either female or male), genital, oral, or anal action (either heterosexual or homosexual), and vernacular vocabularies which, by association, are erotically significant for most males.

On the contrary, not more than 25 per cent of the toilet wall inscriptions made by the females dealt with any of these matters. Most of the female inscriptions referred to love, or associated names ("John and Mary," "Helen and Don"), or were lipstick impressions, or drawings of hearts; but very few of them were genital or dealt with genital action or sexual vernaculars. A brief summary of the material which we have accumulated shows the following:

---

[26] That other collections of graffiti clearly reflect this scarcity of female authors of such material, can be seen by surveying the articles on graffiti in Anthropophyteia 1907(4):316–328; 1908(5):265–275; 1909(6):432–439; 1910(7): 399–406; 1912(9):493–500.

Content of sexual inscriptions

SUBJECT OF INSCRIPTIONS	MADE BY FEMALES	MADE BY MALES
	%	%
Heterosexual	17	21
Genitalia of opposite sex	5	3
Coital contacts	7	8
Oral contacts	2	11
Anal contacts	1	—
Other erotic items	2	3
References to dating	0	5
Homosexual	11	75
Genitalia of own sex	7	15
Oral contacts	1	30
Anal contacts	0	18
Other erotic items	2	8
References to dating	1	21
Erotic, not classifiable as heterosexual or homosexual	5	6
Non-erotic references to love		
With own sex	12	3
With opposite sex	35	3
Sex not specified	9	0
Hearts	6	0
Lips	69	0
Number of inscriptions	331	1048

Again it will be suggested that females are less inclined to make wall inscriptions of any sort, and less inclined to make erotic wall inscriptions, because of their greater regard for the moral codes and the social conventions. In view of our data showing that most females are not erotically aroused by the psychologic stimuli that are of significance to the male, and in view of the data showing that most females are not erotically aroused by observing sexual action, by portrayals of sexual action, or by fantasies about sexual action, there seems little doubt that the average female's lack of interest in making wall inscriptions must depend primarily upon the fact that they mean little or nothing to her erotically. The male usually derives erotic satisfaction from making them, and he may derive even greater satisfaction in anticipating that the inscriptions he makes will arouse other males, amounting sometimes to hundreds and thousands of other males who may subsequently see them.

It is notable that the wall inscriptions in male toilets are concerned with male genitalia and male functions more often than they are concerned with female genitalia or functions. This, at first glance, makes them appear homosexual, but we are not yet ready to accept this interpretation. It is possible that homosexual males are actually more inclined, while heterosexual males are less inclined to make wall inscriptions. It is possible that homosexual males are more inclined because they may be more aroused in making such inscriptions, and because they anticipate how other males will react upon seeing them. The heterosexual male has no such incentive, since he knows that no females will see his writing. But we are inclined to believe that many of the inscriptions that deal with male anatomy and male function are made by males who are not conscious of homosexual reactions and who may not have had overt homosexual experience, but who, nevertheless, may be interested in male anatomy and male functions as elements which enter into heterosexual activities.

But whatever the conscious intent of the inscriber, the wall inscriptions provide information on the extent and the nature of the suppressed sexual desires of females and males. The inscriptions most frequently deal with activities which occur less frequently in the actual histories. This means that the males who make the inscriptions, and the males who read them, are exposing their unsatisfied desires. The inscriptions portray what they would like to experience in real life. Usually the inscriptions are anonymous. They are usually located in restricted, hidden, or remote places. Most of the males who make them would not so openly express their erotic interests in places where they could be identified.

Comparisons of the female and male inscriptions epitomize, therefore, some of the most basic sexual differences between females and males.

25. Discussions of Sex. Males are much more inclined, and females are less inclined to discuss sexual matters with other persons. Striking evidence of this has already been presented in discussing the sources of information which start females masturbating. The data are as follows:

First information on masturbation

SOURCES	FEMALE *	MALE *
	%	%
Self-discovery	57	28
Verbal and printed sources	43	75
Petting experience	12	Very few
Observation	11	40
Homosexual experience	3	9
Number of cases	2675	3999

* The totals amount to more than one hundred per cent because some individuals were simultaneously affected by two or more sources of information.

Note that 57 per cent of the females in the sample had first masturbated as a result of their own discovery that such a process was possible, and that relatively few had started because they had heard of masturbation through verbal sources. Even some of the females who had not started until they were in their thirties or forties had not known that masturbation was possible for a female until they discovered it through their own exploration. On the contrary, most of the males had heard about masturbation, or observed other persons masturbating, before they themselves ever began; and only 28 per cent had learned how to masturbate from their own self-discovery. This is a measure of the extent to which sex is discussed among pre-adolescent and early adolescent males. Such discussions of sex also occur among older males, from adolescence into old age.

For most males, discussions of sex often provide some sort of erotic stimulation. They do not provide anything like the same sort of stimulation for the average female, and in consequence she does not have the same inspiration for engaging in such conversations. Moreover, many of the females in the sample who had overheard discussions of reproductive and sexual functions when they were children, or even when they were adults, had not tried to understand what was being discussed, primarily, as they asserted, because they were "not interested" in sex. We have already recorded (p. 140) that there is frequently a lapse of some years between the time that the female first hears of masturbation, and the time that she attempts to masturbate herself.

On the contrary, from an early age the average male is interested in all that he can learn about sex and searches for sexual information, in part because it may mean something to him erotically. Practically all males who have reached adolescence attempt masturbation almost immediately upon hearing of it. This is further evidence of the importance of psychologic stimulation for the male.

26. Arousal From Sado-Masochistic Stories. Some persons are aroused sexually when they think of situations that involve cruelty, whipping, flagellation, torture, or other means deliberately adopted for the infliction of pain. More individuals are emotionally disturbed when they contemplate such sado-masochistic situations, and they may not recognize such a disturbance as sexual; but at this stage in our knowledge, it is difficult to say how much of the emotional disturbance, or even the more specifically sado-masochistic reactions, may involve sexual elements (p. 88).

A distinctly higher percentage of the males in the sample had responded to sado-masochistic situations in a way which they recognized as sexual.[27] The specific data are as follows:

---

[27] That sado-masochism is less frequent among women is also noted by: [Jacolliot] Jacobus X 1900:347–348. Talmey 1910:136. Forel 1922:236. Krafft-Ebing

EROTIC RESPONSE	BY FEMALES	BY MALES
	%	%
Definite and/or frequent	3	10
Some response	9	12
Never	88	78
Number of cases	2880	1016

That fewer of the females and more of the males had responded, appears again to have depended on the fact that reactions to sado-masochistic stories rely on fantasy. As many females as males seem to react erotically when they are bitten (see below) or when they engage in more specifically sado-masochistic contacts, and this further emphasizes the differences in the psychologic reactions of the two sexes.

It is quite probable that many more males and some more females would respond to such sado-masochistic stimuli if they were to find themselves in sexual situations which were associated with sadism. The development of sado-masochistic responses in a number of our histories had begun in that way.

27. Responses to Being Bitten. It is difficult to know how much of the response of an individual who is being hurt is the product of the physical stimulation, and how much is the product of the stimulation provided by psychologic conditioning, the association of sexual and sado-masochistic phenomena, and the psychologic satisfactions which are to be found in submitting to a sexual partner. It is also very difficult to determine how many of the physical and emotional responses which are manifest in a sado-masochistic situation are sexual and how many are more properly identified as some other sort of emotional response.

During heterosexual petting and coitus, and in homosexual relations, the most frequent manifestation of sado-masochistic responses is to be found in the nibbling and biting which many persons inflict on various parts of the body of a sexual partner. Such behavior is widespread among all of the mammals, and much more widespread in human sexual patterns than most persons comprehend.[28] Definitely

---

1922:129. Kronfeld in Marcuse 1923:314. Bilder-Lexikon 1930(2):538. Negri 1949:206. That sadism is more typical of males and masochism of females is asserted by: Wexberg 1931:182–183. Rosanoff 1938:156. Brown 1940:383. T. Reik 1941:216. Scheinfeld 1944:243. Thorpe and Katz 1948:326–327. Hamilton 1929:458, 461 (an equal number, 28–29 per cent, of males and females reported pleasure from pain being inflicted on them, but one-third of the females as against one-half of the males reported pleasant thrills at some time from inflicting pain on a person or animal).

[28] We have records of biting (usually by the male) as a part of sexual activity in a number of mammalian species, including the baboon, various monkeys,

sexual responses consequent on such biting were recognized by about equal numbers of the males and females in our sample. The specific data are as follows:

Responses to being bitten

EROTIC RESPONSE	BY FEMALES	BY MALES
	%	%
Definite and/or frequent	26	26
Some response	29	24
Never	45	50
Number of cases	2200	567

Twice as many males had responded erotically to being bitten as had responded to sado-masochistic stories. There were more than four times as many females who had responded erotically when they were bitten as had ever responded to sado-masochistic stories. This provides one more body of data to show that males may be aroused by both physical and psychologic stimuli, while a larger number of the females, although not all of them, may be aroused only by physical stimuli.

28. Fetishism. Practically all heterosexual males, as we have already noted, are aroused erotically when they observe the female body or particular parts of it. When the part of the partner's body which brings the erotic response is farther removed from the genital area, as the hair of the head, the feet, and the fingers are, such responses have commonly been identified as fetishes. But the definitions are obviously nebulous, for all of these reactions depend on nothing more than associative conditioning, and it is difficult to draw the line between the sexual responses of the average male when he sees the genitalia or the breasts or some other portion of the partner's body, and his responses to objects which are more remote but still associated with his previous sexual experience.

When an individual responds to objects which are entirely removed from the partner's body, as clothing (especially underclothing), stockings, garters, shoes, furniture, particular types of drapery, or objects which are still more remote from the particular female with whom the sexual relations were originally had, the fetishistic nature of the response seems more pronounced. But in any event, it still depends upon the sort of psychologic conditioning which is involved in most erotic responses.

Persons who respond only or primarily to objects which are remote from the sexual partner, or remote from the overt sexual activities with

---

mink, marten, sable, ferret, skunk, horse, zebra, pig, sheep, rat, dog, guinea pig, chimpanzee, lion, cat, tiger, leopard, rabbit, raccoon, sea lion, shrew, opossum, and bat. Such biting is particularly violent, and even savage, among the Mustelidae (ferret, mink, sable, skunk).

a partner, are not rare in the population. This is particularly true of individuals who are erotically aroused by high heels, by boots, by corsets, by tight clothing, by long gloves, by whips, or by other objects which suggest sado-masochistic relationships, and which may have been associated with the individual's previous sexual activity.

It has been known for some time, and our own data confirm it, that fetishism is an almost exclusively male phenomenon.[29] We have seen only two or three cases of females who were regularly and distinctly aroused by objects that were not directly connected with sexual activity. Our data on the limited number of females who respond to seeing male genitalia or any other portion of the nude or clothed male body, would lead one to expect that females would not be aroused by objects which are still more remote from the sexual partner himself. There seems no question that the differences in the incidences of fetishes among males and females depend upon the fact that the male is more easily conditioned by his sexual experience and by objects that were associated with those experiences.

29. Transvestism. An individual who prefers to wear the clothing of the opposite sex, and who desires to be accepted in the social organization as an individual of the opposite sex, is a transvestite (from *trans,* a transference, and *vesta,* the clothing). But it should be emphasized that transvestism involves not only a change of clothing. The occasional adoption at a masked ball, or in a stage production, of clothing characteristic of the opposite sex is not transvestism in any strict sense, for true transvestism also involves a desire to assume the role of the opposite sex in the social organization.

True transvestism is a phenomenon which involves many different situations and has many different origins.[30] There are persons who are permanent transvestites, who try to identify with the opposite sex in their work as well as in their homes, at all times of the day and through

---

[29] The infrequent occurrence of fetishism among females has also been recognized by: Talmey 1910:136. Hirschfeld 1920(3):1–79 (many case histories, including a few female cases). Krafft-Ebing 1922:24. Forel 1922:240. Hamilton 1929:463 (13 per cent of females, 33 per cent of males). Stekel 1930(2):341. Walker and Strauss 1939:175. Brown 1940:381. Scheinfeld 1944:243. Fenichel 1945:344.

It is notable that fetish magazines currently found on the newsstands are all slanted toward male purchasers.

[30] Transvestism in various pre-literate societies is recorded, for example, for the Navajo, Kwakiutl, Crow, Eskimo (North America); Tanala, Lango, Mbundu (Africa); Uripev, Dyak (Oceania); Chukchee, Yakut, Yukaghir (Siberia); Lushais (India). In many instances the transvestites are respected and thought to possess magical powers; in other instances they are merely tolerated. The great majority of transvestites are anatomic males. Ford 1945:32 points out that "Cases of women adopting the dress and habits of men are much more rare." For further anthropologic data, see: Parsons 1916:521–528 (Zuni). Hill 1935:273–279 (Navajo). Devereux 1937:498–527 (Mohave). Dragoo 1950 ms. (in more than twenty societies in North America). Ford and Beach 1951:130–131 (general, brief discussion).

all of the days of the year. There are persons who are partial transvestites, who adopt their changed roles only on occasion, as at home
in the evening, or occasionally on week ends, or on other special occasions.

Psychologically the phenomenon sometimes depends upon an individual's erotic attraction for the opposite sex. A male, for instance,
may be so attracted to females that he wishes to be permanently identified with them. He wants to have sexual relationships with them, and
he wishes to live permanently with them, as another female might live
with them. The neighbors may believe it to be two females who are
living together, although it is sexually a heterosexual relationship
which is involved.

Sometimes transvestism depends upon an individual's violent reactions against his or her own sex. In such a case, he may or may not be
erotically attracted to the opposite sex. If he is attracted, he may have
heterosexual relationships. But he may so idealize females that he is
offended by the idea of having sexual relationships with them, and
then he may be left without any opportunity for socio-sexual contacts,
because his dislike for individuals of his own sex will prevent him from
having sexual relationships with them.

There are some psychiatrists who consider all transvestism homosexual, but this is incorrect.[31] Transvestism and homosexuality are
totally independent phenomena, and it is only a small portion of the
transvestites who are homosexual in their physical relationships. A
misinterpretation on this point may generate tragedy when psychiatrists insist, as we have known them to do in several cases, that all
transvestites, including those who are basically opposed to everything
connected with their own sex, must frankly accept their "homosexuality" and accept overt homosexual relationships if they wish to resolve
their psychologic conflicts.

On the other hand, some males are transvestites and wish to be
identified with the opposite sex because they are homosexual and because they hope to attract the type of male who would hesitate to
engage in homosexual relationships if the other individual were not
identifiable, to at least some degree, with femininity.

In not a few instances transvestism develops out of a fetishistic interest in the clothing or some part of the clothing of the opposite sex.
The adoption of the clothing of the opposite sex may not modify the
original sexual history of the individual, whether it was heterosexual or
homosexual.

---

[31] The assumption that transvestism is always associated with or an expression of
homosexuality may be noted, for example, in: Krafft-Ebing 1922:398. Forel
1922:251. Thorpe and Katz 1948:314. Allen 1949:146–147,

There are many cases of transvestism which are associated with sado-masochism. Then the masochistic male wishes to be identified as a female in order to be subjugated as males might, conceivably, subjugate a female.

It is clear that transvestism depends very largely upon the individual's capacity to be conditioned psychologically. There are few phenomena which more strikingly illustrate the force of psychologic conditioning. It is, therefore, highly significant to find that an exceedingly large proportion of the transvestites are anatomically males who wish to assume the role of the female in the social organization. At this point we cannot give percentages, although we are attempting to secure a sample which will ultimately allow us to estimate the number of transvestites in the United States; but it is our present understanding that there may be a hundred anatomic males who wish to be identified as females, for every two or three or half dozen anatomic females who wish to be identified as males.[32] This last is particularly interesting because females often assume some of the clothing of males in working around their homes, on farms, in factories, and elsewhere; but we find no evidence that such females are interested in being identified socially with the opposite sex, and such an adoption of male attire has little or nothing to do with transvestism. Males, of course, do not usually wear any part of the female costume unless they are true transvestites.

Transvestism provides one of the striking illustrations of the fact that males are more liable to be conditioned by psychologic stimuli, and females less liable to be so conditioned. The males who wish to be identified as females are in reality very masculine in their psychologic capacities to be conditioned.

30. Discontinuity in Sexual Activity. We have already pointed out that the sexual activities of females are often very discontinuous. Between periods of activity there may be weeks or months and sometimes years in which there is no activity of any sort. This is true of masturbation in the female (p. 148), of nocturnal dreams to the point of orgasm (p. 197), of pre-marital petting (p. 236), of pre-marital coitus (p. 289), of extra-marital coitus (p. 419), and of homosexual experience (p. 456). It is most strikingly true of the female's total sexual outlet. Some females who at times have high rates of outlet, may go for weeks or months or even years with very little outlet, or none at all. But then after such a period of inactivity the high rates of outlet may

---

[32] An example of the sort of unwarranted statement that gets into and is perpetuated in the professional literature, although it is unsubstantiated by any specific data, is the estimate in Allen 1949:145 that transvestism is as common among females as among males.

develop again. Discontinuities in total outlet are practically unknown in the histories of males.

These differences in the continuity of sexual activities may depend upon a variety of factors. They certainly depend in part upon the differences in the way in which females and males respond to psychologic stimuli. Because males are so readily stimulated by thinking of past sexual experiences, by anticipating the opportunity to renew that experience, and by the abundant associations that they make between everyday objects and their sexual experience, the average younger male is constantly being aroused. The average female is not so often aroused. In some instances the male's arousal may be mild, but in many instances the arousal may involve genital erection and considerable physiologic reaction. Nearly all (but not all) younger males are aroused to the point of erection many times per week, and many of them may respond to the point of erection several times per day. Many females may go for days and weeks and months without ever being stimulated unless they have actual physical contact with a sexual partner. Because of this constant arousal, most males, particularly younger males, may be nervously disturbed unless they can regularly carry their responses through to the point of orgasm. Most females are not seriously disturbed if they do not have a regular sexual outlet, although some of them may be as disturbed as most males are without a regular outlet. The failure to recognize these differences in the needs of the two sexes for a regular sexual outlet may be the source of a considerable amount of difficulty in marriage. It is the source of many social disturbances over questions of sex. In establishing sex laws, in considering the sexual needs of females and males in penal and other institutions, in considering the need among females and among males for non-marital sources of sexual outlet, and in various other social problems, we cannot reach final solutions unless we comprehend these considerable differences between the sexual needs of the average female and the average male.

31. Promiscuity. Among all peoples, everywhere in the world, it is understood that the male is more likely than the female to desire sexual relations with a variety of partners. It is pointed out that the female has a greater capacity for being faithful to a single partner, that she is more likely to consider that she has a greater responsibility than the male has in maintaining a home and in caring for the offspring of any sexual relationship, and that she is generally more inclined to consider the moral implications of her sexual behavior. But it seems probable that these characteristics depend upon the fact that the female is less often aroused, as the average male is aroused, by the idea of promiscuity.

An attempt to analyze the reason for the greater promiscuity of the male suggests that it depends upon a variety of psychologic capacities which are not so often found in the female. Several of these we have already discussed. The male is aroused at observing his potential sexual partner, as most females are not. The male is aroused because he has been conditioned by his previous experience, as most females have not. The male is aroused by anticipating new types of experience, new types of sexual partners, new levels of satisfaction that may be attained in the new relationships, new opportunities to experiment with new techniques, new opportunities to secure higher levels of satisfaction than he has ever before attained. In both heterosexual and homosexual relationships, promiscuity may depend, in many instances, upon the male's anticipation of variation in the genital anatomy of the partner, in the techniques which may be used during the contacts, and in the physical responses of the new partner. None of these factors have such significance for the average female.

Male promiscuity often depends upon the satisfactions that may be secured from the pursuit and successful attainment of a new partner. There are some heterosexual males, and a larger proportion of the homosexual males, who may limit themselves to a single contact with any single partner. Once having demonstrated their capacities to effect sexual relations with the particular individual, they prefer to turn to the pursuit of the next partner.

The male's greater inclination to be promiscuous shows up in the record of his petting experience, his experience in pre-marital coitus, in extra-marital coitus, and in homosexual relations. In all of these types of relationships, few females have anywhere near the number of partners that many a promiscuous male may have. The specific data are as follows:

Number of Partners

NUMBER OF PARTNERS	PRE-MARITAL PETTING		PRE-MARITAL COITUS		HOMOSEXUAL CONTACTS	
	Female	Male	Female	Male	Female	Male
	Percent		*Percent*		*Percent*	
1	10	6	53	27	51	35
2–5	32	20	34	33	38	35
6–10	23	16	7	17	7	8
11–20	16	21	4	11	3	6
21–30	8	10	1	4	—	2
31–50	6	11	—	3	—	3
51–100	4	8	—	4	—	3
101+	1	8	—	1		8
Number of cases	2415	1237	1220	906	591	1402

It has sometimes been suggested that the male's capacity to be erotically aroused by *any* female, and even by a physically, mentally, and aesthetically unattractive, lower level prostitute, is a demonstration of the fact that he is not as dependent as females are upon psychologic factors for the achievement of satisfactory sexual relationships. On the contrary, the capacity of many males to respond to *any* type of female is actually a demonstration of the fact that psychologic conditioning, rather than the physical or the psychologic stimuli that are immediately present, is a chief source of his erotic response. As far as his psychologic responses are concerned, the male in many instances may not be having coitus with the immediate sexual partner, but with all of the other girls with whom he has ever had coitus, and with the entire genus Female with which he would like to have coitus.

32. Significance of Sexual Element in Marriage. Our data indicate that the average female marries to establish a home, to establish a long-time affectional relationship with a single spouse, and to have children whose welfare may become the prime business of her life. Most males would admit that all of these are desirable aspects of a marriage, but it is probable that few males would marry if they did not anticipate that they would have an opportunity to have coitus regularly with their wives. This is the one aspect of marriage which few males would forego, although they might be willing to accept a marriage that did not include some of the goals which the average female considers paramount.

Conversely, when a marriage fails to satisfy his sexual need, the male is more inclined to consider that it is unsatisfactory, and he is more ready than the female to dissolve the relationship. We have no statistical tabulation to substantiate these generalizations, but we have discussed the reasons for their marriages, and the reasons for maintaining their marriages, with some thousands of the females and males who have contributed to the present study.

It is too simple to dismiss these differences in female and male attitudes toward marriage as the product of innate moral differences between the sexes. Neither does it suffice to consider that these differences are a product of the female's greater importance in childbearing and in the preservation of the species. Whatever truth there may be in either of these assertions, it seems certain that these differences between female and male approaches to marriage depend primarily upon the fact that the average male is so conditionable that he has a greater need than most females have for a regular and frequent sexual outlet.

33. Social Factors Affecting Sexual Patterns. For males, we found (1948) that social factors were of considerable significance in determining patterns of sexual behavior. In the present volume we have found that social factors are of more minor significance in determining the patterns of sexual behavior among females.

For instance, we found that the educational level which the male ultimately attained showed a marked correlation with his patterns of sexual behavior (Table 175). Thus, the males who had ultimately

Table 175. Correlations Between Social Factors and Patterns of Sexual Behavior

Sexual activity	Educ.		Decade of birth		Age at onset of adol.		Relig.	
	♀	♂	♀	♂	♀	♂	♀	♂
Masturbation								
Accum. incid. (orgasm)	√	−	±	−	x	±	√	
Act. incid. (orgasm)	±	√	x	±	x	√	√	±
Freq., act. med. (orgasm)	x	√	x		x	±	−	√
Percent total outlet	±	√	−		x	x	±	x
Nocturnal dreams								
Accum. incid. (orgasm)	x	√	−		x	x	±	
Act. incid. (orgasm)	x	√	x	x	x	x	±	−
Freq., act. med. (orgasm)	x	±	x	x	x	x	x	x
Percent total outlet	x	±	x		x	x	x	±
Petting								
Accum. incid. (exper.)	x	x	√	±	x	x	−	
Accum. incid. (orgasm)	x	√	√	±	x	x	√	
Act. incid. (orgasm)	x	√	√	±	−	x	±	±
Freq., act. med. (orgasm)	x	−	x		x	x	x	x
Percent total outlet	x	√	±		x	x	x	−
Pre-marital coitus								
Accum. incid. (exper.)	x	√	√	−	−	√	√	
Accum. incid. (orgasm)	−	√	√	−	−	√	√	
Act. incid. (exper.)	±	√	√	−	−	±	√	√
Act. incid. (orgasm)	±	√	√	−	−	±	√	√
Freq., act. med. (exper.)	x	√	x		x	x	±	√
Freq., act. med. (orgasm)	x	√			x	x	±	√
Percent total outlet	±	√	√		−	−	±	√
Marital coitus								
Act. incid. (orgasm)	±	x	√	x	x	x	x	x
Freq., act. med. (exper.)	x	x	√			±	x	√
Freq., act. med. (orgasm)		x	±			±	x	√
Percent total outlet	−	±	±		x		±	−
Extra-marital coitus								
Act. incid. (exper.)	±	±	√		x		√	√
Freq., act. med. (exper.)	x	√	x		x		x	√
Percent total outlet	±	±	−		x		−	√
Homosexual								
Accum. incid. (orgasm)	±	−	x	x	x	√	√	±
Act. incid. (orgasm)	√	√	x	−	x	±	√	√
Freq., act. med. (orgasm)	±	−				x		
Percent total outlet	±	±	x		x	±	−	−
Total outlet								
Accum. incid.	±	x	±	x	x	x	√	x
Active incid.	−	x	±	x	−	x	√	−
Freq., act. med.	−	−	−		x	√	√	√

√ = marked correlation.   ± = some correlation.   − = little correlation.   x = no correlation.   Blanks = no data available.   ♀ = female.   ♂ = male.

gone on into college depended primarily on masturbation and much less frequently on coitus for their pre-marital outlet. On the other hand, the males who had not gone beyond grade school or early high school had drawn only half as much of their pre-marital outlet from masturbation, but they had drawn five times as much of their pre-marital outlet as the upper level males had from coitus. Similarly, kissing habits, breast manipulations, genital manipulations, mouth-genital contacts, positions in coitus, nudity during coitus, the acceptance of nudity or near-nudity during non-sexual activities, and many of the other items in the sexual behavior of a male, are usually in line with the pattern of behavior found among most of the other males in his social group. We have emphasized that such differences do not depend upon anything that is learned in school, for both lower level and upper level males may be together in the same grade school and high school, and the patterns are, for the most part, set soon after the mid-teens and before the average male ever goes on into college. We have emphasized that these differences in patterns of sexual behavior depend upon differences in the sexual attitudes of the different social levels in which the male is raised or into which he may move. This means that he is psychologically conditioned by the attitudes of the social group in which he is raised or toward which his educational attainments will lead him.

In contrast, in connection with most types of sexual activity we have found that patterns of sexual behavior among females show little or no correlation with the educational levels which the females ultimately attain (Table 175). In her pre-marital petting, pre-marital coitus, and extra-marital coitus, and in her total sexual outlet, there are some differences in the incidences and/or frequencies which appear to be correlated with the educational levels of the females, but the apparent differences prove to depend on the fact that marriage occurs at different ages in the different educational groups; and when the pre-marital activities are compared for the females who marry at about the same age, the average incidences and frequencies of these various types of sexual activity prove to be essentially the same in the several educational levels. This appears to mean, again, that females are not conditioned to the extent that males are conditioned by the attitudes of the social groups in which they live.

We have also shown that the age at onset of adolescence and the rural or urban backgrounds do not show as marked a correlation with the patterns of behavior among females as they do among males.

For both the females and males in our sample, degrees of religious devotion did correlate with the incidences of the various types of sexual activity, and devoutly religious backgrounds had prevented some of the females and males from ever engaging in certain types of sexual activity. The incidences of nearly all types of sexual activity except marital coitus were, in consequence, lower among the religiously more devout females and males, and higher among the religiously less devout (Table 175).

The degree of religious devotion, however, had continued to affect those males who finally did become involved in the morally disapproved types of activity, and the median frequencies of such activities were lower among the more devout males and higher among the less devout males (Table 175); but among those devout females who had become involved in morally disapproved types of activity, the average rates of activity were, on the whole, the same as those of the less devout females. This was true, for instance, of masturbation, of nocturnal dreams to orgasm, of pre-marital petting, of pre-marital coitus, and of homosexual contacts among females (Table 175). While religious restraints had prevented many of the females as well as the males from ever engaging in certain types of sexual activity, or had delayed the time at which they became involved, the religious backgrounds had had a minimum effect upon the females after they had once begun such activities.

SUMMARY AND COMPARISONS OF FEMALE AND MALE

We have, then, thirty-three bodies of data which agree in showing that the male is conditioned by sexual experience more frequently than the female. The male more often shares, vicariously, the sexual experiences of other persons, he more frequently responds sympathetically when he observes other individuals engaged in sexual activities, he may develop stronger preferences for particular types of sexual activity, and he may react to a great variety of objects which have been associated with his sexual activities. The data indicate that in all of these respects, fewer of the females have their sexual behavior affected by such psychologic factors.

It was in regard to only three of these items (moving pictures, reading romantic literature, and being bitten) that as many females as males, or more females than males, seem to have been affected. Fewer females than males were affected in regard to twenty-nine of the thirty-three items. There are instances in which the percentages of females who were affected were only slightly below the percentages of males who were affected; but in regard to twelve of these items, the number of females who were erotically aroused was less than half the number of males who were aroused.

There is tremendous individual variation in this regard, and there may be a third of the females in the population who are as frequently affected by psychologic stimuli as the average of the males. At the extreme of individual variation, there were, however, 2 to 3 per cent of the females who were psychologically stimulated by a greater variety of factors, and more intensely stimulated than any of the males in the sample. Their responses had been more immediate, they had responded more frequently, and they had responded to the point of orgasm with frequencies that had far exceeded those known for any male. A few of the females were regularly being stimulated by psychologic factors to the point of orgasm, and this almost never happens among any of the males.

Many of these differences between the sexual responses of females and males have been recognized for many centuries, and there have been various attempts to explain them. It has been suggested that they depend upon differences in the abundance or distribution of the sensory structures in the female and male body. It has been suggested that they depend upon differences in the roles which females and males take in coitus. It has been suggested that they are in some way associated with the different roles that females and males play in connection with reproduction. It has been suggested that there are differences in the levels of "sex drive" or "libido" or innate moral capacities of the two sexes. It has been suggested that the differences depend upon basic differences in the physiology of orgasm in females and males.

But we have already observed that the anatomy and physiology of sexual response and orgasm (Chapters 14 and 15) do not show differences between the sexes that might account for the differences in their sexual responses. Females appear to be as capable as males of being aroused by tactile stimuli; they appear as capable as males of responding to the point of orgasm. Their responses are not slower than those of the average male if there is any sufficiently continuous tactile stimulation. We find no reason for believing that the physiologic nature of orgasm in the female or the physical or physiologic or psychologic satisfactions derived from orgasm by the average female are different from those of the average male. But in their capacities to respond to psychosexual stimuli, the average female and the average male do differ.

The possibility of reconciling the different sexual interests and capacities of females and males, the possibility of working out sexual adjustments in marriage, and the possibility of adjusting social concepts to allow for these differences between females and males, will depend upon our willingness to accept the realities which the available data seem to indicate.

What physicochemical bases there may be for the similarities and differences between the psychosexual capacities of females and males is a matter that we shall undertake to explore in the chapters that follow (Chapters 17 and 18).

Chapter 17

NEURAL MECHANISMS OF SEXUAL RESPONSE

The data which we have now accumulated on the gross physiology and psychology of sexual response and orgasm make it possible to recognize some of the internal mechanisms which may be involved.

Since there are no essential differences between the responses of females and males to tactile and other sensory stimulation (Chapters 14, 15), such responses must depend upon internal mechanisms which are essentially the same in the two sexes. On the other hand, since there are marked differences between females and males in their responses to psychologic stimuli, it seems apparent that those responses must depend upon some mechanism which functions differently in the two sexes.

It is the function of the exploring scientist to describe what he finds, whether or no the observed phenomena are explainable in terms of the known anatomy and known physiologic processes. We have described, as far as we have been able to obtain the data, what happens to the mammalian body when it responds sexually. While it now seems possible to identify some of the internal mechanisms which may account for that behavior, at points we shall find that there is nothing yet known in neurologic or physiologic science which explains what we have found. These are the areas in which, it may be hoped, the neurologist and physiologist may do further research.

It has been important to understand the gross behavior of the sexually responding animal, for too much of the physiologic and experimental work has, so far, been concentrated on explaining the nature of genital responses, and has ignored the fact that all parts of the body may be involved whenever there is sexual response and orgasm. There have been studies of the effects of the stimulation of end organs of touch in genital and perineal areas, studies of the nerves that connect those end organs with lower portions of the spinal cord, studies of the sexual function of that end of the cord, and studies of the nerves that transmit impulses from the cord to the genital and pelvic structures which are involved in a sexual response. In addition, there have been studies of the possible function of certain portions of the brain, particularly of the cerebrum, in connection with sexual response; but, once again, they have been studies of cerebral function in connection with genital response.[1] The neurologic and experimental studies should now be extended in directions which may explain why the whole animal body is involved whenever there is any sort of sexual response.

EVIDENCE OF NERVOUS FUNCTION

There is nothing which needs to be emphasized more than this fact that the entire body of the animal is involved whenever there is any sexual response (Chapters 14, 15). We have pointed out that the tactile or other sensory stimulation of *any* part of the body, and not of the genitalia alone, may initiate these responses. We have pointed out that psychologic stimulation may, in many instances, bring responses that are quite identical with those effected by tactile stimulation. We have pointed out that sexual responses may involve changes in the function of the circulatory system, of the respiratory system, of the sensory capacities of the animal, of all of the glands of the body, and of the muscular activities in every part of the body. We have shown that orgasm is similarly a function of the whole animal body. The internal mechanisms which are responsible for such activity must be mechanisms which can affect all parts of the body. There are three such mechanisms which, conceivably, might accomplish that end.

1. Chain Reactions. The action of any part of an animal's body may be directly responsible for a chain of activities—a series of successive steps in which each act initiates the succeeding act in the chain. Such a chain of responses may be involved, for instance, when the driver of an automobile steers his course along a particular path, and is able to pass other cars without consciously planning the movements of his steering gear. His sensory perception of the objects which lie ahead, his adjustments for the distances which are involved, for the speed of his own car, for the speed of the approaching car, and for the movements of his hands or arms which may steer him safely past the approaching car, may represent such a chain of responses. The initial action is responsible for the next action and that in turn determines the following act, until the ultimate end is achieved.

It has been suggested that sexual activities similarly represent chains of responses. It has been suggested that the stimulation of end organs,

---

[1] For neurologic studies of the genital area see, for instance: Eberth 1904. Marshall 1922:264–272. Stone 1923b:88–90, 104. Semans and Langworthy 1938. Bard 1940:556 ff. Kuntz 1945:304–323. Hooker in Howell (Fulton edit.) 1949:1202–1205. Kuntz 1951:101–106. For studies of the brain in relation to sexual response, see for example: Bard 1934, 1936, 1939, 1940, 1942. Brooks 1937. Rioch 1938. Stier 1938. Klüver and Bucy 1938, 1939. Davis 1939. Maes 1939. Dempsey and Rioch 1939. Beach 1940, 1942a, 1942b, 1943, 1944, 1947a, 1947b. Brookhart, Dey, and Ranson 1941. Brookhart and Dey 1941. Dey, Leininger, and Ranson 1942. Clark 1942. Langworthy 1944.

and the consequent stimulation of the nerves which connect those end organs with the lower end of the spinal cord, and of the nerves which go from the cord to the muscle fibers in the walls of the circulatory system, may directly account for the rises in pulse rate and blood pressure and for the increased peripheral circulation which is responsible for the tumescence of various body structures during sexual response. It has been proposed that these circulatory disturbances are then responsible for the changes which are to be observed in the breathing rate, and that these physiologic disturbances are responsible for the spectacular muscular activities which characterize sexual response. But the present data do not show that these phenomena appear in sequence, one after the other.[2] On the contrary, there is an instantaneous and simultaneous appearance of all of these physiologic changes as soon as the animal is stimulated and begins to respond.

It is not impossible that there are some aspects of the later developments in sexual response—like the ultimate build-up of neuromuscular tensions, the increasing loss of sensory perception, and the ultimate disturbance of the breathing rate as an individual approaches orgasm —which may be products of physiologic developments which appear earlier in the course of the sexual activity. But this cannot be true of most of the phenomena which appear during sexual response and orgasm. A rise in pulse rate, a rise in blood pressure, a rise in breathing rate, a diminution of the capacity for sensory perception, glandular secretions, and a development of neuromuscular tensions over the whole body, appear to develop simultaneously, sometimes within a fraction of a second, as soon as the animal is stimulated and begins to respond.

2. **Blood-Distributed Agents.** The coordination of the functions of separated parts of the body is sometimes effected through blood-circulated agents, such as hormones (Chapter 18). For instance, many of the physiologic aspects of certain emotional reactions, such as anger, may be duplicated by the injection of adrenaline into the blood stream, and it is generally understood that the appearance of raised pulse rates, raised blood pressures, and still other aspects of an angry animal may be a direct product of the secretion of adrenaline from the adrenal glands into the blood stream. But the speed with which sexual responses may occur is far greater than that which could be effected by any blood-circulated substance such as adrenaline. While it may not take more than a few seconds for adrenaline to be carried by the blood over short distances in the animal's body, it takes a longer time for it to circulate to all parts of the body. Sexual responses, how-

---

[2] Beach 1947b:241 also points out the inadequacy of a chain reaction hypothesis in sexual response.

ever, may be initiated, carried through their complex course, and completed within a matter of seconds (p. 605).

It is possible that there is adrenaline secretion during the more advanced stages of any protracted sexual activity, and this in the late stages of sexual response may reenforce some of the physiologic changes which the nervous system has initiated; but adrenaline cannot be responsible for most of the changes which appear as soon as there is sexual stimulation.

3. **Nervous Mechanisms.** Our best reasons for believing that sexual responses must depend primarily upon nervous mechanisms are the speed with which all parts of an animal's body may become involved, the steady and convulsive build-up of neuromuscular tensions as the action develops, the abrupt build-up of tensions at the approach of orgasm, the remarkable rigidity which may develop just before orgasm, the explosive discharge of neuromuscular tensions at orgasm, and the abrupt cessation of tension after orgasm. There are no other means of intercommunication which act as quickly as nervous mechanisms, and no other mechanism that can bring so nearly simultaneous reactions from all parts of the body. The gradual and steady accumulation of neuromuscular tensions during sexual arousal is a known characteristic of some other nervously controlled responses. The explosive discharge which characterizes orgasm is the sort of phenomenon that cannot be ascribed to anything except a neural mechanism.

Finally, the electroencephalograms which are now available (Figure 140, p. 630) show that there are remarkable changes in brain potentials in the course of sexual response, and that it is the development of these and their sudden release at orgasm which provide the most characteristic aspects of sexual response and orgasm.[3] For these several reasons, the search for the mechanisms of sexual response may be concentrated primarily upon the structure and function of the vertebrate nervous system.

TACTILE STIMULATION AND REFLEX ARCS

It is obvious from the record which we have already given, as well as from everyday experience, that physical contacts, touch, and pressure may bring sexual responses only because there are sensory structures in the external surface of the animal's body which respond to such stimulation. These sensory structures are the end organs of touch, and it is on these that many sexual responses depend.

---

[3] Dr. Abraham Mosovich has been kind enough to communicate to us the as yet unpublished results of his electroencephalographic research and has sent us some sample electroencephalograms. See page 630.

We have already pointed out that end organs which are sensitive to such other physical stimuli as light, heat, and sound may also be involved, but we have emphasized that there are no experimental data which show exactly how these other end organs function in connection with sexual response (p. 590).

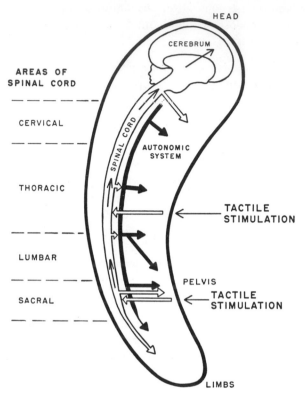

Figure 141. Diagram of neural mechanisms in mammalian sexual response to tactile stimulation

The stimulus received by any such organ is transmitted by afferent (in-going) nerves to the spinal cord. The cord in turn may transmit the impulses by efferent (out-going) nerves to those muscles with which they are directly connected (Figure 141). This may lead to a spontaneous and quite involuntary action of muscles which can be and are ordinarily voluntarily controlled. The prominent muscular action of the pelvis and lower limbs may be accounted for as the direct product of such a simple reflex arc. Because the stimulation of any part of the cord may be extended to all parts of the cord, the reflex arcs may involve not only the particular part of the body which was originally stimulated, but other parts of the body as well. Genital stimulation, for instance, brings not only pelvic responses but responses of the muscles in every other part of the body (see pp. 586, 618 for a further discussion).[4]

A major portion of the experimental work that has been done on the physiology of sexual response has been concerned with these relatively simple aspects of the problem, and the location of those areas of the spinal cord which are concerned with a major portion of the pelvic and lower limb responses is specifically known.

FUNCTION OF THE SACRO-LUMBAR AREA

The experimental work has shown that lower portions of the cord, namely, the sacral and lumbar areas (Figure 141), are the mediating centers upon which genital reflexes and pelvic responses depend.[5] As long as the end organs and the afferent nerves are intact, and as long as the sacro-lumbar areas of the cord and the efferent nerves are intact, it is possible to secure pelvic responses and responses of the lower limbs even though other portions of the cord and considerable portions of the brain of the animal may be damaged. This is demonstrated when the cord is actually cut above the sacro-lumbar area in laboratory experiments with animals. It is also demonstrated by human paraplegics. These are individuals who have had the spinal cord injured or cut at some point above the sacro-lumbar area as the result of an accident, some surgical operation, or some other damage.

An animal that has the cord damaged above the sacro-lumbar area may respond to tactile stimulation of its genitalia, perineum, or other pelvic areas, and may still become tumescent in those areas, develop a genital erection, and reach orgasm.[6] Unfortunately, because the full

---

[4] Impulses originating in tactile stimulation of the pelvic area are transmitted to the sacral area of the cord chiefly by way of the internal pudendal nerve. The efferent impulses include spinal impulses which travel via the internal pudendal nerve to the muscles about the genitalia, causing them to tense. Parasympathetic impulses travel via the erigens nerves to the blood vessels of the genital area, causing tumescence. The striped muscles of the pelvic area and lower limbs are thrown into spasm by spinal impulses from the sacral area; the smooth muscle is thrown into spasm by sympathetic impulses originating in the lumbar area, traveling to the genitalia mainly via the hypogastric nerves. See, for instance: Stone 1923b:89–90, 94, 104. Semans and Langworthy 1938. Kuntz 1945:308–312. Munro et al. 1948:903–910. Hooker in Howell (Fulton edit.) 1949:1203–1204. Whitelaw and Smithwick 1951: 121–130.

[5] That a sacral center mediates tumescence and a lumbar center mediates ejaculation and corresponding muscular contractions in the female is generally accepted in the literature. See: Kuntz 1945:309, 322–323. Talbot 1949:266. However, sacral nerves may play a part in ejaculation according to Munro et al. 1948:910, and lumbar nerves may also be involved in tumescence according to: Kuntz 1945:308–309. Root and Bard 1947:87–89.

[6] Erection and ejaculation in an animal with a severed spinal cord is noted, for example, in: Marshall 1922:264–265. Bard 1940:556. Beach 1942a:213, 215. Munro et al. 1948. Fulton 1949:140. Talbot 1949:266–267 (a concise discussion of the effects of cord damage to sexual function).

extent of the physiologic changes which occur in sexual response has not hitherto been comprehended, there are no good data on the responses which probably occur in the lower limbs of such an experimental animal.

When the human paraplegic receives genital or pelvic stimulation, he does not feel the stimulation or the consequent physiologic changes

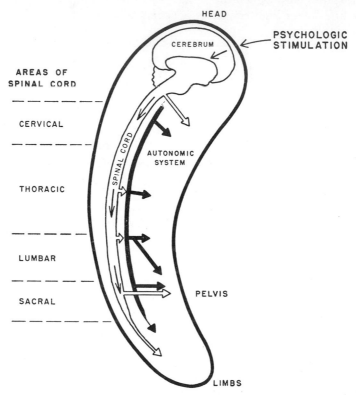

Figure 142. Diagram of neural mechanisms in mammalian sexual response to psychologic stimulation

in those areas, although he may observe them; and he is not conscious of sexual satisfaction when he has coitus or engages in other sexual activities, even though he may come to erection and reach orgasm. This indicates that a brain, and a cord which is intact between the level of stimulation and the brain, are necessary for the attainment of that change of physiologic state which the human animal recognizes as sexual satisfaction. A paraplegic may, however, be conscious of tactile stimulation of portions of the body innervated by nerves which connect with those parts of the cord that are located above the point of damage, and may receive erotic satisfaction from the stimulation of an upper portion of his or her body, even when the pelvis and lower limbs are unresponsive (p. 700).[7]

Psychologic stimulation, depending primarily on the function of the cerebrum (p. 710), may also effect pelvic and lower-limb responses. This also depends, to a considerable degree, on the sacro-lumbar areas of the cord (Figure 142). If those portions of the cord are completely removed in an experimental animal, or seriously damaged in a human subject, or if those areas are separated from the brain by a complete cutting (transection) of the cord above the sacro-lumbar areas, then psychologic stimulation no longer brings pelvic or genital or lower-limb responses.[8]

The cat is one of the experimental animals in which the sacral area of the cord and all of the lumbar area except the uppermost (the first lumbar) segment may be removed without eliminating the animal's responses to the tactile stimulation of genital or other pelvic areas, or its responses to psychologic stimulation. But in the case of this animal it has been demonstrated that such responses are largely eliminated if the first lumbar segment is also removed. This upper end of the lumbar area is connected with the genital area by the hypogastric nerve which is one of the branches of the so-called autonomic system, and this appears to be at least one of the paths by which nervous impulses which are the product of psychologic stimulation are transmitted to the genital area (Figure 142).[9] On the other hand, in man and in some of the other mammals in which there are other connections (additional to the hypogastric nerve) between portions of the spinal cord which are anterior to the sacro-lumbar areas, and other parts of the autonomic nervous system, it is not improbable that there may be some residue of pelvic response when the entire sacro-lumbar area is removed. There is need for a more exact examination of this matter in further work with experimental animals and with clinical cases in the human animal. However, since the human paraplegics who have had the connection between the brain and the sacro-lumbar area completely severed, report failures to achieve erection through

[7] The inability of the true paraplegic to perceive orgasm is noted in Munro et al. 1948:905, 909–910, implied in Talbot 1949:269, and recorded by Dr. L. W. Freeman (verbal communic.). Hyndman and Wolkin 1943:144 add "For . . . orgasm to be sensually appreciated, the spinal connections with the brain must, of course, be intact."

[8] The inability of psychologic stimulation to effect genital response after damage to the cord above the lumbar area is discussed in: Hyndman and Wolkin 1943:143–144. Kuntz 1945:309. Root and Bard 1947:87–88. Talbot 1949: 266–267. Hooker in Howell (Fulton edit.) 1949:1203. Even compression of the cord may produce erectile impotence in humans. Cf. Elsberg 1925:66, 132, 308.

[9] By-passing of a transection of the cord via the hypogastric nerve is described for the cat by Root and Bard 1947:86–89.

psychologic stimulation, it is probable that the major portion of the responses of the pelvic areas and of the lower limbs even in the human species depend upon the integrity of at least the upper segments of the lumbar area, and upon the existence of intact connections between the brain and that portion of the cord.

The importance of the sacro-lumbar area of the cord was one of the first things known about the neurology of sexual response. As early as 1863 it was known that the direct electrical stimulation of certain sacral areas would bring genital erection and other sexual responses from laboratory mammals, and this subsequently was demonstrated for human subjects.[10]

It has also been known for half a century that ejaculation may be effected by the direct stimulation of certain sacro-lumbar areas.[11] Unfortunately, however, most of the neurologists and laboratory experimentalists have taken orgasm and ejaculation to be synonymous phenomena. Since we now understand that this is not so (pp. 634–636), it seems possible that the prostate and other glands which are necessary to effect ejaculation may be brought into action by the direct stimulation of sacral centers without the development of responses that are sexual in any strict sense. Consequently all of this work needs to be reviewed for evidence that a true orgasm may be effected as a result of the direct stimulation of these sacro-lumbar centers. It should be recalled that the mechanical stimulation of the prostate gland via the rectum, as in a prostatic massage, may bring an exudation of semen from the penis and sometimes a propulsive exudation which appears to be an ejaculation, even when there is no genital erection or other evidence of sexual response.

On the other hand, it is also to be noted that the stimulation of the interior of the rectum, of the sort that is involved in a prostatic massage, may also exert pressure upon the perineal nerve masses (page 585), and it is known that this may bring specifically sexual responses with orgasm. This is frequently realized by persons who have been the recipients in anal coitus, and apparently may sometimes be involved in the ejaculatory responses which occur during a prostatic massage.

Both the laboratory experimental work and the work with human subjects have further demonstrated that genital erection and responses

[10] In 1863 Eckhardt found that stimulation of the erigens nerves produced erection in the dog. Also see footnote 4.

[11] For a detailed description of the production of erection and ejaculation through electrical stimulation of the sacral segments, see: Durfee, Lerner, and Kaplan 1940. Also see footnote 4. As early as 1863 Eckhardt noted that tactile stimulation of the penis could not cause erection in a dog whose pudendal nerve was severed, and in 1879 Nikolsky reported contraction of penile blood vessels on cutting the erigens nerves. See Kuntz 1945:308.

to the point of orgasm usually depend upon the integrity of the pudendal and erigens nerves, which are efferent nerves connecting the sacral area of the cord with the muscles of the genital and pelvic areas. If these nerves are accidentally damaged or surgically cut, erection in the male is no longer effected. The effect of damage to the pudendal nerve of the female has not been clearly recorded in the experimental or medical literature.

In the course of mammalian evolution the forepart of the brain has been the portion of the central nervous system which has evolved most elaborately. There are fewer basic differences between the sacro-lumbar areas of the cord in the human animal and the sacro-lumbar areas in the lower mammals. The importance of the sacro-lumbar areas in sexual response explains why we find human sexual behavior much closer to the sexual behavior of the infra-human species, and even of the lower mammalian species, than most persons might have anticipated and than some persons would like to believe.

ROLE OF UPPER PORTIONS OF CORD

In regard to sexual response there is very little precise information concerning the role of those portions of the cord which lie above (anterior) to the sacro-lumbar area. As long as genital and pelvic responses were considered the major portion or even the whole of sexual response, and as long as the demonstrated function of the sacro-lumbar area seemed to account for all genital and pelvic responses, there was a tacit assumption that the thoracic and cervical areas of the cord had little or no direct connection with sexual behavior. The integrity of these upper portions of the cord was obviously necessary for the transmission of psychologic stimulation from the cerebrum to the genital and pelvic areas, but, apart from that, there has been little experimental work to show what role this upper end of the cord may have in sexual response.[12]

If, however, it is understood that tactile stimulation of other portions of the mammalian body quite apart from the genital and pelvic areas may bring some sort of sexual response, and even full and complete sexual response to the point of orgasm, it becomes difficult to believe that the stimulation of the upper end of the trunk of the animal or of the mouth or other portions of the head of the animal is transmitted

---

[12] Bilateral anterior chordotomy, the partial transection of the cord to relieve intractable pain, usually interferes with or prevents tumescence and orgasm in both sexes. The transection is usually done above the lumbar area. Hyndman and Wolkin 1943:143 conclude that the operation ". . . is almost certain to abolish erection and orgasm in the male and orgasm in the female . . . the desire for intercourse is not abolished." Stookey 1943:430 adds, "In the male, ejaculation becomes impossible; erection is not interfered with but orgasm is lost. In the female also there may be a loss of orgasm."

to the sacro-lumbar areas of the cord before it brings response. It is more reasonable to believe that the stimulation of end organs in the upper end of the mammalian body is mediated through thoracic or cervical spinal centers, and that these directly effect sexual response not only of the upper end of the body itself, but of the whole of the animal body which is involved during the sexual response. Because of the complexity of the neural anatomy at this point, and because of the lack of specific experimental work in this area, we can do no more than draw attention to the possibility and hope that additional data may be gathered on the point.

We have already drawn attention (p. 694) to the evidence which suggests that the stimulation of any area of the cord spreads throughout the length of the cord, and that this effects the movement of muscles in the upper portions of the body by way of the spinal nerves which lead out of corresponding portions of the cord. These nerves connect directly with the muscles in the upper portions of the body and are apparently responsible for their action during sexual response and orgasm.

One body of data which shows something of the function of the upper end of the cord comes from a single case of a human female paraplegic in whom an operation had severed the damaged cord above the sacro-lumbar area. While psychologic stimulation did not bring any pelvic reactions from the subject, she claimed that tactile stimulation of the upper end of her body (apparently centered about the breasts) did bring sexual response which led to complete orgasm. There appeared to be a build-up of neuromuscular tensions and the explosive release which characterizes orgasm, although the orgasm involved only the upper parts of the body and did not involve the pelvic area. Because the portion of the body which was involved in orgasm was connected with the brain, the subject was conscious of the sexual arousal and found satisfaction in the orgasm.[13]

There are some other cases in which an awareness of tactile stimulation remains in the intact portion of the body even though no erotic satisfaction is derived from such tactile stimulation. It would be very important to accumulate data on these points from additional cases of true paraplegics.

Unfortunately, the medical literature is badly confused by the fact that many of these supposedly paraplegic cases may have had some injury which did not sever the cord. Some of the reported cases of paraplegics suddenly becoming capable of full sexual function when

---

[13] This case was brought to our attention by Dr. L. W. Freeman of the Indiana University Medical Faculty.

there is a sufficient stimulus, probably depend upon the fact that the cord, although it may have been considerably damaged, was never completely severed.[14] It is doubtful whether any true paraplegic ever maintained voluntary control over the lower portion of his or her body. Consequently it is important to sharply distinguish the records on the sexual performances of supposed paraplegics from the records of individuals in whom the cord is definitely known to have been severed.

ROLE OF AUTONOMIC NERVOUS SYSTEM

While the central nervous system, meaning the brain and the spinal cord, is directly connected by afferent nerves with the peripheral end organs which receive sensory stimuli, and by efferent nerves which transmit impulses to other organs of the body and consequently effect muscular action, the autonomic nervous system (Figures 141, 142) is not directly connected with any peripheral end organs and cannot be brought into direct action by the stimulation of end organs of touch or other types of sense organs. The activities which animals voluntarily undertake are controlled by the central nervous system. There is ordinarily no voluntary control of the action of the autonomic nervous system.

The main trunks of the sympathetic division of the autonomic nervous system lie parallel and close to the spinal cord. Throughout the length of the cord there are nerve connections between it and the autonomic system, and consequently the autonomic system may be brought into action by the stimulation of the cord at various levels. It may also be brought into action by the direct stimulation of blood-circulated substances such as adrenaline. Most of the autonomic nervous system consists of fine and highly branched nerves that spread throughout the body in a fashion that sometimes makes it very difficult for the neurologist to determine with any exactitude what nerves are connected with a given organ.

It is customary to think of the autonomic nervous system as consisting of two main parts, the sympathetic and parasympathetic groups of nerves. Although physiologists and neurologists have become increasingly aware that these two parts do not function independently, and that there is no sharp differentiation of the action of the two at many points, the classification has provided a useful basis for thinking in regard to certain points, and there are some of the body functions

---

[14] Without additional operations or autopsy it is difficult to determine if transection is complete, and information on sexual function is confusing. For example, Talbot, J. Nerv. Ment. Dis. 1952:360–361, states that 20 per cent of a group of paraplegics and quadriplegics experienced erection from psychologic stimulation. Note that Talbot 1949:266–268 states that complete transection precludes all cortical influence but found 8 presumably complete transection cases experiencing erection from psychologic stimuli.

which may depend primarily upon one or the other of the branches of the autonomic system. Anatomically the two portions of the autonomic system are not wholly discrete, for they lie closely parallel at many points and sympathetic nerves may actually fuse at some points with parasympathetic nerves.

Moreover, the stimulation of the sympathetic branch of the system produces a chemical substance (sympathin) which acts as a hormone, producing many of the same results which follow the secretion of adrenaline from the adrenal glands or the injection of the drug adrenaline. The most specific action of sympathin is its effect upon the parasympathetic system, and this is brought into action whenever the sympathetic system is stimulated. Similarly, however, stimulation of the parasympathetic system leads to the secretion of acetylcholine, which has a specific action on sympathetic nerves and brings that portion of the system into play. This accounts for the fact that in many emotional situations the responses of an animal may involve physiologic changes which may be attributed to both sympathetic and parasympathetic controls. This is exactly what we find in regard to the physiology of sexual response; and in the present volume we shall not attempt to suggest which aspects of sexual response may depend upon one or the other portion of the autonomic system.

Actually both portions of the autonomic system are usually involved when any portion of the system comes into action in the course of a sexual response, for the parts of the body which are primarily under autonomic control (such as the heart, the glands, and the smooth muscles) are supplied with both sympathetic and parasympathetic nerve fibers. These two types of nerve fibers act antagonistically on the organ and they may thus exert a slight but constant (tonic) effect on it. A given organ, therefore, will be stimulated or inhibited almost instantaneously depending on (1) the strength of the impulse, and (2) whether the impulse reaches it through the sympathetic or parasympathetic system. Because of the complexity of the interrelationships and the delicate balance which exists here, it is not surprising that some organs may be dominated by the parasympathetic system at the same time that other organs are being controlled by the sympathetic system. It is, moreover, to be remembered that most of the organs which are reached by the autonomic nervous system also have sensory nerves which connect with the central nervous system, and may be affected by reflexes which develop in that part of the nervous system.

Many of the physiologic activities which we have found characteristic of sexual response probably do not represent any direct reaction via a reflex arc. The efferent spinal nerves leading from the sacrolumbar areas can account for only some of the genital, pelvic, and lower-limb responses during sexual activity. Most of the activity must depend primarily upon the action of the autonomic nervous system which is brought into play through nerves which originate in the sacro-lumbar areas and in other parts of the cord. The instantaneous involvement during sexual response of those portions of the body, such as the heart, which are for the most part beyond voluntary control, constitutes strong evidence that the autonomic nervous system is involved.[15]

The following aspects of the gross physiology of sexual response are among those that apparently depend upon the action of the autonomic system:

Increase in pulse rate
Increase in blood pressure
Vasodilation
Increase in peripheral circulation of blood
Tumescence of distensible parts of body
Reduced rate of bleeding
Hyperventilation
Irregular breathing
Increase in genital secretions
Increase in salivary secretion
Increase in lacrimal secretion
Gastro-intestinal activity inhibited
Hair raised
Eye pupil dilated
Ejaculation

Reference to Table 176 will show that more of the elements in sexual response appear to depend on parasympathetic than on sympathetic function.

The autonomic system, like the sacro-lumbar area, is ancient in mammalian heritage, and the similarities between human and infra-human sexual responses probably depend, for the most part, upon the fact that these two are the portions of the nervous system which are chiefly responsible for human sexual responses. The physiology of human sexual response depends only to a minimum degree upon the more highly evolved human brain (p. 708).

THE SEXUAL SYNDROME

We have already pointed out that the most distinctive aspect of any sexual response is the fact that it is a group, a cluster, a syndrome of physiologic elements, all of which usually appear whenever there is

---

[15] Kuntz 1945:313 is one of the few others who have concluded that the entire autonomic system is involved in sexual response.

any sort of sexual response. But nearly all of the elements of sexual response are found in other situations, particularly in other emotional responses and most particularly in anger (Table 176).[16] Actually the sexual elements which are not found in anger are to be found in epilepsy, but there is no other sort of behavioral response which in-

Table 176. Physiologic Elements in the Sexual Syndrome, Anger, Fear, Epilepsy, and Pain

Physiologic element	Neural mech.	Sexual resp.	Anger	Fear	Epi-lepsy	Pain
Increase in pulse rate	symp.	√	√	√	may	√
Increase in blood pressure	symp.?	√	√	√	may	√
Vasodilation	para.	√	may	no	√	
Increased periph. circ. of blood	para.	√	may	no	may	
Tumescence	para.	√	rare	rare	rare	rare
Reduced rate of bleeding	symp.	√	√	√		√
Hyperventilation	symp.	√	√	√		√
Breathing irregularity		√	√	√	may	√
Anoxia		?			√	
Diminished sensory perception		√	√	√	√	√
Increase in genital secretions		√	no	no		
Increase in salivary secretion	para.	√	√	no	√	no
Increase in lacrimal secretion		√				√
Increase in perspiration	para. + symp.	occas.		√		√
Adrenaline secretion	symp.	√ ?	√	√		√
Increase in muscular tensions	spinal symp.	√	√	√	√	√
Increase in muscular capacity		√	√	√		
Involuntary muscular activity	spinal	√	√	√	√	√
Rhythmic muscular movements	spinal	√	no?	no	may	no
Gastro-intest. activ. inhibited	symp.	√ ?	√	√		√
Hair raised	symp.	may	√	√		may
Eye pupil dilated	symp.	√	√	√	√	√
Ejaculation	spinal symp.	√	rare	rare	may	
Involuntary vocalization		√	√	√	√	√

√ = physiologic element is present. **No** = element is absent. **May** = element sometimes but not always present. **Symp.** = sympathetic division of autonomic system. **Para.** = parasympathetic portion of autonomic system. **Blanks** = data not available.

volves all of the elements which may be found in sexual response. One might hypothesize that if certain of the physiologic elements were prevented from developing in a sexual response, or taken away from a sexual response, the individual might be left in a state of anger or fear, or in some other emotional state. The fact that frustrated sexual responses so readily turn into anger and rage might thus be explained. On the other hand, it not infrequently happens, both in the lower mammals and in man, that anger, fighting, and quarrels suddenly turn into sexual responses.

The close relationship of sexual responses and these other emotional states can best be seen by a more detailed examination of the physiology of anger, fear, and epilepsy.

---

[16] The physiology of the emotions is summarized in such sources as: Prince 1914. Cannon 1927. Bard 1934, 1939. Shock in Reymert 1950.

Anger. The closest parallel to the picture of sexual response is found in the known physiology of anger. Table 176 shows fourteen items which usually appear in both situations. There is, of course, some variation under differing conditions, but the items which are usually identical or closely parallel in anger and the sexual syndrome are the following:

Increase in pulse rate
Increase in blood pressure
Vasodilation (sometimes)
Increase in peripheral circulation of blood
Reduced rate of bleeding
Hyperventilation
Anoxia (probably)
Diminution of sensory perception
Adrenaline secretion (probably)
Increase in muscular tensions
Reduction of fatigue and/or increased muscular capacity
Gastro-intestinal activity inhibited (in sex?)
Hair raised (at least in other mammals)
Involuntary vocalization

There are four respects in which the physiology of anger does not fit the known physiology of sex.

1. In sexual response there is an invariable increase in surface temperatures, color, and tumescence during sexual arousal; but in anger there is sometimes (but not always) a vasoconstriction which makes the face of the angry person white, although this may alternate with a flushing of the face which indicates a peripheral flow of blood. Genital tumescence is the more or less inevitable outcome of sexual response in the uninhibited adult animal, short of old age, and while penile erections may sometimes appear in anger, particularly among the infra-human mammals and among pre-adolescent human males, they are not usual.

2. Genital (Cowper's, Bartholin, and cervical) secretions appear with sexual arousal, but apparently not in anger.

3. The most distinctive aspect of sexual physiology is the rhythmic muscular movement which develops when an individual is sexually aroused. These movements include the pelvic thrusts which constitute the copulatory movements among mammals. Such muscular movements do not appear when one is simply angry.

4. Orgasm is a phenomenon which is unique to sexual response. On those rare occasions in which it develops in anger, it is possible that it represents the development of a true sexual response.

Fear. The physiology of fear involves a number of the elements which appear in sexual activity, but fear is not as close as anger is to the sexual syndrome (Table 176). There are nine items in the physiology of fear that are identical with those in a sexual response:

Increase in pulse rate
Increase in blood pressure
Hyperventilation
Diminution of sensory perception
Adrenaline secretion (probably)
Increase in muscular tensions
Reduction of fatigue and/or increased muscular capacity
Hair raised
Involuntary vocalization

On the other hand there are five aspects of the sexual syndrome which are opposites of those found in fear: a peripheral circulation of blood, a vasodilation, genital secretions, salivary secretions, and involuntary and rhythmic muscular movements. The most distinctive aspect of fear which is lacking in a sexual response, is the vasoconstriction which causes the blanching of the face. The rhythmic muscular flow which is so characteristic of a sexual response is lacking in fear. Genital erections only occasionally appear when an individual is afraid, and orgasm is still more rare.[17] In such a case, it is possible that the fear has given way to a sexual response.

Epilepsy. The physiology of epilepsy includes eight or more elements of the sexual syndrome (Table 176).[18] In both epilepsy and sexual response there are:

Increase in pulse rate (sometimes)
Increase in blood pressure
Vasodilation
Anoxia
Diminution of sensory perception
Increase in salivary secretion
Increase in muscular tensions
Rhythmic muscular movements
Involuntary vocalization

The most remarkable parallel lies in the similarity of the spasmodic muscular movements in epilepsy and the tensions and muscular move-

---

[17] Ejaculation from fright was noted as early as Aristotle [384–322 B.C.]: Problems, Bk. IV:877a; Bk. XXVII:949a. We have a few instances in our own case histories.
[18] For the symptoms of epilepsy, see such a standard work as Penfield and Erickson 1941.

ments which are part of the build-up toward orgasm. The extreme rigidity which develops in the build-up to orgasm, and particularly just before orgasm, provides an especially close parallel to the states of tension in epilepsy. On at least some (rare?) occasions orgasm may occur during epilepsy. An even more striking similarity to epileptic movements is to be seen in the more extreme types of spasm which may follow orgasm. Persons who have seen both epileptic seizures and the more extreme types of orgasm have invariably been impressed by the similarities between the two.[19] The electroencephalograms which are now available show a striking resemblance between sexual response and epileptoid reactions (Figure 140). This is true in the period of the build-up toward orgasm, in the rigidity which precedes orgasm, and in the often violent, convulsive movements which follow orgasm.

If the cerebrum is considerably damaged in an accident or by some operation, the body of the individual may become continuously rigid in what is known as a tonic decerebrate rigidity. Such a rigid state is described as a true release phenomenon which results from an interference with the function that the brain ordinarily exercises in controlling muscular tension. The situation in which muscular tensions alternate with movements of the sort which characterize an epileptic seizure has been interpreted to be a "transient decerebrate rigidity."[20] Persons in a state of tonic decerebrate rigidity present the most striking parallel we have seen with certain moments in sexual activity, and particularly in the tensions which immediately precede orgasm. In decerebrate rigidity the body is stretched out to its maximum, the gluteal muscles are tensed and the buttocks tightly appressed, the legs and the arms are usually extended and stiffly held under tension, the feet may be pointed in line with the legs, the toes may be curled or spread, the fingers are flexed and strongly tensed, the back may be arched, and the neck may be so tensed that the head is held at a stiff angle. In all of these respects, tonic decerebrate rigidity matches what may be seen, in a transient state, in both epilepsy and in sexual activity.[21]

---

[19] Some of the earliest writers to draw attention to the similarities between epilepsy and sexual response included Democritus (ca. 420 B.C.), who was quoted as saying that orgasm is like a small epileptic seizure (see: Clement of Alexandria; Paedagogus Bk. II, ch. X, and K. Freeman 1949:306). Aretaeus (2nd–3rd cent. A.D.) cites the similarity in "On the Cure of Chronic Diseases" Bk. I, ch. IV. The latter also noted erection and ejaculation in epilepsy in his "On the Causes and Symptoms of Acute Diseases" Bk. I, ch. V. Erection and ejaculation are sometimes listed as epileptic sequelae in modern medical literature, as in: Hyman 1945:1515.

[20] The concept of the spasms in epilepsy depending on a transient decerebrate rigidity is introduced, for example, in Penfield and Erickson 1941:87.

[21] The postural and muscular similarities existing between decerebrate rigidity and the body just before orgasm are exemplified by the photograph in Penfield and Erickson 1941:fig. 21, p. 86. The rotation of the arm, so characteristic of decerebration, is not, however, a part of the sexual syndrome.

ROLE OF THE BRAIN IN SEXUAL RESPONSE

In its embryonic origin the brain has three main areas: the fore-brain, the midbrain, and the hindbrain. In the evolution of the verte-brates, the forebrain is the portion which has become most highly evolved, reaching its acme of complexity in the primates and some other higher mammals and, of course, particularly in the human ani-mal. The chief contributions which this developed forebrain makes to human sexual behavior are: (1) an increase in the capacity to be psy-chologically stimulated by a diversity of erotic situations; (2) an in-crease in the possibilities of conditioning; and (3) an increase in the capacity to develop inhibitions which interfere with the spinal and autonomic controls of sexual behavior. This curious mixture is what many persons identify as "an intelligent control of the sexual instincts."

The cerebrum of the mammal is derived from the embryonic fore-brain. Sexual and emotional functions have been ascribed to certain areas of the cerebrum, including the frontal lobes, the occipital lobes, the parietal lobes, and the temporal lobes. These four areas constitute the great bulk of the human brain.

Frontal Lobes. Although the frontal lobes occupy a considerable space in the human brain, their exact function has constituted a mys-tery. Accidental damage to the frontal lobes and surgical operations on the frontal lobes have variously been reported as having no effect, or a variety of diverse and often contradictory effects. This has been true, for instance, of the reports on the effects of frontal lobe operations on the sexual function. There were early reports to the effect that frontal lobe operations considerably reduced the "sex drive" of the individual, and optimistic clinical claims that the patterns of sexual behavior might be modified by such operations.[22] The possibilities of such op-erations have, once again, been seized upon by those who are inter-ested in controlling persons whose sexual activities they consider so-cially undesirable, and some clinical reports have encouraged the idea that homosexual could be changed into heterosexual patterns of be-havior, that exhibitionists would lose their compulsions to exhibit, that highly responsive persons might become mild and relatively unrespon-sive. On the other hand, there have been reports of persons whose anxieties and inhibitions were supposed to be released and their sexual responses increased as a result of frontal lobe operations.[23]

---

[22] For a report of reduced sexual response following pre-frontal lobotomy, see, for example: Banay and Davidoff 1942.

[23] For reports of increased sexual response following pre-frontal lobotomy, see: Hemphill 1944. McKenzie and Procter 1946. Kolb 1949 (an excellent dis-cussion). The Columbia Greystone Project is reported in: F. A. Mettler 1949 (Selective partial ablation of the frontal cortex. Hoeber publ.) and Mettler 1952 (Psychosurgical problems. Blakiston publ.). Our data from this project will be published by W. B. Pomeroy in the third volume of the Greystone Series.

We have had the opportunity to make a long-range study of 95 patients who had been subjects for frontal lobe operations. From these patients we secured histories before operation, obtaining a record of their sexual activities for some time prior to the operation. We similarly obtained records from these same patients some time (a median of 3.7 years) after operation. The detailed report is being presented by one of us in connection with the total report on the Columbia-Greystone Brain Research Project. In summary, it may be pointed out that among the females in the sample, the intensities of sexual arousal, the number of items that brought sexual arousal, the frequencies of sexual activities of particular sorts, and the frequencies of total sexual outlet did not show any significant change between a period antedating the institutionalization, and the period when the histories were retaken some years after the operation. The median lapse of time between the pre-institutional and post-institutional histories was 7.0 years.

On the other hand, among the males who had the frontal lobe operations, the frequencies of response to various stimuli and the frequencies of overt sexual activity had dropped in the course of the seven years; but the decline in responsiveness and in frequencies was not significantly different from the decline that may occur in seven years in that portion of the male population that has not had frontal lobe operations. In other words, the decline in male activity after such an operation appears to be the product of aging, rather than a direct effect of the operation. There is no decline in female responsiveness or activity because the female, unlike the male, does not show an aging effect at the ages which were involved in the experimental sample.

The critical review of the previously reported effects of frontal lobe operations, which is included in our detailed report on this material, further substantiates our conclusion that there is no demonstrated relation between the function of the frontal lobes of the human brain and any of the investigated aspects of sexual behavior. There are, inevitably, considerable shock effects from any brain operation as serious as a frontal lobe operation. Immediately following such an operation, a subject's responses and behavior may be seriously modified. Many of the reported effects of frontal lobe operations which are to be found in the clinical literature are in actuality such immediate effects. But in most of the experimental subjects with whom we had the opportunity of working, most of these effects had disappeared within a matter of six months or so; and psychologic tests, psychiatric examinations, and a variety of other tests showed little or no permanent change in the operated sample. Some of the research group working on the project felt that there had been a lessening of emotional tensions in a statistically significant portion of the group, but this did not seem certain to some of the others working on the project, and seems not to have been reflected in any of the data which we have on the sexual behavior of the sample. The samples, however, in both our own and in most of the other studies have been small. Most of the investigators have not secured anything like precise data on the sexual behavior of the patients.

Occipital, Parietal, and Temporal Lobes. Neither is there any clearly demonstrated relation between the functions of the occipital, parietal, or temporal lobes of the mammalian brain, and any aspect of sexual behavior. There is one body of work that reports that operations on the temporal lobes have a depressing effect upon emotional responses in general, but a stimulating effect on sexual responses; but no confirmation of these results by other investigators has yet been published.[24]

Cerebrum. On the other hand, the cerebrum as a whole seems to be significant in the sexual behavior of the mammal. Memory, various aspects of learning, various aspects of motor control, and other behavioral functions are considerably disturbed when there is accidental damage to, or operation on various parts of the cerebrum, and these may considerably affect the animal's sexual function.

Within the last thirty years some dozen different investigators, working with a total of six different species of mammals (rats, cats, dogs, monkeys, rabbits, and guinea pigs), have performed operations on the cortex (the outer layers) of the cerebrum and noted the effects of such operations on the sexual performances of these animals.[25]

Any sort of damage to the cortex may seriously affect an animal's motor coordination, and thus affect its physical capacity to perform effectively as a sexual partner. In addition, the cortical damage may reduce the animal's capacity to react to psychosexual stimuli. The degree of interference is more or less directly proportional to the extent of the damage to the cortex. There are differences in the serious-

---

[24] The relative unimportance, sexually, of the parietal lobes is noted in Beach 1950:263. Lashley reports (verbal communic.) the same finding. Occipital lobe ablations in the cat produce no sexual effect other than that ascribable to blindness, according to Beach 1944:129; 1950:266. Dr. C. C. Turbes (verbal communic.) reports occipital ablations without sexual effects in dogs and monkeys. However, Klüver and Bucy 1939 describe increased sexual activity in male monkeys with bilateral temporal lobectomies; we understand that similar results were obtained with monkeys in research done under Dr. Berry Campbell at the University of Minnesota. On the other hand, Beach 1950:263–264 reports no sexual changes following bilateral temporal ablations in the cat, and Poirier 1952:234 likewise failed to find such sexual effects.

[25] For experiments on the relation of the cerebrum to sexual response, see: Bard 1934, 1936, 1939, 1940, 1942 (cat, dog). Brooks 1937 (rabbit). Rioch 1938 (cat). Klüver and Bucy 1938, 1939 (monkey). Davis 1939 (rat). Maes 1939 (cat). Dempsey and Rioch 1939 (guinea pig). Stone in Allen and Doisy 1939 (rabbit, rat). Beach 1940, 1942a, 1942b, 1943, 1944 (rat, cat). Langworthy 1944 (cat).

ness of the effects on different species of mammals.[26] In general, cortical operations reduce the animal's capacity to recognize (be stimulated by) sexual objects, and very much reduce its aggressiveness in approaching a sexual partner.[27] Since sexual relationships so largely depend on the aggressiveness of the male, and only to a lesser extent on the aggressiveness of the female, damage to the cortex of the male more seriously interferes with his effectiveness as a sexual partner. Although the female with cortical damage may similarly have her aggressiveness reduced, so that she no longer attempts to mount other females or males, it is still possible for an intact male to mount her (if she is in estrus) in effective copulation.[28]

There are a few cases of human males with cerebral damage (the exact nature of which is usually not determined) who similarly have had their responses to psychologic stimuli materially reduced by the injury.[29] They are not aroused by any memory of previous sexual experience, and they find it difficult or impossible to explain why the previous experience was stimulating or satisfying, although they may retain some intellectual realization that the experience was formerly pleasurable. They are not aroused by discussions of sexual activities, by seeing possible sexual partners, or by seeing other sexual objects, and they show no interest in any renewal of sexual experience. However, if such a male still has his sacro-lumbar centers intact, he may still be capable of responding to direct, tactile stimulation, and he may still come to erection, copulate, and reach orgasm. There is one case of a human female who similarly had her psychologic responsiveness reduced by a cerebral injury.[30] Unfortunately few persons with cerebral damage have had their sex histories reported.

---

[26] That the extent of any interference with sexual response is correlated with the extent of cortical lesion is carefully described for the rat by: Beach 1940: 204–205, who reports diminished copulatory activity in male rats with lesions of over 20 per cent of the cortex, and a complete loss of copulatory activity when the lesion exceeds 60 per cent. But Brooks 1937:549–550 reports that male rabbits can copulate effectively with all of the cortex removed, providing the olfactory bulbs are spared.

[27] Localized cortical damage has been reported in a few instances to intensify sexual response, as in: Klüver and Bucy 1939. Langworthy 1944. The first authors stress the "psychic blindness" (inability to visually recognize objects) of the operated animals, but this does not harmonize with the reported "hypersexuality" which, it may be noted, seems to have been chiefly autoerotic. Likewise the frequent and protracted copulation suggests not "hypersexuality," but an inability to achieve orgasm. The seemingly intensified responses reported by Langworthy were complicated by motor defects which interfered with effective copulation.

[28] This is well demonstrated by the work of Beach. See particularly: Beach and Rasquin 1942. Beach 1943. Ford and Beach 1951:240–241.

[29] Stier 1938 describes the sexual effects of brain injury in some 33 human males, and reports that deleterious effects were more pronounced in older males. Goldstein and Steinfeld 1942 give a detailed discussion of a single case. Both papers note a marked reduction in response to psychologic stimuli.

[30] This female case was originally reported by Symonds and is cited in other literature, e.g., Beach 1942a:216.

Although the data on the relation of the cortex to sexual behavior are limited, they do show that this is the part of the nervous system through which psychosexual stimuli are mediated. Since we have shown (Chapter 16) that there are considerable differences in the effectiveness of such psychologic stimuli between females and males, we may believe that this, the most striking disparity which exists between the sexuality of the human female and male, must depend on cerebral differences between the sexes. What the nature of such cerebral differences may be, we do not know. There have been one or two studies which report differences in the biochemistry of the cerebral cortex in female and male animals. The studies are important and highly suggestive, but further investigation is needed before we are warranted in making any generalization.[31]

Since there are differences in the capacities of females and males to be conditioned by their sexual experience, we might expect similar differences in the capacities of females and males to be conditioned by other, non-sexual types of experience. On this point, however, we do not yet have information.

Hypothalamus. While we may explain the similarities of female and male responses to tactile stimulation on the basis of the similarities of spinal and autonomic mechanisms, and while we are inclined to believe that differences between female and male responses to psychologic stimuli may depend on cerebral differences, we still have one of the most significant aspects of sexual response to explain. This is the fact that sexual responses constitute a syndrome of elements most of which are found in other emotional responses, although the combination in which they appear during sexual activity is not duplicated in any other type of behavior. It is still difficult to understand why touching an animal at one time should bring responses which we recognize as sexual, while touching it on some other occasion may make the animal angry or afraid.

It is inevitable that one should assume that such a cluster of responses must depend upon some mediating mechanism, a master switchboard which controls all of the individual elements but brings them together as a unit during sexual response.[32] Perhaps it is not reasonable or necessary to believe that there should be such a mediating

---

[31] For studies of chemical differences that appear to distinguish female from male brains, in both human and infra-human species, see: Weil 1943. Weil and Liebert 1943. Weil 1944.

[32] Such "sex centers" in the cerebrum have been postulated by various students, including: Loewenfeld 1908:597–598. Rohleder 1923:4, 19. Von Bechterew acc. Beach 1940:194. A summary is in Stone 1923b. However, recent and thorough research has discovered no such centers, and Penfield and Rasmussen 1950:26 stress that they were never able to elicit erotic sensations by stimulating the exposed human brain.

mechanism, but the possibility is sufficient to warrant continued search for a central control of the sexual syndrome.

The concept of a master switchboard is encouraged by experimental work which shows that damage to the hypothalamus, a small structure in the brain which lies below the cerebrum, may considerably modify the animal's capacity to be aroused in anger, in fear, and in still other emotional responses. This it seems to do through some control which it exerts on the autonomic nervous system. Nevertheless, those who have done the most extensive research on this particular portion of the brain conclude that there is no evidence—either for or against—that the hypothalamus in any way controls sexual responses. The statement was originally made some twenty years ago, but we are advised that it still represents our present state of knowledge or lack of knowledge on this matter.[33]

We have made considerable progress in understanding the anatomy and the gross physiology of sexual response. After three decades of research done by a score of students of human and infra-human sexual behavior, we are able to identify some of the internal mechanisms which account for the similarities between female and male sexual responses, and have located the portion of the brain which seems responsible for the differences which we have found in the capacities of females and males to respond to psychologic stimuli. With this much of the story pieced together, it should now be possible for the observer of gross behavior, the anatomist, the neurophysiologist, and the student experimenting with mammalian sexual behavior to recognize the areas in which we most need additional research.

---

[33] The role of the hypothalamus in mediating autonomic elements and in the expression of emotion is noted by: Fulton 1949:237, 243–245. The sexual role of the hypothalamus is emphasized by some, as in: Brookhart and Dey 1941. Dey, Leninger, and Ranson 1942. Ford and Beach 1951:240. But Clark 1942 and Bard 1940 report inconclusive results and feel that the evidence is still insufficient for final judgment. Bard 1940:574, 576, states "There are not yet available sufficient experimental facts to warrant any general statement about the relation of the hypothalamus to the excitation and execution of estrual behavior. . . . Further work must be done before any precise statement can be made concerning the relation of the hypothalamus to the central management of sexual behavior." This author recently (verbal communic.) considers the above statements still valid.

Chapter 18

HORMONAL FACTORS IN SEXUAL RESPONSE

We have seen that sexual responses depend upon a basic anatomy which is essentially the same in the female and the male (Chapter 14), and involve physiologic processes which, again, are essentially the same in the two sexes (Chapter 15). Throughout the present volume we have found, however, that there are differences in the sexual behavior of females and males, and we have presented data which suggest that some of these may depend upon differences in capacities to be affected by psychosexual stimuli.

Some of the most striking differences between the sexual patterns of the human female and male are not, however, explainable by any of

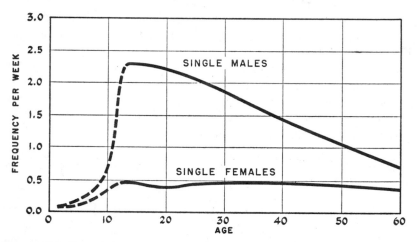

Figure 143. Comparison of aging patterns of total outlet in human female and male

Showing active median frequency of orgasm in total sexual outlet. Data estimated for pre-adolescence are shown by broken line. Data from Table 154 and our 1948:226.

the data which we have yet presented. Throughout the present volume we have emphasized, for instance, the later development of sexual responsiveness in the female and its earlier development in the male. We have pointed out that the male's capacity to be stimulated sexually shows a marked increase with the approach of adolescence, and that the incidences of responding males, and the frequencies of response to the point of orgasm, reach their peak within three or four years after the onset of adolescence (Figure 143). On the other hand, we have pointed out that the maximum incidences of sexually responding females are not approached until some time in the late twenties and in the thirties (Figures 99, 150), although some individuals become fully responsive at an earlier age.

We have pointed out that the frequencies of sexual response in the male begin to decline after the late teens or early twenties, and drop steadily into old age (Figure 143). On the other hand, we have shown that among females the median frequencies of those sexual activities which are not dependent upon the male's initiation of socio-sexual contacts, remain more or less constant from the late teens into the fifties and sixties (Figures 143–145). Nothing that we know about the anatomy or physiology of sexual response, or about the relative significance of psychologic stimuli in females and males, would account for these differences in the development of sexual responsiveness, and for these differences in the aging patterns of the two sexes.

ROLE OF THE HORMONES

In attempting to identify other factors which might affect sexual capacities, it should, again, be emphasized that sexual response is primarily a function of the nervous system. Muscles and blood vessels and other anatomic structures become involved only as a result of the stimulation of the nerves which control those organs. Factors which affect the level of an individual's capacity to respond sexually must be factors which in some way determine the capacities of the nervous system, or some portion of it, to be affected by sexual stimuli.

There is usually considerable variation in an animal's capacity to respond sexually at different periods in its life, and even on different occasions within a short span of time. The newly-born animal's capacity to be sexually aroused may be less than the capacity of the somewhat older animal. Individuals who have reached old age are no longer as capable of responding as they were at an earlier age. The capacity of an animal to respond in a particular sexual situation may be considerably reduced or may totally disappear if the stimulation is continued without interruption for a protracted period of time. Individuals who are physically exhausted, starved, or in ill health are not easily aroused sexually; or if they are aroused, they may not be capable of effective action and may fail to reach orgasm. Such data suggest that anything that modifies the physiologic level at which an animal functions may, through its effect upon the nervous system, modify the general nature of its sexual behavior.

Among the internal factors which may affect the way in which the animal body functions, the best understood are the hormones. These are chemical substances which are produced chiefly in endocrine organs, from which they are ultimately carried by the blood stream to

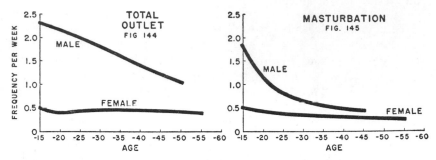

Figures 144–145. Comparison of aging patterns among single females and males

Showing contrasts in active median frequencies of orgasm in female activities which are not primarily dependent on the male. Data from Tables 154 and 23, and our 1948:226, 240.

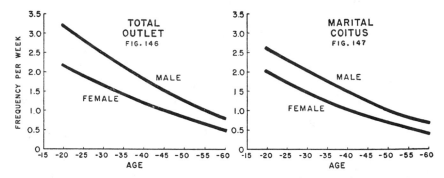

Figures 146–147. Comparison of aging patterns among married females and males

Showing how active median frequencies of orgasm attained in socio-sexual contacts in the female are affected by the patterns of male activity. Data from Tables 154 and 93, and our 1948:226, 241.

every part of the vertebrate body. Because of their accessibility to all parts of the body, hormones may have more effect on bodily functions than any other mechanism except the nervous system.

Discovery of the Hormones. Among all of the hormones that are now known to exist in the vertebrate body, the so-called sex hormones were practically the first to be discovered.

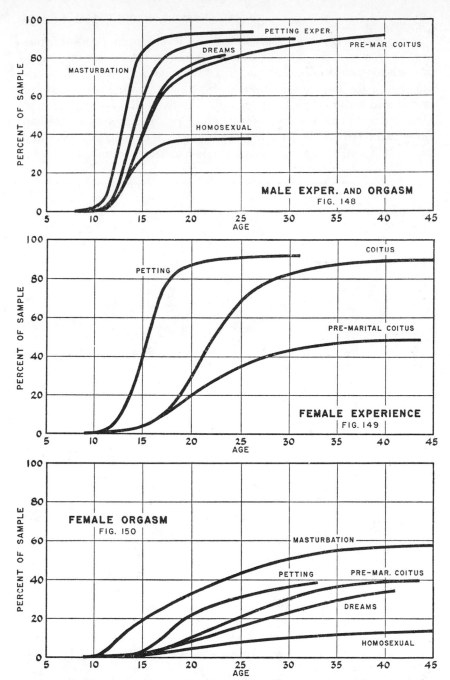

Figures 148–150. Comparisons of Female and Male Experience and Orgasm

Accumulative incidences. For most outlets, male experience and orgasm curves are nearly identical. Female curves showing experience in heterosexual activities are closer to male curves, because the male determines the pattern. Female curves showing orgasm, rise more slowly and do not reach their peak until the mid-twenties or still later. Data from Tables 25, 42, 56, 75, 131, and our 1948:500, 520, 534, 550, 624.

717

It is probable that most races of men, including even the most primitive, have recognized that the testes served two roles—one in connection with reproduction, and one in connection with the growth and function of the body as a whole.[1] Long before it was known that the ovaries and testes produce specific reproductive cells, the eggs and the sperm, it was known that some substance produced by the male had to be transferred to the female tract before she could reproduce; and the inability of a male to contribute to such reproduction after his

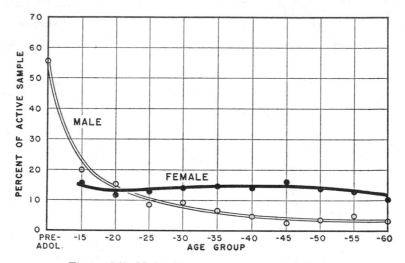

Figure 151. Multiple orgasm in female and male

Active incidences in coitus. For the male the curves show an aging effect, and for the female a plateau extending from the mid-teens into the late fifties. The differences between the two curves more or less parallel the differences between the curves for the total outlet of females and males (Figure 143). Data from Table 176 and our 1948:232.

testes had been removed provided early evidence that they were the source of an essential part of this fertilizing substance.

Although there was, of course, no understanding that a chemical mechanism was involved, both primitive and ancient peoples also recognized that the early physical development of the male animal and its capacity to engage in sexual activity also depended upon its possession of testes. Human male castrates as well as castrates among farm animals were known to the earliest peoples in all parts of the world, and consequently the effects of castration were well understood at an

---

[1] The Trobriand Islanders and certain Australian tribes are said not to be aware of the relationship between coitus and pregnancy, but even they consider that coitus paves the way for subsequent supernatural impregnation. The Trobrianders castrate boars "to improve their condition" and note that such boars cease copulation. This renders suspect Malinowski's statement that the testes are considered to be only ornamental appendages. See: Malinowski 1929:168, 180–181, 190–191. Ashley Montagu 1937:199–202.

Table 177. Multiple Orgasm

Average Number of Orgasms in Each Coital Experience

AGE	TOTAL WITH MULTIPLE ORGASM	NUMBER OF ORGASMS								CASES WITH ANY ORGASM
		1	1-2	2	2-3	3	3-4	4	Over 4	
	%	%				*Percent of females*				
Adol.–15	16	84	2	4	7	1	1	1	0	77
16–20	12	88	4	3	2	1	1	1	—	841
21–25	13	87	4	4	2	1	1	—	1	1770
26–30	14	86	5	3	2	2	1	—	1	1733
31–35	15	85	5	4	2	1	1	1	1	1366
36–40	14	86	5	3	2	2	1	—	1	966
41–45	16	84	6	3	2	1	1	1	2	570
46–50	14	86	5	4	1	1	1	1	1	303
51–55	13	87	6	3	0	1	0	2	1	127
56–60	*10*	*90*	*6*	*4*	*0*	*0*	*0*	*0*	*0*	49

Table based on all females who had had coitus at least 25 times, irrespective of marital status.

Italic figures throughout the series of tables indicate that the calculations are based on less than 50 cases. The dash (—) indicates a percentage smaller than 0.5.

Table 178. Accumulative Incidence: Completion of Menopause

By Educational Level

AGE	TOTAL SAMPLE	EDUCATIONAL LEVEL				TOTAL SAMPLE	EDUCATIONAL LEVEL			
		0-8	9-12	13-16	17+		0-8	9-12	13-16	17+
	%		*Percent*			*Cases*		*Cases*		
40	1	5	1	—	1	930	177	170	252	331
42	4	8	4	2	3	734	146	137	191	260
44	7	15	9	3	5	578	115	110	145	208
46	19	36	25	10	11	461	95	97	109	160
48	31	45	36	21	26	371	82	86	78	125
50	51	72	48	38	48	276	60	71	55	90
52	73	90	63		78	206	50	57		58
54	88					164				
56	97					123				
58	99					102				
60	100					68				

early date.[2] Because the ovaries are within the body cavity, female castrations are more difficult to perform, and were rarely done before

[2] The understanding and practice of castration may have begun as early as 7000 B.C. in the early Neolithic when animals were first domesticated. See: Steinach 1940:3, 25. Turner 1948:324. Many primitives who were at a Neolithic cultural level when first visited by Europeans practiced castration. See, for instance: Malinowski 1929:191 (Trobriand Islanders). Evans-Pritchard 1940:33 (Nuer of Africa). It is interesting to note that in cases of self-castration, as on the islands of Ponapé and Tonga (Westermarck 1922(1):561) and among the Hottentot of Africa (Bryk 1934:123), the males were careful to remove only one of the testes. In addition, there are references to castration in some of the oldest myths of Europe and Egypt. See: Möbius 1903:12. Pritchard 1950:181 (Middle Assyrian laws, 15th century B.C., tablet A, laws 15 and 20, provide castration as a punishment).

the days of modern medicine. Consequently the significance of the ovaries in regulating body functions was not understood at as early a date.

The ancients knew that the effects of castration depended upon the age at which the human or other male was castrated. They knew that when the testes of the human male were removed before the onset of adolescence, the effects were more marked than they were when the castration was performed on a male who was a fully grown adult.[3] The basic biology of these matters did not find an explanation, however, until the middle of the nineteenth century.

In 1835, Graves recognized the relation between thyroid pathologies and the physiologic disturbances which accompany the disease which now bears his name. In 1849, Berthold, studying castrations and testicular implants in fowl, concluded that the testes secreted one or more blood-borne substances which were responsible for the modifications which his experimental castrations had produced. Within the next decade, Addison had noted the deterioration of the adrenal cortex in victims of the disease which bears his name. By the mid-seventies, Gull had identified the role of the thyroid in certain pathologic conditions; by 1887 Minkowski associated acromegaly with pituitary hyperfunction, and two years later (in 1889) von Mering and Minkowski had removed the pancreas and experimentally produced diabetes. The work of Brown-Séquard in 1889 revived interest in the utilization of testicular extracts in clinical practice, and since then there has been a tremendous development of experimental work on the significance of both testicular and ovarian hormones.[4]

The list of endocrine glands which are now recognized in the vertebrate body include the ovaries and testes (or the *gonads,* as the two sets of organs are generically called), the pituitary gland which is located at the base of the brain, the thyroid and parathyroid glands which are located in the throat, and the adrenal glands which are located at the top of the kidneys near the small of the back. The thymus is a gland which reaches its maximum development in the early life of the animal but degenerates considerably after that.[5] The pineal

---

[3] Aristotle (384–322 B.C.), in the Historia Animalium, Bk. IX:631b–632b, has a lengthy discussion of the effects of castration in man and in other male animals, differentiates between pre-adolescent and adult castration, and refers to the removal of the ovaries of sows to lessen their sexual responsiveness.

[4] For brief histories of endocrinology, see: Corner 1942:228–233. C. D. Turner 1948:5–9.

[5] The removal of the thymus and/or injection of thymus extracts are usually without effect; but the development of the gonads at the onset of adolescence is associated with an atrophy of the thymus, and castrates retain the large thymus of childhood. See: Hoffman 1944:275. C. D. Turner 1948:21–22. Selye 1949:679, 683.

gland, in the brain, may be an endocrine organ.[6] The liver and the pancreas, in addition to secreting substances which directly affect digestion, also produce important hormones which influence the development and the maintenance of activities of other organs of the body.[7]

The testes are the chief source of the several hormones known as androgens (the so-called male hormones) in the body of the male. One of the best known androgens is testosterone. The ovaries are the chief source of the so-called female hormones in the female. The most prominent of the female hormones are the estrogens and progesterone.[8] As a group, hormones from the ovaries and testes may be referred to as gonadal hormones.

In recent years, the hormones produced by most of the endocrine glands have been isolated and identified as specific chemical substances. Many of them are closely related compounds of carbon, hydrogen, and oxygen. For instance, the androgens and estrogens, the 17-ketosteroids which are produced by the adrenal glands and by some other structures in the body, and the steroids which are chemicals characteristically found in all animal tissues, are all closely related chemical compounds, even though each may have a different and unique effect on the physiology of the body. Some of the other hormones, such as those produced by the thyroid and the pituitary glands, are totally different in their chemical composition.

Nature of the Hormones. A general knowledge of the hormones has become widespread in the population as a whole, but in regard to certain critical matters this knowledge is quite incorrect. Journalistic accounts of scientific research, over-enthusiastic advertising by some of the drug companies, over-optimistic reports from clinicians who have found a lucrative business in the administration of sex hormones, and some of the discussions among state legislators and public administrators who hope that hormone injections will provide one-package cure-alls for various social ills, have led the public to believe that endocrine organs are *the* glands of personality, and that there is such an exact knowledge of the way in which they control human behavior that properly qualified technicians should, at least in the near future, be able to control any and all aspects of human sexual behavior. It is,

[6] The functions of the pineal gland are poorly known and the data are conflicting, but see: Hoffman 1944:282–284. C. D. Turner 1948:19–21. Selye 1949:595.

[7] It is not fully demonstrated that the liver secretes a hormone, but secretions of the liver inactivate gonadal and probably other hormones. See: C. D. Turner 1948:25. Williams 1950:7.

[8] The estrogenic hormones found in human tissues and fluids are estradiol, estrone, and estriol. Estradiol is thought to be the true hormone and the others to be products derived from it, according to: Smith in Williams 1950:351. Talbot et al. 1952:296.

therefore, important that the general reader understand the nature of the hormones, and understand some of the difficulties that are involved in the accumulation and interpretation of data in the field of endocrinology.

Hormones are products of the physiologic processes that go on in certain of the gland cells that are to be found in the plant or animal body. Any cell which secretes a liquid content which becomes a significant part of the total volume of the cell, or which secretes materials which work their way out of the cell through a permeable cell wall or through some rupture of the wall, may be identified as a gland cell. Many of the cells of the body, and particularly those that line various body cavities, may be considered gland cells even though they are not part of a specific organ which is identifiable as a gland. Consequently, it is not always possible to identify all of the sources of the hormones in an animal's body, even including the androgens and estrogens and the 17-ketosteroids, for part of the hormone may come from cells or groups of cells which lie outside of the specific organs which are known to be the chief sources of these hormones. For instance, the removal of the ovaries or testes (as in a complete castration) may not eliminate all the sources of the sex hormones, and this is one reason that it is difficult to interpret some of the experimental data.[9]

In more complex glands, the secreting cells may pour their products into internal cavities from which ducts may carry them away. This is true, for instance, of the salivary glands. On the other hand, the glandular structures which give rise to the best known of the hormones do not have either internal cavities or ducts. Their secretions are picked up by the blood vessels which enter or surround the glands, and are thus carried away by the blood stream to other parts of the body. The structures are therefore known as ductless glands, or glands of internal secretion, or endocrine (meaning *internally secreting*) organs. There are, however, hormones produced by gland cells in other types of structures, such as the placenta and the duodenal mucosa; and there is some reason for believing that most of the organs in the mammalian body may produce, in actuality, substances which, when circulated through the blood stream, may influence the activities of at least some of the other organs.[10]

The hormones produced by any endocrine gland may affect other endocrine glands as well as organs which are not glandular. For in-

---

[9] For instance, after removal of the testes, the cortex of the adrenal gland enlarges and secretes an additional amount of androgenic (male) hormone in mice and guinea pigs. See: Hartman and Brownell 1949:331. Selye 1949:130–131.

[10] The placenta secretes estrogen, progesterone, and a gonadotropin. The duodenal mucosa secretes several hormones concerned with digestion. See: C. D. Turner 1948:13–16.

stance, the secretions of the testes and ovaries have a direct effect on the anterior lobe of the pituitary and on the adrenal glands, and each of these has a direct effect on the testes and ovaries. Consequently an increase or decrease in the secretory capacity of any one of these glands may be reflected in the activities of the other glands.[11] Some of the other endocrine organs, such as the thyroid, may similarly affect the secretory capacities of the ovaries and testes, and of the pituitary and adrenal glands.

Although the effectiveness of any hormone is usually proportionate to the amount which is available, there is usually a point of optimum effectiveness, and an increase in the amount of hormone beyond that point may have negative effects which, in certain respects, may be as extreme as those obtained when there is an under-supply or complete removal of the source of supply of the hormone.[12]

Usually the amount of hormone produced in an endocrine organ such as a testis or ovary is very small, and the amount that is to be found in the blood or the urine or at any other point in the body is so exceedingly minute that its recovery and chemical identification may be very difficult. Consequently, most of the reports of female and male hormone levels do not rest upon physical or chemical measurements, but upon such indirect evidence as can be obtained by injecting urine or blood extracts into experimental animals, and upon measurements of the changes which are thus effected in the growth or degeneration of some structure (like a rooster's comb) in the experimental animal Difficulties in measurement have been the source of considerable error in much of the reported work, including the studies which have attempted to analyze the relationships of the sex hormones and sexual behavior.[13]

Moreover, when the amount of hormone in an animal's body is determined by measuring the hormone in its urine, it is questionable what relation the amount of excreted material may have to the amount of the hormone that the body is actually utilizing. The hormone in the

---

[11] For the interrelationships between the secretions of the anterior lobe of the pituitary, the ovaries, testes, and adrenal cortex, see: Heller and Nelson 1948: 229–243. C. D. Turner 1948:241–244, 462–468. Hartman and Brownell 1949: ch. 26. Selye 1949:22–23. Burrows 1949:329–343. Williams 1950:21–32. Talbot et al. 1952:385–392.

[12] For instance, both a thyroid deficiency and an excess of thyroid retard sexual maturation. See: Lisser 1942:29–32. Hoffman 1944:239–240. Williams 1950: 122, 175. Talbot et al. 1952:21, 31. See footnotes 37, 66.

[13] As an example of the difficulties encountered in analyses: testicular androgen is metabolized and excreted partly in the form of ketosteroids in the urine, and hence the injection of an androgen such as testosterone propionate may be followed by an increase in urinary ketosteroids. But another androgen, methyl testosterone, may have no effect on the levels of the urinary ketosteroids, or even decrease them. See: Selye 1949:628. Howard and Scott in Williams 1950:337.

urine may merely represent that portion which the body has been unable to utilize. Recent endocrinologic research indicates that this latter may be the correct interpretation, especially when an animal is receiving an over-supply of hormones. In an effort to allow for this, hormonal measures are often made on materials recovered from the blood; but it is not clear that this eliminates the difficulty, for it is still not certain how much of the hormone carried in the blood stream may ultimately be utilized by an animal. Consequently reports on hormonal levels in females and males, or in heterosexual and homosexual males, are acceptable only when allowances are made for possible errors in interpreting the measurements, when a sufficient allowance is made for variation in the same individual on different occasions, when the series of reported cases is of some size, and when the report is based on a statistically adequate experimental group which can be compared with an adequate control group.

GONADAL HORMONES AND PHYSICAL CHARACTERS

Development of Physical Characters in Young Mammals. The most certain effects of the gonadal hormones are their effects on the development of physical characters in the young animal. This includes the development in size and function of many parts of the body, including some of the characters (the secondary sexual characters) which most clearly differentiate adult females from males. Many of these characters do not fully differentiate until the onset of adolescence. The development of these secondary sexual characters, as well as the development of the adult anatomy as a whole, depends upon the animal's possession of intact gonads. This is true of the human female and male, and of the females and males of the lower species of mammals.

If the gonads fail to develop normally—as not infrequently happens when testes of the human male, for instance, are retained in the body cavity and fail to descend into the scrotum—or if the gonads of the pre-adolescent human female or male become diseased, or if they are removed by castration any time before the onset of adolescence, the normal development of adult characters is usually slowed up or completely stopped. And when a castrated animal does reach its full size, its body proportions are not typical of those usually found in the normal adult, *i.e.*, the animal becomes a typical capon, a gelding, or a eunuch in form and structure.[14]

---

[14] The failure of pre-adolescent castrates, either surgical or functional, to develop the secondary sexual characters typical of the adult, is described in such standard works as: Laughlin 1922:435. Lipschütz 1924:6 ff. Pratt in Allen et al. 1939:1267–1268, 1282. Hamilton 1941:1904. Greenblatt 1947:182, 254–257. Mazer and Israel 1951:231. Ford and Beach 1951:170.

In the normal human adolescent, female or male, the genitalia are among the first structures to acquire adult size.[15] When the gonads have been damaged before adolescence, the genitalia may develop even more slowly than the rest of the body and may remain more or less infantile even into later years.

In the human female and male, hair normally begins to develop in the armpits during adolescence. In normal development, pubic hair appears in both sexes, although the pubic hair of the female is ordinarily confined to a more limited triangle while it may spread over a more extensive area in the male. Ultimately, but often not until late in the twenties or thirties, the pubic hair of the male may develop upward along a midline (the *linea alba*) on the abdomen. The normal male also develops hair on his face, on his chest, on his legs, and elsewhere on his body, while such hair is usually absent or scant in the female. But if the testes of the pre-adolescent male are damaged or eliminated, the hair in these several parts of the body may fail to appear at the usual age. If it does subsequently develop in the castrated male, it may appear in a pattern which is in many respects more typical of the very young adolescent. The face and chest and other parts of the body of such a male may remain more or less hairless.[16] While the early castration of a female does not have as marked an effect on the development of her body hair, it may contribute to the appearance of facial hair and other hair developments which are not typical of her sex.[17]

The Adam's apple is characteristic of the adult human male. Associated with this, his voice is rougher and usually at a pitch which is lower than that characteristic of the female. The Adam's apple is ordinarily not developed in the female. The male who is castrated before adolescence fails to develop an Adam's apple and retains a high voice.

In the course of adolescent development the shoulders of a normal male widen more than they do in the normal female. In adult females the hips become characteristically larger and wider than they are in the male. The buttocks in an adult female usually become larger and more elongated, while the buttocks of the adult male remain smaller and are more often rounded. The male who is castrated before adolescence retains body proportions which are closer to those of the juvenile.

The breast of the female normally enlarges in size, and the colored, corrugated (areolar) area surrounding the nipple becomes consider-

---

[15] For data on the growth of the human male genitalia before the rest of the body is fully grown, see: Schonfeld and Beebe 1942:771.

[16] Absence of pubic hair and abnormal hair distribution in males with gonadal insufficiencies are well illustrated in Selye 1949:651–660.

[17] A diminution of axillary and pubic hair, and sometimes hirsutism in females with

ably expanded. The female who has diseased or damaged ovaries does not show such a normal breast development, her voice may become lower in pitch, and she may fail to acquire an adult female body form.

In general, castrations performed on young females and young males of the infra-human species of mammals affect their physical development in ways which are comparable to those just noted for human females and males.

Some of the effects of castration may be partially or largely corrected by the administration of hormones from an outside source. This is true for both females and males, and for both the human and other mammalian species. But injections of hormones have their maximum effect if they are made at an early age. They cannot fully correct the damage done by a castration if they are not administered until some time after adolescence has begun, but they may still have some value even when the therapy is not started until the individual is essentially adult. But the corrective effects of hormonal administrations to young castrates can be maintained only if the treatment is continued throughout the growth period. Otherwise the individual may lapse into its castrated state. If hormonal treatments are continued until the individual has become completely adult—which in the human species means into the middle twenties or sometimes later—then the continued administration of hormones is not so necessary.[18]

Maintenance of Physical Characters in Adults. Damage to the gonads, or a complete castration of a human female or male after physical maturity has been acquired, prevents reproduction, but there are usually minimum effects on other physical characters. Some individuals (particularly some females) who have been castrated as adults may go for years and may even reach old age before they show any marked physical changes. Some females and males, on the contrary, may show more physical deterioration in the course of time. Clinicians commonly report characteristic aging effects on the genitalia of females who have had their ovaries removed.[19] It is generally believed that the deteriorations of old age come on sooner, although the specific data are inadequate on this point.

congenitally absent or undeveloped ovaries are noted in Selye 1949:399–400.
[18] In the abundant literature on the correction of a gonadal insufficiency through the administration of hormones, see, for instance: Kenyon 1938:121–134. Vest and Howard 1938:177–182. McCullagh 1939. Hamilton and Hubert 1940:372. Escamilla and Lisser 1941. Biskind et al. 1941. Kearns 1941. Moore 1942:39. Heller, Nelson, and Roth 1943. Hurxthal 1943. Heller and Maddock 1947:414–418. Beach 1948:38–41, 45. Selye 1949:645–666. Howard and Scott in Williams 1950:328–333. H. H. Turner 1950:32–48.
[19] Menopausal-like involutional changes in the genitalia of castrated adult females, and their control by estrogen therapy, are noted, for example, in: Hoffman 1944:33–35. The lack of regressive changes in some hypogonadal males is discussed in: Heller and Maddock 1947:395.

Castrations may, however, have marked effects on the physiologic well-being of an adult.[20] Since gonadal secretions affect the levels of secretion of the pituitary, adrenal, and thyroid glands, all of which are important in the regulation of the general physiology of an animal, it is inevitable that castrations, even of adults, should have some effect; but this effect is usually minor among human females, and it is not clear that most human males have their physiologic well-being particularly modified by castration if the operation is performed after complete physical maturity has been acquired.

There seem to be more marked effects on the physical characters and on the physiologic well-being of males of lower mammalian species which are castrated as adults.[21]

The effects of castration on an adult animal, such as they are, may be more or less completely corrected by the administration of a sufficient supply of gonadal hormones. This has been demonstrated for laboratory animals, and hormones are often administered in clinical practice to middle-aged and older women who have had their ovaries removed. Usually testosterone is given to a male who is castrated as an adult, and estrogens to a female, but sometimes both hormones are given to individuals of both sexes. It is significant that the corrective administrations of hormones do not need to be kept up indefinitely in an adult, at least in an adult female. In some way the adult human body can adjust in a matter of months to a lack of gonadal hormones, and then it appears to be capable of more or less normal function, even though an important link in the endocrine chain has been eliminated. The capacity of the adult male body to adjust may not be as complete as that of the female. Some adult male castrates appear to adjust to a lack of male hormones for long periods of years; but others show some physical degeneration within a shorter period of years. Until there are further studies of long-time adult male castrates, we are uncertain how to interpret these contradictions in the reported data.[22]

LEVELS OF GONADAL HORMONES AND SEXUAL BEHAVIOR

Much of the confusion concerning the function of the hormones which originate in the ovaries and the testes is a consequence of the

[20] The general physiologic effects of castration are discussed, for instance, in: Möbius 1903:28 ff. Laughlin 1922:435–436. Lipschütz 1924:12–14. Wolf 1934:257–268, 279. Lange 1934. Greenblatt 1947:254–257. Heller and Maddock 1947:393 ff. Ford and Beach 1951:221–225, 229–232.

[21] In animals, adult male castrates show a genital atrophy, an accumulation of fat, and a decrease in metabolism, sexual drive, and aggressiveness. See: Tandler and Grosz 1913:25–41. Rice and Andrews 1951:115–116.

[22] For a brief resumé of the studies on human male castrates, see pages 740–744 of this chapter.

unwarranted opinion that anything associated with reproduction must, *ipso facto,* be associated with an animal's sexual behavior and, contrariwise, that all sexual behavior is designed to serve a reproductive function. Since the glands which produce eggs and sperm also produce hormones, scientists and philosophers alike have considered it logical to believe that these must be the hormones which control sexual behavior. Reasoning thus, men throughout history have castrated criminals as punishment for sexual activity which their gonads were supposed to have inspired, and with the intention of controlling their further sexual activity.[23] In recent years, courts and state legislatures are again considering gonadal operations as a means of controlling sex offenders.[24] There has been some experimentation with hormone injections in an attempt to achieve that end. Castrations and the administration of sex hormones have been carried out under court order and under the direction of physicians and psychiatrists in various parts of the United States, in Denmark, in Holland, and still elsewhere in mental and penal institutions.[25] On the even more amazing assumption that anatomic defects in the genitalia may explain the social misuse of those organs, some of the medical and psychiatric officers in police courts and in penal and mental institutions routinely examine the genitalia of persons committed on sex charges.

But the fact that hormones are produced in the gonads is, without further evidence, no reason for believing that they are the primary

---

[23] For example, in the Middle Assyrian laws, which may date back to the 15th century B.C., tablet A, laws 15 and 20, provide castration as a punishment for certain sexual offenses. See: Pritchard 1950:181.

[24] There are statutes in some ten states providing for involuntary asexualization, or sterilization as a eugenic or therapeutic measure for criminal conduct. In several of these states (*e.g.*, Kansas and Oregon) the practice has been to allow castration as one of the permissible operations. Since the United States Supreme Court decision in Skinner v. Oklahoma 1941:316 U.S. 535, all operations have been "voluntary." In order to circumvent constitutional objections, the California Legislature at its Third Extraordinary Session in 1951 passed a bill, A.B.2367, providing for mandatory life imprisonment for persons convicted of certain types of criminal conduct who did not "consent" to being castrated. This bill was vetoed by Governor Warren on July 18, 1951. A milder version of the same bill, S.B.19, failed to pass in the 1952 regular session of the Legislature. We are informed that a similar proposal was introduced in the 1953 session of the Oregon Legislature. To our knowledge castration proposals were summarily rejected by the commissions on sex offenders in New Jersey and Illinois. See also, Michigan, Governor's Study Commission 1951:4, 6.

[25] For such a use of castration or the administration of hormones, see: Hirschfeld 1928:54. Lange 1934:44, 101. Wolf 1934:16–23. Böhme 1935:10–34. Sand and Okkels 1938:374. Kopp 1938:698–704. Hawke 1950. Tappan 1951:242–246 (Denmark). Bowman 1952:70 (cites Judge Turrentine of San Diego court as stating that "behavior disorders have been well controlled by castration in about 70 men," and that these men failed to become involved again with the law after castration. Since sex offenders are always among the lowest in their rate of recidivism, the Judge's criterion is inadequate.). Bowman 1952:79–80 gives a report from the Swedish authorities on 166 legal castrations between 1944 and 1950. Bowman and Engle 1953:10.

agents controlling those capacities of the nervous system on which sexual response depends. It is unfortunate, as we shall see, that these hormones were ever identified as sex hormones, and especially unfortunate that they were identified as male and female sex hormones, for the terminology inevitably prejudices any interpretation of the function of these hormones.

Estrogen Levels at Younger Ages. It should be borne in mind that estrogens (the female hormones), are to be found in the bodies of both females and males. The ovaries of the female are a chief source of her estrogens. The origins of the estrogens in the male are not so well established, but they seem to be produced, at least in part, by the testes.[26]

Estrogens are reported to occur in about equal amounts in the pre-adolescent human female and pre-adolescent human male until they reach the age of ten (Figure 152). But at about the time of adolescence, the estrogens increase abruptly in the female. There is only a slight increase in estrogens in the male at adolescence.[27] In the adult female there is, in consequence, a much higher estrogen level than in the adult male. There is, of course, wide individual variation in this matter.[28]

There is nothing, however, in the development of sexual responsiveness and activity, either in the female or in the male, which parallels these reported levels of estrogens in the human female or male. At the onset of adolescence there is no upsurge of sexual responsiveness and sexual activity in the female which parallels the dramatic rise in the levels of her estrogens (Figure 152). It is the male who suddenly becomes sexually active at adolescence, but his estrogens stay near their pre-adolescent levels.

Androgen Levels at Younger Ages. Androgens are also found in both females and males. The testes of the male are the chief source of his androgens; but the ovaries of the female apparently produce androgens as well as estrogens, and it is probable that the adrenal glands and still other structures in her body also produce androgens.[29]

---

[26] For data on the two estrogens, estradiol and estrone, found in the testes, see: Selye 1949:54, 84. For data on estrogenic substances from the adrenal cortex, see: Hartman and Brownell 1949:105. Selye 1949:80–81. Kepler and Locke in Williams 1950:203. Thorn and Forsham in Williams 1950:261.

[27] For levels of gonadal hormones in pre-adolescence and adolescence, see Nathanson et al. 1941.

[28] For androgen and estrogen levels in normal adult males and females, see: Gallagher et at. 1937:695–703. Koch 1938:228–230. Heller and Maddock 1947:395–398. Dorfman in Pincus and Thimann 1948:496–508.

[29] The production of androgenic substances by the ovary is noted in: Hoffman 1944:47. C. D. Turner 1948:337. Burrows 1949:123–124. Selye 1949:627. Parkes 1950:108. The adrenal cortex as another source of androgens is noted

In the human species, from about age seven or eight until the middle teens, the androgen levels in the female and the male are about equal (Figure 153). Then the androgen levels begin to rise more markedly in the male, and less so in the female, and it is generally considered that older females have androgen levels that are about two-thirds as high as those of the males.

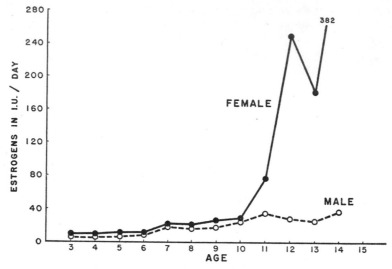

Figure 152. Estrogen levels in pre-adolescent and adolescent female and male

Averages from urinary assays reported by Nathanson et al. 1941.

Since we found a sudden upsurge of sexual responsiveness and overt sexual activity among human males at the beginning of adolescence, there may seem to be some correlation with the androgen picture; but the upsurge of sexual responsiveness in the male is much more abrupt than the steady rise in the levels of his androgens (compare Figures 143 and 153).

As for the female, there seems to be no correlation at all between the levels of her androgens and her slow and gradual development of sexual responsiveness and overt sexual activity (Figures 143 and 153). Although she has nearly as much androgenic hormone as the male in her pre-adolescent and early adolescent years, her levels of sexual response and overt sexual activity at that period are much lower than the levels in the average male. The near identity of the androgen levels in the female and male at the very age at which the two sexes develop

in: Koch 1938:218. Nathanson et al. 1941:862. C. D. Turner 1948:337. Burrows 1949:120. Selye 1949:80, 126–127. Kepler and Locke in Williams 1950:203. Parkes 1950:102. Perloff in Mazer and Israel 1951:124.

such strikingly different patterns of behavior, makes it very doubtful whether there is any simple and direct relationship between androgens and patterns of pre-adolescent and adolescent sexual behavior in either sex.

Levels of Gonadal Hormones in Older Adults. Unfortunately, levels of gonadal hormones seem not to have been established for any ade-

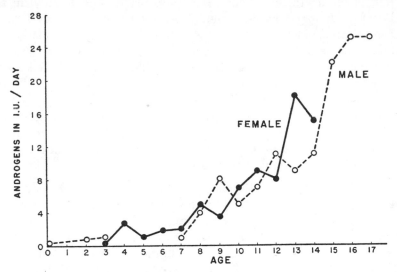

Figure 153. Androgen levels in pre-adolescent and adolescent female and male

Averages from urinary assays reported by Dorfman 1948.

quate series of older human adults, either female or male. There is some reason for assuming that the levels of male hormones drop in the male at advanced ages, and if this were proved to be so it would parallel the drop in the levels of sexual response and overt activity which we have found in the male. On the other hand, there is as much reason for assuming that the levels of male hormone similarly drop in the older female, but such a drop would not correlate with the fact that the frequencies of female response and sexual activity stay on a level from the teens into the fifties or sixties (Figure 143).[30]

GONADAL INSUFFICIENCIES AND SEXUAL BEHAVIOR

Although the importance of the gonadal hormones in respect to the physical growth and development of the young mammal is clearly established by castration experiments, it is more difficult to measure

---

[30] Dorfman in Pincus and Thimann 1948:502–504 differentiates the androgens from the 17-ketosteroid data and shows a decline in androgens with advancing age in both female and male. Ford and Beach 1951:227 state that it is generally agreed that testicular androgens decrease in later life.

the effects of castration on the capacity of an animal to respond sexually. In any case, it is difficult to know how many of the observed modifications of behavior represent the direct consequences of hormonal action, and how many are a product of the fact that the gonads influence other endocrine organs such as the pituitary and the thyroid which may affect the general metabolic level of all physiologic functions, including the functions of the nervous system. Finally, in the case of the human species, it should be noted that there may be pronounced psychologic effects from a castration. This is particularly true of the male because of the great importance which our culture attaches to his genital integrity and sexual potency. Many of the reported effects of castrations on sexual behavior are undoubtedly the product of the social maladjustments in which castrates often become involved. In those cultures where castration is observed as a religious duty, and in religious cults where the priests are regularly castrated, no social opprobrium is attached to such an operation, and the effects of castration do not seem as apparent as they are in our culture.[31]

Castration and Sexual Response in Young Females and Males. The behavioral effects of gonadal insufficiencies, whether they are the product of undeveloped or diseased ovaries or testes, or the product of complete castrations, are most evident in young animals. In many of the lower mammalian species, early castration more or less completely stops the development of all sexual responsiveness in both the female and male.

In the human male, pre-adolescent gonadal insufficiencies regularly delay the development of sexual responsiveness. The responses of a twenty-year-old male whose testes have degenerated because they have failed to descend into the scrotum, or of a male who has been castrated in pre-adolescence, may be on a level with those of the average pre-adolescent boy of eight or ten years of age. Erections and other signs of response occur less frequently in an adult who was an early castrate, arousal is not effected by as large a number of stimuli as in the normal male, and arousal by psychologic stimuli in particular may occur less frequently than in the normal male. Some degree of sexual responsiveness may develop in later years; but the levels of response in the few cases on which we have original data, and in the well known histories of eunuchs who were castrated at an early age, usually do not reach the levels which are typical of the average male.[32]

---

[31] For the social status of castrates in societies in which castration is socially approved, see: Möbius 1903:14, 16, 84.

[32] The effect of pre-adolescent castrations or gonadal under-development in lowering the sexual responsiveness of the human male is also recorded in: Lipschütz 1924:12–13. Commins and Stone 1932:497–499. Pratt in Allen et al. 1939: 1268. Hoffman 1944:623, 625. Beach 1948:23–28. Selye 1949:646, 661. Ford and Beach 1951:231.

There is great need, however, for the accumulation of more data, for there appears to be considerable individual variation in such cases.

Early castrations of males of lower mammalian species similarly may prevent the development of any sexual responsiveness or reduce the levels of response.[33] But in some instances, castrations may have little effect on the development of sexual responsiveness. For instance, there are data on two male chimpanzees who were castrated at a very young age, and these castrations have not prevented the subsequent development of sexual responses comparable to those of normal pre-adolescent or adult chimpanzees.[34]

In lower mammalian females, early castrations have somewhat similar effects on the development of sexual responsiveness.[35] There are, however, practically no data on the effects of such early castrations on the sexual behavior of the human female.

The importance of the gonadal hormones in the development of sexual responses is further confirmed by the fact that when testosterone is administered to an early castrate, whether it is a human or a mammal of some lower species, and whether it is a female or male, the levels of sexual response may be raised to something approaching the normal. The administration of estrogens to a female who was castrated in pre-adolescence has a less marked effect on her behavior, and a still lesser effect (as far as the data are yet available) when administered to males who were castrated at an early age.[36]

Nevertheless, these demonstrations of the importance of the gonadal

---

[33] That an early castration depresses the sex drive of a male animal, although it does not abolish all indications of sexual responsiveness, is noted in: Stone in Allen et al. 1939:1219. Beach 1947a:34–35. Beach 1948:20–23. Rice and Andrews 1951:115. Ford and Beach 1951:229.

[34] At the Yerkes Laboratories at Orange Park, Florida, the male chimpanzee named Don, who is now almost 19 years old, was castrated at approximately 2 years of age (acc. Nissen, verbal communic.). Physically he lies within the norms for adult males. His frequency of erection and sexual interest in females are equal to those of an intact male, but he does not usually reach orgasm and ejaculate. Owing to this inability, he can copulate more frequently than an intact male. Under androgen therapy Don is capable of orgasm and ejaculation, and his behavior and coital frequency then are identical with those of an intact male. The case is also noted in: Clark 1945. Ford and Beach 1951: 231. Beach in Blake and Ramsey 1951:78.

Another male chimpanzee named Dag, now about 8 years old, was castrated at about 2 months of age. Physically Dag falls within the norms, and his frequency of erection and his incidental masturbation are the same as that of intact males of comparable age.

[35] When the females of mammalian species below the primates are castrated at an early age, they never develop sexual receptiveness, according to Beach 1947a: 35.

[36] According to Wilson and Young 1941:781–783, estrogens administered to pre-adolescent guinea pig castrates can produce estrus. Estrogens administered to castrated pre-adolescent male rats show less specific effects; see Ball 1939: 282.

hormones in the development of sexual responsiveness in the young female and male, do not seem to warrant the conclusion that androgens and estrogens have more specific effects upon the development and functioning of the nervous system than they have upon the development and functioning of various other physical structures in the animal body. Quite to the contrary, the retardation of sexual development in a castrate is exactly what might be expected if the gonadal hormones provide, as they appear to provide, simply one of the conditions necessary for the normal growth and development of the body as a whole. Similar damage done to the pituitary, to the thyroid, or to some of the other endocrine organs of a developing animal, may have similarly disastrous effects on the normal course of its development and on the development of its capacity to respond.[37] All of these endocrine organs, as well as many of the other organs in the body, seem necessary for the development of sexual responsiveness in the young animal.

Castration and Sexual Response in Adult Females. There are some contradictions in the reported effects of the castration of a human adult. There appear to be differences in the effects on different individuals. Some of the recorded effects may depend upon the fact that the general level of all physiologic activities may be lowered by a gonadal insufficiency. Again, it is to be noted that the psychologic effects of a castration on an adult, and especially on an adult male, may be more severe than the psychologic effects on a pre-adolescent.

The effects of castration on the sexual behavior of a fully mature female have generally been reported to be minor, or none at all. We have the histories of 123 females who had had ovaries removed, and our examination of these cases confirms the general opinion that there is no modification of sexual responsiveness or capacity for orgasm, following an ovarian operation, which can be clearly identified as the result of such an operation.[38] Some of the sexually most active females in our sample were women in their fifties and sixties who were well

---

[37] Delayed sexual development consequent on insulin deficiencies, on thyroid over- and under-development, on pituitary disturbances, and on adrenal malfunction, are noted, for instance, in: Hoffman 1944:255, 268. Hartman and Brownell 1949:353. Selye 1949:124, 126–127, 524, 737. Williams 1950:42, 122, 173–175. See also footnotes 12, 66.

[38] The lack of any consistent effect of castration of an adult female on her sex drive is also noted in: Hegar 1878:71–72, 74. Canu 1897:ch. 1. Möbius 1903:87 (sex drive remains after late castration). Glävecke acc. Kisch 1907:187–188 (drive reported lessened in two-thirds of 27 castrated women). Commins and Stone 1932:499–501. Havelock Ellis 1936(I,2):11–14. Hoskins 1941:234 (desire often not lessened). Filler and Drezner 1944:123–124 (41 female castrates, 88 per cent reported no change in sex drive, majority under 35 years of age). Huffman 1950:915–917 (68 adult female castrations, ages 26–43, loss of responsiveness reported in 2 cases). Ford and Beach 1951:222–224. Masters in Cowdry 1952:668 (atrophy of uterus, breasts, and vagina; more rapid in younger females; usually decreased sex drive, although exceptions are noted).

past the age of menopause. Some of them had had their ovaries removed ten to fifteen years before.

Of our total sample of 123 castrated (ovariectomized) females (Table 179), twenty-three had not experienced orgasm for a year or two before the operation, and did not experience orgasm after the operation. Of the remaining one hundred cases, forty-one appraised their own record as follows: 54 per cent had not recognized that their loss of ovaries had had any effect on their sexual responses or overt behavior. Some 19 per cent believed that their sexual responses had been increased by their operations, and 27 per cent believed that their sexual responses had been decreased. The record of specific activities on the full hundred cases showed that 42 per cent had not changed in their overt behavior, 15 per cent had increased their activity, and 43 per cent had decreased their activity. However, the median frequencies of orgasm calculated for the whole sample both before and after operation, indicate that over a ten-year period the drop had paralleled the drop in frequencies of total outlet in approximately that same age period, among the females in our total sample. It is to be recalled that the declining frequencies of socio-sexual activities among females are not primarily dependent on an aging process in the female, but upon an aging process in the male which reduces his interest in having frequent coitus (see pp. 353–354). Our cases, therefore, do not provide evidence that females deprived of their normal supplies of gonadal hormones have their levels of sexual responsiveness or their frequencies of overt activity lowered by ovarian operations.

The increases in sexual activity shown in some of our histories may have depended on the fact that some women who have gone through a natural or induced menopause feel more free to engage in sexual activity as soon as they are relieved of the possibility of becoming pregnant.

We have detailed data on 173 cases of females who had gone through natural menopause (Table 179). It is ordinarily considered that there is a considerable reduction in the amount of estrogen secreted by the ovaries after menopause. However, in our sample it would be difficult to identify any reduction of sexual response or activities which could be considered the consequence of any change at menopause. Out of the 173 cases, forty-six had not experienced orgasm for a year or two before menopause, and there was no change in their status following menopause. In the other 127 cases, thirty-one appraised their own record as follows: 39 per cent believed that their sexual responses and activities had not been affected by the menopause, 13 per cent believed that their responses had increased, and 48 per cent believed that their responses had decreased. The detailed record of the activities of the full 127 women, confirmed this distribution of cases (Table 179). Again, however, the decrease in median frequencies in this sample had merely paralleled the decrease in median frequencies in our total sample of females of approximately the same age. Note again that this decrease is primarily dependent upon the male's declining interest in socio-sexual activities.

Table 179. Effect of Castration and of Menopause on Sexual Response and Outlet

Effect	Castr.	Menop.	Castr.	Menop.
	Percent		*Cases*	
Subject's evaluation of effect				
No effect	*54*	*39*	22	12
Increase in response	*19*	*13*	8	4
Decrease in response	*27*	*48*	11	15
Number of cases	41	31	41	31
	Percent		*Cases*	
Effect on total outlet				
No effect	42	42	42	53
Increased frequency	15	5	15	7
Decreased frequency	43	53	43	67
Number of cases	100	127	100	127
	Freq. per week		*Cases*	
Median freq. of total outlet				
1–2 years before	1.0	1.5	100	127
During menopause		1.0		81
1–2 years after	0.7	0.7	100	127
3–4 years after	0.7	0.6	76	90
10 years after	*0.8*	*0.4*	28	38
20 years after		*0.4*		12

Table based on all females available in sample, whose marital status remained constant before and after castration or menopause and who had experienced orgasm within 1 to 2 years before and/or after castration or menopause.

The median age at castration was 38.6 years, the range was 17 to 53 years. The median age at the onset of menopause was 46.3 years, the range was 33 to 56 years.

Some of the decreased frequencies also depended upon the fact that some of these women had seized upon menopause or their ovarian operations as an excuse for discontinuing sexual relationships in which they were never particularly interested. Some of the cases of increased activity were, again, a product of the fact that some of these women had been relieved of their fear of pregnancy after going through menopause.

Castration of Adult Females of Lower Mammalian Species. This lack of effect of castration on an adult human female is not in accord with the reported effects of castrations on adult females of rats, guinea pigs, and some other species of mammals. It is reported that castrations in those species eliminate all evidence of sexual response.[39] Examination of the literature, however, indicates that the chief bases for these reports, persistent as they are, is the fact that the castration of a lower mammalian female puts an end to her periods of estrus—the period during which she will accept coitus from the male. It has always been assumed that she accepts coitus during estrus because she becomes sexually more responsive at that time. But we question whether the

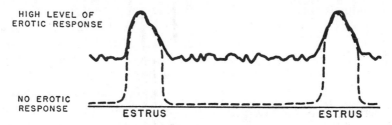

HIGH LEVEL OF
EROTIC RESPONSE

NO EROTIC
RESPONSE

ESTRUS   ESTRUS

Figure 154. Relation of erotic response to estrus in infra-human females

Theoretic diagram. Lighter line shows previous interpretation, darker line shows present interpretation. In both instances, response is at a maximum during estrus; the present data indicate that there is also a considerable capacity for response in periods between estrus.

submission to a male is, in itself, sufficient evidence of erotic arousal. Moreover, we find considerable evidence that lower mammalian females who are not in estrus are frequently aroused erotically.

We have noted that a bull ordinarily gives evidence of his sexual arousal before he ever mounts a cow by showing a development of neuromuscular tensions throughout his body; the muscles on the sides of his abdomen become tensed in a corrugated design, his tail is arched as a result of tensions in that part of his body, he may show a partial erection, and his Cowper's secretions may start flowing before he has touched the cow. Usually a cow which is in estrus does not show similar evidences of sexual arousal until after she is mounted. Then the tensed muscles on the sides of her abdomen, her arched tail, her tumescent genital labia, and her vaginal mucous secretions provide

---

[39] In the earlier work, distinctions were made between the receptivity of estrus and sexual responsiveness, as in: Young and Rundlett 1939:449. But more recent scientific publications have been inclined to consider sexual responsiveness and estrus synonymous, just as most farmers and animal breeders do. See: Williams 1943:125. Ford and Beach 1951:221. Beach in Blake and Ramsey 1951: 75–76 ("Removal of the ovaries in lower mammals is followed by total and permanent loss of female sexual responses . . . the animal's tendency to become sexually aroused and to execute coital reactions is heavily dependent upon hormones from the ovaries." And again, "Removal of the ovaries promptly and permanently abolishes all sexual behavior"). See also Chapter 15, footnote 18.

evidence of her arousal and response. We have also noted (page 450) that cows quite regularly and frequently mount other cows, and that when this occurs, the cow that does the mounting is the one that first shows evidence of erotic arousal, although the cow which is mounted may not give such evidence until after she has been mounted. But the cows that do the mounting are usually not in estrus, while the cows that are mounted are almost always in estrus.

There is, of course, no question that an animal that is in estrus is capable of being aroused erotically, and it is common knowledge that some animals, like female dogs, may become more responsive and actively search for males when they are in estrus; but the data indicate that sexual arousal among infra-human females that arc not in estrus may also occur with some frequency (Figure 154). There are also records of castrated adult female rats and dogs that will sometimes mount other females after castration, just as they did before castration; and this seems clear-cut evidence of sexual responsiveness after castration.[40]

Since reports on the effects of castrations in lower mammalian species usually do not describe those physiologic phenomena which are the best measures of sexual response (Chapter 15), and since there is so much evidence of sexual arousal outside of estrus, we doubt whether the presence or absence of estrus provides a sufficient measure of a lower mammalian female's capacity to respond sexually.

It has been said that the gonadal hormones are more important in controlling the sexual responses of the lower mammalian female, while cerebral controls are more important in the human female.[41] But this, again, seems to be based primarily on the fact that estrus stops after the castration of the lower mammalian female, while responsiveness after castration is retained in the adult human female. If reexamination of the experimental data or further experimental work shows that the lower mammalian female does not actually lose sexual responsiveness as a result of castration, it would mean that the role of the gonadal hormones in the lower mammalian female is, to this extent, about the same as in the human female.

Castration and Sexual Response in Adult Males. Reports on the sexual behavior of human males who have been castrated as fully grown adults have usually been very brief, and the various reports are contradictory in spite of the fact that such operations have been performed with some frequency throughout history. Castrations of adult

---

[40] That castrated female rats and dogs will sometimes mount other females is reported by: Beach and Rasquin 1942. Ford and Beach 1951:142.
[41] This "phylogenetic interpretation" of hormonal control is suggested in: Beach 1947b:293–294. Beach 1948:9–10. Beach 1950:261–269.

males were performed with religious objectives in various ancient groups, and have been performed for that purpose within the present century in certain groups.[31] In various cultures, castrations of adults were performed for the sake of obtaining eunuchs who could be used as household servants, or servants in harems, without the danger of their fathering offspring.[42] Castrations have been most frequently performed as indignities which were inflicted upon enemies captured or killed in battle, and as punishments for certain classes of criminals. Ancient Egyptian drawings, and the derived art of Northern Africa today, depict mounds of severed genitalia gathered from enemies destroyed in battle [43]; and during warfare in probably every part of the world, such mutilation has been considered the supreme subjugation which the conqueror could bestow upon the conquered. There is no doubt that the recurring interest in castration as a legal punishment today is, at least in part, a product of the same sadistic eroticism which has inspired genital mutilation throughout human history.

In more recent decades, both in Europe and in this country, castrations have been rationalized as attempts to modify some aspect of the individual's sexual behavior: to stop masturbation,[44] to transform homosexual into heterosexual patterns of behavior, to control exhibitionists and, in particular, to control adults who sexually "molest" children. Castrations have been used both in Europe and in this country to prevent feeble-minded, criminal, or irresponsible individuals from becoming parents; but simple sterilizations would satisfy that end if there were no other objective in a castration.[25]

Castrations have, of course, been necessarily performed when testes were diseased; and recently castrations of older males have become fairly frequent as a means of reducing their androgen levels, because these may influence cancerous growths or other hypertrophies of the prostate gland. In addition there are a fair number of males who have had to be castrated as a result of war injuries. There has, in consequence, been no shortage of cases for studying the effects of castration

---

[42] For historical accounts of castrations, see such references as: Möbius 1903:12–25. Tandler and Grosz 1913:45–46. Hirschfeld 1948:65–66.

[43] For a description of such mutilations in battle see: Möbius 1903:12–13. We have seen the ancient Egyptian and modern Ethiopian drawings.

[44] For an example of the use of castration to cure masturbation see: Flood [?1901] who reports the castration of 24 males, half of them under 14 years of age, for persistent masturbation and epilepsy, apparently in the Hospital for Epileptics at Palmer, Mass. (See Laughlin 1922:433). Flood concludes: "persistent masturbators . . . unpleasant for a refined woman to see . . . it seemed an absolute necessity to try something which we had not yet tried." See also the account of Dr. Pilcher's castrations of "confirmed masturbators" at the Kansas State Training School at Winfield, Kansas, in: Flood [?1901]:16. Cave 1911:123. Hawke 1950:1 ("Our castrations first started during the administration of Dr. Pilcher who conceived the idea that castration might help control excessive masturbation and pervert sexual acts"). Bowman 1952: 69–70.

on adult males, but there have been very few detailed reports on the sexual behavior of such castrates.

A considerable proportion of the studies have reported, without specific data, that there was an improvement in health as a result of a castration, or an increase or decrease in sex drive, or a generally beneficial effect. Unfortunately some of the reports on which state legislators have recently relied have been in these same general terms, without specific data on the frequencies of response, the intensities of response, the number of items to which the castrated individual responded, the frequencies of erection, the frequencies of masturbatory and overt socio-sexual activities, or the frequencies of total activity to the point of orgasm.

Many of the reports have concerned castrations of older males past the age of fifty, and in many cases between sixty and eighty years of age. Males of such advanced ages normally have their rates so reduced that it would be difficult to determine how much of their inactivity should be credited to a castration. Even at fifty years of age there are 7 per cent of the males who are already impotent and unresponsive sexually, whether they are castrated or not.

The studies that do report frequencies of activity after castration, fail to allow for the fact that most males have their frequencies of sexual activity steadily reduced with advancing age. It means nothing to find that castrated males gradually, over some period of years, show diminished sexual interests and capacities, unless it is shown that the diminution of their activity occurs more rapidly than that which occurs in the population as a whole. It is to be recalled that in our total male sample we found (1948:226) that the average twenty-year-old, married male experienced orgasm with a median frequency of 3.2 per week, but that these frequencies dropped steadily through the years until they had reached 0.8 per week at sixty years of age among males who were not castrated.

Because of the general misunderstanding of the reliability of the evidence on the effects of adult castrations, and because some courts and state legislators have uncritically accepted the published records as justification for their consideration of castration as a means of controlling certain types of sex offenders, it seems appropriate to summarize briefly the data in the published studies. They are here arranged in chronologic order.

STUDIES ON CASTRATION OF ADULT HUMAN MALES

1. Barr 1920. A study of 6 male castrates, most of them with records of low intelligence. Ages from eleven to twenty. Results cannot be evaluated because they are reported in nothing but general terms. They note "an improvement in general behavior" in most instances.

2. Commins and Stone 1932. An extensive review of the literature on the effects of castration on basal metabolism, on the nervous system, on reflex action, on voluntary activity, on sexual behavior in general, and on learning. Deals primarily with lower mammals.

3. Lange 1934. The most extensive and most specific study of the effects of male castration, based on 310 cases which included 242 complete castrates and 68 partial castrates. The data are drawn from a long-time study of 247 cases originating in war injuries, and 63 cases in which there had been a surgical removal of testes following tuberculosis. The following summary applies only to those cases in which there had been complete castrations.

At the time of castration, 10 per cent of the men were under twenty, 50 per cent under twenty-five, and 15 per cent over thirty-five years of age. All but 6 of the cases were observed for fifteen years or longer following castration. The physical changes, which were reported in detail, included regressive effects which appeared chiefly in the earliest and the latest years; but wide individual differences were noted, probably because of the wide age range of the subjects. Data on potency following castration are given on 99 complete castrates: 52 per cent lost potency immediately, 22 per cent lost potency gradually, and 26 per cent still retained their potency at the end of the period of observation. This loss was related to their ages at the time of castration (and hence to their ages at the final report). Some 73 per cent of those retaining potency were under the age of twenty-five at the time of castration. The author points out that the reports of defects due to injury or operation tended to be exaggerated in order to support claims for government compensation.

The sexual desire of many of the subjects had exceeded their potency. The author discusses the fallacy of castration as a cure for sex criminals, since such criminal violence is often the result of the conflict of weakened potency and strong sexual impulses (pp. 44, 101), and he questions the favorable results reported in Switzerland and Denmark on the basis of the selectivity of the groups and the short period of observation of those cases.

4. McCullagh and Renshaw 1934. A study of 12 subjects, 4 castrated between twenty-three and forty, 6 between forty and sixty, and 2 after sixty; observed from six months to twenty-seven years after castration. Partial responses remained in 3 cases, but were entirely lost in 9. There was a shrinking of the penis in 5 cases, a reduction of body and pubic hair in 11 cases, a decrease of energy and endurance in 10 cases, and changes in weight and general appearance. The specific data are, however, still insufficient for final analyses.

5. Wolf 1934. A German study summarizing 162 castrations of human males, many on the basis of fragmentary records from the older literature. Many of the subjects were feeble-minded or mentally deficient. There were 50 cases from the author's own data. The information on the sexual responses of the subjects after operation was quite incomplete. For 72 cases, the effects on responsiveness were minor in 35 per cent, the responses were much reduced in 28 per cent, the responses were completely gone in 37 per cent. However, the data are uninterpretable because there are no correlations with the ages at castration and no exact data on the subsequent frequencies of sexual activity.

6. Kopp 1938. A survey of the status of castration *and sterilization* of criminals in the United States and Europe; but the material is in very general terms, and chiefly historical in interest.

7. Feinier and Rothman 1939. A single male, castrated at twenty-three for tuberculosis of the testes, reported a normal married life and potency which had increased after castration and after recovery from the tuberculosis. At fifty-three (thirty years after the castration) he was having weekly coitus with his wife. The wife corroborated the story. The authors conclude that the only indispensable function of the testes in a fully grown adult is that of procreation, and that sexual responses and potency "are functions of and controlled by the pre-pituitary and psychic centers."

8. Tauber 1940. A good review of the literature, without original data. Reports studies on religious castrations; on castrations of criminals in Germany and Switzerland (where the author feels the data are not reliable); on castrations due to injuries; and on medical castrations. Feels the psychologic aspect of a castration is very important. Concludes that the sexual behavior of male castrates is highly variable, and that the range includes behavior which would be considered normal in non-castrates.

9. Huggins, Stevens, and Hodges 1941. A report on 21 patients castrated to control cancer of the prostate; 3 were between fifty-four and sixty years of age; the others ranged between sixty and eighty-four. Reports sexual drive and potency absent in all cases after operation; but all of the patients were so old that it is impossible to make any critical analysis of the reports on sexual behavior.

10. Engle in Cowdry 1942:489–491. Cites Rössle's study on 125 men castrated under German law for criminal sex offenses, in half of whom sexual responses were "weakened." Ages not given and no records of the specific frequencies of sexual activity. Cites a British report by Hammond of 7 males castrated at ages ranging from thirty to fifty-one, in whom coitus continued after castration, in one case for seventeen years. Concludes that "The evidence suggests then that in men in whom the psychic and neuromotor behavior patterns of sexual activity have been established, complete loss of the testes does not necessarily prevent participation in sexual activity."

11. Hamilton 1943. One male castrated because of cancer at twenty-five years demonstrated normal erections at age forty-three. One male castrated at twenty-six reported marital coitus two to three times a week, at age thirty-nine. Wife confirmed report. Androgen and estrogen levels low, so writer concludes that capacity for erection does not depend upon a supply of androgens from extra-gonadal sources.

12. Stürup 1946a. A psychiatrist's report on 123 males voluntarily castrated in the Danish asylum for psychopathic criminals at Herstedvester. Only general statements on sexual behavior after castration. "Some degree of sexuality is retained in certain cases, at any rate for a number of years, and some cases have been able to achieve a coitus satisfactory to their wives at intervals of about a month. To the majority of cases, however, this does not apply." Insufficient data on ages and on sexual responses and frequencies of activity before and after castration.

13. Stürup 1946b. A discussion of the psychiatric treatment of criminal psychopaths in Denmark. Only a general statement of "good results," without specific data which would allow critical analyses of the results. States that "The detainee must show hyper-sexuality beyond doubt or a stable sexually conditioned criminality, before we use this irreversible treatment."

14. Beach 1948:23–27. Surveys the studies on male castration. Concludes: "Despite the frequency and possibly the accuracy of generalizations regarding the depressing consequences of human castration, the literature is replete with references to complete retention of sexual function in individuals who have been castrated for many years." Then adds: "The frequency of accounts describing the survival of normal sexuality following castration need not obscure the fact that in many, if not the majority of cases, the human male exhibits a gradual loss of mating ability as a result of testicular removal." This last statement, however, ignores the fact that non-castrated males similarly show a gradual loss of mating ability with advancing age.

15. Fuller 1950. No original data. Points out that the medical profession is not agreed on the use of castration as a means of reducing sexual responses. States that there is no assurance that "in man the sexual urge may not persist for years after the castration."

16. Hawke 1950. In a paper delivered before the Illinois Academy of Criminology, Hawke discusses the program of castration employed, under his direction, at the State Training School at Winfield, Kansas, where 330 male castrates furnished material for a nine-year research program. These cases were also the source of physiologic data on castrates in Hamilton 1948:257–322, who gives ages at castration in 57 of these cases. These ranged from eight to twenty-two years, and included 11 boys who were 12 years of age or younger. The cases were largely drawn from a defective delinquent group. The sweeping generalizations as to psychologic improvement, lack of inferiority feelings, increased stability, and lessening of the "social menace" in these cases are not substantiated in the paper by any sufficient data. Only three case histories of individuals, castrated at sixteen, eighteen, and twenty-four, are described in detail, and the only evidence given as to the satisfactory result of these castrations was the fact that they later adjusted to life outside the institution. Hamilton 1948:286–288 presents detailed data, however, showing that a group of these same subjects had difficulty in carrying out their motor activities. Hawke, nonetheless, states that the castrate is "physically a better organism." There do not seem to be any data on the sexual behavior of these subjects which allow reliable analyses of the sexual effects of the castrations.

On the basis of the more reliable of these published studies, and on the basis of the few cases we ourselves have seen, we may generalize as follows: Human males who are castrated as adults are, in many but not in all cases, still capable of being aroused by tactile or psychologic stimuli. They may still be capable of showing essentially all of the physiologic concomitants of sexual response, including the tumescence of all parts of the body and the specifically genital tumescence which may effect normal erection. They may still be capable of developing neuromuscular reactions which include rhythmic pelvic thrusts of the sort necessary for coitus, and they may still be capable of attaining orgasm. The frequency and intensity of response may or may not be reduced by the castration. The psychologic effects of such an operation may make it difficult for some of the males to make socio-sexual adjustments.

Ejaculation may or may not follow orgasm in a castrated human male. In the lower mammals, removal of the testes may cause degeneration of the prostate and seminal vesicles, which are the chief sources of the ejaculate, but there are some recorded instances of a reduced and modified ejaculate in some castrated human males. In most cases there is no ejaculation. The individual variation probably depends on the length of time which has elapsed since the castration and the stage of degeneration of the secreting glands. None of this, however, makes it impossible for a castrated male to have orgasm. We have the history of a male engaging in sexual activity with normal frequencies and with orgasm fifteen years after the castration, and it will be noted that in the literature cited above there are instances of the retention of sexual capacity for similarly long periods, including one case of a male who was normally active thirty years after castration.

Castrations of adult males of lower mammalian species produce, as we have already noted, a more general physical deterioration than is recorded for adult human male castrates. In general, male animals castrated as adults show diminished sexual responses, but the data are insufficient to allow critical analyses.[45] We have already noted that in chimpanzees there are records of adult male castrates who were as active sexually as males who had not been castrated.

In any event, the laboratory experiments on animals, and the data which are at present available on human male castrates, do not justify the opinion that the public may be protected from socially dangerous types of sex offenders by castration laws.

INCREASED SUPPLIES OF GONADAL HORMONES

The administration of an extra supply of male hormone to an animal, female or male, which has intact gonads, may increase its sexual responsiveness. This may appear to contradict the data on the effects of a castration, but the two bodies of data are not actually in conflict.

Excessive Gonadal Hormones in Young Animals. The administration of androgenic hormones to a young, non-castrated male, whether infrahuman or human, ordinarily speeds up its physical development and the development of its sexual responsiveness and overt sexual activity.[46] There are similar results when estrogens are given to young females.[47] There is considerable work on laboratory animals which establishes this fact. In the case of the human male, the clinical administration of testosterone to a pre-adolescent is ordinarily avoided because of the

---

[45] Data on the reduced sexual responses of castrated adult males of lower mammalian species may be found, for example, in: Stone 1927:369 (rats). Commins and Stone 1932:497 (rabbits and rats). Stone in Allen et al. 1939:1246 (rats). Beach 1944c:255 (rats). Beach 1948:21 (summarizes earlier studies). Rice and Andrews 1951:115–116 (farm animals).

[46] Experimental and clinical data on the administration of male hormones to young, non-castrated males are cited in: Beach 1942d. Hoffman 1944:157–159. Heller and Maddock 1947:417. Beach 1948:206–207. Burrows 1949:169. Howard and Scott in Williams 1950:339.

[47] Experimental data on the administration of female hormones to young, lower mammalian females, are cited in: Beach 1948:196, 203–204. Corner 1951: 57–58.

probability that it will start precocious development. But when adolescent development seems to be delayed, and particularly when there seems to be an under-development of the gonads, some physicians do administer testosterone. There may be complications, however, if more than the optimum dose is given, for an excessive supply of gonadal hormones may inhibit the secretory activity of the anterior lobe of the pituitary.

Precocious adolescent development sometimes, although rarely, may occur in children at five or six, or even at two or three years of age. In some of these cases there may be an endocrine imbalance which sometimes involves an androgen disturbance; but there are other cases in which clinical studies fail to show any sort of endocrine disturbance. Such children may show physical developments equal to those of a normal thirteen- or fourteen-year-old. However, the sexual responses and overt activities of such precocious children are ordinarily typical of those among normal pre-adolescent children of the same age. Investigators are inclined to emphasize that such a child masturbates, shows sexual curiosity, or engages in some form of socio-sexual play, and they are likely to conclude that these activities are a product of the precociousness. But it should not be forgotten that such activities are ordinarily found in the histories of normal pre-adolescent children (Chapter 4).

In the several cases which we have of precocious adolescent development, we have rarely found sexual activities which exceeded those ordinarily found among normal children of the same age.[48] We have the history of a five-year-old with the physical development of a four-teen-year-old, but with sexual responses which were normal or even lower than normal for a five-year-old. We have one group of four related cases in which hereditary factors seem to have been involved, for precociousness had appeared among the males of at least two generations in separated branches of the family. We have the history of another boy who turned adolescent at seven, and he was highly responsive and exceedingly active in socio-sexual contacts. Since cases of very early adolescent development are relatively rare, it is highly important that more extensive data be accumulated on the responses and overt sexual activity of such children.

The administration of androgens to a pre-adolescent human female may do considerable damage because of their over-stimulation of

---

[48] Summaries of published cases of precocious adolescent development in which there are data on sexual behavior, may be found in: Doe-Kulmann and Stone 1927:319 (adult sexuality not present in most precocious cases). Singer 1940: 19–22 (summary of published reports on 59 females, 48 males). Stotijn 1946:56 (a Dutch study). Dennis in Carmichael 1946:656–658. Sandblom 1948:110 (one case of a precocious three-year-old male, aggressive sexually).

physical development.[49] There seem to be no data on the effects of such an early administration of androgens on the sexual responsiveness and the overt sexual activity of the human female.

Excessive Androgens in Adults. When an extra supply of androgens is given an adult animal that has not been castrated, there may be an increase in the general level of its physical activity, its aggressiveness, and its frequency of sexual response and overt sexual performance.[50] This is true of laboratory and farm animals, and it is equally true of the human male. It is also true when androgens are given females, whether they are lower mammalian or human females.

When testosterone, for instance, is given the normal human male, there may be an increase in the frequency of his morning erections, the frequency of his erotic response to various stimuli, the frequency of his masturbation, and the frequency of his socio-sexual contacts.[51] This is ordinarily true of adult males of ages ranging at least from the twenties into the fifties or sixties. Testosterone has also been used clinically to increase the levels of sexual response in cases in which a failure to have offspring appears to depend on low rates of coitus. We have several histories of males who had had their coital frequencies increased by such clinical treatment. Sperm counts may also be increased by the administration of testosterone, and this may contribute to the relief of the sterility.[52] The indiscriminate use of testosterone, however, may involve some danger, for if the dose exceeds the amount necessary for optimum effectiveness, pituitary functions may be inhibited, and this may do damage to various structures, including the

---

[49] Discussion of dosages of androgens affecting precocious physical development in young females is found in: Selye 1949:614. Mazer and Israel 1951:126. Talbot et al. 1952:381, 440–441, 484.

[50] Effects of androgens on non-castrate adult male animals is described in: Beach 1942b:181–182, 193–194. Beach 1942c:227–247. Beach 1948:34, 36. Cheng et al. 1950:452 (increased sex activity in male rabbit).

[51] While there is a general use of androgen therapy on intact, normal males in clinical practice, there are few published accounts; but see: Miller, Hubert and Hamilton 1938:538–540. Kenyon et al. 1940:35. Barahal 1940:319 (increased drive in homosexual males). Heller and Maddock 1947:419 (says "normal" men fail to have an increase in sex drive, but on p. 422 agrees that such treatment seems to increase "the power of the sex drive in both normal and homosexual males . . ."). Burrows 1949:169 (excessive masculine urges in "normal" male adults). Perloff 1949:133 ff. H. H. Turner 1950: 38–43 (a survey; indicates contradictions in data).

[52] Surveys and studies on the effect of testosterone on sperm count include: Weisman 1941:240–242 (concludes small doses stimulate sperm production, large doses inhibit it). Heller and Maddock 1947:419 (temporary reduction of sperm). C. D. Turner 1948:344 (considers evidence for increase in sperm inconclusive; lack of sperm if dosage is excessive). H. H. Turner 1950:24–25, 53–54 (no change in sperm production, although recognizes that other reports are contradictory). Cheng et al. 1950:447–452 (increases volume of ejaculate in rabbit, but total number of sperm unchanged). Heckel and McDonald 1952:725–733 (reduces sperm production in 72 men; a return to a higher level after treatment stopped in twenty-three out of forty-five men).

gonads themselves, and there may be negative effects on sexual activities.[53] In laboratory animals, excessive doses of testosterone may reduce the gonads to more or less vestigial structures.

There is some clinical experience in administering testosterone to normal human females, and the results obtained are quite similar to those obtained in males.[54] Once again, the levels of physical activity may be increased, and the general level of aggressiveness may be increased. In the case of the lower mammals, this increased aggressiveness increases the frequency with which the female mounts other animals, either females or males. Because males are normally more aggressive than females, normal females usually find few opportunities to mount males; but females who have been given testosterone may become so aggressive that they succeed in mounting a larger number of males.[55]

The increased responsiveness of a normal female or male who has received an increased supply of testosterone has ordinarily been taken as evidence that the hormone plays a prime part in controlling sexual behavior. Such an interpretation, however, ignores the evidence of the castration experiments on adult females and males. It seems more correct to conclude that androgens, at every level which does not exceed the point of optimum effectiveness, are among the physiologic agents which step up the general level of metabolic activity in an animal's body, including the level of its nervous function and therefore of its sexual activity. For instance, as an example of the effect of testosterone on other physiologic activities, it may be noted that dairy breeders sometimes administer it to cattle in order to increase their food utilization. Thereby the breeder may increase the amount of meat which he secures when he gives the animal a given quantity of food.

There are so many other factors which affect the levels of metabolic activity in a fully mature animal that the loss of the usual supply of androgens, as in a castration, does not make it impossible for an animal to hold its metabolism at something approaching a normal level. This, however, does not preclude the possibility that supplies of male hormones in excess of those normally provided by the gonads, may raise

---

[53] The harmful effects of various doses of testosterone are pointed out in: Moore 1942:40–41. Heller and Maddock 1947:415–416. Ludwig 1950:453, 465 (small doses more injurious than large doses in male rats).

[54] For clinical use of androgens to increase sex drive in human females, see: Geist 1941. Salmon 1941 (survey of animal and clinical experiments). Salmon and Geist 1943. Greenblatt 1947:177–178. Hyman 1946(3):2406. Carter, Cohen and Shorr 1947:361–364 (a comprehensive survey). Beach 1948:62. Selye 1949:619.

[55] Increased aggressiveness among females of lower mammalian species after treatment with testosterone dosage are reported in: Stone 1939. Ball 1940:151–165. Young 1941:135. Birch and Clark 1946 (chimpanzee).

the metabolic levels and consequently the levels of sexual response and performance. But male hormones are not the only agents that step up the levels of activity, including the levels of sexual activity, for the administration of pituitary extracts, of thyroid, and of some other substances may have similar effects. In fact, good health, sufficient exercise, and plenty of sleep still remain the most effective of the aphrodisiacs known to man.

Excessive Estrogens in Adults. What effect the administration of an extra supply of estrogens may have on the sexual behavior of the human or lower mammalian female or male, is a matter which may not be asserted with assurance in our present state of knowledge. Some clinicians assert that they have raised the levels of sexual responsiveness in female patients by administering estrogens, while other clinicians make just as positive statements that they have never secured such a result.[56] Animal breeders and students experimenting with laboratory animals, female and male, give similarly contradictory reports.[57] The contradictions may mean that there is no simple and direct relationship between estrogens and sexual behavior, or they may mean that the effectiveness of an increased supply of estrogens depends upon the concomitance of a variety of factors, including such things as the general metabolic level, the general physical health, the levels of the other hormones in the body, the age, the point in the estrus cycle at which the estrogens are administered, and probably still other factors.

There is a theory that estrogens counteract the effectiveness of androgens. The theory is as yet unsubstantiated by adequate experiment,[58] and is confused by the fact that both androgens and estrogens occur simultaneously in both the female and male bodies. However, some clinicians in this country, in Denmark, and in Holland are using estrogens in an effort to reduce the levels of sexual responsiveness of males convicted as sex offenders.[59] It is possible that estrogens do re-

[56] Various effects of estrogen therapy are reported in: Frank 1940:1509. Soule and Bortnick 1941. Mazer and Israel 1946:34. Greenblatt 1947:177–178. Emmens and Parkes 1947:240–241. Kimbrough and Israel 1948:1217–1219. Perloff 1949:135. Ford and Beach 1951:225–226. Mazer and Israel 1951:33. Masters in Cowdry 1952:669.

[57] For estrogen effects on the behavior and physical structures of mammalian males, see: Clark and Birch 1945:328 (loss of dominance in chimpanzee). Emmens and Parkes 1947:236 ff. (atrophy of testis, prostate, Cowper's glands, spermatogenesis). Beach 1948:61–62. Selye 1949:360 (decreases sexual responsiveness). Goldzieher and Goldzieher 1949:1156 (male impotence). Howard and Scott in Williams 1950:342 (depresses spermatogenesis). Paschkis and Rakoff 1950:137–138 (testicular degeneration). Howard et al. 1950:134. Lynch 1952:734–741 (atrophy of rat testis, depresses spermatogenesis).

[58] The lack of any antagonistic effect between androgens and estrogens is noted in: Koch 1937:206–208. Hartman 1940:449–471 (female monkey). Hoffman 1944:42–43. Burrows 1949:122. Selye 1949:64–65.

[59] The use of estrogens on male sex offenders and others to reduce sex drive is discussed or reported in: Dunn 1940:2263–2264 (a single case, 96 day treat-

duce the amount of androgen which is secreted, but the attempt to control sexual behavior by lowering androgens depends, of course, on a misinterpretation of the role of the androgens in the sexual activities of the male. There are optimistic reports of "good results" from the estrogen injections, but, as usual, the reports are not supported by adequate details of what the "good results" are supposed to be. Since an excessive supply of estrogens may affect many body functions besides sexual behavior, and since an excessive supply may do irreparable damage to other glandular structures, several research endocrinologists assert that they consider the use of estrogens to lower the sexual responsiveness of a male nothing less than medical malpractice.

PITUITARY HORMONES IN SEXUAL BEHAVIOR

Because of the effects which secretions from the anterior lobe of the pituitary gland may have on all of the other endocrine organs, and particularly on the gonads and adrenal glands, the pituitary has often been described as a master gland dominating all of the other endocrine organs in the body. It seems, however, more correct to think of the gonads and the pituitary and adrenal glands as a chain of organs whose secretions have interlocking effects. The effect of the pituitary on the gonads, for instance, seems hardly more significant than the effect of the gonads on the pituitary.

Relation of Pituitary to Physical Characters. Damage to the anterior lobe of the pituitary in a young animal, or in the human female or male before the onset of adolescence, may affect physical development more seriously than a gonadal castration.[60] In the case of the human female or male, the individual remains immature or develops slowly and at a late age, and is abnormal in his or her physical proportions and functions. However, the effects of a pituitary insufficiency in a young animal may be relieved by the administration of pituitary hormones. Because of the general, regulatory function of the pituitary gland, some laboratory students and some clinicians are inclined to depend upon pituitary hormones to correct a gonadal insufficiency.

ment, resulting in loss of sex drive and degeneration of genitalia). Dunn 1941: 643 (later report on same case. Some effects disappeared after stopping therapy, but sexual levels still reduced). Rosenzweig and Hoskins 1941:87–88 (massive doses, no effect on one homosexual male). Greenblatt 1947:279–280. Golla and Hodge 1949 (13 males, uncontrollable sex urge, treated with estrone successfully). Perloff 1949:135. Brown 1950:52–53 (cites 300 male homosexuals, unsuccessful treatment with androgens). Tappan 1951:247–248 (in Holland).

[60] The physical effect of pituitary damage in young animals and human subjects, and subsequent hormonal therapy are discussed in: Pratt in Allen et al. 1939: 1294. Corner 1942:141 (females), 222 (males). Greenblatt 1947:183. Beach 1948:12–17, 22, 208. Selye 1949:262–317. Williams 1950:ch.2. Howard and Scott in Williams 1950:318–319. Ford and Beach 1951:167–169. Dempsey in Stevens 1951:221.

It is reported that the administration of pituitary hormones to a normal pre-adolescent in whom there is neither a pituitary nor a gonadal insufficiency, may induce a precocious adolescent development.[61]

Relation of Pituitary to Sexual Behavior. A pre-adolescent pituitary deficiency affects the sexual behavior of an animal in much the same way that an early castration affects its sexual behavior. Responsiveness develops slowly if at all, and it is probable that the levels of response which are ultimately reached by such an individual are below those which are normal.[62] Since the gonads are among the structures which do not develop normally when there is an early pituitary insufficiency, the effects of the pituitary hormones on sexual behavior may depend upon their regulation of the supply of gonadal hormones, and this interpretation is favored by the fact that the administration of androgens to an animal which has a pituitary deficiency may induce normal sexual behavior. On the other hand, it is also possible that the pituitary hormones directly affect the development and the physiologic function of the nervous system on which sexual behavior depends.[63]

Because the pituitary glands are not located near the organs of reproduction, there are only scattered references to the effects of pituitary deficiencies on sexual behavior. The opinion is generally held that such deficiencies in adults, or the administration of pituitary hormones in cases of deficiencies, or the administration of pituitary hormones to normal adults, does not have as pronounced an effect on sexual behavior as the administration of gonadal hormones.

Pituitary Secretions and Levels of Sexual Response. There are indications that the levels of pituitary secretion may correlate with the fundamental patterns of sexual behavior which we have found in the human female and male. Recently published studies on fowl show that the cells of the anterior lobe of the pituitary in a very young male contain a quite clear cytoplasm, which, however, begins to accumulate granular materials, the so-called mitochondria, soon after the animal

---

[61] Precocious adolescent development resulting from the pituitary treatment of young animals is described in: Smith and Engle 1927 (ablation of thyroid made no difference, showing it was not involved; mice, rats, cats, rabbits, guinea pigs). Young 1941:322. Beach 1948:12–16. Burrows 1949:22–23, 39. Ford and Beach 1951:168–170.

[62] That a lack of pituitary hormone depresses sex drive, is reported by: Burrows 1949:169. Selye 1949:271–282. Williams 1950:43, 46.

[63] Conversely, the effect of the nervous system on the secretory capacity of the pituitary is well-known. Examples of such neural control are in: Hoffman 1944:309–310 (suppression of menses). Hartman 1945:27 (rabbit ovulation). C. D. Turner 1948:364–365 (pseudopregnancy). Durand-Wever 1952:209–211 (gonads deteriorate as a result of fear). Talbot et al. 1952:302–303 (puberty depends on neural mechanisms operating via pituitary).

begins to grow.[64] These mitochondria are associated with the normal physiologic processes that go on in these cells, but as the male animal ages, the mitochondria steadily increase in quantity until the cells of the glands of the older male become more or less filled with the granular inclusions.

The secretory capacity of the cell is inversely proportional to the volume of the granular inclusions in the cell and therefore to the age of the animal, and in the older male bird the cells may, in consequence, lose most of their secretory capacity. The functional significance of the pituitary is therefore steadily lowered as the male becomes more advanced in age.

On the other hand, the cells of the anterior lobe of the pituitary of the female do not accumulate such a quantity of granular material, and cases are reported of ten- and twelve-year-old female birds in which the cells of the anterior lobe of the pituitary are practically as clear of mitochondria as they are in very young females. This means that the secretory capacities of the pituitaries of these females are maintained at a more or less constant level throughout the life of the bird.

This gradual loss of function in the cells of the pituitary of the males, among fowls, parallels the steady decline which we have found in the sexual activities of the human male. The maintenance of pituitary function on a more or less constant level in the females, among fowls, parallels the maintenance of sexual capacity which we have found in the human female. Among all of the biologic phenomena which we are aware of, these differences between female and male pituitary secretion, and the differences which we shall note below in the levels of the 17-ketosteroids among females and males, are the only phenomena that seem to parallel the differences which we find between the sexual activities of the human female and male.

Since cytologic and experimental studies of these differences in female and male pituitary functions are of very recent date, we have no idea whether such a differentiation applies to the human or to any other species of mammal. If the differentiation does hold in the human species, it does not necessarily imply that there is any simple, causal relationship between pituitary secretions and sexual behavior. The relationship may depend upon a whole chain of physiologic phenomena which are initiated by the pituitary hormones; or the pituitary picture may reflect some other physiologic condition of the female on which both pituitary and sexual function depend. In any event there is a parallel between these reported pituitary functions in the bird, and

---

[64] For the relation of age to the mitochondria in the cells of the anterior lobe of the pituitary, see: Payne 1949:197–198. Payne in Cowdry 1952:385.

the data which we have on the sexual behavior of the human female and male. We did not find such a correlation between the levels of gonadal hormones and the patterns of human sexual behavior.

THYROID HORMONES

Thyroid secretions have well known effects upon the general physiologic level of an animal's activities, including its nervous responses. Low levels of thyroid secretion lower the rates of most activities, and high levels raise the rates of activity; but there is no invariable relationship for, once again, the effects depend upon the concomitance of various other factors which may also influence metabolic activities. It is reported that male hormones tend to stimulate thyroid function, but female hormones are said to inhibit their function, thereby reducing metabolic levels.[65]

It is well known that early insufficiencies of thyroid secretions may delay or modify adolescent physical developments and lead to an infantilism of genital structures in both females and males.[66] Cases of such adolescent deficiencies which we have in our histories, show delayed or low levels of sexual response and activity.

There are few published data, but there is a rather widespread clinical understanding that thyroid deficiencies in an older individual may be associated with some lack of responsiveness, and an excess may be associated with rates of sexual activity which are above the average. Not a few physicians administer preparations of thyroid in order to increase the responsiveness of some of their patients. We have some histories of females and a fair number of histories of males to whom thyroid extracts were administered with that express purpose. In some cases, increased frequencies of coitus seem to have been the direct consequence of this therapy, in other cases the record did not seem to indicate that there was any modification of sexual activity, and in some cases a decrease in sexual activity was reported after the thyroid administration. It is, of course, difficult to know how much of the reported change in any particular case was the direct result of the administration of the hormone, how much was the consequence of a change in other physiologic functions, and how much depended on social situations.

Just as some physicians have used testosterone to increase the frequencies of coitus in cases of sterility in which the sterility appeared to be a consequence of low rates of coitus, so there are some who use

[65] Effects of male and female hormones on thyroid function are noted in: Hoffman 1944:240–241 (reciprocal relationship). Williams 1950:115 (estrogen antagonizes thyroid function; testosterone stimulates thyroid and increases metabolic rate).

[66] Delayed adolescence resulting from lack of thyroid is described in: Lisser 1942. Hoffman 1944:239. Williams 1950:173–175. Talbot et al 1952:21, 31.

thyroid to accomplish the same end. Just as with the administration of gonadal hormones, there are reports that such thyroid therapy increases the sperm count and the motility and viability of the sperm, thereby increasing the chances for conception to occur.[67] There is, however, a considerable need for the accumulation of more specific data on these matters, and more carefully controlled experimentation. Since the administration of thyroid extracts may affect a number of other body functions, there is need for caution in the use of these hormones in any attempt to control sexual responses.

ADRENAL HORMONES

The adrenal glands are paired organs lying above the kidneys, which places them in the small of the back of the human animal. They are known to produce a considerable number—perhaps twenty or thirty or more—chemical compounds (steroids) which function as hormones. The possibility that some of these are related to sexual behavior has been considered for some time, but there are still few specific data to establish such a relationship.

Adrenaline. The best known of the secretions of the adrenal glands is adrenaline. This is a product of the central core, the medulla, of the adrenal organ. The role of adrenaline in various types of emotional response, and particularly in the case of fear and fright, was one of the first things known about the glands of internal secretion (p. 692).

Because many of the gross physiologic changes which occur during sexual response are similar to those which may be induced in an animal by injecting it with adrenaline, or by stimulating it so its adrenal glands secrete an extra supply of adrenaline, it has frequently been suggested that adrenaline is responsible for the initiation of sexual response or for some portion of it.

On the other hand, there is a longstanding theory that adrenaline interferes with sexual responses.[68] The theory may have originated in the observation that persons who are frightened during sexual activity may have their activity interrupted. There are, however, no experimental data to establish this inhibitory effect of adrenaline on sexual response.

We have already emphasized (Chapter 17) that sexual reactions may so quickly involve the whole animal body that it is difficult to believe that a blood-circulated agent such as adrenaline could be re-

---

[67] The administration of thyroid in sterility cases is noted in: Siegler 1944:311–313. Smith in Williams 1950:430. Mazer and Israel 1951:461, 488 (to increase sperm count).

[68] The opinion that adrenaline interferes with sexual response, or inhibits erection, is implied or specifically stated in: Cannon 1920:270–271. Kuntz 1945:311.

sponsible for the major body of physiologic changes which constitute sexual response. Nevertheless, many of the physiologic phenomena involved in sexual response, and particularly the activity of the autonomic nervous system during sexual response, may lead to the secretion of adrenaline, and it is quite possible that some of the phenomena seen in the later stages of sexual response may be products of adrenaline secretion (p. 693).

Cortical Hormones. The outer portion of the adrenal organ, its cortex, is the source of a variety of hormones, including androgens, estrogens, and the various compounds known as the 17-ketosteroids. It is understandable that the adrenal cortex should have some of the same functions as the gonads, for the testes, the ovaries, and the cortex of the adrenals originate from a common embryonic cell mass, even though the organs into which they develop may move apart in the adult anatomy. It has generally been considered that the effects of a gonadal castration are not more severe than they are because the adrenal cortex shares some of the responsibility for the production of the same hormones.[69] The importance of the adrenals in this regard, however, may have been overemphasized in the earlier literature.

The 17-ketosteroids are so called because they have a ketone group at the 17 position on the molecule. Some, but not all, of the 17-ketosteroids are androgens. The 17-ketosteroids are supposed to originate in various organs, including the gonads and the adrenal cortex. It has been estimated that the adrenal cortex may produce as much as 60 or 70 per cent of the 17-ketosteroids found in the mammalian body; but the removal of both the testes and the adrenal cortex in a laboratory animal does not wholly deprive it of its 17-ketosteroids, and this indicates that other organs also produce these compunds.[70]

There are suggestions in the literature that the 17-ketosteroids are in some fashion related to levels of sexual responsiveness, and to frequencies of overt sexual activity in a mammal. The suggestions, however, have been theoretic, and there seems to have been no demonstration of such a relationship in either experimental or clinical data. We do find, however, that the reported levels of the 17-ketosteroids in the

---

[69] The compensatory function of the adrenal cortex in castrates is described in: Burrows 1949:189. Dempsey in Stevens 1951:216 (potency of male depressed more severely by destroying adrenals than by castration).

[70] For the relative importance of the cortex in supplying 17-ketosteroids in the body see: Fraser et al. 1941:255 (two-thirds adrenal in male, all from adrenal in female). Dorfman et al. 1947:487 (17-ketosteroids still significant in male and female monkeys 40 days after removal of both gonads and adrenals). Hamburger 1948:31–32. Dempsey in Stevens 1951:215 (one-third gonadal, remainder from adrenal cortex). Engle in Cowdry 1952:712 (two-thirds from adrenal). Maddock et al. 1952:668 (both testes and cortex are important).

human male differ from the reported levels of the 17-ketosteroids in
the human female in a manner which more or less parallels the differences which we have found between the median frequencies of orgasm
at various ages in the two sexes (compare Figures 143 and 155).[71]

It is reported that the 17-ketosteroids increase sharply in the urine
of the developing human male at the approach of adolescence and during early adolescence (Figure 155). They reach a peak in the late teens

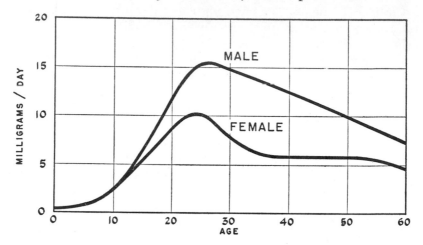

Figure 155. Levels of 17-Ketosteroids in Human Female and Male

Showing aging effect in male, and a prolonged plateau in the female, somewhat
similar to average median frequencies of total outlet among females and males shown
in Figure 143. Data from Hamburger 1948.

or early twenties in the male, but from that point they drop steadily
into old age. Consequently, the levels of sexual activity in the human
male more closely match the levels of the 17-ketosteroids than the
levels of gonadal hormones. We have already noted that there is also
a parallel to the human male behavior curves, in the secretory capacity
of the anterior lobe of the pituitary in one species of laboratory animal.

The levels of the 17-ketosteroids which are reported for the human
female are quite different from those reported for the male (Figure
155). During adolescence and the later teens, there is a sharp rise in
the ketosteroid levels of the female. The curve reaches its peak somewhere in the middle twenties, shows a rather sharp drop in the next

[71] Data on levels of 17-ketosteroids are found in the following sources: Fraser et
al. 1941:237–255 (shows decrease in older ages, both male and female).
Talbot et al. 1943:364. Hamburger 1948:34. Hamilton and Hamilton 1948:
438. Howard et al. 1950:127 ff. Salter, Humm, and Oesterling 1948:302–303,
fig. 3 (decrease with age in male after twenties). Kenigsberg, Pearson, and
McGavack 1949:426–427 (in males increase up to thirties, decrease thereafter.
In contrast to other studies, notes no changes in twenty females aged 17
to 64).

ten years, and then lies on a plateau for some years. It continues on this level through menopause and into the middle fifties, and does not show a further drop until the late fifties or sixties. Another study shows a more or less continuous plateau from ages seventeen to sixty-four, without the teen-age rise which the first-mentioned study showed. This plateau parallels the plateau which we have found in the sexual activities of the female (Figure 143). The chief difference lies in the rise in the 17-ketosteroids reported in one study during the late teens and early twenties, and this rise is not found in the female's sexual performance. This may raise a question as to the significance of the correlation; but it is also clear that a part of the lack of sexual response in the younger American female is a product of cultural restraints on her sexual performance. We have presented evidence for this throughout the present volume, particularly in connection with the data showing the effect of the religious tradition on her behavior.

These correlations between ketosteroid levels and the sexual activities of the human female and male may represent a simple causal relationship, or each of these phenomena may be a product of some other basic physiologic phenomenon, or of a whole complex of physiologic phenomena which are responsible for adrenal function, for pituitary function, and for the capacities of the nervous system to be affected by what we call sexual stimuli.

HORMONES AND PATTERNS OF SEXUAL BEHAVIOR

While the data which we have presented show that hormones may affect the capacity of the central nervous system to be stimulated sexually, and therefore may affect the levels of sexual response, there are no data which warrant the conclusion that an individual's choice of a sexual partner or of a particular type of sexual activity may be directly influenced by any of the hormones. As far as sexual performance is concerned, it is incorrect to think of endocrine organs as the glands of personality.

We have already pointed out that the sexual capacity of an animal depends upon its inherited anatomy and particularly upon its nervous structures and the physiologic capacities of those structures. The capacity of an animal to be aroused by tactile stimuli or psychologic stimuli, and to respond with a development of neuromuscular tensions which produce, among other things, the rhythmic pelvic thrusts which are typical of mammalian coitus, is a capacity which is inherent at birth (Chapter 15).

We have also emphasized (Chapter 16) that all organisms, and particularly such highly evolved organisms as the human animal, are conditioned by their experience, and consequently in the course of time come to respond more readily to particular types of stimuli. Thus, they develop preferences for the repetition of those types of sexual experience which have been most satisfactory, and become conditioned against the repetition of those types of sexual activity which have been unsatisfactory. In addition to being affected by firsthand experience, the individual may be conditioned by the reported experience of his or her friends, and by the social tradition (Chapter 16). Such conditioning seems a sufficient explanation of a preference for a sexual partner who is a blonde or a brunette, or a preference for a sexual partner of the same or of the opposite sex, or for the utilization of one type of technique rather than another in the course of a sexual relationship. It is curious that psychologists and psychiatrists, who are the ones who most often emphasize the importance of psychologic conditioning, so often look for hormonal explanations of any type of sexual behavior which departs from the Hittite and Talmudic codes.

On the unwarranted assumption that homosexuality represents some sort of femininity in an anatomic male, and masculinity in an anatomic female, there have been clinical attempts to redirect the sexual behavior of homosexual males, and occasionally of homosexual females, by giving them gonadal hormones. Recent suggestions concerning the importance of the 17-ketosteroids have led to investigations of the possibilities of using those substances to control behavior. Certain clinicians have developed a lucrative business supplying hormones to patients with homosexual histories, and androgens have been given males who have been discovered in homosexual activity in penal institutions, in the Armed Forces, and elsewhere. Certain of the drug companies have encouraged the use of male hormones for this purpose.

The possibility that hormones might modify homosexual patterns of behavior found some encouragement in early reports on the hormonal injections of laboratory animals. These reports, unfortunately, involved an erroneous use of the term *homosexual*.[72] Among most of the mammals a female in heterosexual coitus typically assumes a crouched position, often with her head drawn down and her haunches raised in a manner which allows the male to mount in coitus. The female rat arches her back convexly (in a *lordosis*) and her ears go into a tremor. The male, on the other hand, typically sits or rises on his hind legs while he effects coitus. The assumption of the crouched position by a male during a sexual relationship, or the assumption of an upright posi-

---

[72] The concept of a "reversal" of "masculinity" or "femininity" in sexual behavior among lower mammals is found, for instance, in: Ball 1937, 1939, 1940. Beach 1938, 1941, 1942b, 1945, 1947b. Young and Rundlett 1939:449 (labelling such a reversal homosexual). Beach corrects this interpretation in: Beach 1948:68. Ford and Beach 1951:41–42.

tion by a female, was recorded in the earlier literature on animal behavior as a *sex reversal* or *homosexual* activity. But this use of the term had no relation to its use in human psychology, where *homosexual* refers to the choice of a partner of the same sex.

We have already noted (p. 747) that rats which are injected with testosterone become more aggressive in all of their behavior, including their sexual behavior, and that females who are given testosterone mount other females and males more frequently than they did before they were given the hormones. But they do this because their aggressiveness has been increased; and when they mount males their behavior is still heterosexual and not homosexual, even though the positions assumed in the coitus have been reversed.

In connection with the clinical treatment of homosexuality there are, of course, reports of "good results," but no adequate data to show that the behavioral patterns of such subjects have ever been modified by hormonal treatments.[73] We have the histories of an appreciable number of males who had received hormonal treatments, but we have never seen an instance in which a homosexual pattern had been eliminated by such therapy. Not infrequently, however, the levels of sexual responsiveness had been raised by the treatment with male hormones, and this, in many instances, had complicated the situation by increasing the capacity of the homosexual individual to be aroused by *homosexual* stimuli. Such failures to attain the desired results in therapy had led to social tragedies in a number of the cases.

SUMMARY AND CONCLUSIONS

Our present understanding of the relations between hormones and the sexual behavior of the human female and male may, then, be summarized as follows:

1. The early development of sexual responsiveness in the human male and its later development in the female, the location of the period of maximum responsiveness for the male in the late teens and early twenties and for the female in the late twenties, the subsequent decline of the male's sexual capacities from that peak into old age, and the maintenance of female responsiveness on something of a level throughout most of her life, are patterns which are not explained by the known

---

[73] For the hormonal treatment of homosexual cases, see: Barahal 1940:329 (7 cases, increased the sex drive of homosexuals, failed to change its direction). Glass, Deuel and Wright 1940. Kinsey 1941 (a critical appraisal of earlier data). Glass and Johnson 1944 (some benefit in 3 cases; no benefit in 8). T. V. Moore 1945:80. Heller and Maddock 1947:419–422 (a well balanced discussion). Perloff 1949:136–139. Howard and Scott in Williams 1950:333. Brown 1950: 52–53 (300 male homosexuals, unsuccessful treatment with androgens). See also footnote 59.

anatomy or physiology of sexual response. Neither are they explained by the known differences in the capacities of females and males to be aroused by psychosexual stimuli.

2. Various hormones may affect the levels of sexual responsiveness in the human female and male because of their effects on the levels of all physiologic activities, including those capacities of the nervous system on which sexual behavior depends.

3. Estrogens, the so-called female hormones, originate primarily in the ovaries and the adrenal cortex. Androgens, the so-called male hormones, originate in the testes, the adrenal cortex, and still other organs. Both estrogens and androgens are present in both females and males. They occur in about equal abundance in human females and males in the pre-adolescent years, but during adolescence the androgens rise to a somewhat higher level in the male, and the estrogens rise to a much higher level in the female. In neither sex, however, does this rise correlate with the levels of sexual responsiveness in the adolescent or older female or male.

4. Gonadal hormones are among the elements necessary for normal physical development in young animals, both female and male. Consequently they are necessary for the development of the capacities of the nervous system and therefore may, indirectly, affect the development of sexual responsiveness in the female and male.

5. In human adults, gonadal hormones may be withdrawn (as in a castration) with minimum effects on physical characters, with a minimum or no effect on the sexual responsiveness of the female, and with little or no effect on the sexual responsiveness of half or more of the males. In a smaller number of cases there may be a slow physical degeneration in the male which may be accompanied by a reduction in his sexual responsiveness.

6. Estrogen and androgen levels, as far as they are known in the normal human female and male, do not correlate with the frequencies of sexual activity in the two sexes. There seem to be no correlations with the aging patterns of the male in his sexual performance, and with the female's maintenance of a level of response throughout most of her life.

7. Increased supplies of androgens given to adult human females or males do raise their levels of sexual response. There is serious danger, however, in the administration of such hormones except under the direction of an experienced clinician.

8. Pituitary hormones are also among the elements necessary for the normal physical development of the female and male, and for the

development of many physiologic capacities, including those capacities of the nervous system upon which sexual behavior depends.

9. The levels of pituitary secretion are known to drop steadily among the males of one species of laboratory animal, while the levels of pituitary secretion in the female of the same species may remain constant for some years. If this is also true of the human species, this would parallel the differences which we find in levels of sexual responsiveness among human females and males. The correlations might represent a causal relationship, or both phenomena might be independent products of more basic physiologic factors.

10. The levels of thyroid secretion sometimes show a direct correlation with the levels of sexual responsiveness. Higher thyroid levels sometimes correlate with higher levels of response, and lower thyroid levels sometimes correlate with lower levels of response; but the correlations are not invariable, for there appear to be other factors which determine the effectiveness of the hormone from the thyroid.

11. Adrenaline, from the medulla of the adrenal glands, does not seem to be involved in the initiation of sexual response. However, as sexual activities progress, the adrenal glands may be stimulated into secretion, and this secretion may be responsible for certain of the phenomena which appear in the later stages of sexual activity. There is no evidence that adrenaline actually inhibits sexual response.

12. The levels of the 17-ketosteroids, which originate largely in the adrenal cortex but also develop in the testes and ovaries and apparently in other organs of the body, show rather striking correlations with the levels of sexual response in the human female and male. In the human male, the 17-ketosteroids drop steadily from a peak in the late teens or twenties into old age, while they remain on a plateau for some period of years in the female. Again, this may represent a direct causal relationship, or (what is more likely) both the 17-ketosteroids and the levels of sexual responsiveness may reflect a more basic and probably more complex physiologic situation.

13. While hormonal levels may affect the levels of sexual response—the intensity of response, the frequency of response, the frequency of overt sexual activity—there is no demonstrated relationship between any of the hormones and an individual's response to particular sorts of psychologic stimuli, an individual's interest in partners of a particular sex, or an individual's utilization of particular techniques in his or her sexual activity. Within limits, the levels of sexual response may be modified by reducing or increasing the amount of available hormone, but there seems to be no reason for believing that the patterns of sexual behavior may be modified by hormonal therapy.

BIBLIOGRAPHY

The following bibliography includes the items which are cited in the footnotes in the present volume, and a limited number of additional references to important general studies on sex. It does not purport to be a general bibliography on human sexual behavior.

Anon. (Madame B——le.). **1707.** The fifteen plagues of a maiden-head. London, F. P., 8p. [reprint].

Anon. **1772.** The fifteen plagues of a maidenhead. *In:* Anon., comp. The merry Andrew, pp. 136–142.

Anon. (Buck, M. S., ed.). **1916** (orig. 6th cent. A.D.). The Greek anthology (Palatine ms). The amatory epigrams. Priv. print., 142p.

Anon., comp. (Paton, W. R., trans.). **1917, 1918** (orig. 1st cent. A.D.). The Greek anthology. In five volumes. Cambridge, Mass., Harvard University Press, v. 3, 456p. v. 4, 422p.

Anon. (Tomita, K., trans.). **ca. 1845.** Hikatsu-sho. Ms, typed, 1 + 83p.

Anon. (Alix (Petrus)). **n.d.** Histoire et psycho-physiologie du vice à travers les siècles et les êtres. Paris, Librairie Mondaine, 160p.

Anon. (Azama Otoko, pseud.) (Tomita, K., trans.). **ca. 1845.** Ikkyū zenshi shoskoku monogatari. Ms, typed, 1 + 24p.

Anon. (Tomita, K., trans.). **ca. 1850.** Jiiro haya-shinan. Ms, typed, 10p.

Anon. (Tomita, K., trans.). **ca. 1840.** Makurabunko. Ms, typed, 11p.

Anon. (?Carrington, Charles). **1896.** Marriage, love and woman amongst the Arabs. Otherwise entitled The book of exposition . . . Translated . . . by an English Bohemian. Paris, Charles Carrington, 1 pl. + xlviii + 285p.

Anon., comp. (Ferdinando Funny, pseud.). **1772.** The merry Andrew: being the smartest collection ever yet published . . . to which is added . . . The fifteen plagues of a maidenhead. London, P. Wickes, 1 pl. + 144p.

Anon. [Burton, R. F., and Smithers, L. C. trans.]. **1888.** Priapeia, or the sportive epigrams of divers poets on Priapus now first completely done into English prose from the original Latin, with notes . . . to which is appended the Latin text. Athens, Erotika Biblion Society, priv. print., xxxiv + 238p.

Anon. (Tomita, K., trans.). **ca. 1885.** Takarabunko. Ms, typed, 20p.

Anon. **1829.** Über die Behandlung der Unarten, Fehler und Vergehungen der Jugend. Graudenz, C. O. Röthe; Berlin, Enslin, [6] + 116p.

Anon. **1772.** The virgin's dream. *In:* Anon., comp. The merry Andrew, pp. 143–144.

Abernethy, E. M. **1925.** Correlations in physical and mental growth. J. Educ. Psychol. 16:458–466, 539–546.

Abraham, K. **1948** (orig. 1927). (Bryan, D., and Strachey, A., trans.). Selected papers of Karl Abraham, M.D. London, Hogarth Press and Institute of Psychoanalysis, 527p.

Achilles, P. S. **1923.** The effectiveness of certain social hygiene literature. New York, American Social Hygiene Association, 116p.

Ackerson, L. **1931.** Children's behavior problems. A statistical study based upon 5000 children examined consecutively at the Illinois Institute for Juvenile Research. I. Incidence, genetic and intellectual factors. Chicago, University of Chicago Press, xxi + 268p.

Adams, C. R. **1946.** Building for successful marriage and family living. *In:* Chivers, W. R., ed. Successful marriage and family living, pp. 30–35.

Adler, O. **1911.** Die mangelhafte Geschlechtsempfindung des Weibes. Anaesthesia sexualis feminarum. Anaphrodisia. Dyspareunia. Berlin, H. Kornfeld, xiv + 231p.

— 1912. Die frigide Frau. Sexual-Probleme 8:5–17.

Aeschines. 1919 (orig. 4th cent. B.C.). (Adams, C. D., trans.). The speeches: against Timarchus, on the embassy, against Ctesiphon. Cambridge, Mass., Harvard University Press, xxiii + 528p.

Alibert. n.d. [ca. 1900?]. Onanism. Onanism amongst men. Its causes, methods, and disorders. Masturbation amongst women. Its causes. Different methods of masturbation. Symptoms. Consequences. Treatment. Paris, Medical Library, 95p.

— 1926. Tribadism and saphism. Paris, priv. print., 86p.

Allen, C. 1949. The sexual perversions and abnormalities. A study in the psychology of paraphilia. London, Oxford University Press, x + 346p.

Allen, E., et al., ed. 1939. Sex and internal secretions. A survey of recent research. Baltimore, Williams & Wilkins Co., xxxvi + 1346p.

Allen, F. L. 1931. Only yesterday. An informal history of the nineteen-twenties. New York, Bantam Books, 413p.

Allendy, R., and Lobstein, H. 1948. (Larsen, E., trans.). Sex problems in school. London, New York, Staples Press, 182p.

Alpert, L. M. 1938. Judicial censorship of obscene literature. Harvard Law Rev. 52:40–76.

American Association of Marriage Counselors. 1952. Premarital sex relations: The facts and the counselor's role in relation to the facts. (Report of a round table meeting held by the Section on Marriage and Family Counseling of the National Council on Family Relations at Lake Geneva, Wisc., Aug. 30, 1951.) Marr. & Fam. Liv. 14:229–238.

Ananga-Ranga. 1935 (orig. 12th cent. A.D.?). (Burton, R. F., trans.). The secret places of the human body. Known as the Ananga-Ranga, or the Hindu art of love. Priv. print., 218p., 10 pl.

Andrews, F. N., and McKenzie, F. F. 1941. Estrus, ovulation, and related phenomena in the mare. Columbia, Mo., University of Missouri (Agricultural Experiment Research Bull. 329), 117p.

Andrews, T. G., ed. 1948. Methods of psychology. New York, John Wiley & Sons; London, Chapman & Hall, xiv + 716p.

Anthropophyteia (Krauss, F. S., ed.). 1904–1913. Jahrbücher für folkloristische Erhebungen und Forschungen zur Entwicklungsgeschichte der geschlechtlichen Moral. Leipzig, Deutsche Verlagsaktiengesellschaft & Ethnologischer Verlag, v. 1–10.

Apfelberg, B., Sugar, C., and Pfeffer, A. Z. 1944. A psychiatric study of 250 sex offenders. Amer. J. Psychiat. 100:762–770.

Apuleius. 1822 (orig. 2nd cent. A.D.). (Taylor, T., trans.). The metamorphosis, or golden ass, and philosophical works. London, Robert Triphook etc., xxiv + 400 + 10p.

— 1915. (Adlington, W., trans.). The golden ass. Being the Metamorphoses of Lucius Apuleius. London, William Heinemann; New York, G. P. Putnam's Sons, xxiv + 608p.

— 1923. (Adlington, W., trans.). The golden ass. London, John Lane, xxxv + 282p., 8 pl., 8 col. pl.

Aretaeus. 1856 (orig. 2nd and 3rd cent. A.D.). (Adams, F., trans.). The extant works of Aretaeus, the Cappadocian. London, priv. print., Sydenham Society, xx + 510p.

Arey, L. B. 1946. Ed. 5. Developmental anatomy. A textbook and laboratory manual of embryology. Philadelphia and London, W. B. Saunders Co., ix + 616p.

Arieff, A. J., and Rotman, D. B. 1942. One hundred cases of indecent exposure. J. Nerv. & Ment. Dis. 96:523–528.

Aristophanes. 1912 (orig. 5th–4th cent. B.C.). Aristophanes. The eleven comedies. London, Athenian Society, priv. print., 2v. v. 1, 392p. v. 2, 476p.

1924. (Rogers, B. B., trans.). Aristophanes. In three volumes. I. The Acharnians. The clouds. The knights. The wasps. II. The peace. The birds. The frogs. Cambridge, Mass., Harvard University Press, 2v. v. 1, xvi + 555p. v. 2, 1 pl. + 443p.

Aristotle. 1910 (orig. 4th cent. B.C.). (Thompson, D. W., trans.). The works of Aristotle. Volume IV. Historia animalium. Oxford, Clarendon Press, xv + n.pag.

1936. (Hett, W. S., trans.). Problems. London, William Heinemann, 2v. v. 1, x + 461p. v. 2, vi + 456p.

Arregui, A. M. 1927. Summarium theologiae moralis, ad recentem codicem iuris canonici accommodatum. Bilbao, El Mensajero Del Corazón de Jesús, xix + 665p.

Asayama, Sin-iti. 1949. Gendai gakusei no seikōdō. (Sex behavior of present-day Japanese students.) Kyoto, Usui Shobo, 346p.

Asdell, S. A. 1946. Patterns of mammalian reproduction. Ithaca, N. Y., Comstock Publishing Co., xi + 437p.

Aurand, A. M., Jr. 1938a. Little known facts about bundling in the New World. Harrisburg, Penna., priv. print., 32p.

1938b. Slants on the origin of bundling in the Old World. Harrisburg, Penna., priv. print., 32p.

Azama Otoko. See Anon. Ikkyū zenshi shoskoku monogatari.

Baber, R. E. 1936. Some mate selection standards of college students and their parents. J. Soc. Hyg. 22:115–125.

1939. Marriage and the family. New York and London, McGraw-Hill Book Co., xii + 656p.

Back, G. 1910. Sexuelle Verirrungen des Menschen und der Natur. Berlin, John Pohl, 2v. v. 1, 7 + x + 544p. v. 2, 545–973p.

Backhouse, E., and Scott, W. B. 1888. Martyr scenes of the sixteenth and seventeenth centuries. London, Hamilton, Adams & Co., 86p., 12 pl.

Bailey, F. R. 1948. Ed. 12. (Smith, P. E., and Copenhaver, W. M., ed.). Textbook of histology. Baltimore, Williams & Wilkins Co., xix + 781p.

Baker, J. R. 1926. Sex in man and animals. London, George Routledge & Sons, xvi + 175p.

Baldwin, B. T. 1921. The physical growth of children from birth to maturity. Iowa City, Ia., The University of Iowa Studies in Child Welfare, Monogr. v. 1, no. 1, 411p.

Ball, Josephine. 1937. Sex activity of castrated male rats increased by estrin administration. J. Comp. Psychol. 24:135–144.

1938. Partial inhibition of sex activity in the intact female rat by injected estrin. Endocrinol. 23:197–199.

1939. Male and female mating behavior in pre-pubertally castrated male rats receiving estrogens. J. Comp. Psychol. 28:273–283.

1940. The effect of testosterone on the sex behavior of female rats. J. Comp. Psychol. 29:151–165.

Ball, J., and Hartman, C. G. 1935. Sexual excitability as related to the menstrual cycle in the monkey. Amer. J. Obstct. & Gynec. 29:117–119.

Ballerini, A. 1890. Opus theologicum morale. . . . Prati, Giachetti, Filii et Soc., v. 2, pp. 678–739, v. 6, var.pag., v. 7, 421–442p.

Banay, R. S., and Davidoff, L. 1942. Apparent recovery of a sex psychopath after lobotomy. J. Crim. Psychopath. 4:59–66.

Banning, Margaret C. 1937. The case for chastity. Readers Digest 31:(Aug.), 1–10.

Barahal, H. S. 1940. Testosterone in psychotic male homosexuals. Psychiat. Quart. 14:319–330.

Barash, M. 1926. Sex life of the workers of Moscow. J. Soc. Hyg. 12:274–288.

Bard, P. 1934. On emotional expression after decortication with some remarks on certain theoretical views. Parts I and II. Psychol. Rev. 41:309–329, 424–449.

1936. Oestrual behavior in surviving decorticate cats. Amer. J. Physiol. 116:4–5.

1939. Central nervous mechanisms for emotional behavior patterns in animals. Res. Publ. Assoc. Nerv. & Ment. Dis. 19:190–218.

1940. The hypothalamus and sexual behavior. In: Fulton, J. F., et al., ed. The hypothalamus and central levels of autonomic function, pp. 551–579.

1942. Neural mechanisms in emotional and sexual behavior. Psychosom. Med. 4:171–172.

Barker, R. G., and Stone, C. P. 1936. Physical development in relation to menarcheal age in university women. Human Biol. 8:198–222.

Barr, M. W. 1920. Some notes on asexualization; with a report of eighteen cases. J. Nerv. & Ment. Dis. 51:231–241.

Barré, M. L., ed. 1839, 1840, 1861. Herculanum et Pompéi. Recueil général des peintures, bronzes, mosaïques, etc. . . . Paris, Firmin Didot Frères, 8v., var.pag.

Barton, G. A. 1925. Ed. 4. Archaeology and the Bible. Philadelphia, American Sunday-School Union, xv + 561p., 122 pl.

Bauer, B. A. 1927. (Haire, N., Jerdan, E. S., and Paul, E. and C., trans.). Woman and love. New York, Liveright Publishing Corp., 2v. v. 1, 7 + 360p. v. 2, xxvii + 396p.

1929. Wie bist Du, Weib? Mit einem besonderen Anhang: Weib, bleibe jung und schön! Hygiene der modernen Frau. Zürich, Viktoria-Verlag, xxiii + 631p.

Bauer, M. 1924. Liebesleben in deutscher Vergangenheit. Berlin, P. Langenscheidt, 390p.

Beach, F. A. 1938. Sex reversals in the mating pattern of the rat. J. Genet. Psychol. 53:329–334.

1940. Effects of cortical lesions upon the copulatory behavior of male rats. J. Comp. Psychol. 29:193–245.

1941. Female mating behavior shown by male rats after administration of testosterone propionate. Endocrinol. 29:409–412.

1942a. Central nervous mechanisms involved in the reproductive behavior of vertebrates. Psychol. Bull. 39:200–226.

1942b. Analysis of factors involved in the arousal, maintenance and manifestation of sexual excitement in male animals. Psychosom. Med. 4:173–198.

1942c. Effects of testosterone propionate upon the copulatory behavior of sexually inexperienced male rats. J. Comp. Psychol. 33:227–247.

1942d. Sexual behavior of prepuberal male and female rats treated with gonadal hormones. J. Comp. Psychol. 34:285–292.

1943. Effects of injury to the cerebral cortex upon the display of masculine and feminine mating behavior by female rats. J. Comp. Psychol. 36:169–199.

1944a. Effects of injury to the cerebral cortex upon sexually-receptive behavior in the female rat. Psychosom. Med. 6:40–55.

1944b. Experimental studies of sexual behavior in male mammals. J. Clin. Endocrinol. 4:126–134.

1944c. Relative effects of androgen upon the mating behavior of male rats subjected to forebrain injury or castration. J. Exper. Zool. 97:249–295.

1945. Bisexual mating behavior in the male rat: Effects of castration and hormone administration. Physiol. Zool. 18:390–402.

1947a. Hormones and mating behavior in vertebrates. Rec. Prog. in Hormone Res. 1:27–63.

1947b. A review of physiological and psychological studies of sexual behavior in mammals. Physiol. Rev. 27:240–307.

1948. Hormones and behavior. A survey of interrelationships between endocrine secretions and patterns of overt response. New York and London, Paul B. Hoeber, xiv + 368p.

1949. A cross-species survey of mammalian sexual behavior. *In:* Hoch, P. H., and Zubin, J., ed. Psychosexual development in health and disease, pp. 52–78.

1950. Sexual behavior in animals and men. Springfield, Ill., Charles C Thomas, from the Harvey Society Lectures (1947–1948), Series 43: 254–280.

1951. Body chemistry and perception. *In:* Blake, R. R., and Ramsey, G. V. Perception, pp. 56–94.

Beach, F. A., and **Gilmore, R. W. 1949.** Response of male dogs to urine from females in heat. J. Mammalogy 30:391–392.

Beach, F. A., and **Rasquin, P. 1942.** Masculine copulatory behavior in intact and castrated female rats. Endocrinol. 31:393–409.

Beauvoir, Simone de. **1949.** Le deuxième sexe. I. Les faits et les mythes. II. L'expérience vécue. Paris, Gallimard, v. 1, 399p. v. 2, 581p.

1952. (Parshley, H. M., trans.). The second sex. New York, Alfred A. Knopf, xxx + 746p.

Becker, H., and **Hill, R.,** ed. **1942.** Marriage and the family. Boston, D. C. Heath & Co., xxxii + 663p.

Becker, J. E. de. **1899.** The nightless city, or the history of the Yoshiwara yukwaku. Yokohama, Z. P. Maruya & Co., 441 + xxv p., 10 pl., 6 col. pl.

Bekker, ?B. **1741** (ex Eng. ed. 15, orig. 1722?). (Crouch, N., ed.). Onania, oder die erschreckliche Sünde der Selbst-Befleckung . . . aus dem Englischen ins Deutsche übersetzet. Leipzig, Johann George Löwe, 16 + 440p.

Belknap, G., and **Campbell, A. 1951.** Political party identification and attitudes toward foreign policy. Pub. Opin. Quart. 15:601–623.

Bell, R. H. **1921.** Some aspects of adultery. A study. New York, Critic and Guide Co., 54p.

Bell, S. **1902.** A preliminary study of the emotion of love between the sexes. Amer. J. Psychol. 13:325–354.

Bender, Lauretta. **1939.** Mental hygiene and the child. Amer. J. Orthopsychiat. 9:574–582.

1952. Child psychiatric technics. Diagnostic and therapeutic approach to normal and abnormal development through patterned, expressive, and group behavior. Springfield, Ill., Charles C Thomas, xi + 335p., 16 pl., 4 col. pl.

Bender, Lauretta, and **Blau, A. 1937.** The reaction of children to sexual relations with adults. Amer. J. Orthopsychiat. 7:500–518.

Bender, Lauretta, and **Cramer, J. B. 1949.** Sublimation and sexual gratification in the latency period of girls. *In:* Eissler, K. R., et al., ed. Searchlights in delinquency, pp. 53–64.

Benedek, Therese. **1952.** Psychosexual functions in women. New York, Ronald Press, x + 435p.

Benedek, T., and **Rubenstein, B. B. 1942.** The sexual cycle in women. Washington, D. C., Nat. Res. Council (Psychosom. Med. Mono. v. 3, no. 1 and 2), viii + 307p.

Bénézit, E. **1948, 1949, 1950, 1951, 1952.** Dictionnaire critique et documentaire des peintres, sculpteurs, dessinateurs et graveurs. . . . Librairie Gründ, v. 1, xvi + 770p., 32 pl. v. 2, 776p., 32 pl. v. 3, 815p., 32 pl. v. 4, 773p., 32 pl. v. 5, 843p., 32 pl.

Bensing, R. G. **1951.** A comparative study of American sex statutes. J. Crim. Law & Criminol. 42:57–72.

Benvenuti, M. **1950.** L'ipersessualità come fattore degenerogeno. Pisa, "Omnia Medica," 209p.

Bergler, E. **1943.** The respective importance of reality and phantasy in the genesis of female homosexuality. J. Crim. Psychopath. 5:27–48.

1944. The problem of frigidity. Psychiat. Quart. 18:374–390.

1948. Lesbianism, facts and fiction. Marr. Hyg. 1:197–202.

1951. Neurotic counterfeit-sex. Impotence, frigidity, "mechanical" and pseudo-sexuality, homosexuality. New York, Grune & Stratton, xii + 360p.

Bernard, J. 1935. Some biological factors in personality and marriage. Human Biol. 7:430–436.

Bernard, W. S. 1938. Student attitudes on marriage and the family. Amer. Sociol. Rev. 3:354–361.

Berrien, F. K. 1935. A study of the drawings of abnormal children. J. Educ. Psychol. 26:143–150.

Bertram, J. G. (Cooper, W. M., pseud.). **1869.** A history of the rod, in all countries, from the earliest period to the present time. (Flagellation & the flagellants). London, John Camden Hotten, x + 544p., xx pl.

Biederich, P. H., and **Dembicki, L. 1951.** Die Sexualität des Mannes. Darstellung und Kritik des "Kinsey-Report." Regensburg, Wien, Franz Decker, 232p.

Bienville, D. T. de. 1771. La nymphomanie ou traité de la fureur utérine . . . Amsterdam, Marc-Michel Rey, xx + 168p.

Bilder-Lexikon (Schidrowitz, L., ed.). **1928, 1929, 1930, 1931.** 1. Kulturge-schichte, 943p. 2. Literatur und Kunst, 944p. 3. Sexualwissenschaft, 917p. 4. Ergänzungsband, 877p. Wien und Leipzig, Verlag für Sexualforschung.

Bingham, A. T. 1922. Determinants of sex delinquency in adolescent girls based on intensive studies of 500 cases. J. Crim. Law & Criminol. 13:494–586.

Bingham, H. C. 1928. Sex development in apes. Baltimore, The Johns Hopkins Press (Comp. Psychol. Monogr. v. 5, Ser. No. 23), 165p.

Birch, H. G., and **Clark, G. 1946.** Hormonal modification of social behavior. II. The effects of sex-hormone administration on the social dominance status of the female-castrate chimpanzee. Psychosomat. Med. 8:320–331.

Biskind, G. R., Escamilla, R. F., and **Lisser, H. 1941.** Treatment of eunuchoidism. Implantation of testosterone compounds in cases of male eunuchoidism. J. Clin. Endocrinol. 1:38–49.

Bissonnette, T. H. 1950. Ferrets. *In:* Farris, E. J., ed. The care and breeding of laboratory animals, pp. 234–255.

Blackwood, B. 1935. Both sides of Buka passage. An ethnographic study of social, sexual, and economic questions in the north-western Solomon Islands. Oxford, Clarendon Press, xxiii + 624p., 80 pl.

Blake, R. R., and **Ramsey, G. V. 1951.** Perception. An approach to personality. New York, Ronald Press Co., viii + 442p.

Blanchard, Phyllis. 1929. Sex in the adolescent girl. *In:* Calverton, V. F., and Schmalhausen, S. D., ed. Sex in civilization, pp. 538–561.

Blanchard, P., and **Manasses, C. 1930.** New girls for old. New York, Macaulay Co., xii + 281p.

Bleuler, E. 1949. Ed. 8 (orig. 1916). Lehrbuch der Psychiatrie. Berlin, Springer, x + 504p.

Bloch, I. (Dühren, E., pseud.). **1900.** Der Marquis de Sade und seine Zeit. Ein Beitrag zur Cultur- u. Sittengeschichte des 19. Jahrhunderts. Berlin und Leipzig, H. Barsdorf, vi + 502p.

     1902–1903. Beiträge zur Aetiologie der Psychopathia sexualis. Pt. I and II. Dresden, H. R. Dohrn, 2v. in 1, xvi + 272 + xviii + 400p.

     1908. (Paul, M. E., trans.). The sexual life of our time in its relations to modern civilization. London, Rebman, xviii + 790p.

     1909 (orig. 1906). Das Sexualleben unserer Zeit in seinen Beziehungen zur modernen Kultur. Berlin, Louis Marcus, xii + 850 + xix p.

     1933. (Wallis, Keene, trans.). Anthropological studies in the strange sexual practices of all races in all ages . . . New York, Anthropological Press, priv. print., ix + 246 + xxiii p.

Blumenthal, A. 1932. Small-town stuff. Chicago, University of Chicago Press, xvii + 416p.

Boas, E. P., and **Goldschmidt, E. F. 1932.** The heart rate. Springfield, Ill., Charles C Thomas, xi + 166p.

Boas, F. 1932. Studies in growth. Human Biol. 4:307–350.

Boas, F., ed. 1938. General anthropology. Boston, D. C. Heath and Co., xi + 718p.

Böhme, A. 1935. Psychotherapie und Kastration. München, J. F. Lehmann, 183p.

Boileau, Jacques. 1700. Historia flagellantium de recto et perverso flagrorum usu apud Christianos, ex antiquis scripturae, patrum, pontificum, conciliorum, & scriptorum profanorum monumentis cum cura & fide expressa. Paris, Joannes Anisson, 18 + 341 + 19p.
 1732 (ed. 1, 1701). Histoire des flagellans, ou l'on fait voir le bon & le mauvais usage des flagellations parmi les chrétiens. Amsterdam, Henry du Sauzet, xxxii + 316p.

Boling, J. L., et al. 1939. Post-parturitional heat responses of new born and adult guinea pigs. Data on parturition. Proc. Soc. Exper. Biol. & Med. 42:128–132.

Bölsche, W. 1926. (Brown, C., trans.). Love-life in nature. The story of the evolution of love. New York, Albert & Charles Boni, 2v. v. 1, 304p. v. 2, 726p.

Bonaparte, M. 1935. Passivity, masochism and femininity. Int. J. Psychoanal. 16:325–333.

Bonnar, A. 1941. c. 1939. The Catholic doctor. New York, P. J. Kenedy & Sons, xvii + 184p.

Bors, E., et al. 1950. Fertility in paraplegic males. A preliminary report of endocrine studies. J. Clin. Endocrinol. 10:381–398.

Boswell, J. 1950. (Pottle, F. A., ed.). London journal, 1762–1763. New York, McGraw-Hill Book Co., xxix + 370p.

Bowman, H. A. 1942. Marriage for moderns. New York and London, McGraw-Hill Book Co., ix + 493p.

Bowman, K. M. 1951. Report of Karl M. Bowman, medical superintendent of the Langley Porter Clinic. In: Brown, R. M. Progress report to the Calif. legislature . . . , pp. 148–160.
 1952. Sexual deviation research. [Report to Assembly Judiciary Committee Subcommittee of Sex Research.] Sacramento, Calif., Assembly of the State of California, 80p.

Bowman, K. M., and Engle, B. 1953. The problem of homosexuality. J. Soc. Hyg. 39:2–16.

Boys' Clubs of America. 1946. Social hygiene in a boys' club. New York, priv. print., 19p.

Brantôme, P. de B. de. 1901, 1902 (orig. 16th cent., ed. 1, 1666). (Allinson, A. R., trans.). Lives of fair and gallant ladies. Paris, Charles Carrington, 2v. in 1. v. 1, xliv + 379p. v. 2, xxiii + 464p.

Brattgård, Sven-Olof. 1950. Personlighetsattityd och sexuellt beteende. En studie på sjukhusmaterial. Svenska Läkartidningen 47:1677–1682.

Braude, J. M. 1950. The sex offender and the court. Fed. Probat. 14(3):17–22.

Brettschneider, R. 1931. Die Rolle der erotischen Photographie in der Psychopathia Sexualis. In: Wulffen, E., et al. Die Erotik in der Photographie, pp. 89–138.

Briffault, R. 1927. The mothers. A study of the origins of sentiments and institutions. New York, The Macmillan Co., 3v. v. 1, xix + 781p. v. 2, xx + 789p. v. 3, xv + 841p.

Brill, A. A. 1946. Lectures on psychoanalytic theory. New York, Alfred A. Knopf, viii + 292 + xiii p.

Brody, M. W. 1943. An analysis of the psychosexual development of a female— with special reference to homosexuality. Psychoanal. Rev. 30:47–58.

Bromley, D. D., and Britten, F. H. 1938. Youth and sex. A study of 1300 college students. New York and London, Harper & Brothers, xiii + 303p.

Brookhart, J. M., and Dey, F. L. 1941. Reduction of sexual behavior in male guinea pigs by hypothalamic lesions. Amer. J. Physiol. 133:551–554.

Brookhart, J. M., Dey, F. L., and Ranson, S. W. 1941. The abolition of mating behavior by hypothalamic lesions in guinea pigs. Endocrinol. 28:561–565.

Brooks, C. McC. 1937. The role of the cerebral cortex and of various sense organs in the excitation and execution of mating activity in the rabbit. Amer. J. Physiol. 120:544–553.

Brower, D., and Abt, L. E., ed. 1952. Progress in clinical psychology. Volume I (Section 1), xi + 328p. (Section 2), xii–xxiii + 329–564p. New York, Grune & Stratton.

Brown, F., and Kempton, R. T. 1950. Sex questions and answers. A guide to happy marriage. New York, McGraw-Hill Book Co., xiv + 264p.

Brown, J. F. 1940. The psychodynamics of abnormal behavior. New York and London, McGraw-Hill Book Co., xvi + 484p.

Brown, R. M. 1950. Preliminary report of the Subcommittee on Sex Crimes of the Assembly Interim Committee on Judicial System . . . Sacramento, California State Legislature, 269p., 1 fold. pl.

> **1951.** Progress report to the legislature . . . by the Assembly Interim Committee on Judicial System and Judicial Process . . . Sacramento, California, Assembly, 170p.

Bruckner, P. J. 1937. How to give sex instructions. A guide for parents, teachers and others responsible for the training of young people. St. Louis, Mo., The Queen's Work, 64p.

Brusendorff, O. 1938. (Rimestad, C., ed.). Erotikens historie, fra Graekenlands oldtil til vore dage. København, Universal-Forlaget, 3v. v. 1, 423p. v. 2, 598p. v. 3, 475p.

Bryk, F. 1933 (orig. 1928). (Sexton, M. F., trans.). Voodoo-Eros. Ethnological studies in the sex of the African aborigines. New York, priv. print., 351p.

> **1934.** (Berger, D., trans.). Circumcision in man and woman. Its history, psychology, and ethnology. New York, American Ethnological Press, 342p.

Buck, W. 1936. Measurements of changes in attitudes and interests of university students over a ten-year period. J. Abnorm. & Soc. Psychol. 31:12–19.

Budge, E. A. W. 1895. The book of the dead. The papyrus of Ani in the British Museum. The Egyptian text with interlinear transliteration and translation, a running translation, introduction, etc. London, British Museum, clv + 377p.

Bühler, C. 1927. Vergleich der Pubertätsentwicklung bei Knaben und Mädchen. In: Stern, E., ed. Die Erziehung und die sexuelle Frage, pp. 155–169.

> **1928.** Männliche und weibliche Pubertätsentwicklunk. In: Marcuse, M., ed. Verhandlungen des I. International Kongresses für Sexualforschung, v. 3, pp. 35–41.

> **1931.** Zum Problem der sexuellen Entwicklung. Ztschr. f. Kinderheilkunde 51:612–641.

Bulliet, C. J. 1932. Modern painting. In: McDermott, J. F., and Taft, K. B., ed. Sex in the arts, pp. 233–252.

Bundesen, H. N. 1951. Toward manhood. Philadelphia and New York, J. B. Lippincott Co., 175p.

Burgess, E. W., and Cottrell, L. S., Jr. 1939. Predicting success or failure in marriage. New York, Prentice-Hall, xxiii + 472p.

Burrows, H. 1949. Ed. 2. Biological actions of sex hormones. Cambridge University Press, xiii + 615p.

Butterfield, O. M. 1939. Love problems of adolescence. New York, Emerson Books, viii + 212p.

> **1940.** Sex life in marriage. New York, Emerson Books, 192p.

Calverton, V. F., and Schmalhausen, S. D., ed. 1929. Sex in civilization. New York, Macaulay, 719p., 1 pl.

Campbell, E. H. 1939. The social-sex development of children. Genetic Psychol. Monogr. 21:461–552.

Canby, H. S. 1934. Sex and marriage in the nineties. Harper's Magazine, Sept., pp. 427–436.

Cannon, W. B. 1920. Bodily changes in pain, hunger, fear and rage. New York & London, D. Appleton and Co., xiii + 311p.

Canu, É. 1897. Résultats thérapeutiques de la castration chez la femme . . . Paris, Ollier-Henry, 188p.

Carmichael, L., ed. 1946. Manual of child psychology. New York, John Wiley & Sons; London, Chapman & Hall, viii + 1068p.

Carpenter, C. R. 1942. Sexual behavior of free ranging rhesus monkeys (Macaca mulatta). J. Comp. Psychol. 33:113–162.

Carpenter, E. 1930 (orig. 1908). The intermediate sex. A study of some transitional types of men and women. London, George Allen & Unwin, 176p.

Carpenter, E., ed. 1902. Ioläus. An anthology of friendship. London, Swan Sonnenschein & Co.; Manchester, priv. print.; Boston, Charles E. Goodspeed, vi + 191p.

Carpenter, N. 1932. Courtship practices and contemporary social change in America. Ann. Amer. Acad. Polit. & Soc. Sci. 160:38–44.

Carter, A. C., Cohen, E. J., and Shorr, E. 1947. The use of androgens in women. Vitamins and Hormones 5:317–391.

Cary, H. N. 1948, ex ?1916. Sexual vocabulary . . . Compiled from manuscript, carbon, and printed materials . . . [from] the files of H. N. Cary . . . Bloomington, Ind., [Institute for Sex Research], Ms, typed, 5v. v. 1–3, n.pag., ca. 262p. ea. v. v. 4, 788–1049p. v. 5, 1050–1396p.

Casañ, V. S. n.d. (ca. ?1900). Conocimientos para la vida privada. I. La prostitución. II. Secretos del lecho conyugal. III. La virginidad. IV. Onanismo conyugal. V. Los vicios solitarios. Barcelona, Maucci, 5v. in 1, 126 + 111 + 95 + 92 + 95p.

Catullus. 1894 (orig. 1st cent. B.C.). (Burton, R. F., and Smithers, L. C., trans.). The Carmina of Caius Valerius Catullus. London, priv. print., xxiii + 313p.

Catullus, et al. 1913 (orig. 1st cent. B.C.). (Cornish, F. W., et al., trans.). Catullus, Tibullus and Pervigilium Veneris. Cambridge, Mass., Harvard University Press, xi + 376p.

Caufeynon, Dr., pseud. of Fauconney, J. [1902.] La masturbation et la sodomie feminine. Paris, Administration de la Vie en Culotte Rouge, 112p.

 1903. Orgasme. Sens genital jadis et aujourd'hui . . . Paris, Charles Offenstadt, 237p.

 1934. Unisexual love. A documentary study of the sources, manifestations, the physiology and psychology of sexual perversion in the two sexes. New York, New Era Press, 164p.

Cave, F. C. 1911. Report of sterilization in the Kansas State Home for Feebleminded. J. Psycho-Asthenics 15:123–125.

Cheng, Peilieu, et al. 1950. Different intensities of sexual activity in relation to the effect of testosterone propionate in the male rabbit. Endocrinol. 46:447–452.

Chesser, E. 1947. Love without fear. How to achieve sex happiness in marriage. New York, Roy, 307p.

Chideckel, M. 1935. Female sex perversion; the sexually aberrated woman as she is. New York, Eugenics Publishing Co., xviii + 331p.

Childers, A. T. 1936. Some notes on sex mores among Negro children. Amer. J. Orthopsychiat. 6:442–448.

Chivers, W. R., ed. 1946. Successful marriage and family living. Atlanta, Ga., Morehouse College, Department of Sociology Publication Number 1, 8 + 47p.

Chlenov. See Feldhusen, F.

Christensen, H. T. 1950. Marriage analysis. Foundations for successful family life. New York, Ronald Press Co., viii + 510p.

 1952. Dating behavior as evaluated by high-school students. Amer. J. Sociol. 57:580–586.

Clark, G. 1942. Sexual behavior in rats with lesions in the anterior hypothalamus. Amer. J. Physiol. 137:746–749.

1945. Prepubertal castration in the male chimpanzee, with some effects of replacement therapy. Growth 9:327–339.

Clark, G., and Birch, H. G. 1945. Hormonal modifications of social behavior. I. The effect of sex-hormone administration on the social status of a male-castrate chimpanzee. Psychosom. Med. 7:321–329.

Clark, L. C., and Treichler, P. 1950. Psychic stimulation of prostatic secretion. Psychosom. Med. 12:261–263.

Clark, LeMon. 1937. Emotional adjustment in marriage. St. Louis, C. V. Mosby Co., 261p.

1949. Sex and you. Indianapolis and New York, The Bobbs-Merrill Co., 203p.

1952. A further report on the virginity of unmarried American women. Int. J. Sexol. 6:27–32.

Clark, W. E., ed. 1937. Two lamaistic pantheons. Cambridge, Mass., Harvard University Press, 2v. v. 1, [Indexes] xxiv + 169p. v. 2, [Plates] 314p.

Clark, W. L., and Marshall, W. L. (Kearney, J. J., ed.). **1940** (ed. 1, 1900). A treatise on the law of crimes. Chicago, Callaghan and Co., lxiii + 724p.

Clement of Alexandria. 1885 (orig. 2nd cent. A.D.). The instructor (Paedagogus). *In:* Roberts, A., Donaldson, J., and Coxe, A. C., ed. The Ante-Nicene fathers, pp. 209–296.

Cleugh, J. 1951. The Marquis and the chevalier. A study of sex as illustrated by the lives . . . of the Marquis de Sade . . . and the Chevalier von Sacher-Masoch . . . London, Andrew Melrose, 255p., 2 pl.

Clinton, C. A. 1935. Sex behavior in marriage. New York, Pioneer Publications, 159p.

Cochran, W. G. 1953. Sampling techniques. New York, John Wiley & Sons; London, Chapman & Hall, xiv + 330p.

Cohen, A. 1949. Everyman's Talmud. New York, E. P. Dutton & Co., xli + 403p.

Colmeiro-Laforet, C. 1952. Lack of orgasm as a cause of sterility. Int. J. Sexol. 5:123–127.

Comfort, A. 1950. Sexual behavior in society. London, Gerald Duckworth & Co., 158p.

Commins, W. D., and Stone, C. P. 1932. Effects of castration on the behavior of mammals. Psychol. Bull. 29:493–508.

Conn, J. H. 1939. Factors influencing development of sexual attitudes and sexual awareness in children. Amer. J. Dis. Child. 58:738–745.

1940. Sexual curiosity of children. Amer. J. Dis. Child. 60:1110–1119.

Cooper, W. M. *See* Bertram, J. G.

Coppens, C. (Spalding, H. S., ed.). **1921.** Moral principles and medical practice. The basis of medical jurisprudence. New York, Benziger Brothers, 320p.

Corner, G. W. 1942. The hormones in human reproduction. Princeton, N. J., Princeton University Press, xix + 265p.

1951. The reproductive cycle of the rhesus monkey. Amer. Scientist 39: 50–74, 109.

1952. Attaining womanhood. A doctor talks to girls about sex. New York, Harper & Brothers, xi + 112p.

Corner, G. W., and Landis, C. 1941. Sex education for the adolescent. Hygeia (July), 18p.

Corpus inscriptionum latinarum, consilio et auctoritate Academiae litterarum regiae borussicae editum . . . 1862–1952. 16v. Berlin, G. Reimer.

Cory, D. W., pseud. **1951.** The homosexual in America. A subjective approach. New York, Greenberg, xvii + 326p.

Cowdry, E. V. (Lansing, A. I., ed.). **1952.** Ed. 3 (ed. 1, 1939). Problems of ageing. Biological and medical aspects. Baltimore, Williams & Wilkins Co., xxiii + 1061p.

Crawley, E. 1927. Ed. 2. (Besterman, T., ed.) The mystic rose. A study of primitive marriage and of primitive thought in its bearing on marriage. New York, Boni and Liveright, 2v. v. 1, xx + 375p. v. 2, vii + 340p.

Crespi, L. P. 1951. Germans view the U. S. reorientation program. I. Extent of receptivity to American ideas. II. Reactions to American democratization efforts. Int. J. Opin. & Attit. Res. 5:179–190, 335–346.

Crisp, K. B. 1939. Growing into maturity. Chicago, J. B. Lippincott Co., 38p.

Crossley, H. M., and Fink, R. 1951. Response and non-response in a probability sample. Int. J. Opin. & Attit. Res. 5:1–19.

Crouch, N. See Bekker, ?B.

Cuber, J. F., and Pell, B. 1941. A method for studying moral judgments relating to the family. Amer. J. Sociol. 47:12–23.

Curtis, A. H. 1946. Ed. 5. A textbook of gynecology. Philadelphia and London, W. B. Saunders Co., 755p.

Daly, M., ed. 1951. Profile of youth. By members of the staff of the Ladies Home Journal. Philadelphia and New York, J. B. Lippincott Co., 256p.

Daniels, G. E., and Tauber, E. S. 1941. A dynamic approach to the study of replacement therapy in cases of castration. Amer. J. Psychiat. 97:905–918.

Davis, C. D. 1939. The effect of ablations of the neocortex on mating, maternal behavior and the production of pseudopregnancy in the female rat and on copulatory activity in the male. Amer. J. Physiol. 127:374–380.

Davis, H. 1946. Ed. 5 (ed. 1, 1935). Moral and pastoral theology, in four volumes. Volume one. Human acts, law, sin, virtue, xix + 361p. Volume two. Commandments of God. Precepts of the Church, x + 463p. Volume three. The sacraments in general, baptism, confirmation, holy eucharist, penance, indulgences, censures, xviii + 504p. Volume four. Extreme unction, holy orders, marriage, the clerical state, the religious state, duties of laypeople, xiii + 432p. New York, Sheed and Ward.

Davis, Katharine B. 1929. Factors in the sex life of twenty-two hundred women. New York and London, Harper & Brothers, xx + 430p.

Dearborn, L. W. 1947. Extramarital relations. In: Fishbein, M., and Burgess, E. W., ed. Successful marriage, pp. 163–173.

——— 1947. Masturbation. In: Fishbein, M., and Burgess, E. W., ed. Successful marriage, pp. 356–367.

——— 1952. The problem of masturbation. Marr. & Family Liv. 14:46–55.

Decurtins, F. 1950. Ärztliches über die Enthaltsamkeit. In: Hornstein, X. von, and Faller, A., ed. Gesundes Geschlechts Leben, pp. 132–142.

Dell, F. 1930. Love in the machine age. A psychological study of the transition from patriarchal society. New York, Farrar & Rinehart, 428p.

Deming, W. E. 1950. Some theory of sampling. New York, John Wiley & Sons, xvii + 602p.

Dempsey, E. W. 1951. Homeostasis. In: Stevens, S. S., ed. Handbook of experimental psychology, pp. 209–235.

Dempsey, E. W., and Rioch, D. McK. 1939. The localization in the brain stem of the oestrus responses of the female guinea pig. J. Neurophysiol. 2:9–18.

Dennis, W. 1946. The adolescent. In: Carmichael, L., ed. Manual of child psychology, pp. 633–666.

DeRiver, J. P. 1949. The sexual criminal. A psychoanalytical study. Springfield, Ill., Charles C Thomas, xvii + 281p.

Deutsch, Helene. 1933. Homosexuality in women. Int. J. Psychoanal. 14:34–56.

——— 1944, 1945. The psychology of women. A psychoanalytic interpretation. Volume one, vii + 399p. Volume two, Motherhood, vi + 498p. New York, Grune & Stratton.

Devereux, G. 1936. Sexual life of the Mohave Indians. An interpretation in terms of social psychology. (Ph.D. dissertation.) Berkeley, Calif., University of California, Ms, ii + 116 + vi p.

774

    1937. Institutionalized homosexuality of the Mohave Indians. Human Biol. 9:498–527.

Dey, F. L., Leininger, C. R., and Ranson, S. W. 1942. The effect of hypophysical lesions on mating behavior in female guinea pigs. Endocrinol. 30:323–326.

Dickerson, R. E. 1931 (c. 1930). So youth may know. New viewpoints on sex and love. New York, Association Press, x + 255p.

    1947. Home study course [in] social hygiene guidance. Lessons I–VI. Portland, Ore., E. C. Brown Trust for Social Hygiene Education, 72p.

Dickinson, R. L. 1933. Human sex anatomy. Baltimore, Williams and Wilkins Co., vii + 145p. + 175 pl.

    1940. Chapter 16. Autoerotism. [From unpublished manuscript entitled The doctor as marriage counselor.] Ms, 27p.

    1949. Ed. 2. Human sex anatomy. A topographical hand atlas. Baltimore, Williams & Wilkins Co., 21 + 145p., 204 pl.

Dickinson, R. L., and Beam, L. 1931. A thousand marriages. A medical study of sex adjustment. Baltimore, Williams & Wilkins Co., xxv + 482p.

    1934. The single woman. A medical study in sex education. Baltimore, Williams & Wilkins Co., xix + 469p.

Dickson, H. R. P. 1949. The Arab of the desert. A glimpse into Badawin life in Kuwait and Sau'di Arabia. London, George Allen & Unwin, 664p., 49 pl., 8 col. pl., + 3 maps + 6 geneal. tab.

Diehl, E. L. T., ed. 1910. Pompeianische Wandinschriften und Verwandtes. Bonn, A. Marcus und E. Weber, 60p.

Dillon, M. S. 1934. Attitudes of children toward their own bodies and those of other children. Child Develop. 5:165–176.

Dinerman, H. 1949. 1948 votes in the making—a preview. Pub. Opin. Quart. 12:585–598.

Döderlein, A., and Krönig, B. 1907. Operative Gynäkologie. Leipzig, Georg Thieme, xvi + 721p.

Doe-Kulmann, L., and Stone, C. P. 1927. Notes on the mental development of children exhibiting the somatic signs of puberty praecox. J. Abnorm. & Soc. Psychol. 22:291–324.

Dollard, J. 1949. (Ed. 1, 1937.) Caste and class in a southern town. New York, Harper & Brothers, xvi + 502p.

Donohue, J. F. 1931. The impediment of crime; an historical synopsis and commentary. Washington, D. C., The Catholic University of America, viii + 110p.

Dorfman, R. I. 1948. Biochemistry of androgens. In: Pincus, G., and Thimann, K. V., ed. The hormones, pp. 467–548.

Dorfman, R. I., et al. 1947. Metabolism of the steroid hormones: Studies on 17-ketosteroids and androgens. Endocrinol. 41:470–488.

Dragoo, D. W. 1950. Transvestites in North American tribes. Ms, 12p.

Dublin, L. I., and Spiegelman, M. 1951. The facts of life, from birth to death. New York, The Macmillan Co., 461p.

Du Bois, C. 1944. The people of Alor. A social-psychological study of an East Indian Island. Minneapolis, University of Minnesota Press, xvi + 654p., 32 pl.

Dubois, J. 1848. The secret habits of the female sex . . . New York, priv. print., 185p., 4 pl.

Dubois-Desaulle, G. 1933. (A. F. N., trans. and ed.) Bestiality. An historical, medical, legal and literary study. New York, Panurge Press, priv. print., 300p.

Dück, J. 1914. Aus dem Geschlechtsleben unserer Zeit. Eine kritische Tatsachenschilderung. II. Der erste Geschlechtsverkehr. III. Die Masturbation. Sexual-Probleme 10:545–556, 713–766.

    1941. Virginität und Ehe. Reihenuntersuchung aus der allgemeinen ärztlichen Praxis. München, priv. print., 11p.

1949. [Two charts received through correspondence:] Sources of first outlet of sexuality. First outlet of sexuality [by age].

Dühren, E. (pseud.). *See* Bloch, I.

Dunn, C. W. 1940. Stilbestrol-induced gynecomastia in the male. J. Amer. Med. Assoc. 115:2263–2264.

1941. Stilbestrol induced testicular degeneration in hypersexual males. J. Clin. Endocrinol. 1:643–648.

Durand-Wever, A.-M. 1952. The influence of the nervous system on the structure and functions of human genital organs. Int. J. Sexol. 5:209–211.

Durfee, T., Lerner, M., and Kaplan, N. 1940. The artificial production of seminal ejaculation. Anat. Rec. 76:65–68.

Duvall, E. M. 1947. Courtship and engagement. *In:* Fishbein, M., and Burgess, E. W., ed. Successful marriage, pp. 32–43.

1950. Facts of life and love for teenagers. New York, Association Press, xx + 360p. (incl. xiv + 16 pl.).

Duvall, E. M., and Hill, R. 1945. When you marry. Boston, D. C. Heath & Co., xiv + 450p.

Duvall, S. M. 1952. Men, women, and morals. New York, Association Press, xvi + 336p.

East, N. 1951. Society and the criminal. Springfield, Ill., Charles C Thomas, x + 437p.

Eberhard, E. F. W. 1924. Die Frauenemanzipation und ihre erotischen Grundlagen. Wien und Leipzig, Wilhelm Braumüller, x + 916p.

1927. Feminismus und Kulturuntergang. Die erotischen Grundlagen der Frauenemanzipation. Wien und Leipzig, Wilhelm Braumüller, xv + 654p.

Eberth, C. J. 1904. Die männlichen Geschlechtsorgane. Jena, Gustav Fischer, xi + 310p.

Edson, N. W. 1936. Love, courtship and marriage. New York, American Social Hygiene Association, Publication No. 932, 18p.

Ehrmann, W. W. 1952. [Correspondence and tabulated data from a study entitled Premarital dating behavior.] Ms, n.pag.

1953. Premarital dating behavior. New York, Dryden Press (in preparation).

Eissler, K. R., et al., ed. 1949. Searchlights on delinquency. New psychoanalytic studies . . . New York, International Universities Press, xviii + 456p.

Elkisch, P. 1945. Children's drawings in a projective technique. Psychol. Monogr., v. 58, no. 1, 31p.

Elliott, G. L., and Bone, H. 1929. The sex life of youth. New York, Association Press, xi + 142p.

Ellis, Albert. 1947. Questionnaire versus interview methods in the study of human love relationships. Amer. Sociol. Rev. 12:541–553.

1948. Questionnaire versus interview methods in the study of human love relationships. II. Uncategorized responses. Amer. Sociol. Rev. 13:61–65.

1949. A study of human love relationships. J. Genetic Psychol. 75:61–71.

1951. The folklore of sex. New York, Charles Boni, 313p.

Ellis, Havelock. 1905. Studies in the psychology of sex. Volume IV. Sexual selection in man. I. Touch. II. Smell. III. Hearing. IV. Vision. Philadelphia, F. A. Davis Co., xi + 270p.

1906. Studies in the psychology of sex. Volume V. Erotic symbolism. The mechanism of detumescence. The psychic state in pregnancy. Philadelphia, F. A. Davis Co., x + 285p.

1910. Ed. 3 (ed. 1, 1900). Studies in the psychology of sex. Volume I. The evolution of modesty. The phenomena of sexual periodicity. Autoerotism. Philadelphia, F. A. Davis Co., xv + 352p.

1910. Studies in the psychology of sex. Volume VI. Sex in relation to society. Philadelphia, F. A. Davis Co., xvi + 656p.

1913. Ed. 2 (ed. 1, 1903). Studies in the psychology of sex. Volume III.

Analysis of the sexual impulse. Love and pain. The sexual impulse in women. Philadelphia, F. A. Davis Co., xii + 353p.

1915. Ed. 3 (ed. 1, 1901). Studies in the psychology of sex. Volume II. Sexual inversion. Philadelphia, F. A. Davis Co., xi + 391p.

1921 (orig. 1897). (Gennep, A. van, trans.). Études de psychologie sexuelle. II. L'inversion sexuelle, 338p. III. L'impulsion sexuelle, viii + 439p. Paris, Mercure de France.

1925. (Gennep, A. van, trans.). Études de psychologie sexuelle. V. Le symbolisme érotique. Le mecanisme de la détumescence. Paris, Mercure de France, 284p.

1926. (Gennep, A. van, trans.). Études de psychologie sexuelle. VI. L'état psychique pendant la grossesse. La mère et l'enfant. Paris, Mercure de France, 212p.

1927. (Gennep, A. van, trans.). Études de psychologie sexuelle. VII. L'éducation sexuelle. Paris, Mercure de France, 220p.

1928. (Gennep, A. van, trans.). Études de psychologie sexuelle. VIII. L'évaluation de l'amour. La chasteté. L'abstinence sexuelle. Paris, Mercure de France, 219p.

1929. Man and woman. A study of secondary and tertiary sexual characters. Boston and New York, Houghton Mifflin Company, vi + 495p.

1934. (Gennep, A. van, trans.). Études de psychologie sexuelle. XVII. Les charactères sexuels physiques secondaires et tertiaires. Paris, Mercure de France, 252p.

1936. Studies in the psychology of sex. New York, Random House, 6v. in 2. v. 1 pt. 1, xxxix + 339p. pt. 2, xii + 353p. pt. 3, xi + 391p. v. 2 pt. 1, x + 285p. pt. 2, xvi + 539p. pt. 3, xvi + 750p.

1952. (Gawsworth, J., ed.). Sex and marriage. Eros in contemporary life. New York, Random House, xiii + 219p.

Ellis, H., and Moll, A. 1911, 1921, ed. 2. 3. Autoerotische Äusserungen des Geschlechtstriebes. B. Erotisches Nachtträumen. In: Moll, Albert, ed. Handbuch der Sexualwissenschaften, pp. 612–616.

Elsberg, C. A. 1925. Tumors of the spinal cord. New York, Paul B. Hoeber, viii + 421p.

Elwin, V. 1947. The Muria and their ghotul. Bombay, Geoffrey Cumberlege, Oxford University Press, xxix + 730p., 1 col. pl.

Emmens, C. W., and Parkes, A. S. 1947. Effect of exogenous estrogens on the male mammal. Vitamins and Hormones 5:233–272.

Enders, R. K. 1945. Induced changes in the breeding habits of foxes. Sociometry 8:53–55.

Engel, G. L. 1950. Fainting; physiological and psychological considerations. Springfield, Ill., Charles C Thomas, xii + 141p.

England, L. R. 1949–1950. Little Kinsey: An outline of sex attitudes in Britain. Pub. Opin. Quart. 13:587–600.

England, L. R. 1950. A British sex survey. Int. J. Sexol. 3:148–154.

Engle, E. T. 1942. The testis and hormones. In: Cowdry, E. V., ed. Problems of ageing, pp. 475–494.

1952. The male reproductive system. In: Cowdry, E. V. Problems of ageing, pp. 708–729.

Engle, E. T., and Shelesnyak, M. C. 1934. First menstruation and subsequent menstrual cycles of pubertal girls. Human Biol. 6:431–453.

Englisch, P. 1931. Sittengeschichte Europas. Berlin, Gustav Kiepenheuer; Wien, Phaidon-Verlag, 442p., 139 pl.

English, O. S. 1947. Sexual adjustment in marriage. In: Fishbein, M., and Burgess, E. W., ed. Successful marriage, pp. 102–116.

English, O. S., and Pearson, G. H. J. 1945. Emotional problems of living. Avoiding the neurotic pattern. New York, W. W. Norton & Co., 438p.

Epstein, L. M. 1948. Sex laws and customs in Judaism. New York, Bloch Publishing Co., x + 251p.

Escamilla, R. F., and **Lisser, H. 1941.** Testosterone therapy of eunuchoids. II. Clinical comparison of parenteral implantation, and oral administration of testosterone compounds in male eunuchoidism. J. Clin. Endocrinol. 1:633–642.

Eulenburg, A. 1902. Sadismus und Masochismus. Wiesbaden, J. F. Bergmann, 89p. **1934.** (Kent, H., trans.). Algolagnia. The psychology, neurology and physiology of sadistic love and masochism. New York, New Era Press, 200p., 10 pl.

Evans, C. B. S. 1941 (orig. 1935). Sex practice in marriage. New York, Emerson Books, 128p.

Evans-Pritchard, E. E. 1940. The Nuer . . . The modes of livelihood and political institutions of a Nilotic people. Oxford, Clarendon Press, xii + 271p., 30 pl.

Everett, M. S. 1948. Preparation for marriage. Chicago, Roosevelt College, 41p.

Exner, M. J. 1915. Problems and principles of sex instruction. A study of 948 college men. New York, Association Press, 39p.
1933. The question of petting. New York, American Social Hygiene Association (Publication No. 853), 14p.

Faegre, M. L. 1943. Understanding ourselves. A discussion of social hygiene for older boys and girls. Minneapolis, Minn., University of Minnesota Press, 44p.

Faller, A. 1950. Befruchtung, Vererbung, Geschlechtsbestimmung, eheliche Vereinigung. *In:* Horstein, X. von, and Faller, A., ed. Gesundes Geschlechts Leben, pp. 221–240.

Famin, César. 1832. Peintures, bronzes et statues erotiques, formant la collection du cabinet secret du Musée Royal de Naples. Paris, Typographie Éverat, 116p., xli pl.

Famin, César (Colonel Fanin, pseud.). **1871** (orig. 1832). The Royal Museum at Naples, being some account of the erotic paintings, bronzes, and statues contained in that famous "Cabinet Secret." London, priv. print., xviii + 122p., 60 col. pl.

Farmer, J. S., and **Henley, W. E.,** comp. and ed. **1890–1904.** Slang and its analogues past and present . . . with synonyms in English, French, German, Italian, etc. . . . [London], priv. print., 7v. v. 1, x + 405p. v. 2, 406p. v. 3, 387p. v. 4, 399p. v. 5, 381p. v. 6, 378p. v. 7, 380p.

Farnham, M. F. 1951. The adolescent. New York, Harper & Brothers, xi + 243p.

Farris, E. J., ed. **1950a.** The care and breeding of laboratory animals. New York, John Wiley & Sons, etc., xvi + 515p.
1950b. Human fertility and problems of the male. White Plains, N. Y., Author's Press, xvi + 211p.

Fauconney, J. *See* Caufeynon, Dr.

Federal Reserve Bulletin. 1946–1953. Annual surveys of consumer finances. Volumes 32–39.

Federn, P. 1927–1928. Die Wiener Diskussion aus dem Jahre 1912. Ztschr. f. psa. Pädagogik 2:106–112.

Fehlinger, H. 1945 (orig. 1921). (Herbert, S. and Mrs. S., trans.). Sexual life of primitive people. New York, United Book Guild, 133p.

Feinier, L., and **Rothman, T. 1939.** Study of a male castrate. J. Amer. Med. Assoc. 113:2144–2146.

Feldhusen, F. 1909. Die Sexualenquete unter der Moskauer Studentenschaft. [Chlenov Study, 1904.] Ztschr. f. Bekämpfung der Geschlechtskrankh. 8:211–224, 245–255.

Fenichel, O. 1945. Ed. 2 (ed. 1, 1924). The psychoanalytic theory of neurosis. New York, W. W. Norton & Company, x + 703p.

Féré, C. S. 1904. The evolution and dissolution of the sexual instinct. Paris, Charles Carrington, xxiv + 358p.

1932. Scientific and esoteric studies in sexual degeneration in mankind and in animals. New York, Anthropological Press, priv. print., xiv + 325p.

Ferenczi, S. 1936. (Bunker, H. A., trans.). Male and female: Psychoanalytic reflections on the "theory of genitality," and on secondary and tertiary sex differences. Psychoanal. Quart. 5:249–260.

Ferguson, L. W. 1938. Correlates of woman's orgasm. J. Psychol. 6:295–302.

Fetscher, R. 1928. Der Geschlechtstrieb. Einführung in die Sexualbiologie unter besonderer Berücksichtigung der Ehe. München, Ernst Reinhardt, 156p.

Fifteen plagues of a maiden-head. See Anon. The fifteen plagues . . .

Filler, W., and Drezner, N. 1944. The results of surgical castration in women under forty. Amer. J. Obstet. & Gynec. 47:122–124.

Finger, F. W. 1947. Sex beliefs and practices among male college students. J. Abnorm. & Soc. Psychol. 42:57–67.

Fink, L. A. 1950. Premarital sex experience of girls in Sidney: A survey of 100 girls. Int. J. Sexol. 4:33–35.

Firth, R. W. 1936. We, the Tikopia; a sociological study of kinship in primitive Polynesia. New York, American Book Co., xxv + 605p.

Fishbein, M., and Burgess, E. W., ed. 1947. Successful marriage. An authoritative guide to problems related to marriage from the beginning of sexual attraction to matrimony and the successful rearing of a family. Garden City, N. Y., Doubleday & Co., xxi + 547p.

Fisher, Mary S. 1938. Romance and realism in love and marriage. In: Folsom, J. K., ed. Plan for marriage, pp. 1–28.

Fletcher, J. [1849]. Summary of the moral statistics of England and Wales. London, priv. print., xi + 228p., xii pl.

Fleuret, F. See Hernandez, L.

Flood, [E.]. [?1901]. Emasculation in twenty-six cases. n.impr., 19p. [Probably address to Mass. Society for Mental Hygiene.]

Folsom, J. K. 1937. Changing values in sex and family relations. Amer. Sociol. Rev. 2:717–726.

——— 1942. Love and courtship. In: Becker, H., and Hill, R., ed. Marriage and the family, pp. 153–189.

Folsom, J. K., ed. 1938. Plan for marriage. An intelligent approach to marriage and parenthood proposed by the staff of Vassar College. New York and London, Harper & Brothers, xii + 305p.

Foras, A. de. 1886. Le droit du seigneur au moyen-age. Étude critique et historique. Chambery, André Perrin, xix + 281p.

Forberg, F. K. 1884 (orig. 1824). (Smithson, J., trans.). Manual of classical erotology (De figuris Veneris). "Manchester, Julian Smithson, priv. print . . ." [Brussels, Charles Carrington], 2v. v. 1, xviii + 261p., 10 pl. v. 2, 250p., 8 pl.

Ford, C. S. 1945. A comparative study of human reproduction. New Haven, Conn., Yale University Press, 111p.

Ford, C. S., and Beach, F. A. 1951. Patterns of sexual behavior. New York, Harper & Brothers, and Paul B. Hoeber, ix + 307p.

Forel, A. 1905. Die sexuelle Frage. Eine naturwissenschaftliche, psychologische, hygienische und soziologische Studie für Gebildete. München, Ernst Reinhardt, viii + 587p.

——— 1922 (ex German ed. 2, 1906). (Marshall, C. F., trans.). The sexual question. A scientific, psychological, hygienic and sociological study. Brooklyn, N. Y., Physicians and Surgeons Book Co., xv + 536p.

Fortune, R. F. 1932. Sorcerers of Dobu. The social anthropology of the Dobu Islanders of the western Pacific. New York, E. P. Dutton & Co., xxviii + 318p., viii pl.

Fortune Quarterly Survey: VII. 1937. Fortune (Jan.) 15:86–87, 150–156, 162–168.

Fortune Survey. 1943. Fortune (Aug.) 28:10–30.

Foster, R. G. 1950 (ed. 1, 1944). Marriage and family relationships. New York, The Macmillan Co., xvi + 316p.

Fowler, O. S. 1875. Sexual science; including manhood, womanhood, and their mutual interrelations; love its laws, power etc. . . . as taught by phrenology. Philadelphia, National Publishing Co., xxx + 930p.

Frank, A. 1952 (orig. 1947). (Mooyaart, B. M., trans.). Anne Frank: The diary of a young girl. Garden City, N. Y., Doubleday & Company, 285p.

Frank, R. T. 1940. The sex hormones: Their physiologic significance and use in practice. J. Amer. Med. Assoc. 114:1504–1512.

Franz, S. I. 1913. The accuracy of localization of touch stimuli on different bodily segments. Psychol. Rev. 20:107–128.

Fraser, R. W., et al. 1941. Colorimetric assay of 17-ketosteroids in urine. A survey of the use of this test in endocrine investigation, diagnosis, and therapy. J. Clin. Endocrinol. 1:234–256.

Freeman, G. L. 1948. The energetics of human behavior. Ithaca, N. Y., Cornell University Press, vii + 344p.

Freeman, K. 1949. The pre-socratic philosophers. A companion to Diels, Fragmente der Vorsokratiker. Oxford, Basil Blackwell, xiii + 486p.

Freud, Anna. 1923. The relation of beating-phantasies to a daydream. Int. J. Psychoanal. 4:89–102.
    1951. Observations on child development. Psychoanalytic study of the child 6:18–30.

Freud, Sigmund. 1910. [Letter to Dr. F. S. Krauss]. Anthropophyteia 7:472–474.
    1910. (Brill, A. A., trans.). Three contributions to the sexual theory. New York, Journal of Nervous & Mental Disease Publishing Co., x + 91p.
    1912. *In:* Wiener psychoanalytische Vereinigung. Die Onanie, pp. 133–140.
    1921. (Paul, E. and C., trans.). Preface to: A young girl's diary. New York, Thomas Seltzer, xvi + 284p.
    1922 (orig. 1910). (Brill, A. A., trans.). Leonardo da Vinci. A psychosexual study of an infantile reminiscence. London, Kegan Paul, Trench, Trubner & Co., 130p., 4 pl.
    1924. (Riviere, J., and Strachey, A. and J., trans.). Collected Papers. London, Hogarth Press and Institute of Psychoanalysis, 4v. v. 1, 359p. v. 2, 404p. v. 3, 607p. v. 4, 508p.
    1924 (orig. 1919). 'A child is being beaten.' A contribution to the study of the origin of sexual perversions. *In:* Collected papers, v. 2, pp. 172–201.
    1933. (Sprott, W. J. H., trans.). New introductory lectures on psychoanalysis. New York, W. W. Norton & Co., 257p.
    1935. (Riviere, J., trans.). A general introduction to psychoanalysis. New York, Perma Giants, 412p.
    1938. (Brill, A. A., ed.). The basic writings of Sigmund Freud. New York, Modern Library, vi + 1001p.
    1949 (orig. 1940). (Strachey, J., trans.). An outline of psychoanalysis. New York, W. W. Norton & Co., 127p.
    1950. (Strachey, J., trans. and ed.). Collected papers. Volume V. London, Hogarth Press and Institute of Psycho-Analysis, 396p.
    1950 (orig. 1931). Female homosexuality. *In:* Collected papers, v. 5, pp. 252–272.

Friedeburg, L. von. [1950]. Ein Versuch ueber Meinung und Verhalten im Bereich der Zwischengeschlechtlichen Beziehungen in Deutschland . . . Allensbach, Institut für Demoskopie etc., 40p. (mimeo.).

Friedjung, J. K. 1923. Die kindliche Sexualität und ihre Bedeutung für Erziehung und ärztliche Praxis. Berlin, Julius Springer, 37p.

Friedlaender, K. F. 1921. (Hirschfeld, Magnus, ed.). Die Impotenz des Weibes. Leipzig, Ernst Bircher (Sexus Monographien no. 2), xii + 88p.

Fromme, A. 1950. The psychologist looks at sex and marriage. New York, Prentice-Hall, xv + 248p.

Fuchs, E. 1909–1912. Illustrierte Sittengeschichte vom Mittelalter bis zur Gegenwart. 1. Renaissance. 2. Die galante Zeit. 3. Das bürgerliche Zeitalter.

München, Albert Langen, 3v. v. 1, 1909, x + 500p., 59 pl. v. 2, 1910, x + 484p., 65 pl. v. 3, 1912, x + 496p., 63 pl.

Fuller, J. K. 1950. Communication from Justin K. Fuller, M.D., Medical Consultant to Department of Corrections. *In:* Kilpatrick, V., et al. Partial report of Assembly Interim Committee on crime and corrections (California), pp. 68–72.

Fulton, J. F. 1949. Ed. 3. Physiology of the nervous system. New York, Oxford University Press, xii + 667p.

Fulton, J. F., ed. 1949. *See* Howell, W. H.

Fulton, J. F., Ranson, S. W., and Frantz, A. M., ed. 1940. The hypothalamus and central levels of autonomic function. Proceedings of the Association for Research in Nervous and Mental Disease . . . 1939. Baltimore, Williams & Wilkins Co. (Research Publication Vol. XX), xxx + 980p.

Furtwängler, A., and Reichhold, K. 1904. Griechische Vasenmalerei. Auswahl hervorragender Vasenbilder. Tafeln, Serie 1 & 2. München, F. Bruckmann.

Gallagher, T. F., et al. 1937. The daily urinary excretion of estrogenic and androgenic substances by normal men and women. J. Clin. Invest. 16:695–703.

Gallonio, A. 1591. Historia delle sante vergini Romane . . . E de' gloriosi martiri papia e mauro soldati . . . Roma, Presso Ascanio, e Girolamo Donangeli, [6] + 350 + [24]p. *Also:* ibid. Trattato de gli instrumenti de martirio e delle varie maniere di martoriare usate da' gentili contro Christiani . . . , [4] + 159 + [9]p., incl. 47 pl.

Gantt, W. H. 1944. Experimental basis for neurotic behavior. Origin and development of artificially produced disturbances of behavior in dogs. New York, London, Paul B. Hoeber, xv + 211p.

1949. Psychosexuality in animals. *In:* Hoch, P. H., and Zubin, J., ed. Psychosexual development in health and disease, pp. 33–51.

1950. Disturbances in sexual functions during periods of stress. *In:* Wolff, H. G., et al., ed. Life stress and bodily disease, pp. 1030–1050.

Ganzfried, S. 1927. (Goldin, H. E., trans.). Code of Jewish law (Kitzur schulchan aruch). A compilation of Jewish laws and customs. New York, Hebrew Publishing Co., 4v. in 1. [ix]p. index. v. 1, 154p. v. 2, 150p. v. 3, 121p. v. 4, 137p.

Gardner, W. U. 1949. Reproduction in the female. *In:* Howell, W. H. (Fulton, J. F., ed.). A textbook of physiology, pp. 1162–1188.

Garnier, P. 1921 (orig. 1889). Anomalies sexuelles, apparents et cachés. Paris, Garnier Frères, 544p.

Geist, S. H. 1941. Androgen therapy in the human female. J. Clin. Endocrinol. 1:154–161.

Gerling, R. 1928. Der Geschlechtsverkehr der Ledigen. Berlin, Orania Verlag, 115p.

Gichner, L. E. 1949. Erotic aspects of Hindu sculpture. U.S.A., priv. print., 1 pl. + 56p.

Gilbert Youth Research. 1951. How wild are college students? [Unsigned article on a survey by Gilbert Youth Research.] Pageant (Nov.), pp. 10–21.

Glass, S. J., Deuel, H. J., and Wright, C. A. 1940. Sex hormone studies in male homosexuality. Endocrinol. 26:590–594.

Glass, S. J., and Johnson, R. H. 1944. Limitations and complications of organotherapy in male homosexuality. J. Clin. Endocrinol. 4:540–544.

Glueck, S., and Glueck, E. T. 1934. Five hundred delinquent women. New York, Alfred A. Knopf, xxiv + 539 + x p.

Goldstein, K., and Steinfeld, J. I. 1942. The conditioning of sexual behavior by visual agnosia. Bull. Forest Sanitarium 1:37–45.

Goldzieher, M. A., and Goldzieher, J. W. 1949. Toxic effects of percutaneously absorbed estrogens. J. Amer. Med. Assoc. 140:1156.

Golla, F. L., and Hodge, R. S. 1949. Hormone treatment of the sexual offender. Lancet 256:1006–1007.

Gollancz, V. 1952. My dear Timothy. An autobiographical letter to his grandson. New York, Simon and Schuster, 439p., [4] pl.

Golossowker. See Weissenberg, S.

Goode, W. J. 1949. Problems in postdivorce adjustment. Amer. Sociol. Rev. 14: 394–401.

Goodenough, W. H. 1949. Premarital freedom on Truk: Theory and practice. Amer. Anthropologist 51:615–620.

Goodland, R. 1931. A bibliography of sex rites and customs. An annotated record of books, articles, and illustrations in all languages. London, George Routledge & Sons, v + 752p.

Gorer, G. 1934. The Marquis de Sade. A short account of his life and work. New York, Liveright Publishing Corp., 264p.

1938. Himalayan village; an account of the Lepchas of Sikkim. London, M. Joseph, 2 pl., 7–510p., 32 pl.

1948. The American people. A study in national character. New York, W. W. Norton & Co., 246p.

Gould, H. N., and Gould, M. R. 1932. Age of first menstruation in mothers and daughters. J. Amer. Med. Assoc. 98:1349–1352.

Grafenberg, E. 1950. The role of urethra in female orgasm. Int. J. Sexol. 3:145–148.

Gray, M. 1951. The changing years. What to do about menopause. New York, Doubleday & Co., 224p.

Greek anthology. See Anon. The Greek anthology.

Greenblatt, R. B. 1947. Office endocrinology. Springfield, Ill., Charles C Thomas, xiv + 303p.

Greulich, W. W. 1944. Physical changes in adolescence. In: Henry, N. B., ed. The forty-third yearbook of the National Society for the Study of Education. Part I, Adolescence, pp. 8–32.

Greulich, W. W., et al. 1938. A handbook of methods for the study of adolescent children. Washington, D. C., Society for Research in Child Development, (Monogr. for the Soc. . . . Vol. 3, No. 1, Ser. No. 15), xvii + 406p.

Griffith, E. F. 1947 (ed. 1, 1935). Modern marriage. London, Methuen & Co., xi + 303p.

Groves, E. R. 1933. Marriage. New York, Henry Holt & Co., xvi + 552p.

Groves, E. R., Groves, G. H., and Groves, C. 1943. Sex fulfillment in marriage. New York, Emerson Books, 319p.

Groves, Gladys H. 1942. Marriage and family life. Boston, Houghton Mifflin Co., x + 564 + iv p.

Gruenberg, B. C., ed. 1922. High schools and sex education. Washington, D. C., U. S. Public Health Service, vii + 98p.

Gruenberg, B. C. 1932. Ed. 3 (ed. 1, 1923). Parents and sex education. For parents of young children. New York, Viking Press, viii + 112p.

Gruenberg, B. C., and Kaukonen, J. L. 1940. Ed. 2. High schools and sex education. Washington, D. C., U. S. Public Health Service (Educational Publication No. 7), xix + 110p.

Gruenberg, Sidonie M., et al. 1943. When children ask about sex. New York, Child Study Association of America, 16p.

Gudden, H. 1911. Pubertät und Schule. München, Aerztliche Rundschau, Otto Gmelin, 31p.

Gurewitsch, Z. A., and Grosser, F. J. 1929. Das Geschlechtsleben der Gegenwart. Ztschr. f. Sexualwiss. 15:513–546.

Gurewitsch, Z. A., and Woroschbit, A. J. 1931. Das Sexualleben der Bäuerin in Russland. Ztschr. f. Sexualwiss. u. Sexualpolit. 18:51–74, 81–110.

Guttmacher, M. S. 1951. Sex offenses. The problem, causes and prevention. New York, W. W. Norton & Co., 159p.

Guttmacher, M. S., and Weihofen, H. 1952. Sex offenses. J. Crim. Law, Criminol. & Police Sci. 43:153–175.

Guyon, R. 1929, 1933, 1934, 1936, 1937, 1938. Études d'éthique sexuelle. I. La
    légitimité des actes sexuels, 399p. II. La liberté sexuelle, 364p. III. Révi-
    sion des institutions classiques (Mariage. Famille.), 392p. IV. Politique
    rationelle de sexualité. La reproduction humaine, 378p. V. Politique ra-
    tionelle de sexualité. Le plaisir sexuel, 325p. VI. La persécution des actes
    sexuels. 1.—Les courtisanes, 432p. Saint-Denis, Dardaillon (and) Dar-
    daillon et Dagniaux.
    1933. (Flugel, J. C. and Ingeborg, trans., Haire, N., ed.). Sex life & sex
    ethics. London, John Lane, xxii + 386p.
    1948. (Flugel, J. C. and Ingeborg, trans.). The ethics of sexual acts. New
    York, Alfred A. Knopf, [25] + 383 + xxvii p.
Guze, H. 1951. Sexual attitudes in the scientific medical literature. Int. J. Sexol.
    5:97–100.

Hafez, E. S. E. 1951. Mating behaviour in sheep. Nature 167:777–778.
Haire, Norman, ed. 1937. Encyclopaedia of sexual knowledge. New York, Eugenics
    Publishing Co., xx + 567p.
Haire, Norman. 1948. Everyday sex problems. London, Frederick Muller, 268p.
    1951. The encyclopedia of sex practice. London, Encyclopaedic Press, 836p.
    (incl. 80 pl., 32 col. pl.)
Hall, G. S. 1904. Adolescence. Its psychology and its relations to physiology, an-
    thropology, sociology, sex, crime, religion and education. New York,
    D. Appleton and Co., 2v. v. 1, xx + 589p. v. 2, vi + 784p.
Hall, W. S. 1920. Sex training in the home. Plain talks on sex life covering all pe-
    riods and relationships from childhood to old age. Chicago, Midland
    Press, 128p.
Hallowell, A. I. 1949. Psychosexual adjustment, personality and the good life in
    a non-literate culture. In: Hoch, P. H., and Zubin, J., ed. Psychosexual
    development in health and disease, pp. 102–123.
Halverson, H. M. 1940. Genital and sphincter behavior of the male infant. Pedag.
    Sem. & J. Genet. Psychol. 56:95–136.
Hamblen, E. C. 1945. Endocrinology of woman. Springfield, Ill., Charles C
    Thomas, xii + 574p.
Hamburger, C. 1948. Normal urinary excretion of neutral 17-ketosteroids with
    special reference to age and sex variations. Acta Endocrinol. 1:19–37.
Hamilton, G. V. 1914. A study of sexual tendencies in monkeys and baboons.
    J. Anim. Behav. 4:295–318.
    1929. A research in marriage. New York, Albert & Charles Boni, xiii + 570p.
    1936. Homosexuality, defensive. [Homosexuality as a defense against in-
    cest.] In: Robinson, Victor, ed. Encyclopaedia sexualis, pp. 334–342.
Hamilton, G. V., and Macowan, K. 1929. What is wrong with marriage. New York,
    Albert & Charles Boni, xxi + 319p.
Hamilton, H. B., and Hamilton, J. B. 1948. Ageing in apparently normal men.
    I. Urinary titers of ketosteroids and of alpha-hydroxy and beta-hydroxy
    ketosteroids. J. Clin. Endocrinol. 8:433–452.
Hamilton, J. B. 1937a. Treatment of sexual underdevelopment with synthetic
    male hormone substance. Endocrinol. 21:649–654.
    1937b. Induction of penile erection by male hormone substances. Endo-
    crinol. 21:744–749.
    1941. Therapeutics of testicular dysfunction. J. Amer. Med. Assoc. 116:
    1903–1908.
    1943. Demonstrated ability of penile erection in castrate men with markedly
    low titers of urinary androgens. Proc. Soc. Exper. Biol. & Med. 54:309–
    312.
    1948. The role of testicular secretions as indicated by the effects of castra-
    tion in man and by studies of pathological conditions and the short life-
    span associated with maleness. Rec. Prog. in Hormone Res. 3:257–322.

Hamilton, J. B., and Hubert, G. R. 1940. Vocal changes in eunuchoidal and castrated men upon administration of male hormone substance. Amer. J. Physiol. 129:P372–P373.

Hamilton, W. J., Boyd, J. D., and Mossman, H. W. 1947. Human embryology. (Prenatal development of form and function.) Baltimore, Williams & Wilkins Co., viii + 366p.

Hammond, W. A. 1887. Sexual impotence in the male and female. Detroit, George S. Davis, 305p.

Hara, Kōzan. 1938. Nihon Kōshoku bijutsu shi. [History of Japanese erotic art.] Tokyo, Kinryūdō, 384p., 16 pl., 1 col. pl.

Hardenbergh, E. W. 1949. The psychology of feminine sex experience. Int. J. Sexol. 2:224–228.

Harper, R. A. 1949. Marriage. New York, Appleton Century Crofts, xi + 308p.

Harper, R. F. 1904. Ed. 2. The code of Hammurabi, King of Babylon. Chicago, University of Chicago Press, xv + 192 + 103 pl.

Hartman, C. G. 1931. On the relative sterility of the adolescent organism. Science 74:226–227.

1936. Time of ovulation in women. Baltimore, Williams & Wilkins Co., x + 226p.

1940. The effect of testosterone on the monkey uterus and the administration of steroidal hormones in the form of Deanesly-Parkes pellets. Endocrinol. 26:449–471.

1945. The mating of mammals. Ann. N. Y. Acad. Sci. 46:23–44.

Hartman, F. A., and Brownell, K. A. 1949. The adrenal gland. Philadelphia, Lea & Febiger, 581p.

Hartwich, A. H., Kaus, G., and Kind, A. 1931. Die Brautnacht . . . Eine Morphologie ihrer Erscheinungsformen. Wien, Verlag für Kulturforschung, 192p., 7 pl., 8 col. pl., + 6 photog. pl.

Harvey, O. L. 1932a. Some statistics derived from recent questionnaire studies relative to human sexual behavior. J. Soc. Psychol. 3:97–100.

1932b. A note on the frequency of human coitus. Amer. J. Sociol. 38:64–70.

Hattwick, LaB. A. 1937. Sex differences in behavior of nursery school children. Child Develop. 8:343–355.

Hawke, C. C. 1950. Castration and sex crimes. [Address delivered to Illinois Academy of Criminology], 8p. mimeo.

Heckel, N., and McDonald, J. H. 1952. The effects of testosterone propionate upon the spermatogenic function of the human testis. Ann. N. Y. Acad. Sci. 55:725–733.

Hediger, H. 1950. (Sircom, G., trans.). Wild animals in captivity. London, Butterworth, ix + 207p., [17] pl.

Hegar, A. 1878. Die Castration der Frauen vom physiologischen und chirurgischen Standpunkte aus. Leipzig, Breitkopf und Härtel, iv + 144p.

Heidel, A. 1946. The Gilgamesh epic and Old Testament parallels. Chicago, University of Chicago Press, ix + 269p.

Heller, C. G., and Maddock, W. O. 1947. The clinical uses of testosterone in the male. Vitamins and Hormones 5:393–432.

Heller, C. G., and Nelson, W. O. 1948. The testis-pituitary relationship in man. Rec. Prog. in Hormone Res. 3:229–255.

Heller, C. G., Nelson, W. O., and Roth, A. A. 1943. Functional prepuberal castration in males. J. Clin. Endocrinol. 3:573–588.

Hellmann. See Weissenberg, S.

Hemphill, F. M. 1952. A sample survey of home injuries. Publ. Health Rept. 67:1026–1034.

Hemphill, R. E. 1944. Return of virility after prefrontal leucotomy with enlargement of gonads. Lancet 247:345–346.

Heneman, H. G., Jr., and Paterson, D. G. 1949. Refusal rates and interview quality. Int. J. Opin. & Attit. Res. 3:392–398.

Henninger, J. M. 1941. Exhibitionism. J. Crim. Psychopath. 2:357–366.
Henry, G. W. 1938. Ed. 3 (ed. 1, 1925). Essentials of psychiatry. Baltimore, Williams & Wilkins Co., xii + 465p.
1941. Sex variants. A study of homosexual patterns. New York, London, Paul B. Hoeber, 2v. v. 1, xxi + 546p. v. 2, vii + 547–1179p.
Henry, Jules. 1949. The social function of child sexuality in Pilaga Indian culture. In: Hoch, P. H., and Zubin, J., ed. Psychosexual development in health and disease, pp. 91–101.
Henry, N. B., ed. 1944. The forty-third yearbook of the National Society for the Study of Education. Part I, Adolescence. Chicago, University of Chicago Press, x + 358p.
Henz, W. 1910. Probenächte. Sexual-Probleme 6:740–750.
Hernandez, L., pseud. [Fleuret, F., and Perceau, L.]. 1920. Les procès de bestialité au XVIe et XVIIe siècles. Paris, Bibliotheque des Curieux, 238p., 4 pl.
Herondas. 1921 (orig. 3rd cent. B.C.). (Buck, M. S., trans.). The mimes of Herondas. New York, priv. print., 119p.
Hesnard, A. 1933. Strange lust: The psychology of homosexuality. New York, Amethnol Press, 256p.
Heyn, A. 1921. Studien zur Physiologie des Geschlechtslebens der Frau. Geschlecht und Gesellschaft 10:405–408.
1924. Über sexuelle Träume (Pollutionen) bei Frauen. Archiv f. Frauenkunde 10:60–69.
Hikatsu-sho. See Anon. Hikatsu-sho.
Hill, W. W. 1935. The status of the hermaphrodite and transvestite in Navaho culture. Amer. Anthropologist 37:273–279.
Himes, N. E. 1940. Your marriage. A guide to happiness. New York, Toronto, Farrar & Rinehart, xiv + 434p.
Hirning, L. C. 1947. Genital exhibitionism, an interpretive study. J. Clin. Psychopath. 8:557–564.
Hirsch, E. W. 1949. Modern sex life. With case histories. New York, Permabooks, xv + 236p.
Hirschfeld, M., ed. 1899–1921. Jahrbuch für sexuelle Zwischenstufen. Unter besonderer Berücksichtigung der Homosexualität. Leipzig, Max Spohr, Volumes 1–21.
Hirschfeld, Magnus (Praetorius, Numa, pseud.). 1911. Homosexuelle Pissoirinschriften aus Paris. Anthropophyteia 8:410–422.
Hirschfeld, M. 1916–1921. Sexualpathologie. Ein Lehrbuch für Ärzte und Studierende. Part 1: Geschlechtliche Entwicklungsstörungen mit besonderer Berücksichtigung der Onanie. Part 2: Sexuelle Zwischenstufen. Das männliche Weib und der weibliche Mann. Part 3: Störungen im Sexualstoffwechsel mit besonderer Berücksichtigung der Impotenz. Bonn, A. Marcus & E. Webers Verlag, 3v. in 1. v. 1, 1916, xv + 211p. v. 2, 1921, x + 279p. v. 3, 1920, xi + 340p.
1920 (ex. 1914 ed.). Die Homosexualität des Mannes und des Weibes. Berlin, Louis Marcus, xvii + 1067p.
1926, 1928, 1930. Geschlechtskunde auf Grund dreiszigjähriger Forschung und Erfahrung bearbeitet. I. Band: Die körperseelischen Grundlagen, xv + 638p. II. Band: Folgen und Folgerungen, 659p. III. Band: Einblicke und Ausblicke, 780p. IV. Band: Bilderteil, 904p. Stuttgart, Julius Püttmann.
1928. Kastration bei Sittlichkeitsverbrechern. Ztschr. f. Sexualwiss. 15:54–55.
1935. (Rodker, J., trans.). Sex in human relationships. London, John Lane, xxii + 218p.
1936. Homosexuality. In: Robinson, Victor, ed. Encyclopaedia sexualis, pp. 321–334.
1940, rev. ed. Sexual pathology. A study of derangements of the sexual instinct. New York, Emerson Books, xii + 368p.

1944. Sexual anomalies and perversions. Physical and psychological development and treatment. A summary of the works of the late . . . Dr. Magnus Hirschfeld. London, Francis Aldor, 630p.

1948, rev. ed. Sexual anomalies. The origins, nature, and treatment of sexual disorders. New York, Emerson Books, 538p.

Hirschfeld, M., and Bohm, E. 1930. Sexualerziehung. Der Weg durch Natürlichkeit zur neuen Moral. Berlin, Universitas Deutsche Verlags-Aktiengesellschaft, 234p.

Hirschfeld, M., and Linsert, R. 1930. Liebesmittel. Eine Darstellung der geschlechtlichen Reizmittel (Aphrodisiaca). Berlin, Man Verlag, x + 395p.

Histoire et psycho-physiologie du vice . . . See Anon. Histoire et psycho-physiologie du vice . . .

Hitschmann, E., and Bergler, E. 1936. (Weil, P. L., trans.). Frigidity in women. Its characteristics and treatment. Washington and New York, Nervous and Mental Disease Publishing Co., v + 76p.

Hoch, P. H., and Zubin, J., ed. 1949. Psychosexual development in health and disease. Proceedings of the thirty-eighth annual meeting of the American Psychopathological Association . . . June 1948. New York, Grune & Stratton, viii + 283p.

Hodann, M. 1929. Onanie. Weder Laster noch Krankheit. Berlin, Universitas-Deutsche Verlags-Aktiengesellschaft, 91p.

1932. Geschlecht und Liebe. Berlin, Büchergilde Gutenberg, 264p.

1937. (Browne, S., trans.). History of modern morals. London, William Heinemann, xv + 338p.

Hoff, H. E. 1949. Cardiac output: Regulation and estimation. In: Howell, W. H. (Fulton, J. F., ed.). A textbook of physiology, pp. 660–680.

Hoffman, J. 1944. Female endocrinology. Including sections on the male. Philadelphia and London, W. B. Saunders Co., xv + 788p.

Hohman, L. B., and Schaffner, B. 1947. The sex lives of unmarried men. Amer. J. Sociol. 52:501–507.

Hollingshead, A. B. 1949. Elmtown's youth. The impact of social classes on adolescents. New York, John Wiley & Sons, London, Chapman & Hall, xi + 453p.

Hooker, C. W. 1949. Reproduction in the male. In: Howell, W. H. (Fulton, J. F., ed.). A textbook of physiology, pp. 1189–1206.

Hooton, E. A. 1942. Man's poor relations. Garden City, N. Y., Doubleday, Doran & Co., xl + 412p., 74 pl., 11 fig.

1946, rev. ed. (Ed. 1, 1931). Up from the ape. New York, The Macmillan Co., 1 pl. + xxii + 788p., 40 pl.

Hoover, J. E. 1947. How safe is your daughter? Amer. Mag. (July), pp. 32–33, 102–104.

Horace. 1914 (orig. 1st cent. B.C.). (Bennett, C. E., trans.). Odes and epodes. Cambridge, Mass., Harvard University Press, xx + 431p.

1926. (Fairclough, H. R., trans.). Satires, epistles and ars poetica. Cambridge, Mass., Harvard University Press, xxx + 509p.

Hornstein, F. X. von, and Faller, A., ed. 1950. Gesundes Geschlechts Leben. Handbuch für Ehefragen. Olten, Switzerland, Otto Walter, 452p.

Horrocks, J. E. 1951. (Carmichael, L., ed.). Psychology of adolescence. Behavior and development. Boston, Houghton Mifflin Co., xxvi + 614p.

Horvitz, D. G. 1952. Sampling and field procedures of the Pittsburgh morbidity survey. Pub. Health Rpt. 67:1003–1012.

Hoskins, R. G. 1941. Endocrinology. The glands and their functions. New York, W. W. Norton & Co., 388p.

Hotchkiss, R. S. 1944. Fertility in men. Philadelphia, J. B. Lippincott Co., xiii + 216p.

Houssay, B. A., et al. 1951. (Lewis, J. T. and Olive T., trans.). Human physiology. New York, McGraw-Hill Book Co., xvi + 1118p.

Howard, J. E., and Scott, W. W. 1950. The testes. *In:* Williams, R. H., ed. Text-book of endocrinology, pp. 316–348.

Howard, P., et al. 1950. Testicular deficiency: a clinical and pathological study. J. Clin. Endocrinol. 10:121–186.

Howell, W. H. 1949. Ed. 16 (ed. 1, 1905). (Fulton, J. F., ed.). A textbook of physiology. Philadelphia and London, W. B. Saunders Co., xl + 1258p.

Hoyer, E. 1929. Das lüsterne Weib. Sexualpsychologie der begehrenden unbe-friedigten und schamlosen Frau. Wien, Leipzig, Verlag für Kulturfor-schung, 256p., 30 pl.

Huffman, J. W. 1950. The effect of gynecologic surgery on sexual reactions. Amer. J. Obstet. & Gynec. 59:915–917.

Huggins, C., Stevens, R. E., and Hodges, C. V. 1941. Studies on prostatic cancer. II. The effects of castration on advanced carcinoma of the prostate gland. Arch. Surgery 43:209–223.

Hughes, W. L. 1926. (Edwards, M. S., ed.). Sex experiences of boyhood. J. Soc. Hyg. 12:262–273.

Huhner, M. 1945. Ed. 3. The diagnosis and treatment of sexual disorders in the male and female including sterility and impotence. Philadelphia, F. A. Davis Co., xiii + 516p.

Hunter, J. 1786. A treatise on the venereal diseases. 12 + 398 + 19p., vii pl.

Hurxthal, L. M. 1943. Sublingual use of testosterone in 7 cases of hypogonadism: Report of 3 congenital eunuchoids occurring in one family. J. Clin. En-docrinol. 3:551–556.

Huschka, M. 1938. The incidence and character of masturbation threats in a group of problem children. Psychoanal. Quart. 7:338–356.

Hutton, I. E. 1942. (Ed. 1, 1932). The sex technique in marriage. New York, Emerson Books, 160p.

Hutton, L. 1935, 1937. The single woman and her emotional problems. Baltimore, William Wood and Co., xv + 173p.

   1950. The unmarried. *In:* Neville-Rolfe, S., ed. Sex in social life, pp. 414–434.

Hyman, H. T. 1946. An integrated practice of medicine. Philadelphia and London, W. B. Saunders Co., 5v. v. 1, xxvii + 1032 + lxiii p. v. 2, xvi + 1033–2010 + xliv p. v. 3, xv + 2011–3095 + xlvii p. v. 4, xvii + 3097–4131 + xlvi p. Index, 4133–4336p.

Hyndman, O. R., and Wolkin, J. 1943. Anterior chordotomy. Further observations on physiologic results and optimum manner of performance. Arch. Neurol. & Psychiat. 50:129–148.

Indiana State Board of Health. n.d. Parents part. [Revised from orig. by U. S. Pub. Health Serv.] Indianapolis, Ind., 13p.

Inge, W. R. 1930. Christian ethics and modern problems. New York, London, G. P. Putnam's Sons, ix + 427p.

Iovetz-Tereshchenko, N. M. 1936. Friendship-love in adolescence. London, George Allen & Unwin, xvi + 367p.

Isaacs, Susan S. F. 1939. Social development in young children; a study of be-ginnings. New York, Harcourt, Brace and Co., xii + 480p.

Ito, P. K. 1942. Comparative biometrical study of physique of Japanese women born and reared under different environments. Human Biol. 14:279–351.

Jackson, L. 1949. A study of sado-masochistic attitudes in a group of delinquent girls by means of a specially designed projective test. Brit. J. Med. Psy-chol. 22:53–65.

Jacobus X. *See* Jacolliot, Louis.

Jacolliot, L. (Jacobus X. . . . French army surgeon). 1900. Medico-legal exam-ination of the abuses, aberrations, and dementia of the genital sense. Paris, Charles Carrington, 19 + 543p.

Jefferis, B. G., and Nichols, J. L. 1912 (ed. 1, 1894). Search lights on health. Light on dark corners. A complete sexual science and a guide to purity and physical manhood. Advice to maiden, wife, and mother. Love, courtship, and marriage. Naperville, Ill., J. L. Nichols, 487p.

Jeffress, L. A., ed. 1951. Cerebral mechanisms in behavior. The Hixon symposium. New York, John Wiley & Sons; London, Chapman & Hall, xiv + 311p., 1 col. pl.

Jenkins, I. 1944. The legal basis of literary censorship. Va. Law Rev. 31:83–118.

Jenkins, M. 1931. The effect of segregation on the sex behavior of the white rat as measured by the obstruction method. In: Warden, C. J., ed. Animal motivation. Experimental studies on the white rat, pp. 179–261.

Jensen, M. B. 1947. A case of sadism expressed through pictorial mutilations. Amer. Psychologist 2:277.

Jiiro haya-shinan. See Anon. Jiiro haya-shinan.

Jonsson, G. 1951. Sexualvanor hos svensk ungdom. In: Wangson, Otto, et al. Ungdomen möter samhället, (Bilaga A), pp. 160–204.

Jordan, H. E. 1934. A textbook of histology. New York and London, Appleton-Century Co., xxvii + 738p.

Justinian, (pseud.), ed. [1939]. Americana sexualis. Chicago, priv. print., 40p.

Juvenal and Persius. 1789 (orig. 1st–2nd cent. A.D.). (Madan, M., trans.). New and literal translation of Juvenal and Persius; with copious explanatory notes, by which these difficult satirists are rendered easy and familiar to the reader. London, priv. print., 2v. v. 1, x + 448p. v. 2, 476 + 20p.

Juvenal and Flaccus. 1817 (orig. 1st–2nd cent. A.D.). (Gifford, W., trans.). The satires of Decimus Junius Juvenalis, and of Aulus Persius Flaccus, translated into English verse. London, W. Bulmer & Co., 2v. v. 1, xi + lxxxii + 384p. v. 2, 163p.

Kadis, A. L. 1952. Latency period. In: Brower, D., and Abt, L. E., ed. Progress in clinical psychology, v. 1, sec. 2, pp. 361–368.

Kahn, F. 1937. Unser Geschlechtsleben. Ein Führer und Berater für jedermann. Zürich und Leipzig, Albert Müller, 393p., 32 pl.

   1939. (Rosen, G., trans.). Our sex life. A guide and counsellor for everyone. New York, Alfred A. Knopf, xxxvi + 459p.

Kahn, S. 1937. Mentality and homosexuality. Boston, Meador Publishing Co., 249p.

Kallmann, F. J. 1952. Comparative twin study on the genetic aspects of male homosexuality. J. Nerv. & Ment. Dis. 115:283–298.

Kantor, J. R. 1924. Principles of psychology. New York, Alfred A. Knopf, 2v. v. 1, xix + 473p. v. 2, xii + 524p.

Karsch, F. 1900. Päderastie und Tribadie bei den Tieren auf Grund der Literatur. Jahrb. f. Sex. Zwisch. 2:126–160.

Karsch-Haack, F. 1906. Forschungen über gleichgeschlechtliche Liebe. 1. Die Mongoloiden. München, Seitz & Schauer, xvi + 134p.

   1911. Das gleichgeschlechtliche Leben der Naturvölker. München, Ernst Reinhardt, xvi + 668p., xiii pl.

Käser, J. 1830. Bemerkungen über die Unzucht und die unehelichen Geburten . . . München, Mich. Lindauer, xii + 74p. + 1 pl.

Katz, D., and Allport, F. H. 1931. Students' attitudes, a report of the Syracuse University reaction study. Syracuse, N. Y., The Craftsman Press, xxviii + 408p.

Kearns, W. M. 1941. Oral therapy of testicular deficiency. Methyl testosterone administered orally to patients with marked testicular deficiency. J. Clin. Endocrinol. 1:126–130.

Keiser, S., and Schaffer, D. 1949. Environmental factors in homosexuality in adolescent girls. Psychoanal. Rev. 36:283–295.

Kelleher, E. J. 1952. The role of psychiatry in programs for the control and treatment of sex offenders. [Speech delivered before the Illinois Academy of Criminology, May, 1952.] Ms, (mimeo.), 10p.

Keller, D. H. 1942. The truth about "self-abuse." New York, Sexology Magazine (Personal Problem Library, v. 2), 16p.

Kellogg, Rhoda. 1953. Babies need fathers, too. New York, Comet Press Books, 256p.

Kelly, G. L. 1930. Sexual feeling in woman. Augusta, Ga., Elkay Co., xviii + 270p.
  1947. Technic of marriage relations. *In:* Fishbein, M., and Burgess, E. W., ed. Successful marriage, pp. 92–101.

Kelly, P. C. M. 1951. The Catholic book of marriage. New York, Farrar, Straus & Young, 299p.

Kempf, E. J. 1917. The social and sexual behavior of infra-human primates with some comparable facts in human behavior. Psychoanal. Rev. 4:127–154.

Kenigsberg, S., Pearson, S., and McGavack, T. H. 1949. The excretion of 17-ketosteroids. I. Normal values in relation to age and sex. J. Clin. Endocrinol. 9:426–429.

Kenyon, A. T. 1938. The effect of testosterone propionate on the genitalia, prostate, secondary sex characters, and body weight in eunuchoidism. Endocrinol. 23:121–134.

Kenyon, A. T., et al. 1940. A comparative study of the metabolic effects of testosterone propionate in normal men and women and in eunuchoidism. Endocrinol. 26:26–45.

Kepler, E. J., and Locke, W. 1950. The adrenals. Part I. Chronic adrenal hyperfunction. *In:* Williams, R. H., ed. Textbook of endocrinology, pp. 180–248.

Kilpatrick, V., et al. 1950. Partial report of Assembly Interim Committee on Crime and Corrections. California State Assembly, House Resolution no. 243, 83p., 16 pl.

Kimbrough, R. A., and Israel, S. L. 1948. The use and abuse of estrogen. J. Amer. Med. Assoc. 138:1216–1220.

Kind, A., and Moreck, C. 1930. Gefilde der Lust. Morphologie, Physiologie und sexual-psychologische Bedeutung der sekundären Geschlechtsmerkmale des Weibes. Wien, Leipzig, Verlag für Kulturforschung, 351p., 14 pl., 26 col. pl.

Kinsey, A. C. 1941. Criteria for a hormonal explanation of the homosexual. J. Clin. Endocrinol. 1:424–428.
  1947. Sex behavior in the human animal. Ann. N. Y. Acad. Sci. 47:635–637.

Kinsey, A. C., Pomeroy, W. B., and Martin, C. E. 1948. Sexual behavior in the human male. Philadelphia and London, W. B. Saunders Co., xv + 804p.

Kinsey, A. C., et al. 1949. Concepts of normality and abnormality in sexual behavior. *In:* Hoch, P. H., and Zubin, J., ed. Psychosexual development in health and disease, pp. 11–32.

Kirkendall, L. A. 1947. Understanding sex. Chicago, Science Research Associates, 48p.

Kisch, E. H. 1907. Das Geschlechtsleben des Weibes in physiologischer, pathologischer und hygienischer Beziehung. Berlin, Urban & Schwarzenberg, viii + 728p.
  1918. Ed. 3 (ed. 1, 1916). Die sexuelle Untreue der Frau. 1. Die Ehebrecherin. Bonn, A. Marcus & E. Weber, viii + 206p.
  1926 (orig. 1910). (Paul, N. E., trans.). The sexual life of woman in its physiological, pathological and hygienic aspects. New York, Allied Book Company, xi + 686p.

Klumbies, G., and Kleinsorge, H. 1950a. Das Herz in Orgasmus. Medizinische Klinik 45:952–958.
  1950b. Circulatory dangers and prophylaxis during orgasm. Int. J. Sexol. 4:61–66.

Klüver, H., and Bucy, P. C. 1938. An analysis of certain effects of bilateral temporal lobectomy in the rhesus monkey, with special reference to "psychic blindness." J. Psychol. 5:33–54.

1939. Preliminary analysis of functions of the temporal lobes in monkeys. Arch. Neurol. & Psychiat. 42:979–1000.

Knight, R. P. 1943. Functional disturbances in the sexual life of women. Frigidity and related disorders. Bull. Menninger Clin. 7:25–35.

Koch, F. C. 1937. The male sex hormones. Physiol. Rev. 17:153–238.

1938. The chemistry and biology of male sex hormones. Baltimore, Williams & Wilkins Co., from the Harvey Society Lecture Series 33:205–236.

Koch, H. L. 1935. An analysis of certain forms of so-called "nervous habits" in young children. J. Genetic Psychol. 46:139–170.

Kogon, E. 1950. (Norden, H., trans.). The theory and practice of hell. The German concentration camps and the system behind them. New York, Farrar, Straus & Co., 307p.

Kolb, L. C. 1949. An evaluation of lobotomy and its potentialities for future research in psychiatry and the basic sciences. J. Nerv. & Ment. Dis. 110: 112–148.

Kopp, Marie E. 1933. Birth control in practice. Analysis of ten thousand case histories of the Birth Control Clinical Research Bureau. New York, Robt. M. McBride & Co., vii + 290p.

1938. Surgical treatment as sex crime prevention measure. J. Crim. Law & Criminol. 28:692–706.

Koran. 1935. Ed. 3 (ed. 1, 1916). (Maulvi, Muhammad Ali, trans. and ed.). The holy Qur-án. Containing the Arabic text with English translation . . . Lahore, India, Ahmadiyya Anjuman-i-Isháat-i-Islam, cxii + 1275p.

Krafft-Ebing, R. von. 1901. Neue Studien auf dem Gebiete der Homosexualität. Jahrb. f. Sex. Zwisch. 3:1–36.

1922 (orig. 1906). (Rebman, F. J., trans.). Psychopathia sexualis, with especial reference to the antipathic sexual instinct. A medico-forensic study. Brooklyn, N. Y., Physicians and Surgeons Book Co., xiii + 617p.

1924. Ed. 16 (orig. 1886). (Moll, Albert, ed.). Psychopathia sexualis. Mit besonderer Berücksichtigung der konträren Sexualempfindung. Stuttgart, Ferdinand Enke, v + 832p.

Krauss, F. S. 1911. Ed. 2 (ed. 1, 1907). Das Geschlechtsleben in Glauben, Sitte, Brauch und Gewohnheitsrecht der Japaner. Leipzig, Ethnolog. Verlag, viii + 226p. + [68] pl.

1931. Japanisches Geschlechtsleben in zwei Bänden. Erster Band: Das Geschlechtsleben in Sitte, Brauch, Glauben und Gewohnheitsrecht des Japanischen Volkes. Leipzig, "Anthropophyteia" Verlag für Urtriebkunde, 432p. + 100 pl. on 95p.

Krauss, F. S., and Satow, Tamio. 1931. (Ihm, Hermann, ed. and trans.). Japanisches Geschlechtsleben, in zwei Bänden. Zweiter Band: Abhandlungen und Erhebungen über das Geschlechtsleben des Japanischen Volkes. Leipzig, "Anthropophyteia" Verlag für Urtriebkunde, 654p.

Krauss, F. S., ed. Anthropophyteia. See Anthropophyteia.

Kroger, W. S., and Freed, S. C. 1950. Psychosomatic aspects of frigidity. J. Amer. Med. Assoc. 143:526–532.

1951. Psychosomatic gynecology: including problems of obstetrical care. Philadelphia and London, W. B. Saunders Co., xvii + 503p.

Kronfeld, A. 1923. Exhibitionismus. In: Marcuse, M., ed. Handwörterbuch der Sexualwissenschaft, pp. 121–122.

1923. Masochismus. In: Marcuse, M., ed. Handwörterbuch der Sexualwissenschaft, pp. 313–314.

1923. Sexualpsychopathologie. Leipzig und Wien, Franz Deuticke, viii + 134p.

Kuhn, M. H. 1942. The engagement. In: Becker, H., and Hill, R., ed. Marriage and the family, pp. 211–233.

Kühn, R. 1932. Die Frau bei den Kulturvölkern. Berlin, Neufeld & Henius, 256p., 77 photog. pl.

Kuntz, A. 1945. Ed. 3. The autonomic nervous system. Philadelphia, Lea & Febiger, 1 pl. + 687p.
> **1951.** Visceral innervation and its relation to personality. Springfield, Ill., Charles C Thomas, viii + 152p.

Lampl-DeGroot, J. 1950. On masturbation and its influence on general development. Psychoanalytic study of the child 5:153–174.

Landes, R. 1938. The Ojibwa woman. New York, Columbia University Press, viii + 247p.

Landis, C., et al. 1940. Sex in development. A study of the growth and development of the emotional and sexual aspects of personality together with physiological, anatomical, and medical information on a group of 153 normal women and 142 female psychiatric patients. New York, London, Paul B. Hoeber, xx + 329p.

Landis, C., and Bolles, M. M. 1942. Personality and sexuality of the physically handicapped woman. New York, London, Paul B. Hoeber, xii + 171p.

Landis, J. T., and Landis, M. G. 1948. Building a successful marriage. New York, Prentice-Hall, xii + 559p.

Landis, P. H. 1945. Adolescence and youth. The process of maturing. New York and London, McGraw-Hill Book Co., xiii + 470p.

Lange, J. 1934. Die Folgen der Entmannung Erwachsener. An der Hand der Kriegserfahrungen dargestellt. Arbeit und Gesundheit 24:51–102 + append.

Langworthy, O. R. 1944. Behavior disturbances related to decomposition of reflex activity caused by cerebral injury. An experimental study of the cat. J. Neuropath. & Exper. Neurol. 3:87–100.

Lanval, M. 1946. L'amour sous le masque. Bruxelles, Le Laurier, 208p.
> **1950.** (Gibault, P., trans.). An inquiry into the intimate lives of women. (L'amour sous le masque.) New York, Cadillac Publishing Co., xii + 243p.

Lashley, K. S. 1916. Reflex secretion of the human parotid gland. J. Exper. Psychol. 1:461–493.
> **1938.** The thalamus and emotion. Psychol. Rev. 45:42–61.
> **1951.** The problem of serial order in behavior. In: Jeffress, L. A., ed. Cerebral mechanisms in behavior, pp. 112–146.

Lasker, G. W., and Thieme, F. P. 1949. Yearbook of physical anthropology, 1948, Volume 4. New York, Viking Fund, v + 217p.

Laubscher, B. J. F. 1938. Sex, custom and psychopathology. A study of South African pagan natives. New York, Robert M. McBride & Co., xv + 347p., 16 pl.

Laughlin, H. H. 1922. Eugenical sterilization in the United States. Chicago, Psychopathic Laboratory of the Municipal Court, xiii + 502p.

Laurent, E. 1904. Sexuelle Verirrungen. Sadismus und Masochismus. Berlin, H. Barsdorf, iv + 271p.

Lazarsfeld, S. 1931. Wie die Frau den Mann erlebt. Fremde Bekenntnisse und eigene Betrachtungen. Leipzig, Wien, Schneider & Co., 331p., 24 pl.

Leach, M., and Fried, J., ed. 1949–1950. Dictionary of folklore, mythology and legend. New York, Funk & Wagnalls Co., 2v. v. 1, xii + 531p. v. 2, 532–1196p.

Lecky, W. E. H. 1881 (orig. c. 1877). History of European morals from Augustus to Charlemagne. New York, D. Appleton and Co., 2v. v. 1, xxiv + 468p. v. 2, xi + 407p.

Lees, H. 1944. The word you can't say. Hygeia 22:336–337, 388–390.

Lenormant, M. F. 1867. Chefs-d'oeuvre de l'art antique. Ser. 2. Monuments de la peinture et de la sculpture. Paris, A. Lévy, 4v. v. 1, 85p. + 122 pl. v. 2, 123p. + 102 pl. v. 3, 107p. + 135 pl. v. 4, 214p. + 168 pl.

Leuba, C. 1948. Ethics in sex conduct. New York, Association Press, 164p.

Levine, M. I. 1951. Pediatric observations on masturbation in children. Psychoanalytic study of the child 6:117–124.

Levy, D. M. 1928. Fingersucking and accessory movements in early infancy. An etiologic study. Amer. J. Psychiat. 7:881–918.

Levy, J., and **Munroe, R. 1938.** The happy family. New York, Alfred A. Knopf, 319p.

Levy, S. S. 1951. Interaction of institutions and policy groups: The origin of sex crime legislation. The Lawyer and Law Notes 5:3–12.

Lewinsky, H. 1944. On some aspects of masochism. Int. J. Psychoanal. 25:150–155.

Lewis, T. 1942. Pain. New York, The Macmillan Co., xiii + 192p.

Licht, H. 1925–1928. Sittengeschichte Griechenlands. Die griechische Gesellschaft. Das Liebesleben der Griechen. Die Erotik in der griechischen Kunst (Ergänzungen zu Band 1 und 2). Dresden und Zürich, Paul Aretz, 3v. v. 1, 1925, 319p., 16 pl. v. 2, 1926, 263p., 16 pl. v. 3, 1928, 279p., 16 pl.
    1932. (Freese, J. H., trans.). Sexual life in ancient Greece. London, George Routledge & Sons, xv + 557p.

Liepmann, W. 1922. Psychologie der Frau. Berlin, Wien, Urban & Schwarzenberg, [12] + 322p.

Limborch, P. 1692. Historia inquisitionis. Cui subjungitur liber sententiarum inquisitionis tholosanae. Amstelodam, Henricum Westenium, 2pts. Pt. 1, [16] + 384 + [12]p. Pt. 2, [8] + 397 + [19]p.
    1816. The history of the Inquisition . . . with a particular description of its secret prisons, modes of torture . . . etc. Abridged (and trans.). London, W. Simpkin & R. Marshall, xvi + 542p.

Lindner, R. M., and **Seliger, R. V.,** ed. **1947.** Handbook of correctional psychology. New York, Philosophical Library, 691p.

Lindsey, B. B., and **Evans, W. 1929.** The companionate marriage. New York, Garden City Publishing Co., xxxiv + 396p.

Linton, R. 1936. The study of man; an introduction. New York, London, D. Appleton-Century Co. (Century Social Science Series), viii + 503p.

Lion, E. G., et al. **1945.** An experiment in the psychiatric treatment of promiscuous girls. San Francisco, City and County Dept. of Public Health, 68p.

Lipschütz, A. 1924. The internal secretions of the sex glands. The problem of the "puberty gland." Cambridge, Heffer & Sons; Baltimore, Williams and Wilkins Co., xviii + 513p.

Lisser, H. 1942. Sexual infantilism of hypothyroid origin. J. Clin. Endocrinol. 2:29–32.

Lisser, H., Escamilla, R. F., and **Curtis, L. E. 1942.** Testosterone therapy of male eunuchoids. III. Sublingual administration of testosterone compounds. J. Clin. Endocrinol. 2:351–360.

Lloyd, J. W. 1931. The Karezza method, or magnetation the art of connubial love. Roscoe, Calif., priv. print., 64p.

Locke, H. J. 1951. Predicting adjustment in marriage: a comparison of a divorced and a happily married group. New York, Henry Holt and Co., xx + 407p.

Loewenfeld, L. 1908. Über sexuelle Träume. Sexual-Probleme 4:588–601.
    1911a. Über die Sexualität im Kindesalter. Sexual-Probleme 7:444–454, 516–534.
    1911b. Über die sexuelle Konstitution und andere Sexualprobleme. Wiesbaden, J. F. Bergmann, 231p.

London, L. S. 1952. Dynamic psychiatry. Vol. 1. Basic principles. Vol. 2. Transvestism—desire for crippled women. Vol. 3. Frustrated women. New York, Corinthian Publications, 3v. v. 1, vi + 98p. v. 2, v + 129p. [incl. 50 pl.]. v. 3, vii + 132p.

London, L. S., and **Caprio, F. S. 1950.** Sexual deviations. Washington, D. C., Linacre Press, xviii + 702p.

Long, H. W., pseud. (Smith, William Hawley). **1922** (orig. 1919). Sane sex life and sane sex living. New York, Eugenics Publishing Co., 151p.

Longus. 1896 (orig. 3rd cent. A.D.). Pastorals of Longus. Athens, Athenian Society, priv. print., xxxii + 227p. Gr. opp. 227p. Eng.

1916 (orig. 3rd cent. A.D.). (Thornley, G., and Edmonds, J. M., trans.). Daphnis & Chloe. London, William Heinemann, xxiii + 247p.

Lorie, J. H., and **Roberts, H. V. 1951.** Basic methods of marketing research. New York, McGraw-Hill Book Co., xii + 453p.

Louttit, C. M. 1927. Reproductive behavior of the guinea pig. I. The normal mating behavior. J. Comp. Psychol. 7:247–263.

1929. Reproductive behavior of the guinea pig. II. The ontogenesis of the reproductive behavior pattern. J. Comp. Psychol. 9:293–304.

Lowry, O. 1938. A virtuous woman. Sex life in relation to the Christian life. Grand Rapids, Mich., Zondervan Publishing House, 160p.

Lucian. 1895 (orig. 2nd cent. A.D.). (Jacobitz, C., trans.). Lucian. The ass, the Dialogues of courtesans, and the Amores. Athens, Athenian Society, priv. print., 225p. Gr. opp. 225p. Eng.

Ludovici, A. M. 1948. Untapped reserves of sadism in modern men and women. J. Sex Educ. 1:95–100.

Ludwig, D. J. 1950. The effect of androgen on spermatogenesis. Endocrinol. 46: 453–481.

Lundberg, F., and **Farnham, Marynia F. 1947.** Modern woman, the lost sex. New York and London, Harper & Brothers, vii + 497p.

Luquet, G. H. 1910. Sur la survivance des caractères du dessin enfantin dans des graffiti à indications sexuelles. Anthropophyteia 7:196–202.

1911. Représentation de la vulve dans les graffiti contemporains. Anthropophyteia 8:210–214.

Lynch, K. M., Jr. 1952. Recovery of the rat testis following estrogen therapy. Ann. N. Y. Acad. Sci. 55:734–741.

Lynd, R. S., and **Lynd, H. M. 1929.** Middletown. A study in contemporary American culture. New York, Harcourt, Brace and Co., xi + 550p.

1937. Middletown in transition. A study in cultural conflicts. New York, Harcourt, Brace and Co., xviii + 604p.

Macandrew, R. 1946. Friendship, love affairs and marriage. An explanation of men to women and of women to men. London, Wales Publishing Co., 150p.

Maccoby, E. E. 1951. Television: Its impact on school children. Pub. Opin. Quart. 15:421–444.

Macfadden, B. 1922. Sex talks to boys. New York, Macfadden Publications (Sex Education Series No. 1), 36p.

Maddock, W. O., et al. 1952. The assay of urinary estrogens as a test of human Leydig cell function. Ann. N. Y. Acad. Sci. 55:657–673.

Maes, J. P. 1939. Neural mechanism of sexual behavior in the female cat. Nature 144:598–599.

Magaldi, E. 1931. Le iscrizioni parietali pompeiane. Naples, Cimmaruta, 148p.

Magoun, F. A. 1948. Love and marriage. New York, Harper & Brothers, xvii + 369p.

Makurabunko. *See* Anon. Makurabunko.

Malamud, W., and **Palmer, G. 1932.** The role played by masturbation in the causation of mental disturbances. J. Nerv. & Ment. Dis. 76:220–233, 366–379.

Malchow, C. W. 1923. The sexual life, embracing the natural sexual impulse, normal sexual habits and propagation, together with sexual physiology and hygiene. St. Louis, C. V. Mosby Co., 317p.

Malinowski, B. 1928. The anthropological study of sex. *In:* Marcuse, M., ed. Verhandlungen des I International Kongresses für Sexualforschung 5:92–108.

1929. The sexual life of savages in Northwestern Melanesia . . . New York, Halcyon House, xxviii + 603p., 96 pl.

Mallett, D. T. 1935. Mallett's index of artists. International-biographical. New York, Peter Smith, xxxiv + 493p.

    1940. Supplement to Mallett's index of artists. New York, Peter Smith, xxxviii + 319p.

Mantegazza, P. n.d. Ger. ed. 3 (orig. 1885). Anthropologisch-kulturhistorische Studien über die Geschlechtsverhältnisse des Menschen. Jena, Hermann Costenoble, x + 434p.

Marañón, G. 1929. Ed. 5. Tres ensayos sobre la vida sexual. Sexo, trabajo y deporte maternidad y feminismo, educación sexual y diferenciación sexual. Madrid, Biblioteca Neuva, 250p.

    1932. (Span. ed. 1, 1930). (Wells, W. B., trans.). The evolution of sex and intersexual conditions. London, George Allen & Unwin, 344p.

Marcuse, M., ed. 1923. Handwörterbuch der Sexualwissenschaft. Enzyklopädie der natur- und kulturwissenschaftlichen Sexualkunde des Menschen. Bonn, A. Marcus & E. Weber, iv + 481p.

Marcuse, M. 1924. Die demi-vierge. Ztschr. f. Sexualwiss. 11:143–153.

    1926. Neuropathia sexualis. In: Moll, Albert, ed. Handbuch der Sexualwissenschaften, v. 2, pp. 843–902.

Marcuse, M., ed. 1927. Verhandlungen des I. Internationalen Kongresses für Sexualforschung . . . 1926. Berlin und Köln, A. Marcus & E. Weber, 5v. in 1, 225 + 249 + 217 + 230 + 183p.

Marinello, G. 1563. Le medicine partenenti alle infermitá. Venitio, Francesco de Franceschi Senese, [16]p. + 258 lvs. (i.e. 516p.) + [16]p.

Marriage, love and woman amongst the Arabs. See Anon. Marriage, love and woman amongst the Arabs.

Marro, A. 1922 (orig. 1900). (Medici, J. P., trans., Marie, A., ed.). La puberté chez l'homme et chez la femme . . . Paris, Alfred Costes, xvi + 536p., 4 pl.

Marshall, F. H. A. 1922. Ed. 2. The physiology of reproduction. London and New York, Longmans, Green, and Co., xvi + 770p.

    1936. The Croonian Lecture. Sexual periodicity and the causes which determine it. Philos. Trans. Roy. Soc. London 226 (Ser. B): 423–456.

Marshall, F. H. A., and Hammond, J. 1944. Fertility and animal-breeding. London, H.M.S.O. (Ministry of Agriculture . . . Bull. no. 39), 42p.

Martial. 1919 (orig. 1st cent. A.D.). (Ker, W. C. A., trans.). Epigrams. I. London, William Heinemann, v. 1, xxii + 491p.

    1920. (Ker, W. C. A., trans.). Epigrams. II. London, William Heinemann, v. 2, 568p.

    1921. (Buck, M. S., trans.). Epigrams. In fifteen books. Priv. print., x + 423p.

Martineau, L. 1886. Ed. 2. Leçons sur les déformations vulvaires et anales produites par la masturbation, le saphisme, la défloration et la sodomie. Paris, Adrien Delahaye et Émile Lecrosnier, iii + 190p.

Martinez, J. A. 1947. El homosexualismo y su tratamiento. Una serie de tres conferencias dictadas en el Tribunal Supremo de la República, bajo los auspicios de la "Asociacion Nacional de Funcionarios del Poder Judicial." Mexico City, Ediciones Botas, 153p.

Maslow, A. H. 1942. Self-esteem (dominance-feeling) and sexuality in women. J. Soc. Psychol. 16:259–294.

Masters, W. H. 1952. The female reproductive system. In: Cowdry, E. V. (Lansing, A. I., ed.). Problems of ageing, pp. 651–685.

Maximow, A. A., and Bloom, W. 1952. Ed. 6. A textbook of histology. Philadelphia and London, W. B. Saunders Co., x + 616p.

May, Geoffrey. 1931. Social control of sex expression. New York, William Morrow & Co., xi + 307p.

Mazer, C., and Israel, S. L. 1946. Ed. 2. Diagnosis and treatment of menstrual disorders and sterility. New York and London, Paul B. Hoeber, xii + 570p.

1951. Ed. 3. Diagnosis and treatment of menstrual disorders and sterility. New York, Paul B. Hoeber, xiv + 583p., 2 col. pl.

McCance, R. A., Luff, M. C., and Widdowson, E. E. 1937. Physical and emotional periodicity in women. J. Hyg. 37:571–611.

McCartney, J. L. 1929. Dementia praecox as an endocrinopathy with clinical and autopsy reports. Endocrinol. 13:73–87.

McCullagh, E. P. 1939. Treatment of testicular deficiency with testosterone propionate. J. Amer. Med. Assoc. 112:1037–1044.

McCullagh, E. P., and Renshaw, J. F. 1934. Effects of castration in adult male. J. Amer. Med. Assoc. 103:1140–1143.

McDermott, J. F., and Taft, K. B., ed. 1932. Sex in the arts. A symposium. New York, Harper & Brothers, xviii + 328p.

McDonald, H. C. 1952. Playtime with Patty and Wilbur. Culver City, Calif., Murray & Gee, 33p.

McKenzie, F. F., and Berliner, V. 1937. The reproductive capacity of rams. Columbia, Mo., University of Missouri (Agricultural Experiment Station Research Bull. 265), 143p. [incl. 20 pl.].

McKenzie, F. F., Miller, J. C., and Bauguess, L. C. 1938. The reproductive organs and semen of the boar. Columbia, Mo., University of Missouri (Agricultural Experiment Station Research Bull. 279), 122p.

McKenzie, F. F., and Terrill, C. E. 1937. Estrus, ovulation, and related phenomena in the ewe. Columbia, Mo., University of Missouri (Agricultural Experiment Station Research Bull. 264), 1 col. pl. + 88p. [incl. 10 pl.].

McKenzie, K. G., and Proctor, L. D. 1946. Bilateral frontal lobe leucotomy in the treatment of mental disease. Canada Med. Assoc. 55:433–441.

McPartland, John. 1947. Sex in our changing world. New York, Rinehart & Co., 280p.

Mead, M. 1939. From the South Seas. Studies of adolescence and sex in primitive societies. New York, William Morrow & Co., xxxv + [3] + 304 + 384 + xiv + 335p.

1949. Male and female. A study of the sexes in a changing world. New York, William Morrow & Co., xii + 477p.

Meagher, J. F. W. 1929. Ed. 2. A study of masturbation and the psychosexual life. New York, William Wood and Co., 130p.

Meagher, J. F. W., and Jelliffe, S. E. 1936. Ed. 3. A study of masturbation and the psychosexual life. Baltimore, William Wood and Co., xii + 149p.

Meibomius, J. H. n.d. (orig. 1761). A treatise of the use of flogging in veneral affairs . . . Also of the office of the loins and reins. Written to the famous Christianus Cassius, Bishop of Lubeck, and Privy-Councillor to the Duke of Holstein. London, n.publ. (facs. repr.), 83p.

Mendelsohn, M. 1896. Ist das Radfahren als eine gesundheitsgemässe Uebung anzusehen und aus ärtzlichen Gesichtspunkten zu empfehlen? Dtsch. med. Wchnschr. 22:381–384.

Menninger, K. A. 1938. Man against himself. New York, Harcourt, Brace and Co., xii + 485p.

Menzies, K. 1921. Ed. 2. Autoerotic phenomena in adolescence. An analytical study of the psychology and psychopathology of onanism. New York, Paul B. Hoeber, viii + 100p.

Merrill, L. 1918. A summary of findings in a study of sexualism among a group of one hundred delinquent boys. J. Delinq. 3:255–267.

Merry Andrew. See Anon., comp. The merry Andrew.

Meyer, F. 1929. Helps to purity. A frank, yet reverent instruction on the intimate matters of personal life for adolescent girls. Cincinnati, O., St. Francis Book Shop (Father Fulgence's Book No. 8), [viii] + 91p., incl. 1 pl.

Michels, R. 1914. (Paul, E. and C., trans.). Sexual ethics. A study of borderland questions. London, George Allen & Unwin, New York, Charles Scribner's Sons, xv + 296p.

Michigan. Governor's Study Commission. (Richards, R. M., chairman.) 1951. Report of the . . . Commission on the deviated criminal sex offender. Lansing, State of Michigan, xi + 245p.

Miller, G. S., Jr. 1931. The primate basis of human sexual behavior. Quart. Rev. Biol. 6:379–410.

Miller, M. M., and Robinson, D. M., trans. and ed. 1925. The songs of Sappho, including the recent Egyptian discoveries. The poems of Erinna. Greek poems about Sappho. Ovid's epistle of Sappho to Phaon. Lexington, Ky., Maxwelton Co., xiv + 436p., 10 pl.

Miller, N. E., Hubert, G., and Hamilton, J. B. 1938. Mental and behavioral changes following male hormone treatment of adult castration, hypogonadism, and psychic impotence. Proc. Soc. Exper. Biol. & Med. 38:538–540.

Mills, C. A. 1937. Geographic and time variations in body growth and age at menarche. Human Biol. 9:43–56.

Mills, C. A., and Ogle, C. 1936. Physiologic sterility of adolescence. Human Biol. 8:607–615.

Mirbeau, O. 1931 (orig. 1899). (Bessie, A. C., trans.). Torture Garden. (Le jardin des supplices). New York, Claude Kendall, 284p., 9 pl.

Möbius, P. J. 1903. Über die Wirkungen der Castration. Halle a. d. S., Carl Marhold, 99p.

Moldau. [1911]. Die Onanie oder Selbstbefleckung. Ihre Ursachen, Folgen und Heilung. Radebeul-Dresden, M. Wolf, 68p.

Moll, A. 1899. Ed. 3 (ed. 1, 1891). Die konträre Sexualempfindung. Berlin, H. Kornfeld, xvi + 651p.

[1909]. Das Sexualleben des Kindes. Leipzig, F.C.W.Vogel, viii + 313p.

1912. The sexual life of the child. New York, The Macmillan Co., xv + 339p.

1931. (Popkin, M., trans.). Perversions of the sex instinct. A study of sexual inversion based on clinical data and official documents. Newark, N. J., Julian Press, 237p.

Moll, A., ed. 1911. Handbuch der Sexualwissenschaften mit besonderer Berücksichtigung der kulturgeschichtlichen Beziehungen. Leipzig, F.C.W.Vogel, xxiv + 1029p.

1921. Ed. 2. Handbuch der Sexualwissenschaften mit besonderer Berücksichtigung der kulturgeschichtlichen Beziehungen. Leipzig, F.C.W.Vogel, xxiv + 1046p.

1926. Handbuch der Sexualwissenschaften. Leipzig, F.C.W.Vogel, v. 1, xxviii + 736p., x pl. v. 2, 737–1280p.

Montagu, M. F. Ashley. 1937. Coming into being among the Australian Aborigines. London, George Routledge & Sons, xxxv + 362p., iv photog. pl.

1946. Adolescent sterility. A study in the comparative physiology of the infecundity of the adolescent organism in mammals and man. Springfield, Ill., Charles C Thomas, ix + 148p.

Moore, C. R. 1939. Biology of the testes. In: Allen, Edgar, et al., ed. Sex and internal secretions, pp. 353–451.

1942. The physiology of the testis and application of male sex hormone. J. Urol. 47:31–44.

Moore, T. V. 1945. The pathogenesis and treatment of homosexual disorders: a digest of some pertinent evidence. J. Personality 14:47–83.

Moraglia, G. B. 1897. Die Onanie beim normalen Weibe und bei den Prostituierten. Berlin, Priber & Lammers, 21p.

Moreck, C. 1929. Kultur- und Sittengeschichte der neuesten Zeit. Das Genussleben des modernen Menschen. Dresden, Paul Aretz, 451p., 32 pl.

Müller, E. 1929. Ein Beitrag zur Sexualforschung in der Volksschule. Ztschr. f. Päd. Psych. 30:467–477.

Munro, D., Horne, H., and Paull, D. 1948. The effect of injury to the spinal cord and cauda equina on the sexual potency of men. N. Eng. J. Med. 239:903–911.

Murdock, G. P. 1949. The social regulation of sexual behavior. *In:* Hoch, P. H., and Zubin, J., ed. Psychosexual development in health and disease, pp. 256–266.

——— 1949. Social structure. New York, The Macmillan Co., xix + 387p.

Nathanson, I. T., Towne, L. E., and Aub, J. C. 1941. Normal excretion of sex hormones in childhood. Endocrinol. 28:851–865.

Naumburg, M. 1947. Studies in the "free" art expression of behavior problem children and adolescents as a means of diagnosis and therapy. New York, Coolidge Foundation, Nervous and Mental Disease Monographs No. 71, xii + 225p.

——— 1950. Schizophrenic art: its meaning in psychotherapy. New York, Grune & Stratton, viii + 247p., viii col. pl.

Neely, W. C. 1940. Family attitudes of denominational college and university students, 1929 and 1936. Amer. Sociol. Rev. 5:512–522.

Nefzawi. n.d. The perfumed garden. A manual of Arabian erotology. Paris, Librairie "Astra," priv. print., 167p.

Negri, V. 1949. Psychoanalysis of sexual life. Los Angeles, Western Institute of Psychoanalysis, 274p.

Nelson, J. 1888. A study of dreams. Amer. J. Psychol. 1:367–401.

Neumann, H. 1936. Marriage and morals. J. Soc. Hyg. 22:102–114.

Neville-Rolfe, S., ed. 1950. Sex in social life. New York, W. W. Norton & Co., 504p.

New York. Law Revision Commission. 1937. Study relating to rape, abduction, seduction, corrupting morals of minors and related sexual offenses contained in the New York Penal Law. Albany, N. Y., J. B. Lyon Co., 116p.

New York. Mayor's Committee for the Study of Sex Offenders. 1944. Report. City of New York, 100p.

Newcomb, T. 1937. Recent changes in attitudes toward sex and marriage. Amer. Sociol. Rev. 2:659–667.

Niedermeyer, A. 1950. Anomalien des Geschlechtstriebes. *In:* Hornstein, X. von, and Faller, A., ed. Gesundes Geschlechts Leben, pp. 143–159.

Niemoeller, A. F. 1935. American encyclopedia of sex. New York, Panurge Press, xiv + 277p.

Nimuendajú, C. 1939. The Apinayé. Washington, D. C., Catholic University of America Press (Anthropological Series No. 8), vi + 189p.

Noldin, H. 1904. Summa theologiae moralis. Volume 3: De sacramentis. Innsbruck, Fel. Rauch (C. Pustet), 798p.

Northcote, H. 1916 (orig. 1906). Christianity and sex problems. Philadelphia, F. A. Davis Co., xvi + 478p.

Norton, H. 1949. The third sex. Portland, Ore., Facts Publishing Co., 112p.

Nowlis, V. 1941. Companionship preference and dominance in the social interaction of young chimpanzees. Compar. Psychol. Monogr. v. 17, no. 1, 57p.

Nystrom, A. 1908. (Swed. ed. 1, 1904). (Sandzen, C., trans.). The natural laws of sexual life. Kansas City, Mo., Burton Co., 260p.

O'Brien, P. 1950. Emotions and morals. Their place and purpose in harmonious living. New York, Grune & Stratton, xiii + 241p.

Ohlson, W. E. 1937. Adultery: A review. Boston Univer. Law Rev. 17:328–368, 533–622.

Orsi, A. 1913. Lussuria e castità. Seguito alla "Donna nuda." Saggio di psicologia. Milano, "La Broderie," 263p.

Ovid. 1921 (orig. 1st cent. B.C.—1st cent. A.D.). (Showerman, G., trans.). Heroides and Amores. London, William Heinemann; New York, G. P. Putnam's Sons, 524p.

——— 1929. (Mozley, J. H., trans.). The art of love, and other poems. London, William Heinemann; New York, G. P. Putnam's Sons, xiv + 382p.

——— 1930. (May, J. L., trans.). The love books of Ovid. Being the Amores,

Ars amatoria, Remedia amoris, and Medicamina faciei femineae of Publius Ovidius Naso. New York, Rarity Press, priv. print., xxxiii + 216p.
1930. (Young, C. D., and Marlowe, Christopher, trans.). The love books of Ovid. A completely unexpurgated . . . edition. Together with the Elegie. Priv. print., 302p., 18 col. pl.

Ozaki, Hisaya. 1928. Edo nan-bungaku kō-i. [Unorthodox thoughts on the light or erotic literature of the Tokugawa period.] Tokyo, Nakanishi Shobō, 578p., 61 pl.

Parke, J. R. 1906. Human sexuality. A medico-literary treatise on the laws, anomalies, and relations of sex with especial reference to contrary sexual desire. Philadelphia, Professional Publishing Company, x + 476p.

Parker, R. A. 1935. A yankee saint. John Humphrey Noyes and the Oneida community. New York, G. P. Putnam's Sons, 322p., 15 pl.

Parker, V. H. n.d. Sex education for parent groups. Outline of four lectures for popular presentation. New York, American Social Hygiene Association (Publication No. A-163), 14p.

Parkes, A. S. 1950. Androgenic activity of the ovary. Rec. Prog. in Hormone Res. 5:101-114.

Parshley, H. M. 1933. The science of human reproduction. Biological aspects of sex. New York, W. W. Norton, xv + 319p.

Parsons, E. C. 1916. The Zuni La' Mana. Amer. Anthropologist 18:521-528.

Paschkis, K. E., and Rakoff, A. E. 1950. Some aspects of the physiology of estrogenic hormones. Rec. Prog. in Hormone Res. 5:115-149.

Patten, B. M. 1946. Human embryology. Philadelphia, Toronto, The Blakiston Co., xv + 776p.

Payne, F. 1949. Changes in the endocrine glands of the fowl with age. J. Gerontol. 4:193-199.
    1952. Cytological changes in the cells of the pituitary, thyroids, adrenals and sex glands of ageing fowl. In: Cowdry, E. V. (Lansing, A. I., ed.). Problems of ageing, pp. 381-402.

Pearl, R. 1930. The biology of population growth. New York, Alfred A. Knopf, xiv + 260p.

Peck, M. W., and Wells, F. L. 1923. On the psycho-sexuality of college graduate men. Ment. Hyg. 7:697-714.
    1925. Further studies in the psycho-sexuality of college graduate men. Ment. Hyg. 9:502-520.

Penfield, W., and Erickson, T. C. 1941. Epilepsy and cerebral localization; a study of the mechanism, treatment and prevention of epileptic seizures. Springfield, Ill., Charles C Thomas, x + 623p.

Penfield, W., and Rasmussen, T. 1950. The cerebral cortex of man. A clinical study of localization of function. New York, The Macmillan Co., xv + 248p.

Pepys, S. 1942 (orig. 1659-1669). (Wheatley, H. B., ed., Bright, M., transcr.). The diary of Samuel Pepys. Transcribed . . . from the shorthand manuscript . . . New York, Heritage Press, 2v. var. pag.

Perceau, L. See Hernandez, L.

Perloff, W. H. 1949. Role of the hormones in human sexuality. Psychosom. Med. 11:133-139.
    1951. The hormonal balance of the normal menstrual cycle. In: Mazer, C., and Israel, S. L. Diagnosis and treatment of menstrual disorders and sterility, pp. 118-128.

Peterson, K. M. 1938. Early sex information and its influence on later sex concepts. [Thesis . . . Master of Arts.] Boulder, Colo., University of Colorado, Ms, vii + 136p.

Petronius. 1913 (orig. 1st cent. A.D.). (Heseltine, M., trans.). Petronius (Satyricon, fragments, poems). London, William Heinemann, 363p.
    1922. (Firebaugh, W. C., trans.). The satyricon . . . unexpurgated translation in which are incorporated the forgeries of Nodot and Marchena,

and the readings introduced . . . by De Salas. New York, Boni & Liveright, priv. print., 2v. v. 1, xxxi + 258p., 36 pl. v. 2, 259–516p., 11 pl.

1927. (?Wilde, Oscar, trans.). The satyricon of Petronius Arbiter . . . Chicago, Pascal Covici, 2v. v. 1, lxxxv + 206p. v. 2, 207–497p.

Pfuhl, E. 1923. Malerei und Zeichnung der Griechen. v. 1, xv + 503p. v. 2, 504–918p. v. 3. Verzeichnisse und Abbildungen, [919]–981p. + 805 fig. on 361 pl. München, F. Bruckmann.

Pillay, A. P. 1950. Premarital sex activities of Indian males. A survey of 381 patients of a sexological clinic. Int. J. Sexol. 4:80–84.

Pilpel, H. F., and Zavin, T. 1952. Your marriage and the law. New York, Toronto, Rinehart & Co., xv + 358p.

Pincus, G., and Thimann, K. V., ed. 1948, 1950. The hormones. Physiology, chemistry and applications. New York, Academic Press, 2v. v. 1, xi + 886p. v. 2, ix + 782p.

Plautus. 1916 (orig. 3rd–2nd cent. B.C.). (Nixon, P., trans.). Plautus. In five volumes. I. Amphitryon. The comedy of asses. The pot of gold. The two Bacchises. The captives. Cambridge, Mass., Harvard University Press, xix + 570p.

Pliny. 1942 (orig. 1st cent. A.D.). (Rackham, H., trans.). Natural history. In ten volumes. II. Cambridge, Mass., Harvard University Press, ix + 664p.

Ploscowe, Morris. 1951. Sex and the law. New York, Prentice-Hall, ix + 310p.

Plutarch. 1905 (orig. 1st–2nd cent. B.C.). (Goodwin, W. W., et al., trans.). Essays and miscellanies. Boston and New York, Little, Brown and Co., 5v. var. pag.

1914, 1916. (Perrin, B., trans.). Lives. In eleven volumes. I, II, IV. London, William Heinemann, v. 1, xix + 582p. v. 2, ix + 631p. v. 4, ix + 467p.

Podolsky, Edward. 1942. Sex today in wedded life. New York, Simon Publications, Section I, xx + 240p.

Poirier, L. J. 1952. Anatomical and experimental studies on the temporal pole of the macaque. J. Comp. Neurol. 96:209–248.

Polatin, P., and Douglas, D. B. 1951. Spontaneous orgasm in a case of schizophrenia. Unpubl. Ms, 13p.

Pomeroy, H. S. 1888. The ethics of marriage. New York and London, Funk & Wagnalls Co., 197p.

Popenoe, P. 1938. Preparing for marriage. Los Angeles, Calif., American Institute of Family Relations, 23p.

1943. Marriage. Before and after. New York, Wilfred Funk, xiv + 246p.

1952. Love: The American way is best. Pageant v. 8 (Sept.), pp. 4–8.

Potter, La F. 1933. Strange loves. A study in sexual abnormalities. New York, National Library Press, ix + 243p.

Pouillet, T. 1897. Ed. 7 (ed. 1, 1876). L'onanisme chez la femme. Ses formes, ses causes, ses signes, ses consequences, et son traitment. Paris, Vigot Frères, 216p.

Powdermaker, H. 1933. Life in Lesu. The study of a Melanesian society in New Ireland. New York, W. W. Norton & Co., 1 pl. + 352p., 12 pl. + 2 folded pp.

Praetorius, Numa. See Hirschfeld, M.

Pratt, J. P. 1939. Sex functions in man. In: Allen, E., et al., ed. Sex and internal secretions, pp. 1263–1334.

Praz, M. 1951. (Ed. 1, 1933). (Davidson, A., trans.). The romantic agony. Translated from the Italian. London, Oxford University Press, xix + 502p.

Priapeia. See Anon. Priapeia.

Priesel, R., and Wagner, R. 1930. Gesetzmässigkeiten im Auftreten der extragenitalen sekundären Geschlechtsmerkmale bei Mädchen. Ztschr. f. d. ges. Anat. 15:333–352.

Priester, H. M. 1941. The reported dating practices of one hundred and six high school seniors in an urban community. Ithaca, N. Y., Cornell University Master's Thesis, 115 + xvii + 5p.

Prince, M. 1914. The unconscious. New York, The Macmillan Co., xii + 549p.

Pringle, H. F. 1938. What do the women of America think about morals? Ladies' Home Journal, v. 55 (May), pp. 14–15, 49, 51–52.

Pritchard, J. B., ed. 1950. Ancient Near Eastern texts relating to the Old Testament. Princeton, N. J., Princeton University Press, xxi + 526p.

Propertius. 1895 (orig. 1st cent. B.C.). (Gantillon, P. J. F., trans.). The elegies of Propertius . . . with metrical versions of select elegies by Nott and Elton. London, George Bell & Sons, viii + 187p.

Pryor, H. B. 1936. Certain physical and physiologic aspects of adolescent development in girls. J. Pediat. 8:52–62.

Public Opinion and Sociological Research Division, SCAP, Japan. 1950. [Abstract of survey on attitude toward foreign countries, etc.]. Int. J. Opin. & Attit. Res. 4:452–453.

Pussep, L. M. 1922. Der Blutkreislauf im Gehirn beim Koitus. In: Weil, Arthur, ed. Sexualreform und Sexualwissenschaft, pp. 61–85.

Quanter, R. 1901. Die Leibes- und Lebensstrafen bei allen Völkern und zu allen Zeiten. Eine kriminalhistorische Studie. Dresden, H. R. Dohrn, 467p.

Rado, S. 1933. Fear of castration in women. Psychoanal. Quart. 2:425–475.

Radvanyi, L. 1951. Measurement of the effectiveness of basic education. Int. J. Opin. & Attit. Res. 5:347–366.

Ramsey, G. V. 1943. The sex information of younger boys. Amer. J. Orthopsychiat. 13:347–352.

——— 1943. The sexual development of boys. Amer. J. Psych. 56:217–234.

Rank, Otto. 1912. [no title]. In: Wiener psychoanalytische Vereinigung. Die Onanie . . . , pp. 107–129.

Rasmussen, A. 1934. Die Bedeutung sexueller Attentate auf Kinder unter 14 Jahren für die Entwicklung von Geisteskrankheiten und Charakteranomalien. Acta Psychiat. et Neurol. 9:351–434.

Rau, H. 1903. Die Grausamkeit, mit besonderer Bezugnahme auf sexuelle Faktoren. Berlin, H. Barsdorf, iv + 248p.

Read, A. W. 1935. Lexical evidence from folk epigraphy in Western North America: a glossorial study of the low element in the English vocabulary. Paris, priv. print., 83p.

Read, J. M. 1941. Atrocity propaganda, 1914–1919. New Haven, Conn., Yale University Press, xiii + 319p.

Reed, C. A. 1946. The copulatory behavior of small mammals. J. Comp. Psychol. 39:185–206.

Reich, Annie. 1951. The discussion of 1912 on masturbation and our present-day views. Psychoanalytic study of the child 6:80–94.

Reich, W. 1942. The discovery of the orgone. Vol. 1: The function of the orgasm. New York, Orgone Institute Press, xxxv + 368p.

——— 1945. The sexual revolution. Toward a self-governing character structure. New York, Orgone Institute Press, xxvii + 273p.

Reichard, G. A. 1938. Social life. In: Boas, F., ed. General anthropology, pp. 409–486.

Reik, T. 1941. Masochism in modern man. New York, Toronto, Farrar & Rinehart, vi + 439p.

Reiman, C. F., and Schroeter, L. W. 1951. Implications of the Kinsey Report upon criminal laws concerning sexual behavior. Unpublished thesis, Harvard Law School, var. pag.

Reisinger, L. 1916–1917. Einige Bemerkungen zur Spezifität des männlichen und weiblichen Geschlechtstriebes. Ztschr. f. Sexualwiss. 3:343–345.

Reiskel, K. 1906. Skatologische Inscriften. Anthropophyteia 3:244–246.

Remplein, H. 1950 (ed. 1, 1948). Die seelische Entwicklung in der Kindheit und Reifezeit. München, Basel, Ernst Reinhardt, 430p.

Reymert, M. L., ed. 1950. Feelings and emotions. The Mooseheart symposium . . .
    New York, McGraw-Hill Book Co., xviii + 603p.
Reynolds, E. L. 1946. Sexual maturation and the growth of fat, muscle and bone
    in girls. Child Develop. 17:121–144.
Reynolds, E. L., and Wines, J. V. 1949. Individual differences in physical changes
    associated with adolescence. In: Lasker, G. W., and Thieme, F. P., ed.
    Yearbook of physical anthropology, 1948, v. 4, pp. 89–110.
Rice, T. B. 1933. In training for boys of high school age. Chicago, American Medi-
    cal Association, Bureau of Health . . . , 48p.
Rice, V. A., and Andrews, F. N. 1951 (ed. 1, 1926). Breeding and improvement
    of farm animals. New York, McGraw-Hill Book Co., xiv + 787p.
Richter, G. M. A. 1936. Red-figured Athenian vases in the Metropolitan Museum
    of Art. New Haven, Conn., Yale University Press, 2v. v. 1, xlvii + 249p.
    v. 2, viii p. + 181 pl.
    1942. Kouroi. A study of the development of the Greek kouros from the
    late seventh to the early fifth century B.C. New York, Oxford University
    Press, xxi + 428p., incl. 483 fig. on 135 pl.
Rickles, N. K. 1950. Exhibitionism. Philadelphia, J. B. Lippincott Co., 198p.
Rioch, D. McK. 1938. Certain aspects of the behavior of decorticate cats. Psychiat.
    1:339–345.
Riolan, Dr. (pseud.). 1927. La masturbation dans les deux sexes. Paris, Librairie
    Artistique et Médicale, 91p.
Roark, D. B., and Herman, H. A. 1950. Physiological and histological phenomena
    of the bovine estrual cycle with special reference to vaginal-cervical se-
    cretions. Columbia, Mo., University of Missouri (Agricultural Experiment
    Station Research Bull. 455), 70p. [incl. 7 pl.].
Roberts, A., Donaldson, J., and Coxe, A. C., ed. 1885. The Ante-Nicene fathers.
    Translations of the writings of the fathers down to A.D. 325. Volume II:
    Fathers of the second century. Buffalo, N. Y., Christian Literature Pub-
    lishing Co., vii + 629p.
Robie, W. F. 1925. The art of love. London, Medical Research Society, 386p.
Robinson, S. 1938. Experimental studies of physical fitness in relation to age. Ar-
    beitsphysiologie 10:251–323.
Robinson, V., ed. 1936. Encyclopaedia sexualis. New York, Dingwall-Rock, xx +
    819p.
Robinson, W. J. 1931. Woman. Her sex and love life. New York, Eugenics Pub-
    lishing Co., 415p.
Rockwood, L. D., and Ford, M. E. N. 1945. Youth, marriage, and parenthood. New
    York, John Wiley & Sons, xiii + 298p.
Rohleder, H. 1902. Ed. 2. Die Masturbation. Eine Monographie für Ärzte, Päda-
    gogen und gebildete Eltern. Berlin, Fischer's medicin. Buchhandlung,
    xxiii + 336p.
    1907. Vorlesungen über Geschlechtstrieb und gesamtes Geschlechtsleben
    des Menschen. Band 1. Das normale, anormale und paradoxe Gesch-
    lechtsleben, xvi + 600p. Band 2. Das perverse Geschlechtsleben des
    Menschen, auch vom Standpunkte der lex lata und der lex ferenda, xvi +
    545p. Berlin, Fischer's medicin. Buchhandlung.
    1918. Ed. 2. Normale, pathologische und künstliche Zeugung beim Men-
    schen. (Monographien über die Zeugung beim Menschen. Band I.) Leip-
    zig, G. Thieme, xvi + 317p.
    1921. Die Masturbation. Eine Monographie für Ärzte, Pädagogen und
    gebildete Eltern. Berlin, Fischer's medicin. Buchhandlung, xxvii + 384p.
    1923, 1925. Vorlesungen über das gesamte Geschlechtsleben des Men-
    schen. Band II. Die normale und anormale Kohabitation und Konzeption
    (Befruchtung), 357p. Band IV. Die homosexuellen Perversionen des
    Menschen, auch vom Standpunkt der lex lata und lex ferenda, 403p.
    Berlin, Fischer's medicin. Buchhandlung.

1927. Die Masturbation. *In:* Stern, E. ed. Die Erziehung und die sexuelle Frage, pp. 279–300.

Roland de la Platière, M. J. P. 1864. Mémoires de Madame Roland. Paris, Henri Plon, [2] + 443p.

Root, W. S., and Bard, P. 1947. The mediation of feline erection through sympathetic pathways with some remarks on sexual behavior after deafferentiation of the genitalia. Amer. J. Physiol. 151:80–90.

Rosanoff, A. J. 1938. Manual of psychiatry and mental hygiene. New York, John Wiley & Sons, xviii + 1091p.

Rosenbaum, J. 1845. Die Onanie oder Selbstbefleckung, nicht sowohl Laster oder Sünde, sondern eine wirkliche Krankheit. Leipzig, Gebauer, iv + 267p.

Rosenthal, H. C. 1951. Sex habits of: European women vs. American women. A digest of two important new surveys . . . Pageant Mag. (March), pp. 52–59.

Rosenzweig, S., and Hoskins, R. G. 1941. A note on the ineffectualness of sex-hormone medication in a case of pronounced homosexuality. Psychosom. Med. 3:87–89.

Ross, R. T. 1950. Measures of the sex behavior of college males compared with Kinsey's results. J. Abnorm. & Soc. Psychol. 45:753–755.

Rossen, R., Kabat, H., and Anderson, J. P. 1943. Acute arrest of cerebral circulation in man. Arch. Neurol. & Psychiat. 50:510–528.

Roubaud, F. 1876. (Ed. 1, 1855). Traité de l'impuissance et de la stérilité chez l'homme et chez la femme . . . Paris, J. B. Baillière et Fils, xvi + 804p.

Rowlands, I. W., and Parkes, F. R. S. 1935. The reproductive processes of certain mammals. VIII. Reproduction in foxes. Proc. Zool. Soc. London 1935: 823–841.

Ruch, T. C. 1949. Somatic sensation. *In:* Howell, W. H. (Fulton, J. F., ed.). A textbook of physiology, pp. 292–315.

Ruland, L. 1934. (Rattler, T. A., trans.). Pastoral medicine. St. Louis and London, B. Herder Book Co., viii + 344p.

Russell, B. 1929. Marriage and morals. New York, Horace Liveright, 320p.

Rutgers, J. 1934. (Haire, N., trans.). The sexual life. Dresden, R. A. Giesecke, 448p.

Sacher-Masoch, L. von. [190–]. Grausame Frauen (Sphinxe). Leipzig, Leipziger Verlag, 112p.

1902. (Beaufort, L. de, trans.). La Vénus a la fourrure. Roman sur la flagellation. Paris, Charles Carrington, xxxvii + 216p.

Sade, D. A. F. de. 1797. Histoire de Justine, ou les malheurs de vertu. Hollande, 4v. v. 1, 347p. v. 2, 351p. v. 3, 356p. v. 4, 366p.

1904. Les 120 journées de Sodome, ou l'École du libertinage. Publié pour la première fois d'après de manuscrit original. Paris, Club des Bibliophiles, 8 + 543p.

Sadger, J. 1921. Die Lehre von den Geschlechtsverirrungen (Psychopathia sexualis) auf psychoanalytischer Grundlage. Leipzig und Wien, Franz Deuticke, 458p.

Sadler, W. S. 1948. Adolescence problems. A handbook for physicians, parents, and teachers. St. Louis, C. V. Mosby Co., 466p.

Sadler, W. S., and Sadler, L. K. 1944. Living a sane sex life. Chicago, New York, Wilcox & Follett Co., xii + 344p.

Salmon, U. J. 1941. Rationale for androgen therapy in gynecology. J. Clin. Endocrinol. 1:162–179.

Salmon, U. J., and Geist, S. H. 1943. Effect of androgens upon libido in women. J. Clin. Endocrinol. 3:235–238.

Salter, W. T., Humm, F. D., and Oesterling, M. J. 1948. Analogies between urinary 17-ketosteroids and urinary "estroid," as determined microchemically. J. Clin. Endocrinol. 8:295–314.

Sanchez, T. 1637. . . . De sancto matrimonio sacramento disputationum . . . Tomus primus (Liber IX). Lugduni, Societas Typographorum, var. pag.

Sand, K., and Okkels, H. 1938. The histological variability of the testis from normal and sexual-abnormal, castrated men. Endokrinologie 19:369–374.

Sandblom, P. 1948. Precocious sexual development produced by an interstitial cell tumor of the testis. Acta Endocrinol. 1:107–120.

Sanger, Margaret H. n.d. What every girl should know. Reading, Pa., Sentinel Printing Co., 91p.

Sappho. See Miller, M. M., and Robinson, D. M.; Weigall, A.; and Wharton, H. T.

Schapera, I. 1941. Married life in an African tribe. New York, Sheridan House, xvii + 364p., 8 pl.

Schbankov. See Weissenberg, S.

Scheinfeld, A. 1944. Women and men. New York, Harcourt, Brace and Co., xv + 453p.

Scheuer, O. F. 1923. [Discussion on] Jungfernschaft [virginity]. In: Marcuse, M., ed. Handwörterbuch der Sexualwissenschaft, pp. 242–244.

Schlichtegroll, C. F. von. 1901. Sacher-Masoch und der Masochismus. Dresden, H. R. Dohrn, 96p.

Schmidt, Karl. 1881. Jus prima noctis. Eine geschichtliche Untersuchung. Freiburg im Breisgau, Herder, xliii + 397p.

Schonfeld, W. A., and Beebe, G. W. 1942. Normal growth and variation in the male genitalia from birth to maturity. J. Urol. 48:759–777 + [2 tables].

Scott, J. C. 1930. Systolic blood-pressure fluctuations with sex, anger and fear. J. Comp. Psychol. 10:97–114.

Sears, R. R. 1943. Survey of objective studies of psychoanalytic concepts. New York, Social Science Research Council, xiv + 156p.

Selling, L. S. 1938. The endocrine glands and the sex offender. Med. Record (May 18), 9p.
    1947. The extra-institutional treatment of sex offenders. In: Lindner, R. M., and Seliger, R. V., ed. Handbook of correctional psychology, pp. 226–232.

Selye, Hans. 1949. Textbook of endocrinology. Montreal, Acta Endocrinologica, xxxii + 914p.

Semans, J. H., and Langworthy, O. R. 1938. Observations on the neurophysiology of sexual function in the male cat. J. Urol. 40:836–846.

Shadle, A. R. 1946. Copulation in the porcupine. J. Wildlife Management 10:159–162 + 1 pl.

Shadle, A. R., Smelzer, M., and Metz, M. 1946. The sex reactions of porcupines (Erethizon d. dorsatum) before and after copulation. J. Mammal. 27:116–121.

Shelden, C. H., and Bors, E. 1948. Subarachnoid alcohol block in paraplegia. Its beneficial effect on mass reflexes and bladder dysfunction. J. Neurosurgery 5:385–391.

Sherwin, R. V. 1949. Sex and statutory law (in all 48 states). New York, Oceana Publications, 2 pts. in 1 v. pt. 1, [6] + 90p. pt. 2, [6] + 74p.
    1950. Some legal aspects of homosexuality. Int. J. Sexol. 4:22–26.
    1951. Sex expression and the law. II. Sodomy: a medico-legal enigma. Int. J. Sexol. 5:10–13.

Shinozaki, Nobuo. 1951. Report on sexual life of Japanese. Tokyo, Research Institute of Population Problems, Ministry of Welfare, 38p.

Shock, N. W. 1950. Physiological manifestations of chronic emotional states. In: Reymert, M. L., ed. Feelings and emotions, pp. 277–283.

Shultz, Gladys D. 1949. Widows: wise and otherwise. A practical guide for the woman who has lost her husband. Philadelphia and New York, J. B. Lippincott Co., 285p.

Shuttleworth, F. K. 1937. Sexual maturation and the physical growth of girls age six to nineteen. Washington, D. C., Nat. Res. Council (Soc. Res. Child Devel. Mono. 12), xx + 253p.

1938a. The adolescent period, a graphic and pictorial atlas. Washington, D. C., Nat. Res. Council (Soc. Res. Child Devel. Mono. 16), v + 246p.

1938b. Sexual maturation and the skeletal growth of girls age six to nineteen. Washington, D. C., Nat. Res. Council (Soc. Res. Child Devel. Mono. 18), vii + 56p.

1939. The physical and mental growth of girls and boys age six to nineteen in relation to age at maximum growth. Washington, D. C., Nat. Res. Council (Soc. Res. Child Devel. Mono. 22), vi + 291p.

1951. The adolescent period: a graphic atlas. Evanston, Ill., Society for Research in Child Development (Monog. Ser. 49, no. 1), n. pag.

Siegler, S. L. 1944. Fertility in women. Causes, diagnosis and treatment of impaired fertility. Philadelphia, J. B. Lippincott Co., vii + 438p.

Simon, C. 1947. Homosexualists and sex crimes. Int. Assoc. Chiefs Police, 8p.

Singer, M. R. D. 1940. Behavior and development in puberty praecox. Charlottesville, Va., University of Virginia (M.A. Thesis), [4] + 79p.

Slater, E., and Woodside, M. 1951. Patterns of marriage. A study of marriage relationships in the urban working classes. London, Cassell & Co., 311p.

Smith, G. F. 1924. Certain aspects of the sex life of the adolescent girl. J. Applied Psychol. 8:347–349.

Smith, G. V. S. 1950. The ovaries. *In:* Williams, R. H., ed. Textbook of endocrinology, pp. 349–449.

Smith, M. B. 1951. The single woman of today. Her problems and adjustment. London, Watts & Co., xiv + 130p.

Smith, P. E., and Engle, E. T. 1927. Experimental evidence regarding the role of the anterior pituitary in the development and regulation of the genital system. Amer. J. Anat. 40:159–217.

Smitt, J. W., ed. 1951. Hvorfor er de sådan? En studie over homosexualitetens problemer. København, Hans Reitzel, 223p.

Snow, W. F. 1941. Women and their health. New York, American Social Hygiene Association (Publication No. A-328), 15p.

Soule, S. D., and Bortnick, A. R. 1941. Stilbestrol. A clinical study in estrogenic therapy. J. Clin. Endocrinol. 1:53–57.

Sparrow, W. S., ed. 1905. Women painters of the world, from . . . Caterina Vigri . . . to Rosa Bonheur . . . London, Hodder & Stoughton, 332p. (incl. 38 pl., 7 col. pl., + unlisted pl.)

Speigel, L. A. 1951. A review of contributions to a psychoanalytic theory of adolescence. Psychoanalytic study of the child 6:375–393.

Spitz, R. A. 1949. Autoerotism. Some empirical findings and hypotheses of three of its manifestations in the first year of life. Psychoanalytic study of the child 3–4:85–120.

1952. Authority and masturbation. Some remarks on a bibliographical investigation. Psychoanal. Quart. 21:490–527.

Spragg, S. D. S. 1940. Morphine addiction in chimpanzees. Comp. Psychol. Monogr. v. 15, no. 7, 132p.

Squier, R. 1938. The medical basis of intelligent sexual practice. *In:* Folsom, J. K., ed. Plan for marriage, pp. 113–137.

Stall, S. 1897. What a young husband ought to know. Philadelphia, Vir Publishing Co., 1 pl. + 300p.

Steinach, E. 1940. (Loebel, Josef, ed.). Sex and life. Forty years of biological and medical experiments. New York, Viking Press, x + 252p.

Steiner, M. 1912. *In:* Wiener psychoanalytische Vereinigung. Die Onanie, pp. 129–132.

Steinhardt, I. D. 1938. Sex talks to girls (twelve years and older). Philadelphia, J. B. Lippincott Co., 221p.

Stekel, W. 1895. Ueber Coitus im Kindesalter. Wiener medizinische Blätter 18 (Apr.18):247–249.

1912. *In:* Wiener psychoanalytische Vereinigung. Die Onanie, pp. 29–45.

1920. Onanie und Homosexualität. (Die homosexuelle Neurose.) Vol. 2 of:

Störungen des Trieb- und Affektlebens. (Die parapathischen Erkrankungen.) Berlin, Wien, Urban & Schwarzenberg, xii + 527p.

1920. Die Geschlechtskälte der Frau. (Eine Psychopathologie des weiblichen Liebeslebens.) Vol. 3 of: Störungen des Trieb- und Affektlebens. (Die parapathischen Erkrankungen.) Berlin, Wien, Urban & Schwarzenberg, xii + 402p.

1922. (Van Teslaar, J. S., trans.). Bi-sexual love, the homosexual neurosis. Boston, Richard G. Badger, viii + 359p.

1923. Ed. 3. Onanie und Homosexualität. (Die homosexuelle Parapathie.) Berlin und Wien, Urban & Schwarzenberg, xii + 600p.

1925. Sadismus und Masochismus, für Ärzte und Kriminalogen dargestellt. Leipzig, Verlag der Psychotherapeutischen Praxis, vi + 765p.

1926. (Van Teslaar, J. S., trans.). Frigidity in woman. New York, Liveright, 2v. v. 1, 304p. v. 2, 314p.

1929. (Brink, L., trans.). Sadism and masochism. New York, Liveright Publishing Corp. 2v. v. 1, 441p. v. 2, 473p.

1930. (Parker, S., trans.). Sexual aberrations. New York, Liveright Publishing Corp., 2v. v. 1, 369p. v. 2, 355p.

1950. (Van Teslaar, J. S., trans.). Auto-erotism. A psychiatric study of onanism and neurosis. New York, Liveright Publishing Corp., vii + 289p.

Stephens, A. O. 1947. Premarital sex relationships. In: Fishbein, M., and Burgess, E. W., ed. Successful marriage, pp. 44–54.

Stern, B. 1933. (Berger, D., trans.). The scented garden. Anthropology of the sex life in the Levant. New York, American Ethnological Press, 443p.

Stern, E., ed. 1927. Die Erziehung und die sexuelle Frage. Berlin, Union deutsche Verlagsgesellschaft, 382p. + xxx pl.

Stevens, S. S., ed. 1951. Handbook of experimental psychology. New York, John Wiley & Sons, xi + 1436p.

Stier, E. 1938. Schädigung der sexuellen Funktionen durch Kopftrauma. Deutsch. med. Wchnschr. 64:145–147.

Stiles, H. R. 1869. Bundling; its origin, progress and decline in America. Albany, Joel Munsell, 139p.

Stockham, A. B. 1901? Karezza, ethics of marriage. Chicago, Stockham Publishing Co., viii + 144p.

Stokes, W. R. 1948. Modern pattern for marriage. The newer understanding of married love. New York, Rinehart and Co., xiv + 143p.

Stone, C. P. 1922. The congenital sexual behavior of the young male albino rat. J. Comp. Psychol. 2:95–153.

1923a. Further study of sensory functions in the activation of sexual behavior in the young male albino rat. J. Comp. Psychol. 3:469–473.

1923b. Experimental studies of two important factors underlying masculine sexual behavior: the nervous system and the internal secretion of the testis. J. Exper. Psychol. 6:85–106.

1927. The retention of copulatory ability in male rats following castration. J. Comp. Psychol. 7:369–387.

1939. Copulatory activity in adult male rats following castration and injections of testosterone propionate. Endocrinol. 24:165–174.

1939. Sex drive. In: Allen, E., et al., ed. Sex and internal secretions, pp. 1213–1262.

Stone, C. P., and Barker, R. G. 1937. On the relationship between menarcheal age and certain measurements of physique in girls of the ages 9 to 16 years. Human Biol. 9:1–28.

Stone, H. M., and Stone, A. S. 1937. A marriage manual. A practical guide-book to sex and marriage. New York, Simon and Schuster, xi + 334p.

1952. Rev. ed. A marriage manual. A practical guidebook to sex and marriage. New York, Simon and Schuster, xiv + 301p.

Stone, L. A. 1924. Sex searchlights and sane sex ethics. Chicago, Science Publishing Co., 1 pl. + xxvii + 606p.

Stookey, B. 1943. The management of intractable pain by chordotomy. *In:* Wolff, H. G., et al., ed. Pain, pp. 416–433.

Stopes, M. C. 1931. Married love. A new contribution to the solution of sex difficulties. New York, Eugenics Publishing Co., xxiii + 165p.

Stotijn, C. P. J. 1946. Pubertas praecox. 's-Gravenhage, Martinus Nijhoff, 62p.

Strain, F. B. 1948. The normal sex interests of children from infancy to childhood. New York, Appleton-Century-Crofts, vii + 210p.

Strakosch, F. M. 1934. Factors in the sex life of seven hundred psychopathic women. Utica, N. Y., State Hospitals Press, 102p.

Stratz, C. H. 1909. Ed. 3 (ed. 1, 1903). Der Körper des Kindes und seine Pflege. Für Eltern, Erzieher, Ärzte und Künstler. Stuttgart, Ferdinand Enke, xviii + 386p., 4 pl.

    1926. Lebensalter und Geschlechter. Stuttgart, Ferdinand Enke, x + 194p., 1 pl.

Sturgis, F. R. 1907. The comparative prevalence of masturbation in males and females. Amer. J. Dermatology (Sept.), pp. 396–400.

    ca. 1908. Notes and reflections on the causes which induce marital infelicity due to the relations of the sexes. n.impr., 32p.

Stürup, G. K. 1946a. A psychiatric establishment for investigation, training and treatment of psychologically abnormal criminals. Acta Psychiat. et Neurol. 21:781–793.

    [1946]b. . . . Treatment of criminal psychopaths. Scandinavian Psychiatrists, Congress 8, Report, 21–33p.

Sullivan, Mark. 1935. Our times; the United States, 1900–1925. Volume 6, The twenties. New York, Charles Scribner's Sons, xx + 674p.

Sundt, E. 1857. Om Saedeligheds-Tilstanden i Norge. Christiania, Norway, J. Chr. Abelsted, iv + 326 + xx p.

Swinburne, A. C. 1952. Lesbia Brandon. An historical and critical commentary, being largely a study (and elevation) of Swinburne as a novelist. London, The Falcon Press, xxxv + 583p.

[?Swinburne, A. C.] et al. 1888. The Whippingham papers; a collection of contributions in prose and verse, chiefly by the author of the "Romance of Chastisement." London, n.publ., var. pag.

Takara bunko. *See* Anon. Takara bunko.

Talbot, H. S. 1949. A report on sexual function in paraplegics. J. Urol. 61:265–270.

    1952. The sexual function in paraplegics. J. Nerv. & Ment. Dis. 115:360–361.

Talbot, N. B., et al. 1943. Excretion of 17-ketosteroids by normal and by abnormal children. Amer. J. Dis. Child. 65:364–375.

    1952. Functional endocrinology from birth through adolescence. Cambridge, Mass., Harvard University Press for The Commonwealth Fund, xxx + 638p.

Talmey, B. S. 1910. Ed. 6. Woman. A treatise on the normal and pathological emotions of feminine love. New York, Practitioners' Publishing Co., xii + 262p.

    1912. Neurasthenia sexualis. A treatise on sexual impotence in men and in women. New York, Practitioners' Publishing Co., xi + 196p.

    1915. Love. A treatise on the science of sex-attraction. For the use of physicians and students of medical jurisprudence. New York, Practitioners' Publishing Co., viii + 438p.

Talmud. 1935–1948. (Epstein, I., and Simon, M., trans. and ed.). The Babylonian Talmud . . . (Volume 1–28.) London, Soncino Press, var. pag.

Tandler, J., and Grosz, S. 1913. Die biologischen Grundlagen der sekundären Geschlechtscharaktere. Berlin, Julius Springer, [4] + 169p.

Tappan, P. W. 1949. Juvenile delinquency. New York, McGraw-Hill Book Co., x + 613p.

1950. The habitual sex-offender. Report and recommendations. New Jersey Commission on the Habitual Sex Offender, 65 + xxi p. + 1 pl.

1951. Treatment of the sex offender in Denmark. Amer. J. Psychiat. 108: 241–249.

Tauber, E. S. 1940. Effects of castration upon the sexuality of the adult male. Psychosom. Med. 2:74–87.

Taylor, W. S. 1933. A critique of sublimation in males: a study of forty superior single men. Genetic Psychol. Monogr. 13, no. 1, 115p.

Terman, L. M. 1938. Psychological factors in marital happiness. New York and London, McGraw-Hill Book Co., xiv + 474p.

1951. Correlates of orgasm adequacy in a group of 556 wives. J. Psychol. 32:115–172.

Terman, L. M., and Miles, C. C. 1936. Sex and personality. New York and London, McGraw-Hill Book Co., xi + 600p.

Theocritus, Bion, Moschus, et al. 1912 (orig. 3rd cent. B.C.). (Edmonds, J. M., trans.). The Greek bucolic poets. London, William Heinemann, xxviii + 527p.

Thieme, U., and Becker, F. 1907–1947. Allgemeines Lexikon der bildenden Künstler, von der Antike bis zur Gegenwart. Leipzig, Wilhelm Englemann, v. 1–4; E. A. Seemann, v. 5–34, 36.

Thorn, G. W., and Forsham, P. H. 1950. The pancreas and diabetes mellitus. In: Williams, R. H., ed. Textbook of endocrinology, pp. 450–561.

Thornton, H., and Thornton, F. 1939. How to achieve sex happiness in marriage. New York, Vanguard Press, 155p.

Thornton, N. 1946. Problems in abnormal behavior. Philadelphia, Toronto, The Blakiston Co., x + 244p.

Thorpe, L. P., and Katz, B. 1948. The psychology of abnormal behavior. A dynamic approach. New York, Ronald Press, xvi + 877p.

Tibullus. See Catullus, et al.

Tinklepaugh, O. L. 1928. The self-mutilation of a male macacus rhesus monkey. J. Mammalogy 9:293–300.

1933. The nature of periods of sex desire in woman and their relation to ovulation. Amer. J. Obstet. & Gynec. 26:333–345.

Tissot, S. A. 1764. Ed. 3 (ed. 1, 1760). L'onanisme. Dissertation sur les maladies produites par la masturbation. Lausanne, Marc Chapius et Cie, xxiv + 264p.

1773–1774. Die Erzeugung der Menschen und Heimlichkeiten der Frauenzimmer. Frankfurt, n.publ., 4v. in 1. v. 1, (1773), 100p. v. 2, (1774), 96p. v. 3, (1774), 95p. v. 4, (1774), 96p.

1775. Ed. 10. L'onanisme. Dissertation sur les maladies produites par la masturbation. Toulouse, Laporte, xvi + 210p.

1777. Ed. 11. L'onanisme. Dissertation sur les maladies produites par la masturbation. Lausanne, Grasset & Cie, xvi + 210p.

1785 (Ex ed. 8). L'onanisme, dissertation sur les maladies produites par la masturbation. Lausanne, Franc. Grasset & Comp., xx + 268p.

Townsend, C. W. 1896. Thigh friction in children under one year of age. Trans. Amer. Pediat. Soc. 8:186–189.

Turner, C. D. 1948. General endocrinology. Philadelphia and London, W. B. Saunders Co., xii + 604p.

Turner, H. H. 1950. The clinical use of testosterone. Springfield, Ill., Charles C Thomas, vii + 69p.

Über die Behandlung der Unarten, Fehler und Vergehungen der Jugend. See Anon. Über die Behandlung der Unarten . . .

Undeutsch, U. 1950. Die Sexualität im Jugendalter. Studium Generale 3:433–454.

U. S. Bureau of the Census. 1943. Sixteenth census . . . 1940. Population. Vol. IV: Characteristics by age, marital status, relationship, education, and citizenship. Pt. 1: U. S. Summary. Washington, D. C., U.S.G.P.O., xii + 183p.

1945. Sixteenth census . . . 1940. Population. Differential fertility, 1940 and 1910. Women by number of children ever born. Washington, D. C., U.S.G.P.O., ix + 410p.

U. S. Bureau of the Census. Sampling staff. [?1947]. A chapter in population sampling. Washington, D. C., U.S.G.P.O., vi + 141p.

U. S. Bureau of the Census. 1952. Current population reports. Population characteristics. Washington, D. C., U.S.G.P.O., (Series P-20, No. 38), 20p.

U. S. Department of Labor. 1949. Family income, expenditures and savings in 1945. Washington, D. C., U.S.G.P.O. (Bull. No. 956), v + 41p.

1952. Family income, expenditures, and savings in ten cities. Washington, D. C., U.S.G.P.O. (Bull. No. 1065), v + 110p.

U. S. Public Health Service. 1930. Sex education in the home. Washington, D. C., U.S.G.P.O., 7p.

1934. Keeping fit. A pamphlet for adolescent boys. Washington, D. C., (V. D. Bulletin No. 55), 15p.

1937. Manpower. Washington, D. C., (V. D. Pamphlet No. 6), 15p.

Urbach, K. 1921. Über die zeitliche Gefühlsdifferenz der Geschlechter während der Kohabitation. Ztschr. f. Sexualwiss. 8:124–138.

Valentine, C. W. 1942. The psychology of early childhood. London, Methuen & Co., xiv + 522p.

Van der Hoog, P. H. 1934. De sexueele revolutie. Amsterdam, Nederlandsche Keurboekerij, 350p.

Van de Velde, T. H. 1926. Het volkomen huwelijk. Een studie omtrent zijn physiologie en zijn techniek. Amsterdam, N. V. Em. Querido, xxiv + 334p. + viii pl.

1930. Ideal Marriage. New York, Covici Friede, xxvi + 323p. + 8 pl.

Van Gulik, R. H. 1952. Erotic colour prints of the Ming Period, with an essay on Chinese sex life from the Han to the Ch'ing Dynasty, B.C. 206–A.D. 1644. Tokyo, priv. print., 3v. v. 1, 242p. v. 2, 210p. v. 3, 50p. + illus.

Vatsyayana. 1883–1925 (orig. betw. 1st and 6th cent. A.D.). (Burton, R. F., and Arbuthnot, F. F., trans.). The Kama Sutra of Vatsyayana. Translated from the Sanscrit by The Hindoo Kama Shastra Society. Benares, New York, Society of the Friends of India, [Guy d'Isère], priv. print., xxi + 175p., 8 pl.

Vecki, V. G. 1920. Ed. 6. Sexual impotence. Philadelphia, W. B. Saunders Co., viii + 424p.

Vest, S. A., and Howard, J. E. 1938. Clinical experiments with the use of male sex hormones. I. Use of testosterone propionate in hypogonadism. J. Urol. 40:154–183.

Vigman, F. K. 1952. Sexual precocity of young girls in the United States. Int. J. Sexol. 6:90–91.

Virgil. 1918 (orig. 1st cent. B.C.). (Fairclough, H. R., trans.). Virgil. I. Eclogues, Georgics, Aeneid I–VI. II. Aeneid VII–XII. Minor poems. Cambridge, Mass., Harvard University Press, 2v. v. 1, xvi + 593p. v. 2, 583p. ea. v., 1 pl.

Virgin's dream. See Anon. The virgin's dream.

Vorberg, G. 1921. Die Erotik der Antike in Kleinkunst und Keramik. München, Georg Müller, priv. print., 34p. + 113 pl.

Vorberg, G., ed. 1926. Ars erotica veterum. Ein Beitrag zum Geschlechtsleben des Altertums. Stuttgart, Julius Püttmann, [3]p., 47 pl.

Waehner, T. S. 1946. Interpretation of spontaneous drawings and paintings. Genetic Psychol. Monogr. v. 33:3–70.

Walker, K., and Strauss, E. B. 1939. Sexual disorders in the male. Baltimore, Williams & Wilkins Co., xiv + 248p.

Wallace, V. H. 1948. Sex in art. Inter. J. Sexol. 2:20–23.

Waller, W. 1937. The rating and dating complex. Amer. Sociol. Rev. 2:727–734.
  1951. (Ed. 1, 1938). The family. A dynamic interpretation. New York, Dryden Press, xviii + 637p.

Walsh, W. T. 1940. Characters of the Inquisition. New York, P. J. Kenedy & Sons, xiii + 301p.

Wangson, O., et al. 1951. Ungdomen möter sämhallet. Ungdomsvårdskommittens slutbetänkande. Stockholm, Justitiedepartementet, Statens Offentliga Wredningar 1951:41, 221p.

Ward, E. 1938. The Yoruba husband-wife code. Washington, D. C., Catholic University of America Press (Anthropological Series No. 6), 1 pl. +[v]–viii + 178p.

Warden, C. J. 1931. Animal motivation. Experimental studies on the albino rat. New York, Columbia University Press, xii + 502p.

Warner, M. P. 1943. The premarital medical consultation. Clinical premarital procedures as an aid to biologic and emotional adjustments of marriage. Med. Woman's J. 50:293–300.

Warner, W. L., and Lunt, P. S. 1941. The social life of a modern community. New Haven, Conn., Yale University Press, xx + 460p.
  1942. The status system of a modern community. New Haven, Conn., Yale University Press, xx + 246p.

Washington Public Opinion Laboratory. (Dodd, S. C., and Bachelder, J. E., director.) 1950. [Abstract of survey on marriage and divorce, etc.] Int. J. Opin. & Attit. Res. 4:467–470.

Wassermann, B. J., ed. 1938. Ceramics del antiguo Peru, de la coleccion Wassermann-San Blas. Buenos Aires, Jacobo Pueser, xxxi pl. + 365 pl.

Weatherhead, L. D., assisted by Greaves, M. 1932. The mastery of sex through psychology and religion. New York, The Macmillan Co., xxv + 246p.

Webster, R. C., and Young, W. C. 1951. Adolescent sterility in the male guinea pig. Fertil. & Steril. 2:175–181.

Weigall, A. 1932. Sappho of Lesbos: her life and times. London, Thornton Butterworth, 319p., 14 pl.

Weil, A., ed. 1922. Sexualreform und Sexualwissenschaft. Vorträge gehalten auf der I. internationalen Tagung für Sexualreform auf sexualwissenschaftlicher Grundlage in Berlin. Stuttgart, J. Püttmann, 288p.

Weil, A. 1943. The chemical growth of the brain of the white rat and its relation to sex. Growth 7:257–264.
  1944. The influence of sex hormones upon the chemical growth of the brain of white rats. Growth 8:107–115.

Weil, A., and Liebert, E. 1943. The correlation between sex and chemical constitution of the human brain. Quart. Bull. Northwestern U. Med. Schl. 17:117–120.

Weisman, A. I. 1941. Spermatozoa and sterility. A clinical manual. New York, London, Paul B. Hoeber, xvi + 314p.
  1948. The engaged couple has a right to know. (A modern guide to happy marriage.) New York, Renbayle House, 256p.

Weiss, E., and English, O. S. 1949. Ed. 2. Psychosomatic medicine. The clinical application of psychopathology to general medical problems. Philadelphia and London, W. B. Saunders Co., xxx + 803p.

Weissenberg, S. 1924a. Das Geschlechtsleben der russischen Studentinnen. [Schbankov Study, 1908. Reported 1922.] Ztschr. f. Sexualwiss. 11:7–14.
  1924b. Das Geschlechtsleben des russischen Studententums der Revolutionszeit. [Hellmann Study, 1923.] Ztschr. f. Sexualwiss. 11:209–216.
  1925. Weiteres über das Geschlechtsleben der russischen Studentinnen. [Golossowker Study, 1922–1923.] Ztschr. f. Sexualwiss. 12:174–176.

Welander, E. 1908. Några ord om de veneriska sjukdomarnas bekämpande. Hygiea N:r 12:1–32.

West, James. See Withers, Carl.

Westbrook, C. H., Lai, D. G., and Hsiao, S. D. 1934. Some physical aspects of adolescence in Chinese students. Chinese Med. J. 48:37–46.

Westermarck, E. 1912, 1917. (Ed. 1, 1906). The origin and development of the moral ideas. London, Macmillan and Co., 2v. v. 1, xxi + 716p. v. 2, xix + 865p.

1922. (Ed. 1, 1891). The history of human marriage. New York, Allerton Book Co., 3v. v. 1, x + 571p. v. 2, xi + 595p. v. 3, viii + 587p.

Wexberg, E. 1931. (Wolfe, W. B., trans.). The psychology of sex: an introduction. New York, Blue Ribbon Books, xxvi + 215p.

Wharton, F. 1932. Ed. 12. (Ruppenthal, J. C., ed.). Wharton's criminal law. Rochester, N. Y., Lawyers Co-operative Publishing Co., 3v. v. 1, viii + 1157p. v. 2, iii + 1159–2446p. v. 3, 2447–3358p.

Wharton, H. T., trans. and ed. 1895 (ed. 1, 1885). Sappho. Memoir, text, selected renderings, and a literal translation. London, John Lane, xx + 217p., 3 pl.

Wharton, L. R. 1947. Ed. 2. Gynecology, with a section on female urology. Philadelphia and London, W. B. Saunders Co., xxi + 1027p.

Whitelaw, G. P., and Smithwick, R. H. 1951. Some secondary effects of sympathectomy. With particular reference to disturbance of sexual function. New Eng. J. Med. 245:121–130.

Whiting, J. W. M. 1941. Becoming a Kwoma. Teaching and learning in a New Guinea tribe. New Haven, Conn., Yale University Press, xix + 226p., 8 pl.

Whitney, L. F. 1950. The dog. In: Farris, E. J., ed. The care and breeding of laboratory animals, pp. 182–201.

Wiener psychoanalytische Vereinigung. 1912. Die Onanie. Vierzehn Beiträge zu einer Diskussion der Wiener psychoanalytischen Vereinigung. Wiesbaden, J. F. Bergmann, iv + 140p.

Wikman, K. R. van. 1937. Die Einleitung der Ehe. Abö, Sweden, Institut für Nordische Ethnologie, xliv + 395p.

Williams, R. H., ed. 1950. Textbook of endocrinology. Philadelphia and London, W. B. Saunders Co., xii + 793p.

Williams, W. L. 1943. The diseases of the genital organs of domestic animals. Worcester, Mass., Ethel W. Plimpton, xvii + 650p., 3 col. pl. incl. 196 fig.

Willoughby, R. R. 1937. Sexuality in the second decade. Washington, D. C., Society for Research in Child Development (Monograph for the Society . . . , Vol. 2, No. 3, Serial No. 10), iii + 57p.

Wilson, J. G., and Young, W. C. 1941. Sensitivity to estrogen studied by means of experimentally induced mating responses in the female guinea pig and rat. Endocrinol. 29:779–783.

Windsor, Edward, pseud. (Malkin, S.). 1937. The Hindu art of love. New York, Falstaff Press, xiv + 276p.

Wirz, P. 1950. Hygiene der Geschlechtsorgane. In: Hornstein, X. von, and Faller, A., ed. Gesundes Geschlechtsleben, pp. 115–132.

Withers, Carl. (West, James, pseud.). 1945. Plainville, U. S. A. New York, Columbia University Press, xviii + 238p.

Wittels, D. G. 1948. What can we do about sex crimes? Sat. Eve. Post. v. 221 (Dec. 11), pp. 30–31, 47–69.

Wolf, C. 1934. Die Kastration bei sexuellen Perversionen und Sittlichkeitsverbrechen des Mannes. Basel, B. Schwabe & Co., xii + 300p.

Wolff, H. G., Gasser, H. S., and Hinsey, J. C., ed. 1943. Pain. Proceedings of the Association for Research in Nervous and Mental Diseases, 1942. Baltimore, Williams & Wilkins Co. (Research Publication Vol. XXIII), xii + 468p.

Wolff, H. G., Wolf, S. G., and Hare, C. C., ed. 1950. Life stress and bodily disease. Proceedings of the Association for Research in Nervous and Mental Diseases, 1949. Baltimore, Williams & Wilkins Co. (Research Publication Vol. XXIX), xxiii + 1135p.

Wolman, B. 1951. Sexual development in Israeli adolescents. Amer. J. Psychother. 5:531–559.

Wood-Allen, M. 1905. (Ed. 1, 1897). What a young girl ought to know. Philadelphia, Vir Publishing Co., 1 pl. + 194p.

Woodside, M. 1950. Sterilization in North Carolina. A sociological and psychological study. Chapel Hill, N. C., University of North Carolina Press, xv + 219p.

Woodworth, R. S., and Marquis, D. G. 1947. Ed. 5 (ed. 1, 1921). Psychology. New York, Henry Holt and Co., x + 677p.

Wright, H. 1937. The sex factor in marriage. New York, Vanguard Press, 172p.

Wulffen, E. 1913. Das Kind. Sein Wesen und seine Entartung. Berlin, P. Langenscheidt, xxiv + 542p.

Wulffen, E., et al. 1931. Die Erotik in der Photographie. Die geschichtliche Entwicklung der Aktphotographie und des erotischen Lichtbildes und seine Beziehungen zur Psychopathia Sexualis. Wien, Verlag für Kulturforschung, 254p., 31 pl.

Yarros, R. S. 1933. Modern woman and sex. A feminist physician speaks. New York, Vanguard Press, 218p.

Yates, F. 1949. Sampling methods for censuses and surveys. New York, Hafner Publishing Co., xiv + 318p.

Yerkes, R. M. 1935. A second-generation captive-born chimpanzee. Science 81: 542–543.

1939. Sexual behavior in the chimpanzee. Human Biol. 11:78–111.

1943. Chimpanzees. A laboratory colony. New Haven, Conn., Yale University Press, xv + 321p.

Yerkes, R. M., and Elder, J. H. 1936a. Oestrus, receptivity, and mating in chimpanzee. Comp. Psychol. Monogr. 13, no. 5, 39p.

1936b. The sexual and reproductive cycles of chimpanzees. Proc. Nat. Acad. Sci. 22:276–283.

Yerkes, R. M., and Yerkes, A. W. 1929. The great apes. A study of anthropoid life. New Haven, Conn., Yale University Press, xix + 652p.

Young, P. V. 1949. Ed. 2. Scientific social surveys and research. New York, Prentice-Hall, xxviii + 621p.

Young, W. C. 1941. Observations and experiments on mating behavior in female mammals. Quart. Rev. Biol. 16:(pt. 1) 135–156, (pt. 2) 311–335.

Young, W. C., et al. 1939. Sexual behavior and sexual receptivity in the female guinea pig. J. Comp. Psychol. 27:49–68.

Young, W. C., and Rundlett, B. 1939. The hormonal induction of homosexual behavior in the spayed female guinea pig. Psychosom. Med. 1:449–460.

Zeitschrift für psychoanalytische Pädagogik. 1927–1928. [Special issue on onanism.] v. 2, no. 4, 5, & 6.

Zell, T. 1921. Geheimpfade der Natur. 1. Die Diktatur der Liebe. 2. Neue Dokumente zur Diktatur der Liebe. Hamburg, Hoffmann & Campe, 2v. v. 1, 307p. v. 2, 288p.

Zikel, Heinz. [1909]. Die Kälte der Frauen. Aerztliche Ratschläge und Beobachtungen aus dem Leben. Berlin und Leipzig, Schweizer & Co., 94p.

Zitrin, A., and Beach, F. A. 1945. Discussion of the paper. In: Hartman, C. G. The mating of mammals, pp. 40–44.

Zuckerman, S. 1932. The social life of monkeys and apes. London, Kegan Paul, Trench, Trubner & Co., xii + 357p., 24 pl.

INDEX

All numbers refer to pages. **Bold face** entries refer to more extended treatment of each subject. Names of authors and titles cited are *italicized*. The letters T and F refer to material in tables and figures respectively. The abbreviation vs. means "in relation to."

Brown-Séquard, 720
Bruckner, 171
Brusendorff, 88
Bryk, 135, 719
Buck, 298
Bucy, 691, 710, 711
Buggery, 483. *See* Anal eroticism.
Bühler, 85, 108, 122, 126, 141, 160
Build-up to orgasm, physiology, 623–625
Bull. *See* Cattle.
Bulliet, 654
Bundesen, 261, 307
Bundling, 232
Burgess, 158, 159, 167, 170, 234, 252, 253, 261, 298, 365, 416, 538
Burlesque shows, erotic response to, 657, 660
Burrows, 723, 729, 730, 745, 747, 749, 751, 755
Butterfield, 170, 228, 253, 256, 625
Buttocks, in sexual response, 160, 254, 589, 618

Calculations, statistical, bases for, **45–57**
Caldwell, Erskine, 244
Calendars, sexual, 84
Calverton, 163
Campbell, B., 25, 710
Campbell, E. H., 126
Canby, 358
Cannon, 606, 615, 704, 754
Canu, 734
Caprio, 86, 88, 448, 503
Carmichael, 124, 125, 746
Carpenter, C., 411, 645, 651
Carpenter, E., 448, 469, 486
Carpenter, N., 244
Carter, 748
Cary, 231
Casañ, 505
Case histories. *See* Histories.
Castration
  correction by hormones, 726, 727, 733
  effects, 720–727, **731–745**
  fear, 377
  historical background, 718, 739
  human female, 734, 736T
  human male, **738–740**
  legal use, 728, 739, 742–745
  mammalian experiments, 736
  previous studies, 730–744
  religious, 367, 732
  sexual behavior and, 731–740
  testosterone therapy, 733
  therapeutic, 739
  young castrates, 732–734
Cat
  biting in sexual activity, 678
  cerebral function, 710
  chimpanzee, in contact with, 503
  coital activity, 283, 629
  conditioned responses, 647
  erection, 605
  homosexual contacts, 449
  human contacts with, 506
  neurologic experiments, 697

Cat, *Continued*
  nocturnal sex dreams, 195
  orgasm in female, 629
  pituitary, 751
  sex play, 229
Catholic. *See* Religious background *and* Moral interpretations.
Catholic code
  animal contacts, 507
  extra-marital coitus, 428
  homosexual, 482, 486
  marital coitus, 366–370
  masturbation, 168
  nocturnal sex dreams, 207
  petting, 260
  pre-marital coitus, 321
Catholic sample, 31T, 34
Cattle
  conditioned response, 647, 669, 737
  erection in bull, 605
  estrual behavior, 651
  homosexual activity, 449
  human contacts with, 503
  masturbation, 135
  orgasm in female, 629
  response to new partner, 411
  sex play, 229, 283
Catullus, 232
Caufeynon, 150, 153, 447, 448, 476, 486, 595, 613
Cave, 739
Census Bureau, U. S., 24, 25
Central nervous system, 617, **694–701, 708–713**
Cerebral cortex, **710–712**
Cerebrum, 192, 630F, 694F, 696F, 707, 708, **710–712**
Cervix, 577T, 584, 607
Chain reactions vs. sexual response, 691
Chaldean code, 322, 428, 482, 507
Chaucer, 671
Cheng, 747
Chesser, 252, 256, 257, 478
Chicken, 503, 751
Chideckel, 448, 458, 505, 506, 583
Childbirth, dreams of, 213, 226T
Childers, 191
Children. *See* Pre-adolescence.
Chimpanzee
  biting in sexual activity, 678
  castration, 733
  cat, in contact with, 503
  estrogen effects, 749
  estrual behavior, 651
  exhibition, 657
  grooming, 655
  homosexual contacts, 449
  masturbation, 135
  orgasm in female, 629
  pre-adolescent sex play, 229, 282, 283, 362
  sympathetic response, 649, 661
Chinchilla, 135, 229, 283
Chione, 13
Chloe, 13
Chordotomy, 699
Christensen, 261, 307, 309, 388

Nocturnal sex dreams, **191–226**
    anthropologic data, 196
    compensatory function, **207–212**
    content, 193, **212–214**, 226T
    defined, 191
    factors, **192–196**
    female vs. male data, 191, 194, 199, **214–215**, 668, 717F
    frequency, 197–206, 198F, 199F, 217T, 224T
    historical record, 191
    incidence, accumulative, 82T, 196, 197F, 201–203, 202F, 204F, 216T, 219T, 222T, 224T, 668
    incidence, active, 197, 198F, 200–205, 205F, 217T, 218T, 220T–224T
    mammals, occurrence in, 195
    moral interpretations, 207–208, 214
    percentage of total outlet, 201, **205–207**, 217T, 218T, 220T–224T, 525, 527F, 530F, 531F, 532, 534F, 535F, 536, 561T–564T
    pre-adolescent, 106
    psychologic significance, 192–195, 212–214, 668
    vs. age, 197–201, 198F, 199F, 206, 217T, 220T–224T, 525, 527F, 530F, 531F, 532, 534F, 535F, 561T–564T
    vs. age at adolescence, 203, 222T, 223T
    vs. coitus, 209–210
    vs. decade of birth, 202, 202F, 219T, 221T
    vs. educational level, 201, 216T, 218T, 226T, 534F, 535F, 563F, 564T
    vs. erotic responsiveness, 210
    vs. marital status, 198F, 200, 206, 210, 217T, 218T, 220T, 221T, 223T, 224T, 530F, 531F, 536, 562T
    vs. masturbation, 200, 210–211
    vs. parental occupational class, 202, 219T, 220T
    vs. religious background, 203–205, 204F, 205F, 224T
    vs. rural-urban background, 203, 222T
    vs. total outlet, 209–212
Noldin, 321, 508
Northcote, 135, 167
Norton, 447, 448, 462
Notonanie, 165
Nudity
    attitudes, 260, 365, 400T
    children, 284
    erotic response, female vs. male, 652
    marital coitus, 365, 400T
    portrayals, commercial, 652, 657
    pre-marital coitus, 312, 400T
Numa Praetorius, 87. *See* Hirschfeld.
Number of cases in sample, **43–45**
Number of partners, 110, 238, 272T, 292, 336T, 409–412, 425, 444T, 458, 492T, **682–684**
Number of sources of outlet, 542, 560T
Nystrom, 191

Objective, scientific, of study, **7**
Objectivity, in interview, 59

O'Brien, 260
Obscenity, 671
Observation, erotic response to, female vs. male
    burlesque, 657, 660
    fetishism, 678
    floor shows, 660
    genitalia, 655–659
    heterosexual, 651, 660, 664
    homosexual, 652–655
    moving pictures, 659, 662
    nudes, 652–655, 663–664
    sexual action, 661–664
Observed data, **89–92**, 569
    clinical studies, 90, 574, 577T
    community studies, 89
    human sexual behavior, 91, 103, 104, 108, 123, 141, 569, 574, 577T, 596, 597F, 602F, 606F, 630F
    mammalian studies, 90–92, 195, 229, 283, 449, 569–570, 598, 598F, 599, 600F, 601F, 605, 629
Occipital lobe operations, 710
Occupational class. *See* Parental occupational class.
Occupations
    females in sample, 33T, 34, 39
    husbands of females in sample, 41
Odors, sexual arousal by, 590
Oesterling, 756
Offenses, sex. *See* Legal aspects.
Ogle, 125
Ohlson, 428
Okkels, 728
Onanie, Die, 170
Onanism, 133. *See* Masturbation.
Oneida Colony, 346, 625
Opossum, 678
Oral techniques
    animal contacts, 505, 600F, 601F
    genital contacts. *See* Mouth-genital activity.
    homosexual, 466, 484, 492T
    kissing, 251, 255F, 280T, 361, 399T, 466, 492T
    mammalian behavior, 229, 587, 677
    petting, 251–253, **255F**, **257–258**, 280T
    pre-coital play, 255F, 257–258, 361, 399T, 427
Oran-utang, 282, 283, 362
Orgasm
    clitoral vs. vaginal, 574–576, 577T, 579–584, 632
    defined, 101, **627–631**
    factors affecting, 101, 132, 357, **376–391**, 401T–408T, 514–516, 594, 626, 668, 684. *See also* 642–689.
    female vs. male, 520, 625–627, 638, **640–641**, 718F, 719T
    first, 512F, 513, 514, 542, 544T
    frequency. *See* Frequency.
    incidence, accumulative. *See* Accumulative incidence.
    incidence, active. *See* Active incidence.
    mammalian female orgasm, 628–631
    multiple, 375, 626, 718F, 719T
    physiology, 594–641, **623–640**